Unjustified Enrichment:
Key Issues in Comparative Perspective

In recent years unjustified enrichment has been one of the most intellectually vital areas of private law. There is, however, still no unanimity among civil-law and common-law legal systems about how to structure this important branch of the law of obligations. Several key issues are considered comparatively here, including grounds for recovery of enrichment, defences, third-party enrichment, as well as proprietary and taxonomic questions. Two contributors deal with each topic, one a representative of a common-law system, the other a representative of a civil-law or mixed system. This approach illuminates not just similarities or differences between systems, but also what different systems can learn from one another. In an area of law whose territory is still partially uncharted and whose borders are contested, such comparative perspectives will be valuable for both academic analysis of the law and its development by the courts.

DAVID JOHNSTON is an advocate and Honorary Professor of Law, University of Edinburgh. His publications include *Roman Law in Context* (1999) and *Prescription and Limitation* (1999).

REINHARD ZIMMERMANN is Professor of Private Law, Roman Law and Comparative Legal History at the University of Regensburg. His publications include *The Law of Obligations: Roman Foundations of the Civilian Tradition* (1990; paperback edition, 1996) and *Roman Law, Contemporary Law, European Law: The Civilian Tradition Today* (2001).

Unjustified Enrichment:
Key Issues in Comparative Perspective

Edited by

David Johnston
Reinhard Zimmermann

CAMBRIDGE UNIVERSITY PRESS
Cambridge, New York, Melbourne, Madrid, Cape Town, Singapore,
São Paulo, Delhi, Dubai, Tokyo, Mexico City

Cambridge University Press
The Edinburgh Building, Cambridge CB2 8RU, UK

Published in the United States of America by Cambridge University Press, New York

www.cambridge.org
Information on this title: www.cambridge.org/9780521808200

© Cambridge University Press 2002

This publication is in copyright. Subject to statutory exception
and to the provisions of relevant collective licensing agreements,
no reproduction of any part may take place without the written
permission of Cambridge University Press.

First published 2002

A catalogue record for this publication is available from the British Library

Library of Congress Cataloguing in Publication data
Unjustified Enrichment: Key Issues in Comparative Perspective / edited by David Johnston
and Reinhard Zimmermann.
    p.   cm.
Includes bibliographical references and index.
ISBN 0 521 80820 0 (hardback)
1. Unjust enrichment.   I. Johnston, David, 1961–   II. Zimmermann, Reinhard, 1952–
K920 .C66 2001
346.02'9 – dc21   2001025953

ISBN 978-0-521-80820-0 Hardback
ISBN 978-0-521-18744-2 Paperback

Cambridge University Press has no responsibility for the persistence or
accuracy of URLs for external or third-party internet websites referred to in
this publication, and does not guarantee that any content on such websites is,
or will remain, accurate or appropriate. Information regarding prices, travel
timetables, and other factual information given in this work is correct at
the time of first printing but Cambridge University Press does not guarantee
the accuracy of such information thereafter.

Contents

List of contributors	*page* viii
Preface	xi
Table of cases	xii
List of abbreviations	xxxiii

I Introduction

1   Unjustified enrichment: surveying the landscape   3
DAVID JOHNSTON AND REINHARD ZIMMERMANN

II Enrichment 'without legal ground' or unjust factor approach

2   Unjust factors and legal grounds   37
SONJA MEIER

3   In defence of unjust factors   76
THOMAS KREBS

III Failure of consideration

4   Failure of consideration: myth and meaning in the English law of restitution   103
GRAHAM VIRGO

5   Failure of consideration   128
ROBIN EVANS-JONES AND KATRIN KRUSE

IV Duress and fraud

6 In defence of unjust factors: a study of rescission
for duress, fraud and exploitation   159
MINDY CHEN-WISHART

7 Fraud, duress and unjustified enrichment:
a civil-law perspective   194
JACQUES DU PLESSIS

V Change of position

8 Restitution without enrichment? Change of position
and *Wegfall der Bereicherung*   227
JAMES GORDLEY

9 Unwinding mutual contracts: *restitutio in
integrum* v. the defence of change of position   243
PHILLIP HELLWEGE

VI Illegality

10 The role of illegality in the English law
of unjust enrichment   289
W. J. SWADLING

11 Illegality as defence against unjust enrichment claims   310
GERHARD DANNEMANN

VII Encroachment and restitution for wrongs

12 Reflections on the role of restitutionary damages
to protect contractual expectations   327
JANET O'SULLIVAN

13 Encroachments: between private and public   348
HANOCH DAGAN

VIII Improvements

14 Mistaken improvements and the restitution calculus   369
ANDREW KULL

15	Enrichment by improvements in Scots law JAMES WOLFFE	384

IX Discharge of another person's debt

16	Performance of another's obligation: French and English law contrasted SIMON WHITTAKER	433
17	Payment of another's debt HECTOR L. MACQUEEN	458

X Third-party enrichment

18	'At the expense of the claimant': direct and indirect enrichment in English law PETER BIRKS	493
19	Searches for silver bullets: enrichment in three-party situations DANIEL VISSER	526

XI Proprietary issues

20	Proprietary issues GEORGE GRETTON	571
21	Property, subsidiarity and unjust enrichment LIONEL SMITH	588

XII Taxonomy

22	Taxonomy: does it matter? EWAN MCKENDRICK	627
23	Rationality, nationality and the taxonomy of unjustified enrichment NIALL R. WHITTY	658
	Index	730

Contributors

PETER BIRKS is Regius Professor of Civil Law in the University of Oxford and Fellow of All Souls College, Oxford.

MINDY CHEN-WISHART is a Lecturer in Law in the University of Oxford and Fellow of Merton College, Oxford.

HANOCH DAGAN is Professor in the University of Tel-Aviv Law School and an Affiliated Overseas Professor in the University of Michigan Law School.

GERHARD DANNEMANN is a University Lecturer in German Civil and Commercial Law in the University of Oxford.

JACQUES DU PLESSIS is Professor of Private Law and Roman Law in the University of Stellenbosch.

ROBIN EVANS-JONES is Professor of Jurisprudence in the University of Aberdeen.

GEORGE GRETTON is Lord President Reid Professor of Law in the University of Edinburgh.

JAMES GORDLEY is Shannon Cecil Turner Professor of Jurisprudence at the School of Law of the University of California at Berkeley.

PHILLIP HELLWEGE is a Research Assistant in the Department of Private Law, Roman Law, and Comparative Legal History in the University of Regensburg.

DAVID JOHNSTON is an advocate at the Scottish bar and an Honorary Professor of Law in the University of Edinburgh.

THOMAS KREBS is a Lecturer in Laws at University College London.

KATRIN KRUSE is a Research Fellow in the Centre for the Study of Civil Law, University of Aberdeen.

ANDREW KULL is Robert Thompson Professor of Law at Emory University, Atlanta.

HECTOR L. MACQUEEN is Professor of Private Law in the University of Edinburgh.

EWAN MCKENDRICK is Professor of English Private Law in the University of Oxford and Fellow of Lady Margaret Hall.

SONJA MEIER is a Lecturer in Law in the University of Regensburg.

JANET O'SULLIVAN is a University Lecturer in the Law Faculty, Cambridge University and a Fellow of Selwyn College.

LIONEL SMITH is an Associate Professor in the Faculty of Law, McGill University, Montreal.

W. J. SWADLING is a Lecturer in Law in the University of Oxford and a Fellow of Brasenose College, Oxford.

GRAHAM VIRGO is a University Lecturer in Law in the Faculty of Law, University of Cambridge.

DANIEL VISSER is Professor of Private Law in the University of Cape Town.

SIMON WHITTAKER is a Lecturer in Law in the University of Oxford and a Fellow of St John's College, Oxford.

NIALL R. WHITTY is a Visiting Professor in the University of Edinburgh.

JAMES WOLFFE is an advocate at the Scottish bar.

REINHARD ZIMMERMANN is Professor of Private Law, Roman Law, and Comparative Legal History in the University of Regensburg.

Preface

This collection of essays has its origin in a conference which we organised at Christ's College, Cambridge in April 1999. The aims of the conference are explained in our introductory chapter. Here it is enough to say that, while unjustified enrichment has clearly been one of the most intellectually vital areas of private law over the last decades, there seemed to us to be scope for comparative exploration of the area in a manner more comprehensive than it had until then received. With this in mind we invited a small group of speakers to Cambridge, where at the time we were both teaching. Our invitations to contributors were perhaps unusually prescriptive, and in particular allowed them no choice of topic. The main reason for this was that for each topic we wished to have two papers, each taking a different perspective. So we are extremely grateful to the contributors both for their enthusiastic participation in the conference and for preparing the papers published here. We would like also to acknowledge the helpful guidance of Peter Birks during the planning phase of the conference. In addition we warmly thank the chairmen who presided over the various sessions of the conference: Lord Goff of Chieveley, Lord Hope of Craighead, Professor Gareth Jones, Lord Rodger of Earlsferry, Professor Peter Schlechtriem and Lord Steyn.

The manuscripts for this book were submitted by the end of 1999; they therefore reflect the law at that date.

Most of the funding for the conference was provided by the Leibniz programme of the German Research Association. In addition, a number of participants were kindly supported by the European Commission through the TMR Programme 'Common Principles of European Law'. We also thank Dirk Schulz and Christian Weinelt in Regensburg for assisting with editing the papers for publication. And we thank Cambridge University Press and Finola O'Sullivan for their willing and generous support of this project, both at the conference and at the stage of publication.

David Johnston
Reinhard Zimmermann

Table of cases

337965 B. C. Ltd v. Tackama Forest Products Ltd (1992) 67 BCLR 2d 1;
    91 DLR 4th 129 (CA)   page 600

ABSA Bank Ltd v. De Klerk 1999 (1) SA 861 (W)   547
ABSA Bank t/a Bankfin v. C. B. Stander t/a C. A. W. Paneelkloppers
    1998 (1) SA 939 (C)   529, 564–6
Aberdeen Railway Co. v. Blaikie, Brothers (1854) 1 Macqueen 461   394
Adam v. Newbigging (1888) 13 App Cas 308   180, 181, 245, 255
Adamson v. The Glasgow Corporation Water-Works Commissioners (1859)
    21 D 1012   253, 409
Addis v. Gramophone Co. Ltd [1909] AC 488   337
Addison v. Ottawa Auto and Taxi Co. (1916) 16 DLR 318   182
Adras Building Material Ltd v. Harlow & Jones GmbH [1995] Restitution
    LR 235   332–4, 354
Agip (Africa) Ltd v. Jackson [1991] Ch 547 (CA);
    [1990] Ch 265   521, 522, 717
Aguilar v. Aguilar (1820) 5 Madd 414   277
Aiken v. Short (1856) 1 H & N 210; 156 ER 1180   41, 503, 651
Air Canada v. British Columbia (1989) 59 DLR (4th) 161   55, 63
Airbus Industrie GIE v. Patel [1999] 1 AC 97   640
Air-Kel (Edms) Bpk h/a Merkel Motors v. Bodenstein en 'n ander 1980 (3)
    SA 917 (A)   219
Alati v. Kruger (1955) 94 CLR 216   180–1
Alfred McAlpine Construction Ltd v. Panatown Ltd (1998) 88 Business
    LR 67   336
Allan v. Gilchrist (1875) 2 R 587   404
Allcard v. Skinner (1887) 36 ChD 145   167, 172, 181
American Home Improvement Co. v. MacIver 201 A 2d 886 (NH, 1964)   231

Ames Settlement, Re [1946] Ch 217	137
Anderson v. Anderson (1869) 8 M 157	404
Anderson v. Blair (1841) 3 D 968	470
Anns v. Merton London Borough Council [1978] AC 728 (HL)	650, 693
Aratra Potato v. Taylor Johnson Garrett [1995] 4 All ER 695	71
Armour v. Glasgow Royal Infirmary 1909 SC 916	715
Armstrong v. Jackson [1917] 2 KB 822	180, 255
Arris v. Stukely (1677) 2 Mod 260; 86 ER 1060	507
Associated Japanese Bank (International) Ltd v. Crédit du Nord SA [1989] 1 WLR 255	250
Astley v. Reynolds (1731) 2 Str 915	301
Atlantic Lines & Navigation Co. Inc. v. Hallam Ltd [1983] 1 Lloyd's Rep 188	175
Attorney-General v. Blake [2000] 4 All ER 385 (HL); [1998] 1 All ER 833; [1998] Ch 439	10–11, 12, 25, 106, 107, 327, 330–4, 341–7, 354
Attorney-General v. Saibo (1923) NLR 321	217
Attorney-General for Hong Kong v. Reid [1994] 1 AC 324 (PC)	576, 581, 663, 666
Attorney-General of Hong Kong v. Humphreys Estate Ltd [1987] AC 114	633
Austin v. Burge 137 SW 618 (Mo App 1911)	233
Ayers v. South Australian Banking Co. (1878) LR 3 PC	582
B. & H. Engineering v. First National Bank of South Africa Ltd 1995 (2) SA 279 (A)	218, 478–9, 536
B. Liggett (Liverpool) Ltd v. Barclays Bank Ltd [1928] 1 KB 48	520
Bainbrigge v. Browne (1881) 18 ChD 188	515
Bank Melli Iran v. Samadi-Rad [1995] 1 Federal Court Reporter 465	173, 189, 190
Bank of Montreal v. Hall [1990] 1 SCR 121; 65 DLR 4th 361	613
Bank of Scotland v. Junior 1999 SCLR 284 (Extra Division)	722
Bank of Scotland v. MacLeod Paxton Woolard & Co. 1998 SLT 258 (OH)	667, 674, 722, 723
Bank Tejarat v. Hong Kong and Shanghai Banking Corp. Ltd [1995] 1 Lloyd's Rep 239	635
Bannatine's Trs v. Cunninghame (1872) 10 M 319	473
Bannatyne v. D. & C. MacIver [1906] 1 KB 103 (CA)	520
Banque Belge pour l'Étranger v. Hambrouck [1921] 1 KB 321 (CA)	515, 718
Banque Financière de la Cité v. Parc (Battersea) Ltd [1999] AC 221; [1998] 1 All ER 737	9, 159

TABLE OF CASES

Banque Worms v. BankAmerica International 77 NY 2d 362;
    570 NE 2d 189 (1991)   504, 538
Barbour v. Halliday (1840) 2 D 1279   392, 396–7
Barclays Bank Ltd v. Quistclose Investments Ltd [1970] AC 567   108
Barclays Bank Ltd v. W. J. Simms Son and Cooke   21, 39, 50–1, 53, 69, 77,
    (Southern) Ltd [1980] QB 677; [1979] 3   137–8, 477–82, 503,
    All ER 522   505–6, 536–8, 704
Barclays Bank plc v. Boulter [1999] 1 WLR 1919   165
Barclays Bank plc v. O'Brien [1994] 1 AC 180   161, 167, 187–8, 504
Barnbugil v. Hamilton (1567) Mor 8915   253
Barnes v. Lozoff 123 NW 2d 543 (1963)   237
Baroness Wenlock v. River Dee Co. (1887) 19 QBD 155   522
Beacon Homes, Inc. v. Holt (1966) 66 North Carolina Rep 467;
    46 SE 2d 434   379
Beattie v. Lord Napier (1831) 9 S 639   401, 421, 578
Bédard v. Bédard Transport Co. [1960] CS 472   598
Bedwell v. Bedwell (1989) 774 SW 2d 953   375
Bell v. Bell (1841) 2 D 1201   404–5, 418
Bell v. Lever Brothers [1932] AC 161   39
Belvoir Finance Co. Ltd v. Stapleton [1971] 1 QB 210   250
Berg v. Sadler & Moore [1937] 2 KB 158   299
Biffin v. Bignell (1862) 7 H & N 877; 158 ER 725   198
Bigos v. Bousted [1951] 1 All ER 92   291, 308
Bilbie v. Lumley (1802) 2 East 469; 102 ER 448   55, 56
Binning v. Brotherstones (1676) M 13401   423–4
Bishop v. Flood 133 Ga App 804; 212 SE 2d 443   551
Blackburn v. Smith (1848) 2 Ex 783   256
Blacklocks v. J. B. Developments (Godalming) Ltd [1982] Ch 183   515
Blum v. Dawkins Inc. 683 So 2d 163 (Florida Districts CA,
    5th District 1996)   552
Boardman v. Phipps [1967] 2 AC 46   666
Bodega Co., Re [1904] 1 Ch 276   41
Bonnington Sugar Refining Co. v. Thomson's Trustees (1878) 6 R 80   246
Boscawen v. Bajwa [1996] 1 WLR 328   14, 666
Bostock & Co. Ltd v. Nicholson, & Sons Ltd [1904] KB 725   255
Boudier, Req. 15 June 1892, S 1893.1.281 note   20, 513, 551, 560,
    Labbé, DP 1892.1.596   578–9, 603, 617, 666, 682
Boulter v. Barclays Bank [1999] 4 All ER 513 (HL)   515–16
Bowmakers Ltd v. Barnet Industries Ltd [1945] KB 65   292, 296
Box v. Barclays Bank plc [1998] Lloyd's Rep Banking 185   108

Boyd & Forrest v. Glasgow & South Western Railway Co. 1915 SC (HL) 20; 1914 SC 472; 1912 SC (HL) 93; 1911 SC 33	175, 184, 252, 253, 282, 407–11
BP Exploration Co. (Libya) Ltd v. Hunt (No. 2) [1979] 1 WLR 783	183, 257
Brand's Trs v. Brand's Trs (1876) 3 R (HL) 16	415
Breunig v. American Family Ins. Co. 173 NW 2d 619 (Wis 1970)	233
Bridgeman v. Green (1757) Wilm 58	515
Bright v. Boyd (1841) 4 Fed Cas 127 (No. 1,875)	370, 375, 378
Brisbane v. Dacres (1813) 5 Taunt 143; 128 ER 641	59
British Steel Corporation v. Cleveland Bridge and Engineering Co. Ltd [1984] 1 All ER 504	633, 701
British Westinghouse Electric and Manufacturing Co. Ltd v. Underground Electric Railways Co. of London Ltd [1912] AC 673	456
Britton v. Turner (1834) 6 New Hampshire Rep 481	379
Brooklyn House Furnishers (Pty) Ltd v. Knoetze and Sons 1970 (3) SA 264 (A)	563
Broun v. Mitchel (1630) 1 BS 68	706
Brown and Davis v. Galbraith [1972] 1 WLR 997 (CA)	502
Brown v. Davis (1987) 514 So 2d 54 (Florida)	376, 502
Brown v. M'Kinally (1795) 1 Esp 279; 170 ER 356	61
Brown v. Nicolson (1629) Mor 8940	253
Buchanan v. Stewart (1874) 2 R 78	398, 399, 709
Buchanan and Carswell v. Eugene Limited 1936 SC 160	428
Building Design 2 Ltd v. Wascana Rehabilitation Centre [1992] 6 WWR 343 (Sask QB)	600
Burnes v. Pennell (1849) 2 HLC 497	282
Butler v. Hayes (1997) 487 SE 2d 229 (Virginia)	376
Butler v. Rice [1910] 2 Ch 277	521
Buzzard Electrical (Pty) Ltd v. 158 Jan Smuts Investments (Pty) Ltd 1996 (4) SA 19 (A)	529, 542–4, 546–7, 563–4
Byfield, Re [1992] 1 All ER 249	495
Byne v. Vivian (1800) 1 Ves Jun Supp 540; 34 ER 911	267
CIBC Mortgages plc v. Pitt [1994] 1 AC 200	504
CTN Cash and Carry Ltd v. Gallaher Ltd [1994] 4 All ER 714 (CA)	163, 704
Caledonia North Sea Ltd v. London Bridge Engineering Ltd 2000 SLT 1123	463, 470–1
Calloway Bank v. Ellis (1922) 215 Mo App 72; 238 SW 844	378
Campbell v. Campbell (1709) M 13432	429
Cano v. Lovato (1986) 105 New Mexico Rep 522; 734 P 2d 762	376

xvi   TABLE OF CASES

Cantiere San Rocco SA v. Clyde Shipbuilding & Engineering Co. Ltd [1924] AC 226; 1923 SC (HL) 105	67, 129–35, 142, 143, 154–5, 254, 266, 430, 659, 699
Caparo Industries plc v. Dickman [1990] 2 AC 605	630
Car and Universal Finance Company Ltd v. Caldwell [1965] 1 QB 525	582, 667
Carmichael v. Castlehill (1698) Mor 8993	246, 253
Carrick v. Carse (1778) Mor 2931	698
Cassell & Co. v. Broome [1972] AC 1027	498
Cavalier Insurance, Re [1989] Lloyd's L Rep 430	71
Chandler v. Webster [1904] 1 KB 493	66, 69, 130, 131, 659
Chase Manhattan Bank NA Ltd v. Israel-British Bank (London) Ltd [1981] Ch 105	77, 290, 668, 669, 724
Cheese v. Thomas [1994] 1 WLR 129	171–2
Chesworth v. Farrar [1967] 1 QB 407	654
Chettiar v. Chettiar [1962] AC 294	294, 296, 298
Chillingworth v. Esche [1924] 1 Ch 97	111, 137
Chisholm v. Alexander & Son (1882) 19 SLR 835	706
Christies's Executrix v. Armstrong 1996 SC 295	463
Cie Immobilière Viger Ltée v. Laureat Giguère Inc. [1977] 2 SCR 67	595, 607, 608
Citadel General Assurance Co. v. Lloyds Bank Canada [1997] 3 SCR 805; 152 DLR 4th 411	589
Citibank v. Brown Shipley [1991] 2 All ER 690	39
Citizens & Southern National Bank v. Modern Homes Constr. Co. (1966) 248 South Carolina Rep 130; 149 SE 2d 326	374
City of New Orleans v. Firemen's Charitable Association (1891) 9 So 486	331, 337–9
Clark v. Woods (1848) 2 Ex 395; 154 ER 545	217
Clarke v. Brodie (1801) Hume 548	709
Clarke v. Dickson, Williams and Gibbs (1858) El Bl & El 148	175, 245, 255
Claxton v. Kay 101 Ark 350; 142 SW 517 (1912)	508
Cleadon Trust Ltd, Re [1939] Ch 286	520–1
Clydesdale Bank v. Paul (1877) 4 R 626	722
Coca-Cola Bottling v. Coca-Cola 988 F 2d 386 (3rd Cir, 1953)	354
Cochrane v. Stevenson (1891) 18 R 1208	415
Commerce Partnership 8098 LP v. Equity Contracting Co. (1997) 695 So 2d 383	551–2
Commercial Bank of Australia v. Amadio (1983) 151 CLR 447	191
Commissioner for Stamp Duties v. Livingston [1965] AC 694 (PC)	516

Commissioner of Customs & Excise v. Randles, Brothers & Hudson Ltd 1941 AD 369	219
Commissioner of Inland Revenue v. First National Bank Ltd 1990 (3) SA 641 (A) 646	213
Commissioner of State Revenue v. Royal Insurance Australia Ltd (1994) 182 CLR 51 (HCA); (1994) 126 ALR 1	63, 312, 500
Commonwealth of Australia v. Verwayen (1990) 170 CLR 394	279
Cooper v. Phibbs (1867) LR 2 HL 149	189–190, 667
Co-operative Insurance Society Ltd v. Argyll Stores (Holdings) Ltd [1997] 2 WLR 898; [1997] 3 All ER 297	345–7, 449, 455
Corpe v. Overton (1833) 10 Bing 252; 131 ER 901	70–1
Countess of Cromertie v. Lord Advocate (1871) 9 M 988	715
Coutts & Co. v. Stock [2000] Lloyd's Rep 14	503
Craddock Bothers v. Hunt [1923] 2 ChD 136 (CA)	508
Cran v. Dodson (1893) 1 SLT 354	396
Craven-Ellis v. Canons Ltd [1936] 2 KB 403	105
Crawfurd v. Royal Bank (1749) Mor 875	674
Crédit Lyonnais v. George Stevenson and Co. Ltd (1901) 9 SLT 93	703
Crédit Lyonnaise Bank Nederland NV v. Burch [1997] 1 All ER 144	167
Crockett v. Sampson (1969) 439 SW 2d 355 (Texas Civil Appeals)	551, 552
Cumming v. Ince (1847) 11 QB 112	198
Cundy v. Lindsay (1878) 3 App Cas 459	250
Curtis v. Hannay (1800) 3 Esp 82; 170 ER 546	255
Custer Builders Inc. v. Quaker Heritage Inc. (1973) 41 App Div 2d 448; 334 NYS 2d 606	550
Cuthbertson v. Lowes (1870) 8 M 1073	406
Dales Service Co. v. Jones 96 Idaho 662; 534 P 2d 1102	550
Dalrymple, Frank & Feinstein v. Friedman and Another (No. 2) 1954 (4) SA 649 (W)	220
Darlington Borough Council v. Witshier Northern Ltd [1995] 1 WLR 68	336
David Securities Pty Ltd v. Commonwealth Bank of Australia (1992) 175 CLR 353	50, 53, 55, 60, 114, 256, 707
Davidson v. Bonafede 1981 (2) SA 501 (C)	221
Dawson v. Stirton (1863) 2 M 196	705
DeAngelo v. Brazauskas (1995) 86 NY 2d 746; 655 NE 2d 165	374
Dearns v. Andree 139 A 695 (Conn 1928)	237
Derry v. Peek (1889) 14 App Cas 337	196
Dies v. British and International Mining and Finance Corporation Ltd [1939] 1 KB 724	10, 123
Diesen v. Samson 1971 SLT 49	341

xviii   TABLE OF CASES

Diplock, Re [1948] Ch 465 524, 634
Dixon v. Monkland Canal Co. (1831) 5 W & S 445 664
Dollar Land (Cumbernauld) Limited v. CIN 131, 385, 387, 388, 390,
   Properties Limited 1998 SC (HL) 90; 1998 SLT 403, 466, 469, 659,
   992; 1997 SLT 260; 1996 SC 331 660, 685, 696
Donoghue v. Stevenson [1932] SC (HL) 31 29
Dorchester upon Medway CC v. Kent CC [1998] *The Times*,
   5 March 1998 120
Douglas v. Douglas' Trs (1864) 2 M 1379 396, 418, 422, 424, 709
Dowling v. McKenny 124 Mass 478 (1878) 236
Dowling & Rutter v. Abacus Frozen Foods Limited, 15 March
   2000 (unreported) 406
Doyle v. Olby [1969] 2 All ER 199 (CA) 231
Duff, Ross & Co. v. Kippen (1871) 8 SLR 299 403-4, 709
Duke of Hamilton v. Johnston (1877) 14 SLR 298 397, 398
Duke of Norfolk v. York Building Co. Annuitants' Trs (1752) Mor 7062 725
Dunbar Bank plc v. Nadeem [1998] 3 All ER 876; [1997]
   2 All ER 253 190, 255
Duncan v. Motherwell Bridge & Engineering Co. Ltd 1952 SC 131 470
Dunnebacke Co. v. Pittman (1934) 216 Wis 305; 257 NW 30 376
Dyer v. Dyer (1788) 2 Cox Eq 92 296, 297

ELCAP v. Milne's Executor 1998 SLT 58 (OH) 699
ERDC Construction v. HM Love & Co. 95 SLT 254 430
Earl of Aberdeen v. Gordon (1708) Mor 9031 268
Earl of Fife v. Wilson (1867) 3 M 323 706
Earthinfo Inc. v. Hydrosphere Resource Consultants Inc. 900 P 2d
   113 (Colorado 1995) 354
East Ham Corporation v. Bernard Sunley & Sons [1966] AC 406 328
Eastwood v. Kenyon (1840) 11 A & E 438; 113 ER 482 97-8
Edinburgh and District Tramways Co. Ltd v. Courtenay
   1909 SC 99 389, 421, 474
Edinburgh Life Assurance Corporation v. Balderston 1909 2 SLT 323 396, 419
Edwards v. Lee's Administrator (1936) 96 SW 2d 1028 498, 510
El Ajou v. Dollar Land Holdings plc [1994] 2 All ER 685 (CA); [1993]
   3 All ER 717 515
Elder v. Clarke (1944) 385 Illinois Rep 335; 52 NE 2d 778 378
Elektrorätefall BGHZ 40, 272 544-5
Ellis v. Fraser (1840) 3 D 264 717
Elphick v. Barnes (1880) LR 5 CP 321 255
Emmerson v. Emmerson (1939) Sh Ct Rep 46 470

TABLE OF CASES   xix

Erlanger v. New Sombrero Phosphate Co. (1878)
   3 App Cas 1218   116, 176, 204
Esgro Inc., Re 645 F 2d 794   556
Esso Petroleum Co. Ltd v. Hall Russell & Co. Ltd 1988 SLT 874 (HL)   463
Express Coach Finishers v. Caulfield 1968 SLT (Sh Ct) 11   396, 502, 717
Extruded Welding Wire (Sales) Ltd v. McLachlan and Brown 1986
   SLT 314   718, 722
Eyre v. Burmester (1864) 4 De G & J 435   722

F. C. Jones (Trustee in Bankruptcy) v. Jones [1997] Ch 159 (CA)   501, 509
Fabian v. Wasatch Orchard Co. 125 P 860 (Utah 1912)   238
Falcke v. Scottish Imperial Insurance Co. (1886)
   34 ChD 234   98, 312, 447, 652
Farmer v. Arundel (1772) 2 Black W 824; 96 ER 485   56
Farquhar v. Campbell (1628) Mor 9022   253
Felder v. Reeth 34 F 2d 744 (9th Cir 1929)   240
Fibrosa Spolka Akcyjna v. Fairbairn Lawson Combe   66–7, 69, 77, 105, 108,
   Barbour Ltd [1943] AC 32   110, 129, 133–5, 151, 155, 257
Fielder v. Starkin (1788) 1 H Bl 17; 126 ER 11   255
First National Bank v. B. & H. Engineering 1993 (2) SA 41 (T)   535–8
First National Bank plc v. Bank of Scotland 1999 SLT (Sh Ct) 10   478
Fisher v. Samuda (1808) 1 Camp 194; 170 ER 925   245
Fleming & Co. (Ltd) v. Airdrie Iron Co. (1882) 9 R 473   255
Fletcher and Fletcher v. Bulawayo Waterworks Co. Ltd 1915 AD 636   426
Fraser v. Hankey & Co. (1847) 9 D 415   409
Friesen (P. H.) Ltd v. Cypress Colony Farms Ltd (1993) 87 Man R
   2d 250 (QB)   606
Frost v. Chief Constable of South Yorkshire Police [1999] 2
   AC 455   640, 641, 655
Frostifresh v. Reynoso 274 NYS 2d 757 (SupCt 1966)   231
Fulton v. Fulton (1864) 2 M 893   473

G. L. Baker Ltd v. Medway Building & Supplies Ltd [1958] 1 WLR 1216   634
Gaertner v. Fiesta Dance Studios Ltd (1972) 32 DLR 3d 639   185
Gagné v. Tremblay [1989] RJQ 1619 (Que Ct)   597, 599
Gamerco SA v. ICM/Fair Warning Ltd [1995] 1 WLR 1226   257, 280
Garriock v. Walker (1873) 1 R 100   488
Gebhardt v. Saunders [1892] 2 QB 452   446
General Property Investment Co. v. Matheson's Trustees (1888) 16 R 282   254
Gibbs v. British Linen (1875) 4 R 630   722
Giffen, Lee & Wagner v. Zellers Ltd (1993) 15 OR 3d 387 (Gen Div)   603

Gilbert v. Hannah (1924) 40 Sh Ct Rep 262	473
Giles v. Edwards (1797) 7 TR 181; 101 ER 920	113, 635
Gilmer v. Galloway (1830) 8 S 420	255
Glasgow Corporation v. Lord Advocate 1959 SC 203	664
Glen v. Roy (1882) 10 R 239	706
Goldberg v. Bank of Alice Brown (Re Goldberg) (1994) 168 BR 382 (Bankr 9th Cir)	555–6, 557–8
Goldcorp Exchange, Re [1995] 1 AC 74	724
Goss v. Chilcott [1996] AC 788	70, 114–15, 302, 635
Gouws v. Jester Pools (Pty) Ltd 1968 (3) SA 563 (T)	529, 562–3, 564, 684
Govender v. The Standard Bank of South Africa Ltd 1984 (4) SA 392 (C)	21, 478–9, 481–2, 534–5
Graham v. Western Bank of Scotland (1864) 2 M 559	246, 253, 282
Graham's Executors v. Fletcher's Executors (1870) 9 M 298	711
Gray's Exor v. Johnston 1928 SC 659	709
Gray's Truck Centre Ltd v. Olaf L. Johnson Ltd, 25 January 1990 (CA, unreported)	502
Green v. Portsmouth Stadium Ltd [1953] 2 QB 190	303–4
Greenwood v. Bennett [1973] 1 QB 195	49, 384, 652, 708
Greisshammer v. Ungerer (1958) 14 DLR 2d 599	185
Grieve v. Morrison 1993 SLT 852	699
Griffith v. Commonwealth Bank (1994) 123 ALR 111	53
Guinness plc v. Saunders [1990] 2 AC 663	268, 270, 279
Guinness Mahon & Co. Ltd v. Kensington and Chelsea Royal London Borough Council [1999] QB 215	68, 82–3, 91, 120, 140, 153, 618
Guldberg v. Greenfield (1966) 259 Iowa 873; 146 NW 2d 298	551
Guthrie & McConnachy v. Smith (1880) 8 R 107	470
Hadley v. Baxendale (1854) 9 Ex 341	455
Haggarty v. Scottish Transport and General Workers Union 1955 SC 109	254, 280
Hambly v. Trott (1776) 1 Cowp 371; 98 ER 1136	501
Hamilton v. Lochrane (1899) 1 F 478	429
Hanson v. Keating (1844) 4 Hare 1	190
Harris v. Nugent (1996) 193 AR 113; 141 DLR 4th 410 (CA)	603
Hart v. O'Connor [1985] AC 1000	166
Hastelow v. Jackson (1828) 8 B & C 221	306–7
Hazell v. Hammersmith and Fulham London Borough Council [1992] 2 AC 1 (HL); [1991] 1 All ER 545; [1990] 3 All ER 33; [1990] 2 QB 697 (CA)	14, 80, 149–50, 303
Head v. Tattersall (1871) LR 7 Ex 7	255, 268, 274, 279

TABLE OF CASES xxi

Heddle v. Baikie (1846) 8 D 376; (1843) 15 Scottish Jurist 559;
(1841) 3 D 370   404
Henderson v. Merrett Syndicates Ltd [1995] 2 AC 145   9, 629, 654
Henry v. Morrison (1881) 8 R 692   674
Heritable Reversionary Co. Ltd v. Millar (1892) 19 R (HL) 43   677
Hermann v. Charlesworth [1905] 2 KB 123   302, 308
Heron v. Stewart (1749) 3 Ross LC 243   583
Hesjedal v. Granville Estate (1993) 117 Sask R 2d 111;
109 DLR 4th 353 (QB)   600
Hoffman v. Sportsman Yachts Inc. (1992) 89 DLR 4th 600 (CA)   614–15
Holiday v. Sigil (1826) 2 C & P 176; 172 ER 81   499
Holman v. Johnson (1775) 1 Cowp 341; 98 ER 1120   294, 310, 315, 316
Home & Colonial Insurance v. London Guarantee (1928)
32 Lloyd's Rep 267   41, 71
Hooper v. Exeter Corporation [1887] 56 LJQB 457   664
Horcal v. Gatland [1984] Industrial Relations Law Reports 288   39
Horne v. Horne's Executors 1963 SLT (Sh Ct) 37   709
Hospital Products v. US Surgical (1984) 156 CLR 41   354
Houldsworth v. City of Glasgow Bank (1880) 7 R (HL) 53; (1879) 6
R 1164   253, 282
Houston & T. C. Ry v. Hughes 133 SW 731 (Texas Civil Appeals 1911)   238–9
Howard v. Wood (1679) 2 Lev 245; 83 ER 530   507
Hudson v. New York & Albany Transportation Co. (1911) 188
F 630 (2nd Cir)   378
Hughes v. Liverpool Victoria Legal Friendly Society [1916] 2
KB 483   299, 301, 306
Huisman v. Soepboer 1994 SLT 682 (OH)   668
Hunt v. Silk (1804) 5 East 449; 102 ER 1142   245, 635
Hussey Seating Co. (Canada) Ltd v. Ottawa (City) (1997) 145 DLR 4th 493
(Gen Div); affirmed (1998) 41 OR 3d 254 (CA)   607

IRC v. Woolwich Building Society [1993] AC 70   28, 59, 64–5, 69, 78–9
92, 124, 127, 135, 630
655, 664–5, 698, 711, 712
Indianapolis Raceway Park Inc. v. Curtiss (1979) 386 NE 2d 724   550
Inland Revenue v. Clark's Trs 1939 SC 11   676
International Sales and Agencies Ltd v. Marcus [1982] 3 All ER 551   634

J. & S. Holdings v. NRMA Insurance (1982) 41 ALR 539   57
J. B. Mackenzie (Edinburgh) Ltd v. Lord Advocate 1972 SC 231   421, 717
Jack v. Pollock (1665) M 13412   424

Jacob v. Allen (1703) 1 Salk 27; 91 ER 26	507
Jacob & Youngs, Inc. v. Kent (1921) 230 New York Rep 239; 129 NE 889	378
Jaggard v. Sawyer [1995] 1 WLR 269	329, 342–4
James v. Bailey (1974) 370 F Supp 469 (DVI)	379
Jamieson v. Watt's Trustee 1950 SC 265	406
Jensen v. Probert (1944) 174 Oregon Rep 143; 148 P 2d 248	374
Johnson v. Agnew [1980] AC 367	245
Johnson v. Unisys Ltd [1999] 1 All ER 854	337
Jones v. Star Credit Corp. 298 NYS 2d 264 (SupCt 1969)	231
Jones Ltd v. Waring & Gillow Ltd, Re [1925] 2 KB 612; rejected [1926] AC 670 (HL)	505
Karon v. Kellogg (1935) 195 Minnesota Rep 134; 261 NW 861	374
Kearley v. Thomson (1890) 24 QBD 742	307–8
Kelly v. Solari (1841) 9 M & W 54; 152 ER 24	38, 68, 506, 718
Kennedy v. Kennedy (1911) 20 Sh Ct Rep 183	470
Kerrison v. Glyn, Mills, Currie & Co. (1911) 81 LJKB 465	49, 651
Kettlewell v. Refuge Assurance Co. [1908] 1 KB 545	185
Kidd v. Rountree (1941) 285 Kentucky Rep 442; 148 SW 2d 275	378
Kinnear v. Brodie (1901) 3 F 540	255, 268, 273, 279
Kiriri Cotton Co. v. Dewani [1960] AC 192	57–8, 64, 185, 290, 301–2
Kirklands Garage (Kinross) Ltd v. Clark 1967 SLT (Sh Ct) 60	718
Kleinwort Benson v. Birmingham City Council [1997] QB 380; [1996] 4 All ER 733 (CA)	68–9, 118, 312, 501, 642
Kleinwort Benson v. South Tyneside Metropolitan Borough Council [1994] 4 All ER 972	68, 284
Kleinwort Benson Ltd v. Lincoln City Council [1999] 2 AC 349; [1998] 3 WLR 1095; [1998] 4 All ER 513	15, 28, 55, 58, 68, 69, 73, 74–5, 80, 83–5, 91–3, 99, 107, 118, 119, 120, 121, 125, 149, 302, 312, 590, 618–19, 640, 649–50, 655, 656, 663, 698
Kleinwort Benson Ltd v. Sandwell Borough Council [1994] 4 All ER 890	81–2, 150, 151
Kommissaris van Binnelandse Inkomste v. Willers 1994 (3) SA 283 (A); [1995] Restitution LR 218	684
Kopelowitz v. West and Others 1954 (4) SA 296 (W) 300	219
Krell v. Henry [1903] 2 KB 740	130, 659
LAC Minerals Ltd v. Corona Resources Ltd [1989] 2 SCR 574; 61 DLR 4th 14	506

TABLE OF CASES   xxiii

Lady Hood of Avalon v. Mackinnon [1909] 1 Ch 476   44, 47
Larner v. London County Council [1949] 2 KB 683   41–4, 46
Lawrence Building Co. Ltd v. Lanark Country Council 1978
    SC 30   412, 474–5, 709
Lechoana v. Cloete 1925 AD 536   394
Lee v. Muggeridge (1813) 5 Taunt 36   97
Leggatt Brothers v. Gray 1908 SC 67   480
Leigh and Sillivan Ltd v. Aliakmon Shipping Co. Ltd [1986] AC 785   650
Leuty v. Hillas (1858) 2 De G & J 110   508
Ligertwood v. Brown (1872) 10 M 832   473
Linden Gardens Trust Ltd v. Lenesta Sludge Disposals Ltd [1994]
    1 AC 85   335–6
Lipkin Gorman (a Firm) v. Karpnale Ltd   28, 106, 168, 169, 173, 227, 250,
    [1991] 2 AC 548 (HL)   514–15, 517, 518, 519, 575, 630, 634–5,
    641–3, 655, 668–9, 703, 712, 717, 722
Lloyds Bank plc v. Independent Insurance Co. Ltd [2000] QB 110;
    [1999] 2 WLR 986 (CA)   125, 478, 482, 503, 650
London County Commercial Reinsurance Office, Re [1922] 2 Ch 67   71
Lord Napier and Ettrick v. Hunter [1993] AC 713   666
Loungnarath v. Centre Hospitalier des Laurentides [1996] RJQ 2498   608
Louth v. Diprose (1992) 175 CLR 621   78, 166
Lumley v. Wagner (1852) 1 De G M & G 604; 42 ER 687   347
Luscar Ltd v. Pembina Resources Ltd (1994) 24 Alta LR 3d 305;
    [1995] 2 WWR 153 (CA)   600, 608
Lynch v. DPP of Northern Ireland [1975] AC 695   200

M. & I. Instrument Engineers Ltd v. Varsada 1991 SLT 106 (OH)   723
Mackay v. Rodger (1907) 15 SLT 42   405
MacKenzie v. Royal Bank of Canada [1934] AC 468   173, 180, 187–8
Macmillan Inc. v. Bishopsgate Investment Trust plc [1996] 1 WLR 387 (CA)   590
Madrid v. Spears (1957) 250 F 2d 51 (10th Cir)   375–376
Magee v. Pennine Insurance Co. Ltd [1969] 2 QB 507   250
Magistrates of Rutherglen v. Cullen (1773) 2 Paton 305   406–7, 417
Magistrates of Selkirk v. Clapperton (1830) 9 S 9   709
Magistrates of Stonehaven v. Kincardineshire CC 1939 SC 760   700
Mahon v. Mahon (1963) 254 Iowa 1349; 121 NW 2d 103   375
Mahoney v. Purnell [1996] 3 All ER 61   172, 255
Maitland v. Gight (1675) Mor 9158   246
Mandell-Vasquez Inc. v. University of Toledo 67 Ohio Misc 2d 24
    (1993, Ohio Ct Cl); 664 NE 2d 740   552

TABLE OF CASES

Manning v. Wingo (1991) 577 So 2d 865 (Alabama) — 376
Mansfield v. Walker's Trs (1833) 11 S 813; affirmed (1835)
   1 Sh & Macl 203; 3 Ross LC 139 — 716, 724–5
Maskell v. Horner [1915] 3 KB 106 (CA) — 61, 704
Mason v. NSW (1959) 102 CLR 108 — 62, 63, 500
Matheson v. Smiley [1932] 2 DLR 787 — 653
McCormick v. Rittmeyer (1869) 7 M 854 — 245, 255
McDowel v. McDowel (1906) 14 SLT 125 (OH) — 401, 425, 709
McFarlane v. Tayside Health Board [1999] 3 WLR 1301 — 645, 648, 655
McGuire v. Makaronis (1997) 144 ALR 729 — 186, 189
McKay v. Brodie (1801) Hume 549 — 709
McKay v. Horseshoe Lake Hop Harvesters, Inc. (1971) 260 Oregon
   Rep 612; 491 P 2d 1180 — 378
McKelway v. Armour (1854) 10 NJ Eq 115 — 380
McKenzie v. Royal Bank of Canada [1934] AC 468 — 191, 255
McWilliam v. Shaw (1576) Mor 9022 — 253
Mellor v. William Beardmore & Co. 1927 SC 597 — 706
Melvil v. Arnot (1782) Mor 8998 — 253
Merkel Motors v. Bodenstein en 'n ander 1980 (3) SA 917 (A) — 219
Merton and Another v. Hammond Suddards and Another [1996]
   2 BCLC 470 — 94
Mesirow v. Duggan (1957) 240 F 2d 751 (8th Cir) — 378
Mess v. Sime's Tr [1899] AC 233; (1898) 1 F (HL) 22, affirming 25 R 398 — 677
Michael v. Carruthers 1998 SLT 1179 — 390
Michigan Central RR v. State 155 NE 50 (Ind 1927) — 239
Middleton v. Newton Display Group Limited, 9 October 1990
   (Glasgow Sheriff Court, unreported) — 407
Miller v. Campbell 1991 GWD 26-1477 (Extra Division) — 698
Miller v. Race (1758) 1 Burr 452 — 94
Ministry of Defence v. Ashman (1993) 66 P & C R 195; [1993]
   2 EGLR 102 — 183, 184, 648
Ministry of Health v. Simpson [1951] AC 251 (HL) — 508, 516, 521
Moffatt v. Kazana [1969] 2 QB 152 — 499
Mogul Steamship Co. v. McGregor, Gow & Co. [1892] AC 25 — 303
Monro v. Findlay (1698) Mor 1768 — 705
Montagu's Settlement Trusts, Re [1987] Ch 264 — 634
Moore's Executors v. M'Dermid [1913] 1 SLT 278 — 42
Morgan v. Ashcroft [1938] 1 KB 49 — 41, 43–4, 46
Morgan v. Morgan's Judicial Factor 1922 SLT 247 — 419
Morgan Guaranty Trust v. Lothian Regional Council — 73, 387, 390, 402, 405,
   1995 SLT 299 — 464–5, 475, 482, 658, 663, 696, 702

Morrisons v. Allan (1886) 13 R 1156   399, 709
Mortgage Corporation v. Mitchells Roberton 1997 SLT 1305   585, 667, 729
Moses v. Macferlan (1760) 2 Burr 1005; 97 ER 676   56, 211, 498–9, 610
Moss v. Penman 1993 SC 300   463
Municipal Council of Johannesburg v. D. Stewart & Co. (1902) Ltd
   1909 SC (HL) 53   263
Munt v. Stokes (1792) 4 TR 561; 100 ER 1176   56
Murphy v. Attorney-General [1982] Irish Reports 241   63
Mutual Finance v. Wetton [1937] 2 KB 389   166
Myers v. Canutt (1951) 242 Iowa 692; 46 NW 2d 72; 24 ALR 2d 1   376

Nadeau v. Doyon [1994] RJQ 2267 (Que Ct)   598
Napier v. Elphingston (1746) M 13434   429
Nasmith v. Nasmith (1681) Mor 13479   473
National Bank of New Zealand Ltd v. Waitaki International Processing
   (NI) Ltd [1999] 2 NZLR 211   642
National Coal Board v. England [1954] AC 403   292
National Pari-Mutuel Association v. R. (1930) 47 TLR 110;
   (1929) 46 TLR 594   664
Naysmith v. Naysmiths (1682) Mor 5319   473
Neate v. Harding (1851) 6 Ex 349; 155 ER 577   499
Nepean v. Ontario Hydro (1982) 132 DLR (3d) 193   55, 62
New Mining and Exploring Syndicate v. Chalmers and Hunter 1912 SC 126   722
Newdigate v. Davy [1693] 1 Ld Raym 742; 91 ER 1397   664
Newton v. Newton 1925 SC 715; 1923 SC 15   398–9, 400, 401–4, 709
Nichols v. Jessup [1986] 1 NZLR 226   167
Nicholson v. Chapman (1793) 2 H Bl 254; 126 ER 536   98, 652
Nicholson v. St Denis (1975) 8 OR 2d 315; 57 DLR 3d 699 (Ont CA)   603
North British Railway Co. v. Tod (1893) 9 Sh Ct Rep 326   488
Nortje en 'n ander v. Pool 1966 (3) SA 96 (A)   419, 684
Norwich Union Fire Insurance v. Price [1934] AC 455   39
Nurdin & Peacock plc v. D. B. Ramsden & Co. Ltd [1999]
   1 WLR 1249   50, 61, 125, 497, 704

Official Custodian for Charities v. Mackey (No. 2) [1985] 1 WLR 1308   508
Ogilvie v. Littleboy (1893) 13 TLR 399   52
Olin v. Reinecke (1929) 336 Illinois Rep 530; 168 NE 676   376
Olwell v. Nye & Nissen 173 P 2d 652 (Wash 1946);
   26 wash 2d 282   348–50, 354, 510
Orakpo v. Manson Investments Ltd [1978] AC 95   9
O'Sullivan v. Management Agency & Music Ltd [1985] QB 428   175, 255

xxvi TABLE OF CASES

Paal Wilson & Co. A/S v. Partenreederei Hannah Blumenthal
  [1983] 1 AC 854   263
Pan Ocean Shipping Co. Ltd v. Creditcorp Ltd   110, 497, 502,
  (The Trident Beauty) [1994] 1 WLR 161;   548–50, 560, 600,
  [1994] 1 All ER 470   603, 607, 614
Panatown Ltd v. Alfred McAlpine Construction Ltd [2000] 4 All ER 97   11
Pao On v. Lau Yiu Long [1980] AC 614   185, 186, 200, 298
Parkinson v. College of Ambulance [1925] 2 KB 1   298–9, 318, 324
Parrish v. Tahtaras 318 P 2d 642 (1957)   237
Paton v. Lockhat (1675) Mor 14232   255
Pattinson v. Luckley (1875) LR 10 Ex 30   510
Pavage Rolland Fortier Inc. v. Caisse Populaire Desjardins de la Plaine
  [1998] RJQ 1221 (SC)   602, 618
Pearce v. Brain [1929] 2 KB 310   70, 250
Penarth Dock Engineering Co. Ltd v. Pounds [1963] 1 Lloyd's Rep 359   328
Pendelton v. Sard (1972) 297 A 2d 889 (Maine); 62 ALR 3d 277   550
Personal Representatives of Tang Man Sit v. Capacious
  Investments Ltd [1996] AC 514   654
Phoenix General Insurance Co. of Greece SA v. Administratia
  Asigurarilor de Stat [1987] 2 All ER 152   310
Phoenix Life Assurance Co., Re (1862) 2 J & H 441; 70 ER 1131   154
Photo Production Ltd v. Securicor Transport Ltd [1980] AC 827   245, 263
Pitt v. Coomes (1835) 2 A & E 459; 111 ER 178   217
Planché v. Colburn (1831) 8 Bing 14; 131 ER 305   238
Port Caledonian, The and The Anna [1903] P 184   186
Portman Building Society v. Hamlyn Taylor Neck [1998] 4 All ER
  202 (CA)   514, 619
Powell v. Mayo (1981) 123 Cal App 3d 994; 177 Cal Rptr 66   374
Power v. Wells (1778) 2 Cowp 818; 98 ER 1379   255
Procter & Gamble Philippine Manufacturing Corp. v. Peter Cremer GmbH
  [1988] 3 All ER 843   183
Property Selection and Investment Trust v. United Friendly plc
  1999 SLT 975   416
Pulbrook v. Lawes (1876) 1 QBD 284   123
Pull v. Barnes (1960) 142 Colorado Rep 272; 350 P 2d 828   380

Quint v. Te Poel, NJ 1959, 546   683

R. v. Ilich (1987) 162 CLR 110   250
R. v. Tower Hamlets [1988] AC 858   62
R. Leslie Ltd v. Sheill [1914] 3 KB 607   170

Raab v. Casper (1975) 51 Cal App 3d 866; 124 Cal Rptr 590	377
Radford v. De Froberville [1977] 1 WLR 1262	341–2
Ramsay v. Brand (1898) 25 R 1212	416
Rankin v. Wither (1886) 13 R 903	398, 399, 402–3, 406, 709
Read v. Goldring (1813) 2 M & S 86; 105 ER 314	446
Redgrave v. Hurd (1881) 20 ChD 1	167
Reedie v. Yeaman (1875) SLR 625	405, 420, 425
Regalian Properties plc v. London Docklands Development Corp. [1995] 1 WLR 212	110–11, 633
Reid v. Lord Ruthven (1918) 55 SLR 616	470, 472, 711
Reid v. Rigby & Co. [1894] 2 QB 40	520
Rigg v. Durward and Thom (1776) Mor 5672, Mor Appendix, 'Fraud' 6	253
Rigg v. Durward Mor Appendix *sub* 'Fraud' No. 2	409
Rillford Investments Ltd v. Gravure International Capital Corp. (1997) 118 Man R 2d 11; [1997] 7 WWR 534 (CA)	601, 615
Robertson v. Beatson McLeod & Co. 1908 SC 921	717
Robertsons v. Strachans (1760) Mor 8087	714
Rogers v. Ingham [1876] 3 Ch 351	59
Rookes v. Barnard [1964] AC 1129 (HL)	498
Rose, Re [1952] Ch 78 (CA)	507
Ross Harper & Murphy v. Banks 2000 SC 500	463
Rover International Ltd v. Cannon Films Sales Ltd (No. 3) [1989] 1 WLR 912 (CA)	68, 105, 123, 141, 616, 701
Rowland v. Divall [1923] 2 KB 500	113, 328
Royal Bank of Scotland v. Ettridge (No. 2) [1998] 4 All ER 705	167, 170, 173
Royal Bank of Scotland v. Holmes 1999 SCLR 297 (OH)	723
Royal Brunei Airlines Sdn Bhd v. Tan [1995] 2 AC 378	635
Rutherford v. Rankine and Lees (1782) M 13422	422
Ruxley Electronics and Construction Ltd v. Forsyth [1996] AC 344 (HL)	335, 340, 378
Sabemo Pty Ltd v. North Sydney Municipal Council [1977] 2 NSWLR 880	633
Sadler v. Scott [1947] 1 DLR 712 (BCCA)	590
St Andrews Magistrates v. Forbes (1893) 31 SLR 225	714
Salvation Army Trustee Co. Ltd v. West Yorkshire Metropolitan County Council (1981) 41 P & C R 179	633
Saronic v. Huron [1979] 1 Lloyd's L Rep 341	60
Sawyer & Vincent v. Window Brace [1943] 1 KB 32	59
Scotland North British and Mercantile Insurance Co. v. Stewart (1871) 9 M 534	277
Scott v. Noble (1994) 99 BCLR 2d 137 (CA)	600

Scott's Executors v. Hepburn (1876) 3 R 816	398, 399
Scott's Trs v. Scott (1887) 14 R 1043	418
Sebel Products Ltd v. Customs and Excise Commissioners [1949] Ch 409	497
Selangor United Rubber Estates Ltd v. Cradock (No. 3) [1968] 1 WLR 1555	634
Selby's Heirs v. Jollie (1795) M 13458	421
Shamia v. Joory [1958] 1 QB 448	507
Sharp v. Pollock's Trustees (1822) 1 S 339	429
Sharp v. Thomson 1997 SLT 636; 1997 SCLR 328	572
Sharp Brothers & Knight v. Chant [1917] 1 KB 771	57
Shaw v. Shaw [1965] 1 WLR 537	304
Sheffield Nickel and Silver Planting Co. Ltd v. Unwin (1877) 2 QBD 218	175
Shetland Islands Council v. BP Petroleum Development Co. Ltd 1990 SLT 82 (OH); 1989 SCLR 48 (OH)	706
Shield Benefit Administrators v. University of Michigan 225 Mich App 467; 571 NW 2d 556 (1997)	504
Shilliday v. Smith 998 SC 725 (1st Division)	92, 385–90, 399–400, 404–6, 418, 427, 465–6, 469, 585, 659, 685, 699
Siboen, The and The Sibotre [1976] AC 104	185
Sinclair v. Brougham [1914] AC 398 (HL)	659
Singh v. Ali [1960] AC 167	293, 294, 296, 297, 582
Singh v. Singh [1993] 2 WWR 59 (CA); (1992) 71 BCLR 2d 336	250, 600
Skeate v. Beale (1841) 11 A & E 983; 113 ER 688	198
Slater v. Burnley Corporation (1888) 59 LT 636	664, 704
Smit v. Abrahams 1994 SA 1 (A)	557
Smith v. Bromley (1760) 2 Doug 696	301, 302, 306
Smith v. Hughes (1871) LR 6 QB 597	166
Smith v. Liquidator of James Birrell Ltd 1968 SLT 174	722
Smith v. Littlewoods Organisation Ltd [1987] AC 241	640
Smith v. Stewart (1983) 10 Ark App 201; 662 SW 2d 202	380
Smith New Court Securities Ltd v. Scrimgeour Vickers (Asset Management) Ltd [1997] AC 254	116, 176
Snepp v. United States 444 US 507 (1980)	350, 360–4
Sodden v. Prudential Assurance Co. Ltd 1999 SCLR 367 (2nd Division)	723
Solle v. Butcher [1950] 1 KB 671	250
Somerville v. Jacobs (1969) 153 W Va 613; 170 SE 2d 805	370
Soues v. Mill (1903) 11 SLT 98	399, 709
South Tyneside Metropolitan Borough Council v. Svenska International plc [1995] 1 All ER 545	68, 284, 642
Southern Cross Commodities Property Ltd v. Martin 1991 SLT 83 (OH)	668
Sowell v. Champion (1838) 6 A & E 407; 112 ER 156	217

TABLE OF CASES xxix

Spence v. Crawford [1939] 3 All ER 271; 175, 176, 204, 252,
1939 SC (HL) 52 253, 255, 276, 279, 582, 583
Spice Girls Ltd v. Aprilia World Service (unreported), 12 June 2000   116
Spiliada Maritime Corporation v. Cansulex Ltd [1987] AC 461   640
Spiro v. Glencrown Properties Ltd [1991] Ch 537   96
Spring v. Guardian Assurance plc [1995] 2 AC 296   628
Standard Bank Financial Services Ltd v. Taylam (Property) Ltd
1979 (2) SA 383 (C)   481
Standard Kredietkorporasie v. JOT Motors (Edms) Bpk h/a Vaal Motors
1986 (1) SA 223 (A)   563
Steam Saw Mills v. Baring Brothers [1922] 1 Ch 244   53
Steel's Tr v. Bradley Homes 1972 SC 48   253
Steinberg v. Scala Ltd [1923] 2 Ch 452   70
Sterling v. Marshall 54 A 2d 353 (DC 1947)   237
Stewart v. Steuart (1878) 6 R 145   00
Stewart's Trs v. Evans (1871) 9 M 810   714
Stock v. Wilson [1913] 2 KB 235   250
Stocznia Gdanska SA v. Latvian Shipping Co. [1998]
1 WLR 574   104–5, 111, 115, 338
Stuarts v. Whiteford and the Duke of Hamilton (1677) Mor 16489   253, 282
Style Financial Services Ltd v. Bank of Scotland 1997 SCLR 633
(OH); 1996 SLT 421 (2nd Division)   722, 723
Sumpter v. Hedges [1998] 1 QB 673   410
Surrey County Council v. Bredero Homes Ltd [1993] 1 WLR
1361; [1993] 3 All ER 705   329, 342, 343–4, 354
Sweeten v. King (1976) 29 NC App 672; 225 SE 2d 598   376
Swindle v. Harrison [1997] 4 All ER 705   648
Sybron Corp. v. Rochem [1984] Ch 111   39
Syme v. Harvey (1861) 24 R 202   415
Symes v. Hughes (1870) LR 9 Eq 475   295, 296, 298

TSB Bank plc v. Camfield [1995] 1 WLR 430   173, 189, 190, 191
Taylor v. Bowers (1876) 1 QBD 291   305–8
Taylor v. Caldwell (1863) 3 B & S 826   256
Taylor v. Forbes (1830) 4 W & S 444; 5 ER 828   722
Taylor (S.A.) Building Ltd v. Von Muenchhausen (1995) 165 NBR 2d 219;
424 APR 219 (CA)   603
Tennent v. City of Glasgow Bank (1879) 6 R 554; (1869) 6 R (HL) 68   246, 253
The Tao Men 1996 (1) SA 559 (CPD)   220
Thienhaus v. Metje & Ziegler Ltd 1965 (3) SA 25 (A) 45   215

TABLE OF CASES

Thom v. Jardine (1836) 14 S 1004	473
Thomas v. Brown (1876) 1 QBD 714	109
Thomas v. Houston Corbett & Co. [1969] NZLR 151 (NZCA)	505
Thomson v. Clydesdale Bank (1893) 20 R (HL) 59	722, 723
Thomson, Jackson, Gourlay, Taylor v. Lochead (1889) 16 R 373	559
Thorpe v. Fasey [1949] Ch 649	175
Tinsley v. Milligan [1994] 1 AC 340; [1992] Ch 310	295–8, 315, 316, 322
Tito v. Waddell (No. 2) [1977] Ch 106	328, 340, 341–2
Tompkins v. Sandeen (1954) 243 Minnesota Rep 256; 67 NW 2d 405	378
Tootal Clothing Ltd v. Guinea Properties Ltd (1991) 64 P & CR 452	96–7
Toronto-Dominion Bank v. Carotenuto (1997) 154 DLR 4th 627 (CA)	603
Towers v. Barrett (1786) 1 TR 133; 99 ER 1014	255
Trade Development Bank v. Warriner & Mason (Scotland) Limited 1980 SC 74	402
Trades House of Glasgow v. Ferguson 1979 SLT 187	463
Transvaal and Delagoa Bay Investment Co. v. Atkinson [1944] 1 All ER 579	210
Tribe v. Tribe [1996] Ch 107; [1995] 3 WLR 913	296, 305, 315–16
Trust Bank van Afrika Bpk v. Western Bank Bpk en Andere NNO 1978 (4) SA 281 (A)	219
Turf Masters Landscaping Ltd v. TAG Developments Ltd (1995) 143 NSR 2d 275; 411 APR 275 (CA)	605, 607
Twinsectra Ltd v. Yardley [1999] Lloyd's Rep Banking 438 (CA)	589
Twyford v. Manchester Corporation [1946] Ch 236	62, 664, 704
United Australia Ltd v. Barclays Bank Ltd [1941] AC 1 (HL)	497, 499
United Building Society v. Snookler's Trustees 1906 Transvaal Supreme Court Reports 623	426
United States v. Francis (1985) 623 F Supp 535 (DVI)	374
Universal Import Export GmbH v. Bank of Scotland 1995 SC 73; 1995 SLT 1318 (2nd Division)	723, 725
Vadasz v. Pioneer Concrete (SA) Pty Ltd (1995) 184 CLR 102	173, 189, 190, 191
Varney (Scotland) Limited v. Lanark Town Council 1974 SC 245	389–90, 413, 474–5, 709
Vickery v. Ritchie (1909) 202 Massachusetts Rep 247; 88 NE 835 (Mass 1909)	240, 375
Vigers v. Pike (1842) 8 Cl & F 562; 8 ER 220	175

Voss v. Forgue (1956) 84 So 2d 563 (Florida)	376
Vulovich v. Baich (1955) 286 App Div 403; 143 NYS 2d 247	379
Wadsworth v. Lydall [1981] 1 WLR 598	455
Walker v. Milne (1825) 3 S 478; (1824) 3 S 123; (1823) 2 S 379	681
Wallace v. Braid (1900) 2 F 754	399
Waltons Stores (Interstate) Ltd v. Maher (1988) 164 CLR 387	279
Webb v. Webb [1994] ECR I-1717	571
Westdeutsche Landesbank Girozentrale v. Islington London Borough Council [1996] AC 669 (HL); [1996] 2 All ER 961 (HL); [1994] All ER 890; [1994] 1 WLR 938 (CA)	15, 60, 68–70, 73, 80, 81–2, 95, 99, 107, 118, 126, 149, 150, 151, 152, 153, 154, 178, 210, 582, 640, 668, 712, 724
Western Bank of Scotland v. Addie (1867) 5 M (HL) 80	252, 253
Westpac Banking Corp. v. Savin [1985] 2 NZLR 41	634
Whincup v. Hughes (1871) LR 6 CP 78	370, 635
White v. Garden (1851) 10 CB 919	175
White v. Jones [1995] 2 AC 207	640, 645
White Arrow Express Ltd v. Lamey's Distribution Ltd (1996) Trading Law Reports 69	335
Wiebe v. Butchart's Motors Ltd [1949] 4 DLR (NS) 838	182
William Lacey (Hounslow) Ltd v. Davis [1957] 1 WLR 932	137, 633
William Whiteley v. R. (1910) 101 Law Times 741	62, 664
Williams v. Bayley [1866] LR 1 HL 200	166
Williamson Shaft & Slope Co., Re 20 BR (1982, BC SD Ohio)	552
Willis Faber Enthoven (Pty) Ltd v. Receiver of Revenue 1992 (4) SA 202 (A)	663
Willmor Discount Corp. v. Vaudreuil (City) [1994] 2 SCR 210	599, 608, 622
Wilson v. Caledonian Railway Company (1860) 22 D 1408	253
Wilson v. Thornbury (1875) LR 10 Ch App 239	52
Windisman v. Toronto College Park Ltd (1996) 28 OR 3d 29; 132 DLR 4th 512 (Gen Div)	600
Wood v. Gordon (1935) 51 Sh Ct Rep 132	709
Wood v. The Northern Reversion Co. (1848) 10 D 254	470
Woolwich Equitable Building Society v. Inland Revenue Commissioners ([1993] AC 70 HL affirming CA); reversing [1989] 1 WLR 137	28, 59, 64–5, 78, 92, 127, 135, 136, 630, 655, 664–5, 698, 711, 712
Works and Public Buildings Commission v. Pontypridd Masonic Hall (1920) 89 LJQB 607	54
Worley v. Ehret (1976) 36 Ill App 3d 48; 343 NE 2d 237	376
Wright v. Blackwood (1833) 11 S 722	255
Wright v. Newton [1835] 2 Cr M & R 124; 150 ER 53	137

Wrotham Park Estate Co. Ltd v. Parkside Homes Ltd [1974]
1 WLR 798   329, 342, 343–5

Yardley v. Arnold (1842) C & M 434; 174 ER 577   507
Yellowlees v. Alexander (1882) 9 R 765   709
Yeoman Credit Ltd v. Apps [1962] 2 QB 508   113
York Buildings Co. v. Mackenzie (1797) 3 Paton 579;   394–6, 408–9, 416,
(1795) 3 Paton 378   418, 419, 424, 583, 709

Zemhunt Holdings Ltd v. Control Securities plc 1992 SLT 151   10, 141, 144–5

Abbreviations

A	Appellate Divison; Atlantic Reporter
A & E	Adolphus & Ellis' Reports
A 2d	Atlantic Reporter, Second Series
ABGB	*Allgemeines bürgerliches Gesetzbuch*
AC	Law Reports, Appeal Cases; Appeal Court
ACJ	Acting Chief Justice
AcP	*Archiv für die civilistische Praxis*
AD	South African Supreme Court Appellate Division Reports
AJ	Acting Judge
al.	alinéa
ALJR	Australian Law Journal Reports
All ER	All England Law Reports
All ER Annual Rev	All England Law Reports Annual Review
ALR	Australian Law Reports
ALR 2d	American Law Reports Annotated, Second Series
ALR 3d	American Law Reports Annotated, Third Series
alt.	alternative
Alta LR 3d	Alberta Law Reports, Third Series
Anm.	*Anmerkung*
App	Appeal Cases
App Cas	Law Reports, Appeal Cases
App Div	Appellate Division; New York Supreme Court Appellate Divison Reports
App Div 2d	New York Supreme Court Appellate Division Reports, Second Series
APR	Atlantic Provinces Reports
AR	Alberta Reports

xxxiii

Ark	Arkansas Supreme Court Reports
Ark App	Arkansas Appeal Cases
art., Art.	article
arts., Arts.	articles
B	Baron
B & C	Barnewall and Cresswell's Reports, King's Bench
B & S	Best and Smith's Queen's Bench Reports
Bankr	Bankruptcy
BC	British Columbia
BC SD	Bankruptcy Court, Southern District
BCCA	British Columbia Court of Appeal
BCLC	Butterworths Company Law Cases
BCLR 2d	British Columbia Law Reports, Second Series
BGB	*Bürgerliches Gesetzbuch*
BGH	*Bundesgerichtshof*
BGHZ	*Entscheidungen des Bundesgerichtshofs in Zivilsachen*
Bing	Bingham's Common Pleas Reports
Black W	Sir William Blackstone's King's Bench Reports
Boston University LR	*Boston University Law Review*
BR	Bankruptcy Reports
BS	Brown's Supplement to Morison's Dictionary of Decisions, Court of Session
Buffalo LR	*Buffalo Law Review*
Bull. Civ.	*Bulletin des arrêts de la Chambre Civile de la Cour de cassation*
Burr	Burrow's King's Bench Reports
Business LR	*Business Law Review*
BW	*Burgerlijk Wetboek*
C	Cape Provincial Division
C & M	Carrington and Marshman's Nisi Prius Reports
C & P	Carrington and Payne's Nisi Prius Reports
C.	*Codex Iustiniani*
CA	Court of Appeal
Cal App 3d	California Appellate Reports, Third Series
Cal Rptr	California Reporter
California LR	*California Law Review*
Camp	Campbell's Nisi Prius Reports
Cap.	*Caput*
CB	Chief Baron; Common Bench Reports by Manning, Granger and Scott

Cels.	Celsus
Ch	Law Reports, Chancery
chap(s).	chapter(s)
ChD	Law Reports, Chancery Division
Chron.	*Chronique*
CILSA	*The Comparative and International Law Journal of Southern Africa*
Cir	Circuit; Circuit Court
Civ.	*Cour de cassation, Chambre civile*
CJ	Chief Justice
Cl & F	Clark and Finnelly's House of Lords Cases
CLJ	*Cambridge Law Journal*
CLR	Commonwealth Law Reports
Cmnd	Command Paper
Columbia LR	*Columbia Law Review*
Com.	*Chambre commerciale de la Cour de cassation*
Cowp	Cowper's King's Bench Reports
Cox Eq	Cox's Equity Cases
CP	Common Pleas
CPD	South African Law Reports, Cape Provincial Division
Cr M & R	Crompton, Meeson & Roscoe's Exchequer Reports
CS	Quebec Reports, Supreme Court
Ct Cl	Court of Claims
D	*Recueil Dalloz*; Dunlop, Bell and Murray's Reports; Dunlop's Session Cases
D.	*Digest*
DC	District of Columbia
De G & J	De Gex and Jones' Chancery Reports
De G M & G	De Gex, Macnaghten and Gordon's Reports, Chancery
DH	*Recueil Dalloz hebdomadaire*
disp.	*disputatio*
Div.	division
DJZ	*Deutsche Juristenzeitung*
DLR	Dominion Law Reports
DLR 2d	Dominion Law Reports, 2nd Series
DLR 3d	Dominion Law Reports, 3rd Series
DLR 4th	Dominion Law Reports, 4th Series
DP	*Recueil Dalloz périodique*

LIST OF ABBREVIATIONS

DS	*Dalloz-Sirey*
DVI	District Court for the District of the Virgin Islands
East	East Report, King's Bench
ECR	European Court Reports
ed(s).	editor(s)
Edinburgh LR	*Edinburgh Law Review*
edn(s)	edition(s)
EGLR	Estates Gazette Law Reports
El Bl & El	Ellis, Blackburn and Ellis's Queen's Bench Reports
ELR	*European Law Review*
ER	English Reports
Esp	Espinasse's Nisi Prius Reports
Ex	Exchequer Reports
F	Federal Reporter; Fraser, Session Cases
F 2d	Federal Reporter, Second Series
F Supp	Federal Supplement
fasc.	fascicle
Fed Cas	Federal Cases
Florida State University LR	*Florida State University Law Review*
Ga App	Georgia Appeals Reports
Gai.	Gaius; Gaius's Institutes
Gen Div	General Division
GmbH	*Gesellschaft mit beschränkter Haftung*
GP	*Gazette du Palais*
GruchB	*Beiträge zur Erläuterung des Deutschen Rechts* (ed. J. A. Gruchot)
GWD	Cases in the Griqualand West Division of the Supreme Court
H & N	Hurlstone and Norman's Exchequer Reports
H Bl	H. Blackstone's Common Pleas Reports
Hare	Hare's Chancery Reports
Harvard LR	*Harvard Law Review*
HC	High Court
HCA	High Court of Australia
HCL	Clark's House of Lords Cases
HGB	*Handelsgesetzbuch*
HL	House of Lords
HLC	House of Lords Cases

HR	*Hoge Raad*, High Court of Justice
HR	Harrison and Rutherford's Common Pleas Reports
HRR	*Höchstrichterliche Rechtsprechung*
Hume	Hume's Decisions (Court of Session, Scotland)
ICLQ	*International and Comparative Law Quarterly*
Idaho	Idaho Supreme Court Reports
Ill App 3d	Illinois Appellate Court Reports, Third Series
Ind	Indiana
Indiana LR	*Indiana Law Review*
Inst.	*Institutiones Iustiniani*
Iowa	Iowa Supreme Court Reports
IR	*Informations Rapides*
Iul.	*Iulianus*
J	Judge
J & H	Johnson and Hemming's Vice Chancellor's Reports
JCP	*Jurisclasseur périodique* (otherwise known as *La Semaine Juridique*)
JhJb	*Jherings Jahrbücher für die Dogmatik des bürgerlichen Rechts*
JJ	Judges
JR	*Juridical Review*
JW	*Juristische Wochenschrift*
JZ	*Juristenzeitung*
KB	King's Bench; Law Reports King's Bench
Law Com	Law Commission
LC	Lord Chancellor
LCCP	Law Commission Consultation Paper
Ld Raym	Lord Raymond's King's Bench Reports
Lev	Levinz's King's Bench and Common Pleas Reports
Lib.	*Liber*
LJ	Lord Justice
LJKB	Law Journal Reports, King's Bench, New Series
LJQB	Law Journal Reports, Queen's Bench, New Series
Lloyd's L Rep	Lloyd's List Law Reports (1919–50)
Lloyd's Rep	Lloyd's List Law Reports (1951–)
Lloyd's Rep Banking	Lloyd's List Law Reports, Banking Law Reports
LQR	*Law Quarterly Review*
LR	*Law Review*
LR	Law Report
LR Ch App	Law Reports, Chancery Appeals

LR CP	Law Reports, Common Pleas
LR Eq	Law Reports, Equity
LR EX	Law Reports, Exchequer
LR HL	Law Reports, English and Irish Appeals
LR PC	Law Reports, Privy Council
LR QB	Law Reports, Queen's Bench
LT	Law Times Reports
M	Macpherson's Session Cases
M & S	Maule and Selwyn's King's Bench Reports
M & W	Meeson and Welsby's Reports, Exchequer
Macqueen	Macqueen's House of Lords Reports
Madd	Maddock's Chancery Reports
Man R 2d	Manitoba Law Reports, Second Series
Mass	Massachusetts Supreme Judicial Court; Massachusetts
Mich App	Michigan Court of Appeals Reports
Michigan LR	*Michigan Law Review*
MLR	*Modern Law Review*
Mo App	Missouri Court of Appeals
Mod	Modern Reports
Mor	Morison's Dictionary of Decisions in the Court of Session
MR	Master of the Rolls
N. C. proc. civ.	Nouveau Code de procédure civile
n., nn.	note, notes
NBR 2d	New Brunswick Reports, Second Series
NBW	Nieuw Burgerlijk Wetboek (New Dutch Civil Code)
NC App	North Carolina Court of Appeals Reports
NE	Northeastern Reporter
NE 2d	Northeastern Reporter, Second Series
New York University LR	*New York University Law Review*
NH	New Hampshire
NJ	*Nederlandse Jurisprudentie*
NJ Eq	New Jersey Equity Reports
NJW	*Neue Juristische Wochenschrift*
NLJ	*New Law Journal*
NLR	New Law Reports of Celyon
no(s).	number(s)
Nomos	*Nomos: Yearbook of the American Society of Political and Legal Philosophy*

North Carolina LR	*North Carolina Law Review*
NS	Nova Scotia
NSR 2d	Nova Scotia Reports, Second Series
NSW	New South Wales
NSWLR	New South Wales Law Reports
NW	North Western Reporter
NW 2d	North Western Reporter, Second Series
NY	New York Court of Appeals Reports
NY 2d	New York Court of Appeals Reports, Second Series
NYS 2d	New York Supplement Reporter, Second Series
NZCA	New Zealand Court of Appeal
NZLR	New Zealand Law Reports
obs.	Observation
OGH	*Oberster Gerichtshof für die Britische Zone*
OGHZ	*Entscheidungen des Obersten Gerichtshofs für die Britische Zone*
OH	Outer House
Ohio Misc 2d	Ohio Miscellaneous, Second Series
Oklahoma LR	*Oklahoma Law Review*
OLG	*Oberlandesgericht*
Ont	Ontario
Ont CA	Ontario Court of Appeal
OR	Official Reports, High Court of the South African Republic; *Obligationenrecht* (Swiss Code of Obligations)
OR 2d	Ontario Reports, Second Series
OR 3d	Ontario Reports, Third Series
Oxford JLS	*Oxford Journal of Legal Studies*
P	Probate, Divorce and Admiralty Division (Law Reports), 1891–; Pacific Reporter
P & C R	Property and Compensation Reports
P 2d	Pacific Reporter, Second Series
Pat App Cas	Craigie, Stewart and Paton's Appeals
Paton	Paton's House of Lords Appeal Cases
Paul.	Paulus
PC	Judicial Comittee of the Privy Council
PD	Probate, Divorce and Admiralty Division (Law Reports), 1875–90
Pomp.	Pomponius
pr.	*Principium*

xl   LIST OF ABBREVIATIONS

QB	Queen's Bench Reports
QBD	Law Reports Queen's Bench Division
QC	Queen's Counsel
Quaest.	*Quaestio*
Que Ct	Court of Quebec
R	Rettie's Session Cases
RabelZ	*Zeitschrift für ausländisches und internationales Privatrecht*
Rep	Reports
Req.	Chamber of Requests of the Cour de cassation
Restitution LR	Restitution Law Review
RG	*Reichsgericht*
RGZ	*Entscheidungen des Reichsgerichts in Zivilsachen*
RJQ	Rapports Judiciaires de Quebec
Ross LC	Ross's Leading Cases in the Law of Scotland (Land Rights)
S	Sirey; Shaw's Session Cases
s(s).	section(s)
SA	South African Law Reports
SALJ	South African Law Journal
Salk	Salkeld's King's Bench Reports
Sask QB	Sasketchewan, Court of Queen's Bench
Sask R 2d	Sasketchewan Law Reports, Second Series
S.C.	Superior Court
SC	Session Cases; Supreme Court
SCC	Supreme Court of Canada
SCLR	Scottish Civil Law Reports
Scot Law Com	Scottish Law Commission
SCR	Canada Law Reports, Supreme Court
SD	Southern District
SE 2d	Southeastern Reporter, Second Series
Sh & Macl	Shaw and Maclean's Scotch Appeal Cases
Sh Ct	Sheriff Court
Sh Ct Rep	Sheriff Court Reports
SLR	Scottish Law Reporter
SLT	Scots Law Times
SLT (Sh Ct)	Scots Law Times, Sheriff Court Reports
So	Southern Reporter
So 2d	Southern Reporter, Second Series
Soc.	*Chambre sociale de la Cour de cassation*

Somm.	Sommaires
Stanford LR	Stanford Law Review
StGB	Strafgesetzbuch
Str	Strange's King's Bench Reports
SupCt	Supreme Court
Supp.	Supplement
SW	South Western Reporter
SW 2d	South Western Reporter, Second Series
T	Transvaal Provincial Division
Tan	Taney's United States Circuit Court Reports
Taunt	Taunton's Common Pleas Reports
Term Rep	Durnford and East's Term Reports
Tex Civ App	Texas Court of Civil Appeals
tit.	title
TLR	Times Law Reports
TR	Durnford and East's Term Reports
trans.	translated, translation
trib.	Tribunal
TS	United Kingdom Treaty Series
TSAR	Tydskrif vir die Suid-Afrikaanse Reg
Tulane LR	Tulane Law Review
Ulp.	Ulpianus
University of British Columbia LR	University of British Columbia Law Review
University of California at Los Angeles LR	University of California at Los Angeles Law Review
University of Illinois LR	University of Illinois Law Review
University of Western Australia LR	University of Western Australia Law Review
US	United States Supreme Court Reports
V-C	Vice-Chancellor
Ves Jun Supp	Hovenden's Supplement to Vesey Junior's Reports
Virginia LR	Virginia Law Review
vol(s).	volume(s)
W	Witwatersrand Local Division
W & S	Wilson and Shaw's Appeal Cases, House of Lords
W Va	West Virginia Supreme Court Reports
Wash 2d	Washington Reports, Second Series
Wilm	Wilmot's Notes and Opinions, King's Bench
Wis	Wisconsin Reports

Wisconsin LR	*Wisconsin Law Review*
WLR	Weekly Law Reports
WM	*Wertpapier-Mitteilungen*
WWR	Western Weekly Law Reports
Yale LJ	*Yale Law Journal*
ZEuP	*Zeitschrift für Europäisches Privatrecht*
ZIP	*Zeitschrift für Wirtschaftsrecht*
ZSS (RA)	*Zeitschrift der Savigny-Stiftung für Rechtsgeschichte, Romanistische Abteilung*

PART I

Introduction

1 Unjustified enrichment: surveying the landscape

David Johnston and Reinhard Zimmermann

I. Preliminary questions

'Unjustified enrichment'. The expression is mysterious. So are the other terms in use for the same subject, 'unjust enrichment' and 'restitution'. What is an enrichment and when is it unjustified? To state that something amounts to unjustified enrichment is merely a conclusion, that because the enrichment is unjustified it should be returned, restored or made over to the person properly entitled to it. That conclusion is in need of supporting normative argument.[1] But what sort of argument?

Some time ago the Roman jurist Pomponius wrote the now-famous words *nam hoc natura aequum est neminem cum alterius detrimento et iniuria fieri locupletiorem*, 'by the law of nature it is right that nobody should be unjustly enriched at another's expense'.[2] Pomponius's maxim encapsulates the key elements of enrichment liability: enrichment, which is unjust, and which is at the expense of the claimant. But it exemplifies a problem that faces modern legal systems, too: formulating the principles of a law of unjustified enrichment in a way which is clear and yet not excessively broad.

There is no doubt that Pomponius's formulation is, as a matter of classical Roman law, much too broad. There were many cases in which unjustified enrichment was simply allowed to rest where it arose. A clear instance is the claim of a possessor in good faith who improved land from which he was later ejected by the true owner. He had a defence (*exceptio doli*) against the true owner's claim so long as he remained in possession, but once out of possession he had no claim at all.

---

[1] See Dagan, below, 360.
[2] D. 50, 17, 206, Pomp. 9 *ex variis lectionibus*; a slightly shortened version appears in D. 12, 6, 14, Pomp. 21 *ad Sabinum*.

Similar considerations arise, for example, in relation to the general principle against unjustified enrichment set out in § 812(1), first sentence, of the German Civil Code: 'Someone who obtains something without legal ground through performance by another or in another way at his expense is bound to make it over to him.'[3] This formulation too is excessively broad: it is not the case that everything that one has without a legal ground (*ohne rechtlichen Grund*) as a result of performance by some other or in another way at his expense can be recovered. The task for German jurisprudence, performed notably by Walter Wilburg and Ernst von Caemmerer, was to identify cases falling within the general principle where the claimant actually did have a cause of action. The four cases they identified from the wording of the first sentence of § 812(1) are now widely accepted: (i) the claimant rendered a performance (*Leistung*) to the defendant which was without a legal basis; (ii) the defendant encroached on the claimant's property (*Eingriff*); (iii) the claimant incurred expense in improving the defendant's property (*Verwendungen*); (iv) the claimant paid the defendant's debt (*Rückgriff*). German law has therefore refined and confined its broad principle so as to cover only particular situations in which enrichment arises. Of these four cases, the first is based on the words 'through performance' (*durch die Leistung*), while the remaining three are sub-categories of enrichment 'in another way' (*in sonstiger Weise*). It is worth emphasising that category (ii) covers cases of enrichment by wrongs; clearly, different considerations may arise in that case from those that do where no wrong is involved.

The task for the common law, especially noticeable in English law, was almost the opposite. It was not a question of refining down existing principles. The question was this: from a vast accretion of cases could any principles be distilled at all? The challenge was taken up first by Robert Goff and Gareth Jones,[4] next (in a more theoretical manner) by Peter Birks;[5] and more recently by Andrew Burrows[6] and by Graham Virgo.[7] While the analyses and presentations of these authors differ on numerous points, for present purposes it is enough to consider the scheme elaborated by Birks. He makes a fundamental distinction between enrichment by wrongs (where the defendant has enriched himself by committing a wrong against

---

[3] 'Wer durch die Leistung eines anderen oder in sonstiger Weise auf dessen Kosten etwas ohne rechtlichen Grund erlangt, ist ihm zur Herausgabe verpflichtet.'
[4] R. Goff and G. H. Jones, *The Law of Restitution* (1st edn, 1966, 5th edn, 1998).
[5] P. Birks, *An Introduction to the Law of Restitution* (1985, revised edn, 1989).
[6] A. Burrows, *The Law of Restitution* (1993).
[7] G. Virgo, *The Principles of the Law of Restitution* (1999).

the claimant) and enrichment 'by subtraction', where the claimant has lost what the defendant has gained.[8] Within the area of enrichment by subtraction, what the claimant must first show is that the defendant's enrichment is at his expense. Next he must establish that the enrichment occurred in circumstances rendering it 'unjust'. Birks therefore sets out to establish a list of 'unjust factors' that support restitution. These include mistake, ignorance, duress, exploitation, legal compulsion, necessity, failure of consideration, illegality, incapacity, ultra vires demands of public authorities, and retention of the plaintiff's property without his consent.

It will be obvious that this is an attempt at systematisation at a quite different level from that of German law. The reason for this is plain: the two systems start out from entirely different points of view. In German law the notion is that a payment or (non-pecuniary) performance made without a legal ground is recoverable, subject to defences. In English law the notion is instead that a payment is recoverable if a ground for its recovery can be demonstrated by the claimant. For example, where money is paid to discharge a non-existent debt, German law presumes that the payment is recoverable (the debt, being non-existent, cannot represent a ground for the recipient to retain the payment). There is no legal ground and therefore the payment must be returned. By contrast, English law requires the claimant to justify why he should get the payment back, for instance because it was made by mistake. In other words, the German approach is objective, the English (mostly) subjective.[9]

As one would expect (perhaps hope) in mature legal systems, the theoretical underpinnings of these two different approaches have not gone unquestioned. Some have thought the German system excessively abstract and that, by making such intensive use of and investing with such juristic nuances the single concept 'transfer' (*Leistung*), it risks obfuscation or even distortion.[10] The late Professor Detlef König expressed his concern that: '[t]he terminology is confusing, almost each statement is disputed, the solution of trivial questions is becoming ever more complicated, and there is a grave danger of a loss of perspective'.[11] On the other hand, the English system of unjust factors has come under criticism for being untidy, excessively complicated, inexhaustive (since new, as-yet-unidentified

---

[8] Birks, *Introduction*, 99 ff., 313 ff.
[9] Recovery of payments made in response to ultra vires demands by public authorities is an instance of an objective ground for recovery.
[10] B. Kupisch, 'Rechtspositivismus im Bereicherungsrecht', 1997 JZ 213; cf. Visser, below, 527–8.
[11] *Ungerechtfertigte Bereicherung: Tatbestände und Ordnungsprobleme in rechtsvergleichender Sicht* (1985), 15–16.

unjust factors may be recognised), and involving unnecessary duplication of other areas of the law.[12]

Against this background, the aim of the conference from which the present collection of papers derives was not to seek a single right answer. Nor was it to advance further on the quest towards some Holy Grail of universal significance in enrichment law. It was instead partly to see how far civil-law and common-law systems in fact arrive at the same and how far at different solutions to the same problems; and how far, even where their destination is the same, they arrive at it by the same or different doctrinal routes. In part, too, it was to see if, from their very different perspectives, the civil and common law might cast light upon one another and suggest possible solutions or approaches to recognised problems or deficiencies. An added interest derived from examining how mixed systems of law deal with these issues. This is particularly so in the case of Scotland, where there is a lively debate about how the law of unjustified enrichment is or ought to be structured.

To take stock of these various matters, it seemed necessary to embark on a treatment of the law of unjustified enrichment that was reasonably comprehensive. With this in mind, we asked two speakers to comment on the same themes, each from a comparative perspective but one as a representative of a common-law system and the other of a civil-law or mixed legal system. It was not possible to do this in any systematic way, so although we speak of 'common' law and 'civil' law, we do not mean to imply that the law of the United States of America and England are just the same, or that no relevant distinctions can be taken between French and German law. Indeed, the various Continental systems differ from one another in important respects, not least because some take an abstract and some a causal approach to the question of transfer of ownership.[13] All we claim is that on each of our topics we have attempted to gain a perspective from a representative of each of what are usually thought to be two different legal traditions. While the emphasis in this volume, owing to the contributors' own backgrounds, is mainly on the laws of England, Germany and Scotland, some attention is also paid to French, Dutch and Israeli law and to the laws of United States jurisdictions.

To focus attention on unjustified enrichment in this way seemed to us appropriate not least because of current interest in the possible emergence

---

[12] See, e.g., R. Zimmermann, 'Unjustified Enrichment: The Modern Civilian Approach', (1995) 15 *Oxford JLS* 403, 416.

[13] See Du Plessis, below, 194–5.

of a European private law.[14] While there is an 'institutional' dimension to this – notably emerging from directives of the Council of the European Union, decisions of the Court of Justice of the European Communities, and also from conventions such as the United Nations Convention on Contracts for the International Sale of Goods – it remains important to remember that law in Europe has always been shaped by the combined work of judges, legislators and professors.[15]

Within a Community inspired in the first place by the idea of a common market, the law of contract was bound to be the first area of private law to be affected by the quest for transnational legal rules. This is reflected not only in a recent textbook that deals with the rules of modern national legal systems as local variations on a common European theme, but also in the *Principles of European Contract Law*, in effect a restatement of European contract law, and in the concerns of the Trento Common Core project.[16] Contractual liability, however, can be closely interlinked with delictual liability: both regimes can apply to one and the same set of facts; their rules must be well co-ordinated with one another. It was logical, therefore, that attention should soon turn to the attempt to identify common rules and principles and a common framework within the law of delict (or tort).[17]

Since, alongside contract and delict, unjustified enrichment is nowadays recognised as an independent source of rights and obligations,[18] and since it is closely related to the law both of contract and delict, it makes sense to start thinking about common principles of the law of unjustified enrichment. There have been earlier attempts to do this.[19] Equally, the first volume of Peter Schlechtriem's comparative treatise on the law

---

[14] See, e.g., Arthur Hartkamp, Martijn Hesselink *et al.* (eds.), *Towards a European Civil Code* (2nd edn, 1998); Peter-Christian Müller-Graff (ed.), *Gemeinsames Privatrecht in den Europäischen Gemeinschaften* (2nd edn, 1999).

[15] See R. C. van Caenegem, *Judges, Legislators and Professors* (1987).

[16] H. Kötz, *European Contract Law* (trans. T. Weir, 1997), vol. I; O. Lando and H. Beale (eds.), *Principles of European Contract Law: Parts I and II* (2000). Cf. also the *Unidroit Principles of International Commercial Contracts* (1994). From the Trento Common Core project, see R. Zimmermann and S. Whittaker (eds.), *Good Faith in European Contract Law* (2000); J. Gordley (ed.), *The Enforceability of Promises in European Contract Law* (2001).

[17] C. von Bar, *The Common European Law of Torts*, vol. I (1998), vol. II (2000); J. Spier and O. A. Haazen, 'The European Group on Tort Law ("Tilburg Group") and the European Principles of Tort Law', (1999) 7 *ZEuP* 469, with references to volumes already published within the scope of that project.

[18] See section II, below.

[19] P. Russell (ed.), *Unjustified Enrichment: A Comparative Study of the Law of Restitution* (1996); E. Clive, 'Restitution and Unjustified Enrichment', in: Hartkamp and Hesselink, *European Civil Code*, 383 ff.

of restitution and unjustified enrichment in Europe is about to appear; and unjustified enrichment is to be included in Christian von Bar's ambitious European civil code project.[20] None the less, in the conference from which the present volume derives the aim was to present a more systematic comparative discussion of the law of unjustified enrichment than had yet been offered. That is also the aim of this book.

The conference began as it ended, with general questions: can the law best be understood by focusing on a general ground for restitution or on a series of specific factors? What is the most illuminating way of structuring the subject-matter of unjustified enrichment? Between these two extremes, for two days attention was directed to the main contexts in which issues of enrichment arise: failure of consideration; fraud and duress; improvements; payment of another's debt; infringement of another's right; cases involving three parties; then to the defences of change of position and illegality; and finally to the question of redressing unjustified enrichment by means of a proprietary remedy. In this introductory chapter little more is attempted than the merest sketch of the main issues, with some accompanying observations about what they may point to.

II. A little history

Roman law, and systems that have adopted its general principles, have never been in any doubt that within the law of obligations there was an area quite separate from contract and from delict (or tort), part of which was occupied by the law of unjustified enrichment. This goes back at least to the second-century jurist Gaius, who categorised obligations as arising from contract, delict or in another manner.[21] Almost four centuries later, Justinian's *Institutes* recognised a division of all obligations into those arising from contract, from delict, as if from contract (*quasi ex contractu*), and as if from delict (*quasi ex maleficio*).[22] Obligations arising from unjustified enrichment were among those arising 'as if from contract', on the basis no doubt that they involved nothing resembling a wrong, while some of them closely resembled contract.[23] While this categorisation goes back to

---

[20] P. Schlechtriem, *Restitution und Bereicherungsausgleich in Europa: Eine rechtsvergleichende Darstellung* (2000). On the European civil code project, see Christian von Bar, 'The Study Group on a European Civil Code', in: P. Gottwald, E. Jayme and D. Schwab (eds.), *Festschrift für Dieter Henrich* (2000), 1.
[21] Gaius, D. 44, 7, 1 pr. The Latin is rather obscure: '*proprio quodam iure ex variis causarum figuris*'.
[22] Justinian, *Institutes*, III, 13, 2.
[23] Notably loans of money and payments made in error: see Gaius, *Institutions*, III, 91.

Roman times, it is right to give some credit for further analytical effort in elevating unjustified enrichment into a legal category of obligations on the same level as contract and delict to the late scholastics of the sixteenth century.[24]

By contrast, it is well known that until comparatively recently English law regarded the notion of a law relating to unjustified enrichment as foreign. In *Orakpo v. Manson Investments Ltd*,[25] Lord Diplock intoned that 'there is no general doctrine of unjust enrichment recognised in English law. What it does is to provide specific remedies in particular cases of what might be classified as unjust enrichment in a legal system that is based upon the civil law.' But matters have moved on a good deal since then: witness the speech of Lord Steyn in *Banque Financière de la Cité v. Parc (Battersea) Ltd*:[26] 'Unjust enrichment ranks next to contract and tort as part of the law of obligations [as] an independent source of rights and obligations.'

III. Demarcation disputes

If the position of unjustified enrichment as an autonomous area of the law of obligations is now secure, what exactly is the extent of that area? The issue is one of demarcating the area as against other areas of the law of obligations, as well as against property law.[27] Two main questions seem to arise: first, which issues properly fall within each of these areas of the law, it being understood that at least in some systems there is no barrier to concurrent claims based on different principles of law;[28] secondly, the significance of the measure of recovery.

On the second question, the position seems to be this: what remedies based on unjustified enrichment have in common is that they seek recovery from the defendant of the amount by which he has been enriched, rather than the amount which the claimant may have lost. The converse does not necessarily follow. That is, it does not follow that any remedy

---

[24] See, esp., the work of J. Gordley, e.g. 'The Purpose of Awarding Restitutionary Damages', (2000) 1 *Theoretical Inquiries in Law* 39, 40; also his 'The Principle against Unjustified Enrichment', in: H. Schack (ed.), *Gedächtnisschrift für Alexander Lüderitz* (2000), 213, 215 ff.

[25] [1978] AC 95 at 104.   [26] [1999] AC 221 at 227.

[27] For valuable comments on this, see the essays collected in *Acta Juridica* 1997, also published as D. Visser (ed.), *The Limits of the Law of Obligations* (1997).

[28] For example, in English law concurrent claims in contract and tort: *Henderson v. Merrett Syndicates* [1995] 2 AC 145; for Germany, see Max Vollkommer in: Othmar Jauernig (ed.), *Bürgerliches Gesetzbuch* (9th edn, 1999), § 241, nn. 14 ff.

whose measure is the quantum of the defendant's enrichment must be based on unjustified enrichment. There are some (probably exceptional) cases in other areas of the law where the measure of the claim is the defendant's enrichment.

1. Contract

English law traditionally contains remedies given for unjustified enrichment to parties in contractual relationships by requiring that, for any such remedy to be available, the contract must be at an end.[29] Where a party to a contract fails to perform his obligations as required, the injured party's remedy is generally a contractual one: so a breach of contract will generally be redressed by damages assessed according to the particular contract. In short, breach of contract is a wrong, and one that is redressed outside the law of unjustified enrichment. The same will apply also to cases where a person has been wrongfully induced to enter into a contract or to do so on unfair terms: these are matters which will be addressed where appropriate by setting the contract aside or by rendering certain of its terms unenforceable. Likewise, where a contract has failed or been frustrated, the consequences are matters best resolved by reference to the contract.[30] In general it makes good sense to say that, where parties have entered into a contract that distributes the risks of various events between them, it is just to them to apply the contractual allocation, and that it would be wrong to reallocate the risks on the basis of the law of unjustified enrichment. That is why it makes sense to speak of the remedy in unjustified enrichment as being in this context subsidiary.[31]

The measure of damages is itself a question of contract. Usually the remedy will be the amount of compensation which would put the party wronged by a breach in the position as if the breach had not occurred. Sometimes other measures of damages may be suggested. To ask whether a contracting party should be entitled against a contract breaker to an award of money representing the contract breaker's gain is still to ask a question about the proper scope of the law on damages for breach of contract, even though some would describe this as 'restitutionary damages'. At the time of the conference, *Attorney-General v. Blake* was under appeal

---

[29] See, e.g., Virgo, below, 109.
[30] Recoverability of any transfers or deposits may involve the law of unjustified enrichment: see, e.g., *Dies v. British and International Mining and Finance Corporation Ltd* [1939] 1 KB 724; *Zemhunt (Holdings) Ltd v. Control Securities plc* 1992 SLT 151.
[31] See Smith, below, 599 ff.

to the House of Lords. Since the papers were submitted for publication, judgment has been given.[32] The case concerned publication of a volume of memoirs by the former British secret service agent and Russian double-agent George Blake, in which he breached his undertaking to the Crown not to divulge any official information gained by him as a result of his employment, either during it or afterwards. The Court was concerned with the Crown's right to royalties due to be paid to Blake. The Crown had suffered no financial loss, so the question was whether it could seek to deprive Blake of his enrichment. The House of Lords disapproved the Court of Appeal's attempt to identify general situations in which restitutionary damages might be available.[33] 'Exceptions to the general principle that there is no remedy for disgorgement of profits against a contract breaker are best hammered out on the anvil of concrete cases.'[34] On the rather special facts of *Blake*, a majority of the House recognised the Crown's right to restitutionary damages, although Lord Nicholls preferred to describe it as an 'account of profits'. (The description of the remedy indicates that much significance was attached by the majority to the fact that the undertaking given by Blake was akin to a fiduciary obligation, breach of which is conventionally recognised as being capable of resulting in an account for profits.) Lord Hobhouse, who dissented, rejected the Crown's entitlement to restitutionary damages. He accepted that Blake had made a gain but held that this was not at the expense of the Crown or by making use of any property or commercial interest of the Crown either in law or equity. These seem to be considerations arising under the law of unjustified enrichment: conventionally, they would provide grounds for seeking a remedy within that area of the law. But it may be doubtful whether they strictly arise where the question before the court is the measure of damages for breach of contract.

---

[32] [2000] 4 All ER 385. The speeches of Lords Nicholls (at 390) and Steyn (at 403) both refer to the paper in the present volume by O'Sullivan, then unpublished. (It is the same paper that is referred to by Lord Goff in *Panatown Ltd v. Alfred McAlpine Construction Ltd* [2000] 4 All ER 97 at 124.)

[33] Cf. the criticisms made by O'Sullivan, below, 340 ff., 343 ff.

[34] At 403 *per* Lord Steyn. German law does recognise a remedy for the disgorgement of gains in certain cases of breach of contract (§ 281 BGB) but it is now increasingly debated whether the rule might have to be extended. See, on the one hand, Johannes Köndgen, 'Immaterialschadensersatz, Gewinnabschöpfung oder Privatstrafen als Sanktion für Vertragsbruch? Eine rechtsvergleichende Analyse', (1992) 56 *RabelZ* 696; on the other hand Raimund Bollenberger, *Das stellvertretende Commodum: Die Ersatzherausgabe im österreichischen und deutschen Schuldrecht unter Berücksichtigung weiterer Rechtsordnungen* (1999).

This is not, however, the only demarcation problem between contract and unjustified enrichment. German law, for instance, has long been troubled by the question to which of these fields the rules relating to restitution after termination of contract (§§ 346 ff. BGB) systematically belong. The Convention on the International Sale of Goods (Articles 81 ff.) and the Principles of European Contract Law (Articles 9:305 ff.), too, contain restitution rules, which do not, formally, belong to the law of unjustified enrichment.

2. Delict or tort

Where a person infringes another's right, for example by encroaching on his land or infringing her intellectual property rights, the question arises how the remedies arising are to be categorised. In German law this depends on whether the use of the other's property is wrongful (that is, negligent or intentional) or not. If it is, then there may be liability in delict.[35] If it is not, there is no liability in damages, but there may still be liability as a matter of the law of unjustified enrichment.[36] This helpfully focuses the question that, depending on the facts of the particular case, there may be two different principles at work. Where the defendant can be shown to have committed a wrong, there may be liability in damages for the wrong (the damages to be assessed according to the rules of delict or tort). Quite separate from this is the bare fact that the defendant has used or enjoyed property which is, or ought properly to be, the claimant's. That in itself need not involve any wrong: the liability turns purely on the objective fact of having benefited from something to which the claimant was entitled. As Lord Hobhouse said in *Attorney-General v. Blake* in a somewhat different context, the claimant 'gets the money because it was his property or he was in some other way entitled to it'.[37]

Take, for example, the case of mistaken improvement of another's land. Here it is clear that liability can be justified in enrichment terms only so far as the improvement can be described as an enrichment. But it is equally clear, at least from the American cases, that sometimes the liability may exceed the quantum of the enrichment. To the extent that it does, some principle other than the reversal of unjustified enrichment must be at work.[38] So Andrew Kull suggests that the additional liability must be based on fault. It is a damages claim not an enrichment claim.

---

[35] § 823(1); § 687(2) BGB. In addition, there may be a gain-based remedy, i.e. the *Eingriffskondiktion*. The plaintiff may avail himself of either remedy.
[36] Under the *Eingriffskondiktion*: §§ 812(1), 816, 951 BGB.
[37] At 409.   [38] See Kull, below, 380 ff.

It is important to note, too, that the measure of the enrichment claim itself reflects considerations of policy: the defendant might, for example, be made liable for the market value of his use or enjoyment of the plaintiff's thing; or he might be deprived of all profits that he made from it. The second would embody a policy of deterrence, since it would have the consequence that no defendant could ever derive any benefit from using the claimant's property. The first, on the other hand, would not necessarily deter, since it would not necessarily deprive the defendant of all gain derived from the claimant's property.[39]

3. Property

Apart from cases based on use or enjoyment of another's property, the question of a remedy based on unjustified enrichment is particularly important if property has passed to the recipient. It is clear that if property has remained throughout with the transferor, the transferor's main remedy is in civilian terms a proprietary one. So, for example, the reason that only a claim in unjustified enrichment may arise in the case of failure of consideration is that the failure of consideration generally will not prevent title in the money or goods transferred passing to the recipient, so excluding the transferor's proprietary claim.[40]

In civilian systems the question which remedies are available to the transferor will depend (among other things) on whether the particular legal system takes an abstract or causal approach to transfer of ownership: clearly, if property has passed there is room for an enrichment-based remedy; if it has not, there may be both a proprietary and an enrichment-based remedy.[41] In English law there has been some dispute about whether the owner's property-based action is properly to be treated as an instance of the reversal of unjustified enrichment. On one view it is not obvious that vindication of property rights really has anything at all to do with reversing unjustified enrichment; and, if this is entirely a matter of the law of property, there is no reason why the claimant should be required to prove in the ordinary way that the defendant was unjustly enriched at his expense.[42] From a civilian perspective, matters are complicated by the absence from English law of a *rei vindicatio* and by the recognition by English law of equitable as well as legal titles in property. None the less, the fundamental issue is quite recognisable: can the claimant establish that he

---

[39] See Dagan, below, 351; cf. also Gordley, 'Purpose'.   [40] See Virgo, below 108.
[41] Cf. Gretton, below, 573.   [42] For recent discussion, Virgo, *Principles*, 592 ff.

has a proprietary interest (whether legal or equitable) in the defendant's property? It is to answering that question that the rules on 'tracing' are directed. Tracing 'is the process by which the plaintiff traces what has happened to his property, identifies the persons who have handled or received it, and justifies his claim that the money which they handled or received (and, if necessary, which they still retain) can properly be regarded as representing his property'.[43] Once money or other property has been traced, the question will arise what the claimant's proper remedy is (if any). The rules of tracing are necessarily more complex than those of *rei vindicatio*, since they are concerned not just to identify the claimant's original property but the property which now represents the value of his original property. With these very significant differences, however, it remains the case that the aim – of establishing that the claimant has a proprietary interest in the defendant's property – is as comprehensible in civilian as in common-law terms.

IV. Circumstances for reversing enrichment

1. Cases involving enrichment by transfer

The great divide between the civilian and common-law approaches to enrichment by transfer is, as indicated earlier, between the traditional civilian approach, which focuses on the single question whether there is or is not a legal ground for retention of a transfer or performance; and the approach more recently developed in English law that requires the claimant to point to a particular 'unjust factor' or ground for restitution to support his or her claim.

The explanatory force of the 'unjust factors' approach has been placed under some pressure by a number of decisions in the English courts. Here it is enough to glance only at recent events in the long-running interest-rate swaps litigation. Since the decision of the House of Lords in *Hazell v. Hammersmith and Fulham London Borough Council*[44] that interest-rate swaps contracts were ultra vires local authorities, in the ensuing flurry of litigation between banks and local authorities fundamental issues of the law of unjustified enrichment in the United Kingdom have been addressed.

Had these cases arisen in German law, for example, the question would have been formulated as: is the underlying contract valid or void? The conclusion, if the contract were void, would be that there was no ground

---

[43] *Boscawen v. Bajwa* [1996] 1 WLR 328, 334 *per* Millett LJ.   [44] [1992] 2 AC 1.

for the recipient of transfers made under the contract to retain them. Although in certain cases judges in the English courts have made reference to 'no consideration' or 'absence of consideration',[45] concepts which seem closely to resemble lack of a legal ground for retention, in general the emphasis has been placed on the claimant's having to demonstrate a ground for recovering the transfer. So long as a mistake of law was not a good ground for recovery, claimants were forced to analyse their claims in some other way, notably by pleading that there had been a failure of consideration. This approach is no longer necessary now that recovery of payments made under mistake of law is possible.[46] But that development in the law has created tensions in the emerging analytical framework of the English law of unjustified enrichment. The reason is simple enough: when a person makes a payment in a subjective belief as to the law which is at the time correct although, owing to the declaratory theory of adjudication, it has since turned out to be mistaken, to describe this as a 'mistake' is to use that word in a most unusual sense.[47] It would seem more straightforward just to say that there is no legal reason for the recipient to retain the payment. Following this decision, it is at least possible that even in English law the emphasis may shift away from the mind of the person making the payment towards the objective question whether the obligation he sought to discharge was valid. If so, this might be 'the beginning of the end of the system of unjust factors'.[48]

This leads on to a more general consideration of the role of legal reasons for retaining transfers. That question can be focused more sharply by some examples.

(a) Failure of consideration
Suppose payments are made under a contract to a person who has promised to do something in return but does not do so. So long as the contract remains in force, it governs relations between the parties to it. But if it is once set aside, questions under the law of unjustified enrichment will arise. Once again (to take German law as an example), if the contract is set aside there is no ground for retention of the payment, which must therefore be recoverable in unjustified enrichment. As a matter of English

---

[45] *Westdeutsche Landesbank Girozentrale v. Islington London Borough Council* [1994] 4 All ER 890 at 930 *per* Hobhouse J; *Guinness Mahon & Co. Ltd v. Kensington and Chelsea Royal London Borough Council* [1999] QB 215.
[46] *Kleinwort Benson Ltd v. Lincoln County Council* [1999] 2 AC 349.
[47] See Meier, below, 74.   [48] See Krebs, below, 76.

law, however, the mere setting aside of the contract does not entitle the claimant to recover: it remains necessary for him to provide a reason why he should do so. Here the unjust factor on which the claimant will rely is 'failure of consideration'. The orthodoxy is that the failure must be total. There is reason to think that the general insistence of English law on total failure of consideration rests on borrowing from the civilian scheme of things, in particular on the translation of *causa* as 'consideration'.[49] In the Roman and civilian tradition the conception is that a payment is made in order to discharge an obligation (*solvendi causa*):[50] it therefore follows that if there is no obligation, there is no cause for the payment.

The requirement that, to be relevant, a failure of consideration must be total is capable of working injustice. The English courts have, therefore, in appropriate cases been willing to categorise consideration as a collateral benefit, or to apportion it between different parts of a contract, so as to be able to conclude that the consideration had in fact wholly failed and maintain the integrity of the doctrine while reaching more satisfactory results.[51]

It is now widely accepted that, in order to avoid some of the analytical artificialities consequent upon an insistence on total failure of consideration, it would make good sense to recognise partial failure of consideration as a ground for recovery.[52] The consequence would be that, whenever a person transfers a benefit to a defendant in the expectation of receiving something in return and that expectation is not fully satisfied, he could make a claim for restitution, subject to making counter-restitution to the claimant.[53] This development would result in a law more similar to the civilian approach: if the claimant has not received all that he bargained for, and the contract has been discharged, there is no ground for the defendant to retain what he received.

(b) Mistake

In the law of unjustified enrichment the focus is usually on mistakes about legal liability. But there are other kinds of mistakes, and if all that is considered is whether the motives of the person making payment are mistaken, it is clear that the recipient of any payment or service is highly insecure in his receipts. In order to keep the notion of mistake within reasonable bounds, it is therefore necessary to evolve criteria that determine whether a mistake is relevant for the purposes of unjustified

---

[49] See Evans Jones and Kruse, below, 131 ff.
[50] R. Zimmermann, *The Law of Obligations: Roman Foundations of the Civilian Tradition* (1990), 748 ff.
[51] See Virgo, below, 112 ff. [52] See Virgo, below, 116 ff. [53] See Virgo, below, 118.

enrichment or not.[54] But the elaboration of such criteria necessarily has regard to matters other than the subjective intention of the person making payment. This is clear, for example, from the fact that in English law the mistaken payment of a debt which actually exists does not ground a claim for restitution. As Sonja Meier argues,[55] this appears to suggest that English law already has regard to the objective facts underlying the mistake, in particular whether there is a legal ground for retention of the payment or not.

(c) Fraud and duress

The traditional view has been that civilian systems treat fraud and duress only as reasons why a contract underlying a transfer is invalid and why it therefore cannot represent a ground (or *causa*) for retaining the property transferred. This, however, appears to be less than the whole truth.

To approach the question in German law: the first question will be whether there is a remedy for recovery on the basis of a transfer (*Leistung*) to the recipient or on the ground of an interference (*Eingriff*) with his property. Unless the property was actually seized or taken, it will be difficult to say that there is an *Eingriff*. For that reason, in the case of fraud, it makes more sense to say that the transfer to the recipient was intentional, although the intention was, of course, vitiated by the fact of the recipient's fraud. The fraud serves as the reason why the underlying transaction or contract can be set aside, with the consequence that there is no legal ground for the retention of the property, and it must be made over to the claimant.

In the case of duress there is scope for a much more sophisticated inquiry about whether the transferor actually had an intention to transfer or not. One possible approach is at any rate to follow the Roman jurist Paul: *coactus volui*, he explained, of a legal act done under duress: there is an intention even if it is one which is compelled.[56] On that analysis, duress falls to be analysed in the same way as fraud.

The approach of the common law is different. The difficulty is that, it being taken for granted that the contract can be set aside on grounds of duress or fraud, it is still necessary to identify on what unjust factor the transferor should rely in order to claim recovery. There are various possibilities, notably failure of consideration (the transferor did not receive the counterperformance for which he bargained) or mistake or ignorance.

---

[54] See Meier, below, 46 ff.   [55] Below, 53–4.
[56] D. 4, 2, 21, 5, Paul 11 *ad edictum*. For discussion of other possible views, see Du Plessis, below, 196 ff.

This may suggest that a preferable analysis would be simply to say that, the contract having been set aside, there is no ground for retention of the property.

None the less, such an analysis may itself face difficulty in certain situations.[57] Suppose in German law that a payment which is actually due is handed over to the recipient but only under compulsion. If the payment is due, then regardless of the way in which it was induced, there appears to be no ground for recovery: there is still a legal ground for retention. So the question arises whether it may be appropriate to recognise circumstances for granting a remedy where the method employed is objectionable even though it is not possible to say that the transfer is undue or that the property is held without legal ground. The main point, however, is that this example suggests that analysis purely in terms of legal grounds may not be exhaustive of all the problems that may arise.

It would in any event be misleading to say that (for example) German law has no regard to things other than the presence or absence of a legal ground. In particular, the measure of recovery and the defences available are affected by other factors.[58] So, for instance, the broad ground for recovery where the defendant has no legal ground for retention is qualified (i) so that there is a defence if the claimant knew that the transfer was not due and (ii) so that that defence is unavailable in the event of duress. Conversely, the defendant's entitlement to plead the defence of change of position is excluded in the event that he is in bad faith.

What these examples appear to suggest is that, at least in the case of mistakes of law, the 'unjust factor' approach faces some difficulty. On the other hand, the general principle that there should be no retention without a legal ground is workable, provided due account is taken, so far as the question of making defences available is concerned, of factors such as the state of mind of the parties.

2. Three-party situations

The description of third-party enrichment as 'the most notoriously difficult of all enrichment constellations'[59] has clearly struck a chord with those wrestling with that issue, since it is often quoted. The difficulties arise both in identifying who is enriched at whose expense, and also in trying to ensure that remedies based in unjustified enrichment do not subvert contractual provisions made between the various parties.

---

[57] See Du Plessis, below, 213 ff.   [58] See Chen-Wishart, below, 192.
[59] The phrase is from Zimmermann, *Law of Obligations*, 874.

(a) Payment of another's debt

German law provides a useful analysis of the question. If a person pays a debt someone else owes, without the debtor's instructions and without intending to act as his *negotiorum gestor*, it is clear that he has no recourse against the debtor in mandate or *negotiorum gestio*.[60] Nor, however, does he have an intention of transferring anything to the debtor. Nor indeed is there an encroachment on the debtor's property. Accordingly there can be no *condictio* based on either a *Leistung* or an *Eingriff*. This is why the law recognises a special category of *condictio* (*Rückgriffskondiktion*) by which the person paying can have recourse against the debtor for releasing him from his obligation to the third party.

The first question will be whether the debtor's debt to his creditor was discharged by the payment made to the creditor by the third party.[61] If it was not, then the creditor will be enriched: he has not only the payment made by the third party but also retains his right of action against the debtor. Here the third party, who made the payment in order to discharge the debtor's debt, is likely to have a right of action against the creditor based (on the English approach) on failure of consideration or (elsewhere) on the argument that the creditor has no cause to retain the payment.[62]

If the debt was discharged, the question arises what remedy the third party has against the debtor. In English law, the original debt will be discharged only if the third party acts on behalf of the debtor and with the intention of discharging him; it is less clear whether he needs actual authority from the debtor. It will be for the third party to plead an 'unjust factor' to support his claim against the debtor. In French law the third party will be subrogated to the creditor's claims, but only if he acted on behalf of the debtor or had an interest in the transaction. Otherwise, he will have to make out an independent right of recourse against the debtor.[63]

Here a similar policy can be detected in various legal systems, that of attempting to ensure that the debtor is not prejudiced by the substitution of a new third-party creditor for his original creditor. So the appearance of the third party ought not to affect the defences available to the debtor against the original creditor. English law achieves this by taking a restrictive approach to the circumstances in which the third party can discharge the debt. French law protects the debtor's interests by subrogating the third party to the creditor's claim, so preserving the debtor's original

---

[60] §§ 670, 683 BGB.
[61] This is the position in German law (unless the debtor has to perform in person): § 267(1) BGB.
[62] See MacQueen, below, 469 ff.   [63] See Whittaker, below, 439 ff.

defences. German law maintains that counter-rights or defences by the debtor against the creditor may reduce or even wipe out any enrichment received by the former as a result of the third party's performance.

(b) Other cases

The same notions are to be found in the broader areas of what may be called 'three-party' or 'indirect' enrichment. Here German law employs the so-called Canaris principles:[64] the parties must retain their defences against one another; each must be protected against defences arising from the relationship between the other two parties; and each party must bear the risk of insolvency of the party with whom he dealt.[65] Similarly, English law insists that there can be no claims for indirect enrichment if these involve 'leapfrogging' the claimant's contractual counterparty.[66] This ensures that the risk of his insolvency or dishonesty rests on the person who contracted with him.

These policies seem to explain the broad agreement[67] between the systems examined in this volume about cases in which it is not possible to sue a third party for enrichment. So, for example, if an employer in a construction contract is enriched by the work done by the sub-contractor, the sub-contractor has no claim in enrichment but must proceed in contract against the contractor; or if the insurance company which is supposed to pay the garage for repairs to a car fails to pay, the garage cannot sue the owner of the car.

What is harder to explain is the underlying principles and their limits. Here Daniel Visser is surely right to emphasise that the search for a single right answer is likely to be fruitless, and that to focus on a single approach to these complex situations (for instance, the *Leistung* of German law) may lead to excessive analytical complexity.[68] Instead, he proposes that in addition to asking the standard questions (is the defendant enriched? is the enrichment unjustified? is it at the claimant's expense?), the relevant policy factors have to be identified and applied to the facts of each case. These include the existence of a contractual relationship; who should bear the risks of contracting; avoiding double claims; maintaining contractual defences; security of receipts; and subsidiarity.

---

[64] See chap. 19, below.
[65] See, e.g., R. Zimmermann and J. du Plessis, 'Basic Features of the German Law of Unjustified Enrichment', [1994] *Restitution LR* 14, 31–6.
[66] See Birks, below, 502 ff., 512 ff.
[67] As well as general disquiet about the *Boudier* decision (Req. 15 June 1892, DP 1892.1.596, note Labbe, S 1893.1.281).
[68] See Visser, below, 530 ff.

As an example take the facts of *Barclays Bank Ltd v. W. J. Simms Son and Cooke (Southern) Ltd*:[69] there the bank's customer drew a cheque on the bank in favour of a building company. Owing to the receivership of the company the customer then stopped the cheque. But the bank paid anyway, by mistake. The German approach to this kind of question is to identify the payment by cheque as involving the (intended) discharge of two different debtor-creditor relationships (the bank and its customer; the customer and his creditor) and then to ask which of these relationships is vitiated. The purpose of doing so is to identify where the enrichment lies, by identifying where there is a lack of cause for retention of the sum received. That would seem to suggest that, if there is no doubt that the customer owes the building company, the problem is one between the bank and its customer.

So far as the actual decision in this case is concerned, a curiosity is that the judge did not mention enrichment at all but was concerned purely to identify that the payment was made by the bank under a mistake (an 'unjust factor'). However, it is far from clear that the recipient (the building contractor) was in fact enriched, rather than merely receiving payment for work already done.[70] It is true, of course, that if the payment did not discharge the customer's debt (since it was not authorised by him), then the building company would both have been paid and retain its claim against its creditor (the bank's customer). To that extent one can detect an enrichment. But there remains an oddity in the result if the payee of the cheque had given value and was in good faith. It may be thought that a preferable result would be to subrogate the bank to whatever claims its mistaken payment has discharged.[71]

3. Cases where is no transfer

All the cases mentioned so far in this section have been cases where there is a transfer, directly or indirectly, to the defendant. The basis of claims for use or enjoyment of another's property was discussed in section III. There remains the question of mistaken improvements to another's property.

This is the classic case of enrichment without a transfer by claimant to defendant. The point was noted by the Roman jurist Julian:[72] according to Roman law, anything built on land belongs by the doctrine of *accessio*

---

[69] [1980] 1 QB 677. Cf. also *Govender v. The Standard Bank of South Africa Ltd* 1984 (4) SA 392 (C).
[70] Kull, 'Rationalizing Restitution', (1995) 83 *California LR* 1191, 1229 ff.
[71] *Ibid.*, citing Uniform Commercial Code §§ 3-418 and 4-407. Such claims might include any asserted by either party under the contract in issue.
[72] D. 12, 6, 33, Julian 39 digesta.

to the owner of the land. Someone who mistakenly builds on another's land automatically loses ownership of the building materials as they accede to the land. But there is no transfer (*Leistung*) from one party to the other.

The particular enrichment-based remedy must be shaped according to the way in which the improvement has come about, whether by enhancing the value of the land; by discharging a liability associated with the land that would properly fall on the landowner; or by anticipating expenditure which would otherwise have to be borne by the landowner.[73] The difficult case is the first, simply because the enhancement of the value of the land may well be inseparable from it.

Improvements cases raise fundamental questions about what amounts to enrichment. This is so in more than one sense. (i) The true landowner may not want the building at all but regard it as an obstruction on his land. Is he enriched?[74] (ii) The cost of building may well exceed the value of what is built: what is the measure of the enrichment? (iii) The true landowner may not be able to pay the amount of any enrichment that he is found to derive from the building. Does this affect the remedies available?

It may be that it is largely because of concern about this last point that English law in principle rejects the claim of the mistaken improver. But civilian systems do not, and neither do the laws of United States jurisdictions. What emerges from looking at those systems is that, while a claim in principle is recognised, there is intricacy in structuring the remedies and their proper extent so as to arrive at equitable results. For instance, in German law (and probably also in Scots law) a good deal turns on the nature of the improvement: compensation can be claimed for expenditure which was either necessary or increased the value of the property, provided it was made in good faith, but not for other purely voluntary or 'voluptuary' expenditure.[75] From the perspective of the remedy to be granted, the United States cases illustrate great flexibility on the part of the courts. Consideration of all the circumstances may lead the courts to resolve the question by the grant of a lien; partition of the land; exchange; forced payment for the added value; or tender to the improver at the unimproved value.[76]

---

[73] See Wolffe, below, 411 ff.
[74] A question nowadays sometimes mysteriously described as 'subjective devaluation'.
[75] D. Verse, 'Improvements and Enrichment: A Comparative Analysis', [1998] *Restitution LR* 85; Wolffe, below, 425–6.
[76] See Kull, below, 375 ff.

So far as the measure of the claim is concerned, the following principles can be identified, at least in the United States: (i) the liability of the innocent recipient must not leave him worse off; (ii) nor may it exceed the cost to the claimant of providing the improvements; (iii) the cost of providing the benefit so far as it exceeds the value to the recipient rests on the claimant, unless reallocated on the basis of fault; (iv) a defendant who takes the benefit owing to conscious wrongdoing will be liable to disgorge the whole benefit, without limitation to the claimant's cost.[77] Application of these principles serves to protect the improver in the degree appropriate to his state of mind.

V. Defences

It is obvious that the adequacy of each system depends on its working as a whole. The very broad ground for recovery of transfers in German law is workable in practice not just because of recognition of the particular cases in which the broad ground for recovery applies but also because defences to enrichment claims have been elaborated. Conversely, in English law at least until recently the need for elaboration of defences was more limited, owing to the fact that the claimant had in any event to bear the burden of proving a ground for restitution.

It is clear that different systems may reach the same result, even if they arrive there by different routes.[78] For instance, in English law a claimant can recover on the ground of mistake, but if there was no mistake he will not succeed. In German law, on the other hand, while a mistaken payment is in principle recoverable, if there was no mistake on the part of the claimant then the defendant has a defence.[79]

1. Change of position

Where a defendant has been enriched, he may still be able to plead the defence of change of position. The effect of the defence is to reduce the quantum of enrichment recoverable by the claimant from the amount originally received to the amount still retained. Clearly, it is crucial to identify what conduct on the part of the defendant counts as a relevant change of position. For example, it is plain that if the defendant has paid his electricity bill out of the enrichment received, he has not relevantly changed his position, since he would have had to pay the bill anyway. What is needed therefore is to establish a causal connection between

---

[77] See Kull, below, 371–2; cf. above, section III. 2.
[78] See esp. Dannemann, below, 311–12.   [79] § 814 BGB.

the enriching event and losses sustained by the defendant,[80] such as, for example, sums that he would not otherwise have expended and which he cannot now recover.

By contrast with pleas of estoppel or personal bar (which might bar a claimant's recovery where he had knowingly allowed the defendant to rely on receipt of the payment or performance), this defence does not depend on the claimant's knowledge of or acquiescence in the conduct relied upon by the defendant. It is therefore particularly important to confine the defence within appropriate bounds. Partly this is a matter of identifying whether the basis of the claim is truly unjustified enrichment or something else.[81] The reason for doing so is that, where the claimant seeks to recover from the defendant solely on the basis that the defendant has been enriched out of his (the claimant's) resources, it makes sense to ask what the extent of the defendant's actual enrichment is.[82] This is why, for example, it is possible to object to the availability of the defence of change of position when the situation is one of 'unwinding' a mutual contract, for instance on grounds of invalidity.[83] In such a case it may reasonably be maintained that the aim should be to restore the status quo before the void contract was entered into: in short, *restitutio in integrum*. This aim is frustrated by allowing one of the parties to plead what are for these purposes extraneous reasons why he is no longer or not so extensively enriched.

Apart from this, even in a situation which is purely one of unjustified enrichment and therefore open to the application of this defence, there may be situations where it is not appropriate on policy grounds to admit the defence. Where there is a loss, it is obvious after all that one of the parties must bear it, and change of position is simply a means for the defendant to transfer some of the loss on to the claimant. So, where the purpose of a legal rule such as undue influence is to protect a person or class of persons, to allow the defendant to claim change of position would be to transfer the loss to the claimant who is meant to be protected.[84] The defence should therefore in such cases be unavailable.

2. Illegality

In both the common law and civil law the illegality of the claimant's own conduct can defeat his claim. There appears to be no real difference

---

[80] R. Nolan, 'Change of Position', in: P. Birks (ed.), *Laundering and Tracing* (1995), 135, 145 ff.
[81] See Gordley, below, 229 ff. [82] See Gordley, below, 239 ff.
[83] See Hellwege, below, 284. [84] See Chen-Wishart, below, 170–1.

between the positions adopted here by the different systems. Perhaps this is because this defence does not depend on how the grounds for claims in unjustified enrichment are structured.[85] To keep the defence within reasonable bounds it is important to be clear about the policies it is intended to serve. The principal consideration is what is prohibited by the norm which constitutes the illegality. In order to further rather than frustrate the purposes of the prohibitory norm, the courts must deny a claim for the value of services (*quantum meruit*) that are rendered illegal by the norm in question. But the same reasoning does not apply to performances which can be returned: indeed in some cases the very best way of achieving the purpose of the norm will be to allow a claim for return of the performance; this might be so, for example, if denying recovery would have the same effect as validating a bargain which the norm had declared illegal. In general, therefore, it appears that the right approach will be to ask whether allowing or refusing relief in unjustified enrichment would create, maintain or prevent the situation which the prohibitory norm seeks to avoid.[86] Similarly, where it is a question of asserting claims to property rights, the question will be whether the claimant needs to rely on illegal conduct or found on it in the evidential basis of his case; if not, illegality should not prevent an assertion of these rights.[87] Subsidiary matters of policy may arise if no clear answer emerges from considering this principal issue.

VI. Classification

Clear thought and principled development of the law, as well as the eradication of inconsistencies, are much assisted if clarity about the underlying structure of the law can be attained.[88] Recently Lord Steyn began a speech, '[i]n law classification is important. Asking the right questions in the right order reduces the risk of wrong decisions.'[89]

To illustrate the importance of clear classification, one can hardly do better than resort to the categorisation of animals identified by Jorge Luis Borges in 'a certain Chinese encyclopaedia'. There 'animals are divided into (a) belonging to the Emperor, (b) embalmed, (c) tame, (d) sucking pigs, (e) sirens, (f) fabulous, (g) stray dogs, (h) included in the present classification, (i) frenzied, (j) innumerable, (k) drawn with a very fine camelhair

---

[85] See Dannemann, below, 310.   [86] See Dannemann, below, 319 ff.
[87] See Swadling, below, 292 ff. (The approaches taken in law and in equity are somewhat different.)
[88] See McKendrick, below, 632 ff.   [89] *Attorney-General v. Blake* [2000] 4 All ER 385 at 402.

brush, (l) *et cetera*, (m) having just broken the water pitcher, (n) that from a long way off look like flies'.[90] Some of these categories are obscure ((f), (j), (n)); some are alarming in their affront to logic ((h), (l)). But what is perhaps most disturbing about this taxonomy is its sheer disregard for the use of a single classifying factor. The result is that the same animal can fall into several parts of the taxonomy at the same time. What about the law of unjustified enrichment in various legal systems?

1. Scotland

At the risk of only modest exaggeration one might say that the structure of the law of unjustified enrichment in Scotland has until recently been as illuminating as Borges's taxonomy. Traditionally Scots law has used both the terminology of the Roman *condictiones* and its own classification in terms of repetition, restitution and recompense. These two systems of classification overlapped, *condictio* terminology being used to describe the different kinds of remedy for recovery of money ('repetition') or other property ('restitution'). But a more coherent structure is now emerging.[91] It has become clear that the various Roman *condictiones* are not to be viewed as causes of action related solely to recovery of sums of money or other property.[92] They are instead descriptive of the bases on which recovery may be sought. The significance of this is that recovery of unjustified enrichment in relation to services can be sought on exactly the same basis. For example, where services have been performed in circumstances where the purpose or consideration for which they were performed has failed, there should be a claim for the enrichment resulting. This would traditionally be described as a claim in recompense, but the ground on which it rests is precisely the same as that on which a sum of money or other property can be recovered: in short, the *condictio causa data causa non secuta*. In other words, it can now be recognised that claims for enrichment by services lie in precisely the same circumstances as claims for enrichment by transfers.[93] It is true that they will raise different questions about quantification, but that is a separate issue from asking on what grounds recovery of enrichment should be available.

Prior to this common-law rationalisation it had been thought that the only hope for system was legislation or codification. It remains to be seen whether that will yet prove to be correct. A draft code is to hand if called

---

[90] See M. Foucault, *The Order of Things* (English trans., 1970), xv.
[91] Cf. Endnote in Wolffe, below, 427 ff.   [92] *Shilliday v. Smith* 1998 SC 725.
[93] Cf. for English law Virgo, below, 122-3.

upon.[94] But not everyone agrees that, even if codification is necessary, the draft indicates how it should be done.[95] It is at any rate cause for great satisfaction that the law has now been placed by the courts on a coherent theoretical basis.

2. Germany

The theoretical structure of the law is well established. If there is a deficiency in the system, it appears to lie in its extreme abstraction. German scholars have themselves pointed out the great difficulty of establishing what are or should be the factors that limit the operation of the single general principle of recovery, absence of a legal ground.[96] Certainly to arrive at acceptable results using but a single concept involves acrobatics both linguistic and intellectual. While the German analysis copes well with two-party situations, it is perhaps no accident that it has strained to deal with three-party situations within its traditional framework. As Daniel Visser explains in this volume:

> Not unlike the way in which linear mathematics can cope very adequately with simple structures such as planets in a stable orbit around a star, but non-linear chaos theory is necessary to explain the eddies that form in the water flowing under a bridge, and in the same way that the former seeks precise prediction while the latter attempts to describe the general pattern or character of a system's behaviour, two-party situations in law can often be solved with direct, clear rules whereas the best we can do in three-party situations is mostly to lay down the general pattern along which a solution should proceed.

Progress in such matters may well depend on jettisoning absolute dogmatic precision in favour of more flexibility.

3. England

Recent developments in the courts have, as already noted, stretched the existing explanatory structure of unjust factors supporting restitutionary claims. There are indications here and there that English law recognises as a ground for recovery of enrichment the fact that there is no reason for it to be in the hands of the recipient. One of these is the case of recovery

---

[94] See the 'Draft Rules on Unjustified Enrichment' prepared by Dr E. Clive and originally published as an appendix to Scottish Law Commission Discussion Paper no. 99, *Judicial Abolition of the Error of Law Rule and its Aftermath* (1996).
[95] See Whitty, below, 693.
[96] König, *Ungerechtfertigte Bereicherung*; P. Schlechtriem, *Schuldrecht: Besonderer Teil* (5th edn, 1998), 310.

of payments made to satisfy ultra vires demands for payment of tax.[97] There the conventional 'unjust factor' analysis can rely on the subjective point that the intention of the person paying is vitiated. But regardless of questions of intention, in this instance it is absolutely certain that there is no underlying obligation. That fact might be thought to have great explanatory force.

Another case, already mentioned, is the need following upon *Kleinwort Benson Ltd v. Lincoln County Council*[98] to describe as a 'mistake' a subjective belief as to the law which is at the time of payment correct although has since turned out to be mistaken.[99] Again, it may be thought that the absence of a legal ground for retaining a payment in these circumstances has significant explanatory force. From the Borgesian perspective with which this section began, it may be that the real cause for analytical concern is not that the taxonomy appears to be incomplete but that it fails to recognise the critical category: absence of a legal ground.

VII. Convergence and divergence: the future

In the law of unjustified enrichment there are some fundamental differences between civil-law and common-law systems. But that is not the whole truth. For example, the treatment of mistaken improvements differs greatly as between English law on the one hand and civil-law systems and the laws of United States jurisdictions on the other. It is evident from this example that the difference is not founded on the divide between civil and common law. It seems, rather, to rest on a different view of the equities of protecting the recipient of the improvements.

Yet there is a certain amount of common ground. In common-law and civil-law systems alike, the scope of defences recognised appears to be broadly similar. Illegality is put to service in very much the same way. Change of position, late to arrive in English law,[100] seems to be available in essentially the same circumstances as in German law.

The operative policies of the law are also regularly the same. Although different methods are employed – for instance, in cases of payment of another's debt English law takes a narrow view of when a third party can discharge a debt, while French law subrogates the third party to the creditor's claim – the general aim appears to be the same: to avoid prejudice to the debtor by substitution of a new creditor who would not,

---

[97] *Woolwich Equitable Building Society v. Inland Revenue Commissioners* [1993] AC 70.
[98] [1999] 2 AC 349.   [99] See Meier, below, 74–5.
[100] *Lipkin Gorman (a Firm) v. Karpnale Ltd* [1991] 2 AC 548.

without these restrictions, be subject to the same defences as the original creditor. This – protection of what might in other legal contexts be called the legitimate expectations of the debtor – is the general context in which the various systems considered have regard to such things as that the parties should retain their defences against one another; each must be protected against defences arising from the relationship between the other two parties; and each party must bear the risk of insolvency of the party with whom he dealt. Similarly, English law insists that there can be no claims for indirect enrichment if these involve 'leapfrogging' the claimant's contractual counterparty. This ensures that the risk of his insolvency or dishonesty rests on the person who contracted with him. The same kinds of considerations explain why unjustified enrichment always seems to raise the issue of subsidiarity.

It seems clear, therefore, that the substantial differences between the civil- and common-law approaches to unjustified enrichment are in the underlying structure of the subject. Even here the consequences of abolition in England (and Scotland) of the rule against recovery of payments made under error of law, as well as occasional (though controversial) hints of absence of consideration as a ground for recovery in English law may suggest that the gulf is narrowing. Much less controversial has been the progress of partial failure of consideration towards acceptance by legal scholars and perhaps eventually by the courts. Recognition of this as a ground for restitution would itself bring English law closer to the civilian test of whether the purpose for which the payment was made had been fulfilled. Yet in spite of these developments it can hardly be doubted at present that the difference of approach is a fundamental one.

In their results, however, the two approaches often differ less. This is confirmation of the fact that it is the whole picture of the law that matters, not just the grounds for recovery but also the defences recognised and the circumstances in which they are made available. For that reason it is clear that a necessary concomitant of any rapprochement of English law towards a general principle of recoverability of transfers retained without a legal ground would be a fundamental reworking of the limits on that principle, what might be described as 'just factors'.[101]

What is clear is that the system of grounds for restitution or 'unjust factors' in English law is in a state of development. Nothing could be less surprising. Ever since Lord Macmillan pronounced that the categories of negligence are never closed,[102] more and more legal categories have been

---

[101] See Krebs, below, 88. [102] *Donoghue v. Stevenson* [1932] SC (HL) 31 at 70.

discovered to be open. In the common law that is scarcely to be regarded as a ground for criticism, let alone as a fatal flaw. Although it may be true at a general level that there is a divergence of approach between codified and uncodified systems of law, this does not explain why the structure of the English law of unjustified enrichment is so different from that found elsewhere. The piecemeal recognition in English law (at least by some judges and jurists) of situations in which it seems analytically convincing to focus on the absence of a legal ground is reminiscent of the rise of the *condictio sine causa* in Roman law. Originally developed as a special *condictio* to provide a remedy for cases not covered by the existing scheme of *condictiones*, it ultimately came to be seen as a general remedy (*condictio sine causa generalis*) and lack of a cause as the overarching principle which justified recovering a payment or performance. Since history has a remarkable tendency to repeat itself, it is tempting to speculate that we may yet see this development again.

Bibliography

Jack Beatson, *The Use and Abuse of Unjust Enrichment* (1991).
Peter Birks, 'English and Roman Learning in Moses v. Macferlan', (1984) 37 Current Legal Problems 1–28.
Peter Birks, *An Introduction to the Law of Restitution* (1985; revised edn, 1989).
Peter Birks and Grant McLeod, 'The Implied Contract Theory of Quasi-contract: Civilian Opinion Current in the Century Before Blackstone', (1986) 6 Oxford JLS 46–85.
Peter Birks and Charles Mitchell, 'Unjust Enrichment', in: Peter Birks (ed.), *English Private Law* (2000), vol. II, chap. 15, 525–635.
Peter Birks and Francis Rose (eds.), *Lessons of the Swaps Litigation* (2000).
Raimund Bollenberger, *Das stellvertretende Commodum: Die Ersatzherausgabe im österreichischen und deutschen Schuldrecht unter Berücksichtigung weiterer Rechtsordnungen* (1999).
Andrew Burrows, *The Law of Restitution* (1993).
Andrew Burrows (ed.), *Essays on the Law of Restitution* (1991).
Andrew Burrows and Ewan McKendrick, *Cases and Materials on the Law of Restitution* (1997).
Eric Clive, 'Restitution and Unjustified Enrichment', in: Arthur Hartkamp, Martijn Hesselink *et al.* (eds.), *Towards a European Civil Code* (2nd edn, 1998), chap. 25, 383–94.
W. R. Cornish, Richard Nolan, Janet O'Sullivan and Graham Virgo (eds.), *Restitution: Past, Present and Future: Essays in Honour of Gareth Jones* (1998).
Hanoch Dagan, *Unjust Enrichment* (1997).
Brice Dickson, 'Unjust Enrichment Claims: A Comparative Overview', (1995) 54 CLJ 100–26.

Joachim Dietrich, *Restitution: A New Perspective* (1998).
J. E. du Plessis, *Compulsion and Restitution – A Historical and Comparative Study of the Law of Restitution or Unjustified Enrichment* (unpublished Ph.D. thesis, University of Aberdeen, 1997).
Izhak Englard, 'Restitution of Benefits Conferred Without Obligation', in: *International Encyclopedia of Comparative Law* (1991) vol. X, chap. 5.
Essays in Honour of Wouter de Vos (1992) (= *Acta Juridica* 1992).
Robin Evans-Jones, 'From "Undue Transfer" to "Retention without a Legal Basis"', in: Robin Evans-Jones (ed.), *The Civil Law Tradition in Scotland* (1995), 213–52.
Robin Evans-Jones, 'Unjustified Enrichment', in: Kenneth Reid and Reinhard Zimmermann (eds.), *A History of Private Law in Scotland* (2000), vol. II, chap. 14, 369–421.
Robin Evans-Jones and Phillip Hellwege, 'Some Observations on the Taxonomy of Unjustified Enrichment in Scots Law', (1998) 2 *Edinburgh LR* 180–217.
Jorge Fabrega Ponce, *El enriquecimiento sin causa*, 2 vols. (1996).
Daniel Friedmann, 'Restitution of Benefits Gained by Breach of Contract', in: Herbert Hausmaninger, Helmut Koziol *et al.* (eds.), *Developments in Austrian and Israeli Private Law* (1999), 93–101.
Daniel Friedman and Nili Cohen, 'Payment of Another's Debt', in: *International Encyclopedia of Comparative Law* (1991), vol. X, chap. 10.
Paolo Gallo, 'Unjust Enrichment: A Comparative Analysis', (1992) 40 *American Journal of Comparative Law* 431–65.
Paolo Gallo, *Arrichimento senza causa e quasi contratti (I rimedi restitutori)* (1996).
W. M. Gloag and R. C. Henderson, *The Law of Scotland* (10th edn, 1995, eds. W. A. Wilson and Angelo Forte), chap. 29, 470–85.
Lord Goff of Chieveley and Gareth Jones, *The Law of Restitution* (5th edn, 1998).
James Gordley, 'The Principle Against Unjustified Enrichment', in: H. Schack (ed.), *Festschrift für Alexander Lüderitz* (2000), 213–31.
Thomas Krebs, *Restitution at the Crossroads: a Comparative Study* (1999).
Manfred Heemann, *Action for Money Had and Received: Zur Geschichte des englischen Bereicherungsrechts* (1996).
Phillip Hellwege, 'The Scope of Application of Change of Position in the Law of Unjust Enrichment: A Comparative Study', [1999] *Restitution LR* 92–117.
David Ibbetson, *A Historical Introduction to the Law of Obligations* (2000), chap. 14, 264–93.
Peter Jaffey, *The Nature and Scope of Restitution* (2000).
Michael Jewell, 'The Boundaries of Change of Position – A Comparative Study', [2000] *Restituton LR* 1–69.
Dagmar Kaiser, *Die Rückabwicklung gegenseitiger Verträge wegen Nicht- oder Schlechterfüllung* (2000).
Detlef König, *Ungerechtfertigte Bereicherung: Tatbestände und Ordnungsprobleme in rechtsvergleichender Sicht* (1985).
Markus Krebs, *Die Rückabwicklung im UN-Kaufrecht* (2000).

Berthold Kupisch, *Ungerechtfertigte Bereicherung: geschichtliche Entwicklungen* (1987).
Karl Larenz and Claus-Wilhelm Canaris, *Lehrbuch des Schuldrechts* (13th edn, 1994), vol. II/2, second section, 127–348.
Ewa Letowska, 'Unjust Enrichment in Eastern European Countries', in: *International Encyclopedia of Comparative Law*, vol. X (1995), chap. 4.
Werner Lorenz, in: *J. von Staudingers Kommentar zum Bürgerlichen Gesetzbuch* (13th revised edn, 1999), §§ 812–22.
Geoffrey MacCormack, 'The *Condictio Causa Data Causa Non Secuta*', in: Robin Evans-Jones (ed.), *The Civil Law Tradition in Scotland* (1995), 253–76.
Michael Martinek, 'Der Weg des Common Law zur allgemeinen Bereicherungsklage – Ein später Sieg des Pomponius?', (1983) 46 *RabelZ* 294–335.
Sonja Meier, *Irrtum und Zweckverfehlung: Die Rolle der unjust-Gründe bei rechtsgrundlosen Leistungen im englischen Recht* (1999).
Sonja Meier, 'Mistaken Payments in Three-party Situations: A German View of English Law', (1999) 58 *Cambridge Law Journal* 567–603.
Sonja Meier, 'Nach 196 Jahren – Bereicherungsanspruch wegen Rechtsirrtums in England', 1999 *JZ* 555–64.
George E. Palmer, 'History of Restitution in Anglo-American Law', in: *International Encyclopedia of Comparative Law* (1989), vol. X, chap. 3.
Dieter Reuter and Michael Martinek, *Ungerechtfertigte Bereicherung* (1983).
Francis Rose (ed.), *Failure of Contracts* (1997).
Konrad Rusch, 'Restitutionary Damages for Breach of Contract: A Comparative Analysis of English and German Law', (2001) 118 *South African Law Journal* 59–86.
Paul W. L. Russell (ed.), *Unjustified Enrichment: A Comparative Study of the Law of Restitution* (1996).
Frank Schäfer, *Das Bereicherungsrecht in Europa: Einheits- und Trennungslehren im gemeinen, deutschen und englischen Recht* (2001).
Peter Schlechtriem, *Restitution und Bereicherungsausgleich in Europa: Eine rechtsvergleichende Darstellung* (2000).
H. C. F. Schoordijk, *Onverschuldigde betaling en ongerechtvaardigde verrijking bij zogenaamde driehoeksverhoundingen* (1999).
Eltjo J. H. Schrage, 'Restitution in the New Dutch Civil Code', (1994) *Restitution LR* 208–21.
Eltjo J. H. Schrage, 'Unjustified Enrichment: Recent Developments from a Comparative and Historical Perspective', (1999) 46 *Netherlands International LR* 57–86.
Eltjo J. H. Schrage (ed.), *Unjust Enrichment: The Comparative Legal History of the Law of Restitution* (2nd edn, 1999).
Ingeborg Schwenzer, 'Restitution of Benefits in Family Relationships', in: *International Encyclopedia of Comparative Law* (1997), vol. X, chap. 12.
William Swadling (ed.), *The Limits of Restitutionary Claims: A Comparative Analysis* (1997).

William Swadling and Gareth Jones (eds.), *The Search for Principle: Essays in Honour of Lord Goff of Chieveley* (1999).
Theoretical Enquiries in Law, vol. I (2000).
Ungerechtfertigte Bereicherung: Grundlagen, Tendenzen, Perspektiven: Symposium zum Gedenken an Detlef König (Symposium Detlef König: edited by the Institut für ausländisches und internationales Privat- und Wirtschaftsrecht der Universität Heidelberg, 1984).
Dirk A. Verse, 'Improvements and Enrichment: A Comparative Analysis', [1998] Restitution LR 85–103.
Dirk A. Verse, *Verwendungen im Eigentümer-Besitzer-Verhältnis* (1999).
Graham Virgo, *The Principles of the Law of Restitution* (1999).
Daniel Visser (ed.), *The Limits of the Law of Obligations* (1997) (= Acta Juridica 1997).
Daniel Visser, *Unjustified Enrichment* (2001).
Ernst von Caemmerer, 'Bereicherung und unerlaubte Handlung' in: *Festschrift für Ernst Rabel* (1954), vol. I.
Niall R. Whitty, 'Indirect Enrichment in Scots Law', [1994] *Juridical Review* 200–29, 239–82.
Niall R. Whitty, 'Die Reform des schottischen Bereicherungsrechts', (1995) 3 ZEuP 216–41.
Reinhard Zimmermann, 'Unjustified Enrichment: The Modern Civilian Approach', (1995) 15 *Oxford JLS* 403–29.
Reinhard Zimmermann, *The Law of Obligations: Roman Foundations of the Civilian Tradition* (1996), chap. 26, 834–901.
Konrad Zweigert and Hein Kötz, *An Introduction to Comparative Law* (trans. Tony Weir, 3rd edn, 1998), chaps. 38 and 39, 537–94.

PART II

Enrichment 'without legal ground' or unjust factor approach

2 Unjust factors and legal grounds

Sonja Meier

One of the major differences between the English and Continental law of unjust enrichment seems to be the justification for the claim in restitution. Whereas German law founds the claim on the lack of a legal ground (*Rechtsgrund*), English claims in restitution are said to rest on a specific 'unjust factor', such as mistake, compulsion or failure of consideration. This chapter concentrates on the role of unjust factors and legal grounds in a specific area of unjust enrichment, namely where the claimant willingly conferred a benefit – in particular, money – on the defendant. It does not deal with cases of encroachment, payment of another's debt, improvement of another's property or restitution for wrongs.

I. Restitution for mistake and the *condictio indebiti*

1. Liability mistake and *condictio indebiti*

The Roman unjustified enrichment claim that attracts the greatest interest today is the *condictio indebiti*. It required that the claimant conferred a benefit on the defendant in order to discharge a liability that, however, did not exist. The action did not lie when the claimant knew that the liability did not exist. Whether there was also a requirement that the claimant had to be mistaken is disputed.[1] It may be that in classical law a mistake by the claimant was presumed if he performed in terms of a non-existent liability, and that the defendant had to rebut this presumption by showing that the claimant knew that the liability did not exist. But at least in post-classical law, the claimant, in order to avail himself of the *condictio indebiti*, had to show that he mistakenly assumed the liability to exist.

I would like to thank Niall Whitty for commenting upon an earlier draft of this paper.

[1] See R. Zimmermann, *The Law of Obligations: Roman Foundations of the Civilian Tradition* (paperback edn, 1996), 849 ff.

With this *error* requirement, there originated the long-lasting dispute as to whether a mistake of law would be sufficient.

In this shape – performance in discharge of a liability that did not exist and the need for a mistake about the existence of the liability – the *condictio indebiti* was taken over into the European *ius commune*. In some countries, it can still be found in its original form; in others – among them Germany – the *condictio* underwent changes. Whereas the first draft of the German Civil Code still incorporated all the traditional *condictiones*, among them the *condictio indebiti*, the second draft, which became the final version, made a significant change in recognising a general enrichment action in the shape of a *condictio sine causa*. Thus, we read in § 812(1), first sentence, BGB: 'A person who, either by way of transfer from another person, or in any other manner, receives something without legal ground, is bound to return what he has received.' A special provision for the *condictio indebiti* was thought to be unnecessary as it was held to be covered by the general enrichment action: a person effecting a transfer in order to discharge an obligation that does not exist effects such transfer without legal ground. But what if the claimant knew that the liability did not exist? § 814 BGB provides: 'What has been given in order to discharge an obligation cannot be recovered if the person performing knew that he was not bound to effect that performance.' Instead of a mistake requirement, the code introduced a defence of knowledge and thereby eventually turned back to the position of classical Roman law.

In England, restitution for mistake was originally for recovery of money paid in the mistaken assumption of a liability to pay – the so-called 'liability mistake'.[2] In the classic case of *Kelly v. Solari*[3] directors of an insurance company had paid the insurance sum to the defendant although the policy had lapsed by reason of non-payment of the premium. They contended that they had, when paying, forgotten the lapse of the policy. The court remitted the case to the jury in order to find out whether this contention was true. Recovery had to be barred if the directors knew of the lapse, or if they had paid without reference to the question of liability. But if the directors had paid because they mistakenly assumed they were liable to pay, recovery was to be allowed. Since then, recovery for liability mistake (of fact) has always been an uncontroversial example of restitutionary liability.

---

[2] See P. Birks, *An Introduction to the Law of Restitution* (1985, revised edn 1989), 149 ff.; A. Burrows, *The Law of Restitution* (1993), 95 ff.; Lord Goff of Chieveley and G. Jones, *The Law of Restitution* (5th edn, 1998), 181 ff.

[3] (1841) 9 M & W 54; 152 ER 24.

The European *condictio indebiti* and the old English action to recover for a liability mistake thus have two similarities: (i) the claimant performs in order to discharge a liability that does not, however, exist; (ii) the claimant does not know that there is no liability. Regarding the second point, there are differences in detail. Modern German law works with a defence of knowledge, while the European *ius commune* and English law required the claimant positively to show a mistake. That mistake, in England, had to be a mistake of fact. This requirement also fitted into the European tradition where recovery for mistake of law had, for a long time, been excluded or at least disputed. Thus one can say that the English action to recover for a liability mistake, established in the nineteenth century, was an English form of the *condictio indebiti*.[4]

2. Liability mistake and contractual mistake

In England, 'liability mistakes' leading to restitution have always been distinguished from mistakes in the formation of a contract.[5] The latter have, in one way or another, to be fundamental and shared by the other party to render a contract void or voidable. For liability mistakes, there is no such requirement: no contract is destroyed; instead, the claimant asks for the return of something the defendant has never been entitled to have. There is, however, a relationship between the two mistakes: if the claimant paid the defendant under a contract, there is no restitution for mistake unless the mistake is able to avoid the contract.[6] Even a mistaken payment cannot be recovered if it is made under a contract that is still valid. (This proposition is also self-evident on the Continent: the contract, unless invalidated, provides a legal ground preventing every action in unjust enrichment.) Hence, two questions have to be distinguished: is the contract invalidated on account of the parties' mistake? And if a contract is invalid, can the parties recover what they transferred? Regarding mistakes at law, the following distinction is made in

---

[4] Birks, *Introduction*, 153.
[5] Goff and Jones, *Law of Restitution*, 179; Burrows, *Law of Restitution*, 97 ff.; S. Stoljar, *The Law of Quasi-contracts* (2nd edn, 1989), 20–1; *Citibank v. Brown Shipley* [1991] 2 All ER 690 at 700–1. The contrary dictum of Lord Wright *in Norwich Union Fire Insurance v. Price* [1934] AC 455 at 461–2, may be explicable on the special facts of the case, involving an apparent notice of abandonment, acceptance of which would exclude claims for recovery.
[6] *Bell v. Lever Brothers* [1932] AC 161; *Horcal v. Gatland* [1984] Industrial Relations Law Reports 288; *Sybron Corp. v. Rochem* [1984] Ch 112; Goff J in *Barclays Bank v. Simms* [1980] QB 677 at 695; Goff and Jones, *Law of Restitution*, 48; Birks, *Introduction*, 160; Burrows, *Law of Restitution*, 94.

Peter Birks's *Introduction to the Law of Restitution*: on the one hand the fundamental mistake rendering the contract void, on the other hand the liability mistake providing a ground to recover.[7] With respect to mistake in equity or misrepresentation, the distinction is blurred, as the courts in case of a rescission automatically order restitution. If restitution seems too difficult, rescission is denied. But, analytically, the questions whether a mistake has been induced, or is sufficiently fundamental to override the bargain, and whether restitution is practically possible are distinguished.

3. Other mistakes

It soon emerged that recovery could not be restricted to liability mistakes. If the claimant, intending to discharge an existing debt, mistakenly overpays the defendant or pays the amount twice, the need to recover has always been acknowledged. But suppose the obligation the claimant intends to discharge is, for certain reasons and with the claimant's knowledge, not enforceable. If he now, in discharging this obligation, overpays the defendant or pays him twice, the need to recover the overpayment should be the same. The problem is that the claimant did not assume that he was liable to pay.

How does German law deal with this situation? As already mentioned, the draftsmen of the code incorporated the *condictio indebiti* into a *condictio sine causa*. For conscious transfers by the claimant, this means that the reason why the claimant effects a transfer to the defendant need not necessarily be the discharge of a pre-existing obligation. Rather, the claimant may create and discharge the obligation in one act. Or he may intend to discharge a claim that is for certain reasons not legally enforceable, like a so-called natural obligation or a claim that is statute-barred. Or he may honour a formless promise to make a gift. (A promise to make a gift, if accepted, is a contract according to German law; as long as it has not been executed it is, however, void unless notarial authentication has been obtained.[8]) If the obligation, the natural obligation or the promise of gift do not exist, or if the claimant overpays the defendant on such obligation, natural obligation or promise, he can recover under the *condictio sine causa*.[9] Obligations, natural obligations and gifts are *causae*, legal grounds which, though they may not be legally

---

[7] Birks, *Introduction*, 159 ff.   [8] § 518 BGB.
[9] See D. Reuter and M. Martinek, *Ungerechtfertigte Bereicherung* (1983), 126 ff.; W. Lorenz, in: *J. von Staudingers Kommentar zum Bürgerlichen Gesetzbuch* (13th edn, 1994), § 812, n. 78.

enforceable, are still able to determine whether a recipient may retain a benefit transferred to him. The claim for unjust enrichment based on a transfer (*Leistungskondiktion*) is justified by the fact that the legal ground the claimant had in mind did not exist.[10]

In England, the problem was whether restitution for mistake was confined solely to liability mistakes. This was indeed a position maintained for a long time.[11] The reason seems to be not only a quest for certainty but also the view that someone giving away money without being obliged to do so deserves, as a mere volunteer, less protection. But such a view disregards the fact that, independently of whether I intend to pay my debt or to honour a non-enforceable promise, mistaken overpayments, or double payments, or payments to wrong recipients, equally cause a – partial – failure of my plans. I intended to pay a certain sum to a certain recipient. In one case I felt liable to do it, in the other case I did not. But this does not concern the amount of the overpayment. At any rate I never intended the recipient to have that money.

The first two-party constellation of a non-liability mistake where recovery was allowed seems to be *Larner v. London County Council*.[12] During the Second World War, London County Council passed a resolution to pay all employees who went to war the difference between their war-service pay and their civil pay. Larner, one of the employees, failed to notify the Council of changes in his war-service pay; as a result, the Council overpaid him. When the Council later tried to recover the overpayments, Larner contended that, since he had not given any consideration for the Council payments, there was no enforceable agreement: therefore the Council did not labour under a liability mistake. Nevertheless, the Court of Appeal allowed recovery. What was the reason? Commentators speak of a moral obligation: according to them, *Larner* shows that the mistaken assumption of a moral obligation can be assimilated to a mistaken assumption of liability and thus lead to recovery.[13] But the concept of a moral obligation is

---

[10] For accounts in English, see R. Zimmermann, 'Unjustified Enrichment: The Modern Civilian Approach', (1995) 15 *Oxford JLS* 403; R. Zimmermann and J. du Plessis, 'Basic Features of the German Law of Unjustified Enrichment', [1994] *Restitution LR* 14; K. Zweigert and H. Kötz, *Introduction to Comparative Law* (trans. T. Weir, 3rd edn, 1998), 540 ff.

[11] *Aiken v. Short* (1856) 1 H & N 210 at 215; 156 ER 1180; *Re Bodega Co.* [1904] 1 Ch 276 at 286; *Home & Colonial Insurance v. London Guarantee* (1928) 32 Lloyd's L Rep 267 at 269; *Morgan v. Ashcroft* [1938] 1 KB 49 at 66.

[12] [1949] 2 KB 683.

[13] Goff and Jones, *Law of Restitution*, 187; Burrows, *Law of Restitution*, 98; P. Matthews, 'Money Paid Under a Mistake of Fact', (1980) 130 *NLJ* 587, 588; D. Friedmann, 'Valid, Voidable, Qualified and Non-existent Obligations: An Alternative Perspective on the Law of Restitution', in: A. Burrows (ed.), *Essays on the Law of Restitution* (1991), 247, 257.

a vague one: is it the obligation to honour all promises given or is it only the obligation to honour promises made for reasons of national policy?

In German law the promise by the Council would be part of the contract of employment and therefore enforceable. The mistake would then be an ordinary liability mistake. In English law, it is the consideration doctrine that makes the difference. The Council and Larner (by his application) had agreed that Larner was to be entitled to a certain sum. But for the consideration doctrine, there would be a contract, and therefore a liability mistake entitling the Council to restitution. Does the lack of consideration matter? The promise could not be enforced by an action, but it may nevertheless have been able to determine whether and to what extent Larner was entitled to keep the money. This was also the opinion of Denning LJ: 'It may be that... there was in strictness no consideration for the promise. But that does not matter. It is not the question here of enforcing the promise by action. It is a question of recovering overpayments made in the belief that they were due under the promise but not in fact due.'[14]

The result in *Larner* could be easily explained if it were to be acknowledged that the doctrine of consideration only governs the enforceability of promises, for if an agreement cannot be enforced, it does not follow that its existence has to be ignored completely by the law. It may be used to explain whether and to what extent the recipient was entitled to the sum and to what extent there was a mistaken payment that can be recovered. In other words, an agreement without consideration, although not enforceable, could for restitutionary purposes be assimilated to an ordinary contract. The mistaken assumption of such an agreement or the overpayment under such an agreement would then, like a liability mistake, found an action to recover.

There are other cases where the obligation the claimant intends to discharge is for certain reasons not enforceable:[15] the claimant may, for

---

[14] [1949] 2 KB 683 at 688.

[15] For example, the Scottish case of *Moore's Executors v. M'Dermid* [1913] 1 SLT 278. A debtor arranged with his creditors to discharge his debts by part payment. But one creditor, the defendant, did not agree and was paid in full. After the debtor's death, his executors, in terms of his will, paid the outstanding part of the debts to his creditors and, by mistake, also paid (again) the defendant creditor. This is another example of a mistaken assumption of an obligation that is for certain reasons (discharge by arrangement) not recognised as a liability. In Scotland, the problem was similar: the defendant contended that the *condictio indebiti* did not lie as the executors did not intend to discharge an existing obligation. With this contention, however, he was unsuccessful; the defendant, according to Lord Ormidale, 'gives to the word "due" a much too limited and technical meaning': *ibid.* at 279.

instance, overpay the defendant on a claim that is statute-barred. In *Morgan v. Ashcroft*[16] the plaintiff by mistake paid a betting debt to the defendant twice over. The betting contract, though not illegal, was void. The court denied recovery, *inter alia*, for lack of a liability mistake. Today writers agree that the result is either wrong or has to be explained by a special defence of gaming and wagering.[17] Here the contractual debt was not enforceable because of the Gaming Act, ultimately because of a general policy not to enforce bets. Regarding a mistaken overpayment, however, should the betting debt not be treated like an ordinary debt? In German law, betting debts are natural obligations: they are not enforceable but, if paid, form a justification for the defendant to retain the money.[18] If, however, the betting debt the payer has in mind did not exist at all, the payer can recover.

In recovery of mistaken payments, there seems to be no decisive difference whether the obligation the claimant intended to discharge, and which in truth did not exist, is enforceable or not. Consequently, it might have been possible to enlarge the category of mistakes leading to restitution in such a way as to encompass not only liability mistakes but also mistaken assumptions about other obligations that are for certain reasons not enforceable. But this is not what happened.[19] Perhaps the consideration doctrine prevented lawyers from giving any legal effect to gratuitous agreements, although, as noted above, it is questionable whether this doctrine extends beyond the question of enforceability of promises. Perhaps it was thought that an agreement that is able to determine whether the defendant may retain what he received necessarily has to be enforceable. The very idea of a concept of 'legal ground', by contrast, is that though an obligation may not be enforceable, it may nevertheless be able to determine whether and to what extent the defendant may retain the benefit transferred to him.

4. Lack of differentiation

The English development went another way: all mistakes that were neither contractual mistakes nor liability mistakes were thrown together into a diffuse category of non-liability mistakes. In *Morgan v. Ashcroft*, Sir Wilfrid Greene held that the mistaken assumption of a betting debt could not found a claim to recover because the payer never thought he was liable

---

[16] [1938] 1 KB 49.   [17] Birks, *Introduction*, 425; Burrows, *Law of Restitution*, 464.
[18] § 762(1) BGB.
[19] But see Stoljar, *Law of Quasi-contracts*, 20, 23, 31; P. Watts, 'Mistaken Payments and the Law of Restitution', [1993] *Lloyd's Maritime and Commercial Law Quarterly* 145, 147–8.

to pay. 'In that case the payment is intended to be a voluntary one and a voluntary payment it is whether the supposed fact be true or not.' The judge argued: 'If a father, believing that his son has suffered a financial loss, gives him a sum of money, he surely could not claim repayment if he afterwards discovered that no such loss has occurred.'[20] From a German point of view, the example of the father is surprising since it does not fit cases of mistake in unjust enrichment. In German law, father and son concluded a contract of gift. As an executed gift, it is valid even without notarial authentication. If the father now wants to recover what he has given, he has to invalidate the underlying contract. Thus, the question is whether the father's mistake is able to invalidate the gift. As it is a unilateral mistake concerning the father's motive, and not known to the son, the contract remains valid. The father cannot, therefore, recover: not because he did not think he was liable to pay, but because his mistake concerned merely his motives for making a gift. In English law, gifts are not recognised as binding contracts. But the quality of mistake remains the same: it concerns the reasons for a decision to enter into a certain transaction with another person and thus resembles a mistake in the formation of a contract. Suppose, in the example mentioned, that the son gave a (minimal) consideration in return for his father's financial help: the father's mistaken assumption about the son's financial situation would then be a unilateral mistake in the formation of a contract, not a liability mistake. The contract would remain valid, and therefore the father could not recover.

The mistakes in *Larner* and in *Morgan*, by contrast, are of a different nature. The claimant intends to perform a specific obligation that is for a certain reason not enforceable, because of the consideration doctrine or because of a policy against betting. Were it not for this, the mistake would be an ordinary liability mistake. One can conceive of similar examples. The claimant promises a gift of £100 to the defendant, without establishing a deed under seal to this effect, and then the claimant mistakenly pays the amount twice over or to the wrong person. Or the claimant intends to discharge an obligation, knowing that this obligation is time-barred, and later it turns out that the obligation did not exist at all. These examples differ from the case of the father who does not believe in a specific obligation to pay a fixed sum to his son, or from the case of *Lady Hood of Avalon v. Mackinnon*,[21] where a mother made a gift to her daughter, forgetting that she had already made an even larger gift at her daughter's marriage. She

---

[20] [1938] 1 KB 49 at 65–6.   [21] [1909] 1 Ch 476.

Table 2.1. *Types of mistake*

(A) Forming the intention to give something	(B) Executing this intention
(A1) Mistake in formation of contract	(B1) Mistaken assumption of contractual or other liability
(A2) Mistake in formation of gratuitous or otherwise unenforceable agreement or decision to make a gift	(B2) Mistaken assumption of gratuitous agreement or other non-enforceable obligation

could recover for mistake. The mistake was not that she had assumed to be under a specific duty but it concerned the motives for making a gift.

Regarding mistakes that may found a claim in restitution, the differentiation shown in Table 2.1 can be made.

(A1) If the claimant mistakenly concludes a contract and then discharges his obligation under that contract, he can only recover if the contract is set aside. Therefore, the question is whether the mistake is serious or fundamental enough to invalidate the parties' agreement (*Bell v. Lever Brothers*[22]).

(B1) On the other hand, there may not be a mistake in the formation of the contract but in its execution: the claimant pays too much, or twice over, or to the wrong recipient, or he mistakenly assumes a contract that does not exist. Similarly, the claimant may mistakenly execute, not a contractual, but another enforceable obligation, such as a liability arising in tort or a statutory obligation. All these cases are covered by the term 'liability mistake'.

(A2) The claimant may mistakenly enter into an agreement that is for certain reasons not recognised as a contract, such as lack of consideration or lack of form. The nature of mistake is essentially the same as in (A1): but for the lack of consideration or of the required form there would be a straightforward contractual mistake. Mistaken decisions to make a gift (as in the example of the father or in the case of *Lady Hood v. Mackinnon*) also belong to this category. Although gifts are not recognised as bilateral contracts, the essential nature of the mistake remains the same: it causes the decision to transfer a benefit to the defendant, and this decision can, under certain circumstances (for example, deed under seal), be binding.

---

[22] [1932] AC 161.

(B2) Like a binding contract, an unenforceable agreement can be executed by mistake: the claimant intends to discharge his 'obligation' under an unenforceable agreement but mistakenly pays the defendant too much, or twice over, or there is no agreement at all. Examples are *Larner v. LCC* or *Morgan v. Ashcroft*. Similarly, the claimant may mistakenly perform on another obligation that is not enforceable, such as an obligation that is time-barred. In (A2) there are mistakes that would be liability mistakes were it not for the fact that the obligation the claimant intends to discharge is not legally enforceable.

In German law, a payment caused by a mistake under category (B) is a transfer without legal ground whereas mistakes under category (A) are dealt with in the law of contract. The view changes drastically when looking at English law. Here, mistakes in (A1) (contractual mistake) and (B1) (liability mistake) are well-known and clearly defined categories in contract and restitution. The other mistakes, (A2) and (B2), are thrown together and called 'non-liability mistakes'. The distinction developed in line 1 of the table, above, is not taken over. Thus, the category of 'non-liability mistakes' embraces not only mistaken overpayments on gifts or non-enforceable obligations but also the execution of a gift that was itself mistakenly made. No distinction is made whether a claimant who agreed to pay a certain sum to his partner to help him in a financial difficulty had overestimated his own financial capacity or whether he mistakenly paid the amount twice.

5. Which mistakes lead to restitution?

The question arises which of these non-liability mistakes should lead to restitution. In his *Introduction to the Law of Restitution*, Peter Birks gives three reasons why it is the liability mistake that originally and indisputably gave rise to a restitutionary remedy.[23] First, there is the fear of too much restitution for mistake. Liability mistakes form a specific single category, excluding trivial or collateral errors. Secondly, restitution for liability mistake does not, unlike restitution for contractual mistakes, destroy bargains between the parties. Thirdly, there are rarely problems of counter-restitution, that is, problems that occur because the claimant asking for restitution has himself received a benefit from the defendant that he may not easily be able to restore. But differentiating between the four categories, as described above, may lead to different results. Problems of

---

[23] Birks, *Introduction*, 148 ff.

counter-restitution usually emerge if the parties exchange benefits under a real or assumed contract. Therefore, these problems arise not only in cases of contractual mistakes but also in cases of liability mistakes, if the liability that the claimant mistakenly assumed was a contractual liability. Conversely, mistakes in (A2) and (B2) usually concern gratuitous transfers or agreements without consideration. Problems of counter-restitution can therefore be found in the categories (A1) and (B1) rather than in (A2) or (B2).

Next, there is the problem of upholding the parties' bargains. So far as contractual mistakes are concerned, only fundamental mistakes are taken into account because, if benefits transferred under a contract have to be retransferred on account of such a mistake, the bargain between the parties will be disturbed. Conversely, restitution for a liability mistake does not interfere with bargains, as the parties never agreed on the transfer that the claimant mistakenly made. But the same is true for mistakes under (B2). If the claimant mistakenly assumes an 'obligation' that is for certain reasons not enforceable or if he overpays the defendant in discharge of such an obligation, allowing restitution will not undermine any agreement between the parties since there was never any agreement about the transfer of wealth actually made. Matters are different with mistakes under (A2). If A and B agree that A is to pay 100 to B, and if A later contends that he entered the agreement mistakenly (because he was mistaken about his own financial situation, about B's character or about the tax advantages associated with the payment), allowing restitution would undermine the parties' agreement. It is true that the agreement does not amount to a contract, but this does not mean that B's reliance on the agreement is not worthy of a certain level of protection. This reliance has to be distinguished from the reliance on the receipt as such, which is common to all restitutionary cases and which can be catered for by the defence of change of position. B relied not only on the receipt but on an executed agreement. While his protection need not be as strong as in the case of contracts mistakenly entered into, there is at least a need to balance A's interest to recover the mistaken transfer against B's interest in upholding the agreement. This need does not arise if there is no agreement about the transfer in issue, namely in cases of (B1) and (B2). Here, leaving aside possible defences, there is no argument against recovery. The same holds true with regard to gifts. If A wants to recover a gift made to B because his decision to make the gift was influenced by a mistake (category (A2), example: *Lady Hood v. Mackinnon*), recovery is not self-evident: A's interest has to be balanced against B's reliance on an executed gift. The matter is different if A mistakenly overpays B on a gift or pays to the wrong person, at least if the recipient had no reason to expect a voluntary gift (B2): here, recovery should be possible.[24]

Finally, the mistaken assumption of an obligation that is, for specific reasons, not enforceable forms a clearly defined category excluding trivial errors, just as does the liability mistake. In the result, applying Birks's policy factors, it would seem to be sensible always to allow restitution for mistakes in (B1) and (B2). Conversely, in (A2) it has to be considered whether the reliance on an agreement not amounting to a formal contract or on an executed gift should be protected in the same way as the reliance on a contract, or not at all, or somewhere in between. In other words: there must be a decision whether the mistakes in (A2) have to be as fundamental as in the case of a contractual mistake, or less fundamental, or whether perhaps even every mistake may be taken into account. This is a policy decision.

The suggested approach of differentiating between various types of mistakes that are to be dealt with in different ways has not, however, been adopted in English law. In truth, it is a kind of legal-ground analysis. The mistakes in (B1) and (B2) are assumptions of liabilities or certain non-enforceable obligations that do not exist: the legal ground is lacking, restitution is unproblematic. In the case of a mistake under (A1) or (A2), it must be asked whether the contract, agreement or gift can be upheld in spite of the mistake. Contracts, other agreements or gifts are regarded as prima facie legal grounds, preventing restitution, unless they are set aside as a result of a sufficiently fundamental mistake. In the latter case, it is the destruction of the legal ground on account of the mistake, not the mistake itself, that triggers restitution.

English law, as has been said above, did not accept a notion of legal ground. Such notion had been implicit in the action allowing recovery for liability mistakes, which presupposes a conscious transfer in relation to an assumed legal ground (the liability) that does not, in fact, exist. When it emerged that the notion of liability mistake is too narrow, it could have been extended to a wider notion of mistakes covering the mistaken assumption not only of a liability but also of other legal grounds: a mistake about the *causa*. But this was not done. Instead, the word 'liability' was dropped, and with it all references to a legal ground. The mistake alone remained as justification for recovery.

---

[24] Cf. I. Englard, 'Restitution of Benefits Conferred Without Obligation', *International Encyclopedia of Comparative Law* (1991), vol. X, chap. 5, § 14.

6. Restitution for vitiation of the claimant's will

'For it is perfectly sensible, even if too simple, to start with the proposition that what is given by mistake should be given back.'[25] Stripped of its reference to a legal ground, the notion of mistake is so wide that the action to recover for mistake covers the most diverse constellations, breaking down the borderlines between the Continental *condictiones*. If a person makes a gift to his son, he may be mistaken about his son's financial situation or he may mistakenly have paid the amount twice: in both cases there is a mistaken payment. Restitution for mistake may also cover the payment on a *future* obligation, which does not, however, come into existence, as long as the claimant paid under a mistake about the present (overlooking the fact that the recipient had committed an act of bankruptcy).[26] Restitution for mistake also covers improvements on another person's property by a claimant believing the property to be his own[27] – a case Roman and Continental law have always regarded as being completely different. The common ratio of all these restitutionary actions is the vitiation of the claimant's decision: the transfer is, in one way or another, not based on his free and unimpaired will. The claimant's will may also be vitiated by reasons other than mistake, for example by duress, undue influence or by the claimant's minority. In this way, other unjust factors such as duress, inequality and incapacity have joined mistake. Restitution for mistake thus fits into a larger system that proceeds from the premise that restitution in most cases is intended to allow for the recovery of a benefit the claimant did not really mean the defendant to have. In Birks's terminology: either the claimant's will was qualified (the transfer is meant to be conditional – for example, dependent on the rendering of counterperformance; unjust factor: failure of consideration), or it was vitiated by mistake, duress or inequality. Restitution is based, not on the lack of legal ground, but on the lack of the claimant's consent.

7. Recovery for every causal mistake?

As a result, restitution was now simply founded on the claimant's mistake as such. But the problem of which mistakes should lead to recovery remained unsolved. Ultimately, the view gained ground that every mistake that has caused a transfer should lead to restitution. It was first proposed

---

[25] Birks, *Introduction*, 148; similarly Burrows, *Law of Restitution*, 95.
[26] *Kerrison v. Glyn, Mills, Currie & Co.* (1911) 81 LJKB 465; cf. Goff and Jones, *Law of Restitution*, 183.
[27] See the discussions of *Greenwood v. Bennett* [1973] QB 195 in Birks, *Introduction*, 155; Burrows, *Law of Restitution*, 121; and Goff and Jones, *Law of Restitution*, 246 ff.

by Goff and Jones, and concisely formulated in Goff J's (as he then was) famous judgment *Barclays Bank v. Simms*.[28]

If a person pays money to another under a mistake of fact which causes him to make the payment, he is *prima facie* entitled to recover it as money paid under a mistake of fact. His claim may, however, fail if... the payment is made for good consideration, in particular if the money is paid to discharge, and does discharge, a debt owed to the payee... by the payer or by third party by whom he is authorised to discharge the debt.[29]

This 'causal mistake approach' has found more and more supporters.[30]

A prima facie entitlement to recover for every kind of mistake as long as it caused the payment may, however, unreasonably endanger the position of the recipient. Goff J's defence of 'good consideration' protects the recipient in the large group of cases where the payer intends by his payment to discharge an obligation: if the obligation is successfully discharged, recovery is excluded. But is there a similar safeguard if the payer did not intend to discharge an obligation? In *Barclays Bank v. Simms*, Goff J mentioned four examples where a requirement of a liability mistake would exclude restitution but where recovery should be possible:

---

[28] [1980] QB 677. *Barclays Bank v. Simms* was a three-party constellation (the plaintiff bank had mistakenly paid to the defendant a countermanded cheque), and Goff J cited other English three-party cases to support his proposition. However, these authorities do not support the causal mistake approach. In some cases the claimant paid the defendant in order to discharge a third person's debt. In these cases, English and German law allow recovery from the recipient if (and only if) the debt is not discharged by the payment (because it did not exist or because it could for other reasons not be discharged). If the mistake leading to restitution had to be defined, it would not be a causal mistake but a mistake about whether the payment can discharge a debt. In other cases the claimant paid primarily because of an (assumed) order by a third person to pay a certain sum to the defendant (the claimant usually being a bank). The claimant may by his payment have intended to discharge a liability towards the third person or to acquire a contractual right of reimbursement. The need for recovery arises only if his purpose fails, either because the contract does not exist or because the claimant's payment was not governed by a valid mandate. His mistake leading to restitution will therefore concern his relationship to the third person. For details, see S. Meier, 'Mistaken Payments in Three-party Situations: A German View of English Law', (1999) 58 *CLJ* 567.

[29] [1980] QB 677 at 695.

[30] Burrows, *Law of Restitution*, 100, 104–5; Goff and Jones, *Law of Restitution*, 180, 191; C. Needham, 'Mistaken Payments: A New Look at an Old Theme', (1978) 12 *University of British Columbia LR* 159, 220–1; A. Tettenborn, 'Mistaken Payments and Countermanded Cheques', (1980) 130 *NLJ* 273; M. Bryan, 'Mistaken Payments and the Law of Unjust Enrichment', (1993) 15 *Sydney LR* 461, 472 ff.; the Australian High Court in *David Securities Pty Ltd v. Commonwealth Bank of Australia* (1992) 175 CLR 353; Neuberger J in *Nurdin & Peacock plc v. D. B. Ramsden & Co. Ltd* [1999] 1 WLR 1249 at 1272 ff.

(1) A man, forgetting that he has already paid his subscription to the National Trust, pays it a second time. (2) A substantial charity uses a computer for the purpose of distributing small benefactions. The computer runs mad, and pays one beneficiary the same gift one hundred times over. (3) A shipowner and a charterer enter into a sterling charterparty for a period of years. Sterling depreciates against other currencies; and the charterer decides, to maintain the goodwill of the shipowner but without obligation, to increase the monthly hire payments. Owing to a mistake in his office, the increase in one monthly hire payment is paid twice over. (4) A Lloyd's syndicate gets into financial difficulties. To maintain the reputation of Lloyd's, other underwriting syndicates decide to make gifts of money to assist the syndicate in difficulties. Due to a mistake, one syndicate makes its gift twice over.[31]

All these cases are examples of mistakes in the execution of an intention to give something – (B2). The payer does not mistakenly form an intention to give something but merely executes his intention more often than he intended to. There is a good reason to pay the sum once, but all further payments lack even a prima facie reason. It seems uncontroversial to allow recovery in such cases. The problem with the causal mistake approach lies somewhere else: it allows recovery for *every* kind of causal mistake, that is, for every mistake that has influenced the payer's decision to give something at all (A2). In consequence, recovery has to be allowed in the following examples (always assuming the payer would not have paid if he had known the real facts). A gives a donation to a charity because he mistakenly assumes that both the mayor and the pastor of his village also made a donation and because he does not want to stand aside. B gives money to an environmental organisation, not knowing that the organisation occasionally takes part in illegal demonstrations. C pays a time-barred debt to his creditor, not knowing that that creditor won in the lottery the day before. The charterer D from Goff J's example (3) who increased the hire payments overrated his own financial situation, or he did not know that the shipowner is a close friend of his archenemy or belongs to a religious community of which the charterer disapproves. In other words: every mistake, even if it merely concerns the payer's motive, leads to a prima facie claim to recover as long as it has caused the payment. The recipient cannot be protected by the restitutionary defences (submission, change of position) as long as he did not request the payment and did not change his position to his detriment. He is always in danger of having to return the money on account of every kind of mistake the payer may have made.

[31] [1980] QB 677 at 697.

It is true that a recipient of a gratuitous benefit is a mere volunteer and therefore need not be protected in the same way as a party to a commercial contract.[32] It is not unusual to be more liberal in allowing recovery in cases of gifts. But it does not follow that the recipient of a gratuitous benefit need not be protected at all, as long as he did not change his position. An executed gift can undoubtedly not be recovered because of a later change of mind by the donor. Here, the recipient is protected even if he still holds the benefit in his hand. It is highly questionable whether the situation should be so drastically different as soon as there is some mistake on the part of the donor. If, in the case of a mistake, the interests of the donee are disregarded, why should they not be disregarded in the case of a change of mind? The difference between a mistake in motive and a later change of mind may be very slight.

Moreover, the older case law on the recovery of gifts seems to suggest that the only mistakes that can lead to recovery are those that are, in one way or another, 'serious'. In *Ogilvie v. Littleboy* Lindley LJ said:

> Gifts cannot be revoked, nor can deeds of gift be set aside, simply because the donors wish they had not made them and would like to have back the property given... In the absence of all such circumstances of suspicion [sc.: fraud, undue influence, fiduciary relation, induced mistake] a donor can only obtain back property which he has given away by showing that he was under some mistake of so serious a character as to render it unjust on the part of the donee to retain the property given to him.[33]

This passage is cited with approval in Goff and Jones.[34] But if the mistake has to be serious, not every causal mistake can lead to recovery. In *Wilson v. Thornbury*,[35] for instance, the plaintiff gave to the defendant £300 on the occasion of her marriage. Both parties assumed that the marriage of the defendant caused the loss of an annuity and a life interest she had in a certain house, and the sum was intended to compensate her for that loss. When it turned out that the defendant was in fact the owner of the house and had therefore lost only the annuity as a result of her marriage, the plaintiff tried to recover his gift, but without success. The payment was 'simply a voluntary gift founded upon a common mistake, and cannot now be recovered'.[36] It is difficult to see whether the courts have changed their attitudes since then and, if so, when.

---

[32] Goff and Jones, *Law of Restitution*, 190.
[33] (1897) 13 TLR 399 at 400.
[34] Goff and Jones, *Law of Restitution*, 190.
[35] (1875) LR 10 Ch App 239.
[36] Ibid. at 249, *per* James LJ.

It is submitted that the causal mistake approach neglects the interests of the recipient in an unacceptable way. It does not offer any formula for excluding the most far-reaching mistakes concerning the payer's motives: they have to be taken account of as long as the payer can prove that he would not have paid but for his mistake. The action to recover for mistake had been unduly restricted for a long time, but there is now the danger of restitutionary overkill.[37]

8. Mistake and legal ground

If there is a need to restrict restitution for mistakes concerning the payer's motives, it must be admitted that not every mistake causing the payment may lead to restitution. Therefore, it is necessary to find criteria for distinguishing between relevant and irrelevant mistakes. This task has never as yet been undertaken. The reason is not difficult to see. It is not possible to differentiate mistakes in restitution without resorting to a legal-ground analysis.

English law has already known a kind of legal ground. If the claimant mistakenly pays on an existing obligation (his mistake concerning something else, such as his own or the recipient's financial position), he cannot, in spite of his mistake, recover.[38] This proposition is remarkable for a system that founds the right to recover solely on the claimant's mistake. It is certainly possible to say that restitution is always based on the claimant's mistake, and that the discharge of an obligation is merely a defence against a prima facie right to recover.[39] It is also possible to say that an enrichment brought about in the discharge of an obligation is not unjust.[40] At any rate, the claimant's mistake is only one of several criteria to determine whether an enrichment has to be returned, and it is questionable whether it is the most important one. If the claimant paid in order to discharge an obligation, the first question for the court is often whether and to what extent there was an obligation. Only in so far as there is no obligation does the next question arise – whether the claimant

---

[37] See also Watts, 'Mistaken Payments', 147–8.
[38] *Steam Saw Mills v. Baring Brothers* [1922] 1 Ch 244; Goff and Jones, *Law of Restitution*, 48; Birks, *Introduction*, 160; Friedmann, 'Obligations', 247 ff.
[39] Goff J in *Barclays Bank v. Simms* [1980] QB 677 at 695; Mason CJ, Deane, Toohey, Gaudron, McHugh JJ in *David Securities v. Commonwealth Bank* (1992) 175 CLR 353 at 381; *contra*: Matthews, 'Money Paid Under a Mistake', 587; P. A. Butler, 'Mistaken Payments, Change of Position and Restitution', in: P. Finn (ed.), *Essays on Restitution* (1990), 87, 99.
[40] Brennan J in *David Securities v. Commonwealth Bank* (1992) 175 CLR 353 at 392; Lee J in *Griffith v. Commonwealth Bank* (1994) 123 ALR 111 at 122–3.

can recover for mistake.[41] An obligation that has been discharged, by excluding restitution, assigns the benefit that has been transferred finally to the recipient's estate. Finally assigning benefits to a recipient is exactly the function of a legal ground.

If, then, obligations perform the function of a legal ground, it may be asked whether English law should not recognise other legal grounds as well. As mentioned before, the need to distinguish between mistakes that trigger a right to recover and those that do not requires a kind of legal-ground analysis. It is not enough to focus merely on a transfer of a certain benefit by the claimant to the defendant. Rather, it has to be asked what purpose the claimant had in mind. To appreciate the role of a specific mistake, one has to appreciate its influence on a specific transaction. To take again the example of the father who gives money to his son in the mistaken belief that the latter has made a financial loss, there may be different opinions on whether the father should, under these circumstances, recover. The crucial point is whether a donation should be upheld or not. Denying recovery is to say that the donation remains valid, despite the donor's mistake. Allowing restitution is to say that the donor's mistake is able to invalidate an executed donation the son may have relied upon. It is not possible to appreciate the role of a specific mistake without looking to the specific transaction that has been based on it. Depending on the transaction, the same incorrect assumption can be more or less important: mistakes about the private way of life or the religious beliefs of the recipient will more likely be a reason for the recovery of a gift by the recipient's fiancé than for the recovery of a payment by the recipient's business partner in order to maintain the recipient's financial reputation. Matters are different if the claimant mistakenly pays too much, twice over, or to the wrong recipient. As long as the recipient cannot reasonably expect a gift, or rely on another reason for the payment, there is no reason not to allow recovery (leaving aside special defences). But if there is an agreement by the parties about the transfer in issue, or a donation (at least in the reasonable view of the recipient), it has to be asked whether the claimant's mistake may, by giving rise to a right to recover, invalidate the agreement or donation. The advantage of this approach is to reveal the real reasons behind the legal decision. If a certain mistake is held not to give rise to a right of recovery, it is because, in order to protect the interests of the recipient, a certain transaction (agreement or donation) should be upheld.

---

[41] See, e.g., *Works and Public Buildings Commission v. Pontypridd Masonic Hall* (1920) 89 LJQB 607.

II. Mistake of law

The German Civil Code dispensed with a requirement of a mistake for the *condictio indebiti* and thereby also jettisoned the old problem of how to deal with mistakes of law. The right to recover is only barred by positive knowledge that the liability does not exist; a mistake of law, however, excludes such knowledge. In England the old rule barring restitution if the claimant's mistake is merely one of law[42] was abolished only recently.[43] It had been increasingly criticised since there seemed to be no difference in principle between mistakes of fact and of law: since both mistakes vitiate the claimant's intention to give, both mistakes, it was thought, should trigger a right to recover.[44] The mistake of law rule was not based on the nature of this type of mistake, but rather on a number of policy reasons. Thus, for example, restitution had to be barred if the defendant had detrimentally changed his position in reliance on the receipt, or if the claimant, by paying, had submitted to an honest claim.[45] As long as there were no special defences covering those situations, the task had to be fulfilled by the mistake of law rule. Most importantly, however, the rule was necessary in view of the fact that modern English law does not recognise legal grounds other than (enforceable) obligations.

Every legal system knows obligations that are not legally enforceable but nevertheless are able to provide a justification for the recipient to keep the benefit transferred in fulfilment of the obligation.[46] The classic example is a claim that is time-barred. The debtor cannot legally be forced to perform; however, if he performs, the law approves of the transfer and does not intervene to undo it. The transfer is upheld even if the

---

[42] Founded in *Bilbie v. Lumley* (1802) 2 East 469; 102 ER 448.
[43] *Kleinwort Benson v. Lincoln City Council* [1998] 3 WLR 1095; cf. *Air Canada v. British Columbia* (1989) 59 DLR (4th) 161 (Canada); *David Securities v. Commonwealth Bank* (1992) 175 CLR 353 (Australia); and R. Zimmermann and P. Hellwege, '"Error iuris non excusat" und das "law of restitution"', in: U. Hübner and W. Ebke (eds.), *Festschrift für Bernhard Großfeld* (1998), 1367.
[44] Dickson J in *Nepean v. Ontario Hydro* (1982) 132 DLR (3d) 193 at 206 ff.; Goff and Jones, *Law of Restitution*, 214–15; Burrows, *Law of Restitution*, 116 ff.; Stoljar, *Law of Quasi-contracts*, 48 ff.; Needham, 'Mistaken Payments', 170 ff; W. Knutson, 'Mistake of Law Payments in Canada: A Mistaken Principle?', (1979) 10 *Manitoba Law Journal* 23; J. McCamus, 'Restitutionary Recovery of Moneys Paid to a Public Authority under a Mistake of Law', (1983) 17 *University of British Columbia LR* 233.
[45] For details, see Zweigert and Kötz, *Comparative Law*, 567 ff.; S. Meier, *Irrtum und Zweckverfehlung: Die Rolle der unjust-Gründe bei rechtsgrundlosen Leistungen im englischen Recht* (1999), 123 ff.
[46] Cf. Engand, 'Restitution of Benefits', §§ 21 ff.; Stoljar, *Law of Quasi-contracts*, 28 ff.; P. Birks, 'The English Recognition of Unjust Enrichment', [1991] *Lloyd's Maritime and Commercial Law Quarterly* 473, 494, nn. 89, 91.

transferor mistakenly assumed the obligation to be legally enforceable. Since the result of the transfer is approved of, the transferor's mistake of law is irrelevant. German law has different devices to exclude restitution in such cases. The code provides expressly that a payment to discharge a time-barred claim cannot be recovered even if the claimant overlooked the time bar (§ 222(2), first sentence); recovery is also excluded if the claimant has fulfilled a moral duty (§ 814). More importantly, German law took over from Roman law the notion of a 'natural obligation', which, despite not being legally enforceable, forms a legal ground preventing restitution. A modern German example is the contract of betting (§ 762).

The Roman natural obligations were in Lord Mansfield's mind[47] when he, in *Moses v. Macferlan*, said about the action to recover money:

> It lies only for money which, *ex aequo et bono*, the defendant ought to refund: it does not lie for money paid by the plaintiff, which is claimed from him as payable in point of honour and honesty, although it could not have been recovered from him by any course of law; as in payment of a debt barred by the Statute of Limitations, or contracted during his infancy, or to the extent of principal and legal interest upon an usurious contract, or for money fairly lost at play: because in all these cases, the defendant may retain it with a safe conscience, though by positive law he was barred from recovering.[48]

In similar terms, De Grey CJ said in 1772:

> But the proposition is not universal, that whenever a man pays money which he is not bound to pay, he may by this action recover it back. Money due in point of honour or conscience, though a man is not compellable to pay it, yet if paid, shall not be recovered back: as a bona fide debt, which is barred by the Statute of Limitations.[49]

If the claimant had performed such a moral or natural obligation, mistakenly believing it to be enforceable, recovery could, until 1802, be prevented by the argument that he had merely paid what in 'honour and conscience' he was bound to pay.[50] After *Bilbie v. Lumley*[51] the courts could resort to the mistake of law rule to exclude recovery. This explanation, however, obscures the true reason why recovery is excluded: not because of the nature of the mistake, but because of the obligation on which the claimant paid: an obligation which provided the defendant with a justification to keep the benefit.

---

[47] See P. Birks, 'English and Roman Learning in *Moses v. Macferlan*', (1984) 37 *Current Legal Problems* 1, 16 ff.
[48] (1760) 2 Burr 1005 at 1012; 97 ER 676.
[49] *Farmer v. Arundel* (1772) 2 Black W 824 at 825–6; 96 ER 485.
[50] Cf. *Munt v. Stokes* (1792) 4 TR 561 at 563; 100 ER 1176.   [51] (1802) 2 East 469.

Similarly, there are cases where a statute prevents the defendant from demanding a certain payment from the claimant. If the claimant, not knowing about the statute, pays none the less, there is the question whether he can recover. This is principally a problem of interpretation of the statute. In *Sharp Brothers & Knight v. Chant*[52] the statute had a partly retroactive effect and was therefore construed restrictively: a right to recover, according to the court, would have required an express provision in the statute. The plaintiff tenant could therefore not recover rent payments which, under the statute, he could never have been compelled to pay. His mistake of law was held to be irrelevant. Thus, the statute was construed merely as excluding the enforceability of the claim for a higher rent. A different result was reached in *Kiriri Cotton Co. v. Dewani*:[53] here the plaintiff could recover a premium he had paid to his landlord in contravention of a Ugandan statute, although the statute did not mention a right to recover (only criminal sanctions) and although the plaintiff's mistake was one of law. The statute aimed at the protection of the plaintiff, which could best be served by a right to recover. In the Australian case *J. & S. Holdings v. NRMA Insurance*[54] the parties had agreed on a loan with 16 per cent interest, overlooking a statute that rendered clauses providing for more than 12 per cent interest void. The statute (unlike the Ugandan one) did not render the agreement illegal; moreover, it expressly provided for a right to recover in certain cases (such as usury) without mentioning such a right in the case of the 12 per cent limit. The court therefore held that the statute did not serve a protective function and that the plaintiff, since his mistake was merely one of law, could not recover. In the result, the 12 per cent limit was held merely to restrict the enforceability of interest claims.

A statute restricting the right to demand a certain payment may thus either be regarded as serving a protective function, in which case the payer can recover, or it may not be so regarded, in which case there is no recovery. In terms of the 'unjust factor' language, one may say that in *Sharp Brothers* and in *J. & S. Holdings v. NRMA Insurance* the plaintiff lacked an unjust factor (as there was only a mistake of law) whereas the result in *Kiriri Cotton* has to be explained by a special unjust factor. This unjust factor focuses on the vulnerable position of the claimant as the reason for recovery and may be called 'inequality'.[55] But this approach cannot obviate the central problem of determining in which cases the

---

[52] [1917] 1 KB 771.   [53] [1960] AC 192.   [54] (1982) 41 ALR 539.
[55] Birks, *Introduction*, 167, 209–10.

contravention of a statute triggers a right to recover. This can only be determined by way of interpreting that particular statute. Does it merely exclude the enforceability of a claim, or does it require the benefit to be retransferred? In the first case, one may refer to a non-enforceable obligation that nevertheless furnishes the defendant with a right to retain the benefit.

The difference between the question whether there is an enforceable liability and whether the defendant may retain the benefit is crucial with regard to mistakes of law. In restitution, the central question is whether the defendant may retain the benefit, not whether there is an enforceable liability. Therefore, the mistaken assumption on the part of the claimant that he is bound to transfer the benefit is irrelevant, as long as the defendant has a good reason to keep it; or, as the civil law would put it, as long as there is a legal ground for the transfer. Various cases are conceivable where the defendant obtained the benefit 'justly' although he could not have forced the claimant to transfer it. If, prior to *Kleinwort Benson v. Lincoln CC*,[56] the claimant contended that he had assumed an enforceable obligation, the mistake of law rule was able to prevent restitution. Now that the rule has been abolished, other ways have to be found to achieve that result. One suggestion has been to work with a defence of submission to an honest claim.[57] But what exactly are the 'honest claims' that give the defendant a right to retain the benefit? It is necessary to name and explain them. This is nothing other than a legal-ground analysis.

III. Doubts and submission

If the claimant pays on an obligation that does not, in actuality, exist, German law bases recovery on the lack of obligation, providing merely for a defence if the claimant positively knew that the obligation did not exist. In contrast, the English claim in restitution requires an unjust factor, most often a mistake by the claimant. Does the requirement of an unjust factor have a limiting effect in that it would restrict recovery of payments made on non-existent obligations? Is there any practical difference between German and English law in this area? Leaving the burden of proof aside, in both systems recovery is allowed if the payer did not

---

[56] [1999] 2 AC 349.
[57] P. Birks, 'Konkurrierende Strategien und Interessen: Das Irrtumserfordernis im Bereicherungsrecht des common law', (1993) 1 *Zeitschrift für Europäisches Privatrecht* 554, 571.

know of the lack of obligation whereas recovery is excluded if he knew that there was no obligation. But what about the cases where the payer entertains doubts about his obligation? It might be argued that here the requirement of an unjust factor is vitally important. However, a closer view reveals that the cases of doubt do not justify an approach requiring a specific reason for restitution.

In these cases, the defendant usually demands payment from the claimant, but the claimant's liability is doubtful, and the parties are arguing about it. Eventually, the claimant pays, only to find out later that he was not liable. Despite there being no compromise in the true sense of the word, there is a good case for preventing the claimant from recovering. In both English and German law there are policy-motivated restrictions on the right to recovery. According to German law, the claimant has paid on a non-existent obligation. His doubts do not amount to a positive knowledge of the lack of obligation, which would exclude his prima facie claim to restitution. However, the courts have invoked the principle of good faith to deny recovery in cases where the defendant is entitled to infer from the claimant's conduct that the claimant intended a final payment, independently of whether his obligation existed.[58] The focus is on the intention of the claimant, as it could be perceived by the defendant. Thus, the claimant may always, by an express reservation, keep his right to recover open.[59]

In English cases where there are doubts as to the claimant's liability there is a policy of 'submit or litigate': the claimant, if he wants to contest his liability, has to refuse payment, thereby enabling the defendant to institute legal proceedings that finally decide the point. If he submits to the demand he cannot later bring proceedings to recover and thereby choose his own time for litigation.[60] In order to exclude restitution, the mistake of law rule was a welcome tool.[61] Those who criticised the mistake of law rule contended that the denial of recovery had to be explained by a special submission principle.[62] This is even more important now after

---

[58] RGZ 97, 140; RGZ 144, 89; BGHZ 32, 271, 278-9; see Lorenz in: *J. von Staudingers Kommentar*, § 814, n. 5; Reuter and Martinek, *Ungerechtfertigte Bereicherung*, 186.
[59] BGHZ 83, 278, 282; Lorenz in: *J. von Staudingers Kommentar*, § 814, n. 6.
[60] Cf. *Brisbane v. Dacres* (1813) 5 Taunt 143 at 152 (Gibbs J), 159-60 (Chambre J), 160-1 (Heath J); *Rogers v. Ingham* [1876] 3 Ch 351; *Maskell v. Horner* [1915] 3 KB 106; Lord Goff in *Woolwich Equitable Building Society v. IRC* [1993] AC 70 at 165.
[61] See, e.g., *Rogers v. Ingham* [1876] 3 Ch 351; *Sawyer & Vincent v. Window Brace* [1943] 1 KB 32.
[62] Goff and Jones, *Law of Restitution*, 214-15; S. Arrowsmith, 'Mistake and the Role of the "Submission to an Honest Claim"', in: Burrows, *Essays*, 17 ff.; Butler, 'Mistaken Payments', 102 ff.

the abolition of the mistake of law rule, in view of the fact that there still seems to be the need to restrict recovery in cases of open doubts.[63]

It has been suggested that a claimant paying in spite of doubts about his liability does not labour under any mistake and can therefore not recover.[64] But if the claimant had known the true legal situation he would not have made the payment.[65] If ignorance of a certain set of facts can count as a mistake of fact, why should ignorance of the true state of his indebtedness not be regarded as a mistake of law? It has been said that doubts on the part of the claimant should exclude the possibility of relying on a mistake, either because there can be no mistake if there are doubts,[66] or because there is a mistake but the claimant assumed the risk of being mistaken and thus cannot rely on it.[67] Another proposal has been to apply a balance of probabilities test: if the claimant pays in the belief that the facts are probably not what in truth they are (for example, he is 51 per cent mistaken) he may recover on account of mistake, otherwise his doubts preclude restitution.[68] But what about the claimant who strongly denied his liability and in the end was convinced by the defendant that he has to pay? This seems a typical submission case, although when the claimant paid he was 100 per cent convinced of the wrong state of affairs. Should one focus instead on another, earlier, moment? But why?

A general problem with all these approaches is that they focus solely on the claimant's mind in their inquiry as to how doubts and the notion of mistake relate to each other. The typical fact situation (and the real problem) is, however, that the question of liability is doubtful *between the parties*: they are arguing about the point, and in the end one of them gives way. The claimant may be convinced that he is not liable and subsequently (say, because of wrong advice) change his mind. Why

---

[63] Cf. Law Commission of England and Wales, *Restitution: Mistakes of Law and Ultra Vires Public Authority Receipts and Payments*, Report No. 227 (1994), §§ 2.34–2.35; *David Securities v. Commonwealth Bank* (1992) 175 CLR 353 at 372.

[64] Needham, 'Mistaken Payments', 178; Mocatta J in *Saronic v. Huron* [1979] 1 Lloyd's L Rep 341 at 363; Brennan J in *David Securities v. Commonwealth Bank* (1992) 175 CLR 353 at 397.

[65] Arrowsmith, 'Mistake', 23; Dawson J in *David Securities v. Commonwealth Bank* (1992) 175 CLR 353 at 403.

[66] *Maskell v. Horner* [1915] 3 KB 106 at 117–18, 123, 126.

[67] Arrowsmith, 'Mistake', 26 ff.; Law Commission, *Restitution*, § 2.31; and the majority of the High court in *David Securities v. Commonwealth Bank* (1992) 175 CLR 353 at 373–4; Hobhouse J in *Westdeutsche Landesbank Girozentrale v. Islington London Borough Council* [1994] 4 All ER 890 at 934.

[68] Burrows, *Law of Restitution*, 102.

must he be regarded as having had doubts? What these subjective approaches fail to take into account is the position of the other party, who merely notes that the claimant is paying after arguments about his liability have been exchanged, and who may therefore assume that the claimant has overcome his initial objections. The reason why English writers focus solely on the claimant's state of mind is that they try to integrate the submission problem into the system of unjust factors, which in turn focuses solely on the claimant's will. Arguably, however, the submission cases do not turn on the claimant's will but on a special policy of protecting the recipient's reliance on the claimant's payment after the dispute. Thus, claimants have been prevented from recovery even if they protested against the demand and reserved their right to recovery.[69] To speak of a voluntary payment in these circumstances is a mere fiction. There may be good policy reasons to deny recovery under these circumstances, but the results should not be explained by reference to a system focusing on the claimant's will.

What is therefore needed is a submission principle in the form of a defence, balancing the interests of claimant and defendant and not concealing its policy-motivated origin.[70] This is even more important if restitution can be founded on every kind of causal mistake. For then the mistaken assumption of the claimant need not concern his liability as such; he may be positively mistaken (without any doubts) about a certain fact, for example wrongly assume a judicial decision to his disadvantage, and therefore doubt his being liable. If restitution can rest on every mistake, he should, in spite of his doubts, recover; if, however, his doubts should be taken into consideration, a special defence would be needed. In the recent case of *Nurdin & Peacock plc v. D. B. Ramsden & Co. Ltd*[71] the plaintiff paid the defendant in spite of doubts about his liability. Neuberger J held that he was entitled to recover for mistake of law because the plaintiff had wrongly assumed he was entitled to recover if the liability turned out not to exist. If this proposition is followed, one can hardly speak any more of a policy protecting a recipient who reasonably believes in a final payment, and many 'submission cases' will now have to be decided differently. The result of *Nurdin* was probably correct, as the defendant knew that the plaintiff paid under reservation of a right to recover. This factor should be emphasised in formulating a submission defence taking the interests of *both*

---

[69] Cf. *Maskell v. Horner* [1915] 3 KB 106 at 120, 122, 126; *Brown v. M'Kinally* (1795) 1 Esp 279; 170 ER 356; Goff and Jones, *Law of Restitution*, 57.
[70] Cf. Lionel Smith, 'Restitution for Mistake of Law', [1999] *Restitution LR* 148, 157.
[71] [1999] 1 WLR 1249.

parties into account instead of concentrating on some diffuse mistake on the part of the claimant.

IV. Ultra vires demands

If a public authority unlawfully (ultra vires) exacts taxes or other levies from a citizen, the question arises whether the citizen can recover his payment. Whereas in the Continental legal systems, which separate public law from private law, this problem is seen as one of administrative law, the English lawyer will ask whether the citizen has an action in the law of restitution. The older case law of the twentieth century required the citizen to show an unjust factor that would have founded a claim to recover if the payment had been made to a private individual – most notably, mistake or compulsion.[72] As a result, the right to recover was gravely restricted: in order to establish compulsion, the claimant had to show more than the mere threat by the authority to institute criminal proceedings; and if the claimant had paid because he believed the tax to be lawful, he stumbled over the mistake of law rule. Behind this restrictive attitude lay the fear of a disruption of the public finances that would ensue if it turned out that an authority had for a long time and in a vast number of cases misapplied the law so that a multitude of litigants might now demand their money back – the so-called 'floodgates argument'.[73] The requirement of an unjust factor served to ward off this danger, for the traditional unjust factors giving a right to recovery were mistake of fact and compulsion (established, for example, by a threat to seize the claimant's property), which typically concerned individual cases where there was no danger of fiscal chaos.

The restrictive attitude towards recovery that appeared to reward public authorities for their unlawful behaviour attracted considerable criticism

---

[72] See, e.g., *William Whiteley v. R.* (1910) 101 Law Times 741; *National Pari-Mutuel Association v. R.* (1930) 47 TLR 110; *Twyford v. Manchester Corp.* [1946] Ch 236; *Mason v. NSW* (1959) 102 CLR 108; *Nepean v. Ontario Hydro* (1982) 132 DLR (3rd) 193; *R. v. Tower Hamlets* [1988] AC 858.

[73] In Germany, the floodgates problem is catered for by rules of administrative and tax law requiring the citizen to lodge objections against administrative acts within one month. This can be done by a rather simple procedure finally ending before an administrative court. The principal safeguard for the public purse is that the administrative act, if no objection has been lodged against it in time, is deemed to be lawful. It may, however, still be revoked by the public authority. See *Abgabenordnung*, §§ 172 ff., §§ 347 ff.; *Verwaltungsgerichtsordnung*, §§ 68 ff.; *Verwaltungsverfahrensgesetz*, § 49; *Bundesverfassungsgerichtsgesetz*, § 79(2).

emphasising the infringement of the principle 'no taxation without Parliament' and of the rule of law.[74] If the public purse was to be protected at all, it was argued, this had to be done by special defences or time limits. The path towards a general right to recover the unlawfully exacted money was, however, controversial. One possibility consisted in abolishing the mistake of law rule.[75] But what if the payer, when paying, merely had doubts as to the lawfulness of the demand, or if he knew of its unlawfulness but none the less paid in order to avoid unfavourable consequences? Liberalising the requirements of compulsion[76] did not exclude the danger of gaps, and an assumption that all ultra vires payments are made under compulsion[77] would have been of a somewhat fictitious nature, particularly if the citizen did not entertain the slightest doubts about the lawfulness of the demand. None of these approaches offered a satisfactory explanation of why unlawful demands by the state should be treated differently from unlawful demands by private individuals: after all, pressure might also be exerted by a big private company. More importantly, the focus on the involuntariness of the payment obscured the true reason for recovery. The involuntariness was presumed because the demand was unlawful – but then it is the unlawfulness of the public demand, not the involuntary payment, that founds the right to recover. Even lawful tax demands, after all, are often only involuntarily honoured.

Because of the deficiencies of the traditional unjust factors it was proposed to base the right to recover on the ultra vires demand as such.[78] This

---

[74] Birks, *Introduction*, 294 ff.; Birks, 'Restitution From the Executive. A Tercentenary Footnote to the Bill of Rights', in: Finn, *Essays*, 164; McCamus, 'Restitutionary Recovery'; Ronald Collins, 'Restitution From Government Officials', (1984) 29 *McGill Law Journal* 408; W. R. Cornish, ' "Colour of Office": Restitutionary Redress Against Public Authority', [1987] *Journal of Malaysian and Comparative Law* 41; Stoljar, *Law of Quasi-contracts*, 64 ff.; A. Burrows, 'Public Authorities, Ultra Vires and Restitution', in: Burrows, *Essays*, 39 ff.

[75] B. Crawford, 'Restitution: Mistake of Law and Practical Compulsion', (1967) 17 *University of Toronto Law Journal* 344; McCamus, 'Restitutionary Recovery'; Dickson J (dissenting) in *Nepean v. Ontario Hydro* (1982) 132 DLR (3rd) 193 at 201 ff.; Burrows, 'Public Authorities', 52. This solution was finally adopted in Canada: *Air Canada v. British Columbia* (1989) 59 DLR (4th) 161; and in Australia, cf. *Commissioner of State Revenue v. Royal Insurance Ltd* (1994) 126 ALR 1.

[76] Kitto J in *Mason v. NSW* (1959) 102 CLR 108 at 129; Burrows, 'Public Authorities', 42 ff.

[77] Cf. J. Beatson, 'Duress as a Vitiating Factor in Contract', (1974) 33 *CLJ* 97, 110 ff.; Collins, 'Restitution'. This solution was adopted in Ireland: *Murphy v. Attorney-General* [1982] *Irish Reports* 241 at 316.

[78] P. Birks, 'Restitution From Public Authorities', (1980) 33 *Current Legal Problems* 191; Birks, 'Tercentenary Footnote'; Cornish, ' "Colour of Office" ' 41.

approach was finally endorsed by the House of Lords in *Woolwich Equitable Building Society v. IRC*.[79] 'In the end', as it was put by Lord Goff, 'logic appears to demand that the right of recovery should require neither mistake nor compulsion, and that the single fact that the tax was exacted unlawfully should *prima facie* be enough to require its repayment.'[80] But what, the commentators asked, was the exact unjust factor?[81] Some passages in the judgment stating that, because of the unlawfulness of the demand, the money was paid 'for no consideration',[82] sounded alarming.[83] This formulation seemed to resemble the civil-law concept of *sine causa*, flying in the face of the fact that the English action in restitution did not rest on a lack of legal ground. However, the Law Lords made it clear that the new right to recover should only apply in cases of ultra vires demands by public authorities. Therefore, a new unjust factor, '*ultra vires* demand', might be added to the list of existing unjust factors.[84] In order to fit the new right into a comprehensive system of unjust factors (and loyal to the English tradition not to create special legal rules against public authorities), Peter Birks has suggested an unjust factor of 'transactional inequality'.[85] It gives a right for recovery in specific situations where the law protects an individual from being compelled to submit to a certain demand. Thus, the citizen is to be protected against having to pay unlawful taxes or other levies, just as in *Kiriri Cotton* the law protects the tenants from having to pay premiums for leases. The protection is made complete by a right to recover that does not require mistake or compulsion.

It is true that the allusions to 'no consideration' do not say anything about the special situation of unlawful demands by public authorities and the special reasons for and against protecting the ratepayer.[86] But, however it is named, the new unjust factor created in *Woolwich* has a distinctive character compared with the traditional ones: one of its core

---

[79] [1993] AC 70.   [80] *Ibid.* at 173.

[81] E. McKendrick, 'Restitution of Unlawfully Demanded Tax', [1993] *Lloyd's Maritime and Commercial Law Quarterly* 88, 93; G. Virgo, 'Restitution of Overpaid Tax', (1993) 52 *CLJ* 33–4.

[82] [1993] AC 70 at 166 (Lord Goff), at 197–8 (Lord Browne-Wilkinson).

[83] P. Birks, '"When money is paid in pursuance of a void authority..." – A Duty to Repay?', [1992] *Public Law* 580, 587–8; McKendrick, 'Restitution', 95; Burrows, *Law of Restitution*, 351–2; J. Beatson, 'Public Law, Restitution and the House of Lords', (1993) 109 *LQR* 1, 2.

[84] Birks, *Introduction*, 294 ff.; J. Beatson, 'Restitution of Taxes, Levies and Other Imposts: Defining the Scope of the *Woolwich* Principle', (1993) 109 *LQR* 401, 410 ff.

[85] Birks, 'Tercentenary Footnote', 175–6, cf. his *Introduction*, 208 ff.

[86] P. Birks, 'No Consideration: Restitution After Void Contracts', (1993) 23 *University of Western Australia LR* 233.

elements is that the obligation the claimant intends to discharge does not exist. The tax demand being unlawful means that the claimant pays on a (tax) liability that in fact does not exist. The same holds true for the unjust factor 'transactional inequality'. If the law protects the individual from having to fulfil a certain demand and therefore provides him with a right to recover, then the individual has paid on an obligation that does not exist. In other words: the *Woolwich* unjust factor (and generally the unjust factor 'transactional inequality') requires a performance without legal ground and then dispenses with the need to find an express element of vitiated intention. Thus, there are now certain areas where payment on the basis of a legal ground that does not exist triggers, without more, restitution. This may be the background to the allusions to 'no consideration' and to Lord Goff's well-known passage in the *Woolwich* judgment:

> The law might have developed so as to recognise a *condictio indebiti* – an action for the recovery of money on the ground that it was not due. But it did not do so. Instead... there developed common law actions for the recovery of money paid under mistake of fact, and under certain forms of compulsion. What is now being sought is, in a sense, *a reversal of that development, in a particular type of case.*[87]

It is no accident that the reversal happened in the case of ultra vires demands, even apart from the special need to protect the citizen. It is because the legal ground, which the payer has in mind and which turns out to be lacking, is always an enforceable obligation. There is no need to conceive of other legal grounds, because a case where the citizen pays without obligation but nevertheless 'justly' is hardly conceivable. If the legal ground is always an obligation, there is no danger in founding restitution on the lack of legal ground. In other words, restitution for no consideration is tolerable as long as everyone knows exactly what consideration is.

V. Contractual payments and defective contracts

1. Valid contracts: the basis of performance

For valid contracts, there seems to be universal agreement that contractual payments cannot be recovered unless the counterperformance is, in some or other way, defective. Thus, both English and German law provide for a right to recover a contractual payment in cases of frustration or fundamental breach by the other party. Both legal systems also share

---

[87] [1993] AC 70 at 172 (emphasis added).

the proposition that neither frustration nor fundamental breach is able to invalidate a contract with retroactive effect. In these circumstances, the right to recover can be construed in different ways. A rescission for breach may, for instance, be regarded as having the effect of changing the contents of the contract by creating a right of the person rescinding to recover his performance. The right to recover would thus be a contractual one. This solution is employed by the German Civil Code.[88] But recovery might equally be regarded as a matter of unjust enrichment. It might then be said that either the failure of counterperformance itself or the rescission by the payer terminating the contract *in futuro* has the effect of bringing the payer's own contractual obligation to an end. The right to recover might thus be founded on the fact that an event after payment would have extinguished the payer's liability if it had not already been extinguished by the payment: in other words, the reason for the payment has fallen away subsequently.[89]

The key decision in English law, *Fibrosa Spolka Akcyjna v. Fairbairn Lawson Combe Barbour Ltd*,[90] concerned a case of frustration. In *Chandler v. Webster*[91] it had been held that an obligation to pay, which was due before the time of frustration, was not affected by the frustrating event. Outstanding payments, therefore, still had to be made, and payments previously made could not be recovered. This is an unsatisfactory result, and so it was right for the House of Lords to overrule *Chandler v. Webster*. But what the House did not do was to state that, contrary to *Chandler v. Webster*, the frustrating event invalidates the obligation to pay, and to base the right of recovery on the fact that the obligation had fallen away.[92] Instead, it was held that the right to recover rests, without regard to the underlying obligation, directly on the failure of counterperformance. Though it is generally agreed that recovery requires a termination of the contract, it is not the termination itself but the failure of counterperformance – or failure of consideration – that justifies recovery. In Lord Wright's words: 'The payment was originally conditional. The condition

---

[88] §§ 325(1), first sentence, 326(1), second sentence, 327, first sentence, 346 BGB. For details, see R. Zimmermann, 'Restitution After Termination for Breach of Contract in German Law', [1997] *Restitution LR* 13; G. Dannemann, 'Restitution for Termination of Contract in German Law', in: Francis Rose (ed.), *Failure of Contracts* (1997), 129; B. Markesinis, W. Lorenz and G. Dannemann, *The Law of Contracts and Restitution* (vol. I of B. Markesinis, *The German Law of Obligations*, 1997), 641 ff.

[89] See, for German law, §§ 323(1), (3), 325(1), third sentence, 812 BGB.

[90] [1943] AC 32. [91] [1904] 1 KB 493.

[92] Cf. W. W. Buckland, 'Casus and Frustration in Roman and Common Law', (1933) 46 *Harvard LR* 1281 ff.

of retaining it is eventual performance. Accordingly, when that condition fails, the right to retain the money must simultaneously fail.'[93] This is (as their Lordships well knew[94]) the model of the Roman *condictio causa data causa non secuta*,[95] which, however, was in Roman law (and still is in modern German law[96]) only applicable if there was no contractual obligation at all. This was because the basis of a contractual payment was the contract itself, not the counterperformance; hence, the counterperformance could only then be regarded as the basis of the payment if there was no contract, not even the mistaken assumption by the payer of a contract.[97]

2. Void contracts: the problem of the correct unjust factor

It does not seem to matter, in cases of payments made on valid contracts, whether the focus is on the underlying contractual obligation (as in Roman and modern civil law) or on the payer's expectation of counterperformance (as in modern English law): the results do not seem to differ. Turning to void contracts, however, the different attitudes towards the basis of contractual payments are crucial. If, as is the case in German law, the basis of the payment is the intended discharge of a contractual obligation, there is a right to recover if the underlying contract turns out to be void.[98] In England, the proposition that the basis of a contractual payment is the receipt of the counterperformance seems to hold true also

---

[93] [1943] AC 32 at 65. Restitution for failure of consideration can be fitted into the system of unjust factors by regarding it as a case of qualified intention: the claimant specifies the basis of his giving by indicating that he wants the defendant to have the benefit only in certain circumstances (namely, if the counterperformance is forthcoming). See Birks, *Introduction*, 219.

[94] In *Fibrosa* all judges referred to the Scottish case of *Cantiere San Rocco SA v. Clyde Shipbuilding & Engineering Co.* [1924] AC 226, a case of frustration where the House of Lords had directly applied the *condictio causa data*, which was translated with 'action to recover something for a consideration which has failed': at 235, 251.

[95] P. Birks, 'Restitution and the Freedom of Contracts', (1983) 36 *Current Legal Problems* 141, 156–7; Birks, *Introduction*, 223; Birks, 'No Consideration', 209–10.

[96] RGZ 66, 132; 108, 329, 335; Reuter and Martinek, *Ungerechtfertigte Bereicherung*, 147; Lorenz in: *J. von Staudinger's Kommentar*, § 812, n. 105.

[97] Zimmermann, *Law of Obligations*, 842 ff., 857 ff.; R. Evans-Jones, 'Unjust Enrichment, Contract and the Third Reception of Roman Law in Scotland', (1993) 109 *LQR* 663.

[98] It may be different if both parties consciously perform on a void contract in the expectation that the other party will perform its non-enforceable obligation: then the basis of performance is the expectation of counterperformance; hence, there can be recovery under the *condictio causa data causa non secuta* (§ 812(1), sentence 2, alt. 2 BGB) if the counterperformance fails: RGZ 98, 237, 240; BGH 1961 WM 967; BGH 1971 JZ 556; BGH 1976 NJW 237; BGH 1980 NJW 451.

in cases of void contracts. Thus, there are statements to the effect that payments made on a void contract can be recovered if there is a failure of consideration (that is, counterperformance).[99] But the matter does not rest there. A performance on a void contract may also be recovered if the payer has overlooked the invalidity on account of a mistake of fact. The mistaken assumption of a valid contract has always been a subspecies of the classic liability mistake.[100] Thus, English law has recognised that, independently of the counterperformance, the basis of a contractual payment may also be the contractual obligation itself. As a result, there seem to be two unjust factors – mistake of fact and failure of consideration – and therefore two bases (or two assumptions) underlying a contractual payment – the assumption of a valid contract and the expectation of the counterperformance. Since recovery for failure of the first basis was restricted by the mistake of law rule, attention was bound to shift to the second one.

A completely different approach was suggested by the courts of first and second instance in the recent swaps litigation. Beginning with Hobhouse J's (as he then was) judgment in *Westdeutsche Landesbank Girozentrale v. Islington LBC*, it was said that the correct unjust factor in cases of void contracts is 'no consideration': recovery rested, independently of the receipt of the counterperformance, on the sole fact that the underlying contract was void.[101] The judgments attracted massive criticism among academic writers who accused the courts of introducing the civilian concept of *sine causa*, which does not fit into English law.[102] Finally, in *Kleinwort Benson v. Lincoln City Council*,[103] the House of Lords held that a payment on a void contract may be recovered if the payer overlooked the invalidity on account of a mistake of law. The fate of the 'no consideration' approach is

---

[99] Birks, 'No Consideration', 195; Burrows, *Law of Restitution*, 304; Goff and Jones, *Law of Restitution*, 499 ff.; P. J. Millett, 'Restitution and Constructive Trusts', (1998) 114 *LQR* 399, 414; but see Guenter Treitel, *The Law of Contract* (9th edn, 1995), 950.

[100] *Kelly v. Solari* (1841) 9 M & W 54, 152 ER 24; *Rover International Ltd v. Cannon Films Sale Ltd (No. 3)* [1989] 1 WLR 912.

[101] [1994] 4 All ER 890 at 924 ff.; see also *Kleinwort Benson v. South Tyneside Metropolitan Borough Council* [1994] 4 All ER 972 at 984; *South Tyneside MBC v. Svenska International plc* [1995] 1 All ER 545 at 556 ff.; *Kleinwort Benson v. Birmingham City Council* [1997] QB 380; *Guinness Mahon & Co. Ltd v Kensington & Chelsea Royal LBC* [1999] QB 215 (here the unjust factor was confusingly called 'total failure of consideration').

[102] Birks, 'No Consideration', 195; D. Cowan, 'Banks, Swaps, Restitution and Equity', [1993] *Lloyd's Maritime and Commercial Law Quarterly* 300; W. Swadling, 'Restitution for No Consideration', [1994] *Restitution LR* 73; A. Burrows, 'Swaps and the Friction Between Common Law and Equity', [1995] *Restitution LR* 15; Millett, 'Restitution and Constructive Trusts', 413–14.

[103] [1999] 2 AC 349.

unclear.[104] All in all, the foundations of the right to recover payments on void contracts seem to be in a certain state of confusion.

First, what exactly is the unjust factor 'no consideration'? Are its critics correct in holding that with such an unjust factor all gifts have to be recovered and that the judges in *Westdeutsche*, like those in *Chandler v. Webster*, have confused different notions of 'consideration'? In English law, the word 'consideration' has a whole variety of meanings. In contract law, it is usually the promise of a counterperformance; in the law of restitution it has been used to stand for, *inter alia*, the rendering of counterperformance,[105] a future state of affairs contemplated and communicated as the basis of a transfer,[106] and the discharge of a debt.[107] In *Chandler v. Webster*, the consideration (that did not fail) was the underlying obligation, not the valid promise of counterperformance. All that mattered in that case was whether the obligation on which the claimant was paying was due before the frustrating event and thus continued to exist, independently of the fate of the other party's promise, which was not mentioned at all. Likewise, 'consideration' in *Westdeutsche* was not the validity of the promise of counterperformance (as had been suggested by the plaintiff) but either the obligation the plaintiff intended to discharge or the entire underlying contract as such, demanding and justifying the plaintiff's payment. 'Consideration' is here a certain kind of legal ground, and 'no consideration' is, like ultra vires demands in terms of *Woolwich*, an unjust factor focusing on the lack of the legal ground the claimant had in mind.[108] (The last qualification may be important: recovery is justified by the fact that the contract that, in the minds of the parties, underlay the payment, was not valid; that is, the consideration which is absent must be something the parties had in mind; therefore there is no question of recovering all gifts.)

3. Restitution after full execution?

A further question is whether it is correct to allow recovery even if there is no failure of consideration. As there now seems to be general agreement

---

[104] It seems to be approved of by Lords Browne-Wilkinson and Lloyd (calling it 'total failure of consideration') and rejected by Lord Goff; see *Westdeutsche Landesbank Girozentrale v. Islington London Borough Council*, [1996] AC 669 at 683 (Lord Goff), 710–11. (Lord Browne-Wilkinson); *Kleinwort Benson v. Lincoln City Council* [1998] 3 WLR 1095 at 1126 (Lord Goff), 1135 (Lord Lloyd).
[105] *Fibrosa Spolka v. Fairbairn* [1943] AC 32 at 48, *per* Viscount Simon LC.
[106] Birks, *Introduction*, 223.
[107] Goff J in *Barclays Bank v. Simms* [1980] 1 QB 677 at 695; Matthews, 'Money Paid Under a Mistake'.
[108] See, especially, Leggatt LJ in *Westdeutsche Landesbank v. Islington LBC* [1994] 4 All ER 890 at 969; Saville LJ in *Kleinwort Benson v. Birmingham City Council* [1997] QB 380.

about the right to recover in cases of a partial failure of consideration (at least if both performances consist in money, as in the swaps cases),[109] the crucial case is that of a void contract that has been fully executed. If failure of consideration (that is, counterperformance) was the correct unjust factor, recovery would be excluded. But what is then the role of a void contract in English law: is it a reason for restitution or does it merely exclude the enforceability of contractual claims? It has been suggested that a claimant has no reason for restitution if he got everything he bargained for: he would merely take advantage of the fact that the contract turns out to be void in order to escape a bargain he regrets.[110] However, the problem is that the claimant may take advantage of the invalidity as long as he has not yet performed: he may always refuse to perform, even if he has already received the entire counterperformance. Why is the contract regarded as valid as regards recovery, but as invalid as regards enforceability? Why are there different rights of penitence, dependent on the state of contractual performance? And what is the difference between a void and an unenforceable contract?

So far as the case law is concerned, there seems to be no general principle that restitution after defective contracts requires a failure of consideration. Rather, there are different lines of authority, depending on the reason why the contract is defective.[111] In several cases restitution is possible without having regard to the counterperformance. This is explained, by academic writers, by a long list of unjust factors such as mistake, fraud, undue influence, inequality, minority, ultra vires and illegality, which merely reflect the reason why the contract is void or voidable.[112] The policy rendering a contract invalid is, very often, also a policy requiring a right to recover. But instead of introducing a double inquiry, it may be easier to hold that, as a general principle, an invalid contract triggers restitution and then consider possible exceptions.

One exception are contracts made by minors. The courts have excluded recovery by the minor if he has received the counterperformance.[113] On the other hand, recovery seems to be possible as long as the minor has

---

[109] Lord Goff in *Westdeutsche Landesbank v. Islington LBC* [1996] AC 669 at 682–3; *Goss v. Chilcott* [1996] AC 788 at 798 (PC); Birks, 'No Consideration', 213–14; A. Burrows, 'Restitution of Payments Made Under Swap Transactions', [1993] *NLJ* 480.

[110] Birks, 'No Consideration', 199, 206 ff.; Swadling, 'Restitution', 85; Millett, 'Restitution and Constructive Trusts', 414; Goff and Jones, *Law of Restitution*, 656–7.

[111] For details, see S. Meier, 'Restitution after Executed Void Contracts?', in: Peter Birks (ed.), *Lessons of the Swaps Litigation* (2000), 168.

[112] Cf. Zimmermann, 'Unjustified Enrichment', 416.

[113] *Steinberg v. Scala Ltd* [1923] 2 Ch 452; *Pearce v. Brain* [1929] 2 KB 310.

not received anything, even though the other party is ready and willing to perform.[114] This state of the law, restricting the minor's protection to cases where he has not yet performed, cannot be explained on account of a failure of consideration (since the minor does not complain about the other party's unwillingness to perform). In fact, it cannot be rationally explained at all and is therefore criticised by academic writers who favour a right in the minor to recover independently of the receipt of the counterperformance, based on an unjust factor such as inequality or minority.[115]

More interesting are those cases where the contract lacks the form required by a statute or is tainted by another, rather technical, defect. If both parties have performed their obligations, there are good reasons to hold that the legal defect does not necessarily require an unwinding of performance and counterperformance, and that it may be more convenient to leave the parties in their actual positions. This may be the reason why the Statute of Frauds[116] and similar English acts[117] have held the contract to be merely unenforceable rather than void. Thus recovery after full execution was prevented, because recovery in the case of a valid (though unenforceable) contract always requires some kind of defect with regard to the counterperformance. Another device is used by German law, which provides for the possibility of 'curing' the defect: contracts lacking a statutory form are usually void,[118] but nevertheless are often held to be valid after full performance has been made.[119] This has the result that restitution after full execution is prevented. A similar policy seems to explain those English cases where the contract has been held to be void for lack of form or another technical defect, but where recovery has been made dependent on a failure of consideration. Restitution of a fully executed contract was thus prevented.[120] Many of these cases concerned insurance

---

[114] *Corpe v. Overton* (1833) 10 Bing 252; 131 ER 901; which seems not to have been overruled by *Steinberg*, cf. [1923] 2 Ch 452 at 460–1.
[115] Goff and Jones, *Law of Restitution*, 641–2; see also Goff and Jones (3rd edn, 1986) 439 ff.; Burrows, *Law of Restitution*, 324–5; Birks, *Introduction*, 216–17; S. Arrowsmith, 'Ineffective Transactions, Unjust Enrichment and Problems of Policy', (1989) 9 *Legal Studies* 307, 316–17; G. Treitel, 'The Infants Relief Act, 1874', (1957) 73 *LQR* 194, 202 ff.
[116] Statute of Frauds (1677), abolished 1954.
[117] Law of Property Act 1925, s. 40, and Law of Property Act (1949) s. 2, rendered contracts for sale of land unenforceable if not in writing. Now, these contracts are rendered void: Law of Property Act 1989, s. 2.
[118] § 125 BGB.
[119] See, e.g., §§ 313, second sentence, BGB (contracts for sale of land), 518(2) BGB (contracts of gift).
[120] *Re London County Commercial Reinsurance Office* [1922] 2 Ch 67; *Home & Colonial Insurance v. London Guarantee* (1928) 32 Lloyd's Rep 267; *Re Cavalier Insurance* [1989] 2 Lloyd's Rep 430; cf. also *Aratra Potato v. Taylor Johnson Garrett* [1995] 4 All ER 695.

contracts. Here a unilateral right on the part of the insured to recover the premiums, without counter-restitution, seemed to be unfair; mutual restitution, however, including recovery of the insurance sum by the insurer, seemed to run counter to the purpose of the invalidating statute. Therefore, the courts held that recovery required a failure of consideration, and that the claimant's assumption of a valid contract was merely an irrelevant mistake of law.

Whereas in German law there exists a well-defined notion of a void contract, always triggering a right in restitution (unless the invalidity is 'cured'), in English law the word 'void' has no such technical meaning. It is thus necessary to distinguish those kinds of defective contracts where restitution is always possible and others where restitution does not take place after the contract has been fully executed. This can best be done by a kind of legal-ground analysis, crystallising certain types of defective contracts that may, once they have been executed, provide a legal ground for the performance. A system of unjust factors may perform a similar task by establishing for every ground of invalidity whether it will also serve as a ground for restitution. But then it will concentrate on the legal transaction underlying the transfer rather than on the claimant's state of mind. Generally speaking, it would be better not to confuse defects in contracts that are grave enough to require an unwinding of performances with the reasons why a transfer without any justification should be recovered (for example, liability mistake).

Wagers are another example of contracts that are void but do not trigger a right to recover. It is as yet unclear whether this can be better explained by the assumption that a wager is a kind of legal ground in the form of a natural obligation[121] or by a defence of wagering. In any case, it cannot be explained by a system of unjust factors focusing on the claimant's will.[122] May a person recover for failure of consideration, contending that he won the wager and was not paid by the loser? Or can a person, having lost, recover for mistake of fact because he did not know that the other party was a professional gambler? Or perhaps even for a mistake of law if he assumed the contract to be binding?

4. Mistake of law and the re-emergence of the *condictio indebiti*

Confusion has increased since contractual payments have become recoverable on account of a mistake of law. The idea behind this unjust factor seems to be that claimants who knowingly perform on a void contract

---

[121] Cf. above, 55–6. [122] This is suggested by Birks, 'No Consideration', 220–1.

should be excluded from restitution (provided they have received the entire counterperformance).[123] This policy is not, in principle, objectionable; however, it does not apply to all cases of invalid contracts. Knowledge of the invalidity should not bar recovery on the part of a victim of compulsion, undue influence or illegal exploitation, or on the part of a minor, or (presumably) on the part of a local authority in the case of an ultra vires contract. German law, providing for a defence against the *condictio indebiti* if the claimant knew that he was not obliged to perform (in which case he has to resort to the *condictio causa data causa non secuta*[124]), does not apply that defence in those cases. In *Westdeutsche Landesbank v. Islington LBC*, where recovery was said to rest on the void contract itself, the judges arguably provided for a defence of voluntary payment if the claimant knew the contract was void,[125] a defence which might also be applied in a flexible manner. But if the unjust factor is the mistake of law as such, it can cover only those cases where knowledge of the invalidity really matters. For the other cases, the usual unjust factors are still needed.

Even in those cases where knowledge of the invalidity should bar recovery, it may be asked whether the unjust factor mistake of law can really perform this function. *Kleinwort Benson v. Lincoln City Council* may be compared with the Scottish decision *Morgan Guaranty Trust v. Lothian Regional Council*[126] where recovery after a void swap was also allowed by abolishing the mistake of law rule. Abolition of the mistake of law rule, in Scottish law, means that the mistake of law does not bar the *condictio indebiti*, that is, a performance without legal ground may be recovered if the claimant, labouring under a mistake of law, assumed the legal ground to exist.[127] Conversely, in England it is solely the mistake itself that is regarded as the reason for restitution. Taking the causal mistake approach seriously, it need not be a mistake about the validity of the contract. Therefore, a bank, knowing the swap to be void, and having received the entire counterperformance, should nevertheless be able to recover if it had miscalculated the tax effects of the swap, or if it had forgotten that it had received a better offer from another municipality, and if it would not have entered the swap had it not been mistaken. Such an expansion of restitution after

---

[123] Burrows, 'Swaps', 17.   [124] See above, n. 98.   [125] See [1994] 4 All ER 890 at 893.
[126] (1995) SLT 299.
[127] It is still unclear whether the Scottish *condictio indebiti* requires proof of *error* or whether transfer without legal ground suffices with knowledge as a defence. See N. Whitty, 'Some Trends and Issues in Scots Enrichment Law', [1994] JR 127; Whitty, 'Die Reform des schottischen Bereicherungsrechts', (1995) 3 *Zeitschrift für Europäisches Privatrecht* 216 ff.; R. Evans-Jones, 'From "Undue Transfer" to "Retention Without a Legal Basis"', in: his (ed.), *The Civil Law Tradition in Scotland* (1995), 213.

void contracts is highly inconvenient and, at any rate, nowhere discussed; rather, it seems that mistake of law is usually conceived of as a mistake about the validity of the contract. But then restitution for mistake of law comes close to the *condictio indebiti*.

There are indeed some indications in *Kleinwort Benson v. Lincoln CC* that the true reason for restitution might be the void contract rather than the claimant's mistake. First, if restitution were based on mistake, one may reasonably ask whether recovery should be possible after full execution, when the sole reason why the claimant would not have entered the swap had he known its invalidity was fear for the counterperformance.[128] According to Lord Goff, however, full execution could not prevent recovery, for otherwise 'effect would be given to a contract which public policy has declared to be void'.[129] Is it, then, really the mistake of the parties that justifies recovery?

Secondly, in *Kleinwort Benson* the Lords faced the problem of judicial change in the law.[130] May a claimant who pays in accordance with the previously held view recover if this view is later overruled? The traditional declaratory theory according to which the new decision merely declares what has always been the law was said by all Lords to rest on a fiction: in reality, the new decision changes the law. None the less, Lords Goff and Hoffmann held that a claimant acting under the previously held view was labouring under a mistake of law. This can hardly be reconciled with the common-sense meaning of the word 'mistake'. Interestingly, therefore, Lord Hoffmann stated that account had to be taken of the principle of unjust enrichment and then it had to be decided whether the claimant 'should be treated for the purpose of some legal rule as having made a mistake'.[131] And indeed, the problem of recovery after a judicial change in the law cannot be solved by asking what constitutes a mistake. This inquiry merely obscures the decisive policy question whether a transfer made in accordance with the earlier view of the law should be regarded as final – in other words, whether an established line of cases, even if it is later overruled, should be able to constitute a legal ground. It is not *per se* objectionable that Lord Hoffmann and Lord Goff abandoned the ordinary meaning of the word 'mistake'. This step, however, necessitates

---

[128] Birks, 'No Consideration', 230, n. 137.   [129] [1998] 3 WLR 1095 at 1127.
[130] See S. Meier and R. Zimmermann, 'Judicial Development of the Law, *Error Iuris*, and the Law of Unjustified Enrichment – A View From Germany', (1999) 115 *LQR* 556.
[131] [1998] 3 WLR 1095 at 1137.

abandoning the proposition that the reason for restitution for mistake is the vitiated intention of the claimant.[132]

Thirdly, there is the speech of the Scottish judge sitting in *Kleinwort Benson*, Lord Hope, according to whom the mistake has the function of demonstrating that a transfer without legal ground is not voluntary.[133] This is exactly the model of the *condictio indebiti*. Even though the English judges may object to this passage, it may well be, as shown above, that restitution for mistake of law is in truth restitution on grounds of the void contract. While English lawyers may refuse to base restitution openly on the lack of legal ground the claimant has had in mind – for example, in the form of an unjust factor of 'no consideration' – the very same proposition would seem to enter the stage again through the back door of mistake of law.

[132] See P. Birks and W. Swadling, 'Restitution', [1998] *All ER Annual Rev* 390, 397 ff.
[133] [1998] 3 WLR 1095 at 1146.

3 In defence of unjust factors

Thomas Krebs

I. Introduction

The English law of unjust enrichment has always insisted that a claimant asking for restitution must show that there is a good reason why restitution should be available to him. It has differed from its more ancient Continental counterparts in that the ground for restitution was not an abstraction like 'lack of juridical reason for the enrichment', but a pragmatic, positive requirement or 'unjust factor', as Peter Birks has called it.

One question that lies at the heart of the recent swaps litigation is whether there can be restitution in English law for the mere reason that money was paid pursuant to a contract which has subsequently turned out to be void. If this question is answered in the affirmative, it will mean that the English law of unjust enrichment has come close to adopting the civil-law *condictio indebiti* – the claim to restitution on the basis that money was paid which was not due. In this chapter, it is argued that that would be the beginning of the end of the system of 'unjust factors'. The English law of unjust enrichment would move considerably closer to civilian legal systems.

Before the question can be faced, it is necessary to look very briefly at the two different approaches. The leading textbook in comparative law, Konrad Zweigert and Hein Kötz's *An Introduction to Comparative Law*, identifies 'the entrenched position of the institution of unjustified enrichment' as one of the distinctive features of German law.[1] For this reason amongst others, German law will serve as a model of the civilian approach.

I am grateful to Professor Ewan McKendrick for his comments on an earlier draft.
[1] K. Zweigert and H. Kötz, *An Introduction to Comparative Law* (trans. T. Weir, 3rd edn, 1998), 71.

1. The common-law approach to unjust enrichment

In the latest edition of their book *The Law of Restitution*, Lord Goff of Chieveley and Gareth Jones write: 'If money has been paid under a contract which is or becomes ineffective, the recipient is evidently enriched. It is a distinct question whether that enrichment is an *unjust* enrichment.'[2]

This 'distinct question' is answered by English law by reference to a list of what Birks has called 'unjust factors' – factors that render an enrichment unjust in the eyes of the law. It is characteristic of these unjust factors that they give us an immediately intelligible reason why restitution should follow. Birks has identified three families of unjust factors:[3] the 'I did not mean to give' family of claims, 'unconscientious receipt' and 'policy-motivated restitution'. Where the claimant was mistaken in making the payment, as in *Barclays Bank v. Simms*[4] (where a bank honoured a cheque which had been countermanded), or in *Chase Manhattan Bank v. Israel-British Bank*[5] (where a payment had, by mistake, been made twice), it is readily apparent that the defendant's enrichment is unjust and should be reversed. Similarly, where the claimant is forced to part with his money because of the defendant's illegitimate pressure, the latter's enrichment will be considered 'unjust' by the law – this time, 'duress' is the unjust factor.

In cases of 'failure of consideration' payment is made on a certain condition, normally that the defendant will counterperform. Where that counterperformance fails, as it did in the famous *Fibrosa* case,[6] it is clear that restitution should be available to the disappointed claimant.[7]

It is controversial whether there exists an additional family of claims called 'unconscientious receipt' or 'free acceptance'. The reason for restitution here is argued to be the fact that the defendant exploited the

---

[2] Lord Goff of Chieveley and Gareth Jones, *The Law of Restitution* (5th edn, 1998), 499.
[3] See P. Birks and R. Chambers, *Restitution Research Resource* (2nd edn, 1997), § 113.
[4] *Barclays Bank Ltd v. W. J. Simms Son and Cooke (Southern) Ltd* [1980] 1 QB 677.
[5] *Chase Manhattan Bank NA Ltd v. Israel-British Bank (London) Ltd* [1981] Ch 105.
[6] *Fibrosa Spolka Akcyjna v. Fairbairn Lawson Combe Barbour Ltd* [1943] AC 32.
[7] A complete account of Birks's taxonomy should not fail to mention 'ignorance', where a benefit is taken from the claimant without his knowledge, and 'helplessness', which is the more extreme form of duress in which the claimant is incapable of preventing the defendant's enrichment – for example, by being tied to a chair: see P. Birks, *An Introduction to the Law of Restitution* (1985, revised edn, 1989), 140 ff.

claimant's weakness in some way,[8] or freely accepted a benefit which he knew was not proffered gratuitously.[9]

Classifications and taxonomies often contain a residual category 'others', and this taxonomy is no exception. In some cases, restitution is available even though the case does not fit either of these two broad categories. Invariably, this is because the law pursues a policy favouring restitution in this kind of case. It will be necessary to discuss 'policy-motivated restitution' in more detail later. For now, the well-known case of *Woolwich v. IRC* may serve as an example.[10] The Woolwich Equitable Building Society had been assessed for taxes which, in its view, the Inland Revenue had no power to raise. It nevertheless paid under protest. It then successfully challenged the tax, showing that the assessment had been ultra vires and void. The Revenue repaid the overpaid tax, but refused to pay interest on it. The Woolwich therefore had to show that, as soon as it paid over the money, it had a restitutionary claim against the Revenue, which would naturally attract interest. The difficulty was that the Woolwich had not made a mistake – it had known the assessment was ultra vires from the start, and had said so. Nor could it be seriously contended that the payment had been made under duress: any pressure exerted was the pressure of due legal process, and as such it was not 'illegitimate'. The Woolwich nevertheless succeeded. The principle 'no taxation without Parliament', the policy in favour of the legality of government and the rule of law strongly favoured restitution.[11]

Within this taxonomy there is no room for 'restitution of moneys paid under void transactions'. Nullity as such does not lead to restitution, although this does not mean that restitution will not be available in circumstances in which a payment is made under a void transaction. In the majority of cases some unjust factor will be available: thus, if the defendant has not yet performed, the claimant might be able to rely on failure of consideration. Even where this is not the case, policy-motivated restitution may well be available. The *Woolwich* case is an example in point: the Revenue's claim was void, but it was not that voidness which led to

---

[8] For example, *Louth v. Diprose* (1992) 175 CLR 621 (High Court of Australia). It is arguable that some duress cases should equally be categorised as belonging in this category.
[9] See P. Birks, 'In Defence of Free Acceptance', in: A. Burrows (ed.), *Essays on the Law of Restitution* (1991), 109.
[10] *Woolwich Equitable Building Society v. IRC* [1993] AC 70.
[11] Professor Birks had strongly argued that claimants in the Woolwich's position should succeed on this ground: see P. Birks, 'Restitution from the Executive: a Tercentenary Footnote to the Bill of Rights', in: P. Finn (ed.), *Essays on Restitution* (1990), 161.

restitution, but the policy favouring constitutional legality. Often, and this is an important point to grasp at the outset, the policy favouring nullity will also favour restitution. That is not to say, however, that this will always be the case in English law.

2. The German approach to unjust enrichment

It is striking that German law refers to 'unjustified' rather than 'unjust' enrichment. This is more than a mere semantic difference. Although one should not fall into the error of supposing that in German law it is the defendant who has to show that he is entitled to keep the enrichment, the starting point in German law is that all enrichments are prima facie unjust, unless they can be justified. The fact that it is the claimant who has to show that the defendant's enrichment cannot be justified does not change this fundamental characteristic of German law, which is inherent in the formulation of the general provision of unjust enrichment in § 812(1) of the German Civil Code, the *Bürgerliches Gesetzbuch* (BGB):

Wer durch die Leistung eines anderen oder in sonstiger Weise auf dessen Kosten etwas ohne rechtlichen Grund erlangt, ist ihm zur Herausgabe verpflichtet...

[He who obtains something through somebody else's performance or in another way at his expense without a legal cause, is obliged to make restitution to the other...]

By § 812(1), first sentence, an enrichment is considered unjust if it lacks a 'legal cause'. In most cases, this will mean that a benefit has been transferred under a supposed legal transaction. That transaction turns out to have been void, either because it was void from the beginning, or because it has since been avoided *ab initio*. In such cases, § 812(1), first sentence, provides that the recipient has to return the benefit to the transferor.

The problem with § 812(1), first sentence, is, however, that it is considerably wider than this. As Basil Markesinis, Werner Lorenz and Gerhard Dannemann point out, the main dilemma with general provisions 'is that with them one tends to get more than one has bargained for: their wording will often cover more than it should. The main attention within legal systems based on general clauses will, therefore, be geared towards excluding certain categories from the application of the general rule.'[12] The section has thus been narrowed down considerably, first by jurists, then by judges who adopted the proposed academic solutions. German law today

---

[12] B. S. Markesinis, W. Lorenz and G. Dannemann, *The German Law of Obligations*, vol. I, *The Law of Contracts and Restitution* (1997), 713.

differentiates between 'enrichments by performance' and 'enrichments in another way'. Both have precisely defined requirements, which it has taken German jurists almost half a century to work out, and even today there is considerable controversy over whether the distinction is appropriate, and where precisely it lies.

This chapter concentrates on 'enrichments by performance'. While it is argued in Germany that in these cases restitution will follow because the purpose of the transfer, namely the discharge of an obligation, has failed,[13] it is clear that in practice restitution will normally follow where a benefit has been transferred pursuant to an obligation which has later turned out to be void.

II. The swaps litigation

After this brief overview of the different approaches to unjust enrichment in England and Germany, it is now time to consider the swaps litigation. It is argued in this chapter that the effect of that litigation has been to move English law appreciably closer to German law.

Many readers will be, in Lord Goff's words, 'seasoned warriors in the continuing battle of the swaps'.[14] They may forgive me for the brief explanation of the background which follows. Interest swaps are traded on the financial markets. Two parties lend each other a notional sum on terms that one pays interest at a fixed, the other at a floating, rate. Both are speculating that interest rates will develop in their favour. Local authorities widely engaged in interest-rate swaps from the early 1980s onwards. In *Hazell v. Hammersmith and Fulham London Borough Council*[15] the House of Lords held that such transactions were ultra vires local authorities and that any swaps that local authorities had entered into were therefore wholly void. The consequence was a wave of litigation in which losing parties to interest-rate swaps sought restitution of their losses. In this chapter, I am mainly concerned with the first and the last of these cases, namely with *Westdeutsche Landesbank Girozentrale v. Islington LBC*[16] and *Kleinwort Benson v. Lincoln City Council*.[17]

---

[13] See D. Reuter and M. Martinek, *Ungerechtfertigte Bereicherung* (1983), 110.
[14] *Kleinwort Benson v. Lincoln London Borough Council* [1999] 2 AC 349 at 367.
[15] [1992] 2 AC 1.
[16] *Westdeutsche Landesbank Girozentrale v. Islington London Borough Council* [1994] 4 All ER 890 (QBD and CA) at 924 (references will be to the *All England Law Reports*, as both first instance and Court of Appeal decisions are conveniently reported together there); varied [1996] AC 669 (HL).
[17] [1999] 2 AC 349.

The cases that reached the Commercial Court can be broadly divided into those which concerned 'interrupted swaps' and those which concerned 'closed swaps'. In interrupted swaps the risks had not been allowed to run their full course. One party was ahead when the blow of *Hazell* fell, but there was no telling whether the roles of winner and loser might not have been reversed as the swap continued, sometimes over several more years. Closed swaps had been fully performed, winners and losers conclusively determined. The risks had run their course, the parties had got what they had bargained for.

Litigants asking for restitution of moneys paid pursuant to interest-rate swaps involving local authorities were faced with a number of problems. In most cases payments had been made both ways. The losing party had got at least something from the winner. This made it more difficult to argue that there had been a total failure of consideration, which would otherwise have been the obvious ground on which restitution could have been based. The problem was compounded in cases involving closed swaps. In these cases there had been no failure of consideration at all. The parties had got exactly what they had bargained for. It was, furthermore, difficult to base the claim for restitution on the ground of mistake. If there had been a mistake at all, and this is a question of some controversy, it had been one of law, and only the House of Lords could depart from the long-standing rule that there could be no restitution in English law based on mistake of law only. It was thus tempting to argue that restitution should be awarded for the simple reason that the interest-rate swaps under which the money had been paid had been declared void by the House of Lords. This approach avoided all of the above difficulties at a stroke.

1. 'No consideration'

Westdeutsche Landesbank Girozentrale v. Islington LBC was the first swaps case to reach the High Court. Two cases, *Westdeutsche* itself and *Kleinwort Benson v. Sandwell BC*[18] were heard together by Hobhouse J. In *Westdeutsche*, the relevant swaps had all been interrupted. One swap in *Sandwell*, however, had been fully completed. Irrespective of whether the swaps had been completed or not, Hobhouse J ordered restitution because there had been 'no consideration' for the payments, the swaps agreement having been void from the start. In other words, he based restitution on the nullity of the underlying transaction alone, without looking for substantive reasons for

---

[18] [1994] 4 All ER 890.

restitution, thus putting Birks's taxonomy into doubt and moving English law considerably closer to the *Leistungskondiktion*.

Birks has since shown[19] that restitution in interrupted swaps can be explained on the ground of failure of consideration: the risks have not run their course, the parties did not get what they bargained for. The requirement that a failure of consideration must be total can be avoided by ordering restitution of the net balance of payments, as Hobhouse J indeed did in *Westdeutsche* itself. When Islington Council appealed to the Court of Appeal, this analysis was confirmed, although in a somewhat half-hearted fashion, and while arguably endorsing the 'no consideration' approach at the same time. As Sandwell Council did not appeal, the Court of Appeal did not get the opportunity to decide the crucial question whether restitution was available in completed swaps until much later, in *Guinness Mahon & Co. Ltd v. Kensington and Chelsea Royal London BC*.[20]

In a completed swap, there can be no question of restitution based on failure of consideration. While the mistake of law bar was still in place, the only conceivable ground for restitution was one of policy: the ultra vires doctrine pursues a policy in favour of a responsible administration of public finances. This policy is best realised by making sure that any ultra vires transactions entered into by local authorities are reversed, at least where the local authorities are the losers. A legal system committed to the rule of law, however, cannot countenance the possibility of compelling the unsuspecting banks to repay their winnings to the local authorities while not putting them in a position likewise to recoup their own losses.[21] The policy underlying the ultra vires doctrine in this type of case could thus have justified ordering restitution in all cases. This argument, however, was never seriously advanced.[22] Once Hobhouse J had ordered restitution on the ground of 'no consideration', it was no longer necessary to discuss the policy underlying the nullity in these particular cases. 'No consideration' was far more convenient.

In *Guinness Mahon v. Kensington and Chelsea LBC* the Court of Appeal confirmed that 'absence of consideration' was available as a ground for restitution in cases of completed swaps. Thus, there is now unequivocal Court

---

[19] P. Birks, 'No Consideration: Restitution after Void Contracts', (1993) 23 *University of Western Australia LR* 195.
[20] [1999] QB 215.
[21] Not surprisingly, the banks had been the overall winners of the swaps entered into with local authorities – *Hazell* turned them into the overall losers!
[22] It is referred to in the bank's skeleton argument in *Westdeutsche* and some of the other lead cases, but since in those cases the *banks* were asking for restitution, the argument was perceived to be a weak one.

of Appeal authority that nullity as such can trigger restitution. It is nevertheless open to doubt whether this line of authority will in future need to be relied on. This is because of the recent case of *Kleinwort Benson v. Lincoln CC*, to which the discussion will now turn.

2. Mistake of law

'Absence of consideration' was unlikely to assist the claimants in the latest and probably last instalment of the swaps saga. Some of the payments had been made more than six years before issue of the writ. The only hope was recovery on the ground of mistake, because section 32(1)(c) of the Limitation Act 1980 meant that time would only have begun to run when the mistake could have been discovered, in other words when *Hazell* was decided.

As mentioned above, the obstacle in the way of such a claim was the long-standing rule that there could be no restitution for the sole reason that a transfer had been made under a mistake of law. A mistaken belief in the legal capacity of the local authority was, after all, clearly a mistake of law rather than fact. Only the House of Lords could abrogate that rule, and by a three to two majority it did.[23] Their Lordships' disagreement did not concern the question whether the rule should be abolished or not: they were unanimous in their condemnation of it. However, Lords Browne-Wilkinson and Lloyd felt that the bank could not be described as having paid the money under a mistake at all: at the time the payment was made the law was indeed what they thought it was, and most lawyers would have advised them that they were liable to pay. It was only later, when the Divisional Court declared swap transactions ultra vires local authorities, that the law was changed. While both Law Lords accepted that the decision of an English court was to some extent retrospective, they both felt that 'retrospection cannot falsify history'.[24] The 'paradigm case' on which they relied is one in which the House of Lords overrules a line of Court of Appeal authority. In that situation, according to Lord Lloyd,[25] prior to the House of Lords ruling, the law was as the Court of Appeal had said previously. The House of Lords is unable to change this. 'The House of Lords can say that the Court of Appeal took a wrong turning. It can say what the law should have been. But it cannot say that the law

---

[23] [1999] 2 AC 349. The way in which the case reached the House of Lords was unusual. In the Commercial Court, Langley J made a consent order dismissing the claim but granting a certificate for an appeal directly to the House of Lords. In this way, their Lordships did not have the benefit of reasoned judgments below.

[24] At 517 (Lord Browne-Wilkinson), 548 (Lord Lloyd).   [25] At 548.

actually applied by the Court of Appeal was other than what it was.'[26] The majority, however, took the view that the declaratory theory of judicial decision meant that the law applicable at the time of the payment indeed had been what the House of Lords now declared it to be. It followed from this that at the time of the payment the payer was labouring under a mistake of law.

The question what constitutes a mistake in this context will exercise the minds of unjust enrichment and contract lawyers for some time to come. It will also be of great interest to legal philosophers. This is not the place to discuss the question in any detail. Whatever view one takes on this issue, however, the result of the decision of the majority is that where the law is changed by judicial decision this may well have restitutionary consequences. The emphasis is taken away from the state of mind of the payer and is transferred to the validity or otherwise of the obligation he sought to discharge by making the payment. Restitution follows, not so much because the payer was mistaken, but because the obligation he sought to discharge has now been declared void.

This was always going to be one difficulty with abolishing the mistake of law bar. Birks had foreseen it. He had argued that, where both parties had got precisely what they had bargained for, in other words where they could no longer be prejudiced by their mistake of law, restitution should not be available – the mistake, if any, had been 'spent'.[27] He thus focused on mistake, not on the nullity as such. Had his argument been accepted, it would have been necessary, in cases of 'spent' mistakes, to ask *why* the underlying transaction had been void, and whether the policy favouring nullity also favoured restitution. Restitution in such cases would thus have been policy based, not mistake based. The House of Lords unfortunately rejected Birks's analysis without discussing it in any detail, and apparently without realising that there was much more to it than the question of at what point in time the cause of action in money had and received arose.

In consequence, whenever a payment is now made under a void contract, a defendant will face an uphill struggle if he is to convince the court that the claimant was not labouring under a 'mistaken' belief in the validity of the contract. The result will be that in the overwhelming majority of cases nullity by itself will be sufficient to trigger restitution. While the dismantling of the mistake of law bar has no doubt taken the wind out of the sails of the 'no consideration' doctrine, the end result is

---

[26] *Ibid.*   [27] P. Birks, 'No Consideration', 230, n. 137.

very much the same, with nullity by itself leading to restitution of any benefits received pursuant to a void transaction.

Lord Goff, true to form, referred to comparative law in order to justify his reasoning. German law took pride of place in his analysis:

> It is of some interest that, in German law, recovery is not dependent on proof of mistake (whether of fact or law) by the claimant. Para. 812(1) of the BGB (*Bürgerliches Gesetzbuch*) confers a right to recover benefit obtained without legal justification (*ohne rechtlichen Grund*)...Para. 814 of the BGB, however, provides that a person cannot reclaim a benefit conferred by him if he knew that he was not bound to confer it; but it seems that the burden rests on the recipient to prove the existence of such knowledge (a striking contrast with the common law, which requires the plaintiff to prove mistake)... For present purposes, however, the importance of this comparative material is to reveal that, in civil law systems, a blanket exclusion of recovery of money paid under a mistake of law is not regarded as necessary. In particular, the experience of these systems assists to dispel the fears expressed in the early English cases that a right of recovery on the ground of mistake of law may lead to a flood of litigation, while at the same time it shows that in some cases a right of recovery, which has in the past been denied by application of the mistake of law rule may likewise be denied in civil law countries on the basis of a narrower ground of principle or policy. (At 374–5.)

There is much in this brief extract to stimulate the thought processes of a comparative lawyer. In particular: if it is true that the decision in *Kleinwort Benson v. Lincoln CC* means that a claimant no longer needs to prove a mistake properly so called, but that the voidness of the transaction itself triggers restitution, the words of Lord Goff assume a new significance. Is it truly possible to conclude from the experience of German law that restitution for lack of legal ground will not lead to a flood of litigation in a common-law system? The remainder of this chapter will examine this question.

III. Invalidity in German law

In German as in English law, there are a number of reasons why a supposedly valid obligation might later turn out to be void. As a general rule, the use of the word *nichtig* ('void') triggers the application of §§ 812–22, the law of unjust enrichment. This might be thought to mean that the voidness of the obligation itself is the *reason* for restitution, or at least that it is the mistaken belief in the validity of the obligation which could be described as the 'unjust factor'. In a seminal essay, which to this day can be described as the basis of the modern German law of unjust enrichment, Ernst von Caemmerer pointed out that this is not so. He wrote: 'The actual reasons for restitution lie outside the law of unjust enrichment. The law of restitution would otherwise be overburdened.'[28] Whether an obligation is valid, void or voidable is determined by the general law. Where the general law determines that an obligation is void, or can be rendered void by one party's unilateral act, restitution is the consequence. The general law is drafted with that consequence in mind. Generally, when the law uses the word *nichtig*, it is aware that this might have restitutionary consequences. Where restitution is not intended, the word *nichtig* can be avoided or 'disarmed', by making it clear that though an obligation is wholly void, any payments made under it are to be irrecoverable.

1. Anfechtung (Rescission)

One way in which a transaction can end up void is because one or other of the parties decides to exercise a right of rescission. According to § 142(1), if a transaction is rescinded, it becomes void *ab initio*, or, as a German lawyer would say, void '*ex tunc*'. A party may have a right to rescind on the grounds of mistake (§ 119(1)), duress (§ 123(1)) or fraudulent misrepresentation (§ 123(1)). There are significant differences between English and German law in terms of what mistakes count, what kind of threat is unlawful and amounts to duress, and when rescission is possible for misrepresentation. These differences are not considered here. Where both systems are largely similar is in the mechanism by which these vitiating factors are translated into reasons for restitution. If a party was coerced into contracting by duress, and paid out money under that contract, he will be able to extricate himself from the contract by rescinding it. In English law, rescission has the automatic consequence of restitution, although it is a matter of debate in what way this is to be conceptualised. In German law, rescission renders the contract void *ab initio*, which in turn triggers § 812(1). Restitution follows. The duress that caused the contract to be voidable is also the underlying reason for restitution.

2. Illegality

Illegality is a particularly good example of the point I am trying to make. Where a party has contracted to do an act which is illegal, the law cannot

---

[28] E. von Caemmerer, 'Bereicherung und unerlaubte Handlung', in: H. Dölle, M. Rheinstein and K. Zweigert (eds.), *Festschrift für Ernst Rabel* (1954), vol. I, 333, 343.

be seen to enforce that contract. If it did, this would give rise to an inherent contradiction within the legal system. It is therefore imperative that obligations to do an illegal act will not be enforced by the law. To that extent at least, such obligations must be invalid.

If an illegal contract has already been performed, on the other hand, the law is no longer faced with the danger of an inherent contradiction: it is not faced with the difficulty that giving the contract validity will imply using the legal process for illegal purposes. The question that must now be faced is whether the illegality should lead to restitution. This question is a complex one and need not be fully discussed for present purposes.[29] For now it suffices to point out that German law is sufficiently flexible to examine the nature and purpose of the infringed law in deciding whether or not restitution should follow. § 134 reads: 'A transaction which contravenes a legal prohibition is void, unless the contrary appears from the legal provision in question.'

In order to decide whether or not a transaction should be held void, the court will thus be able to look at the relevant statute and ask whether its purpose would be furthered by awarding restitution. For example, German law makes it an offence for a shop to trade after opening hours as laid down by federal statute. If this rule is breached, it would make little sense to hold the contract of sale void, requiring the parties to make restitution to each other. The purpose of the statute – namely, to prevent the exploitation of shop assistants – would not be furthered by such a rule. On the contrary, the unwinding of the contract would require them to work even longer hours.[30] On the other hand, German law also makes it an offence for an unlicensed craftsman to contract for work. His customer also commits an offence by engaging him. These rules attempt, with very limited success, to prevent the evasion of VAT and income tax. That purpose is best served by rendering such contracts absolutely void. The worker cannot be sure that he will be paid, and a restitutionary claim will not be available to him.[31] The aim is to dissuade him from entering into such illicit bargains.

The voidness of an illegal contract, particularly if it has already been executed, is thus not a foregone conclusion. It depends on a myriad of policy considerations. The judge retains a great degree of flexibility. Again, the word *nichtig* could only be used as long as the judge retained that

---

[29] See the contributions by Dannemann and Swadling to this book.
[30] See D. Medicus, *Allgemeiner Teil des BGB* (7th edn, 1997), n. 648.
[31] But see BGHZ 111, 308, 312 ff.

flexibility; otherwise, restitution might have to be awarded in circumstances in which it might not be appropriate.

It should further be pointed out that the law of unjust enrichment itself contains a special provision concerned with illegality and immorality. Broadly, this focuses on the legality and morality of the receipt of the benefit. If the receipt itself is contrary to law or morals, § 817, first sentence, provides an independent restitutionary 'unjust factor'. Restitution is wholly barred, however, where both parties were guilty of infringing law or morals (§ 817, second sentence). This provision will be examined in greater detail in the chapter by Gerhard Dannemann, below. For present purposes, however, it demonstrates, at least in the area of illegality, that saying that restitution will follow when a performance has been made under a void transaction is not very informative.

To summarise: the German legislature is well aware of the restitutionary consequences of rendering a transaction or obligation void. The code attempts not to use the word *nichtig* where such consequences are not desired.

3. 'Just factors'

Sometimes, however, performances are made under transactions which are void, but where restitution is for one reason or another not desired by the legal order. This is an effect of the very wide negative formulation of § 812(1), focusing on the lack of legal ground. In order to identify such cases, German law has had to construct a typology of factors barring restitution. They may be called 'grounds for retention' or indeed, slightly cynically, 'just factors'.

(a) Formalities

Formality requirements may be imposed by the law in the interest of the parties themselves or in the public interest. The parties themselves may benefit because they are prevented from taking ill thought-out, hasty steps which might have serious consequences, and because a formal transaction is easier to prove subsequently. The frequent requirement of notarial attestation also ensures the provision of appropriate legal advice, so that the parties are prevented from entering blindly into a transaction the consequences of which they do not fully understand. Formalities also benefit the state: transactions are recorded in order to keep public registers up to date and to levy taxes and fees. Generally, § 125, first sentence, provides that where legal formality requirements are not complied with, the transaction is absolutely void.³² This general rule, however, does not apply across the board. In particular, in certain cases the provision imposing the formality requirement makes sure that § 125, first sentence, will have no restitutionary consequences.

§ 313 requires that land contracts must be attested by a notary. If they are not, they should be void according to § 125, first sentence. The second sentence of § 313, however, provides that where the land contract has been fully performed and the new owner registered at the land registry (*Grundbuchamt*), the lack of form is 'cured' and the contract becomes binding. Full performance is therefore seen as a factor militating against restitution. Registration itself is a formal act, and the purpose of § 313 is thus largely achieved by registering the new owner's title.³³ Unwinding the transaction at this stage would mean compromising the integrity of the register, which is a further reason to bar restitution.

Similarly, § 518(1) provides that gift promises require attestation by a notary. If they are not attested, they are thus void according to § 125. However, § 518(2) provides that, again, lack of form is cured by full performance, which must be a relief to all children on their birthdays. Again, once the gift promise has been fully performed, and the gift has been handed over, there are obvious and strong reasons militating against restitution: these reasons make § 518(2) necessary.

A final example is provided by § 766. This rule lays down the requirement that a guarantee or surety agreement must be in writing, otherwise § 125 will apply. The purpose of this requirement is that, since the surety does not have to pay any money at the time of agreeing to guarantee the main debt, he should be warned against the potential adverse consequences of that step.³⁴ The second sentence of § 766 again provides that, once the surety pays up and satisfies the creditor, the lack of formality is cured. There is no longer any need to warn the surety at that stage. Indeed, even if the surety mistakenly believes he is bound by the guarantee, this will not help him.³⁵ The payment is, in other words, a ground of retention which trumps the prima facie voidness of the guarantee. The fact that the obligation was void at or just before the time of payment does not trigger restitution.

---

[32] This can lead to hard cases, which have indeed led to bad law: the courts have tried to temper the inflexibility of the rule in cases in which its application would lead to 'simply unacceptable results': OGHZ 1, 217; BGHZ 85, 315.
[33] See K. Larenz, *Lehrbuch des Schuldrechts* (14th edn, 1987), vol. I, 73.
[34] BGH 1993 *NJW* 1127, 1262.
[35] See Karl Larenz and Claus-Wilhelm Canaris, *Lehrbuch des Schuldrechts* (13th edn, 1994), vol. II/2, 5.

(b) Natural obligations

§ 762(1) provides that a bet does not give rise to an obligation. This is commonly justified not by moral objections but by the inherent dangers of gambling contracts.[36] The provision goes on, however, to say that any performances under a bet cannot be recovered on the basis that no obligation existed. The second sentence of § 762(1) thus effectively disapplies § 812(1).

§ 656, which applies to marriage brokerage, is in almost identical terms. Again, it provides that a promise to pay in consideration of marriage brokerage services does not give rise to an obligation, and again it goes on to say that if such a promise is nevertheless honoured, the fact that no obligation existed cannot be relied on to demand restitution of any payments made.

These so-called 'natural obligations'[37] are good examples of cases in which German law considers that even the strongest form of invalidity, the total absence of an obligation, should not lead to restitution if performances are made. It would go too far to discuss the policies underlying these rules; it is enough to point out that the legislature was quite clearly aware that both forms of 'natural obligation' would be caught by the very wide § 812(1) unless it was made clear that the latter provision should not apply. Although they are not obligations properly so called, 'natural' obligations thus form *legal grounds*; in other words, they entitle the recipient to retain the benefit conferred – they are reasons for retention.

(c) Time-barred claims

Time-barred claims, often also placed in the category of 'natural obligations', are not void, but unenforceable. Again, the code makes careful use of terminology in § 222(1): 'After the limitation period has expired, the debtor is entitled to refuse to perform.' Given that the word *nichtig* is not employed, it is arguable that § 812(1) would not have applied in any event. § 222(2) nevertheless puts it beyond doubt that where a time-barred claim is satisfied, the fact that the limitation period had expired does not entitle the payer to restitution, even where he was unaware that the claim was time-barred and thus unenforceable. The time-barred claim, though not enforceable, nevertheless constitutes a legal ground, a reason for retention.

---

[36] Max Vollkommer, in: Othmar Jauernig (ed.), *Bürgerliches Gesetzbuch* (9th edn, 1999), § 762, n. 1.

[37] For criticism of the term see Larenz, *Lehrbuch*, 21.

4. The Wilburg/von Caemmerer typology

If a widely formulated ground for restitution based on mistake of law has a saving grace, it is that it is clearly restricted to cases in which the claimant made a conscious decision to transfer the relevant benefit to the defendant. It cannot be said to extend to cases in which the benefit accrued to the defendant in any other way. However, the Court of Appeal in *Guinness Mahon* enthusiastically endorsed the 'absence of consideration' approach, and although *Kleinwort Benson v. Lincoln CC* may have stolen the thunder of that idea for the time being, it is still lurking at the back of the minds of legal advisers looking for a way to frame the otherwise hopeless claims of their clients.

Peter Schlechtriem, in his textbook on the law of obligations, writes: 'The more abstract the requirements for enrichment claims, the more difficult becomes the necessary limiting exercise; this is especially true if one assumes one basic general requirement for all enrichment claims.'[38] He writes in the context of three-party situations, a particular problem area in German enrichment law,[39] but his comment is of more general validity. To base restitution on the absence or otherwise of a 'legal ground' invites confusion. In particular, if the abstraction is rendered, as has been done so far in this chapter, as 'basis in the law of obligations' – that is, as an obligation by which the transferor is compelled to render a specific performance – one will run into problems when the enrichment is based not on a performance, but has come about in 'another way', as § 812(1) puts it. Cases which English lawyers would now categorise as falling into the group of 'restitution for wrongs', or cases in which the claimant was wholly unaware that the defendant was enriching himself at his expense (called cases of 'ignorance' by Birks), simply do not involve a supposed obligation. Some other criteria must be found in order to decide when restitution should be available. This is not the place to go into that discussion. It should merely be pointed out that § 812(1) as it was interpreted in the early decades of the twentieth century, just after the enactment of the BGB, represented an open invitation to dispense palm-tree justice, and was in fact interpreted as such. It is only due to the self-denying discipline of the *Reichsgericht* and the brilliance of two academics that this did not happen. Professors Wilburg and von Caemmerer, in 1934 and 1957 respectively, developed a typology based on the way in which the enrichment was obtained that was accepted by the *Bundesgerichtshof* as late as

---

[38] P. Schlechtriem, *Schuldrecht Besonderer Teil* (4th edn, 1995), 310.
[39] Concerning three-party situations in English law, see the contribution by Peter Birks to the present volume.

the 1960s. It was only then that German enrichment law was put on a secure intellectual and typological footing.

The development of the Wilburg/von Caemmerer typology, presented as an example for English law by Reinhard Zimmermann,[40] took several decades. It is not obvious to me that English law would simply adopt this typology wholesale, were it to accept a similarly broad general requirement for restitution. It is to be hoped that the potential time bomb of restitution for 'absence of consideration' has been defused by *Kleinwort Benson v. Lincoln CC*. However, the 'absence of consideration' idea is still out there, has never been expressly disapproved by the House of Lords, and is thus, in Birks's words, left 'lying casually around',[41] to be relied on by a litigant who is not even able to rely on the new and very broad unjust factor 'mistake of law', for the simple reason that he never made a conscious transfer in the first place.

IV. Invalidity in English law

I do not propose to argue that English law, contrary to Zimmermann's allegation, is 'distinguished by its elegance'. I do argue, however, that English law serves its purpose: to identify those cases in which restitution should be available by requiring the claimant to prove that his claim falls within one of the established categories. In other words, the claimant has to show that there is a reason, recognised by the law, why he should have restitution.

Before the swaps litigation, the fact that a benefit was transferred under a void or non-existent obligation did not by itself trigger restitution. Lord Goff has recognised the superficial attractiveness of the proposition that where money is paid under a void contract it ought to be recoverable. One objection to this 'simple call of justice' he saw in the structure of the English law of restitution: 'That law might have developed so as to recognise a *condictio indebiti* – an action for the recovery of money on the ground that it was not due. But it did not do so. Instead, as we have seen, there developed common law actions for the recovery of money paid under a mistake of fact, and under certain forms of compulsion.'[42]

It has been argued above that *Westdeutsche* in effect introduced the *condictio indebiti* into English law. It is arguable that *Kleinwort Benson v.*

---

[40] R. Zimmermann, 'Unjustified Enrichment: The Modern Civilian Approach', (1995) 15 *Oxford JLS* 403.
[41] Birks, 'No Consideration', 231.   [42] *Woolwich Building Society v. IRC* [1993] AC 70 at 172.

Lincoln CC achieved very much the same result by dressing the *Leistungskondiktion* in English sheep's clothing: by interpreting mistake of law to encompass cases where the 'mistake' arose by subsequent overruling of existing law alone, in effect placing the emphasis on the invalidity of the obligation rather than the mistake of the claimant.

The great beauty of German law, as seen above, is that the law of unjust enrichment works in tandem with the general law. The word *nichtig* works, if the simile is not too far-fetched, like a catalyst, referring the claimant to the law of unjust enrichment wherever it occurs. This result can be achieved within the framework of a coherent codification, namely by the careful use of the word *nichtig*, by providing a number of 'reasons for retention' (which I have called 'just factors'), and last but not least by developing a typology which has successfully limited the potentially very wide general clause in § 812(1), dispelling fears of palm-tree justice.

Outside the law of rescission, there is no such working in tandem in English law. In most cases, even following *Kleinwort Benson v. Lincoln CC*, there will be a certain duplication of inquiries. It is clear that where a contract is valid, the law of restitution can have no role to play.[43] The contract must therefore be shown to be void before the claimant can begin to establish a restitutionary claim. The 'unjust factor' upon which the claimant relies will often be the same as the vitiating factor upon which he relied to show that the contract was void. Thus, if the contract is void for mistake, it is likely that the mistake will also be relied upon as an unjust factor. Yet does this really matter? Elegance is not the be-all and end-all of the law. It is unlikely that where a contract is void for mistake much argument would be directed at the question whether that mistake should also trigger restitution: it would appear that that would be the obvious conclusion.

Where contracts turn out to be invalid, failure of consideration will often be relied upon as an unjust factor. The contract being void, it is no longer possible to compel the defendant to fulfil his part of the bargain. The restitutionary claim enables the claimant at least to get back his own performance.

Some contracts are rendered void or voidable for policy reasons that favour restitution. In such cases the reason for restitution is that restitution favours the policy in question. One example is section 127 of the Insolvency Act 1986. That section, re-enacting section 522 of the Companies

---

[43] This has been pointed out by Sonja Meier in her book on the English law of unjust enrichment *Irrtum und Zweckverfehlung* (1999), 99. She argues that English law here employs legal-ground reasoning without realising it.

Act 1985, provides that in a winding up by the court any disposition of the company's property made after the commencement of the winding up is void unless the court orders otherwise. It is not possible nor is it necessary to analyse the effects of the section here. One effect of the section might be that an alienee never obtains the property in the benefit transferred. This may be so, for instance, where the property in goods is supposed to pass at the time of contracting. The contract and the transfer of property are void from the beginning and the company (whether through liquidator, administrator or administrative receiver) will be able to recover the goods. Whether the company's claim to the goods is characterised as restitutionary is a difficult question, given that the property in the goods remains the company's throughout. Where money is paid by the company after the commencement of the winding up, however, the company's right under section 127 is clearly restitutionary. This is so because it is one of the characteristics of money that it is fully negotiable.[44] Once the payment passes into currency the company's title is lost.

Where a transaction transfers good title, notwithstanding section 127, the transferee will be subject to a claim to make restitution of the benefit obtained to the company, unless the court orders otherwise.[45] It is difficult to explain this using mainstream unjust factors. 'Mistake' may sometimes work, because the company may not have been aware of the presentation of the winding-up petition at the time of the payment, but this will only be so in some cases. Likewise, 'failure of consideration' will only explain restitution in rare instances. Instead, the reason for restitution must be the policy of the bankruptcy laws to ensure the *pari passu* distribution of the company's assets amongst creditors.[46] Section 127 has this in common with other rules designed to protect the interests of creditors, in particular section 238 (transactions at an undervalue), section 239 (preferences) and

---

[44] *Miller v. Race* (1758) 1 Burr 452.
[45] See *Merton and Another v. Hammond Suddards and Another* [1996] 2 BCLC 470. In that case, somewhat contrary to the argument taken in this paper, His Honour Judge Kolbert sitting as a High Court judge said, in interpreting section 127: 'I take the view that there is much to be said for a plain interpretation of a provision in plain language, especially as "void" is a word of unmistakable meaning. Once an argument enters even marginally upon the proposition that "void" bears any meaning other than "of no effect", or the court is urged that "void" really means "voidable", that is, that a disposition takes effect until challenged and cancelled or avoided, the court should be very wary of accepting that argument.'
[46] Although it may sometimes have the opposite effect, namely when assets have come into the hands of the liquidator and are claimed by an administrative receiver on behalf of a secured creditor: see *Merton v. Hammond Suddards* [1996] 2 BCLC 470.

section 423 (transactions defrauding creditors).[47] Sometimes, restitution will favour that policy. In such cases, the court will refuse to ratify the disposition. In others, the disposition might have been beneficial to the company, and thus to the company's creditors. In such a case, the court may ratify the disposition under section 127. The court's power is similar to the German court's discretion under § 134 BGB to uphold an illegal transaction, refusing to declare it void where restitution would not favour the policy pursued by the infringed rule of law.[48]

It is tempting, however, to conclude that the word 'void' will always have similar consequences, that it will always imply not only that an obligation cannot be relied on to found a claim to performance or compensation, but that it will also always have restitutionary consequences. In other words, one might be tempted to generalise that the policy underlying the decision to render a transaction void will also favour restitution in all cases. Hobhouse J drew that conclusion in *Westdeutsche*: the ultra vires doctrine rendered the swaps transactions void. Hobhouse J relied on nullity as such in granting the banks restitution. This made it unnecessary to analyse the ultra vires doctrine itself. Hobhouse J explicitly held that the ultra vires doctrine could not possibly assist the banks.[49] He thus never asked himself whether the policy underlying it, namely the aim of protecting the integrity of public finances, made restitution necessary. Therefore, although it is possible to defend the outcome of *Westdeutsche* on that basis,[50] the problem is that the inquiry was never undertaken.

In English law, it is not always possible to conclude that where an obligation is void, the policy that underlies the nullity will also favour restitution. For example, under section 2 of the Law of Property (Miscellaneous Provisions) Act 1989, a contract for the sale or other disposition of an interest in land can only be made in writing, all the terms must be contained in one document, or, where contracts are exchanged, in each, and the relevant documents must be signed by or on behalf of each party to the contract. It must follow that where these formalities are not complied with, the agreement in question is void and of no effect. Where one party refuses to perform such an agreement, the courts will not assist the other by ordering specific performance or by awarding him damages. The question in the present context is, however, whether such an agreement, once performed, will subsequently have to be reversed, or will be reversible at the instance of one party or the other. If restitution must

---

[47] See Birks, *Introduction*, 308.   [48] See above, 86–8.
[49] [1994] 4 All ER 890 at 915.   [50] See above, 82.

necessarily follow where performances have been exchanged pursuant to a void contract, that should clearly be the result.

Tootal Clothing Ltd v. Guinea Properties Ltd[51] concerned a lease under which the tenant was to carry out certain shop-fitting works to the demised premises. The landlord, Guinea Properties, was to contribute to the costs of these works. Its obligation to do so, however, was contained in a separate document. Having taken possession of the property, and having completed the works, the tenant sued for recovery of the landlord's contribution. The landlord argued that the agreement was void and unenforceable because under section 2 of the 1989 Act all the relevant terms should have been in one document. This argument succeeded at first instance before Douglas Brown J, dealing with the question as a preliminary issue. He held 'without any enthusiasm at all' that section 2 applied to the contract and that therefore all the terms of the contract had to be incorporated in one document. In the Court of Appeal, Scott LJ, with whom Boreham J and Parker LJ agreed, held that Guinea's defence missed the point of section 2 of the 1989 Act. If the argument was sound, the result would be that executed agreements would have to be unravelled. It was therefore necessary to ask what policy was pursued by section 2. This question had been addressed previously by Hoffmann J (as he then was) in *Spiro v. Glencrown Properties Ltd*.[52] He had held that section 2 'was intended to prevent disputes over whether the parties had entered into a binding agreement or over what terms they had agreed'. As such, argued Scott LJ, section 2 was of relevance only to executory contracts. He continued: 'If parties choose to complete an oral land contract or a land contract that does not in some respect or other comply with section 2, they are at liberty to do so. Once they have done so, it becomes irrelevant that the contract they have completed may not have been in accordance with section 2.'[53]

While *Tootal Clothing* did not concern a restitutionary claim, the conclusion that section 2 had no relevance to executed contracts was necessary to avoid the conclusion that Douglas Brown J had felt compelled to draw at first instance.

For present purposes, *Tootal Clothing* can be interpreted in two ways: on the one hand it can be argued that the case clearly demonstrates that nullity as such will not lead to restitution where both parties have obtained what they bargained for; in other words, where there has been no failure of consideration or other substantive reason for restitution. On the other

---

[51] (1991) 64 P & CR 452. [52] [1991] Ch 537 at 541. [53] (1991) 64 P & CR 452 at 455.

hand, it is arguable that lack of formality renders a contract unenforceable rather than void, or that the lack of formality is 'cured' by subsequent performance. This would mirror the position in German law.

The traditional inquiry in English law would be turned right around. Instead of asking for reasons why an enrichment should be reversed, the defendant, enriched pursuant to a void contract, would have to show reasons justifying retention. English law, however, is not contained in a coherent code. Nor is language always used with the same degree of precision in English statutes as in the German Civil Code. When the word 'void' is used in English law, it is far from clear that the policy underlying nullity can be made to extend to restitution of benefits conferred. The simple truth is that English law lacks the system of 'just factors' which the fathers of the BGB were able to draft into their code. In the wake of *Kleinwort Benson v. Lincoln CC*, this is likely to give rise to a number of problems.

One obvious difference between English law and German law is that English law still insists on the presence of some consideration before a promise will be enforced as a contract. In the well-known case of *Eastwood v. Kenyon*[54] a guardian decided to improve his young ward's matrimonial prospects by renovating a house which belonged to her. He raised the necessary funds on a promissory note. The scheme bore fruit, and soon the ward was engaged to be married. The bridegroom, feeling morally obliged to do so, promised to pay the promissory note. Once the couple were married, however, he changed his mind. When sued upon his promise it was held that, contrary to Lord Mansfield's view,[55] a moral obligation was not sufficient consideration to support a promise. Any consideration furnished by the guardian was past consideration, and as such no consideration at all. Change the facts slightly: what if the defendant had already honoured his promise, in the mistaken belief that he was bound to do so? English law has never had to address this question, because the mistake of law bar has prevented it from arising. Now, following *Westdeutsche* and *Kleinwort Benson v. Lincoln CC*, the husband, in a restitutionary claim against the guardian, would be able to rely on two compelling arguments in favour of recovery: first, he could say that, in paying, he had made a mistake of law. Unknown to him, his promise did not bind him. He should therefore recover. Secondly, he could argue, the contract which he thought

---

[54] (1840) 11 A & E 438; 113 ER 482.
[55] Expressed in *Lee v. Muggeridge* (1813) 5 Taunt 36 at 46, when he was still Sir James Mansfield CJ.

compelled him to pay never came into being because the three requirements of contractual liability – offer, acceptance and consideration – were never present. There should thus be restitution based on 'absence of consideration'.

Restitution in such a case, however, is not desirable. The general policy of the law should be that people should honour their promises, the doctrine of consideration being merely a means to make sure that promises will not be *enforced* that were not given seriously, with intention to give rise to legal relations. English law will thus have to deal with this case in some way, following the recent developments in the law of unjust enrichment. Sonia Meier suggests that the only way to deal with this situation is a wholesale adoption of the *condictio indebiti*. She argues that the underlying promise, though not binding as a contract, would still be sufficient to give rise to a legal ground. In other words, payment in accordance with an unenforceable promise will have to be considered a 'just factor', a reason for retention. As Meier rightly recognises, this would constitute the final acceptance by English law that the German solution is superior.

The modified *Eastwood v. Kenyon* raises another question, addressed in German law by § 814: the defendant was under a moral obligation to reimburse the claimant. The latter, although he had spent his money 'voluntarily', had spent it on improving his ward's property. English law would probably deny him a restitutionary claim against the ward based on some kind of 'moral compulsion' or necessity: for example, *Nicholson v. Chapman*[56] and *Falcke v. Scottish Imperial Insurance Co.*[57] It is nevertheless easy to see why the ward's later husband would feel obliged to his wife's former guardian and reimburse him for his expenditure. Should he be able to reclaim that reimbursement on the basis that he paid for 'no consideration' or because he had believed[58] himself legally obliged to pay? Again, English law might have to make an exception to the general rule, might have to recognise yet another 'just factor'.

'Restitution for nullity', whether it be referred to as restitution for 'absence of consideration' or restitution for mistake of law, will give rise to problems in English law, problems which go further than the obvious difficulty that all gifts might become recoverable. English law does not yet have the mechanisms which have enabled German law to function correctly. It will most likely have to develop them now.

---

[56] (1793) 2 H Bl 254; 126 ER 536. [57] (1886) 34 ChD 234.
[58] In German law, that belief might well have been right, because German law recognises claims based on *negotiorum gestio*: cf. §§ 677 ff.

V. Conclusion

Comparative law can be a powerful tool of legal analysis. Superficial comparative law, however, can be dangerous. The comparative lawyer must never lose sight of the bigger picture. Just because a legal rule operates well in one legal system does not necessarily mean that it will operate equally well in another. This is particularly true of the law of unjust enrichment. We may admire the German solution, we may be struck by its elegance, impressed by its logical coherence. But we must not be blinded by our own enthusiasm. The two legal systems, the two legal cultures are fundamentally different. These differences reflect differences in legal history and in cultural and intellectual development. I cannot put it any better than Tony Weir in his brilliant translation of Zweigert and Kötz's *Introduction to Comparative Law*:

If we may generalize, the European is given to making plans, to regulating things in advance, and therefore, in terms of law, to drawing up rules and systematizing them. He approaches life with fixed ideas, and operates deductively. The Englishman improvises, never making a decision until he has to: 'we'll cross that bridge when we come to it'. As Maitland said, he is an empiricist. Only experience counts for him; theorizing has little appeal; and so he is not given to abstract rules of law. Convinced, perhaps from living by the sea, that life will controvert the best-laid plans, the Englishman is more at home with case-law proceeding cautiously step-by-step than with legislation which purports to lay down rules for the solution of all future cases.[59]

It fits in well with these broad general differences that German law should lay down a general provision of unjust enrichment, designed to operate within a coherent code, made possible by the rigorous and uniform use of terms such as *nichtig*, while English law, less confident about the coherence of the legal system as a whole, should put its trust in less abstract, less well-defined 'unjust factors'. The German law of unjust enrichment operates *deductively*, its starting point is a wide general principle, which is limited and narrowed down both by the codification itself and by subsequent academic analysis and interpretation. English law, on the other hand, has chosen to extend the incidence of restitution for unjust enrichment little by little, case by case, always, until now, on the basis that there must be some good reason why restitution should be available. In *Kleinwort Benson v. Lincoln CC* and in *Westdeutsche Landesbank v. Islington LBC* the English courts have for the first time chosen a different approach. The new rule in English law is that whenever a payment is made under a void

---

[59] Zweigert and Kötz, *Introduction*, 70.

transaction, restitution will be available. The rule is very wide, and very indiscriminate. It no longer asks whether there is a good reason for restitution. The rule does fit well into a Continental legal system. Our own system is likely to have problems with it. The rule is so wide that it will need to be narrowed down. Litigants will be encouraged by it to come to court with cases which previously would have been struck out as disclosing no reasonable cause of action. Now such cases are likely to proceed to trial until a new taxonomy of unjust enrichment is found. German law may be instructive in shaping that taxonomy.[60] It is nevertheless a shame that the English law of restitution, having just settled down, having just established its place on the English legal map, should now be thrown into renewed turmoil.

---

[60] Zimmermann and Meier go so far as to suggest that the only way forward for English law is now to resort to a legal-ground analysis: see R. Zimmermann and S. Meier, 'Judicial Development of the Law, *Error Iuris*, and the Law of Unjustified Enrichment – A View from Germany', (1999) 115 *LQR* 556; cf. also S. Meier, 'Nach 196 Jahren – Bereicherungsanspruch wegen Rechtsirrtums in England', 1999 *JZ* 555; R. Zimmermann, 'Rechtsirrtum und richterliche Rechtsfortbildung', (1999) 7 *Zeitschrift für Europäisches Privatrecht* 713.

PART III

Failure of consideration

4 Failure of consideration: myth and meaning in the English law of restitution

Graham Virgo

The doctrine of failure of consideration is of vital importance to the modern law of restitution in common-law jurisdictions, but it is a doctrine about which there remains a great deal of uncertainty. By concentrating on the main principles and themes underlying this doctrine and by comparing it with equivalent civil-law concepts, it is possible to identify the ambit of the doctrine and resolve some of the uncertainties. The doctrine also provides a useful case study by reference to which the differences of approach in the application and understanding of the law of restitution in common-law and civil-law jurisdictions can be assessed. There are eleven issues concerning the doctrine of failure of consideration that deserve particular attention.

I. The meaning of consideration

The main reason why the doctrine of failure of consideration has caused a great deal of confusion derives from the fact that the notion of 'consideration' has two different meanings. First, there is the contractual sense whereby 'consideration' refers to the parties' promises in the contract. The mutual promises are the *quid pro quo* by virtue of which the contract becomes contractually binding. Alternatively, there is the restitutionary sense of 'consideration', which is not concerned with the existence of the promises under the contract as such but is more concerned with the performance of those promises.

Even as regards this restitutionary sense of 'consideration' there are different interpretations depending on the context in which the promise is made.

103

1. Receipt of a benefit by the claimant

Usually the question whether consideration has been provided will be determined by reference to whether the claimant has received any benefit from the defendant which the defendant had promised to provide pursuant to the contract. If such a benefit has been received it constitutes consideration for the law of restitution. So, for example, if the claimant entered into a contract to buy a car from the defendant and paid £10,000 for a car which the defendant did not deliver, it follows that no consideration has been provided, because the claimant did not receive the benefit that he or she expected to receive.

2. Performance by the defendant

It is possible, however, as recently recognised by the House of Lords in *Stocznia Gdanska SA v. Latvian Shipping Co.*,[1] to conclude that consideration has been provided even though the claimant has not received any benefit from the defendant. For example, if, as occurred in the *Stocznia* case itself, the defendant agreed to build and deliver a ship to the claimant, once the defendant has started to build the ship this will be treated as the provision of consideration even though the claimant had not received any benefit. As Lord Goff said: 'the test is not whether the promisee has received a specific benefit, but rather whether the promisor has performed any part of the contractual duties in respect of which the payment is due'.[2]

Although usually the performance of a promise by the defendant will result in a benefit being received by the claimant, this will not always be the case, as Lord Goff acknowledged.[3] As long as the claimant has transferred a benefit to the defendant on the understanding that he or she will do something in return, such as build a ship, it follows that if the defendant has started to build the ship then some consideration will have been provided. It is important, therefore, to determine what condition was attached by the parties for the transfer of the benefit. To identify this condition it will usually be necessary to consider the terms of the contract, if there is one, by reference to which the transfer was made. So, for example, if the contract was simply a contract to sell a ship to the claimant, the fact that the defendant has started to build the ship will not constitute the provision of consideration, because the building

---

[1] [1998] 1 WLR 574.   [2] *Ibid.* at 588.   [3] *Ibid.*

of the ship was not the performance that the claimant expected.[4] If, however, as occurred in the *Stocznia* case, the contract was both to build and to deliver the ship, the defendant's building of the ship will constitute the provision of consideration. Ultimately, the terms of the agreement between the parties will determine the nature of the consideration.

3. Consideration without performance

Even though Lord Goff suggested that consideration refers to the performance of contractual duties by the defendant, it is possible to conceive of cases where consideration will have been provided without any performance by the defendant. For example, the claimant may transfer a benefit to the defendant which is conditional on performance by a third party, such as the grant of planning permission by a local authority.

In the light of these different interpretations of 'consideration', the restitutionary sense of that word is preferably defined simply as the condition by reference to which the claimant transfers a benefit to the defendant.[5] It is not sufficient that the claimant simply imposes such a condition in his or her own mind; at the very least that condition must have been communicated to the other party.[6]

II. The meaning of failure of consideration

The doctrine of failure of consideration in the common law can be interpreted in three different ways.[7]

1. Failure of promise

If the claimant and the defendant enter into a contract which is invalid for some reason, such as the parties being mistaken as to some fundamental issue at the time the contract was made,[8] then the defendant's promised performance will fail *ab initio*. If the defendant's promise is not

---

[4] This is illustrated by *Fibrosa Spolka Ackyjna v. Fairbairn Lawson Combe Barbour Ltd* [1943] AC 32, which concerned a contract to sell machinery. Whilst the machinery was being manufactured by the defendant it became impossible to deliver it because of the outbreak of the Second World War. It was held that no consideration had been provided by the defendant, presumably because the condition which attached to the payment of money to the defendant by the plaintiff was simply the delivery of the machinery and did not include its manufacture.
[5] *Rover International Ltd v. Cannon Film Sales Ltd (No. 3)* [1989] 1 WLR 912 at 923 (Kerr LJ).
[6] *Craven-Ellis v. Canons Ltd* [1936] 2 KB 403.
[7] S. Stoljar, 'The Doctrine of Failure of Consideration', (1959) 75 *LQR* 53.
[8] See J. Beatson, *Anson's Law of Contract* (27th edn, 1998), chap. 8.

valid then there is no contract to be performed and so the consideration for the contract can be said to have failed. Whether the defendant's promised performance has failed from the outset is a contractual question which will usually not have any implications for the law of restitution, save where the claimant has transferred a benefit to the defendant in purported performance of the contract.[9]

2. Failure of performance

This will occur where the contract is valid but the defendant does not do what he or she promised to do. This generally has nothing to do with the law of restitution, since the claimant will sue the defendant for breach of contract and seek a compensatory remedy, although exceptionally restitutionary relief may be available founded on the defendant's wrongdoing in breaching the contract.[10]

3. Collapse of bargain

Where a bargain has collapsed it follows that the contractual regime will cease to be applicable. It is in this situation that the law of restitution is most important to return the parties to the position which they occupied before the contract had been made and usually this will be on the ground that there has been a total failure of consideration.

III. The place of failure of consideration on the map of restitution

There has been a great deal of controversy amongst restitution scholars in the common-law world about the nature of the law of restitution. Although the orthodox view is that the law of restitution is only about the reversal of unjust enrichment,[11] this is in fact a somewhat simplistic approach.[12] The preferable view is that the law of restitution is concerned with the award of remedies that are assessed by reference to benefits obtained by the defendant rather than by losses suffered by the claimant.

---

[9] This is considered at section VIII, below.
[10] *Attorney-General v. Blake* [2001] AC 268.
[11] This was recognised by the House of Lords in *Lipkin Gorman (a Firm) v. Karpnale Ltd* [1991] 2 AC 548. See also Lord Goff of Chieveley and G. Jones, *The Law of Restitution* (5th edn, 1998), 3 and P. Birks, *An Introduction to the Law of Restitution* (revised edn, 1989). Birks has since rejected this quadration between the law of restitution and unjust enrichment: see his 'Misnomer', in: W. R. Cornish, R. Nolan, J. O'Sullivan and G. Virgo (eds.), *Restitution: Past, Present and Future* (1998), chap. 1.
[12] See G. Virgo, *Principles of the Law of Restitution* (1999), chap. 1.

The award of these remedies will be triggered by three different principles. First, where the defendant has obtained a benefit as the result of committing a restitution-yielding wrong. Secondly, where the defendant has obtained property in which the claimant has a proprietary interest and the claimant wishes to vindicate his or her proprietary rights. Thirdly, where the defendant has been unjustly enriched at the expense of the claimant. When the doctrine of failure of consideration is considered it is important to distinguish between each of these different principles.

1. Restitution for wrongs

The doctrine of failure of consideration is of no significance where the claimant seeks a restitutionary remedy following the defendant's commission of a wrong, most notably where the defendant has breached a contract. This is because the claim is founded on the breach of contract, which does not depend on proof that there has been a failure of consideration. It is only necessary to show that the defendant has done what he or she promised not to do or has failed to do what he or she promised to do. This provides the cause of action for the claim. The only question to consider then is whether or not restitutionary relief is available.[13]

2. Proprietary restitutionary claims

Where there has been a failure of consideration this will not usually have any proprietary consequences because it will not prevent legal title from passing to the defendant and it will not create an equitable title. This was recognised by the House of Lords in *Westdeutsche Landesbank Girozentrale v. Islington LBC*.[14] In this case the claimant bank had entered into an interest-rate swap transaction with the defendant local authority. This was ultra vires the local authority and so was null and void. The bank sought restitution of the money that it had paid to the local authority on the ground that there had been a failure of consideration.[15] Although the bank was able to establish that the consideration had indeed failed, it needed to establish that it had a proprietary claim to recover the money rather than merely a personal claim, since this affected the nature of the interest which could be awarded. But the House of Lords held that, where a

---

[13] *Attorney-General v. Blake* [2001] AC 268 where the House of Lords recognised that restitutionary damages are exceptionally available for breach of contract.
[14] [1996] AC 669. See also R. Chambers, *Resulting Trusts* (1997), 157–63.
[15] Specifically that there had been an absence of consideration. See section VIII, below. Today the claimant would be able to recover the money by reason of a mistake of law. See *Kleinwort Benson Ltd v. Lincoln CC* [1999] 2 AC 349.

claimant pays money in the expectation that he or she will receive something in return which is not forthcoming, this will not vitiate the claimant's intention that title in the money should pass. Neither will it be sufficient to create an equitable interest in the money.

The only possible exception to this is where the consequence of the failure of consideration is that the property transferred to the defendant is held on trust for the claimant. This is called a *Quistclose* trust after the name of the case which first recognised it.[16] It raises many complex issues, including when this type of trust will be recognised. The traditional view is that it will only be recognised where money has been transferred for a particular purpose which can no longer be fulfilled.[17] Recently, however, it has been suggested that such a trust will be recognised if the purpose has not been carried out.[18] This would dramatically widen the ambit of the trust, although the judge in that case did emphasise that the *Quistclose* trust could only be recognised where the parties intended the property to be held on trust if the purpose had not been satisfied. It follows that this should be characterised as an express trust. The consequence of recognising a trust in such circumstances is that the defendant will hold legal title to the property on trust for the claimant, who has an equitable proprietary interest in it. Although the claimant will be able to recover the property, this *Quistclose* trust cannot be considered to be founded on the doctrine of failure of consideration because it arises by virtue of the parties' intention rather than by operation of law.

3. Unjust enrichment

It follows that the doctrine of failure of consideration is only relevant as a ground of restitution for the purpose of establishing that the defendant has been unjustly enriched. Failure of consideration should be considered to operate as a ground of restitution because, when the claimant transfers a benefit to the defendant subject to a condition, the claimant's intention that the defendant should retain the benefit is qualified. When the condition is not satisfied this qualified intent can be considered to be vitiated, albeit retrospectively. If the claimant did not intend the defendant to receive the enrichment then the defendant should be required to make restitution of its value to the claimant. That this is the reason why failure of consideration should operate as a ground of restitution was recognised by Lord Wright in *Fibrosa Spolka Akcyjna v. Fairbairn Lawson Combe Barbour*

---
[16] *Barclays Bank Ltd v. Quistclose Investments Ltd* [1970] AC 567.
[17] *Ibid.* See also Chambers, *Resulting Trusts*, chap. 3.
[18] *Box v. Barclays Bank plc* [1998] Lloyd's Rep Banking 185.

Ltd:[19] 'There was no intent to enrich [the defendant] in the events which happened... The payment was originally conditional. The condition of retaining it is eventual performance. Accordingly, when that condition fails, the right to retain the money must simultaneously fail.'

IV. The contract must cease to be operative

It is a fundamental principle of the law of restitution that, if the claimant wishes to recover a benefit which has been transferred to the defendant pursuant to a contract, the claimant must first establish that the contract has ceased to be operative. This is because the law of restitution is subordinate to contract and so must not be used to subvert contractual obligations and the contractual allocation of risk. This is a major limitation on the success of restitutionary claims which are grounded on failure of consideration since, if the contract continues to operate, it is not possible to conclude that the consideration for the benefit received by the defendant has failed.

The claimant can establish that the contract has ceased to operate in three different ways:

1. There never was a contract. This may be because no contract was ever made or, if one had been made, that contract was, for some legal reason, void *ab initio*.
2. The contract is no longer operating. This may be because the contract has been breached by one party and the other party has accepted this as repudiating the contract. Or it may be because the contract has been frustrated. In either case it does not matter that the consequence of the breach or the frustration is not to treat the contract as void *ab initio* but only as repudiated from the time of the breach or the frustrating event.[20]
3. The defendant is no longer ready, able or willing to perform his or her side of the bargain. Where the contract is unenforceable, the claimant can establish that it is no longer operating simply by showing that the defendant is not ready, able or willing to perform his or her side of the bargain.[21] It is not, however, necessary to establish this in any other case. So, for example, where the defendant has breached a contract and the claimant has accepted this breach, it is enough for the claimant to establish that the contract has ceased to be operative; it is not necessary to show in addition that the defendant is not ready, able or willing to perform the contract.

---

[19] [1943] AC 32 at 64–5.
[20] *Fibrosa Spolka Ackyjna v. Fairbairn Lawson Combe Barbour Ltd* [1943] AC 32.
[21] *Thomas v. Brown* (1876) 1 QBD 714.

The general requirement that the contract must cease to be operative before the claimant can establish that the defendant has been unjustly enriched illustrates an important distinction between common-law and civilian restitutionary claims. At common law the fact that the contract has ceased to operate is merely a precondition which must be satisfied before examining the nature of the restitutionary claim. Once this has been established it is then necessary to consider whether the defendant has been unjustly enriched. It is not possible to conclude that the defendant's enrichment is unjust simply because the benefit was transferred in respect of a contract that has ceased to operate.[22] The notion of injustice for the purposes of an unjust enrichment claim is defined much more rigidly by reference to principles such as failure of consideration. For civilian lawyers, however, the fact that the contract has ceased to operate with the effect that the defendant is no longer entitled to the benefit which he or she had received from the claimant is the main factor that will trigger a restitutionary claim.[23]

Even though a restitutionary claim at common law which is founded on the defendant's unjust enrichment can only succeed if the contract has ceased to operate, it does not follow that the contractual regime is totally irrelevant to restitutionary claims.[24] For example, it has already been seen that the identification of the relevant consideration will often depend on the terms of the contract, namely what the defendant had promised to do for the claimant. Similarly, the terms of the contract may be relevant to the valuation of the enrichment which the defendant had received. Most importantly, the contract may have allocated the risk of loss to one of the parties. If this has happened it is not for the law of restitution to subvert this allocation of risk by, for example, allowing the claimant to recover benefits from the defendant when the claimant had been intended to bear the risk that the condition might not be satisfied. So, for example, if the claimant and the defendant entered into

---

[22] Save perhaps where the contract was void *ab initio*. See section VIII, below. Note also that if the ground of partial failure of consideration is recognised as a general ground of restitution then it will be sufficient to establish a claim for restitution that the contract has ceased to operate and that the defendant has received some benefit under it. See section VII, below.

[23] K. Zweigert and H. Kötz, *An Introduction to Comparative Law* (trans. T. Weir, 3rd edn, 1998), 537. See also R. Zimmermann, 'Restitution After Termination of Contract', [1997] *Restitution LR* 13.

[24] *Fibrosa Spolka Ackyjna v. Fairbairn Lawson Combe Barbour Ltd* [1943] AC 32. See also *Pan Ocean Shipping Co. Ltd v. Creditcorp Ltd (The Trident Beauty)* [1994] 1 WLR 161, where the common-law restitutionary regime was excluded by the terms of the contract which continued to apply even though the contract had been discharged for breach.

an agreement to purchase land which was subject to contract and the claimant paid the defendant some money in respect of this agreement then, if no contract is made, the claimant will not be able to recover the money, because he or she bore the risk that no contract would be made.[25]

V. The significance of failure of consideration

'Failure of consideration' is a phrase which is rarely used within the law of restitution. It is certainly not a phrase which can be used to establish that the defendant has been *unjustly* enriched. Rather, it should properly be regarded as a neutral phrase that requires the addition of words to make sense of it. Alternatively, failure of consideration can be considered to be a general principle on which three specific grounds of restitution are founded, namely total failure of consideration, partial failure of consideration and absence of consideration.

VI. Total failure of consideration

The most important ground of restitution that is founded on the principle of failure of consideration is total failure of consideration. Although the continued existence of this ground is a matter of some controversy (because of the apparently stringent requirement that the consideration must have failed totally before the defendant can be considered to have been unjustly enriched), it has recently been affirmed by the House of Lords.[26]

1. Meaning of total failure of consideration

The significant feature of this ground of restitution is that it can only be established if no part of the condition by reference to which the claimant has transferred a benefit to the defendant has been satisfied. The stringency of this requirement is illustrated by *Hunt v. Silk*,[27] which first recognised it. In this case the claimant leased a house from the defendant for £10 on condition that the defendant executed the lease and arranged for

---

[25] *Regalian Properties plc v. London Docklands Development Corp.* [1995] 1 WLR 212. Cf. *Chillingworth v. Esche* [1924] 1 Ch 97 where the claimant recovered a deposit from the defendant even though it had been paid in respect of an agreement which was subject to contract. This was presumably because it was not possible to allocate the risk of loss to the payer of the deposit.
[26] *Stocznia Gdanska SA v. Latvian Shipping Co.* [1998] 1 WLR 574.
[27] (1804) 5 East 449; 102 ER 1142.

certain repairs to be done to the property within a limited period of time. The claimant paid the money and took immediate possession of the property, but the defendant failed to execute the lease or to repair the premises as he had promised. The claimant remained in possession of the property for two days after the time by which the defendant should have executed the lease and effected the repairs. The claimant then sought to recover the money which he had paid to the defendant, but was unable to do so because he had remained in possession of the property after the time the defendant was expected to have done what he had promised to do. It followed that the claimant had received a benefit and so it was not possible to conclude that the consideration for the payment had failed totally.

It might be argued in a case such as this that there was a total failure of consideration because, even though there had been a part-performance of the contract, since the defendant had allowed the claimant to gain possession of the property this part-performance was irrelevant because the contract had been discharged for breach. But the common law does not analyse the failure of contracts in this way. If the effect of setting a contract aside was to render that contract void *ab initio* then it would appear that the consideration had failed totally, since all benefits that the claimant had received could be wiped away. But that was not the case. The claimant only accepted that the contract had been discharged for breach and such a discharge only operates prospectively and not retrospectively. Since the claimant had received some benefit under the contract it was not possible to wipe this away by discharging the contract for breach.

2. Methods of establishing total failure of consideration

Despite the apparent rigidity of the total failure requirement the English courts have in fact developed a number of ways of weakening the requirement, to ensure that the claimant can obtain restitution on this ground despite having received some benefits from the defendant. There are three methods which are especially worthy of note.

First, the nature of the contract may be such that the receipt of a benefit by the claimant will not constitute the provision of consideration. The best example of this is where the contract which the parties have made is characterised as an entire contract. This is a contract where the risk that the agreement will not be performed is allocated to the performer. Consequently, if the defendant has been paid in advance but fails fully to perform as he or she had promised to do, it follows that the claimant can recover the advance payment by virtue of total failure of consideration even though he or she has received some benefit under the contract.[28] Although this might seem unjust, it is consistent with the fundamental principle that where the contract has allocated the risk of loss it is not for the law of restitution to subvert that allocation. In the context of an entire contract the notion of consideration is defined to mean only full performance of the contract.

Secondly, even though the claimant may have received a benefit from the defendant under the contract this may be discounted if it can be characterised as a collateral benefit. In other words, the benefit received was not a benefit for which the claimant had bargained. This is illustrated by *Rowland v. Divall*,[29] where the claimant had bought a car from the defendant and, having used it for over four months, he discovered that it had been stolen. He was compelled to return the car to its owner and then sought to recover the purchase price from the defendant on the ground of total failure of consideration. The claim succeeded even though the claimant had used the car for a substantial period of time. This was because the period of use was characterised as a collateral benefit since the real benefit for which the claimant had bargained was lawful possession of the car with good title, and he had not received this at all.[30]

This case can be contrasted with *Yeoman Credit Ltd v. Apps*,[31] where the defendant had entered into a hire-purchase agreement with the claimant by virtue of which the defendant obtained possession of a car in an unroadworthy condition. Despite its condition he drove the car for six months. But he failed to keep up with the hire payments and the claimant recovered the car. The claimant sued the defendant for those hire payments which were in arrears and the defendant counterclaimed for recovery of the hire payments which had been made, on the ground of total failure of consideration. This counterclaim failed because the defendant had obtained some benefit from the use of the car. *Rowland v. Divall* was distinguished because, in that case, the contract was one of purchase for which the claimant had bargained for good title, whereas in *Yeoman Credit* the contract was one of hire-purchase, so the defendant had only bargained for the use of the car and this he had obtained, albeit that the quality of the use was not what he had expected to receive. Comparing these two cases emphasises the importance of having regard to the nature of the contract when determining what the consideration is and whether or not it has failed totally.

---

[28] *Giles v. Edwards* (1797) 7 TR 181; 101 ER 920.   [29] [1923] 2 KB 500.
[30] See also *Rover International Ltd v. Cannon Film Sales Ltd (No. 3)* [1989] 1 WLR 912.
[31] [1962] 2 QB 508.

Thirdly, where the claimant has received a benefit under the contract this will not necessarily prevent the consideration from failing totally if it is possible to apportion the consideration between different parts of the contract. This was recognised by the Privy Council in *Goss v. Chilcott*.[32] The facts of this case were complex but the restitutionary claim basically involved the recovery of a loan on the ground of total failure of consideration. The dispute in the case arose from the fact that the defendants had made two payments of interest to the claimant in respect of the loan. Did this mean that the consideration had not failed totally? The Privy Council decided that it was possible to recover the capital sum from the defendants because no part of the capital had been repaid to the claimant. In other words, it was possible to treat payments in respect of capital and interest separately. This is a perfectly acceptable conclusion because, although the defendants' obligation to pay interest and capital arose under the same transaction, the obligations arose for different reasons; interest payments being payments for the use of the capital rather than the return of the capital. To the extent that it was possible to say that the money paid by the defendants related either to interest or to capital and that only interest had been repaid, this decision is correct. But Lord Goff went on to say that:

> even if part of the capital sum had been repaid, the law would not hesitate to hold that the balance of the loan outstanding would be recoverable on the ground of failure of consideration; for at least in those cases in which apportionment can be carried out without difficulty, the law will allow partial recovery on this ground...[33]

This is more difficult to justify. Where, for example, the claimant lends £1,000 to the defendant who repays £400, can it really be said that, as regards the outstanding amount, the consideration had failed totally? Surely it would only be possible to apportion the consideration in this way if, for example, the contract of loan itself provided for repayment by instalments.[34] So if, for example, two out of five instalments had been paid, it could be concluded that the consideration had failed totally in respect of the final three instalments, which would then be recoverable. But in *Goss v. Chilcott* the whole loan was repayable three months after it was made; it was only the interest payments that were payable in instalments. There is therefore no justification for saying that, if the defendants had repaid part of the loan, then the consideration would have failed totally

---

[32] [1996] AC 788.   [33] *Ibid.* at 798.
[34] See *David Securities Pty Ltd v. Commonwealth Bank of Australia* (1992) 175 CLR 353 at 383 (High Court of Australia).

in respect of the outstanding sum, simply because there was nothing in the loan transaction to suggest that consideration could be apportioned in this way.

Even though the dictum of Lord Goff was not relevant to the decision and it was given in the Privy Council, it is a clear indication of judicial dissatisfaction with the total failure requirement,[35] which could lead to the eventual recognition of a general ground of partial failure of consideration.

VII. Partial failure of consideration

Partial failure of consideration has not been recognised as a ground of restitution in its own right.[36] If it had been recognised it would mean that the claimant would be able to recover benefits which had been transferred to the defendant whenever the condition for the transfer of the benefit had not been fully satisfied. This would, however, be subject to the claimant making counter-restitution for the value of all benefits which he or she had received.

There is, however, some evidence for partial failure of consideration being recognised in the law of restitution, albeit not explicitly. For example, the cases that have allowed restitution on the ground of total failure of consideration even though the claimant had received some benefit from the defendant, because that benefit was collateral or could be apportioned, are in effect cases where the consideration has only partly failed. Further, where the claimant has transferred benefits to the defendant under a contract which is subsequently frustrated, he or she is able to recover those benefits from the defendant even though the claimant had received some benefits from the defendant under the contract. It is acceptable to analyse this claim as grounded on partial failure of consideration, but it does not follow that a new independent ground of restitution has been recognised, because restitutionary claims in respect of frustrated contracts exist by virtue of a statutory scheme[37] which is not simply concerned with the restitution of benefits but also encompasses loss apportionment.[38] But,

---

[35] This dissatisfaction is apparent from Lord Goff's judgment in the case. In the light of this it is surprising that he affirmed the requirement that the consideration must fail totally in *Stocznia Gdanska SA v. Latvian Shipping Co.* [1998] 1 WLR 574 at 590.
[36] This was affirmed by the House of Lords in *Stocznia Gdanska SA v. Latvian Shipping Co.*, ibid.
[37] The Law Reform (Frustrated Contracts) Act 1943.
[38] See especially E. McKendrick, 'Frustration, Restitution and Loss Apportionment', in: A. Burrows (ed.), *Essays on the Law of Restitution* (1991), 169.

apart from these two situations where restitutionary claims can be analysed with reference to notions of partial failure of consideration, that ground of restitution is not recognised in English law.

Whether partial failure of consideration should be recognised as a ground of restitution in its own right is a matter which has received a great deal of academic interest recently. Most commentators are in favour of replacing 'total failure' with 'partial failure'.[39] Two reasons in particular can be identified to support this view.

First, the major obstacle to recognising a ground of partial failure of consideration has related to the ability of the court to require the claimant to make counter-restitution to the defendant. In the vast majority of cases where consideration has only failed partially this is because the claimant has received a benefit from the defendant. It would be unjust to require the defendant to make restitution to the claimant in such circumstances without requiring the claimant to make counter-restitution to the defendant. Such counter-restitution is essential because the prime function of the law of restitution is to restore the parties to the position which they occupied before the transaction was made. Unfortunately, the ability of the courts to require counter-restitution has developed very slowly. The attitude of the common-law courts was that, if the claimant had received a benefit from the defendant, this could only be restored to the defendant in specie and only, apparently, where the transaction was void for a fraudulent misrepresentation. It followed that if the claimant had received a benefit which had been dissipated or by its nature could not be restored, such as a service, then counter-restitution was not possible and so the claim for restitution would fail. The attitude of equity became much more generous in such circumstances, because equity was much more prepared to require the claimant to restore the value of the benefit which had been received if the benefit itself could not be restored.[40] There is some evidence that this approach might also be adopted at common law.[41] If so, it would follow that, in every case where the claimant had not received everything which he or she had expected to receive under a contract that was no longer operating, the claimant could recover the benefits which had been transferred to the defendant but the claimant would

---

[39] See, in particular, P. Birks, 'Failure of Consideration', in: F. Rose (ed.), *Consensus Ad Idem* (1996), 179 and E. McKendrick, 'Total Failure of Consideration and Counter-restitution', in: P. Birks (ed.), *Laundering and Tracing* (1995), chap. 8. See also *Spice Girls Ltd v. Aprilia World Service* (Arden J.) (unreported) 12 June 2000.

[40] See *Erlanger v. New Sombrero Phospate Co.* (1878) 3 App Cas 1218.

[41] *Smith New Court Securities Ltd v. Scrimgeour Vickers (Asset Management) Ltd* [1997] AC 254 at 262 (Lord Browne-Wilkinson).

need to make counter-restitution of the value of all benefits which the defendant had provided. It will only be in the most exceptional circumstances that it will not be possible to value the benefit received from the defendant; but where this is the case it should follow that the claimant's restitutionary claim would be barred.

Secondly, where the claimant has transferred a benefit to the defendant and he or she has received part of the expected consideration in return, restitution can still be justified as a matter of principle. In such circumstances the claimant's intention that the defendant should retain the benefit is contingent on the complete fulfilment of a condition and, if that condition is not completely satisfied, the claimant's intention that the defendant should retain the benefit can be treated as vitiated.

In an important article on the doctrine of failure of consideration[42] Stoljar concludes, having analysed in detail the history of the doctrine, that the requirement that failure must be total is a myth, although some of the older cases can be interpreted as suggesting that the failure must be material. The total failure requirement appears to have developed in the nineteenth century by virtue of the rules on pleading and proof. But those rules no longer exist, so the total failure requirement should no longer be necessary either.[43]

If the courts do eventually recognise partial failure of consideration as a ground of restitution in its own right this would have a liberating effect on the law in this area. It would, for example, mean that much of the artifice of the total failure requirement can be avoided, because it would no longer be necessary to show that benefits which the claimant had received were collateral or could be apportioned. It would not necessarily mean, however, that the ground of total failure of consideration would disappear, since it would still be advantageous for the claimant to assert that the consideration had failed totally. If this could be established, he or she would not need to make counter-restitution to the defendant. But, crucially, if the claimant could not establish this, it would no longer follow that the restitutionary claim failed automatically unless a different type of ground of restitution was available, such as mistake or duress. Instead, the claimant would be able to fall back on partial failure of consideration.

If partial failure of consideration was recognised as a ground of restitution in its own right, it would share many of the characteristics of total

---

[42] Stoljar, 'Doctrine of Failure of Consideration'.
[43] See also Goff, 'Reform of the Law of Restitution', (1961) 24 MLR 85, 90.

failure. Most importantly, it would still be essential for the claimant to establish that the contract had ceased to operate before the restitutionary claim could be brought. Further, the claimant could not successfully rely on this ground of restitution if the risk of the consideration partially failing had been placed by the contract on him or her.

The true significance of recognising a ground of partial failure of consideration would be that the nature of the claimant's claim for restitution would change. This is because all that the claimant would need to show, once it has been established that the defendant had indeed been enriched and that this was at the claimant's expense, is that the contract had ceased to operate and that the claimant had not received all the benefits which he or she had expected to receive under the contract. This is much more like the approach that is applied to restitutionary claims following the termination of contracts in civilian jurisdictions, especially Germany.[44]

VIII. Absence of consideration

In those cases where the claimant alleges that the consideration has totally or partially failed, the issue before the court concerns the failure of the condition by reference to which the claimant transferred a benefit to the defendant, where this failure arises from the collapse of the contract. Absence of consideration uses consideration in a different sense, since it is not concerned with the collapse of the bargain but rather with the failure of the promise.[45] In other words, it will only arise where a benefit has been transferred in respect of a contract which is null and void, so that the benefit which the claimant expected to receive under the contract was never owed because no obligation to benefit the claimant existed as a matter of law.

Although it remains a matter of some controversy, it appears that absence of consideration is indeed a ground of restitution in its own right, as was recognised by the Court of Appeal in *Westdeutsche Landesbank Girozentrale v. Islington LBC*.[46] In this case a bank had entered into an interest-rate swaps transaction with a local authority which was subsequently found to be void since it was beyond the capacity of the local

---

[44] Zimmermann, 'Restitution after Termination'.
[45] Stoljar, 'Doctrine of Failure of Consideration'.
[46] [1994] 1 WLR 938. This ground of restitution was also recognised by the trial judge, Hobhouse J: [1994] 4 All ER 890. See also *Kleinwort Benson Ltd v. Birmingham CC* [1997] QB 380 at 393 (Evans LJ) and 394 (Saville LJ).

authority to enter into the transaction. The bank had paid more to the local authority than it had received and so the bank sought to recover this extra money. It was unable to rely on the ground of mistake because its mistake had been one of law and this did not ground restitutionary claims at the time. Equally, it could not rely on the ground of total failure of consideration because, as regards most of the swaps transactions, it had been paid some money in the course of the transaction so that the consideration had not failed totally.[47] Nevertheless, the bank's claim for restitution succeeded because the swaps transactions were null and void *ab initio*, so that the local authority could never have provided consideration for the bank's payments.

This recognition of the ground of absence of consideration was not overruled by the subsequent decision of the House of Lords in the same case.[48] Unfortunately that decision is of little assistance in determining the interpretation of this ground of restitution because the case was primarily concerned with the bank's equitable claim for restitution. Nevertheless, the judgments of Lords Goff and Browne-Wilkinson do provide some indication as to whether absence of consideration is a valid ground of restitution. Although Lord Goff declined to express any concluded view, he did say that there was considerable force in the criticisms which have been expressed concerning the validity of absence of consideration as a ground of restitution and he would have preferred that the ground of restitution was failure of consideration.[49] Since the consideration had not failed totally, he presumably meant that the ground should have been partial failure of consideration. Lord Browne-Wilkinson, on the other hand, did appear to recognise the validity of absence of consideration as a ground of restitution, although he used the language of total failure of consideration. But how could the consideration have failed totally when the bank had received payments from the local authority? The only way that this could be characterised as a failure of consideration is if the consideration is treated as failing as a matter of law rather than fact. Failure of consideration at law would mean that, even though the claimant had received some benefit from the defendant, this should be discounted because the transaction was null and void by operation of law so that the consideration had not been validly provided by the defendant.

---

[47] As regards two transactions, however, the bank had not received any money from the local authority and so it was able to recover the money which it had paid, on the ground of total failure of consideration.

[48] *Westdeutsche Landesbank Girozentrale v. Islington LBC* [1996] AC 669 (HL).   [49] *Ibid.* at 683.

At the very least the decision of the House of Lords is ambiguous as to whether absence of consideration exists as a ground of restitution in its own right. However, a subsequent decision of the Court of Appeal suggests that it does exist. In *Guinness Mahon and Co. Ltd v. Kensington and Chelsea Royal Borough Council*[50] the bank's claim to recover money paid to a local authority in respect of a swaps transaction succeeded even though the transaction had been fully performed. Although the judges tended to analyse the ground of restitution as total failure of consideration, they acknowledged that consideration had been provided by the local authority but that it was irrelevant because of the assumption that any benefit which the claimant had received was not validly received since the transaction was considered to be null and void from the start.[51]

The identification of the most appropriate ground of restitution where the claimant has transferred a benefit to the defendant pursuant to a void transaction remains highly controversial. Analysis of the case law suggests that three grounds of restitution are potentially applicable, namely total failure of consideration, absence of consideration and mistake. With the recognition by the House of Lords in *Kleinwort Benson v. Lincoln City Council*[52] that a mistake of law can ground a restitutionary claim, it will be much easier to establish that the defendant has been unjustly enriched in respect of transactions which are held to be void. Consequently, there will be much less need for a ground of absence of consideration. But such a ground may sometimes still be of some significance where an operative mistake cannot be established, for example because the claimant suspected that there was no liability to pay the money.[53] Even though the ground of absence of consideration would be applicable in such circumstances, the preferable view is that such a ground of restitution should not be recognised because it confuses the contractual sense of consideration with its restitutionary sense.[54] Whereas consideration in the law of

---

[50] [1999] QB 215. This decision was commended by Lord Hope in *Kleinwort Benson Ltd v. Lincoln CC* [1999] 2 AC 349 at 416. In *Dorchester upon Medway CC v. Kent CC* (1998) *The Times*, 5 March, Sullivan J specifically relied on absence of consideration as the ground of restitution to recover an ultra vires payment.

[51] See P. Birks, 'No Consideration: Restitution after Void Contracts', (1993) 23 *University of Western Australia LR* 195, 206, who argues that restitution should not be available once the transaction had been fully executed. But if the transaction is null and void then the fact that it has been fully performed should be irrelevant to the success of the restitutionary claim.

[52] [1999] 2 AC 349.

[53] Though restitution of payments made in such circumstances may be defeated by the bar of voluntary submission to an honest claim.

[54] See, for example, W. J. Swadling, 'Restitution for No Consideration', [1994] *Restitution LR* 73, 85.

restitution is concerned with the condition which attaches to the transfer of a benefit to the defendant, the contractual notion of consideration is the defendant's promise, which is required for a contract to be valid. Consequently, if the contract is void as a matter of law then the defendant's promise fails, so that there is no contractual consideration, but there is no failure of performance, so that there is no restitutionary failure of consideration. In other words, it does not follow from the fact that the contract is void that restitutionary relief should result automatically, since some reason must be identified to require the defendant to make restitution to the claimant, typically that the claimant's intention to transfer a benefit to the defendant can be considered to be vitiated. This is a strong argument and, whilst it can be countered by saying that the transfer of a benefit to the defendant is conditional on the transaction being valid so that if the contract is invalid the claimant's intention can be considered to be vitiated, this notion of vitiation of intention is highly artificial.

The better view is that the award of restitution in cases such as the interest-rate swaps cases has nothing to do with absence of consideration and everything to do with the reason why the transaction is void in the first place. Absence of consideration is merely the symptom. It is necessary to look behind this to determine why the consideration was absent. In many of the cases where a contract is found to be null and void the reason for this is because one of the parties lacks capacity to enter into the contract. Where, for example, the claimant lacks capacity to enter into a contract, the reason why the contract is null and void is to protect the claimant, such as a minor, or a public authority. This policy of protection should be carried through into the law of restitution, so if the party who lacks capacity to enter into the contract has transferred a benefit to the other party then restitution should be grounded on the incapacity. This is illustrated by those cases arising from the swaps litigation where the local authority sought restitution from a bank. Since the local authority lacked capacity to enter into such a transaction, because of a policy that it should not take unnecessary risks with local taxpayers' money, it is right that the bank should make restitution of the money it had received, even if the swaps transaction had been executed. The policy behind the decision to make the transaction void must be followed through into the restitutionary claim, where the policy can be vindicated most effectively. This was explicitly recognised by Morritt LJ in the *Guinness Mahon* case:[55]

---

[55] [1999] QB 215 at 229. See also *Kleinwort Benson Ltd v. Lincoln CC* [1999] 2 AC 349 at 416 (Lord Hope).

'the *ultra vires* doctrine exists for the protection of the public'. But that does not mean that 'the court should apply the law of restitution so as to minimise the effect of the doctrine. If... there is no claim for money had and received in the case of a completed swap then practical effect will be given to a transaction which the doctrine of *ultra vires* proclaims had no legal existence.' As this dictum makes clear, emphasis on the reason why the transaction is void explains why restitution is available in respect of fully executed transactions. The recipient of the benefit has no better right to receive or retain the benefit after the transaction was executed than he or she did before.

If this analysis is correct it follows that the approach adopted by the common-law and civilian systems is broadly similar. Both systems emphasise the fact that the benefit which was received by the defendant was not due to it. But comparison of the two systems also identifies a crucial difference, namely that civilian lawyers are only concerned with the fact that the benefit was not due to the defendant.[56] Common-law systems are more conservative and so need to identify reasons why the benefit was not due to the defendant, to ensure that this reason is consistent with the grant of restitutionary relief.[57]

IX. Other types of enrichment

A further feature of claims grounded on failure of consideration, primarily total failure of consideration, is that this ground only appears to be relevant where the benefit which the claimant seeks to recover is money. This is because total failure of consideration originated as a ground of restitution in the action for money had and received. But, with the abolition of the forms of action, there is no longer any reason why this ground of restitution should be inapplicable where the enrichment received by the defendant takes the form of goods or services.[58] It is clearly possible for consideration to fail totally where the defendant has been enriched by the receipt of goods or services, but restitutionary claims in respect of such enrichments are still founded on the opaque actions of *quantum valebat* and *quantum meruit*. But where the claimant alleges that the defendant has been enriched by services, it cannot assist the claimant simply to assert that the action is *quantum meruit*. The elements of this action need to be unpacked. When this occurs the only reasonable conclusion

---

[56] Zweigert and Kötz, *Introduction*, 557. [57] See section XI, below.
[58] Birks, 'Failure of Consideration', 185–6.

is that the action is actually one founded on unjust enrichment. It must therefore be shown that the defendant was enriched, that this was at the claimant's expense and that there is a ground of restitution which is applicable. Total failure of consideration should be such a ground. The state of the authorities is such that it is not yet possible to assert with confidence that restitution will lie where consideration has failed regardless of the type of enrichment involved. There are, however, a few cases which implicitly support the proposition that restitutionary remedies are available where consideration has failed even where the enrichment takes the form of goods or services.[59]

X. The relevance of fault

A matter of some importance in the modern law of restitution concerns the significance of the parties' fault. It is clear that, if the reason why the contract is no longer operating was because of the fault of the claimant in breaching it, then this will not prevent the claimant from bringing a restitutionary claim founded on the ground of total failure of consideration.[60] But should the claimant's fault be relevant in determining whether the restitutionary claim should succeed? In particular, as Robin Evans-Jones suggests,[61] should the fact that the claimant has been acting in bad faith bar his or her restitutionary claim? The preferable view is that it should not, for the following reasons.

First, the notion of bad faith is notoriously difficult to define. Even if it can be defined with any clarity it is clear in English law that the wrong of breaching a contract is not characterised as involving bad faith. Breach of contract is not considered as particularly wrongful in English law, otherwise specific performance of contracts would be generally available. Instead, where the claimant breaches a contract usually the only consequence is that he or she is required to compensate the defendant for any loss suffered. Therefore, where the claimant has breached a contract this is not serious enough in itself to defeat the claimant's claim for restitution.

Secondly, it must not be forgotten that the restitutionary question only arises once the claimant's repudiatory breach has been accepted by the defendant so that the contract ceases to operate; or the contract ceases to

---

[59] See, in particular, *Pulbrook v. Lawes* (1876) 1 QBD 284 and *Rover International Ltd v. Cannon Film Sales Ltd (No. 3)* [1989] 1 WLR 912.
[60] *Rover International Ltd v. Cannon Film Sales Ltd (No. 3)* [1989] 1 WLR 912. See also *Dies v. BIMFC Ltd* [1939] 1 KB 724.
[61] See Robin Evans-Jones's contribution to the present volume, 128 ff.

operate for some other reason. Once that occurs, the secondary question is what remedy should be available for the other party. But if the claimant has provided benefits to the defendant then why should the claimant not be allowed to recover those benefits by virtue of a failure of consideration, subject to the obligation to compensate the defendant for loss suffered? It is vitally important to maintain the distinction between the contractual and the restitutionary regimes. Once the breach has been accepted we have left the contractual regime and are into the restitutionary one.

It is, however, not enough to show that the contract has been discharged, since it is still necessary to identify the elements of the unjust enrichment claim. The significance of this can be illustrated by the following example. The claimant has agreed to buy a car from the defendant for £5,000. The claimant pays the defendant £3,000 in advance, but he then realises that the car was only worth £2,000 so he refuses to accept delivery of it and asks for his money back. This is a breach of contract by the claimant. There is no reason why the claimant cannot recover the money if he or she compensates the defendant for loss suffered. The defendant will obtain expectation damages of £3,000 (that is, the profit on the car) and the claimant will be able to recover the £3,000 which he has paid, so there is no point in the claimant suing the defendant. But if the values are changed a point will be reached where it is worth the claimant suing the defendant for restitution despite the claimant's obligation to make restitution to the defendant. It follows that it is only in the most exceptional circumstances that the question of the claimant's fault will be relevant, but, where it is, there is no obvious reason why the fault that triggers a contractual remedy for the defendant should defeat a restitutionary remedy for the claimant.

XI. Relationship with other grounds of restitution

It is a characteristic of the common law of restitution that a number of different grounds of restitution may be applicable on the same facts, unlike civilian systems which have discrete claims for different fact situations.[62] Most importantly, in a case where the claimant might rely on the ground of total failure of consideration he or she may instead rely on mistake of fact or of law.[63] So, for example, where the claimant has paid money to

---

[62] Zweigert and Kötz, *Introduction*, 539.
[63] Other alternative grounds of restitution include the incapacity of the claimant in transferring the benefit to the defendant or the incapacity of the defendant in receiving the benefit, at least where the defendant is a public authority. See *IRC v. Woolwich Building Society* [1993] AC 70.

the defendant in respect of a transaction which is subsequently held by the courts to be null and void the claim for restitution may be founded either on the ground of absence of consideration, since the defendant could never validly provide consideration for the payment, or on the ground of mistake of law, because the decision to treat the transaction as void operates retrospectively, so when the claimant paid the money he or she will have been mistaken.[64]

Some commentators have argued that the ground of mistake should not be treated as an independent ground of restitution in its own right, but is preferably treated as being founded on the principle of failure of consideration.[65] This is because the traditional interpretation of the ground of mistake is that the mistake must relate to the claimant's liability to pay the defendant. It follows that, if the claimant believes that he or she is liable to pay the defendant, then the claimant will believe that the payment to the defendant should discharge liability. But if there is no liability in the first place then the expected consideration for the payment will fail and so the ground of restitution should be that of failure of consideration and not the mistake. But, in fact, the two grounds of restitution are distinct. This is because the notion of mistake as a ground of restitution is not confined to a mistake as to the claimant's liability to pay the defendant; it is sufficient that the mistake was a cause of the payment, or transfer of other benefit, to the defendant, but for which the benefit would not have been transferred. This is strongly supported by the decision of the House of Lords in *Kleinwort Benson Ltd v. Lincoln CC*,[66] where the ground of mistake of law was specifically recognised, rather than failure of consideration. Some of the judges also endorsed the causation test of mistake. This has also been recognised in other recent decisions.[67]

The reason why it matters whether there is an alternative ground of restitution to that of failure of consideration is because this may affect the operation of the bars to restitutionary claims, especially limitation periods. This was the reason why the claimant in *Kleinwort Benson v. Lincoln CC*[68] wanted to found its claim on mistake rather than absence of

---

[64] *Kleinwort Benson Ltd v. Lincoln CC* [1999] 2 AC 349.
[65] P. Matthews, 'Money Paid Under Mistake of Fact', (1980) 130 *NLJ* 587 and 'Stopped Cheques and Restitution', [1982] *Journal of Business Law* 281. See also P. A. Butler, 'Mistaken Payments, Change of Position and Restitution', in: P. Finn (ed.), *Essays on Restitution* (1990), chap. 4.
[66] [1999] 2 AC 349.
[67] See *Nurdin and Peacock plc v. D. B. Ramsden and Co. Ltd* [1999] 1 WLR 1249 and *Lloyds Bank plc v. Independent Insurance Co. Ltd* [2000] QB 110.
[68] [1999] 2 AC 349.

consideration. The usual limitation period for restitutionary claims is six years,[69] but where the claim is grounded on mistake the limitation period does not begin to run until the claimant either did realise or should have realised that a mistake had been made. Consequently, if the claimant paid money to the defendant thirty years ago in circumstances when he or she had made a mistake and he or she has only just realised that a mistake had been made then, assuming that a reasonable person would not have realised earlier that a mistake had been made, time would begin to run now for purposes of a restitutionary claim. This is the main advantage of founding a claim on mistake rather than failure of consideration.

XII. Conclusion: common-law and civilian approaches compared

This analysis of the common-law approach to restitutionary claims founded on failure of consideration has identified a number of specific differences between the common-law and civilian systems. It suggests that the fundamental distinction between the two systems is essentially that the common law focuses on the claimant whereas civilian systems focus on the defendant. This is illustrated by claims founded on mistake. At common law a mistake will only ground a restitutionary claim if it caused the claimant to transfer a benefit to the defendant. In civilian systems, however, the claim would simply be grounded on the fact that the benefit was not due to the defendant. The focus then shifts to the defendant to establish a reason why restitution should not be made. The same difference of approach is also apparent in respect of claims concerning failure of consideration. At common law it is necessary to show that the claimant had not received any of the expected benefit whereas civilian systems would simply be concerned with whether the benefit that had been received by the defendant was due to him or her and, if the expected consideration had not been provided, it would follow that the benefit was not due to the defendant and so restitution would need to be made.

Whether one system is preferable to another is a difficult question to answer because, although the problems are the same, the traditions and jurisprudence of the two systems are so different. But, from an English lawyer's perspective, the common-law approach is preferable to the civilian for the following reasons.

First, the common law places the burden of establishing the defendant's unjust enrichment firmly on the claimant, whereas the claimant in civilian systems only has to show that the benefit was not due to the defendant

---

[69] See *Westdeutsche Landesbank Girozentrale v. Islington LBC* [1994] 4 All ER 890 at 943 (Hobhouse J).

and the defendant must identify why it was due.[70] But why should the burden effectively shift to the defendant to show why restitution should not be made rather than be placed on the claimant to establish why restitution should be made? It is the claimant who is bringing the claim and who, as a matter of justice, should bear the burden of establishing it. This is a big advantage of the unjust enrichment principle since it requires the claimant to establish that the defendant has been enriched at the claimant's expense and that there is a ground of restitution to justify restitution. Without this ground of restitution the claim cannot be established.

Secondly, the restrictive approach of the common law to unjust enrichment claims means that the defendant's receipt of the benefit is secure save in the exceptional cases where the claimant establishes that the defendant's enrichment is unjust. This principle of security of receipt is important in the development of the law of restitution, especially in the commercial field where parties generally need to be certain that benefits which have been transferred have been validly transferred and will not be upset too readily.

Finally, the common law is still not confident about restitution. This is particularly true in England where the development of the subject has been slow and piecemeal. This difference between the restitutionary tradition in England especially and civilian jurisdictions is crucial. As lawyers become more confident with the law of restitution it is possible to see restitutionary relief being made more widely available, especially if there are carefully defined defences to restrict such claims in appropriate circumstances. Such a development in the subject can be seen in Canada and Australia. There are signs of such developments in England as well.[71] The development of the law of restitution can be viewed as a continuum, with England at one end of the spectrum and civilian systems at the other. But the gap between the two is gradually being reduced and this reduction is likely to speed up. Probably the most important change in English law which would reduce this gap substantially is if the requirement of total failure of consideration were replaced by partial failure of consideration. It would mean that whenever the claimant had transferred a benefit to the defendant in the expectation that he or she would receive something in return and that expectation was not fully satisfied then a ground for a restitutionary claim could be identified, conditional on the claimant making counter-restitution to the defendant. This would dispense with a myth and provide meaning to this otherwise complex area of law.

---

[70] Zweigert and Kötz, *Introduction*, 541.
[71] See especially *Woolwich Equitable Building Society v. IRC* [1993] AC 70.

5 Failure of consideration

Robin Evans-Jones and Katrin Kruse

I. Introduction

'Consideration' is a feature both of the English law of contract and of the law of restitution. We are told that in the law of contract it is the *quid pro quo* in an agreement that makes it binding as a contract. Within the law of restitution its meaning is different: Graham Virgo says that 'failure of consideration is not a ground of restitution in its own right but rather a general principle which underlies the existence of a number of particular grounds of restitution'.[1] He then proceeds to discuss three possible grounds of recovery: total failure of consideration, partial failure of consideration and no consideration. In this restitutionary context 'consideration' is understood generally as 'the condition which formed the basis for the plaintiff transferring a benefit to the defendant'.[2]

The separation between the contractual and restitutionary meanings of 'consideration' has not always been so clearly made. Although the background is rather complex, there is evidence to suggest that the influence of the civil law was an important factor in leading to this separation of meanings in English law when it was finally unequivocally reached. In a series of decisions known collectively as the 'Coronation' cases, English law provided a result which came, in time, to be regarded as unsatisfactory by leading English lawyers. The result that was reached in the 'Coronation' cases proceeded on the assumption that there was no distinction between

---

[1] G. Virgo, *The Principles of the Law of Restitution* (1999), 323. One might question whether it is completely correct to say that 'failure of consideration' is a general principle underlying various grounds of restitution. 'Failure of consideration' is, in fact, a proper cause of action which might, although the matter is disputed, apply in two forms/modes: total and partial failure of consideration. If it is recognised, absence of consideration would then, however, be a separate cause of action.
[2] *Ibid.*, 325.

the contractual and restitutionary meanings of 'consideration'. An opportunity to change the result was presented in 1923 in a Scottish case, *Cantiere San Rocco SA v. Clyde Shipbuilding and Engineering Co. Ltd*.[3] *Cantiere* was heard by the House of Lords sitting as the highest court of appeal for both Scotland and England. In this capacity the House of Lords has often sought to achieve similar results in both jurisdictions. A motivating factor has been the perception that, notwithstanding their separate jurisdictions, Scotland and England are part of the single union state of Britain. Especially in commercial matters it was, and still is, thought that similar results are desirable in both countries. In the *Cantiere* appeal before the House of Lords the *condictio causa data causa non secuta* (claim in relation to a performance made for a future lawful purpose outside contract which fails) was used to break apart the approach of the 'Coronation' cases, which had been followed as precedents in the lower Scottish courts. English law was later brought into line with *Cantiere* as regards its result in the later decision of the House of Lords in *Fibrosa Spolka Akcyjna v. Fairbairn Lawson Combe Barbour Ltd*.[4] It was in *Fibrosa* that English law unequivocally made the distinction between the contractual and restitutionary meanings of 'consideration' by founding on the *condictio causa data causa non secuta* as this had earlier been understood in *Cantiere*.

Our intention is, first, to examine the process by which the *condictio causa data causa non secuta* influenced the conception of 'consideration' in English law. Secondly, we will examine certain functional difficulties that seem to us to arise in relation to 'failure of consideration' as a cause of action. Some of these difficulties may arise precisely from the fact that it was from the *condictio causa data causa non secuta* that English law drew its inspiration in this context.

II. The *condictio* and consideration

1. *Cantiere San Rocco SA v. Clyde Shipbuilding and Engineering Co. Ltd*

This case concerned a sale of marine engines to be manufactured and supplied by the defenders. Payment of the price was to be made in instalments; the first on signature of the contract and the remainder at specified stages in the construction of the engines. After payment of the first instalment, but before construction of the engines had commenced, the outbreak of war rendered further performance of the contract legally

---

[3] 1923 SC (HL) 105.   [4] [1943] AC 32.

impossible. The point at issue was whether the pursuers could recover the sum that they had paid as the first instalment. The issue, though seemingly simple, was one which had to be resolved by the House of Lords.

It was accepted at all levels of the appeal that, had the contract been void *ab initio* or had the performance failed as a result of the fault of the sellers, the pursuers would have been entitled to recover what they had paid, provided in the latter case that they had chosen first to rescind the contract. However, the non-performance of the contract was not attributable to the sellers' fault and the effect of the outbreak of war was merely to discharge the parties from further performance of their duties and not to render the contract void. This being the case, one approach to the issue of recoverability of the first instalment of the price was that everything done in fulfilment of the contract up to the moment of frustration was rightly done. In effect there was said to be a general rule that losses arising from performance of a contract up to the moment of frustration should lie where they fall. The main authority for this approach was *Chandler v. Webster*,[5] one of the 'Coronation' cases of English law.

In that case a house owner let seats to view a Coronation procession for a sum of £141, payable before the procession. £100 was paid in advance and £41 was still outstanding when the procession was cancelled due to the king's illness. The parties sued each other, the house owner for the balance of £41 and the other party for recovery of his £100. The Court of Appeal held that the house owner was entitled to retain what he had received. Consistent with the reasoning that this payment was 'rightly' made in fulfilment of an existing obligation, it was also held that the house owner was entitled to the balance of £41 because the obligation in respect of this sum was also referable to the time before the frustration and therefore still properly exigible. As it was understood at the time, there had been no failure of consideration as a ground of restitution. Sufficient consideration had been given to conclude a contract and the consideration had not failed in view of the continuing validity of the contract.

When *Cantiere* was heard on appeal before the Court of Session, recovery of the price was denied mainly on the authority of the 'Coronation' cases. The alternative approach to the issue of recoverability found in the pleadings, which was subsequently to be approved by the House of Lords, was that the pre-payment was recoverable in principle on the grounds that it had been given for a consideration that had failed. The inspiration

---

[5] [1904] 1 KB 493; see also especially *Krell v. Henry* [1903] 2 KB 740.

for recoverability was found in the *condictio causa data causa non secuta* of Roman and Scots law.

2. Analysis of the 'Coronation' cases

Frustration does not annul a contract but merely discharges the obligation to make future performance. In such circumstances, according to the 'Coronation' cases, losses should be allowed to lie where they fall at the moment of frustration. This approach did not preclude readjustment of the relations of the parties. The critical inquiry concerned what performance had been made in fulfilment of obligations properly enforceable up to the moment of frustration. If, by chance, P had paid a sum in advance which was not in fact exigible until after the frustrating event, he could claim it back. The approach of the courts appears to have been one of allocating risk under a valid, albeit unenforceable, contract. The result was harsh where, for example, P had agreed to pay the full price in advance for the manufacture of certain goods since he would lose the money without being entitled to the goods. However, it was open to him either to insure or to provide for an alternative allocation of losses expressly in the contract.

Although 'total failure of consideration' appears as a concept in the pleadings in the 'Coronation' cases, very little is said about it in the judgments. The emphasis, in what is regarded as the *locus classicus* for the approach of the 'Coronation' cases,[6] is that the validity of the contract excluded a claim for 'total failure of consideration'. The reasoning was that, if the contract still subsists, regulation of the relationship of the parties is achieved by reference to the contract and not by reference to the law of restitution.[7] Thus Collins MR observed in *Chandler*:[8]

the doctrine of failure of consideration does not apply. The rule adopted by the Courts in such cases is I think to some extent an arbitrary one, the reason for its adoption being that it is really impossible in such cases to work out with any certainty what the rights of the parties in the event which has happened should be.

---

[6] *Per* Collins MR at 499.
[7] This is the approach adopted by the House of Lords in the recent Scottish Appeal, *Dollar Land (Cumbernauld) Ltd v. CIN Properties Ltd* 1998 SC (HL) 90; 1998 SLT 992, with the difference that on this occasion the relationship between the parties was expressly regulated by the terms of the contract. See further, H. MacQueen, 'Contract, Unjustified Enrichment and Concurrent Liability: A Scots Perspective', [1997] *Acta Juridica* 176.
[8] [1904] 1 KB 493 at 499.

3. Further analysis of *Cantiere*

The cause of action expressed by the *condictio causa data causa non secuta* lies within the law of unjustified enrichment. Thus *Cantiere* differed from the 'Coronation' cases in the fundamental respect that it established a claim for unjustified enrichment on the grounds of failure of consideration where a contract had been frustrated. *Cantiere* also cleared up doubts concerning the nature of the consideration in a reciprocal contract and the circumstances in which its failure was 'total'.

The foundation of the pursuers' claim in *Cantiere* was the *condictio causa data causa non secuta* of Roman law. This is a claim where something is given for a *causa* that fails. It was assumed by the House of Lords that the failure of *causa* was no different from a failure of consideration. In fact the House of Lords' understanding of the *condictio causa data causa non secuta* was not fully consistent with either Roman or Scots law. The English-law claim on total failure of consideration was in part the model on which the House of Lords understood the *condictio*. Thus, when dealing with the *condictio causa data causa non secuta*, Lord Shaw was concerned to demonstrate that the consideration had 'entirely' failed.[9] The failure of 'consideration' from a restitutionary point of view was seen to consist of the non-supply of the engines, the actual *supply* of the engines being the reciprocation for which the buyer had paid the price.[10] Therefore at a restitutionary level price and *res* were regarded as the reciprocal considerations within a normal contract of sale and consideration had failed totally if one was not supplied for the other.

The House of Lords was of the view that on these facts it was not possible to split up the consideration[11] by attributing part of it to the signing of the contract and the remainder to the delivery of the *res*. Each party was seen to perform in consideration of the full performance by the other party. Any difficulties concerning the coincidence between frustration and (total) failure of consideration were thereby resolved. Frustration of a sale which has not been fully performed will normally give rise to a claim of (total) failure of consideration, since anything short of full performance (payment of the price and delivery of the *res*) is normally a total failure.

The effect of the decision in *Cantiere* was to introduce a rule of general application to frustrated contracts in Scots law: what is transferred in fulfilment of the contract is recoverable subject to any counterclaim by the other party for expenses that he had incurred in performing his side of the

---

[9] 1923 SC (HL) 105 at 117.   [10] *Ibid.*   [11] *Ibid., per* Lord Shaw.

bargain. Instead of following the general rule of contemporary English law that losses should lie where they fall, the House of Lords applied the law of unjustified enrichment to strike a balance between the parties. It was, and remains, unclear from the terms of the decision whether this balance was to be struck strictly according to the principles of 'enrichment' or whether the defenders were entitled to counterclaim for losses which they had incurred even if the other party had not been enriched thereby. The general rule that *res perit domino* was inapplicable to a case of this kind because no *res* had ever come into existence to which risk could attach.

4. Fibrosa Spolka Akcyjna v. Fairbairn Lawson Combe Barbour Ltd

It was twenty years before the House of Lords was provided with the opportunity to bring English law into conformity with Scots law as expressed in its decision in *Cantiere*. As Lord Macmillan observed in *Fibrosa*, '[t]he mills of the law grind slowly'.[12] The facts of *Fibrosa* were similar to those of *Cantiere*. A contract of sale was concluded for the supply of machinery. As required, part of the price had been paid in advance before the contract was frustrated by the outbreak of war. At issue was whether the advance payment could be recovered or not.

The decision of the House of Lords in *Cantiere* had a very significant influence on *Fibrosa*. *Cantiere* regulated the interests of parties to a frustrated contract by reference to a claim in the law of unjustified enrichment, effectively on the ground of total failure of consideration. The principle of recoverability in such circumstances broke apart the approach represented by the 'Coronation' cases, which *Fibrosa* over-ruled.

Whereas 'failure of consideration' was barely mentioned in the judgments in the 'Coronation' cases, it was the essential factor on which the decision in *Fibrosa* was made to turn. In approaching the case from this point of view *Fibrosa* had to confront a central problem of definition. A considerable degree of uncertainty as to what constituted the consideration for payment was apparent in the 'Coronation' cases and in *Cantiere*, when it was before the Court of Session. The problem was that in English law 'consideration' is a term which has different meanings depending on whether it is used in a contractual or restitutionary sense. Viscount Simon in *Fibrosa* distinguished these meanings in the following manner:[13]

... in the law relating to the formation of contract, the promise to do a thing may often be the consideration, but when one is considering the law of failure of consideration and the quasi-contractual right to recover money on that ground,

[12] [1943] AC 32 at 58.   [13] *Ibid.* at 48.

it is, generally speaking, not the promise which is referred to as the consideration, but the performance of the promise ...

The 'Coronation' cases were seen to have confused these meanings. By excluding a claim for total failure of consideration because of the validity of the contract they ascribed the consideration to the promise and not to its performance. The conception of failure of consideration in the restitutionary sense as depending on performance of the promise reflects the influence of *Cantiere*. According to the House of Lords in *Cantiere* the price was paid for the *supply* of the engines. That this conclusion was reached from an understanding of the operation of the *condictio causa data causa non secuta* in Roman law, albeit accommodated to the requirement of English law that the failure of consideration must be 'total', is made clear by Lord Shaw:[14]

The consideration as a whole stands with reference to the price and every part of the price. It is an admitted fact in the case that that consideration has entirely failed. Therefore, this, as I say, would be a typical case of restitution under the Roman law and one for the application of the maxim *causa data causa non secuta*. The *condictio* under that head would have been, in my humble opinion, plainly applicable. If not applicable to this and to similar cases of outstanding simplicity, then the whole chapter of the Roman law devoted to that *condictio* need never have been written.

The significant feature of the *condictio causa data causa non secuta* is its formulation in terms of '*dare*'. *Dare* emphasises the failure of the actual *performance* of the bargain because, within a sale for example, it focuses, not on the existence of the promise, but on its execution. The price is *given* in consideration of the object of the sale, which is then not forthcoming.

By understanding the *condictio causa data causa non secuta* as it did,[15] the House of Lords in *Cantiere* found the justification for applying a claim of unjustified enrichment to frustrated contracts on the basis of failure of consideration. In its use of unjustified enrichment (restitution) in this context and in its principal result, *Cantiere* was the model for *Fibrosa*. The importance of this change in conception is observed by Goff and Jones:[16]

the so-called rule in *Chandler v. Webster* rested on the misconception that there could be no total failure of consideration unless the contract was void *ab initio*.

---

[14] 1923 SC (HL) 105 at 117.
[15] This notion of the *condictio causa data causa non secuta* was not fully consistent with how it is generally understood in the civil-law tradition.
[16] *The Law of Restitution* (5th edn, 1998), 511–12.

Severely criticised by judge and jurist, the fallacy underlying *Chandler v. Webster* was exposed in *Fibrosa*.

III. The operation of the unjust factors and the *condictiones*

Total failure of consideration is one of a range of causes of action (or unjust factors) recognised by the English law of restitution. The number of unjust factors remains open-ended: new causes of action are continuously capable of recognition. These causes of action do not operate as a 'system'. First, one cause of action can overlap with and does not necessarily exclude another: a claim based upon 'mistake' may also be conceived as based upon 'total failure of consideration'. Secondly, recognised causes of action sometimes have to be supplemented by new causes of action because facts arise in which there is no existing claim but it is thought that restitution should be allowed.[17] The new claim is free standing with respect to previously recognised causes of action; the causes of action do not cohere like the *condictiones* of the civil law, where new fact situations give rise to a claim only if they conform to the principle that what is retained without a legal basis is recoverable (*condictio sine causa*). The new claim is an ad hoc reaction to a novel fact situation. Ad hoc responses unguided by a single unifying principle are likely to leave gaps in circumstances in which it is thought that a claim of restitution should properly be allowed.

In the civil law all claims arising from deliberately conferred enrichment are united by the principle that what is retained without a legal basis (*sine causa*) is recoverable. The following are the main applications of the general principle:

(i) undue performance, that is a performance made to discharge a legally recognised duty that fails (*condictio indebiti*);
(ii) performance made to create an obligation or gift which fails (*condictio obligandi/donandi causa*);
(iii) performance which fails because its purpose is immoral or illegal (*condictio ob turpem vel iniustam causam*);
(iv) performance made for a purpose (discharge of a legal duty), which succeeds temporarily but which then fails (*condictio ob causam finitam*);
(v) performance made for a future lawful purpose outside contract which fails (*condictio causa data causa non secuta*); and
(vi) residual causes of action (*condictio sine causa*).

The principle 'retention without a legal basis' both unites all the individual nominate claims and provides flexibility by providing a residual

---

[17] *Woolwich Building Society v. IRC* [1993] AC 70.

cause of action for cases which do not fall within the nominate claims but which nevertheless conform to the general principle. As Reinhard Zimmermann has observed, it was 'the general principle that had justified the granting of specific enrichment actions and [that] could now be used to expand, but at the same time suitably contain, the range of claims'.[18]

Compared with the unjust factors of English law the *condictiones* are systematic. Each nominate claim is directed to a specific fact situation. There is no overlap between them, and they are comprehensive of cases which conform to the general principle. This difference can be important. Scots law, a jurisdiction in which the *condictiones* apply, received from English law the rule that payments in mistake of law are irrecoverable. The consequences of applying this rule to the *condictio indebiti* were potentially far more severe in Scotland than was the corresponding rule in England. Once the *condictio indebiti* was barred in cases where there had been an error of law, there was no other claim to which those who had acted to discharge a debt could turn, even though their payment was undue. But, since one unjust factor does not exclude another, the plaintiff in English law who could rely upon a cause of action other than 'mistake' could avoid the consequences of the rule.[19]

IV. The width of the restitutionary meaning of consideration in English law

We have argued that the civil law (at least as it was understood in *Cantiere*) had an important influence on English law in separating the restitutionary from the contractual meaning of consideration. We will now look at the range of applications of 'failure of consideration' in the English law of restitution. The cause of action provided by the civil law in similar circumstances will also be identified. Our purpose in making this comparison is, at the first level, to highlight the extraordinary breadth of 'failure of consideration' as a cause of action in English law. Some difficulties which result from this breadth in conception will then be examined.

There is a failure of consideration most importantly:

(1) within a valid contract (a) where there has been a failure to perform duties whether because of breach or frustration.[20] In the civil law, once the contract has been rescinded, the claim would be a *condictio ob*

---

[18] *The Law of Obligations, Roman Foundations of the Civilian Tradition* (paperback edn 1996), 852.
[19] *Woolwich Equitable Building Society v. IRC* [1993] AC 70.   [20] Virgo, *Principles*, 325.

causam finitam or *condictio sine causa* depending on the circumstances;[21] (b) where there is a suspensive or resolutive condition that fails. 'P pays 100 in advance for your car *if he can find a garage.*' If he fails to find a garage he can reclaim the advance payment.[22] In the civil law the pre-payment would be conceived as having been made to discharge a duty that fails (*condictio indebiti* or a *condictio ob causam finitam*[23]).

(2) Outside contract the 'consideration' can be (a) a future purpose: for example, P gives X in exchange for your making him your heir. Such circumstances are dealt with by the civil law with the *condictio causa data causa non secuta*; (b) the conclusion of a contract as distinct from the *quid pro quo* within a contract:[24] for example, P gives 100 subject to contract (*condictio obligandi causa*);[25] (c) the conclusion of a valid gift. Here P gives 100 in view of your impending marriage (*condictio donandi causa*).[26] Consideration may also fail where a transfer is made under a mistake (*condictio indebiti* or *condictio sine causa*).

P. Matthews and P. A. Butler have argued that 'failure of consideration' is wide enough to encompass cases which have traditionally been dealt with under the separate cause of action 'mistake'. In their view, failure of consideration can no longer merely be interpreted as the failure of the bargained-for counter-performance. It should be afforded a much broader connotation that comes close to the civilian notion 'failure of purpose'. They substantiate this approach by reference to *Barclays Bank Ltd v. W. J. Simms Son and Cooke (Southern) Ltd.*[27] The plaintiff's customer had drawn a cheque upon the bank that was sent to the payees. When the customer found out that the payees had been put into receivership he stopped the

---

[21] This is an over-simplification based more directly on the position in Scots law. In German law rescission is akin to a contractual right: it is a *vertragsähnliches Recht*. As such it does not trigger restitutionary remedies but displaces these because of its 'speciality'; cf. D. Reuter and M. Martinek, *Ungerechtfertigte Bereicherung* (1983), § 19 I.

[22] Another example of the failure of a (suspensive) condition is the case of *Wright v. Newton* [1835] 2 Cr M & R 124; 150 ER 53. Cf. Parke B (at 54): This was a contract with a condition that the landlord's consent should be obtained. It must be taken as if the landlord never consented, and that the condition was not performed.

[23] In German law in the case of failure of a resolutive condition it is a *condictio ob causam finitam*; BGH 1959 *Monatszeitschrift für Deutsches Recht* 658; H. Thomas, in: Palandt (ed.), *Bürgerliches Gesetzbuch* (55th edn, 1996), § 812, n. 76.

[24] See the 'anticipated contract cases' which A. Burrows, *The Law of Restitution* (1993), 293 ff. explains on the basis of 'failure of consideration': *William Lacey (Hounslow) Ltd v. Davis* [1957] 1 WLR 932.

[25] *Chillingworth v. Esche* [1924] 1 Ch 97. In German law, these cases are called '*Vorleistungsfälle*'; See Reuter and Martinek, *Ungerechtfertigte Bereicherung*, § 5 III 1(c)(aa). In this context the '*causa*' of the transfer in question does not lie in the extinction of a debt (*solvendi causa*) because the performance was rendered with a view to receiving the expected counterperformance.

[26] *Re Ames Settlement* [1946] Ch 217.   [27] [1980] QB 677.

cheque. Despite his order the bank mistakenly paid the cheque. When the bank discovered its mistake, it sought to recover from the payees. Although Goff J (as he then was) held that the money was recoverable on the ground of the plaintiff's mistake of fact, Matthews and Butler argue that recovery should instead have been granted on the ground of 'failure of consideration'. They then follow slightly different lines of argumentation. Matthew's position is that regard has to be paid to the purpose that the bank pursued towards its customer. Only if this purpose proved to have failed would the bank be entitled to recover. According to Matthews, the real intention of Barclays Bank was not to fulfil a presumed obligation towards Simms, who was the recipient of the money. Although its payment was obviously engendered by the obligation between the drawer of the cheque and Simms, the bank was aware of the fact that it did not owe any payment to the latter.

The bank's only concern is to pay a sum of money to the payee in order to secure a consideration from its own customer ... The bank cares only that there should be authority to pay, so as to be able to debit the drawer's account. If there is no actual authority, the bank fails to secure the consideration for which payment is made ...[28]

Matthews's view is developed by Butler. Butler agrees that mistaken payments do not constitute a ground of restitution separate from 'failure of consideration'. But, in contrast to Matthews, he does not look for any consideration or purpose in the relationship between Barclays Bank and the drawer of the cheque. He focuses on the relationship between the bank and Simms as the receiver of the money. In his view 'consideration' in this context has to be understood as a state of affairs which both of these parties assumed to be present and which constituted the condition under which Simms should be allowed to keep the payment. This condition was that the bank in fact possessed authorisation from their customer to make the payment. As this condition was not fulfilled due to the customer's stop-order, the consideration for payment on the cheque failed:[29]

Where payment is made by a paying bank to a payee it is done so conditionally on the basis of an assumption common to the payer and payee that the payer is paying with the customer's authority. If that assumption is incorrect the money is recoverable for failure of consideration.

---

[28] P. Matthews, 'Stopped Cheques and Restitution', [1982] *Journal of Business Law* 281, 284.
[29] P. A. Butler, 'Mistaken Payments, Change of Position and Restitution', in: P. D. Finn (ed.), *Essays on Restitution* (1990), 87 ff., 121.

It is clear from the above survey that 'failure of consideration' is a broad-ranging cause of action that spans a range of claims which are distinguished one from the other by the civil law. In fact, in its different guises 'failure of consideration' covers effectively the whole range of the individual *condictiones*. In this respect, as a conception, at one level, it looks similar to the general principle that what is retained without a legal cause (consideration) is recoverable. Certainly the House of Lords in *Cantiere* drew no distinction between '*causa*' and 'consideration'. However, there are important differences between failure of cause and failure of consideration. Certainly, the civilian understanding of 'cause' in this context is not without its difficulties. It is normally conceived as the 'purpose' underlying the transfer which gave rise to the enrichment.[30] Most commonly, an enrichment is held to be without a legal basis or cause if it was made to discharge a legally recognised duty (*solvendi causa*) and this purpose (*causa*) failed. The appropriate claim in such circumstances is the *condictio indebiti*. Wherever a person makes a performance under a valid contract or where he pays a debt he is deemed to have acted to discharge the obligation in question (*solvendi causa*). The question whether there is a failure of cause is determined objectively from whether there has been a failure to discharge a duty, mostly whether the payment in question was undue.

The 'consideration' is the 'condition' on which a benefit was transferred. The consideration fails if the condition is not performed. However, where the consideration is the reciprocation in a bargain there can often be considerable uncertainty as to its content. This uncertainty arises for different reasons. (i) Different people sometimes attribute different significance to different parts of the reciprocation in a bargain. It has been argued that in a void contract of insurance the consideration for the payment of the premium is the assumption of risk by the insurance company, whereas assumption of risk is not part of the consideration in a swaps contract;[31] but others view the assumption of risk in a swaps contract as part of the 'consideration'.[32] (ii) Some argue that consideration is purely factual: 'Did the plaintiff get what he wanted?' If he did get what he wanted there is no

---

[30] Supporters of this so-called 'subjective approach' are Reuter and Martinek, *Ungerechtfertigte Bereicherung*, § 4 II 4(a); D. Medicus, *Schuldrecht II* (7th edn, 1995), § 126 I; H. Ehmann, 'Über den Begriff des rechtlichen Grundes', 1969 *NJW* 400.

[31] Cf. P. Birks, 'No Consideration: Restitution after Void Contracts', (1993) 23 *University of Western Australia LR* 195, 221.

[32] Cf. E. McKendrick, 'The Reason for Restitution' in: P. Birks and Francis Rose (eds.), *Lessons of the Swaps Litigation* (2000), 84.

failure of consideration.[33] Others give consideration a more technical content. Even if the plaintiff got what he wanted, the consideration still fails if performance of the reciprocation was not legally obligatory.[34] (iii) Some see 'consideration' in any transaction which is not purely gratuitous, so if I act to discharge a duty to someone and this fails there is a failure of consideration. Likewise, some argue that payments made in mistake as to liability are better explained as instances of failure of consideration.

The identification of what constitutes 'consideration' is clearly crucial to the question whether that consideration has failed. On the one hand difficulties in identification lead to uncertainty as to whether there is a cause of action. For example, different views were held concerning whether there was a failure of consideration in respect of benefits transferred under fully executed swaps.[35] On the other hand, reflecting the fluid nature with which causes of action are conceived in the law of restitution, Virgo has suggested that there are *five* possible causes of action for the recovery of benefits transferred under swaps agreements.[36]

V. The theoretical basis for the operation of total failure of consideration as a ground for restitution

1. English law

The theoretical justification for 'failure of consideration' as a ground of recovery is that the intention of the transferor is vitiated[37] or at least qualified.[38] He did intend the transferee to receive the benefit at the time of transfer but his intention is qualified by future events. For example, when P paid you the price of X he intended you to receive it. However, there is *subsequently* a failure of consideration if you fail to deliver X. The transferor 'qualifies his intent that [the other party] should be enriched by specifying what must be or become the case in order for his intent to

---

[33] Cf. Birks, 'No Consideration', 207 and 214 ('... a plaintiff who has received all that he expected under the contract has no substantial ground for restitution').

[34] Cf. McKendrick, 'Reason for Restitution', 102 ('... although the parties have, as a matter of fact, obtained the benefits for which they contracted (in the sense that the relative payments have been made), as a matter of law, they have not received the benefit for which they contracted').

[35] 'Failure of consideration' has, for example, been proposed as a basis for recovery with regard to the fully executed swaps in the case of *Guinness Mahon & Co. Ltd v. Kensington and Chelsea Royal London Borough Council* [1999] QB 215. Its applicability in these kinds of cases has, however, been rejected by Birks, 'No Consideration', 195.

[36] See Virgo, *Principles*, 396 ff.   [37] *Ibid.*, 323.

[38] *Ibid.*, 323 speaks of the intention of the plaintiff being vitiated, not just qualified.

become absolute'.[39] By contrast where 'mistake' is the cause of action the vitiation is operative at the time of transfer. For example, P paid you the price under a contract that was void *ab initio*. When P *actually made* the payment he was operating under a mistake as to liability. Notwithstanding their differences when viewed in these terms the common feature of both causes of action is that they fall within the group of 'didn't mean it' unjust factors.[40]

Our purpose now is to test the theoretical justification for total failure of consideration as a cause of action. We will do so by reference to cases of breach of contract. Broadly stated, there is a failure of consideration where the reciprocation under a contract is not performed due to the other party's fault. Following rescission of the contract by the innocent party, the plaintiff can recover what he has transferred even where he himself brought about the failure of consideration.[41] It seems rather odd in such a case to see the basis of the cause of action as resting on the qualification of the plaintiff's intention. How can the right to restitution be seen to depend on the fact that he 'didn't mean it' if the failure of consideration was brought about through his own deliberate attempt to ensure that consideration was not given under the contract? A further question is whether the issue of restitution should be affected by considerations of fault. Should P, for example, be allowed to recover what he gave for a purpose which he subsequently prevented from being achieved through, say, his own bad faith?

In transactions that do not generate obligations the circumstances in which the law attributes fault to P will be relatively few. He is not at fault, for example, if he withdraws from an engagement to be married. The civil law nevertheless draws a limit to the idea that P is not at fault when he prevents reciprocation under an extra-contractual agreement. This limit is drawn by reference to bad faith. Legal consequences are attributed to the fact that a person was at fault in preventing the reciprocation or purpose of a bargain. Thus a person who raises a *condictio causa data causa non secuta* will be unsuccessful where the failure of purpose was brought

---

[39] P. Birks, *An Introduction to the Law of Restitution* (1989), 261.   [40] Ibid., 140.
[41] Burrows, *Law of Restitution*, 272; *Rover International Ltd v. Cannon Film Sales Ltd (No. 3)* [1989] 1 WLR 912. Note that Scottish law also seems to recognise the right of a contract breaker to recover in restitution. See the *obiter* statement made by Lord Morison in *Zemhunt (Holdings) Ltd v. Control Securities plc* 1992 SLT 151 at 155H: 'a breach of contract by the payer of part of the price which is sought by him to be recovered, following rescission of the contract by the payee on the ground of that breach, does not *per se* affect the equity of the claim for restitution'.

about by his bad faith.[42] From the point of view of the civil law, in such circumstances, fault is a proper consideration when determining whether restitution should be allowed or not. The plaintiff who was in bad faith in preventing the achievement of a particular end should not be entitled to found on that bad faith to recover what he transferred.[43]

Within contract the circumstances in which P is at fault when he prevents the reciprocation under the contract will be more numerous. He will be at fault, for example, where he either deliberately or negligently prevents the reciprocation from being performed. The divide between agreements which are, or are not, contracts is of importance in this context only in so far as within contract the circumstances in which restitution should be denied as a matter of principle would seem potentially to be much greater. It does not affect the issue that in principle restitution should be denied in some circumstances where the pursuer himself is at fault in bringing about the failure of reciprocation under an agreement. Peter Birks[44] suggests that, '[i]f the essence of the matter is that the money is recoverable because the condition for retaining it fails, it is hard to see how the failure or fulfilment of that condition can ever depend on the character of the remoter causes behind the happening or the failure to happen of the events contemplated'. However, later[45] he says that '[a]n

---

[42] A rule to this effect is contained in § 815 BGB, which states that a plaintiff's right to recovery under the *condictio causa data causa non secuta* (§ 812(1), 2nd sentence, alt. 2 BGB) is generally excluded under two circumstances: (a) if the extra-contractual purpose which was aimed at by the particular transfer in question was impossible right from the beginning and the plaintiff was aware of this impossibility or (b) if he actively prevented the realisation of the extra-contractual purpose in bad faith ('*wider Treu und Glauben*'); Thomas, in: *Palandt*, § 815, nn. 1–3.

[43] For Roman law, see D. 12, 4. A considerable number of the texts discuss what should happen where the cause fails through no fault of the transferee. This is a different question from that concerning what happens when the cause is prevented by the transferor. See J. Erskine, *An Institute of the Law of Scotland* (8th edn, 1871), III, 1, 10 who, drawing on D. 12, 4, 5, says that '[i]f it has become impossible that the cause of giving should exist by any accident not imputable to the receiver, no action lies against him, unless he hath put off performing it when it was in his power to perform'. This statement caused difficulty, and was effectively disapproved by the House of Lords in *Cantiere*. The reason is that it places the risk of the non-fulfilment of the cause on the transferor. This is odd because the non-fulfilment of the *causa* should in principle entitle the transferor to recover. In other words Erskine reverses what the House of Lords saw should be the proper allocation of risk. The further implication of Erskine's statement is that if the transferor bears the risk of non-fulfilment of the *causa*, a fortiori he will not be entitled to recover if he prevents the fulfilment of the *causa* in bad faith.

[44] Birks, *Introduction*, 234.   [45] *Ibid.*, 236.

unwilling buyer is not in a position, as against a willing seller, to bring about a total failure of consideration'. This suggests that the mere failure of the condition of a transfer is not the ground of restitution. Only if the failure of consideration is accepted by the buyer is restitution possible. But this in turn raises the question whether the ground of restitution should not more naturally be attributed to the rescission in such a case. It is not in the hands of the unwilling party to bring about the failure of consideration; something else is required which, prima facie at least, is referable to actions by the innocent party, namely the rescission or discharge of the contract.

It is worth restating that 'failure of consideration' is the primary cause of action where the reciprocation under an agreement (whether a contract or not) is not forthcoming. The theoretical justification for 'total failure of consideration' operating as a ground of restitution is that the will of the plaintiff was qualified. The transferor has made a *non-voluntary*[46] enrichment of the other party in that the circumstances under which he specified that the transfer was to be made have not come about. English law experienced some difficulty in allowing a plaintiff who brings about the failure of consideration to found upon this failure to claim restitution. Birks[47] says that '[t]he cases do not clearly admit the notion of a plaintiff-precipitated failure of consideration'. The right of such a plaintiff is, however, now generally recognised.

2. Scots law

Can anything be learned about this issue from the experience of Scots law? The claims which Scots law allows in these general circumstances are based on the *condictiones*. However, under the influence of English law it made an important change in the twentieth century. Traditionally Scots law allowed a *condictio sine causa* to the pursuer who sought restitution following a breach of contract. Under the influence of English law Scots law substituted for the *condictio sine causa* the *condictio causa data causa non secuta*. The reason is attributable to the decision of the House of Lords in *Cantiere*, where 'causa' was assimilated to 'consideration'.

Is there any significance attached to the change in Latin terms? In the civilian tradition a performance is made under a contract, not to receive the reciprocation, but to discharge the obligations created by the contract.

---

[46] Ibid., 219. [47] Ibid., 235.

Therefore the *condictio sine causa* in these circumstances expresses the fact that what was given to discharge a duty should no longer be deemed to have done so (it is a *condictio ob causam finitam*). By contrast the *condictio causa data causa non secuta*, which traditionally applies only in respect of transactions that lie outside contract, focuses upon the fact that there has been a failure of the purpose for which a benefit was transferred. If the transferor is responsible for the failure of purpose, in certain circumstances it is thought right that he should not be entitled to recover. In Scots law, following the decision in *Cantiere*, this claim was applied to cases where the reciprocation (or consideration) had not been given under a contract. A problem with this substitution is that by presenting the issue of restitution as being dependent on the failure of consideration (*causa non secuta*) the question was raised in the case law whether the pursuer who himself prevented the achievement of the *causa* should be able to recover what he transferred.

By contrast the *condictio sine causa* presents the same issue in terms of whether what was transferred should still be deemed to discharge the duty for which it was given. The answer to this question in turn depends on the status of the contract under which the benefit was transferred. Only if this has been rescinded can what was transferred be deemed no longer to discharge the duty under the contract since it has now been discharged. In short, the *condictio causa data causa non secuta* as applied by Scots law in this context focused upon the issue of consideration for the failure of which the person seeking restitution might be responsible. By contrast, the *condictio sine causa* focuses upon the contract, the continued status of which following a repudiation lies in the hands of the innocent party.

The difficulty that can arise when the claim for restitution following rescission is conceived in terms of 'failure of consideration' is illustrated by *Zemhunt Holdings Ltd v. Control Securities plc*.[48] The pursuers bought property at an auction and made a deposit of £165,000. They failed to pay the balance of the price on time with the result that the defenders, as they were entitled to do in terms of the contract, rescinded and kept the full amount of the deposit even although it must have exceeded their loss. The pursuers sought to recover what they had paid with the *condictio causa data causa non secuta*. Conceived in these terms, the issue arose, as Lord Clyde put it, whether 'the *condictio* can be available to one who is himself in breach of contract'.[49] The Lord Ordinary (Lord Marnoch) was firmly of the

---

[48] 1992 SLT 151. [49] *Ibid.* at 156.

view that 'that question, as a matter of principle, falls to be answered in the negative'.[50]

Rescission of contract is a right that attaches to the innocent party. If that party wishes to keep the contract alive, no issue of restitution arises even although there has been failure of reciprocation under the contract. If the right to rescind is exercised, its effect is to terminate performance of the contract. The innocent party says, in effect, that, given the circumstances, he will no longer be bound by his own obligations under the contract. In such circumstances there is a corollary. The innocent party should not be allowed to say that 'I will no longer be bound by my obligations' while keeping the party in breach tied to his obligations under the contract. This would amount to a breach of mutuality.[51] Rescission imports restitution as a matter of principle.

The presentation in Scots law of restitution following breach of contract as dependent on failure of consideration (*causa data causa non secuta*) misplaces the source of the right to restitution. If the right to restitution depends on 'failure of consideration', it seems right to question whether the person who is responsible for the failure can rely on it to claim restitution. Why should a person who was perhaps in bad faith be entitled to found his right to restitution on the consequences of that bad faith? By contrast the right to restitution can more naturally be seen to depend on the rescission of the contract. This means that the breach by the guilty party creates the right in the innocent party to rescind instead of a right in the guilty party to recover, which seems to be a preferable way to view the problem. If, following rescission, the contract breaker were not able to claim restitution the failure of consideration which he caused would be given a double effect: (i) to create the right in the other party to rescind and (ii) that right having been exercised, to bar the right to restitution notwithstanding that following the rescission mutuality would no longer be given under the contract.

A question which remains to be answered is this: why should a contract breaker always be entitled to restitution following rescission, while a person who has transferred a benefit under an extra-contractual transaction sometimes should not? The answer lies in the fact that in the former case the innocent party is protected by the contract: rescission is one of a range of options, of which a claim for damages is the most important, exercisable at his will depending on the circumstances. Outside contract

---

[50] 1991 SLT 653 at 655.
[51] See J. A. Dieckmann and R. Evans-Jones, 'The Dark Side of *Connelly v. Simpson*', [1995] JR 90.

the innocent party's only protection is a right to keep the benefit where the transferor was in bad faith.

There is a further difficulty arising from treating 'failure of consideration' as the cause of action following upon breach and rescission of contract. Virgo notes that: 'It has sometimes been suggested that awarding restitution to a plaintiff who has entered into a losing contract may subvert the allocation of risks under the contract where the risk of the contract being a bad bargain has been allocated to the plaintiff.'[52] Virgo concludes: 'The better view is that, where it is clear that the contract has allocated the risk of loss to the plaintiff, then the law of restitution should not be used to subvert this allocation of risk even though the contract has been discharged by the plaintiff for breach.'[53] There is arguably a difficulty with this approach. A breach has occurred which was sufficiently serious to amount to a failure to give mutuality under the contract. In effect the innocent party has said that 'I do not want to stand by this contract.' Yet it is suggested by Virgo that the plaintiff will still be bound by the contract, which has been justifiably rescinded. His rescission, if he were the innocent party, is a right that encourages performance by the defendant in terms of the contract. But it seems that the defendant is allowed to keep the contract alive in terms of the allocation of risk notwithstanding the fact that he has failed to observe its terms to an extent that justifies rescission.

The approach advocated by Virgo can be explained by the fact that the cause of action 'failure of consideration' is dissociated from the failure of the contract itself. As a result, as in the case just mentioned, central features of the contract (allocation of risk) are left to govern the relationship of the parties notwithstanding the fact that the contract has been discharged.

VI. Total failure of consideration

In English law, if the failure of consideration is not total, restitution is barred in principle. Birks gives the following example:[54]

Suppose you want to have a cottage restored. You contract with me for the job to be done for £15,000; you pay £5,000 in advance. Then you suddenly repudiate when I have only taken off the old roof and begun clearing up the inside of the shell. Even if I accept your repudiation and thus discharge the contract, you

---

[52] Virgo, *Principles*, 351.   [53] *Ibid.*   [54] Birks, *Introduction*, 237.

will not get back your £5,000, because you have had the benefit of some of my work. The consideration has not totally failed.

The requirement that the failure of consideration be total underlines the separation between the fact that a contract has been set aside and causes of action in the law of restitution. A contract may be set aside but restitution denied because, as in this example, the failure of consideration was not total.

There are possible oddities associated with the requirement that the failure of consideration be total. Using the example given by Birks, the contractor may retain your £5,000 where you have benefited to *some degree* from his work. He may therefore make a substantial profit out of your repudiation. However, the fact that he gained a windfall and you suffered a penalty depended on the chance that you paid in advance. Otherwise he would have been restricted to a claim of damages.

1. Reaction against total failure of consideration

There has been a reaction against the idea that the failure of consideration must be total to operate as a ground for restitution. The argument has been advanced that in practice the English courts allow restitution on the basis of a partial failure of consideration.[55] There are those who argue for the express recognition of partial failure of consideration as a ground of restitution.

2. Civil law

In the civil law the pursuer must prove that the transferee holds without a *causa*. The actual cause of action is established by the lack of *causa*; one does not establish a claim on the basis of a 'partial' lack of *causa*. Where the parts of the *causa* are separable, although my purpose may only have been partly achieved, the claim is based on the 'total' failure of *causa*. If P pays 100 to discharge a duty but in fact the debt was only for 50, although one might say that he partially achieved his purpose to discharge the notional debt of 100, he establishes his cause of action by showing that there was no *causa* for the excess of 50. Where the *causa* is not divisible the problem is different. Part-performance, for example, of a future 'purpose' outside contract is no performance. The purpose has failed totally. The problem is how to assess who pays what following part-performance in circumstances in which the *causa* (the purpose) has failed totally. Similarly, in the civil law the right to restitution following a breach of contract depends on

---

[55] Virgo, *Principles*, 373.

the rescission of the contract. Once the contract is rescinded the *causa*, notwithstanding that the contract has been partly performed, fails totally.

English law in this context, like the civil law, is concerned to regulate the relationship of parties to a transaction which has been partially performed. However, the civil law differs from the common law in not identifying the part-performance itself as the cause of action. Are there any difficulties associated in the identification of part-performance as the cause of action? In this context we distinguish between transactions within and without contract. Where a transaction involves a non-contractual reciprocation that is not fully performed it seems relatively unproblematic to allow restitution on the basis of the part-performance. Anything less than full performance is non-performance; the problem concerns the measure of recovery. However, there is difficulty in applying the same reasoning when the benefit has been transferred under a contract.

English law allows a person who has precipitated the failure of contractual consideration to claim restitution. But how does one determine from the terms of the new cause of action just how 'partial' the failure must be to ground a claim for restitution? Before restitution can be claimed, the contract must have been set aside.[56] So it is not any partial failure of consideration that grounds a right to restitution – only if the contract has been set aside can one claim restitution on the basis of partial failure of consideration. This seems to amount to saying that the right to restitution effectively depends on the contract having been set aside.

Partial failure of consideration has no independent existence from 'failure of contract'. In this respect the position is different from that which applied to 'total' failure of consideration. In that case the content of the cause of action was not determined solely by reference to the contract, since a failure of consideration sufficient to set the contract aside was not necessarily sufficient to ground a cause of action in restitution. In other words, it might seem that (i) partial failure of consideration is a reaction to difficulties associated with the cause of action 'total failure of consideration'; (ii) the content of partial failure of consideration seems to coincide with the proposition that 'the contract has been set aside'; and (iii) if, generalising from the case of partial failure of consideration, it were to be recognised that failure of 'consideration' and 'discharge of the contract' are the same, the failure of consideration would be 'total' notwithstanding the fact that it had been part-performed. This conclusion

---

[56] See Birks, *Introduction*, 46–7; Goff and Jones, *Law of Restitution*, 37–8; Burrows, *Law of Restitution*, 251.

brings one round full circle to Virgo's argument[57] that in practice the English courts have operated an artificial understanding of what amounts to a 'total' failure of consideration because it has been deemed to be 'total' where the contract has been part-performed but discharged.

VII. Swaps

Many problems surrounding 'failure of consideration' as a basis for restitutionary recovery can be illustrated by reference to the so-called swaps cases. However, before going into any detail about the extent to which the 'failure of consideration' principle was utilised in this context, a few words should be said on the general commercial background of these transactions.

1. Definition and background

Generally speaking, a 'swaps contract' denotes the agreement of two parties that over a stated number of years one of the parties will make to the other a series of payments. The exact amount of each payment is calculated by reference to the differences between a fixed rate of interest and the current market rate of interest from time to time upon a notional principal sum.[58] A swaps contract, therefore, represents a futures contract in that its financial outcome hinges on the future movement of certain interest rates. That is also why this type of transaction is frequently described as an 'interest-rate swap'.

Interest-rate swaps contracts made their initial appearance in commercial life at the beginning of the 1980s. In about 1982 they also came to be used by local authorities. For the latter the swaps constituted a welcome means by which to evade the strict governmental controls to which any local financial activity at that time was generally subject. Furthermore, swaps offered new possibilities for debt management by enabling the local authorities to obtain a certain lump-sum payment as an immediate source of cash while their obligation to make counterpayments still remained speculative. However, in the case of *Hazell v. Hammersmith and Fulham London Borough Council*[59] the House of Lords decided in 1991 that

[57] Virgo, *Principles*, 373.
[58] See Hobhouse J in *Westdeutsche Landesbank Girozentrale v. Islington LBC* [1994] 4 All ER 890 at 895; Lord Goff of Chieveley in *Kleinwort Benson Ltd v. Lincoln CC* [1999] 2 AC 349, 365; Birks, 'No Consideration', 200; A. Burrows, 'Restitution of Payments made under Swap Transactions', (1993) *NLJ* 480; A. Burrows, 'Swaps and the Friction between Common Law and Equity', (1995) 3 *Restitution LR* 15.
[59] [1992] 2 AC 1 (HL); [1991] 1 All ER 545; [1990] 2 QB 697 (CA); [1990] 3 All ER 337.

swaps transactions, although lawful in themselves, lay outside the powers of local authorities and were therefore void. The judges were of the opinion that any participation of a local authority in such a contract could no longer be regarded as an exercise of their statutory right to lend or to borrow money.[60]

The decision in *Hazell v. Hammersmith* precipitated a flood of litigation. Well over 200 actions were commenced, all with a view to establishing that sums previously paid by or to a local authority under any such swaps agreement could be recovered from the recipient. Since the courts were not in a position to try each and every individual action that had been instigated after the *Hazell* case, certain characteristic actions were selected for trial. The most important of these lead actions were *Westdeutsche Landesbank Girozentrale v. Islington London Borough Council*[61] and *Kleinwort Benson Ltd v. Sandwell Borough Council*,[62] which were both heard by Hobhouse J, sitting as a judge of first instance. The two cases also had in common that it was the banks that sought restitution of the balance of the money which they had paid to the local authorities.

2. The decisions in *Westdeutsche* and *Kleinwort Benson v. Sandwell*

The facts in *Westdeutsche* and *Kleinwort Benson v. Sandwell* were similar. In both cases payments had been made by each of the parties under the agreement, the larger sums having been paid by the banks to the local authorities involved. The principal factual difference between the two cases was that *Kleinwort Benson v. Sandwell* concerned four separate swaps agreements, one of which had run its full course by the time litigation commenced. In both cases, the plaintiff banks raised a restitutionary claim for the recovery of the amount by which they were out of pocket and in each case the claim was made at common law as well as in equity.

Both claims succeeded before Hobhouse J. Although the outcome of his decision was never really called into doubt, his reasoning has been exposed to heavy criticism. We will turn to a critical analysis of his judgments in more detail in due course. Before doing so, it is helpful to draw attention to the conceptual problems that Hobhouse J had to face. The main problem for a restitutionary claim in these circumstances was that it did not fall squarely within any of the recognised grounds of restitution.

---

[60] As to the exercise of the borrowing power of local authorities, see the Local Government Act 1972.
[61] [1996] AC 669 (HL); [1994] 1 WLR 938 (CA); [1994] 4 All ER 890.
[62] [1994] 4 All ER 890.

FAILURE OF CONSIDERATION

Hobhouse J was not in a position to award restitution on the basis of 'mistake'. The reason was that the parties were under a mistaken belief as to the existence of a valid transaction. This amounted to a 'mistake of law' for which, at the time, no restitutionary recovery was allowed.[63] Furthermore, Hobhouse J saw no possibility of allowing a restitutionary claim on the basis of 'total failure of consideration'. This was because nearly all of the swaps agreements had been, if not wholly, then at least partially performed. Instead of relying on any of the recognised grounds of recovery, he founded his decision on the basis that there had been 'no consideration' for the respective payments since the underlying agreements were ultra vires and therefore void.[64]

In *Westdeutsche* the local authority appealed without success.[65] The Court of Appeal upheld Hobhouse J's judgment with essentially the same reasoning.[66] The case then came to be heard by the House of Lords which, unfortunately, was not asked to consider the exact ground on which the plaintiff banks were entitled to restitution. But Lord Goff expressed the view that 'it may be right to regard the ground of recovery as failure of consideration'.[67]

Ever since its formal recognition by Hobhouse J and the Court of Appeal, the notion 'absence of consideration' has been the subject of academic debate. In response academics have offered four alternative grounds on which restitution could have been awarded in the swaps cases. In the following section, these grounds of recovery are considered in more detail in so far as they relate to failure of consideration.

3. Absence of consideration and no consideration

'Consideration' in its restitutionary sense usually denotes the actual performance of the 'condition' of a bargain.[68] If this performance fails there is generally said to have been a total failure of consideration. However, this

---

[63] See Hobhouse J in *Westdeutsche Landesbank v. Islington LBC* [1994] 4 All ER 890 at 931 ('I am bound by authority to hold that a mistake of law does not give a right to recover money at common law as money had and received').

[64] See Hobhouse J in *Ibid.* at 930 ('I consider that the correct analysis is absence of consideration and not failure of consideration'), at 936 ('The essential basis upon which they are entitled to recover is that the sums were paid without consideration under contracts which were *ultra vires* the defendants and were void ab initio'), and at 956 ('There was no consideration for the making of the payment').

[65] Note that no appeal was brought in respect of the *Sandwell* case because it was decided by Hobhouse J on precisely the same grounds as *Westdeutsche*.

[66] See Leggatt LJ [1994] 4 All ER 890 at 969.   [67] [1996] AC 669 at 683.

[68] See the classical statement of Viscount Simon in *Fibrosa Spolka Akcyjna v. Fairbairn Lawson Combe Barbour Ltd* [1943] AC 32 at 48.

conception of 'consideration' is problematic as most of the swaps cases were characterised by the fact that money had already been advanced by both parties to the agreement. In other words there had always been at least a part-performance of the other side of the bargain. For this reason Hobhouse J favoured another definition of the term 'consideration'. He was of the opinion that, for restitutionary purposes, 'consideration' described the existence of a valid contract as the basis for a contractual exchange. This meant that 'consideration' was present only if there had been a legally valid obligation to perform by each party. Thus, where a contract was void all payments made under it had been made for 'no consideration'.[69]

Hobhouse J's analysis serves to dilute the distinction between the contractual and restitutionary meanings of consideration. It is, in fact, a clear step towards assimilating these two notions once more. While it used to be only in a contractual context that 'consideration' expressed a valid promise or the contractual *quid pro quo*, Hobhouse J's conception of the restitutionary term 'consideration' as a legally valid promise to perform appears to be nothing but the other side of the same (contractual) coin. His conception of 'absence of consideration' is so wide that it can encompass many of the other recognised grounds of recovery.[70] It is resonant of the principle of the civil law that what is held 'without a legal ground' is recoverable. Birks's concern with such developments has been expressed in the following terms:[71]

If the common law is drawn into an enrichment law in which an enrichment is unjust when it is obtained or retained 'without consideration (in the eye of law)', or, in Latin, *sine causa*, it will have at the same time to learn what civilian systems mean by insufficient legal cause and it will have to learn how the civilian systems relate unjust enrichment and property.

4. Failure of consideration

The severe criticism of absence of consideration as a ground for restitution in the swaps cases led to the suggestion that English law should have

---

[69] Cf. Hobhouse J in *Westdeutsche Landesbank v. Islington LBC* [1994] 4 All ER 890 at 924 ('In the case of *ultra vires* transactions such as those with which I am concerned where there is not and never has been any contract, I prefer to use the phrase "absence of consideration"').
[70] See McKendrick, 'Reason for Restitution,' 106 ('... ground of recovery which is so broad that it has the potential to swallow up most of the existing grounds of restitution').
[71] Birks, 'No Consideration', 233.

adhered to the recognised claim of failure of consideration.[72] The difficulty was how to establish a claim on this ground since the plaintiffs in most cases had already received part of the expected interest payments. The requirement that the 'failure of consideration' be 'total' seemed to represent an impenetrable obstacle to a restitutionary claim on this ground. This in turn led to attempts to redefine the cause of action. Instead of interpreting 'consideration' in its restitutionary sense as the expected contractual counterperformance, it was suggested that 'consideration' had a broader meaning, denoting the general basis upon which a particular payment had been effected.[73] According to this view, which interestingly draws upon the *condictio causa data causa non secuta* for its inspiration, the failure of the contractual performance is not synonymous with 'failure of consideration'. Instead, it is but a 'species of a wider ground of recovery, namely that the basis upon which the payment was made has failed'.[74] The parties render their total performance in a transaction on the condition of receiving the total performance of the other party. Without a total performance the basis of the transaction fails.

An immediate difficulty was that failure of consideration so conceived did not ground restitution where a swap had run its full course, since the parties had obtained exactly what they had bargained for.[75] By contrast, if the ground of restitution was 'no consideration', restitution would be allowed where the swap had been fully executed. The former approach has not been followed. In its recent decision in *Guinness Mahon & Co. Ltd v. Kensington and Chelsea Royal London Borough Council*[76] the Court of Appeal held that, even if the swap had been completed, there was a 'failure of consideration'. Two considerations support this decision: first of all, it is difficult to see why one should distinguish between a transaction that is 99 per cent or 100 per cent completed. In the first instance restitution for failure of consideration would be allowed, in the second instance it

---

[72] The view that 'failure of consideration' would have been the appropriate ground for recovery is, for example, held by P. Birks, 'The English Recognition of Unjust Enrichment', (1991) *Lloyd's Maritime and Commercial Law Quarterly* 473, 494; also his 'No Consideration', 228 (' "Failure of consideration", properly understood, can explain ' "all cases of restitution where the defendant has not completed his part" '), Burrows, *Law of Restitution*, 304; also his 'Restitution of Payments'. See also the dissenting opinion of Dillon LJ in *Westdeutsche* [1994] 4 All ER 890 at 959 ('the only recognised category which Westdeutsche can hope to invoke is that of "money paid for a consideration which has wholly failed"').

[73] See McKendrick, 'Reason for Restitution', 100; Birks, (1993) 23 *University of Western Australia LR* 195 at 209f.

[74] See McKendrick, 'Reason for Restitution', 100.

[75] See *ibid.*, 102; Birks, 'No Consideration', 207, 214, 228.   [76] [1999] QB 215.

would be denied. The second consideration is that although, as a matter of fact, the parties got what they bargained for, as a matter of law they had not received the benefit for which they contracted. It is said that, as a matter of law, the bank had bargained for 'an obligation on the other party to make counter-payments over the whole term of the agreement'.[77] This statement seems to suggest that there would always be a failure of consideration whenever the contractual obligations of either party are not legally enforceable.[78] The critical point with regard to a statement to this effect is that it dilutes the distinction made in *Fibrosa* between the contractual and the restitutionary meanings of 'consideration', since consideration is given only when there was a legally enforceable obligation to perform. In other words, there is a failure of consideration notwithstanding full performance of what the parties had agreed if this was not in fulfilment of a valid contract.

VIII. Conclusions

We have argued in this chapter that an understanding of the civil law led in *Fibrosa* to the separation of the contractual from the restitutionary meaning of failure of consideration. The understanding that there could not have been a failure of consideration where the contract was valid had led to a result in the 'Coronation' cases that was thought, in time, to be unacceptable. In *Cantiere* the *condictio causa data non secuta* was used to produce a different result in Scotland from that in England. At the time of the decision in *Cantiere*, English law continued to be governed by the authority of the 'Coronation' cases. The critical feature of the *condictio*

---

[77] Lord Browne-Wilkinson in *Westdeutsche Landesbank v. Islington LBC* [1996] AC 669 at 711. See further McKendrick, 'Reason for Restitution'.

[78] This view has, for example, been held by Birks when examining the case of *Re Phoenix Life Assurance Co.* (1862) 2 J & H 441; 70 ER 1131. In this case policies had been issued to the insured by Phoenix Life Assurance Co. Losses were incurred on some of the policies. The company was then wound up in 1860. The marine insurance business was held to have been ultra vires the company. Although the insured were not able to claim on the marine policies, they were held entitled to recover the premiums which they had paid. Despite the fact that judgment was given on the ground that there had been 'no consideration' for the premiums, the case has since been rationalised as a claim based upon a 'total failure of consideration'. Birks supported this case on the basis that 'because the insurance company never bore the risk, the consideration totally failed'. He thus draws a distinction between whether, as a matter of fact, a person gets what he bargained for or whether, as a matter of law, 'the nullity of the contract means that there was no legal nexus between his getting it and his own performance': Birks, 'No Consideration'. It must, however, be noted that Birks does not seem to apply the same reasoning in the 'swaps' cases.

as formulated in *Cantiere* was that it emphasised that, irrespective of the validity of the contract, consideration failed if actual performance was not forthcoming. *Cantiere* was the model when the House of Lords in *Fibrosa* achieved for England the same result as it had earlier reached for Scotland. An underlying aim for the House of Lords in these two decisions was to achieve a similar result in the area in question throughout Britain.

It is certain that in reaching its decisions in *Cantiere* and *Fibrosa* the House of Lords saw no distinction between failure of cause in the *condictio* and failure of consideration. In the law of contract consideration is the *quid pro quo* in an agreement that makes it binding as a contract. In a restitutionary context 'consideration' has to be broadened as a notion beyond '*quid pro quo*' to 'the condition on which a benefit is transferred'. For example, if P donates X in anticipation of Q's marriage, the marriage is not the *quid pro quo* of the gift but it can be conceived as the 'condition' on which the gift was made. The decision in *Fibrosa* entrenched into English law the point that, while consideration is necessary to conclude a contract, it is its performance which is relevant to restitution.

In its contractual guise the presence of consideration is intimately connected with the validity of the contract; without consideration there is no contract. However, this is not true of consideration in its restitutionary sense. Notwithstanding the fact that following a breach the contract must first be discharged before restitution can be claimed, failure of consideration in this context is independent of the invalidity or unenforceability of the contract. (It is worth remembering that in *Fibrosa* the contract was still valid.) It was precisely to draw a clear distinction from the 'Coronation' cases that restitution was given notwithstanding the validity of the contract. The unenforceability of the contract in cases of frustration could have been assimilated to invalidity of the contract but this was not done. So the cause of action focused on the failure of the *quid pro quo* rather than on the failure of the contract itself.

It is interesting that 'no consideration' has recently appeared as a distinct cause of action from 'total failure of consideration', denoting the fact either that something was not due or that it was transferred under a contract that was void. Similarly, there are those who now argue for recognition of 'partial failure of consideration' as a cause of action. It seems that what amounts to a sufficient failure can only be determined by reference to the fact that the contract has been discharged. A further problem with '(total) failure of consideration' is that it seems to misplace the source of the right of action where the contract has been discharged. This leads to confusion. Why should the claimant be entitled to restitution where she has precipitated the failure of consideration in bad faith? At the very least it is difficult to understand how, in such circumstances 'total failure of consideration' can be classified within the so-called 'didn't mean it' unjust factors.

Once restitutionary claims for failure of consideration within and outside contract are assimilated, drawing on the wider conception of 'consideration' formulated to cover both sorts of claim, restitution will be available within a contract where the 'condition' of the contract was not performed. 'Condition' conceived in such general terms is a broader notion than *quid pro quo*. Hence the possibility arises of restitution within a valid contract in a broader range of circumstances than failure to perform the bare *quid pro quo*. As it has been operated in English law, 'failure of condition' covers the whole range of the *condictiones*. Most transactions are made on the basis of some sort of 'condition', which explains the extraordinary width of the concept. However, the 'condition' under which a transaction is effected may be conceived very differently by different parties. This explains the extraordinary uncertainty of the concept. In terms of its formulation, 'failure of condition' comes closest to the *condictio causa data causa non secuta* of the civil law. Notwithstanding the fact that theoretically this claim is given a very narrow range of application in German law, the debates on its proper application in Germany[79] illustrate precisely the difficulty of determining its limits. Yet, while the limits of the *condictio causa data causa non secuta* should and can be drawn by reference to the restricting concept of 'cause', 'condition' in English law seems to have no such fixed point by which it can be suitably contained.

---

[79] See Reuter and Martinek, *Ungerechtfertige Bereicherung*, § 5 III.

PART IV

Duress and fraud

6 In defence of unjust factors: a study of rescission for duress, fraud and exploitation

Mindy Chen-Wishart

I. Introduction

A fundamental difference between the English and the German laws of unjust enrichment is the way in which each establishes that enrichment is 'unjust' and so reversible. § 812(1) of the German Civil Code (the BGB) states that a person who, through an act performed by another, or in any other way, acquires something at the expense of that other person without legal ground is bound to render restitution. This general enrichment action has been described as 'probably the most outstanding feature of the German law of unjustified enrichment'.[1] More recently English law has also recognised the general principle of restitution to reverse unjust enrichment[2] but, in contrast, it is 'engaged in crystallising the principles into rules adapted to the different types of case so as to meet the specific interests involved in them'.[3] An influential classification proposed by Peter Birks sets out the specific factors that can make the plaintiff's transfer of

---

My gratitude to Professors Peter Birks, Jane Stapleton and Richard Sutton, Dr Gerhard Dannemann and Mr Dominic O'Sullivan for generous discussions which have clarified my thinking and saved me from errors although, doubtlessly, many persist. I am also grateful to Professors Reinhard Zimmermann and David Johnston for providing me with the occasion for embarking on comparative study and to the Law Faculty at Otago University for hosting me during a sabbatical when the text was finalised.

[1] Reinhard Zimmermann and Jacques du Plessis, 'Basic Features of the German Law of Unjustified Enrichment', [1994] *Restitution LR* 14.
[2] *Banque Financière de la Cité v. Parc (Battersea) Ltd* [1998] 1 All ER 737 at 740; [1998] 2 WLR 475. The House of Lords recognises that unjust enrichment claims comprise a four-stage inquiry: (i) is the defendant enriched? (ii) was this enrichment at the plaintiff's expense? (iii) was the enrichment unjust? (iv) does the defendant have any defences?
[3] Konrad Zweigert and Hein Kötz, *Introduction to Comparative Law* (trans. Tony Weir, 3rd edn, 1998), 565.

159

wealth to the defendant 'unjust' in the eyes of English law.[4] Thus, while the German approach appears to yield restitution whenever defendants cannot advance a legal cause for retention, English law leaves defendants with their enrichments unless the plaintiffs can show why they should not keep them.

Many commentators observe that this apparent structural divergence probably yields no significant differences at the level of actual outcomes.[5] Konrad Zweigert and Hein Kötz explain why 'too much should not be made of the apparent differences':

[I]t is manifest that an approximation will take place in the theoretical treatment of these areas of law. The unduly abstract detail of the German code will be loosened by a typology of enrichment claims and in the Common Law general rules will be developed to give form and structure to the unduly concrete details of the case-law. Each system has a great deal to learn from the other.[6]

Reinhard Zimmermann will concede this only so far. While he acknowledges 'a significant rapprochement of patterns of liability', he notes that 'there are still considerable differences as to the question of how best to organize this area of the law'.[7] In short, he regards the English multiple unjust factors approach as inferior to the German single ground of absence of cause, and considers it 'hardly conceivable that a legal system engaged with the task of rationally organizing its law of unjustified enrichment should take its lead from English jurisprudence'.[8]

This essay begs to differ. In defence of the unjust factors approach it will be argued that practical and important details of the restitutionary response rest on the nature and the effect of the operative unjust factor. In other words, the particular reason why the transfer was without legal cause and the impact of that on the value of the benefit transferred can and, to a significant extent, do explain how the initial entitlement to restitution is worked out in practice. Even German unjust enrichment law is not indifferent to the unjust factors. In both systems of law, reference to the unjust factors explains the operation of certain features of the current law and, it is further argued, lights the way to important and desirable future developments. There is undoubtedly room for development in the

---

[4] Peter Birks, *An Introduction to the Law of Restitution* (1989, revised paperback edn). See also Andrew Burrows, *The Law of Restitution* (1993).
[5] See for example, Reinhard Zimmermann, 'Unjustified Enrichment: The Modern Civilian Approach', (1995) 15 *Oxford JLS* 403, 414.
[6] Zweigert and Kötz, *Introduction*, 565.
[7] Zimmermann, 'Unjustified Enrichment', 414.
[8] *Ibid.*, 416.

nascent English law of unjust enrichment and lessons can certainly be learned from German law. But it is not in replacing the unjust factors approach by the single absence of cause approach that progress lies. On the contrary, it is by taking the unjust factors and the policies behind them even more seriously that the wisdom of certain aspects of German unjust enrichment law is thrown into sharp relief. By the same token, it seems that certain features of the German law can benefit from greater sensitivity to the unjust factors. As Zweigert and Kötz exhort, '[e]ach system has a great deal to learn from the other'.

These claims will be advanced with particular reference to a group of unjust factors coming under the headings of duress and fraud.[9] Fraud will be taken to include constructive fraud. Constructive fraud, in turn, encompasses the specific unjust factors of non-fraudulent misrepresentation, undue influence, unconscionability and the constructive notice doctrine introduced by *Barclays Bank plc v. O'Brien*[10] (collectively these will be referred to as 'exploitation'). The emphasis is on how restitution on these grounds operates on rescission of contract. Rescission is described as 'one of the commonest remedies in the law of restitution...[and] one of the most difficult to analyse'.[11] It operates *simultaneously* to set aside the contract and to effect mutual restoration of any transfers made under it. In English law the question whether rescission belongs to the law of unjust enrichment and should therefore conform to its principles remains one of the unresolved questions on the borderline between the laws of contract and unjust enrichment.[12] The question is a serious and important one and, while that debate is sidestepped here, the assumption made is that at least the restitutionary part of rescission properly belongs within the wider body of law on giving back.[13] The present claim is that taking the unjust factors seriously can enlighten and inform the operation and development of unjust enrichment law in general and of the law of rescission in particular.

---

[9] These being my terms of reference for a paper presented at the Symposium on the Comparative Law of Unjust Enrichment, Cambridge, April 1999, from which this and the other papers in this collection have emerged.
[10] [1994] 1 AC 180. This doctrine protects plaintiffs who have been wrongly induced by someone to whom they are emotionally attached, typically the plaintiff's husband, to guarantee his debt, and typically by putting up the family home as security.
[11] Burrows, *Law of Restitution*, 31–2.
[12] See Peter Birks, 'Foreword' in: Andrew Skelton, *Restitution and Contract* (1998), iv.
[13] For discussion see, for example, *ibid.*; D. P. Visser, 'Rethinking Unjustified Enrichment: A Perspective of the Competition between Contractual and Enrichment Remedies', [1992] *Acta Juridica* 203.

Section II of this essay addresses the major criticisms of the unjust factors approach. Section III discusses the nature of duress, fraud and exploitation. It asks why the law intervenes when it does so in the name of these unjust factors. Section IV looks at how the nature of these unjust factors colours the availability of the change of position defence (the enrichment surviving). In particular, the protective policies underlying certain unjust factors can explain why disqualification from this defence should be extended from bad-faith defendants to some innocent defendants. In Section V it is argued that the logic of the unjust factors points to the desirability of dissolving certain bars to rescission in English law and of making the change of position defence available to *plaintiffs* who must make counter-restitution. Section VI considers how the unjust factors may affect the valuation of the enrichment received by either party. Sensitivity to the impact of particular unjust factors on the enrichment received can overcome the problem of subjective devaluation. It also provides the best justification for the controversial remedy of partial rescission.

II. Criticisms of the unjust factors approach

Zimmermann[14] criticises the unjust factors approach as untidy, uncertain in scope, not comprehensive, involving needless duplication and generally irrelevant to the restitutionary response.

1. Untidy, uncertain and not comprehensive?

The first objection, untidiness, is premised on the basic division in German unjust enrichment law between enrichment by performance (the *Leistungskondiktion*) and enrichment in another way (the *Eingriffskondiktion*) and the observation that all the English unjust factors except ignorance involve enrichment by performance. But this assumes no particular significance in English law, which operates no such division. It is only 'untidy' from the point of view of German law. The second and third criticisms, that the identified unjust factors are uncertain in scope and not comprehensive since they can be added to, may also be swiftly dealt with. Under German law, a restitutionary award must be prefaced by a plaintiff showing that his intentional transfer was without cause. Essentially, one of the recognised factors that vitiate the declaration of intention (or will) detailed in contract law must be made out.[15] It is doubtful whether the operation of these vitiating factors is more certain in German law than

---

[14] Zimmermann, 'Unjustified Enrichment', 416.
[15] See further B. S. Markesinis, W. Lorenz and G. Dannemann, *The German Law of Obligations*, vol. I, *The Law of Contracts and Restitution* (1997), 725–6.

in English law. And as for the unjust factors being not comprehensive, the possibility of adding new causes of action[16] is a general feature of the common law and, many would say, part of its commendable strength and adaptability. Moreover, the distinction between recognising a new unjust factor and interpreting an established one can be very fine indeed.

2. Unnecessary duplication?

In substance, Zimmermann's criticism is that where restitution follows rescission of contract, English law seems to have to inquire into the unjust factors twice, once to vitiate the contract and again to ground the restitutionary claim. This 'unnecessary duplication' is contrasted with the 'internal economy' of the preferred civilian analysis. But this criticism is not a crippling one. Certainly, as far as rescission for duress, fraud or exploitation is concerned it makes no practical difference which approach is applied. The scope of these vitiating factors in contract law coincides with their manifestation as unjust factors in unjust enrichment law.[17] Even if it does not, as with the ground of mistake, a plaintiff under *either* system must satisfy the vitiating factor before any claim for restitution can be made. Since the scope of mistake as a vitiating factor in contract is narrower than its scope as an unjust factor in unjust enrichment, satisfaction of the former will automatically satisfy the latter. Nothing is saved by the apparently more economical German approach and nothing is added by the apparent duplication of the English approach. In English law the vitiating factor *simultaneously* sets aside the contract and furnishes the ground for restitution. In German law it avoids the contract and so removes the 'cause', which would otherwise justify the transfer and deny restitution. The German restitutionary claim is therefore necessarily based on the unjust factor, although this is obscured by the single ground of absence of cause. The unjust factor vitiating the plaintiff's declaration of intention is the first domino which triggers the rescission of the contract which, in turn, creates the absence of cause which, in turn, provides the ground for restitution.

3. Unjust factors irrelevant?

This last criticism appears more serious. Zimmermann prefers the economy of the single catch-all ground because:

[w]hy there was no legal ground for this specific transfer is entirely irrelevant. The underlying contract the transfer attempted to discharge may not have come

---

[16] See *CTN Cash and Carry Ltd v. Gallaher Ltd* [1994] 4 All ER 714 at 720 *per* Sir Donald Nicholls VC.
[17] See further Markesinis, Lorenz and Dannemann, *Law of Contracts*, 187–91, 204–11.

into existence; it may have been invalid for a whole variety of reasons ... All this has to be determined according to the law of contract. The law of restitution does not have to concern itself with these issues.[18]

He considers the English approach not 'to be a scheme distinguished by its elegance'.[19] While elegance in structuring the law is not the exclusive or even highest aim of a legal system, the criticism is a potent one if there are no valid reasons for retaining the reference to particular unjust factors. If that is so, then there can be no objection to the more elegant and economical German approach. But, while the unjust factors may be irrelevant to the prima facie right to restitution, the claim here is that they do affect important details of the restitutionary response, that they should matter even more in both systems than they currently do, and that they can inform important and desirable developments in unjust enrichment law. It seems an obvious, logical and sensible starting point to say that the reasons *why* the law intervenes should indicate *what* results it seeks to generate and *how* that is achieved. The first step is to consider the reasons for restitution in cases of duress, fraud and exploitation.

III. Duress, fraud and exploitation: a proposed taxonomy

When transactions are rescinded on these grounds in English law, what is the pathology to which the law is responding? Birks's taxonomy of the unjust factors in English law[20] draws a basic distinction between autonomous unjust enrichment (typically by subtraction from the plaintiff) and unjust enrichment by wrongdoing against the plaintiff (typically non-subtractive). He locates duress, fraud and exploitation within autonomous unjust enrichment and, more specifically, under the heading of 'vitiated consent'. The plaintiff's defective consent to the transfer is said to be the touchstone of restitutionary liability; the presence or absence of fault on the defendant's part is immaterial, hence restitutionary liability here is said to be strict. This strict liability is said, in turn, to justify conceding a change of position defence to innocent defendants. German law also regards these factors as invalidating the plaintiff's declaration of will.[21]

---

[18] Zimmermann, 'Unjustified Enrichment', 415–16.
[19] Ibid., 416.
[20] Birks, *Introduction*, 140–355. See further elaboration in Burrows, *Law of Restitution*, chaps. 3–13.
[21] See for example Markesinis, Lorenz and Dannemann, *Law of Contracts*, 205 and Zweigert and Kötz, *Introduction*, 423–4, 428.

However, this apparently exclusive focus on the quality of the plaintiff's consent can paint a somewhat misleading picture of the balance of the law's concerns. It is clear that, in determining whether these grounds are satisfied, the defendant's conduct and the fairness of the outcome are also factored into the equation. Fuller discussions of the juristic nature of these unjust factors are given elsewhere[22] and a few points will suffice for present purposes.

The plaintiff's defective consent alone is not sufficient to set aside contracts for duress, fraud or exploitation. In the first place contract law is rarely concerned with a plaintiff's actual subjective consent. Quite apart from problems of proof, the law's proper concern to protect transactional security and the defendant's reasonable expectations means that the legal test of consent is objective. Thus, any defect in the plaintiff's actual consent in deviating from its objective manifestation will not, alone, justify rescission and restitution. Secondly, it seems uncontroversial that unjust enrichment law should not only be concerned about why a plaintiff should get restitution, but also why a defendant should have to render restitution. In both German and English law the defendant's interest is only defeated if additional factors supplement the plaintiff's defective consent. With duress, fraud and exploitation, these take the form of the defendant's unconscientious conduct or knowledge of the plaintiff's defective consent and/or a manifest disproportion in the values exchanged to the disadvantage of the plaintiff in certain circumstances. These considerations necessarily shape the corresponding unjust factors when restitution is sought. The point is brought home most recently and most forcefully by the House of Lords in *Barclays Bank plc v. Boulter*,[23] which held that, in a claim based on the *O'Brien* doctrine, it is insufficient for the plaintiff simply to plead the misrepresentation or undue influence affecting the quality of his consent; he must also specifically plead the defendant's notice of this.[24]

Lastly, where the plaintiff's defective consent results from duress, fraud or exploitation by a third party (rather than the defendant), relief does

---

[22] See Mindy Chen-Wishart, *Unconscionable Bargains* (1989); also her 'The O'Brien Principle and Substantive Unfairness', (1997) 56 *CLJ* 60; also her 'Controlling the Power to Agree Damages', in: Peter Birks (ed.), *Wrongs and Remedies in the Twenty-first Century* (1996), 271 ff.
[23] [1999] 1 WLR 1919.
[24] The view that these unjust factors nevertheless remains plaintiff-sided, albeit 'inhibited' on policy grounds, creates an unnecessary distortion. See Peter Birks and Chin Nyuk Yin, 'On the Nature of Undue Influence', in: Jack Beatson and Daniel Friedmann (eds.), *Good Faith and Fault in Contract Law* (1995), chap. 3.

not automatically follow.[25] Again, something else is required – that is, that the defendant knows (actually or constructively) that the plaintiff's consent has been wrongfully induced by the third party. Such knowledge can be seen as negating the reasonableness of the defendant's reliance upon the plaintiff's apparent consent and so renders its protection unwarranted.

Instead of 'vitiated consent' per se, a tripartite division is suggested which, it is submitted, reveals the nature of these unjust factors more precisely and in a way that illuminates the restitutionary response.

1. Unconscientious procurement

This describes defendants who deliberately and actively exert pressure or lie to induce the plaintiffs' consent (hence defective) to the contract and to its performance. The law will not assist in the enforcement or retention of benefits obtained by such active taking of advantage. Located here are cases of deceit or actual fraud, all kinds of duress, some cases of actual undue influence[26] and of active unconscionable conduct.[27]

2. Unconscientious receipt

Here the defendant takes no active advantage but she nevertheless accepts benefits from the plaintiff in 'unconscientious circumstances' (namely, with knowledge of his defective consent or that he belongs to a protected class) and fails to respond reasonably, generally by recommending independent advice or disclosing certain material features of the transaction. This is regarded in English law as constructive fraud or as comprising passive victimisation. It includes cases of presumed undue influence and most cases of unconscionable bargains.[28]

---

[25] Although exceptionally in German law third-party duress *can* rescind the contract. See generally Reinhard Zimmermann, *The Law of Obligations: Roman Foundations of the Civilian Tradition* (paperback edn 1996), 661.

[26] For example *Williams v. Bayley* [1866] LR 1 HL 200 and *Mutual Finance v. Wetton* [1937] 2 KB 389, where some active pressure is applied by threatening to prosecute, or to expose some harmful information to, the plaintiff's loved one.

[27] In *Hart v. O'Connor* [1985] AC 1000 the Privy Council indicates that victimisation by the defendant may be active or passive. The former requires positive conduct by the defendant, which unconscientiously induces the plaintiff's transfer. *Louth v. Diprose* (1992) 175 CLR 621 provides a colourful example. See further Chen-Wishart, *Unconscionable Bargains*, 71–9.

[28] It would also logically account for the relief given in cases of unilateral mistake of terms known to the defendant, *Smith v. Hughes* (1871) LR 6 QB 597; and of knowing receipt.

However, many cases justified on this rationale are not true members of this category. They occur where no meaningful independent evidence exists of the plaintiff's personal bargaining disability or of the defendant's knowledge of that disability. Instead, these elements are largely inferred from the serious disparity in the values exchanged (substantive unfairness), and from the plaintiff's membership of an identifiably vulnerable group.[29] This yields the third category of cases.

3. Protection of vulnerable groups from improvidence

The dual features of this category are manifest disadvantage to the plaintiff in the substance of the transaction and the plaintiff's membership of a class identified by the law as warranting special protection. This is the proper home of the *O'Brien cases*;[30] some cases of presumed undue influence;[31] unconscionable bargains;[32] and non-fraudulent misrepresentations.[33] In the last case, unconscientiousness is said to attach not to the defendant's procurement or receipt of the benefit, but to his attempt to retain or enforce the benefit once the misrepresentation is known. In the contractual context, the relevant harm against which plaintiffs are protected is better described as that inherent in an inappropriate, unwanted or disproportionately disadvantageous contract, rather than the more abstract harm of the defendant's 'abuse of superior bargaining power', which is not actionable per se and more or less undetectable without an uneven exchange. The protected classes are identified largely by reference to circumstances that attract a high incidence of disproportionate outcomes:[34] wives of, and others in a sexual or emotional relationship with, primary debtors (the *O'Brien* doctrine); those who place

---

[29] For example, the *O'Brien* doctrine treats a lender as having *constructive* notice of the surety plaintiff's defective consent where it knows that the plaintiff is in a 'sexual or emotional relationship' with the primary debtor and where the suretyship is manifestly disadvantageous to the plaintiff. Normally there is no actual or even constructive knowledge in any meaningful sense and knowledge here is really deemed and fictional.

[30] *Barclays Bark plc v. O'Brien* [1994] 1 AC 180; *Royal Bank of Scotland v. Ettridge (No. 2)* [1998] 4 ALL ER 705. See for example, *Crédit Lyonnaise Bank Nederland NV v. Burch* [1997] 1 All ER 144; Chen-Wishart, 'The *O'Brien* Principle'.

[31] For example *Allcard v. Skinner* (1887) 36 ChD 145.

[32] For example, *Nichols v. Jessup* [1986] 1 NZLR 226, noted in Mindy Chen-Wishart, 'Unconscionable Bargains', [1987] *New Zealand Law Journal* 107.

[33] For example, *Redgrave v. Hurd* (1881) 20 ChD 1.

[34] For fuller discussion see Chen-Wishart, *Unconscionable Bargains*, 108–12, also in *Wrongs and Remedies*, 293–4.

a very high degree of trust in the other contract party (undue influence); those with less personal competence who deal with substantial portions of their assets (unconscionable bargains) and those who have been lied to, albeit non-fraudulently (misrepresentation).

These three categories are largely reflected in the German law.[35] § 123 BGB provides for rescission on the grounds of fraud or threats and § 138 BGB voids transactions against public policy and those which are obviously disproportionate and exploitative of the disadvantaged party's 'need, carelessness or inexperience'.[36]

It is now possible to test the claim that these unjust factors, explained along this tripartite classification, infuse the details of the law's restitutionary response. Their most obvious impact is in the availability of the change of position defence.

IV. Unjust factors and the change of position defence (value surviving)

The defendant's restitutionary liability may be measured by the enrichment initially received or be limited to that which survives in the defendant's hands when the claim is made. English law regards this as a question of defences and asks whether the defendant has relevantly and innocently 'changed his position' so as to justify a reduction of his restitutionary liability.[37] German law treats this as an aspect of the quantification of the enrichment to be returned.[38] In both jurisdictions the applicable measure is influenced by the nature of the unjust factor initially triggering restitution.

---

[35] See, for example, Markesinis, Lorenz and Dannemann, *Law of Contracts*, 187–91, 204–11.

[36] § 138(2) reads: 'A legal transaction is also void whereby a person exploiting the need, carelessness or inexperience of another, causes to be promised or granted to himself or to a third party in exchange for a performance, pecuniary advantage which exceed the value of the performance to such an extent that, under the circumstances, the pecuniary advantages are in obvious disproportion to the performance.' Translated in Markesinis, Lorenz and Dannemann, *Law of Contracts*, 825.

[37] *Lipkin Gorman (a Firm) v. Karpnale Ltd* [1991] 2 AC 548. The scope of the defence is still uncertain and the possibility that it may extend beyond instances of loss of enrichment, to those where supervening events make full restitution unjust, is not ruled out.

[38] *Wegfall der Bereicherung*; § 818(3) BGB: 'The obligation to provide return or compensation for the value is excluded to the extent that the recipient is no longer enriched.' Translated in Markesinis, Lorenz and Dannemann, *Law of Contracts*, 895.

1. Defendants in bad faith

Both jurisdictions lay down just one clear disqualification: defendants in bad faith (those who know of the plaintiff's restitutionary entitlement[39]) are barred from discounting the enrichment spent, lost or given away and must account for all of the enrichment received. Whether the defendant should be regarded as in bad faith must be influenced by the operative unjust factor. The clearest cases are defendants tainted by unconscientious procurement. Where fraud, duress or actual undue influence involving pressure is found, the defendant should normally have to account for any depletion of the enrichment received. The same applies to defendants tainted by unconscientious receipt.

The reason for the invalidity of the transfer also affects the extent of the defendant's restitutionary liability in German law. Where duress or fraud under § 123 BGB are triggered, German law in practice disqualifies defendants from the value-surviving measure. Defendants are treated as having knowledge of their 'lack of a legal cause at the time of receipt' (§ 819(1) BGB) since 'innocent fraud is impossible and innocent duress very difficult at least'.[40] Moreover, § 819(2) BGB automatically disqualifies the defendant from change of position where the unjust factors are illegality (detailed in § 134 BGB) or immorality (§ 138 BGB),[41] the latter largely corresponding with my third category (as defined in Section III, above). Notably this also shuts out innocent defendants in this category, on which more will be said below.

2. Minors in bad faith

The impact of unjust factors is highlighted in the case of minority. Here the strong policy of protection underlying minority (which can operate as an unjust factor or as a defence in English law) dissolves the general bar against defendants in bad faith. Necessaries aside, a defendant minor can appeal to change of position and return only what value survives even

---

[39] See *Lipkin Gorman (a Firm) v. Karpnale Ltd* [1991] 2 AC 548 and § 819(1) BGB: 'If the recipient knows of the lack of a legal cause at the time of the receipt, or if he later learns of this lack, he is obliged to provide restitution from the time of the receipt or from the time when he obtains this knowledge as if an action for restitution had been pending at that time.' Translated in Markesinis, Lorenz and Dannemann, *Law of Contracts*, 895.

[40] I am indebted to Gerhard Dannemann for clarifying this point. See also Zweigert and Kötz, *Introduction*, 557: 'In practice... the recipient cannot escape on the ground that his enrichment has ceased to exist if the underlying contract was tainted by his deceit or duress.'

[41] But it must have been the very acceptance of the performance which offended against the law or good morals in order for change of position to be ruled out as a defence.

if he has acted fraudulently.[42] This prompted Zweigert and Kötz to generalise that 'the extent of liability in restitution may be affected by the purpose and power of the rule which justifies the claim'.[43] Even more relevant to this inquiry, they add that: 'in all legal systems liability depends on considerations appropriate to the particular type of case, and that *these considerations... oust or temper the abstract rules of liability preformulated in general terms*'.[44] In short, the unjust factors, which express these considerations, matter.

3. Defendants in good faith: presumed undue influence

The disqualification of defendants in bad faith from change of position should, in principle, leave those in good faith in the third category within the fold. They should be liable only for the value surviving. However, it is noted above that where the unjust factors are illegality or immorality § 819(2) BGB automatically disqualifies defendants (whether or not they know of the plaintiffs' restitutionary entitlement) from change of position. In English law the defence seems generally invisible in undue influence and *O'Brien* cases,[45] although very often the defendants cannot be described as unconscientious without seriously distorting and denaturing the substantive sense of the word. The reason again lies in policies underlying the unjust factors and can be summed up in the phrase 'anti-subversion'. Just as the policy underlying minority would be subverted if minors in bad faith were shut out from change of position, so the policies underlying other unjust factors may be subverted if innocent defendants are permitted unlimited access to the defence.[46] Change of position is said

---

[42] See, for example, *R. Leslie Ltd v. Sheill* [1914] 3 KB 607 where a minor fraudulently misrepresented his age to obtain a loan, which he completely dissipated. The Court of Appeal rejected the suggestion that the minor should repay the amount he received but accepted that, in principle, equity could compel restitution of any enrichment still surviving in the minor's hands. For German law see Zweigert and Kötz, *Introduction*, 557, 590-1, 593.

[43] Zweigert and Kötz, *Introduction*, 594. [44] *Ibid.*, 591 (emphasis added).

[45] In *Royal Bank of Scotland v. Ettridge (No. 2)* [1998] 4 All ER 705, the Court of Appeal offers no reasons other than that there is no hint of change of position in *O'Brien* itself.

[46] See M. Bryan, 'Change of Position: Commentary', in: Mitchell McInnes (ed.), *Restitution: Developments in Unjust Enrichment* (1996), 75, 79-80, arguing that change of position should not be available for all 'innocent' defendants in undue influence and unconscionability cases. He points out that security of receipts is not the only operative policy where a legal or equitable wrong has been committed; that the civil law protects many interests and promotes many values and that the 'effectiveness of the law in furthering these interests and values could be blunted by an overgenerous application of the change of position' defence; further, that allowing change of position 'may defeat not only the demands of restitution but also the equitable concern with transactional imbalances of power which inform' these areas of the law.

to be aimed at protecting the security of receipt of defendants in good faith, by shielding them from the loss that they would suffer if called on to account for the enrichment which is no longer in their possession to return. However, this can only be done by transferring the loss to the plaintiffs and denying them the protection which the third category of unjust factors aim to confer.[47] That protection, of vulnerable plaintiffs from improvidence, would be subverted, perhaps fatally, if defendants could freely reduce their restitutionary liability in this way. Thus anti-subversion explains the general unavailability of change of position in presumed undue influence cases. But one limited exception is detectable in English law. In balancing the parties' equities, it seems that in respect of at least one type of loss-generating expenditure, the balance can tip in favour of the innocent defendant. That is, loss resulting from the innocent defendant's expenditure in attempted performance for the plaintiff's purposes, when this expenditure yields no counter-restitution from the plaintiff. Limiting change of position to this type of loss minimises the risk of subverting the protective policy underlying undue influence.

This describes the reduction allowed in *Cheese v. Thomas*.[48] There, the plaintiff contributed £43,000 towards the purchase of a house for £83,000 in the name of the defendant, his great-nephew, in order to provide himself with a suitable home for the rest of his life. Presumed undue influence was found, although the court was at pains to emphasise the good faith of the great-nephew. When the house realised significantly less than the original purchase price in a mortgagee's sale, the loss was divided proportionately so that the plaintiff obtained restitution of the £43,000 less 43/83 of the loss suffered in the sale. It has been argued that this result is best interpreted as an instance of the court allowing change of position to an innocent defendant, albeit intuitively.[49] A further refinement should now be added.

In *Cheese v. Thomas* change of position was not triggered simply by the defendant's good faith. The purpose of the expenditure, which occasioned the eventual loss, must also be factored into the equation. The court used the language of 'joint venture' to describe an expenditure which was, to a significant extent, for the plaintiff's benefit. In so far as loss eventuates

---

[47] See generally John Dawson, 'Erasable Enrichment in German Law', (1981) 61 *Boston University LR* 303, 306.
[48] [1994] 1 WLR 129.
[49] Mindy Chen-Wishart, 'Undue Influence, Manifest Disadvantage and Loss Apportionment', (1994) 110 *LQR* 173; Lord Goff of Chieveley and Gareth Jones, *The Law of Restitution* (5th edn, 1998), 367, 822 and Peter Birks, 'Change of Position: The Nature of the Defence and its Relationship to Other Restitutionary Defences', in McInnes (ed.), *Restitution: Developments in Unjust Enrichment*, 49, 56–7.

from expenditure of this character, it is not inequitable for a defendant to reduce his restitutionary liability even though the protective policy would generally bar him from doing so. Consistently, in *Mahoney v. Purnell*,[50] another case of innocent presumed undue influence, the defendant was fixed to the value received since his loss had resulted from expenditure in support of his own venture, quite independent of the plaintiff's purposes.

Allcard v. Skinner[51] also supports this formulation. There the non-contractual transfer from the novice nun to the Mother Superior was vitiated by presumed undue influence. While the claim for restitution was eventually defeated by laches and affirmation, it was made clear that, in any event, the novice nun would only have recovered so much of the funds transferred which 'had not been spent in accordance with the wishes of the Plaintiff but remained in the hands of the Defendant'.[52] Cotton LJ opposed making the morally blameless Mother Superior 'liable for money spent for the charitable purposes with which the Plaintiff and Defendant were at the time of the expenditure associated, and which the Plaintiff was at the time willing and anxious to promote'.[53]

Thus, in *Cheese* and *Allcard*, if the great-nephew, or perhaps more uncharacteristically the Mother Superior, had dissipated the plaintiffs' money on their own purposes, say on high-risk investments or throwing extravagant parties, these would not have come within the category of expenditure qualifying for change of position in cases of 'innocent' undue influence.

4. Defendants in good faith: *O'Brien* cases

In general, even innocent defendant lenders[54] cannot discount their restitutionary liability to plaintiff sureties by the extent of their loss, that is, the un-repaid loans advanced to the principal debtors. Anti-subversion

---

[50] [1996] 3 All ER 61, the plaintiff agreed, *inter alia*, to cancel his 50 per cent of shares in a company for an annuity of £20,000 a year for ten years payable by that company. The company was sold shortly after for £3.3 million but the sum was lost on another venture. May J awarded the difference in money value between what the plaintiff transferred and what he received. See comment by Peter Birks, 'Unjust Factors and Wrongs: Pecuniary Restitution for Undue Influence', [1997] *Restitution LR* 72, and J. D. Heydon 'Equitable Compensation for Undue Influence', (1997) 113 *LQR* 8.
[51] (1887) 36 ChD 145.
[52] *Ibid.* at 186 *per* Bowen LJ; see also Kekewich LJ at 164, and Lindley LJ at 180.
[53] *Ibid.*, Cotton LJ at 171.
[54] In *O'Brien*-type cases lenders normally have no actual or even constructive knowledge of the principal debtor's equitable wrong in any meaningful sense. Knowledge is deemed where the lender is aware that the plaintiff has a 'sexual or emotional relationship' with the primary debtor and that the plaintiff is securing a debt of the latter.

can also account for the apparent invisibility of change of position. The *O'Brien* doctrine is a protective response to a very specific but common situation, typically that of sureties who place the family home at risk to benefit their spouses' or partners' shaky business ventures. It would hardly make sense to negate that intended protection by invariably allowing lenders to shift the loss entailed in making the loans to the sureties via change of position. The law does not contradict itself by giving with one hand in circumstances which will almost invariably allow it to be taken back with the other.

This provides another explanation for *MacKenzie v. Royal Bank of Canada*,[55] where the court refused to set off the defendant's un-repaid loan to the principal debtor against its restitutionary liability to the plaintiff surety. Since the loan moved towards the primary debtor, the case is traditionally explained in terms of the plaintiff receiving no benefit, thus triggering no obligation to make *restitutio in integrum* (in modern terms 'counter-restitution').[56] Quibbles on the benefit point aside,[57] this explanation nevertheless does not account for why the defendant could not appeal to the quite independent defence of change of position. The answer lies in the strong and specifically targeted protection underlying the *O'Brien* doctrine. The disqualification of such innocent defendants seems to bear out Lord Goff's prediction in *Lipkin Gorman*[58] that the defence was 'likely to be available only on comparatively rare occasions'. The Court of Appeal recently confirmed this result in *Royal Bank of Scotland v. Ettridge (No. 2)*,[59] conceding 'difficulties with [the change of position] analysis, not least that there is no trace of it in *O'Brien*'. Nevertheless, it may be that one small exception has been allowed, although its recognition as such is obscured by its particular presentation.

5. Partial rescission

Exceptional change of position may provide one justification for the controversial remedy of partial rescission (with partial restitution) in *O'Brien* cases.[60] Where the plaintiff's transfer is affected solely by the primary debtor's misrepresentation about the extent of the risk being assumed,

---

[55] [1934] AC 468.
[56] See, for example, Guenter Treitel, *The Law of Contract* (10th edn, 1999), 352.
[57] The plaintiff can be said to have benefited in the sense of achieving a desired end for which she would have had to pay, see discussion below at 187-8.
[58] [1991] 2 AC 548 at 580.   [59] [1998] 4 All ER 705.
[60] The remedy was adopted in *Vadasz v. Pioneer Concrete (SA) Pty Ltd* (1995) 184 CLR 102 and *Bank Melli Iran v. Samadi-Rad* [1995] 1 Federal Court Reporter 465, but was disapproved in *TSB Bank v. Camfield* [1995] 1 WLR 430. See further discussion below at 189-91.

then holding the plaintiff to the risk represented and accepted may be justifiable. Thus where the lender lends in reliance on the surety's apparent but tainted consent to assume the risk of the principal debtor's non-repayment, it is inequitable for her to deny her untainted consent to assume a *lower* risk. This can be put in the language of change of position: while a plaintiff in an *O'Brien* case generally need not concede anything to the lender's change of position, where her consent is tainted only by a misrepresentation about the extent of the risk assumed, she should not be able to deny the defendant's change of position to the extent of that lower risk represented to her if she would have willingly agreed to it.

Of course, the force of this argument disappears where undue influence colours the whole transaction. Then there may be no untainted decision by the surety to assume any *part* of the risk and so no reason for departing from the general protective policy barring change of position. An alternative and preferred rationalisation for partial rescission is suggested later, based on the plaintiff's obligation to make counter-restitution.[61]

V. Unjust factors and counter-restitution

Where both parties have commenced performance of a contract which is subsequently rescinded, restitution must be accompanied by counter-restitution. The plaintiff who wants back must also give back. In principle, this means that the defendant's restitutionary liability is reducible twice, first by reference to the loss of the enrichment received from the plaintiff (unless disqualified), and second by reference to the reciprocal enrichment conferred on the plaintiff in attempted performance. The operation of the second reduction is also influenced by the unjust factors. Two questions arise. First, how do the unjust factors enlighten us about the proper *mode* of counter-restitution: should it be confined to return in kind or extended to include return in moneys-worth? Secondly, do the unjust factors throw any light on the measure of the *plaintiff's* counter-restitution: specifically, should change of position be available here?

1. Counter-restitution impossible?

(a) The mode of counter-restitution and the effect of exact counter-restitution being impossible

English and German law agree that the plaintiff must make counter-restitution of any benefit received as a condition of obtaining restitution on rescission. But they diverge on the permissible mode of that counter-

---

[61] See below at VI, 4.

restitution. German law adopts a common approach to restitutionary and counter-restitutionary liability since, on rescission, either party can bring a restitutionary claim to retrieve the transfers, which are now without cause.[62] In both cases, while return in kind is regarded as the norm, where that is impossible translation into money is expressly allowed.[63] Here, English law has much to learn.

In English law the starting point is that the mutual restoration necessary for rescission must be proprietary. Money aside,[64] what must be restored is a *thing*. Moreover, it should be the *exact* thing. Traditionally this has the astonishing effect that rescission can be barred where return in kind to the plaintiff was never possible (as with services),[65] or has become impossible (as where the property is completely dissipated through use or consumption or been sold on to a third party).[66] But if the property in question still exists, albeit depreciated, partly consumed or otherwise dealt with, rescission can be granted although there seems to be no facility for making a money adjustment even against fraudulent defendants.[67] Rescission is also barred where counter-restitution of substantial property[68] (although curiously not services[69]) to the defendant is impossible. These are

---

[62] English law confers no such automatic entitlement on the defendant in the absence of an unjust factor in his favour (although failure of consideration has been posited, see Burrows, *Law of Restitution*, 133–4). Rather, counter-restitution is generally regarded as a condition of rescission and the concomitant restitution.

[63] § 818(2) BGB: 'If due to the nature of what has been obtained, return is impossible, or if the recipient for another reason is not in the position to return what he has obtained, he must compensate for the value.' Translated in Markesinis, Lorenz and Dannemann, *Law of Contracts*, 895.

[64] In the case of money, mutual restitution essentially becomes a personal claim for the sum transferred rather than for the precise notes or coins.

[65] *Boyd & Forrest v. Glasgow & South Western Railway* 1915 SC (HL) 20, where the plaintiff was induced to build a railway by misrepresentation as to the rock strata, the plaintiff's claim for rescission and for *quantum meruit* exceeding the contract price failed because, *inter alia*, restitution of the plaintiff's services was impossible.

[66] *White v. Garden* (1851) 10 CB 919.

[67] Thus in *Spence v. Crawford* [1939] 3 All ER 271 rescission was allowed and restitution of the shares sold by the plaintiff ordered although the fraudulent defendant had dealt with the shares.

[68] *Ibid*. For example, rescission was barred in *Clarke v. Dickson, Williams and Gibbs* (1858) El Bl & El 148 where the plaintiff bought shares in a partnership but converted it into a limited liability company; and in *Vigers v. Pike* (1842) 8 Cl & F 562 where the plaintiff bought a mine and sought to rescind after it had been worked out. See also *Sheffield Nickel and Silver Planting Co. Ltd v. Unwin* (1877) 2 QBD 218; *Thorpe v. Fasey* [1949] Ch 649.

[69] See *O'Sullivan v. Management Agency & Music Ltd* [1985] QB 428 where a partly performed contract to manage a popular singer was rescinded. The defendant had to account for their profits but credit was given to them for their skill and labour in promoting the plaintiff and making a significant contribution to his success. See also *Atlantic Lines & Navigation Co. Inc. v. Hallam Ltd* [1983] 1 Lloyd's Rep 188 at 202.

embodied in three of the traditional bars to rescission: restitution impossible; counter-restitution impossible; and attachment of third-party rights to the subject of the restitutionary claim. The rigidity of this position has been relaxed somewhat so that some money adjustments have been permitted where precise return in kind is impossible,[70] particularly in the case of bad faith defendants[71] (so that on this limited level, the unjust factors matter). Even so, such monetary substitution is only possible where the 'substantial identity of the subject matter of the contract remains'.[72] In practice then, these bars can continue to block restitutionary claims.

(b) English position unsatisfactory

To describe this state of affairs as unsatisfactory puts the matter mildly. The unjust factors of duress, fraud and exploitation express strong policies in favour of restitution, namely protecting vulnerable plaintiffs and refusing to assist unconscientious defendants. Those policies are subverted when these bars are triggered. If the defendant has been unjustly enriched at the plaintiff's expense then, affirmation and undue delay aside, the law should automatically allow the plaintiff to avoid the contract and claim restitution, if necessary in money's worth. The plaintiff should not have to show additionally that both parties can still return substantially what they received. This is the straightforward position in German law.

---

[70] In *Erlanger v. New Sombrero Phosphate Co.* (1878) 3 App Cas 1218 at 1278 Lord Blackburn held that a Court of Equity can give relief by way of rescission whenever by the exercise of its powers it can do what is practically just by directing accounts, ordering equitable compensation and making allowances when it cannot restore the parties precisely to their pre-contractual position. More recently, in *Smith New Court Securities Ltd v. Scrimgeour Vickers (Asset Management) Ltd* [1997] AC 254 at 262, Lord Browne-Wilkinson suggested, obiter, the possibility of allowing *substitute* in species restitution in the case of a fungible asset such as shares in a public company. He said that since 'identical shares can be purchased on the market, the defrauded purchaser can offer substantial restitutio in integrum which is normally sufficient'. Ewan McKendrick identifies the potential problem of the plaintiff profiting by acquiring the substitute shares more cheaply than it sold them and suggests a solution. See his 'Total Failure of Consideration and Counter-restitution: Two Issues or One?' in: Peter Birks (ed.), *Laundering and Tracing* (1995), 217, 233–6. This unnecessary complication is avoidable if counter-restitution can be worked out wholly in money.

[71] Where a contract has been induced by fraud, the courts are particularly ready to give the victim rescission – *Spence v. Crawford* [1939] 3 All ER 271 at 288–9 *per* Lord Wright: 'The court will be less prepared to pull a contract to pieces where the defendant is innocent, whereas in the case of fraud the court will exercise its jurisdiction to the full in order, if possible, to prevent the defendant from enjoying the benefit of his fraud at the expense of the innocent plaintiff. Restoration, however, is essential to the idea of restitution ... The court can go a long way in ordering restitution if the substantial identity of the subject matter of the contract remains.'

[72] *Ibid.* at 289.

The English position can leave admittedly unjust situations unremedied; the discredited contract and its admittedly unsupportable terms are left standing and the plaintiff is sent away empty-handed (aside from any possible rights in tort[73]). The defendant retains the unjust enrichment and the plaintiff can be made liable in damages for breach of this unfair contract, even if specific performance of it can be resisted. This makes English law's ability to reverse unjust enrichment on rescission, being confined to the return of money and substantially subsisting property, embarrassingly feeble. It is too easily derailed from the task of conferring the protection underlying the unjust factors. The position is indefensible. The way out is clear.

(c) Mutual restitution in money

English unjust enrichment law must recognise, as German law does, that *all* forms of benefits are returnable, if necessary by translation into money. Currently non-contractual claims for goods and services (*quantum meruit* and *quantum valebat*) can be personal claims (that is, for money's worth). Claims for the return of money, even on rescission of contract, can be personal (the exact notes and coins transferred need not be traced). It is then an unjustifiable and intolerable asymmetry to insist that non-money claims on rescission be confined to the vehicle of proprietary claims. If English law is prepared to make small money adjustments to *supplement* a plaintiff's counter-restitution of substantially subsisting property, then it should be prepared to make big adjustments, even to the extent of wholly *substituting* for the benefit that is unreturnable in kind. The same arguments apply to the mode of effecting the defendant's restitutionary liability. Impossibility of precise return in kind by either party should not bar rescission.

If mutual restitution can be monetised, it will usually yield a net balance to the plaintiff. This outcome not only gives teeth to the unjust factors where precise return is impossible, it can also be described as a fitting response to the consequences of contracts induced by duress, fraud or exploitation. For plaintiffs, these unjust factors generally yield inappropriate or disproportionately unfavourable exchanges, while defendants are left with disproportionately favourable or otherwise undeserved advantages. In theory, the law can respond in two ways. First, it can undo the

---

[73] Compensation is available for deceit and negligent misrepresentation and under the Misrepresentation Act 1969 in English law. But contracts induced by duress or exploitation suggest no obvious torts. In so far as there is a tort (e.g. of deceit or intimidation) the plaintiff can recover all his losses including the value of his own performance towards the defendant (in German law see §§ 249, 823(2) BGB).

exchange and take the parties 'back to zero'. The precise mutual return in kind envisaged here is the traditional mode of restitution mandated by rescission. It is the most sure-fire way of negating inappropriate exchanges or eliminating disproportionate ones and it has the added attraction of avoiding the need to value the mutual performances.

The second method is simply to eliminate the difference or disproportion between the values transferred. Here, unjust enrichment signifies *excessive* enrichment and only that *part* is returned. That there is no enrichment save in the difference can be clearly seen in the award of the difference between the parties' mutual payments in the famous swaps case *Westdeutsche Landesbank Girozentrale v. Islington LBC*.[74] To adopt this approach on the rescission of contract might alarm traditionalists steeped in the idea that the law has no mandate to reshape contracts but only to set them aside. One reply is that eliminating the difference meets head on the problem of disproportion raised by the rescission of executed contracts. Moreover, even the adjustment of continuing contracts is not unknown in English contract law, although rarely conceded as such.[75] A less controversial reply is that working out the balance and eliminating the difference may be the only constructive response where going 'back to zero' is impossible. This is the *Saldo*, which German law uses in effecting mutual restitution on rescission.

2. Mutual restitution and value surviving

One reason for barring a defendant in good faith from the defence of change of position is to avoid subverting the policies underlying certain unjust factors. Another reason lies in the logic of the German *Saldotheorie*.

(a) *Saldotheorie*

The idea behind the German *Saldotheorie*[76] is that the law's concern to protect innocent defendants' security of receipt via change of position must be heavily qualified by the *mutuality* inherent in contractual performance. The receipt of contractual performance is conditional and not absolute in

---

[74] [1996] AC 669.
[75] The most obvious examples are rescission on terms in mistake cases; the adjustment of extortionate credit bargains; doctrines which allow particular terms of the contract to be struck out leaving the rest of the contract on foot (restraint of trade, penalties, forfeitures and particular exclusion and exemption of liability clauses); the awarding of damages in lieu of rescission under section 2(2) of the Misrepresentation Act 1969; and the controversial possibility of *partial* rescission which has already been discussed above at Section IV, 5. and on which more will be said at Section VI, 4.
[76] See generally Markesinis, Lorenz and Dannemann, *Law of Contracts*, 764–6; Zimmermann and Du Plessis, 'Basic features', 40–2; Visser, 'Rethinking Unjustified Enrichment', 203.

nature; it is premised on the recipient's own transfer given in exchange. This mutuality persists through the contract's invalidity and a defendant cannot deny it by seeking full counter-restitution while not giving full restitution. This reasoning applies equally to the plaintiff so that, prima facie, neither party can reduce their liability to account for the value received from the other if full restitution of the value conferred on the other is sought. Thus, if the plaintiff pays $10,000 for a car which is worth only $6,000, on rescission the plaintiff must give credit for the $6,000 of value received even if the car is subsequently written off. Likewise, the defendant must give credit for the $10,000 received even if the money has been given to charity or lost in a fire. This would yield a net award of $4,000 to the plaintiff.

(b) *Saldotheorie*, unjust factors and the plaintiff's change of position

The *Saldotheorie* puts the risk of the loss of enrichment on the recipient while the change of position defence puts that risk on the transferor. In German law it is apparent that the nature of the unjust factor triggering rescission influences the allocation of that risk. Even fraudulent minors are not shut out of the change of position defence. But so strong is the protective policy underlying minority that it can also displace the *Saldotheorie*, so minors in bad faith need only return the enrichment surviving yet can claim back the full enrichment transferred even from adults in good faith who have lost some of that enrichment.

The *Saldotheorie* is similarly displaced where it would protect defendants who are in bad faith or undeserving from the loss of their transfers in the plaintiffs' hands. In the example given, a strict application of the *Saldotheorie* would require the plaintiff to account fully for the $6,000 value of the car even if its total loss is attributable to the defendant's fraud (say, in misrepresenting the condition of the brakes). To counter this potential unfairness, it has been held that where fraud, duress or immorality (analogous to exploitation in English law) vitiates the contract, defendants are required to return the value received while plaintiffs need only account for the value surviving. This is the *Zweikondiktionenlehre*.[77] But while this solution meets one type of unfairness it can create another because of its insufficient sensitivity to how the plaintiff lost the enrichment. One case illustrates the problem.[78] The plaintiff bought a used car relying on

---

[77] See Zimmermann and Du Plessis, 'Basic Features', 42; Markesinis, Lorenz and Dannemann, *Law of Contracts*, 765.

[78] BGH 14 October 1971, BGHZ 57, 137, 141 ff. cited in Markesinis, Lorenz and Dannemann, *Law of Contracts*, 765.

the defendant's fraudulent misrepresentation that it had never been in an accident. Three weeks later, the car was wrecked through the plaintiff's negligence. The damage was not attributable to the car's previous accident yet, because of the fraud, the *Bundesgerichtshof* allowed the plaintiff to rely on change of position while also recovering the full price paid for the car. The injustice of this result indicates that the availability of change of position to plaintiffs should not only depend on the nature of the operative unjust factor but, analogous to the defendant's change of position,[79] must also be sensitive to how the loss was occasioned.

(c) Should English law recognise change of position for the plaintiff?

In cases of fraud, duress or exploitation, English law largely disqualifies defendants from change of position. If mutual restitution by money substitute is allowed, the position would largely mirror the German *Saldotheorie*. This would be a positive development. But should English law go further and admit the German exceptions to the *Saldotheorie*, which essentially permit plaintiffs to reduce their counter-restitution by reference to their change of position? The notion may raise some eyebrows but it deserves serious consideration.

First, if the aim of restitution is to remove defendants' unjust enrichment and the aim of counter-restitution is to remove plaintiffs' unjust enrichment[80] then, as a matter of symmetry, change of position should be potentially available to neither or to both in working out mutual restitution. Secondly, the plaintiff's change of position is already implicitly recognised in cases where counter-restitution is satisfied by the return of severely depreciated property.[81] Moreover, it seems that plaintiffs at fault are disqualified from relying on this type of change of position. In *Alati v. Kruger*,[82] the plaintiff rescinded his purchase of a fruit shop for

---

[79] See discussion above, 170–3.

[80] See *MacKenzie v. Royal Bank of Canada* [1934] AC 468. This is not uncontroversial since counter-restitution is usually said to be aimed at restoring the defendant to his *status quo ante* – that is, his position before the contract was made – which is suggestive of a tortious measure.

[81] For example, in *Adam v. Newbigging* (1888) 13 App Cas 308 at 330 the partnership contract was rescinded although it was by then 'worse than worthless'. The Court said that to bar rescission 'would be to say that where a losing and insolvent business is sold by means of the representation that it is solvent and profitable, rescission could never be obtained if the loss were increased prior to the discovery of the true state of affairs'. See also *Armstrong v. Jackson* [1917] 2 KB 822, where a contract for the purchase of shares was set aside on return of the shares and account given for the dividends received despite a substantial intervening fall in their value, from £3 to 5 shillings.

[82] (1955) 94 CLR 216 at 225.

fraudulent misrepresentation as to its average takings and abandoned the shop after the hearing but before the judgment. He obtained restitution and was permitted to return the deteriorated business without compensation to the defendant since 'it was not due to any fault on the [plaintiff's] part'. The High Court of Australia noted that 'even at common law the necessity to return property in its original condition was qualified so as to allow incidents for which the buyer was not responsible, such as those to which the property was liable ... from its inherent nature (cf. *Adam v. Newbigging* ...)'.[83] But such change of position is limited. Fullager J explained that:

> a purchaser remaining in possession after giving notice of rescission is under a duty to take reasonable care to preserve the property, so that what he has received from the other party may, so far as reasonably practicable, be restored to the other party... If he commits a breach of this duty and deterioration results, one of two consequences may follow... The court may find, having regard to the conduct of the purchaser, that it would not be equitable to decree rescission. *Or ... the court may make it a condition of the decree that the purchaser shall compensate the vendor in respect of the deterioration of the property.*[84]

If plaintiffs are admitted to change of position, what types of loss should count? Loss of the actual receipt which is causally attributable to the unjust factor should be allowed,[85] as should such loss occasioned by external factors.[86] As a matter of symmetry with good-faith defendants,[87] it may also be appropriate to allow plaintiffs to write off expenditure in attempted performance for the defendant's benefit or in accordance with the defendant's wishes. Suppose the mother superior in *Allcard v. Skinner* had sold a donated vehicle to the plaintiff (a religious zealot) for an exorbitant price: on rescission for presumed undue influence, if she is permitted to write off the sums spent on the charitable purposes subscribed to by the plaintiff, then it would seem distinctly unbalanced not to allow the plaintiff to write off his loss from crashing the vehicle while delivering food to the poor and needy, consistent with the mother superior's instructions.

On the other hand, the German experience indicates the desirability of being responsive to how the loss occurred. For example, it could be suggested that plaintiffs should not be able to discount loss or depreciation

---

[83] Ibid. at 225. [84] Ibid. at 228 (emphasis added).
[85] See above, nn. 81 and 83 and accompanying text.
[86] As in *Alati v. Kruger* (1955) 94 CLR 216, where devaluation of the fruit shop to be returned was due to the opening of a supermarket nearby.
[87] See above, 170–2.

caused by their own negligence or intended use (aside from the exceptional expenditure in favour, or consistent with the wishes, of the defendant just mentioned). This is one explanation[88] for the outcome in *Wiebe v. Butchart's Motors Ltd*,[89] where a contract for the sale of a car induced by the seller's misrepresentation was rescinded on condition that the buyer pay the seller $600 for the deterioration of the car, which had been used continuously since the sale.

VI. Unjust factors and valuation of the enrichment received

Enrichment may be primary (that initially received) or secondary (that derived *from* the initial enrichment, such as the fruits, profits and the user value). The restitution of secondary enrichment raises extremely difficult issues since it overlaps with questions of tracing proprietary rights, restitution for wrongs and whether such derivative enrichments are 'at the plaintiff's expense'. These knots will not be untangled here. The point to be advanced can be made with reference to the primary enrichment received; doubtless a similar exercise with secondary enrichments is possible.

1. Subjective devaluation

If English law accepts the possibility of mutual restitution in money's worth, particularly where restitution in kind is impossible, the issue becomes purely one of valuation. The potential difficulties in this exercise may be one reason for barring rescission once exact restoration is impossible. But this cannot justify the retention of these bars. Courts are constantly called upon to monetise things that are difficult to monetise, such as arms and legs and nervous shock in tort actions. Valuing the benefits conferred by mutual performances is problematic, but no more problematic.

One solution would be simply to impose the objective value. This is largely the German approach.[90] However, a recipient who cannot return in kind should be entitled to say 'Had it not been for the unjust factor I would not have wanted the transfer at its objective price, or indeed,

---

[88] Another is that the proper measure of counter-restitution includes not only the primary enrichment transferred but also the secondary enrichment derived from its user.

[89] [1949] 4 DLR (NS) 838; see also *Addison v. Ottawa Auto and Taxi Co.* (1916) 16 DLR 318.

[90] Markesinis, Lorenz and Dannemann, *Law of Contracts*, 760–2.

at all. It is not worth that to *me*.' This problem is described by Birks as that of 'subjective devaluation'.[91] German law has been criticised for being insufficiently sensitive to its claim. Indeed, the indiscriminate imposition of objective values in unjust enrichment claims 'could seriously disturb the equilibrium which the law of contract attempts to establish between the parties, by denying the existence of a contractual obligation. In other words, restitution would stop to remedy the unjust situations which other areas of law have created, and end up creating unjust situations which other areas of the law aim to prevent.'[92]

Unjust enrichment law should not impose a forced sale at the objective value despite the rescission of the contract and so undermine the logic of the unjust factors. In the valuation exercise, it is German law's turn to learn from English law. English courts and academics have utilised a number of tests to overcome the plea of subjective devaluation.[93] Sensitivity to the impact of particular unjust factors can reveal which of these different tests are appropriate in determining the existence and the value of the relevant benefit to their recipients.

2. Valuing the defendant's enrichment

Where the defendant's receipt results from the plaintiff's attempted contractual performance, the existence of enrichment to the defendant can be established by the 'bargained-for' or 'reprehensible seeking out' tests. The defendant has sought the benefit by contracting for it or otherwise unconscientiously procuring or accepting it. Her consent is untainted and she is not the intended beneficiary of any unjust factor so she must be taken to value its receipt. But how much she values that receipt cannot be determined by reference to the value fixed in the vitiated contract, otherwise the policy underlying the contractual invalidity would be subverted. The defendant cannot be heard to say: 'To *me*, it is only worth the little I agreed to pay.' The defendant's unconscientious procurement or receipt of that benefit (in the first or second categories), should fix her to its objective value.

---

[91] Birks, *Introduction*, 109–14. This terminology was first used judicially by Hoffmann LJ in *Ministry of Defence v. Ashman* (1993) 66 P & CR 195.

[92] Markesinis, Lorenz and Dannemann, *Law of Contracts*, 761–2.

[93] See generally *BP Exploration Co. (Libya) Ltd v. Hunt (No. 2)* [1979] 1 WLR 783; *Ministry of Defence v. Ashman* (1993) 66 P & CR 195; *Procter & Gamble Philippine Manufacturing Corp v. Peter Cremer GmbH* [1988] 3 All ER 843; and see Goff and Jones, *Law of Restitution*, 16–33; Birks, *Introduction*, 114 ff.; Burrows, *Law of Restitution*, 7–16; discussing tests such as 'incontrovertible benefit', 'bargained-for', 'reprehensible seeking out' and 'free acceptance'.

On the other hand, there may be a case for allowing innocent defendants (in the third category) subjectively to devalue their receipts. In non-contractual contexts the devaluation should stop at the 'incontrovertible benefit', that is, the realised, or readily realisable, benefit received or the saving of necessary expense by the defendant. For example, in *Ministry of Defence v. Ashman*[94] the defendant lost the right to occupy the plaintiff's premises when her husband, a member of the Royal Air Force, moved out. Although she stayed on with her children, she could not be said to have reprehensibly sought out, or freely accepted, the benefit as she had nowhere else to go pending rehousing by the local authority. She was undoubtedly benefited since the court found that she would otherwise have had to pay for alternative accommodation. However, the value to her was fixed by reference to the cost of the council housing for which she had applied. This was a quarter of the market rental of the plaintiff's property and was fixed as the 'incontrovertible benefit' to her for which she had to account to the plaintiff.

In the context of failed contracts, whether void, discharged, terminated or rescinded, the prices contained in such contracts can nevertheless provide evidence of the value which the innocent defendant attached to the plaintiff's transfer on the 'bargained-for' test. For example, in *Boyd & Forrest v. Glasgow & South Western Railway*[95] the plaintiff's claim to rescind an executed contract to build a railway, on the ground of the defendant's innocent misrepresentation, was denied for the ludicrous reason that the plaintiff's services in building the railway could not be returned. Consistent with what has been argued, rescission should be granted and restitution by way of a *quantum meruit* limited by the contract price awarded.[96]

Even in contractual situations, where the 'incontrovertible benefit' clearly exceeds the 'bargained-for' price, it may be a moot point which measure is more consistent with the reason for restitution underlying the operative unjust factor. For example, if an innocent mother superior, believing she was aiding a young convert's discipleship, engages her to work for trifling pay around the convent, on a finding of presumed undue influence, restitution of the 'incontrovertible benefit' which the young convert's labours conferred may be appropriate. The value of the crooked

---

[94] (1993) 66 P & CR 195. [95] 1915 SC (HL) 20.
[96] Burrows, *Law of Restitution*, 136, and see 269 in respect of the valuation of the plaintiff's claim where failure of consideration follows discharge of the contract for breach.

fence she builds or her shabby laundering services may be much less than the notional hourly market rate of her labour but it may also exceed the paltry contract rate.

3. Valuing the plaintiff's enrichment

The existence and value of the plaintiff's enrichment is more complicated. The law should be responsive to the impact of the operative unjust factor on the value of the defendants' transfers to the plaintiffs since they are the unjust factors' intended beneficiaries. First, the unjust factor could make the transfer wholly inappropriate or unwanted by the plaintiff. For example, the plaintiff may obtain something that she would never have wanted had she known the truth[97] or not been unfairly pressurised; or the benefit may be wholly inappropriate to her circumstances, even at market value.[98] If this is so, counter-restitution should only be required of the 'incontrovertible benefit' conferred on the plaintiff. Secondly, the plaintiff could have obtained something which he clearly values, but the unjust factors indicate that he should not have had to pay for it. For example, when a contract modification is set aside for duress, the plaintiff need not pay the extra sum promised since he is entitled to the defendant's performance without paying more.[99] There are other examples.[100] In such cases, the plaintiff's enrichment is non-existent or not 'unjust'.

---

[97] For example, in *Kettlewell v. Refuge Assurance Co.* [1908] 1 KB 545 the defendant's fraudulent misrepresentation induced the plaintiff to pay insurance premiums for four years; rescission was allowed although counter-restitution of the benefit from the defendant (the insurer was on risk and would have had to pay if the risk had eventuated) was impossible. No payouts were made. If it had been otherwise, the plaintiff should have had to make an allowance of her incontrovertible benefit.

[98] For example, in *Gaertner v. Fiesta Dance Studios Ltd* (1973) 32 DLR 3d 639, the plaintiff, a young woman, contracted for 551 hours of dancing lessons owing to her gullibility and loneliness.

[99] Of course, the concern to protect the plaintiff from the pressure applied by a defendant's threat to breach the original contract may be outweighed by other policy considerations such as the prevention of waste. The concern to ensure that projects are brought to fruition without undue waste even if more must be paid has manifested itself in a higher degree of coercion being required which is then deemed not to have been met in certain cases, for example, *The Siboen and the Sibotre* [1976] AC 104 and *Pao On v. Lau Yiu Long* [1980] AC 64.

[100] This accounts for *Kiriri Cotton Co. v. Dewani* [1960] AC 102, where the plaintiff paid an illegal premium to obtain a tenancy. Since the illegality seeks to protect those in need of rental accommodation, the plaintiff could recover the premium without giving up the tenancy.

Lastly, the unjust factor may have resulted in the plaintiff paying too much for something that he undoubtedly values. Where there is no evidence of how much less the plaintiff values the receipt, it may be appropriate to lower the value to the market price. This is one explanation for the salvage cases tucked away in the Admiralty jurisdiction, where exorbitant prices charged for rescue services are substituted by reasonable awards.[101] Similar considerations may colour the adjustment of extortionate credit contracts permitted in English law[102] and the outcome in the recent decision of *McGuire v. Makaronis*.[103] Where there *is* some indication what lower value the receipt held for the plaintiff, it may well be defensible to hold him to that, whether on the 'incontrovertible benefit' or the 'bargained-for' tests, along the lines discussed as being appropriate for innocent defendants.[104]

Taking into account available evidence of the value of the receipt *to* the plaintiff explains two other phenomena. First, where a contract modification is set aside for duress, it accounts for why the plaintiff must still pay what was agreed under the original contract for the defendant's performance. Even if that original contract is not automatically revived to regulate the defendant's entitlement in contract,[105] it is nevertheless evidence of the plaintiff's untainted valuation of the defendant's performance for which counter-restitution should be made. This counter-restitution can be seen as being effected by partial rescission of the modified contract. Partial rescission is the second phenomenon illuminated by this approach to valuation.

---

[101] For example, see *The Port Caledonia and The Anna* [1903] P 184 where a reasonable sum of £200 was substituted for the contract price of £1,000.

[102] Sections 137–40 of the Consumer Credit Act 1974 allow English courts to reopen extortionate credit agreements to do justice between the parties. The German practice of partial rescission in usury cases leaving an interest-free loan seems justifiable only in the interest of deterrence.

[103] (1997) 144 ALR 729. There, solicitors provided bridging finance to clients on the security of their home without disclosing their interest in the mortgage. The High Court agreed with the lower court that the mortgage should be set aside but required the clients to repay the money with interest, not at the contract rate, but at the commercial rate.

[104] See above, nn. 94–6.

[105] The Court in *Pao On v. Lau Yiu Long* [1980] AC 64 regarded as grossly unfair to the defendants the plaintiff's argument that they were not bound to pay anything for the defendant's performance because (i) the original contract was put to an end by the modification and not binding, and (ii) the modification was tainted by duress and also not binding. This no doubt contributed to the court's finding that no economic duress vitiated the modification.

4. Partial rescission again
(a) Subjective devaluation of counter-restitution
This controversial remedy may be supportable as an expression of exceptional change of position.[106] But an even better explanation of partial rescission is simply as a *means* of effecting counter-restitution of the subjectively devalued enrichment of the plaintiff, on particular facts. The reversal of unjust enrichment involved in counter-restitution can be achieved by negating the impact of the unjust factors. If an unjust factor has induced the plaintiff to pay too much for the benefit received, she should be able to devalue it subjectively to that which she would have been prepared to pay (in the absence of the unjust factor) and make counter-restitution of that. Where the unjust factor is *solely*[107] a misrepresentation as to the price the plaintiff is paying (or, in an *O'Brien* case, the risk being assumed) in return for the defendant's performance, the represented price or risk which the plaintiff agreed to, may evidence her actual valuation of the defendant's performance. If so, holding the plaintiff to that representation is a defensible expression of her counter-restitution on rescission.

(b) Valuing counter-restitution where performance moves to a third party
In principle, this way of subjectively devaluing the plaintiff's counter-restitution should hold even if the defendant's performance moves towards a third party rather than to the plaintiff. *MacKenzie v. Royal Bank of Canada*[108] takes the contrary position, denying the existence of any benefit to the plaintiff in such circumstances, so that no counter-restitutionary obligation is said to arise. But is this reasoning sound? If a plaintiff buys a car or piano lessons for her son, on rescission (say) for innocent misrepresentation, it would seem offensive to allow the plaintiff to recover all her money without giving any allowance for the value of the car or the lessons simply because the plaintiff did not personally receive them.[109] Yet that is the logical outcome of *MacKenzie*. Even though the defendant's performance does not move towards the plaintiff, she can still be said to

---

[106] See above, 173–4.
[107] In *O'Brien* situations this will often not be the case. Even if the operative unjust factor is this sort of misrepresentation, there will often be overtones of undue influence or breach of fiduciary duty owed to the plaintiff or the misrepresentations about the extent of the risk assumed will imply other facts, namely about the health and viability of the business being supported.
[108] [1934] AC 468.
[109] Although, in theory at least, the defendant may appeal to change of position.

have benefited since she has achieved the very end she sought[110] and for which she would have had to pay.

This view of benefit is consistent with contract law's conception of valuable consideration. More importantly in this context, it is also a corollary of the idea of subjective devaluation. The issue is the value or benefit of the defendant's performance to the plaintiff. The fact that the plaintiff has chosen to route that performance towards a third party does not in itself extinguish the benefit to the plaintiff. This can be expressed in restitutionary language: the plaintiff has received the incontrovertible benefit of saving expenses, expenses which she would have had to incur to achieve her desired end. This approach also respects the conditionality inherent in contractual exchanges expressed by the *Saldotheorie*. A's retention of B's performance is premised on A's own counterperformance. Thus, A cannot deny this conditionality by claiming restitution of his own performance while denying counter-restitution of B's performance, simply because the latter moved to a third party, designated by A. This is consistent with the view of the English Law Commission[111] and with section 1(6) of the Law Reform (Frustrated Contracts) Act 1943 in English law, which allows one party to claim, for the value of benefits conferred, against a second party who has promised to pay for the work benefiting a third party.

It can be objected that *O'Brien* itself appears to regard the plaintiff who receives no direct transfer as being 'manifestly disadvantaged'. But closer inspection shows that the doctrine distinguishes clearly between appearances and reality. The appearance of manifest disadvantage, because the plaintiff receives no direct transfer, along with the appearance of a surety/primary-debtor relationship which is at risk of abuse, give rise to a finding of constructive notice on the defendant's part which facilitates the plaintiff's restitutionary claim consistent with the underlying protective policy. But no relief is available unless an independent unjust factor (which may require actual manifest disadvantage) actually taints the dealing between the surety and the primary debtor. The policy of protection may warrant easing the plaintiff's evidentiary burden against the lender, by presuming the relevant knowledge where the plaintiff appears to receive no direct benefit. But it should not extend to absolving the plaintiff from giving counter-restitution where there is untainted

---

[110] But it would be otherwise if the impact of the unjust factor was to render the defendant's transfer valueless to the plaintiff, as where the defendant is unqualified to teach piano or the car is not roadworthy.

[111] Report No. 121, 'Law of Contract: Pecuniary Restitution on Breach of Contract' (1983), § 2.47.

evidence that the plaintiff does attribute a particular value to the defendant's transfer.

(c) What the cases say

Support for this position can be found in the outcome of some cases. In the Australian High Court's decision in *Vadasz v. Pioneer Concrete (SA) Pty Ltd*,[112] the defendant misrepresented that the guarantee sought from the plaintiff only covered the company's future indebtedness when it in fact also extended to its past indebtedness. Only the latter part of the guarantee was rescinded.[113] The same result was arrived at by the English High Court in *Bank Melli Iran v. Samadi-Rad*,[114] an *O'Brien* type of case. On the reasoning that she who sought equity must also do equity, the Court required the plaintiff, as a condition of relief, to recognise the security to the extent of the lesser amount misrepresented to her as her maximum liability.

The real objection seems to be the packaging of this as 'partial rescission', with its suggestion that the defendant is only making partial restitution. In *TSB Bank plc v. Camfield*[115] the Court of Appeal unanimously denied this possibility. There, a husband innocently misrepresented to his wife that the charge over their home to support his overdraft was limited to £15,000. The defendant was fixed with constructive notice of this and, at first instance, the charge was partially rescinded to leave a subsisting charge against her for £15,000 because the wife was 'quite prepared to risk' that sum.[116] But the Court of Appeal set aside the charge in its entirety on the reasoning that rescission 'is an all or nothing' process and the right 'of the representee, not that of the court'. Further, that if the rescission was lawful, it was not the Court's proper role to 'grant equitable relief to which terms may be attached'.[117]

Rejection of partial rescission in these terms does not necessarily prevent acceptance of rescission as total and as the right of the plaintiff, but still requiring the plaintiff as a condition of rescission to make counter-restitution of the value of the defendant's performance (if necessary on terms). This is quite different from any suggestion of imposing terms to do some vague and arbitrary justice rejected in *Camfield*. Moreover, it should

---

[112] (1995) 184 CLR 102.
[113] But note that *McGuire v. Makaronis* (1997) 144 ALR 729 at 744 distinguishes *Vadasz* where fraud was assumed on the basis that the 'scope of rescission may be determined by the nature and extent of the conduct giving rise to the equity for rescission'.
[114] [1995] 1 Federal Court Reporter 465.   [115] [1995] 1 WLR 430.   [116] *Ibid.* at 433.
[117] *Ibid.* at 439.

be unobjectionable for counter-restitution to be effected by fixing a charge on what is to be recovered by the plaintiff, akin to the imposition of a lien in *Cooper v. Phibbs*.[118] The result is the same (retaining a partial charge on the security rescinded), but the reasoning falls squarely within the traditional view of rescission and the principles of unjust enrichment, both of which require counter-restitution on restitution. This approach has the added advantage of enabling an outcome which Nourse LJ concedes in *Camfield* as one marked by 'morality, perhaps justice in an abstract sense'.[119]

Partial rescission as a means of effecting counter-restitution is suggested in *Vadasz*. The High Court of Australia said that 'the justification for not setting aside the transaction in its entirety or in doing so subject to conditions' is 'to prevent one party obtaining an unwarranted benefit at the expense of the other'.[120] In *Samadi-Rad*,[121] the English High Court approved Wigram V-C's statement in *Hanson v. Keating*:[122]

The equity of the obligor [plaintiff] is to have the entire transaction rescinded. The court will do this so as to remit both parties to their original position: it will not relieve the obligor [plaintiff] from his liability, leaving him in possession of the fruits of the illegal [vitiated] transaction he complains of. I know of no case which cannot be explained upon this or analogous reasoning... the court can never lawfully impose arbitrary conditions upon a plaintiff... but can only require him to give the defendant that which... is the right of the defendant in respect of the subject of the suit.

In *Samadi-Rad*, effecting counter-restitution was accepted as '[t]he basis on which the court can, without rewriting the parties' bargain, impose terms as a condition to recognising the wife's claim to relief'.[123]

Of course, such partial rescission is only warranted if the court is satisfied that the plaintiff would have contracted on the basis represented. This was so in *Vadasz*. The High Court said: '[I]t cannot be maintained that the appellant would not have entered into the guarantee had it been confined' in the way that he was led to believe. 'Rather, the evidence is that he would have done so, if not happily, because it was the only way to secure' the defendant's desired performance.[124] On the other hand, if the court finds that the plaintiff would not have agreed in the absence of

---

[118] (1867) LR 2 HL 149. The contract was rescinded for mistake and a lien was granted over the fishery returned to the plaintiff in response to the money spent by the defendants improving the property.
[119] [1995] 1 WLR 430 at 437.   [120] (1995) 184 CLR 102 at 114.
[121] [1995] 1 Federal Court Reporter 465 at 476.   [122] (1844) 4 Hare 1 at 6.
[123] [1995] 1 Federal Court Reporter 465 at 477.   [124] (1995) 184 CLR 102 at 115.

the unjust factor, then the plaintiff should only be obliged to account for any incontrovertible benefit received,[125] which may be nil.

In *Commercial Bank of Australia v. Amadio*,[126] the plaintiffs' son misrepresented to them that his overdraft, which they were securing, was limited to $50,000 and for six months only. The High Court of Australia set aside the security in its entirety as an unconscionable bargain. Deane J had considered 'setting aside the guarantee/mortgage only to the extent . . . in excess of $50,000', but he concluded that the plaintiffs would not have entered the transaction at all had they known their son's true financial position.[127] The same explanation accounts for the total rescission in *MacKenzie v. Royal Bank of Canada*.[128] The bank had misrepresented to the plaintiff that her shares, which had secured previous loans to her husband, were already lost and that her signing the new guarantee 'offered the only means of salving them'.[129] In the absence of this misrepresentation, the plaintiff would never have entered the contract at all. *Camfield* bears the same interpretation. The charge was set aside completely because 'had the true nature of the legal charge been known to the wife she would not have entered into the charge and the enjoyment of her home would never have been at risk'.[130] These are not cases where the plaintiffs would have valued the benefits even at the lower risks represented. In *O'Brien* situations such misrepresentations often imply further misrepresentations about the viability and health of the business which the charge is supporting. Moreover, the whole situation is often coloured by undue influence.

VII. Conclusion

Unjust factors are irrelevant only in so far as the absence of cause for the transfer, for any reason, should prima facie admit the plaintiff to a restitutionary claim. But that is just the beginning. In working out the precise details of the restitutionary response, the nature of the unjust factors, embodying the reasons for restitution, come to the fore. First, they explain why the change of position defence is not available to unconscientious defendants and why that disqualification should extend to some innocent defendants. Secondly, they point to the logic of dissolving certain bars to

---

[125] The quantification problems may be extremely complex, see *Dunbar Bank plc v. Nadeem* [1998] 3 All ER 876 at 885 and 887, but the principle is clear.
[126] (1983) 151 CLR 447.
[127] *Ibid.* at 481. See discussion in *Vadasz v. Pioneer Concrete (SA) Pty Ltd* (1995) 184 CLR 102 at 115.
[128] [1934] AC 468.   [129] *Ibid.* at 474 and 476.
[130] *TSB Bank plc v. Camfield* [1995] 1 WLR 430 at 439.

rescission in English law and of extending change of position to reduce the plaintiff's counter-restitution. Thirdly, in valuing enrichment, they signal the need in English and German law to allow the parties, especially plaintiffs, subjectively to revalue their enrichments to reflect the impact of the unjust factors. Lastly, this process of revaluation can offer a justification for the remedy of partial rescission.

Even German law, with its single ground of absence of cause, is not indifferent to the unjust factors.[131] The precise reason for invalidating a transfer affects when a defendant's restitutionary liability is reducible to the enrichment surviving (analogous to the English change of position), and when the *Saldotheorie* should be ousted, in favour of the *Zweikondiktionentheorie*, to allow for the plaintiff's change of position. The call for German law to show greater sensitivity to the unjust factors in valuing the enrichments received has also been discussed above. Moreover, it is evident that the single-ground approach can generate restitutionary liability which is both overinclusive and underinclusive, necessitating further qualifications to generate satisfactory outcomes. I will conclude with two examples from the field of duress.

The general enrichment action would logically confer a claim on one who makes an undue transfer even if it is made deliberately and without mistake. This necessitates the first qualification: §814 BGB bars restitution if the plaintiff knew at the time of performance that there was no obligation to perform. This bar essentially functions as the unjust factor of mistake in English law. But, since this no-mistake bar operates as a *general* defence to a *general* action, a further complication arises necessitating a further qualification. Plaintiffs induced to make transfers under duress usually know that they are not legally obliged to do so and a straightforward application of § 814 BGB would bar restitution here. Without an unjust factors approach 'other mechanisms have been found in order to ensure that § 814 BGB does not defeat restitution in most cases of duress and imbalance of bargaining power ... thus, ... the defence of knowledge only applies to performance which has been made voluntarily, i.e. without pressure having been applied, and for this reason will not defeat restitution cases of compulsion'.[132]

A second example illustrates how inappropriate outcomes can result from a failure to acknowledge the unjust factors. The general ground of absence of cause confers no restitutionary action where 'the transaction which took place was based on a valid legal cause but has, nevertheless, led

---

[131] See generally Zweigert and Kötz, *Introduction*, 557.
[132] Markesinis, Lorenz and Dannemann, *Law of Contracts*, 763.

to an unjust shift of wealth between two people'.[133] Thus, where a debtor pays because the creditor has threatened him with physical violence if he does not, the creditor's retention would *not* be without cause and yet retention of the proceeds of this sort of self-help is surely objectionable. With such non-contractual acts of fulfilment, other means have to be found to generate an appropriate restitutionary response. Exploring the possibilities,[134] Jacques du Plessis notes that, while it could be argued that fraud or duress affect the determination of the purpose of a transfer, thereby leading to its failure to fulfil an obligation, there are difficulties in interpreting this as 'failure of the purpose of the transfer'. Equally he notes that as long as there has been some form of transfer or 'giving' rather than 'taking', an analysis based on *Eingriff* or encroachment is problematic. He concludes that it might even be necessary to identify a further type of enrichment claim, based on the idea that any due transfer obtained in an improper manner is retained without legal ground.[135]

In a survey of the German law of unjustified enrichment, Zimmermann and Du Plessis conclude that 'by adopting a general enrichment action the fathers of the BGB created a catalyst which eventually led to a completely new, but more rational, division of enrichment claims'. Nevertheless, they concede that 'greater clarity' can 'be obtained of the basic policies underlying the law of unjustified enrichment'.[136] The claim here is more emphatic. The details of the restitutionary response should be closely tailored to the initial reasons for granting restitution. These reasons are accessible only by a proper understanding of the unjust factors that invalidate the particular transfer, whether legally due or not, and which bring the case to the door of unjust enrichment law. English and German law already show a degree of responsiveness to the unjust factors. Both can, and should, be more responsive still.

---

[133] *Ibid.*, 719. [134] See his contibution to the present volume, pp. 194 ff.
[135] See chap. 7, below, 213–18. [136] Zimmermann and Du Plessis, 'Basic Features', 43.

7 Fraud, duress and unjustified enrichment: a civil-law perspective

Jacques du Plessis

I. Introduction

Fraud and duress are the two classical improper means of influencing human conduct. When they are used to induce a person to confer a benefit on another, it is only natural to respond that the benefit, or a substitute, should be restored. The purpose of this contribution is to examine how the law of unjustified enrichment in certain civil-law systems deals with this duty to provide restitution.[1] Particular attention will be paid to the position in German, Dutch and South African law, although comparisons will at times be made with the position in the common law. The reason for the choice of these systems is that they represent quite distinct lines of development within the civilian tradition. Both German and Dutch law show how codification impacted on the development of the civil law.[2] In the case of German law, the recognition of a single codified general enrichment action has given rise to a complete realignment of enrichment remedies.[3] The relevant Dutch law is also codified, but in certain respects its approach

---

[1] For a comparative overview of the treatment of fraud and duress in the law of unjustified enrichment, see Izhak England, 'Restitution of Benefits Conferred Without Obligation', in: *International Encyclopedia of Comparative Law* (1991), vol. X, chap. 5, §§ 5-81 ff., 5-92 ff.

[2] On early nineteenth-century thought, which was still characterised by specific codified grounds of recovery, and rather haphazard judicial reform, see Eltjo Schrage and Barry Nicholas, 'Unjust Enrichment and the Law of Restitution: A Comparison', in: Eltjo J. H. Schrage (ed.), *Unjust Enrichment* (1995), 22 ff.; Reinhard Zimmermann, 'Unjustified Enrichment: The Modern Civilian Approach', (1995) 15 *Oxford JLS* 403, 409.

[3] See Reinhard Zimmermann and Jacques du Plessis, 'Basic Features of the German Law of Unjustified Enrichment', [1994] *Restitution LR* 14, 24 ff.; B.S. Markesinis, W. Lorenz and G. Dannemann, *The German Law of Obligations*, vol. I, *The Law of Contracts and Restitution* (1997), 711 ff., 717 ff.

is quite different – most notably its separation of the payment that is not due from the general enrichment action and its adherence to a causal system of the transfer of ownership. It can, therefore, act as an interesting foil for German law.[4] Finally, there is South African law, which is remarkable in that it has retained significant aspects of the relevant civil law in uncodified form.[5] For example, in the case of contracts concluded under fraud and duress it still makes use of the familiar civilian regime of rescissionary actions and *restitutio in integrum*. It should then be apparent that these three systems provide divergent responses to the questions when and how there has to be restitution of what has been obtained under fraud and duress.

The outline of this chapter is as follows. So as to avoid any terminological confusion, the first section will deal briefly with the exact relationship between the common-law concepts of fraud and duress and certain civilian counterparts. Thereafter, the focus will shift to the effect of fraud and duress. The German and Dutch codes stipulate that they impact on the validity of certain declarations of intent and legal or juristic acts. A distinction will then be drawn between their effect on declarations or acts which are aimed at creating contractual obligations, fulfilling obligations and transferring ownership. In each case, it will be necessary to determine whether fraud and duress could influence the availability of relief based on unjustified enrichment. In this regard, specific attention will have to be paid to the nature and measure of the appropriate remedies. Since fraud or duress could also amount to a delict, it is further necessary to examine how the law of delict could provide alternative or additional relief. The conclusion seeks to evaluate the results of this overview, taking special account of the extent to which fraud or duress are factors that influence the availability of relief based on unjustified enrichment.

---

[4] On the historical background, see Eltjo J. H. Schrage, 'The Law of Restitution: The History of Dutch Legislation', in: Schrage, *Unjust Enrichment*, 323 ff.; J. J. Hallebeek and E. J. H. Schrage, *Ongerechtvaardigde Verrijking – Grepen uit de Geschiedenis van de Algemene Verrijkingsactie van het NBW* (1989); for a comparison between the German and Dutch systems, see M. W. Scheltema, *Onverschuldigde betaling* (1997), 12 ff.

[5] However, this is not to say that English law did not have a profound influence on extending the grounds for relief beyond *metus* and *dolus* (see Gerhard Lubbe, 'Voidable Contracts', in: Reinhard Zimmermann and Daniel Visser (eds.), *Southern Cross: Civil Law and Common Law in South Africa* (1996), 261 ff., especially on the reception of the English law of negligent misrepresentation and undue influence). Given the restricted definition of fraud and duress, which will be accepted for present purposes, these developments need not be considered here.

II. The meaning of fraud and duress

The concepts of 'fraud' and 'duress' are peculiar to the common law.[6] This implies that their meanings are determined by common-law rules, and that strictly speaking it is impossible to talk of the German law of 'duress' (just as it would be impossible to talk about the English law of *Drohung*). However, these terms can also be interpreted more broadly, in a colloquial sense, to describe certain 'fact patterns'.[7] In other words, they can be used to describe a core of factual situations that all legal systems have to respond to. In the analysis of different approaches to the law of unjustified enrichment, it is this core meaning which will be of interest.

1. Fraud or fraudulent misrepresentation

At common law, 'fraud' is proved when it shown that 'a false representation has been made, (1) knowingly, or (2) without belief in its truth, or (3) recklessly, careless whether it be true or false'.[8] To a certain extent, the definition resembles that of *arglistige Täuschung* in German law.[9] The latter notion also describes the situation where a person makes a representation that is false. However, in German law, the person making the representation has to know that it is false and intended to induce a mistake, thereby moving the victim to make a declaration of intent; recklessness does not suffice.[10] A closely related notion is that of *bedrog* under the new Dutch Civil Code (BW). It is present 'where a person induces another to perform a certain legal act by intentionally providing inaccurate information, by intentionally concealing a fact which he was bound to disclose, or through

---

[6] See Konrad Zweigert and Hein Kötz, *An Introduction to Comparative Law* (trans. Tony Weir, 3rd edn, 1998), 424 ff. For a historical overview of fraud and duress in the Western law of contract, see James Gordley, 'Contract in Pre-commercial Societies and in Western Theory', in: *International Encyclopedia of Comparative Law*, vol. VII, chap. 2, §§ 2-64 ff.; Reinhard Zimmermann, *The Law of Obligations: Roman Foundations of the Civilian Tradition* (paperback edn, 1996), 651 ff.

[7] See England, 'Restitution of Benefits', § 5-3.

[8] *Derry v. Peek* (1889) 14 App Cas 337 at 374. Fraud could give rise to an action for damages when it meets the requirements of the tort of 'deceit' (see Jack Beatson, *Anson's Law of Contract* (27th edn, 1998), 239; G. H. Treitel, *The Law of Contract* (10th edn, 1999), 317). On the more extended meaning of fraud in equity (as opposed to common law), see Beatson, *Anson's Law of Contract*, 261. The comparable civil-law rules relating to fraud as a delict are dealt with at Section III, 4, below.

[9] See Markesinis, Lorenz and Dannemann, 207 ff.

[10] § 123(1) BGB does not define the concept; but see Karl Larenz, *Allgemeiner Teil des Deutschen Bürgerlichen Rechts* (7th edn, 1989), § 20, IV, (a); Ernst Kramer, in: *Münchener Kommentar zum Bürgerlichen Gesetzbuch* (3rd edn, 1993), vol. I, § 123, nn. 5 ff.

any other artifice'.[11] As far as South African law is concerned, the meaning of 'fraud' has long been uncertain, due to a strange convergence of civil- and common-law influences. At first it was equated with the very broad civilian concept of *dolus malus*, which covered all sorts of cases involving intentional deception, cheating or circumvention.[12] However, under the influence of the common law, 'fraud' later came to be interpreted more restrictively, along lines very similar to that of the English law as set out above. Thus, in all these systems, fraud, or its equivalent, at least consists in knowingly or intentionally making a false representation. Although it could still cover gross negligence under common law, it is clear that it certainly does not cover mere negligent or innocent misrepresentation. It is as a descriptor of the basic 'fact pattern' of particularly serious types of misrepresentation that the concept of 'fraud' will be used here.[13] The differences in where the cut-off point lies can for present purposes be regarded as of secondary importance.[14]

However, a difference which is especially important in the context of the law of unjustified enrichment is the way in which these different systems perceive the relationship between fraud and certain other improper ways of obtaining consent. In English contract-law texts, fraud is viewed as a species of misrepresentation,[15] and therefore as a specific means of inducing an error. It is also not traditionally grouped together with duress. This stands in contrast to the position in German and Dutch law, which reflect

---

[11] Art. 3: 44(3) BW; also see A. S. Hartkamp, *Mr. C Asser's Handleiding tot de Beoefening van Het Nederlands Burgerlijk Recht – Verbintenissenrecht* (1997), vol. II, nn. 199–204, where it is indicated that the expression 'through any other artifice' (*door een andere kunstgreep*) should be interpreted restrictively. *Bedrog* essentially requires an intention to deceive.

[12] See Lubbe, 'Voidable Contracts', 265 referring to the definition of *dolus malus* in Ulp. D. 4, 3, 1, 2.

[13] See generally Zweigert and Kötz, *Introduction*, 425 ff. In some systems, 'specially deceptive practices' are required, but as Zweigert and Kötz point out, '[e]ven so, it is admitted on all hands that a simple lie can constitute deceit' (*ibid.*, 425).

[14] In the English common law and in South African law, these differences were particularly important in determining whether a claim for damages would be available: traditionally, such a claim could only succeed in those cases of misrepresentation which amounted to fraud; rescission, on the other hand, could be obtained even in the event of innocent misrepresetation; see Lubbe, 'Voidable Contracts', 270 ff.

[15] See generally Treitel, *Law of Contract*, 317 ff.; Anthony Guest (ed.), *Chitty on Contracts* (28th edn, 1999), vol. I §§ 6-001 ff., 6-045. The law of misrepresentation covers all cases of error induced by misrepresentation. In fact, it has been said that the term 'mistake' could be used to refer only to those cases of error not caused by misrepresentation; see Zweigert and Kötz, *Introduction*, 421.

the traditional civilian preference for linking these notions.[16] There, innocent and negligent misrepresentation are generally dealt with in the context of the law relating to error, whereas the more serious cases of fraudulent representation (the terrain of the law of *arglistige Täuschung* and *bedrog*) are grouped with duress.[17] But why view fraud in this light? If it in any event causes an error, and if error is a ground for relief, why not simply deal with it as a special case of error? Apart from obvious historical considerations, it would seem that the answer lies in the feature of fraud identified earlier, namely that the means used to induce error in these cases are so seriously improper that the normal rules applying to the restitution of transfers made in error are inappropriate. It is recognised that the victim deserves special protection. This could be provided, for example, by not requiring that his error be material or fundamental. In other words, he could be allowed to escape from liability even though the fraud simply caused an error in motive.[18] It also means that he should be provided with a fuller spectrum of remedies, and that he should be able to recover more than the person who merely acted under an innocent or negligent misrepresentation. But these are issues more relevant to the effect of fraud than its content, and will be returned to later on.

2. Duress or unlawful threats

The (originally Norman French) term 'duress' is derived from the common law. Traditionally, it only covered the situation where a person was unlawfully subjected to actual or threatened personal physical harm.[19] This means that in some other cases where a person was subjected to pressure, relief had to be provided on different grounds – usually 'undue influence' in equity.[20] However, the scope of duress has broadened over the years so as also to accommodate harm to economic interests, and nowadays the difference between the two concepts is rather indistinct. German and Dutch law, on the other hand, have avoided these problems. Although a

---

[16] On the historical background to the law of *dolus* and *metus* see Zimmermann, *Law of Obligations*, 664 ff.

[17] On the relationship between error and misrepresentation in English law, as opposed to German and Dutch law, see Michael H. Whincup, *Contract Law and Practice: The English System and Continental Comparisons* (3rd edn, 1996), §§ 11.49, 11.56 ff.

[18] Zweigert and Kötz, *Introduction*, 425; Engländ, 'Restitution of Benefits', § 5-81. See further Larenz, *Allgemeiner Teil*, § 20; Hartkamp, *Mr. C Asser's Handleiding*, n. 199.

[19] See Beatson, *Anson's Law of Contract*, 271–2; Treitel, *Law of Contract*, 375; *Skeate v. Beale* (1841) 11 A & E 983; *Cumming v. Ince* (1847) 11 QB 112 at 120; *Biffen v. Bignell* (1862) 7 H & N 877.

[20] See Treitel, *Law of Contract*, 375, 378; Zweigert and Kötz, *Introduction*, 428.

traditionally narrow conception of *metus* required that at times additional relief had to be provided on different grounds,[21] it is recognised nowadays that duress covers all cases where a person is unlawfully subjected to actual or threatened harm.[22] Because the fear has to emanate from the person who made the threat, there can be no duress if the pressure is (merely) the consequence of some situation of need or distress.[23] No distinction is drawn between forms of duress according to the nature of the interests (for example, physical or economic) harmed.[24] The key question is simply whether the threat is unlawful. South African law again bears the imprint of both civil- and common-law influences: it received the civil law of *metus* (translated as 'duress'), which was flexible enough to accommodate a broad range of threats of harm, but under the influence of the common law it somehow adopted a restrictive approach to providing relief in what could be termed cases of 'economic duress'. It further felt the need to supplement the law of *metus* with the common law of undue influence. Curiously though, the justification for this development was not sought in the civil law of *metus* (and especially 'reverential fear' or *metus reverentialis*). In fact, it was with reference to the idea that in civil law *restitutio in integrum* would be provided in cases of *dolus* (interpreted in the broad sense indicated above) that the reception of undue influence from the common law was facilitated.[25]

As in the case of 'fraud', it is not necessary to analyse the meaning of 'duress' in great detail. However, one important observation needs to be made. It deals with the much-disputed basis for providing relief.[26] Is the victim protected because his mental ability to make a decision is affected by the duress, or is it because of some other ground, such as an unlawful limitation of the freedom of choice through subjecting a person to threats of harm? Civilians as early as Paulus have held that the basis for relief is not a defect in mental ability: what is willed under compulsion, none

---

[21] Most notably the law of the *condictiones* (see Jacques E. du Plessis, *Compulsion and Restitution* (unpublished Ph.D. thesis, University of Aberdeen, 1998), 16 ff., 40 ff., 60 ff., 121 ff., 134 ff.; John P. Dawson, 'Economic Duress and the Fair Exchange in French and German Law', (1937) 11 *Tulane LR* 345, 348.

[22] See Zweigert and Kötz, *Introduction*, 428. On *Drohung* in German law see Kramer in: *Münchener Kommentar*, § 123, n. 33; and in Dutch law art. 3:44(2) BW.

[23] See Zweigert and Kötz, *Introduction*, 428; Kramer in: *Münchener Kommentar*, § 123, n. 33. In cases of *vis absoluta*, where the person is being physically overpowered, he obviously does not act at all. See Zweigert and Kötz, *Introduction*, 428; Kramer in: *Münchener Kommentar*, § 123, n. 32.

[24] On the historical background see Zimmermann, *Law of Obligations*, 659.

[25] See Lubbe, 'Voidable Contracts', 286 ff.

[26] For a historical overview, see Gordley, 'Contract in Pre-commercial Societies', §§ 2–4 ff.

the less is willed (*coactus volui, tamen volui*).[27] The victim could be quite rational, and not even be afraid: his problem is that he cannot freely decide what he wants to do because the available choices have been restricted unlawfully.[28] The emphasis is then on the nature of the methods used to influence his will, and not on a deficiency in the will itself. In the common law, by contrast, it has been said that duress 'overbears' the victim's will,[29] thereby influencing his mental ability to make a decision. However, some common lawyers have criticised this approach; after all, if all that has to be proven is an 'overborne will', even the victim of lawful pressure should be able to escape liability on grounds of duress.[30]

From the overview above it should be apparent that fraud and duress deal with serious violations of individual autonomy. In the case of fraud, the victim's freedom of choice cannot be exercised properly, because he was made to act on wrong information 'conveyed' in a particularly unacceptable manner, while in the case of duress his freedom of choice is restricted by actual or threatened harm. It then stands to reason that these violations justify a strong measure of protection – stronger at least than the case where the actions are prompted by a spontaneous error or the sorts of pressures which are part of daily life. It will now be considered how the law of restitution or unjustified enrichment can fulfil this function.

III. The effect of fraud and duress

In the course of the eighteenth century, German legal scholars devised the concepts of the 'declaration of intent' (*Willenserklärung*) and the 'legal transaction' (*Rechtsgeschäft*).[31] In essence, a declaration of intent is a declaration

---

[27] Paul. D. 4, 2, 21, 5. See Zimmermann, *Law of Obligations*, 652 ff.; Du Plessis, *Compulsion and Restitution*, 6 ff.
[28] See Du Plessis, *Compulsion and Restitution*, 161 ff.
[29] See *Pao On v. Lau Yiu Long* [1980] AC 614.
[30] See *Lynch v. DPP. of Northern Ireland* [1975] AC 695 B–C; Patrick S. Atiyah, 'Economic Duress and the "Overborne Will"', (1982) 98 *LQR* 197; Nicholas Seddon, 'Compulsion in Commercial Dealings', in: P. D. Finn, *Essays on Restitution* (1990), 138, 142 ff.; Beatson, *Anson's Law*, 273 ff.
[31] See Werner Flume, *Allgemeiner Teil des Bürgerlichen Rechts* (3rd edn, 1979), vol. II, §§ 2, 4. Flume indicates that the Roman concepts such as *actus* and *negotium* could not fulfil such a function. The notions were never received in South African law, whose civilian roots lie in seventeenth- and eighteenth-century Roman-Dutch law. Modern introductory textbooks on South African law refer to concepts such as 'legal act' or 'juristic act' (*regshandeling*), but only as pedagogical tools; see, for example, H. R. Hahlo and E. Kahn, *The South African Legal System and its Background* (1968), 100 ff.

indicating that certain legal consequences are intended[32] and it is essential for the validity of many legal transactions, of which the contract is but one.[33] These concepts (which were unknown in Roman law, and which are still of scant relevance in modern South African law) have influenced other civil-law codes. Dutch law, for example, recognises similar concepts, most notably that of the 'legal act' (*rechtshandeling*).[34] These are acts that produce a legal effect or consequence because they were intended to do so.[35] This intention has to be manifested in a declaration. The important point for present purposes is that in these systems fraud and duress could affect the validity of all declarations of intent and legal transactions or acts,[36] by rendering them voidable.[37] This means that the person entitled to annul can decide whether to uphold the validity of the legal act. The effect of annulment is retrospective, so that the legal relationship of the parties is restored to the state in which it was before the act was performed.[38]

But let us move from the general to the particular. Of all the types of declarations of intent or acts that can be influenced by fraud and duress, the present concern is with those relevant when determining liability based on unjustified enrichment. For present purposes, the most important of these are declarations or acts aimed at (1) creating contractual obligations, (2) achieving fulfilment or performance of all types of obligations and (3) transferring ownership. As far as the difference between the

---

[32] See, generally, Larenz, *Allgemeiner Teil*, § 19, and the authorities quoted there.
[33] Cf. Zweigert and Kötz, *Introduction*, 348 ff.
[34] See A. R. Bloembergen, *Rechtshandeling en Overeenkomst* (1995), 2 ff. on the notion of a *rechtshandeling* and Flume, *Allgemeiner Teil*, §§ 2, 4 on the influence of the German Civil Code on Meijers's draft of the New Dutch Civil Code, and also on its influence on the position in France, Italy and Greece.
[35] See art. 3:33 BW and generally Hartkamp, *Mr. C Asser's Handleiding*, n. 2.
[36] § 123(1) BGB. The reason why a declaration of will, and not only a juristic act, is affected is that the compilers of the BGB wanted to provide maximum protection to a person acting under duress (Benno Mugdan, 'Denkschrift zum BGB', in: Benno Mugdan (ed.), *Die gesammten Materialien zum Bürgerlichen Gesetzbuch für das deutsche Reich* (1899), vol. I, 834).
[37] See § 123(1) BGB; art. 3:44(1) BW; Arthur S. Hartkamp and Marianne M. M. Tillema, *Contract Law in the Netherlands* (1995), §§ 36, 99. On the historical background regarding the consequences of voidability as opposed to voidness, see Zimmermann, *Law of Obligations*, 660, 671 ff. It is only in certain cases of fraud that the error it causes is so material that the act should be regarded as void (see section II, 1, above, on the relationship between misrepresentation and error). In the case of absolute duress or *vis absoluta* (e.g. where a person's hand is held and thus forced to make a signature) there obviously is no declaration of intent at all. This renders any act affected by it automatically void.
[38] See § 142(1) BGB; art. 3:53 BW.

first two categories is concerned, attention is usually focused on the situation where a contract is concluded and restitution is sought of what was performed thereunder. This is, of course, an important category of cases, but it should not be ignored that fraud and duress can also influence the conferring of a benefit outside a contractual context. For example, they may move a person to perform *ex lege* obligations, or even to engage in acts that do not involve performance at all, such as to make a bequest, declare a dividend or grant a licence. These cases do not concern the validity of a contract between the victim and the wrongdoer, but rather some other act whose validity is suspect. As far as the difference between the second and third categories is concerned, it is important from a civilian perspective to distinguish between the intention to fulfil an obligation (that, is to perform), and the intention to transfer ownership. The position in practice normally would be that the person who intends to transfer ownership of something does so in order to fulfil an obligation, but this need not be the case – he might, for example, intend to make the transfer now with a view towards creating a loan agreement or donation in the future. A question that is of particular importance in this regard is the extent to which fraud or duress may prevent ownership from passing in the first place, and so entitle the owner to vindicatory relief, rather than relief based on unjustified enrichment. The last category therefore deals with the borderline between the laws of property and unjustified enrichment. But first consider the borderline between the laws of unjustified enrichment and contract.

1. The effect of fraud and duress on the validity of contracts
(a) Rescission and *restitutio in integrum*
In the civilian systems under review, the question whether fraud and duress affect the validity of a contract has not traditionally been the concern of the law of unjustified enrichment. From a historical perspective, this is perfectly understandable. In Roman times, the praetor did not try to counteract fraud or duress through developing the law of the *condictiones*.[39] He dealt with the problem head-on by exercising his extraordinary powers to order *restitutio in integrum*, thus ensuring that both parties were restored to their previous position, and by awarding an *actio quod metus causa*, which apparently was aimed at inducing the victim to make restitution through

---

[39] A possible, and problematic, exception is the extorted *stipulatio*; see Pomp. D. 12, 5, 7; Du Plessis, *Compulsion and Restitution*, 23 ff.

FRAUD, DURESS AND UNJUSTIFIED ENRICHMENT   203

subjecting him to fourfold damages if he did not.[40] The fact that restoring parties *in integrum* generally took place in the context of rescission of contracts explains how in some systems *restitutio in integrum* came to be regarded as 'contractual' in nature, something tailor-made for cases of improperly obtained consent. This is still the position in modern South African law, which (mainly due to differences in the measure of recovery) expressly rejects the idea that a duty of restitution in cases of fraud or duress is based on unjustified enrichment.[41]

However, other modern civilian systems view matters rather differently. Already at the end of the nineteenth century, the compilers of the German code regarded it as unnecessary to recognise a remedy styled *restitutio in integrum*.[42] Where a declaration of intent was rescinded on grounds of fraud or duress, any juristic act of which this declaration of intent formed part would be invalid. If such a juristic act was supposed to act as the legal ground or *causa* of a transfer, that legal ground would be regarded as never having existed.[43] It is only here that the law of unjustified enrichment would enter the scene.[44] By determining that the contract is invalid, the law regarding the validity of declarations of intent and legal transactions has already done the hard work of indicating that a performance is retained without legal ground. The law of unjustified enrichment only

---

[40] See Berthold Kupisch, *In integrum restitutio und vindicatio utilis bei Eigentumsübertragungen im klassischen römischen Recht* (1974); Zimmermann, *Law of Obligations*, 656 ff.; Du Plessis, *Compulsion and Restitution*, 13 ff.

[41] For an exposition of these views and criticism, see D. P. Visser, 'Rethinking Unjustified Enrichment: A Perspective of the Competition between Contractual and Enrichment Remedies', [1992] *Acta Juridica* 203, 211.

[42] The reasons for not incorporating a provision dealing with *restitutio in integrum* mainly relate to problems with its application in earlier times, and changed procedural views and institutions (Benno Mugdan, 'Motive', in: Mugdan, *Die gesammten Materialien*, vol. II, 566 ff.). It was considered unnecessary because the provisions on unjustified enrichment could perform this role satisfactorily (see Visser, 'Rethinking Unjustified Enrichment', 215 ff.). The *actio quod metus causa* likewise was dropped because general provisions were adopted on delict and unjustified enrichment, and there was a desire not to burden the code with unnecessary provisions (Mugdan, 'Motive', 423). The same was true of the *condictio ex iniusta causa*, which was used in the German *ius commune* law to reclaim illegally extorted bestowments (see Detlef König, *Ungerechtfertigte Bereicherung: Tatbestände und Ordnungsprobleme in rechtsvergleichender Sicht* (1985), 47).

[43] On the retrospective operation of rescission, and exceptions thereto, see Theo Mayer-Maly, in: *Münchener Kommentar zum Bürgerlichen Gesetzbuch* (3rd edn, 1993), vol. I, § 142, n. 14 ff.

[44] See Manfred Lieb, in: *Münchener Kommentar zum Bürgerlichen Gesetzbuch* (3rd edn, 1997), vol. V, § 812, nn. 144, 148; Zimmermann, 'Unjustified Enrichment', 407; Englard, 'Restitution of Benefits', § 5-9.

has to regulate what has to be restored in so far as this has not already been done by specific rules of the law of contract. However, this still leaves the problem of ensuring some reciprocity in the restitution of what the parties performed. One solution is simply to say that rescission would not be granted if *restitutio in integrum* is impossible.[45] Such an approach could operate rather harshly on the victim, and therefore cannot be followed without exception. In this regard, it is of interest that Dutch law recognises the qualification that the victim may be protected by allowing 'equitable monetary adjustments'.[46]

However, in modern German law, the situation is viewed somewhat differently. In essence, the inability to provide restitution does not preclude rescission; the victim can obtain rescission, but the entitlement to and measure of enrichment-based relief is affected in three ways. First, under § 814 BGB the victim is not entitled to relief, if at the time of performance of a contract he knew that he was not obliged to perform. Thus, if he knew that the validity of the contract was tainted by fraud, but still performed, his enrichment claim would be barred. It can justifiably be asked why he did not refuse to perform when he had the chance. (It is obvious that the victim of duress has to be treated differently: it is precisely because of the compulsion that he cannot refuse even if he knows that he is not obliged to perform. Duress indicates that an enrichment remedy should not be barred.) In this regard it has been argued that the reason for excluding a claim where the transferor knew that the transfer was not due is to prevent him from acting contrary to his previous conduct (*venire contra factum proprium*).[47] Secondly, under § 819(1) BGB, the wrongdoer is not entitled to plead loss of enrichment or change of position if he was aware that he was not entitled to keep the enrichment. In other words, he cannot plead that his liability should be restricted to what remains in his hands, instead

---

[45] See, for example, in the context of Scots law, Du Plessis, *Compulsion and Restitution*, 92 ff., 167 ff.

[46] Art. 3:53 BW. On the position in the common law, see the contribution of Mindy Chen-Wishart to this volume. Although *restitutio in integrum* is regarded as a condition to rescission (see *Erlanger v. New Sombrero Phosphate Co.* (1878) 3 App Cas 1218 at 1278), it is also acknowledged that the innocent party's right to rescind is not automatically barred due to his own inability to provide restitution (Robert Goff and Gareth Jones, *The Law of Restitution* (5th edn, 1998), 273 ff.; Treitel, *Law of Contract*, 350-1; England, 'Restitution of Benefits', §§ 5-74, 5-88).

[47] See Peter Schlechtriem, in: Othmar Jauernig (ed.), *Bürgerliches Gesetzbuch* (7th edn, 1994), § 814, nn. 1, 5; see further Markesinis, Lorenz and Dannemann, *Law of Contracts*, 736. On the influence of duress on the recoverability of undue transfers outside the contractual context, see section III, 2, (a) and (b), below.

of the full extent of what he received. Thirdly, the wrongdoer is not protected by the *Saldotheorie*, which seeks to ensure reciprocity in the return of transfers.[48] Although the BGB seems to have been drafted in a way which indicates that one is dealing with separate claims (this is the way in which the old 'doctrine of the two enrichment claims' or *Zweikondiktionenlehre* also understood it), the *Saldotheorie* 'combines the legal fates' of these claims through a process of adjustment.[49] In essence, whenever a person's performance has been destroyed while being retained by his contracting partner, he can raise the *Saldotheorie* against the partner's enrichment claim. The defendant/enrichment debtor can only counterclaim to the extent that he is able to provide restitution. If he lost something worth more than his counterclaim, he in effect has no claim. However, since the wrongdoer who defrauds another is not entitled to the protection of the *Saldotheorie*, the victim should be entitled to reclaim his full performance.[50]

(b) The nature of enrichment-based remedies
(i) Leistungskondiktion and its scope of application
Against the background of the rescissory actions and *restitutio in integrum*, it can now be investigated what type of enrichment-based remedy will provide the victim with relief. In German law the code itself is rather unhelpful. All § 812(1), first sentence BGB states is that a person who obtains something without legal ground at the expense of another through a transfer by that person or in any other way is liable to return it. However, it will be noticed that in the code a distinction is drawn between obtaining something through a transfer (*Leistung*), and obtaining it in any other way. Nowadays, this distinction is regarded as crucial.[51] A typology has been developed that places all enrichment claims involving a *Leistung* or transfer

---

[48] See England, 'Restitution of Benefits', §§ 5-90, 5-278 ff.; Dieter Medicus, *Schuldrecht II: Besonderer Teil* (9th edn, 1999), § 129; Zimmermann and Du Plessis, 'Basic Features', 40 ff.
[49] See Medicus, *Schuldrecht II*, § 129.
[50] See BGHZ 53, 144; England, 'Restitution of Benefits', § 5-279. However, some adjustment based on contributory fault is possible. For criticism of the view that fraud should be an exception to the *Saldotheorie* in cases where there is no causal link between the misrepresentation and the harm giving rise to the law of enrichment, see Markesinis, Lorenz and Dannemann, 765.
[51] See the pioneering works of Walter Wilburg, *Die Lehre von der ungerechtfertigten Bereicherung nach österreichischen und deutschem Recht* (1934), and Ernst von Caemmerer, 'Bereicherung und unerlaubte Handlung', in: *Festschrift für Ernst Rabel* (1954), vol. I, 333 ff.; Markesinis, Lorenz and Dannemann, 717 ff.

in the domain of a remedy called the *Leistungskondiktion*. All other cases are classified under three other categories, of which the most notable is the *Eingriffskondiktion* or enrichment claim based on encroachment.[52]

For present purposes, the *Leistungskondiktion* is of particular importance. According to the prevailing view, this remedy is available when someone has made a *Leistung* – that is, intentionally enlarged another's estate with a specific purpose in mind[53] – and this purpose for some reason or another then failed. As Dieter Reuter and Michael Martinek put it, 'in the case of the *Leistungskondiktion* the lack of the legal ground for the *Leistung* lies in the failure of its purpose'.[54] Since the *Leistungskondiktion* unites various cases of retention without legal ground brought about by a transfer, it is not surprising that German authors have found it convenient to categorise the fields of application of this remedy along the lines of the *condictiones* of Roman law.[55] According to the prevailing view, the *Leistungskondiktion* in its *condictio indebiti* guise would then be applied when the purpose of a transfer failed because the intended discharge of a debt did not materialise.[56] After all, the *condictio indebiti* is the civil-law remedy *par excellence* for the recovery of an *indebitum*, or transfer which is not due or owed. However, there is also a minority opinion, which regards the emphasis on the purpose of the transfer as unnecessary. To the supporters of this view, the legal ground for a *Leistung* is simply the relationship of indebtedness to which it pertains.[57] A contract of sale, for example, provides such a relationship when the *Leistung* takes the form of a payment of the purchase price. Whether it was intended to achieve the purpose of payment is not relevant if the relationship of indebtedness existed in any event. Thus, if the purchaser in this example accidentally pays the purchase price twice, but also happens to owe the seller a separate debt

---

[52] On these various remedies, see Markesinis, Lorenz and Dannemann, 717 ff., 740 ff., 752 ff.

[53] See BGHZ 40, 272 (277); BGHZ 58, 184 (188).

[54] Dieter Reuter and Michael Martinek, *Ungerechtfertigte Bereicherung* (1983), 125.

[55] See Dieter Medicus, *Bürgerliches Recht* (18th edn, 1999), n. 689; Reuter and Martinek, *Ungerechtfertige Bereicherung*, 125 ff.; Hans-Georg Koppensteiner and Ernst Kramer, *Ungerechtfertigte Bereicherung* (2nd edn, 1988), 49 ff.; for criticism see Markesinis, Lorenz and Dannemann, 719.

[56] See Medicus, *Bürgerliches Recht*, n. 689; Koppensteiner and Kramer, *Ungerechtfertige Bereicherung*, 50; Reuter and Martinek, *Ungerechtfertige Bereicherung*, 126 ff.

[57] See Karl Larenz and Claus-Wilhelm Canaris, *Lehrbuch des Schuldrechts* (13th edn, 1994), vol. II/2 § 67 III 1. It might seem as if this approach is unable to deal with the *datio ob rem*, which is not supported by an obligation at the time of transfer. However, such a *datio* is still supported by an underlying understanding as to the basis on which it is to be held by the recipient. This is regarded as sufficient to justify the retention of what has been given by the recipient.

(say, under an agreement of loan), the seller can set off the purchaser's enrichment claim based on the second payment against his own claim for payment of the loan.[58] The second payment would then no longer be retained without legal ground. This consequence cannot be explained with an analysis based on the failure of the purpose of the second payment. In fact, it indicates that such an analysis is unnecessary.

(ii) Leistungskondiktion in cases of fraud and duress
To return to the original inquiry, namely to establish what enrichment remedy should be used to recover transfers made where a contract was rescinded due to fraud or duress. As far as fraud is concerned, the appropriate remedy would be the *Leistungskondiktion*. Under the prevailing view, it should be available because a transfer has been made with the purpose of fulfilling an obligation under a contract, and the purpose failed because the contract was rescinded. And under the minority view, it should be available simply because rescission removed the relationship of indebtedness or *causa* for the transfer. Hence, in terms of both theories, the transfer is not due, and is retained without legal ground, rendering it recoverable with the *Leistungskondiktion*.[59]

In the case of duress, the situation is somewhat more complicated. First, it has to be determined whether a *Leistung* is being dealt with at all. In this regard, it is necessary to return briefly to a question raised in treating the content of duress, namely whether it 'overbears' the will or merely 'deflects' it. If the 'overborne will' theory is followed, it seems as if the relevant concept is an *Eingriff* or 'encroachment' by the wrongdoer, rather than with a *Leistung* as defined above. Put in very simple terms, there is no longer a 'giving' but rather a 'taking' of the benefit. If so, then the *Eingriffskondiktion* would have to be awarded.[60] However, as indicated above, the preferable approach is that duress does not destroy consent, but instead improperly influences or 'deflects' it. To what extent, then, would the *Leistungskondiktion* be an appropriate remedy? Here the prevailing and minority views have to be contrasted.

According to the prevailing approach, the benefit had to be conferred with a specific *purpose* in mind, and this purpose then had to fail. The problem is to determine what the purpose of the transfer was. One possibility is that the purpose was to fulfil the obligations created by the extorted contract, and that this purpose then failed due to the rescision.

---
[58] See § 387 BGB.
[59] See Lieb, in: *Münchener Kommentar*, § 812, nn. 137 ff.
[60] Du Plessis, *Compulsion and Restitution*, 72 ff., 159 ff.

The *Leistungskondiktion* in its *condictio indebiti* guise should then be available. However, it seems rather artificial to say that a person who is so averse to being bound that he has to be illegally forced to enter into a contract would really have the purpose to fulfil obligations under such a contract. A more convincing view seems to be that the purpose of the transfer is temporarily to avert the harm which would flow from non-fulfilment. The problem is that if the victim then succeeds in averting harm through making the transfer, its purpose has in fact been achieved, which means that it is precisely the type of situation where the *Leistungskondiktion*, as traditionally understood, should *not* be awarded. However, the minority approach to the *Leistungskondiktion* completely avoids these problems: the mere fact that the declarations of intent required for the conclusion of a contract have been rescinded means that no relationship of indebtedness or *causa* can exist. Hence, as in the case of fraud, the retention is without legal ground, and the question whether the 'purpose' of the transfer has been fulfilled is irrelevant.[61] Under the minority view, the *Leistungskondiktion* should therefore be available to reclaim the transfer made in fulfilment of a contract concluded under duress.

(iii) The approach of Dutch law
In modern Dutch law a different picture emerges. Unlike a number of other civilian systems,[62] it has consciously grouped together things that are *given* without legal ground in art. 6:203 BW. This article, which is distinct from the general provision dealing with unjustified enrichment,[63] provides that all undue payments are to be restored, even though no shift of wealth (in other words, no enrichment) took place. Thus, even though the 'payment' remained the property of the payer, it is still recoverable under this provision. The reason is that Dutch law, contrary to German law, subscribes to a causal system of the transfer of property. The purpose is to simplify life for the claimant. All he has to do is prove that something not due was given and received. Proof of ownership is not required,[64] and loss of enrichment or change of position is no defence either.[65] One instance where a payment is recoverable under this section is where an initially

---

[61] See Lieb, in: *Münchener Kommentar*, § 812, n. 138.
[62] See, e.g., on the German, Swiss and Greek codes, E. J. H. Schrage, 'Restitution in the New Dutch Civil Code', [1994] *Restitution LR* 208, 209. On the background to the code see C. J. van Zeben and J.W. du Pon (eds.), *Parlementaire Geschiedenis van het Nieuwe Burgerlijk Wetboek*, vol. VI, *Algemeen Gedeelte van het Verbintenissenrecht* (1981), 802 ff.
[63] Art. 6:212 NBW.
[64] Van Zeben and Du Pon, *Parlementaire Geschiedenis*, 803.
[65] Schrage, 'Restitution', 209, n. 8.

valid obligation is rescinded on grounds of fraud or duress.[66] Because Dutch law follows a causal system of transfer, there is also a concurrence with vindicatory remedies, based on ownership.[67] The practical difference is that the latter remedy can only be used to obtain restitution in *natura* of a thing. If it is lost or damaged, the remedy is useless. On the other hand, in the case of insolvency, the owner can use his vindicatory remedy to reclaim his property, and will not be left with a mere personal claim.

(iv) The common-law approach
The crucial point in these civilian jurisdictions is that fraud and duress are merely grounds which indicate that a contract is invalid. This renders performances under the contract undue, and (in German law at least) results in the performances being retained without legal ground or *sine causa*. Ultimately, relief could then be provided in unjustified enrichment.

But this is, of course, not the only way of viewing the function of fraud and duress. It can be argued that it is not necessary to work with models that employ concepts such as 'undue' or 'retention without legal ground'. Why not simply say that where a contract is concluded under fraud and duress, there should be restitution of any performance made in fulfilment of such a contract? Here the views of common lawyers who follow the 'unjust factors' approach to the law of restitution are of interest.[68] Since other contributions deal with this approach at length, this is only a brief overview of what unjust factors have to be relied on in claiming restitution where a contract has been concluded under fraud or duress. This is not the easiest of tasks.[69] For example, fraud as such does not seem to be an unjust factor (in fact, the word 'fraud' does not even feature in

---

[66] Art. 3:44 BW; Hartkamp and Tillema, *Contract Law*, §§ 102 ff., 328. Additional provisions apply if the recipient is in bad faith: he then is, among other things, liable for all damage and payment of interest from the time the obligation arose.

[67] See section III, 3, below. On the relationship between these remedies see Scheltema, *Onverschuldigde betaling*, 80 ff., 130 ff.

[68] It should be noted that these factors are not determined by the law of contract, but by the law of restitution itself. It is obvious that the law of restitution, thus conceived, has a much greater role to play in common-law systems than the law of unjustified enrichment in civilian systems. As Brice Dickson puts it, '[r]ather than being a particular head of recovery with a small part to play in the law of obligations it is supposedly a great unifying principle underlying the whole range of restitutionary remedies' ('Unjust Enrichment Claims: A Comparative Overview', [1995] 54 *CLJ* 100, 101; also see Steve Hedley, 'Unjust Enrichment', [1995] 54 *CLJ* 578).

[69] See Andrew Burrows, *The Law of Resitution* (1993), 106 (he refers to the 'quicksilver requirement'). For criticism of the 'unjust factors' approach from a comparative perspective see Zimmermann, 'Unjustified Enrichment', 414.

the index of one of the basic textbooks).[70] Some argue that the appropriate unjust factor is in fact error or mistake, since, as seen above, all misrepresentations induce error.[71] However, the reprehensible manner in which the error has been induced in the case of fraud requires exceptional protection for the victim. Fraud therefore needs to be dealt with separately from other cases of error. Others argue that in cases of mistake of fact (and presumably also those cases where the mistake was induced by fraud), the restitutionary ground of 'failure of consideration' is more appropriate. The problem here, though, is that there are different views on what this expression is supposed to mean.[72] Another possible unjust factor (more relevant to situations not involving a contract) is ignorance. Ignorance apparently would be the appropriate unjust factor where a third party obtained something without knowledge of the claimant as a consequence of another's fraud.[73] As for duress, it can be brought home under the unjust factor of 'compulsion',[74] but for a civil lawyer (at least), its relationship with some of the other cases of compulsion seems rather remote.[75] Finally, there is the idea that the use of an improper method of obtaining consent could amount to a 'wrong', although the exact relationship with compulsion as an unjust factor is not clear: one will have to look at the way the judge deals with the claim.[76]

---

[70] Burrows, *Law of Restitution*,

[71] See Peter Birks, *An Introduction to the Law of Restitution* (1985, revised edn, 1989), 167 ff.

[72] See Burrows, *Law of Restitution*, 108 ff. On the idea that in the case where a contract has been avoided on grounds of mistake (and presumably fraud), the unjust factor is 'failure of assumptions', see Andrew Tettenborn, *The Law of Restitution in England and Ireland* (2nd edn, 1996), 16, 135 ff., 139. On the dangers involved in introducing 'absence of consideration' as an unjust factor see Peter Birks, 'No Consideration: Restitution after Void Contracts', (1993) 23 *University of Western Australia LR* 195, 231 ff. (as quoted in Andrew Burrows and Ewan McKendrick, Cases and Materials on the Law of Restitution (1997), 294 ff.; cf. also the speech of Lord Goff of Chieveley in *Westdeutsche Landesbank Girozentrale v. Islington LBC* [1996] 2 All ER 961 (HL) at 967 ff.).

[73] Cf. *Transvaal and Delagoa Bay Investment Co. v. Atkinson* [1944] 1 All ER 579, which deals with the situation where the person committing the fraud knew that cheques were signed routinely.

[74] See Birks, *Introduction* 174–84. Burrows, *Law of Restitution*, 161, seems to regard the relationship between duress and compulsion more loosely; he merely states that duress can be distinguished from 'other autonomous unjust factors that, to a greater or lesser extent, also deal with compulsion, such as legal compulsion, necessity and exploitation'. Tettenborn, *Law of Restitution*, 14–15, 77 ff. avoids the generic concept 'compulsion' and simply regards duress as a 'factor qualifying voluntariness'.

[75] See Du Plessis, *Compulsion and Restitution*, 210 ff. The most notable example is the treatment of 'moral compulsion'. From a civilian perspective the idea that the good Samaritan or *negotiorum gestor* acts under compulsion seems rather unusual.

[76] Birks, *Introduction*, 318 ff.

Altogether this is not a model that is manifestly clear or user-friendly. However, if these difficulties of approach are disregarded for the moment, and it is simply assumed that fraud and duress can generally be regarded as (at least) belonging under the unjust factors of 'mistake' and 'compulsion', one important concluding observation can be made. It has been said that these unjust factors can be brought home under the generic term of 'non-voluntariness', which covers the situation where one person did not intend another to have something. It has also been said that this is the field of the *condictio* marked out by Lord Mansfield in the eighteenth-century decision of *Moses v. Macferlan*.[77] As seen above, the *Leistungskondiktion* in modern German law also covers the field of the *condictio*, through unifying all cases where a person failed to achieve a certain purpose when making a transfer to another. Thus, it seems that on a very broad level there are certain similarities between organising concepts of the civil law of unjustified enrichment and the common law of restitution.

But there is one crucial difference. The moment we ask '*why* was it not intended that another should have it?' – in other words, the moment we start subdividing these categories – the responses vary dramatically. The civil lawyer immediately responds that one important reason why it was not intended that another should have something is because it was not due. The case where a transfer was not due because a contract was rescinded on grounds of fraud or duress just happens to be one of many, and the civilian enrichment lawyer is not interested in devising long lists of all these cases. This is not to say that fraud or duress are irrelevant when determining whether certain rules modifying the measure of recovery should apply, but this does not detract from their primary function. On the other hand, the response of some common lawyers to the same question would be that the reason why restitution should be provided is that the victim was mistaken or compelled. To them the 'due/undue' distinction simply masks underlying reasons for providing restitution – reasons which should be the legitimate concern of enrichment lawyers. However, for present purposes it is not necessary to deal at length with these differences. They are not only dealt with in greater theoretical detail by other contributions, but from a practical perspective they do not seem to matter very much: both ultimately result in enrichment-based or restitutionary relief being provided where a contract was rescinded on grounds of fraud or duress.

---

[77] Peter Birks, 'Restitution: A View of Scots Law', [1985] *Current Legal Problems* 57, 67. The reference is to *Moses v. Macferlan* (1760) 2 Burr 1005 at 1009.

2. The effect of fraud and duress on the validity of a performance[78]

Where a transfer has been made in fulfilment or performance of a contract concluded under fraud or duress, its recoverability is dealt with in terms of the principles set out above. However, as stated at the outset, not all transfers are aimed at the performance of contractual obligations. What impact then do fraud and duress have on the recoverability of these transfers? In the civil-law systems under review, the answer depends on two issues, namely whether the transfers were in fact due, and whether achieving fulfilment or performance requires the type of act or declaration which can be rescinded.

(a) Undue transfers: *the condictio indebiti*

It has been indicated above that one of the most important features of the civil law of unjustified enrichment is that it awards an enrichment remedy if something was given that turned out not to be due. This notion has a certain rational appeal, for why, if something was not owed, should the recipient be entitled to retain it? However, a number of systems recognise that the mere fact that something not due was given does not automatically entitle the transferor to an enrichment remedy. It is not necessary here to recount the centuries-old debate on whether the claimant who seeks relief with the *condictio indebiti* had to prove a factor (such as error) that justifies the departure of the *indebitum* from his hands, or whether it is up to the recipient to argue that recovery should be barred because of the transferor's knowledge that it was due.[79]

To focus solely on the modern systems under review, it is clear that the approaches diverge considerably. South African law, which has retained the *condictio indebiti* in uncodified form, does not only require proof of an undue transfer, but also further factors such as excusable error or certain

---

[78] On the nature of performance in German law in general see Joachim Gernhuber, *Die Erfüllung und ihre Surrogate sowie das Erlöschen der Schuldverhältnisse aus anderen Gründen* (2nd edn, 1994), §§ 5 ff.; Helmut Heinrichs, in: *Münchener Kommentar zum Bürgerlichen Gesetzbuch* (3rd edn, 1994) vol. II, § 362, n. 2; Josef Esser and Hans-Leo Weyers, *Schuldrecht* (7th edn, 1991), vol. II, 429 ff.; Karl Larenz, *Lehrbuch des Schuldrechts* (14th edn, 1987), vol. I, § 18; for Dutch law, see arts. 6:27–51; 6:111–26 BW; Hartkamp, *Mr. C Asser's Handleiding*, n. 184. The effect of fraud on various methods of performance, such as the Continental counterparts of negotiable instruments, documentary credits, or credit or charge cards, which could involve a host of a additional (collateral) agreements, regulating the rights of third parties or stopping the process of payment, cannot be considered here (see in the context of German law, Gernhuber, *Die Erfüllung*, § 9 II; Larenz, *Lehrbuch*, § 18 IV).

[79] See Zimmermann, *Law of Obligations*, 834 ff., 848 ff., 866 ff.

forms of compulsion (under the influence of the English law of 'payments made under duress of goods').[80] In German law, the approach is more indirect: proof of error or compulsion is not required, but (as seen above in the case of a performance under a contract rescinded on grounds of fraud) knowledge on the part of the transferor that no debt is due could be raised as a defence barring recovery. The relevance of fraud is then to indicate that the victim acted in error, and consequently could not have known that no debt was due. It will further be recalled that the bar to recovery based on knowledge could not apply in cases of duress: it cannot be said that the victim acted contrary to his previous conduct if such conduct was compelled.[81] In Dutch law, the protection of the transferor is greater: even knowledge that no debt is due does not bar recovery. And yet, even here, the fact that the performance has been obtained through fraud and duress is not irrelevant. Since it influences the question whether the recipient would be considered to be in bad faith, and hence in default, it may give rise to increased liability.[82] All in all, it is clear that outside the contractual context too, fraud and duress influence the relief which the law of unjustified enrichment can give a person who made an undue transfer.

(b) Due transfers

If a due transfer (irrespective of the source of the obligation) is obtained through fraud or duress, the instinctive reaction is that there can be no liability based on unjustified enrichment, since there is no enrichment. After all, if the transfer merely takes the place of the obligation, the recipient's net worth remains the same. However, this would only be the case if the transfer in fact succeeded in validly discharging the obligation. The question that therefore now arises is whether fraud or duress might in fact influence the validity of performance. To answer this question it needs to be established whether performance involves some declaration of intent or act that could be rescinded. Unfortunately, in the civilian

---

[80] See *Commissioner for Inland Revenue v. First National Bank Ltd* 1990 (3) SA 641 (A) 646 ff.; J. G. Lotz, 'Enrichment', in: W. A. Joubert (ed.), *The Law of South Africa* (1st reissue, 1996), vol. IX, § 79. On the problems surrounding the determination of the key requirements of the *condictio indebiti* in another mixed jurisdiction, namely Scots law, see Robin Evans-Jones, 'Unjust Enrichment, Contract and the Third Reception of Roman law in Scotland', (1993) 109 *LQR* 643; also his 'Some Reflections on the Condictio Indebiti in a Mixed Legal System', (1994) 111 *SALJ* 759; Du Plessis, *Compulsion and Restitution*, 202 ff., 221 ff.

[81] See section III, 1, (a) above.

[82] See Schrage, [1994] *Restitution LR* 208, 215 and the treatment of arts. 6:205, 6:84 ff. BW.

systems under consideration, no unanimity exists on this point. Classical Roman law knew the doctrine of *solutio*, but this simply entailed that you did what you had obliged yourself to do.[83] There was no refined analysis as to whether *solutio* is a unilateral or bilateral act, or with what intention it has to be made. In the *ius commune*, no particular doctrinal approach prevailed either.[84] It is not surprising then that the position in modern civilian systems is anything but settled.[85]

Here only a brief review of the main approaches to the nature of performance will be attempted. Particular emphasis will be placed on the position in German law, where the debate has reached a considerable degree of sophistication. First, there is the traditional approach that performance requires *agreement* between the parties that a transfer is intended to fulfil a specific obligation.[86] Since such an agreement would require valid declarations of intent, fraud or duress could conceivably affect the validity of performance. However, this approach has difficulties in accommodating performance through rendering a service or omission, where

---

[83] See Ulp. D. 50, 16, 176; 12, 6, 63; 46, 3, 54; 46, 3, 80 pr.; J. A. C. Thomas, *Textbook of Roman Law* (1976), 343; Zimmermann, *Law of Obligations*, 748 ff.

[84] Most Roman-Dutch authors did not expressly require an agreement whereby performance extinguishes the obligations; see Hugo de Groot, *Inleidinge tot de Hollandsche Rechts-geleertheyd* (ed. Robert Warden Lee, 2nd edn, 1953), III, XXXIX, 8; Johannes Voet, *Commentarius ad Pandectas* (1827, 1829), XLVI, III, 1 (translated by Percival Gane, *The Selective Voet, being the Commentary on the Pandects* (1957), vol. VII, 93). In fact, it even was said that a third party could pay on behalf of an unaware or unwilling debtor (see ibid., XLVI, III, 1). However, the seventeenth-century German author Wolfgang Adam Lauterbach and, following in his footsteps, the eighteenth-century Roman-Dutch author Willem Schorer seem to have believed that proper performance does require the consent of both parties (see Lauterbach, *Collegium theoretico-practicum* (1723 ff.), Lib. XLVI, Tit. III, nn. 3, 4; Willem Schorer, *Aantekeningen over de inleydinge tot de Hollandsche rechtsgeleerdheid* (translated into Dutch by J. E. Austen, 1784–6), III, XXXIX, 7.

[85] In fact, Wolfgang Fikentscher regards the legal nature of fulfilment as belonging to the most contentious areas in the whole of the law of obligations: *Schuldrecht* (9th edn, 1997), § 268. The compilers of the German Civil Code were careful to avoid making an explicit choice, and preferred to leave it in the hands of legal scholarship to come up with an answer (see Mugdan, 'Motive', 81). On German law in general, see Helmut Heinrichs, in: Palandt (ed.), *Bürgerliches Gesetzbuch* (59th edn, 2000), § 362, nn. 5–7; Heinrichs, in: *Münchener Kommentar*, § 362, nn. 5–14; Larenz, *Lehrbuch*, § 18 I. In the law of the Netherlands, uncertainty also prevails (see Hartkamp, *Mr C Asser's Handleiding* vol. I, n. 186).

[86] On this theory, which is known as the *Vertragstheorie* in German law, and which really represents a continuation of the views which were popular in the last stages of the *ius commune*, see Larenz, *Lehrbuch*, § 18 I sub 2; Heinrichs, in: *Münchener Kommentar*, § 362, n. 6 with footnote 12; Gernhuber, *Die Erfüllung*, § 5 II 3; cf. also RGZ 60, 24 (28). In the Netherlands, such an approach was advanced by M. H. Bregstein, *Ongegronde Vermogensvermeerdering* (Ph.D. thesis, 1927), 278.

it is rather artificial to work with the idea of 'acceptance'.[87] One might argue (as modern South African law does[88]) that these cases are merely exceptions to the rule, but this still leaves the problem that the creditor might refuse to accept performance. An approach currently more popular maintains that performance requires only that the debtor indicates the purpose for which the benefit is conferred.[89] It is not quite clear whether this determination of the purpose of the transfer is itself a juristic act. Apparently it is only aimed at 'assigning' the transfer to a debt, and not at achieving the legal consequence of fulfilment.[90] However, it does seem as if some declaration of will is made, which at least would be voidable in cases of error.[91] Although this approach also suffers from defects,[92] it does have one notable advantage. It will be recalled that, for purposes of the German law of unjustified enrichment, a *Leistung* is defined as the conscious conferment of a benefit with a certain purpose in mind. This approach adopts essentially the same definition for purposes of defining *Leistung* in the context of performance, and therefore streamlines the application of this concept in different branches of law. However, this view does not enjoy general acceptance.

The approach which currently prevails in German law rejects any notion that performance requires an 'intention to fulfil' or an indication as to the 'purpose' of a transfer. All that is required is for a benefit to be conferred.[93] In other words, the debtor simply has to bring about performance in a

---

[87] For other difficulties see Gernhuber, *Die Erfüllung*, § 5 II 3. On the rejection of this approach in Dutch law, see Hartkamp, *Mr C Asser's Handleiding*, n. 187.

[88] See J. C. de Wet and A. H. van Wyk, *Kontraktereg en Handelsreg* (5th edn, 1992), vol. I, 183, 263, n. 73; Gerhard Lubbe and Christina Murray, *Farlam & Hathaway, Contract: Cases, Materials and Commentary* (1988), 716; Schalk van der Merwe et al., *Contract: General Principles* (1993), 359, referring to *Thienhaus v. Metje & Ziegler Ltd* 1965 (3) SA 25 (A) 45. On related attempts at modification through the *beschränkte Vertragstheorie* in German law see Larenz, *Lehrbuch*, § 18 I sub 3; Heinrichs, in: *Münchener Kommentar*, § 362, n. 7 with footnote 13; Gernhuber, *Die Erfüllung* § 5 II 4.

[89] On the *Theorie der finalen Leistungsbewirkung* see Larenz, *Lehrbuch*, § 18 I; Heinrichs, in: *Münchener Kommentar*, § 362, n. 10 with footnote 16; Gernhuber, *Die Erfüllung* § 5 II 8.

[90] Larenz, *Lehrbuch*, § 18 I; but see Hans Wieling, 'Empfängerhorizont: Auslegung der Zweckbestimmung und Eigentumserwerb', 1977 JZ 291.

[91] Cf. Dieter Medicus, *Schuldrecht I: Allgemeiner Teil* (11th edn, 1999), § 23 IV 3 (he refers to BGHZ 106, 163, 166); Heinrichs, in: *Burgerliches Gesetzbuch*, § 362, n. 5.

[92] The mere fact that an indication of the purpose of the transfer occasionally is important (e.g. where there are several debts and it has to be determined which of them the debtor wants to fulfil) does not imply that such an indication always should be required; see Heinrichs, in: *Münchener Kommentar*, § 362, n. 13; Larenz, *Lehrbuch*, § 18 I.

[93] See Larenz, *Lehrbuch*, § 18 I; Medicus, *Schuldrecht I*, § 23 IV 3; Gernhuber, *Die Erfüllung*, § 5 II 6.

'real' or factual sense. Thus, in the case of sale, performance would take place if ownership was transferred to the purchaser.[94] The 'allocation' or 'assignment' of the transfer to the fulfilment of a specific debt is automatic.[95] Unsurprisingly, this approach, too, has been subject to criticism. It fails to show which obligation is to be fulfilled if there is a plurality of debts; it has also been doubted whether it is acceptable to design a theory around the exceptional case (such as *omissio*) where a purely factual performance would indeed suffice, instead of the commoner case (such as delivery) where transfer does require some juristic act.[96]

In the light of the above, it should therefore be clear that the contentious nature of performance leaves the question unanswered whether a due transfer obtained through fraud or duress is recoverable with enrichment-based remedies. However, the question can be asked from a policy perspective. Should the victim merely be satisfied with a delictual claim, based on the violation of his dignity and physical integrity, or with the cold comfort of the criminal sanction? On the one hand, there is the policy objective that one should not waste the time of the courts by reclaiming what has to be transferred in any event. This is encapsulated in the ancient civilian maxim of *dolo facit qui petit quod redditurus est*, which essentially states that in such a case a person acts with *dolus*.[97] But this maxim makes no distinction as to the way in which the defendant obtained what now has to be returned. Presumably it is aimed against the type of 'technical' reliance on a right in a way that violates bona fides or good faith.[98] On the other hand, there is ample civilian authority which supports the policy objective that where a person takes the law into his own hands, and disturbs the peace, he should be made to return what he has obtained, irrespective of whether he is entitled to it or not. Here the relief which for centuries has been provided to possessors of property, regardless of the validity of their title, is particularly relevant.[99] All

---

[94] § 929 BGB. The same holds true for cession: § 398 BGB (*Abtretung*).

[95] Obviously, specific rules apply in the case of appropriation of performance; see § 366 (1) BGB.

[96] Fikentscher, *Schuldrecht*, § 270.   [97] Paul. D. 44, 4, 8 pr.; D. 50, 17, 173, 3.

[98] See Zimmermann, *Law of Obligations*, 668. The accompanying example in Paul. D. 44, 4, 8, 1 indicates a more restricted scope of application for the maxim. It reads as follows: '[t]hus, if an heir has been condemned not to claim from the debtor, the debtor can employ the defence of fraud, as well as bring an action based on the will'.

[99] See, from a South African perspective, the treatment of the *mandament van spolie* in C. G. van der Merwe and M. J. de Waal, *The Law of Things and Servitudes* (1993), §§ 73 ff. Although the roots of the *mandament* lie in Canon law, Roman law knew possessory interdicts, which fulfilled related functions.

in all, the notion that enrichment-based remedies can be provided where a due transfer is obtained through improper means therefore cannot be dismissed out of hand.[100]

On the assumption that such a claim should be allowed, it may be asked in conclusion what civil-law remedy could most conveniently be used toward this end. In the light of the fact that we are dealing with a due transfer, any modern version of the *condictio indebiti* seems inappropriate. Another possibility is to have recourse to a long but almost forgotten line of civilian authority which regards the application of extortion as so improper that it gives rise to illegality, and hence to another *condictio*, the *condictio ob turpem vel iniustam causam*. However, the references in the *ius commune* to this remedy ultimately derive from a text dealing with a transfer that is undue, because it was made pursuant to an extorted stipulation.[101] In modern German law, one of the (last remaining) fields of application of the *Leistungskondiktion* in its *condictio ob turpem vel iniustam causam* guise are in fact 'extortion-related' situations, but this again applies to payments which are not due.[102] It may further be argued that duress amounts to a type of *Eingriff* or encroachment, but (as pointed out before) in cases of extortion we are still dealing with a *Leistung* or 'giving', rather than the type of 'taking' that an encroachment would require. Ultimately, the solution may well be to recognise a whole new field of application of the *Leistungskondiktion*, based on retention of a transfer without legal ground due to impropriety of the method used to obtain it. Such a development seems rather unlikely in the light of the approach currently favoured to the nature of performance in German law.

As far as South African law is concerned, the *condictiones indebiti* and *ob turpem vel iniustam causam* would be inappropriate for reasons similar to those mentioned when dealing with the German law. However, South African law does recognise the *condictio sine causa specialis*. In essence, it is a residual category, covering cases of *sine causa* retention that do not fall

---

[100] Cf. the Sri Lankan case of *Attorney-General v. Saibo* (1923) NLR 321, where a payment made in consequence of an unlawful threat of detention of some boats by the customs authorities was held to be recoverable, even though it was due. Incidentally, in that case it was held that this position also conforms with the position in English law; see Chief Justice Bertram's discussion of *Sowell v. Champion* (1838) 6 A & E 407; 112 ER 156; *Clark v. Woods* (1848) 2 Ex 395; 154 ER 545 and *Pitt v. Coomes* (1835) 2 A & E 459; 111 ER 178.
[101] Pomp. D. 12, 5, 7.
[102] See Larenz and Canaris, *Lehrbuch*, § 68 I 6; du Plessis, *Compulsion and Restitution*, 146 ff., but also see *Attorney-General v. Saibo* (1923) NLR 321 at 324.

under the established *condictiones*.¹⁰³ In so far as the debt-extinguishing agreement required for performance can be rescinded, it can be argued that we are dealing with a case of *sine causa* retention that warrants the provision of relief by way of this enrichment remedy.

3. The effect of fraud and duress on the validity of the transfer of ownership

It has been seen that fraud and duress may affect the ability of a transfer to fulfil an obligation, depending on which theory of performance is followed. It is now necessary to go one step further and inquire whether fraud or duress might affect the validity of the transfer itself. Here one encounters the difficult problem of the relationship between the laws of property and unjustified enrichment. In this regard the difference between systems that follow the abstract and causal approaches to the transfer of ownership is fundamental. This distinction cuts across the boundaries of the civil-law/common-law division. For example, German law and South African law follow the abstract approach, while Dutch law and English law regard the transfer of ownership as causal. What are the implications for the choice of remedy where a transfer has been obtained as a consequence of fraud or duress?

According to the abstract system, the validity of a transfer is not affected by the invalidity of any underlying obligation that the transfer is supposed to fulfil. In this regard German law draws a clear distinction between a *Verpflichtungsgeschäft* – that is, a juristic act (such as a contract of sale) that gives rise to an obligation to transfer – and a *Verfügungsgeschäft* – that is, a juristic act by means of which a right (such as ownership) is directly affected (i.e. transferred, encumbered, changed or nullified). The rescission of a declaration of will under § 123 BGB (the provision dealing with fraud and duress) may influence the validity of both these juristic acts. If ownership has passed (that is, the *Verfügungsgeschäft* was valid), the claimant would have to use remedies based on unjustified enrichment.¹⁰⁴ Vindicatory or ownership-based remedies are not available if the transfer (and more specifically the real agreement required for transfer) is valid. However, if the *Verfügungsgeschäft* itself is invalid, ownership cannot pass, and

---

¹⁰³ See *B & H Engineering v. First National Bank of South Africa Ltd* 1995 (2) SA 279 (A); Du Plessis, *Compulsion and Restitution*, 223.

¹⁰⁴ See section III, 1, (b) above. As Dernburg so graphically pointed out, the function of the law of unjustified enrichment is to heal the wounds inflicted by the abstract system (*Bürgerliches Recht* (3rd edn, 1906), vol. II/2, 677 ff. as quoted by Zimmermann, *Law of Obligations*, 867).

the owner should then be able to institute a vindicatory claim against the recipient in terms of § 985 BGB. This paragraph holds that an owner can demand that a possessor return his property.[105] The problem, of course, is to determine whether someone who has transferred something under fraud or duress is still the owner. The key to this problem lies in § 935(1) BGB.[106] In essence this provides that acquisition of ownership is not possible if something has been stolen from the owner, gone missing, or otherwise been lost (*abhanden gekommen*). Since one way in which something can become 'lost' is through duress (but not fraud),[107] the claimant can rely on this section of the code to prove that ownership has not passed, and that the possessor should return his property in terms of § 985 BGB. However, not all cases of duress are regarded as sufficiently serious to affect the validity of a *Verfügungsgeschäft*, and it is difficult to determine where the border lies. According to the *Bundesgerichtshof*,[108] one would have to prove that there was duress through irresistible physical violence or equivalent psychological compulsion.[109]

If one turns to the position in modern South African law, it generally seems very similar to that prevailing in German law: it also favours the abstract system,[110] and therefore excludes vindicatory remedies where there has been a transfer of ownership. However, there has been some support for a causal system, especially where something has been obtained as a consequence of fraud.[111] This is no doubt due to the influence of Roman-Dutch law, which maintained that valid title could not pass under a contract induced by fraud, and that a *rei vindicatio* had to be used to effect recovery.[112] But these views have not received general recognition,

---

[105] Cf. Dieter Giesen, *BGB Allgemeiner Teil: Rechtsgeschäftslehre* (1991), n. 303; Esser and Weyers, *Schuldrecht*, § 49 III.
[106] On this paragraph, see generally, Friedrich Quack, in: *Münchener Kommentar zum Bürgerlichen Gesetzbuch* (3rd edn, 1997), vol. III, § 935. It does not apply to money, bearer instruments, or things sold by public auction (cf. § 935(2) BGB).
[107] See Quack, in: *Münchener Kommentar*, § 935, n. 9.
[108] BGHZ 4, 10 (34 ff.).
[109] This view has been criticised by Jürgen F. Baur and Rolf Stürner in their edition of Fritz Baur, *Lehrbuch des Sachenrechts* (17th edn, 1999), 610–11 (they favour a broader approach to cover all situations of *Drohung*).
[110] See the majority judgment in *Commissioner of Customs & Excise v. Randles, Brothers & Hudson Ltd* 1941 AD 369; *Trust Bank van Afrika Bpk v. Western Bank Bpk en Andere NNO* 1978 (4) SA 281 (A); *Air-Kel (Edms) Bpk h/a Merkel Motors v. Bodenstein en 'n ander* 1980 (3) SA 917 (A); Van der Merwe and De Waal, *Law of Things*, §§ 13, 166–8.
[111] See *Kopelowitz v. West & Others* 1954 (4) SA 296 (W) 300; Van der Merwe and De Waal, *Law of Things*, § 167.
[112] For a critical assessment see J. Scholtens, 'Justa Causa Traditionis', (1957) 74 *SALJ* 280, 285 ff.

especially since they seem to reflect some confusion between the different effects of voidness and voidability on the validity of a contract itself as opposed to the real agreement needed to effect delivery under the contract.[113] It is only if fraud (and presumably duress) affect the validity of the real agreement that a *rei vindicatio* may be awarded.[114]

Dutch law subscribes to the causal system, which means that there is no transfer of ownership if the causa is invalid. As seen above, a curious feature of this system is that the transfer can be recovered not only with a modern version of that central remedy available to the owner, the *rei vindicatio*, but also with a specific remedy used for the recovery of undue payments.[115] The relationship between these remedies is somewhat complex: in contrast to German law, some overlapping seems inevitable,[116] but there are important cases where only the one remedy would be available. For example, only the claim based on undue payment would be available if a payment of money can no longer be identified. Furthermore, if there has been a disposition to a third party, the victim will have to use the vindicatory action against the third party. If the third party is protected because he was bona fide, the victim will only be left with an action based on undue payment against the recipient.[117] It is also important to stress that the sections of the Burgerlijk Wetboek that deal with recovery of undue payments do not form part of the provisions relating to liability based on unjustified enrichment. One is therefore dealing with something more complex than the terrain usually covered by the *condictio indebiti*.[118]

4. Fraud and duress as delicts

The laws of delict and unjustified enrichment are both aimed at correcting imbalances. In the case of delict, the correction takes the form of an award of damages as compensation for a civil injury or harm, while in the case of the law of unjustified enrichment, it takes the form of a restitutionary award, aimed at taking away or 'skimming off' the enrichment.[119]

---

[113] See *ibid.*, 288 ff.
[114] See the analysis of *Dalrymple, Frank & Feinstein v. Friedman and Another (2)* 1954 (4) SA 649 (W) at 664 provided by C. G. van der Merwe, *Sakereg* (2nd edn, 1989), 312, and approved of in *The Tao Men* 1996 (1) SA 559 (CPD). Also see Du Plessis, *Compulsion and Restitution*, 121, n. 65.
[115] See Scheltema, *Onverschuldigde betaling*, 130 ff. on the relationship between arts. 6:203 ff. BW and art. 5:2 BW.
[116] See the explanation by Prof. Meijers in Van Zeben and Du Pon, *Parlementaire Geschiedenis*, 813.
[117] Scheltema, *Onverschuldidge betaling*, 81.
[118] *Ibid.*, 138 ff.
[119] See Zimmermann, 'Unjustified Enrichment', 403.

Defining how exactly transfers obtained through fraud or duress should be dealt with under such a division has never been simple. There is a strand of civilian authority which, out of rather overenthusiastic loyalty to the *coactus volui* principle, regards the relief in the case of duress as delictual. In essence, the argument is that what is willed under duress is none the less willed; duress would therefore not affect the validity of a contract, and would not give rise to the remedy of *restitutio in integrum*.[120] This means that it would be up to the law of delict to effect restitution of the transferred object.[121] However, civilian systems nowadays avoid such an exclusionary approach, and prefer to award delictual relief in conjunction with enrichment-based or contractual remedies. This gives rise to some uncertainty with regard to concurrence of actions. In South African law, for example, the measure of the duty to provide full restitution (*restitutio in integrum*) is close[122] to the measure of damages in cases of delict, where the aggrieved party has to be placed in the position in which he would have been if the delict had not been committed.[123] The German law of duress also recognises delictual relief. A person who is entitled to rescind a declaration of will through *Anfechtung* is not only entitled to cancel a contract by relying on *culpa in contrahendo*,[124] but can also claim damages because of blameworthy conduct during negotiations.[125] The claim for damages is subject to § 249 BGB, which aims at putting the threatened person in the position he would have been in, had someone not

---

[120] See James Gordley, 'Natural Law Origins of the Common Law of Contract', in: John Barton (ed.), *Towards a General Law of Contract* (1990), 398. Some Roman law textbooks also classify *metus* and *dolus* as praetorian delicts (see Thomas, *Textbook*, 373 ff.).

[121] See James Dalrymple, 1st Viscount Stair, *Institutions of the Law of Scotland* (tercentenary edn by D. M. Walker, 1981), Book I, Title 9, 4; Du Plessis, *Compulsion and Restitution*, 55 ff.

[122] But obviously not identical; see Van der Merwe et al., *Contract*, 106. Cf. also M. A. Lambiris, *Orders of Specific Performance and Restitutio in Integrum in South African Law* (1989), 333, n. 60. For example, *restitutio in integrum* does not cover consequential loss.

[123] Cf. *Davidson v. Bonafede* 1981 (2) SA 501 (C), where it is acknowledged that delictual relief might take the form of 'restitution' of the purchase price. According to Marais AJ, 'in the end, it seems to me to be a question of degree as to whether any particular financial adjustment which falls to be made is one which is an integral element in the granting of *restitutio in integrum*, or is one which is collateral to it, and so should form the subject of a distinct claim for damages' (at 511G). On the relationship between *restitutio in integrum* and enrichment remedies in South African law, see Visser, 'Rethinking Unjustified Enrichment', 215 ff.

[124] Jauernig, *Bürgerliches Gesetzbuch*, § 123, n. 5; Giesen, *BGB*, nn. 303, 307. But cf. Hans Brox, *Allgemeiner Teil des BGB* (20th edn, 1996), nn. 425, 413.

[125] On *culpa in contrahendo* in general, cf. Larenz, *Lehrbuch*, § 9 I; Friedrich Kessler and Edith Fine, 'Culpa in Contrahendo, Bargaining in Good Faith, and Freedom of Contract: A Comparative Study', (1964) 77 *Harvard LR* 401 ff.

influenced his ability to decide freely.[126] Furthermore, if the duress is covered by the provisions of the criminal code dealing with coercion (§ 240 StGB – *Nötigung*) and extortion (§ 253 StGB – *Erpressung*), it would also be possible to claim delictual damages under § 823(2) BGB, which provides that a person incurs delictual liability if he infringes a statute intended for the protection of others. Finally, a delictual claim may be brought under § 826 BGB, which provides that a person who intentionally causes damage to another in a manner contrary to morality is bound to compensate that person for the damage.[127] This also seems to be the position in Dutch law, which imposes delictual liability if an act was contrary to proper social conduct.[128]

IV. Conclusions

Although civil-law systems have traditionally recognised that something obtained through *dolus* or *metus* (loosely translated as fraud or duress) has to be restored, they have not been particularly consistent or clear as to the exact legal basis of this obligation. None the less, it would seem that the modern tendency is to base the duty primarily on the need to prevent unjustified enrichment (rather than on contract or sui generis grounds) and to provide complementary or supplementary relief through the laws of property and delict.

If the conclusions of this chapter are restricted to the law of unjustified enrichment, it is apparent that fraud or duress are relevant in the following contexts. First, through influencing the validity of certain acts, they can remove the legal ground or basis for the retention of a benefit or transfer. The classic case is where a contract is invalidated through rescission. In some systems, it is specifically recognised that in such a case the purported performance is retained without legal ground because it is no longer due or owing – in other words, because it is an *indebitum*. However, the mere fact that a transfer is not due does not automatically give rise to relief based on unjustified enrichment. There are situations where the circumstances surrounding the making of the undue transfer are such that its recovery cannot be allowed. This leads to the second function of fraud and duress.

---

[126] On the concurrence between the various claims, cf. Giesen, *BGB*, n. 307.
[127] Cf. *ibid.*, n. 303 and Medicus, *Bürgerliches Recht*, n. 626; Brox, *Allgemeiner Teil*, n. 425. Generally see Larenz and Canaris, *Lehrbuch*, § 68 I 1 c).
[128] See Hartkamp and Tillema, *Contract Law*, § 105; especially on the obligation to pay damages, arts. 6:162, 6:95 ff. BW.

There is a long-standing controversy as to whether the person who made an undue transfer must prove a further ground (most notably error, but also compulsion) in order to succeed, or whether it is up to the defendant to raise a defence (based usually on the knowledge that no debt was due), which indicates that it was intended that the recipient could retain the undue transfer. Whatever the preferable approach may be, the fact patterns of fraud and duress are also relevant in this context, in that they assist in determining whether enrichment-based liability should be imposed. Fraud fulfils this function by indicating that someone acted in error (that is, wrongly believed a debt was due), while duress shows that there was no indication that a transfer could be retained. They therefore show that, in both instances, the victim's frame of mind was of such a nature that relief should not be barred.

However, there is a further related but distinct function of these improper methods of obtaining consent. Even when it has been determined that enrichment liability should be imposed in principle, it may still influence the exact measure of such liability. While some civilian systems generally prefer to hold the recipient liable only to the extent that he is still enriched, it stands to reason that such protection should not be accorded to the recipient who used fraud or duress to obtain the transfer. His unacceptable conduct and lack of bona fide belief in being entitled to retain what he received should render him liable for the full value of what he received.

Three final observations may be made. The first is that it is simplistic to state that civilian systems only regard the fact patterns covered by fraud and duress as relevant so far as they indicate that contracts are invalid, and that contractual performances are therefore retained without legal ground. While fraud or duress may not be 'unjust factors' directly regarded as grounds for recovery in unjustified enrichment, they certainly matter for the rules regulating the restriction and extent of enrichment-based relief.

The second observation is that, although the civilian tradition generally places strong emphasis on the recoverability of undue transfers, the possibility cannot be discounted that fraud or duress could also render due transfers recoverable. Much depends on whether rescission of performance of the due transfer is possible from a doctrinal perspective, and whether policy considerations in any event justify providing relief. If this is so, then fraud and duress could indeed be regarded as 'factors' that justify enrichment-based relief.

The last observation is that if there is one aspect of the treatment of fraud and duress in the civil law which deserves criticism, then it is the lack of clarity surrounding the essential features of some of the specific enrichment remedies. The prevailing view in German law regarding the nature of the *Leistungskondiktion* is particularly problematic. Although it is said that this remedy should be awarded where a transfer has been obtained through duress, it is not clear what the purpose of such a transfer is supposed to be, and how this purpose is supposed to fail. These problems are avoided by minority approaches to the *Leistungskondiktion*, as well as by Dutch law, which do not focus on any purpose of a transfer and simply provide relief based on the absence of a legal ground.

PART V

Change of position

8 Restitution without enrichment? Change of position and *Wegfall der Bereicherung*

James Gordley

I. Introduction

In German law,[1] American law[2] and, more recently, English law, it is a defence to an action for unjust enrichment that the defendant is no longer enriched.[3] Nevertheless, many German scholars want to limit this defence. My former teacher, John Dawson, thought it leads to senseless results in Germany,[4] which American courts avoid only by refusing to apply it. In the United States, he said, 'we would not as in Germany, conceive of enrichment as a variable that can be recovered only as long as it lasts'.[5]

I do not like to quarrel with Dawson. I spent my early professional life believing he was infallible. This once, however, he may have been mistaken. At any rate, I do not think this defence leads to senseless results as long as it is confined to its original scope, using it to resolve the problems it was originally meant to resolve.

II. The original scope of the doctrine

These problems become clear if the origin of the doctrine is examined. The drafters of the German Civil Code took the doctrine from the nineteenth-century pandectists, Windscheid and Savigny. Savigny seems to have taken it from members of the seventeenth- and eighteenth-century natural law

---

[1] § 818(3) BGB.
[2] Restatement of the Law of Restitution, Quasi Contracts and Constructive Trusts (1937), § 142.
[3] *Lipkin Gorman (a Firm) v. Karpnale Ltd* [1991] 2 AC 548.
[4] John P. Dawson, 'Erasable Enrichment in German Law', (1981) 61 *Boston University LR* 271–314.
[5] John P. Dawson, 'Restitution Without Enrichment', (1981) 61 *Boston University LR* 563, 564.

227

school such as Grotius and Pufendorf. They took it from a group centred in Spain in the sixteenth century and known to historians as the 'late scholastics'. The late scholastics had been discussing the implications of Aristotle's concept of commutative justice as it had been interpreted by Thomas Aquinas. As Robert Feenstra has pointed out,[6] their efforts gave rise to the modern idea of unjust enrichment as a separate body of law coeval with contract and tort.

According to Aristotle, while distributive justice gives each citizen a fair share of whatever resources a community has to divide, commutative justice preserves each person's share. In involuntary transactions, one who took or destroyed another's resources has to give back an equivalent amount. In voluntary transactions, parties have to exchange resources of equivalent value.[7] This distinction between involuntary and voluntary transactions not only resembles the one now drawn between tort and contract, but seems to have been its lineal ancestor. Our distinction goes back to Gaius.[8] Modern scholars believe that he took it from Aristotle.[9]

In any event, Thomas Aquinas explained that when one person had acquired or interfered with another's property, he might be liable for two different reasons. First, he might be liable because of the way in which he did so (*acceptio rei*): he might have acted wrongfully, against the owner's will, in which case he was liable whether or not he still had the property; or he might have acted with the owner's consent, in which case whether he was liable depended on the kind of voluntary agreement they had made.[10] Secondly, he might be liable merely because he had another's property, regardless of how he had come by it (*ipsa res accepta*). According to Aquinas, commutative justice required that he give it back.[11]

In this last case, according to the late scholastics, and then Grotius and Pufendorf, a person who no longer has another's property should

---

[6] Robert Feenstra, 'Grotius' Doctrine of Unjust Enrichment as a Source of Obligation: Its Influence on Roman-Dutch Law' in: E. J. H. Schrage (ed.), *Unjust Enrichment* (1995), 197.

[7] *Nicomachean Ethics*, V, 9, 1130b–1131a.   [8] Gai. 3, 88.

[9] Reinhard Zimmermann, *The Law of Obligations: Roman Foundations of the Civilian Tradition* (1990, paperback edn, 1996), 10–11; Max Kaser, *Das Römische Privatrecht* (2nd edn, 1971), vol. I, 522; Anthony Honoré, *Gaius* (1962), 100; Helmut Coing, 'Zum Einfluß der Philosophie des Aristoteles auf die Entwicklung des römischen Rechts', (1952) 69 *Zeitschrift der Savigny-Stiftung für Rechtsgeschichte (Romanistische Abteilung)* 24, 37–8.

[10] *Summa theologiae* II–II, Quaest. LXII, art. 6. According to Aquinas, if the transaction was purely for the benefit of the person who received the property – for example, a gratuitous loan – then compensation is due even if the property has been lost; if it was purely for the benefit of the owner – for example, a deposit – then compensation is not due except if the loss was caused by grave fault.

[11] *Summa theologiae* II–II, Quaest. LXII, art. 6.

still be liable if he has become richer by having once had it.[12] Such a person is liable only to the extent that he is still enriched. Thus he is not liable if he consumed another's property or gave it away[13] except to the extent that he saved money he would otherwise have spent. He is not liable if he bought and then resold another's property except if he made a profit.[14]

They reached this conclusion by first setting aside every other reason that the plaintiff might recover until all that is left is the defendant's enrichment by means of the plaintiff's resources. It is a defence that the defendant is no longer enriched, but only if he no longer had the plaintiff's property and is not liable because of the way he had initially acquired it, whether wrongfully or with the plaintiff's consent. The thesis of this chapter is that the doctrine is correct provided that it is confined to its original scope. It should be applied when the only reason the plaintiff should recover is that he has been enriched out of the defendant's resources.

III. Cases outside the proper scope of the doctrine

The trouble in Germany arose, I believe, by oversimplifying this approach: by thinking that a plaintiff who can neither find his property in the defendant's hands, nor recover in tort or contract, must recover in unjust enrichment, and if so, can recover only to the extent that the defendant is enriched. German courts did so because of the structure of their code. They supposed that the plaintiff must make out his claim under §§ 812–22 BGB, which govern unjust enrichment, unless he can reclaim his property under § 985 BGB, the modern version of the *rei vindicatio*, or recover in tort, or recover in contract. At that point, they either had to live with the consequences of the doctrine of *Wegfall* or invent some excuse for not applying it. But could it not be that the reasons for allowing the

---

[12] Luis de Molina, *De iustitia et iure tractatus* (Venice, 1614), disp. 718, n. 2; Leonard Lessius, *De iustitia et iure ceterisque virtutibus cardinalis* (Paris, 1628), lib. II, cap. 14, dubitatio IV, n. 3; Hugo Grotius, *De iure belli ac pacis libri tres* (Amsterdam, 1646), II, X, 2, 1; Samuel Pufendorf, *De iure naturae ac gentium libri octo* (Amsterdam, 1688), IV, XIII, 6. For a defence of this principle, see James Gordley, 'The Principle against Unjustified Enrichment' in: K. Luig, H. Schack and H. Wiedemann (eds.), *Gedächtnisschrift für Alexander Lüderitz* (2000), 13.

[13] Lessius, *De iustitia*, lib. II, cap. 14, dubitatio I, n. 5 ('For example, if he spent ten gold pieces of another's property and only saved five of his own because he would only have consumed five otherwise, he is only liable for five because he appears to have become richer only to that extent'); Grotius, *De iure*, II, X, 5; Pufendorf, *De iure*, IV, XIII, 9.

[14] Molina, *De iustitia*, disp. 718, n. 2; disp. 721, n. 6; Lessius, *De iustitia*, lib. II, cap. 14, dubitatio I, n. 4; Grotius, *De iure*, II, X, 8; Pufendorf, *De iure*, IV, XIII, 8.

plaintiff to reclaim his property from a bona fide purchaser extend beyond the case governed by § 985 BGB in which the purchaser still has the property? Might it not matter whether the one party wronged or injured the other even if the plaintiff's action is not in tort? Might it not matter that a party did consent even if he did not enter into an enforceable contract? If so, then the oversimplification leads in the wrong direction, to a consideration merely of whether the defendant was enriched. What should be considered instead is the responsibility of a bona fide purchaser, or of a person who commits a wrong or injury, or of a person who makes a voluntary decision even if it does not result in an enforceable contract.

1. The bona fide purchaser

In Germany, as elsewhere, an owner can reclaim his stolen car from a bona fide purchaser. The reason, we now recognise, is not simply that the thief had no title to give. It concerns the buyer's ability to protect himself by dealing with someone who is reputable or at least amenable to a lawsuit. It may be that, for the same reason, the owner should recover from a bona fide purchaser who has resold the car. If so, all one needs to say to justify this result is to say that the bona fide purchaser can still sue whoever originally sold the car to him. German courts, however, see the remedy in unjust enrichment, and then explain away the requirement that the defendant be enriched by claiming that the money he paid the thief was not causally related to his enrichment.[15] As Dawson has pointed out, that claim is inconsistent with the loose approach they take to causation in other cases.[16] As Werner Lorenz has observed, it is not helpful because it obscures the reason the plaintiff is allowed to recover, which has nothing to do with whether the defendant is enriched.[17]

2. Wrong or injury

Suppose, next, that one of the parties committed a wrong or injury. Four types of cases are examined below: (a) the defendant wrongfully induced the plaintiff to contract, (b) the defendant exploited the plaintiff's need or ignorance to contract on unfairly advantageous terms, (c) the defendant wrongfully appropriated a benefit that he should have obtained by

---

[15] BGHZ 14, 7, 9–10; BGHZ 9, 333, 335–6; BGHZ 55, 176, 180 (two bulls sold to butcher who cut them up, thereby acquiring title).
[16] As noted by Dawson, 'Erasable Enrichment', 294.
[17] Werner Lorenz, in: *J. von Staudingers Kommentar zum Bürgerlichen Gesetzbuch* (13th edn, 1994), § 818, n. 38.

contract, and (d) one party injured the other by disavowing the contract after he had changed his position in reliance upon it, and yet the party committing the injury is not at fault because he is a minor, an insane person, or otherwise incompetent.

(a) Wrongfully inducing the other party to contract
Suppose the defendant fraudulently induced the plaintiff to buy a car, and that the car has been destroyed. Lord Denning once said in a fraud case,[18] and I have argued elsewhere,[19] that a person who commits an intentional wrong should be liable for its unforeseen consequences. If so, then the reason that the plaintiff should recover the purchase price is because the defendant committed a wrong, not because he was enriched. German courts have reached this result by saying that the remedy is in unjust enrichment, but then creating an exception to the requirement that the defendant be enriched. Rather than entering by one door only to exit by another, it would be better to say that the remedy is not one for unjust enrichment.

(b) Unfair terms
In another type of case, the wrong was to obtain unfair terms by exploiting the plaintiff's ignorance or necessity. The plaintiff cannot then claim that, but for the wrong, he would not have contracted at all. He would have done so but on better terms. The appropriate remedy, it would seem, would be to enforce the contract but on fair terms, which, in fact, is done in the United States.[20] If this result were thought to be too hard on a defendant who might not have contracted at all on such terms, he could be given the option to reject these terms and rescind the contract. That, in fact, was done under the *ius commune* when a remedy was given for *laesio enormis* or gross disparity in price.[21] German courts face the difficulty that § 138 BGB prescribes only one remedy when a contract is one-sided: the

---

[18] *Doyle v. Olby* [1969] 2 All ER 199 at 122 (CA).
[19] James Gordley, 'Responsibility in Crime, Tort and Contract for the Unforeseeable Consequences of an Intentional Wrong: A Once and Future Rule?', in: P. Cane and J. Stapleton (eds.), *The Law of Obligations: Essays in Celebration of John Fleming* (1998), 175–208.
[20] Uniform Commercial Code § 2-302. See *Jones v. Star Credit Corp.* 298 NYS 2d 264 (SupCt 1969); *Frostifresh v. Reynoso* 274 NYS 2d 757 (SupCt 1966), reversed as to damages, 281 NYS 2d 964 (App 1967); *American Home Improvement Co. v. MacIver*, 201 A 2d 886 (NH, 1964).
[21] James Gordley, 'Just Price', in: P. Newman (ed.), *The New Palgrave Dictionary of Economics and the Law* (1998), vol. II, 410.

contract is void.[22] Consequently, they apply the law of unjust enrichment to return the parties, so far as possible, to their original position. In one case, a seller had been forced by his necessity to sell at too low a price, and the buyer had resold at a profit. The seller later became insolvent. The court awarded the seller the difference between the resale price and the initial purchase price.[23] Supposedly, that was the amount by which the buyer had been enriched. Dawson believes that the seller should recover the initial purchase price and that the buyer should have to line up with the seller's other creditors to recover anything at all.[24] If, as suggested here, the seller should merely recover the difference between a fair price and the unfair purchase price, then both approaches are wrong. One source of the difficulty is the rigidity of § 138 BGB. But another is the assumption of both the German courts and Dawson that the problem is one of unjust enrichment rather than of devising a remedy for a certain type of wrong.

(c) Wrongful appropriation of a benefit which one should have obtained by contract

In another type of case, the wrong was knowingly to appropriate something instead of obtaining it by contract. Here, German courts not only do not apply the doctrine of *Wegfall* but they do not even require that the defendant ever have been enriched. In a famous case, the defendant managed to take a trip to New York (and back again, when he was refused entry) without paying the plaintiff airline for his ticket. The court required him to pay even though he was not enriched by that amount.[25] When a railroad that put more traffic across a plaintiff's land than its right-of-way, the court required it to pay the amount it would have had to pay had it acquired the right in the normal way. The railroad was not allowed to say that it would not have done so, had it expected to pay that amount.[26] A motorcycle manufacturer that used a picture of a well-known actor in its advertising, taken without his consent, was made to pay the licence fee that would usually be paid to a celebrity.[27] American courts have reached similar results by holding that a contract has been formed.

---

[22] See generally Reinhard Zimmermann, *Richterliches Moderationsrecht oder Totalnichtigkeit?* (1979).
[23] RG, 1915 JW 918, 919.
[24] Dawson, 'Erasable Enrichment', 290 (at least, that seems to be what he means: he says the seller should get 'direct recovery').
[25] BGH, 1971 NJW 609.   [26] RGZ 97, 310.   [27] BGHZ 20, 345.

According to the Second Restatement of Contracts, the offeree's 'silence and inaction operate as an acceptance' where he 'takes the benefit of offered services with reasonable opportunity to reject them and reason to know that they were offered with the expectation of compensation'.[28] For example, a person who reads newspapers delivered to him without his request is deemed to have bought them even if he clearly did not intend to do so.[29] In such cases, to say a contract was formed is a fiction since the defendant did not consent. Nevertheless, they are not cases of unjust enrichment in the ordinary sense since it does not matter whether the defendant was enriched. He is liable because he wrongfully attempted to appropriate a benefit instead of contracting for it. He is not allowed to better his position by refusing to contract.[30]

(d) Injury caused by an incompetent party

A related question is what to do when an incompetent party has injured someone by entering into a contract with a person who changes his position in reliance on it. The competent party cannot ask a court to enforce the contract and thereby protect his right to the bargain that he has made. He has not made a valid bargain because the incompetent party cannot give consent. Nevertheless, should he be able to recover any loss he has suffered from the incompetent party? The question is like the one in tort law about whether insane people or minors should have to pay for the physical damage that they do. The answer is not obvious. On the one hand, they are not at fault. On the other, because of their condition, they have caused someone else a loss. Not surprisingly, different legal systems have given different answers although the most frequent approach is that they are held liable in tort. In the United States, the insane are liable in most jurisdictions[31] but not all.[32] Children are not liable if they used the care to be expected of a child of similar age.[33] In French law until recently

---

[28] Restatement (Second) of Contracts, § 69 (1981).
[29] *Austin v. Burge*, 137 SW 618 (Mo App 1911).
[30] On the damages awarded in such cases, see James Gordley, 'The Purpose of Awarding Restitutionary Damages: A Reply to Professor Weinrib', (2000) 1 *Theoretical Inquiries in Law* 39, 55–7.
[31] Restatement (Second) of Torts, § 283B (1963); W. Page Keeton, Dan B. Dobbs, Robert E. Keeton and David G. Owen, *Prosser and Keeton on the Law of Torts* (5th edn, 1984), 176–8; Stephanie I. Splane, 'Tort Liability of the Mentally Ill in Negligence Actions', (1983) 93 *Yale LJ* 153, 155–6.
[32] E.g., *Breunig v. American Family Ins. Co.* 173 NW 2d 619 (Wis 1970).
[33] Restatement (Second) of Torts, § 283A (1963); Keeton et al., *Prosser and Keeton on Torts*, 179–82.

neither children nor the insane were held liable. They are today. They are said to be at fault by an 'objective' standard even for actions they could not help.[34] In Germany and Italy, they are not liable on account of fault but special provisions allow the court to award damages that are 'equitable' considering the financial resources of the parties.[35] Thus, where an incompetent has caused a loss by entering into a contract, one might expect legal systems to differ but that, most often, they would have to bear it themselves.

In the United States and Germany, however, the problem is approached as one of unjust enrichment. Yet, this approach has not prevented American and German courts from protecting, albeit only partially, a party who has suffered a loss by contracting with an incompetent. In the United States, sometimes the contract is enforced, and, when it is not, the right of the incompetent to recover for unjust enrichment is conditioned on the return of whatever benefits he received.[36]

In Germany, protection was traditionally given by applying the so-called *Saldotheorie*. The claims in unjust enrichment of each party are aggregated so that the defendant may deduct the value of whatever he gave the plaintiff from the value of whatever the plaintiff had given him. For example, in one case in which the doctrine was first applied, the incompetent party, who was supervising the construction of a building, purchased steel girders in his own name. They were incorporated into the building which later was seized and sold to satisfy the demands of creditors. After he died, his heirs sued to recover the purchase price in unjust enrichment. They recovered an insignificant amount because the court allowed the defendant to deduct the value of the girders.[37] Dawson pointed out that if one wants an incompetent person to bear a loss that he occasioned, this is hardly a logical way to do so.[38] The competent party is protected only when he is a defendant. He is protected if the incompetent party seeks money damages but not if title to a moveable has not passed, and the incompetent party recovers it by self-help or without suing in unjust enrichment to do so. Dawson also claimed that to give even this limited protection was inconsistent with the doctrine of *Wegfall*, since the disappearance of the

---

[34] The insane became liable when a 1968 statute changed the law. Law of 3 January 1968, now art. 489(2), *code civil*. See Patrizia Petrelli, 'La responsabilità civile dell'infermo di mente nell'ordinamento francese', (1991) 37 *Rivista di diritto civile* 77–86. Children were held to the standard of care of a child of their own age until the decision of 9 May 1984, by the Cour de cassation meeting in assemblée plénière: DS 1984.525. See Henri Mazeaud, 'La "faute objective" et la responsabilité', DS 1985. Chron.13 at 86–95.
[35] §§ 827–9 BGB; arts. 2046–7, *codice civile*.   [36] Dawson, 'Erasable Enrichment', 298, n. 91.
[37] RG *GruchB* 55, 963.   [38] Dawson, 'Erasable Enrichment', 299.

plaintiff's enrichment – for example, by the incorporation of the girders in the building – is ignored.[39] He is quite right that the real question is whether the competent party should be protected against the loss that the incompetent one would otherwise cause him. But that is why the real basis for liability is not that the incompetent has been enriched but rather that the competent should be protected. Since it does not matter whether the incompetent was enriched, there is no reason why the doctrine of *Wegfall* should apply.

3. Consent

A contract may be void, and yet one of the parties may still have made a decision voluntarily which should affect his rights. Examined below are (a) the decision to enter into a contract that turns out to be void and (b) the decision to employ a third party whose actions have prejudiced the other party to the void contract.

(a) The decision to enter into a contract that proves to be void

Suppose that the defendant has received the plaintiff's property voluntarily, even though the transaction is not an enforceable contract: for example, he buys the plaintiff's goods but the contract is void for defect in form. Suppose that these goods are now valueless because they were destroyed or because they were specially made for the defendant, who does not want them any more. If the contract is void, it follows that neither party can claim the benefit of his bargain. It does not follow that the transaction must be regarded as involuntary for all purposes. It might be that the risks should still fall where they do whenever resources are exchanged voluntarily. If the goods are destroyed by chance, the risk falls on the buyer; if they are destroyed because they were defective when delivered, the risk falls on the seller; if they were specially made to the buyer's order, the risk falls on him that neither he nor anyone else will want them. If so, then these results are appropriate because the reason for declaring the contract void does not extend to all the consequences a voluntary transaction normally carries with it. Once again, they have nothing to do with whether the defendant is enriched.

Again, German courts arrive at these results, but to do so they find a way around the requirement that the defendant must be enriched. If the goods were destroyed by chance after delivery, German courts again apply

---

[39] Ibid., 298.

the *Saldotheorie*. The claims of buyer and seller in unjust enrichment are aggregated so that the seller returns the purchase price less the value of the goods he had delivered and which the buyer is unable to return to him. Thus, while the risk of destruction falls on the buyer, the seller does not receive the benefit of his bargain, as he would if the contract were enforceable. If the goods are worthless because they were defective, the *Saldotheorie* has been construed to allow the buyer to recover the purchase price,[40] an explanation that German authors regard as artificial even though they approve of the result.[41] In one case, where goods were specially made to the buyer's order and were worthless, the seller was allowed to deliver them and keep the purchase price.[42] Having done so, he was supposedly no longer enriched.

Nevertheless, since courts have to bob and weave to come to the right result, it is not surprising that, in some of the cases to which Dawson objected, they came to the wrong one. In one case, for example, the defendant employed the plaintiff to drill a hole on his land to the depth of 800 metres. The plaintiff could not even recover his costs, because, the court said, the hole was worthless, and therefore the defendant had not been unjustly enriched.[43] Although the case is an old one, Dawson argued that there is no logical escape from this result under German law.[44] There is not if we imagine that the defendant is liable solely because he has been enriched. We should say instead that even if the contract is void, those who order holes to be dug should bear the normal risks of doing so.

Moreover, it is worth noting that American courts have sometimes made the same mistake, not in asking whether enrichment has disappeared, but in asking whether the defendant was ever enriched at all. In one case, the defendant had contracted for the plaintiff to carve and erect a stone monument. The contract was unenforceable. The plaintiff was allowed to recover in unjust enrichment for having dug a hole for the monument but not for the work he had done carving the stone, supposedly because the hole benefited the defendant but the carving did not since it had not been finished and the stone had not been erected.[45] According to the approach I am suggesting, he should have recovered for both, since

[40] RGZ 94, 253, 255. [41] Lorenz: in *Staudinger*, § 831, n. 46.
[42] RGZ 118, 185, 188. Here, the machines had not yet been delivered, and so the court did not apply the *Saldotheorie*; rather, it allowed the manufacturer to transfer the machines to the buyer in satisfaction of his claim for unjust enrichment.
[43] RG, 1911 JW 756. [44] Dawson, 'Erasable Enrichment', 312–13.
[45] *Dowling v. McKenny* 124 Mass 478 (1878).

what matters is that the defendant voluntarily agreed for him to build the monument.

Those familiar with the German literature will have noticed that this approach is like that of Werner Flume. He believed that a person who had voluntarily decided to contract should not escape the normal consequences simply because the contract is unenforceable.[46] But Flume rested this conclusion on a claim about causation. He tried to distinguish between events the defendant himself had caused and those that were caused by the receipt of the plaintiff's asset.[47] Consequently, he had to say, for example, that if the defendant gave away property he believed he had received as a gift, the cause was the receipt of the property rather than the defendant's decision to give it away.[48] That seems forced. Moreover, Flume spent the bulk of his article arguing that the defence of *Wegfall der Bereicherung* was an ill-advised nineteenth-century innovation. Thus his solution seems to be an attempt to domesticate a defence he disliked. In my view, the defence is perfectly sound provided we remember that from its very origins, it was meant to apply only when the plaintiff's claim was based simply on the fact that the defendant was enriched.

Although Dawson liked Flume's article, he said: 'I know of no way that an American approach could make use of this peculiar formula, which enforces promises ("commitments") made in contracts found to be void.'[49] In fact, it is the best description of what American and English courts do. If, under a void contract, the seller altered a house at the buyer's request, he recovers the reasonable value of the alterations even if they lower its market value.[50] If the defendant contracted for the plaintiff's services as an architect, he pays the value of these services even if he never uses the plaintiff's plans.[51] If the defendant contracted for the plaintiff's

---

[46] 'Wenn jemand mit seinem Willen einen gegenseitigen Vertrag schließt, so fällt er damit – auch wenn der Vertrag nichtig ist – die vermögensmäßige Entscheidung, daß er statt des Vermögenswerts seiner Gegenleistung die ihm zu erbringende Leistung haben will. Die Konsequenzen dieser Entscheidung muß er tragen, denn er ist es, der die Entscheidung gefällt hat': Werner Flume, 'Der Wegfall der Bereicherung in der Entwicklung vom römischen zum geltenden Recht', in: Rechts- und Staatswissenschaftliche Fakultät zu Göttingen (ed.), *Festschrift für Hans Niedermeyer* (1953), 103, 165.
[47] Ibid., 154.
[48] 'Zwar ist der Empfänger des Erwerbs sine causa in diesen Fällen auch durch sein Verhalten ursächlich für die Vermögensminderung geworden. Das Verhalten des Empfängers wurde aber ursächlich bestimmt durch den Erwerb sine causa': Ibid., 158.
[49] Dawson, 'Erasable Enrichment', 303, n. 110.   [50] *Dearns v. Andree*, 139 A 695 (Conn 1928).
[51] E.g., *Barnes v. Lozoff* 123 NW 2d 543 (1963); *Parrish v. Tahtaras* 318 P 2d 642 (1957); *Sterling v. Marshall* 54 A 2d 353 (DC 1947).

services marketing his products, he pays their value whether or not they were successful.[52] In a famous early English case, a publisher who commissioned a book and then decided before it was written not to publish it had to pay the author for a manuscript that was never completed.[53] Dawson himself says that, in such cases, the 'responsibilities and risks continue to be those assigned by or inherent in the contract itself'.[54] That comes close to saying that it does not matter if the defendant was enriched when he voluntarily decided to acquire the plaintiff's resources.

In that respect, voluntary acquisition differs from what Peter Birks calls 'free acceptance'. For Birks, the defendant's 'free acceptance' of a performance, knowing that the plaintiff expected to be paid, proves that the defendant was enriched by the amount that he expected the plaintiff to charge.[55] But the defendant is often liable for that amount even if, in retrospect, he can show he was not enriched, as when he commissions architectural drawings that he later decides not to use, or, as Birks notes, when he does not receive the performance he commissioned, as in the case of the publisher.[56] In such cases, the defendant should be liable because it does not matter whether he was enriched or not.

(b) The decision to employ a person whose actions prejudice the other party

Closely related are cases in which the loss is due to the conduct of a third party whom the defendant hired, or to the fact that this party is insolvent or cannot be sued. Here, the defendant's decision to hire this party was voluntary, whether his contract with the plaintiff was voluntary or not. That decision should carry its normal consequence: the loss falls on the defendant. When the plaintiff paid money to the defendant's agent who then embezzled it, the defendant has sometimes escaped liability on the grounds that he was not enriched,[57] although in one case the court avoided this result by noting that he could sue his admittedly judgment-proof agent.[58] As Dawson notes, he should be liable. In one American case, a railroad that negligently overpaid a contractor recovered the

---

[52] *Fabian v. Wasatch Orchard Co.* 125 P 860 (Utah 1912). I mention these cases because Palmer regards them as typical: George E. Palmer, *The Law of Restitution* (1978), vol. II, § 16.3.
[53] *Planché v. Colburn* (1831) 8 Bing 14, cited with approval in Peter Birks, *An Introduction to the Law of Restitution* (1985), 232.
[54] Dawson 'Restitution Without Enrichment', 584.
[55] Birks, *Introduction*, 114–16.   [56] *Ibid.*, 232.
[57] See RG, 1933 HRR n. 1843 (1932); RGZ 65, 292, 297–8 (1907).
[58] OLG Frankfurt am Main, 1929 JW 791.

entire amount although, because of the error, the contractor had passed on some of the money by overpaying his sub-contractors who subsequently disappeared.[59] Dawson agrees with the result, and believes it shows that the doctrine of *Wegfall* is wrong.[60] But all one needs to say is that the contractor's decision to hire the sub-contractors was voluntary, and it should carry its normal consequences when the sub-contractors disappear.

Sometimes German courts have used the doctrine of *Wegfall* to reach an appropriate result. In one case, the buyer of meat paid the defendant's agent, believing with good reason that the agent was in fact the seller. The agent became insolvent, and the contract was declared void for mistake as to the identity of the parties. When the owner sued the buyer in unjust enrichment, the court allowed him to deduct the money he paid to the agent.[61] Dawson objected,[62] but this is precisely the result that should be reached if the hiring of the agent is to have its normal consequence.

IV. Cases within the proper scope of the doctrine

Sometimes, then, we should not be troubled that the defendant is not enriched. He may have purchased the plaintiff's goods from a third party, committed a wrong, or voluntarily accepted plaintiff's performance, or voluntarily hired a third party for whom he should be responsible. In other cases, however, the plaintiff has done none of these things, and we should resist the temptation to allow the plaintiff to recover. In one American case, the plaintiff delivered a carload of coal to the wrong party, the defendant, who consumed it. Its market value was $6.85 a ton but the defendant had a contract with another supplier to buy coal at $3.40 a ton. Quite properly, the plaintiff was allowed to recover only $3.40 a ton.[63] Dawson agreed this case is different, because, he said, a mistake like this 'carries one beyond the realm of contract, even the illusion of contract'.[64] To put it another way, the defendant never decided to acquire coal at such a price, and so it mattered, to this court, whether he was actually enriched. Yet Dawson is not sure the defendant should only have had to pay the lower price.[65] Why? What reason could there be for him to owe the plaintiff money except that he was enriched?

---

[59] *Houston & T. C. Ry v. Hughes* 133 SW 731 (Tex Civ App 1911).
[60] Dawson, 'Restitution Without Enrichment', 573.
[61] RGZ 98, 64; see also BGH, 1974 *NJW* 1132.   [62] Dawson, 'Erasable Enrichment', 291.
[63] *Michigan Central RR v. State* 155 NE 50 (Ind 1927).
[64] Dawson, 'Restitution Without Enrichment', 598.   [65] *Ibid*.

Indeed, I do not see why the defendant who has not been enriched should pay even if his role was a more active one than simply to burn the coal the plaintiff delivered. In a celebrated American case, the defendant hired the plaintiff to build him a Turkish bathhouse. Due to an architect's error, the defendant expected to pay about $23,000, which was approximately what the bathhouse added to the value of his land, and the defendant expected to charge about $33,000, which was approximately the fair value of the work. The court allowed the plaintiff to recover the higher figure.[66] Dawson liked the result and noted that it would not have been reached under German law.[67] He did not like the result[68] in a German case in which an officer, who was immune from suit, seized and sold to satisfy a judgment goods that belonged to the plaintiff rather than the judgment debtor. When the plaintiff sued the judgment creditor who had received the proceeds, the creditor was allowed to deduct the costs of the judicial sale.[69] Nor did Dawson like the result[70] in another German case in which the lessee of the plaintiff's land, without authority to do so, agreed to sell the defendant a right of way so he could build a private railway leading from his industrial plant to the autobahn. When the owner sued for unjust enrichment, the defendant was allowed to set off its expenses constructing and maintaining the railway.[71] The results would be different in the United States, Dawson claimed, where American courts have not applied the defence of change of position unless the defendant altered his position after being enriched. I agree with the way German law would resolve all of these cases: I do not see why the defendant should be held for more than he ever agreed to pay unless he was enriched by that amount.

Dawson's favourite example of the good sense of the common law is the rule that the innocent converter who takes and sells another's property is liable for its value even if he sells it for less.[72] I do not see the wisdom of this solution. It seems to be a relic of an age in which justice was done in a rough and ready fashion by writs – in this case, lumping people together as innocent converters without sorting through the differences in their circumstances and asking whether such differences should matter.

---

[66] *Vickery v. Ritchie* 88 NE 835 (Mass 1909).
[67] Dawson, 'Restitution Without Enrichment', 594, 597.
[68] Dawson, 'Erasable Enrichment', 252.   [69] BGHZ 32, 240.
[70] Dawson, 'Erasable Enrichment', 293.   [71] RG, 1932 JW 1044.
[72] Palmer, *Law of Restitution*, vol. II, § 2.2. For example, in *Felder v. Reeth* 34 F 2d 744 (9th Cir 1929), the defendant was liable for $3,000, the value of the chattel he converted, even though he sold it for $550.

Dawson agrees that the defendant should have a defence of change of position when he lost all or part of the amount by which he was enriched by acting in reliance on a belief induced by the plaintiff's conduct. Indeed, he believes that in American law, 'the purpose of reimbursing loss through reliance will explain the defence of change of position'.[73] Consequently, he has a quite different reason than I do for believing that the plaintiff should recover the value of services performed under a void contract whether or not they enriched the defendant. My reason is that the defendant voluntarily decided that these services should be performed for him. Dawson's reason is that the plaintiff relied on the defendant's statements. He also has a different reason for believing that the defendant should be able to deduct expenses he incurred only because he believed that he could keep some benefit that the plaintiff conferred upon him.[74] My reason is that, having spent this money only in that belief, the defendant was not enriched by the full amount of the benefit. Dawson's reason is that the defendant relied on a belief induced by the plaintiff's conduct in conferring the benefit. In all these cases, according to Dawson, the defendant should not have the defence of change of position, even though the enrichment disappeared, because he did not rely on a belief that the plaintiff's conduct had induced.

I do not see why reliance should matter. The reason, for Dawson, is not that the plaintiff foresaw that the defendant might rely. Dawson says that he should be liable even if the reliance could not have been foreseen.[75] The reason cannot be that the plaintiff was at fault for the conduct that induced the reliance. Nor can it be that the plaintiff consented that the defendant's services be performed even though the contract was void. Reliance matters for Dawson even if the plaintiff was not at fault and did not consent.

Dawson seems to think that the ultimate principle at stake, and the principle that is violated by the defence of *Wegfall* in Germany, is that risks should be assigned to the party who is the proper one to bear them.[76] Does this mean that we should analyse who that party is and place the risks on him? Not according to Dawson. He is critical, and rightly so, of German jurists such as Wilburg and Flessner who take that approach. They think that when a loss must fall on either the plaintiff or the defendant, the law must consider which of the two is the appropriate person to bear

---

[73] Dawson, 'Restitution Without Enrichment', 569.   [74] *Ibid.*, 574–5.   [75] *Ibid.*, 569.
[76] This suggestion seems to me to be implicit in his criticisms of the German doctrine. See Dawson, 'Erasable Enrichment', 292, 293, 298, 303 and his 'Restitution Without Enrichment', 574, 584, 596, 599.

it. Flessner wants to assign liability by asking about spheres of risk, the ability to bear burdens and the purposes of allocating them, and the causal connections between activities and losses.[77] By this approach, it would seem that a feather could tip the balance.[78] As Dawson notes, it leads into a 'maze' in which one soon becomes 'lost and bewildered'.[79] In a similar vein, Flume asked what Wilburg could possibly mean by assigning liability to conduct that is 'contrary to commercial usage [*verkehrswidrig*] although it is neither culpable nor contrary to law'.[80] Dawson's test is admittedly less difficult to apply: the defence of change of circumstances is available only if the defendant relied on a belief induced by the plaintiff's conduct. But Dawson does not explain how this test is related to the ultimate question that Dawson, like Wilburg and Flessner, seems to think is decisive: which is the appropriate party to bear a risk? Among parties who are equally innocent, neither of whom has decided that a risk should be taken, it is hard to see how that question could be answered.

It is, indeed, unfortunate if an innocent plaintiff has suffered a loss. According to an ancient principle, however, before he can shift the loss on to the defendant he must give some reason why the defendant should bear it instead. If the only reason is that the defendant has become richer through the use of his resources, then, it would seem, his claim should fail if the defendant has not become richer.

[77] Axel Flessner, *Wegfall der Bereicherung* (1978), 112, 162.
[78] *Ibid.*, 94; Walter Wilburg, *Die Lehre von der ungerechtfertigten Bereicherung* (1934), 18–21, 143–4.
[79] Dawson, 'Erasable Enrichment', 305.   [80] Flume, 'Der Wegfall der Bereicherung', 151.

9 Unwinding mutual contracts: *restitutio in integrum* v. the defence of change of position

Phillip Hellwege

This contribution addresses the question how the defence of change of position can apply when a mutual contract is unwound. The following hypothetical case, illustrated in Figure 9.1, should make the problem clear. A and B have agreed to swap A's cow for B's horse. Both have fully performed their respective obligations. A has transferred his cow to B and B has transferred his horse to A. Then the horse ceases to exist. Neither A nor B were at fault. The horse was lost due to some supervening event. They now find out that there is some reason why the contract could be unwound: A was mistaken when he entered into the contract, fraudulently induced or forced by B to enter into the contract, the horse was defective, B did not have title to the horse, A was a minor, or the contract was simply void. In all these cases A may have a right to claim back the cow from B and B may claim back the horse from A. But how does it affect A's claim for the cow that B has already given the horse to A and that A is not able to give it back? How does it affect B's claim that the horse has ceased to exist? Is the defence of change of position the proper legal tool to help to solve these questions? The defence could come into play at two different points of analysis. First, one could argue that B has changed his position by giving his horse to A and is therefore no longer liable to refund the cow – at least in so far as the value of the horse corresponds to the value of the cow. Secondly, one could apply the defence in B's claim against A, because A has lost the horse. The conclusion of this essay is that the defence of change of position should not play any role in these fact patterns. However, in order to arrive at this conclusion it is first necessary to discuss the different tools and methods of unwinding contracts, their problems and their justification. Only as a final step is the function of the defence of change of position fully discussed.

243

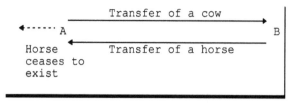

Figure 9.1. *Unwinding of a mutual contract.*

One final preliminary remark is required. This essay addresses only *how* a mutual contract is to be unwound. It does not deal with *why* and *when* a contract is to be unwound. Thus, it will be presupposed that the mistake, fraud, frustration or breach of contract gives the right to ask that the contract be unwound. This is not to deny that the question *why* and *when* a contract is unwound is itself problematic.

I. Distinction I: stages, methods, factors and categories

So far only the word 'unwinding'[1] has been used. The terms 'unjustified enrichment', 'restitution', 'rescission', 'termination', 'frustration', '*quantum valebat*', '*quantum meruit*' and '*quantum lucratus*' have been intentionally avoided because each of them is for the purpose of this essay not broad enough. 'Unwinding' is used in its broadest sense, including the different stages or steps of unwinding a contract *in toto* and including different methods for doing so.

1. Different steps or stages of unwinding a contract *in toto*

When asking what effect one of the above factors – error, fraud, fear, force, minority, breach, frustration, voidness – may have, one must distinguish *what* is affected. There is first the effect on the contract itself: if one says that a contract is rescinded for mistake, what is meant is that the contract is avoided *ab initio*. If it is terminated, at the choice of the innocent party the contract loses its force *ex nunc*. If it is frustrated, the contract loses its force *ex nunc* automatically. For lack of a better term, this effect will be called 'unwinding the contract as agreement'. It only describes the effect on the contract.

The second effect is that on the transfer of property. In our example, A and B have not only agreed on a contract (that A should be obliged

---

[1] The term 'unwinding contracts' is used by Joseph M. Perillo, 'Restitution in a Contractual Context', (1973) 73 *Columbia LR* 1208.

to give his cow and that B should be obliged to transfer the horse), they have already executed the contract. It would only be half the business of unwinding the contract if A were allowed to rescind the contract and leave all the consequences of the contract in force. Thus, the proprietary consequences of the execution of the contract have to be unwound as well. So, minority can prevent property from passing; a mistake usually does not affect the transfer of property. Property or the value of the property has to be claimed back. This effect will be called 'unwinding the proprietary consequences of the contract'. It only describes the effect on the transfer of property.

The third and final effect is that on the factual consequences of the contract. In the example above, not only has A transferred property to B but A is also now in possession of the cow. If the contract is unwound for mistake, the process of unwinding the contract would be incomplete if we said to A that he was able to avoid the contract *ab initio* and that he was able to claim back the property of his cow from B. He also wants the possession of the cow back. This effect will be called 'unwinding the factual consequences of the contract'. It only describes the effect on the fact of possession.

Throughout this contribution 'unwinding the contract *in toto*' is used in such a way that it includes all three steps: unwinding the contract as agreement, its proprietary consequences, and its factual consequences (Figure 9.2). The legal term used to include these three steps is that of 'rescission' or '*Anfechtung*'.[2] However, these terms have been narrowed down in today's terminology: they never include the question of unwinding the factual consequences of the contract: rescission is only the avoidance of a legal act, usually a contract, *ex tunc* (for example) for mistake at the instance of one party.[3] Other terms used in earlier English and Scots literature and cases are '*restitutio in integrum*', 'restitution *in toto*' or

---

[2] For German law see, e.g., Ferdinand Regelsberger, *Pandekten* (1893), vol. I, § 174. For Scots law see, e.g., *McCormick v. Rittmeyer* (1869) 7 M 854 at 856 *per* Lord President Inglis. For English law see, e.g., *Clarke v. Dickson, Williams and Gibbs* (1858) El Bl & El 148 at 153 *per* Crompton J; *Adam v. Newbigging* (1888) 13 App Cas 308 at 323 *per* Lord Watson; *Hunt v. Silk* (1804) 5 East 449 at 452 *per* Lord Ellenborough CJ; *Fisher v. Samuda* (1808) 1 Camp 194, n. (a)[2] of the reporter of the case, Campbell.

[3] For English law see, e.g., *Johnson v. Agnew* [1980] AC 367; *Photo Production Ltd v. Securicor Transport Ltd* [1980] AC 827. For Scots law see, e.g., W. M. Gloag and C. Henderson, *The Law of Scotland* (10th edn, 1995), §§ 7.2, 13.4. In Scots law 'rescission' is used also in cases in which English law uses the term 'termination'. For German law see § 142 BGB.

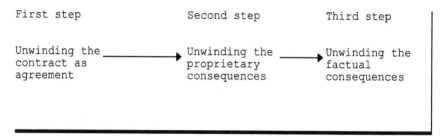

Figure 9.2. *Three steps to unwind mutual contracts* in toto.

'total restitution'.[4] However, these terms have to be avoided as well. Today, *restitutio in integrum* is looked upon as a requirement for rescission.[5] 'Restitution' needs to be avoided because it suggests that the term 'restitution' requires that something is given back. There are problems with looking upon the rescission of the contract – the first step in the analysis – as a kind of restitution.[6]

2. Different methods

There are also different methods to unwind a contract. A factor on the basis of which a contract can be unwound – such as mistake, fraud, fear

---

[4] See, e.g., G. Campbell and H. Paton (eds.), *Baron David Hume's Lectures*, Stair Society, vol. V (1939), 300 ff.; *Carmichael v. Castlehill* (1698) Mor 8993 at 8995; *Graham v. Western Bank of Scotland* (1854) 2 M 559 at 564 per Lord Ordinary Kinloch; *Tennent v. City of Glasgow Bank* (1879) 6 R 554 at 557 for the defender; *Maitland v. Gight* (1675) Mor 9158; *Bonnington Sugar Refining Co. v. Thomson's Trustees* (1878) 6 R 80 at 98 per Lord Ormidale.

[5] For English law see, e.g., P. S. Atiyah, *An Introduction to the Law of Contract* (5th edn, 1995), 410 ff.; Andrew Burrows, *The Law of Restitution* (1993), 32, 132 ff.; *Chitty on Contracts* (28th edn, 1999), vol. I, §§ 6-112 ff.; Lord Goff of Chieveley and Gareth Jones, *The Law of Restitution* (5th edn, 1998), 273 ff., 365 ff.; Ewan McKendrick, *Contract Law* (3rd edn, 1997), 247–8; G. H. Treitel, *The Law of Contract* (10th edn, 1999), 295, 350 ff.; Graham Virgo, *The Principles of the Law of Restitution* (1999), 32 ff. For Scots law see, e.g., W. M. Gloag, *The Law of Contract* (2nd edn, 1929), 59, 539 ff.; Gloag and Henderson, *Law of Scotland*, § 7.4; Hector L. MacQueen, 'Unjustified Enrichment and Breach of Contract', [1994] *JR* 137, 148; Hector L. MacQueen, 'Contract, Unjustified Enrichment and Concurrent Liability: A Scots Perspective', [1997] *Acta Juridica* 176, 198; W. W. McBryde, *The Law of Contract in Scotland* (1987), §§ 9-73–9-74, 10-63 ff., 15-43, 26-05; T. B. Smith, *A Short Commentary of the Law of Scotland* (1962), 790; D. M. Walker, *The Law of Contracts and Related Obligations in Scotland* (2nd edn, 1985), §§ 5.34, 14.114.

[6] See Peter Birks, *An Introduction to the Law of Restitution* (1989), 172; Burrows, *Law of Restitution*, 32; Phillip Hellwege, 'The Scope of Application of Change of Position in the Law of Unjust Enrichment: A Comparative Study', [1999] *Restitution LR* 92, 104 ff.; Virgo, *Principles*, 29.

or force – can confer on one party a power or, in German terminology, a *Gestaltungsrecht*. A *Gestaltungsrecht* is a power to create, change or destroy a legal status by a unilateral act of one party.[7] The right to rescind is such a power: one party to the contract is allowed to avoid the contract *ab initio* at his option. The other party's agreement to avoiding the contract is not needed. Thus, the first method for unwinding a contract is conferring a power on one of the parties. However, all three steps of unwinding contracts cannot be achieved with this method. Only legal acts can be unwound through a unilateral power to rescind. It is possible to rescind a contract ('unwinding the contract as an agreement') and it is also possible to rescind the transfer of property ('unwinding the proprietary consequences of the contract'). However, it is not possible to rescind the transfer of possession by this method ('unwinding the factual consequences of the contract').

Another method of unwinding a contract may be called the 'obligational method'. It occurs when there is an obligation on one party to unwind the contract; the other party has a corresponding right against the first party to claim that the contract be unwound. It is obvious that 'unwinding the factual consequences' and 'unwinding the proprietary consequences' may be achieved with this method. If in the above example A has entered the contract under a mistake, he can first rescind the contract ('first method'). Then he can claim back the property and the possession of the cow by using a *condictio indebiti* in German and Scots law and by using the unjust factor 'mistake' in English law. Thus, the proprietary and the factual consequence of the contract are unwound by applying the 'obligational method'. But the contract as an agreement can also be unwound in this way. The right of the buyer of a defective object to unwind the contract is called in German law *Wandelung*. The *Wandelung* falls into two parts: first, the buyer has a right against the seller to claim that the seller has to agree to termination of the contract.[8] Then both parties have the right to claim back their respective performances.[9] In this example all three consequences are achieved by the 'obligational method'.

A third method of achieving the unwinding of a contract is what may be called a 'judicial method'. Thus, in English law the rescission of a contract for mistake in equity is not achieved by conferring on the mistaken

---

[7] See, e.g., Karl Larenz, *Allgemeiner Teil des Deutschen Bürgerlichen Rechts* (7th edn, 1989), 220.
[8] §§ 463, 465 BGB.   [9] §§ 346, 467 BGB.

party a right to rescind the contract but by the court rescinding the contract.[10]

There is a further method of unwinding contracts. The factor – for example, the mistake or the frustrating event – may have automatic effect. A fundamental mistake might prevent *consensus in idem*. The contract is *ipso iure* void. Logically, only legal acts can be *ipso iure* void, so with this method only the contract as an agreement or the proprietary consequences of the contract can be unwound. If B was, in the above example, below the age of seven, both the contract and the transfer of property would – at least in German law – be *ipso iure* void.[11] However, B is still in possession of the cow. A has to claim back the possession of the cow. In English, Scots and German law this factual consequence of the contract is unwound by the 'obligational method': A has a *condictio indebiti* or a *vindicatio*, an *actio in quantum locupletior factus est pupillus*, or an action based on the unjust factor 'minority' against B.

Arguably, one could mention a final method of unwinding contracts: granting a defence to the defendant. The pandectists regarded it as a method of rescinding the contract if the defendant had an *exceptio* against the action of the plaintiff, such as an *exceptio quod metus causa* or an *exceptio doli*.[12]

3. Reasons for unwinding contracts

The reasons why a contract can be unwound have already been enumerated. As an adaptation of the English legal term 'unjust factor', these reasons for unwinding contracts will be called 'unwinding factors'. For the

---

[10] See Atiyah, *Introduction*, 228–9; McKendrick, *Contract Law*, 264 ff.; Treitel, *Law of Contract*, 285 ff. A Scots example of this method is the remedy of reduction. Modern German law does not know the 'judicial method'. Before enactment of the BGB it was the rule that a contract was rescinded by a court and not by the exercise of a unilateral power of one of the parties, which was confined to the narrow exception of *relative Nichtigkeit* and was regarded not as rescission but as a kind of voidness; see, e.g., Albrecht Schweppe, *Das Römische Privatrecht in seiner Anwendung auf Teutsche Gerichte* (3rd edn, 1822), §§ 996 ff.; Johann Nepomuk von Wening-Ingenheim, *Lehrbuch des Gemeinen Civilrechts* (5th edn, 1837), vol. I, §§ 144–5; Johann Friedrich Ludwig Göschen, *Vorlesungen über das gemeine Civilrecht* (1838), vol. I, § 84; Friedrich Carl von Savigny, *System des heutigen Römischen Rechts* (1841), vol. IV, 536 ff.; Ludwig Ritter Arndts von Arnesberg, *Lehrbuch der Pandekten* (14th edn, 1889), § 79; and Ludwig Mitteis, 'Zur Lehre von der Ungiltigkeit der Rechtsgeschäfte', (1889) 28 *JhJb* 85.

[11] See §§ 104, n. 1, 105(1) BGB.

[12] See, e.g., Schweppe, *Römische Privatrecht*, §§ 998 ff.; Savigny, *System*, 536–7; Eduard Böcking, *Pandecten des römischen Privatrechts aus dem Standpuncte unseres heutigen Rechtssystems oder Institutionen des gemeinen deutschen Zivilrechts* (2nd edn, 1853), § 119; Mitteis, 'Zur Lehre von der Ungiltigkeit,' 131, 162.

purpose of this essay it is not appropriate simply to use the term 'unjust factor'. Although the aim is unwinding the contract *in toto*, the reasons for unwinding its various consequences may be distinct. In English law, the reason why a contract is terminated for breach is the breach itself. However, the reason why the proprietary and factual consequences of the contract are unwound is not the breach but the unjust factor 'total failure of consideration'.[13] In Scots and German law, the reason for rescission of a contract is (for example) a mistake. However, the reason for unwinding the proprietary and factual consequences of the contract is that the respective performances were made *sine causa*.[14] Under German law, if A was below the age of seven both the contract and the transfer of property would be void. Thus, the reason for unwinding the contract as obligation and the proprietary consequences of the contract would be his lack of capacity. However, in order to unwind the factual consequences of the contract A may use a *vindicatio*.[15] The reason for unwinding the factual consequences would therefore be the retention of A's property by B. In this essay 'unwinding factor' is used to denote the reason that stands at the outset of this analysis, such as the breach of contract, mistake or incapacity. The fact that the second and third step of unwinding contracts might have different reasons or unjust factors will be disregarded. This is because the purpose of this chapter is to examine how contracts are unwound *in toto*

---

[13] See Peter Birks, 'Restitution and the Freedom of Contract', (1983) 36 *Current Legal Problems* 141, 149 ff.; Birks, *Introduction*, 221; Peter Birks, 'The Independence of Restitutionary Causes of Action', (1990) 16 *University of Queensland Law Journal* 1, 19 ff.; Lionel D. Smith, 'The Province of the Law of Restitution', (1992) 71 *Canadian Bar Review* 672, 673–4; see also Sonja Meier, *Irrtum und Zweckverfehlung* (1999), 257 ff., 272 ff.

[14] For German law see §§ 812 ff. BGB. In Scots law it is a matter of controversy whether the *condictio indebiti* is based on the notion of 'undue' or 'mistake'. But those who regard it as based on the mistake of the performing party mostly do not regard this mistake as the same as the mistake which renders the contract voidable. The mistake on which the *condictio indebiti* is based is arguably a mistaken belief in liability. On this view the reasons for rescission and for unwinding the proprietary and factual consequences of the contract are distinct. See, e.g., Robin Evans-Jones, 'From "Undue Transfer" to "Retention without a Legal Basis"', in: his (ed.), *The Civil Law Tradition in Scotland* (1995), 213 ff.; Robin Evans-Jones and Phillip Hellwege, 'Swaps, Error of Law and Unjustified Enrichment', (1995) 1 *Scottish Law & Practice Quarterly* 1, 7 ff.; Robin Evans-Jones and Phillip Hellwege, 'Some Observations on the Taxonomy of Unjustified Enrichment in Scots Law', (1998) 2 *Edinburgh LR* 180, 208–9; For the view that the same mistake supports both rescission and unwinding the proprietary and factual consequences of the contract, see W. J. Stewart, *The Law of Restitution in Scotland* (1992); Peter Birks, 'Six Questions in Search of a Subject – Unjust Enrichment in a Crisis of Identity', [1985] *JR* 227 ff.; Peter Birks, 'Restitution: A View of Scots Law', (1985) 38 *Current Legal Problems* 57 ff.

[15] § 985 BGB.

and how the defence of change of position then comes into play. The emphasis is on the reasons that precipitate the unwinding of contracts *in toto*.

4. Different categories

So far I have distinguished different methods of unwinding contracts, different steps in unwinding contracts *in toto*, and different unwinding factors. The picture is complicated further by the fact that the different steps in the process of unwinding contracts may fall into different legal categories. There is the law of property and the law of obligations. Within the law of obligations are to be found the law of contract, of unjustified enrichment and of delict. Additionally, German law also has a General Part of the BGB.

If A was under a substantial mistake, then in English law A has a right to rescind the contract.[16] Rescission is part of the law of contract:[17] the unwinding of the contract as an agreement, and of its proprietary and factual consequences, is regulated only by the law of obligations. In German law, rescission belongs to the General Part of the BGB. Only the unwinding of the proprietary and factual consequences of the contract is governed by the law of unjustified enrichment. However, a mistake may in rare cases also prevent property from passing or may allow the mistaken party to rescind also the transfer of property.[18] Then in English law B's claim against A to give up possession of the horse may be regulated by the tort of conversion, in German law by the *vindicatio* that is part of the law of property.

---

[16] See, e.g., *Solle v. Butcher* [1950] 1 KB 671; *Magee v. Pennine Insurance Co. Ltd* [1969] 2 QB 507; *Associated Japanese Bank (International) Ltd v. Crédit du Nord SA* [1989] 1 WLR 255; Atiyah, *Introduction*, 228–9; McKendrick, *Contract Law*, 264 ff.; Treitel, *Law of Contract*, 285 ff.

[17] According to some it is part of the law of unjustified enrichment: see references in n. 6.

[18] Property usually passes; for the English position see, e.g., *Singh v. Ali* [1960] AC 167; *Stock v. Wilson* [1913] 2 KB 235; *Belvoir Finance Co. Ltd v. Stapleton* [1971] 1 QB 210; *Lipkin Gorman (a Firm) v. Karpnale Ltd* [1991] 2 AC 548; *Pearce v. Brain* [1929] 2 KB 310. Exceptionally, the unwinding factor prevents property from passing: for English law see, e.g., *Cundy v. Lindsay* (1878) 3 App Cas 459; *R. v. Ilich* (1987) 162 CLR 110; Peter Birks, 'Trusts Raised to Reverse Unjust Enrichment: The *Westdeutsche* Case', [1996] *Restitution LR* 3, 24; Peter Birks, 'No Consideration: Restitution after Void Contracts', (1993) 23 *University of Western Australia LR* 195, 197–8; William J. Swadling, 'Restitution for no Consideration', [1994] *Restitution LR* 73, 80 ff.; Sarah Worthington, 'The Proprietary Consequences of Contract Failure', in: Francis D. Rose (ed.), *Failure of Contracts: Contractual, Restitutionary and Proprietary Consequences* (1997), 67, 68–9. On the Scottish position see: Kenneth G. C. Reid, 'Transfer of Ownership', in: his (ed.), *The Law of Property in Scotland* (1996), §§ 599, 614; William M. Gordon, 'Transfer of Ownership', in: Reid, *Law of Property in Scotland*, §§ 615, 617; David M. Walker, *Principles of Scottish Private Law* (1989), vol. III, 435. On German law see, e.g., Fritz Baur, Jürgen F. Baur and Rolf Stürner, *Lehrbuch des Sachenrechts* (17th edn, 1999), § 5 IV.

In the last subsection it was noted that the reason for unwinding the proprietary or factual consequences may be different from the reason the contract as an agreement is unwound. Equally, the reason for unwinding the factual consequences may be different from that for unwinding the proprietary consequences. These different steps in unwinding a contract *in toto* may fall into different legal categories. Thus, if the reason for unwinding the factual consequences of the contract is B's retention of A's property then this step of unwinding the contract is part of the law of property.

5. Summary

The different methods of unwinding contracts can be combined to achieve the goal of unwinding a contract *in toto*. One method may be used to unwind the contract as an agreement, the next to unwind its proprietary consequences and a third to unwind its factual consequences. For different unwinding factors, the combination of methods may be different. Finally, the different steps in unwinding the contract may fall into different legal categories. Thus, there are four distinctions and they all come into play at the same time. A few examples should clarify what has been said so far (see Table 9.1).

Table 9.1 shows that a fifth factor has an impact on the analysis. It is the nature of the benefit received by one party. If chattels are exchanged,

Table 9.1. *Methods for unwinding contracts*

	Unwinding factor	Unwinding the contract as agreement	Unwinding the proprietary consequences	Unwinding the factual consequences
German law	Breach of contract	Unilateral power (law of contract)	Obligational method (law of contract)	Obligational method (law of contract)
English law	Breach of contract	Unilateral power (law of contract)	Obligational method (law of unjust enr.)	Obligational method (law of unjust enr.)
German law	Defective goods (*Wandelung*)	Obligational method (law of contract)	Obligational method (law of contract)	Obligational method (law of contract)
Scots law, contract of sale	Incapacity	Automatic void (law of contract)	Automatic void (law of property)	Obligational method (law of property)
Scots law, contract of services	Incapacity	Automatic void (law of contract)	Obligational method (law of unjust enr.)	
English law	Fundamental mistake	Automatic void (law of contract)	Automatic void (law of property)	Obligational method (tort law)

unwinding the contractual performances may take place in the law of property. If services are rendered under the contract, that will never be the case but the whole process of unwinding the contract is regulated only by the law of obligations. Furthermore, with services there is not the familiar three-step analysis. We need only distinguish two steps: first, what impact the unwinding factor has on the contract as agreement; secondly, the performances have to be unwound. Here it is not appropriate to speak of proprietary or factual consequences. The benefit is the service itself. What has to be unwound is the transfer of wealth.[19] For the most part this chapter will disregard the case of services rendered under a contract.

II. Distinction II: four basic models for unwinding mutual contracts

The various distinctions identified in the last section may require further explanation. This section deals with how these distinctions affect the outcome of a case. Prima facie it is surprising that the unwinding of a mutual contract *in toto* should be affected by the method of unwinding it or by the particular step in question, by the reason why the contract is to be unwound, by the benefit in question, or by how the whole problem is categorised. This section investigates the various unwinding factors in Scots, English and German law. This is not a full account of each jurisdiction; in some cases the account given may be an oversimplification. For each jurisdiction and for each unwinding factor two questions are of interest: How does it affect A's rights that he has lost the horse he received from B? How does it affect B's rights that the horse has ceased to exist?

1. Scots law
(a) Mistake, fraud, force and fear
In the given example, if A is mistaken when he enters into the contract, he might be able to rescind the contract. One requirement of rescission is that *restitutio in integrum* must be possible and offered by the rescinding party.[20] Thus, at the first step – unwinding the contract as agreement – account is already taken of the fact that unwinding the proprietary and

---

[19] Wealth is used here in a wider sense than by Jack Beatson, *The Use and Abuse of Unjust Enrichment: Essays on the Law of Restitution* (1991), 29 ff.
[20] For example *Boyd & Forrest v. Glasgow and South Western Railway Co.* 1914 SC 472; 1915 SC (HL) 20; *Western Bank of Scotland v. Addie* (1867) 5 M (HL) 80; *Spence v. Crawford* 1939 SC (HL) 52.

factual consequences of the contract must be possible. If unwinding the contract *in toto* is not possible, because, say, the horse has ceased to exist, the contract will stand and even the first step of unwinding the contract will not be allowed. So with error, fraud, fear and force, there needs to be a total and mutual unwinding or there is no unwinding. A different question is whether it is enough that A, instead of transferring back the property and possession of the horse, makes good its value. This may be looked upon as a substitute for the second and third steps of unwinding the contract. One could still say that there is mutual and total restitution if B gives back the cow and A makes good the value of the horse instead of handing it back in specie.[21]

(b) Minority

The same was at one stage true when the contract was unwound because B was a minor: *restitutio in integrum*, the mutual and total restoration of the parties, was the goal of unwinding the contract.[22] Today, however, Scots law would probably end up with a different solution: the contract and the transfer of property would be void.[23] The factual consequences of the contract would probably be unwound by B's using a proprietary claim against A. If A lost the horse without fault, B has no claim against A. Whether A can claim back the cow from B without making up for the value of the horse is unclear. However, since in Scots law the requirement of *restitutio in integrum* is today only applied when a legal act is rescinded,[24] it should follow that A can claim back the cow without being able to give back the horse.

---

[21] Cases that did not require exact *restitutio in integrum* are, e.g., *Rigg v. Durward and Thom* (1776) Mor 5672, Mor Appendix 'Fraud' 6; *Stuarts v. Whiteford and the Duke of Hamilton* (1677) Mor 16489; *Adamson v. Glasgow Corporation Water-Works Commissioners* (1859) 21 D 1012; *Wilson v. Caledonian Railway Company* (1860) 22 D 1408; *Graham v. Western Bank of Scotland* (1864) 2 M 559; *Tennent v. City of Glasgow Bank* (1879) 6 R 554; (1879) 6 R (HL) 68; *Houldsworth v. City of Glasgow Bank* (1879) 6 R 1164; (1880) 7 R (HL) 53; *Steel's Tr v. Bradley Homes* 1972 SC 48; *Spence v. Crawford* 1939 SC (HL) 52. Cases which require *restitutio in integrum* to be exact are, e.g., *Boyd & Forrest v. Glasgow and South Western Railway Co.* 1915 SC (HL) 20; *Western Bank of Scotland v. Addie* (1867) 5 M (HL) 80; *Houldsworth v. City of Glasgow Bank* (1879) 6 R 1164 per Lord Deas.

[22] *Barnbugil v. Hamilton* (1567) Mor 8915; *Melvil v. Arnot* (1782) Mor 8998; *Carmichael v. Castlehill* (1698) Mor 8993; *McWilliam v. Shaw* (1576) Mor 9022; *Farquhar v. Campbell* (1628) Mor 9022; *Brown v. Nicolson* (1629) Mor 8940.

[23] Reid, 'Transfer of Ownership', § 599; Walker, *Principles*, vol. III, 435.

[24] See Gloag, *Law of Contract*, 59, 539 ff.; Gloag and Henderson, *Law of Scotland*, § 7.4; MacQueen, 'Unjustified Enrichment', 148; MacQueen, 'Scots Perspective', 198; McBryde, *Law of Contract*, §§ 9-73–9-74, 10-63 ff., 15-43, 26-05; Smith, *Short Commentary*, 790; Walker, *Law of Contracts*, §§ 5.34, 14.114.

(c) Frustration

The frustrating event has an automatic effect on the contract. The parties are excused from performing the contract *ex nunc*. The proprietary and factual consequences of the contract are unwound by using a *condictio causa data causa non secuta*.[25] B's *condictio causa data causa non secuta* against A is of no value. Since A lost the horse without fault, he is not liable to restore either the horse or its value. But A's *condictio causa data causa non secuta* against B for the cow is still valid. How is it taken into account that B himself has rendered a performance to A? According to modern Scots law, *restitutio in integrum* does not apply.[26] Instead, an equitable adjustment should be found between the parties. It is not clear exactly what that implies in this example. Can A recover the cow without giving back the horse or without making up its value? Or does he have to make up the whole value of the horse in order to claim back the cow? For modern Scots law the truth probably lies between these two extremes. The loss is split between the parties.[27]

(d) Voidness

According to modern Scots law, the same is true where the contract is unwound for voidness. The contract itself is void *ipso iure*, so only the proprietary and factual consequences need to be unwound. The parties may claim back their respective performances with a *condictio indebiti*. This is the 'obligational method'. Again, *restitutio in integrum* is said not to apply.[28] If B claims back the horse from A, he will fail, because the horse ceased to exist. But A is not allowed to claim back the cow he has given B without it being taken into account that B himself has rendered some performance to A. In this group of cases the courts have asked whether the focus should be on the enrichment of the pursuer by the counterperformance or on the expenses the defender incurred in rendering the counterperformance. The courts have given no answer in principle. Again, all that is required is that the result is equitable.[29]

---

[25] *Cantiere San Rocco SA v. Clyde Shipbuilding and Engineering Co. Ltd* 1923 SC (HL) 105.

[26] See the references in n. 24 and also *Cantiere San Rocco SA v. Clyde Shipbuilding and Engineering Co. Ltd* 1923 SC (HL) 105 at 111 *per* Earl of Birkenhead, at 126 *per* Lord Dunedin.

[27] See Lord Cooper of Culross, 'Frustration of Contracts in Scots Law', in: *Selected Papers 1922–1954* (1957), 128.

[28] See the references above in n. 24 and *General Property Investment Co. v. Matheson's Trustees* (1888) 16 R 282.

[29] *Haggarty v. Scottish Transport and General Workers Union* 1955 SC 109 at 112–13 *per* Lord Sorn.

Some reasons for unwinding the contract render not only the contract void but also the transfer of property. A mistake may in exceptional cases have this result. Only the factual consequences of the contract have to be unwound in this case. Since the transfer of property is void, A's claim ('obligational method') against B is proprietary in nature. A can claim back his performance. B cannot claim back anything.

(e) Defective goods

This group of cases demonstrates something very similar to *restitutio in integrum*. If A wants to unwind the contract he needs to reject the goods.[30] If the horse has ceased to exist, A will only be successful if it was destroyed through the fault of B. This would be the case if destruction of the horse was caused by the exact defect that allowed A to unwind the contract.[31] In all other cases A remains bound to the contract. As in the case of *restitutio in integrum*, A is in principle only allowed to unwind the contract if the proprietary and factual consequences of the contract can be unwound as well. Similarly, it has been suggested that it is sufficient to offer the value of the goods received if unwinding the proprietary and factual consequences in specie is impossible.[32]

2. English law

(a) Mistake, fraud, fear and force, undue influence

As in Scots law, it is a requirement that *restitutio in integrum* should be possible and be offered before the contract can be rescinded.[33]

(b) Defective goods

In this group of cases, A can only terminate the contract if he rejects what he received under the contract.[34] This requirement of rejection is very similar to the requirement of *restitutio in integrum*.

---

[30] *Paton v. Lockhat* (1675) Mor 14232.
[31] *Gilmer v. Galloway* (1830) 8 S 420; *Wright v. Blackwood* (1833) 11 S 722; *Fleming & Co. (Ltd) v. Airdrie Iron Co.* (1882) 9 R 473; *Kinnear v. Brodie* (1901) 3 F 540.
[32] *McCormick v. Rittmeyer* (1869) 7 M 854 at 858 *per* Lord President Inglis.
[33] See, e.g., *Clarke v. Dickson, Williams and Gibbs* (1858) El Bl & El 148; *MacKenzie v. Royal Bank of Canada* [1934] AC 468; *O'Sullivan v. Management Agency & Music Ltd* [1985] QB 428; *Mahoney v. Purnell* [1996] 3 All ER 61; *Dunbar Bank plc v. Nadeem* [1997] 2 All ER 253; *Spence v. Crawford* 1939 SC (HL) 52; *Adam v. Newbigging* (1888) 13 App Cas 308 at 323; *Armstrong v. Jackson* [1917] 2 KB 822.
[34] See, e.g., *Power v. Wells* (1778) 2 Cowp 818; *Towers v. Barrett* (1786) 1 TR 133; *Fielder v. Starkin* (1788) 1 H Bl 17 and n. (a) to this case in 126 ER 11; *Curtis v. Hannay* (1800) 3 Esp 82; *Head v. Tattersall* (1871) LR 7 Ex 7; *Elphick v. Barnes* (1880) LR 5 CP 321; *Bostock & Co. Ltd v. Nicholson & Sons Ltd* [1904] KB 725 and for the modern law *Chitty on Contracts* (27th edn, 1994), vol. II, §§ 41-323 ff.

(c) Other breaches of contract

In this group of cases the case law has gone down a different route. A may terminate the contract for the breach. However, he can only unwind the proprietary and factual consequences of the contract if there is a total failure of consideration.[35] Thus, if B is in breach, A can only claim back the cow from B if he never received any part of the performance from B. The questions posed at the beginning of this section therefore do not arise. If A's claim to have the proprietary and factual consequences of the contract unwound is already excluded by receipt of the horse, then the problem of how A's loss of the horse affects the process of unwinding the contract is never reached. A loses his rights immediately through receipt of the horse.

Today, however, English law is moving towards a solution that is very similar to the requirement of rejection and that of *restitutio in integrum*. A has to offer counter-restitution if he wants the proprietary and factual consequences of the contracts to be unwound.[36]

(d) Frustration

Let me modify the hypothetical example: A and B have a contract of sale. B has transferred the horse to A; the full price is already payable but A has so far paid only half. A and B are from different countries and the contract is frustrated by an outbreak of war between them. The war destroys the horse. The frustrating event has automatic effect on the contract. The parties are excused from future performances *ex nunc*.[37] The only question is how the proprietary and factual consequences of the contract are to be

---

[35] See, e.g., *Blackburn v. Smith* (1848) 2 Ex 783.

[36] See Peter Birks, 'Failure of Consideration', in: Francis D. Rose (ed.), *Consensus ad Idem: Essays on the Law of Contract in Honour of Guenter Treitel* (1996), 179, 180 ff., 193 ff.; Birks, 'No Consideration', 211; Andrew Burrows, 'Restitution – Where Do We Go From Here?', (1997) 50 *Current Legal Problems* 95, 100 ff.; John W. Carter, 'Restitution and Contract Risk', in: Mitchell McInnes (ed.), *Restitution: Developments in Unjust Enrichment*, (1996), 137, 154; Goff and Jones, *Law of Restitution*, 503; Mitchell McInnes, 'The Structure and Challenges of Unjust Enrichment', in: his (ed.), *The Structure and Challenges of Unjust Enrichment*, 17, 45 ff.; Ewan McKendrick, 'Total Failure of Consideration and Counter-restitution: Two Issues or One?', in: Peter Birks (ed.), *Laundering and Tracing* (1995), 217, 230–1; Ewan McKendrick, 'Frustration, Restitution, and Loss Apportionment', in: Andrew Burrows (ed.), *Essays on the Law of Restitution* (1991), 147, 152; Andrew Skelton, *Restitution and Contract* (1998), 27 ff.; *David Securities Pty Ltd v. Commonwealth Bank of Australia* (1992) 175 CLR 353 at 383.

[37] See *Taylor v. Caldwell* (1863) 3 B & S 826.

unwound. At common law, the traditional view is that B can only ask that the contract be unwound when there is a total failure of consideration.[38] However, as where the contract is unwound for breach, it seems sufficient if B makes counter-restitution in order to enable him to claim back his performances.[39] If B has already received part of the price, he needs to give it back.

This example would also be governed by section 1(2) of the Law Reform (Frustrated Contracts) Act 1943: A could claim back the price he paid to B, but B could deduct expenses he incurred 'before the time of discharge in, or for the purpose of, the performance of the contract... if [the court] considers it just to do so having regard to all the circumstances of the case'. In the example, B has incurred expenses: he has transferred the horse to A. According to some, section 1(2) and 1(3) of the Law Reform (Frustrated Contracts) Act 1943 are nothing but a defence of change of position.[40] Thus B could claim that the value of the horse be deducted from A's claim for the price. Others prefer a different reading of section 1(2). They emphasise the words 'if it is just to do so' and argue that an equitable solution to the case has to be found. Some argue that this implies that the loss has to be split between the parties.[41] In this example this probably implies that B can deduct half the value of the horse from A's claim for the price. Still others argue that all that section 1(2) does is give the judge a broad discretion to find a just solution between the parties.[42]

(e) Other cases
So far, it has been presupposed that the reason for unwinding the contract does not render the transfer of property void. However, in exceptional cases a mistake (for example) may render not only the contract but also

---

[38] See *Fibrosa Spolka Akcyjna v. Fairbairn Lawson Combe Barbour Ltd* [1943] AC 32.
[39] See references in n. 36.
[40] *BP Exploration Co. (Lybia) Ltd v. Hunt (No. 2)* [1979] 1 WLR 783 at 800, 804 *per* Goff J.
[41] See McKendrick, 'Total Failure', 159, 168 ff.; G. H. Treitel, *Frustration and Force Majeure* (1994), § 15-054; Virgo, *Principles*, 374 ff. Cf. the British Columbia Frustrated Contracts Act 1974, s. 5(3); the New South Wales Frustrated Contracts Act 1978, s. 13; and the South Australian Frustrated Contracts Act 1988, s. 7(2); see on these Acts, e.g., Peter D. Maddaugh and John D. McCamus, *The Law of Restitution* (1990), 417 ff.; Keith Mason and J. W. Carter, *Restitution Law in Australia* (1995), §§ 1245 ff., 1253 ff.; McKendrick, 'Total Failure', 165 ff.; Andrew Stewart and J. W. Carter, 'Frustrated Contracts and Statutory Adjustment: The Case for a Reappraisal', (1992) 51 *CLJ* 66, 82 ff.
[42] *Gamerco SA v. ICM/Fair Warning Ltd* [1995] 1 WLR 1226 at 1236-7 *per* Garland J.

the transfer of property void. Then only the factual consequences of the contract need be unwound. The tort of conversion will govern this. If B is still the owner of the horse, A will be liable for its value.

3. German law
(a) Mistake, fraud, fear and force

The first step (unwinding the contract as agreement) is achieved by giving the mistaken party the power to rescind the contract.[43] The proprietary and factual consequences of the contract are unwound through the law of unjustified enrichment.[44] Both parties have a *condictio indebiti* to claim back their respective performances. It is a matter of controversy what happens if one of the parties is not capable of returning what he has received.

There is the *Zweikondiktionenlehre*.[45] According to this theory, A can claim the cow back from B, but B cannot claim anything back from A because A has changed his position. The only argument, which is a strong one, in favour of this solution is that it is the one the draftsmen of the German Civil Code apparently had in mind.

The *Zweikondiktionenlehre* has not attracted much support. Modify the example slightly:[46] B sold his horse to A. A intentionally destroyed the horse after receiving it, in reliance on the validity of the contract. He knew that the destruction of the horse was at his own expense. Now he finds out that the contract may be rescinded. If he could claim back the price without himself being liable for the horse or its value, he would be able to shift the loss caused by his own intentional act onto B. The courts and academics sought to avoid this result, on two bases.

---

[43] §§ 119, 142, 143 BGB.   [44] §§ 812 ff. BGB.
[45] Paul Oertmann, 'Bereicherungsansprüche bei nichtigen Geschäften', 1915 *DJZ* 1063; Paul Oertmann, *Kommentar zum Bürgerlichen Gesetzbuch und seinen Nebengesetzen, Bürgerliches Gesetzbuch, Zweites Buch, Recht der Schuldverhältnisse, Zweite Abteilung,* §§ 433–853 (5th edn, 1929), § 818 Anm. 3 a α; Paul Oertmann, 'Noch einmal die Bereicherungsansprüche aus nichtigen Geschäften', [1919] *Das Recht* 329 ff.; K. Schneider, 'Zur Bestimmung des Umfanges der Bereicherung nach Erfüllung eines nichtigen Vertrages', (1912) 61 *JhJb* 179; Heinrich Siber, *Schuldrecht* (1931), 446–7; Andreas von Tuhr, 'Zur Lehre von der ungerechtfertigten Bereicherung', in: F. Bernhoft, P. F. Gerard et al (eds.), *Aus Römischem und Bürgerlichem Recht: Festschrift für Ernst Immanuel Bekker* (1907), 291, 306 ff.
[46] Cf., e.g., Claus-Wilhelm Canaris, 'Die Gegenleistungskondiktion', in: B. Pfister (ed.), *Festschrift für Werner Lorenz* (1991), 19, 20; Karl Larenz and Claus-Wilhelm Canaris, *Lehrbuch des Schuldrechts: Besonderer Teil* (13th edn, 1994), vol. II/2, § 73 III 1 a.

First, the *Saldotheorie*.[47] Its main thesis is that B is not enriched by the price which he has received from A. B's enrichment is the balance (= *Saldo*) of all the benefits and disadvantages from the transaction.[48] So B is only enriched by the price which he received from A minus the value of the horse. Another line of argument in support of this theory is that B can rely on the defence of change of position.[49] He has changed his position by transferring his horse to A. However, the *Saldotheorie* has been criticised heavily.

Today's literature prefers another route to achieve similar results. The argument is that the applicability of the defence of change of position has to be restricted when a mutual contract is unwound.[50] The difference from the *Saldotheorie* is as follows: with the *Saldotheorie* B's claim

---

[47] For example A. Bolze, 'Der Anspruch auf Rückgabe aus einem nichtigen Geschäft', (1890) 76 *AcP* 233; A. Bolze, 'Zum Anspruch auf Rückgabe aus einem nichtigen Geschäft', (1894) 82 *AcP* 1; Hans Albrecht Fischer, 'Bereicherung und Schaden', in: *Festschrift für Ernst Zitelmann* (edited by Juristische Fakultät der Rheinischen Friedrich-Wilhelms-Universität zu Bonn, 1913), 1, 3 ff.; Maenner, 'Bereicherungsansprüche', 1916 *DJZ* 282; Gerhard Weintraud, *Die Saldotheorie: Ein Beitrag zur Lehre vom Gegenstand des Bereicherungsanspruchs* (1931); Ernst von Caemmerer, 'Bereicherung und unerlaubte Handlung', in: H. Dölle, M. Rheinstein and K. Zweigert (eds.), *Festschrift für Ernst Rabel* (1954), vol. I, 333, 384 ff.; Hans G. Leser, *Von der Saldotheorie zum faktischen Synallagma: Ein Beitrag zur Lehre vom Wegfall der Bereicherung* (1975); Hans G. Leser, *Der Rücktritt vom Vertrag: Abwicklungsverhältnis und Gestaltungsbefugnisse bei Leistungsstörungen* (1975), 110 ff. The case law follows the *Saldotheorie*: see, e.g., RGZ 54, 137; RGZ 94, 253; RGZ 86, 343; RGZ 139, 208; BGHZ 1, 75; BGHZ 53, 144; BGHZ 57, 137; BGHZ 72, 252.

[48] See, e.g., Bolze, 'Anspruch auf Rückgabe', 243 ff.; Fischer, 'Bereicherung', 1 ff.

[49] See, e.g., RGZ 54, 137; BGHZ 57, 137, 149; BGHZ 72, 252; Weintraud, *Saldotheorie*, 2–3, 47, 56 ff., 66–7; Georg Heiman-Trosien, in: Mitglieder des Bundesgerichtshofes (eds.), *Kommentar zum Bürgerlichen Gesetzbuch mit besonderer Berücksichtigung der Rechtsprechung des Reichsgerichts und des Bundesgerichtshofes, Kommentar herausgegeben von Mitgliedern des Bundesgerichtshofes*, vol. II, 5th part, §§ 812–31 (12th edn, 1989), § 812, n. 61.

[50] For example Werner Flume, 'Der Wegfall der Bereicherung in der Entwicklung vom römischen zum geltenden Recht', in: Rechts- und Staatswissenschaftliche Fakultät zu Göttingen (ed.), *Festschrift für Hans Niedermeyer* (1953), 103, 151 ff.; Werner Flume, 'Die Entreicherungsgefahr und die Gefahr bei Rücktritt und Wandlung', 1970 *NJW* 1161; Werner Flume, 'Die Saldotheorie und die Rechtsfigur der ungerechtfertigen Bereicherung', (1994) 194 *AcP* 427; Werner Flume, 'Aufwendungen und Erträge bei der Rückabwicklung nichtiger gegenseitiger Verträge als Problematik der Rechtsfigur der ungerechtfertigten Bereicherung', in: Wolfgang Schön, in collaboration with Werner Flume, Horst Heinrich Jakobs, Eduard Picker and Jan Wilhelm (eds.), *Gedächtnisschrift für Brigitte Knobbe-Keuk* (1997), 111 ff.; Canaris, 'Die Gegenleistungskondiktion', 19 ff.; Larenz and Canaris, *Lehrbuch*, § 73 III 4 a; Manfred Lieb, in: *Münchener Kommentar zum Bürgerlichen Gesetzbuch* (3rd edn, 1997), vol. V, § 818, n. 106; Detlef König, 'Ungerechtfertigte Bereicherung', in: Bundesminister der Justiz (ed.), *Gutachten und Vorschläge zu Überarbeitung des Schuldrechts* (1981), vol. II, 1515, 1547–8.

against A will fail, because A can rely on the defence of change of position. However, A's claim against B will equally fail because B has changed his position by giving his horse to A.[51] Under the new theory A's claim against B will be successful, because B cannot rely on the defence of change of position with regard to the horse he has given to A. Equally, B's claim against A will be successful, because A cannot rely on the defence of change of position either. A has to make good the value of the horse.

(b) Breach of contract

If B breaches the contract, A may terminate it.[52] The unwinding of the proprietary and factual consequences of the contract is not governed by the law of unjustified enrichment, but by a special set of rules, the *Rücktrittsrecht*.[53] According to § 351 BGB the right to terminate may be lost if A was at fault when losing the horse. As with *restitutio in integrum* in English and Scots law, the first step of unwinding the contract is only allowed if the second and third steps of unwinding the contract are still possible or if the impossibility is not due to A's fault.

(c) Incapacity

If A is below the age of seven, both the contract and the transfer of property are void.[54] The unwinding of the factual consequences is governed by the law of property.[55] A has a *vindicatio* against B. He can claim back the cow. It does not affect his claim that he is himself not able to hand back the horse. B also has a *vindicatio* against A. This claim will fail, since A has lost the horse.

4. **Four basic models for unwinding mutual contracts**

This multitude of solutions to one and the same problem can be reduced to four basic models.

(a) Model I: total failure of consideration

The first model is that provided by the unjust factor 'total failure of consideration'. A is not able to claim back the cow, which he transferred to B once he has received B's counterperformance. Total failure of consideration only operates at the stage of unwinding the proprietary or factual consequences of the contract.

---

[51] It is assumed that the value of the horse corresponds to the price that A has paid.
[52] For example §§ 325(1), 326(1), 636(1) BGB.
[53] §§ 346 ff. BGB.   [54] §§ 104, 105(1) BGB.   [55] §§ 985 BGB.

(b) Model II: *Zweikondiktionenlehre*

The second model is that of the *Zweikondiktionenlehre*. A can claim back the cow that he transferred to B. It does not affect his rights that he is himself not able to hand back the horse received from B. On the other hand, B will fail with his claim against A, because the horse has ceased to exist. This is the model for the parties' proprietary claims to get back their respective performances. The loss of the horse falls on B.

(c) Model III: *Saldotheorie, restitutio in integrum,* counter-restitution

The third model does not allow A to claim back his cow unless he himself renders restitution to B either in specie or by making good the value of the horse. There are different tools to achieve this result. *Restitutio in integrum* is a requirement of rescission. Thus, if A is not able or willing to hand back the horse or its value, he will not be able to rescind the contract. It is a requirement for unwinding the contract as agreement that unwinding the proprietary and factual consequences is also possible. So *restitutio in integrum* presupposes at the outset that the aim is to unwind the contract *in toto*. § 351 BGB works similarly for termination for breach under German law. With counter-restitution, A can claim back the cow only if he is himself able and willing to give back the horse or its value. A can only claim that the proprietary and factual consequences be unwound, if he is willing and able to unwind the proprietary and factual consequences of the contract. Thus, counter-restitution seeks to safeguard that the proprietary and factual consequences of the contract are unwound equally for both parties: the contract is either unwound in its totality or not at all. The *Saldotheorie* functions very similarly. In this model, the loss of the horse falls on A.

(d) Model IV: splitting the loss

Finally, the loss is in some situations split between the parties.

5. Summary

The question whether a given contract is unwound *in toto* following model I, II, III or IV depends on: (a) whether a given unwinding factor is classified as belonging to the law of contract, unjustified enrichment, tort or the law of property; (b) the method for unwinding the contract; (c) the unwinding factor; and (d) what kind of benefit is at issue.

III. Is there a justification for having four models for unwinding mutual contracts?

There is an obvious problem about having more than one model for unwinding mutual contracts in one legal system. An illustration proves the point. In the revised example, B has transferred the horse to A. A was already liable to give the cow to B but did not do so. A and B are from countries that are now at war with one another. The contract is frustrated. Performance by A is legally impossible. B wants his horse back. In the meantime the horse is destroyed in the war. According to some, the most just solution is to split the loss between A and B. This solution seems to be justified by the facts that neither A nor B was at fault; that the frustrating event came about; and that the horse was destroyed.[56] Compare this with another hypothetical case: A and B have fully executed a contract. A was induced to enter the contract by fraudulent misrepresentation by B. A wants to rescind. A has to offer *restitutio in integrum*. Because there was fraud, *restitutio in integrum* need not be exact but A has to make good the value of the horse. There is a discrepancy between these two cases. In the first case the loss is split because neither was at fault for the frustrating event or the destruction of the horse. In the second case the loss falls on A, although this time the reason why the contract can be unwound is B's improper behaviour.

Different models of unwinding mutual contracts will result in discrepancies. It seems to be a better approach to have only a single mode of unwinding mutual contracts, which applies to all unwinding factors. The American literature seems to have accepted such a unified approach.[57] German law is searching for it; but in the English and Scottish literature arguments have been put forward against such an approach. I will try to show that there is no justification for having different models and legal institutions for unwinding mutual contracts.

1. Rescission for mistake, fear and force, fraud and undue influence on the one hand and breach of contract on the other

One requirement of rescission is that *restitutio in integrum* is possible and offered. A party seeking to unwind the proprietary and factual consequences

---

[56] Maddaugh and McCamus, *Law of Restitution*, 408; McKendrick, 'Total Failure', 168–9; Stewart and Carter, 'Frustrated Contracts', 101; Virgo, *Principles*, 389.
[57] Frederic Campbell Woodward, *The Law of Quasi Contracts* (1913), § 23; William A. Keener, *A Treatise on the Law of Quasi-Contracts* (1926), 138, 302–3; George E. Palmer, *The Law of Restitution* (1978), vol. I, § 3.11.

of a contract following breach used to have to prove that there had been a total failure of consideration. According to modern authors it is sufficient for this party to make counter-restitution. These instances belong to model III. That they are related is accepted by modern English writers;[58] yet there are still two distinct sets of rules governing the unwinding of mutual contracts, with the associated risk that the two legal institutions might develop differently. This risk could be avoided by also requiring *restitutio in integrum* where a contract is unwound following breach.

Modern commentators are opposed to applying *restitutio in integrum* in such a way. What are their arguments? The inapplicability of *restitutio in integrum* is explained on the ground that termination for breach works only prospectively whereas rescission (for example, for mistake) avoids the contract retrospectively.[59] Termination does not even avoid the contract *ex nunc* but only excuses the parties from their future performances. *Restitutio in integrum* implies that both parties are put into their *status quo ante contractum*. Thus, *restitutio in integrum* cannot apply if the contract is not avoided *ab initio*. These arguments appear to be attractive. But they are not a justification for having two sets of rules for unwinding contracts. The reason why English and Scots law regard termination for breach as prospective is only to safeguard the applicability of contractual arbitration, limitation and exemption clauses.[60] This rationale should not affect in any way how mutual contracts are unwound. Nor is it an argument for excluding the application of *restitutio in integrum*. As seen in the previous section, in German law one of the problems in unwinding mutual contracts is the different rules applying in the events of breach (*Rücktrittsrecht*) and of rescission (law of unjustified enrichment). The problems were less pressing as long as termination for breach was understood to put an end to the contract. The rules applying to restitution after breach were then understood only to be *leges speciales* of the law of unjustified enrichment

---

[58] Birks, 'Failure of Consideration', 180, 195; Peter Birks, 'Overview: Tracing, Claiming and Defences', in: his (ed.), *Laundering and Tracing*, 289, 336; McKendrick, 'Total Failure', 217-18. See also Virgo, *Principles*, 32 ff.; Peter Birks, 'Restitution without Counter-restitution', [1990] *Lloyd's Maritime and Commercial Law Quarterly* 330, 333-4.
[59] For example MacQueen, 'Unjustified Enrichment', 148. G. H. Treitel, *Remedies for Breach of Contract* (1988), 383, thinks that this difference between rescission and termination has little significance. See also Mason and Carter, *Restitution Law*, §§ 1433, 2331.
[60] *Municipal Council of Johannesburg v. D. Stewart & Co. (1902) Ltd* 1909 SC (HL) 53; *Photo Production Ltd v. Securicor Transport Ltd* [1980] AC 827; *Paal Wilson & Co. A/S v. Partenreederei Hannah Blumenthal* [1983] 1 AC 854, 917. See also *Chitty on Contracts*, §§ 14-022, 16-019, 25-046; Hector L. MacQueen, 'Remedies for Breach of Contract: The Future Developments of Scots Law in its European and International Context', (1997) 1 *Edinburgh LR* 200, 210; McBryde, *Law of Contract*, § 14-73; A. M. Shea, 'Discharge from Performance of Contracts by Failure of Condition', (1979) 42 *MLR* 623.

and so it was possible to resort to the law of unjustified enrichment as a subsidiary set of rules where the special rules for restitution following breach of contract were silent. It was only later that it was decided that termination for breach does not affect the existence of the contract. The only reason for this change of approach was to preserve some of the innocent party's contractual claims for damages. The unfortunate side-effect was that the law of unjustified enrichment was no longer applicable, even as a subsidiary set of rules.[61] But here, too, the fact that termination for breach does not affect the existence of the contract does not support the conclusion that there have to be two sets of rules governing the unwinding of contracts.

Although termination for breach does not avoid the contract *ab initio*, the parties can still claim that the proprietary and factual consequences of the contract should be unwound. The application of *restitutio in integrum* could be restricted to these two steps of unwinding mutual contracts. In the case of rescission it is a requirement of the first step of unwinding a mutual contract that *restitutio in integrum* is possible and has been offered. In the case of unwinding a mutual contract following a breach of contract, it is a requirement of A's claim to have the proprietary and factual consequences unwound that he himself offers to unwind the proprietary and factual consequences (for example, he offers to give back the horse or its value).

Another argument has been put forward to suggest that there is a fundamental difference between unwinding contracts following rescission and following termination for breach. This, too, is based on the fact that rescission works retrospectively and termination prospectively. A right to rescind a contract is granted in those cases in which there is a defect in the process of the formation of the contract. This is why rescission operates retrospectively. The contract should lose its force in every respect. However, in the case of breach of contract the reason for unwinding the contract appears only after the formation of the contract. That is why termination does not work retrospectively and why the parties have to be bound by the contractual allocation of risk.[62] However, for three reasons this argument is not conclusive:

(a) Termination works only *ex nunc* (not *ex tunc*), not to safeguard the allocation of risk but the applicability of contractual arbitration, limitation and exemption clauses.

[61] See especially Heinrich Stoll, 'Rücktritt und Schadensersatz', (1929) 131 AcP 141 ff. and also Leser, *Rücktritt*, 164 ff.; Reinhard Zimmermann, 'Restitution after Termination for Breach of Contract in German Law', [1997] *Restitution LR* 13, 17 ff.

[62] For example Carter, 'Restitution and Contract Risk', 142, 156 ff.

(b) Where a contract is terminated because the object sold is defective, the reason for unwinding the contract already existed at the time the contract was formed. The party buying the defective object is also in error as to its quality. If one explained the subsistence of the contractual allocation of risk after termination by the fact that the breach appeared only after the formation of the contract, then one would need to make exceptions in these cases.

(c) The contract is the reason why one party may keep the performance of the other party. In German and Scots law, a claim in unjustified enrichment usually only lies if the performances were made *sine causa*. The contract first needs to be discharged before a claim in unjust enrichment lies. In English law it is a defence to a claim in unjust enrichment that the contract is still undischarged. In the case of breach of contract, all three jurisdictions allow claims to have the proprietary and factual consequences of the contract unwound. Since the contract loses its force for some purposes but remains in force for others, it is a matter of careful analysis whether for the purpose of contractual allocation of risk the contract should subsist even after termination. It is submitted that there is no reason why it should.[63] If the proprietary and factual consequences of the contract may be unwound, then the allocation of risk should equally be unwound.

2. Rescission and termination on the one hand, frustration on the other

Unwinding mutual contracts after rescission and after termination follows model III. If the contract is unwound after frustration, Scots law seems to prefer model IV. It is unclear which model governs the unwinding of the contract following frustration in English law: one has to distinguish between common law and the Law Reform (Frustrated Contracts) Act 1943. The models discussed in the case law and the literature are models I, III and IV. Again, the question arises as to whether there is a justification for having a different model for unwinding mutual contracts following rescission and termination on the one hand and frustration on the other. The most obvious route for English and Scots law would be to apply *restitutio in integrum* to this group of cases, too. The arguments against applying *restitutio in integrum* in the event of frustration are twofold: (a) because the contract is not avoided *ex tunc*, and the parties are only excused from

---

[63] See also Peter Birks, 'Restitution after Ineffective Contracts: Issues for the 1990s', (1990) 2 *Journal of Contract Law* 227, 232; Claus-Wilhelm Canaris, 'Der Vorrang außerbereicherungsrechtlicher, insbesondere dinglicher Wertungen gegenüber der Saldotheorie und dem Subsidiaritätsgrundsatz', 1992 JZ 1114, 1115.

further performance *ex nunc*,[64] an argument which has been considered already; (b) because frustration operates automatically, whereas *restitutio in integrum* applies only if the contract is discharged – as it is with rescission – at the option of one of the parties to the contract. But this latter argument is less convincing than it appears at first sight. First, it is a serious issue whether frustration would not operate better at the choice of one party rather than automatically.[65] Secondly, whether or not frustration should operate automatically has nothing to do with how the contract is unwound. What effect frustration has on the contract should therefore not affect the mode in which the contract is unwound. Thirdly, different methods of unwinding contracts were distinguished above. All of them aim at the same end: unwinding the contract. The choice of one particular method for unwinding the contract is not in itself a reason to reach different results when doing so. The choice of method may be motivated by very different reasons: logically, the factual consequences of a contract cannot be unwound by conferring on one of the parties a power to rescind; nor can the factual consequences of a contract be *ipso iure* void. Only the 'obligational method' will work. If the frustrating event renders it impossible to fulfil future obligations, then it makes sense to say that frustration operates automatically. If the law wishes to safeguard the mistaken party by giving him the choice to fulfil the contract if he wishes to be bound by it, then it makes perfect sense to confer on him a power to rescind the contract. The choice of method is in itself no reason for adopting different models for unwinding mutual contracts. Furthermore, there are no policy reasons why unwinding contracts after frustration should operate differently from doing so after rescission.

Although the frustrating event affects the contract *ipso iure*, it is still up to the parties whether to seek to have the proprietary and factual consequences of the contract unwound. *Restitutio in integrum* could be applied so that it is a requirement of claiming back one's own performance that mutual *restitutio in integrum* be possible. *Restitutio in integrum* would thus not be a requirement of the first step of unwinding contracts but of the second and third steps.

---

[64] *Cantiere San Rocco SA v. Clyde Shipbuilding and Engineering Co. Ltd* 1923 SC (HL) 105 at 111 *per* the Earl of Birkenhead, at 126 *per* Lord Dunedin; McBryde, *Law of Contract*, § 15-40 ff.

[65] See the discussions by, e.g., Atiyah, *Introduction*, 242; Treitel, *Law of Contract*, 848; Treitel, *Frustration*, §§ 15-012 ff.; D. G. Goldberg, 'Is Frustration Invariably Automatic?', (1972) 88 *LQR* 464 ff.; Cooper, 'Frustration of Contracts', 128; D. M. Walker, *Principles of Scottish Private Law* (1989), vol. II, 139.

3. Void contracts

The last two subsections argued that: (a) there is no reason for having different models for different unwinding factors; (b) the most obvious way of unifying the approach to unwinding mutual contracts is to expand the applicability of *restitutio in integrum*. This subsection deals with contracts void *ipso iure*. Here it is not possible to regard *restitutio in integrum* as a requirement for the first step of unwinding contracts *in toto*; it would need to be a requirement of unwinding the proprietary and factual consequences of the contract. However, there may be policy considerations preventing the application of *restitutio in integrum* in this way. This point was raised by Vesey, the reporter of the annuity case *Byne v. Vivian*:[66]

> That a defendant, whose annuity has been set aside, on whatever grounds, cannot resist an account of sums received by him in respect of such an invalid contract, seems well settled by the principal case; and as the plaintiff in this case had by his bill offered to account, on his part, for the consideration actually received by him...there could be no doubt as to the propriety of directing the whole account to be taken. But if no such offer had been made by the plaintiff, it may be questioned whether the Court could have imposed terms upon him, as a condition of relief against an instrument repudiated by the policy of the legislature...

The argument is that if the legislator decided that a contract should be void, the courts cannot require additional steps (such as an offer of counter-restitution) as conditions of unwinding the proprietary and factual consequences of the contract. But there are several reasons in favour of applying *restitutio in integrum* even here.

(a) In Scots law *restitutio in integrum* is a requirement of the remedy of reduction, which may – in some special cases – be the correct remedy even if a legal act is already void.[67]

(b) In English and German law, even when a contract is unwound for voidness, it is model III that is applied. In English law, this is achieved by the requirement of counter-restitution. In German law it is achieved by the *Saldotheorie*.

(c) The concept of voidness as we know it today is relatively young.[68] In the old case law there is no strict distinction between a contract being

---

[66] (1800) 1 Ves Jun Supp 540 at 540–1.
[67] Viscount Stair, *The Institutions of the Law of Scotland* (tercentenary edn by D. M. Walker, 1981), Book I, Title 9, 36. Whether this is true for today's Scots law is unclear: Stair Memorial Encyclopaedia (1992), vol. XIII, § 35. See also Smith, *Short Commentary*, 790.
[68] Manfred Harder, 'Die historische Entwicklung der Anfechtbarkeit von Willenserklärungen', (1973) 173 *AcP* 209; Reinhard Zimmermann, *The Law of Obligations: Roman Foundations of the Civilian Tradition* (paperback edn, 1996), 680 ff.

void and one being rescindable. The terms voidness and rescission were used interchangeably. This is especially true for German law. In German law, today's rescission developed from the concept of relative voidness of the *Pandektistik*.[69]

(d) The line between cases in which a factor avoids the contract *ipso iure* and those in which it renders it only rescindable is drawn differently in Scots, English and German law. In German law, a mistake only rarely prevents *consensus ad idem*. On the other hand, in Scots and English law a fundamental mistake may do so. But this difference should not influence how the contract is unwound.

(e) Even if *restitutio in integrum* were in principle a requirement of unwinding the proprietary and factual consequences of a void contract, a legal system might make exceptions to this rule. In our example A may under certain circumstances be allowed to claim back the cow without making counter-restitution. Such exceptions have been allowed in English[70] and German law[71] and they have been discussed in Scots law.[72] If insistence on *restitutio in integrum* being possible and offered would subvert the policy underlying the voidness of the contract, such an exception should be allowed.

4. Proprietary unwinding

Sometimes claims to unwind contracts can also have a proprietary base. In German law, this was the *vindicatio*. In English law proprietary restitutionary claims come to mind. The results achieved with these claims belong to model II: A can claim back the cow from B; in A's claim against B no account is taken of the fact that B has already performed and that he will fail in his own claim against A. Is there is a justification for following different models for unwinding contracts only because the claims in question are categorised differently?

(a) A possible justification would be that claims to unwind contracts are categorised as proprietary to secure special protection for one of the

---

[69] Harder, 'Die historische Entwicklung', 209 ff.
[70] *Head v. Tattersall* (1871) LR 7 Ex 7; *Guinness plc v. Saunders* [1990] 2 AC 663.
[71] Pre-BGB see, e.g., Ferdinand Mackeldey, *Lehrburch des heutigen Römischen Rechts* (12th edn, 1842), § 207.c.12; Schweppe, *Römische Privatrecht*, § 991; Johann Nepomuk von Wening-Ingenheim, *Lehrbuch des Gemeinen Civilrechts* (5th edn, 1838), vol. III, Book VI, § 11; Johann Adam Seuffert, *Praktisches Pandektenrecht* (4th edn, 1872), vol. III, § 665.8; Friedrich Heinrich Theodor Vering, *Geschichte und Pandekten des Römischen und Heutigen Gemeinen Privatrechts* (4th edn, 1875), § 134 VII; Heinrich Dernburg, *Pandekten* (1884), § 143.5. For today's law, see Lieb, in: *Münchener Kommentar*, § 818, nn. 91–2, 106.
[72] Lord Bankton, *An Institute of the Laws of Scotland* (Stair Society, vols. 41-3, 1993-5), vol. I, p. 182, n. 83 and p. 184, n. 94; John Erskine, *An Institute of the Law of Scotland* (3rd edn, 1793), Book I, Title VII, 41; Campbell and Paton, *Hume's Lectures*, 300 ff.; *Earl of Aberdeen v. Gordon* (1708) Mor 9031; *Kinnear v. Brodie* (1901) 3 F 540.

parties. Modifying the example can make this point clear. A lacks capacity. The contract is void. The transfer of property is also void. A has a *vindicatio* to claim back his cow. B has to bear the loss of the horse transferred to A. But categorising the claim as proprietary does not favour only A. If B has lost the cow, he can claim back his horse from A, and A has to bear the loss of the cow transferred to B.

(b) If categorisation of claims as proprietary depended on a policy of special protection for one of the parties, such policy considerations would have to determine whether an unwinding factor also renders the transfer of property void. However, at least in German law this is not the case.[73]

(c) The claim to have the factual consequences unwound can in German and in Scots law be categorised as proprietary only as long as the transferred chattel exists.[74] Once the obligor has lost the chattel for whatever reason, he is not any longer liable in property. However, if he is still enriched he will be liable in the law of unjust enrichment. In our example, if B has sold the cow to C, then he will be liable for the price that he received from C.[75] Both in Scots and German law this claim would belong to the law of unjustified enrichment. This claim would not have the advantages of the proprietary claim. Again, the policy consideration would here need to influence the claim in unjustified enrichment. Otherwise the protection would be incomplete.[76]

(d) If A instead of transferring a cow rendered a service to B, B would only be liable in the law of unjustified enrichment. If *restitutio in integrum* only applied in the law of unjustified enrichment, but not in the law of property, then A would need to make good the value of the horse or its value in order to be able to claim the value of his services. Now the risk of loss of the horse would be on A not B. But neither the categorisation of A's claim nor the nature of the benefit that A conferred on B should influence the question on whom the risk of the horse falls. So the special protection of one of the parties cannot explain why the contract

---

[73] For example § 138(2) BGB states that a legal act is void if: (a) the party doing the act was in a situation of special need or if he is mentally inadequate, (b) if this necessity or inadequacy has been exploited, and (c) if there is a manifest disadvantage. § 138(2) BGB renders not only the (obligatory) contract but also the transfer of property void. This is not justified by special protection of the weaker party but merely with a literal – and historically doubtful – interpretation of § 138(2) BGB; see Reinhard Zimmermann, 'Sittenwidrigkeit und Abstraktion', 1985 *JR* 48.

[74] Owing to the law of tracing the same may not be true of English law.

[75] For German law see § 816(1) BGB. For Scots law, Stair, *Institutions*, Book I, Title VII, 11.

[76] Problems arising when a proprietary claim changes into a claim for unjustified enrichment have been much discussed in German law: see, e.g., Dieter Bremecker, *Die Bereicherungsbeschränkung des § 818 Abs. 3 BGB bei nichtigen gegenseitigen Verträgen* (1982), 58 ff.; Flume, 'Der Wegfall', 164, 171; Jürgen Kohler, *Die gestörte Rückabwicklung gescheiterter Austauschverträge* (1989), 166; Leser, *Saldotheorie*, 25–6, 62–3; Oertmann, 'Bereicherungsansprüche', 1063; Oertmann, 'Noch einmal', 335–6; Bernhard Rengier, 'Wegfall der Bereicherung', (1977) 177 *AcP* 418, 434 ff.; von Tuhr, 'Zur Lehre', 307–8.

should be unwound differently when the unwinding factor belongs to the law of property.

(e) In Scots and English law, that *restitutio in integrum* has to be possible is not the only bar to rescission. Another is the intervention of third-party rights.[77] If B has sold the cow to C and C has acquired title bona fide then A is barred from rescinding the contract. This bar only makes sense if at one stage rescission affected not only the validity of the contract but also the transfer of property. C's rights are not affected in any way if A is only able to rescind the contract as an agreement. C's rights would only be affected if A's rescission had the effect that now A and not C was the owner of the cow. So one must assume that at one stage in the development of Scots and English law rescission also avoided the transfer of property *ab initio*. And yet *restitutio in integrum* is a requirement of rescission. Therefore, the question who owns the cow should not in any way influence how the contract is unwound.[78]

5. Summary

This section of the paper may be summarised as follows. There seems to be no reason why the distinctions identified in the first section of this paper should influence how a mutual contract is unwound. One model for unwinding mutual contracts *in toto* should be adopted.

But it needs to be chosen carefully. Take a further example. The contract is void. A and B have fully executed their respective obligations. If A claims back the cow from B, A has to make counter-restitution. Thus, the risk of destruction of the horse is on A. If on the other hand only B has performed, it is B who might want to claim back the horse. However, the defence of change of position will be open to A. He can say that he has lost the horse. The risk of destruction of the horse is now on B. Hence, even within model III there can be different results depending on whether the contract has been fully executed or performed by only one of the parties.

IV. Which model should a unified approach adopt?

1. Are there external arguments for a particular model?

The previous section of this chapter concluded that there should be only one model regulating the unwinding of mutual contracts. Model III, *restitutio in integrum*, would be the obvious choice for English and Scots law,

---

[77] For Scots law see, e.g., Gloag, *Law of Contract*, 533 ff.; Gloag and Henderson, *Law of Scotland*, § 7.5; Walker, *Law of Contracts*, § 33.44; Walker, *Principles*, vol. II, 159. For English law see, e.g., Atiyah, *Introduction*, 414; Virgo, *Principles*, 34. In English law this bar to rescission has been criticised: see, e.g., Peter Birks, 'Unjust Factors and Wrongs: Pecuniary Rescission for Undue Influence', [1997] *Restitution LR* 72.

[78] See already *Guinness plc v. Saunders* [1990] 2 AC 663 at 698.

because it is most consonant with these two systems. But are there more fundamental reasons for selecting one model over another? Does equity (for example) demand the adoption of model III? At first sight it is surprising that most of the arguments raised in English, German and Scots law are intended to justify the choice of model III. Why are no fundamental arguments discussed in favour of model II? Is model III perhaps the more equitable? The truth is probably less obvious. It is that model III needs special justification. In model II the risk of loss of the horse is on B. A can claim back his cow from B. It does not influence A's claim that he himself is unable to make counter-restitution. B cannot claim back his horse from A, since A has lost it. On the other hand, under model III whether A is able and willing to make counter-restitution (in specie or in value) is relevant. The claims of A and B are therefore interdependent.[79] If the parties have undertaken reciprocal obligations, a party can only ask for counterperformance if he himself offers performance. In German law, if one of the obligations ceases to exist due to supervening impossibility then the other party will be freed from his obligation, too. The requirements of *restitutio in integrum* and of counter-restitution reach very similar results, not at the stage of performance but at that of unwinding the failed contract. But if the contract between A and B is void, there are immediately problems explaining how their rights to unwind the contract can be reciprocal. The mutuality principle gets its justification from the existence of the contract. But how is the principle of mutuality justified in the process of unwinding the contract? This problem has forced judges and academics to give special reasons for following model III.

(a) The will of the parties
In German law, the will of the parties has been presented as an argument pro model III and contra model II.[80] As long as the contract is in force,

---

[79] In German law the reciprocity of performance and counterperformance is called *Synallagma*. The reciprocity of the claims to have the contract unwound is called *faktisches Synallagma*. The closest translation is 'factual reciprocity', an attempt to express that reciprocity at the stage of unwinding the contract is based not on the contract but on the factual exchange of performance and counterperformance. Cf. Ernst Christian Westphal, *Lehre des gemeinen Rechts vom Kauf-, Pacht-, Mieth- und Erbzinscontract, der Zession, auch der Gewähr des Eigenthums und der Mängel* (1791), § 492, and see also §§ 503, 519.
[80] See, e.g., Bolze, 'Der Anspruch', 241; Leser, *Saldotheorie*, 48; Josef Esser, *Schuldrecht: Besonderer Teil* (4th edn, 1971), vol. II, § 105 II 2; Karl Larenz, *Lehrbuch des Schuldrechts: Besonderer Teil* (12th edn, 1981), vol. II, § 70 III; Heiman-Trosien, in: *Reichsgerichtsräte-Kommentar*, § 818, n. 61; Dieter Reuter and Michael Martinek, *Ungerechtfertigte Bereicherung* (1983), 606; Flume, 'Der Wegfall', 154–5; Hans-Martin Pawlowski, *Rechtsgeschäftliche Folgen nichtiger Willenserklärungen* (1966), 46.

the mutuality principle is based upon the contract and thus upon the will of the parties. German academics have argued that if the contract is void or rescinded that does not change the fact that the parties wanted their rights – even at the stage of unwinding the contract – to be reciprocal and the mutuality principle, with all its consequences, to apply.

There is, however, an immediate problem. If A was mistaken and rescinded the agreement, or if the agreement was void, how can one assume that that fact does not affect the will of the parties that their obligations should be reciprocal? No satisfactory answer has yet been given to this question.[81]

(b) The reliance of the parties

In German law, some have argued that reciprocal rights to have the contract unwound are based on the mutual reliance of the parties.[82] They have relied on the fact that their obligations are reciprocal: this matters even at the stage of unwinding the contract. For a number of reasons this explanation is not satisfactory.

> (i) What is the basis for reliance? It cannot be the contract (as some have argued) because the contract is void or has been avoided *ab initio*. Others argue that the basis is the factual exchange of performances. But this explanation has difficulty in explaining cases in which only one party has performed his obligations.
> (ii) In English and Scots law *restitutio in integrum* is also a requirement of A's rescission of the contract, if A was fraudulently induced by B to enter into the contract. In this case, the reciprocity of A's and B's rights cannot be explained by the mutual reliance of A and B. B has committed fraud and therefore cannot legitimately rely on anything.
> (iii) It has never been shown why reciprocal rights to unwind the contract are the correct response to the mutual reliance of A and B. Usually a claim for reliance damages is the more natural response.

(c) Execution of the contract

Some have argued that actual execution of the contract is enough to explain the mutuality of rights to unwind the contract.[83] The supporters of

---

[81] See, e.g., Bremecker, *Die Bereicherungsbeschränkung*, 69; Kohler, *Die gestörte Rückabwicklung*, 188–9, 193–4.
[82] See, e.g., Leser, *Saldotheorie*, 48; Esser, *Schuldrecht*, § 105 II 2; Hans Josef Wieling, *Bereicherungsrecht* (2nd edn, 1998), 72.
[83] See Bolze, 'Der Anspruch', 241; Leser, *Saldotheorie*, 48; Esser, *Schuldrecht*, § 105 II 2; Heiman-Trosien, in: *Reichsgerichtsräte-Kommentar*, § 818, n. 61.

this approach talk of the *'normative Kraft des Faktischen'* – the normative power of facts. However, this approach will not do either. First, it would be necessary to distinguish between cases in which a contract is fully executed and those in which it is only half executed. Secondly, as seen above, in model III the risk of loss of the horse is usually on A, with one exception: if the horse is lost owing to B's fault. For example, if the horse is lost owing to a defect that already existed at the time of the transfer of the horse, A can claim back his cow, although he is not able to give back the horse. If the reciprocal rights to unwind the contract are based on its actual execution, then there is no explanation for this exception to the rule, since here too the contract was executed. A more fundamental problem of this theory is that the question in issue is: on whom is the risk of destruction of the horse? That cannot be answered by looking only to one fact.

(d) *Casum sentit dominus/res perit domino*

Some answer the question who has to bear the loss by appealing to the brocard *casum sentit dominus* or *res perit domino*.[84] The risk of loss of the horse falls in our example on A because A is the owner. Again, there are problems with this explanation:

(i) Some unwinding factors prevent the transfer of property. In German law, if B was a minor, he could not transfer property to A, so B would remain owner. Should the loss now fall on B?

(ii) Some legal systems (such as Austrian law) do not know the principle of abstraction, so if the contract is void, so is the transfer of property. Under the brocard *casum sentit dominus*, the loss of the horse will regularly be on B.

(iii) As argued earlier, the question whether or not property passes should not affect how a mutual contract is to be unwound. Whether voidness, rescission, termination or frustration have proprietary effects is a matter based on policy considerations that have nothing to do with unwinding contracts.

(iv) In the example used here, if A rescinds the contract as an agreement he might still be the owner of the horse. Even if *casum sentit dominus* were the right starting point, there would still be problems. Following rescission of the contract, the law decides that A is unjustly enriched at B's expense. That is why B can usually claim back the horse, although

---

[84] See *Kinnear v. Brodie* (1901) 3 F 540 at 542 (sheriff), at 544 (contra, on appeal); also Campbell and Paton, *Hume's Lectures*, 300–1; Malte Diesselhorst, *Die Natur der Sache als außergesetzliche Rechtsquelle, verfolgt an der Rechtsprechung zu Saldotheorie* (1968), 83; Zimmermann, *Law of Obligations*, 332.

A is still its owner. If B is in the end entitled to the horse, why should he not bear the loss?[85]

(e) *Commodum eius esse debet, cuius periculum est*

For the same reasons, the brocard *commodum eius esse debet, cuius periculum est* (the benefit ought to go to the person who bears the risk) seems to be the wrong starting point.

(f) Identity of control and risk

Under this theory, the risk of loss is on A, not because he is usually the owner but because he had control over the horse. This theory avoids the criticisms levelled at the rule *res perit domino*. Just as model III is reminiscent of the mutuality principle in unwinding the contract, this theory is parallel to the problem of passing of risk, at least in German law. § 446 BGB states that in the case of a contract of sale the risk passes with delivery and not immediately when the contract is formed or when the property passes. The core of § 446 BGB is therefore that the party who has control over the object also has to bear the loss. This principle is also applied to unwinding mutual contracts. However, this line of argument is not open to English and Scots law, since they do not accept that under a valid contract the risk usually passes with delivery; it does so with the transfer of property.[86]

(g) *Venire contra factum proprium*

Some argue that model III is justified by the rule *venire contra factum proprium nulli conceditur* or *venire contra factum proprium nemini licet*.[87] In German law this rule is based on the principle of good faith (§ 242 BGB), a principle that also applies at the stage of unwinding a contract. This

---

[85] See *Head v. Tattersall* (1871) LR 7 Ex 7 at 14 *per* Cleasby B, and Walter Wilburg, in: Heinrich Klang (ed.), *Kommentar zum allgemeinen bürgerlichen Gesetzbuch* (2nd edn, 1951), vol. VI, §§ 1431 ff. ABGB, X C 4 e; Walter Wilburg, *Die Lehre von der ungerechtfertigten Bereicherung nach österreichischem und deutschem Recht* (1934), 157.

[86] *Chitty on Contracts*, §§ 41–146 ff.; Gloag and Henderson, *Law of Scotland*, § 16.18.

[87] ('Nobody is allowed to derogate from his own act.') See, e.g., Gustav Boehmer, 'Rechte und Pflichten des Käufers einer gestohlenen Sache', 1953 *JZ* 392, 393–4; Ludwig Enneccerus, Heinrich Lehmann, *Recht der Schuldverhältnisse* (15th edn, 1958), § 39 II 1 e; Rengier, 'Wegfall der Bereicherung', 438–9; Ernst Wolf, 'Vertretenmüssen und Verschulden', (1954) 153 *AcP* 97, 131, 135 ff.; Zimmermann, 'Restitution after Termination', 19.

rule means that a person may not act in a self-contradictory manner if another person has already relied on the first act. The rule applies where A acts in such a way that B is induced to believe that A will abide by his act; B legitimately relies upon A's act and makes expenditure in reliance upon it. If A then wants to depart from his original act, the rule will bind him to it. The requirements are very similar to those of estoppel by representation in English law and personal bar in Scots law. Despite the importance of these doctrines in the law of unjustified enrichment, it has never been suggested that *restitutio in integrum* or counter-restitution is simply an application of estoppel or personal bar. Instead, *restitutio in integrum* and counter-restitution on the one hand and estoppel and personal bar on the other are, according to English and Scots law, distinct defences. English and Scots law seem to be right about this: model III cannot be justified by reference to the rule *venire contra factum proprium nulli conceditur*.[88]

The first requirement is an act by A, such as (a) exchanging the cow for the horse; (b) taking the horse; (c) using the horse; (d) using the horse in such a way as to make its loss possible, even if it was not A's fault. However, all of these acts will legitimately induce in B only the belief that A thinks the contract cannot be rescinded or terminated, will not be frustrated and is not void. They cannot legitimately induce in B the belief that A will keep the horse at his own risk even if the contract can be rescinded, and so forth. For A to claim back the horse without making counter-restitution is not self-contradictory. Furthermore, B has made no reliance expenditure in these instances. Finally, even where there has been fraudulent misrepresentation by B, *restitutio in integrum* is still a requirement in English and Scots law. But in this case B's reliance does not deserve to be protected by the law.

This essay has been assuming that the rationale of the present rule is to protect B's reliance. It has, however, been argued that the rule may be supported by the rationale of preventing somebody from shifting his own loss on to another person.[89] If A were allowed to claim back his

[88] See Hans Walter Dette, *Venire contra factum proprium nulli conceditur: Zur Konkretisierung eines Rechtssprichworts* (1985), 105 ff.; Joachim Klink, *Eine Sphärentheorie für Ausgleichsmodi im Synallagma* (1981), 46–7; Ernst Mezger, 'Rechte und Pflichten des Käufers einer gestohlenen Sache', 1953 JZ 67, 68; Reinhard Singer, *Das Verbot widersprüchlichen Verhaltens* (1993), 14 ff., 36–7; Dagmar Kaiser, in: J. von Staudingers *Kommentar zum Bürgerlichen Gesetzbuch* (13th edn, 1995), § 351, nn. 29 ff.
[89] Arndt Teichmann, in: *Soergel, Kommentar zum Bürgerlichen Gesetzbuch* (12th edn, 1990), § 242, n. 315.

cow without making counter-restitution, he would be able to shift the loss of the horse on to B. But this approach is incorrect, since it presupposes without argument that the loss of the horse falls naturally on A not B.

(h) *Exceptio doli*

In Roman law one can unwind a contract only if one offers back what one has received under it:[90] this is model III. It has been suggested that the Roman means of employing model III was the *exceptio doli*.[91] Much the same has been said in German law.[92] Accordingly, B would have an *exceptio doli* if A did not offer to make counter-restitution. Among Romanists this theory has not been found convincing[93] and it is of no assistance to modern English, Scots or German law.

(i) Avoiding unjust enrichment

One of the most frequently cited justifications of model III in English, Scots[94] and German law,[95] but also in American law[96] and among Romanists,[97] is that it prevents unjust enrichment of A. If A could both claim the cow back from B and keep the horse, he would be unjustly enriched. As long as the horse exists, this justification of the rule of counter-restitution seems to be correct. However, the hard case is the one in which A has lost the horse. If the horse has ceased to exist, A is no longer enriched, because he has changed his position. If avoiding the unjust enrichment of A were the only justification of the rule, then A should be successful against B once he has lost the horse. So this explanation of model III only works as long as a given jurisdiction employs the concept

---

[90] See, e.g., Berthold Kupisch, *In integrum restitutio und vindicatio utilis bei Eigentumsübertragungen im klassischen römischen Recht* (1974), 109 ff.; Wilhelm Felgentraeger, *Antikes Lösungsrecht* (1933), 104 ff.; Max Kaser, 'Zur in integrum restitutio, besonders wegen metus und dolus', (1977) 94 ZSS (RA) 101, 137, 164; Ernst Levy, 'Zur nachklassischen restitutio in integrum', (1951) 68 ZSS (RA) 360, 367; Zimmermann, *Law of Obligations*, 656–7.

[91] Levy, 'Zur nachklassischen', 367.   [92] Bolze, 'Anspruch auf Rückgabe', 242.

[93] Kupisch, *In integrum restitutio*, 109 ff.; Kaser, 'Zur in integrum restitutio', 137, 164.

[94] MacQueen, 'A Scots Perspective', 198; Mason and Carter, *Restitution Law*, § 1434; McKendrick, 'Frustration', 232; *Spence v. Crawford* [1939] 3 All ER 271 at 288–9.

[95] Arndts, *Lehrbuch*, § 124; Friedrich Christian Glück, *Ausführliche Erläuterungen der Pandecten, Fünften Theils erste Abteilung* (1798), 453 ff.; Christian F. Mühlenbruch, *Lehrbuch des Pandekten-Rechts* (2nd edn, 1839, reprint 1983), vol. I, § 162; Georg Friedrich Puchta, *Pandekten* (9th edn, 1863), § 106; Seuffert, *Praktisches Pandektenrecht*, § 665.

[96] Palmer, *Law of Restitution*, § 3.12.   [97] Kaser, 'Zur in integrum restitutio', 137, 164.

of 'received enrichment' and not 'surviving enrichment'. Once the defence of change of position is recognised, this explanation of model III will no longer do.

(j) The loss lies where it falls
Some apply the maxim 'the loss lies where it falls' and argue that in the current example the loss fell on A and he should not be able to shift it on to B without good reason. But the argument is flawed. Under model II loss of the horse falls on B. It will lie there unless B has a good reason to shift it on to A. With model III the loss of the horse falls on A. It will lie on A unless there is some justification for shifting it on to B. These two models start from opposite ends. The maxim 'the loss lies where it falls' is of no argumentative value when deciding whether to follow model II or model III.

(k) He who seeks equity must do equity
In English and Scots law, this principle is mentioned as being at the root of model III.[98] It seems to mean that a person seeking to unwind a contract should himself be in a position to give back what he received. The reference to equity is helpful as long as both the horse and the cow are in existence. However, equity is not of much help once the horse has ceased to exist.

(l) Summary
In England, Scotland and Germany, but also in America and among Romanists, there are a number of arguments that seem to suggest that model III is preferable. But none of these arguments were compelling enough to justify the conclusion that model III is the right choice for unwinding mutual contracts.

2. Are there internal arguments for a particular model?
The question I am concerned to answer in this subsection is whether or not any of these models achieve equitable results and provide the tools to deal with different possible fact patterns.

(a) Model I
I will not spend any time on total failure of consideration. It is now accepted in English law that total failure of consideration should be

[98] *Aguilar v. Aguilar* (1820) 5 Madd 414 at 416 n. 1; Scotland *North British and Mercantile Insurance Co. v. Stewart* (1871) 9 M 534 at 537.

interpreted in such a way that all that is needed is counter-restitution. The case law is starting to follow the lead of legal academics. Model I is slowly being replaced by model III.[99]

(b) Model II

Model II is that of the *Zweikondiktionentheorie*. A can claim back the cow. It does not affect A's claim against B that he himself is not able to give back the horse. B cannot claim anything from A, since A can rely on the defence of change of position: he has lost the horse. Thus, the risk of loss of the horse is usually on B. If that were the end of the story, the results would be in many, though not in all, cases unjust. However, German law offers a number of tools whereby B can shift the loss on to A.

(i) If A rescinds the contract for mistake, he has to make good B's reliance damage: § 122 I BGB. In reliance on the validity of the contract, B has transferred the horse to A. A has to make good B's reliance damage either by transferring back the horse or by making good its value. It is no defence to the claim for damages that A has lost the horse.

(ii) If the contract is void for impossibility (§ 306 BGB) and one party knew or ought to have known that, then the other party can claim back his or her reliance expenditures (§ 307 BGB). Thus, if A was to give two cows in exchange for B's horse and A has so far transferred only one, while the other was already dead when the contract was formed, then the contract is void. A can claim back the one cow that he has already delivered to B for impossibility. It does not affect his claim that he cannot offer the horse back. However, if he knew or ought to have known that the cow was dead, he is liable to make good B's reliance damage.

(iii) If the contract is void for illegality (§ 134 BGB) and A knew or ought to have known of the illegality, B can claim his reliance damages from A (§§ 309, 307 BGB).

(iv) Similar results may be achieved with *culpa in contrahendo*, with § 826 BGB, and with §§ 823 II BGB, 263 StGB. Therefore, although in principle the risk of loss of the horse is on B, B can shift it on to A in all cases in which A is either responsible for the unwinding factor or in which he knew or ought to have known of the unwinding factor before B transferred the horse to A.

(v) Furthermore, B can always shift the loss on to A where A knew or ought to have known that he was not entitled to the horse and was at fault in dealing with the horse in such a way that it ceased to exist: §§ 989, 990 BGB; §§ 989, 292, 818 IV, 819 I BGB; §§ 989, 347, first sentence, BGB.

---

[99] See the references in n. 36, above.

The results achieved with model II are therefore acceptable, but only if backed up by legal tools with which B can shift the loss on to A. German law offers these tools, as shown. English law does not have comparable actions to claim reliance damage, such as on grounds of *culpa in contrahendo*. For this reason, model II is not open to English law.[100]

(c) Model III

As already seen, model III may be achieved by a number of means, of which counter-restitution, *restitutio in integrum* and the *Saldotheorie* are the most important. All of these aim to unwind the contract *in toto*. A's claim against B and B's claim against A are not looked upon as distinct, but as just two steps in the same story: unwinding the proprietary and factual consequences of the contract. The conclusion which model III draws from this is that A is within his rights to have the contract unwound only if he offers counter-restitution to B either in specie or in value. As a consequence, the risk of the loss of the horse is on A not on B.

There are, however, exceptions to this rule:

(i) If to allow A to unwind the contract only on offering counter-restitution would subvert the policy consideration that renders the contract void, then A need not make counter-restitution.[101]

(ii) If loss of the horse is attributable to B, A is again able to claim back the cow without making counter-restitution. The most important case is where A wants to have the contract unwound because the horse is defective, but the horse ceased to exist owing to this same defect.[102]

(iii) Furthermore, the *Saldotheorie* does not apply where B has fraudulently induced A to enter into the contract.[103] English and Scots law do not know this exception. A even has to offer *restitutio in integrum* to B if he wants to rescind the contract for fraudulent misrepresentation.[104]

The results achieved by model III are acceptable.

[100] Model II might be open to Australian law which has claims for reliance damages comparable to those of German law: *Waltons Stores (Interstate) Ltd v. Maher* (1988) 164 CLR 387; *Commonwealth of Australia v. Verwayen* (1990) 170 CLR 394; Justine Munro, 'The New Law of Estoppel', (1993) 23 *Victoria University of Wellington Law Review* 271; Michael Spence, 'Australian Estoppel and the Protection of Reliance', (1997) 11 *Journal of Contract Law* 203; Michael Spence, *Protecting Reliance: The Emergent Doctrine of Equitable Estoppel* (1999).

[101] See, e.g., *Guinness plc v. Saunders* [1990] 2 AC 663; Erskine, *Institute*, Book I, Title VII, 41.

[102] *Kinnear v. Brodie* (1901) 3 F 540; *Head v. Tattersall* (1871) LR 7 Ex 7; RGZ 94, 253.

[103] BGHZ 53, 144. See Dernburg, *Pandekten*, § 143.5; Vering, *Geschichte und Pandekten*, § 134 VII; von Wening-Ingenheim, *Lehrbuch*, Book VI, § 11.

[104] For example *Spence v. Crawford* 1939 SC (HL) 52.

(d) Model IV

Under model IV the loss is split between the parties. This is the most flexible approach. It can take into account the special circumstances of each case. Prima facie it is the most attractive model. However, there are a number of problems with it.

(i) First, there needs to be a catalogue of factors that can be taken into consideration when apportioning the loss. Some might tend to argue that this should be left to the judge.[105] He will best be able to work out which factors should influence the loss apportionment in a given case. However, one should be able to agree on a catalogue of factors which should and those which should never influence the result of a given case. If this cannot be done in principle, how is the judge expected to do so? In German, Scots and English legal literature as well as in the case law a number of factors have been suggested: responsibility for the unwinding factor; responsibility for the loss; policy considerations of the unwinding factor; which party can better bear the loss; for whose benefit the contract was made.[106]

(ii) It is not enough just to enumerate the different factors. One has to decide how these factors come into play.[107] The law faces a similar problem with contributory negligence: if the loss of the plaintiff has been caused not only by the defendant but also by his own negligence, his claim for damages may be reduced.[108] In the case of contributory negligence both the acts of the plaintiff and the acts of the defendant have caused the loss. However, the problem here is slightly more complicated. If B induced A to enter into the contract by fraudulent misrepresentation and A killed the horse, then A is responsible for the loss of the horse; B is responsible for the unwinding factor. Each is responsible for a different fact. How should these two responsibilities be weighed against one another? If B had not fraudulently induced A to enter into the contract, A would never have received the horse, and would never have been in a position to kill it. Should the loss therefore be on B? One possible answer is that B's misrepresentation only influences the loss apportionment, if the fact misrepresented to A caused the loss.[109] B fraudulently tells A that the horse is fit for work and in fact it is not. If A kills the horse, the loss will be on him. If the horse only dies because it was not fit for work, the loss will be on B. If A

---

[105] *Haggarty v. Scottish Transport and General Workers Union* 1955 SC 109 at 114–15 *per* Lord Sorn; *Gamerco SA v. ICM/Fair Warning Ltd* [1995] 1 WLR 1226 at 1236–7 *per* Garland J; Axel Flessner, *Wegfall der Bereicherung. Rechtsvergleichung und Kritik* (1970), 156 ff.; Edgar Deplewski, *Die Risikoverteilung im nichtigen Synallagma* (1976), 164 ff.

[106] Flessner, *Wegfall*, 115 ff.; Deplewski, *Die Risikoverteilung*, 85 ff.

[107] Kohler, *Die gestörte Rückabwicklung*, 249; Rengier, 'Wegfall der Bereicherung', 428.

[108] Law Reform (Contributory Negligence) Act 1945; § 254(1) BGB.

[109] See Canaris, 'Die Gegenleistungskondiktion'.

by using the horse breaches his *diligentia quam in suis* and the horse dies, but a horse which was fit for work would have been able to manage this situation, the loss may be split.

It is therefore already difficult to explain how only two factors may influence the loss apportionment.

(iii) It is not yet clear which loss is to be apportioned. Let me again modify the hypothetical case. B transferred his horse to A. The value of the horse at the time of performance was £400. The value of the cow that B was to get in exchange was £300. B has made a bad bargain. Before A performs his side of the bargain the horse declined in value. It is now worth only £200. Finally, the contract is frustrated and the frustrating event also kills the horse. Since neither party is responsible for the frustrating event and since neither party is responsible for the death of the horse, it can be assumed that the loss is best split equally between the parties. But is it the loss of £200, £300 or £400 which is to be split?

In conclusion, model IV is unattractive for English and Scots law, because it is not at all clear how it functions. Leaving all these questions to the discretion of the judge would be capitulation to the problems of principle.

3. Summary

In English and Scots law, the unwinding of mutual contracts should be further developed on the basis of model III. This should apply regardless of the unwinding factor, how the claim is categorised, and which method is adopted to unwind the contract.

V. The meaning of *restitutio in integrum*

Model III needs a name. For English and Scots law, counter-restitution or *restitutio in integrum* seem to be suitable candidates. I would suggest that *restitutio in integrum* is the most appropriate.[110] But what is meant by *restitutio in integrum* needs to be carefully defined. The term has been used at different times in Scottish and English legal history in different senses: (i) to denote an action;[111] (ii) to describe the plaintiff's aim in bringing the

---

[110] Virgo, *Principles*, 32 ff. apparently prefers counter-restitution.
[111] See the old cases of unwinding contracts for minority. See also Percival Gane's 'Translator's note', in: *The Selective Voet: Being the Commentary on the Pandects by Johannes Voet* (1989), IV, 1. This was also the pandectist sense of the term: see, e.g., Mackeldey, *Lehrbuch*, § 207.c.1; Puchta, *Pandekten*, § 100; Friedrich Carl von Savigny, *System des heutigen Römischen Rechts* (1848), vol. VII, 93–4, 98 ff.; Alois Brinz, *Lehrbuch der Pandekten* (2nd edn, 1873), § 115.

action (to be put *in integrum*);[112] (iii) to refer to a requirement of rescission (the defendant needs to be put *in integrum*);[113] (iv) as a synonym for 'total restitution' or that both parties have to be put into their *status quo ante contractum*.[114] This last sense is to be preferred because it describes the unwinding of a mutual contract in its totality: A asks for *restitutio in integrum* and in order to be successful has to offer *restitutio in integrum*.

Restitutio in integrum means that someone is put back into his *status quo ante*. Is it ever possible that both parties are put back into their *status quo ante*? If *restitutio in integrum* or *status quo ante* is understood too literally, then this will rarely be so.

First, if one party has incurred any expenditure in reliance on the contract, one of the two parties will have to bear this loss. This party will be worse off than he was before the contract so not returned exactly to his *status quo*. But *restitutio in integrum* has always disregarded reliance expenditure. *Restitutio in integrum* only means that both parties have to give back benefits received under the contract.

Secondly, if one party has lost what he received, exact *restitutio in integrum* will be impossible. But the preferable view is that *restitutio in integrum* need not be exact. In the example used in this chapter it is sufficient that A makes good the value of the horse if he wants to claim back the cow. Literally, neither A nor B is put back into his *status quo ante*. B only gets the value of the horse and not the horse in specie. A is financially worse off.

Thirdly, if the contract is terminated or frustrated, it will stay in force for some purposes; to that extent the parties are not put back into their *status quo ante contractum*. This must be disregarded as well.

All that *restitutio in integrum* means is that both parties have to give back what they received under the contract either in specie or in value.

VI. *Restitutio in integrum* v. the defence of change of position

Having now determined how a mutual contract is unwound, I can properly discuss the question how the defence of change of position can be applied in this context. There are two questions: (i) is *restitutio in integrum* merely an application of the defence of change of position? (ii) are the two distinct?

---

[112] See the Scottish cases on minority and, e.g., *Burnes v. Pennell* (1849) 2 HLC 497 at 515 per Lord Campbell.

[113] See, e.g., *Houldsworth v. City of Glasgow Bank* (1879) 6 R 1164 at 1173 per Lord Deas.

[114] See, e.g., *Stuarts v. Whiteford and the Duke of Hamilton* (1677) Mor 16489 at 16493; *Boyd & Forrest v. Glasgow and South Western Railway Co.* 1914 SC 472 at 496 per Lord Dundas; *Graham v. Western Bank of Scotland* (1864) 2 M 559 at 564 per Lord Ordinary Kinloch.

Can they be applied in the same case, or is the defence only applicable where *restitutio in integrum* does not apply?

I have already observed that there are two possible applications of the defence in the example. First, B could rely on the defence of change of position. He could say to A: 'In reliance on the contract I have given you my horse. I have thereby changed my position. Give it back, before you get your cow back.' On the other hand, A could rely on the defence. He could argue: 'I have received your horse, but now it has ceased to exist. I have therefore changed my position.' It would be nonsensical to allow both parties to rely on the defence in this way. In each case only the fate of the horse is in question. If A and B are both allowed to rely on the defence, no policy decision has been taken as to who should bear the loss. If A is the plaintiff, the loss would be on him, because the defence is open to B. If B is the plaintiff, the loss would be on him, because the defence is open to A.[115] There would also be a cumulative risk on the plaintiff.[116] If A can claim that the contract should be unwound, the loss of the cow will be on him, because B can rely on the defence of change of position; equally the loss of the horse will be on him, because B can rely on the defence of change of position.

1. Should B be able to rely on the defence?

B has given the horse to A. That could count as a change of position. The question is whether *restitutio in integrum* is nothing but this defence of change of position. For a number of reasons the answer has to be a clear 'No':

  (a) It is thought that the defence of position only applies to parties who change their position in the honest belief of their entitlement to the enrichment. Thus, if B were fraudulent, he would not be able to rely on the defence. But the case law is very clear that *restitutio in integrum* works in favour even of a party who is fraudulent.[117]

  (b) The problem of anticipatory reliance comes into play: B might have given his horse before he received the cow from A. B therefore relied not

---

[115] Bremecker, *Die Bereicherungsbeschränkung*, 69–70; Oertmann, 'Bereicherungsansprüche', 1065; Oertmann, 'Noch einmal', 335; Pawlowski, *Rechtsgeschäftliche Folgen*, 41–2; Schneider, 'Zur Bestimmung', 179–80.

[116] Bremecker, *Die Bereicherungsbeschränkung*, 66–7; Deplewski, *Die Risikoverteilung*, 13, 23; Kohler, *Die gestörte Rückabwicklung*, 168–9; Leser, *Saldotheorie*, 14–15.

[117] Peter Birks, 'Change of Position and Surviving Enrichment', in: William Swadling (ed.), *The Limits to Restitutionary Claims: A Comparative Analysis* (1997), 36, 55 ff.; Peter Birks, 'Change of Position: The Nature of the Defence and its Relationship to other Restitutionary Defences', in: McInnes (ed.), *Structure and Challenges*, 49, 66; McKendrick, 'Total Failure', 239.

on his enrichment but on the expectation of A's performance. The case law indicates that anticipatory reliance might not be sufficient for a successful defence of change of position.[118] However, for the application of *restitutio in integrum* it is totally irrelevant who performed first.[119]

(c) In addition, the following arguments have been put forward in German legal literature. Take the following modification of the example: B has given the horse to A, but A has not yet transferred the cow to B. The defence of change of position fails in this situation because B never received an enrichment from which he could deduct his own performance. However, the principle of *restitutio in integrum* is capable of dealing with this case. A has to render *restitutio in integrum* if he wants to rescind the contract, not just if he wants to claim his cow back.

(d) Finally, A does not have to offer *restitutio in integrum* to B if the horse ceases to exist due to B's fault. This exception cannot be explained on the basis of the defence of change of position.

2. Should A be able to rely on the defence?

Should A be able to rely on the defence in a claim by B? He has lost the horse. Again, the answer needs to be 'No'.

(a) With *restitutio in integrum* the parties either have to restore what they received in specie or they have to make up its value regardless of whether they are still enriched. Hence, with *restitutio in integrum* it is of no concern whether A changed his position or not.

(b) Suppose that the contract in our example is void. The contract is fully performed. The loss of the horse is on A. He can only claim back the cow if he makes good the value of the horse. However, if only B has performed the contract, then the loss of the horse would be on B, if A were able to rely on the defence of change of position. Yet whether the contract has been fully performed or not should not influence the allocation of risk. It is most consistent with *restitutio in integrum* that in this case, too, A should make good the value.

VII. Summary

1. In the unwinding of mutual contracts, our particular concern was with the question of what effect it should have on A's claim against B that A is himself unable to give back what he received under the contract. In English, German and Scots law the answer to this question depends on a number of factors: (i) the unwinding factor; (ii) categorisation of the unwinding factor; (iii) the method for unwinding

---

[118] *South Tyneside Metropolitan Borough Council v. Svenska International plc* [1995] 1 All ER 545.
[119] Burrows, *Law of Restitution*, 429.

the contract *in toto*; (iv) whether the contract as agreement, the proprietary consequences of the contract, or the factual consequences of the contract need to be unwound; and (v) the nature of the performance. It was argued that none of these factors should influence the answer to the problem. A unified approach needs to be found.
2. For English and Scots law, the most appropriate candidate for such an approach is *restitutio in integrum*.
3. *Restitutio in integrum* means that the party who seeks to unwind the contract needs to give back what he received under it. Offering *restitutio in integrum* is a requirement for each step of unwinding the contract. If one party at his choice can unwind the contract as agreement (as is the case with rescission), then *restitutio in integrum* is a requirement for rescission. If the contract is (for example) *ipso iure* void, then *restitutio in integrum* is a requirement for the claim to have the proprietary and factual consequences of the contract unwound. If the contract and the transfer of property are void, then *restitutio in integrum* is a requirement for claiming that the factual consequences of the contract should be unwound.
4. With *restitutio in integrum* the parties have to give back what they received in specie or by making good its value. Only in very exceptional cases will attention be paid to the fact that one party has lost what he received and that that party is no longer enriched. Only two such exceptions exist: where requiring a party to offer *restitutio in integrum* would subvert the policy underlying the unwinding factor; or where loss of what was received is attributable to the other party. The most prominent example of this second exception is where the object received ceased to exist owing to an inherent defect.
5. The defence of change of position and *restitutio in integrum* are two distinct legal institutes. Furthermore, the one is not compatible with the other. In the example used here, with *restitutio in integrum* the rule is that A has to give back the horse or its value regardless of whether or not he is still enriched. The risk is usually on A. With the defence of change of position one would have to start from the other end. It would be the rule that A had only to give back his surviving enrichment. The risk of the horse would be on B. Thus, *restitutio in integrum* and the defence of change of position exclude each other. *Restitutio in integrum* governs the unwinding of mutual contracts. Hence, the defence of change of position should not be applicable to unwinding mutual contracts. If it were allowed, there would be a risk of subverting the results achieved by *restitutio in integrum*. Furthermore,

the defence of change of position is limited to the law of unjustified enrichment. But not every step of unwinding a mutual contract is governed by the law of unjustified enrichment. In German law, unwinding a contract following a breach of contract is regulated by the law of contract. This would mean that in the process of unwinding a mutual contract the defence might sometimes be applicable and sometimes not. That would contradict the thesis of this chapter, that the process of unwinding mutual contracts should be governed by only one set of rules. It is therefore preferable to exclude the defence of change of position altogether.

PART VI

Illegality

10 The role of illegality in the English law of unjust enrichment

W. J. Swadling

I. Introduction

When English unjust enrichment lawyers talk of 'illegality', they generally do so in the context of the unravelling of partly performed illegal contracts. Two parties enter into an illegal contract. What generally happens is that one pays for a service to be performed but fails to receive the agreed exchange. Can that party recover the value he has transferred to the non-performing recipient? The law in this area is complex and difficult to state with any accuracy.

There are a number of reasons why the judges do not find it easy to come to an agreed answer to this problem. The consequence of a finding of illegality in English law is that the contract is null and void. No action may be brought for compensation for non-performance, nor will an order for specific performance be available. With such a harsh attitude taken to contractual performance, the pressure falls entirely on the law of unjust enrichment to sort out the mess. And the difficulties are only exacerbated by the fact that English law adopts an extremely wide view as to what amounts to an illegal contract.[1] Not only does it include contracts to commit crimes, as, for example, a contract to kill or to injure another person, but also contracts of which performance, though not illegal in any criminal sense, will not be enforced for various reasons of public policy. Examples are marriage brokerage contracts, contracts to commit civil wrongs, contracts to indemnify another against liability for unlawful acts, contracts in restraint of marriage, contracts promoting sexual immorality, contracts of insurance where there is no insurable risk, contracts purporting to oust the jurisdiction of the courts, trading with the enemy, and contracts

---

[1] For a general account of illegality in the context of contractual undertakings, see G. Treitel, *The Law of Contract* (10th edn, 1999), 392–452.

restricting personal liberty. The merits of the plaintiff who pays a hit-man to murder a business rival are clearly different from one who pays a premium on an insurance policy in which he has no insurable interest.

A further difficulty is caused by the fact that in many cases the role contractual illegality is playing is ambiguous. Though in some it clearly provides a defence to what would be an otherwise valid claim for restitution of unjust enrichment, in others the illegality, at least at first sight, appears to provide a ground of claim in itself. In other words, the illegality gives rise to a liability to make restitution of an unjust enrichment which, in the absence of the illegality, would not be present. Unfortunately, this distinction – between illegality as a defence to a claim for restitution of unjust enrichment and illegality as a cause of action in unjust enrichment – is not always cleanly drawn, either in the case law[2] or the academic literature. The cases on illegality as defence and illegality as cause of action tend simply to be run together, making an already difficult subject almost impossible to comprehend. This essay, adopting the scheme first suggested by Peter Birks,[3] proceeds on the basis that the role of illegality in unjust enrichment claims cannot be understood unless a separation is first made between cause of action and defence. The test that will be adopted here to decide on which side of the line any particular case falls is as follows. If the illegality is put aside, will the plaintiff still have a good cause of action? If the answer to that question is yes, then the illegality is operating as a defence. But where, conversely, the removal of the illegality would cause the claim to fail, the illegality goes to the existence of a cause of action, and is not operating as a defence.

But there is yet another difficulty of a similar nature. Little attempt is made by the majority of writers, both judicial and academic, to distinguish between claims based on the unjust enrichment of the defendant and those in which plaintiffs are seeking to enforce rights not generated by the unjust enrichment of the defendant – more particularly, property rights not generated by the unjust enrichment of the defendant.[4] Claims

---

[2] The worst offender in this regard is probably the decision of the Privy Council in *Kiriri Cotton Co. v. Dewani* [1960] AC 192, discussed below (at 302).

[3] P. Birks, *An Introduction to the Law of Restitution* (revised edn, 1989), 299-303, 424-32.

[4] This is not to deny the possibility, at least in English law, of property rights being generated by the defendant's unjust enrichment, as witness the decision of Goulding J in *Chase Manhattan Bank NA Ltd v. Israel-British Bank (London) Ltd* [1981] Ch 105 (recipient of a mistaken payment said to hold it on constructive trust for the payee). On the question whether it is correct for the courts to create property rights as a response to unjust enrichment, see W. J. Swadling, 'Property and Unjust Enrichment', in: J. W. Harris (ed.), *Property Problems: From Genes to Pension Funds* (1997).

for the enforcement of property rights generated by the defendant's unjust enrichment and claims for the enforcement of property rights not generated by unjust enrichment are clearly two different things,[5] for they are rights generated by different causative events, and to which different defences may or may not be available. As will be shown below, it was precisely this failure to distinguish between the two species of rights in *Bigos v. Bousted*[6] that led the court into error.

The aims of this essay are relatively modest. What it does not purport to do is to provide an answer to the difficult question, 'when will illegality bar an otherwise valid claim for restitution of unjust enrichment?'.[7] What it instead seeks to do is much more basic. First, it will demonstrate the need to keep distinct the operation of the defence of illegality where the claim is one to the enforcement of property rights not generated by unjust enrichment from one where the claim is to the restitution of unjust enrichment. Secondly, it will ask whether, in the law of restitution of unjust enrichment, illegality really does have the bivalent role ascribed to it above, namely that it operates both as a defence and as a cause of action ('unjust factor'). It will be seen that, though well established as a defence to claims for restitution of unjust enrichment, the authority for saying that illegality also operates as a cause of action is weak. The so-called 'repentance' cases apart, the decisions in which illegality looks to be operating as an unjust factor can all be explained on alternative grounds. And what is more, even the repentance cases themselves provide no authority for claims in unjust enrichment, for they are in the main concerned with claims in respect of property rights not generated by unjust enrichment, and, moreover, are cases in which the illegality of the transaction is operating, albeit unsuccessfully, as a defence, not a cause of action. The conclusion which will be drawn is that in English law illegality operates only as a defence to claims for restitution of unjust enrichment and never as a cause of action.

II. Illegality as defence

The defence of illegality is not unique to claims for restitution of unjust enrichment. We have already seen that it will bar claims in respect

---

[5] Though this is something which the word 'restitution' tends to disguise: see P. Birks, 'Misnomer', in: W. R. Cornish *et al.* (eds.), *Restitution: Past, Present and Future* (Oxford, 1998).
[6] [1951] 1 All ER 92.
[7] Those seeking an answer to this question should consult P. Birks, 'Recovering Value Transferred Under an Illegal Contract', (2000) 1 *Theoretical Inquiries in Law* 155.

of compensatory damages for the non-performance of contractual promises. It can also bar claims for compensatory damages for torts[8] and, more controversially, for the enforcement of property rights not generated by unjust enrichment. Since cases in the latter category are often run together with claims for restitution of unjust enrichment, it is to those that we must first turn.

1. Illegality as a defence to claims for the enforcement of property rights not generated by unjust enrichment

This is a complex issue. In order to make any sense of the law in this area it is necessary to examine separately the position at law from that obtaining in equity.

(a) Common-law property rights

So far as the common law is concerned, illegality does not operate as a defence to claims for the enforcement of property rights not generated by the defendant's unjust enrichment. The reason seems to be that, unlike claims for the enforcement of purely executory contractual rights, the owner does not seek to extract his rights from any illegal act, but rather from rights which were in existence before the illegal act occurred. In asserting such rights, therefore, the holder has no need to rely on any unlawful conduct on his part. An example is *Bowmakers Ltd v. Barnet Instruments Ltd.*[9] Machine tools were delivered pursuant to an unlawful hire-purchase agreement. Not all the instalments under the agreement were paid by the purchaser and the seller brought conversion when his demand for the return of the tools was not met. The purchaser defended the claim by pointing to the illegality of the hire-purchase agreement. The Court of Appeal held that this was no defence. Du Parcq LJ, delivering the judgment of the Court, said:

a man's right to possess his own chattels will as a general rule be enforced against one who, without any claim of right, is detaining them, or has converted them to his own use, even though it may appear either from the pleadings, or in

---

[8] In *National Coal Board v. England* [1954] AC 403 at 429, Lord Asquith said: 'If two burglars, A and B, agree to open a safe by means of explosives, and A so negligently handles the explosive charge as to injure B, B might find some difficulty in maintaining an action for negligence against A.' For a general account of the defence of illegality in tort, see W. V. H. Rogers, *Winfield & Jolowicz on Tort* (15th edn, 1998), 866–71.

[9] [1945] KB 65.

the course of the trial, that the chattels in question came into the defendant's possession by reason of an illegal contract between himself and the plaintiff, provided that the plaintiff does not seek, and is not forced, either to found his claim on the illegal contract or to plead its illegality in order to support his claim.[10]

The same result was reached in *Singh v. Ali*.[11] The plaintiff haulier wanted to acquire a lorry but knew that, because he did not satisfy certain government conditions, he would not be granted a haulier's permit by the relevant authorities. He therefore entered into an agreement with the defendant haulier, who did satisfy those conditions, under which the defendant would buy the lorry, register it in his own name and sell it on to the plaintiff, all the while concealing the second sale from the authorities by keeping the registration unchanged. The defendant did acquire such a lorry, registered it in his own name, and sold and delivered it to the plaintiff. The parties later fell out, and the defendant seized the lorry from the plaintiff, who thereupon sued him in detinue. The defendant set up the illegality of the second sale as a defence. The trial judge, Smith J, held that the defence succeeded, that there was a 'moral estoppel' generated by the illegal design which prevented the plaintiff from recovering. The Judicial Committee of the Privy Council disagreed. Although the transaction between the plaintiff and the defendant was illegal, property in the lorry passed through the act of delivery. The plaintiff could assert his title to the lorry against all the world, not because he had any merit of his own, but because there was no one who could assert a better one. As Lord Denning explained:

The court does not confiscate the property because of the illegality – it has no power to do so ... The parties to the fraud are, of course, liable to be punished for the part they played in the illegal transaction, but nevertheless the property passes to the transferee.[12]

That must be right. As Lord Denning makes clear, it is not for the civil court to punish the plaintiff for his illegal conduct. In any case, the 'punishment' that would be meted out might bear no relation to the seriousness of the conduct involved. As *Singh v. Ali* demonstrates, a fairly minor criminal infringement, which might attract a fine of only a few hundred pounds from a criminal court, could well be visited with a confiscation of property worth many thousands of pounds were the court to allow

---

[10] *Ibid.* at 71. [11] [1960] AC 167. [12] *Ibid.* at 177.

illegality to operate as a defence to the enforcement of property rights not generated by unjust enrichment.

(b) Equitable property rights

The position here is more complex. Until recently, the exact opposite to that which obtained at common law prevailed. Applying the maxim 'he who comes to equity must do so with clean hands', the courts refused relief to a plaintiff who was party to an illegal design where what was claimed was an equitable, as opposed to a legal, property right. An example is provided by *Chettiar v. Chettiar*,[13] a decision of the Privy Council on appeal from the Court of Appeal of Malaya of almost the same vintage as *Singh v. Ali*, with Lord Denning once again delivering the opinion of the Board. There, a father owned 139 acres of land. In order to evade administrative regulations as to its use, he transferred forty acres into his son's name, on the express understanding that the son was to hold it for him on trust. The father later contracted to sell the land and asked his son for a power of attorney to do so. The son refused and the father sought a declaration that the son held the land for him on trust, founding his claim not on the express trust[14] but on the resulting trust which is presumed in the case of gratuitous transfers of property rights.[15] The trial judge, who had also decided *Singh v. Ali* at first instance but who had been reversed on appeal, held that the plaintiff's possible turpitude was 'no reason for denying him the orders which he seeks'. The Judicial Committee of the Privy Council, however, disagreed:

> In *Singh v. Ali* the plaintiff founded his claim on his right of property in the lorry and his possession of it. He did not have to found his cause of action on an immoral or illegal act. He was held entitled to recover. In the present case the father has of necessity to put forward, and indeed, assert, his own fraudulent purpose ... He is met therefore by the principle stated long ago by Lord Mansfield 'No court will lend its aid to a man who founds his cause of action upon an

---

[13] [1962] AC 294.
[14] It is unclear why a claim was not made on the basis of the express trust. One probable reason is that there was no written evidence of the declaration, a statutory requirement in English law by virtue of the Law of Property Act 1925, s. 53(1)(b), and its predecessor, the Statute of Frauds 1677, s. 7. If the 1677 statute had not been in force in Malaya at the time the case was decided, it would have only been because it had been replaced by a more modern piece of legislation to the same effect.
[15] 'If a man seised of land make a feoffment thereof and it appeareth not to what use the feoffment was made, nor it is not upon any bargain or other recompence, then it shall be taken to the use of the feoffor, except the contrary can be proved': Christopher St Germain, *Dialogues between a Doctor of Divinity and a Student of the Common Law* (1532), Second Dialogue, Chapter XXI.

immoral or an illegal act', see *Holman v. Johnson* (1775) 1 Cowp 341, 343. Their Lordships are of opinion that the courts should not lend their aid to the father to obtain a re-transfer from the son.[16]

Being entirely at odds with the attitude taken by the common law, and with its tendency to impose a disproportionate punishment on the plaintiff, it is not surprising that the equitable position is subject to a number of exceptions. The first is that relief will be given where the purpose for which the illegal trust was created fails to take effect. So, in *Symes v. Hughes*[17] the plaintiff, who was in financial difficulties, conveyed leasehold property to a widow with whom he was 'on intimate terms' to hold for him on trust, the intention being to keep the leasehold property out of the hands of his creditors should he become bankrupt. Not surprisingly, the conveyance made no mention of the trust, instead falsely declaring that the widow had given valuable consideration for the transfer. Although he did become bankrupt three years later, the widow had in the meantime conveyed the lease to her son-in-law. After her death, the plaintiff sought a reconveyance from the son-in-law, alleging that the latter took the lease with notice of the former's equitable interest. Lord Romilly MR held that the plaintiff's claim was not defeated by the illegality. He said that where the purpose for which the assignment was given was not carried into execution, and nothing was done under it, the mere intention to effect an illegal object when the assignment was executed did not deprive the assignor of his right to recover the property from the assignee.[18]

A further inroad into the confiscatory attitude of equity was made much more recently by a majority of the House of Lords in *Tinsley v. Milligan*,[19] where the clean hands rule was held to be confined to the situation in which the plaintiff somehow had to plead his own illegality as part of the evidential basis of his case. If he could plead his case without mentioning the illegality, then even though that illegality might later be disclosed during the trial of the action, the plaintiff would still be given equitable relief.

In *Tinsley v. Milligan* the plaintiff and the defendant bought a house with joint funds. In order to enable both parties to make fraudulent claims to welfare benefits, the property was conveyed into the name of the plaintiff alone, although the agreement between the parties was that it would

[16] [1962] AC 294 at 303.
[17] (1870) LR 9 Eq 475.   [18] *Ibid.* at 479.
[19] [1994] 1 AC 340. The minority, Lords Goff of Chieveley and Keith of Kinkel, adhered to the old position that once the court was apprised of the illegality it should automatically refuse relief.

be held by her on trust for the two of them. Fraudulent claims were in fact made by both parties, but, having now made her peace with the authorities, and having fallen out with the plaintiff, the defendant sought a declaration that the plaintiff held the property on trust for them both. As in *Chettiar v. Chettiar*, she relied not upon the express trust but on the presumed trust that arose through the device of a purchase money resulting trust.[20]

A majority of the House of Lords allowed the plaintiff's claim. Lord Browne-Wilkinson said that she won her case simply because it was not necessary on the pleadings for her to rely in any way on the illegality. He said that the common-law principle enunciated in *Bowmakers Ltd v. Barnet Industries Ltd*[21] should apply with equal force to claims in equity:

> English law has one single law of property made up of legal and equitable interests. Although for historical reasons legal estates and equitable estates have differing incidents, the person owning either type of estate has a right of property, a right *in rem* not merely a right *in personam*. If the law is that a party is entitled to enforce a property right acquired under an illegal transaction, in my judgment the same rule ought to apply to any property right so acquired, whether such right is legal or equitable.[22]

His Lordship said that the mere fact of her contribution to the purchase price of the house was enough to give the plaintiff an interest under a resulting trust and her motive for leaving her name off the title could not affect that result.

But the differences between common law and equity have not been completely eradicated, as the subsequent case of *Tribe v. Tribe*[23] shows. There recovery was allowed, but only under the *Symes v. Hughes* principle.[24] Had the illegal purpose been achieved, the plaintiff's interest would have been forfeit, something which, as *Singh v. Ali*[25] demonstrates, could not have happened at common law. In *Tribe v. Tribe* a father owned 459 out of 500 shares in a family-run clothing company. The father also held a lease of two shops, which the company occupied as licensee. The shops were in a state of disrepair and, worried about his liability under the repairing covenants and that he might, in order to meet those liabilities, be forced

---

[20] '... the trust of a legal estate, whether freehold, copyhold, or leasehold; whether taken in the names of the purchasers and other jointly, or in the names of others without that of the purchaser; whether in the one name or several; whether jointly or successive – results to the man who advances the purchase-money': *per* Eyre CB in *Dyer v. Dyer* (1788) 2 Cox Eq 92 at 93.
[21] [1945] KB 65. See discussion at 292–3, above.   [22] [1994] 1 AC 340 at 371.
[23] [1996] Ch 107.   [24] (1870) LR 9 Eq 475.   [25] [1960] AC 167.

to dispose of his shares in the family company, the father transferred the shares to his son to hold for him on trust, the purpose of the trust being to keep the shares out of the hands of the father's creditors. But the crisis passed, the matter being settled with the landlords by a surrender of the lease in the one case and a purchase of the reversion in the other. At no stage did the fact that the shares were in the hands of the son affect the outcome of the settlements. The father later sought the return of the shares from his son, not on the basis of the express trust,[26] but by arguing that the gratuitous nature of the conveyance gave rise to a resulting trust in his favour. Not surprisingly, the son in turn argued that a presumption of advancement (gift) operated in his favour,[27] which could only be rebutted by the father leading evidence of his illegal purpose, which *Tinsley v. Milligan*[28] prevented him from doing.

The Court of Appeal found for the father. *Tinsley v. Milligan* was a liberalising decision, and was certainly not to be seen as abolishing the *Symes v. Hughes* exception, with the result that because the father had not in fact defrauded his creditors he would be allowed to lead evidence of the illegal purpose in order to rebut successfully the presumption of advancement in favour of his son. Any other result, said the court, would have been nonsensical. As Nourse LJ remarked:

If Miss Milligan was able to recover against Miss Tinsley even though she had succeeded in defrauding the Department of Social Security over a period of years, it would indeed be a cause for concern if a plaintiff who had not defrauded his creditors in any way was prevented from recovering simply because the defendant was his son.[29]

It will thus be apparent that there are a number of difficulties with the operation of the illegality defence where a claim is made to the enforcement of equitable property rights not generated by the unjust enrichment of the defendant. If, as Lord Denning pointed out in *Singh v. Ali*,[30] a common-law court has no power to confiscate such property rights because of illegality, the question which then arises is why the position in equity should be any different. For as *Chettiar v. Chettiar* illustrates, the

---

[26] Although there are no formality requirements attaching to a declaration of trust of personalty, this tactic probably explained by the fact that the writ was issued before the decision of the House of Lords in *Tinsley v. Milligan* [1994] 1 AC 340 had been handed down.

[27] '...the circumstance of one or more of the nominees being a child or children of the purchaser, is to operate by rebutting the resulting trust': *per* Eyre CB in *Dyer v. Dyer* (1788) 2 Cox Eq 92 at 93.

[28] [1994] 1 AC 340.   [29] [1996] Ch 107 at 122.   [30] [1960] AC 167 at 177.

potential for confiscation still exists, the reasoning in that case being left untouched by *Tinsley v. Milligan*. Secondly, the operation of the illegality defence in equity is arbitrary. Recovery depends upon who is forced to play the illegality card. As Millett LJ pointed out in *Tribe v. Tribe*, the rule that the plaintiff wins so long as he does not have to rely on his own illegality:

> ... is procedural in nature and depends on the adventitious location of the burden of proof in any given case. Had Mr Tribe transferred the shares to a stranger or distant relative whom he trusted, albeit for the same dishonest purpose, it cannot be doubted that he would have succeeded in his claim.[31]

As it was, Mr Tribe only succeeded because he was able to bring himself within the *Symes v. Hughes* exception. Had his illegal design succeeded, his interest would have been forfeited to his son.

2. Illegality as a defence to claims for restitution of unjust enrichment

The illegality of a contract will sometimes operate not only to prevent enforcement of that contract, but also to disqualify the plaintiff's right to restitution of benefits transferred pursuant to it, in what would otherwise be a valid claim based on more familiar unjust factors such as mistake or failure of consideration. The operation of the defence is governed by two overlapping maxims, *ex turpi causa non oritur actio* (no disgraceful matter can ground an action) and *in pari delicto potior est conditio defendentis* (where the guilt is shared the position of the defendant is the stronger). As noted above, the exact limits of the defence are the subject of much conjecture and this essay will not be entering into that debate. All that need be done is to note that illegality undoubtedly does sometimes have the effect of barring what would otherwise be valid claims for the restitution of unjust enrichments.

An example of a claim in respect of a mistaken payment barred by illegality is provided by *Parkinson v. College of Ambulance*,[32] where the secretary of a charity fraudulently misrepresented to the plaintiff that either he or the charity was in a position to undertake that the plaintiff could be got a knighthood in return for a large donation to the charity. The plaintiff made the donation but did not receive the promised knighthood. He sued to recover the money which he had paid on the ground that the payment had been induced by fraud (a species of mistake). Lush J refused

---

[31] [1996] Ch 107 at 134.   [32] [1925] 2 KB 1.

the claim. Although it was true that the plaintiff had been defrauded, he knew that the contract into which he was entering was illegal and one which he ought not to have made. He could not therefore claim that he was not *in pari delicto* with the defendant. He had only himself to blame for his loss. Applying the test set out above,[33] the illegality is here clearly operating as a defence since, if the illegality is put aside, the plaintiff would undoubtedly have had a good cause of action based on his mistaken transfer.

The same is true of cases involving a failure of consideration, an example being *Berg v. Sadler & Moore*.[34] The plaintiff tobacconist had been put on a stop-list by the Tobacco Trade Association. He tried to get supplies by putting up another person to buy them with his money, an action that amounted to a criminal offence. After the money had been paid over but before the goods were delivered, the defendant wholesalers realised what was happening. They declined either to deliver the goods or to return the money. The Court of Appeal refused the tobacconist restitution of the moneys he had paid. Since, in the absence of the illegality, the plaintiff would have had a claim for restitution of unjust enrichment based on a total failure of consideration, the illegal nature of the design is clearly operating as a defence here, too.

But the mere fact that the contract is illegal will not always operate as a bar. An exception is implicit in the wording of one of the maxims used in this area. If the rule is *in pari delicto potior est conditio defendentis*, then, in cases where the plaintiff does not share the defendant's guilt, recovery ought to be allowed. So, for example, in *Hughes v. Liverpool Victoria Legal Friendly Society*,[35] the plaintiff was induced by a fraudulent misrepresentation to pay premiums on policies on lives in which she had no insurable interest. The contract of insurance, since it did not relate to an insurable interest, was an illegal one.[36] The plaintiff sought recovery of the premiums which she had paid but was met with the defence of *in pari delicto*. She succeeded none the less. The Court of Appeal held that, as the victim of a fraud, she was innocent and so entitled to say that she was not *in pari delicto* with the defendant who by a false representation had induced her to believe that the transaction was an innocent one and one that was enforceable in law. Once again, therefore, illegality is operating as a defence, though this time it is found to have no application to the facts of the case in hand.

---

[33] Above, 290.   [34] [1937] 2 KB 158.   [35] [1916] 2 KB 483.
[36] Life Assurance Act 1774, s. 1.

III. Illegality as cause of action

Unjust enrichment apart, nowhere in any other branch of English private law does illegality per se provide a plaintiff with a cause of action he would not otherwise have. Although illegality operates in contract and tort to bar what would otherwise be valid claims, it never creates a cause of action in itself. Nor does illegality ever give rise to property rights, at least not property rights not created as a response to unjust enrichments. But, it is said, this is not the case in claims for the restitution of unjust enrichment. Lord Goff of Chieveley and Gareth Jones, for example, while acknowledging that it in general it operates as a defence, assert that 'there are situations where a plaintiff is able to rely on illegality itself as the ground to support his restitutionary claim'.[37] This is also the view of Andrew Burrows, who devotes separate chapters to 'Illegality as a ground of restitution' and 'Defences', one of which is illegality.[38] The question which will now be addressed, and the point which is the main focus of this essay, is whether this is right. Does illegality, or, more accurately, 'transfer of benefits pursuant to an illegal contract', ever constitute a ground of restitutionary claim?

What should be immediately obvious is that the ground as formulated does not allege any vitiation or qualification of the plaintiff's consent to the transfer. If it comes anywhere, therefore, it has to come under some head of policy-motivated restitution. But before addressing the question whether it does fall under that heading, we must first clear away two potential distractions. The first is that there are some cases that are claimed as examples of restitution for illegality but which can be explained on more orthodox grounds, as cases in which the unjust factor is the vitiation of the plaintiff's consent to the transfer. The second is that an illegal contract is a void contract, and there is an argument which says that a void contract is itself a ground of claim.

1. Illegality within vitiated consent

There are some cases that are claimed as examples of illegality operating as a cause of action but which, on closer examination, are better explained as examples of restitution for vitiated consent. Some are clearer than others.

---

[37] *The Law of Restitution* (5th edn, 1998), 607.
[38] A. S. Burrows, *The Law of Restitution* (1993), chaps. 11 and 15.

A clear case is *Smith v. Bromley*,[39] where the ground of claim was duress. The plaintiff's brother was bankrupt. The defendant, his chief creditor, had taken out a commission against him, but afterwards, finding no dividend likely to be paid, refused to sign his certificate unless he was paid £40 and given a credit note for a further £20. The plaintiff paid the money and the defendant signed the certificate. When the plaintiff sought to recover the money, the defendant argued that the consideration for the payment was illegal and that the plaintiff was party to that illegality. Lord Mansfield nevertheless allowed recovery. The case was, he said, analogous to *Astley v. Reynolds*[40] (a case of duress of goods), and, the plaintiff not being *in pari delicto*, the illegality presented no bar to her claim.[41] The fact pattern of this case is, therefore, exactly the same as that in *Hughes v. Liverpool Victoria Legal Friendly Society*.[42] Illegality is being raised as a defence, though a defence which fails on the particular facts of the case because the parties are not *in pari delicto*. In no way is the illegality of the transaction operating as a cause of action.

Next, there is a group of cases in which the ground of claim can also be explained as non-voluntary transfer, though this is admittedly more controversial. I will call these cases the 'protected class' cases.[43] In *Kiriri Cotton Co. v. Dewani*,[44] a landlord charged a premium for the grant to a tenant of a seven-year lease. By virtue of section 3(2) of the Uganda Rent Restriction Ordinance, a landlord committed an offence in demanding or receiving such a premium. But the ordinance was poorly drafted, and both parties honestly and reasonably believed that the provision did not apply to their transaction. The tenant went into possession, but, upon discovering that the restriction did in fact apply to his lease, sought the return of the premium. In his defence, the landlord argued that the tenant's claim was barred because he was guilty of aiding and abetting a criminal offence. He also denied the existence of any ground of claim, the mistake on the

---

[39] (1760) 2 Doug 696; Goff and Jones, *Law of Restitution*, 613 would appear to claim this as an example of illegality as a cause of action, though it must be admitted that their treatment of it is ambiguous.
[40] (1731) 2 Str 915.
[41] The case has parallels in the Roman law, where the *condictio ob turpem vel iniustam causam* would have been available to such a litigant.
[42] [1916] 2 KB 483, discussed above (at 299).
[43] Although the plaintiff in *Smith v. Bromley* was in a protected class, this fact went to the inapplicability of the defence (because she was not *in pari delicto*) rather than to the cause of action itself, which in this case was duress.
[44] [1960] AC 192.

part of the tenant being a mistake of law.[45] The Privy Council nevertheless allowed recovery. Lord Denning, who gave the opinion of the Board, said that the issue was whether the plaintiff was *in pari delicto* with the defendant. He said that he was not, because '[t]he duty of observing the law is firmly placed by the Ordinance on the shoulders of the landlord for the protection of the tenant; and if the law is broken, the landlord must take the primary responsibility'. From that it followed that the plaintiff won. 'Seeing, then, that the parties are not *in pari delicto*, the tenant is entitled to recover the premium by the common law.'[46]

It is not immediately obvious why a finding that the parties were not *in pari delicto* should lead to the conclusion that the tenant could recover his premium. As seen above with the case of *Smith v. Bromley*,[47] a finding that a plaintiff is not *in pari delicto* gives a reason why illegality should not bar an otherwise valid claim; but it gives no positive reason why a claim which is bad from the start should be allowed. Indeed, *Kiriri Cotton Co. v. Dewani* is a prime example of the phenomenon referred to above,[48] of a court failing to distinguish between illegality as defence and illegality as cause of action. But if one looks closely, there is in fact a ground of restitution contained in the decision which is independent of the illegality. A better explanation of the case is that, like *Smith v. Bromley*, this too was a case of non-voluntary transfer. Housing was in short supply in Uganda, with the result that landlords had the upper hand and tenants were vulnerable to exploitation. And while the market is normally left to mediate in such situations, statute had recognised the transactional inequality by forbidding this particular type of bargain. The law having decreed that the tenant was not capable of bargaining as an equal, restitution followed because of his lack of free will to the bargain. An alternative explanation, again within non-voluntary transfer, is mistake. Though the mistake was one of law, the fact that the statute was passed for the protection of the tenant against the landlord meant that the usual restrictions on recovery for mistake of law were removed.

But, since there was no evidence of a mistake, mistake of law cannot explain the case of *Hermann v. Charlesworth*.[49] Nor can failure of consideration do so, even if the requirement that the failure be 'total' is removed.[50]

---

[45] It was not until 1998 that English law allowed recovery for mistake of law: *Kleinwort Benson Ltd v. Lincoln City Council* [1999] 2 AC 349.
[46] [1960] AC 192 at 205.   [47] (1760) 2 Doug 696.   [48] At 290.   [49] [1905] 2 KB 123.
[50] As Lord Goff of Chieveley recently did in *Goss v. Chilcott* [1996] AC 788, at least in cases in which no computational difficulties were involved in valuing the benefits received by the plaintiff.

In this case a woman who had entered into a marriage brokerage contract with the defendant was able to recover the fee she had paid, despite the fact that the defendant had partly performed the agreement. Indeed, the Court of Appeal said that even if there had been full performance, the plaintiff would still have been allowed to recover.[51] This can again be explained as a case of transactional inequality, the rule that such contracts are illegal being for the protection of single women as a vulnerable class.

2. Void contracts

An illegal contract is a void contract.[52] There is an argument which says that 'void contract' is in itself a ground of restitution. That proposition is demonstrably wrong, but this is not the place to chase that hare. The only point to make is that illegal contracts and void contracts are not coterminous. A contract may be void for many reasons other than illegality – for example, for incapacity[53] or for want of formality.[54] So, if restitution follows because of a contract's invalidity, it must be the invalidity and not the illegality which is the trigger.

3. Illegality per se

Having cleared away those potential distractions, we now reach the heart of the inquiry. The first point to note is that it is clear that 'payment under an illegal contract' is not per se a ground of restitution. This can be illustrated by reference to two cases: *Green v. Portsmouth Stadium Ltd* and *Shaw v. Shaw*.

In *Green v. Portsmouth Stadium Ltd*[55] the plaintiff bookmaker paid £2 for entry to a greyhound track. This was almost four times the amount the owner of the track was allowed by statute to charge, the overcharging in fact amounting to a criminal offence on his part. The Court of Appeal held that there was no ground on which the plaintiff could recover his overpayment. Denning LJ said:

there is no allegation that the plaintiff was under any mistake of fact, nor is there any allegation that he was under a mistake of law; nor that he was

---

[51] [1905] 2 KB 123 at 133–4 (Collins MR), 136 (Mathew LJ) and 138 (Cozens-Hardy LJ).
[52] *Mogul Steamship Co. v. McGregor, Gow & Co.* [1892] AC 25 at 39 *per* Lord Halsbury.
[53] As in *Hazell v. Hammersmith and Fulham LBC* [1992] 2 AC 1, where an interest-rate swaps agreement between a local authority and a merchant bank was held to be beyond the powers of the local authority.
[54] As in the case of contracts for the sale of interests in land which are not in signed writing: Law of Property (Miscellaneous Provisions) Act 1989, s. 2.
[55] [1953] 2 QB 190.

oppressed or imposed upon in any way. We must assume on this pleading that the bookmaker knew perfectly well that the only lawful charge was 11s. 3d.; nevertheless he voluntarily chose to pay £2 to the stadium, and he now seeks to recover it back. He does not claim, and cannot claim, for money paid on a consideration that has wholly failed, for he has had the consideration. He has gone on the track and conducted his bookmaking operation there. The only ground on which he claims the money is that there was a breach of the statute in charging him too much.[56]

No orthodox ground of unjust enrichment having been found, the next question was whether the statute made bookmakers a protected class. The Court of Appeal held that it did not. The statute was passed for the regulation of racecourses via the criminal law; it did not create a 'bookmakers charter'. That being the case, the Court held that the breach of the statute did not, standing alone, give rise to a claim for repayment.

In *Shaw v. Shaw*,[57] the plaintiff sought to recover £4,000 paid for a flat in Majorca. The contract of sale was illegal, as the Treasury consent required under the Exchange Control Act 1947 had not been obtained. The defendant's application to have the claim struck out as disclosing no cause of action was granted by the Court of Appeal. Lord Denning MR said:

It has long been settled that no person can found a cause of action upon his own illegal act ... If the plaintiff is to overcome this bar, he must [put] forward some reason why he should not be defeated by his own illegality. To take a simple illustration: supposing the flat in Majorca had not been conveyed to him and that it had not been handed over to him in return for the £4,000, then I can well see that he could make out a claim. He could say that the money had been paid over on a consideration which had wholly failed, but he does not attempt to do that. On this pleading, it may well be that he has got the flat and yet still wants his money back. He bases himself on nothing but the illegal payment. To my mind, it is clearly bad.[58]

The starting point, therefore, is that 'payment under an illegal contract' is not in and of itself a ground of restitution. Indeed, given that it entails no defect or qualification of consent, nor any inherent policy reason why restitution should issue, any other conclusion would be absurd.

But though 'payment under an illegal contract' is not per se a ground of restitution, there are said to be two classes of case in which, were the illegality to be removed, the claim would fail. Thus, the argument goes, the illegality is operating as an ingredient of a cause of action. The

[56] *Ibid.* at 195.   [57] [1965] 1 WLR 537.   [58] *Ibid.* at 539.

two classes of case are the 'protected class' cases and the 'repentance' cases.

The 'protected class' cases were dealt with above, where it was shown that they properly belong under the heading of vitiated consent, for in them there is a deemed transactional inequality. The 'repentance' cases are more difficult to explain. In these there is said to be a policy-motivated head of claim in unjust enrichment concerned with encouraging the renunciation of unlawful contracts. But why should the availability of an unjust enrichment claim be considered as encouraging the renunciation of illegal designs? The reason given is that if money, goods or services have changed hands pursuant to a still executory illegal contract and restitution is not available, the transferor will have no incentive to repent. If he cannot get restitution he will be more likely to go ahead with the unlawful design, for he will have nothing to lose; whereas if he knows that if he repents he can recover his outlay, he will be more likely to do so. Though plausible, this explanation suffers from the obvious difficulty that it somewhat unrealistically assumes a fairly sophisticated knowledge of the law of restitution on the part of participants in illegal designs.[59]

But it is not the rationale of the principle that is in question, but its existence. That there is such a principle is said to stem from a dictum of Mellish LJ in *Taylor v. Bowers*, where he said that: 'If money is paid, or goods delivered for an illegal purpose, the person who has so paid the money or delivered the goods may recover them back before the illegal purpose is carried out.'[60] This 'repentance principle' must, however, be read in context.

In *Taylor v. Bowers* itself, the plaintiff, fearing his own insolvency, handed over the possession of goods to a friend to keep them out of the hands of his creditors. The delivery was dressed up as a sale, with fictitious bills of exchange given by the friend in return. But there was no intention to transfer property in the goods to the friend, who as a result became only a bailee. Two meetings of the plaintiff's creditors were held, but no compromise was effected. The friend later sold the goods to the defendant,

---

[59] Cf. the comment of Millett LJ in *Tribe v. Tribe* [1996] Ch 107 at 133–4, that '[i]t is, of course, artificial to think that anyone would be dissuaded by the primary rule [that no court will lend its aid to a man who founds his cause of action on an illegal act] from entering into a proposed fraud, if only because such a person would be unlikely to be a studious reader of the law reports or to seek advice from a lawyer whom he has taken fully into his confidence'.
[60] (1876) 1 QBD 291 at 300.

who knew of the fraudulent arrangement. The plaintiff brought detinue against the defendant, and, in his defence, the defendant pleaded the illegal nature of the original bailment. The Court of Appeal held that the defence of illegality failed. The fraudulent purpose not having been carried out, the plaintiff was not relying on the illegal transaction, but was entitled to repudiate it, and recover his goods from the friend, and the defendant had no better title than the friend, as he knew how the latter had become possessed of the goods.

The point to note about this case is that all three judges in the Court of Appeal treated the illegality of the bailment as a possible defence, but held it inapplicable on the facts, the reason for the inapplicability being that the illegal purpose had not been carried out. In other words, the case is in the same mould as *Smith v. Bromley* and *Hughes v. Liverpool Victoria Legal Friendly Society*. In no sense was the illegality itself treated as the cause of action. The cause of action was instead one based on the plaintiff's continuing property rights in the goods. Ironically, this comes out most clearly in a passage in Mellish LJ's judgment, where he says:

I think the only question open upon this rule is, assuming that the plaintiff had never really intended to part with his goods to Alcock or to Bowers, whether he was precluded from recovering the goods from Bowers on the ground that he could not do so without proving the illegal transaction to which he was a party.[61]

There is, however, a dictum similar to that of Mellish LJ in the earlier case of *Hastelow v. Jackson*.[62] There, Littledale J said: 'If two parties enter into an illegal contract, and money is paid upon it by one to the other, that may be recovered back before the execution of the contract, but not afterwards.'[63] But, again, this statement has to be read in context. A and B had deposited equal sums with a stakeholder to abide the event of a boxing match between them. The match was played and B was adjudged the winner. A did not accept the result and told the stakeholder not to pay over his stake to B. The stakeholder nevertheless paid it to B, and A sued the stakeholder for money had and received. He won. But the court made it clear that the question was simply one of want of authority. Before paying the money over to B, A's consent to the payment had been withdrawn. As Bayley J said: 'if a stakeholder pays over money without authority

---

[61] *Ibid.* at 298–9.
[62] (1828) 8 B & C 221. Although there are earlier statements to similar effect, all those before this case are obiter: R. Merkin, 'Restitution by Withdrawal from Executory Illegal Contracts', (1981) 97 *LQR* 420, 423.
[63] (1828) 8 B & C 221 at 226.

from the party, and in opposition to his desire, he does so at his own peril'.[64] The case is not, therefore, one in which the plaintiff's repentance of an illegal design is founding a cause of action in unjust enrichment.

But the biggest problem for those who argue that *Taylor v. Bowers* is authority for the proposition that repentance from an illegal design is a cause of action in unjust enrichment is that it is not actually a case involving restitution of unjust enrichment. The court was clear that property in the goods had not passed to the friend. The claim was not therefore made on the basis of rights arising from unjust enrichment but from rights arising in some other way, presumably, in this case, the consensual purchase of the goods by the plaintiff at some time prior to the bailment. Thus, even if the principle which it lays down is correct, *Taylor v. Bowers* provides no authority for repentance as a ground of claim in unjust enrichment.

A case that did involve restitution for unjust enrichment, and in which the claim actually failed, was *Kearley v. Thomson*.[65] The defendants were solicitors to the petitioning creditor in certain bankruptcy proceedings, and had incurred costs, which were to be paid out of the estate. The plaintiff, a friend of the bankrupt, offered to pay the defendants a sum of money for these costs, which had not been paid owing to want of assets, on their undertaking not to appear at the public examination of the bankrupt, and not to oppose his order of discharge. The defendants, with the consent of their client, agreed to this, and received the money. They did not appear at the public examination of the bankrupt, but, before any application for his discharge had been made, the plaintiff brought an action to recover back the money from them.

The Court of Appeal[66] held that the money was not recoverable. Fry LJ, who gave the only reasoned judgment, doubted the validity of the dictum of Mellish LJ in *Taylor v. Bowers*, but anyway distinguished it on the ground that in the instant case the illegal purpose had been partly carried out. Fry LJ thought the better rule was that there should be no recovery, whether the contract was executed or executory. In other words, and keeping an eye on the distinction between illegality as a cause of action and illegality as a defence, he said that even in the case of a total failure of consideration, where the illegal purpose had in no part been carried out, the illegality of the contract should operate as a defence to an otherwise valid claim.

So far, then, the repentance principle, if seen as a principle dictating restitution of unjust enrichment, would seem to have little, if any, support. It forms no part of the decision in *Taylor v. Bowers*, which was

---

[64] *Ibid.* at 225. [65] (1890) 24 QBD 742. [66] Lord Coleridge CJ, Lord Esher MR and Fry LJ.

in any case not a claim for restitution of unjust enrichment, and its correctness was doubted by Fry LJ in *Kearley v. Thomson*. Unfortunately, however, it was applied in *Bigos v. Bousted*.[67] Bousted had deposited a share certificate as security for a loan of money to be made in contravention of exchange controls. The loan was never made and Bousted sought the return of his certificate. He argued that, though the contract was an illegal one, as it was still executory he was allowed a *locus poenitentiae* and was, therefore, entitled to claim the return of the certificate. He failed. Pritchard J held that Bousted could not succeed because he could not bring himself within the repentance principle. The parties were *in pari delicto* at the time of making the agreement, and Bousted was not entitled to seek the aid of the court to recover the certificate. Bousted had not withdrawn from the agreement because of repentance but rather because the illegal contract had been frustrated by the lender's refusal to perform.

Despite the doubts cast upon the validity of Mellish LJ's dictum, it was said by Pritchard J to have been approved by the decision of the Court of Appeal in *Hermann v. Charlesworth*.[68] But, as seen above,[69] *Hermann v. Charlesworth* was not a case explicable on any principle of repentance, for the court would have allowed recovery even had Miss Hermann contracted a valid marriage: the better explanation of the case is that it was a claim in respect of money transferred pursuant to vitiated consent. *Bigos v. Bousted* is clearly different. As a claim to a common-law property right not generated by unjust enrichment, the correct principle to be applied was that contained in *Singh v. Ali*, which would have led to recovery by the plaintiff, however unrepentant he may have been.

IV. Conclusion

While there is no doubt that in English law illegality can operate as a defence to a claim for restitution of unjust enrichment, the argument which has been made is that there is no support in the case law for the proposition that illegality can found a claim in unjust enrichment. Most of the cases normally cited in favour of illegality as a cause of action can be explained as cases of transfers under an impaired consent, including the 'protected class' cases. That leaves only the repentance cases, which turn out on closer examination not to be concerned with claims for restitution of unjust enrichment at all but with actions for the enforcement of the

---

[67] [1951] 1 All ER 92. [68] [1905] 2 KB 123. [69] At 302–3, above.

plaintiff's property rights generated by events other than the defendant's unjust enrichment. As such, they can tell us nothing about the role of illegality within the law of unjust enrichment. When those cases are extracted from the law of unjust enrichment, there remains no authority for saying that illegality operates as a cause of action in the English law of unjust enrichment.

11 Illegality as defence against unjust enrichment claims

Gerhard Dannemann

As a defence, illegality implies that the plaintiff's own illegal or immoral conduct can defeat a claim in unjust enrichment which would otherwise lie. Whether or not illegality can also serve as a ground for restitution is a different question, which is treated elsewhere in this book.[1] The present article will concentrate on situations where both parties are responsible for the illegality, as one-sided illegality will frequently not render a contract void,[2] with the result that no action will lie in the first place because the enrichment was supported by a *causa* (in civil-law terminology) or by consideration (in the language of the common law).

There is, interestingly, no divide between common law and civil law as regards the illegality defence. This has largely to do with the fact that this defence can be traced back to Roman law in all legal systems under consideration.[3]

I am grateful to Jeroen Kortmann, who has helped me much in my attempts to understand the Dutch law of unjust enrichment.

[1] See William Swadling's contribution to this volume.

[2] If only one party has violated a statutory provision, a contract will normally not be void: BGH 1984 *NJW* 230; for an English translation, see Basil Markesinis, Werner Lorenz and Gerhard Dannemann, *The German Law of Obligations*, vol. I, *The Law of Contracts and Restitution* (1997), case 29; see also *ibid.*, 178 ff.; similarly for English law, see *Phoenix General Insurance Co. of Greece SA v. Administratia Asigurarilor de Stat* [1987] 2 All ER 152 at 176 *per* Kerr LJ. Transgressions of legal or moral norms committed by one party will normally make a contract void only where this is necessary to protect the other party or a third party, and will thus call for restitutionary solutions which reinforce this protection. See generally Markesinis, Lorenz and Dannemann, *Law of Contracts*, chap. 3(1).

[3] This is not surprising for Continental Roman-law based systems. In English law, Roman-law influence appears particularly from Lord Mansfield's speech in *Holman v. Johnson* [1775] 1 Cowp 341; 98 ER 1120, which contains the *nemo auditur turpitudinem suam allegans* rule in nearly literal English translation, and where further references are made to *ex dolo malo non oritur actio* and the rule that *potior est conditio defendentis* if both parties are equally to blame.

I. Illegality and other unjust enrichment defences

It could be argued that, next to change of position, illegality is the only other defence which is specific to unjust enrichment claims and which does not depend on how grounds of restitution are structured.[4] In many other cases, one system's ground of restitution, put in the negative, is the other's defence against such a claim. Three examples should suffice:

(i) If one party intentionally enriches another party, mistake will be a ground of restitution in the common law.[5] Most civilian systems will grant restitution if the enrichment is not supported by a legal cause. But lack of mistake concerning such a *causa* will then operate as a defence, as, for example, in § 814 of the German Civil Code (*Bürgerliches Gesetzbuch, BGB*).[6]

(ii) A similar point can be made for the defence of bona fide purchase for value.[7] This common-law defence operates where the plaintiff has enriched a first recipient, who then sells this enrichment to the defendant. The defence of bona fide purchase for value serves to protect the reliance which the defendant has placed in his or her contract with the previous recipient of the enrichment. In German law, the concept of performance, which identifies both plaintiff and defendant to an action, serves to restrict the wide general clause and effectively keeps unjust enrichment claims within failed contractual relationships. Thus, a plaintiff must usually sue the first recipient of the enrichment rather than a party who subsequently acquired the enrichment bona fide.[8] Again, the main exception that German law allows is telling. In a number of

---

[4] Even change of position and illegality can be phrased as elements of a ground for unjust enrichment, namely if surviving enrichment is understood to be the primary object of an unjust enrichment claim, or if illegality is constructed through the *nemo auditur* rule (see below, 315–16). On the other hand, it is still the defendant who has to show that the initial enrichment has not survived, and even the *nemo auditur* rule is applied only to defeat claims which would otherwise lie.

[5] See, generally, Peter Birks, *An Introduction to the Law of Restitution* (paperback edn, 1989), 146 ff.; Andrew Burrows, *The Law of Restitution* (1993), chap. 3; Lord Goff of Chieveley and Gareth Jones, *The Law of Restitution* (5th edn, 1998), chaps. 4–9.

[6] See, generally, Markesinis, Lorenz and Dannemann, *Law of Contracts*, 736 ff.; Gerhard Dannemann, *Unjust Enrichment by Transfer: Some Comparative Remarks* (2001) 79 Texas L Rev 1837–67, at 1850ff.

[7] Birks, *introduction*, 439 ff.; Burrows, *Law of Restitution*, 472 ff.; Goff and Jones, *Law of Restitution*, chap. 41.

[8] BGHZ 40, 272 (= Markesinis, Lorenz and Dannemann, *Law of Contracts*, case 134). However, this applies to performance-based restitution claims only. A plaintiff claiming under restitution for wrongs (or *Eingriffskondiktion*) can sue a defendant who has acquired the enrichment from the interferer bona fide and for value, as long as title has not passed to this defendant. See BGHZ 55, 176 (= Markesinis, Lorenz and Dannemann, *Law of Contracts*, case 133). See generally, Markesinis, Lorenz and Dannemann, *Law of Contracts*, 731 ff.

situations, a plaintiff can jump outside the failed contractual relationship and recover from a third party if this third party has acquired the initial enrichment without providing value in return.[9] The English counterdefence that the bona fide acquisition was not for value thus becomes, in German law, an exceptional ground of restitution against a third party.

(iii) If an enrichment was imposed on the owner against his or her will, this can amount to a defence in German law (*aufgedrängte Bereicherung*).[10] However, if the same cases were to be decided under common-law rules, there would be either no ground of restitution to start with, or no initial enrichment under the rules of subjective valuation.[11] The rationale behind this German defence is served by restrictions on the grounds of restitution in the common law.

Both the civil and common law have some other defences against unjust enrichment claims which, however, are doubtful, of very limited relevance, or not particularly enrichment related; these can be ignored for the purposes of the present article.[12]

II. The reasons behind the illegality defence

The following example might help to illustrate the rationale which the illegality defence is meant to serve. An instigator pays £1,000 to a thug

---

[9] §§ 816, 822 BGB. See Markesinis, Lorenz and Dannemann, *Law of Contracts*, 748–9 and 766.

[10] The leading case is BGHZ 23, 61 (= Markesinis, Lorenz and Dannemann, *Law of Contracts*, case 141).

[11] In BGHZ 23, 61, the plaintiff had erected a building on his landlord's property in full knowledge that he was not entitled to do so; there would be no ground of restitution for his claim for a *quantum meruit* in the common law. See Markesinis, Lorenz and Dannemann, *Law of Contracts*, 762; for subjective valuation, see Birks, *Introduction*, 109–14 and *Falcke v. Scottish Imperial Insurance Co.* (1886) 34 ChD 234 at 248.

[12] These include in particular: (i) § 814, 2nd alt., BGB (plaintiff barred from recovery because of moral (as opposed to legal) obligation towards defendant – this could also become a defence in English law now that *Kleinwort Benson Ltd v. Lincoln City Council* [1999] 2 AC 349 has paved the way for restitution based on mistake of law); (ii) passing on in the common-law world (which might be described as being on its way out after *Commissioner of State Revenue v. Royal Insurance Australia Ltd* (1994) 126 ALR 1 at 11–18 (per Mason CJ); *Kleinwort Benson Ltd v. Birmingham City Council* [1997] QB 380; see Peter Birks, 'The Law of Restitution at the End of an Epoch', (1999) 28 *University of Western Australia LR* 21, n. 18); (iii) impossibility of counter-restitution (this is becoming less important; also it is doubtful whether this is a defence (Birks, *Introduction*, 415), or whether the reverse is part of a ground of restitution (Burrows, *Law of Restitution*, 420)); (iv) estoppel (which is much more closely linked with change of position, and therefore falls outside the scope of the present article); (v) incapacity (which – from a comparative view – appears as a particular reason for making a contract void and thus to be related to grounds of restitution).

who in return beats up a victim. The instigator then seeks to recover his payment in unjust enrichment. English, German and most other laws will agree that this claim must be disallowed. For this, one or several of the following reasons are normally given: (i) no one will be allowed to found his action on his own illegal conduct;[13] (ii) courts would be tainted if they were to assist one villain in his claim against the other;[14] (iii) the claim must be disallowed in order to deter from, or even punish, illegal or immoral conduct.[15]

The same victim now sues the thug in tort for injuries suffered. In turn, the thug sues the instigator for contribution to his tortious liability towards the victim. This action can only succeed if the thug can show that he committed the tort in execution of his agreement with the instigator. The thug must therefore plead his own illegal conduct. Furthermore, in allowing the thug's action, the courts will assist one villain against the other. Additionally, by reducing the thug's overall liability, contribution equally diminishes the deterrent effect of his tortious liability. So all the above reasons why illegality can be raised against a claim in unjust enrichment should prevent a joint tortfeasor's claim in contribution. Yet English, German and most other laws agree that the action for contribution must be allowed.[16]

It looks therefore as if these three explanations of the illegality defence do not stand up to scrutiny. At the very least, they are formulated too widely, so that there must be something which makes these arguments work in an enrichment environment, but not in tort. At the same time, these arguments must be of fundamental importance, as the very purpose of the law of unjust enrichment is to prevent losses from lying where they fall.

---

[13] *Nemo auditur turpitudinem suam allegans*; see below, 315–16. Claim must not be founded on illegality.

[14] Reinhard Zimmermann, *The Law of Obligations: Roman Foundations of the Civilian Tradition* (1990, paperback edn 1996), 846; OGHZ 4, 57, 60; Burrows *Law of Restitution*, 463; Andrew Tettenborn, *Law of Restitution in England and Ireland* (2nd edn, 1996), 257. See also Konrad Zweigert and Hein Kötz, *An Introduction to Comparative Law* (trans. Tony Weir, 3rd edn, 1998), 576.

[15] RGZ 105, 270, 271–2 argued that the defence was intended as a punishment (and justified its operation even against a plaintiff who was of unsound mind and thus without contractual capacity, provided that the defendant could still be liable in tort under § 827 BGB); BGHZ 39, 87, 91 ('Strafcharakter'); see Zweigert and Kötz, *Introduction*, 576.

[16] German law: the instigator and the thug are considered joint tortfeasors under §§ 830, 840 BGB; whoever compensates the victim can sue any other joint tortfeasor for contribution using the victim's claim, which is assigned to the compensating tortfeasor by operation of the law under § 426 BGB. English law: sections 1 and 2 of the Civil Liability (Contribution) Act 1978.

It has been suggested in the past that, when assessing the merit of the illegality defence, it is of paramount importance to keep an eye on the policy rationale behind those rules that make a particular contract, performance or transaction illegal.[17] I further suggest that this rationale might help in reducing the above three general principles to their useful role for justifying illegality as a defence against an unjust enrichment claim.

The reason why a party should not be allowed to rely on its own illegal conduct is that people should not be rewarded for their own illicit behaviour. This is why an unpaid thug cannot recover a *quantum meruit* from the instigator, but why the same unpaid thug could still sue the instigator for contribution to his tortious liability towards the victim.

The second argument – that of the dignity of the courts preventing them from assisting one villain against the other – has, in my view, been inflated out of proportion. If the argument held true, courts would either have a terrible reputation, or else a rather low case load. The law is not against divorcing couples from hell, does not prevent lawsuits between neighbours from hell, and does not prohibit litigation between legacy hunters or between rogues who fiddle company mergers to their own advantage. What could taint courts, though, is if they were forced to allow an action the success of which offends acknowledged legal or public policy. To allow an action for a *quantum meruit* for having beaten up a victim would have the same effect as declaring that the agreement between the thug and the instigator is a valid contract. This is why courts would indeed endanger their reputation if they allowed such an action. To allow an action by the thug against the instigator for contribution, on the other hand, does not counteract the policy which makes such agreements void.

Finally, the deterrence argument needs some fine tuning. In any lawsuit, whoever wins will feel encouraged, and whoever loses will feel discouraged. If both parties are to blame, one may have to consider carefully which party, if any, needs to be deterred more. It is easy to state in a lawsuit between two villains that the action must be disallowed because the plaintiff needs to be deterred from illegal conduct – just as easy, in

[17] Dieter Fabricius, 'Einschränkung der Anwendung des § 817 S. 2 BGB durch den Zweck des Verbotsgesetzes?', 1963 *JZ* 85–91; similarly Dieter Reuter and Michael Martinek, *Ungerechtfertigte Bereicherung* (1983), 209; Detlef König, 'Empfiehlt es sich, das Bereicherungsrecht im Hinblick auf seine Weiterentwicklung in Rechtsprechung und Lehre durch den Gesetzgebern neu zu ordnen?', in: Bundesministerium der Justiz (ed.), *Gutachten und Vorschläge zur Überarbeitung des Schuldrechts* (1981), vol. II, 1515–90, 1522 (§ 1.1(2)(d) of a proposed legal reform act), 1542; Werner Lorenz, in: *J. von Staudingers Kommentar zum Bürgerlichen Gesetzbuch* (13th revised edn, 1999), § 817, n. 2.

fact, as it is to state the exact opposite, namely that the action must be allowed because the defendant needs to be deterred. Where both parties need to be deterred equally, deterrence as justification of either outcome becomes meaningless. The tortious action for contribution, on the other hand, distributes the deterrence between the culprits, as both are made to pay for the consequences of their wrongdoing.

III. The mechanisms

Turning now to the mechanisms that various unjust enrichment laws employ to operate the illegality defence, I will deal with the *nemo auditur* approach, the *in pari delicto* approach and the discretionary approach.

1. Claim must not be founded on illegality

The first mechanism is procedural and, technically speaking, not a defence but a limitation in making a claim. A plaintiff can only succeed if he or she can present a claim on the basis of facts which do not include the plaintiff's illegal or immoral conduct – *nemo auditur turpitudinem suam allegans*.[18] This is the position of English law from *Holman v. Johnson* to *Tinsley v. Milligan*,[19] and commonly associated with the general maxim of *ex turpi causa non oritur actio*.[20] But the same rule has, in a much more general form, entered the reformed Czech and Slovak Civil Code of 1992.[21] It is not, however, the main basis of the illegality defence in German law.[22]

This mechanism has two main difficulties.[23] First and foremost, it can counteract the very policy which makes an agreement between parties illegal. In *Tribe v. Tribe*,[24] a father transferred his assets to his son as the father's creditors were closing in. The father's claim against his son for restitution of his assets would have been barred by the illegality defence, had it not been for the fact that all creditors were paid and the father

---

[18] See Zimmermann, *Law of Obligations*, 865, n. 196.
[19] *Holman v. Johnson* [1775] 1 Cowp 341; 98 ER 1120 at 1121; *Tinsley v. Milligan* [1994] 1 AC 340 at 354 *per* Lord Goff, 376 *per* Lord Browne-Wilkinson.
[20] See, e.g., Graham Virgo, 'The Effect of Illegality on Claims for Restitution in English Law', in: W. Swadling (ed.), *The Limits of Restitutionary Claims: A Comparative Analysis* (1997), 141–85.
[21] Section 40a, second sentence, Obcanský zákoník: 'A person who has caused a juridical act to be invalid may not raise the issue of invalidity.' Translation taken from: *The Civil Code* ('Obcanský zákoník') (translated by Trade Links, Prague, 1993).
[22] But see Reuter and Martinek, *Ungerechtfertigte Bereicherung*, 205 and 214.
[23] See also William Swadling's contribution to this volume.   [24] [1995] 3 WLR 913.

was considered to have withdrawn from the illegal purpose. I would argue that by allowing the illegality defence in cases involving concealed assets, these assets will be even further removed from the reach of the creditors. This might put the seal on the very situation which the law wants to prevent.[25]

Secondly, this rule can produce rather arbitrary results.[26] In a recent German case, the plaintiff was a company which had first prepared and then audited the defendant's accounts in violation of a statute that requires complete separation of these functions.[27] Such a plaintiff is able to plead its case for a *quantum meruit* for the auditing without the slightest reference to their previous work on the accounts. In this case, the plaintiff, as the professional auditors, seem more blameworthy than their clients. Should this be of no relevance, and should the decision really hang on the fact that the prohibitory norm contains a requirement (previous preparation of accounts) which is not a necessary element in plaintiff's pleading? The best thing to be said about the *nemo auditur rule* is probably that it will more often lead to the right than to the wrong result, but that is no praise for a rule of law, especially when it additionally has a somewhat unfortunate inclination towards favouring the cleverer amongst two villains.

2. In pari delicto or turpitudine rule

The second mechanism for the illegality defence has two names, both of which are in Latin. In English Latin, it reads *in pari delicto potior est conditio defendentis*, and in German Latin *in pari turpitudine melior est causa possidentis*.[28] Two villains sue each other over an illegal or immoral deal: losses will lie where they have fallen. English law recognises this defence next to the *nemo auditur* rule.[29] It is also contained in § 817, second sentence BGB, but is limited there to situations where the enrichment was given for a purpose which violated a statutory prohibition or offended

---

[25] See also below, 319, for further examples.
[26] For a similar view, see A. S. Hartkamp, *Mr C Asser's handleiding tot de beoefening van het Nederlands burgerlijk recht, Verbintenissenrecht* (1998), vol. III, n. 346.
[27] BGH 1992 NJW 2021 (violation of § 319(2) n. 5, (3) n. 2 HGB).
[28] This should imply that English law caters for defendants in actions concerning illegality, whereas German law is concerned with those who are in possession of an enrichment obtained through an immoral transaction. In fact, however, no such distinctions are being attributed to the different choice of words in either law.
[29] *Holman v. Johnson* [1775] 1 Cowp 341; 98 ER 1120; *Tinsley v. Milligan* [1994] 1 AC 340, 354–5; Virgo, 'Effect of Illegality'; Birks, *Introduction*, 424 ff.; Burrows, *Law of Restitution*, 461 ff.

good morals. Courts will also require that the claimant was aware of the illegality.[30] The Austrian and Italian Civil Codes and the Swiss Code of Obligations contain similar rules.[31] The German provision is surrounded by many disputes and uncertainties. It has been called 'one of the most dreaded perils in the sea of legal doctrine'.[32] I will limit my presentation of it to some aspects which are of particular relevance in the comparative context.

The discussion below deals first with cases where one party performed for the sake of a counterperformance which never came about. Within this category, one can further distinguish: (a) cases where the claim is for a *quantum meruit*, as in the auditor's case; (b) for restitution of money paid in expectancy of a counterperformance under an illegal or immoral agreement; and (c) for restitution where a performance can be returned in kind.

(a) Recovery for one-sided performance

Two more cases may serve to illustrate *quantum meruit* claims. The first concerned payment for a series of advertisements for what was described as 'Die schönen Stunden zu zweit' (Those lovely hours *entre deux*), garnished with the additions 'just call me', 'habla español' and 'parla italiano'.[33] The reader may already have guessed the nature of the services offered in this way. The judgment by the *Bundesgerichtshof*, anxious to avoid any doubt on this point, illuminates the reader with a graphic reproduction of the offending article and probably makes legal history by placing this particular type of advertisement within an official case reporter. The Court explains at some length why this was indeed an advertisement for prostitution and thus amounted to a petty criminal offence, and why the contract was void in consequence. There are nearly three pages on why the defendant's reliance on illegality against the claim for the agreed prize did not offend good faith, and only one paragraph on the defence in § 817, second sentence, BGB, which was held to apply both in word and in spirit, in particular in order to deter publishers from offending. (Deterrence of the client who ran the brothel was apparently not an issue.)

Both the auditor and the advertisement cases were preceded by a much more controversial decision, which concerned a builder who claimed a

---

[30] RGZ 161, 57.
[31] Austria: § 1174 ABGB; Italy: Art. 2035 *codice civile*; Switzerland: Art. 66 OR. Arguably, the Swiss Code of Obligations contains the best-worded version of this rule.
[32] Zimmermann, *Law of Obligations*, 864; similarly Reuter and Martinek, *Ungerechtfertigte Bereicherung*, 199.
[33] Reported in BGHZ 118, 182.

quantum meruit for a job that parties had agreed to keep secret from the taxman.[34] The Court held that this action should, in principle, be defeated by the *in pari turpitudine* rule, but set this rule aside on the grounds of good faith. It is somewhat puzzling that the Court held honour amongst thieves to be stronger than a provision of the Civil Code.[35] More particularly, however, the Court argued that denying the claim was not really necessary to enforce the relevant tax and social legislation, and that it was unjust that the client, who would normally have the stronger bargaining position, should be allowed to keep the windfall. One wonders, of course, whether the same rationale would not apply to the auditor and the publisher in the other two cases, but the *Bundesgerichtshof* ruled in each of these cases that the builder was to be distinguished, though, unfortunately, without indicating any reasons for this distinction.

There are also cases where one party has paid in advance for an illegal performance. One couple paid DM 15,000 under an illegal adoption agreement whereby the defendant was to procure, within two-and-a-half weeks, an unnamed child from the Philippines.[36] The *Oberlandesgericht* Oldenburg barely touched upon good faith and the purpose of the prohibitory norm to arrive at the conclusion that courts are not meant to sort out the consequences where both parties have acted immorally or unlawfully. And in a mirror case to *Parkinson v. College of Ambulance Ltd*,[37] the *Bundesgerichtshof* held that a plaintiff who had paid $50,000 in order to obtain the title of honorary consul of Sierra Leone was barred from recovering when the title failed to come through.[38]

With the exception of the builder case, it is noteworthy that all these judgments devote comparatively little space to the *in pari turpitudine* rule itself. They rush to their conclusion as if they were a little embarrassed to deny a claim on such a tedious ground.[39] It is also noteworthy that good faith, purpose of the prohibitory norm, and reliance on one's own illegal conduct are used to explain each other, and rather interchangeably. I do

---

[34] BGHZ 111, 308, 312; English translation in Markesinis, Lorenz and Dannemann, *Law of Contracts*, case 136.

[35] The judgment has been criticised as being *contra legem* by several authors, e.g. Lorenz in Staudinger, § 817, n. 10; Karl Larenz and Claus-Wilhelm Canaris, *Lehrbuch des Schuldrechts* (13th edn, 1994), vol. II/2 § 68 III. 3. g.

[36] OLG Oldenburg, 1991 NJW 2216.   [37] *Parkinson v. College of Ambulance Ltd* [1925] 2 KB 1.

[38] 1994 NJW 187. Unlike in *Parkinson*, though, the recipient was not a charitable institution so that the payment could hardly be classified as a gift.

[39] The same is not true for OGHZ 4, 57, 60 ff., which contains a long discussion of § 817, second sentence, BGB.

believe, though, that a common rationale can, after all, be found behind these judgments.

The main argument flows indeed from the prohibitory norm, and it is that no claim should lie for the *quantum meruit* of an act which is in itself illegal, for otherwise restitution would ensure that illegal conduct pays. This clearly explains the advertisement case, but also the auditor case, as the purpose of the statute was to keep the functions of accountants and auditors completely separate. Similarly, no claim should lie for the *quantum meruit* of an act which, although not illegal in itself, should not be linked with a counterperformance in money – because this would enforce via restitution the very link which the prohibitory norm tries to prevent. This could explain why prostitutes or merchants in knighthoods are not allowed to claim a *quantum meruit* for their services.

On the other hand, the builder's work was not in itself illegal. Neither was it illegal to build against payment. What was illegal was that no tax or social insurance contributions should be paid from these earnings. Going back to the wording (and perhaps the history)[40] of § 817, second sentence, BGB, one could also doubt whether in this case performance was indeed made for an illegal or immoral purpose.

Neither does the rationale apply to performances that can be returned. On the contrary, allowing a restitutionary claim in kind may be the best or even the only way of enforcing the policy rationales which may prohibit certain currency deals or restrict trade with national heritage objects, endangered species, toxic substances, drugs or arms. The same is true for agreements for the illegal concealment of assets. This is where an application of the *in pari turpitudine* rule is likely to produce the most disastrous results.

Can the same argument be applied to the recovery of money paid in anticipation of counterperformance? In principle, allowing restitution should remove any unwanted link between the illicit act and payment. But allowing recovery would favour the illicit client over the illicit contractor. Those who create demand for illicit acts are, generally speaking, neither less dangerous nor less blameworthy than those who commit them. The person who orders a murder deserves no better treatment than a contract killer. I wonder whether the illegality defence is not used in this context to create a limited amount of equality between those who commit and those who pay for illegal acts. It is the intended

---

[40] For the history of the *in pari turpitudine* rule, see Zimmermann, *Law of Obligations*, 846–7.

link between payment and counterperformance which could ultimately justify the application of the illegality defence in these cases. It is also, arguably, this link which Roman law had in mind when it constructed this particular defence as a bar to a *condictio ob rem*.[41] However, these cases show perhaps more than any others that illegality is a difficult rule, and that there may be cases where a fully satisfactory result is not feasible. It is noteworthy that the new Dutch Civil Code will generally allow the recovery of money paid in advance under an illegal contract, but not recovery for a *quantum meruit* that should not be valued in money.[42]

There is one particular problem with the *in pari turpitudine* approach, which concerns enrichments that were meant to be temporary by both parties, and in particular loans or securities. Under a narrow application of *nemo auditur*, there can be recovery after the stipulated time has elapsed, because the illegal purpose of the loan or security need not to be pleaded. However, the *in pari turpitudine* approach creates some difficulties, as this defence could preclude any recovery of a loan or security given for an illegal purpose. For loans, German courts have frequently avoided this result by ruling that it is not the money loaned itself, but rather the temporary use of this money, which constitutes the enrichment, so that § 817, second sentence, BGB would not prevent recovery after the stipulated time for the loan has elapsed.[43]

(b) Recovery after mutual performance

An equally difficult application of the *in pari turpitudine* rule relates to void, but fully executed, agreements. Denying restitution has essentially

---

[41] Zimmermann, *Law of Obligations*, 846–7 and 863–5.
[42] Art. 6:211(1) BW; Eltjo Schrage, 'Restitution in the New Dutch Civil Code', [1994] *Restitution LR* 208, 214. See also references at n. 48, below.
[43] However, this concerns mainly usury cases, where only one party (the loan shark) has acted illegally or immorally (see RGZ 161, 52, 57; Reuter and Martinek, *Ungerechtfertigte Bereicherung*, 216; Lorenz in: *Staudinger*, § 817, n. 12). A different solution was found in BGH 1990 ZIP 915, concerning a bank loan given in the full knowledge that it would be used to finance a brothel ship in the Mediterranean. It helped that the money went through a probably bona fide middlewoman and that § 817, second sentence, BGB contains a loophole: it does not provide that the illegality defence will also operate if the plaintiff, but not the defendant, acted immorally. The bank was thus awarded the unjustified enrichment of the middlewoman, which consisted in her claim against the operator-to-be of the brothel ship. See Lorenz in: *Staudinger*, § 817, n. 11. Lorenz argues that not allowing restitution in this case would have legalised a situation which is frowned upon by the legal order.

the same effects as ruling that the contract is valid,[44] but one must also inquire whether undoing the contract will serve the prohibitory norm better than keeping matters as they are. Again, where restitution in kind is possible without further illegality or violation of interests or rights of third parties, this may well be a better way of enforcing the prohibitory rule than allowing the illegality defence.

On the other hand, illicit work or services can normally not simply be returned. Putting a price tag on them results in the same problems which, in my view, can justify the illegality defence in the first place. Not allowing a *quantum meruit* but allowing restitution for money paid leads to the same imbalance between those who commit illegal acts and those who instigate them with their payment. This may explain why in some situations the prohibitory norm can be served best by leaving both enrichments where they are.

3. Discretionary approach

Next to the *nemo auditur* and *in pari delicto* rules, there is a third approach which has been chosen, in particular, by legislation in New Zealand and Israel – namely, to leave the decision as to whether or not the illegality defence should apply to the courts to be decided on the merits of each case. Both statutes give very broad discretion.[45] The New Zealand legislation invites the courts specifically to consider the conduct of the parties, the object of any statute breached and the gravity of the penalty provided, and any other matter which the court thinks proper, but to refrain from granting relief if this would not be in the public interest.[46]

To a certain extent, both German and Dutch law have taken a discretionary approach. Dutch law has essentially limited the illegality defence to cases where a performance cannot be returned, but leaves the

---

[44] Similarly Zimmermann, *Law of Obligations*, 864.
[45] Section 31 of the Israeli Contracts (General Part) Law 1973, whereby courts may relieve a party from restitution claims under section 21 in cases involving contracts which are void on the grounds of illegality or immorality (s. 30) 'if it deems just to do so and on such conditions as it sees fit'. Quoted from (and see): Nili Cohen, 'Illegality: The Case for Discretion', in: W. Swadling (ed.), *The Limits of Restitutionary Claims: A Comparative Analysis* (1997), 186–211, 188.
[46] The Illegal Contracts Act 1970, s. 7(3): '(3) In considering whether to grant relief under subsection (1) of this section the Court shall have regard to – (a) The conduct of the parties; and (b) In the case of a breach of an enactment, the object of the enactment and the gravity of the penalty expressly provided for any breach thereof; and (c) Such other matters as it thinks proper; but shall not grant relief if it considers that to do so would not be in the public interest.'

decision whether this performance ought not to be valued in money to the courts, and makes restitution of any counterperformance in a mutually executed transaction subject to reason and equity.[47] In addition, the *Hoge Raad* (the highest Dutch court) has held that unjust enrichment claims are, quite generally, subject to the general good-faith provision in Article 6:2 BW.[48] Modern German law should be named in this context because, as the illicit labour case demonstrates, German courts are forever prepared to set aside fairly clearly worded rules on grounds of equity and good faith.[49] Indeed, Dieter Reuter and Michael Martinek's influential book urges German courts to develop their own case law by deciding each case on its merits, using the purpose of the prohibitory norm as the guiding principle.[50] Finally, the public conscience test developed by Nicholls LJ in the Court of Appeal's judgment in *Tinsley v. Milligan* is a value judgment based on the adverse consequences of refusing or granting restitutionary relief. This attempt to introduce a discretionary approach to English case law was, however, rejected by the House of Lords in the same case.[51]

The obvious advantage of a discretionary approach is that it enables courts to avoid results which are unjust to one party or unwise as a matter of legal policy. But its obvious drawback is the legal uncertainty it creates. On the other hand, this uncertainty needs to be placed in its context. While I would not go as far as stating that legal uncertainty is an appropriate response to parties who place themselves outside of the legal order, one might still feel less concerned about this uncertainty than in many other cases where, for example, English, German or French

---

[47] Schrage, 'Restitution in the New Dutch Civil Code', 214; Art. 6:211 BW provides that the claim for the counterperformance 'is also barred so far as it would offend reason and equity'. Translation taken from: Schrage, 'Restitution', 204.

[48] 1992 NJ n. 787, in a case involving an illegal form of temporary employment business: claim for *quantum meruit* for work performed denied. The *Hoge Raad* held (at 3.3) that unjust enrichment claims could generally be denied on grounds of reason and equity (*redelijkheid en billijkheid*) under Art. 6:2(2) BW. See also Hartkamp, *Mr C Asser's handleiding*, n. 348, and Hugo J. van Kooten, 'Artikel 6:211 en de Engelse *law of restitution*', (1994) 43 *Ars Aequi* 311–20.

[49] It is noteworthy, though, that any element of discretion or balancing of culpability was rejected by OGHZ 4, 57, 60 ff. This was an action for return of the purchase price of a radio which was bought on the fraudulent representation of being brand new; the buyer's action failed because both parties had violated a maximum price regulation in force at the time.

[50] Reuter and Martinek, *Ungerechtfertigte Bereicherung*, 210–11.

[51] *Tinsley v. Milligan* [1992] Ch 310 (CA) at 319 *per* Nicholls LJ; [1994] AC 340 at 358–63 *per* Lord Goff, at 364 *per* Lord Browne-Wilkinson.

law have not hesitated to adopt statutory provisions of almost scandalous vagueness.[52]

IV. Conclusions

I have some sympathy with the Dutch approach. It does not defeat a claim for restitution in kind where it is possible. It limits the discretion to two fairly precise issues, namely: (i) If a performance under an illegal agreement cannot be returned, ought it to be valued in money? (ii) If an illegal agreement has been fully performed by both parties, should restitution be allowed? There is one main point in the Dutch approach where I have my doubts: it seems to allow, quite generally, those who instigate illegal activity by payment to recover as long as the illegal activity itself has not been performed.[53] And while Article 6:2 BW is available as an emergency brake even in this situation, its use will be hampered by the fact that the *Hoge Raad* has so far refused to balance the respective wrongdoings of the parties concerned.[54]

Here, as generally when discretion is to be used within the illegality defence, I suggest the first and foremost consideration should be whether either allowing or refusing restitutionary relief would create, maintain or prevent the very situation which the prohibitory norm wants to avoid. Only if this does not provide a clear indication for the outcome can notions of deterrence help to find the right solution. This requires in particular a balancing of which party needs to be deterred more. The relevant factors include the culpability of both parties and any actual harm created by, or danger generally associated with, their behaviour. This will still leave a few situations – in particular as concerns recovery of an advance payment for illicit conduct – where this test fails to produce an unequivocal result.

---

[52] English law has, *inter alia*, a statutory provision which, quite simply, makes it an offence to publish any material that tends to 'deprave and corrupt' readers (Obscene Publications Act 1959, ss. 1(1), 2). British law requires for the purpose of naturalisation as a British citizen, that the applicant 'is of good character' (British Nationality Act 1981, Sched. 1, s. 1(1)(b)). French law provides general tortious liability for all damage caused to another by fault (art. 1382, *code civil*). Within the German law of obligations, almost any desired result can be achieved via the good-faith provision in § 242 BGB as applied by German courts: see Markesinis, Lorenz and Dannemann, *Law of Contracts*, chap. 7.

[53] For Hartkamp, *Mr C Asser's handleiding*, n. 348, this is a welcome consequence of Art. 6:211 BW.

[54] 1992 NJ n. 787. But see also van Kooten, 'Artikel 6:211', 315, who believes that Art. 6:211 BW permits courts to allow or deny a claim on a balance of the wrongdoing of each party.

Various ideas have been voiced, all of which present their own difficulties: that the money should be taken from the defendant and given to charity[55] or forfeited;[56] or that apportionment might be better than an all-or-nothing approach.[57]

I would like to float one more idea. If the policy reasons for defeating and allowing the action hold the balance, perhaps one should deny recovery of advance payments made for an illegal purpose, but make the defendant pay for the costs of the action for recovery in consideration of the facts that the action does not fail because the defendant has a right to keep the money, and that the defendant has also been culpable of illegal conduct.[58] This would at least ensure that both parties lose something. There is just a hint of such an approach in *Parkinson v. College of Ambulance Ltd*.[59] In this case, an action for recovery of a donation made with the express purpose of obtaining a knighthood was defeated on grounds of illegality. The Court observed that the second defendant had denied fraud, had administered cross-examination to the plaintiff, and had refused to be examined himself. In the view of the Court, all this amounted to oppressive behaviour. Accordingly, an order was made to deprive him of his costs.

---

[55] Zweigert and Kötz, *Introduction*, 576–7 trace this idea back to Thomas Aquinas.

[56] I 16 §§ 173 Prussian Code of 1794; Zweigert and Kötz, *Introduction*, 577.

[57] Some of the wording of the judgment of the *Bundesgerichtshof* in the builder case (BGHZ 111, 308, 312; English translation in Markesinis, Lorenz and Dannemann, *Law of Contracts*, case 136) suggests that the deductions which the Court imposed on the builder's claim for a *quantum meruit* amount to partial recovery. The Court stated that the enrichment claim 'must at any rate be subject to certain restrictions' (at 313). On the other hand, on 314 the 'very considerable deductions' that need to be made are dressed up as reflecting the lower economic value of an illicit labour job. Perhaps the Court was equally anxious to avoid either full recovery in the given case, or the official introduction of partial recovery into the law of restitution.

[58] Additionally, the defendant could be allowed to avoid being burdened with the costs of the proceedings, e.g. by paying the sum into court on first demand. Depending on the merits of the case, the judgment could then award this sum to the plaintiff, have it returned to the defendant, or give the money to a charitable purpose. To what extent such mixed substantive and procedural law solutions are feasible does, of course, depend much on the applicable procedural law.

[59] [1925] 2 KB 1 at 17.

PART VII

Encroachment and restitution for wrongs

12 Reflections on the role of restitutionary damages to protect contractual expectations

Janet O'Sullivan

I. Introduction

This chapter considers the suggestion made by the English Court of Appeal in *Attorney-General v. Blake*[1] that a restitutionary measure of damages for breach of contract might exceptionally be justified, in cases where the normal compensatory measure of damages is deficient or unsatisfactory. In the words of Lord Woolf MR, delivering the judgment of the Court:

> [i]f the court is unable to award restitutionary damages for breach of contract, then the law of contract is seriously deficient. It means that in many situations the plaintiff is deprived of any effective remedy for breach of contract, because of a failure to attach any value to the plaintiff's legitimate interests in having the contract duly performed.[2]

It will be suggested that a restitutionary measure of damages for breach of contract cannot be justified solely on this basis and that it would be more transparent, accurate and appropriate to tackle deficiencies in the compensatory measure directly.

II. Background

Until *Blake*, English law was tolerably clear. The role of restitution in cases of contractual default was limited to autonomous 'subtraction' claims, such as the paradigm case of the recovery of money on the ground of total failure of consideration, following discharge of a contract for repudiatory

---

[1] *Attorney-General v. Blake (Jonathan Cape Ltd, third party)* [1998] 1 All ER 833. Since this chapter was written, the House of Lords has affirmed the decision of the Court of Appeal on different grounds, reported [2000] 4 All ER 385.

[2] *Ibid.*, [1998] 1 All ER 833 at 845.

breach.[3] Moving outside this area into 'restitution for wrongs', in the light of repeated judicial assertions that damages for breach of contract are compensatory only,[4] there seemed no prospect of a restitutionary measure for contractual damages (that is, damages based not on the plaintiff's loss but on the defendant's gain).

It was certainly true that many academic commentators were critical of this state of affairs, unhappy that a party in breach of contract should be entitled to make and retain profit (or save expense) by the breach, with the innocent party confined to the recovery of compensation for losses. There was pressure for change, although its advocates generally stopped some way short of proposing a restitutionary measure for all breaches of contract. So Gareth Jones[5] advocated a general right to restitutionary relief but with a judicial discretion to refuse it in appropriate cases, while Peter Birks[6] argued for the restitutionary measure for cynical breaches where a loss-based award would be inadequate.

As to the case law on contractual remedies, English authorities favouring a restitutionary measure for breach of contract were sparse and unpromising. First, there were some exceptional cases where a restitutionary measure was justified on a basis other than simple breach of contract. So, for example, in cases where the breach of contract also involved a wrongful interference with the plaintiff's property, damages assessed by reference to the defendant's gains have been awarded.[7] Secondly, elsewhere in the law reports occasional examples can be found of a rough and ready resort to the amount of the defendant's gain as one way of approximating the quantum of the plaintiff's loss,[8] but such cases contain no principled examination or adoption of restitutionary principles.

More promising at first glance is the significant line of cases where damages are awarded in lieu of an injunction for breach of a restrictive covenant concerning land use, despite the breach causing no diminution

---

[3] See, for example, *Rowland v. Divall* [1923] 2 KB 500.
[4] One typical example is the statement by Megarry J in *Tito v. Waddell (No. 2)* [1977] Ch 106 at 332 that 'it is fundamental to all questions of damages that they are to compensate the plaintiff for his loss or injury by putting him as nearly as possible in the same position as he would have been in had he not suffered the wrong. The question is not one of making the defendant disgorge what he has saved by committing the wrong, but one of compensating the plaintiff.'
[5] G. Jones, 'The Recovery of Benefits Gained from Breach of Contract', (1983) 99 *LQR* 442.
[6] P. B. H. Birks, 'Restitutionary Damages for Breach of Contract: *Snepp* and the Fusion of Law and Equity', [1987] *Lloyd's Maritime and Commercial Law Quarterly* 421.
[7] *Penarth Dock Engineering Co. Ltd v. Pounds* [1963] 1 Lloyd's Rep 359.
[8] See, for example, *East Ham Corporation v. Bernard Sunley & Sons* [1966] AC 406 at 434 *per* Lord Cohen.

in value to the plaintiff's adjoining property. In such cases, damages can be assessed on the basis of the hypothetical amount that the plaintiff would have required for consenting to the breach, had the defendant bothered to ask in advance for such consent. So in *Wrotham Park Estate Co. Ltd v. Parkside Homes Ltd*[9] the defendant was bound by a restrictive covenant not to develop land adjoining the plaintiff's property without the plaintiff's consent, but had constructed fourteen houses in breach of the covenant. Brightman J refused the plaintiff's request for a mandatory injunction to compel the defendant to destroy the houses, but instead awarded damages (representing a reasonable sum for release of the covenant), which he calculated as 5 per cent of the defendant's anticipated profits. The judge regarded this measure as compensatory, as did the Court of Appeal in the more recent case of *Jaggard v. Sawyer*.[10]

However, the notion that this measure represented the amount the plaintiff would have bargained for and received for release of the covenant was often somewhat fictitious, ignoring the fact that the particular plaintiff would very likely never have consented to release the covenant at any price. This led some commentators[11] to deride the loss-based reasoning as strained and to assert that a restitutionary explanation of the *Wrotham Park* award was more natural. The restitutionary explanation gained some judicial support, although even its judicial proponents did not regard it as heralding a general measure of gain-based recovery for breach of contract. So in *Surrey County Council v. Bredero Homes Ltd*,[12] Steyn LJ described *Wrotham Park* as an exceptional example of restitutionary recovery, which he regarded as not justified in general or on the facts of *Bredero* itself. Subsequently, the orthodox explanation of *Wrotham Park* as an example of compensatory principle was reasserted in *Jaggard v. Sawyer*.

All in all, then, there was nothing in the case law before *Blake* to suggest a principled acceptance of a restitutionary measure of damages for breach of contract. In addition, the Law Commission for England and Wales decided against such a reform, recommending that the current exceptional categories should remain, with further development on a case-by-case basis if the courts thought fit.[13] There the law rested until December 1997.

---

[9] [1974] 1 WLR 798.
[10] [1995] 1 WLR 269 at 281 *per* Sir Thomas Bingham MR, and at 291 *per* Millett LJ.
[11] See, for example, W. Goodhart, 'Restitutionary Damages for Breach of Contract: The Remedy That Dare Not Speak its Name', [1994] *Restitution LR* 3, 7.
[12] [1993] 1 WLR 1361.
[13] Law Commission, *Aggravated, Exemplary and Restitutionary Damages* (LCCP No. 132, 1993).

III. The Court of Appeal's decision in *Attorney-General v. Blake*

The *Blake* case concerned the efforts of the British Crown to prevent the infamous Soviet double agent, George Blake, from reaping the financial rewards of the publication of his memoirs. Blake, a former member of the Secret Intelligence Service, was tried and imprisoned in Britain, but escaped to Moscow where he wrote his autobiography. This was published in 1990 and sold well. The Crown, anxious to prevent the payment of royalties to Blake, brought proceedings against the book's publishers (Jonathan Cape) seeking an injunction and an account of profits. The Crown's private-law claim based on breach of fiduciary duty failed, but the alternative public-law claim succeeded. Hence, the Court of Appeal granted an injunction on the basis that Blake's publication (in breach of the Official Secrets Act) was a criminal offence, relying on the Court's inherent jurisdiction to grant such relief to further the public-policy objective that a criminal should not benefit from his crime.

For the purposes of this chapter, the interest in the case lies not in its substantive result, but in a short passage in which the Court suggested that restitutionary damages for breach of contract would in principle have been available. Blake was undoubtedly in breach of contract, having covenanted to observe the Official Secrets Act both during and after his employment, but orthodox English contractual remedies were of no use to the Crown, which had not sought an injunction preventing publication and which could establish no tangible loss from the breach to justify compensatory damages. Yet for some reason, the Crown ignored the broad hints dropped by the Court of Appeal during argument and decided not to ask for restitutionary damages,[14] so that the Court's comments on the matter were necessarily sketchy and made without the benefit of argument.

The principal feature of the Court of Appeal's comments on restitutionary damages was its emphasis on the role of restitutionary damages as limited to cases where the compensatory measure is inadequate and does not fully protect the plaintiff's interest in performance. Beyond this 'negative justification', no positive independent justification for restitutionary damages was offered. Indeed, in the Court's view, the restitutionary measure should be regarded as an exceptional one. 'The difficult question is not whether restitutionary damages should ever be available for breach

---

[14] The Court 'invited submissions' on this point but 'the Attorney General decided that the Crown did not desire to advance such a claim in this court...': [1998] 1 All ER 833 at 843-4.

of contract, but in what circumstances they should be made available.'[15] Some guidance was given as to what is needed for the necessary exceptional circumstances to arise.

First, more is required than merely a cynical or deliberate breach by the defendant: 'The fact that his breach is deliberate and cynical is not by itself a good ground for departing from the normal basis on which damages are awarded.'[16] It is unclear from this whether deliberate breach is a *necessary* condition, although the use of the words 'by itself' and the tenor of the Court's later comments[17] suggest that it is. Likewise, just because a breach gave the defendant the opportunity of making his profit is not a sufficient condition justifying a restitutionary measure.[18]

Having explained what will not suffice for an exceptional award of restitutionary damages, the Court went on to enunciate two sorts of contractual breach which would attract restitutionary damages, as follows:

(i) Skimped performance: 'This is where the defendant fails to provide the full extent of the services which he has contracted to provide and for which he has charged the plaintiff.'[19] The celebrated US case of *City of New Orleans v. Firemen's Charitable Association*[20] was given as an example.

(ii) Breach of a negative stipulation: 'Where the defendant has obtained his profit by doing the very thing which he contracted not to do.'[21] This was the category which, the Court indicated, covered the facts of *Blake* precisely, since Blake 'promised not to disclose official information and he did so for profit. He earned the profits by doing the very thing which he had promised not to do.'[22]

Having described the two sorts of breach attracting restitutionary damages, the Court explained the characteristics that they share, namely that:

in both the profits in question are occasioned directly by the breach, which do not merely provide the opportunity to make them; and in both compensatory damages are an inadequate remedy if regard is paid to the objects which the plaintiff sought to achieve by the contract.[23]

---

[15] *Ibid.* at 845.
[16] *Ibid.* The Court went on to explain why: 'It is not only that the line cannot easily be drawn in practice; it is rather that the defendant's motives will normally be irrelevant.'
[17] In particular, the citation with approval of Professor Birks's article ('Restitutionary Damages'), which argues that those who commit cynical, deliberate breaches of contract should be liable to make restitution.
[18] [1998] 1 All ER 833 at 846.   [19] *Ibid.* at 845.
[20] (1891) 9 So 486. (See below, 337–40.)   [21] [1998] 1 All ER 833 at 846.
[22] *Ibid.*   [23] *Ibid.*

Beyond this, no further principled argument in favour of a restitutionary measure was proffered. So the Court of Appeal regarded restitutionary damages as exceptional and as justified, not by their own intrinsic merit, but as a back-up device to redress the deficiencies in the compensatory measure.

This certainly accords with the intuition that many writers have that, although a restitutionary measure does have a principled basis[24] and should thus not be confined to isolated exceptions, it would none the less be inappropriate to allow a restitutionary measure in cases where the plaintiff's expectation is fully protected on breach. For most English commentators, the impetus for a restitutionary measure comes primarily from the sense that, in certain cases, the compensatory measure is deficient. This is seen particularly in the critical reaction to the Israeli Supreme Court decision in *Adras Building Material Ltd v. Harlow & Jones GmbH*,[25] which concerned a contract to sell 7,000 tons of steel to a purchaser. The seller had imported sufficient steel and had delivered all but 1,762 tons of it when the Yom Kippur war broke out, pushing up the market price of steel. The seller duly accepted a higher offer for the remainder of the steel from a third party, despite the purchaser's protests. The market price of steel subsequently fell to its pre-war ordinary price. The purchaser, however, did not bring the contract to an end and mitigate its loss by purchasing substitute steel on the market: instead, it claimed the seller's profits in an action for restitution, based on the Israeli Unjust Enrichment Law 1979. The Israeli Supreme Court, by a majority, allowed the purchaser's claim to the seller's profits, despite acknowledging that the steel had never been appropriated to the purchaser's contract and that the contract between the parties had not been terminated.

English commentators have overwhelmingly rejected the reasoning and result in *Adras*, which seems, to English eyes, to subvert both the exclusivity of the contractual remedial regime whilst the contract remains in force *and* the requirement of mitigation of loss.[26] So, for example, Richard

---

[24] Although Birks has recently accepted that unjust enrichment principles do not provide the justification for instances of restitutionary damages for breach of contract, tort and other wrongs: see P. H. B. Birks, 'Misnomer', in: W. R. Cornish, R. Nolan, J. O'Sullivan and G. Virgo (eds.), *Restitution: Past, Present and Future* (1998), chap. 1.

[25] [1995] *Restitution LR* 235.

[26] The case should be viewed in the light of the significant differences between the English and Israeli contractual systems, particularly the requirement in Israel of good faith in the performance of contractual obligations and the fact that specific performance is the primary remedy for breach of contract.

O'Dair[27] (in a detailed economic examination of the theory of efficient breach) has argued for the availability of restitutionary damages if the parties would have agreed to an express clause providing for them if their contract had been negotiated in sufficient detail, which are essentially situations where the normal measure of compensatory damages does not fully protect the plaintiff's interest in contractual performance. However, in his view, the economic arguments for restitutionary damages do not extend to all breaches of contract, since:

on the one hand it is difficult to believe that wealth maximisation is the ethical basis of contract law. On the other hand, there is something very attractive about the rules of law which it seems to explain, such as the denial of restitutionary damages following a breach of contract for the sale of goods in a highly liquid market and the mitigation principle.[28]

A further criticism of a general restitutionary measure in an *Adras* situation is based on principles of reciprocity. As I have argued elsewhere, 'if the market [in *Adras*] had continued to rise... the plaintiff would have been able to demand the difference between the contract price and the then market value, even though that exceeded the defendant's gain, and thus reciprocity must surely require like treatment for the plaintiff when the market falls back to the level of the contract price'.[29] Likewise, Sir William Goodhart QC, although arguing for a very broad recognition of restitutionary damages in contract, none the less expressed unease about allowing it to supplement the compensatory measure where the latter operates to produce complete protection of expectations.[30] He would exempt cases following the *Adras* fact pattern on the basis that 'there seems no adequate reason why the reduction or elimination of a loss as a result of the plaintiff's mitigation should open the way to a claim for restitutionary damages', and suggests more generally that restitutionary damages should not be available 'if the plaintiff has in fact been able to obtain satisfactory substitute performance from another source or could have obtained it and has acted unreasonably in failing to do so'.[31]

---

[27] D. R. F. O'Dair, 'Restitutionary Damages for Breach of Contract and the Theory of Efficient Breach: Some Reflections', (1993) 46(2) *Current Legal Problems* 113.
[28] *Ibid.*, 134.
[29] J. O'Sullivan, 'Loss and Gain at Greater Depth: The Implications of the *Ruxley* Decision', in: F. Rose (ed.), *Failure of Contracts* (1997), chap. 1.
[30] 'Restitutionary Damages for Breach of Contract – The Remedy that Dare Not Speak Its Name', [1995] *Restitution LR* 3.
[31] *Ibid.*, 10.

But this reasoning, and the treatment of restitutionary damages in *Blake*, prompts a moment's pause. If restitutionary damages for breach of contract have an intrinsic justification of their own, going beyond a 'gap-filling' role to bolster the imperfect protection currently offered to contractual expectations, then the quantum of the plaintiff's loss should be irrelevant to the restitutionary measure. The reason the plaintiff receives no compensatory damages should not matter, be it because of successful mitigation or because the common law does not adequately protect certain genuine losses. Yet no such intrinsic justification is offered by the Court in *Blake*.

It is this feature of the reasoning that will be considered in this chapter. Reflection on a purely 'back-up' role for restitutionary damages prompts the response: if there is something deficient about the operation of the compensation principle, and this is the *only* impetus for a restitutionary measure, then this deficiency should be rectified directly. The great merit of recent restitution scholarship in England has been its drive to remove artificiality in legal reasoning and labelling, yet here the opposite approach is being advocated. This retreat into restitutionary notions to solve compensatory problems suggests tolerance of deficiencies in the compensatory measure and an unjustified defeatism about the prospects of any direct improvement. Yet, as parallel developments in English law show, this defeatism is far from justified.

IV. Deficiencies in the orthodox compensatory measure

In recent years, concerns about deficiencies in the compensatory measure in the English law of contract have arisen because of its perceived failure to recognise that the plaintiff's interest lies in the *performance* of the contract. The 'performance interest'[32] tends not to be accorded sufficient weight in the English remedial system, which generally assumes that a plaintiff is neutral as between damages (assessed by reference to market value) and performance itself.[33] This English deficiency is evident first in the exceptional status of the remedy of specific enforcement of a contract, which is countenanced only in exceptional cases. Secondly, the 'performance interest' is undervalued by the practice of measuring the plaintiff's loss by

---

[32] A term that is preferable to 'expectation interest' in this context: see D. Friedmann, 'The Performance Interest in Contract Damages', (1995) 111 *LQR* 628.

[33] B. Coote, 'Contract Damages, *Ruxley* and the Performance Interest', (1997) 56 *CLJ* 537.

reference to the exchange or market value of performance,[34] even in a non-commercial context where he contracted for reasons other than the realisation of profit.[35]

However, English law is beginning to recognise this deficiency in the remedial regime for breach of contract and to attack it directly, as the following three examples illustrate. First, the House of Lords has recognised in *Ruxley Electronics and Construction Ltd v. Forsyth* that, although the measure of damages for defective building work which fully respects the performance interest (namely the cost to the plaintiff of curing the defect) is not invariably appropriate, the plaintiff's interest in performance should none the less be valued and compensated, even where it exceeds the market value of performance.[36] In *Ruxley*, their Lordships were prepared to award damages for loss of amenity to a householder for whom a swimming pool had been constructed which was slightly shallower than the contract required, even though there was no difference in market value between the work as performed and as it should have been performed. The plaintiff's 'consumer surplus' was regarded as worthy of protection as part of his expectation from performance, albeit not an expectation shared by the arbiters of the market.[37]

The second example of this trend is found in the obiter comments of Lord Griffiths in *Linden Gardens Trust Ltd v. Lenesta Sludge Disposals Ltd*.[38] Here, the employer under a building contract assigned the property to a third party before the contract was fully performed: defects came to light and the original employer sued for damages (there being an absolute prohibition on assignment contained within the building contract itself). The defaulting contractor argued that the employer had suffered no loss, having disposed of the building for full value. The majority of the House of Lords, whilst accepting the orthodox argument that the employer had suffered no loss, none the less rejected the argument and, by extending an existing exception to privity principles to this case, allowed the employer to recover substantial damages for the benefit of the

---

[34] See, for example, *White Arrow Express Ltd v. Lamey's Distribution Ltd* (1996) Trading Law Reports 69 at 73.

[35] See D. Harris, A. Ogus and J. Phillips, 'Contract Remedies and the Consumer Surplus', (1979) 95 *LQR* 581 and E. McKendrick, 'Breach of Contract and the Meaning of Loss', (1999) 52 *Current Legal Problems* 37.

[36] [1996] AC 344.

[37] Lord Mustill explicitly regarded the loss of amenity award as reflecting the plaintiff's subjective performance interest. Lord Lloyd regarded it instead as an exceptional example of damages for disappointment. See further O'Sullivan, 'Loss and Gain'.

[38] [1994] 1 AC 85.

third-party owner. Lord Griffiths suggested a more radical route to the same result, which involved challenging the notion that the employer had suffered no loss: it had, after all, not received the contractual performance to which it was entitled. He reasoned that the 'promisee had suffered financial loss because he had to spend money to give him the benefit of the bargain which the defendant had promised but failed to deliver'.[39] His Lordship gave an example of a matrimonial home owned by the wife, which requires a new roof. The husband (the sole earner) contracts with a builder to do the work, but it is done defectively, such that the husband has to call in and pay another builder to do the work. As Lord Griffiths opined:

[i]s it to be said that the husband has suffered no loss because he does not own the property? Such a result would in my view be absurd and the answer is that the husband has suffered loss because he did not receive the bargain for which he had contracted with the first builder and the measure of damages is the cost of securing the performance of that bargain by completing the roof repairs properly by the second builder.[40]

Lord Griffiths's approach has subsequently received judicial[41] and academic[42] support and is likely to prove a significant development in the search for adequate protection of the contractual performance interest.

The third (and related) example of recent attempts to improve the deficient protection of the performance interest is seen in the recent legislation to reform the doctrine of privity so as to permit non-contracting parties to enforce contractual promises made for their benefit.[43] The privity principle has long been regarded as defeating the expectations, not just of third parties, but also of the contracting parties themselves, who will henceforth be able to confer a legally enforceable benefit to a third party by contract.

So deficiencies in the compensatory measure are being tackled directly by the English courts and by Parliament, but of course the process is by

---

[39] Ibid. at 96.   [40] Ibid. at 97.

[41] Notably by Steyn LJ in *Darlington Borough Council v. Witshier Northern Ltd* [1995] 1 WLR 68 and by the Court of Appeal in *Alfred McAlpine Construction Ltd v. Panatown Ltd* (1998) 88 Business LR 67.

[42] Coote, 'Contract Damages' and McKendrick, 'Breach of Contract'.

[43] The Contract (Rights of Third Parties) Act 1999, introduced following the recommendation of the Law Commission's Report *Privity of Contract: Contracts for the Benefit of Third Parties* (Law Com No. 242, 1996).

no means complete.[44] It remains to be considered whether the addition of restitutionary damages for breach of contract will make a useful, albeit indirect, contribution to the process. This article will suggest that restitutionary damages are a blunt and unsuitable instrument for remedying defects in the compensatory measure, and cannot be justified in this role.

V. Restitutionary damages to protect contractual expectations?

In general terms, three difficulties with the *Blake* approach to restitutionary damages can be identified. First, it is surely neater and more transparent to reform deficiencies in the compensatory measure directly, if that is the sole justification for remedial changes. Secondly, the restitutionary approach articulated in *Blake* will not necessarily cure the ills of an inadequate compensatory measure in the examples given by the Court of Appeal, since those ills are not necessarily dependent on or connected with any gain having been made by the defendant. Thirdly, it is clear that there are significant (perhaps even greater) deficiencies in the measure of compensatory damages, with performance undervalued and undercompensated, in areas other than the two exceptional examples given in *Blake*. These observations can be explained by considering the two *Blake* examples in more detail.

1. Skimped performance of services

This category was described by the Court of Appeal in *Blake* as follows: 'This is where the defendant fails to provide the full extent of the services which he has contracted to provide and for which he has charged the plaintiff.'[45] The Court gave as an example the well-known US case of *City of New Orleans v. Firemen's Charitable Association*.[46] In this case, the plaintiff paid the defendant to provide a fire-fighting service for a number of years, with the contract specifying how many men and horses should be kept available and how much hosepipe. At the end of the contract period, the plaintiff discovered that that the defendant had failed to keep available the specified men, horses or length of hosepipe, thereby saving itself over

---

[44] Problems remain, including the lack of a principled basis for assessing Ruxley 'loss of amenity' awards, and the reluctance of the courts to award damages for non-financial loss resulting from breach of employment contracts: see *Addis v. Gramophone Co. Ltd* [1909] AC 488 and *Johnson v. Unisys Ltd* [1999] 1 All ER 854.
[45] [1998] 1 All ER 833 at 845.   [46] (1891) 9 So 486.

$40,000. However, as the plaintiff could not demonstrate that the defendant's breach had prevented it extinguishing any fires, the Supreme Court of Louisiana held that the plaintiff had suffered no loss and was thus not entitled to damages. For the Court of Appeal in *Blake*, 'justice surely demands an award of substantial damages in such a case, and the amount of expenditure which the defendant has saved by the breach provides an appropriate measure of damages'.[47]

It is undoubtedly true that, as the Court observed, justice requires that the Supreme Court's refusal to award substantial damages should be reconsidered.[48] However, the Court of Appeal in *Blake* did not pause to consider whether the conclusion that the plaintiff suffered no loss is correct, moving immediately to a clarion call for restitutionary damages. The Supreme Court of Louisiana stressed that the defendant's breach did not prevent any fires being extinguished, so that the plaintiff lost nothing through incineration. But this fact was in reality irrelevant, since the plaintiff was not alleging breach of a warranty that fires would be extinguished or any similar guarantee of success.[49] The plaintiff's claim was simpler: I did not get the performance which I was promised and for which I paid.

It seems clear that the principal reason for feeling unease at the result in *City of New Orleans* is that the plaintiff did not get what he paid for and only secondarily that the defendant made a profit as a result. This emphasis is inherent in the very word, 'skimped', chosen by the Court of Appeal to describe this sort of case. The conclusion that the plaintiff in a *City of New Orleans* situation (who did not get the level of service he bargained and paid for) has suffered no loss reveals an extremely restrictive conception of loss, disregarding the plaintiff's performance interest entirely. In a pure services case of this kind it is difficult to apply standard rules of loss quantification: the breach was 'once and for all' so it cannot be 'cured' or disposed of by way of mitigation, but such features do not negate the character of the loss. If anything, they enhance it. So it is in the definition of loss that the defect in *City of New Orleans* is found, and that definition which should therefore be the target of reform.

---

[47] [1998] 1 All ER 833 at 845.
[48] Arguably the greatest difficulty of facts of this kind is English law's refusal to countenance the return of part of the price paid, on the basis of partial failure of consideration: see, for example, *Stocznia Gdanska SA v. Latvian Shipping Co.* [1998] 1 WLR 574. This vitally important issue is, however, beyond the scope of this article.
[49] I am most grateful to Lord Hope of Craighead for this point, made in discussions following the original presentation of this paper.

The narrowness of the concept of loss adopted in *City of New Orleans* (and seemingly endorsed by the Court of Appeal) can be seen if it is contrasted with the treatment of contracts involving the provision of goods. There is no denial of the genuineness of the plaintiff's loss when the defendant provides inferior goods, just because the plaintiff does not want the goods for resale or other profitable purposes, but for personal use or consumption. Likewise, if the defendant delivers goods of inferior quality, it is no defence to an action for damages for breach of warranty that they nonetheless 'do the job' that the plaintiff intends for them, or that the plaintiff did not notice the difference until it is too late to reject the goods.[50] An example might be a contract for the purchase of vintage champagne, which the seller breaches by supplying sparkling wine: no one doubts that the plaintiff has suffered a loss, even if he or his guests consume the sparkling wine happily without noticing the difference.

It is therefore surprising to find the Court of Appeal in *Blake* assuming that the 'no loss' conclusion in a skimped services case like *City of New Orleans* correctly represents modern English law, and equally surprising that the solution proposed is one which focuses not on the plaintiff's loss but the defendant's gain. For, looked at from the opposite angle, would a restitutionary measure attack the gist of the compensatory inadequacy which the Court took as its justification? It seems on reflection to be unlikely: the general unease that the conception of loss adopted in *City of New Orleans* was inappropriately narrow would exist, even if the defendant had made no appreciable saving from breach. The plaintiff's performance interest would be equally deserving of protection, whatever the particular circumstances of the defendant's breach.

So a plaintiff in a 'skimped performance' case would still have been overcharged and suffered a loss even if, to take a modern example, all the security men engaged to guard his factory had sat around drinking tea and playing cards, instead of providing the contractually specified security services, or if the notorious New Orleans firemen had taken the opportunity to go on a training course for the duration of the plaintiff's contract, using all the specified equipment for this purpose instead. Yet if the defendant's saving is not at the root of the impetus for substantial damages, restitutionary damages begin to appear as a somewhat haphazard way to remedy inappropriately narrow conceptions of loss in the contractual context.

---

[50] Sale of Goods Act 1979, s. 53(3). A buyer can 'recover the difference between the actual value of the goods and their value as warranted, even where he buys for use': P. S. Atiyah, *The Sale of Goods* (by J. Adams, 9th edn, 1995), 495.

Thus the first two objections to the reasoning in *Blake*, identified above, can be levelled at the example and analysis of skimped performance. Likewise, the skimped performance example illustrates the third objection, namely that it is difficult to justify *restricting* the example on the reasoning offered by the Court. There are significant deficiencies in the compensatory measure, with performance undervalued and undercompensated, in related areas outside the 'skimped performance' category as defined by the Court.

For one thing, it is by no means clear what the term 'skimped performance', as used by the Court of Appeal, is meant to encompass. Is it confined to pure services with no end product (like the *City of New Orleans* situation) or could it be used where corners are cut in building work (perhaps by using less expensive materials than those specified) or the provision of goods made to order? What of the case where a building or other contractor saves or makes money by not finishing the specified performance? There will generally be a satisfactory compensatory measure based on the cost of cure in such an example, but not necessarily.[51]

A good example of an unsatisfactory compensatory measure in a case of this kind is the decision in *Tito v. Waddell (No. 2)*,[52] yet it is not clear whether this would fit into the skimped performance category. If not, it is a narrow and extremely exclusive category (essentially the *City of New Orleans* 'pure services' model only). Yet if it is within the category, it is open to the same observations concerning the performance interest that have already been made.

They are that, once again, the unease felt about *Tito v. Waddell (No. 2)* is summed up in the objection that the judge's small award of damages (based on the difference in economic value between the unplanted and planted island) failed fully to protect the islanders' performance interest, their 'consumer surplus'.[53] Their expectation was performance, not the economic value of performance, and damages should therefore have been calculated by reference to the amenity value *they* placed on their paradise home. Once again, this is a deficiency in the compensatory measure, best

---

[51] *Ruxley Electronics and Construction Ltd v. Forsyth* [1996] AC 344.

[52] [1977] Ch 106. Here, the plaintiffs were the residents of Ocean Island, who had agreed to allow the British Phosphate Commissioners to mine for phospate on the island, on condition that the island be restored to its former state at the end of the licence period. In breach of contract, the defendant did not carry out its replanting obligation. Megarry J (at 328-38) refused to award to islanders the cost of curing the breach (estimated at A$73,140 per acre) but confined them to the diminution in the market value of the island, a tiny fraction of the cost of replanting.

[53] Harris, Ogus and Phillips, 'Contract Remedies', 592-4.

addressed directly, rather than one necessarily related to the defendant's saving.

The Court in *Blake* indicated that it is often possible to resolve problems of skimped performance by 'presuming that the plaintiff has suffered a loss of an amount corresponding to the amount by which he has been overcharged' and to justify it by 'invoking the notion of the consumer surplus', but concluded that it 'would surely be preferable, as well as simpler and more open, to award restitutionary damages'.[54] This, with respect, reveals a misunderstanding of the notion of consumer surplus, which represents part of the plaintiff's expectation, not necessarily linked to the defendant's gain. The argument reflects a general trend to regard a restitutionary analysis as *inevitably* a simpler and less convoluted way of explaining exceptional loss-based awards such as the cost of cure or the consumer surplus.

This is not so. A restitutionary analysis *can* explain exceptional awards protecting the performance interest (such as damages based on the cost of cure), but only coincidentally. Likewise, the consumer surplus concept is relevant to valuing the plaintiff's performance interest, regardless of any gain to the defendant. This is evident from the paradigm instance of the consumer surplus cited in textbooks, the loss of wedding photographs through the photographer's default,[55] as well as from the *Ruxley* context of defective building work intended to increase the plaintiff's pleasure, privacy or amenity rather than his economic position.

This lack of equivalence is sometimes overlooked by those eager to advocate a restitutionary measure for contract damages. For example, in the article cited with approval in *Blake*,[56] Peter Birks noted the suggestion made by Donald Harris, Anthony Ogus and Jennifer Phillips that expectation awards should include protection of the plaintiff's consumer surplus, but remarked: 'This subtlety is not necessary; open recognition of the possibility of restitutionary damages would give the plaintiff the enrichment of the defendant – i.e. the saving made by him in not keeping his promise.'[57] This observation was made in the context of *Tito v. Waddell (No. 2)* and of *Radford v. De Froberville*,[58] the latter being a case in which the defendant's failure to build a wall, which he had covenanted with the plaintiff to build, made no difference to the

---

[54] [1998] 1 All ER 833 at 845–6.   [55] See the Scots case *Diesen v. Samson* 1971 SLT 49.
[56] Birks, 'Restitutionary Damages', 421.
[57] *Ibid.*, 432. See also 423, describing the notion of the consumer surplus as 'sophisticated manipulation' of the compensatory principle.
[58] [1977] 1 WLR 1262.

market value of the plaintiff's property, but where the cost of cure was awarded.[59]

Yet it is only in this precise sort of case where the consumer surplus can, coincidentally, be equated with the saving to the contractor, because the contractor has done absolutely nothing. The majority of cases where a consumer surplus or cost of cure award is merited will not involve the same equivalence. Put the other way round, just because there is no saving to a contractor does not mean that there is no justification for fuller protection of the plaintiff's unfulfilled expectation.

A more vivid illustration would be to imagine that the replanting had been done, but done dreadfully, by the defendants in *Tito v. Waddell (No. 2)*: presumably the island would once again have experienced nothing but a small diminution in economic, market value but this time there would be no appreciable saving to the contractor either. But the plaintiff's performance interest, its consumer surplus, would still have been unfulfilled and undercompensated by a measure of damages tied to the diminution in market value. It is this recurrent feature of English law which merits a judicial solution[60] and which only coincidentally involves examination of the defendant's gains.

2. Making profit by doing the very thing promised not to do

The second category of case regarded by the Court in *Blake* as meriting a restitutionary award is 'where the defendant has obtained its profit by doing the very thing which he contracted not to do'.[61] Beyond this description, the Court gave no examples of cases it regarded as falling within the category.

In some ways this category is less problematic than the first, since it bears a superficial resemblance to the restrictive covenant line of cases discussed above.[62] However, this makes it all the more surprising to find the category created with no mention of that line of authority. Indeed, the only reference is to *Wrotham Park*, described a little earlier in the judgment as a case where 'the defendant's gain (or saving of expense) is used as a

---

[59] Opposite results were reached in the two cases because of evidence in *Radford v. De Froberville* that the plaintiff intended to build the wall. In contrast, Megarry V-C decided that the plaintiffs in *Tito v. Waddell (No. 2)* had no intention to replant and could thus not claim the cost of doing so. This reasoning is described by Birks as an 'important artificiality': 'Restitutionary Damages', 431.
[60] One possible solution might be a *Ruxley* 'loss of amenity' award.
[61] [1998] 1 All ER 833 at 846.
[62] *Wrotham Park* (see n. 9, above); *Bredero* (see n. 12, above) and *Jaggard v. Sawyer* (see n. 10, above).

measure of the plaintiff's loss',[63] accompanied by the observation that, because of the equivalence of loss and gain, it is matter of controversy whether the 'reasonable sum' awarded is restitutionary or compensatory. The Court went on to criticise those who insist that it is restitutionary but regard the measure as exceptional based only on the proprietary nature of claim,[64] on the basis that 'the measure of damages cannot depend on whether the proceedings are between the original parties to the contract or their successors in title'.[65] Beyond this eminently sensible observation, there is no further reference to the restrictive covenant cases and the Court's attitude to them is impossible to glean. Is the Court in *Blake* suggesting that the cases are adequately explained in compensatory terms or, as seems more likely,[66] that they should be regarded as examples of restitutionary relief within this second category?

The puzzle is this. The second category – cases of making a profit by doing the very thing promised not to do – would encompass not just *Wrotham Park* (where damages based on a reasonable sum to release the covenant were awarded) but also *Bredero* (where such damages were denied).[67] The Court of Appeal in *Jaggard v. Sawyer* provided an explanation of the seemingly inconsistent result in *Bredero* in compensatory terms. This was essentially that substantial damages are awarded in lieu of an injunction because the plaintiff's rights derived from the covenant have been expropriated by the denial of injunctive relief. However, in *Bredero* the plaintiff itself rendered its rights under the covenant valueless by not seeking an injunction, suing only after the defendant had disposed of the additional

---

[63] [1998] 1 All ER 833 at 844.
[64] The defendant in *Wrotham Park* was not the original party to the covenant but was a subsequent owner of the adjoining land, which was burdened by the restrictive covenant as to the use of the land by virtue of its registration under the Land Charges Act 1972. In contrast, the *Bredero* defendant was the original covenantor.
[65] [1998] 1 All ER 833 at 845.
[66] Although the Court seemed to regard the disgorgement of *all* the defendant's profits as the appropriate restitutionary measure for cases in the second category, which may suggest that the restrictive covenant cases (awarding merely a notional licence fee) were not intended to fall within this second category.
[67] The reasoning in *Bredero* itself is unconvincing; the judgments were unreserved and the judges did not speak with one voice, although all decided against substantial damages. Dillon LJ opted not to follow *Wrotham Park* on the basis that it was probably wrongly decided and could in any event be distinguished as an example of statutory compensatory damages in lieu of an injunction, a remedy which had not been sought by the plaintiff in *Bredero*. In contrast, according to Steyn LJ *Wrotham Park* was correct but represented an example of an exceptional restitutionary measure (based on 'invasion of property rights'), which was not justified on the facts of *Bredero*. Rose LJ agreed with both judgments.

houses (whereupon injunctive relief was impossible).[68] As Richard Nolan has argued:

the local authorities had lost the chance to bargain away the threat of injunctive enforcement of the covenant through their own deliberate delay in bringing proceedings. In such circumstances, it is perfectly plausible to say that the local authorities were the authors of their own loss: they were responsible for their own loss of opportunity.[69]

Millett LJ's reasoning in *Jaggard v. Sawyer* is certainly consistent with the orthodox view of contractual performance in terms of economic value only. Moreover, on this view, *without* the availability of an injunction to give 'bargaining' value to the covenant, the 'lost opportunity to bargain' justification for substantial damages has a tendency to circularity: the covenant only has economic value if substantial damages will be awarded and damages will be awarded because the covenant is valuable.[70] However, as academic commentators have noted,[71] the *Jaggard v. Sawyer* justification of the result in *Bredero* is open to the criticism that the availability of one sort of remedy – damages – should not be dependent on whether the plaintiff has sought an entirely different, specific remedy. Arguably, a compensatory award can be justified without reference to whether a specific remedy has been sought or is available, on the basis that, either way, the plaintiff's performance interest should be respected. This broader approach regards the right to contractual performance as valuable whether or not an injunction is sought to protect it directly and would, of course, serve to justify substantial damages in *Bredero* as well as in *Wrotham Park*.

Despite academic arguments of this kind, it is clear that the prevailing judicial explanation of the restrictive covenant cases is in compensatory not restitutionary terms, and for this reason the second *Blake* category calls at least for some explanation. One such explanation might involve the familiar argument that a restitutionary justification for the restrictive covenant cases avoids the artificiality inherent in the 'lost opportunity to

---

[68] 'It is the ability to claim an injunction which gives the benefit of the covenant much of its value. If the plaintiff delays proceedings until it is no longer possible for him to obtain an injunction, he destroys his own bargaining position and devalues his right': *Jaggard v. Sawyer* [1995] 1 WLR 269 at 291 *per* Millett LJ.

[69] R. Nolan, 'Remedies for Breach of Contract: Specific Enforcement and Restitution', in: Rose (ed.), *Failure of Contracts*, chap. 3.

[70] Cf. R. Sharpe and S. M. Waddams, 'Damages for Lost Opportunity to Bargain', (1982) 2 *Oxford JLS* 290, 293.

[71] See, for example, L. Smith, 'Disgorgement of the Profits of Breach of Contract', (1994) 24 *Canadian Business Law Journal* 121, 137; Goodhart, 'Restitutionary Damages', 11–12.

bargain' analysis,[72] particularly in circumstances where it is clear that the plaintiff would not have agreed to release the covenant at any price.[73] This justification is not examined in *Blake* at all. Indeed, it is sidestepped by the Court's indication that the entirety of the defendant's profits should be disgorged.[74] More fundamentally, there is no recognition of the fact that the full disgorgement of profits proposed for a second category case is inconsistent with the *Wrotham Park* 'reasonable licence fee' measure.[75]

A further difficulty concerns the *scope* of the second category. It could be interpreted widely, or be confined very specifically to breaches of negative stipulations. As Mindy Chen-Wishart has pointed out:

> [a]rguably all breaches of contract involve the defendant doing something he had contracted not to do, namely depart from the contractual undertaking. But such an interpretation would take in the first case and make restitution generally available for breach of contract, contrary to the clear intention of the court. Thus, a plaintiff must establish the breach of a negative promise.[76]

Once again, this prompts the reflection that, if the impetus for a restitutionary measure comes from a desire to protect the performance interest from an inadequate compensatory measure, it is odd to confine relief to such cases. Consider, for example, the disputed 'anchor tenant' leasehold covenant in *Co-operative Insurance Society Ltd v. Argyll Stores (Holdings) Ltd*,[77] for which the House of Lords refused specific performance. It was phrased as a positive covenant ('to keep the demised premises open for retail trade') but could equally have been drafted in negative form ('not to close the business'). The failure of English law to enforce covenants to trade may be regarded by civilians as a paradigm example of the deficiency in the protection of the performance interest. Presumably the defendant closed the shop to minimise losses, which an accountant at least would regard

---

[72] See, for example, A. Burrows, *The Law of Restitution* (1993), 399 and P. Jaffey, 'Restitutionary Damages and Disgorgement', [1994] *Restitution LR* 30, 33–4.

[73] Although of course the same artificiality applies equally to a restitutionary justification, where recovery is explained as representing the saving to the defendant of the amount it would have had to pay for the release of the covenant.

[74] [1998] 1 All ER 833 at 846.

[75] This suggestion is problematic. A strict requirement of factual causation should serve to limit recovery to the saving to the defendant of the amount it would have had to pay for the release of the covenant: E. A. Farnsworth, 'Your Loss or My Gain? The Dilemma of the Disgorgement Principle in Breach of Contract', (1985) 94 *Yale LJ* 1339, 1343–50.

[76] M. Chen-Wishart, 'Restitutionary Damages for Breach of Contract', (1998) 114 *LQR* 363, 365.

[77] [1997] 3 All ER 297.

as making a profit, so might cases of this kind be included within the *Blake* second category?

As authority currently stands, they could not be so included. The approaches of the House of Lords in *Argyll* and the Court of Appeal in *Blake* could not have been more different, despite their obvious similarity in the sense that loss to the plaintiff would be difficult, even impossible, to quantify in orthodox terms.[78] First, the House of Lords in *Argyll* regarded the deliberate nature of the defendant's breach as irrelevant: it could not, as the Court of Appeal thought, justify departure from the orthodoxy that positive covenants to trade are protected only by compensatory damages, not an order for specific performance.[79] In contrast, although the Court in *Blake* accepted that a cynical, deliberate breach is not a sufficient condition for restitutionary damages, it impliedly regarded it as a necessary condition (at least under the second category).[80]

More significant is the House of Lords' emphasis in *Argyll* on the need to ensure that contractual remedies provide nothing more than compensation for the plaintiff. A prima facie entitlement to specific performance in this sort of case was therefore objectionable because a plaintiff could use it to hold out for more than the value of its loss and receive a windfall at the defendant's expense. As Lord Hoffmann said:

There is a further objection to an order requiring the defendant to carry on a business... That is that it may cause injustice by allowing the plaintiff to enrich himself at the defendant's expense. The loss which the defendant may suffer through having to comply with the order (for example, by running a business at a loss for an indefinite period) may be far greater than the plaintiff would suffer from the contract being broken.[81]

Of course, completely the opposite approach was suggested in *Blake*, which countenanced stripping the entirety of the defendant's profit and transferring it to the plaintiff. This may well be justifiable as a response to a *criminal* breach of the Official Secrets Act (and this was the final decision in *Blake*) but is less justifiable for breaches of negative stipulations generally. Is such a generous windfall to the plaintiff the most appropriate way

---

[78] In *Argyll*, the plaintiff landlord would not have suffered any immediate financial loss from the closure of the 'anchor' supermarket in its shopping mall because, although fewer customers might have been drawn into the mall thereafter, the landlord's rental income from the remaining tenants would not change initially. The closure would only have an adverse impact on rental income at the next rent review for each of the remaining leases (which would most likely only permit 'upwards' review), by which time the defendant's breach would be extremely difficult to single out as the cause of identifiable financial loss.
[79] [1997] 3 All ER 297 at 307.   [80] Above, 331.   [81] [1997] 3 All ER 297 at 304–5.

to protect the plaintiff's performance interest here, when the equivalent was denied in *Argyll*?

This contrast seems particularly glaring when one considers that, in England, specific relief is virtually always available for breach of a negative stipulation,[82] yet not for breach of a positive stipulation (such as the trading covenant in *Argyll*). This would tend to suggest that the deficiencies in orthodox contractual remedies are *greater* in the case of positive stipulations. In other words, if restitutionary remedies are justified only where the usual remedial scheme is deficient, a plaintiff (such as the Crown) who could in theory have sued for an injunction, but chose not to, is arguably less deserving of a restitutionary remedy than a plaintiff without any possibility of specific relief.

VI. Conclusion

This chapter has advanced one modest thesis,[83] namely that restitutionary damages cannot be justified as filling gaps where a compensatory measure offers inadequate protection of the plaintiff's performance interest. That is not to say that there may not be an *independent* justification for a restitutionary measure for breach of contract in certain circumstances,[84] merely that any such justification cannot be derived from the compensatory basis offered in *Blake*. Once again, it is important to remember that one of the huge benefits of recent English restitutionary scholarship has been the stripping away of legal fictions and the quest for appropriate categorisation of remedies and causes of action. It is with this in mind that I remain uneasy at the promotion of restitutionary answers to compensatory problems.

---

[82] See, for example, *Lumley v. Wagner* (1852) 1 De G M & G 604.

[83] For a thorough and convincing examination of a number of other restitutionary issues raised by the judgment, see Chen-Wishart, 'Restitutionary Damages'.

[84] Arguments might be founded on the role of restitutionary damages to protect 'facilitative institutions', which could be said to include 'contract' (cf. I. M. Jackman, 'Restitution for Wrongs', (1989) 48 *CLJ* 302) or on the undesirability of distinguishing between invasion of property and contractual rights. The latter argument, raised in discussion following presentation of this paper, is problematic, since, unlike tangible property, contractual rights are artificial, legal constructs. If the prevailing legal regime regards contractual rights as carrying an entitlement to protection of expectations only, then it is fallacious to reason that, since they resemble other forms of property, they must necessarily also carry an entitlement to disgorgement of gains (awarded on interference with proprietary rights).

13 Encroachments: between private and public

Hanoch Dagan

I. The egg-washing machine

The celebrated case of *Olwell v. Nye & Nissen*[1] has become one of the legends of the law of restitution. Olwell sold his interest in an egg-packing corporation to Nye & Nissen. By the terms of the sale, he was to retain full ownership in an egg-washing machine formerly used by that corporation. Olwell stored the machine in a space adjacent to the premises occupied by Nye & Nissen. Nye & Nissen, without Olwell's knowledge or consent, took the egg-washer out of storage and used it for the next three years in the regular course of its business. Olwell was not materially damaged, since the egg-washing machine was not injured by Nye & Nissen's operation during that period, and Olwell never claimed any title to it. Hence, Olwell sued Nye & Nissen in quasi-contract, waiving his conversion suit. He sought to recover the profits that inured to Nye & Nissen as a result of its wrongful use of the machine.

The Supreme Court of Washington held that, though no material harm had been done, Nye & Nissen was none the less liable for the benefit it had captured. More precisely, given the scarcity of labour immediately after the outbreak of World War II, the Court held that the captured benefit itself was the amount Nye & Nissen saved in labour costs by using Olwell's machine.[2]

In a recent paper, Professor Ernest Weinrib severely criticised the *Olwell* Court.[3] In Weinrib's view the Court committed two interrelated conceptual

I am grateful to Elizabeth Milnikel for research assistance and Trudy Feldkamp for secretarial support.

[1] 173 P 2d 652 (Washington 1946).

[2] None the less, the Supreme Court eventually reduced the judgment that was based on this calculation, because it exceeded the amount prayed for by the plaintiff.

[3] Ernest J. Weinrib, 'Restitutionary Damages as Corrective Justice', (1999) 1 *Theoretical Inquiries in Law* 1.

errors. First, 'the Court rejected the correct benefit', that is, the value of use or the rental value of the machine. Secondly, 'in focusing on the expense of hand-washing the eggs, the Court accepted the wrong benefit'. Indeed, in Weinrib's view, cases of unauthorised use justify only the measure of recovery of fair market value, as opposed to any measure based on the actual profit that the defendant derived from the encroachment.[4]

Weinrib insists that his objection is not technical; rather, it is based on the most fundamental attributes of the restitutionary doctrine governing cases of encroachment. For Weinrib, this doctrine is premised on the Aristotelian notion of corrective justice. Corrective justice, explains Weinrib,

> requires that the remedy reflect the wrong and that the wrong consist in a breach of duty by the defendant with respect to the plaintiff's right. The role of damages within this framework is to make good the failure of the defendant to carry out his or her duty to the plaintiff. Basing the damages in *Olwell* on the cost of hand-washing the eggs implies that the defendant was under an obligation to the plaintiff to wash the eggs by hand. This is absurd. The plaintiff had a right in the machine but no right in hand-washed eggs. The only relevant duty that the defendant owed the plaintiff was not to use the machine. Accordingly, the damages should have been set at the value of the use.[5]

To be sure, Weinrib does not deny that but for the encroachment 'the defendant would have had the eggs washed by hand'. But he insists that 'that is no concern of the plaintiff'. In other words, for Weinrib 'whatever the alternatives to using the machine and however probable their employment, none of them forms the basis for calculating the damages, because in principle none is directly relevant to the injustice between the parties'. In *Olwell*, because 'the injustice consists in the unauthorized use of the plaintiff's property, the damages are to be calculated with reference to the value of the use'. The benefit of the savings gained by using the plaintiff's property rather than an alternative is 'external to the juridical relationship' and therefore irrelevant.

Olwell is an important case for Weinrib. For him, it demonstrates the way in which failing to take the adjective 'private' in 'private law' seriously leads to grave mistakes. To respect the central idea of private law, which makes private law 'a moral possibility', the defendant's liability must be restricted to the plaintiff's entitlement. Likewise, the bilateral logic, inherent in private law, requires that the specific remedy be 'the

---

[4] For the purposes of this article, 'encroachments' can be loosely defined as invasions to or derogations from other people's entitlements.
[5] Weinrib, 'Restitutionary Damages', 20.

notional equivalent at the remedial stage of the right that has been wrongly infringed'. *Olwell* violates this injunction, explains Weinrib, because it resorts to factors that are extrinsic to the relationship between the plaintiff and the defendant. Depriving the defendant of its net profits promotes the *social* purpose of deterrence, which cannot be accommodated within the correlative nature of private-law justifications.

Is the *Olwell* plaintiff indeed entitled, as a conceptual matter, only to the fair market value of the unauthorised use of his egg-washing machine? Is deterrence necessarily extrinsic to the juridical relationship between plaintiff and defendant? Can the restitutionary doctrine governing encroachments be strictly private, isolated from any broader, public considerations?

This article seeks to demonstrate that the answer to these three questions is negative. It shows that the choice between the measure of recovery applied by the *Olwell* Court and the one supported by Weinrib is normative, rather than conceptual. It claims that deterrence may be intrinsic to the relationship between plaintiff and defendant, although it concedes that it is not necessarily the case that it is. Finally, it maintains that although private law is not just another mode of regulation, indistinguishable from a host of other public-law regimes, it cannot be a socially isolated segment of law. The restitutionary doctrine governing encroachments lies between private and public.

I hope to vindicate these claims through an analysis of three distinct questions of restitution in encroachment settings. Section II discusses the broad category of cases of unilateral appropriation of another's resource. Section III deals with the availability of restitutionary damages in the context of breaches of contract. Finally, the article concludes with a discussion of another celebrated case, *Snepp v. United States*,[6] the leading case on restitutionary damages for breach of fiduciary duties.

II. Appropriation of another person's resource

The doctrine of restitution for wrongs covers a wide variety of appropriation cases: these cases involve encroachments to land and chattels; copyright, trademark and patent; trade secrets, contractual relations and performances, and pre-contractual expectations; individual reputation and dignity; commercial attributes of personality; and even identity and physical integrity.

---

[6] 444 US 507 (1980).

Not all encroachments lead to the same measure of recovery. On the contrary, different measures of recovery apply to different resources.[7] Thus, there are resources with respect to which the sheer appropriation triggers a rather severe measure of recovery, which allows the plaintiff to choose between the fair market value of the resource or of its unauthorised use and the net profit gained by the invader. In American law, this is the case respecting encroachments that invade the plaintiff's identity, physical integrity or land. On the other hand, there are resources the invasion of which triggers pecuniary recovery only if the defendant employed improper means. Thus, the sheer appropriation of trade secrets or pre-contractual expectations triggers no liability. In between these poles there are several other interesting points. Thus, the appropriation of copyright allows the plaintiff to choose between the fair market value of the copyright at issue and a proportional part of the defendant's profits. On the other hand, the appropriation of patents allows a plaintiff only the measure of recovery of fair market value.[8]

This diversity of measures of recovery respecting divergent resources is neither chaotic nor unprincipled. Rather, it reflects the differing degrees to which a community perceives those resources as constitutive of their possessor's identity. Thus, the more closely a resource is attached to its holder's identity in her society, the greater is the degree of protection accorded to such a resource, and vice versa.

Studying the normative underpinnings of the various possible measures of recovery in cases of appropriation helps to refine this point. These measures range from requiring that the plaintiff receive compensation for the harm she has suffered (a rare measure of recovery in American law) to awarding the plaintiff the profits realised by the defendant at the plaintiff's expense, and they also include several intermediate possibilities, the most frequently used of which is the fair market value of the resource involved. My claim is that the legal choice among these pecuniary remedies is not a matter of legal technicality or of pure conceptual analysis. Instead, it requires a choice between competing values.[9]

For example, the measure of profits deters non-consensual invasions, thereby vindicating the cherished libertarian value, control. Entitling the

---

[7] This fact was first illuminated in Daniel Friedmann, 'Restitution of Benefits Obtained through the Appropriation of Property or the Commission of a Wrong', (1980) 80 *Columbia LR* 504, 512–13, 556–7.
[8] For a fuller account see Hanoch Dagan, *Unjust Enrichment: A Study of Private Law and Public Values* (1997), chap. 4.
[9] This is an abbreviated account of a long discussion in *ibid.*, chap. 2.

resource-holder to any net profit the invader may acquire from the appropriation takes the sting out of the forced transfer. It thus discourages potential invaders from circumventing the bargaining process and appropriating the protected interest without first securing its holder's consent. Therefore, a profits remedy implies that transfers are legitimate only by obtaining the plaintiff's *ex ante* consent, thus vindicating the plaintiff's liberty to control her entitlement.

Prescribing a remedy of fair market value is importantly different. It does not seek to deter appropriations – at times, it may even encourage them. Fair market value is what the defendant would presumably have had to pay to the plaintiff had she not circumvented the bargaining process, even if the plaintiff's consent to the transfer is taken for granted. The fair market value of an entitlement measures – since no better proxy is available – its (objective) level of well-being or utility to its holder. Thus, fair market value is aimed at securing (merely) the utility that is embodied in the appropriated resource. An award of fair market value vindicates the utilitarian value of well-being.

Finally, recovery limited to compensation for the harm suffered responds to the claim of the appropriator to a share of the entitlement of the resource-holder, as long as the former does not actually diminish the latter's estate. A harm-based measure of recovery vindicates the value of sharing; it is a form of limited institutionalised altruism, a legal device that calls for other-regarding action and seeks to inculcate other-regarding motives.

Consider now the three claims I set out to vindicate in section I, relating to the egg-washing case. First, consider the choice between profits and fair market value as a remedy. Weinrib's complaint to the *Olwell* Court is based on the claim that different measures of recovery *must* apply to unauthorised alienation and unauthorised use. Weinrib insists that profits from beneficial unauthorised *alienation* should be available to plaintiffs because they are intrinsic to the concept of property, whereas when unauthorised *use* is at issue, only the value of this use is within the ambit of the plaintiff's entitlement. This is, I concede, a possible interpretation of the owner's bundle of rights. But it is by no means necessary. The concept of property is much too indeterminate and value-laden to yield such a precise conclusion. Property is an essentially contested concept which can be, and has been, modified in accordance with human needs and values.[10]

---

[10] See Jeremy Bentham, *The Theory of Legislation* (trans. R. Hildreth, ed. C. K. Ogden, 1931), 111–13; Fredrick G. Whelan, 'Property as Artifice: Hume and Blackstone', (1980) 22 *Nomos* 101.

Different conceptualisations of the owner's entitlement would yield other conclusions.[11]

Furthermore, there are good reasons why the law adopts other conceptualisations of the owner's entitlement that yield different conclusions. Thus, as seen above, it may well be the case that respecting certain resources we want to preserve the owner's control not only against possible unauthorised alienation, but also against unauthorised use. By the same token, for other resources we may want to limit the owner's entitlement to the well-being embodied in the holding.

It is important to emphasise that according a resource-holder the net profits derived from an encroachment, as opposed to another remedy, is by no means dependent on external factors. An effective deterrence of encroachments should not be deemed extrinsic to the parties' relationship. Rather, such a profit-based award vindicates the resource-holder's control, which is part and parcel of the content and meaning of her entitlement. In other words, where we opt for structuring the entitlement of the holders of a certain resource around the model of libertarian rights, deterrence is an entailment of the entitlement to control, and is thus intrinsic, rather than extrinsic, to the parties' relationship. On the other hand, if we decide to structure the entitlement on the utilitarian model, the only legitimate claim of the plaintiff respecting the resource is to the well-being that it embodies, and therefore to the fair market value of its use or alienation.

The choice between fair market value and profits – between preserving well-being and deterring encroachments – is normative, not conceptual. Both measures of recovery, and many others, may be within the entitlement of the resource-holder, and thus cannot be ruled out by reference to the central characteristic of private-law litigation, that it is limited to facts of the two-party relationship.

Implicitly I have by now already vindicated my third main claim: that the restitutionary doctrine governing encroachment cases lies between private and public.[12] It is affected by the structure of private law as a drama between a particular plaintiff and a particular defendant, which requires correlativity between the defendant's liability and the specific measure of recovery imposed on her on the one hand, and the plaintiff's entitlement on the other hand. This does not, however, entail the isolation

---

[11] See Kenneth J. Vandevelde, 'The New Property of the Nineteenth Century: The Development of the Modern Concept of Property', (1980) 29 *Buffalo LR* 325; Joseph W. Singer, 'Legal Realism Now', (1988) 67 *California LR* 467, 491.

[12] For an extended discussion of this point see Hanoch Dagan, 'The Distributive Foundation of Corrective Justice', (1999) 98 *Michigan LR* 138.

of the doctrine from public values. The *ex ante* entitlements from which this correlativity must be measured are best analysed through a public lens. Only an open discussion of the underlying social values can explain – and maybe even justify – the law of encroachments.

To be sure, this discussion does not necessarily vindicate *Olwell*. *Olwell* may well be a mistake. But if it is such, it is not a result of a conceptual confusion. Rather, it may seen mistaken on the view that an owner of a chattel – or at least an owner of a commercial chattel such as an egg-washing machine – should not have been accorded an entitlement to control her resource; that, for example, a protection of the well-being embodied in such a resource is more appropriate. In order to criticise *Olwell*, in other words, it is necessary to resort to explicit normative persuasion.

III. Breach of contract

The question whether restitutionary damages can supplement traditional contract remedies for breach of contract is situated at the frontier of contractual and restitutionary liability. The traditional common-law approach to the issue excluded the promisor's profits from breach as a remedy for most breaches of contract.[13] But recently this approach has been destabilised. The Israeli Supreme Court has led a movement to revolutionise this area of the common law[14] – a movement that has enjoyed some sympathy in various jurisdictions.[15] The revolutionary approach advocated in Israel would enable promisees to pursue the profits derived by promisors through a breach of contract as an alternative pecuniary remedy. The new approach would make the profits remedy available without distinguishing cases that involve a breach of fiduciary duties or the sale of 'unique goods' (such as land), while the traditional common-law approach allowed for such a remedy only in those circumstances. The new approach would allow a profits remedy even if the promisor's profits could not be said to approximate to the promisee's lost profits.

[13] See, e.g., *Surrey County Council v. Bredero Homes Ltd* [1993] 3 All ER 705; *Coca-Cola Bottling v. Coca-Cola* 988 F 2d 386 at 409 (3rd Cir, 1953); *Hospital Products v. US Surgical* (1984) 156 CLR 41 at 67–76, 118–19, 136–50.
[14] *Adras Building Material Ltd v. Harlow & Jones GmbH,* easily available in [1995] *Restitution LR* 235 (the decision is from 11 February 1988).
[15] See *Attorney-General v. Blake* [2000] 4 All ER 385; [1998] 1 All ER 833 at 844–6; *Earthinfo Inc. v. Hydrosphere Resource Consultants Inc.* 900 P 2d 113 (Colorado 1995). In both jurisdictions, however, it is still emphasised that the mere breach of contract is not sufficient to make the defendant accountable for benefits thereby obtained. Furthermore, *Earthinfo* is a case of restoring benefits conferred by the plaintiff, rather than benefits derived from the breach. Hence, the rule it announces respecting the latter issue is not binding.

Analysed in the framework of the discussion of the previous section, the traditional rules seem clearly preferable. Commercial goods, with respect to which no restitutionary damages are available, are held for instrumental purposes, and are, thus, fungible resources that are not constitutive of their holder's identity.[16] Unique goods – such as land – are very different. Traditionally, land has been one of the most prominent objects of property rights in Western culture, accorded a unique status as a symbol of the self and as a resource closely linked to personal freedom, rank and power.[17] Furthermore, while there is no doubt that contracts are significant forms of wealth in modern industrialised societies, they are also the consummate example of a characterless good. At most, one can speak of an expectation on the part of the promisee that she will develop a personal connection to the promissory resource; but such an expectation – and even the justified reliance it may entail – cannot be equated with an existing constitutive connection to a resource.[18]

These two distinctions – between commercial goods and unique goods, and between contractual rights and property rights – seem to vindicate the traditional rules. These rules reject any claim for the defendant's actual profits as a result of the breach of a regular contract. However, where unique goods (notably land) are at stake, an important exception is invoked and restitutionary damages are available.[19]

The unilateral appropriations framework of analysis just employed cannot be exclusive in the context of the debate over the availability of restitutionary damages for breach of contract. The contractual background is significant and it should therefore not be omitted from this discussion. Is it possible to find – if attention is focused on the ramifications of this

---

[16] Menachem Mautner, '"The Eternal Triangles of the Law": Toward a Theory of Priorities in Conflicts Involving Remote Parties', (1991) 90 *Michigan LR* 95, 123–4.

[17] Herbert McClosky and John Zaller, *The American Ethos: Public Attitudes toward Capitalism and Democracy* (1984), 138; Lynton K. Caldwell, 'Land and the Law: Problems in Legal Philosophy', 1986 *University of Illinois LR* 319, 320; Russell W. Belk, 'Possessions and the Extended Self', (1988) 15 *Journal of Consumer Research* 139, 153; Clare Cooper, 'The House as Symbol of the Self', in: Harold M. Proshansky et al. (eds.), *Environmental Psychology: People and Their Physical Settings* (2nd edn, 1976), 435, 437–8; E. Doyle McCarthy, 'Toward a Sociology of the Physical World: George Herbert Mead on Physical Objects', (1984) 5 *Studies in Symbolic Interaction* 105, 116–17; Margaret Jane Radin, 'Property and Personhood', (1982) 34 *Stanford LR* 957, 992, 1013.

[18] See Margaret Jane Radin, 'Residential Rent Control', (1986) 15 *Philosophy & Public Affairs* 350, 360–2.

[19] Law Commission, *Aggravated, Exemplary and Restitutionary Damages* (LCCP No. 132, 1993), 159; George E. Palmer, *The Law of Restitution* (1978 and Supp. 1997) § 4.9(a); P. D. Maddaugh and J. D. McCamus, *The Law of Restitution* (1990), 434–5; see also S. W. Waddams, 'Profits Derived from Breach of Contract: Damages or Restitution', (1997) 11 *Journal of Contract Law* 115, 121.

aspect of the issue – a doctrinal solution that will be isolated from public values? Is the contractual setting perhaps more amenable to a fruitful conceptual analysis for choosing between the measures of recovery of fair market value and profits than the appropriations setting was?

I suggest that the answer to these questions is, again, negative.[20] More precisely, I maintain that a principled resolution of these difficult questions can be founded only on a normative, public choice between an instrumental conception of contract (which supports the traditional rule) and a more co-operative alternative (which, actually, endorses a norm different from the Israeli revolutionary rule and from the traditional rule).

Consider first the connection between the instrumental conception of contract and the traditional common-law rule.[21] The traditional contract remedies, which are aimed at compensating the promisee for her loss, require information that tends to be available to the promisee-plaintiff. In contrast, the data required for establishing restitutionary damages are much less accessible to her. In order to recover the promisor's profits,

---

[20] The discussion that follows summarises my conclusions in Hanoch Dagan, 'Restitutionary Damages for Breach of Contract: An Exercise in Private Law Theory', (1999) 1 *Theoretical Inquiries in Law* 115.

[21] The conventional economic justification of the traditional rule is that the promisor is likely to derive more utility than the promisee from the entitlement to the profits of the breach since the promisor is generally in a better position to exploit opportunities to redirect the promissory resource. By dissociating the opportunity for profitable reallocation from the legal entitlement to utilise it, the Israeli rule structures the renegotiation between the promisor and promisee as a bilateral monopoly entailing heavy transaction costs that reduce the surplus from the reallocation and, thus, the promisor's expected gain (indeed, in extreme cases, the promisor may even forgo the efficient reallocation altogether). This analysis is premised upon the rationale that the incentive for (that is, the expected benefit from) attaining efficient resource allocation, and hence for searching for alternative buyers, should be assigned to the party in the best position to find them. It further assumes that the promisor, presumed to be in the business of selling this particular type of promissory resource, is such a 'best finder'. However, this is not necessarily the case. While there are, of course, cases in which such an assumption is valid (where the promisor is a merchant and the promisee a consumer), none the less, there are also numerous instances in which the promisee in fact has access to the market, and this access is not inferior – and, at times, may even be superior – to that of the promisor. See Alan Schwartz, 'The Case for Specific Performance', (1979) 89 *Yale LJ* 255, 284–7; Daniel Friedmann, 'The Efficient Breach Fallacy', (1989) 18 *Journal of Legal Studies* 1, 5; G. M. Cohen, 'The Fault Line in Contract Damages', (1994) 80 *Virginia LR* 1225, 1292–1304. The more common example of such a case is where the promisor is a producer and the promisee a wholesaler or a retailer, such that it is at least questionable as to whether the promisor, rather than the promisee, is the best finder of efficient reallocations. Less frequent examples are those that involve a consumer who sells merchandise to a merchant dealing in second-hand goods; in such a case, it is quite obvious that the promisee, and not the promisor, is the best finder.

the promisee is required to submit evidence regarding another's affairs. Furthermore, restitutionary damages require that difficult judgments be made regarding causation as well as attribution of specific profits (and, presumably, also costs) to one specific transaction out of all the undertakings of the promisor.[22] Contractual rights that rely on information that can be verified only at a prohibitively high cost are inefficient. They entail high litigation costs that are burdensome *ex post* and, even more significantly, create an *ex ante* uncertainty that commercial parties dislike.[23] An instrumental conception of contract that understands the contractual relationship in the classical, adversarial model of self-interested exchange would yield to this preference for maximising the material surplus of the contract. Thus, as argued above, it would resist any attempt to apply a profits remedy to breaches of contract.[24]

---

[22] E. Allan Farnsworth, 'Your Loss or My Gain? The Dilemma of the Disgorgement Principle in Breach of Contract', (1985) 94 *Yale LJ* 1339, 1350; Sidney W. DeLong, 'The Efficiency of a Disgorgement as a Remedy for the Breach of Contract', (1989) 22 *Indiana LR* 737, 772–3; J. Standen, 'The Fallacy of Full Compensation', (1995) 73 *Washington University Law Quarterly* 145, 171; Law Commission, *Aggravated, Exemplary and Restitutionary Damages*, 170; Waddams, 'Profits', 120.

[23] Alan Schwartz, 'Relational Contracts in the Courts: An Analysis of Incomplete Agreements and Judicial Strategies', (1992) 21 *Journal of Legal Studies* 271, 279–80; Hugh Collins, *The Law of Contract* (2nd edn, 1993), 367.

[24] The conventional approach to the impact of proof difficulties in the context discussed here leads to the opposite conclusion – i.e. to preferring the Israeli rule. That approach perceives the profits from breach as a substitute for the losses for which traditional contract remedies fail to compensate due to proof difficulties. See, e.g., Lord Goff of Chieveley and Gareth Jones, *The Law of Restitution* (5th edn, 1998), 518. This claim is correct, in so far as it warns against contingencies of undercompensation and also insists that there are cases (for example, where both parties operate in similar markets and with comparable skills) in which the profits that the promisor obtained from her breach can help in assessing the promisee's lost profits. In such instances, award of profits is an appropriate remedy for the difficulty of undercompensation. Indeed, as noted above, common-law jurisprudence has expressed no hesitancy in granting such an award, without subscribing to the Israeli revolutionary rule. Such a recovery, however, should not be available in any case where the promisor's profits are not a good – or even reasonable – proxy of the promisee's loss, and thus not a suitable solution for undercompensation. In such cases (such as where the promisor sells in a different market or where by the time the promisee covers in the market, the market price equals the contract price) liquidated damages are more appropriate than restitutionary damages. Only liquidated damages can credibly solve in these circumstances the difficulties to the promisee of proving the promisor's profits, and thus the problem of potential undercompensation to the promisee: liquidated damages would allow a promisee to assess (*ex ante*) the circumstances in which she may be undercompensated due to loss that can be verified *ex post* only at a prohibitively high cost. See Alan Schwartz, 'The Myth that Promisees Prefer Supracompensatory Damages: An Analysis of Contracting for Damage Measures', (1990) 100 *Yale LJ* 369.

This, however, is not the only possible conception of contract. A counter-vision of modern contract law perceives the contractual relationship (even in commercial settings) not only as a locus of competition or an instrument for the allocation of risks and the production of wealth, but also as a zone of mutual co-operation and confidence, dependence and vulnerability. This conception of the contractual relationship requires the parties to protect one another and care for each other. To be sure, the contractual parties are not required to prioritise the interests of the other side. But the pursuit of their self-interest must be constrained; they must respect the legitimate interests of their fellow contractors; their obligations to their contractual partners may deviate from those to which they explicitly committed themselves.[25]

This counter-vision of the contractual relationship rejects both the traditional rule limiting the promisee to the fair market value measure of recovery, and the revolutionary Israeli rule that allows a promisee to recover her promisor's net profits from the breach. The traditional rule must be rejected because it ignores the injunction to share both unexpected difficulties and unexpected benefits as they arise over the course of the contractual relationship. When the opportunity to sell at the better price materialises, the proper thing for the promisor to do, under this conception of contract, is to contact the promisee, make sure profits expected from breach are greater than the promisee's expected loss, and – if indeed it turns out that the alternative transaction is more efficient – share these profits with the promisee. The traditional rule is inappropriate because it implicitly sanctions the promisor's unilateral pursuit of her own interests, irrespective of the existing relationship she has already established with her contractual partner. It thus undermines the conception of contract as an area of interpersonal trust, solidarity and sharing.[26]

However, the co-operative conception of contract also entails rejecting a rule that entitles the promisee, as a matter of course, to the net profits the promisor derived from the breach. Such a rule would absolutely

---

[25] John Adams and Roger Brownsword, *Key Issues in Contract* (1995), 200–2, 215, 217, 220, 223–5, 301–3; Roberto M. Unger, 'The Critical Legal Studies Movement', (1983) 96 *Harvard LR* 561, 632, 639, 641–4; Hugh Collins, 'The Transformation Thesis and the Ascription of Contractual Liability', in: T. Wilhelmsson (ed.), *Perspectives of Critical Contract Law* (1993), 293, 306–7; J. M. Fineman, 'Critical Approaches to Contract Law', (1983) 30 *University of California at Los Angeles LR* 829, 837; Robert W. Gordon, 'Unfreezing Legal Reality: Critical Approaches to Law', (1987) 15 *Florida State University LR* 195, 206–8.

[26] Adams and Brownsword, *Key Issues*, 228–31, 302; Duncan Kennedy, 'Form and Substance in Private Law Adjudication', (1976) 89 *Harvard LR* 1685, 1734; Ian R. Mcneil, 'Efficient Breach of Contract: Circles in the Sky', (1982) 68 *Virginia LR* 947, 968–9; M. J. Trebilcock, *The Limits of Freedom of Contract* (1993), 142.

deter profitable deviations from the contract. A promisee who stubbornly insists on performance, where non-performance will not harm her in any way and performance would cause the promisor to lose a profitable opportunity, must be perceived – from the perspective of a co-operative understanding of contract – as abusing her rights. The Israeli rule grants a promisee a position of threatening leverage that can enable her to demand that the promisor purchase her release at a prohibitively high price and, at times, may even impede efficient reallocation of the promissory resource altogether. A rule that enables people to prevent others from improving their situations without any detrimental effect on anyone else cannot be required by (or correspond to) the values of trust, solidarity and sharing.[27]

While rejecting both the measures of fair market value and net profits, the co-operative conception of contract requires a third alternative. The appropriate measure of recovery according to this conception cannot be a rule of 'all or nothing', as are the two rules considered thus far, since any such binary rule is antithetical to the prescriptions of sharing unexpected difficulties and benefits. Hence, the co-operative conception of contract requires a third rule, which divides between the parties the efficiency gain of the reallocation (that is, the difference between the promisor's gain from the breach and the promisee's expectation interest).[28] This third possibility does not give the promisee the power to veto the beneficial alternative transaction and thus does not encourage her to take a threatening 'hold-out' stance. At the same time, this alternative does not disregard the parties' special commitment toward one another as contractual partners, and thus it requires that the promisor consider the interests of the promisee. In addition to compensating the promisee for her expectation interest, the promisor is required to share with her the unexpected benefits that arise over the course of their contractual relationship.[29]

---

[27] See, similarly, Robert W. Gordon, 'Macaulay, Macneil, and Discovery of Solidarity and Power in Contract Law', [1985] *Wisconsin LR* 565–9; Anthony T. Kronman, 'A New Champion for the Will Theory', (1981) 91 *Yale LJ* 404, 416.

[28] Other authors have also proposed such a division. See Daniel Friedmann, 'Good Faith and Remedies for Breach of Contract', in: Jack Beatson and Daniel Friedmann (eds.), *Good Faith and Fault in Contract Law* (1995), 399, 411–12; William Goodhart, 'Restitutionary Damages for Breach of Contract', (1995) 3 *Restitution LR* 3, 12–13.

[29] Implementing this approach can take two main forms: a precise rule that prescribes that in cases of this sort the parties should divide the reallocation profits into equal shares between them, or else a vague standard that would leave to the discretion of the court the decision as to how the reallocation profits are to be divided amongst the parties. The choice between these two types of norms requires difficult normative judgments which cannot be adequately addressed here. For my discussion of these issues see Dagan, 'Restitutionary Damages', 151–2.

Indeed, even turning from the framework of analysis of unilateral appropriations to the framework of analysis of contractual relationship, there are still difficult normative questions. Social values are required in order to establish the entitlements of the parties against which infringements are measured. Appreciating the significance of the pre-existing entitlements of the parties is crucial for analysing the restitutionary doctrine governing encroachments in particular, and of private law in general. These entitlements cannot be deduced logically from concepts or just presupposed by the analyst. Setting these entitlements requires instead explicit normative discussion.

IV. Agents as unauthorised authors

It is possible to reach similar conclusions by analysing the third, and last, sub-field of encroachment law: the doctrine governing breaches of fiduciary duties. Consider, for example, the celebrated United States Supreme Court case of *Snepp v. United States*.[30] Snepp was a CIA agent who published a book about certain CIA activities without submitting it to a pre-publication review. This was an unequivocal violation of an express term of the employment agreement he had signed. The Supreme Court approved the imposition of a constructive trust on the benefits gained thereby so that the CIA would receive all the profits from the book.[31] The premise of this remedial response was the 'extremely high degree of trust' reposed in Snepp, which he had breached.[32] Given the fiduciary relationship between Snepp and the CIA, the Court held, there should be a remedy that 'is tailored to deter those who would place sensitive information at risk'.[33]

Justice Stevens, with whom Justices Brennan and Marshall joined, dissented. The dissent expressed three major objections to the Court's holding. First, Justice Stevens insisted that restitutionary damages were misplaced because Snepp was not unjustly enriched (and constructive trusts – he added – have nothing to do with deterrence).[34] Snepp's profits did not derive in any way from his breach: they were not the product of Snepp's failure to submit the book to a pre-publication review. On the contrary, had he performed this duty, the Government would have been obliged to give its clearance, and the very same profits would have been gained.

Justice Stevens's second objection was that the CIA's protected interest, namely the confidentiality of its classified information and sources,

---

[30] 444 US 507 (1980). [31] *Ibid.* at 515–16. [32] *Ibid.* at 510. [33] *Ibid.* at 515.
[34] See *ibid.* at 521 and 523.

was not compromised: the Government had conceded that Snepp's book did not contain any such information. The failure to submit it to prepublication approval should not be regarded, said the dissent, as a breach of Snepp's fiduciary duty as long as no confidentiality had been breached. These circumstances were but a garden-variety breach of contract, which, unlike breaches of fiduciary duties, did not justify any *profits*-based recovery.[35] A breach of a covenant that *supports* a fiduciary duty should not be regarded as a breach of that duty.

Finally, the dissenters' last concern was that restitutionary damages would 'enforce a species of prior restraint on a citizen's right to criticize his government'.[36] The remedy is risky, Justice Stevens maintained, because the reviewing agency may 'misuse its authority to delay the publication of a critical work or to persuade an author to modify the content of his work beyond the demands of secrecy'.[37]

The debate between the majority and the dissent in *Snepp* provides a good opportunity to evaluate two of the claims of this article: that deterrence is not necessarily external to the relationships between plaintiff and defendant, and that encroachment law is situated *between* private and public.

The starting point of any analysis of fiduciary law must be that the fiduciary's duty of loyalty is constitutive of the fiduciary relationship, in which one person's interests are entirely subject to another's discretion. This duty of loyalty 'becomes for purposes of this relationship an entitlement of the beneficiary'.[38] A second step must be a normative choice of the extent to which the beneficiary has control over her entitlement to the fiduciary's loyalty and, thus, of the beneficiary's capacity to deter breaches of such loyalty. Such deterrence, again, does not impact the relationship between fiduciary and beneficiary from the outside.[39] Rather, it is just the remedial correlative of a normative judgment that no derogation from the beneficiary's entitlement to the fiduciary's loyalty should be allowed.

Therefore, the availability of a *profits*-based recovery must be a function of the deterrence issue. However, as Robert Cooter and Bradley Freedman

---

[35] See ibid. at 518–19.   [36] Ibid. at 526.   [37] Ibid. at 526.
[38] Weinrib, 'Restitutionary Damages', 33.
[39] Contra, ibid. at 33–4: 'Since the meaning of this duty of loyalty is that the fiduciary cannot profit from the relationship, gains can be regarded as the material embodiment of the breach of duty... Seen in this light, the fiduciary's liability to disgorge profits is not an example of a policy of deterrence impacting the relationship from the outside, but is rather the remedial consequence that reflects the nature of the obligation owed by the fiduciary to the beneficiary.'

have demonstrated, deterrence in the context of fiduciary relations turns out to be intricate.[40] Two structural characteristics of the various categories of fiduciary relationships make deterrence difficult.[41]

(i) The beneficiary's interests are subject to the fiduciary's discretion; the fiduciary should control and manage the asset in the beneficiary's best interest.

(ii) The asset's management involves risk and uncertainty and thus requires continual recalculations to determine the most productive course of action.

This need for dynamic management precludes the possibility of dictating the behaviour of the fiduciary by specific and easily enforceable rules. Furthermore, the standard prescribed by the duty of loyalty – that the fiduciary should not appropriate the beneficiary's asset or some of its value – is also difficult to enforce, since profitable misappropriation is likely to be difficult to prove.

The asymmetrical information concerning acts and results inherent to the fiduciary relationship makes it difficult for the beneficiary to distinguish bad luck from the fiduciary's misappropriation.[42] Due to the hardships of detection and proof, the beneficiary's control over her entitlement to loyalty – embodied by the profits remedy for breaches – may be insufficient.[43] The beneficiary's entitlement (and not any other reason that is exogenous to the parties' relationship) requires some 'reinforcement' of the profits remedy if it is to vindicate control. In response, fiduciary law can grant the beneficiary control over entitlements that are not as central to the fiduciary relationship as loyalty, such as reporting requirements or the appearance of propriety.

Indeed, fiduciary law creates a cluster of presumptive rules of conduct that restrict the permissible scope of the fiduciary's behaviour whenever possible conflicts of interest arise between the beneficiary and the fiduciary.[44] This bundle of rules – the most fundamental of which are

---

[40] See Robert Cooter and Bradley J. Freedman, 'The Fiduciary Relationship: Its Economic Character and Legal Consequences', (1991) 66 *New York University LR* 1045.

[41] See *ibid.*, 1046–7.   [42] See *ibid.*, at 1051.

[43] Cooter and Freedman argue that the reduced probability of enforcement reduces the deterrent effect of a profits remedy, because the probable gain from breach is always greater than the probable liability. See *ibid.*, 1052. In so far as the probability of enforcement is related to factors extrinsic to the parties, it should not influence liability under the correlativity thesis. However, the difficulties of enforcement in the context under discussion are inherent to the fiduciary relationship, and thus may properly influence the normative definition of the beneficiary's entitlement.

[44] See Cooter and Freedman, 'Fiduciary Relationship', 1053–4.

the rule against conflict of interest and the rule against secret profits – facilitates the proof of appropriation by inferring disloyalty from its appearance, either through conclusively presuming appropriation or by requiring the fiduciary to prove that she did not misappropriate the principal's asset. Thus, these rules raise the enforcement probability and help to solve the deterrence problem. In order properly to vindicate the beneficiary's entitlement in the fiduciary's loyalty, the law treats these ancillary duties as themselves fiduciary duties and gives the beneficiary the right to a strong remedy for breaches of these entitlements.

At this point one can appreciate the inadequacy of the dissent's first two objections. If Snepp was obliged to notify the CIA before publishing information for profit, and if this obligation is to be perceived as an ancillary duty for which a profits remedy is appropriate, Snepp's profits embody the breach of that duty and Snepp has in fact been unjustly enriched.

Thus, once it is appreciated that deterrence may be an internal entailment of the beneficiary's entitlement, and that effective deterrence requires some ancillary rules of presumptive and strict liabilities governing certain aspects of fiduciaries' conduct, one can no longer dismiss out of hand the possible availability of a profits recovery for breaching a 'merely' ancillary obligation. And once this recovery may be a required entailment of the beneficiary's entitlement, the 'no unjust enrichment' argument becomes wholly question-begging. To say that the fiduciary has not been unjustly enriched is to assume that the beneficiary is not entitled to the profits gained by the breach of such ancillary obligation, thus posing the very question the 'principle against unjust enrichment' purports to resolve.[45]

This does not mean that any breach of the fiduciary's obligations should trigger restitutionary damages. Deciding which obligations should be deemed ancillary to the fiduciary's duty of loyalty, and whether they should be backed up by a conclusive presumption of appropriation or by shifting the balance of proof to the fiduciary, requires a detailed analysis, which is not necessary here.[46] For the purposes of this article, it is enough to emphasise that these are questions regarding the *initial* allocation of entitlements between fiduciaries and beneficiaries, and are thus

---

[45] I discuss elsewhere, in some detail, the broader claim that 'unjust enrichment' is but a conclusion merely in need of supportive normative arguments. See Dagan, 'Restitutionary Damages', 126–32.
[46] For an economic analysis of this question, see Cooter and Freedman, 'Fiduciary Relationship', *sub* III.

both distributive (that is, public) and – at the same time – internal to the relationships between each fiduciary and her beneficiary.

This conclusion can facilitate a better understanding of the debate in *Snepp*, but it cannot yield a value-free resolution thereof. The relationship of agents such as Snepp with the CIA are deemed fiduciary, due to the trust the agent enjoys respecting the CIA's confidential information. Since the agent's duty of loyalty is aimed, first and foremost, at preserving and vindicating the CIA's control over the dissemination of such information, it seems that the obligation to submit materials to pre-publication review is a reasonable (ancillary) rule of conduct that can secure this control.

This, however, does not necessarily tilt the scales in favour of restitutionary damages in cases like *Snepp*. A difficult question still remains as to whether the breach of this ancillary duty should lead to a conclusive presumption of appropriation (as the majority's view implies), or merely to a shift of burdens that would require the fiduciary to prove that she did not misappropriate. (If proof of misappropriation is required, no restitutionary damages seem appropriate in *Snepp*, given the Government's admission that no confidential information has been revealed.) I believe that the most informative consideration for the resolution of this question lies in the dissent's third concern, namely a normative judgment respecting prior restraint on the free speech of the CIA agents (this concern does not apply – it is important to emphasise – in many other fiduciary cases).[47]

Indeed, just as in cases of the appropriation of resources such as land, patents or copyright, or in cases of breach of contract, the important correlativity between the defendant's liability (and the applicable measure of recovery) and the plaintiff's entitlement cannot absolve us from the difficult public decisions we need to make in order to set the entitlements in the first place. There is no way to isolate private law from public values.

V. Conclusion

Encroachments raise complex questions for the doctrine and theory of the law of restitution. This article focused on the choice of pecuniary remedy

---

[47] A court making this normative decision might also consider the unusual situation in *Snepp*, where the beneficiary is more powerful relative to the fiduciary than in most such relationships. Perhaps such a powerful beneficiary does not need control over its fiduciaries' ancillary duties, because it is better positioned than other beneficiaries to detect and to prove breach.

for cases of appropriation of another's resource, breach of contract and breach of fiduciary duties. This seemingly technical question turned out to require important value choices. However, since these normative choices shape the parties' *ex ante* entitlements, they do not deprive restitutionary cases of their nature as encounters between a particular plaintiff and a particular defendant. As the title of this article claims, the restitutionary doctrine governing encroachments lies between private and public.

PART VIII

Improvements

14 Mistaken improvements and the restitution calculus

Andrew Kull

I. The measure of recovery

Mistaken improvements are interesting because they give rise to some of the most revealing real-life restitution claims in respect of non-money benefits. Such claims expose the underlying structure of restitution in a way that money claims usually do not, because they implicate important questions that are usually elided by a claim in respect of a money payment: what ought to be accounted a benefit, and how should it be measured? The observation that the mistaken improver sometimes recovers in circumstances where the benefit to the defendant, on any measure, is doubtful at best, leads to the even more fundamental question of what 'restitution' is really about after all.

The inherent attraction of the resulting problems may be judged by the fact that even in English law – where, according to the best authorities, actual instances of restitutionary recovery in favour of a mistaken improver are virtually non-existent[1] – there is nevertheless a highly developed theoretical account of what the shape and the justification of the remedy ought to be, if only it did exist.[2] The American law of mistaken improvement, by comparison with the English, offers less theory and more practice. Not only is mistaken improvement a relatively common phenomenon with us – it is customary to attribute the incidence

---

Mark Gergen's helpful criticism is gratefully acknowledged.

[1] See Lord Goff of Chieveley and Gareth Jones, *Law of Restitution* (5th edn, 1998), 240 (in English law, there can be no recovery for mistaken improvement 'if the land owner has not acted unconscionably').

[2] See, e.g., *ibid.*, 18–22 (free acceptance), 240–5 (acquiescence; incontrovertible benefit); Peter Birks, *Introduction to the Law of Restitution* (1985, revised edn 1989), 109–32 (subjective devaluation; free acceptance; incontrovertible benefit; realisation in money); Andrew Burrows, *Law of Restitution* (1993), 9–14.

of the problem to the chaotic land titles of an earlier day, as well as to the difficulties of surveying the wide open spaces – but the improver's claim is far more likely to succeed. American courts are prepared to draw on a wide choice of remedies in such cases, making available a set of outcomes at least as varied, and as nuanced, as those reached under German law,[3] with some additional possibilities besides. The fact that the American law of mistaken improvement should resemble the German so much more than it does the English is curious in itself, inasmuch as the American law has been freely constructed on a common-law foundation, without reference (in the last century at least) to the more liberal civil-law tradition.[4]

The vast difference between English and American law on this subject is largely to be explained by one critical difference in judicial approach. On the issue of mistaken improvements, modern American judges have accepted the messy proposition that '[i]n cases involving the right to recover for improvements placed by mistake upon land owned by one other than the improver, the solution of the questions involved depends largely upon the circumstances and the equities involved in each particular case'.[5] The quotation is from a 1969 opinion of the Supreme Court of West Virginia, but it makes a fair translation of the statement of the civilian Celsus: that in this context, *bonus iudex varie ex personis causisque constituet*.[6] As a concession to reality this seems fairly modest, but it makes all the difference. A judge who will say this much (in English or in Latin) has abandoned the judicial perfectionism that elsewhere obstructs the claim of the mistaken improver: the familiar, self-protective reaction of the common law that consists in refusing to decide a question to which a judicial answer must inevitably be approximate.[7] Because the true benefit to the landowner from an unrequested improvement is ultimately unknowable, the only way to exclude any possibility of prejudice to an innocent owner is to deny any relief to the improver. This constricted approach may still have

---

[3] For everything that is said or implied in this article about German law, I am indebted to the valuable paper by Dirk A. Verse, 'Improvements and Enrichment: A Comparative Analysis', [1998] *Restitution LR* 85.

[4] Justice Story's influential opinion in *Bright v. Boyd* (1841) 4 Fed Cas 127 (No. 1,875) (Cir Decisions, Maine), favouring more liberal relief for the mistaken improver, included a direct appeal to the authority of Roman law.

[5] *Somerville v. Jacobs* (1969) 153 W Va 613 at 629; 170 SE 2d 805 at 813–14.

[6] ('A good judge will decide differently according to the parties and circumstances in issue.') Cels. D. 6. 1. 38, quoted in Verse, 'Improvements and Enrichment', 88.

[7] A familiar example of the same phenomenon is the denial of relief for interrupted contractual performance, where restitution would necessitate the judicial apportionment of a pre-paid sum: *Whincup v. Hughes* (1871) LR 6 CP 78.

predominated in a majority of US jurisdictions during the first half of the twentieth century, to judge by the 1937 *Restatement of Restitution*,[8] but it imposes a reticence that is thoroughly out of character for contemporary American judges, who are perfectly prepared, in most legal settings, to go ahead and make such order as justice may seem to require.

Not surprisingly, therefore, the restrictive approach of the older common law of improvements is usually replaced, in the current tendency of the American decisions, by a recognition that substantial justice in a case of mistaken improvement depends simultaneously on questions of enrichment, expenditure, relative fault and relative hardship; and that the suitability of one remedy or another, among the wide variety available, is likewise determined by the circumstances of the particular case. If the American law of improvements offered remedial flexibility and nothing more, it might constitute merely an elaborate compilation of palm-tree justice: admirable or not, but of questionable relevance for any more rigorous law of restitution. In fact, as the cases will demonstrate, the results reached with this remedial array are kept within predictable bounds by important rules that determine the scope of liability in restitution in cases of improvements as in all others.

Let me suggest, purely as a hypothesis and by way of experiment, that the measure of recovery in restitution can be accurately described by a fairly simple calculus. A successful restitution claimant is entitled the highest value he can establish for a non-contractual benefit conferred, consistent with four general rules. (Only the first three of these rules will be relevant to the problem of mistaken improvement. The fourth rule has been included, out of context, merely to yield a scheme that will cover every restitution claim.)

- Proposed Rule 1 states that the restitutionary liability of *an innocent defendant* must never be such as to leave him worse off than if the transaction as a whole had not taken place.[9]
- Proposed Rule 2 states that the restitutionary liability of *an innocent defendant* may not exceed the cost to the plaintiff of providing the benefit in question. (In other words, the restitutionary liability of an

---

[8] *Restatement of Restitution* (1937), § 42(1) (allowing a claim for improvements only to the extent of a set-off against liability for mesne profits).

[9] The same proposition has been advanced from the perspective of German law: '[A]n enrichment claim may not exceed the factual gain; it must not leave the recipient worse off than he was before the transfer of the benefit. That is, it must not leave the recipient with a loss. If that it correct ... the plaintiff in unjust enrichment can recover just as much as he can skim off without causing a loss to the defendant' (Verse, 'Improvements and Enrichment', 96).

innocent defendant may not leave the plaintiff better off than if the transaction as a whole had not taken place.)
- Proposed Rule 3 states that the loss resulting from *an inefficient transfer* – that is, the extent to which the cost of conferring a non-contractual benefit exceeds the value realised by the recipient – will be left with the transferor (this much follows from Proposed Rule 1), except in so far as it is reallocated to the recipient on the basis of fault.
- Proposed Rule 4 states that a defendant who has obtained a benefit by means of *conscious wrongdoing* will be liable to disgorge it, including any portion of the benefit that exceeds the plaintiff's cost.

Some combination of these rules operates to yield the measure of recovery in respect of a non-contractual transfer, wherever there is an appreciable divergence between the cost of the transfer to the plaintiff and benefit thereby realised by the defendant. This latter condition will be satisfied, given the fundamental intransitivity of value between one person and another, by every restitution claim in respect of a non-money benefit.

The discussion that follows will not attempt a defence of these proposed rules in comprehensive terms. My contention is merely that the mistaken-improvement decisions furnish an extensive set of real-world controversies, on facts that facilitate a comparison of outcomes, permitting the testing of the usefulness of Proposed Rules 1–3 in predicting the measure of recovery for non-money benefits.

II. Benefit and loss

Mistaken improvement might serve as the archetype of the inefficient transfer: a transfer in which benefits are conferred upon a person who does not value them at the market rate (the market consisting of people who want the benefits), or even at their cost of production. The familiar economics of the building trades make it highly likely that a mistaken improvement will be inefficient in this sense, inasmuch as the benefit of *any* improvement will usually be less than its cost – if the benefit is appraised from the standpoint of someone who has not chosen to spend his own money to have the work performed.

Recognition of the fact that a mistaken improvement will usually constitute an inefficient or loss-producing transfer leads to the observation that any adjudication of liability as between improver and landowner is simultaneously performing two distinct functions. To the extent that a benefit to the landowner is identifiable – and Proposed Rule 1 requires, in effect, that the benefit be 'incontrovertible'[10] – a liability in restitution

---

[10] On the test of 'incontrovertible benefit' see Goff and Jones, *Law of Restitution*, 22–5.

obliges the landowner to pay for a benefit received. This is the aspect of the remedy that squares with ordinary ideas of what restitution is about. At the same time, however, to the extent that the identifiable benefit to the landowner falls short of the cost to the improver, the effect of the same adjudication is no longer to impose a liability in respect of a benefit, but rather to allocate a loss. To the extent that the improver recovers less than his costs, the resulting loss – the value dissipated in the inefficient transfer – is allocated to the improver. To the extent that the landowner is made liable for any amount exceeding the identifiable (that is, 'incontrovertible') benefit to him, an analogous loss is allocated to the landowner. If the defendant's liability is fixed anywhere in the range between his incontrovertible benefit and the improver's cost, the effect of the judgment is to split the loss between the parties.

In fact, judgment in a typical case of mistaken improvement gives effect not only to these two basic determinations – identification of benefit and concomitant allocation of loss – but to a third as well. The American decisions oblige us to recognise that the availability of restitution in this context will depend significantly on a court's determination of relative fault and relative hardship between the parties. This makes the improvement cases even more distinctive, because considerations of fault and hardship have no bearing on the availability of a claim of restitution based on a money payment.[11] Acknowledging a role for fault and hardship in the improvement cases creates a puzzle, moreover, since such comparisons find no obvious place in restitution's theoretical structure.

III. Restitution and the forced exchange

1. Valuation and liquidity

The difficulties attending restitution for non-money benefits stem from the related problems of valuation and liquidity. Even if it were established, in other words, how much a given benefit was actually worth to the defendant in some absolute sense, a judgment requiring the defendant to pay that value in cash might well impose an extraneous cost. If it does, a liability in that amount leaves the defendant even with the world on a balance-sheet test, but worse off than if the whole transaction had never taken place – thereby violating Proposed Rule 1. By contrast, if and to the extent that a restitutionary remedy can be devised that solves or obviates the problems of valuation and liquidity in the circumstances of

---

[11] It is conceded that fault and hardship may be relevant to the availability of an affirmative defence.

a particular case, then and to that extent the law has identified what is usually regarded as an incontrovertible benefit.

Liquidity limits the availability of restitution because it is harder to require a defendant to take money out of his pocket than to deduct the same amount from the defendant's share of money that is already on the table. Valuation is self-evidently a problem because of Proposed Rule 1. These fundamental limits are reflected even in the narrowest common-law response to mistaken improvement, where it has long been conceded that the improver's claim in restitution may be asserted defensively, in set-off against his liability to the owner for use and occupation. Because the value of the improvement is typically far greater than the improver's liability for use and occupation, restricting the improver to a defensive claim also makes it unimportant to value the improvement with precision. Seen in this light, the older common law already permitted a claim for improvements, limited in such a way that both liquidity and valuation might be safely ignored.

The first steps beyond this barrier, allowing the improver to assert an affirmative claim, will predictably be taken in circumstances where the issues of valuation and liquidity may be resolved without judicial intervention. This will be the case when the landowner has realised the value of a mistaken improvement in money, by a voluntary sale or lease of the property improved.[12] Specific restitution of the improvement, where feasible, likewise obviates both problems of valuation and liquidity, so long as the landowner is indemnified against damage from the removal of the improvement.[13] In the rare circumstance where the improvement is the very thing that the landowner was planning to pay to have constructed, valuation and liquidity problems might potentially be resolved under the heading of saved expense.[14] Finally, given the right facts – probably involving a mistake about the existence of a contract – the landowner's own appraisal of a mistaken improvement (what Michael Garner calls

---

[12] See, e.g., *Powell v. Mayo* (1981) 123 Cal App 3d 994; 177 Cal Rptr 66 (property sold by improver before co-tenant's interest comes to light; improver entitled to cost of improvements or their proceeds, whichever is less); *United States v. Francis* (1985) 623 F Supp 535 (DVI) (improver develops property to which he has no title; lender to improver, whose mortgage is void, awarded repayment from rents received by true owner in respect of improvements).

[13] See, e.g., *DeAngelo v. Brazauskas* (1995) 86 NY 2d 746; 655 NE 2d 165; *Jensen v. Probert* (1944) 174 Oregon 143; 148 P 2d 248; *Citizens & Southern National Bank v. Modern Homes Constr. Co.* (1966) 248 South Carolina 130; 149 SE 2d 326.

[14] See *Karon v. Kellogg* (1935) 195 Minnesota 134; 261 NW 861 (restitution from owner for value of necessary repairs, where work performed by agreement with occupant).

'subjective revaluation'[15]) might furnish a definitive answer to the valuation question while obviating any concern about liquidity.[16]

2. Remedial techniques

Outside of these fortunate and largely fortuitous circumstances, however, in which the problems of valuation and liquidity essentially take care of themselves, the identification of incontrovertible benefit will usually require a greater degree of judicial intervention. American courts, when inclined to do so, attack this problem with a variety of remedial techniques. If liquidity rather than valuation is the problem – so that the issue is a benefit 'realisable' rather than 'realised' in money – one relatively modest approach is to grant the improver an equitable lien on the property, securing a claim to any added value attributable to the improvement that might be realised on a subsequent sale.[17] Instances of this sort of deferred relief are still rare for cases of mistaken improvement, but the remedy is closely analogous to the relief frequently afforded the improving co-tenant: no affirmative right to contribution, in other words, but a right to the improvements themselves, or to their realised value, on an eventual partition.[18]

Except where the owner has acted voluntarily, as by a sale or lease of the improved property, the *present* realisation in money of a non-money benefit requires that the owner be subjected to a forced exchange. The simplest approach is to make the owner liable to the improver for the value added by the improvement, possibly giving the improver a lien on the property as security.[19] A judgment in this form makes the owner an involuntary purchaser at a price fixed by appraisal. Alternatively, a forced exchange may take the form of a court-ordered transfer that unlocks the

---

[15] Michael Garner, 'The Role of Subjective Benefit in the Law of Unjust Enrichment', (1990) 10 *Oxford JLS* 42–65.
[16] In *Vickery v. Ritchie* (1909) 202 Massachusetts 247; 88 NE 835, a builder constructed a Turkish bathhouse on the owner's property at a cost of $50,000. Both parties believed that the work was done pursuant to a valid contract. By a fraud of the architect, however, the builder's copy of the purported contract reflected a price of $52,000, while the owner's copy called for payment of $24,000. The construction of the bathhouse increased the value of the property by $20,000. Consistent with 'subjective revaluation', the owner's liability on these facts should be $24,000. See *Restatement of Restitution* (1937), § 155, Illustrations 3 and 4. The Massachusetts court gave the builder the value of his labour and materials in *quantum meruit*.
[17] *Bedwell v. Bedwell* (1989) 774 SW 2d 953 (Tennessee Appeals)(improver obtains equitable lien, foreclosure deferred pending voluntary sale by elderly owner); *Madrid v. Spears* (1957) 250 F 2d 51 (10th Cir) (equitable lien securing payment to improver from anticipated rents and profits).
[18] *Mahon v. Mahon* (1963) 254 Iowa 1349; 121 NW 2d 103.
[19] *Bright v. Boyd* (1841) 4 Fed Cas 127 (No. 1,875)(Cir Decisions, Maine).

value represented by the improvement (so to speak) by putting it into the hands of someone who values it more highly than does the landowner. Where a claim arises from an improver's mistake about which of two adjacent lots in the subdivision was his, one possible remedy is to order that the improver and the landowner exchange lots.[20] In other circumstances a court will sometimes direct that the improved property be sold, as on partition, the improver to receive from the sale proceeds either the added value attributable to the improvement or the cost of the improvement, whichever is less.[21] (This last condition is necessary to satisfy Proposed Rule 2.[22]) By the most common and most characteristic of the forced-exchange remedies, the landowner is presented with a choice: either pay the improver the added value of the property attributable to the improvement, or tender the improved property to the improver at its unimproved value. Some version of this buy/sell remedy is not merely authorised, it is (ostensibly at least) conferred upon the improver as an entitlement, by the 'betterment acts' of some twenty-eight US jurisdictions.[23]

3. The betterment acts

In the American view, it is impossible to judge the propriety of such a remedy for mistaken improvement except in the light of particular circumstances. So in the familiar (if strictly hypothetical) case of the homeowner who returns from a weekend excursion to find that a builder – perhaps mistaking the address – has constructed a garage behind his house, the short answer is that in such a case a remedy by forced exchange is inconceivable.[24] At the other extreme, however, suppose that unimproved

---

[20] *Brown v. Davis* (1987) 514 So 2d 54 (Florida); *Voss v. Forgue* (1956) 84 So 2d 563 (Florida); *Olin v. Reinecke* (1929) 336 Illinois 530; 168 NE 676.

[21] *Manning v. Wingo* (1991) 577 So 2d 865 (Alabama); *Sweeten v. King* (1976) 29 NC App 672; 225 SE 2d 598. Cf. *Butler v. Hayes* (1997) 487 SE 2d 229 (Virginia) (denying an allowance, on partition, for the value of improvements where the improver acted in the knowledge of competing interests).

[22] American decisions hold uniformly and explicitly that the recovery for value added by mistaken improvement may not exceed the improver's costs. *Madrid v. Spears* (1957) 250 F 2d 51 (10th Cir); *Myers v. Canutt* (1951) 242 Iowa 692; 46 NW 2d 72; 24 ALR 2d 1; *Worley v. Ehret* (1976) 36 Ill App 3d 48; 343 NE 2d 237; *Cano v. Lovato* (1986) 105 New Mexico 522; 734 P 2d 762.

[23] The statutory provisions are identified and compared by Kelvin H. Dickinson, 'Mistaken Improvers of Real Estate', (1985) 64 *North Carolina LR* 37–75.

[24] For a real-life case approaching the textbook illustration, see *Dunnebacke Co. v. Pittman* (1934) 216 Wisconsin 305; 257 NW 30, denying restitution to a builder who (in the mistaken belief that he had been asked to do so) constructed a massive breakwater on lakefront property during the owners' absence. There was conflicting evidence about whether or not the improvement added value to the land; owners were found not liable because they had demanded that the wall be removed. The court suggested that

property is held by its owner purely for investment, so that the owner has no expectations regarding its use other than a general expectation of capital appreciation; that the value added by the improvement is many times the value of the unimproved tract; that a forced exchange of the property subjects the owner to no measurable hardship, while the hardship to the improver would be substantial should relief be denied; and, finally, that the improver has done nothing by way of bad faith or carelessness to forfeit the natural sympathy of the court. If these favourable circumstances are united, as in real life they may be, it becomes difficult to deny relief merely because it necessitates a forced exchange.

Most of the American betterment acts are nineteenth-century legislation. They respond to the intolerable injustice that resulted when an honest yeoman, by a mistake about title or boundaries for which he was in no way responsible, spent years of labour cultivating Blackacre and building a modest dwelling for his family, only to discover that the few acres he had cleared and improved were part of a larger tract of wilderness belonging to an absentee speculator. As previously noted, the betterment acts typically give the improver a right to force the landowner to make a buy/sell election; the statutes do not (with one exception) qualify this right in terms of the nature of the property, the owner's expectations or other equitable considerations.[25] If the statutes are taken at face value, in other words, the forced exchange should be equally available to redress the mistaken cultivation of untamed wilderness and the mistaken construction of a garage behind a suburban house. Yet it will be impossible to find a reported case in which a buy/sell election was imposed on the suburban

the owners might be liable in quasi-contract if they had been aware of the improver's mistake, or if they had manifested an intention to retain the improvement.

[25] The California statute is a very significant but isolated exception. By this legislation, the court is authorised to 'effect such an adjustment of the rights, equities, and interests of the good faith improver, the owner of the land, and other interested parties (including, but not limited to, lessees, lienholders, and encumbrancers) as is consistent with substantial justice to the parties under the circumstances of the particular case. The relief granted shall protect the owner of the land upon which the improvement was constructed against any pecuniary loss but shall avoid, insofar as possible, enriching him unjustly at the expense of the good faith improver ... In determining the appropriate form of relief under this section, the court shall take into consideration any plans the owner of the land may have for the use or development of the land upon which the improvement was made and his need for the land upon which the improvement was made in connection with the use or development of other property owned by him': *California Civil Procedure Code* § 871.5 (1999). Unlike the other betterment acts, California's is a relatively modern enactment (1968); it is the product of a conscious effort to reform the law of mistaken improvement to provide more flexible remedies in the full range of circumstances where the improver has a valid claim on restitution principles. See generally *Raab v. Casper* (1975) 51 Cal App 3d 866; 124 Cal Rptr 590.

homeowner, notwithstanding that a statute purports to give that right to the improver. A remedy that does substantial justice in one factual setting would be grossly inequitable in another. Being realistic about it, one must acknowledge (with Celsus) that the remedy in restitution depends on the circumstances of the particular case.

4. Qualification of Proposed Rule 1

On the strictest accounting it is plain that no forced exchange could ever satisfy the test of Proposed Rule 1. If the owner *wanted* to sell the tract at the unimproved price, there would be no need for judicial intervention. A defendant who is required to buy or sell at a price fixed by an appraiser will not be left indifferent by a liability in restitution. But such an accounting is manifestly too strict. The test of Proposed Rule 1 applies to the judgment on its face – adjudged liability must not exceed adjudged benefit – while ignoring in many instances the transaction costs of the remedy. Liability in respect of non-money benefits often requires the defendant to pay on the basis of an appraisal. Nor are the forced-exchange remedies unique in their potential requirement that an innocent recipient reach into his pocket to pay cash for unrequested benefits conferred. A vendor of land may be obliged to pay for the purchaser's improvements when the transaction is later set aside.[26] An owner who recovers land previously conveyed under an invalid judicial sale may be liable for improvements by the purchaser.[27] The contract doctrine of 'substantial performance' disguises a claim in restitution that may likewise require an innocent recipient to pay for something he did not want.[28] More directly, a claim for unjust enrichment asserted in terms by a party in breach of

---

[26] *Calloway Bank v. Ellis* (1922) 215 Mo App 72; 238 SW 844 (lender to purchaser/improver obtains lien on improved property in the hands of vendor, after conveyance from vendor to purchaser held void); *Elder v. Clarke* (1944) 385 Illinois 335; 52 NE 2d 778 (vendor liable for improvements where conveyance avoided for incapacity); *Tompkins v. Sandeen* (1954) 243 Minnesota 256; 67 NW 2d 405 (same, vendor disaffirms contract unenforceable for indefiniteness). Compare *McKay v. Horseshoe Lake Hop Harvesters, Inc.* (1971) 260 Oregon 612; 491 P 2d 1180 (owner liable for improvements where owner and improver shared mistaken belief that improver held under ninety-nine-year lease).
[27] The decision in *Bright v. Boyd* (1841) 4 Fed Cas 127 (No. 1,875) (Cir Decisions, Maine), usually identified as the source of the more liberal American approach to mistaken improvers generally, allowed a claim for improvements made by a purchaser at a void judicial sale. For further examples see *Hudson v. New York & Albany Transportation Co.* (1911) 188 F 630 (2nd Cir); *Mesirow v. Duggan* (1957) 240 F 2d 751 (8th Cir); *Kidd v. Rountree* (1941) 285 Kentucky 442; 148 SW 2d 275.
[28] *Ruxley Electronics and Construction Ltd v. Forsyth* [1996] AC 344 (HL) (swimming pool too shallow); *Jacob & Youngs, Inc. v. Kent* (1921) 230 New York 239; 129 NE 889 (builder obtains materials from wrong manufacturer).

contract may put an innocent defendant to the same necessity, and at the instance of a contractual wrongdoer besides.[29]

In all such cases, the hardship to the defendant consists in being obliged to submit to a forced exchange of what are objectively determined to be equivalent values. Restitution will sometimes impose this much cost on the defendant where the alternative would be very much more costly to the plaintiff. Proposed Rule 1 must evidently be qualified to this extent. The qualification is relatively slight, because even the unquantifiable costs of the forced-exchange remedy are taken into account in determining the relief to which the plaintiff is entitled. This accounting may be observed, in the mistaken-improvement cases, in the fact that the availability of a remedy depends a great deal on what might be called the equities of the parties. So a mistaken improver who has acted negligently – not even bothering to obtain a proper survey before building his cabin, for instance – is much less likely to obtain relief in restitution than one who paid for a survey that was erroneously performed.

This sounds like common sense, but in a restitution context the distinction is less obvious than it seems. Note that the position of the landowner (including the extent to which he may be enriched by the improvement) is prima facie identical in the two cases supposed above (mistaken cultivation of wilderness and mistaken construction of a garage). And yet the cases make it clear that the success of the improver's claim depends not simply on the fact of benefit to the landowner, but on the improver's own equitable position. The idea forms a pervasive theme of the American cases, variously expressed in the language of good faith, negligence and notice. The improver's claim of title must be 'honest and reasonable', not 'frivolous, presumptuous or merely conjectural';[30] his mistake must be a 'bona fide' or 'reasonable' one;[31] restitution will be denied to an improver who has acted 'recklessly and upon a belief of ownership which is completely without foundation'.[32] In short, the plaintiff's negligence may well be a bar to restitution in respect of a mistaken improvement. This makes a sharp contrast to the rule governing restitution for a mistaken payment, where the plaintiff's exercise of care is strictly irrelevant. The difference in this regard between mistaken payment and mistaken improvement

[29] *Britton v. Turner* (1834) 6 New Hampshire 481 (labourer abandoning employment before completion of contract term permitted to recover in restitution for value of part-performance).
[30] *Vulovich v. Baich* (1955) 286 App Div 403 at 405; 143 NYS 2d 247 at 250.
[31] *Beacon Homes, Inc. v. Holt* (1966) 66 North Carolina 467 at 472, 474; 46 SE 2d 434 at 438, 439.
[32] *James v. Bailey* (1974) 370 F Supp 469 at 472 (DVI).

reflects the degree to which an effective restitutionary remedy in the two settings will necessarily be burdensome to the defendant.

5. The position of the defendant

Conversely, the courts' readiness to grant restitution by means of a forced exchange is plainly affected by their assessment of any appreciable (if unquantifiable) consequences to the defendant. Remedy by forced exchange is much more likely if the improved tract is a small corner of a large holding, or a tract whose sale does not affect the owner's potential uses of the remainder.[33] By the same token, if the landowner has participated in the improver's mistake – for example, by unwitting acquiescence in an erroneous survey – relief by forced exchange is more likely to be granted; not necessarily on a theory of estoppel, but simply because the owner's mistake reveals that he had no expectation of ownership in the tract that the plaintiff has mistakenly improved.[34]

Even where a court is satisfied that a forced exchange achieves substantial justice, such a remedy threatens to impose an unquantifiable injury on an innocent defendant. How significant is the resulting anomaly in terms of restitution principle? We may deny that there is any anomaly at all if we can accept a composite justification of a restitution remedy by forced exchange. The justification of such a remedy is mostly, but not entirely, a matter of avoiding unjustified enrichment. At the margin, and to the extent the enrichment explanation fails, the remedy serves the distinct, utilitarian purpose of avoiding disproportionate hardship.

To recapitulate: the radical remedy of a forced exchange is justified only in part by the objective of reversing the unjustified enrichment of the landowner at the expense of the improver. Naturally it does that much. To the extent that the remedy outruns the enrichment, imposing a residual if unquantifiable cost on the defendant, a justification must be found elsewhere. Other instances of forced exchange offer the most direct analogies: eminent domain, or the laws that sometimes permit private parties to obtain property from unwilling sellers.[35] These forced transactions

---

[33] Such factors are discussed in *Smith v. Stewart* (1983) 10 Ark App 201; 662 SW 2d 202.

[34] *Pull v. Barnes* (1960) 142 Colorado 272; 350 P 2d 828; *McKelway v. Armour* (1854) 10 NJ Eq 115.

[35] Nineteenth-century railway construction could not have occurred in developed countries without laws permitting the builders to acquire a right-of-way from unwilling sellers. See R. W. Kostal, *Law and English Railway Capitalism 1825–1875* (1994), 144-80. To take a modern-day instance, statutes in some of the western United States permit the owner of a landlocked parcel to compel the sale of an easement permitting access. See, e.g., *Washington Revised Code Annotated* § 8.24.010 (1999) (authorising condemnation of a 'private way of necessity').

compromise property rights in order to avoid the disproportionate hardship (both public and private) resulting from the owner's refusal to sell, while they realise value that will not otherwise be realised if the parties are left to their own devices. German writers advance a different analogy, closer in some respects if more remote in others: they compare the burden imposed on a landowner by a forced sale of improved property to the burden imposed on tort or contract plaintiffs by the duty to mitigate damages.[36] Like the innocent landowner, the aggrieved party is constrained to engage in a transaction he has not freely chosen, for the purpose of minimising the aggregate loss resulting from the other party's infringement.

In the case of mistaken improvements, as in these other instances, the law will sometimes impose an unquantifiable hardship on an innocent party for the sake of avoiding an appreciably greater hardship to another party. Taken in isolation, the utilitarian objective of minimising aggregate hardship has nothing to do with the restitutionary objective of reversing unjustified enrichment. Taken in remedial context, the two objectives are pursued simultaneously. This is only a problem if the aim is to find a single explanation of everything accomplished by a given remedy in restitution.

IV. Allocation of loss: landowner at fault

A passive landowner who stands by in the knowledge that a mistaken improvement is being made will be liable to pay for it, without any quibbling over incontrovertible benefit. The familiar question is how such a liability can best be explained.

One response is to say, in effect, that the landowner will be deemed to have received a benefit that he has not in fact received. Lord Goff and Gareth Jones suggest that '[i]n such a situation it is unconscionable for the landowner to deny that he has received a benefit'.[37] Peter Birks puts the same thought more ornately when he says that in such circumstances it would be 'unconscientious' of the recipient to evade the 'objective valuation' of a benefit (and the consequent liability in restitution) 'by an appeal to the argument from the subjectivity of value'.[38] Such statements recall the rule offered by the 1937 *Restatement of Restitution* for the liability of a defendant who has obtained services by 'consciously tortious conduct': 'Where a person is entitled to restitution from another because the

---

[36] See Verse, 'Improvements and Enrichment', 95–6.
[37] Goff and Jones, *Law of Restitution*, 20.
[38] Peter Birks, 'In Defence of Free Acceptance', in: A. Burrows (ed.), *Essays on the Law of Restitution* (1991), 105, 128.

other has obtained his services ... by fraud, duress or undue influence, *the measure of recovery for the benefit received* by the other is the market value of such services *irrespective of their benefit to the recipient*.'[39]

The awkwardness about all these formulations is that they insist on denominating as a 'benefit' something that they simultaneously concede is not in fact a benefit.[40] This is not an approach that is either rhetorically or logically attractive, and it would not be undertaken – it seems fair to say – by anyone who was not irrevocably committed to describing these particular instances of liability as benefit-based.

My own preference, as will be evident from the preceding discussion, is for a more candid recognition that the legal response in such a case is partly benefit-based and partly based on something else. To the (unknowable) extent that the acquiescent landowner is in fact benefited by the improvement, he is made liable for the benefit. To the extent that the landowner's liability exceeds the benefit, the effect of the remedy is evidently compensation for the improver's loss by means of a liability based on fault.[41] The nature of the landowner's fault in such circumstances might be identified in a variety of ways: as tacit misrepresentation, or constructive fraud, or by analogy to the doctrine of 'last clear chance'. In purely descriptive terms, the landowner is at fault because he has failed to make use of an appropriate opportunity to avoid a non-consensual transfer and the injury resulting therefrom.

V. Conclusion

The American law of mistaken improvement encompasses certain instances of liability not based on benefit. A landowner who bears responsibility for the improver's mistake will be liable to indemnify the improver; responsibility in this context can include a failure to correct the improver's error when correction would have been easy. Any landowner who

---

[39] *Restatement of Restitution* (1937), § 152 (emphasis added). On the specific issue of 'standing by', the *Restatement* comments elsewhere that '[a] landowner who has knowledge that another, in the mistaken belief of ownership, is making improvements upon the land is liable to the other for the value of improvements made after the landowner has had a reasonable opportunity to notify the other of his mistake and fails to do so': § 40, comment d.

[40] This objection is not new. See, e.g., J. Beatson, *Use and Abuse of Unjust Enrichment* (1991), 32–9.

[41] That such is the effect seems all the more evident if it is accepted that the improver's recovery should be set at the greater of cost or benefit, wherever the owner has either 'encouraged the improver to act as he did' or else 'simply stood by without protest': Goff and Jones, *Law of Restitution*, 245.

is subjected to a forced exchange bears significant costs of the remedy afforded the improver. In all likelihood, such a remedy will be conditional on the court's finding that it will not result in substantial prejudice to the owner; but the uncompensated cost to the owner is real, none the less. These outcomes are anomalous only if we insist that every aspect of every liability forming part of 'restitution' must be referable to the defendant's receipt of a benefit. Conversely, such results present no theoretical problem if they are properly seen as having a composite basis: partly the defendant's unjustified enrichment, partly something else. When the landowner 'stands by' or actively induces the mistaken improvement, a liability in the amount of the improver's costs is based partly on enrichment, partly on indemnification. When even an innocent landowner is subjected to a forced exchange, the liability is based partly on enrichment, partly on the extraneous legal objective of avoiding a disproportionate hardship and the resulting economic waste.

The difficulty that remains is the familiar one of defining what is meant by a liability in restitution. If the subject is seen from John Dawson's iconoclastic perspective – he once described restitution law as comprising 'a great variety of disrupted, derailed, or otherwise irregular transactions' for which the remedies in American law 'do not depend in any way on showing that someone has been or will be "enriched"'[42] – the observation that a landowner might be liable in restitution, in excess of any incontrovertible benefit, is scarcely worth making. But even if 'restitution' is defined to refer exclusively to liability for benefits, the cases only require an acknowledgement that a restitutionary liability will not always be discovered in its unalloyed form. It follows that a single judgment may simultaneously give effect to a liability in restitution and to something else besides.

---

[42] John Dawson, 'Restitution Without Enrichment', (1981) 61 *Boston University LR* 563, 565, 577.

15 Enrichment by improvements in Scots law

James Wolffe

I. Introduction

An 'improvement' presupposes an asset which is improved. The obvious example is improvement to land or buildings by the construction of new works (an addition to a house, say, or a new building on land) or by repair, renovation or upgrading. Such work may be carried out by someone other than the owner of land in a variety of contexts: by a building contractor in implement of a contract with the owner of the land (a contract that may turn out to be void or unenforceable by the contractor for one reason or another); by the fiancé of the owner in anticipation of their marriage (which may not take place); by someone with a right of occupation of the land such as a tenant or life-renter; by someone who, though not the true owner of the land, believes that he is the owner. These are only some of the possible cases – and they are all capable of giving rise to questions for enrichment law.

This article examines how Scots law deals with some of the issues which arise when someone is enriched by improvements. The subject merits exploration in its own right. Recent important developments in Scottish enrichment law justify a reappraisal of the older texts. The exercise may be of some interest beyond Scotland – not least because improvements are treated very differently in English law (where improvers are generally not accorded an enrichment claim)[1] on the one hand and

---

[1] Lord Goff of Chieveley and Gareth Jones, *The Law of Restitution* (5th edn, 1998), 240–51, particularly at 241; see, however, the Torts (Interference with Goods) Act 1977, s. 6; and *Greenwood v. Bennett* [1973] 1 QB 195; for a challenge to the English law position see R. J. Sutton, 'What Should be Done for Mistaken Improvers?', in: P. D. Finn (ed.), *Essays on Restitution* (1990), 241–96.

in civilian legal systems (which generally favour improvers' claims)[2] on the other. The aim is neither to give a detailed statement of the law in Scotland nor to engage in a detailed comparative survey, but to discuss certain general themes which emerge from a consideration of the Scottish materials, glancing from time to time at texts from certain other jurisdictions.

II. Enrichment law in Scotland

1. *Shilliday v. Smith*

The starting point for explaining the structure of enrichment law in Scotland is now the opinion of the Lord President, Lord Rodger of Earlsferry, in *Shilliday v. Smith*.[3] The pursuer, in anticipation of her marriage to the defender, had paid over £7,000 to tradesmen to carry out work on the defender's house (which was the intended matrimonial home). She had also paid the defender more than £1,800, which he had spent on repairs to the house. The relationship had broken down, and the pursuer sought to recover both these sums from the defender. The Lord President said this:

at the most general level the pursuer's case depends on the defender's alleged unjust enrichment at her expense ... While recognising that it may not cover all cases, for present purposes I am content to adopt the brief explanation which Lord Cullen gave in *Dollar Land (Cumbernauld) Limited v. CIN Properties Limited*[4] at 348-9; a person may be said to be unjustly enriched at another's expense when he has obtained a benefit from the other's actings or expenditure, without there being a legal ground which would justify him in retaining that benefit.[5] The

---

[2] Within that generality, however, civilian systems are not uniform in their approach to particular issues: Dirk A. Verse, 'Improvements and Enrichment: A Comparative Analysis', [1998] *Restitution LR* 85.

[3] 1998 SC 725. This opinion has been described as a 'brilliant synthesising judgment' by Peter Birks: P. B. H. Birks, 'Rights, Wrongs and Remedies', (2000) 20 *Oxford JLS* 1, 11. Lord Rodger's analysis of the nature of repetition, restitution and recompense has been approved in the House of Lords: *Dollar Land (Cumbernauld) Limited v. CIN Properties Limited* 1998 SC (HL) 90 at 98-9 *per* Lord Hope of Craighead.

[4] 1996 SC 331.

[5] This formula – also used by Lord Hope in *Dollar Land* – aligns Scots law in a general sense with the civilian tradition as it has been explained by Reinhard Zimmermann and others: see especially Reinhard Zimmermann and Jacques du Plessis, 'Basic Features of the German Law of Unjustified Enrichment', [1994] *Restitution LR* 14; Reinhard Zimmermann, 'Unjustified Enrichment: The Modern Civilian Approach', (1995) 15 *Oxford JLS* 403.

significance of one person being unjustly enriched at the expense of another is that in general terms it constitutes an event which triggers a right in that other person to have the enrichment reversed.

As the law has developed, it has identified various situations where persons are to be regarded as having been unjustly enriched at another's expense and where the other person may accordingly seek to have the enrichment reversed. The authorities show that some of these situations fall into recognisable groups or categories. Since these situations correspond, if only somewhat loosely, to situations where remedies were granted in Roman law, in referring to the relevant categories our law tends to use the terminology which is found in the Digest and Code. The terms include *condictio indebiti*, *condictio causa data causa non secuta* and – to a lesser extent – *condictio sine causa*. It is unnecessary in this case to examine all the groups and it is sufficient to note that the term *condictio causa data, causa non secuta* covers situations where A is enriched because B has paid him money or transferred property to him in the expectation of receiving a consideration from A, but A does not provide that consideration. The relevant situations in this group also include cases where B paid the money or transferred the property to A on a particular basis which has failed to materialise – for example in contemplation of a marriage which does not take place. The pursuer in this action contends that the defender should be regarded as having been unjustly enriched in a manner which falls within this general category and that his enrichment should therefore be reversed.

Once he has satisfied himself that he has a relevant case, anyone contemplating bringing an action must then determine how the court is to reverse the defender's enrichment if it decides in the pursuer's favour. This will depend on the particular circumstances. The person framing the pleadings must consider how the defender's enrichment has come about and then search among the usual range of remedies to find a remedy or combination of remedies which will achieve his purpose of having that enrichment reversed.

Elementary examples make this clear. For instance, if A has been unjustly enriched because he has received a sum of money from B, the enrichment can be reversed by ordering A to repay the money from B. B's remedy will be repetition of the sum of money from A. On the other hand, if the unjust enrichment arises out of the transfer of moveable property, the enrichment can be reversed by ordering A to transfer the property back to B. An action of restitution of the property will be appropriate. If A has been unjustly enriched by the transfer from B to him of heritable property, then reduction of A's title will be required. The remedy will be an action of reduction. If A is unjustly enriched by having the benefit of B's services, the enrichment can be reversed by ordering A to pay B a sum representing the value of the benefit which A has enjoyed. An action of recompense will be appropriate. So repetition, restitution, reduction and recompense are simply examples of remedies which the courts grant to reverse an unjust enrichment, depending on the way in which the particular enrichment has arisen: see *Morgan Guaranty Trust Company of New York v. Lothian Regional Council*,[6] *per* Lord President Hope at 155B–D.[7]

2. From the 'three Rs' to *Shilliday*

The background to Lord Rodger's judgment is well known. An earlier Lord President, Viscount Stair, distributed enrichment law across two separate titles of his *Institutions of the Law of Scotland*:[8] that on 'restitution' and that on 'recompense or remuneration'. The title on restitution concerned 'The obligations, whereby men are holden to restore the proper goods of others';[9] the title on recompense 'that bond of the law of nature, obliging to do one good for another'.[10] Neither treated only of enrichment law. Under restitution, Stair dealt with the obligation of a non-owner to restore goods to their true owner[11] as well as the obligation to restore things 'which coming warrantably to our hands, and without any paction of restitution...the cause cease by which they become ours'.[12] In the latter context Stair referred to the *condictio causa data causa non secuta*, the *condictio indebiti*

---

[6] 1995 SC 151.
[7] See also *Dollar Land (Cumbernauld) Ltd v. CIN Properties Ltd* 1998 SC (HL) 90 at 99 *per* Lord Hope of Craighead. The Lord President omitted relief from his list. It is sometimes suggested that claims of relief are not properly to be regarded as founded on unjustified enrichment: cf. Robin Evans-Jones and Philip Hellwege, 'Some Observations on the Taxonomy of Unjustified Enrichment in Scots Law', (1998) 2 *Edinburgh LR* 180, 189. But, if a defender has been enriched by the discharge or partial discharge of a debt or other liability which he (the defender) owes to a third party, that enrichment may in appropriate circumstances be reversed by ordering payment to the pursuer of the amount of the enrichment (which may be the whole or a proportionate part of the debt according to circumstances). The pursuer's action in such a case has traditionally been denominated one of relief. The term 'relief' is also used in an extended sense to apply to any action which seeks to recover an amount paid by the pursuer to discharge a liability of his own, whatever the basis of liability. So, for example, the term is sometimes applied to claims for damages for breach of contract where the loss caused to the pursuer by the defender's breach of contract was a liability incurred by the pursuer to some third party. That some actions seeking 'relief' in this extended sense are clearly not enrichment claims (not least because the liability discharged was not a liability of the defender) does not affect the proposition that actions by a pursuer who has discharged a liability of the defender may be regarded as enrichment claims.
[8] James Dalrymple, Viscount Stair, *Institutions of the Law of Scotland* (1st edn, Edinburgh, 1681, 2nd edn, Edinburgh, 1693).
[9] *Ibid.* Book I, Title 7, 1.   [10] *Ibid.* Book I, Title 8, 1.
[11] *Ibid.* Book I, Title 7, 1–5.   [12] *Ibid.* Book I, Title 7, 7.

and the *condictio sine causa*. He included within restitution the obligation to restore which arises 'when any party payeth that which he supposeth is due...; if thereafter it appear that it was not due to that other'. Under 'recompence or remuneration', Stair included obligations of gratitude (generally unenforceable), obligations *negotiorum gestorum* and 'generally the obligations of recompense of what we are profited by the damage of others without their purpose to gift, or (as the law expresseth it) in *quantum locupletiores facti sumus ex damno alterius*'.[13] In this last category, Stair instanced improvements, the obligations of pupils and minors,[14] the action *de in rem verso*, contribution under the Rhodian law, and obligations of relief among co-obligants. Later writers, while making some variations to the scheme – in particular by distinguishing between repetition (repayment of money) and restitution (return of things) – did not depart from it in essentials.[15]

In two seminal articles published in 1985,[16] Peter Birks identified the damaging consequences of this division in so far as it related to unjustified enrichment. He identified the main division in this scheme (that between restitution/repetition and recompense) as one 'between benefits susceptible of exact return and benefits susceptible only of substitutional return after a valuation in money'.[17] He pointed out that such a division gave rise to the impression that the cause of action differs depending on the form in which an enrichment was received while, provided value has in fact been received, its form is morally and legally neutral.[18] Lord Rodger's judgment in *Shilliday* is consistent with this aspect of Birks's diagnosis. The characterisation of the 'three Rs' – restitution, repetition and recompense – as 'remedies' has also been accepted in the House of Lords (in the speech of Lord Hope of Craighead in *Dollar Land (Cumbernauld) Limited v. CIN Properties Limited*[19]) and Scots enrichment law appears now to be committed, in principle, to enrichment neutrality – that is, to the proposition that the

---

[13] *Ibid*. Book I, Title 8, 3.
[14] On which see Alan Rodger, 'Recovering Payments under Void Contracts in Scots Law', in: W. Swadling and G. Jones (eds.), *The Search for Principle: Essays in Honour of Lord Goff of Chieveley* (1999), 1.
[15] See generally Evans-Jones and Hellwege, 'Some Observations', 180 ff.
[16] P. B. H. Birks, 'Restitution: A View of the Scots Law', (1985) 38 *Current Legal Problems* 57; P. B. H. Birks, 'Six Questions in Search of a Subject – Unjust Enrichment in a Crisis of Identity', [1985] *JR* 227.
[17] Birks, 'Restitution', 62–3. For further discussion of the precise nature of the distinction implied in the institutional scheme see Evans-Jones and Hellwege, 'Some Observations', 180–9.
[18] Birks, 'Restitution', 63.   [19] 1998 SC (HL) 90 at 98.

grounds upon which an enrichment may be reversed are unaffected by the nature of the enrichment and apply consistently irrespective of the nature of the enrichment. Terms which were previously used as if they quadrated with or at least described grounds of liability are now identified as 'remedies'.[20]

3. Analysing enrichment law after *Shilliday*

It follows that for a long time Scots lawyers have been asking themselves the wrong questions. For example, in *Edinburgh and District Tramways Co. Limited v. Courtenay*, Lord President Dunedin said this:

I do not think it is possible – it certainly would not be easy – but I do not think it is possible, to frame a definition of recompense which shall by itself in terms at once include all classes of cases which fall within the doctrine and at the same time successfully exclude those which do not. A very much greater framer of definitions than any of us can hope to be – Mr George Joseph Bell – tried it, and I am afraid that he failed...[21]

It can now be seen that to seek such a definition may be no more useful than to attempt a definition of damages which by itself includes all cases that give rise to a liability to pay damages. In *Varney (Scotland) Limited v. Lanark Town Council*[22] Lord Fraser picked up the challenge laid down by Lord President Dunedin. He observed:

Nothing has happened since 1909 which would seem to make the framing of such a definition any easier, and the best we can do is, in my opinion, to identify the factors which are essential to the success of a case based on recompense and to see whether they are present in this case.[23]

Following *Shilliday*, it would be wrong to describe a case as 'based on recompense': 'recompense' is the response, not the ground of liability. Equally one cannot assume that all cases which give rise to the 'remedy' of recompense are necessarily based on the same grounds. Lord Fraser went on to characterise the factors essential to a 'case based on recompense' in the following way:

Three factors are, in my opinion, clearly essential. The first of these is that the defenders must have received benefit, that is they must be *lucrati* by the action of

---

[20] This proposition merits further analysis: see the Endnote below, 427–30.
[21] 1909 SC 99 at 105.   [22] 1974 SC 245.   [23] *Ibid.* at 258.

the pursuer... Secondly, the pursuers must have incurred a loss... In the third place there must have been no intention of donation on the part of the pursuers towards the defenders... From that point on the matter becomes less clear, but I think the fourth and last factor was stated by junior counsel for the pursuers with as much accuracy as is possible for a general statement, as being to the effect that the whole circumstances of the case must be such that it would be equitable for the pursuers to be reimbursed by the defenders on the basis of *quantum lucrati*.[24]

Lord Fraser's dictum has been approved in the House of Lords as the 'correct way in which to subject the facts to analysis'.[25] It is now clear that when these features require an enrichment to be reversed it should not matter in what form the enrichment has been enjoyed.[26]

That is not to say that one can necessarily analyse any specific case solely by reference to statements of general principle such as Lord Fraser's. The Lord President's opinion in *Shilliday* reminds us that Scots law has identified various situations where persons are to be regarded as having been unjustly enriched at another's expense. While unjust enrichment at another's expense may be the unifying feature of the cases, it is necessary to anchor the analysis in texts which tell us how Scots law has instantiated that general principle in particular circumstances.

---

[24] *Ibid*.

[25] *Dollar Land (Cumbernauld) Limited v. CIN Properties Limited* 1998 SC (HL) 90 at 99 *per* Lord Hope of Craighead.

[26] Lord Fraser's formulation implies that the pursuer must shoulder the onus of showing that, in the whole circumstances of the case, it would be equitable for a remedy to be granted. By contrast, in *Morgan Guaranty Trust Company of New York v. Lothian Regional Council* 1995 SC 151 (which concerned a *condictio indebiti* claim for repayment of money) it was held that once the pursuer has established that he has paid a sum which was not due and (normally at least) that it was paid in error, the onus shifts to the defender to plead any equitable circumstances going to defeat the claim. Formally, the two propositions are not necessarily inconsistent: it may be that in a *condictio indebiti* case, a pursuer satisfies the burden implied by Lord Fraser simply by showing that he has paid a debt which was not due and explained how he came to do so (normally by proving that he did so in error). Applying the principle of enrichment neutrality, the same approach should apply when a pursuer seeks to show that he improved the defender's land in the erroneous belief that he was under a contractual obligation to do so. But when the ground of liability is different, the pursuer may clearly have to prove other matters in order to make out his claim. There is a danger that the discrepancy between Lord Fraser's formulation and the statement of the law in *Morgan Guaranty* will be explained on the basis that the former was uttered in a case seeking recompense, the latter in a case seeking repetition (e.g. *Michael v. Carruthers* 1998 SLT 1179 at 1187). Applying the principle of enrichment neutrality, that would not be a sound basis of distinction.

III. Enrichment by improvement in Scots law

1. Three texts
Certain themes in the law on enrichment by improvements in Scotland (some of which will come to be considered in more detail later) can be illustrated by considering three key texts.

(a) Stair

At Book II, Title 1 of his *Institutions* (which deals with 'rights real or dominion') Stair says this:

> It is a rule in the Roman law, which we follow, *inaedificatum solo cedit solo*; for thereby all buildings of houses, walls, wells, dykes, &c. and generally all things fixed to the ground, or walls, are accounted as parts of the ground...; and thence, not only the materials of others become the owners of the ground, on which they are builded, and for preserving of policy, cannot be demolished, as hath been said of constructure: but likewise he that builds with his own materials upon another man's ground, the same accresce to the ground, and if the owner of these materials knew the ground to be another's, the Roman law gave him no recompense therefor, but presumed it to be done *animo donandi*, which is rather penal, in hatred of these who encroach upon the ground of others, than from any sufficient ground of presumption; and therefore our custom doth allow a recompense to the builder, in so far as the heritor was profited thereby, in that he might get a greater rent for that building... But building of houses by tenants for their own use, though at their removing they leave the land in better condition than at their entry, they get no satisfaction therefor without paction.[27]

In his discussion of recompense Stair mentions improvements simply as an illustrative example:[28]

> The other obligation of recompense is for that whereby we are enriched by another's means, without purpose of donation, which is only presumed in a few cases, as he who even[29] *mala fide* buildeth upon another man's ground, or

---

[27] Stair goes on to deal with improvements by life-renters and apprisers.

[28] Book I, Title 8, 6. The illustration may have occurred to Stair relatively late in the development of the text: it does not appear in the equivalent passage in a 1676 manuscript of the *Institutions* in my possession.

[29] The punctuation and syntax at this point vary in different editions, with a subtle effect on the meaning. The first edition (Edinburgh, 1681) is as follows: 'The other Obligation of Recompense, is, for that whereby we are enriched by anothers Means, without purpose of Donation, which is only presumed in few Cases, even he who *mala fide*, buildeth upon another Man's Ground, or repaireth unnecessarily his House, is not presumed to do it, *animo donandi*, but hath Recompense by the owner, *in quantum lucratus*.' Brodie's edition (Edinburgh, 1826) follows Stair's own second edition; More's edition (Edinburgh, 1832) the first (with a change in the punctuation).

repaireth unnecessarily his house, is not presumed to do it, *animo donandi*, but hath recompense by the owner in *quantum lucratus*[30] ...

The following points may be noticed:

(i) The law on enrichment by improvements is, for Stair, a response to the proprietary effects of the law of accession. If someone's property is taken away from them by the law of accession, enrichment law, on Stair's analysis, steps in to provide recompense.[31]

(ii) Stair is prepared to allow even a mala fide improver a claim and is prepared to allow such an improver a claim even in respect of unnecessary expenses. This was controversial and ultimately came to be departed from.

(iii) Stair links the question whether or not the improver should be allowed a claim to the question whether or not he could be taken to have intended donation. He construes Roman law as applying a presumption of donation to the mala fide improver,[32] and denies, in the passage at *Institutions*, Book I, Title 8, 6, that it is proper to make such a presumption.[33]

(iv) Stair denies any claim to a tenant. This has consistently been asserted to be the position in Scots law.[34]

---

[30] Stair founds here on a text of Paul. D. 5, 3, 38. The text concerns *hereditatis petitio* and was explained by Lord Murray, the Lord Ordinary, in *Barbour v. Halliday* (1840) 2 D 1279 in the following terms: 'A *mala fide* possessor was obliged by the civil law to account for whatever profit might have been reaped from the subject. It would be obviously unjust in the proceedings under a *petitio hereditatis*, which included whatever belonged to the *hereditas jacens*, to oblige a *mala fide* possessor to account for all profits which he might have made, but never actually received, and not be allowed in that accounting the outlay from which such profits may have arisen.'

[31] As Kenneth Reid has put it, '[e]nrichment law is like a dog snapping at the heels of property law': 'Unjustified Enrichment and Property Law', [1994] JR 167, 168.

[32] What did Stair mean by the mala fide improver? He cannot have meant that *anyone* who improved land knowing that it belonged to someone else would have a claim, since in Book II, Title 1, 40 he expressly excluded the case of a tenant. He may simply have meant that someone who occupies land on the basis of a title of ownership, but is aware that it is open to challenge, has a claim: cf. Brodie's note to Book II, Title 1, 40 in his edition (Edinburgh, 1826) of Stair's *Institutions*. Or he may have meant that any possessor or occupier (other than those expressly excluded in Book II, Title 1, 40) would have a claim whatever their state of knowledge. The judges in *Barbour v. Halliday* (1840) 2 D 1279 appear to have understood Stair to be stating this stronger proposition.

[33] He was not consistent on this point. In *Institutions*, Book IV, Title 45, 17 he wrote: 'What is wittingly built or wrought upon the ground of another is presumed to be a donation.'

[34] Interestingly, this was not the position in Roman-Dutch law until the issue of two Placcaeten in 1658 and 1696, which, in the case of lessees of rural tenements, denied a claim for improvements unless effected with the consent of the landowner-lessor. The Placcaeten continue to apply in South African law.

(b) Bankton

In his *Institutions*, published in 1751,[35] Bankton sets out a somewhat different version of the law:

When one builds on another's ground, the building follows the ground, and belongs in property to the proprietor of the ground, it being a rule, that *Inaedificatum cedit solo*: and thus likewise reparations made upon another's house accrue to the proprietor of the house, as to things fixed thereto, for its perpetual use; but at the same time, regularly, the owner of the ground or house is naturally liable to make satisfaction to the builder or repairer, even without paction, so far as he profited thereby.

By the civil law, in this case, even a person that built or repaired *bona fide*, believing the ground or house to be his own could only recover the Necessary and Profitable expenses, by retaining the possession till he was reimbursed; but, if he lost the possession, he had no remedy; he might only remove the materials, without prejudicing the subject, in Voluptuary expenses, i.e. such repairs as are only for pleasure, but yield no profit. A *mala fide* possessor, or one that built or repaired, when he knew the subject was not his own, had Retention for the necessary expenses in accounting for the rents and profits, provided only the subject were thereby improved in its value; and, as to other expenses, he might remove the materials, with the above limitation.

But our law not only allows Retention to every *bona fide* builder and repairer, but action likewise to both, for Necessary expenses, i.e. such as save the house from perishing or growing worse; and Profitable ones, whereby the subject is meliorated, and affords a greater rent; but not as to Voluptuary expenses laid out only for decorement; and, in every case where expenses are not refunded, the removal of materials, fixed for the perpetual use of the subject, is likewise refused: but the foresaid rule admits of this limitation, That tenants of a country farm are bound to keep the houses in such repair as they got them; and if they either make new reparations, or additional buildings, they get no allowance of expense, at expiration of their tacks, even tho' they leave the houses and land in better condition than at their entry...[36]

The following points may be noticed:

(i) Once again, the enrichment remedy is identified as a response to the law of accession.
(ii) Bankton treats retention as the improver's primary remedy. This is consistent with Roman law. It is implicit that Bankton has in mind an improver who was in occupation of land, and who therefore could insist on remaining in occupation until his claim for improvements

---

[35] Andrew McDouall, Lord Bankton, *An Institute of the Laws of Scotland in Civil Rights* (Edinburgh, 1751).
[36] Bankton, like Stair, goes on to consider the case of the life-renter.

had been met. This right of retention probably remains part of Scots law.[37]

(iii) It appears to be implicit in his treatment that Bankton envisages that at least some improvers have the right to remove the materials, at least provided this does not prejudice the subjects. He states that this remedy was available in Roman law. In his treatment of Scots law, he excludes a right of removal in those cases where the improver has no pecuniary claim, which tends to imply that he considered that improvers with a pecuniary claim could also have such a right.

(iv) Bankton regards as of some importance the distinction between necessary, profitable and voluptuary expenses. This is a distinction which is familiar in other civilian systems.[38] Although, apart from Bankton's treatment, it makes only fleeting appearances in Scottish texts,[39] it is probably part of Scots law.

(c) *The York Buildings Company v. Mackenzie*[40]

The third 'text' is a case, one that illustrates the operation of the law in a common situation and has been treated throughout the history of the law as a 'prominent example' of the 'doctrine' of recompense,[41] namely that situation which arises when someone 'in *bona fide* builds on another's ground believing it to be his own'.[42] Estates in Scotland of the York Buildings Company were sold under authority of the court. Mackenzie was the common agent in the sale. He purchased the estates himself, the sale was approved by the court, and he received a Crown charter. After he had been in possession of the estates for eleven years, the company brought an action to reduce the sale. The House of Lords, in a decision which is

---

[37] *Stair Memorial Encyclopaedia of the Laws of Scotland* (1993), vol. XVIII, §§ 173–4; but see George Joseph Bell, *Principles of the Law of Scotland* (10th edn by W. Guthrie, 1899), § 937.

[38] For example South African law (see, e.g., *Lechoana v. Cloete* 1925 AD 536) and French law (e.g. F. Terré and P. Simler, *Droit Civil: Les Biens* (4th edn, 1992), 319–20). Paul. D. 50, 16, 79, 2 illustrates the concept of voluptuary expenses.

[39] A. Bayne, *Notes for the Use of Students of the Municipal Law in the University of Edinburgh* (Edinburgh, 1731), 38, deploys the same three-part distinction. Baron David Hume, *Lectures, 1786–1822* (ed. G. C. H. Paton, 1952), vol. III, 171, uses the concept of voluptuary expenses without using the term. See further below, 398 ff., 424–5.

[40] (1795) 3 Paton 378; (1797) 3 Paton 579; see also the discussion of this case in *Aberdeen Railway Co. v. Blaikie, Brothers* (1854) 1 Macqueen 461.

[41] Bell, *Principles*, § 538.

[42] *Ibid.* (the last five words in this quotation were added by Guthrie). Rankine has pointed out that the accounting did not treat Mackenzie in all respects as a bona fide possessor in the strict sense, but this does not deprive the example of its utility in the present context: John Rankine, *The Law of Landownership in Scotland* (4th edn, Edinburgh, 1909), 90–2.

a leading authority on the rule against self-dealing by fiduciaries,[43] held that the claim was made out. It was therefore necessary to unravel the consequences of Mackenzie's occupation of the subjects over a period of eleven years. On the one hand he had occupied the estate and enjoyed rental income from it. But on the other he had considerably improved it, erecting a fine mansionhouse[44] and other buildings, sinking coalmines and laying out plantations and policies. He had also granted leases to tenants. The order which the House of Lords approved is worth quoting at length:

it is hereby declared that the decreet of sale, and the charter under the great seal, proceeding on the said decree of sale in favour of the defender... ought to be set aside and voided, to such extent and degree, and in manner hereafter provided, and the defender ought to refund to the pursuer all the rents and profits which he hath received out of the estate in question, and an adequate consideration for the enjoyment of such part thereof as he occupied himself: But without prejudice to the title of the defender to reclaim all such sums of money as he hath paid for the original price thereof, and also for the permanent improvement of the same, with the interest thereof, to be computed from the time when the same were advanced... and likewise without prejudice to the titles and interests of the lessees and others, who may have contracted with the defender *bona fide* and before the dependence of the present process... And it is further ordered, that an account be taken of the several sums of money which the defender hath actually paid as the original price of the said estates, and also of such further sums of money as he had actually laid out for the benefit and improvement of the said estates, and that interest be computed... upon the said several sums... and that one of the said accounts be set against the other... and that either party do pay to the other such sum of money as shall

---

[43] The case is sometimes cited for the proposition that the constructive trust is part of Scots law: e.g. P. Hood, 'What is so Special about Being Fiduciary?', (2000) 4 *Edinburgh LR* 308, 320, n. 82. *York Buildings Co. v. Mackenzie* does not support that proposition if it is taken to imply that the 'trust property' is sheltered in the event of the 'trustee's' insolvency. Lord Thurlow stated as follows: 'It is undoubtedly clear that no man can be trustee for another, but by contract: it is equally clear, that under circumstances, a man may be liable to all the consequences in his own person which a trustee would become liable to by contract' ((1795) 3 Paton 378 at 393). A trustee may be liable if he breaches his fiduciary obligations. An agent may also be liable if he breaches his fiduciary obligations. This is because both are fiduciaries. It does not follow that an agent *is* a trustee, constructive or otherwise. It is noteworthy that Lord Thurlow speaks of 'the consequences in his own person': this would be consistent with the proposition that the obligations which arise do not have proprietary effects.

[44] The architect was Robert Adam. The house, Seton House, has been described as 'the most perfectly executed of the castle type which he [Adam] developed in Scotland over the last fifteen years of his life' and to mark 'the high point in Adam's synthesis of neo-classical geometry and picturesque diversity': Colin McWilliam, *The Buildings of Scotland: Lothian* (1978), 428–9.

be found due on the balance of the accounts, if nothing be due to the defender or upon payment of what shall be so found due, that the defender do re-convey the said estates to the pursuers...

This is a very striking example of the willingness of Scots law, in the process of mutual accounting which takes place when someone who has been in occupation of land for a period of time is dispossessed by the true owner, to value benefits in kind, and in particular benefits of the nature of improvements to the owner's property. It is also noteworthy that Mackenzie was not required to reconvey the property unless and until he had been paid any balance found owing to him.[45]

2. Improvements by bona fide possessors of land and cognate cases[46]

(a) The legal position of mala fide improvers

It is a feature of modern civilian legal systems – in contrast to English law[47] – that they favour the claims of the person who, while occupying land belonging to someone else, improves it.[48] It will already be clear that Scots law is in this respect firmly in the civilian camp. Stair was prepared to grant a remedy even to a mala fide improver.[49] His view may not be

---

[45] When an order to similar effect was made in the case of *Douglas v. Douglas' Trs* (1864) 2 M 1379, the owner elected not to take the property: at 1388.

[46] See generally Rankine, *Law of Landownership*, 86–94; for a more recent treatment see *Stair Memorial Encyclopaedia*, vol. XVIII, §§ 131–4, 167, 172–3. The history is discussed in some detail in H. L. MacQueen and W. D. H. Sellar, 'Unjust Enrichment in Scots Law', in: E. J. H. Schrage (ed.), *Unjust Enrichment: The Comparative Legal History of the Law of Restitution* (1995), 305–10. Although the authorities deal mainly with heritable property, there is no reason in principle why the same ground of liability should not apply to moveables (cf. *McCarthy Retail Ltd v. Shortdistance Carriers CC*, 16 March 2001, Supreme Court of Appeal of South Africa) – although there is a curious dearth of Scottish examples: cf. the unsuccessful claims in *Cran v. Dodson* (1893) 11 SLT 354 and *Express Coach Finishers v. Caulfield* 1968 SLT (Sh Ct) 1. There is authority for applying the same rule to improvements to incorporeal assets: *The Edinburgh Life Assurance Corporation v. Balderston* (1909) 2 SLT 323.

[47] See Goff and Jones, *Law of Restitution*, 241.

[48] See Verse, 'Improvements and Enrichments', The Roman texts include Inst. II, 1, 30; Cels. D. 12, 1, 38; Iul. D. 12, 6, 33; see also Pomp. D. 12, 6, 51. For the later history, see J. Hallebeek, 'Developments in Mediaeval Roman Law', in: Schrage (ed.), *Unjust Enrichment*, 59; Reinhard Zimmermann, *The Law of Obligations: Roman Foundations of the Civilian Tradition* (paperback edn, 1996), 875–6. The issues typically arise, as is exemplified by the *York Buildings Co.* case, in the context of recovery of possession by the owner. The BGB has a detailed regime regulating such cases: §§ 994–1003.

[49] Cf. modern South African law, which apparently gives a remedy to mala fide possessors and occupiers (except tenants): see, e.g., C. G. van der Merwe and M. J. de Waal, *The Law of Things and Servitudes* (1993), §§ 90–102; S. Eiselen and G. Pienaar, *Unjustified Enrichment: A Casebook* (1993), chap. 5. Visser's view is that the matter remains uncertain in South African law (and he clearly disapproves of the equation

unconnected with his theoretical starting point that '[t]he obligation of remuneration or recompense is that bond of the law of nature, obliging to do one good deed for another'.[50] one who deliberately bestows a benefit on another is perhaps more worthy of gratitude than one who does so by mistake. But then, as Stair remarked, 'because the complaints of ingratitude are so frequent and unclear, everyone esteeming highly of the demerit of his own actions, therefore most of them are laid aside without any legal remedy'.[51] Later writers doubted whether Stair was correct[52] and in 1840 the First Division repudiated his position in the case of *Barbour v. Halliday*.[53] Halliday went to America, leaving the title deeds to some land in the custody of his father and brother. Halliday's brother, without having authority to do so, handed the title deeds to Barbour in security of a debt owed to Barbour by one McIntyre (the original seller of the land to Halliday). Barbour purported to sell the ground to Gordon, who built a house on it at the cost of £200 or £300. Gordon became apprehensive about the want of a good title and Barbour agreed to take the subjects back, reimbursing Gordon for his outlays. Gordon granted Barbour a disposition. Halliday returned from America and, not surprisingly, insisted on his right to the ground with the house built on it. He succeeded in having Barbour evicted, but Barbour raised an action seeking reimbursement for the improvements on the land, contending that Halliday was liable *in quantum lucratus*. At first instance, Lord Murray examined Cujacius, Vinnius and Robert-Joseph Pothier as well as the Scottish writers, and concluded that Scots law was to the same effect as the law stated by Pothier, 'that the matter is judged of according to the circumstances of the case'. He seems to have envisaged that a distinction fell to be drawn between someone who (like Barbour) took advantage of the long absence of a proprietor and other cases where the possessor might have a good title which he knew was defective or defeasible (and would therefore be in bad faith, but would be looked on more favourably). On appeal, the First Division took a more robust position: stating unequivocally that

of mala fide possessors and occupiers with bona fide possessors and occupiers) although he recognises that 'there is powerful backing amongst academic writers in favour of treating the *mala fide* possessor in the same way as the *bona fide* possessor': D. Visser, 'Unjustified Enrichment', in: R. Zimmermann and D. Visser (eds.), *Southern Cross: Civil Law and Common Law in South Africa* (1996), 543–7. The medieval debate on the position of the *mala fide* improver is described in Hallebeek, 'Developments in Medieval Roman Law'.

[50] *Institutions*, Book I, Title 8, 1.   [51] *Ibid*.

[52] John Erskine, *An Institute of the Law of Scotland* (ed. J. Badenoch Nicolson, 1871), Book III, Title 1, 11; Bell, *Principles*, § 538; but see Bayne, *Notes*, 38; Brodie's note to Book II, Title 1, 40 of his edition (the fourth, 1826) of Stair's *Institutions*.

[53] (1840) 2 D 1279; followed in *Duke of Hamilton v. Johnston* (1877) 14 SLR 298.

'if the meliorations were made *mala fide*, the party who makes them has no claim for recompense'.[54]

Barbour did not, however, necessarily exclude mala fide improvers from any redress. There remained two possibilities. The first was that the mala fide improver, though excluded from an active claim, might nevertheless set up the value of meliorations as a deduction from any accounting which the true owner might require of him for profits. In *Barbour*, Lord Murray had explained the *Digest* text upon which Stair had founded, to this effect.[55] But in *Scott's Executors v. Hepburn*,[56] which concerned a meliorations claim by the executors of a tenant (which the Lord Ordinary was prepared to contemplate could be pled as a counterclaim to the landlord's claim to enforce repairing obligations), Lord President Inglis said this:

> his Lordship thinks that though this is a claim which cannot be made in an ordinary action, it may be pleaded by way of compensation. Now, that is rather a puzzling idea. I confess I am not acquainted with a kind of claim which cannot be enforced by ordinary action, but may be pleaded in compensation.[57]

Another possibility was that mala fide improvers would continue to have a claim in respect of improvements which could be characterised as 'necessary'. Text-writers have certainly asserted that *Barbour* did not touch such a claim and the mala fide improver's claim for necessary expenses may well remain part of the modern law.[58]

(b) Liability for improvements that are not necessary

By contrast, when someone carries out improvements on someone else's land which cannot be characterised as necessary improvements, the state of the improver's knowledge appears to be critical to whether or not he may have a financial claim against the owner. In the context of this type of liability it has been said that error is essential to liability.[59] In *Newton v.*

---

[54] At 1284 *per* Lord Mackenzie; see also at 1285 *per* Lord Fullerton. Lord Fullerton left open the possibility that Barbour had the right to remove the buildings. The same reservation was expressed by Lord President Inglis in *Duke of Hamilton v. Johnston* (1877) 14 SLR 298.

[55] See note 30, above.   [56] (1876) 3 R 816.

[57] *Ibid.* at 825-6. The irony is that such reasoning perhaps led to the extrapolation from D. 5, 3, 38 of an active claim for the mala fide improver in the first place.

[58] Bell, *Principles*, § 538, n. (g); Rankine, *Law of Landownership*, 89-90; *Stair Memorial Encyclopaedia*, § 172. This may perhaps be best regarded as an extension of *negotiorum gestio*: cf. Zimmermann, *Law of Obligations*, 875-6.

[59] E.g. *Buchanan v. Stewart* (1874) 2 R 78 *per* Lord Neaves; *Rankin v. Wither* (1886) 13 R 903 at 908 *per* Lord Young. Lord Young observed that error is essential to a case in recompense. This must be wrong. Error may be necessary before the remedy of

Newton[60] a husband had improved property belonging to his wife in the erroneous belief that he owned it. The wife argued that he could not have a claim unless he could produce an apparent title to the property. The argument was rejected: 'The test... is not whether there was a title or not, but whether there was *bona fides* on the part of the pursuer.'[61] The Lord Justice Clerk described 'the mental attitude' of the pursuer as the 'de quo' of the case. *Newton* was explained by the Lord President in *Shilliday* in the following terms:

> The critical factor in the pursuer's ground of action was his mistake about the title: he recovered because his wife was benefiting from sums which he would not have spent if he had been aware of the true position.[62]

If the improver knows the true state of things, he will not have a claim, whether or not he possesses on an apparent title of ownership or occupies the land on some title less than ownership such as a lease.[63] On the other

---

recompense is granted in this particular class of case. It does not follow that error is necessary if some other ground of liability consistent with the improver knowing the true state of ownership can be identified – e.g. under the *condictio causa data causa non secuta*: *Shilliday v. Smith* 1998 SC 725 at 731 *per* the Lord President (Lord Rodger).

[60] 1925 SC 715.

[61] *Ibid.* at 722. Arguably, this represented a change in the law: contrast Rankine, *Law of Landownership*, 78, 88. Indeed there is some authority to the effect that an improver who has an apparent title has no claim if circumstances should have put him on inquiry as to the defeasibility of his title: *Soues v. Mill* (1903) 11 SLT 98. See further below (n. 71). The issue has also caused trouble in Roman-Dutch law: see texts referred to in Van der Merwe and De Waal, *The Law of Things*, § 92, n. 1.

[62] 1998 SC 725 at 731.

[63] For example Stair, *Institutions*, Book II, Title 1, 40; *Scott's Executors v. Hepburn* (1876) 3 R 816. The law in respect of life-renters is somewhat more complex, although here, too, the basic rule is that a life-renter has no claim against the fiar for improvements: *Wallace v. Braid* (1900) 2 F 754; but see Erskine, *Institute*, Book III, Title 1, 11; Gloag and Henderson, *The Law of Scotland* (10th edn, 1995), 482. The reason for excluding these cases is usually said to be that such persons can be taken to have carried out improvements for their own benefit: e.g. Stair, *Institutions*, Book II, Title 1, 40; *Buchanan v. Stewart* (1874) 2 R 78; *Rankin v. Wither* (1886) 13 R 903; *Wallace v. Braid* (1900) 2 F 754. The suggested rationalisation is not a particularly satisfactory basis for distinguishing these cases from the person who improves land mistakenly believing that he owns it – the latter person likewise carried out the improvements for his own benefit. Rather, the critical point is that the improver's expectation that the improvements will enure to his estate is defeated because of his error as to the true state of affairs. This point is perhaps supported by the case of the life-renter who improved land erroneously believing that he was the fiar (and therefore had a claim): *Morrisons v. Allan* (1886) 13 R 1156. Stair, of course, had to rationalise the exclusion of such cases when he was prepared to allow that mala fide improvers had a claim: now that only *bona fide* improvers have a claim it is possible to discern a common feature in all the cases, namely error as to the true state of ownership.

hand, if he is labouring under some mistake about the true state of affairs and would not have carried out the works if he had known the truth,[64] then he may have a claim against the owner.

Phillip Hellwege has criticised the Lord President's explanation of *Newton* by reference to mistake (or at least to mistake or error on its own).[65] He puts his argument in this way:

> The legal context is property, not unjustified enrichment. If mistake were enough, then the *bona fide* possessor should have an active claim against the owner... This is not the case in Scots law. The right of the *bona fide* possessor does not simply accrue when he mistakenly improves the property of another but only when he is dispossessed of that property and a court will only allow the owner to take possession after he has recompensed the possessor. Finally, the rights of the possessor are part of broader considerations concerning how to balance the interest between the possessor and the owner. The claim of the *bona fide* possessor is thus not only dependent on his mistake... The right of the possessor arises because and when he is dispossessed of the thing which he improved.

It is true that most of the cases have concerned the adjustment of the respective rights of the parties on dispossession of the possessor and that the regime applicable when that arises is the context in which the claim of the bona fide possessor is typically discussed.[66] Indeed, the model which Hellwege describes is the focus of many of the texts. There are, however, at least three reasons for doubting whether modern Scots law is as Hellwege describes it.

(i) It is difficult to accommodate either the facts or the reasoning of *Newton* itself within Hellwege's description of the law. Mr Newton arranged for title to the property to be taken in his wife's name in 1918. He carried out the improvements in that year. His claim in respect of the improvements was raised after failure of a previous action for declarator that his wife owned the property in trust for him.[67] Its basis was not that he had been dispossessed, but simply that he had carried out the improvements in the erroneous belief that he was the owner.[68]

---

[64] *Shilliday v. Smith* 1996 SC 725 at 731 *per* the Lord President (Lord Rodger).
[65] Phillip Hellwege, 'Rationalising the Scottish Law of Unjustified Enrichment', 2000 *Stellenbosch Law Review* 50, 61–4.
[66] E.g. Rankine, *Law of Landownership, Stair Memorial Encyclopaedia*, vol. XVIII, §§ 167–73; cf. the special regime in §§ 994–1003 BGB.
[67] *Newton v. Newton* 1923 SC 15.
[68] His wife had granted a deed purporting to reconvey the subjects to him in 1921. This deed was reduced because of failure to comply with essential formalities: 1923 SC 15 at 18. But the improvements were carried out in 1918 and therefore not in reliance on this purported title. Nothing appears to have been made of the reduction of this deed in the context of the improvements claim.

(ii) There is at least one case that would suggest that the error need not be as to the improver's title to the land:[69] if this is correct it would not fit with Hellwege's analysis. Captain McDowel granted a ninety-nine-year lease to his wife over some land on an entailed estate. He then entered into contracts for the construction of considerable additions to the house on the property. While work was in progress he died. Ownership of the estate passed to his son. Twenty-two years later it transpired that the lease in favour of the widow had been void. The widow, suing as executrix of her husband, sought recompense from the son for the improvements to the estate. She was successful. Lord Mackenzie said this: 'I am of opinion that it has been proved that there was a *bona fide* belief on the part of Captain McDowel that he had given a valid title to his wife, and that but for that belief he would not have entered into the contracts for adding to Craig Lodge.' The case is, on one view, rather odd. Mrs McDowel, who was dispossessed, could not assert the claim in her own right because she was not the improver. The claim was accordingly pursued by her as executrix of Captain McDowel. But Captain McDowel (whose claim was being pursued) knew that he was improving his own land. He knew that ownership of the land (and any accessions to it) would pass to his son. The son received no more than he was entitled to as heir. But the case may have achieved a practical result. The son did obtain a benefit – namely, vacant possession of the property – and Mrs McDowel may have received some compensating benefit for the loss of the lease through the executry's claim.

(iii) If Hellwege's analysis were to be correct, then the improver's claim would be against the proprietor in possession at the date of dispossession. There is, however, some authority for the proposition that the improver's claim is against the person who was proprietor when the improvements were carried out, and does not transmit against singular successors at least where they are in good faith and gave full value for the property.[70]

(c) The basis of the owner's liability

There are, however, unresolved puzzles. Thus, although *Newton* asserted that subjective error on the part of the improver sufficed as the basis for a claim, in one subsequent case the court held that a sub-tenant whose lease was reduced at the instance of a heritable creditor was in bad faith, not because it knew of the existence of the heritable creditor, but because it had taken the sub-lease without inquiries which would have disclosed

---

[69] *McDowel v. McDowel* (1906) 14 SLT 125. [70] *Beattie v. Lord Napier* (1831) 9 S 639.

that the sub-lease would be reducible at the heritable creditor's instance.[71] More generally, what is one to make, following *Newton*, of the older authorities to the general effect that a possessor could only have a claim if he had an apparent title? Moreover, can it really be said that an improver cannot bring into account the improvements in circumstances where he is evicted by someone who was not the true proprietor when the improvements were carried out? How is such a proposition to be squared with the improver's right of retention (assuming that to remain part of Scots law)?

It is tempting to seek to explain the role of error in the analysis on the basis that the true owner receives and retains a benefit without any legal ground. The bona fide possessor and cognate cases[72] involve someone improving another's land without being under any legal obligation to do so. It might be said that the owner retains the benefit without any legal ground for doing so. But would this not be the case whether the improver was in good or in bad faith? One might seek to return to Stair's discussion of the role of donation in the analysis in order to rationalise the case law – an approach that has been approved in the context of *condictio indebiti* claims in relation to money.[73] It might be said that, if the improver knows the true state of ownership he may be taken to have intended to donate the improvement to the true owner of the land (in which case the owner has a legal ground for retaining the benefit). If he believes that he himself is the true owner when he is not, this negatives any presumption of donation (and the owner therefore retains the benefit without a legal ground). It is questionable, however, whether such an analysis convincingly explains the particular ground of liability under consideration.

In reality an absence of any intention of donation is not inconsistent with full knowledge of the circumstances. In *Rankin v. Wither*[74] a husband who had improved his wife's property in full knowledge of the state of ownership sought to argue that the improvement *was* a donation – because

---

[71] *Trade Development Bank v. Warriner & Mason (Scotland) Limited* 1980 SC 74, in particular at 98 *per* Lord President Emslie and at 104 *per* Lord Cameron. The consideration of good faith for the purposes of the meliorations claim in this case may have been affected by an association with the issue of good faith for the purposes of the 'rule against offside goals'. The two concepts need not necessarily be identical. The improver's claim was in any event rejected on the basis of longstanding authority that an improver has no claim against a heritable creditor.

[72] But not *McDowel*.

[73] *Morgan Guaranty Trust Company of New York v. Lothian Regional Council* 1995 SC 151 at 165 *per* Lord President Hope, and at 170 *per* Lord Clyde.

[74] (1886) 13 R 903.

he could then argue that it was revocable as a donation between spouses. The argument was rejected on the basis that the intention to make a donation had not been proved. If the improver in fact had no intention of donation, notwithstanding that he knew the true state of affairs, then, in principle, if the matter is merely one of presumption, he would be entitled to give evidence that he did not intend donation, evidence which would (if believed) entitle him to a remedy. But the rule, for example, refusing a claim to a tenant has the flavour of an absolute exclusionary rule of law[75] rather than a rule founded on a presumption which the tenant could seek to rebut by, for example, asserting that he did not understand the law of accession.[76] It appears that the ground of liability which applies in these cases is not adequately or at least completely explained by the 'retention without legal ground' formula:[77] 'retention without legal ground' may be necessary, but it is not sufficient for liability. Indeed, if *McDowel* was correctly decided, 'retention without legal ground' may not be a necessary condition of liability in these cases.

Whatever may be the basis of the particular ground of liability which is at issue in the bona fide possessor and cognate cases, commitment to enrichment neutrality would require that when a defender has been enriched in circumstances falling within that ground of liability, the enrichment should be reversed whatever its nature (i.e. the *bona fide* possessor cases should not be regarded as peculiarly about improvements). There is a neat proof of this thesis in the facts of *Duff, Ross & Co. v. Kippen*.[78] A partnership carried on business in Clydebank in the bona fide belief that the business premises were owned by it. On that basis the firm spent more than £234 on (i) paying the half-yearly ground annual and various assessments due on the property, and (ii) making alterations and repairs. In fact the property was owned by a third party and leased to one of the partners. The business folded and the sole surviving partner advanced a claim against the owner, *inter alia*, for £234 'expended by him on the works while in the bona fide belief that they belonged to his firm'. The Lord Ordinary found the whole sum due and his decision was affirmed on appeal. No distinction was drawn between the two modes of enrichment.

---

[75] Cf. *Dollar Land (Cumbernauld) Limited v. CIN Properties Limited* 1998 SC (HL) 90. That improvements are carried out by a tenant under a lease does not constitute a 'legal ground' for the improvements unless they are improvements which are required to be carried out in terms of the lease.
[76] That the error is one of law should not matter following *Morgan Guaranty*.
[77] It may be noted that the Lord President in *Shilliday* expressly envisaged that there might be cases not covered by the 'retention without legal ground' formula.
[78] (1871) 8 SLR 299.

It would have been astonishing if any such distinction were to be drawn. If it is morally justifiable to require a defender owner in such circumstances to pay for improvements to his property which he did not request, it is equally (if not more) justifiable to require him to pay for the discharge of his liabilities.[79] *Anderson v. Anderson*[80] may be another example. The pursuer and his three siblings inherited a farm. The pursuer managed it in the genuine (but mistaken) belief that he had made an arrangement with his siblings by which the farm was handed over to him for his own benefit. He was allowed recompense. The ground of liability fits neatly with the bona fide possessor cases at least as the doctrine in those cases was applied in *Newton*. But the defenders' enrichment did not take the form of improvements: rather, it was probably expenditure saved.[81]

3. Improvements and other grounds of liability

Most improvements done by one person to another's land are probably done deliberately, in full knowledge of the situation – pursuant to a building contract or because of some other relationship between the improver and the owner. It follows that one would expect to find (consistent with the enrichment neutrality thesis) instances of liability in respect of improvements in the 'fact situations' gathered under the *condictiones*.

(a) *Condictio causa data causa non secuta*

Shilliday was (in part) about enrichment by improvements, reversed because the facts fell within those situations dealt with in Scots law under the rubric of the *condictio causa data causa non secuta*. Like *Duff, Ross & Co.* it proves the enrichment neutrality thesis because more than one mode of enrichment was at issue, but only one ground of liability. There is a tract of improvements cases which, in light of *Shilliday*, can now also be seen to fall into the category *condictio causa data causa non secuta*.[82] In *Bell v. Bell*[83] a son sued his father, alleging that they had entered into an arrangement whereby the son was to be allowed to build a dwelling house on land

---

[79] Cf. § 995 BGB.   [80] (1869) 8 M 157.   [81] See further below, 411–13.
[82] It would be fair to observe that the judges who decided these cases did not have this basis of liability clearly in their minds: the opinions exhibit a degree of uncertainty as to how the claims were to be categorised. Treating them as falling within the group of cases treated under the rubric of the *condictio causa data causa non secuta* (at least as that rubric was explained in *Shilliday*) appears to be a satisfactory explanation.
[83] (1841) 2 D 1201; see also *Heddle v. Baikie* (1841) 3 D 370; (1846) 8 D 376; (1843) 15 Scottish Jurist 559; and *Allan v. Gilchrist* (1875) 2 R 587 at 590–1 *per* Lord Deas (who explains *Heddle* under reference to the Session Papers).

belonging to the father and that the defender would, whenever required, grant him title to the land. The son built the house but the father transferred the land to his daughter. The son was entitled to 'repetition' of the amount which he had spent.[84] Although the case has been characterised as one based on fraud,[85] it appears satisfactorily classifiable within the 'fact situation' known as the *condictio causa data causa non secuta*,[86] as it was explained in *Shilliday*.[87] Likewise, in *Mackay v. Rodger*,[88] the pursuers were allowed a proof of their claims for recompense when they averred that they had spent £900 erecting buildings on land belonging to their sister under an arrangement with her (never reduced to writing) that each of them would be entitled to a proportionate interest in the new buildings and that the land had now passed to the sister's heir on her death. *Reedie v. Yeaman*[89] presents a somewhat different situation, which may nevertheless be seen as a *condictio causa data causa non secuta* case. A husband and wife executed a mutual *mortis causa* disposition and settlement by which each conveyed to the survivor his or her property. The disposition

---

[84] 'Repetition' is inapt since it properly refers to repayment of money by the recipient thereof.

[85] See the opinions of Lord Gillies and Lord Mackenzie; also the reference to the case in *Allan v. Gilchrist* (1875) 2 R 587 (not itself a *condictio causa data causa non secuta* case) at 592 *per* Lord Deas. The use of 'fraud' in this context may hark back to the *exceptio doli* in favour of the good-faith builder in Inst. II, 1, 30.

[86] Birks treats *Bell* and *Mackay v. Rodger* (1907) 15 SLT 42 as cases of 'free acceptance': 'Restitution', 73. Birks's own analysis of that concept has undergone development, however, and it might be consistent with his more recently expressed views to recognise these as cases of 'non-reciprocation': see P. B. H. Birks, 'In Defence of Free Acceptance', in: A. Burrows (ed.), *Essays on the Law of Restitution* (1991). In *Shilliday* the Lord President noted that the defender knew that the pursuer was expending money on his house (as will no doubt be the situation in this class of cases), but this does not seem to be at the root of the decision: 1998 SC 725 at 730D–E.

[87] In *Shilliday* the contention that the expenditure needed to be conditional in a technical sense was rejected. It was sufficient that the expenditure was incurred in contemplation of a marriage which failed to materialise. The pursuer in *Shilliday* knew full well that she was incurring expenditure on the defender's property. She may be taken to have appreciated that it would become the defender's property albeit that she expected that title would be transferred into joint names at some later date. These circumstances would be enough, in other contexts in the law of unjustified enrichment, to require the pursuer to make averments rebutting donation: *Morgan Guaranty Trust Company of New York v. Lothian Regional Council* 1995 SC 151 at 165 *per* Lord President Hope and at 170 *per* Lord Clyde. But if there was donation the retention was not 'without legal ground' unless the donation was in the strict sense conditional, so that the ground fell away upon the condition not being purified. This is not to suggest that *Shilliday* was wrong in its approach to the *condictio causa data causa non secuta*; rather, the problem may lie in the tendency to infer donation when a party acts in full knowledge of the circumstances: see above, 402–3.

[88] (1907) 15 SLT 42.   [89] (1875) SLR 625.

was revocable. The husband spent money building additions to a house which belonged to his wife. Without telling her husband, the wife revoked the disposition and settled the property on her sons. After her death, the husband sought recompense from the sons and was successful because of the specialty created by the mutual disposition.[90]

(b) *Condictio indebiti*

Improvement works carried out by someone under the erroneous belief that he is under an obligation to execute them can be treated simply as a case of the *condictio indebiti*, with the consequence that the party who receives the benefit of the works may be required to pay for them to the extent that he is enriched. For example, if a building contractor were to carry out works in implement of a supposed contract with the owner of the land which turned out to be void,[91] he should be entitled to recompense from the owner of the land.[92] Examples are rare but an old House of Lords case, *Magistrates of Rutherglen v. Cullen*,[93] may be one. Cullen contracted with the magistrates of Rutherglen to build a bridge across the Clyde according to a specified plan. It transpired that if the bridge was executed according to the plan it would not be a sufficient one. In order to make an adequate bridge it would be necessary to construct elaborate foundation work not shown on the plan and, indeed, to enlarge the abutments shown on the plan. The Court of Session found that neither party had this in view when they entered into the contract and held that neither party was bound by the contract. Cullen was ordered to repay moneys advanced by the magistrates. The court also declared that he was entitled to remove the materials and works already used or prepared by him, unless by a particular date the magistrates should 'agree to take the materials not used off his hands, or to make use of the work already wrought'. In that event the materials and works were to be valued and the value deducted from the moneys to be repaid by Cullen. The House of Lords affirmed this order. The case has been treated as one founded on essential error[94] but might also be regarded as one of impossibility

---

[90] The other grounds advanced failed; see also *Rankin v. Wither* (1886) 13 R 903.
[91] See generally *Stair Memorial Encyclopaedia of the Laws of Scotland* (1994), vol. III, § 27.
[92] Subject to the specialties that may arise if the contract is void for illegality: see *Cuthbertson v. Lowes* (1870) 8 M 1073; *Jamieson v. Watt's Trustee* 1950 SC 265; *Dowling & Rutter v. Abacus Frozen Foods Limited*, 15 March 2000 (unreported) *per* Lord Wheatley.
[93] (1773) 2 Paton 305.
[94] W. W. McBryde, *The Law of Contract in Scotland* (1987), 179. The rubric in the Scots Revised Reports is 'Essential Error'.

ab initio.[95] For present purposes its interest is to illustrate the availability of a remedy[96] when works have been executed in implement of a supposed but void contract. *Middleton v. Newton Display Group Limited*[97] may be a more recent example. A painting contractor agreed to carry out work for a sub-contractor engaged in constructing structures at Glasgow Garden Festival. The sheriff held that the agreement between the parties was entered into under mutual error as to the nature of the work involved, that the contract was void, and that the defenders having benefited from the pursuers' work were obliged to recompense the pursuers.[98]

(c) The problem of the voidable contract: *Boyd & Forrest v. Glasgow & South Western Railway*

There is an impediment to achieving the same result when improvement works have been carried out under a contract which is voidable (for example because it was induced by a misrepresentation that did not vitiate the parties' consent) rather than void. An enrichment remedy cannot be granted unless the contract has been reduced: while the contract subsists the benefit of the work is not retained without legal ground. But it is a precondition to reduction of a voidable contract that *restitutio in integrum* be possible.[99] Observations in the House of Lords in a Scottish appeal, *Boyd & Forrest v. Glasgow & South Western Railway*,[100] would, if they correctly represent the law, effectively exclude reduction of a voidable contract if, in implement of the contract, construction works have been executed. A railway company let a contract for the construction of a railway line. The contractors came across much more rock than they expected but nevertheless proceeded with the work and completed it. Because of the hard strata, the work cost the contractor a great deal more than it had anticipated. The contractor alleged that a journal of bores which had been produced before entering into the contract had in certain respects misstated the position (and that he had only discovered this after the works had been completed).

---

[95] Cf. Robert-Joseph Pothier, *Contrat de Louage*, in: his *Oeuvres* (1835), § 395.
[96] See further below, 427-30, on the nature of the remedy.
[97] Glasgow Sheriff Court, 9 October 1990 (unreported).
[98] The sheriff awarded a reasonable price for the work done calculated on a *quantum meruit* basis. Strictly speaking, this cannot be correct. The pursuer was a sub-sub-contractor. The defender was enriched by the pursuer's work either by the discharge of its own obligations to the main contractor or by the saving of expenditure which it would otherwise have incurred in discharging those obligations. The quantum in fact awarded might approximate to the latter amount – but there is nevertheless a missing step in the analysis.
[99] W. M. Gloag, *The Law of Contract* (2nd edn, 1929), 533, 539-42. [100] 1915 SC (HL) 20.

During the extensive litigation which ensued,[101] it was decided that there had been no fraud, but the contractor nevertheless argued that the contract was inapplicable because it had entered into the contract under essential error induced by the company's innocent misrepresentation.[102] The House of Lords held that there had been no misrepresentation and that, the contractor had failed to prove that it had been induced to enter into the contract by the alleged misrepresentation. In any event, said the judges, the impossibility of *restitutio in integrum* barred reduction of the contract:

> I do not find myself able fully to comprehend that view of the case which would treat the situation as one equivalent to possible reduction by a process of adjustment of accounts. The railway is there, the bridges are built, the excavations are made, the rails are laid, and the railway itself was in complete working two years before this action was brought. Accounts cannot obliterate it, and unless the railway was obliterated, *restitutio in integrum* is impossible.[103]

This reasoning would extend to any case involving a building or construction contract once works have commenced on site. Although in a formal sense the *Boyd & Forrest* approach to *restitutio in integrum* is not an impediment to enrichment neutrality – because it prevents an enrichment cause of action ever coming into existence – in a practical sense it involves an asymmetry of result between building and construction works and other types of benefit: the *restitutio in integrum* requirement as interpreted in *Boyd & Forrest* is likely to exclude reduction (and consequently enrichment claims) as a matter of course in construction contracts[104] but to apply much less frequently in other cases.

This result was far from inevitable. As seen above, Scots law has been quite prepared to contemplate the valuation of construction works in the balancing of accounts which takes place when an owner recovers possession from a bona fide possessor. The contrast in approach between *Boyd & Forrest* and the *York Buildings Co.* case is striking: the more so since it is now well established that a transaction by a fiduciary which infringes the prohibition on self-dealing is not void but (like a contract induced by

---

[101] 1915 SC (HL) 20; 1914 SC 472; 1912 SC (HL) 93; 1911 SC 33 1051.

[102] On the inter-relationship (and confusion) between error and misrepresentation in this case see McBryde, *Law of Contract*, 194–6.

[103] 1915 SC (HL) 20 at 36 *per* Lord Shaw of Dunfermline; see also at 23 *per* Earl Loreburn, at 28–9 *per* Lord Atkinson and at 42–3 *per* Lord Parmoor.

[104] This was one of the reasons why the Second Division had held that the difficulties with *restitutio in integrum* did not bar the remedy sought: 1914 SC 472 at 506 *per* Lord Salvesen.

misrepresentation, such as that in *Boyd & Forrest*) voidable.[105] More than fifty years before *Boyd & Forrest*, the Court of Session had been prepared to contemplate reduction and an appropriate financial adjustment in a very similar case, *Adamson v. The Glasgow Corporation Water-Works Commissioners*.[106] Adamson had entered into a contract for the construction of a tunnel and reservoir. He alleged that he had been misled by the information (including a schedule of bores) that had been provided to him before entering into the contract. He abandoned the works when they were partially complete. He raised an action, concluding for reduction of the contract on the ground of essential error induced by misrepresentation. Notwithstanding that the works had been partially carried out the Court approved an issue to go to the jury to that effect, with a consequential issue directed to the question whether or not Adamson had provided work and materials in a particular amount.[107] Although *Adamson* concerned partially completed works rather than completed works, an application of the *Boyd & Forrest* approach to *restitutio in integrum* would have barred Adamson's claim. It would no doubt be undesirable to allow a contractor who discovers in the course of the works that he was induced to enter into the contract by a misrepresentation to continue with the works and only then seek to reduce the contract in order to claim a larger sum of money than the contractual price. But any attempt to do this can be forestalled by doctrines other than the requirement of *restitutio in integrum*.[108] The question is whether it is right to preclude reduction and a consequent enrichment claim where the contractor does, upon discovering the misrepresentation, immediately seek to avoid the contract, and in cases (which one imagines will be relatively rare) where a contractor only discovers that he has been materially misled after the works have been completed.[109]

---

[105] *Fraser v. Hankey & Co.* (1847) 9 D 415; see generally the cases mentioned by McBryde, *Law of Contract*, 155-6.
[106] (1859) 21 D 1012.
[107] The judgments exhibit a degree of uncertainty as to the legal basis of the financial claim. It might be said that *Adamson* arose before trial, when a question as to whether or not the contract was void on the ground of essential error, rather than merely voidable, could be said to be live, but this very ground of distinction illustrates the artificiality of a rule which in principle permits reduction and a balancing of accounts when a building contract is void, but refuses it if the contract is merely voidable.
[108] See Gloag, *Law of Contract*, 542-8; McBryde, *Law of Contract*, 625-6; *Rigg v. Durward* Mor Appendix *sub* 'Fraud' No. 2.
[109] *Boyd & Forrest* is itself an illustration of how difficult it will be for a contractor legitimately to complain of having been induced into a contract by a misrepresentation as to, say, ground conditions, after the works have been completed.

Lord Atkinson's speech in *Boyd & Forrest* presents an even more radical challenge to enrichment neutrality between building and construction works and other types of benefit. Although he refrained from expressing a formally concluded view, the tenor of his remarks makes plain that he would have refused a remedy even if the contract had fallen to be reduced:

> Now, where a special contract... has been entered into to execute, for a lump sum, the works therein mentioned, the right to be paid on a *quantum meruit* does not arise out of that contract, but out of a new contract springing into existence on the extinction of the old one. The two contracts cannot co-exist... This new contract must be proved by those who rely upon it. The mere taking advantage, or enjoying the benefit, of the work, does not, as it appears to be assumed in this case, necessarily prove its existence. It does prove its existence if the thing takes place under circumstances from which a promise to pay may be implied. In cases dealing with works done on real property, no such implication arises in most cases, since it is impossible for the owner of the land to rid himself of the works unless he destroys them, which would in many cases be as impossible as in the present case, or he gets rid of the land on which they have been executed, which in this case the defenders cannot do. In *Pattinson v. Luckley* [(1875) LR 10 Ex 330 at 334], Lord Bramwell points out this difference. He said: 'In the case of goods sold and delivered it is easy to show a contract from the retention of the goods; but that is not so where work is done on real property.' In *Sumpter v. Hedges* [[1898] 1 QB 673]... Collins LJ, as he then was... laid down the law thus: 'There are cases in which, though the plaintiff has abandoned the performance of a contract, it is possible for him to raise the inference of a new contract to pay for the work done on a *quantum meruit* from the defendants having taken the benefit of that work, but in order that that may be done, the circumstances must be such as to give an option to the defendant to take, or not to take, the benefit of the work done. It is only where the circumstances are such as to give that option that there is any evidence on which to ground the inference of a new contract. Where, as in the case of works done on land, the circumstances are such as to give the defendant no option whether he will take the benefit of the work or not, then one must look to other facts than the mere taking the benefit of the work in order to ground the inference of a new contract... The mere fact that a defendant is in possession of what he cannot help keeping, or even has done work upon it, affords no ground for such an inference.'... The law of Scotland does not, as far as I have been able to ascertain, differ from the law of England on this subject. Having regard to the view I take upon the other questions raised in this case, it is unnecessary for me to pronounce a definite opinion on this point. I wish, however, to guard against being supposed to acquiesce in the assumption that the mere use and enjoyment of the works executed proves, in such a case as the present, the entering into a contract to pay for them on a *quantum meruit* basis.[110]

[110] 1915 SC (HL) 20 at 25–6.

The underlying fallacy in these observations is the assumption that the basis of payment in such circumstances would be implied contract. Lord Atkinson is quite correct that the mere use and enjoyment of the works executed does not prove the existence of an implied contract – but that is beside the point when liability to reverse an unjustified enrichment is capable of being imposed by law. In so far as Lord Atkinson asserts that the *mere* use and enjoyment of improved property does not impose liability, such a statement would be unexceptionable. It is not the mere use and enjoyment of improved property which imposes liability, but its use and enjoyment in circumstances where the enjoyment of that benefit is unjustified. In such circumstances Scots law has never had difficulty granting a remedy: ample illustration has already been given of that. Inasmuch as Scots law differs in this respect from English law, Lord Atkinson's researches had failed him. As to the proposition that the owner of land which has been improved has no option whether or not to accept the benefit of the improvements, this cannot be treated as a universal truth: in cases where the works have not been authorised by the owner at least, the latter may be entitled to insist that they be removed.[111] In any event, as seen above, this factor has not been regarded in Scots law as a sufficient reason to refuse a remedy in improvements cases.

IV. Improvements and enrichment

1. Modes of enrichment

Someone may be said to have been enriched by an event if his stock of wealth – the overall value of his patrimony,[112] taking account both of assets and liabilities – has been increased[113] as compared with the

---

[111] See further below, 415–16. This option would not have been available to the railway company in *Boyd & Forrest* – after all, the company had invited the contractor to come onto its land in order to carry out the very works in issue.

[112] As the term is explained in G. L. Gretton, 'Trust and Patrimony', in: H. L. MacQueen (ed.), *Scots Law into the 21st Century: Essays in Honour of W. A. Wilson* (1996), 182 ff.

[113] This observation has deliberately been framed in such a way as not to exclude the possibility that someone may be enriched in other ways: e.g. by the provision of pure services which do not increase his stock of wealth in any of the ways about to be mentioned. Whether or not receipt of pure services can properly be regarded as an enrichment is controversial: see J. Beatson, *The Use and Abuse of Unjust Enrichment* (1991), 29–44; and for an answer Birks, 'In Defence of Free Acceptance', 132–5. The observation has also been framed so as not to predetermine the question of whether or not all increases in the value of the patrimony fall to be treated as enrichments as a matter of law.

position if the event had not taken place.[114] The overall value of someone's patrimony may be increased by an event (as compared with the position if the event had not taken place) in one of four ways:

  (i) by adding a new asset (whether a thing or money) to the patrimony;
  (ii) by discharging a liability of the patrimony;
  (iii) by increasing the value of an asset which already forms part of the patrimony;[115] and
  (iv) by preserving or maintaining in the patrimony an asset (whether a thing or money) which would (had the event not taken place) have been lost to it.

The last category perhaps requires a little more explanation. It would include preventing the destruction of tangible things: for example where 'goods are thrown overboard to lighten ships in danger of shipwreck, whereby the loss of all is prevented'.[116] It would also include the anticipation of expenditure which the defender would otherwise have incurred (but which he is not under an obligation to incur).[117]

The mode of enrichment is – or at least should be (assuming that it is regarded by the law as a recoverable type of enrichment) – critical in determining not only the method of reversing the enrichment but also the quantum of any pecuniary claim (leaving aside for present purposes any limitation to the amount expended by the pursuer). If the defender has been enriched by the addition of a new thing to his patrimony, the enrichment may be reversed by simply requiring him to redeliver the thing. If he has been enriched by the addition of money to his patrimony, he may be required to repay the same amount. If he has been enriched by the discharge of a liability to pay money, the enrichment may be reversed by requiring him to pay the pursuer the amount of the liability (or an

---

[114] As Stair observed: 'We are enriched either by accession of gain or by prevention of loss': *Institutions*, Book I, Title 8, 8; but contrast Baron Hume: 'It is not sufficient that, by means of his neighbour's money, he is less a loser, than he would otherwise have been. He must have a real benefit, or return of profit, into his own pocket': *Lectures*, vol. III, 167.

[115] This can, in principle, include maintaining the value of the asset if, in the absence of the event in question, the value of the asset would have declined.

[116] Stair, *Institutions*, Book I, Title 8, 8.

[117] The issue here is not whether or not the defenders would have been obliged to make the expenditure, but whether or not they would in fact have done so if the pursuer had not saved them from having to do so in *Lawrence Building Co. Ltd v. Lanark Country Council* 1978 SC 30 (in which the pursuer's construction company sought to recover the cost of constructing sewers from a local authority). Lord Maxwell, the Lord Ordinary, was prepared to contemplate that proof that the defenders would in fact have constructed the sewers if the pursuers had not done so might be sufficient to constitute enrichment: *ibid.* at 37.

appropriate proportion thereof). If he has been enriched by the discharge of a liability to do something, he may be required to pay the amount it would have cost him to discharge his liability. If the value of his existing assets has been increased, the enrichment may be reversed by requiring him to pay the amount of the increase. If he has been enriched by anticipating expenditure which he would otherwise have incurred (assuming that this counts as an enrichment), this can be reversed by requiring him to pay the amount of the expenditure saved.

'Improvements' in a practical sense – such as building or repair works that enhance land, buildings or moveable property – are capable of operating to increase a patrimony in any of the four ways described. They may involve the addition to a patrimony of physical assets – as when building materials built into a house pass into the ownership of the owner of the house (one might call these cases 'improvements by accession'). Equally, one person may, by carrying out improvement works, discharge someone else's liability. For example, if a building contractor by constructing a sewer fulfils a public authority's statutory duty to do so, the latter has been enriched by discharge of its liability.[118] Likewise, when a sub-contractor carries out building work on a building which a main contractor is building for a client, the main contractor is enriched by the discharge *pro tanto* of his obligations to the client. It goes without saying that improvements often enhance the value of assets. From time to time improvement works on an asset may also anticipate expenditure – if it can be proved that the owner of the asset would have carried out those works at his own expense if they had not been carried out by the improver.

2. Improvements by accession: some general considerations

Improvements to land and buildings often – indeed characteristically – involve accession of moveables to the land. Building a house, for example, may involve the affixation to the site of concrete, bricks, stone, timber and other materials. By virtue of the law of accession, in such circumstances ownership of the moveable is transferred to the owner of the land or building to which it is attached. The physical corpus of the moveable is transferred into the patrimony of the owner of the land or building.

If ownership of a corporeal moveable is transferred (without accession) from one person to another in circumstances in which it can be said that the latter retains it without a legal ground for doing so and the moveable is still in the hands of the latter, the former is entitled to delivery of the

---

[118] *Varney (Scotland) Limited v. Lanark Town Council* 1974 SC 245.

moveable – to restitution, in Stair's language. For example, if ownership of the moveable were transferred by the pursuer to the defender in implement of a supposed legal obligation which was not in fact due (if the moveable were still to be in the defender's hands), the pursuer would be entitled to delivery: the case falls into the category called *condictio indebiti*. In principle, it should make no difference if, in implement of a supposed legal obligation which was not in fact due, the pursuer were to build the moveable into the defender's building, thereby transferring ownership: the mode by which ownership was transferred to the defender (which happens to be accession) does not affect the moral – and should not affect the legal – ground for imposing a liability on the defender.[119]

The mode of transfer of the property, however, has remedial consequences. If the defender has been enriched by transfer to him of some piece of moveable property which remains entire in his hands, the enrichment may be reversed quite simply by ordering redelivery of the moveable. This may not be satisfactory if the moveable has acceded to the ground. Even if the moveable is detachable from the ground, why should the defender be put to the expense of detaching and removing the moveable? To impose upon him that burden would go beyond simply reversing the benefit that he is unjustifiably retaining. One answer might be that the pursuer should be entitled to insist that the defender remove and redeliver the moveable provided the pursuer pay the expense of doing so. Another might be that the pursuer should be entitled to insist on being allowed to come upon the defender's ground to detach and remove the moveable. These responses might be satisfactory in certain circumstances. But detachment and removal might involve damage to other property of the defender. One could, of course, impose on the pursuer a liability for any damage caused to the defender by removal of the moveable, but this is unsatisfactory on two counts. The cost to the pursuer in insisting on this right might well be so high as to deter him from doing so – and would be so for arbitrary reasons related to the degree of attachment. Equally, why should a defender be required, perhaps, to dismantle his property even in part, even if he is to receive financial compensation? In claims relating to improvements by accession, it will therefore frequently be more appropriate to require the defender to pay a money equivalent than to return the moveable itself.

---

[119] It is worth observing (though the point may be an obvious one) that it is not the fact of accession which gives rise to liability. Accession is simply the way in which the benefit comes into the defender's hands. It is only when accession occurs in circumstances giving rise to an obligation to reverse the enrichment that liability arises.

These concerns will not, however, be equally engaged in every case. The nature of improvements by accession is such that, in certain cases, remedial strategies other than a money payment may be possible.

(a) If accession, in a legal sense, has not taken place then there will have been no transfer of ownership: the owner of the moveable will be entitled to remove it simply because he remains its owner. In certain cases the Scottish law of accession[120] may be capable of being applied in such a way that an enrichment remedy does not need to be considered. For example, in *Cochrane v. Stevenson*[121] it was held that a picture painted on canvas and inserted as a panel above a fireplace in a dining room was moveable, even though its removal left exposed a stone and lime wall. In so far as this result can be achieved through the law of accession, the question of a right to remove such items[122] does not require to be addressed.

(b) One way in which an enrichment by accession could be reversed, in certain cases, would be by permitting the improver to detach the accessory (a *ius tollendi*) where this does not damage the property to which it is attached. Stair took the view that it would be against public policy to allow a right of removal[123] but Bankton appears to have contemplated that improvers might have such rights.[124] Certain types of improvements – garden statuary, for example, and wall decorations[125] – may particularly lend themselves to this remedy. Such a remedy is, moreover, likely to be of particular interest to an improver if he is given no financial remedy – as in the case of voluptuary expenses. The only established *ius tollendi* in Scots law is the right of tenants to remove tenants' fixtures, a right whose juridical basis is uncertain,[126] but which counterbalances to some extent

---

[120] See generally *Stair Memorial Encyclopaedia*, vol. XVIII, §§ 578–87.
[121] (1891) 18 R 1208.
[122] One writer states that there is a right to remove voluptuary expenses: Bayne, *Notes*, 38. Bankton seems to be against such a right: *Institute*, Book I, Title 9, 42; see above. Given that there is no financial claim in relation to voluptuary expenses, a right of removal (always provided that this can be done without damage to the property) might seem an equitable solution in such a case.
[123] *Institutions*, Book II, Title 1, 40; see above. It has been said that 'improvements... cannot be removed because they belong to the owner of the principal thing': *Stair Memorial Encyclopaedia*, vol. XVIII, § 173. This reason precludes the improver from removing the accessory by virtue of any right of ownership. It does not preclude the existence of a *ius tollendi*.
[124] *Institute*, Book I, Title 9, 42; see above, 393–4.
[125] Which may well be properly classifiable as voluptuary expenses: cf. Paul. D. 50, 16, 79, 2. Bankton would not appear to allow removal of these: *Institute*, Book I, Title 9, 42.
[126] See Reid, 'Unjustified Enrichment', 184. At one time the very fact that the improvements were made by a tenant was regarded as a factor indicating that accession had not taken place: e.g. *Syme v. Harvey* (1861) 24 R 202; but see *Brand's Trs v. Brand's Trs* (1876) 3 R (HL) 16; *Stair Memorial Encyclopaedia*, vol. XVIII, § 575.

the absence of any financial claim for meliorations. A right of removal is likely to be of much less interest to an improver who has, for example, constructed a building. The enrichment in such a case may be much more than the sum of the values of the component moveables.

(c) Looking at matters from the owner's point of view, he may wish to reject the improvement either by insisting that the improver detach the moveables and take them away or by detaching them himself and returning them to the improver. A question arises whether or not he should have an unlimited discretion to do this. In some cases it is obvious that he should be permitted to do so: for example, if the 'improvement' is in fact a wrongful encroachment on his land.[127] In other cases the equities may lie the other way: it would be inconsistent with the approach that was taken in *York Buildings Co.* and like cases to permit the owner simply to insist that the possessor remove buildings that he may have erected on the subjects. Some civilian systems make express provision in this regard. Article 936 of the Italian Civil Code, for example, provides as follows:[128]

When the plantings, structures or works have been performed by a third person with his materials, the owner of the land has the right to keep them or to require him who made them to remove them.

If the owner prefers to keep them, he shall pay at his choice the value of the materials and labour or the increase in value of the land.

If the owner of the land demands that they be removed, they shall be removed at the expense of him who made them. He can in addition be required to pay damages.

The owner cannot require the third person to remove the plantings, structures or works, when they were made with his knowledge and without opposition or when they were made by the third person in good faith.

The issue is undeveloped in Scots law but the possibility that a broadly similar approach might be taken is suggested by a dictum of Lord President Robertson uttered under reference to building works that were materially disconform to contract:[129]

If the deviations [from contract] are material and substantial, then the mere fact that the house is built would not prevent the proprietor of the ground from rejecting it and calling on the contractor to remove it, and he might do so if not barred by conduct from insisting in his right. If this right were so insisted in, then the contractor would of course have right to the materials,

---

[127] *Stair Memorial Encyclopaedia*, vol. XVIII, §§ 175–9; see also *Property Selection and Investment Trust v. United Friendly plc* 1999 SLT 975.

[128] *The Italian Civil Code*, trans. M. Beltramo, G. E. Longo and J. H. Merryman. See, similarly, Article 555 of the French Civil Code.

[129] *Ramsay v. Brand* (1898) 25 R 1212 at 1214.

but he would have no right to payment. If, on the other hand, the proprietor made the best of it and let the house stay, the only claim which the contractor could[130] have would be a claim of recompense; and this, be it observed, would be not for *quantum meruit* the builder, but for *quantum lucratus est* the proprietor.[131]

(d) Quite apart from rights of the parties, in certain cases the court itself might use the possibility of detachment and removal as a means of equitably adjusting the interests of the parties. An example of this may be found in *Magistrates of Rutherglen v. Cullen* but, again, this is an undeveloped possibility in Scots law.

3. Other modes of enrichment by improvements

Stair and Bankton regarded the improver's claim as a response to the law of accession.[132] It has been taken to be the modern law that '[b]y improvements are meant such permanent additions to the property as have by the law of accession become a part thereof'.[133] In fact the accession theory does not adequately explain all (or indeed many of) the cases. It is axiomatic that an improver could only justify a claim by reference to the theory that his property has been transferred to someone else by the operation of the law of accession if and in so far as: (i) the improvement involved the accession to the ground of corporeal moveables; and (ii) he previously owned the corporeal moveables.[134] An improver who improves

---

[130] The use of the word 'could' suggests that the Lord President was not committing himself on whether or not the builder would actually have had such a claim. The availability of an enrichment claim to the contract-breaker in Scots law has been recognised, despite there being few actual examples of such claims: see H. L. MacQueen, 'Unjustified Enrichment and Breach of Contract', [1994] *JR* 137, 149–66.

[131] There is a question of characterisation here: is the owner being allowed to waive or defeat an enrichment liability which would exist if he did not insist on removal? or is he, rather, assuming a liability by accepting the improvement? If Lord President Robertson's dictum does stand for the proposition that a contractor may have an enrichment claim in respect of work which does not conform to contract, then the answer to this question could be quite significant for the overall shape of the subject: the works are not provided in implement of a purported obligation (although they may have been intended to implement the obligation, they failed to do so). The contractor knew that he did not own the ground. What then is the basis of liability in such a case?

[132] Stair, *Institutions*, Book II, Title 1, 40 (quoted above, 391–2); Bankton, *Institute*, Book I, Title 9, 42 (quoted above, 393–4); see also Bell, *Principles*, § 538. Both the French and the Italian Civil Codes include enrichment provisions among the articles on accession: art. 555 of the French Civil Code; arts. 936 and 937 of the Italian Civil Code.

[133] *Stair Memorial Encyclopaedia*, vol. XVIII, § 173.

[134] Stair's statement of law is accordingly wholly consistent in limiting the claim to a person 'that builds with his own materials upon another man's ground': *Institutions*, Book II, Title 1, 40.

land by, for example, draining it by removing soil rather than by importing materials to the site would have no claim on this theory. Equally, an improver who affixes someone else's materials to the ground – or who pays someone else (such as a building contractor) to affix another's materials to the ground – could not found a claim on the accession theory. Indeed, in such circumstances the only person who might have a claim on the accession theory would be the former owner of the moveables.[135] But on the face of it there is no reason why an evicted possessor should not be entitled to bring into account, when the owner seeks to resume possession of the land, work which he has paid others to do (for example, construction of buildings and other works), or work which does not involve accession at all (for example, ditching and draining).[136] Indeed, it is apparent that most of the Scottish cases involving claims for the cost of building and improving houses are likely to be about payments made to contractors for carrying out the work (presumably with their own materials or those of sub-contractors rather than with the materials of the pursuer himself)[137] – a claim which cannot be justified as a response to the effects of accession. The point is not confined to the context of recovery of possession cases (and could not be, consistent with adhering to the commitment to enrichment neutrality): *Shilliday v. Smith* itself concerned payments made by the pursuer to someone else to carry out works.

What is the mode of enrichment in such cases? There would appear to be two possibilities: enhancement of value of the defender's asset, or anticipation of expenditure that he would himself have carried out.[138] Although the cases do not always analyse the position particularly clearly, the focus normally appears to be on improvement of the land rather than on anticipation of expenditure. This is consistent with the measure of

---

[135] Consistently with this observation the Italian Civil Code provides, in Book III (Property rights), Title II (Ownership), Section 2 (Accession, specification, union and commixtion), separately for the cases: (i) of a third party who makes plantings, structures or works on the land with his own materials (art. 936); and (ii) of someone who does so with someone else's materials (art. 937). In the latter case it is the owner of the materials who has a claim under article 937.

[136] The improvements in *Douglas v. Douglas' Trs* (1864) 2 M 1379 included draining a farm: at 1383.

[137] E.g. *York Buildings Co. v. Mackenzie* (1795) 3 Paton 378; (1797) 3 Paton 579 (Seton House was built by Adam and Thomas Russell to plans by Robert Adam: McWilliam, *Buildings of Scotland*, 429); *Bell v. Bell* (1841) 2 D 1201 (the expense of erecting a dwelling house); *Scott's Trs v. Scott* (1887) 14 R 1043 (expense of erecting a steading).

[138] In particular circumstances, improvement works may also discharge liabilities to the defender: see above, 411–13.

liability in such cases:

> The recompense due in such cases is measured by the enhanced permanent value of the subjects at the time when the true owner resumes possession, arising (apart from any natural increment of value) from improvements executed during the subsistence of bona fide possession; but it cannot exceed the sum originally expended.[139]

If enhancement of the value of existing assets of the defender is a recoverable mode of enrichment, it should follow as a matter of principle that there need not have been any physical change wrought on the land at all for a claim to be capable of being made.[140] A possible example appears in the *York Buildings Co.* case.[141] Among the items claimed by Mackenzie was the cost of making up title to the land. This was allowed because this had been a necessary first step to a reordering of the estate – in particular to dealing with areas occupied by rentallers and areas of runridge – which was said to have been 'particularly beneficial'.[142] A further corollary is that claims may be made in respect of the enhancement of value of non-corporeal assets – for example if someone who has taken an assignation of a life policy (which turns out to be void) has paid premiums which have enhanced its value.[143]

The value of an asset is capable of being affected by many circumstances. Acceptance that a person may be regarded as enriched when his existing assets have been increased in value might be discouraged by a concern that this could open the way to open-ended liability – or at least to arguments that liability should be imposed in circumstances where the increase in value is simply an effect of legitimate market activity. There are perhaps two separate points in play here: first, a concern that it may be difficult to disentangle the recoverable enhancement in the value of an asset from increments in value which arise owing to other causes, such as the ordinary

---

[139] Bell, *Principles*, § 538; see also Rankine, *Law of Landownership*, 93. The limit to the expenditure incurred is an established feature of Scots law in this area: contrast German law as described by Verse, 'Improvements and Enrichment'. In practice, a perusal of the cases suggests that the increase in value is often less than the amount expended. It follows that in principle an improver requires to prove both so that the court is provided with the means of properly quantifying the claim.

[140] Contrary to the position in South African law: *Nortje en 'n ander v. Pool NO* 1966 (3) SA 96 (A).

[141] (1795) 3 Paton 378; (1797) 3 Paton 579.

[142] (1797) 3 Paton 579 at 584 *per* Lord Chancellor Loughborough. He also observes that '[a] considerable part of that expense will not be needed again. Whoever makes up a title in future, it will not be necessary to take it up by decree of the Court.' This looks like enrichment by anticipation of expenditure.

[143] Cf. *Edinburgh Life Assurance Corporation v. Balderston* (1909) 2 SLT 323; see also *Morgan v. Morgan's Judicial Factor* 1922 SLT 247.

operation of the market; and, secondly, a concern that liability may be imposed in circumstances where it should not be. The first concern raises no issue of principle: the Scottish texts certainly recognise the need to exclude any increases in value which are not directly due to the improvement but which arise because of general changes in the market.[144] There may be evidential difficulties, but these may be more likely to create problems for the pursuer, who must prove the amount of the increase in value due to the improvement, than for the defender. A further counter to the possibility that pursuers might claim in respect of changes in value which simply reflect vagaries of the market can be created by insisting, as the Scottish texts do, that the increase in value be 'permanent'.[145] The second issue, a concern that liability should not be imposed inappropriately, exercised Lord Kames[146] and Baron Hume.[147] It should be dealt with, however, not by foreclosing a particular type of enrichment from consideration, but by addressing the preconditions for liability. This requires attention to be paid, not only to the circumstances in which liability may arise, but more particularly to the formulation and application of appropriate requirements of directness between the pursuer's expenditure and the increased value of the asset. The Scottish texts contain both positive requirements of directness and negative rules excluding indirect and incidental benefits.[148] Kames and Hume express the positive requirement of directness thus:

[M]y loss... is intimately connected with his gain, because in effect my money goes into his pocket.[149]

---

[144] Rankine, *Law of Landownership*, 93; for a practical example (albeit the approach might appear somewhat rough and ready to modern eyes), see the quantification of the claim in *Reedie v. Yeaman* (1875) SLR 625 at 628.

[145] See Bell, *Principles*, § 538. This may be a difficult requirement to overcome in respect of non-corporeal 'improvements'. But that there are examples where a permanent increase in value can be attributed to an 'improvement' has already been illustrated.

[146] Henry Home, Lord Kames, *Principles of Equity* (4th edn, Edinburgh, 1800), 101–23.

[147] Hume, *Lectures*, vol. III, 170–1.

[148] Such tests are in any event essential if liability is capable of being imposed on the basis of the general formula 'unjustified enrichment of the defender at the expense of the pursuer'. In deploying this formula, there may be a temptation to find liability simply on the basis that the defender has been enriched and that there is a causal connection between the defender's enrichment and loss on the part of the pursuer. In fact the 'at the expense of' element of the formula involves more than mere causal connection. Unless this is appreciated there is a risk that justified concerns about appropriately limiting enrichment liability will be met by inappropriately limiting the grounds of liability (the 'unjustified' element) or by inappropriately limiting the type of enrichment which may be recovered.

[149] Kames, *Principles of Equity*, 101.

The maxim only applies to that connection between the loss and gain which is the most intimate of any – viz., where the very money that is lost by the one passes into the pocket, and goes to the use, of the other.[150]

A claim in respect of the enhanced value of an asset of the defender should therefore generally be capable of being made out only if the pursuer has spent money or done work specifically in order to improve or increase the value of the asset in question. This proposition is fortified by the general rule against recovery of incidental enrichment,[151] which normally precludes a claim where the increase in value is merely the side effect of activities directed to some other end.[152] Liability is further controlled and limited by the general rule against recovery of indirect enrichment,[153] which normally precludes a claim where the defender's benefit arises incidentally out of a transaction between the pursuer and a third party. Thus a sub-contractor who does work on a client's land will not usually have an enrichment claim against the owner:[154] the owner has not been enriched (because he is liable to the main contractor), and indeed any enrichment has not been at the sub-contractor's expense (he has a claim for payment against the main contractor). Similarly, someone who does work on land has no claim against a creditor who has a security over the property.[155] The rule against indirect enrichment may be supported by the proposition that the improver's claim is a personal one, which does not affect subsequent purchasers of the ground.[156]

4. Subjective devaluation

(a) The requirement of a positive benefit for the owner

To make a defender pay for improvements which he has not asked for (or at least freely accepted) is an infringement of his autonomy, of his

---

[150] Hume, *Lectures*, vol. III, 171.
[151] *Edinburgh and District Tramways Co. Ltd v. Courtenay* 1909 SC 99.
[152] This rule would exclude, if the requirement of a direct connection between the pursuer's expenditure and the defender's enrichment did not, my claim against my neighbour if I increase the value of his house by obtaining planning permission to develop a supermarket on my land.
[153] See N. Whitty, 'Indirect Enrichment in Scots Law', [1994] JR 200, 239 ff.
[154] *J. B. Mackenzie (Edinburgh) Limited v. Lord Advocate* 1972 SC 231.
[155] *Selby's Heirs v. Jollie* (1795) M 13458; see also *Cran v. Dodson* (1893) 1 SLT 354.
[156] *Beattie v. Lord Napier* (1831) 9 S 639. It may be rather difficult to apply this proposition to the recovery of possession cases: in them the issue of accounting arises between the person who seeks to vindicate his title and the possessor. The question as to what happens if the vindicating owner has acquired ownership from someone else, who happened to be owner at the time when the improvements were carried out, has not been explicitly addressed.

freedom to dispose of his stock of wealth as he wishes. For this reason, the defender should, so it is said, be entitled to engage in 'subjective devaluation': that is, to assert that, whatever the objective market value of the benefit which he enjoys, *he* does not value it.[157] Indeed, looking at the matter in the context of recovery of possession cases, to require an owner to pay for improvements which he did not ask for (and may not have known about) as a condition of recovering land is to impose upon him a price for recovering his own property – a price which may be a high one and one which he may ill be able to afford.[158] The argument has been advanced in Scotland. In *Rutherford v. Rankine and Lees* the pursuer (who was seeking reduction of the defenders' title) is recorded as having argued that to allow the defenders' claim for recompense for improvements 'would oblige the proprietor, either to purchase what was useless to him, or unsuitable to his circumstances, or part with his property against his inclination'.[159] The court disagreed: the defenders were entitled to 'what the pursuer was actually *lucratus* by these meliorations'. This formulation begs the question whether or not it suffices, for a person to be regarded as 'actually *lucratus*', that his land has been enhanced in value without more.[160] Common-law commentators argue that only if the defender can

[157] P. B. H. Birks, *An Introduction to the Law of Restitution* (1985; paperback edn, 1989), 109–28; see also M. Garner, 'The Role of Subjective Benefit in the Law of Restitution', (1990) 10 *Oxford JLS* 42; Birks, 'In Defence of Free Acceptance'; A. S. Burrows, *Understanding the Law of Obligations* (1998), chap. 4; Verse, 'Improvements and Enrichment'.

[158] It has been observed in this context that 'the easiest way to ruin someone is to enrich him': G. Pacchioni, *Trattato della gestione d'affari altrui secondo il diritto romano e civile* (1893), as quoted by Verse, 'Improvements and Enrichment', 87. The risk is not a theoretical one. In the seventeenth century legislation was enacted in the Netherlands to counter a practice on the part of lessees of effectively depriving lessors of their land by exercising a lien in respect of claims for improvements more costly than the owner could afford to compensate: see Van der Merwe and De Waal, *The Law of Things*, § 98, n. 3. The sums involved in improvements cases may be very large: e.g., in *Douglas v. Douglas' Trs* (1864) 2 M 1379 the improver spent more than £23,000 (at mid-nineteenth-century values) on an estate which, it was suggested, might be worth £50,000 (after the improvements). The person entitled to it declined to take the estate upon the court holding that he would have to give credit for the whole cost of the estate, including the improvements.

[159] (1782) M 13422 at 13423.

[160] The Session Papers (Faculty Collection Skene Papers No. 39) do not disclose what transpired after the decision reported in Morison's dictionary. It is interesting to notice, however, that at an earlier stage in the case the Lord Ordinary, Lord Covington, had required the defenders to specify the sums expended by them on the improvements, the present value of the building and an account of the rents at which it was let. On 17 February 1781 on reporting the case he recommended a voluntary sale by roup as the best way of ascertaining the just and true value of the subjects.

be regarded as having been unequivocally enriched should a remedy be given to the improver (and a mere increase in the value of the asset is not enough):[161] it is said that the enhancement value must have been turned into money by sale of the land[162] or that the court must find it to be 'reasonably certain that he will realise the positive benefit'.[163] Dirk Verse, drawing on the experience of German law (which in this respect appears to take an approach similar to that of the common law), has noted that the enhanced value of land may be 'realised' not only by sale, but also by increased rental.[164] Where property is held (or ready to be held) under tenancy, the capitalised value of the additional income is, as Verse describes German law, held to be the owner's enrichment.[165]

The earlier Scottish authorities can be read in a manner broadly consistent with a similar approach. Stair said this:

our custom doth allow a recompense to the builder, insofar as the heritor was profited thereby, *in that he might get a greater rent for that building*...[166]

Likewise, Bankton observed that:

our law not only allows Retention to every *bona fide* builder and repairer, but action likewise to both, for Necessary expenses, i.e. such as save the house from perishing or growing worse; and Profitable ones, whereby the subject is meliorated, *and affords a greater rent*...[167]

In *Binning v. Brotherstones*,[168] the pursuer reduced the defender's title to a tenement. The defender asserted a right of retention until his claim for

---

[161] Unless – in Birks's formulation – the defender has debarred himself from relying on subjective devaluation by free acceptance: Birks, 'In Defence of Free Acceptance'.
[162] Birks, *Introduction*, 121–4.
[163] A. S. Burrows, *The Law of Restitution* (1993), 10. Goff and Jones, *Law of Restitution*, 23, however, take the view that 'it is sufficient...that the benefit is realisable; it should not be necessary to demonstrate that it has been realised. It may not be unreasonable, in some circumstances, to compel a person to sell an asset which another has mistakenly improved.' They go on to observe, however, that '[i]t is long established [in English law] that subject to the application of the equitable doctrine of acquiescence a landowner is not obliged to make restitution to the mistaken improver even though the land can, of course, be sold or mortgaged'.
[164] Verse, 'Improvements and Enrichment', 94–8.   [165] *Ibid*. 94.
[166] *Institutions*, Book II, Title 1, 40 (emphasis added).
[167] *Institute*, Book I, Title 9, 42 (emphasis added). Erskine's approach, while not entirely clear, appears to suggest that it is only in the case of improvements by a life-renter or adjudger that the claim is 'restricted' to expenses which bring a higher rent to the owner: *Institute*, Book III, Title 1, 11.
[168] (1676) M 13401.

improving the tenement had been satisfied. The court held that the defender:

> ought to have no satisfaction for what expenses he gave out to keep the tenement in as good condition as he got it, but only for other meliorations, as would be profitable to the pursuer, *by raising of the rent of the tenement*.[169]

(b) Objective approach

This trend appears to have fallen out of sight and Scots law appears in practice now to align itself with French and Italian law in taking an objective approach to the enrichment question.[170] It is clearly not the law in Scotland that an improver can only justify a claim if he has in fact already realised the enhanced value of the asset by sale or rent. After all, in the *bona fide* possessor cases, the improver's claim typically comes to be considered when the owner has not yet recovered his land – and indeed payment of the possessor's claim for improvements may be a precondition of recovery of the land.[171] In *York Buildings Co.*, Lord Loughborough spoke of the claim in respect of the construction of Seton House and making plantations in terms that anticipate the argument from subjective devaluation:

> It would be singular indeed if these were to be deemed no permanent improvement. It is not according to the fancy of the owner or of the builder that the improvement upon the estate is to be estimated; but it cannot be said that these are no improvements. The only question is the quantum.[172]

In practice, in more recent cases, the pursuer does not appear to have been required to show that the owner was likely in fact to realise the enhanced value of the land by sale or by rent.[173] In *Newton v. Newton*,[174] for example, the pursuer averred that the defender would 'be in a position to obtain a materially greater price...than she would have obtained had [the improvements] not been carried out',[175] but this does not appear to

---

[169] Emphasis added. See also *Jack v. Pollock* (1665) M 13412. This was, however, a case of improvements by a life-renter, as to which see Erskine, *Institute*, Book III, Title 1, 11.

[170] For French and Italian law, see Verse, 'Improvements and Enrichment'.

[171] See above; and note especially the form of the orders in *York Building Co. v. Mackenzie* (1797) 3 Paton 579 and *Douglas v. Douglas' Trs* (1864) 2 M 1387.

[172] (1797) 3 Paton 579 at 584.

[173] Having regard, however, to the lack of explicit discussion of the issue and to the older authorities, the point may remain capable of being argued.

[174] 1925 SC 715.   [175] *Ibid.* at 717.

have formed any part in the judgment upholding the pursuer's claim and, so far as the reports disclose, Mrs Newton does not appear to have been intending to sell the property. Increased rental value is quite often referred to in the cases,[176] but apparently merely as a means of ascertaining the market value and not on the basis that the realisation of an actual money gain is a prerequisite of the claim.[177]

This is not necessarily objectionable. Provided the grounds of liability are appropriately defined, the equities are not by any means all in favour of the owner. After all, he has the right and power to prevent works on his land which he does not want. It is difficult to imagine that works that will permanently enhance the value of the land could often be executed without either active involvement on the owner's part, or the owner standing by in full knowledge that the works are being done, or negligence on the owner's part in the protection of his own rights. John Rankine states the balance of equities as reflected in Scots law on *bona fide* possessors as follows:

> It is obviously fair and equitable that he who has possessed a piece of property in the honest belief that it was his own, and has at his own expense, and on that footing, enhanced the value of the subject, should not be compelled to give it up to the true owner, who in the meanwhile has been ignoring or neglecting his rights, without some remuneration for the improvements.[178]

Even if an objective approach is taken to quantum, the court may not be wholly precluded from recognising, in certain cases, the force of the argument for subjective devaluation. It may be entitled to deny that what has been done counts as an 'improvement' for the purposes of a claim – by praying in aid the concept of 'voluptuary' expenses. Hume observed: 'Tis essential... to the claim that the improvements are not of a fanciful sort, or such as are suited only to the particular taste and humour of the late possessor...'[179] Bankton's description of voluptuary expenses tends to suggest that the term would not include improvements (even if they could be regarded as purely decorative and 'suited only to the particular taste and humour of the possessor') that enhanced the value of the land.

---

[176] For example *Reedie v. Yeaman* (1875) SLR 625; *McDowel v. McDowel* (1906) 14 SLT 125.
[177] Rankine observed that 'where the subjects have been all along let, the safest guide will be the actual rise in rent': *Law of Landownership*, 93.
[178] *Ibid.*, 86.
[179] Hume, *Lectures*, vol. III, 171. For examples of 'voluptuary' expenses see Paul. *D.* 50, 16, 79, 2.

There is South African authority to the same effect.[180] This approach to the definition of voluptuary expenses, if correct, would deprive the concept of any useful content as a mechanism for limiting improver's claims. Hume's more expansive approach would, on the other hand, enable the court to exclude certain claims which would otherwise be admissible on the basis that the value of the land had been enhanced. Another possibility, available where the improvement takes the form of moveables acceding to land, would be to allow the owner, at least in certain circumstances, to reject the enrichment, either by himself detaching the moveables and returning them to the improver, or by insisting that the improver do so.[181] The power of the court in South African law to permit the owner to waive the enrichment by removing acceding moveables where that could be done without damage and where the owner would not have effected the improvement himself has been justified on grounds suggestive of the argument for subjective devaluation.[182] The recognition of a like power in Scots law could similarly protect owners in certain cases.

A particular category of owner – namely one who can be characterised as a consumer – may be protected at least from certain improvers' claims by legislation which is in prospect. Article 9 of Directive 97/7/EC on the Protection of Consumers in respect of Distance Contracts provides as follows:

Member States shall take the measures necessary to

- prohibit the supply of goods and services to a consumer without their being ordered by the consumer beforehand, where such supply involves a demand for payment;
- exempt the consumer from the provision of any consideration in cases of unsolicited supply, the absence of a response not constituting consent.

The United Kingdom Government construes the Directive as providing that in effect 'any such goods and services are treated as a gift to the consumer' and intends to implement this Directive by amending the Unsolicited Goods and Services Act 1971 to that effect.[183]

---

[180] *United Building Society v. Snookler's Trustees* 1906 Transvaal Supreme Court Reports 623 at 627.
[181] See above, 415–16.
[182] *Fletcher and Fletcher v. Bulawayo Waterworks Co. Ltd* 1915 AD 636.
[183] Department of Trade and Industry, 'Distance Selling Implementation of EU Directive 97/7 on the Protection of Consumers in respect of Distance Contracts', November 1999, Section 7; Department of Trade and Industry, 'Simplification of the Unsolicited Goods and Services Act 1971', December 1999, Section 6.

V. Endnote: The redundancy of the 'three Rs'

The characterisation of the 'three Rs' – restitution, recompense and repetition – as 'remedies' raises a fundamental question as to the continuing value of using those terms at all. As Peter Birks has demonstrated, the term 'remedy' does not have a single meaning.[184] What analytical space do terms such as 'recompense' occupy? *Shilliday* has exposed the error of believing that they quadrate with particular grounds of action. Nor do they describe in a practical sense what the pursuer will ask the court to do. In an action seeking return of a particular piece of moveable property, the pursuer will conclude for delivery. The response to the enrichment is not 'restitution' but an order for delivery. In an action seeking substitutional return of a sum of money paid to the defender, the pursuer will simply conclude for payment, the amount of the claim being measured by the amount of money received by the defender. The term 'repetition' adds nothing. Likewise, in a claim based on improvements enhancing the value of an asset of the defender, the pursuer will conclude for payment, the amount being measured (subject to defences) by the enhancement in value of the asset or the pursuer's expenditure, whichever is less. The words 'recompense', 'repetition' and 'restitution' do not add anything to the practical analysis of cases. The methodology endorsed by the Lord President in *Shilliday* involves: (i) identifying a ground of action; (ii) identifying the nature of the benefit enjoyed; and (iii) formulating a conclusion habile to reverse the enrichment having regard to the nature of that benefit. The conclusion is not framed by reference to the terms under discussion.[185]

The mere fact that a term does not occupy any analytical space in the practical analysis of cases does not necessarily mean that it has no value. It might, for example, provide a handy expression for responses which are common to different grounds of action. As shown above, Stair used 'restitution' to describe both the right of an owner to the return of his own property from a person into whose hands it has come and the right of someone who has lost ownership of property but who has a personal right to demand its return by reason of unjustified enrichment. But it is unnecessary to use the term 'restitution' to describe what these two situations have in common. What they have in common is that in each the pursuer will invite the court to order delivery of the item. The grounds of action will be different in each case. The pleadings which set out the

[184] Birks, 'Rights, Wrongs and Remedies'.
[185] Reduction, also referred to by Lord Rodger, is different, because the very thing which the pursuer will ask the court to do is to reduce the writ at issue.

orders sought, the facts founded upon and the pleas-in-law upon which the action will proceed need not use the word 'restitution' at all. There may be a common response – but it is not necessary to use the word 'restitution' to describe it. Indeed, the very fact that the term brings together heterogeneous situations poses a danger for clarity of understanding.

A term might also have value because it brings together in a handy expression a congeries of features which have a particular relationship with one another. 'Relief' might be regarded as an example. In a case to which the term in its technical sense applies, the pursuer has two rights (depending on whether or not the pursuer has already discharged the obligation from which he is entitled to be relieved): (i) to insist that the defender discharge the obligation (or the appropriate part of it) from which the pursuer is entitled to be relieved; and (ii) if the defender has not done so and the pursuer has fulfilled the obligation himself, to payment of the appropriate amount.[186] It is useful to have a term that implicitly describes these rights which flow sequentially from the underlying obligation.[187] It has been suggested that 'restitution' performs a similar function, describing: (i) the right to delivery; and (ii) the right to payment of value of the thing if the defender no longer has possession of it.[188] The same justification cannot be advanced for the terms 'recompense' or 'repetition'.

It might be suggested that 'recompense' is a convenient term, being applicable to any claim for payment measured by reference to a benefit (other than receipt of money or a thing) which the defender has enjoyed, irrespective of the specific measure of the value, which will depend on whether the benefit is the saving of expenditure or enhancement of the value of some asset of the defender (and will be limited by the pursuer's expenditure). But it is not necessary to use the term 'recompense': one could simply use 'payment of an amount equal to the benefit enjoyed by the defender' or, for those who like Latin tags, 'payment *quantum lucratus*'. It is not clear that there is in fact a stable usage limiting 'recompense' to claims for payment of the value of the benefit received by the defender. Stair's title is, after all, 'recompence or *remuneration*' and includes the claim of a

---

[186] *Buchanan and Carswell v. Eugene Limited* 1936 SC 160 at 181–2 *per* Lord Murray.
[187] There are, however, problems arising from the loose use of the word 'relief' to include any case in which the pursuer seeks an amount measured by the amount of some liability discharged by the pursuer – for example where a purchaser seeks, as part of his damages for breach of contract by a seller, the amount of damages which he has had to pay a sub-purchaser. The ground of liability is quite different from an action of relief in the strict sense: see above, 387.
[188] See A. J. W. Steven, 'Recompense for Interference in Scots Law', [1996] *JR* 51, 58; but *quaere* whether this is an entirely stable usage.

gestor for his expenses whether or not the defender has been enriched.[189] The digests of cases edited by William Morison and Patrick Shaw both include under the rubric 'recompense' cases that are clearly claims founded in contract for payment *quantum meruit*.[190] In Scots usage, payment *quantum meruit* is measured not by the benefit to the defender but by reference to a fair price for the work done by the pursuer.[191] It is often explicitly contrasted with the measure *quantum lucratus*[192] – correctly, because the two measures do not necessarily coincide. Taking improvements to land by a building contractor as an example, a fair price for the work will usually be assessed by reference to comparative rates and prices for similar work. This may well not produce the same result as the increase in the value of the land as a result of the work. If one were to analyse the defenders' benefit as expenditure saved, it might often be the same as, or similar to, the fair price for the work done, but it will not necessarily be so in all cases.

Moreover, it distorts the underlying nature of a claim for payment *quantum meruit* so to characterise it. Take for example someone who does work under a contract which does not specify the price: he is entitled to payment of a fair price for the work done, not because the defender has been saved some expenditure, but because the defender has promised to pay him for the work. It is not difficult to imagine a case in which payment *quantum meruit* is due but the defender has not been enriched. For example, if someone who proposes to purchase a house specifically requests a contractor to carry out work on the house without specifying the price, and the contractor does the work but the purchase is never concluded, the 'purchaser' has a contractual obligation to pay the contractor a reasonable price for the work done but will never enjoy the benefit of it.[193] The fundamental point is this: if the term 'recompense' can properly be used to encompass a claim for payment *quantum meruit* (and there is

---

[189] It might be possible to regard this as the value of an enrichment by anticipation of expenditure which the defender would have incurred anyway (as a matter of probability). The problem with such an analysis is that there is no inquiry into the position in this regard. Moreover, the very reason why the gestor intervenes is that the defender would not (as a matter of probability) by reason of absence or otherwise incur the expenditure himself.

[190] For example *Campbell v. Campbell* (1709) M 13432; *Napier v. Elphingston* (1746) M 13434; *Sharp v. Pollock's Trustees* (1822) 1 S 339.

[191] Which might itself be measured in a number of different ways, depending on the nature of the work and the circumstances.

[192] For example Gloag, *Law of Contract*, 328.

[193] This is probably the best explanation of *Hamilton v. Lochrane* (1899) 1 F 478. Although the rubric describes it as a case of 'recompense', the defender was not enriched: see Lord Moncreiff's opinion.

usage to suggest that it can),[194] then it cannot be said that recompense is limited to payment by reference to the value of the benefit enjoyed by the defender. If that is the case, then the word does not succeed even in usefully grouping like cases and excluding unlike cases: to say that the pursuer is entitled to 'recompense' does not disclose, even at the level of generality, the standard by which payment is to be measured. If this is correct, use of the term may not only be redundant to the analysis, but may actively hinder a clear appreciation of the issues.

[194] I myself have previously suggested that payment *quantum meruit* may be one possible way of valuing a claim in recompense: 'Contract and Recompense: ERDC Construction v. HM Love & Co.', (1997) 4 *Edinburgh LR* 469. The suggestion is consistent with the usage of the word 'recompense' mentioned in the text. But the analysis presented in the article may not have been entirely correct. The article was concerned with the right of a building contractor to payment *quantum meruit* when he rescinds the contract in response to a material breach on the part of the client. It was suggested that, since the contractor was disabled from suing under the contract by its premature termination, the remedy must be founded on unjustified enrichment. The conclusion may not follow: an alternative would be a specific right within the law of contract entitling the innocent contractor on premature termination to payment *quantum meruit*. This would have the merit of distorting neither the notion of unjustified *enrichment*, by suggesting (as I did in the article cited) that payment *quantum meruit* is a measure available in certain claims founded on unjustified enrichment, nor the fundamental moral basis of the innocent contractor's right to payment – namely that he carried out work in implement of a contract for which he is entitled to be paid a reasonable price irrespective of any benefit enjoyed by the party in breach. This characterisation of the remedy may, however, not be available. Scots law has sought to deploy the law of unjustified enrichment to adjust the parties' positions in the context of frustration – which likewise involves premature termination of the contract: *Cantiere San Rocco SA v. Clyde Shipbuilding & Engineering Co. Ltd* 1923 SC (HL) 105 (as to which see Robin Evans-Jones, 'Unjust Enrichment, Contract and the Third Reception of Roman Law', (1993) 109 *LQR* 663; also his 'The Claim to Recover what was Transferred for a Lawful Purpose outwith Contract (*Condictio Causa Data Causa Non Secuta*)', in: D. Visser (ed.), *The Limits of the Law of Obligations* (1997)). This discussion merely emphasises the point made here: that it does not advance the argument to describe the contractor's remedy as one of recompense; it remains necessary to attend closely to the underlying basis of the obligation on the one hand, and to the precise measure of recovery on the other; use of the term 'recompense' assists neither inquiry.

PART IX

Discharge of another person's debt

16 Performance of another's obligation: French and English law contrasted

Simon Whittaker

'Performance' of obligations by persons other than those who bear them, far from being exceptional, is an everyday occurrence under both the French and English systems of law. It is the purpose of this article to explain how this is the case in particular in relation to contractual (and private-law[1] obligations and to explain how this relates to more general issues of performance (whether voluntary or enforced), damages (notably, the rules clustered around the notion of mitigation) and restitutionary recovery. As my title indicates (and, indeed, as the structure of the French law requires), I shall discuss the performance of obligations in general and not merely those to pay money. The juxtaposition of two provisions of the French Civil Code forms the starting point of the discussion: the first, article 1236, is the obvious one, as it deals with the situations in which the law permits the performance of another's obligation by a third party; the second, article 1144, is less obvious, as it provides for judicial authorisation of a creditor of a contractual obligation to have the debtor's obligation performed at the debtor's expense.

I. A note on terminology

In the following discussion, it seems helpful to set out the French terminology and explain its usefulness for analysis of the two situations. Here, it is necessary to distinguish carefully between *obligation, prestation*

I wish to express my gratitude for comments on an earlier draft of this paper made by participants at the colloquium held in Cambridge in April 1999.

[1] This article will discuss the French private-law position and not raise in its discussion of English law the question whether its treatment of the performance of public-law duties by third parties differs from its treatment of private-law contractual duties.

433

and *paiement*. In French discussions, the term *obligation* itself may bear two significances: it may describe the totality of the relationship between the two parties, the duty-bearer (known as *débiteur*, whether or not the obligation concerns a sum of money) and the right-holder (known as *créancier*, equally generally).[2] However, *obligation* may also bear the meaning which is most common to the English word obligation – that is, to describe the duty itself, *la dette*, the correlative of which is the creditor's personal right, the *droit de créance*. French law takes analysis of obligation a stage further and asks what is the subject-matter of this duty and answers that it is the *prestation*, the 'thing to be done' (or 'thing not to be done') with which the obligation is concerned.[3] So, for example, in a building contract, for the builder it is the work, for the employer the paying of the price. Thus, the well-known French classification of obligations into those to do, not to do and to transfer property (*de faire, de ne pas faire* and *de donner*[4]) is a classification according to the nature of the *prestation*.[5]

French lawyers use *paiement* to describe what a common lawyer would see as payment of another's debt, but the term is potentially misleading. First, *paiement* is not restricted to the ordinary French (and English) meaning of the payment of a money sum: *paiement* may relate to obligations to do or not to do more generally. Beyond this, there are two ways in which it is used.[6] In the ordinary situation of *paiement* by the debtor of an obligation, *paiement* refers both to performance and its resulting discharge of the debtor: as Ph. Malaurie and L. Aynès put it, '*paiement* is the extinction

---

[2] F. Terré, Ph. Simler and Y. Lequette, *Les obligations* (6th edn, 1996), 1.

[3] The relationship between *obligation* and *prestation* is usually found in French texts in their analysis of the requirement of *objet* for the validity of a contract: see arts. 1126–30, *code civil*; Terré, Simler and Lequette, *Les obligations*, 215 ff. and B. Nicholas, *The French Law of Contract* (2nd edn, 1992), 114–15.

[4] See arts. 1101, 1136 and 1142, *code civil*.

[5] Nicholas, *French Law of Contract*, 115 explains that there is a further level to the analysis, according to which the subject-matter of a *prestation* is said to be *la chose*. So, for example, in the case of sale, 'a seller's obligation is, among other things, the *prestation* consisting in the conveyance of the thing, and . . . the *objet* of that *prestation* is the thing (*chose*) itself'.

[6] A further and different significance is to be found in relation to *paiement de l'indu*, where *paiement* is to be understood as referring only to the performance of obligations to transfer property, whether moveables (including and typically money) or immoveables. This more restricted usage results from French law's treatment of restitutionary recovery in respect of 'undue services' as a matter for *enrichissement sans cause* rather than *répétition de l'indu*: see S. Whittaker, 'Obligations', in: J. Bell, S. Boyron and S. Whittaker (eds.), *Principles of French Law* (1998), chap. 10, 407.

of the obligation by its performance'.[7] However, while *paiement* usually entails the discharge of the debtor, it does not always do so.[8] Recognising this qualification, many jurists follow Charles Aubry and Charles-Henri Rau in defining *paiement* as 'the accomplishment of the *prestation* which forms the subject matter of the obligation'.[9]

This definition of *paiement* is very helpful, as it emphasises that when one talks of performance of another's obligation it is not performance in a full sense at all; for, in my view, in a full sense only a debtor can perform an obligation as only he bears the duty. What another person may do is the 'accomplishment' of the very thing which is the subject-matter of the debtor's obligation; it is then for the law to decide whether this is to be treated in law (either for some or for all purposes) as equivalent to performance by the debtor. In both English and French law, a typical situation where the law does indeed assimilate the accomplishment of the *prestation* by a third party to performance by the debtor is where the third party is the debtor's agent, for both systems recognise the idea of representation of one person by another; but a legal system may treat other third-party *paiements* as performance of the debtor's obligation (as French law indeed does).[10]

It is also this idea that *paiement* in the context of non-debtor 'performance' consists of no more than the actual accomplishment of the subject-matter of the debtor's obligation which leads me to juxtapose article 1136 with article 1144, as the latter provides a legal mechanism by which a creditor may himself or through a third party have the subject-matter of the debtor's obligation achieved. In this context, however, French discussions acknowledge this idea by use of the expression *exécution en nature* to describe both the obvious case of performance of an obligation by a debtor after order by a court and also creditor or third-party performance after authorisation by a court.

---

[7] '*Le paiement est l'extinction de l'obligation par son exécution*': Ph. Malaurie and L. Aynès, *Droit civil, Les obligations* (8th edn, 1997), 557. R.-J. Pothier termed this *le paiement réel*, i.e. 'l'accomplissement réel de ce qu'on s'est obligé *de donner ou de faire*': *Traité des obligations*, in: *Oeuvres de Pothier* (Paris, 1821), no. 494.

[8] See below, 439 ff. Use of the verb '*acquitter*' is no more conclusive: it normally refers to the discharge of the debtor, but art. 1236, *code civil*, uses it as regards *paiement* by third parties who benefit from subrogation where the debtor is discharged only vis-à-vis the creditor.

[9] 'L'accomplissement de la prestation qui forme la matière de l'obligation': C. Aubry and C. Rau, *Cours de droit civil français d'après la méthode de Zachariae* (6th edn by E. Bartin, 1936) vol. IV, § 315, 220.

[10] Below, 437 ff.

II. 'Parties au paiement': article 1236, code civil

1. The texts

Article 1236 of the Civil Code describes the general rules as to *paiement* by a third party:

An obligation may be discharged by any person who has an interest in doing so, such as a joint debtor or a surety.

The obligation can even be discharged by a third party who has no interest in doing so, provided that the third party acts in the name of and in order to discharge the debtor or provided that, if he acts in his own name, he is not subrogated to the rights of the creditor.[11]

Article 1237 then qualifies this:[12]

An obligation to do cannot be discharged by a third party contrary to the wishes of the creditor, where the latter has an interest in it being performed by the debtor himself.[13]

This framework of rules is clearly derived from the Roman position, via Robert-Joseph Pothier.[14] The position in the modern French law is somewhat more complex than these provisions suggest, particularly as regards the relationship between *paiement* by a third party and restitutionary recovery.[15] In all, three questions are addressed: who may perform an obligation? what is the effect of performance on the original obligation? what recourse by the third party is recognised?

---

[11] 'Une obligation peut être acquittée par toute personne qui y est intéressée, telle qu'un coobligé ou une caution.
'L'obligation peut même être acquittée par un tiers qui n'y est point intéressé, pourvu que ce tiers agisse au nom et en l'acquit du débiteur, ou que, s'il agit en son nom propre, il ne soit pas subrogé aux droits du créancier.' Although I have translated '*acquitter*' as 'to discharge', as has been noted, this does not mean that the obligation is necessarily altogether extinguished, for where the third party is subrogated to the creditor's rights, the debtor's obligation is discharged only *vis-à-vis* the creditor himself: see above, n. 8.

[12] There is a further qualification that in order to constitute valid *paiement*, the payer must be the owner of the thing and capable of alienating it (art. 1238, *code civil*) but this need not detain us.

[13] 'L'obligation de faire ne peut être acquittée par un tiers contre le gré du créancier, lorsque ce dernier a intérêt qu'elle soit remplie par le débiteur lui-même.'

[14] Pothier, *Traité des obligations*, nos. 495–500.

[15] See Whittaker, 'Obligations', 398–403 on the difficulties of using the terminology of 'restitution' in the French context.

2. Who may perform?

In principle any person may perform another person's obligation: as it is often put, 'in principle the personality of the *solvens* is a matter of indifference'.[16] The third-party need not for this purpose even purport to act in the name of the debtor in offering the *prestation*, as long as he offers the creditor exactly the subject-matter of the debtor's obligation. While in French law a typical context for third-party performance of an obligation is the case where the debtor asks a third party to perform the *prestation* for him, there is no need for the third party to have the debtor's consent or authority to act in this way (though the issue of consent does affect the possible recourse which a third party may have against the debtor).[17]

However, this general principle is qualified by article 1237 of the code, which disallows third-party performance where the creditor has an interest in performance by the debtor himself. In general, the issue of a creditor's interest is a matter for the *juges du fond* and they have interpreted the matter generously from the point of view of the creditor.[18] The creditor's 'interest' for this purpose is typically found in the fact that the creditor in entering the contract with the debtor relies on the latter's skill or other personal characteristics, of which he should not be deprived by third-party intervention. However, it may be found in other elements, so that, for example, where a person sells property in return for an annual payment (*rente viagère*), the seller (creditor) may have a legitimate interest in refusing payment of the *rente* by a third party even if the buyer (debtor) is insolvent, as non-payment of the *rente* would otherwise entitle him to terminate the contract and recover his property.[19] Also on this basis, the courts have allowed a landlord of a farm to refuse to accept the payment of rent by the father of the tenant farmer where both the tenant and his father's attitude suggested that the father did not treat his previous assignment of the farm as final: the landlord was justified in fearing that the father's payments could later be used as evidence in support of his 'abusive allegations'.[20] Related to this is the position taken by French courts as regards the parties' exclusion of third-party performance: while the Civil Code does not require that the third party acts with the consent

---

[16] Malaurie and Aynès, *Droit civil, Les obligations*, 559.   [17] Below, 439 ff.
[18] J. Issa-Sayegh, 'Extinction des obligations, Paiement: Caractères généraux. Parties. Effets', in: *Juris-Classeur civil*, art. 1235 à 1248, fasc. 64 à 67, no. 59, 11.
[19] Civ. 24 Jun. 1913, DP 1917.1.38.   [20] Civ. (3) 23 Feb. 1972, Bull. Civ. III, no. 126, 92.

of the debtor, French courts accept that if both the debtor and creditor agree (whether in advance or subsequently) that only the debtor should perform, then this agreement will be given effect, subject to its being 'legitimate'.[21] On the other hand, the creditor may not oppose performance by a third party simply on the basis that it is useless or even dangerous to the debtor.[22]

This law, then, is expressed in terms of what a third party may do, and whether a creditor may refuse third-party performance if the due *paiement* is tendered. But what does this mean in practice? Modern French law possesses no notion of *mora creditoris* to categorise the situation where the creditor wrongly refuses due performance.[23] Instead, where the *prestation* consists of the supply of money or property, French law possesses a procedure by which tender of what is due may be formally offered to the creditor and then 'consigned' to the relevant approved depositary.[24] If the creditor does not then accept the formal tender, after the appropriate procedures and a decision of the court, the debtor is discharged by operation of law.[25] This procedure applies as much to third-party *paiement* as to *paiement* by the debtor.[26] Moreover, more generally, it would seem that tender of a conforming *prestation* by a third

---

[21] Issa-Sayegh, 'Extinction', 10; B. Starck, H. Roland and L. Boyer, *Droit civil, Les obligations*, vol. III, *Régime général* (5th edn, 1997), 63; Req. 7 Jun. 1937, DH 1937.427 (where the third party was held able effectively to intervene despite the agreement of the debtor and creditor to the contrary, as it was found by the lower court that the agreement had been 'fraudulent'); Civ. 29 May 1953, D 1953.516 (where the third party had an interest in intervening and the parties no legitimate interest in refusing intervention).

[22] Issa-Sayegh, 'Extinction', 10, citing Aubry and Rau, *Cours de droit civil français*, no. 316, 221, n. 2 (who disagree with Pothier in this respect on the basis that article 1236 does not so restrict third-party *paiement*).

[23] Cf. Pothier, *Traité des obligations*, no. 500, who does indeed refer to putting the creditor *en demeure*. On the rejection of this idea in the modern law, see Terré, Simler and Lequette, *Les obligations*, 1004, n. 1 noting the contrary position in German law found in § 293 BGB. For criticism of this rejection, see C. Robin, 'La mora creditoris', [1998] *Review trimestrielle de droit civil* 607.

[24] This procedure is known as 'offres réelles avec consignation' and is provided for by arts. 1257–8 *code civil* and arts. 1426 ff., *Nouveau code de procédure civile*.

[25] Art. 1257 al. 1, *code civil*. According to Henri, Léon and Jean Mazeaud, *Leçons de droit civil*, vol. II/1, *Obligations, théorie générale* (8th edn by François Chabas, 1991), 954, n. 3 following J. Courrouy, 'La consignation d'une somme d'argent est-elle un payement?' [1990] *Review trimestrielle de droit civil* 23, even after *consignation* and court approval, the debtor's discharge does not mean that there is *paiement* nor is there therefore an end to the relationship of *obligation* between the parties.

[26] Terré, Simler and Lequette, *Les obligations*, 1004.

party would prevent any attempt to enforce performance against the debtor.[27]

3. The 'liberating effect' of performance and recourse by the third party

Article 1236 sets out the 'liberating effect' of third-party performance, an issue which in French law is intimately related to the question of recourse by the third party. In the following discussion it should be recalled that there is no general requirement that any of the *paiements* in question be effected with the debtor's consent: instead, the primary distinction is between performance by a third party with or without an interest in doing so.

(a) Performance by interested third parties

Where the third party whose performance is accepted by the creditor has an interest in so acting, then the debtor is discharged *vis-à-vis* the creditor, but not *vis-à-vis* the third party, who is subrogated by operation of law into the legal position of the creditor.[28] French law therefore uses the idea of relative discharge to reconcile the third party's intention to discharge the debtor, the creditor's satisfaction and the technique of subrogation. Article 1236 gives two examples of such an interest: where the third party is jointly obligated with the debtor and where he is the debtor's surety (*caution*). As to the latter, it is to be noted that a surety who performs the obligation for the debtor (typically, but not exclusively, by paying a sum of money) may recover from and is subrogated to the creditor's rights against the debtor whether or not the surety entered the contract of suretyship at the request of the principal debtor.[29] However, the form of article 1236 makes clear that a third party may have an interest in performing another's obligation, even where he is not himself a joint debtor or surety. A common example of this in French practice is the situation where A

---

[27] Such a denial could be based on the idea that a creditor's failure to accept tender of due performance would constitute breach of his *obligation de loyauté* and that this breach would mean that the creditor would not be allowed to terminate the contract for non-performance, nor to rely on the debtor's own non-performance as a defence (the *exception d'inexécution*) nor recover damages: see Robin, 'La mora creditoris', 611–12, 625 ff.

[28] Subrogation by operation of law is known as *subrogation légale*. Subrogation may also take place by agreement, this being known as *subrogation conventionnelle*.

[29] Arts. 2028 al. 1 and 2029, *code civil*. Where joint debtors are liable *solidairement* (i.e. jointly and severally), payment in full by one gives rise to a right of recourse against the others to the limits of their own part share: art. 1214, *code civil*.

buys from B property that is subject to a mortgage or lien owed by B to C: here, A has an interest in paying the debt owed by B to C so as to avoid the threat of dispossession by C.[30]

The technique of subrogation has both advantages and disadvantages from the point of view of the third party.[31] The main advantage is that he may take advantage of any security which the creditor enjoyed in relation to performance of the obligation; but the disadvantages include the possibility of being met with a defence or right of set-off which the debtor enjoyed against the creditor and the possibility of the right expiring according to the prescription period applicable to the creditor's claim.[32] This being the case, it is interesting that French law at times allows a third party who possesses a subrogated claim also to have recourse against the debtor on the basis of his own independent right. This is the case with sureties, whose claims arise simply on payment and without any need to satisfy the conditions of *gestion d'affaires* or *enrichissement sans cause*.[33]

(b) Performance by non-interested third parties

As regards performance by non-interested third parties, the position has proved more controversial and remains more complex. Article 1236 itself distinguishes here between those third parties who perform 'in the name of and to discharge the debtor' (*au nom et en l'acquit du débiteur*) and those who perform to discharge the debtor but in their own name:[34] the former are to benefit from subrogation to the creditor's rights against the debtor by operation of law and so their performance in general discharges the debtor *vis-à-vis* the creditor, but not *vis-à-vis* the third party. Article 1236 also provides that performance by a third party to discharge the debtor but in the third party's own name will discharge the debtor, but will not give rise to any subrogation to the creditor's rights: here, then, the original obligation is entirely extinguished. However, in order for even relative discharge to occur, the third party must perform out of his own resources

---

[30] A lien (*droit de rétention*) has been held opposable against third parties even if they are not themselves liable on the debt: Civ. (1) 7 Jan. 1992, Bull. Civ. I, no. 4, 3.

[31] Starck, Roland and Boyer, *Régime général*, 41 ff.

[32] M. Cabrillac and Ch. Mouly, *Droit des sûretés* (3rd edn, 1995), 195.

[33] *Ibid.*, 195 and see Civ. 25 Nov. 1891, DP 1892.1.261.

[34] Two further situations are not dealt with in the text. First, where a third party pays another's (false) debt, thinking the debt genuine, the third party may recover his *paiement* from the creditor as being undue: arts. 1235 al. 1 and 1376, *code civil*. Secondly, where a third party pays another's (true) debt in his own name thinking himself the debtor (which he is not), then he may not recover against the true debtor (see Whittaker, 'Obligations', 411 and cases there cited), but he may recover from the creditor: Starck, Roland and Boyer, *Régime général*, 128.

(*de ses propres derniers*), a condition which arises in the context of payments in money. Thus, if a third party purports to pay a debtor's debt out of his own funds, but is found to have paid out of the creditor's funds, then the obligation is not discharged.[35]

However, the terms of article 1236 do not give a complete picture of the modern law.

First, French lawyers do not consider that article 1236 prevents the effectiveness of an express condition that on performance for the debtor a third party is to be subrogated to the creditor's rights:[36] such a *subrogation conventionelle* leads to the same position as does subrogation by operation of law, the debtor being discharged only *vis-à-vis* the creditor and remaining bound to the original obligation to the third party.

Secondly, quite apart from any subrogated rights, a third party in this situation may have an independent right of recourse against the debtor. In this respect, there has recently been a fluctuation in the attitude of the Cour de cassation. The traditional view was that third-party performance could give rise to a right of recourse if an independent ground for such a right could be established on the facts, notably by way of *mandat* (if the performance was authorised by the debtor), *gestion d'affaires* or *enrichissement sans cause* (if the performance was not so authorised).[37] However, in 1990 the Cour de cassation took a radical departure and declared that where a third party knowingly pays another's debt out of his own resources without being bound to do so, the sole fact of *paiement* gives rise to an independent right of recourse.[38] This jurisprudence was the subject of much juristic criticism: quite apart from other considerations, the mere discharge of the debtor in these circumstances clearly cannot always allow the third party to recover, for the latter may have acted from a spirit of generosity to the debtor, which should clearly rule it out.[39] More importantly, the new approach allowed recovery in situations where the conditions of *gestion d'affaires or enrichissement sans cause* were not satisfied, but these conditions

---

[35] Issa-Sayegh, 'Extinction', no. 62, 11, citing Com. 14 Nov. 1975, D 1976 IR 26.
[36] Aubry and Rau, *Cours de droit civil français*, 222, n. 9; art. 1250 al. 1, *code civil* provides that *subrogation conventionelle* must be expressly provided for and made at the same time as performance of the debtor's obligation.
[37] Aubry and Rau, *Cours de droit civil français*, 220; M. Planiol and G. Ripert, *Traité pratique de droit civil français*, vol. VII, *Obligations* (2nd edn, 1954), 552. *Paiement* may also be made to the creditor under a contract between the debtor and the third party such as insurance.
[38] Civ. (1) 15 May 1990, JCP 1991.II.21628, note Bruno Petit; D 1991.538, note G. Virassamy.
[39] Petit, JCP 1991.II.21628, 36.

should be retained as they encapsulate a fair and proper balance of the interests of the parties in question and their avoidance sacrifices the interests of the debtor.[40] Perhaps in response to these criticisms, only two years later, the Cour de cassation changed its mind and implicitly returned to the traditional position.[41] In this case, the claimant had paid the 'residence tax' of his handicapped stepdaughter who lived with him over a period. After her death, he claimed to be reimbursed for these sums from her estate. The Cour de cassation declared that 'it is for a person who has knowingly discharged another person's debt without being subrogated to the creditor's rights, to show that the cause from which this payment arises implies for the debtor an obligation to reimburse the payer in respect of sums paid'. This being the case, the lower court was entitled to reject the claimant's claim on the ground that he had not established on what basis he had paid the tax. Subsequent decisions of the Cour de cassation have taken the same line.[42]

What then is the present position? Clearly, where a third party performs in order to discharge the debtor out of a spirit of generosity, then he cannot later change his mind and claim reimbursement from the debtor, and the form of the 1992 judgment suggests that it will be for a third party to show that it was not done out of a sense of philanthropy to the debtor.[43] This rule holds good whether or not the performance was effected in the third party's own name or the debtor's. It is also clear that this change in approach by the courts does not threaten the established independent claims of interested third-party performers, such as the surety, for in such a case the relationship of suretyship itself constitutes the cause from which his performance arises, even if the suretyship was undertaken against the principal debtor's wishes.[44]

Beyond this, a distinction should be made on the basis of whether or not the third party's performance was authorised by the debtor.

If performance is rendered in the name of the debtor and with his authority, then a contract of *mandat* arises between them,[45] with a resulting right of reimbursement in the third party as the debtor's mandatory.[46] On the other hand, if the debtor did not give any authority for the third party to act in his name and perform his obligation or if the third party did not act in the debtor's name (even though he acted in order to discharge

[40] Cf. *Ibid.*, 37.   [41] Civ. (1) 2 Jun. 1992, D 1992 Somm. 407, note Philippe Delebecque.
[42] Civ. (1) 23 Feb. 1999, *pourvoi* no. 95-18.860 (unreported).
[43] Delebecque D 1992 Somm. 407.   [44] Cabrillac and Mouly, *Droit des sûretés*, 194.
[45] Art. 1984, *code civil*.   [46] Art. 1999, *code civil*.

him), then the third party may be able to recover on the basis of *gestion d'affaires* or, if not, *enrichissement sans cause*.[47]

For a right of recourse to arise in the third party as the debtor's *gérant d'affaires*[48] there are two conditions that are particularly significant in this context:[49] first, *gestion d'affaires* arises only when the third party's performance is 'useful' (*utile*) to the debtor, a condition which is placed in the 'sovereign power of assessment' of the lower courts. Now, it may be thought that the performance of another's obligation is always 'useful' to him, but it may not be, for by being liable to the third party directly and independently of the original obligation, the debtor may lose the benefit of any defences which he might have possessed against the original creditor: in such a circumstance it would not be useful for a third party to perform to the prejudice of the debtor.[50] It is on this ground also that it is rare for *gestion d'affaires* to be successfully invoked by a bank who pays a debt of a third party for which the bank no longer had a mandate, since intervention by a bank in such a situation contradicts the principle against conducting a client's affairs without authority.[51] Secondly, while

---

[47] Again, in the case of payment in money this assumes that the third party paid from his own resources. In this respect, the presumption is that a person who pays in his own name does so from his own resources, but this presumption may be rebutted. Thus, if the court finds that the third party paid with the debtor's own resources, clearly he cannot be reimbursed: Req 18 Feb. 1901, DP 1901.1.303.

[48] Art. 1375, *code civil*. For an early application of *gestion d'affaires* in this context, see Civ. 8 Jan. 1862, DP 1863.1.75. For an introduction to *gestion d'affaires* in English, see Whittaker, 'Obligations', 403-6.

[49] *Gestion d'affaires* may arise whether or not the *gérant* acts in the name of the *maître d'affaires*, though if he acts in his own name in entering legal transactions with third parties, any recourse of the latter is in principle available only against the *gérant* (unauthorised manager) and not the *maître d'affaires*: J. Flour and J.-L. Aubert, *Les obligations*, vol. II, *Le fait juridique* (6th edn, 1994), no. 17, 22. Tribunal de grande instance, Strasbourg, 9 July 1954, GP 1954.2.350 is an example of its application, where no mention is made of whether the performance was or was not made in the debtor's name. Cf. Issy-Sayegh, 'Extinction', no. 67, 12 and Starck, Roland and Boyer, *Régime général*, 63, who both assert that performance by a third party other than in the name of the debtor can give rise to recovery only on the basis of *enrichissement sans cause*.

[50] Cf. Virassamy, D 1991.538, 541 and M. Billiau obs. JCP 1992.I.3632, no. 6 who criticise the position there taken by the Cour de cassation on the ground that this issue is thereby avoided. The issue of utility is judged from the point of view of the would-be *gérant* to whom intervention must *appear* to be useful: B. Starck, H. Roland and L. Boyer, *Droit civil, Les obligations*, vol. I, *Le contrat* (6th edn, 1998), 750; Flour and Aubert, *Le fait juridique*, 16.

[51] Ph. Derouin, 'Le paiement de la dette d'autrui, Répétition de l'indu et enrichissement sans cause', D 1990 Chron. 1.

gestion d'affaires does not rest on any authority in the debtor, in French law it will not arise if the debtor has made clear his lack of consent[52] as long as this is deemed to be legitimate.[53]

Recovery by the third party on the basis of *enrichissement sans cause* is possible where the conditions of neither *mandat* nor *gestion d'affaires* are fulfilled.[54] An example may be found in a decision of the Cour de cassation in 1984 in which the former husband of a child's mother had paid her maintenance in respect of the child's upkeep after divorce.[55] After the child's mother and natural father obtained the child's legitimation (the effect of which was retroactive), the former husband successfully sued the child's natural father on the ground that his payments to the mother enriched the natural father *sans cause*, since his own obligation to maintain the child had been retroactively put to an end on legitimation. Of the conditions for recovery on the ground of *enrichissement sans cause*,[56] the most significant hurdle in the context of performance of another's obligation appears to be that the performance was made without fault on the part of the third party.[57] In common with the position more generally, a distinction is to be drawn here between a third party who acts in bad faith (notably where his intervention constitutes a deliberate breach of an applicable rule[58]) and where he acts merely negligently.[59]

---

[52] Malaurie and Aynès, *Droit civil, Les obligations*, 530 (concerning *gestion d'affaires* generally) and Com. 21 Nov. 1978, Bull. Civ. IV no. 271, 223 (where the lack of consent stemmed from a prior contract term between the debtor and the third party).

[53] A. Bénabent, *Droit civil, Les obligations* (4th edn, 1994), 217. An example of a refusal being illegitimate may be found in Civ. (1) 11 Feb. 1986, GP 1986.2, Somm. 507, note A. Piédelièvre in which a son paid the monthly installments of his father's loan, despite the father's opposition; the court accepted that this was a case of *gestion d'affaires*, for the father's opposition was not justified by the family's interest.

[54] The principle of the subsidiarity of the *action de in rem verso* rules it out only where the law provides an effective remedy or where such a remedy is barred by a legal obstacle: Whittaker, 'Obligations', 416–17.

[55] Civ. (1) 1 Feb. 1984, D 1984.388. It is to be noted that the subsidiary nature of the *action de in rem verso* did not prevent the former husband's recovery, despite his possessing a claim for *répétition de l'indu* from his former wife (who was insolvent).

[56] On which see Whittaker, 'Obligations', 413 ff.

[57] Virassamy, D 1991.541; Petit, JCP 1991.II.21628, 37.

[58] E.g. Civ. (1) 3 Apr. 1979, D 1979 IR 408 (where the third party was held to act 'dans son propre intérêt et à ses propres risques').

[59] Derouin D 1990 Chron. 1, 201–2 and see, for a general affirmation of the availability of recovery on the basis of *enrichissement sans cause* despite the claimant's negligence: Civ. (1) 11 Mar. 1997, D 1997.407, note Marc Billiau. It would seem that the effect of the latter decision is that the payer's negligence does not bar recovery on the ground of *enrichissement sans cause*, but this leaves the possibility of set-off by the debtor on the ground of a claim for delictual fault based on the third party's negligence under art. 1382, *code civil* (on this in general terms, see Billiau, *ibid.*, 409).

4. Summary of French law

The French position in relation to article 1236 may therefore be summarised as follows.

First, a creditor may not reject tender of due performance by a third party to the obligation unless the creditor has an interest in doing so or the debtor has agreed or does agree with the creditor that the third party should not perform. There are, on the other hand, no exceptions to this rule on the ground that the debtor has not authorised the third-party performance nor on the ground that the creditor considers that the debtor would be prejudiced by his acceptance of due tender.

Secondly, if the creditor accepts tender of due performance by a third party, then the debtor is thereby discharged vis-à-vis the creditor himself.

Thirdly, where the creditor accepts third-party performance, if the third party has an interest in performing or if he pays 'in the name of and to discharge the debtor' then, while the debtor is discharged vis-à-vis the creditor, he still owes the same obligation to the third party who is subrogated to the creditor's rights. Again, there is no distinction in this respect according to whether the third party intervenes with or without the debtor's authority.

Fourthly, where the tender of performance of another's obligation by a third party in order to discharge the debtor is accepted by the creditor, that third party will possess an independent recourse against the debtor (quite apart from any subrogated rights he may have) if he can establish a recognised legal ground for so doing whether this is *mandat*, some other relationship from which the performance arose (as with *caution*), *gestion d'affaires* or *enrichissement sans cause*. In this way, while French law does not make the debtor's authority a condition either for discharge of an obligation by the third party nor of the latter's recovery, the debtor's interests are by no means left unprotected.

5. The position in English law contrasted

At this stage, it may be helpful to recall the position in English law, which differs significantly from its French counterpart.

First, in English law the question whether a creditor of an obligation must accept tender of performance by a third party is dealt with in terms of 'vicarious performance'.[60] In this respect, in general the creditor may not reject tender of performance by a third party who performs on behalf

---

[60] See G. H. Treitel, *The Law of Contract* (10th edn, 1999), 699 ff.

of the debtor and with his authority, the exceptions to this position being made for the cases where the nature of the obligation is 'personal' in the sense that the creditor relies on the skill and judgment of the debtor and where the terms of any contract from which the obligation arises exclude performance by a third party.[61] As regards tender of performance, it may be thought that the whole notion of vicarious performance is predicated on the idea that the third party performs on behalf of the debtor and that therefore a creditor should not be required to accept tender of 'performance' by a third party who acts other than on behalf of the debtor.[62] This does not mean, however, that the debtor has actually to have authorised the 'purportedly vicarious performance' at the time of tender, and there is authority which suggests that a creditor is not justified in refusing due performance if tendered on behalf of the debtor.[63]

Secondly, the effect of tender of due performance in English law is in general to relieve the debtor of liabilities for failure to perform. Due tender is assimilated to performance itself and will give rise to the plea of tender as a defence to any subsequent action against him for failure to perform: there is no need in English law for a doctrine such as *mora creditoris*.[64] Where the obligation in question is one to pay money, then a successful plea of tender will not of itself discharge the debt, but if the creditor sues, the debtor's payment into court and proof of continued willingness to pay since tender will bar any claim for interest or damages after tender.[65]

Thirdly, at least as regards payment of another's money debt,[66] where the creditor accepts tendered performance by a third party, the generally accepted position is that the debtor is discharged only if the third party acts on behalf of the debtor with the intention to discharge him and with his authority (whether actual or subsequent by ratification).[67] Exceptions to this position are made where the payment is effected under compulsion of law (that is, to avoid the threat of the legitimate application of legal

---

[61] Ibid., 700-1. Cf. *Chitty on Contracts* (28th edn, 1999), §§ 20-079-20-081, which accepts the substance of this position, but does not distinguish sharply between the two.
[62] Below, 447-8.   [63] *Read v. Goldring* (1813) 2 M & S 86.
[64] G. H. Treitel, *Remedies for Breach of Contract, A Comparative Account* (1988), 41; *Chitty on Contracts*, § 22-083.
[65] *Chitty on Contracts*, § 22-084.
[66] Some contend that as a matter of authority, the performance of obligations other than to pay money does discharge a debt without the authority of the debtor: A. Burrows, *The Law of Restitution* (1993), 223, citing *Gebhardt v. Saunders* [1892] 2 QB 452.
[67] P. Birks, *An Introduction to the Law of Restitution* (revised edn, 1989), 189-90; Lord Goff of Chieveley and G. Jones, *The Law of Restitution* (5th edn, 1998), 16-17.

process) and, less certainly, necessity.[68] On the other hand, it has been argued by some that payment of another's debt should be held to discharge the debt even where the debtor gave no authority.[69]

Fourthly, there is a similar division of opinion as to possible restitutionary consequences of the payment of another's debt. Those who hold that authority is required for discharge, allow restitution from the debtor in favour of the payer only where discharge has occurred and where there is an independent unjust factor, such as mistake or necessity, but they argue that in the absence of discharge, the payer may recover from the creditor on the ground of failure of consideration.[70] Those who argue for discharge in the absence of debtor authority also argue for the existence of a wider area of restitutionary recovery from the debtor and, conversely, a narrower one from the creditor.[71]

It has been said that the original purpose of the common-law rule was the concern to protect a debtor from the imposition of an undesired creditor, but, assuming this is so, the present free assignability of rights (even with its formalities) suggests that this is no longer a convincing legal policy. Apart from this concern and from disagreements about the proper interpretations of the (admittedly complex) common-law authorities,[72] the dispute between these two positions centres to a considerable extent on the availability of possible restitution against the creditor in the absence of discharge of the debtor and, of course, on the general concern of English law to discourage officious intermeddling.[73] A further concern of those who support the traditional English position is that it protects the position of the debtor, for if the third party is able by payment to gain an independent restitutionary right against the debtor, then the latter may lose the benefit of any defences and, what is more, lose counterclaims which he may have against the creditor.[74]

[68] See P. Birks and J. Beatson, 'Unrequested Payment of Another's Debt', chap. 7 with a postscript by J. Beatson, in: J. Beatson, *The Use and Abuse of Unjust Enrichment, Essays on the Law of Restitution* (1991).
[69] D. Friedmann, 'Payment of Another's Debt', (1983) 99 *LQR* 534; Burrows, *Law of Restitution*, 222-3.
[70] See, especially, Birks and Beatson, 'Unrequested Payment', 201-2. Goff and Jones, *Law of Restitution*, 129 take a different view again, accepting the general position as regards discharge, but arguing for restitution against the debtor by means of subrogation in all cases except those involving maliciously officious intervention.
[71] Friedmann, 'Payment of Another's Debt', 539; Birks and Beatson, 'Unrequested Payment', 201-2.
[72] For their analysis see Birks and Beatson 'Unrequested Payment'.
[73] For the leading authority on this approach see *Falcke v. Scottish Imperial Insurance Co.* (1886) 34 Ch D 234.
[74] Birks and Beatson, 'Unrequested Payment', 203.

The differences between the English and French positions in this area stem partly from their different authoritative bases and historical sources. However, they are also based on the well-known different positions taken in particular to the intervention of a person in the interests of another but without his consent: in French law, the officious intermeddler is discouraged by the more subtle restrictions on the availability of recovery under *gestion d'affaires* and *enrichissement sans cause*, rather than on any broader exclusionary rule. And where the third party has an 'interest' in paying, then he is not thought to be intermeddling: it is his own affair (even if it was not previously) and he can recover either by way of legal subrogation or personally and independently without the benefits or the disadvantages that subrogation entails. Furthermore, French law protects the debtor's rights of defence or counterclaim against the creditor in two ways: first, by using the technique of subrogation, where the third party's claim is subjected to the same constraints as the creditor's and secondly, as regards claims on the basis of *enrichissement sans cause*, by setting the measure of restitution at the lowest value as between the 'impoverishment' of the claimant and the 'enrichment' of the defendant,[75] for the debtor's enrichment by the third party would be less than the latter's impoverishment if the debtor would not have had to pay (as much) to the creditor.

However, in turning to the second situation of this discussion, it will be seen that English law does sometimes consider it not merely not officious but actually a 'duty' for a person other than a debtor of an obligation to perform or have performed the obligation: this is the light in which I suggest the English law of mitigation of damage may be viewed.

III. The faculté de remplacement: article 1144, *code civil*

1. Article 1144, *code civil*, and the nature of performance of contractual obligations

Again the starting point is a provision of the French Civil Code. But here it refuses to allow intervention by the non-debtor without judicial authorisation. The provision in question relates to much wider questions about the nature of performance of contractual obligations and this requires a brief introduction.

Many common lawyers are aware that French law takes a very different attitude from that of English law to the primary remedy for breach

---

[75] See generally, Whittaker, 'Obligations', 418 ff.

of contract:[76] French lawyers accept that a creditor of a contractual obligation has a right to performance by the debtor.[77] This is put in terms of the availability of *exécution en nature* (or performance in kind), a type of court order that may be backed up by the threat of the payment of a money sanction (or *astreinte*) in respect of the time when the court order is not obeyed, when the order is termed *exécution forcé en nature*. Such a direct order of *exécution en nature* is ruled out by French law only when performance by the debtor is impossible, including not merely physical impossibility but also 'moral impossibility', which notably includes the position where the debtor's obligation is too personal to be enforced against him.[78]

This system is certainly a triumph of juristic interpretation and judicial invention. Judicial invention, because until 1972 *astreintes* had no legislative basis and were justified (entirely unconvincingly) on the basis that they were a form of damages;[79] juristic interpretation, because the terms of the Civil Code suggest quite the opposite position and strikingly announce in article 1142 that 'every obligation to do or not to do gives rise to damages in the case of its non-performance by the debtor.'[80] Clearly, this provision was enacted in the Civil Code because its drafters were sufficiently imbued with enlightenment thinking that they thought it contrary to personal liberty for an individual to be ordered to perform his private-law obligations. However, it is not this provision which is of principal concern here, but rather article 1144, which originally stated that '[t]he creditor may also, in the case of non-performance, be authorised to have the obligation performed at the expense of the debtor.'[81] This option for a creditor is known generally as the *faculté de remplacement*.

To a common lawyer, this is a rather odd provision: why should the court be involved in these circumstances? How does this relate to the Civil Code's provisions on non-performance? However, the reason why I wish to

---

[76] See the observations of Lord Hoffmann in *Co-operative Insurance Society Ltd v. Argyll Stores (Holdings) Ltd* [1997] 2 WLR 898 at 902–3.
[77] Bénabent, *Droit civil*, 177.
[78] See, generally, Nicholas, *French Law of Contract*, 216 ff.; Whittaker, 'Obligations', 348.
[79] The legal basis for the imposition of *astreintes* is now to be found in Loi no. 91-650 of 9 July 1991, arts. 33–7.
[80] 'Toute obligation de faire ou de ne pas faire se résout en dommages et intérêts, en cas d'inexécution de la part du débiteur.' Somewhat oddly, though, art. 1184, *code civil*, which is concerned with the availability of judicial termination of a bilateral contract on the ground of the debtor's serious non-performance, assumes that the injured party can force the debtor to perform his obligation if this is possible: art. 1184 al. 2.
[81] 'Le créancier peut aussi, en cas d'inexécution, être autorisé à faire exécuter lui-même l'obligation aux dépens du débiteur.'

include it in this discussion is that article 1144 clearly provides a system of control for the actual achievement of the debtor's *prestation* (and in this sense performance) by someone other than himself, this someone being either the creditor himself or a third party. Originally, the provision, which was included in the Civil Code only on the suggestion of the Tribunal d'appel of Montpellier,[82] was seen as a qualification on the principle laid down in article 1142, as it provides a judicial mechanism by which the creditor of a contractual obligation may receive the exact performance (*prestation*) that is due to him, even if this does not come from the debtor himself. This being the case, those jurists who believed that the nature of obligations argued in favour of a court being able (in principle) to order their performance, saw support for their view in article 1144 (and in article 1143, which concerns judicial orders of destruction of things made in contravention of a negative obligation). As a result, article 1142 came to be seen as providing for the exception (where performance is physically or morally impossible) and article 1144 came to be seen as an example of *exécution en nature* which applied to *obligations de faire*, even though article 1144 does not involve the debtor in being ordered to perform his obligation. Here, then, *exécution en nature* is 'performance in kind' only from the point of view of the creditor.

2. Significant features of article 1144, code civil

There are three particular further features of article 1144 to which I wish to draw attention.

(a) *Mise en demeure*

First, in principle a creditor must put the debtor on notice to perform (*mise en demeure*) and then go to court to ask for authorisation to have the debtor's obligation performed by someone other than the debtor. It is available to a creditor only as regards obligations whose performance by a person other than the debtor is properly possible; this excludes obligations which are personal to the debtor or which concern the supply of ascertained property owned by the debtor.[83] Before 1991, a creditor might have been so authorised by a court and then find himself without

---

[82] P. Wéry, *L'exécution forcée en nature des obligations contractuelles non pécuniaires* (1993), 88, notes that the *faculté de remplacement* was not discussed by Pothier as a general mechanism: *ibid.*, 66–7.

[83] Ph. Simler, 'Classification des obligations, Distinction des obligations de donner, de faire et de ne pas faire', *Juris-Classeur civil*, arts. 1136 à 1145, 28. For an example of a contract of supply of ascertained property, see Com. 20 Jan. 1976, D 1976 Somm. 36.

actual recourse against the debtor (if the latter became insolvent). In that year article 1144 was amended to provide that the court may order the debtor to provide the money in advance of the commissioning of the performance by a third party.[84] While recourse to court may seem an unnecessarily delaying element in the process, French civil procedure does possess an accelerated procedure for urgent cases before the *juge des référés*, a procedure much used in relation to article 1144 of the Civil Code.[85]

(b) The requirement of judicial decision

Secondly, while it has been argued that as a form of *exécution en nature* the creditor should have a right to demand authorisation,[86] the courts recognise in themselves a discretion as to whether or not it should be awarded.[87] In practice what this means is that instead of authorising third-party performance, a court may give time to the debtor to perform himself,[88] may order the debtor to perform the contract (if appropriate, backed up with *astreintes*) or simply award the creditor damages.[89] If the creditor is authorised to have the obligation performed at the debtor's expense, then, once this has occurred, the debtor is released from his obligation (even though the contract is not terminated).[90] Clearly, this discretion gives the courts considerable power to control the situations in which the creditor may substitute a third party's performance for the debtor's. For, as P. Wéry has observed, when a third party is substituted to performance, the debtor is ousted from his own obligation, from the performance of which he may have been counting on benefiting.[91]

In this respect, there is a clear relationship with the Civil Code's attitude to termination of bilateral contracts on the ground of a party's breach (*résolution*), for article 1184 provides that the injured party must in principle ask the court to terminate the contract and it expressly recognises in the court a discretion to give the debtor more time to perform if

---

[84] Loi no. 91-650 of 9 July 1991, art. 82.
[85] Y. Chartier note to Tribunal de grande instance, Dunkerque, 3 Oct. 1984, GP 1985.1.154.
[86] For the competing views, see Wéry, *L'exécution forcée*, 326 ff. especially at 333.
[87] Simler, 'Classification des obligations', no. 139, 29 'Le juge saisi d'une telle demande d'autorisation apprécie son opportunité'. Wéry, *L'exécution forcée*, 329–30 notes Civ. 20 Dec. 1820 S 1819–1821.349 as the first decision to this effect, the Court stating that 'les articles invoqués du Code civil et particulièrement l'article 1142 [sci. 1144] sont conçus en termes facultatifs qui laissent aux juges le pouvoir d'adopter le mode d'indemnité qui leur paraît le plus juste et le plus favorable à l'intérêt des parties.'
[88] Simler, 'Classification des obligations', no. 136, 28.
[89] *Ibid.*, no. 139, 29, citing Req 23 Mar. 1909, DP 1910.1.343.
[90] Wéry, *L'exécution forcée*, no. 188, 261.   [91] *Ibid.*, no. 199, 274.

appropriate, even when the seriousness of the debtor's breach would otherwise justify the termination of the contract.[92] The Cour de cassation has held that where the debtor offers to perform, the lower courts will normally refuse *résolution* unless they consider the offer to perform too late.[93] The *faculté de remplacement* therefore has in common with *résolution judiciaire* the ousting of the debtor from his own performance and both are subjected to judicial control. In my view, what unites articles 1144 and 1184 is a concern to protect the debtor's interest in performing, an interest which in the context of the procedure of *offres réelles* is even sometimes put in terms of the debtor's right to perform.[94]

The principal (and very important) exception to the requirement of judicial decision in relation to termination of a contract for non-performance is the recognition of express contract terms (known as *clauses résolutoires*), which give the injured party a right to terminate the contract. Such a term has the advantage from the injured party's point of view of avoiding the judicial discretion which goes with the need to have recourse to court, and not merely the delay and expense of doing so.[95] However, there is no mention in the French texts of a practice or discussion as to the effectiveness of *clauses de remplacement*, by which a party is contractually entitled to have the debtor's obligation performed without recourse to court,[96] and there are instead three other types of exception: first, a creditor need not go to court in cases of urgency (that is, greater urgency than even the accelerated civil procedures can satisfy); secondly, in cases of commercial sales, both seller and buyer may go into the market and sell or buy if they are let down by the other party; and thirdly, legislation allows specific instances where the creditor may arrange a substitute performance of his own volition.[97] Of the latter two, it can be said that

---

[92] Art. 1184 al. 3, *code civil*.   [93] Civ. (1) 17 May 1954, GP 1954.2.82.
[94] For an older example, see M. Planiol, *Traité élémentaire de droit civil* (6th edn, 1912), vol. II 150. For more recent use, see Terré, Simler and Lequette, 1004; F. Kernaleguen, 'Offres de *paiement* et consignation', *Juris-Classeur civil*, art. 1257 à 1264, 3; Robin, 'La mora creditoris', 608. For the procedure of *offres réelles*, see above, 438.
[95] Terré, Simler and Lequette, *Les obligations*, 485. The courts have recognised that such a contractual right to terminate must be exercised in good faith, on which see Whittaker, 'Obligations', 353. Such a clause in a consumer contract is subject to a test of fairness under art. L 132-1 *Code de la consommation* (implementing in French law Council Directive 93/13/EC of 5 April 1993 concerning unfair terms in consumer contracts).
[96] Cf. the position in Belgian law, where *clauses de remplacement* are current both in private and administrative law contracts: Wéry, '*L'exécution forcée*, no. 204 ff., pp. 281 ff.
[97] For these, see Simler, 'Classification des obligations', nos. 140-1, 29. A special legislative example may be found in arts 1792-6 al. 4, *code civil* relating to the *garantie de parfait achèvement* in *contrats d'entreprises*.

either commercial needs (and commercial practice) or other special considerations justify the potentially prejudicial effect on the debtor's right to perform. The exception on the ground of urgency is more interesting; while the French case law here is far from systematic, the general view is that it will apply only where the expenses thereby incurred by the debtor in securing substitute performance are 'urgent, indispensable and effected in the most economical way'.[98] What this means in practice is that if the creditor of an obligation considers the matter to be urgent and wishes to procure substitute performance elsewhere, he may do so, but risks (i) being told subsequently by a court when he seeks to recover his expenses from the debtor as damages that the situation was not in fact urgent or that the expenses were not indispensable or sufficiently economical and (ii) the debtor deciding in the meanwhile to tender performance himself (though the latter possibility may be avoided if the creditor is able to exercise a right to terminate the contract arising under an express contract term).[99] The French courts are therefore able to verify whether the debtor should in the circumstances be deprived of his right to perform; this is effected either by prior or subsequent judicial control.

In this way, French courts are able in the context of article 1144 to protect the debtor's interest by reference to criteria similar but by no means identical to those found in article 1236 and *paiement* by a third party. The judicial discretion in relation to the *faculté de remplacement* may be seen as performing a similar function to the requirement of 'utility' as regards recovery by a third party in *gestion d'affaires*, discharge having been effected under article 1236: in both situations, a central concern is the need to protect the debtor's interests, while at the same time relieving him from further performance.[100] In both, the debtor's attitude is significant: if the debtor forbids *paiement* by a third party, then the latter cannot recover under *gestion d'affaires*; if the debtor offers to perform himself, a court will not authorise *remplacement* nor is it likely to think justifiable a creditor's unilateral recourse to substitute performance.

However, there are clearly considerable differences between the respective domains of articles 1236 and 1144. Article 1236 is concerned with the effect on performance of any type of obligation by a third party (whether or not authorised by the debtor): while there is no exclusion of third-party

---

[98] Soc. 7 Dec. 1951, D 1952.144 and see Malaurie and Aynès, *Droit civil, Les obligations*, 592–3.
[99] There may be a further way in which the creditor may avoid this latter difficulty, for it has been said that the urgency (if it is exists) also justifies rejection by the creditor of any offer by the debtor to perform: Simler, 'Classification des obligations', no. 140, 29.
[100] See above, 443–4.

intervention at the request of the creditor, the system which it creates applies only to performance undertaken in order to discharge the debtor *vis-à-vis* the creditor by use of the third party's own resources (and not the creditor's).[101] As to consequential recourse, under article 1236 it is the third party who may be entitled to recover in respect of the substitute performance, whereas in the case of article 1144 it is the creditor, for the cost of obtaining substitute performance by the third party.

Article 1236 of the Civil Code distinguishes between performance by interested and non-interested third parties, this accounting in part for the different grounds of recourse, either by way of subrogation by operation of law or an independent right of recourse.[102] Moreover, if recovery after *paiement* under article 1236 is based on *gestion d'affaires*, then the third party must be found to be acting on the basis of a limited altruism: not entirely in his own interest, but, on the other hand, not so generously as to be not looking for any indemnity. While the law governing the *faculté de remplacement* recognises that the creditor does have an interest in procuring a substitute performance in the absence of performance by the debtor, it denies the creditor a right to do so; instead, the creditor's interest in procuring substitute performance is balanced by the courts against the debtor's interest in performing himself.

(c) *Obligations de faire*

Finally, while *paiement* for the purposes of article 1236 is not restricted to payments of money, this is the performance typical of third parties who act neither from their own interest nor with the debtor's authority and also the typical context in which the availability of recourse by the third party based on *gestion d'affaires* (or, indeed, *enrichissement sans cause*) arises. By contrast, the *faculté de remplacement* is restricted to contractual *obligations de faire*. While they may sometimes include obligations to pay money,[103] in practice article 1144 is concerned with substitute performances for obligations to deliver generic property other than money and obligations to perform services. French law treats the enforcement of money obligations to a distinct regime, providing for the recovery of interest at a legally determined rate but also giving a discretion to courts to allow the debtor time to pay.[104] So it is not meaningless to suggest that

---

[101] Above, 440-1.   [102] See above, 439 ff.
[103] Simler, 'Classification des obligations', no. 91, 20.
[104] Art. 1153, *code civil* (as amended) provides the general rules for payment of interest for delay in payment of a money sum: exceptions are made where the debtor is in bad faith and in the context of commercial law and suretyship. Arts. 1244-1–1244-3 *code civil* (as amended in 1991) give to the court a general discretion to allow a debtor

a creditor of a money obligation should be able to obtain 'performance' from a third party by way of a loan (at agreed interest), with the expenses thereby incurred by the creditor to be paid by the debtor, but such a procedure would disrupt this legal regime, which balances the interests of creditor and debtor of sums of money.

3. The position in English law contrasted

English law knows no technical equivalent of the *faculté de remplacement* and its starting point for the remedies available on breach by a debtor of his obligation is fundamentally different. As with French law, English law recognises the right of a creditor of a money obligation to have it enforced, this being put in contractual terms as a matter of the action for the agreed contract price – 'specific performance' at common law. However, while there is nothing to stop a creditor of a money obligation from going into the market and obtaining 'substitute performance' from a third party by way of a loan at interest, English law has traditionally taken a restrictive attitude to recovery of such an expense against the debtor. The general common-law rule is that no interest is recoverable for delay in payment of a debt,[105] but interest may be stipulated and the courts enjoy by statute a considerable power as to the award of interest.[106] Moreover, the courts have accepted that a creditor may be able to recover damages for breach of contract for loss incurred by obtaining money at interest owing to the debtor's lateness in paying, as long as this loss was 'within the reasonable contemplation of the parties' given the debtor's knowledge of the creditor's particular circumstances.[107]

As regards all other positive obligations, English law's starting point is in damages. It is still generally true that specific performance is not available where damages are an adequate remedy, although a somewhat more flexible approach has at times been taken, depending on the circumstances.[108] Now in many cases damages are indeed an adequate remedy, because the

---

of a money obligation time to pay (a *délai de grâce*) of up to two years, this discretion being exercised taking into consideration the situation of the debtor, the needs of the creditor, the relative good or bad faith of the parties and their circumstances more generally (such as age or health): Starck, Roland and Boyer, *Régime général*, 89 ff.

[105] Treitel, *Law of Contract*, 924 ff.

[106] As regards interest on judgment debts, this is now contained in the Supreme Court Act 1981, s. 35(A). As regards interest on commercial debts before judgment, see the Late Payment of Commercial Debts (Interest) Act 1998.

[107] These phrases describe the so-called second limb of the test of remoteness of damage of the rule in *Hadley v. Baxendale* (1854) 9 Ex 341. An example of recovery in this type of situation may be found in *Wadsworth v. Lydall* [1981] 1 WLR 598.

[108] See Treitel, *Law of Contract*, 949 ff. and see *Co-operative Insurance Society Ltd v. Argyll Stores (Holdings) Ltd* [1997] 2 WLR 898 at 903 *per* Lord Hoffmann.

law allows a creditor to go out into the market and obtain a substitute performance for the debtor by way of mitigation of his own damage when it is reasonable to do so; indeed, if he does not do so, he will lose the right to compensation for the loss which he suffers as a result of the debtor's breach.[109] In this way English law gives a direct incentive to a creditor to obtain third-party performance of a debtor's obligation and, if a creditor does mitigate in this way, he does indeed receive what he was owed under the obligation (the *prestation*, in French terms), although he does not receive it from the debtor.

The advantage of the English approach here, by contrast with the French, is that the creditor does not even in principle have to wait for judicial authorisation to obtain third-party performance and this avoids the inconvenience, expense and delay of judicial proceedings. On the other hand, the disadvantage is that, having engaged a third party, a creditor risks not being able to recover the costs of substitute performance. Such a failure to recover may be caused by the debtor's insolvency: there is no possibility, as there is in French law, of being granted an amount of money in advance from the debtor to cover the cost of obtaining a substitute. Moreover, a creditor who mitigates his loss also risks a court subsequently considering his action unreasonable. The absence of prior authorisation should not disguise the fact that in English law there is judicial control of the creditor's substitution of a third party (or himself) for the debtor, but it is effected a posteriori by a court seised with a claim by the creditor to recover expenses in the form of damages.[110] The test here is one of reasonableness, to be assessed at the time of breach (or reasonable notice of breach) rather than in its result. This means that, while the purpose of the law of mitigation is to reduce the creditor's losses, if the creditor's purported acts of mitigation were reasonable at the time, he will be able to recover their cost, even if the result increased his own losses.[111]

Here there is again a certain analogy with the traditional requirements of *gestion d'affaires*: in mitigating, the creditor acts not merely in his own

---

[109] *British Westinghouse Electric and Manufacturing Co. Ltd v. Underground Electric Railways Co. of London Ltd* [1912] AC 673. Another way of looking at mitigation is in causal terms, so that it can be said that any losses suffered by a creditor after an unreasonable failure to mitigate are caused by this failure to mitigate, rather than by the debtor's breach.

[110] Of course, this does not mean that all creditors have to go to court to recover compensation in this way, but any settlement agreed to between the debtor and the creditor is made on the basis of judicial attitudes to mitigation.

[111] *Chitty on Contracts*, § 27-098.

interest, but in the interest of the debtor (to reduce his liabilities)[112] and the application of the reasonableness test could be thought to operate somewhat like the criterion of utility for the *gérant*'s intervention. What is clear, however, is that in English law there is no need for the debtor's consent before the creditor is entitled to mitigate (and thereby have the debtor's obligation performed by a third party), although a debtor's own later offer of due performance may be relevant to the reasonableness of the creditor's mitigation.[113]

IV. Conclusion

Even if in English law a third party cannot effectively discharge another's money obligation without the latter's authority, a creditor of a non-money obligation may do so and then recover from the debtor its cost, whether the debtor approves or not, subject to the 'reasonableness' of his doing so. In French law, by contrast, a third party may perform the debtor's *prestation* even without his consent, but may recover from him only if he can establish a legal ground for doing so, whether *gestion d'affaires* or *enrichissement sans cause*. On the other hand, in French law in general a creditor of a contractual obligation to do may not have the obligation performed by a third party without prior authorisation by the court. In both these situations, French courts protect the debtor's right to perform. In all, under both systems, it is clear that contractual obligations are very frequently 'performed' by third parties: either at the request of the debtor (whose agents therefore 'vicariously perform' the debtor's obligation) or at the request of the creditor (on breach and for reward by the creditor, either with or without the need to have recourse to court).

[112] Cf. D. Harris, *Remedies in Contract and Tort* (1988): '[i]t is in the interests of contract-breakers (as well as of society) that P [the promisee], the person in the best position to minimise the loss, should be encouraged to try to do so. P should be indemnified against his expenses in any reasonable attempt to mitigate, since such attempts are usually successful.'

[113] *Chitty on Contracts*, § 26-054.

17 Payment of another's debt

Hector L. MacQueen

I. The problem

A parent picks up the unpaid bills of her student child at the end of the university term. A football club pays off the gambling and other debts incurred by one of its star players. In my absence from home at an enrichment conference, my neighbour in my Edinburgh tenement flat pays my share of the bill for work carried out in the tenement garden, the underlying contract with the gardener providing that each resident is to be liable only for a pro-rata share. At least two potential enrichment questions arise. If the creditors take no further action against the student or the footballer or me, we three debtors will benefit by the savings made through not having to pay our debts. The creditors will be enriched, however, if, despite the interventions of the parent, the club and the good neighbour, they also continue to seek and recover payment from, respectively, the student or the footballer or me. In both situations, the gain is made at the expense of the payer. Can the respective payers recover either their own expenses or the debtors' enrichments?

II. Terminology

In the rest of this account the following terminology will be used: the person who pays another's debt will be called the payer (P); the recipient of the payment will be termed the creditor (C); and the person whose debt is paid by P will be known as the debtor (D).

I am very grateful to Eric Clive and George Gretton for valuable comments on an earlier draft. Any remaining errors, whether of fact or law, ground recovery only against me.

III. The general comparative position

The problem of payment of another's debt is an area of the law of unjustified enrichment or restitution in which the basic solutions of the Continental systems and the common law appear to be different. The study by Daniel Friedmann and Nili Cohen in the *International Encyclopaedia of Comparative Law* states:

> It has been suggested that under continental law a person who pays another's debt is generally entitled to restitution from the debtor. The rule does not of course apply where payment was made in accordance with a contract with the debtor, in which case the rights of the payer will be governed by the contract, or where the payment was intended as a gift to the debtor... Historically it was the doctrine of *negotiorum gestio* which provided the major vehicle for allowing reimbursement from the debtor... [R]estitution will be allowed by virtue of the general rule which treats the payment of another's debt as an established category of unjust enrichment... Unlike the continental legal systems, the common law does not recognise a general principle which entitles a person who pays another's debt to restitution. Its starting point was that no person can make himself the creditor of another's debt against his will or without his consent.[1]

Friedmann and Cohen go on after this passage to point out that there are specific situations in which recovery from the debtor is allowed in the common law: by way of rights of indemnity or contribution in cases of liability *in solidum*; when payments are made under compulsion of law; in cases of agency of necessity; and where the doctrine of subrogation applies.

Elsewhere in the *International Encyclopaedia of Comparative Law*, Samuel Stoljar's study of *negotiorum gestio* (unauthorised management or administration of another's affairs in his absence) notes of the situation where P, acting without authorisation, pays the debt of D to C that it:

> affords an excellent illustration of the different conceptions obtaining, respectively, in the civil and the common law. At common law a stranger, paying another's debt purely voluntarily and without (what is called) compulsion or coercion, has no legal recovery, while in the civil law, payment of another's debt has been one of the great instances of *negotiorum gestio*.

Stoljar notes that P's recovery from D was one of the main examples of the *actio negotiorum gestorum contraria* in Roman law, provided that D did not have a clear interest that the payment should not be made, and that this has continued to the present day in civilian systems such as Germany and

---

[1] D. Friedmann and N. Cohen, 'Payment of Another's Debt', in: *International Encyclopedia of Comparative Law* (1991), vol. X, chap. 10, §§ 9–10.

France, so long as P acts with the intention of managing D's affairs and his intervention is useful. The common law, on the other hand, 'though far from inhospitable to ideas of *negotiorum gestio*, has nevertheless remained, and largely still remains, deeply reluctant to assist, let alone encourage, the unsolicited payer'.[2]

The different approaches to payment of another's debt thus nicely illustrate the contrasting general characteristics of Continental enrichment law, together with *negotiorum gestio*, and common-law restitution, together with its refusal to recognise any principle akin to *negotiorum gestio*. The Continental approach is that the benefit or service must be paid for unless there is some legal ground for its retention such as a valid contract or a gift. It is interventionist and paternalistic, in that one who acts in the interests of another, even if not asked to do so, is seen to deserve some protection from the law. The common-law approach is that the enrichment need not be reversed unless there is some additional 'unjust factor' in the case. It is individualistic and concerned to protect the security of transactions. A person who meddles in the affairs of another without that other's consent or authorisation acts at his own risk.

The discrepancy in approach to payment of another's debt reflects other fundamental differences between the two great legal traditions. The most significant for present purposes concerns the basic question: in what circumstances does a third-party payment discharge a debt? Unless D's debt is discharged, there can be no question of his being enriched at P's expense. Friedmann and Cohen give the following overview:

> On the issue whether an unauthorized third party may discharge the debt there is a fundamental divergence between the Continental and the Anglo-American legal systems ... [U]nder the Continental legal systems, where performance need not be made in person, a third party has the power to fulfil the debtor's obligation irrespective of whether he has an interest in discharging the obligation. The Anglo-American legal system adopts a completely different approach. Its basic position is that a third party has no power to tender performance, unless he is authorized by the debtor to do so. Therefore, if a stranger offers to pay another's debt, the creditor is not bound to accept it. This rule does not, however, apply to

---

[2] S. J. Stoljar, 'Negotiorum Gestio', in: *International Encyclopedia of Comparative Law* (1984), vol. X, chap. 17, §§ 93–133 (quotations at §§ 93, 104). See also generally D. H. van Zyl, *Negotiorum Gestio in South African Law* (1985) and R. Zimmermann, *The Law of Obligations: Roman Foundations of the Civilian Tradition* (1990, paperback edn 1996), 433–50, for historical and comparative discussion. See further, for critical analysis of the Anglo-American opposition to *negotiorum gestio*, H. Dagan, 'In Defense of the Good Samaritan', (1999) 97 *Michigan LR* 1152.

instances where the unauthorized payment was made by a third party who had a sufficient interest (as defined by the particular jurisdiction) in the discharge of the debt. In such an instance, the third party has presumably the power to tender performance, and in any event his payment, if accepted, discharges the obligation.[3]

The Continental rule springs ultimately from Roman law,[4] and can also be linked conceptually with the assignability of debt. Once the Roman-Dutch school had taken the *ius commune* beyond the idea that obligations were strictly personal to debtor and creditor and had enabled the creditor generally to transfer his rights freely to third parties,[5] it became apparent that the debtor had no right to a particular creditor, and the possibility of a third party paying the debt and having a corresponding enrichment claim against the debtor became logical.[6] The common law, on the other hand, did not recognise general assignability until the fusion of law and equity in the later nineteenth century, and the further step of allowing discharge at the hand of an unauthorised third person who would then have a restitutionary claim against the original debtor has not been taken since.

Reference to assignation does, however, raise one key problem if P has a right of action against D. Had C assigned to a third party, D could plead against the assignee any defences good against the original C – *assignatus utitur iure auctoris*. The intervening P is not an assignee, however, and the obligation under which he claims against D is quite independent of the original debt. What then becomes of D's defences in the original debt? Another version of the same issue arises from the fact that probably any prescriptive period relating to the original debt will have commenced before that for the enrichment claim. However, enrichment claims bring with them their own defences, such as change of position, and, if taken against P, these may help to protect D from the unavailability of defences

---

[3] Friedmann and Cohen, 'Payment of Another's Debt', § 4.
[4] Gai. D. 3, 5, 38; Gai. D. 46, 3, 53; Inst. 3, 29 pr.
[5] R. Zimmermann, 'Roman-Dutch Jurisprudence and its Contribution to European Private Law', (1992) 66 *Tulane LR* 1685, 1703–4.
[6] Note too that in some legal systems a party may seek specific implement of a contract by a third party, this being at the direct expense of the original debtor in the obligation and saving the creditor from having to make a damages claim in respect of the extra cost of the third party (e.g. in France, art. 1144, *code civil*). Scots law could, it is suggested, adopt this approach under the very general provisions about orders which can be granted in lieu of specific implement under the Law Reform (Miscellaneous Provisions) (Scotland) Act 1940, s. 1(2).

against C. Nevertheless, there is an unresolved tension here in systems recognising P's claim.[7]

The basic common-law position, that there is no discharge by unauthorised third-party intervention, raises sharply the question of the relationship between P and C. At first sight, it would appear that if the payment does not discharge the debt, the reason for, or purpose of, the payment falls away, and that as a result of this 'total failure of consideration' P should be entitled to restitution from C. But it has been persuasively argued that, if C in fact takes no action against D, then the purpose of P has been fulfilled, and in consequence there is no failure of consideration. So once again, before recovery is possible, there must be an additional 'unjust factor' in P's favour, such as mistake or duress.[8] The problem of the P-C relationship can also arise in Continental law, however, where P acts under mistake or involuntarily, under duress. Given that the payment may otherwise have discharged D's debt, such cases can give rise to very complex questions about who is enriched and who is impoverished by the payment.[9]

Finally, the division between the common law and the Continental systems on the subject of payment of another's debt raises sharply the question how the problem should be addressed in any future system of European private law. Can the mixed legal system of Scotland, which has not hitherto attracted much attention from comparative lawyers working on this topic, provide any guidance as to possible modes of reconciliation?

IV. Scots law

Scottish enrichment law evidently springs from civilian rather than common-law sources. There has been influence from English law from time to time over the last 200 years, but by and large the field is a good example of Roman-Scotch law, built up essentially in an indigenous way after an initial reception from the *ius commune*. Much the same is true of the institution of *negotiorum gestio*, which was long ago received in Scotland and, perhaps thanks to a fairly limited case law, is still

---

[7] Friedmann and Cohen, 'Payment of Another's Debt', §§ 22, 23.
[8] See generally D. Friedmann, 'Payment of Another's Debt', (1983) 99 *LQR* 534;
J. Beatson, *The Use and Abuse of Unjust Enrichment* (1991), 177 ff. For a recent perspective see S. Meier, 'Mistaken Payments in Three-party Situations: A German View of English Law', (1999) 58 *CLJ* 567.
[9] See further below, section IV.

clearly civilian, although sometimes confused with the English 'agency of necessity'.[10]

The topic of payment of another's debt has attracted little attention from writers on Scots law, reflecting the absence of significant case law on the topic. There are two major published studies, both of which appeared in the 1990s. The first was an article by Robin Evans-Jones,[11] the second the relevant parts of the two-volume Discussion Paper produced by the Scottish Law Commission in 1993 and entitled 'Recovery of Benefits Conferred under Error of Law'.[12] Just as 'the hand of Esau was less distinctive than that of the Downing Professor',[13] so the Discussion Paper bears the unmistakable imprimatur of Niall Whitty. In what follows, my debt to him and Evans-Jones will be readily apparent to all those who know their work.[14]

Excluded from consideration in this chapter are the following issues: (i) where D and P are jointly and severally liable to C; (ii) where P is D's agent; (iii) cautionary obligations; (iv) rights of relief;[15] and (v) subrogation (the scope of which in Scots law beyond insurance is unclear[16]). The concern is mainly with the unauthorised intervention of a third-party performance to C which is or can be attributed to D's debt and which is outside the scope of the above doctrines.

---

[10] See generally H. L. MacQueen and W. D. H. Sellar, 'Unjust Enrichment in Scots Law', in: E. J. H. Schrage (ed.), *Unjust Enrichment: The Comparative History of the Law of Restitution* (1995). On negotiorum gestio, see now N. R. Whitty's treatment of the topic, 'Negotiorum Gestio', in: *Stair Memorial Encyclopaedia* (1996), vol. XV, §§ 87–142; also R. D. Leslie, 'Negotiorum Gestio in Scots Law: The Claim of the Privileged Gestor', [1983] JR 12.

[11] 'Identifying the Enriched', 1992 SLT (News) 25.

[12] Discussion Paper No. 95 (1993), vol. I, especially §§ 3.85–3.109; and vol. II, especially §§ 2.25–2.40, 2.157–2.191.

[13] J. H. Round writing in 1895 of F. W. Maitland, Downing Professor of the Laws of England at the University of Cambridge 1888–1906: quoted in H. E. Bell, *Maitland: A Critical Examination and Assessment* (1965), 62.

[14] I have also greatly benefited from studying an unpublished research paper on the subject written by Philip Simpson for the Scottish Law Commission, kindly brought to my attention by Niall Whitty.

[15] Relief is recognised as an instance of recompense (i.e. unjustified enrichment) in *Moss v. Penman* 1993 SC 300; *Christie's Executrix v. Armstrong* 1996 SC 295; *Caledonia North Sea Ltd v. London Bridge Engineering Ltd* 2000 SLT 1123 at 1141F–G, per Lord President Rodger. Cf. *Trades House of Glasgow v. Ferguson* 1979 SLT 187 at 192, and *Ross Harper & Murphy v. Banks* 2000 SC 500 at 505.

[16] See *Esso Petroleum Co. Ltd v. Hall Russell & Co. Ltd* 1988 SLT 874 (HL); *Caledonia North Sea Ltd v. London Bridge Engineering Ltd* 2000 SLT 1123. Subrogation in Scots law appears to operate by force of law, and is much narrower in scope than, for example, French law with its doctrines of *subrogation conventionelle* and *subrogation légale*. See further Friedmann and Cohen, 'Payment of Another's Debt', §§ 17–21, and the opinion of Lord President Rodger in the *Caledonia North* Sea case at 1138L–1141C.

1. The impact of the general enrichment action

A necessary preliminary, however, is to trace the emergence in recent Scottish cases of a general enrichment concept. The traditional accounts of unjustified enrichment in Scots law have divided it up into three actions: repetition, restitution and recompense. The last of these, recompense, is said to be 'subsidiary' in that it is excluded where another remedy is available. It seems clear that, whatever the origins of this division, in modern practice it has been based upon the nature of the remedy provided under the heading in question (rather than, for example, upon the nature of the benefit sought to be recovered). The taxonomy was much criticised. In *Morgan Guaranty Trust Company of New York v. Lothian Regional Council*[17] Lord President Hope said:

> As a general rule it would appear that restitution is appropriate where the demand is for the return of corporeal property, repetition where the demand is for the repayment of money and recompense where the defender has been enriched at the pursuers' expense in the implement of a supposed obligation under a contract other than by the delivery of property or the payment of money. Recompense will be available as a more broadly based remedy, in cases where the benefit was received by the defender in circumstances other than under a contract or a supposed contract... But the important point is that these actions are all means to the same end, which is to redress an unjustified enrichment upon the broad equitable principle *nemo debet locupletari aliena jactura*. Thus the action of repetition, to take this as an example, may be based upon the *condictio causa data causa non secuta*, the *condictio sine causa* or the *condictio indebiti* depending upon which of these grounds of action fits the circumstances which give rise to the claim. The nature of the benefit received by the defender and the circumstances on which the pursuer relies for his claim ought, in a properly organised structure for this branch of the law, to provide all that is needed for the selection of the appropriate remedy. The selection is distorted if there is introduced into the structure a rule [i.e. the error of law rule] which is essentially one of expediency rather than of equity between the parties... It becomes wholly disorganised if that rule is applied to one of the remedies within the system and not to others, with the result that a pursuer is driven to seeking another less appropriate remedy to escape from it.[18]

Morgan Guaranty held that an action of repetition based upon the *condictio indebiti* was the appropriate remedy for recovery of money paid under

---

[17] 1995 SC 151.
[18] *Ibid.* at 155. It is to be noted that the definitions of the 'three Rs' in this dictum are incomplete, especially that of recompense.

a contract void as ultra vires;[19] that the pursuer's error of law could be a basis of claim (over-ruling previous authority); and that the error did not have to be excusable before a claim could be made. The nature of the error and its avoidability would, however, play a part in judging the overall equities of the situation, it being for the defender to show that the remedy should be refused on grounds of equity. Equity (in a broad general sense) remains an important controlling factor for the Scottish courts as a result. However, the court left uncertain the question whether error had always to be shown before an action of repetition could be successful. There has been academic argument that error as such is not a requirement; rather, the pursuer's knowledge that he was not obliged to make the transfer in question is a defence for the recipient.[20]

In *Shilliday v. Smith*,[21] Lord President Rodger said:

A person may be said to be unjustly enriched at another's expense when he has obtained a benefit from the other's actings or expenditure, without there being a legal ground which would justify him in retaining that benefit. The significance of one person being unjustly enriched at the expense of another is that in general terms it constitutes an event which triggers a right in that other person to have the enrichment reversed. As the law has developed, it has identified various situations where persons are to be regarded as having been unjustly enriched at another's expense and where the other person may accordingly seek to have the enrichment reversed. The authorities show that some of these situations fall into recognisable groups or categories. Since these situations correspond, if only somewhat loosely, to situations where remedies were granted in Roman law, in referring to the relevant categories our law tends to use the terminology which is found in the Digest and Code... So repetition, restitution, reduction and recompense are simply examples of remedies which the courts grant to reverse an unjust enrichment, depending on the way in which the particular enrichment has arisen.[22]

---

[19] This is controversial: see, however, A. Rodger, 'Recovering Payments under Void Contracts in Scots Law', in: W. Swadling, and G. Jones (eds.), *The Search for Principle: Essays in Honour of Lord Goff of Chieveley* (2000), 1 ff.

[20] See R. Evans-Jones and P. Hellwege, 'Swaps, Error of Law and Unjustified Enrichment', (1995) 1 *Scottish Law and Practice Quarterly* 1; R. Evans-Jones, 'From "Undue Transfer" to "Retention without a Legal Basis" (the *Condictio Indebiti* and *Condictio ob Turpem Vel Iniustam Causam*)', in R. Evans-Jones (ed.), *The Civil Law Tradition in Scotland* (1995); R. Evans-Jones and P. Hellwege, 'Some Observations on the Taxonomy of Unjustified Enrichment in Scots Law', (1998) 2 *Edinburgh LR* 180.

[21] 1998 SC 725. [22] Ibid. at 727, 728.

Shilliday was approved by the House of Lords in *Dollar Land (Cumbernauld) Ltd v. CIN Properties Ltd*,[23] and Lord Hope of Craighead said that there was:

a desire that the law of unjustified enrichment should develop in a uniform way, and a concern that if the law continues to express the remedies in terms of restitution, repetition and recompense it will inhibit that development. I sympathise with the desire that the law of unjustified enrichment should be unified... These actions were all means to the same end, which is to address an unjustified enrichment upon the broad equitable principle *nemo debet locupletari aliena jactura*. It is an important part of this reasoning to recognise that the obligation to redress the enrichment arises not from contract, but from the separate duty which arises in law from the absence of a legal ground to justify its retention... On the other hand it does not seem to me to be inconsistent with the broad principle of the law of unjustified enrichment for the various situations in which redress may be sought to be expressed in terms of remedies... For my part I see no harm in the continued use of these expressions to describe the various remedies, so long as it is understood that they are being used merely to describe the nature of the remedy which the court is being asked to provide in order to redress the enrichment. The event which gives rise to the granting of the remedy is the enrichment. In general terms it may be said that the remedy is available where the enrichment lacks a legal ground to justify the retention of the benefit. In such circumstances it is held to be unjust.[24]

Following these three cases and the judicial dicta from them just quoted, it would seem that Scots law has now moved to a position where in principle enrichment is unjustified and should be reversed if its retention is supported by no legal ground such as contract or gift. The traditional remedies and their civilian bases survive in this generalisation, but do not exhaust the ways in which the courts may reverse unjustified enrichment. As far as possible, rules which limit or exclude recovery should be the same across the whole field of unjustified enrichment. A critical question is whether the specific requirement of error to found an action of repetition has been swept away by the move to the 'no legal ground for retention' approach.

Going alongside these judicial developments, there has been much academic debate about a general enrichment action in Scots law. David Sellar, in part aided and abetted by me, has argued that the remedy of recompense, already said to be available only if there is no other remedy, can be developed as a subsidiary general action.[25] We were encouraged in this argument by parallels with French, Italian and Dutch law, in which

---

[23] 1998 SC (HL) 90.   [24] *Ibid.* at 98.
[25] See MacQueen and Sellar, 'Unjust Enrichment'; W. D. H. Sellar, 'Unjust Enrichment', in: *The Laws of Scotland: Stair Memorial Encyclopaedia* (1996), vol. XV, §§ 73–86.

the main enrichment action corresponds to the *condictio indebiti*, and there is in addition a subsidiary general enrichment action. But this approach has been strongly rejected by Robin Evans-Jones and Niall Whitty, both of whom appear to favour a development of the law along German lines, centred round the concept of enrichment by transfer or performance (*Leistung*) between pursuer and defender, the claim being typically that the transfer was undue, and retention being justified only if some legal ground supports the transfer.[26] The heart of this would be the *condictio indebiti*, or the action of repetition in the traditional taxonomy of Scots law, and would correspond to the *Leistungskondiktion* of German law. In addition, it is argued, Scots law can be recast to recognise other aspects of the German approach: the interference action (*Eingriffskondiktion*),[27] the action for improvements to another's property (*Verwendungskondiktion*),[28] and the subject-matter of this paper, the 'recourse' action arising from performance of another's obligation (*Rückgriffskondiktion*). The difference between the two positions could therefore be summarised crudely as follows: the Sellar/MacQueen position would see the remedies of repetition and restitution, based on the civilian *condictiones*, as relatively narrowly defined (that is, probably confined to cases of mistaken payments and transfers for purposes which fail), with the main vehicle of future development in the enrichment field being the general action of recompense; while for Evans-Jones and Whitty, the principal category of enrichment law is the *condictio indebiti* (or action to recover an undue transfer), represented in modern Scots law by repetition and restitution.[29] In this view, recompense needs to be broken down into further categories in order to make its role in enrichment law more precise and predictable. The view of the courts, that enrichment should be reversed where its retention is supported by no legal ground, has so far taken no account of, or position in, these debates, although it is implicitly closer to the Evans-Jones/Whitty stance.

[26] The most recent statements of the two authors' views are: (i) Evans-Jones and Hellwege, 'Some Observations', and (ii) Niall Whitty's contribution to the present volume.
[27] See further A. J. M. Steven, 'Recompense for Interference in Scots Law', [1996] *JR* 51.
[28] As to which see the contribution to this volume by James Wolffe.
[29] Evans-Jones also argues that the *condictio causa data causa non secuta* should be treated much more narrowly than it is in modern Scots law, while the *condictio ob turpem causam* has been largely subsumed in the *condictio indebiti*: see, in addition to the articles cited at n. 20 above, R. Evans-Jones and D. McKenzie, 'Towards a Profile of the Condictio ob Turpem vel Injustam Causam in Scots Law', [1994] *JR* 60, and R. Evans-Jones, 'The Claim to Recover What Was Transferred for a Lawful Purpose outwith Contract (Condictio Causa Data Causa Non Secuta)', [1997] *Acta Juridica* 139.

In German law, payment of another's debt is seen to be a special category of enrichment for the following reasons:

(i) Unless P intended to manage D's affairs in making the payment to C, *negotiorum gestio* (*Geschäftsführung ohne Auftrag*) provides no remedy in this situation.[30] Since nevertheless P's payment discharges the debt, D is enriched at P's expense and is thus prima facie within the scope of § 812 BGB, which spells out the principle that one who is enriched at another's expense, whether by way of transfer or in another way, is bound to restore the enrichment to him.

(ii) The transfer or performance involved in the payment of another's debt does not take place directly between P and D, but between P and C. D's enrichment is therefore not enrichment by transfer, but, as § 812 BGB expresses it, 'in another way'.

(iii) In paying C, P may, or may not, think that he is obliged to do so. If P knows that he is not obliged to pay C, then, even though his performance may be directed towards D and D is enriched thereby, recovery from D may be barred under § 814 BGB, by which it is a defence against a *Leistungskondiktion* that 'what has been performed for the purpose of fulfilling an obligation cannot be claimed back if the person who performed knew that he was not obliged to perform, or if the performance corresponded with a moral duty or with respect to decency'. If, however, P pays C as the result of a mistaken belief that he is obliged to do so, he has no *Leistungskondiktion* against D, because he did not perform towards D.

(iv) The case is not one of interference with another's property, because there the claim is against rather than by the intervener. It is also pretty clear that the case is not one of improvement to another's property, or of D's erroneous payment to someone other than his true C. Therefore, if there is to be recovery from D in either of the situations under which P pays C, it requires a special *condictio* – that is, the *Rückgriffskondiktion* – under which neither the *Leistung* requirement nor the knowledge defence of § 814 BGB is relevant.

Despite this conceptual clarity, however, I was struck by the following comment in a recent text on German law:

Psychology tells us that persons who suffer from mania for cleaning – a recognized mental disorder apparently more commonly found in Germany – will have one dirty corner in their otherwise sparkling bright, spotless and germ-free house. If German law can properly be criticized for being unduly concerned with conceptual consistency, the *Rückgriffskondiktion* or restitution by way of recourse can be held out as an example of the dirty corner where some unfinished business is hidden away and seems to defy the general concept. Perhaps the

---

[30] For the German rules on *negotiorum gestio* see §§ 677–87 BGB.

Rückgriffskondiktion is best described as a mixture of potential, rare cases which genuinely fall outside the *Leistungskondiktion*, and of other cases which are placed within enrichment in another way in order to avoid the defence of § 814 BGB, or in order to find a different defendant.[31]

Returning to Scots law, it may be noted that recompense does most if not all of the work required to reverse enrichments falling outside the *Leistungskondiktion* under German law. It would appear from the latest Report of the Scottish Law Commission that, at any rate for the time being, the further development of Scottish enrichment law is to be left to the courts and the text-writers.[32] It undoubtedly surpasses the powers of the courts to reorganise enrichment law all at once on German lines, and in the meantime, therefore, much will depend on the ability of the academic analysis of general enrichment principles to provide convincing solutions to the specific problems with which practitioners and the courts will be confronted.

The question which thus requires discussion is whether the *Rückgriffskondiktion* is really a by-product of the language of the BGB, or whether the known elements of Scots law also require the recognition of a specific category of recourse action within its newly identified principle requiring the reversal of enrichment unjustified because its retention is supported by no legal ground. The Scottish debates already referred to, in particular those about the roles of repetition and recompense, and about whether error is a ground of action or knowledge a defence, clearly have some significance here. It looks as though recompense can cover much of the ground dealt with as 'enrichment in another way' in § 812 BGB; and the error/knowledge debate takes Scots lawyers directly into the terrain of the knowledge defence under § 814 BGB.

2. Discharge of debt by third-party payment

Before turning to the enrichment issues, however, it is necessary to know whether, and if so when, an unauthorised third-party payment can discharge a debt. If it does not, D cannot be enriched by P's action; P's only

---

[31] B. S. Markesinis, W. Lorenz and G. Dannemann, *The German Law of Obligations*, vol. I, *The Law of Contracts and Restitution* (1997), 753.
[32] 'Report on Unjustified Enrichment, Error of Law and Public Authority Receipts and Disbursements' (Scot Law Com. No. 169: February 1999). The Report observes (at § 5.15) that, as a result of *Shilliday* and *Dollar Land*, the law is now 'based on a unifying principle of rule to the effect that an enrichment of one person at the expense of another falls to be redressed if there is no legal justification or ground for the retention of the enrichment', adding that this provides 'an excellent basis for further judicial or statutory refinement of the Scottish law on this subject'.

claim, if any, will be against C. Scots law on this question is, remarkably, unclear despite nearly three centuries of discussion. There was a conflict of view amongst the authoritative writers of the eighteenth and early nineteenth centuries. Citing and following Justinian's *Institutes*,[33] the institutional writers Bankton and Bell were for the third-party payment constituting discharge. Bankton wrote: 'Payment may be made for one that is ignorant of it, or even against his will, because he cannot hinder the creditor to take his payment where he can get it.'[34] Bell observed:

Payment, to the effect of extinguishing the obligation, may be made not only by the debtor himself, but by anyone acting for the debtor: or even by a stranger, where the debt is pecuniary, and due, and demanded; or where any penal effect may arise from delay; or where the creditor has no interest in demanding performance by the proper debtor.[35]

By way of contrast, Lord Kames[36] and Baron Hume[37] took the view that third-party payment does not discharge a debt until the payment is ratified by the debtor.

There is little case law addressing the issue. The leading decision appears to be *Reid v. Lord Ruthven*,[38] where P had paid the debts owed by D to C (a bank). P sued D. Lord Anderson (whose opinion was approved without significant comment by the First Division) stated: 'In the first place, according to our law the defender's obligation to the bank is discharged. To this effect the law of Scotland follows the civil law...'[39] So far as I have been able to discover, there is no other similarly clear judicial statement, although a number of cases appear to proceed on the basis that there is discharge in these circumstances.[40] In *Caledonia North Sea Ltd v.*

---

[33] Inst. 3, 29 pr. ('Every obligation is discharged by performance or, with the consent of the creditor, by a substituted performance. It makes no difference who performs, whether the debtor or someone else for him. The discharge is complete even when a third party performs, with or without knowledge of the debtor, or even against his will').
[34] *An Institute of the Law of Scotland in Civil Rights* (1751), Book I, Title XXIV, 1.
[35] *Principles of the Law of Scotland* (10th edn, 1899), § 557.
[36] *Principles of Equity* (5th edn, 1825), 330, 331.
[37] *Lectures on the Law of Scotland* (ed. by G. C. H. Paton, 1952), vol. III, 16, 17.
[38] (1918) 55 SLR 616.   [39] *Ibid.* at 618.
[40] See, e.g., *Anderson v. Blair* (1841) 3 D 968; *Wood v. The Northern Reversion Co.* (1848) 10 D 254; *Guthrie & McConnachy v. Smith* (1880) 8 R 107; *Emmerson v. Emmerson* (1939) Sh Ct Rep 46; *Kennedy v. Kennedy* (1911) 20 Sh Ct Rep 183; *Duncan v. Motherwell Bridge & Engineering Co. Ltd* 1952 SC 131. I owe my knowledge of these cases to Philip Simpson's research paper, cited at n. 14 above.

London Bridge Engineering Ltd[41] Lord President Rodger raised the issue, but deliberately left the question open.[42]

The topic is generally not addressed in modern texts on contract or debt. The *Stair Memorial Encyclopaedia* states in its treatment of *negotiorum gestio*, however, that 'the better view is that the unauthorised payment of a debt by a third party discharges the debt'.[43] The reasons for preferring this view are not expressed by the author, but it is one with which I agree, subject to a reservation to be expressed more fully later on in this article. The first reason in support of the proposition of discharge is the practical: it is very unlikely that C will continue to seek payment from D; having got his money, he will normally rest content. Second is the systemic: the conclusion aligns Scots law with other systems in the civilian tradition, and is consistent with the general assignability of money debts in Scots law. A third reason is that there is more clear authority in favour of the view than there is against it. My reservation concerns the case of payment made by a bank in respect of a cheque despite a previous countermand: it would seem that this does not discharge the debt which the cheque was originally drawn to meet.[44]

What, if any, controls are there upon a third party intervening to discharge another's debt? It appears from Bell's statement quoted above that P may or may not have the consent of D; if he does not have that consent, there is discharge only in certain circumstances, in particular if the debt is a money one which is due and being demanded by C. Is C bound to accept P's performance? In French and German law, C may refuse P where D must perform in person,[45] and something similar must underlie Bell's statement that P's payment extinguishes the obligation 'where the creditor has no interest in demanding performance by the proper debtor'.[46] Again, in German law, if D objects to P's performance, C may, but need not, decline to accept it,[47] a position with which may be compared Bankton's view that P may make payment even against D's will, 'because he cannot hinder the creditor to take his payment where he can get it'.[48] Thus, the observation of Friedmann and Cohen about German law – 'the third party's performance may be declined only where both the creditor and

---

[41] 2000 SLT 1123.
[42] *Ibid.* at 1144L–1145A (noting the position in English law and saying '[i]t is not altogether clear whether the same rule applies in Scotland').
[43] Vol. XV, § 97. [44] See further below, section V. [45] Art. 1237 *code civil*; § 267(1) BGB.
[46] *Principles*, § 557. [47] § 267(2) BGB. [48] *Institute*, Book I, Title XXIV, 1.

the debtor object to it'[49] – probably holds good for Scots law as well. German and French law both also allow third-party performance to be effective discharge without regard to the consent of either C or D where P is performing to protect his own interest – for example, because D's non-payment may enable C to take action in execution against property in which P has some right.[50] Possibly this situation is covered by Bell's remark about discharge occurring through P's payment 'where any penal effect may arise from delay'.[51]

A final point is that P in paying C may intend a gift to D. If so, then clearly there can be no recovery from D by P, since D's retention of the benefit is justified by the donation.

3. *Negotiorum gestio*: P v. D

Reid v. Lord Ruthven, already cited, provides authority for the proposition that the unauthorised payer of another's debt may be a gestor entitled to payment of his expenses by D under the rules of *negotiorum gestio* in Scotland. The matter is expressed as follows by Niall Whitty in the *Stair Memorial Encyclopaedia*[52] (including the footnotes of the original):

In Roman law,[53] the *gestor* could recover money paid to discharge another's debt provided that the debtor did not have a clear interest that payment should not be made.[54] In certain circumstances a third party can recover even where the discharge was against the debtor's wishes[55]... In Scots law, *negotiorum gestio* may consist in the payment of a single, ordinary unsecured debt due by the *dominus*[56] or a debt secured over the property of the *dominus* by a voluntary heritable

---

[49] Friedmann and Cohen, 'Payment of Another's Debt', § 3. The authors argue in the same place that this is also the position in French law.
[50] Art. 1236, *code civil*; § 268 BGB; Friedmann and Cohen, 'Payment of Another's Debt', §§ 3, 45, 46.
[51] *Principles*, § 557. [52] Whitty, 'Negotiorum gestio', §§ 97, 98.
[53] Stoljar, 'Negotiorum Gestio', § 96. This was one of the main examples of the *actio negotiorum gestorum contraria*.
[54] Labeo D. 3, 5, 42 (43) ('nisi quid debitoris interfuit eam pecuniam non solvi').
[55] See Inst. 3, 29 pr.; and Bankton, Institute, Book I, Title XXIV, 2. But this is a form of 'impure *gestio*' resulting in a gestor's enrichment claim, rather than an *actio negotiorum gestorum contraria*.
[56] In *Reid v. Lord Ruthven* (1918) 55 SLR 616 at 618, Lord Anderson observed, citing J. Erskine, *An Institute of the Law of Scotland* (8th edn, 1871), Book III, Title III, 52 and 53, and Bell, *Principles*, §§ 540, 541: 'When a third party intervenes without the debtor's knowledge or consent and payment is accepted by the creditor, the third party's right to recover payment from the debtor seems to me to be based on the principle *negotiorum gestio*.'

security, or by an adjudication for debt whose legal is about to expire.[57] The general management of the estate of the *dominus* will invariably involve paying his book debts.[58]

In Roman law, the *actio negotiorum gestorum contraria* lay in respect of aliment [that is, the legal obligation of support between certain family members] furnished to children.[59] Scots law, so far as not indigenous, derives from Roman law[60] and not from the English doctrine of agency of necessity. In Scots law, the normal common-law basis of recovery of the cost of aliment provided is recompense for the redress of unjustified enrichment,[61] but an action based on *negotiorum gestio* has been recognised, albeit *obiter*, and more clearly where the defender is a relative liable to maintain the alimentary creditor[62] than where the defender is the alimentary creditor himself.[63]

The limits of recovery under the principles of *negotiorum gestio* are rather unclear.[64] The *dominus* (that is, D in the situation with which this article is concerned) must be absent, ignorant of the fact that his affairs are being managed, or incapacitated. The gestor (that is, P in this situation) must act for the benefit of the *dominus* and with the intention of claiming his expenses (which distinguishes *negotiorum gestio* from donation); but the fact that P also intends his own benefit does not preclude his recovery of his expenses. That will happen only if there is no intention at all to benefit D: if, for example, in the problem discussed here P thought he was paying his own rather than another's debt. Again, the intervention must be useful to the *dominus* – that is, discharge the debt. If, however, the intervention was against the wishes or will of the *dominus*, the gestor's claim may be limited to the enrichment of the *dominus* as distinct from

---

[57] Viscount Stair, *The Institutions of the Law of Scotland* (tercentenary edn by D. M. Walker, 1981), Book I, Title VIII, 3; Bankton, *Institute*, IV, 45, 66. See also *Nasmith v. Nasmith* (1681) Mor 13479; and *Naysmith v. Naysmiths* (1682) Mor 5319.
[58] See, e.g, *Fulton v. Fulton* (1864) 2 M 893 at 901 *per* Lord Neaves: ('Anyone who ultroneously collects money for another, and who discharges the claim and docquets accounts on his behalf is a *negotiorum gestor*'); and *Bannatine's Trs v. Cunninghame* (1872) 10 M 319.
[59] C. 2, 18, 11 and 15.
[60] See, e.g., Stair, *Institutions*, Book I, Title VIII, 2; Bankton, *Institute*, Book I, Title IX, 22 and 23; *ibid.*, Book IV, Title XLV, 69; Erskine, *Institute*, Book III, Title III, 92.
[61] *Thom v. Jardine* (1836) 14 S 1004 at 1006 *per Lord* Fullerton; 'Aliment and Financial Provision' (Scot Law Com. Consultative Memorandum No. 22, 1976), § 2.80.
[62] *Thom v. Jardine* (1836) 14 S 1004 at 1006 *per* Lord Fullerton (action by mother against father of natural child for aliment); *Ligertwood v. Brown* (1872) 10 M 832 at 833 *per* Sheriff Guthrie Smith (obiter), at 834, 835 *per* Lord Ardmillan (obiter), and at 836 *per* Lord Kinloch (obiter).
[63] *Gilbert v. Hannah* (1924) 40 Sh Ct Rep 262.
[64] For what follows, see Whitty, 'Negotiorum Gestio'.

his own expenses. This may be a distinction without a difference in the case of payment of another's debt, since the expense of paying the debt is the same as the saving in not having to pay the debt.

4. Recompense: P v. D

As already noted, Kames and Hume held that payment of another's debt did not discharge that debt until it was ratified by the debtor. Once such ratification had been made, however, Kames held that P had a claim of recompense against D.[65] Presumably had he taken the view that discharge resulted from unauthorised third-party payment, he would have regarded the case for P's recovery as a fortiori. But none of the other authoritative writers, not even those who held that there is discharge by unauthorised third-party payment, directly address the resultant question of liability between P and D.

Where P knows that his payment to C was not due by him to C, it seems clear that this knowledge means that generally he has no claim against D (or indeed C) in repetition or the *condictio indebiti*,[66] either because he was not in error in making the undue payment, or because his knowledge gives D (and C) a defence. By contrast, however, the situation would appear to fall well within most of the classic definitions of recompense, such as Bell's: 'Where one has gained by the lawful act of another, done without any intention of donation, he is bound to recompense or indemnify that other to the extent of the gain.'[67] There are a number of cases about aliment where a third party who has supported the alimentary creditor has been held to have a claim in recompense against the alimentary debtor.[68] The well-known cases of *Varney (Scotland) Ltd v. Lanark Town Council*[69] and *Lawrence Building Co. Ltd v. Lanark County Council*[70] may also be instances of performance (as distinct from payment) of another's obligation in which the performer sought recompense from the party obliged. In both cases, a building company fulfilled the statutory obligation of a local authority to construct sewers, in order to connect a development carried out

---

[65] *Principles of Equity*, 331.   [66] See further below, 476-7.

[67] *Principles*, § 538. Lord President Dunedin famously stated that this definition of recompense 'will not do', because it makes no reference to the requirement that the claimant have made a loss (*Edinburgh and District Tramways Co. Ltd v. Courtenay* 1909 SC 99 at 105-6). Even with this qualification, payment of another's debt seems well within the scope of recompense.

[68] See 'Aliment and Financial Provision' (Scot Law Com. Consultative Memorandum No. 22, 1976), § 2.80.

[69] 1974 SC 245.   [70] 1978 SC 30.

by the builders to the existing system of public sewers. Recovery was denied in *Varney*, because the parties had been in dispute about the liability to construct the sewers before the builders unilaterally commenced and completed the work. Since the builders had had available a remedy to compel performance of a statutory duty, and recompense was only available where there was no other remedy, the action was found irrelevant. The claim was held relevant, however, in *Lawrence*, where the element of dispute was absent, and the problem arose after construction of the sewers, when as a result of statutory reorganisation of local government the former local authority was succeeded by a new one which refused to pay for the work that had been done. The cases are special, inasmuch as the obligation was statutory, the debtor was a public body and the creditor in the obligation was the public (or at least the ratepayers in the area of the local authority). But they none the less illustrate the potential relevance of recompense in cases of performance of another's obligation, including payment of another's debt.

In its 1993 Discussion Paper, the Scottish Law Commission proceeded on the basis that recompense could provide P with a claim against D where the payment discharged the debt.[71] The point was, however, explored primarily in the context of the Commission's study of the error of law bar to recovery and the consequences of abolition of that rule. It noted that error was not an essential in all cases of recompense, and that there was authority supporting recovery in cases of unauthorised payment of another's debt both where P acted in the interests of another and where he acted in his own interests. Where error was required, error in law was not enough; the error had to be one of fact. But this bar should be removed (and now has been, thanks to the *Morgan Guaranty* case).

The classic case of error would be where P paid believing that he himself was the true debtor, a circumstance which might well lead him to want his money back from the creditor once the truth emerged. This would entitle him to a *condictio indebiti* against C. But if action against C was barred – by, say, C's change of position – then P might resort to a claim of recompense against D. If, however, an action was available against C, then there could be an issue of choice of remedies between repetition from him or recompense against D. Recompense is subsidiary in Scots law, however, whereas repetition is not:

---

[71] For the remainder of this paragraph and the next two paragraphs, see vol. I, §§ 3.85–3.109.

It would follow that the third party would be bound to raise a *condictio indebiti* first against the creditor. Only if that action failed would he be entitled to maintain the payment as a valid discharge and bring an action of recompense against the debtor.[72]

The Discussion Paper also draws attention to the logical difficulty inherent in this solution: if P sues C, he is affirming that the payment is invalid and the underlying debt therefore not discharged, whereas action against D can only succeed if there has been enrichment of that party by discharge of his debt.

A matter that published discussion has not touched upon is that of defences. Can D plead against the recompense-seeking P the defences he would have had against C or C's assignee? Had C assigned the debt to P, these defences would have been available. Can P be better off by not taking an assignation? Perhaps the general control upon enrichment recovery provided by 'equity' in Scots law may help to provide just solutions in these questions.[73]

Another issue that appears to have been overlooked in the literature to date is the relationship between the seemingly alternative claims of recompense and *negotiorum gestio*. The subsidiary nature of recompense would suggest, however, that it should only be deployed where the requirements of *negotiorum gestio* are not met.

5. The *condictio indebiti* (repetition): P v. C; P v. D

This article has already touched upon the territory of the *condictio indebiti*, which, it will be recalled, is concerned with direct transfers of value between the parties. As already noted, where P pays in the erroneous belief that he is paying his own debt, he can recover from C by way of the *condictio indebiti*. More complex, however, is the situation where P knows that he is not indebted to C, but pays because he is in error in some other respect: either about his own relationship with D or about D's relationship with C. The following propositions have been put forward as representing the present law of Scotland in this regard by Evans-Jones and the Scottish Law Commission:

(i) If P believes he owes D and D owes C, and P on D's instructions pays C, P may sue D if the debt P–D did not exist.
(ii) If P owes D and D believes he owes C, and P on D's instructions pays C, D may sue C if the debt D–C did not exist.

---

[72] Ibid., § 3.107.
[73] Friedmann and Cohen, 'Payment of Another's Debt', § 23, see a useful role for a general 'equity' control on P's recovery from D.

(iii) If, on a background of beliefs that P owes D who owes C, P pays C on D's instructions, but neither of the debts exists, P may sue C under the *condictio indebiti*. Evans-Jones suggests that P may recover only as D's representative.[74]

The rationale for this complex analysis is, as Evans-Jones puts it, 'identifying the enriched' and, one might add, identifying the impoverished. In all the cases given, P pays C; but the correct identities of gainer and loser vary. It is crucial to observe that, by contrast with the earlier discussion, in which P was unauthorised by D, here P is acting in consequence of an at least putative debt which he believes is owed to D. The 'instructions' referred to in the summary above occur either when D assigns to C the rights he believes he has against P, or when D delegates to P the duty of paying C. P's payment may thus be D's way of discharging his debt to C, or D's discharge of P. In example (i), although C receives the payment, it is D who is enriched at P's expense by virtue of the discharge of his (D's) debt. In example (ii), C is enriched because he receives payment of that which he is not owed, but the party who suffers the corresponding loss is D rather than P, because D's claim against P has been discharged by P's payment to C. In example (iii), however, C gains at P's expense; since no debts existed, none are discharged. Careful analysis rooted in the general principle that unjustified enrichment should be reversed seems to come to the correct answer in each case. And in each case the enriched person has no legal ground for retaining the enrichment against the claim of the impoverished one.

V. Scots law and *Barclays Bank v. Simms*: P v. C case?

In the English case of *Barclays Bank Ltd v. W. J. Simms Son and Cooke (Southern) Ltd*,[75] the bank (P) mistakenly paid out to the payee (C) of a countermanded cheque. The bank's mistake lay in overlooking its customer's (D) stop instruction. Since the bank had failed to comply with its customer's instructions, it could not debit his account. It claimed restitution from the payee. Robert Goff J (as he then was) held that the bank could get restitution for mistake, which had caused payment. The D–C debt had not been discharged, since the bank had acted without mandate. The payee had thus given no consideration for what it had received, was enriched, and had no change of position defence.

---

[74] Evans-Jones, 'Identifying the Enriched', summarised at 29; Discussion Paper No. 95, vol. II, §§ 2.163–2.191 summarised at the last paragraph.
[75] [1979] 3 All ER 522 *per* Goff J.

The reasoning in *Barclays Bank v. Simms* was affirmed by the Court of Appeal in *Lloyds Bank plc v. Independent Insurance Co. Ltd*,[76] although a different result was reached on the facts. The bank paid its customer's creditor in the mistaken belief that cheques previously paid into the customer's account represented cleared funds sufficient to cover the transfer. It was held that the bank could not get restitution from the payee: the authorised payment discharged the customer's debt to the payee, so there was no unjust enrichment.

Barclays Bank v. Simms has not attracted much attention in Scotland, although it is accepted and applied in banking practice.[77] Both the *Stair Memorial Encyclopaedia*[78] and Wallace and McNeil's *Banking Law*[79] also accept it as correct. In his text on debt, the late Professor W. A. Wilson stated: 'Where countermand is made before presentation of the cheque for payment or after presentation but before payment has been made, the banker cannot in safety make the payment.'[80] It is not clear whether this comment implies that the payment would be at the banker's risk and irrecoverable. The only explicit discussion is in the 1993 Discussion Paper of the Scottish Law Commission.[81]

It has recently been accepted in a case concerned with the liability of a collecting bank for negligence that a Scottish court may usefully look to South African decisions, because there too the Bills of Exchange Act 1882 has been engrafted upon a basically civilian scheme of obligations, including the law of delict and unjustified enrichment.[82] The problem of payment upon a countermanded cheque has been addressed by the South African courts.[83] One decision appears to follow *Barclays Bank v. Simms*. This is *Govender v. The Standard Bank of South Africa*.[84] Another, more recent, case – *B. & H. Engineering v. First National Bank of South Africa Ltd*[85] – does not.

---

[76] [2000] QB 110 (CA).

[77] This at least is the position of both the Bank of Scotland and the Royal Bank of Scotland as disclosed to me in personal correspondence with their respective legal departments.

[78] Vol. IV, § 206.   [79] 10th edn (1991), 137-8.   [80] *Debt* (2nd edn, 1992), § 6.8.

[81] Vol. II, §§ 2.8-2.11; see further below, 481-2.

[82] *First National Bank plc v. Bank of Scotland* 1999 SLT (Sh Ct) 10 (a case about the liability for negligence of a collecting bank to an issuing bank). See the comment by S. Miller, 'The Liability of the Collecting Bank in Scots Law', (2000) 4 *Edinburgh LR* 87.

[83] For fuller discussion, see D. H. van Zyl, 'Unauthorised Payment and Unjust Enrichment in Banking Law', in: F. D. Rose (ed.), *Restitution and Banking Law* (1998); see also the contribution of D. P. Visser to this volume.

[84] 1984 (4) SA 392 (C).   [85] 1995 (2) SA 279 (A).

In *Govender v. The Standard Bank of South Africa*, the bank paid a payee of a cheque, overlooking the drawer's preceding countermand. The bank sought repayment. It was held that in principle the bank had an enrichment action against the payee, albeit on the facts there was no enrichment here. The debate in the case was about whether the appropriate action was a *condictio indebiti* or the residual *condictio sine causa*. The significance of the point was that the negligence of the bank in making the error could be a defence in the *condictio indebiti*, but not in the *condictio sine causa*. Since the performance of the bank was directed to its customer, not to the drawee, so, it was argued, the *condictio indebiti* was inapplicable, and if there was to be enrichment recovery, it had to be under the *condictio sine causa*. Rose-Innes J held that the error was not unreasonable and that the *condictio indebiti* might therefore be used, but that the *condictio sine causa* was the more appropriate action.

A different result was reached, however, in *B. & H. Engineering v. First National Bank of SA*. Again a bank made payment on a previously stopped cheque. It was held that the bank's payment discharged the debt owed to the payee of the cheque, who was therefore not enriched by the payment, since he had now lost his claim against the drawer. It was accepted, however, that had there been enrichment of the cheque payee, the bank's action would have been the *condictio sine causa*.

The debate about the appropriate action in these cases takes us back to the German analysis already discussed, about whether payment of another's debt is a transfer reversible under the *Leistungskondiktion* or requires, as German law has generally concluded, a different category. Generally speaking, however, payment through a bank does not involve the bank as such in paying and discharging its customer's debt. If D instructs his debtor P to pay his creditor C, in law P's performance is to D rather than C, while D is making performance to C through the medium of P. If either the D/P or the D/C relationship turns out to be void or otherwise legally ineffective, claims of restitution can only be made through the performance relationships: that is, P can only recover from D, and D from C. P, having made no performance to C, has no action against him. The classic example of this is the customer–banker–payee triangle. 'P [the bank] in transferring the amount to C's [the payee's] bank account has no intention of paying another's debt... [The] bank (P) neither knows nor is it interested in knowing why D had given this instruction to transfer money from his account to C's account.'[86]

[86] Markesinis, Lorenz and Dannemann, *Law of Contracts*, 374–5.

However, there is a crucial exception to the above analysis in Germany: 'where there had been no valid instruction by D in regard to the payment made by P'.[87] Thus P can recover from the wrong recipient or the recipient who has been paid twice (or more). 'The same must apply to the case where D had revoked his instruction, but P inadvertently made payment to C (e.g. payment by a bank of a stopped cheque).'[88] The federal Supreme Court has not indicated whether recovery is on the basis of enrichment by performance or 'in some other way'. The German courts, however, deny recovery by the bank where the payee did not know of the drawer's revocation (that is, for recovery the payee must be in bad faith) and the payment has discharged the drawer's obligation. If the bank is unable to recover from the payee for these reasons, it can use the *Rückgriffskondiktion* to recover instead from the drawer.[89]

What then of Scots law? Payment by cheque discharges the underlying obligation of payment from the time the cheque is received by a creditor; but the discharge is conditional upon the cheque being honoured.[90] Presentation of the cheque is by statute an assignation of funds if there are funds available.[91] The banker's duty and authority to pay are determined by a countermand. A countermand means that the banker is to be treated as having no funds available for payment of the cheque.[92] The paying banker cannot debit his customer in respect of payment following a forgery of the drawer's signature or, in the absence of drawer negligence, fraudulent increases in the amount of the cheque. The holder of the cheque not paid by virtue of a countermand can sue the drawer or any indorsers on the cheque, while the underlying payment obligation is also revived.

---

[87] Ibid., 375. Note that at 734–5 the authors say that 'this is, however, not necessarily an exception to the general rule. This was a case of performance towards the recipient, and the only question was whether this was performance by the bank or by the account holder. As this is generally to be determined from the recipient's perspective, the bank should be the right plaintiff. For if the recipient knew that the bank was mistaken, he also knew that the bank shifted its own and not the account holder's wealth onto him. It is true that this deprives the recipient from raising defences against the bank which might arise from his relationship with the account holder, but this type of recipient did not seem particularly worthy of protection... It would thus seem that the Bundesgerichtshof attaches more importance to whether or not the recipient was *mala fide* rather than to the person who was performing from the perspective of the recipient.'

[88] Ibid., 375.

[89] Ibid., 375–6, 734–5. See for further analysis Meier, 'Mistaken Payments'.

[90] *Leggatt Brothers v. Gray* 1908 SC 67.

[91] Bills of Exchange Act 1882, s. 53(2).   [92] Ibid., s. 75A.

It seems clear, therefore, that a bank which pays on a countermanded cheque is paying without instruction, and it must be very dubious, despite the general principle that an unauthorised third-party payment of a debt can discharge a debtor, whether the customer's debt should be treated as discharged by such payment. In general, the reason for countermand will be some claim which the drawer wishes to make against the payee, in which the ability to withhold payment will bring helpful and legitimate pressure to bear upon the payee. While the right to claim would still exist after the discharge, it would have to be made good by costly action of some kind; and in the event of the payee's insolvency (the situation which in fact occurred in *Barclays Bank v. Simms*), such action might be of very limited utility. Insult would be added to injury if the bank, having discharged the debt, could make an enrichment or *negotiorum gestio* claim against the drawer. The latter claim provides particular difficulties: it could be argued that the bank's payments are intended to protect the interests of the drawer even though they are against his express instructions, and that if the debt is discharged the actions of the bank have been useful to the drawer. The bank as gestor therefore has an enrichment claim against the drawer. The *Stair Memorial Encyclopaedia* states that enrichment actions against a *dominus prohibens* seem likely to be allowed 'only in narrow categories of case', and draws attention to the need for 'safeguards to protect a debtor-*dominus* who has a right of retention or lien, or of compensation (set-off)'.[93] Whitty notes the South African case of *Standard Bank Financial Services Ltd v. Taylam (Property) Ltd*,[94] which holds that the gestor must show just cause for disregarding the wishes of the debtor-*dominus*. The requirement of utility to the *dominus*, the content of which is far from clear in Scots law,[95] may also restrict the bank's ability to claim that it is a gestor for the drawer.

If the bank is unable to claim against its customer, the only way it can recover its payment is from the payee-recipient. Since the payment was not due and was made in error, the relevant remedy in Scots law appears to be repetition. In its 1993 Discussion Paper, the Scottish Law Commission took on board the arguments in the *Govender* case in South Africa and commented as follows:

In Scots law, though there are many references to performance *sine causa* or retention *sine causa* in the sources, it is common practice to refer simply to an (innominate) action of repetition in cases where the nominate *condictiones* (*indebiti, causa*

---

[93] Whitty, 'Negotiorum gestio', § 139.   [94] 1979 (2) SA 383 (C).
[95] Whitty, 'Negotiorum gestio', §§ 117–22.

data causa non secuta, and less certainly *ob turpem vel iniustam causam*) are regarded as inapplicable. One might therefore expect the bank's action in Scotland to be an innominate action of repetition equivalent to a *condictio sine causa (specialis)* ... Another open question is whether the pursuer in a *condictio indebiti* must erroneously believe that the debt was legally due by him, with the effect that if he erroneously believes that the debt was legally due by a third party, his remedy is an innominate action of repetition. The definitions of the Institutional writers do not confine the *condictio indebiti* to errors as to the payer's own liability.[96]

But in this context, at least, a more general enrichment approach seems preferable to rather sterile arguments about which *condictio* is appropriate. Assuming no discharge of the basic debt, for the reasons already given above, the position is that the recipient has received value at the expense of another who was under no liability to him in making the transfer. Prima facie, retention of that enrichment is unjustified, there being no legal basis upon which the transfer can be retained. The recipient may have a defence with regard to the excusability of the bank's error as an equity issue, but will have the burden of showing that as inequitable. Here it should be borne in mind (following *Morgan Guaranty*) that the defences should as far as possible be the same across the whole field. If the payee has to repay the bank, it should also be remembered that the underlying debt still exists, entitling the payee to take action against the drawer, albeit subject to the counterclaims of that party. The end result seems entirely fair and equitable, with the balance of equities favouring recovery by the bank from the payee.

What of the *Lloyds Bank v. Independent Insurance*[97] case? This was a case where D instructed P to pay C in discharge of a debt that D owed to C. P's error was that its debt to D was less than the amount which D had instructed it to pay to C. It would seem here that C is not enriched, since he has merely received what he was owed by D through the medium of P. It is D who is enriched, because his debt has been discharged at the expense of P, who therefore has a claim against him for the amount of that enrichment. There is no question of *negotiorum gestio*, because P did not act in D's absence and without D's authority.

VI. The Clive Code

The foregoing discussion suggests that the Scots law on payment of another's debt is at best undeveloped. In a system in which case law is a key source, the absence of court decisions dealing with the matter has thrown

[96] Vol. II, § 2.10. [97] [2000] QB 110.

the burden of exposition on text writers, who have had to speculate within a framework of principles and rules the scope of which is contested, and on law reform bodies, which have treated the subject within exercises devoted to other objectives. So those who wish to create a European private law will not find very much or detailed inspiration in current Scottish solutions to this problem. Indeed, it is the Scots who have been looking to Europe, and in particular Germany. Yet the European analysis will be assisted to some extent by the confirmation from Scotland that the proper approach to the relationship between P and D lies through the institutions of *negotiorum gestio* and enrichment actions lying outside ones based on transfers between the parties. Finally, there is also much understanding to be gained from one Scottish source dealing with the law as it might be rather than as it is.

In 1996 the Scottish Law Commission published a set of Draft Rules on Unjustified Enrichment prepared by Dr Eric Clive, then one of the Commissioners.[98] The Rules (henceforth the Clive Code) provide for a general enrichment action, working on the basis that an enrichment of one at the expense of another is unjustified and, therefore, reversible unless justified by legal cause or public policy. Payment or performance of another's debt or obligation is clearly included within the scope of the Clive Code. Enrichment is defined as the acquisition of an economic benefit, and includes acquiring money or other property and 'being freed, in whole or in part, from an obligation'.[99] The enrichment is at the expense of another person if it is:

the direct result of (a) a payment, grant, transfer, incurring of liability, or rendering of services by the other person...(ii) in fulfilment of an obligation of the enriched person...[100]

Such an enrichment will be unjustified unless justified by legal cause such as contract or gift, or by public policy.[101] The category of public

---

[98] 'Judicial Abolition of the Error of Law Rule and its Aftermath' (Scot Law Com. Discussion Paper No. 99, 1996), Appendix: Draft Rules on Unjustified Enrichment and Commentary. The Rules and commentary represent Dr Clive's personal views and are not necessarily those of the Scottish Law Commission. The rules are reprinted in full in: F. D. Rose (ed.), *Blackstone's Statutes on Contract, Tort & Restitution* (8th edn, 1997), 444 ff. An abbreviated version of the rules and commentary has also been published by Clive in A. Hartkamp et al. (eds.), *Towards a European Civil Code* (2nd edn, 1998), 383-94. This version omits the special rules on payment of another's debt, for which see further below. Clive is now a Visiting Professor at the Edinburgh Law School.
[99] Rule 2(2)(c). It also includes '(a) acquiring money or other property'.
[100] Rule 3(1)(a)(ii). Rule 3(1)(a)(i) covers the direct performance 'to the enriched person'.
[101] Rules 4-6.

policy includes:

(1) work or expenditure undertaken or incurred for one's own benefit, or for the benefit of a third party, or for the benefit of the public at large, and when the undertaker could reasonably have been expected to know that there would be a benefit to the enriched person and to have accepted the risk that the enriched person would not pay for the benefit;[102] and
(2) the voluntary and deliberate conferring by the other person of a benefit on the enriched person, in the knowledge that it is not due and in acceptance of the risk that the enriched person may choose not to pay or do anything in return.[103]

But these rules of public policy do not apply to prevent recovery where the other person has, in circumstances where it was reasonable to do so, (a) paid a monetary debt due by the enriched person, or (b) fulfilled an alimentary obligation due by the enriched person.[104] Clive argues that only the payment of a monetary debt or aliment should be seen as escaping from the limitations of public policy, and that performance of non-monetary obligations should not be so exempt:

[T]here are policy considerations in favour of encouraging the satisfaction of monetary debts and alimentary obligations, and no policy considerations operating the other way. In the case of a monetary debt, the debtor cannot normally prevent his creditor from assigning and has not normally a strong interest in who the creditor is. The position is different in the case of many other obligations. It would be unacceptable if, say, a stonemason who had failed to win a contract to repair some stonework which was accessible from a public road could perform the obligation of the mason who had won the contract and then claim payment from him under the law on unjustified enrichment.[105]

The amount of redress for payment or performance of another's obligation is 'the amount paid, with interest from the date of payment'.[106] The court is, however, given general powers to refuse or modify an award on various grounds. These include such classic enrichment defences as the recipient's change of position before he knew redress was due, the culpability or negligence of the claimant, and, finally, because 'for any other reason, it would be inequitable or contrary to public policy to make a full award or grant decree unconditionally'.[107] A further rule likely to be of interest when a third party discharges a debt, and in particular a non-monetary obligation of the kind described above, allows the court to refuse or to modify an award where the enriched person has received the

[102] Rule 6(1)(a). [103] Rule 6(1)(b). [104] Rule 7(5)(a) and (b). [105] Commentary, 66.
[106] Schedule, Part I, 4. [107] Rule 10.

benefit passively, without a reasonable opportunity of refusal; the benefit cannot be converted into money or money's worth; and a full award would be inequitable.[108] A party who has been saved the expense of performing an onerous non-monetary obligation may well argue that the 'benefit' has in reality produced a loss if, had the expenditure been incurred, a profit would have been earned; thus the benefit cannot be converted into money or money's worth.[109]

The issue of whether a debt may be discharged by a third-party payment is beyond the scope of the Clive Code, although the commentary notes that there can be enrichment only if there is first discharge.[110] Nor does it deal with *negotiorum gestio*, since in essence that is not an enrichment action. But the position of the gestor is to some extent protected by provision that the public-policy exclusions quoted above do not apply where a person has, 'in circumstances where it was reasonable to do so...(c) incurred expenditure or performed services necessary for preserving the life, health or welfare of the enriched person, or (d) incurred expenditure or performed services urgently necessary for preserving the property of the enriched person or preventing it from being dangerous'.[111] The code will thus be generally congruent with a system in which obligations may be discharged by third persons and *negotiorum gestio* or some equivalent is recognised.

VII. Conclusions

This article began with the observation that payment of another's debt was an area upon which the common law and the Continental law appear to be divided, and raised the question whether the mixed system of Scots law might provide guidance towards a European solution to the problem. The analysis has shown that in Scotland the question has been addressed almost entirely in academic writings, and that these have been much influenced by the approach of German law. That approach in turn owes much to academic elaboration of the sometimes rather open-ended language of the enrichment provisions of the BGB. A European solution is therefore likely to require something of a fresh start, albeit that there is clearly much to be learned from the experience to date of the various legal systems in Europe.

---

[108] Rule 10(2). This is described as the defence of 'subjective devaluation' in Commentary, 79; it is there elaborated only in the context of improvements to another's property.
[109] Alternatively, it could be argued that there was no enrichment under Rule 2.
[110] Commentary, 64 (note 62).   [111] Rule 7(5)(c) and (d).

The first and foremost point upon which both Scots law and any European proposal need to take a clear position concerns the discharge of a debt by a third person. If the view is taken that there can be no discharge in such circumstances, then the question of the act of P being of benefit to D does not arise. However, it seems probable that the alternative view, favouring discharge, will be preferred, at least with regard to money debts, because this solution is congruent with the general assignability of such debts and the fact that a money debtor has no particular interest in who his creditor is. Ole Lando and Hugh Beale's *Principles of European Contract Law* follow this line, further providing that, unless the contract requires personal performance by D, C cannot refuse P's performance if it is with D's consent, or if P has a legitimate interest in performance and D has failed to perform or clearly will not perform when performance falls due.[112] However, these principles are not confined to money debts. The question what happens if C accepts performance by P when D has not given his consent and P has no legitimate interest in performing is left unanswered by the *Principles*; the logic would seem to be that the debt is not discharged, but it is rather unlikely that C would seek, or could obtain, performance from D. The real significance of this for present purposes, however, is that P would have no claim against D either.

Only if there is discharge does the question of P's claim against D arise. There is, however, an issue here, which is the relationship between, on the one hand, a rule allowing discharge by a third party and, on the other, such matters as the formalities of assignation (for example, writing, or intimation in those systems which require it for the completion of the transfer, such as Scotland) and the defences against the original creditor, which in an assignation would continue to be available to the debtor. Third-party discharge certainly has the ability to undermine the requirements of formality, and commonly does so in France, for example; this may have far-reaching implications in insolvency with regard to priority of claims.[113] An appropriate solution with regard to the defences may be a provision that the discharge of the debt cannot make D's position worse than it would have been had there been an assignation. So far as the current Scots law of enrichment and the Clive Code are concerned, however,

---

[112] O. Lando and H. Beale (eds.), *The Principles of European Contract Law, Parts I and II* (2000), art. 7:106.

[113] Given that assignation may no longer need to be in writing in Scotland, it may be rather hard to tell whether P's claim against D arises as a result of a transfer from C or simply by virtue of P's payment to C; a point for which I am indebted to George Gretton.

the only solution seems to lie in the application of considerations of equity. While no doubt more precise rules may emerge in time from this process, D does for the moment seem exposed to an unfortunate amount of uncertainty under these provisions.

As already noted, Clive argues that the position with regard to non-monetary obligations may also be problematic. Why should an unauthorised third-party performance deprive a willing debtor of the opportunity and, indeed, right to make a profitable performance to the creditor and at the same time subject that debtor to a claim from the third-party intervener? On the other hand, the provision on discharge in the *Principles of European Contract Law* does extend to non-monetary obligations. Clive's stonemason example would be dealt with under these rules, either by saying that the employer, having chosen one stonemason rather than another, was entitled to personal performance from the stonemason of his choosing, or by holding that the first stonemason had not given his consent to the second's actions, or that the latter had no legitimate interest in performing the work. Thus in such circumstances there would be no discharge by the unauthorised intervention. The employer could require the second stonemason to remove his unasked-for work; while if he kept it, he might leave himself open to the first stonemason's claim for damages for breach of contract and, perhaps, the second stonemason's enrichment claim. On balance, therefore, it seems possible to include non-monetary obligations within the scope of carefully drawn rules about third-party discharge and the claims then arising, so that D is not exposed to the risk of discharge at another's hand and a consequential enrichment or *negotiorum gestio* claim when he himself is ready, willing and able to perform.

Once P has discharged D's debt, two approaches are possible with regard to the consequential rights and duties of the parties. The first is through *negotiorum gestio*; the other through the law of unjustified enrichment.

An approach through the law of *negotiorum gestio* is in many ways a more persuasive overall solution to the problems arising from payment of another's debt. The concern with P's state of mind in paying or performing is to find whether he had the intention to benefit or protect D's interests, and this is regardless of whether that was his sole motive in acting. Thus P's knowledge of what he is doing, instead of being a potential difficulty for recovery forcing special treatment within enrichment law, becomes part of the basic grounds for recovery in *negotiorum gestio*. The problem of the unwanted non-monetary performance can be addressed in two ways: through the requirement that the intervention be of reasonable utility to D (that is, that it discharge the debt, which, as seen above, is unlikely to be the case where D was ready, willing and able to perform), and by the limitation of P's recovery to D's enrichment (as opposed to P's expenses, albeit that this is probably a distinction without a difference) when the performance was against D's wishes.

None the less, *negotiorum gestio* does leave gaps in the protection of P. There may be cases where D is neither absent, ignorant of P's management, or *incapax*, but allows P to act, perhaps himself declining to deal with whatever the problem may be;[114] or P may perform solely in the furtherance of his own interests, for example, thinking that he is discharging his own debt, as when he thinks he owes D and pays C following an assignation of that debt by D. There is a residual role for enrichment law, therefore, bearing in mind that P will only have a claim if his performance has succeeded in discharging D's debt. The conceptual difficulties of bringing the situation within the scope of repetition and the *Leistungskondiktion* in Scotland and Germany respectively if P acts knowingly (that is, wishing to pay D's debt to C and aware that he does not owe C) are solved in each jurisdiction by moving to other categories within their enrichment laws, namely recompense and the *Rückgriffskondiktion*. It is also striking that the Clive Code, which seeks a unified approach to enrichment, none the less has to make specific provision for the claim arising on payment of another's debt.[115]

Taken all in all, therefore, this article suggests that it is not possible to treat enrichment law as an absolutely unified field in which the same rules can be applied to all situations, unless the scope of enrichment law is actually narrowed down considerably, so as to exclude payment of another's debt from its ambit. But that would be to go too far. This article also demonstrates the need, in developing any system of law (whether Scottish or European) to deal with the problem of payment of another's

---

[114] As, for example, in the Scottish cases of *Garriock v. Walker* (1873) 1 R 100 (owner of cargo of whale blubber took no action when it began to putrefy; master of ship had it unloaded, cleaned and put into casks, to owner's profit) and *North British Railway Co. v. Tod* (1893) 9 Sh Ct Rep 326 (railway company incurred expense of tending owner's injured colt when the latter had declined to take responsibility), neither of which could be dealt with under *negotiorum gestio* in consequence of the owner's presence and knowledge of the management of his property. I am grateful to Professor Clive for drawing these cases to my attention.

[115] Note that the more concise version of Clive's code printed in Hartkamp, *Civil Code*, omits the special rules on payment of another's debt. The result is that if P voluntarily and deliberately pays D's debt to C, to D's enrichment, knowing that the payment is not due and accepting the risk that D might choose not to make reimbursement, he cannot recover under enrichment (although this is without prejudice to recovery under *negotiorum gestio* rules).

debt, to take careful account of legal institutions such as the rules on discharge of obligations and *negotiorum gestio* as well as enrichment law. Clear rules on when a third party may extinguish another's debt and on when a person may make a claim in respect of his unauthorised management of another's affairs, coupled with a recognition that enrichment law is subsidiary to *negotiorum gestio*, should leave only limited need for enrichment claims in this field, as well as going some way towards meeting the traditional common-law concern not to give undue scope for officious intermeddling in other people's business.[116]

[116] As this article was completed in December 1999, I received a copy of a position paper on *negotiorum gestio* prepared by Professor Christian von Bar as part of the work of the Study Group towards a European Civil Code based at Osnabrück. The paper brings payment of another's debt within the scope of *negotiorum gestio*, and proposes that unjustified enrichment should play a subsidiary role. I am grateful to Professor von Bar for allowing me to refer to this unpublished work.

PART X

Third-party enrichment

18 'At the expense of the claimant': direct and indirect enrichment in English law

Peter Birks

I. Introduction

Some time ago a study by Jack Dawson compared the German and American positions on the requirement of 'directness' in the law of unjust enrichment.[1] It is not at all easy to come up with a satisfactory short statement of that requirement, but, broadly speaking, its effect is to restrict liability to the first or immediate enrichee and to forbid leapfrogging the proper defendant in order to sue remoter recipients who, on one argument or another, might also be said to have been enriched at the claimant's expense. Dawson's study concluded that German law had chosen to insist rather strictly on directness, while American law, although agreeing with German law in a number of important and recurrent situations, had never committed itself to the same dogma. Proceeding in a characteristically pragmatic manner, it had allowed a variety of claims which could not have satisfied any requirement that the enrichment must have come directly from the claimant.

This subject has preoccupied German jurists but has been very little visited by English lawyers. Niall Whitty's recent study of the Scots law, heavily influenced by German and other civilian writing, has served to draw English attention to the deficiency.[2] More recently still, Sonja Meier, who has made a speciality of comparison between the German and English law of unjust enrichment,[3] has written an important and helpful article

---

[1] J. P. Dawson, 'Indirect Enrichment', in: E. von Caemmerer, S. Mentschikoff and K. Zweigert (eds.), *Ius Privatum Gentium: Festschrift für Max Rheinstein* (1969), vol. II, 789–818.
[2] N. R. Whitty, 'Indirect Enrichment in Scots Law', [1994] *JR* 200 (Part I) and 239 (Part II).
[3] Sonja Meier, *Irrtum und Zweckverfehlung* [Mistake and Failure of Purpose] (1999), reviewed by Thomas Krebs, [1999] *Restitution LR* 271–82; cf. her 'Restitution after Void Contracts', in: P. Birks and F. Rose (eds.), *Lessons of the Swaps Litigation* (2000), 168–213.

493

in the *Cambridge Law Journal*, which once again reminds us of the need to take this subject much more seriously.[4]

This is not a subject in which it is easy to draw comparisons with civilian systems. Their law of unjust enrichment turns on the absence of legal ground for the enrichment (*sine causa / ohne rechtlichen Grund*) and hence on the science of nullity which has to underpin that approach. The science of nullity is heavily in evidence in the discussion of indirect enrichment. The common law, by contrast, looks for down-to-earth reasons for restitution, which are intelligible on the Clapham omnibus. This humdrum search for unjust factors can claim the merit of having coped unobtrusively and interstitially with the problems in which civilian jurists have found themselves inextricably entangled. An unkind observer might say that the English have simply failed to notice the difficulties. Our leading textbook, reflecting the pragmatism that is shared with American law, devotes only three pages exclusively to this matter, under the heading of the sub-principle that the enrichment must be obtained at the claimant's expense.[5] Two other influential books both accept that, subject to exceptions, English law is committed to the requirement of directness, though neither finds it necessary to spin a conceptual web to catch every case.[6] As it happens, both invoke the word 'privity'.[7] This is an unwanted echo of the old implied contract theory of unjust enrichment, which both authors quite rightly regard as once and for all repudiated. Though the word can barely be given meaning outside contract, both agree that in some sense the English law of unjust enrichment is and ought to be hemmed in by a notion of privity.[8] There is no doubt that the common law needs to tidy up its thinking on this subject, though it cannot do it in the structurally alien language of sufficient and insufficient cause.

This article takes the view that the exceptions are arguably stronger than the rule. If that is right, the Burrows–Virgo position is not wrong, but its emphasis is misleading. Furthermore, the supposed rule, especially when dressed up in its borrowed contractual clothing, proves difficult to tie in to any convincing rationale. Rule and exceptions must swap places.

---

[4] Sonja Meier, 'Mistaken Payments in Three-party Situations: A German View of English Law', (1999) 58 *CLJ* 567–603.

[5] Lord Goff of Chieveley and Gareth Jones, *The Law of Restitution* (5th edn, 1998), 37–40.

[6] A. Burrows, *The Law of Restitution* (1993), 45–54; G. Virgo, *The Principles of the Law of Restitution* (1999), 106–13.

[7] '[A] clumsy way of expressing a requirement of directness...rejected almost everywhere': Dawson, 'Indirect Enrichment', 801.

[8] Professor Tettenborn has attempted a more principled explanation of this restriction: A. Tettenborn, 'Lawful Receipt – A Justifying Factor', [1997] *Restitution LR* 1.

English law is not in principle averse to leapfrogging, though there is a recurrent situation, as Dawson's study recognised, in which it is outlawed. It is relatively easy to explain the rationale behind that prohibition. Almost more important than working out what the rule is, and how many exceptions it might admit, is the need for a stable technique for handling the relevant fact situations. The method proposed and used in this paper involves the rigid separation of two inquiries.

The first inquiry is directed to discovering what the English law of unjust enrichment might understand by the requirement of 'privity' or 'directness' to which it is supposed to subscribe. Who counts as a direct recipient or, in the contractual language, who satisfies the requirement of privity? This inquiry will identify the immediate enrichee. No leapfrogging question can arise till that job is done. The second inquiry then asks when, if ever, English law allows a claimant to leapfrog the immediate enrichee in order to sue someone who received from or through him – a remoter recipient – at his expense.

Burrows rightly says that the requirement of directness cannot be treated as a logical implication of the requirement that the defendant must have been enriched at the expense of the claimant.[9] The claimant and defendant in an action in unjust enrichment must necessarily be linked by that phrase. It is by bringing himself within that phrase that the claimant connects himself to the enrichment in question and identifies himself as having a prima facie title to sue.[10] Hence the phrase must be satisfied in every case. Directness is superadded. The defendant may have been *immediately* enriched at the claimant's expense, or he may have been *remotely* enriched at his expense, where 'remotely' means 'after and through the immediate enrichee'.

It follows that this entire discussion turns on the scope of 'at the expense of'. The first inquiry is directed to identifying the party immediately enriched at the expense of the claimant and the second inquiry is directed to the question whether it is possible to sue a party remotely enriched at his expense. It requires to be emphasised that the ground for restitution – the unjust factor – is not in question. The questions whether the defendant was enriched and, if so, whether he was enriched at the expense of the plaintiff are essential but preliminary. Before liability can be imposed, it must be shown that the enrichment was unjust. Even then the defendant may not be liable: he may be able to establish some defence. This article is concerned only with immediate and remote enrichment

---

[9] Burrows, *Law of Restitution*, 47.   [10] *Re Byfield* [1992] 1 All ER 249 at 256.

at the plaintiff's expense. Nevertheless, it needs also to be said that the ground for recovery of remote enrichment is unlike any other, in being parasitic on the ground for recovery from the immediate enrichee.[11]

The organising role of 'at the expense of' might be said to have been dissolved in German law. Superficially, it has been. The reason is to be found in the tantalising wording of § 812 BGB:

Wer durch die Leistung eines anderen oder in sonstiger Weise auf dessen Kosten etwas ohne rechtlichen Grund erlangt, ist ihm zur Herausgabe verpflichtet. [Anyone who receives something without legal ground through a performance made by another or in some other way at that other's expense incurs an obligation to that other to make restitution.]

This wording has led to a very strong differentiation between the *Leistungskondiktion* (the claim in unjust enrichment where the enrichment is conferred on the defendant by a performance by the claimant) and the *Nichtleistungskondiktionen* (claims in unjust enrichment where the enrichment arises at the expense of the claimant in some way other than through a performance by the claimant). Although the words 'at the expense of another' (*auf Kosten [eines anderen]*) do expressly appear in relation to the latter and by implication carry back to the former, the learning on the meaning of this phrase has tended to be mediated through discussion of the nature of a *Leistung* and of other modes of enrichment. Thus where there is a *Leistung* the connection between claimant and defendant is automatically established, and the phrase 'at the expense of' has no further role.[12]

It is a difficult question, and one of great importance to the common law, whether rationality ultimately requires this distinction between enrichment by performance and enrichment in other modes. Suffice it to say here that, without any equivalent text on which to hang it, English law has not so far found it necessary to draw any such line. If and so long as it is not insisted upon, the discussion of the essential link between the claimant and the defendant must focus immediately on 'at the expense of'. It is certainly true, however, that in the discussion a line similar but not identical to that between performance and other modes may increasingly assert itself in English law, namely the line between ordinary and interceptive subtractions.

---

[11] Briefly touched on at the end, see 523, below.
[12] The useful discussion in B. S. Markesinis, W. Lorenz and G. Dannemann, *The German Law of Obligations*, vol. I, *The Law of Contracts and Restitution* (1997), 722-4 appears to assume, as was previously thought, that in English law 'at the expense of' required a 'corresponding loss'. This now appears to be incorrect. See 500-1, below.

II. Eliminating the 'wrong' sense of 'at the expense of'

An unjust enrichment is an enrichment at the expense of another which has to be given up to that other for a reason, that reason being neither a contract nor a wrong. Obligations to give up a gain received can arise from a contract[13] or from a wrong.[14] Such obligations are indeed restitutionary and belong in the law of restitution, but they do not arise from unjust enrichment.[15] This is a study of unjust enrichment. It is not concerned with any other grounds for restitution. One particular sense of 'at the expense of' blurs this distinction. A preliminary task is therefore to ensure that it is not used.

If C pays D, the money is received by D at C's expense in the sense that it comes from C. This is a simple illustration of the subtractive sense of the phrase or the 'from' sense. A mistaken payment from C to D is sometimes described as 'a subtractive enrichment' merely to emphasise that it falls within the 'from' sense of the crucial phrase. However, 'at the expense of' can be used to mean that the enrichment has been obtained by a wrong to the person wronged. C is beaten up by D. D was paid £5,000 by X to do it. Here D is enriched at C's expense in the sense that he has obtained the money by doing a wrong to C. This is the 'wrong' sense of 'at the expense of'. It is the 'wrong' sense in that C relies on a wrong to connect him to D's enrichment. And it is the wrong sense in that it cannot be admitted to the law of unjust enrichment. Where a plaintiff identifies himself as the victim of a wrong by invoking the phrase 'at the expense of' in this 'wrong' sense, he is relying on the wrong and, albeit in the language of unjust enrichment, asking the court to decide that the wrong is one which yields an entitlement to a gain-based award. The law of unjust enrichment cannot answer that question. A claimant who does rely on that sense, whether because the facts allow him no other or because he chooses to analyse the facts in such a way as to make that sense available to him, defines himself out of the law of unjust enrichment. He is talking about a wrongful enrichment and his claim is made in the law of wrongs.

---

[13] *Sebel Products Ltd v. Customs and Excise Commissioners* [1949] Ch 409; *Nurdin & Peacock plc v. D. B. Ramsden & Co. Ltd* [1999] 1 WLR 1249. Contractual restitution displaces the law of unjust enrichment: *Pan Ocean Shipping Co. Ltd v. Creditcorp Ltd (The Trident Beauty)* [1994] 1 WLR 161 (HL).

[14] *United Australia Ltd v. Barclays Bank Ltd* [1941] AC 1 (HL).

[15] P. Birks, 'Misnomer', in: W. R. Cornish et al. (eds.), *Restitution: Past, Present and Future* (1998), 1. Virgo, *Principles*, is the first textbook not to assume that unjust enrichment and restitution are one and the same.

Where the facts amount to a wrong, the law of unjust enrichment will have nothing to say unless the wrongful enrichment is susceptible of alternative analysis as an unjust enrichment. That is, the claimant may be able to dispense with the wrong and present the facts as an unjust enrichment without placing any reliance on them in their character as a wrong. Whether this can be done often or rarely depends in large measure on the breadth of the interpretation which the courts will give the subtractive sense of 'at the expense of'. The subtractive sense is amenable to broader or narrower interpretation. A very broad interpretation will bring a large number of cases of restitution for wrongs within the range of alternative analysis as cases of unjust enrichment.

Some scholars do not believe that the common law ever gives gain-based awards for wrongs;[16] that is, they think that restitution for wrongs is an illusion. Every case which looks like restitution for a wrong as such is really a reanalysis of the facts as an unjust enrichment. On this view it is never *qua* wrong that the story yields restitution but only *qua* unjust enrichment. There is no need to go so far. The law of wrongs is not confined to compensating loss. Every jurisdiction that awards exemplary damages proves as much.[17] For example, *Edwards v. Lee's Administrator*[18] is perfectly satisfactorily analysed as an example of restitution – that is, gain-based recovery – for trespass. The finder of a scenic cave made a fortune through tourism. A third of the cave lay under his neighbour's land. Deep down under the surface, doing no harm, every party of tourists trespassed. The victim of the wrong, who had no access to the cave from his land, was awarded one third of the profits.

The great case of *Moses v. Macferlan* itself is only explicable as a case of restitution for the wrong of breach of contract.[19] Every other explanation leads to the conclusion that the court ignored and contradicted a judgment which had not been quashed. Macferlan had promised Moses not to sue him to enforce the endorser's liability on certain promissory notes. Macferlan did sue. Moses paid up. Lord Mansfield did not doubt that Moses could have brought an action for breach of contract (general

---

[16] J. Beatson, 'The Nature of Waiver of Tort', in his: *The Use and Abuse of Unjust Enrichment* (1991), 206–43; D. Friedmann, 'Restitution for Wrongs', in: Cornish *et al.*, *Restitution*, 87–126.

[17] This was the foundation of the school of thought which successfully restricted punitive damages in English law: *Rookes v. Barnard* [1964] AC 1129 (HL); *Cassell & Co. v. Broome* [1972] AC 1027. Note, however, the non-doctrinaire position of Lord Wilberforce in the latter case, which has now prevailed in Law Commission, *Aggravated, Exemplary, and Restitutionary Damages* (Law Com Report No. 247, 1997), 98–138.

[18] 96 SW 2d 1028 (1936).   [19] (1760) 2 Burr 1005.

assumpsit). The only question was whether he could bring the restitutionary action for money had and received instead. It was held that he could.[20]

Although it is impossible and unnecessary to deny the existence of restitutionary awards for wrongs *qua* wrongs, it is none the less true that if a broad interpretation of 'at the expense of' is adopted a great many of the cases that seem to exemplify restitution of wrongful enrichment – restitution for wrongs as such – become susceptible of alternative analysis as cases of unjust enrichment. Moreover, as demonstrated below, the law does increasingly appear to be adopting a broad interpretation.

Eliminating the wrong sense of 'at the expense of', leaves the 'subtractive' or 'from' sense. A claimant in unjust enrichment must identify himself as the person from whom the defendant was enriched. The case law on the interpretation of this sense of the phrase provides the answer to the first of the two principal inquiries.

III. The first inquiry: identifying the immediate enrichee

The central model is very simple. It consists of a performance made by one person to another. For example, C pays D by mistake. In practice nearly every case is like that. However, to find the limits one must move out from that simple model, to see what is minimally required. English law certainly agrees with German law that there is no actual requirement of a performance. Those who take and find are subjected to the same liability as those who are mistakenly paid. If I drop my money in the street, the finder who pockets it has always been exposed to the same action for money had and received as a mistaken payee.[21] Here there is a shift of wealth from P to D in which P plays no active role. If there is a difference from the German approach, it is, as already noticed, that no fuss whatever is made, as it is in German law, about the line between performance (*Leistung*) and acquisition in other ways. It is possible to formulate a tentative proposition that identifies the immediate enrichee and covers both *Leistung* and *Nichtleistung*: the immediate enrichee is the first recipient from the claimant. This notion

---

[20] It is only by bringing to bear the analysis used in relation to waiver of tort in *United Australia Ltd v. Barclays Bank Ltd* [1941] AC 1 (HL) that it becomes apparent that *Moses v. Macferlan* was indeed an action for breach of contract brought to recover the contract-breaker's gains. Prior to that decision of the House of Lords the line between restitution of unjust enrichment and restitution for wrongs was never clearly drawn.

[21] *Holiday v. Sigil* (1826) 2 C & P 176; 172 ER 81; *Neate v. Harding* (1851) 6 Ex 349; 155 ER 577; *Moffatt v. Kazana* [1969] 2 QB 152.

of a first recipient seems at first sight clear enough, but there are some complications.

1. Corresponding loss

Shorn of complications, the question is whether there must be a plus and minus relationship, a minus to the would-be claimant corresponding with the plus which is the enrichment of the defendant. In ninety-nine out of a hundred cases there will have been a correspondence of that kind. In Canada it is now constantly said that a claim in unjust enrichment requires a corresponding impoverishment on the part of the plaintiff. That seems to commit the law to the view taken in some civilian jurisdictions that the arithmetic sense of subtraction must be satisfied. There must be a minus to the plaintiff.[22] German law takes the other view. German authors remind their readers that this is enrichment law, not impoverishment law.[23]

Recent cases in Australia and in England have opted for the German position. The context of these holdings to the effect that an impoverishment of the claimant is not required has been the rejection of any defence of passing on. Defendants have tried to resist claims by showing that a plaintiff in unjust enrichment, who did indeed suffer a loss corresponding to their enrichment, has since made good that loss by passing the burden on to others. An ultra vires tax is imposed on sellers of certain goods. Sellers then raise their prices. Can they still recover? Statute apart, the answer in Australia was negative.[24] Claims in unjust enrichment are not

---

[22] This position is defended in Mitchell McInnes, 'The Canadian Principle of Unjust Enrichment: Comparative Insights into the Law of Restitution', (1999) 37 Alberta Law Review 1, 22; also 'At the Plaintiff's Expense: Quantifying Restitutionary Relief', (1998) 57 *CLJ* 471.

[23] H.-G. Koppensteiner and E. A. Kramer, *Ungerechtfertigte Bereicherung* (2nd edn, 1988), 84, 85, citing a famous dictum of Esser: 'Wir haben es mit Bereicherungs- und nicht mit Entreicherungsrecht zu tun' [Our business is with enrichment law, not impoverishment law]. Cf. also: '[H]ier kommt es nur auf die Bereicherung des Schuldners an; ob der Gläubiger entreichert ist, ist von keinerlei Bedeutung...Es wäre also ein schwerer Fehler, einen Bereicherungsanspruch mit der Begründung zu verneinen, der Gläubiger habe keinen Nachteil erlitten' [In this area of law only the enrichment of the person liable is relevant. Whether the enrichment-creditor has been impoverished is of no significance...It would therefore be a serious mistake to withhold a claim founded on unjust enrichment on the ground that the enrichment-creditor had suffered no detriment]. Cf. also H. J. Wieling, *Bereicherungsrecht* (1993), 1–2.

[24] *Commissioner of State Revenue v. Royal Insurance Australia Ltd* (1994) 182 CLR 51 (HCA), where Mason ACJ adopted the view of Windeyer J in *Mason v. NSW* (1959) 102 CLR 108 at 146.

about recouping loss. So long as the plaintiff can be identified, it is not necessary for him to prove impoverishment.

This was followed in England. A bank engaged in an interest swap. It turned out that the swap was void. The bank therefore had a prima facie right to restitution of the money it had paid out. But it had hedged. It had made a back-to-back swap with another counterparty, reversing out the risk. Overall it had lost nothing. However, the Court of Appeal held that the defendant had no defence: it could not rely on the claimant bank's hedge. The action was not about the claimant's impoverishment but the defendant's unjust enrichment.[25] The Court of Appeal thus accepted that the reason there is no defence of passing on is that corresponding loss is, as the German jurists hold, beside the point.

These utterances are somewhat weakened by their context. The defence of passing on could have been rejected on a number of grounds. Nevertheless, they are strengthened by support from a quite different quarter. Suppose that I use your bicycle while you are on holiday. By the time you come back, I have returned it. Let it be that there is no perceptible wear and tear attributable to me. It is clear that I must pay the value of my user. Yet you have suffered no loss. I have taken three weeks' riding 'from' you, but I have inflicted no corresponding impoverishment on you.[26]

There is another substantial piece of evidence against the requirement of a corresponding impoverishment. You have my money. You invest it and roll the investment over ten times. You produce a five-fold increase. We will recur to this below, but at this point we need only note that it is hard to turn a blind eye to the fact that if, as is the case, I can claim the yield of your successful investment, my recovery will give me five times the amount of the value which I lost at the beginning of the story.[27] In short, I recover without showing any corresponding loss.

2. Externalities of performance not conclusive

This second complication arises in some cases in which the claimant wishes to say that he conferred the benefit in question on the defendant and where the physical externalities might seem to support that contention. The externalities are not conclusive. In particular, they are not conclusive where the would-be claimant in unjust enrichment, C, confers the benefit on D under a contract made with X for its conferment. This is a

---

[25] *Kleinwort Benson v. Birmingham City Council* [1996] 4 All ER 733 (CA).
[26] *Hambly v. Trott* (1776) 1 Cowp 371; 98 ER 1136. Lord Mansfield's example used horses, not bicycles.
[27] *F. C. Jones (Trustee in Bankruptcy) v. Jones* [1997] Ch 159 (CA), discussed at 509–10, below.

not uncommon configuration. A contractor building on the land of D will, for example, often sub-contract aspects of the work. The externalities will then suggest that a sub-contractor's carpentry is a benefit conferred by the carpenter on the owner of the site and that the owner might therefore be said to be enriched at the carpenter's expense. However, at least in the common case in which the sub-contracting carpenter does indeed have a good contract with the head contractor, the owner is only a remote recipient of that benefit; the immediate recipient is the head contractor. It is for him that the carpenter has worked. In such circumstances an action in unjust enrichment, if any there be, will lie to the head contractor, for it is at that party's expense that the recipient owner has been directly, or immediately, enriched. The carpenter could only reach the owner as a remote recipient. On these facts he will not be allowed to leapfrog the head contractor.[28]

Two situations need to be considered. There is first the common case in which a person in the position of the sub-contractor, the would-be claimant C, does indeed have a valid contract with the person in the situation of the head contractor. Secondly there is the rarer case in which that contract is merely putative: in the eyes of the law there is no contract between C and X.

(a) D benefits from performance of a valid contract between C and X

Suppose a garage, C, does work on a car which has been damaged in a crash. The car's owner, D, is the ultimate beneficiary of the work. However, in almost all cases the garage will be doing the work under a contract with an insurance company. It has been held that if after the work is done and the customer has taken the car back into his possession, the insurance company becomes insolvent, the unpaid garage has no claim against the owner. The work is done for the insurance company. The garage has to take the risk of the insolvency of the insurance company with which it validly contracted. It cannot say to the customer that the customer was directly enriched at its expense, and it cannot leapfrog the insurance company.[29]

---

[28] 522–3, below.
[29] *Brown and Davis v. Galbraith* [1972] 1 WLR 997 (CA); *Gray's Truck Centre Ltd v. Olaf L. Johnson Ltd* (CA, 25 January 1990, unreported); *Kirklands Garage (Kinross) Ltd v. Clark* 1967 SLT (Sh Ct) 60; *Express Coach Finishers v. Caulfield* 1968 SLT (Sh Ct) 11. Cf. Whitty, 'Indirect Enrichment', 211–17. Though superficially similar, *Pan Ocean Shipping Ltd v. Creditcorp Ltd (The Trident Beauty)* [1994] 1 WLR 161 (HL) is not of this kind. Pan Ocean were obliged to pay the owners of The Trident Beauty freight in advance under a charter which included its own regime for restitution in the event of the freight not being earned. They had contracted out of the law of unjust enrichment. The right to receive the advance freight was assigned to Creditcorp. Pan Ocean paid the assignees, and the

In *Lloyds Bank plc v. Independent Insurance Co. Ltd*[30] the bank paid its customer's creditor a large sum with its customer's authority but by reason of a grave mistake as to the funds available to the customer. The case reaffirms that a bank, C, cannot recover from the payee, D, in those circumstances, despite its indubitably causative mistake. The dominant reason given by the Court of Appeal is that on these facts the bank gets what it paid for. It gets good consideration in the form of the discharge of a debt owed to D by the bank's customer, X.

That cannot be the right reason. On the one hand it is very doubtful that the receipt of good consideration is really a bar to such a claim and, on the other, it is inconceivable that the result would have been any different if the payee had been a donee. A father, for instance, will often enough ask his bank to send money to his son. Suppose that he sets up a standing order for £500 per month. If the bank inadvertently allows the father's account to slide into overdraft, it cannot look to the son for repayment, even though the son be a mere donee. The true reason is that in these circumstances the payment is not the bank's payment. It is the customer's payment, and the immediate enrichee is the customer. Where the customer has insufficient funds, the authority to pay is simultaneously a request to lend. In most cases it might indeed be said that the payee gives good consideration to the customer, in the form of the discharge of the customer's debt. But that is superfluous. A bank that pays to the order of a customer is paying the customer who is paying the payee.[31] If the customer is out of funds the payment is a loan to the customer. The payment is not received immediately at the expense of the bank.[32] The payee is at most a remote recipient at its expense.

These cases show that if C makes a valid contract with X for a performance the cost of which is to be borne by X, and C's performance of that

---

freight was never earned. The claim based on failure of consideration failed because of the contracting out, not because it was not received at Pan Ocean's expense. There was no unjust factor, no more than there would have been if the right had not been assigned. Cf. G. J. Tolhurst, 'Assignment, Equities, *The Trident Beauty* and Restitution', (1999) 58 *CLJ* 546, 561, 564. Burrows prefers an explanation closer to that given above, namely that Pan Ocean could not be allowed to succeed without undermining the contract of assignment between the shipowners and Creditcorp, but that argument depends on the prior determination of the exact nature of the right assigned: A. S. Burrows, 'Restitution from Assignees', [1994] *Restitution LR* 52, 55–6. Cf. 523, below.

[30] [2000] QB 110. [31] Cf. *Coutts & Co. v. Stock* [2000] Lloyd's Rep 14 at 17 (Lightman J).

[32] This explanation also applies to the leading case of *Aiken v. Short* (1856) 1 H & N 210; 156 ER 1180, the facts of which were materially identical. The 'good consideration' explanation derives from the necessity of upholding the result in that case despite the liberalisation of the test for restitution-yielding mistake: *Barclays Bank Ltd v. W. J. Simms Son and Cooke (Southern) Ltd* [1980] QB 677.

contract enures to the benefit of D, C cannot say that D has been immediately enriched at his expense. It is X who has been enriched at C's expense, while D has received his benefit from X. Later this configuration of facts is revisited – there is a doctrine which allows leapfrogging: where a first recipient is unjustly enriched at another's expense and a second recipient is then enriched because of the first enrichment, it is possible, under certain restrictions, to leapfrog the first recipient and attack the second recipient instead. When we have introduced that doctrine we will need to say exactly why it does not apply to this kind of case. These defendants can be attacked neither as first recipients nor, through the first recipient, as remote recipients.[33]

(b) D benefits from a putative contract between C and X

The law as considered so far turns on the validity of the transaction between C and X: D appears to be enriched immediately from C but is actually enriched from X. In English law the picture changes dramatically in the case in which C thinks he has a contract with X but in truth has none. If C is a bank which mistakenly pays a stopped cheque, the payee D receives directly at the bank's expense. The mistake then provides the unjust factor, and C can therefore recover from D. That is *Barclays Bank Ltd v. W. J. Simms Son and Cooke (Southern) Ltd.*[34] In such a case the bank intends to pay on the credit of its customer, just as in the case discussed above, but the putative contract with the customer cannot turn the payment into the customer's payment. Again, in the very common but more complex *O'Brien* situation,[35] in which C, being in a domestic or confidential relationship with X, gives security to D for X's business indebtedness, there is either no contract at all between C and X or the contract to provide security will be voidable for undue influence or misrepresentation. For that reason, if for no other, it cannot be said that the security is obtained by D from X. Here D's security is taken directly at P's expense.

In German law, and indeed in American law,[36] different results are reached. The German law agrees with the English law on the common case

---

[33] Below, 523–4. [34] [1980] QB 677.
[35] *Barclays Bank plc v. O'Brien* [1994] 1 AC 180; *CIBC Mortgages plc v. Pitt* [1994] 1 AC 200.
[36] American law is substantially the same as the German law as described below in relation to the brewery case: American Law Institute, *Restatement of Restitution* (1937), 14 (1); *Bank Worms v. Bankamerica International* 77 NY 2d 362; 570 NE 2d 189 (1991); cf. *Shield Benefit Administrators v. University of Michigan* 225 Mich App 467; 571 NW 2d 556 (1997). There is a very useful discussion, critical of the English position, in A. Kull, 'Rationalising Restitution', (1995) 83 *California LR* 1191, 1228–32. It is important to notice that C (the bank) is entitled to be subrogated to the claims of D against X: see Kull at 1229.

discussed above,[37] but it treats the putative case in exactly the same way: it would deny Barclays any claim in unjust enrichment against Simms. This derives from its commitment to assessing the matter from the standpoint of a reasonable person in the shoes of D, the defendant recipient of the enrichment. If it would appear to such a person that the *Leistung* (performance) was in substance made by X, C can have no claim in unjust enrichment.[38] In one case hot-water tanks and kitchen equipment were supplied to a building site by a supplier, C, which believed its contract was with the site owner, when in fact the order had been placed by the head contractor, X. That equipment was then installed in the new building. The supplier had no claim in unjust enrichment against the site owner, D. A reasonable person in D's position would have regarded the performance – the supply of equipment – as procured by X through a contract with C. The result would have been different if it could have been shown that D knew that C had no such contract and a person with that knowledge would have known that the *Leistung* was C's own.[39]

Again, in a case substantially identical to *Barclays v. Simms*,[40] the claimant bank, C, had neglected a stop put on a standing order in respect of rent due from its customer, X, to the defendants, D.[41] X was a brewery in dispute with D, the landlords of one of its taverns. It had indicated to the landlords that it would stop its payments of rent and it had told its bank not to pay. The bank went on paying for many months. The tenant brewery failed to notice. The bank had no right to restitution from the landlords. Even taking the notice issued by the tenants into account, a reasonable person in the position of the landlords would have thought

---

[37] BGHZ 27, 317 discussed by Dawson, 'Indirect Enrichment', 805: hirer contracts for repair of locomotive but does not pay; owner recovers the locomotive after repair. No claim by repairer against owner. Cf. n. 29 above, and n. 92 below.

[38] Meier, 'Mistaken Payments', 579–80 astutely identified the Court of Appeal's decision in *Re Jones Ltd v. Waring & Gillow Ltd* [1925] 2 KB 612 as an English application of this approach, rejected in the House of Lords [1926] AC 670. With the HL decision, she compares *Thomas v. Houston Corbett & Co.* [1969] NZLR 151 (NZCA).

[39] BGHZ 40, 272; English translation in Markesinis et al., *Law of Contracts*, 789; cf. BGHZ 36, 30, Dawson, 'Indirect Enrichment', 806.

[40] [1980] QB 677.

[41] BGHZ 89, 376; English translation in Markesinis et al., *Law of Contracts*, 794. In this case the court refuses to deal with the case in which the bank's authority was, not terminated, but absent *ab initio*. As to that case the German law remains unclear, although Zimmermann and du Plessis say that 'most writers' would now allow the bank in that situation to recover from its immediate payee – the same result as in *Barclays Bank Ltd v. W. J. Simms Son and Cooke (Southern) Ltd*: R. Zimmermann and J. du Plessis, 'Basic Features of the German Law of Unjustified Enrichment', [1994] *Restitution LR* 14, 34. Meier, 'Mistaken Payments', 572–3 clearly takes the view that the case where there never was a valid order is to be treated as different from that in which a valid order is given and subsequently revoked, as by stopping a cheque.

that the performance was that of the tenants. It therefore had to be treated as their performance, not the bank's.

It is extremely difficult for an English lawyer, no doubt because of a series of different presuppositions, to come to terms with the notion that in this context the honest and reasonable belief of the recipient should be decisive. In a simple two-party case such as *Kelly v. Solari*,[42] where a widow had to make restitution when it turned out that her husband had after all not been insured, the innocence of the recipient is irrelevant until the receipt has generated some change of position. It then becomes relevant, since recipients in bad faith are disqualified from pleading that defence. However, if the German or American approach were applied to *Barclays v. Simms*, the bank's claim would have to be denied unless the builders knew that it had no mandate to pay. It is not clear how or why, in this context, liability might be confined to the knowing recipient. American law, but not German, appears to dress the matter up in terms of a defence and the limits placed upon it. There is said to be a defence of 'discharge for value',[43] but that 'defence' does no more than restate the proposition that a claimant in this *Barclays* situation cannot recover from the defendant payee. In short, the defence still needs to be explained. It is not an example of, or even a cousin of, bona fide purchase from a third party. There is no acquisition from a third party in such a case. The only possible third party, X, has either never dealt with or has cancelled its dealing with the would-be claimant, C.

3. Interceptive subtraction

The idea of interception appears to have a role, at least in Canada, in determining the response to wrongful enrichment. It is important not to be distracted by that.[44] The question here is whether in the law of unjust enrichment it is possible to say that value has been obtained from another when the asset in question had never been reduced into that other's ownership or possession. The answer is yes, but it is complicated by the fact that the law often ensures that the property passes before the interception actually happens. The subtraction then ceases to be interceptive.

Suppose that, intending a loan to C, I throw down a bundle of notes from an upper window, expecting C to catch them. D physically intercepts

---

[42] (1841) 9 M & W 54. [43] American Law Institute, *Restatement of Restitution* (1937), § 14(1).
[44] *LAC Minerals Ltd v. Corona Resources Ltd* [1989] 2 SCR 574; 61 DLR 4th 14 shows that one who abuses confidential information to acquire an asset may be turned into a trustee if the court finds, as a matter of fact, that it was his intervention that prevented the benefit going through to the plaintiff.

them, jumping up before C can get them. The property at law will not have passed to C, since C never took possession. But equity raises a perfectionary beneficial interest in C at the moment at which I have done all that lies in me to do to transfer the legal title.[45] The physical interception comes a second or two later, C already has a proprietary interest in the notes, and the subtraction from him is not interceptive. Again, suppose that I give D £100 to give to C. One might say that that money is now on its way to C. However, if D absconds with it, the question whether D is enriched at my expense or, interceptively, from C admits of no natural answer. The law therefore adopts an inevitably artificial criterion. The claim stays with me until you have attorned to C, which means until you have informed him that you are holding for him. Thereafter, the claim against you goes round to him. But your attornment passes the property in the £100 to C, with the result that when you pocket the money the subtraction is no longer interceptive. You are taking what is already his.

The problem is not always short-circuited in this way. In *Shamia v. Joory*[46] there was no identified fund, so that no property could pass. The defendant owed money to a third party, was told to pay the claimant, and attorned. The plaintiff, though not owner, was able to claim the sum. It is sometimes said that the case was wrongly decided for the very reason that no property could pass. But it is defensible as an instance of interceptive subtraction. The attornment, though it could not pass the property in any specific thing, nevertheless served as an indication that the sum in question had been finally destined to go to the plaintiff. Accordingly, in withholding it the defendant had enriched himself by subtraction from the plaintiff.

There are quite a few cases of this kind, where money destined to C is intercepted by D. One large group has become obsolete. If D usurped an office which ought to have been occupied by P and received money due to the office-holder, C could bring money had and received against D.[47] Similarly, and not obsolete, a self-appointed executor or administrator who receives what was due to the estate is liable to make restitution to the incoming rightful personal representative.[48] Similarly, if D receives rent

---

[45] *Re Rose* [1952] Ch 78 (CA). The word 'perfectionary' indicates that the goal at which the right aims is the perfection of the intent of the transferor.
[46] [1958] 1 QB 448.
[47] *Arris v. Stukely* (1677) 2 Mod 260; 86 ER 1060; *Howard v. Wood* (1679) 2 Lev 245; 83 ER 530. Although these provide a root for waiver of tort, they do not need to be analysed as instances of wrongful enrichment.
[48] *Jacob v. Allen* (1703) 1 Salk 27; 91 ER 26; *Yardley v. Arnold* (1842) C & M 434; 174 ER 577.

which was due to C, he will have to account to C.[49] Of the same kind but rather more difficult are the cases, discussed by Robert Chambers, of land intended to be conveyed to C being mistakenly conveyed to D. In such a case P has been allowed to claim against D.[50]

Lionel Smith has argued that it is a condition for the recognition of an interceptive subtraction that the plaintiff must have lost his right to sue the person who paid the interceptor.[51] Accordingly, if an executor pays the wrong people, those who ought to have been paid cannot be said to have suffered an interceptive subtraction, because they are no less entitled to be paid by the executors after the misdirection than they were before. In *Ministry of Health v. Simpson*[52] the executors of Caleb Diplock had paid to charities sums which ought to have gone to the next of kin. The next of kin recovered directly from the charities. Smith's view is that this could not be justified in terms of interceptive subtraction, unless by understanding the Court to have complied with the requirement that the next of kin's continuing claim against the executors be discharged by insisting on prior exhaustion of all possible remedies against them. Smith's argument is powerful. However, it might be said to overlook the regularity with which the law allows an election between inconsistent rights.

It was inexcusable to leave the Diplock executors bearing the loss. Even now when restitution for mistake of law has finally become possible, it would be pointlessly wasteful to insist on two actions rather than one. The next of kin's action against the mistakenly paid charities should have been allowed, without a requirement of exhaustion of remedies against the executors, on the basis of interceptive subtraction: the charities had taken money that was destined to the next of kin. That analysis is factually attractive, even if it is inconsistent with the view that the plaintiffs had an undiminished right against the executors. It makes good sense to give the next of kin an election.

---

[49] *Official Custodian for Charities v. Mackey (No. 2)* [1985] 1 WLR 1308, where Nourse J acknowledged the principle but found it not to apply on the particular facts.

[50] *Leuty v. Hillas* (1858) 2 De G & J 110; *Craddock Bothers v. Hunt* [1923] 2 ChD 136 (CA); R. Chambers, *Resulting Trusts* (1997), 127. Cf. Dawson, 'Indirect Enrichment', 801, citing, *inter alia*, a case in which a reward was paid to the wrong person and the person to whom it should have gone sued, to achieve what Dawson calls 'a short-circuit of liabilities that are ultimately interconnected': *Claxton v. Kay* 101 Ark 350; 142 SW 517 (1912).

[51] L. D. Smith, 'Three-party Restitution: A Critique of Birks's Theory of Interceptive Subtraction', (1991) 11 *Oxford JLS* 481.

[52] [1951] AC 251 (HL).

With the possible exception of the Diplock saga, all the cases of interceptive subtraction discussed above are cases in which there is no doubt that the plaintiff has suffered a loss by virtue of the interception. The only question is whether it is possible for the plaintiff to connect that loss with the defendant's gain without relying on the 'wrong' sense of 'at the expense of'. In other words, can it be said that the gain which caused the loss came 'from' the plaintiff rather than 'by doing the plaintiff wrong'? We have already noticed that the courts seem to be inclining to the German view that a loss is not necessary. If that is taken seriously, the scope of interceptive subtraction enlarges quite considerably, and something that was formerly inexplicable can also be explained. The next task is therefore to contemplate interceptive subtraction freed from a requirement of loss.

It seems to be perfectly clear that if D invests C's money and doubles it, C is entitled to the doubled proceeds. This is the case encountered above.[53] D invests £10,000 and gets £20,000. That £20,000 was not C's before D received it, but C can trace from the £10,000 to the £20,000, and C can claim the £20,000. There is no need to spend time here on the exact nature of the entitlement, *in rem* or *in personam* or both. C has suffered no 'corresponding loss'. The outcome does not depend on the commission of a wrong. There is no doubt about any of these propositions. They underlie the operation of the presumption which produces the trust that operates when one party buys an asset with resources provided by another. And they have recently been seen in action in a case which was decided entirely at law, namely *F. C. Jones (Trustee in Bankruptcy) v. Jones*.[54]

Only very contrived arguments can conclude that C suffered a loss of £20,000. The loss was £10,000, plus the value of money over time. Further, there is no avoiding the necessity of accepting that the £20,000 earned from C's £10,000 cannot be said to be obtained *from* C unless the notion of an interceptive subtraction is accepted. That money came to D when D sold out the investment. It was never in C's ownership or possession. The only way to explain these results is (a) to accept that loss is not necessary and (b) to say that C's ownership of the £10,000 carries with it the wealth-creating opportunities inherent in that £10,000, so that when the potential is realised all that is actually earned through the £10,000 is regarded as having been destined to C all along. The earning opportunity is C's. Anyone who takes the opportunity intercepts what is already attributed in law to C.

---

[53] 501, above.   [54] [1997] Ch 159 (CA).

This step requires us to revisit the Kentucky cave case.[55] That case is a paradigm of restitution in the law of wrongs: restitution for the wrong as such. It could easily be reanalysed in unjust enrichment if what was at issue were the value of the user itself. Far below the ground the taking of that user caused no loss, but it was none the less taken from Mr Lee in the simple sense: it was user of land that was his.[56] The question now is whether an unjust enrichment analysis can reach even the money paid by the tourists. The answer must be that it can. If investment of the whole value of another's asset – selling it – can later give that other the traceable substitute, exactly the same must apply to the investment of the user of another's asset – hiring it out. Mr Edwards exploited the user of Mr Lee's land and turned it into money. If the right of ownership attributes the earning opportunities of an asset to its owner, the same must be true of the earning opportunities inherent in the user of the land. Hence, it must be true that Mr Lee could have secured his award without relying on the facts in their character as a trespass but analysing them instead as an unjust enrichment at his expense in the subtractive sense. The law attributes the earning opportunities inherent in a thing to that thing's owner, and their realisation by a non-owner is an interception of money destined for the owner. There is no need for the connection between such a claimant and such an enrichment to be established by reliance on a wrong.

The logic seems irresistible: if without relying on wrongdoing one can have the proceeds of the sale and the assets thereby obtained, one must be similarly entitled to the gains made by hiring it out. Whether the law has really come so far is open to debate. It has travelled blind and may not care for the destination. It may turn back. Strong renewed insistence on 'corresponding impoverishment' would immediately narrow the law of unjust enrichment. However, the *Jones* case[57] will be an obstacle to any turning back. It seems to show that the English law is committed to the broad notion of 'at the expense of', which includes the relatively weak form of interceptive subtraction that has just been outlined.

German law gives rather uncertain guidance in this matter. Some preliminary propositions are secure. First, since German law gives no

---

[55] *Edwards v. Lee's Administrator* 96 SW 2d 1028 (1936); see 498, above.
[56] Cf. *Olwell v. Nye & Nissen* 26 Wash 2d 282; 173 P 2d 652 (1946) where this difference was centrally in issue and the court preferred profits to rental. The defendant had wrongfully used the plaintiff's egg-washing machine.
[57] [1997] Ch 159 (CA).

gain-based awards for wrongs as such,[58] the species of restitution seen in the Kentucky cave case has to be explained within the law of unjust enrichment or not at all. It is not a question of alternative analyses, one in the law of wrongs and one in the law of unjust enrichment. Secondly, among the *Nichtleistungskondiktionen* (claims arising other than from a performance by the claimant) the *Eingriffskondiktion* (the claim arising from an encroachment on or intrusion into the rights of another) would be appropriate in principle for this case.[59] The idea that some rights do, and some do not, attribute wealth to the holder of the right is familiar to German jurists under the label *Zuweisungstheorie* or *Zuweisungsgehalt eines Rechts* – the doctrine of allocation, or the allocation-potential of a right.[60] It is used to discriminate between gainful encroachments upon rights which do, and which do not, give rise to a claim in unjust enrichment. On the other hand, it seems that majority opinion among German jurists does not take the attribution doctrine to the point of attributing to the owner the earning opportunities inherent in the thing owned. In the Kentucky cave case the German law of unjust enrichment would apparently give only reasonable rental, not the profits actually made, a view which seems to belong to a strictly subtractive interpretation.[61]

It is no doubt only an outsider's want of understanding that suggests that this is not a logical sticking-point in a system which insists that enrichment law is not impoverishment law. And it is all the more illogical in light of acceptance of the principle that the defendant must surrender that which he obtains in substitution for the plaintiff's thing; § 816 (1), first sentence, BGB, says:

Trifft ein Nichtberechtigter über einen Gegenstand eine Verfügung, die dem Berechtigten gegenüber wirksam ist, so ist er dem Berechtigten zur Herausgabe des durch die Verfügung Erlangten verpflichtet. [If a person who is not entitled makes a disposition of a thing, and that disposition binds the person entitled,

---

[58] There is an exception in intellectual property: Markesinis *et al.*, *Law of Contracts*, 742 (Dannemann).
[59] *Ibid.*, 743–9 (Dannemann); Zimmermann and Du Plessis, 'Basic Features', 26–9.
[60] Werner Lorenz, in: *J. von Staudingers Kommentar zum Bürgerlichen Gesetzbuch* (13th revised edn, 1999), § 812, n. 23. Lorenz there admits that the courts have had to proceed pragmatically. It is not easy to say in advance what will be attributed by which right.
[61] Dannemann, in Markesinis *et al.*, *Law of Contracts*, 747, points out that German law would none the less award the profits on a not-wrong analysis, treating the matter, not as an unjust enrichment, but as an abnormal or aggravated form of *negotiorum gestio* under § 687(2) BGB, which contemplates the case of a person who manages another's business as his own, in full knowledge that it is not his own. Cf. Whitty, 'Indirect Enrichment', 274–81.

he comes under a duty to make restitution to that person of that which he received by virtue of the disposition.]

That does not go to the lengths of the *Jones* case but it does make it difficult to account for reluctance to do the same in the case which may be compendiously called 'hire', where a person not entitled makes an irredeemable disposition of time and user. Logical or not, the German position may possibly offer some comfort to those reluctant to admit that facts of the Kentucky cave kind do admit of dual analysis, not only as a wrongful enrichment, but also as an unjust enrichment at the expense of the plaintiff and, in particular, that the profits received from the tourists can be analysed as interceptively subtracted from the plaintiff landowner.

4. Summary

The immediate enrichee is in general easily identified as the person who was the first recipient from the claimant. That first recipient may have received by virtue of a performance by the claimant or without any performance, as where he was a finder or taker. The word 'from' generally does, but need not, connote a corresponding loss to the claimant. The subtraction need not be arithmetic. There are two cases in which the reasonable observer might be deceived. First, where the would-be claimant confers the benefit on D under a contract with a third party, that benefit is received by D immediately at the expense of the third party, so that, if D can be attacked at all, it must be as one who received through the immediate enrichee. Secondly, a benefit which D receives directionally from a third party may nevertheless be immediately received at the expense of C if D can be said to have intercepted it on its way to C. In particular the law takes the view that earning opportunities inherent in assets are attributed to the owner of the asset, so that earnings from the asset are interceptively subtracted from its owner.

This first inquiry into 'at the expense of' has allowed the identification of the necessary connection between the plaintiff and the defendant and, more particularly, to say who counts as the immediate enrichee. If there were a strict requirement of 'directness' or 'privity', this would identify the only possible defendant in an action to recover unjust enrichment.

IV. The second inquiry: leapfrogging the immediate enrichee

It will often happen that the first recipient passes the enrichment on to a second recipient. He may do this specifically, by handing over the very *res* received, or he may do it abstractly, by handing over some other *res* in reliance on his receipt. The second inquiry is directed to discovering whether a claimant can leapfrog the first recipient and sue the second recipient, and so on down the chain of remoter recipients thereafter. It is a very important question, because the first recipient may be immune from suit or not worth suing, and the remote recipient may have the longer purse.

1. Fears

The draftsmen of the BGB were alive to the dangers of allowing leapfrogging claims. They feared that third parties would be drawn into liabilities engendered by transactions with which they had nothing to do. Precisely because they saw it as an instrument to that end, they expressly rejected the *actio de in rem verso*, the claim arising from wealth turned to the advantage of the defendant which had been developed by civilian scholars from very slight Roman beginnings. The early years of the BGB then reinforced the requirement of 'directness'.[62]

To some extent the responsibility for these fears may lie with the French Cour de cassation in its notorious *Boudier* decision in 1892.[63] The claimant there supplied manure to a tenant farmer. Before the next crop was harvested the tenant fell into financial problems and lost his lease. The claimant, not having been paid by the tenant to whom he had sold the manure, successfully leapfrogged the tenant and recovered from the landlord, the advantage having accrued to him. This application of the *actio de in rem verso* was crucial in supplementing the exiguous provisions of the French *Code civil* in relation to unjust enrichment. However, it is not the first or last leading case to be roundly condemned on the facts. It exemplifies one kind of leapfrogging which cannot be allowed.[64] Provided such specific restrictions are maintained, the dangers of allowing leapfrogging claims are rather less than has often been supposed.

A discussion of this topic must start by putting agency on one side. Agency causes many very difficult problems in the law of unjust enrichment, but agents can for the purpose of this particular discussion be

---

[62] Dawson, 'Indirect Enrichment', 790–6; Zimmermann and du Plessis, 'Basic Features', 31.
[63] Req. 15 June 1892, S 1893.1.281 note Labbé, DP 1892.1.596. This case and subsequent attempts to restrict it are discussed in K. Zweigert and H. Kötz, *An Introduction to Comparative Law* (trans. T. Weir, 3rd edn, 1998), 545–8.
[64] Above 502, and below, 523–4.

identified with their principals. If P makes a mistaken payment to D's agent, and then sues D for restitution, that is not a case of leapfrogging.[65]

Agency aside, there are two arguments which make a prima facie case for reaching a second or more remote recipient. One is based on property and the other on causation. The proprietary argument says to the remote recipient, 'You received my property!', and the causation argument says, 'You would not have received your enrichment from X but for X's having been enriched from me!' Neither stands any chance of success against a second or more remote recipient who is in a position to plead the defence of bona fide purchase for value without notice or who took through such a person. A defendant who cannot use that defence may be able to fall back on change of position. This is not the place to investigate the range of those defences, but it is important to notice that, because of them, these leapfrogging arguments do not threaten any general disruption. If and so far as these arguments can succeed, they will generally prevail only against remote recipients who are either not innocent or are mere donees who have not changed their position. Thus only a rather narrow band of remote recipients is vulnerable.

2. The proprietary argument

There is no doubt that a proprietary connection does support leapfrogging of a kind. In *Lipkin Gorman (a Firm) v. Karpnale Ltd*[66] a partner in a firm of solicitors who was addicted to gambling fed his addiction from the firm's client account. He gambled the money away at the defendant's casino. There was no point in suing the gambler. He was penniless and in prison. The firm leaped over him and succeeded in recovering from the casino. Although, as is shown below, the facts were more complex, the model from which the House of Lords worked was this. If X steals C's money or finds it and then gives it gratuitously to D, D becomes indebted to C in the sum that he receives. D has received C's money, albeit from a third party.

In the *Lipkin Gorman v. Karpnale* case, the casino was treated as a donee, because the gambling contracts of a licensed casino are all void, though not illegal. The payments made by the gambler were received innocently, but not for value. Had the gambler been addicted to champagne and caviar at the Ritz, the Ritz would have been perfectly safe, having given value

---

[65] *Portman Building Society v. Hamlyn Taylor Neck* [1998] 4 All ER 202 at 207 (Millett LJ). Cf. H. Dörner, 'Change of Position and *Wegfall der Bereicherung*', in: W. J. Swadling (ed.), *The Limits of Restitutionary Claims: A Comparative Analysis* (1997), 64, 66.

[66] [1991] 2 AC 548 (HL).

bona fide within valid contracts. As an innocent donee, the casino, a second recipient, was allowed to plead change of position. Its liability was thereby somewhat reduced.

(a) What interests suffice?
Ownership clearly suffices to make the connection between plaintiff and defendant. However, it is clear that lesser interests are also sufficient. There is no doubt that a power to rescind and revest suffices, for such a power can indubitably be exercised against third parties who are not bona fide purchasers. If C transfers a *res* to X under undue influence or misrepresentation, and X makes a gift of it to D, C can exercise the power in respect of the *res* in D's hands.[67] There are some indications that even an unexercised power will suffice. In *El Ajou v. Dollar Land Holdings plc*[68] the plaintiff was the victim of fraud with a power to rescind. It is tolerably clear that Millett J regarded that power as sufficient in itself to make the proprietary connection, even though it had not been exercised against any specific property. In the *Lipkin Gorman* case itself, which was ultimately contested only at law, close analysis shows that the general property in the money was in the gambler, not in the firm, and that the most that could be said was that the plaintiff firm held a power to revest in itself the money which went to the casino. And the power was never exercised.[69] If these indications are correct, weak or inchoate interests can satisfy the requirement of a proprietary connection.

It is an inference from *Boulter v. Barclays Bank*[70] that the House of Lords thinks that the power held by a person who has parted with an asset voidably is not a proprietary right of any kind: 'In such a case the defrauded owner retains no proprietary interest in the chattel, and it is therefore

---

[67] *Bridgeman v. Green* (1757) Wilm 58 at 65; *Bainbrigge v. Browne* (1881) 18 ChD 188 at 197 (CA). Compare the right to rectify and reclaim: *Blacklocks v. J. B. Developments (Godalming) Ltd* [1982] Ch 183. Whitty, 'Indirect Enrichment', 252–3 creates a special exceptional category 'Defender's indirect enrichment procured at pursuer's expense by fraud or comparable act of third party' and has real difficulty in explaining it. A system that can extend the property argument as in the text above does not encounter that difficulty.

[68] [1993] 3 All ER 717 (Millett J) reversed on one point as to attribution of knowledge [1994] 2 All ER 685 (CA).

[69] The firm never identified a fund in the hands of the casino, being content to stop at the moment of the receipt. Contrast *Banque Belge pour l'Étranger v. Hambrouck* [1921] 1 KB 321 (CA), where a fund was identified in the hands of the remote donee, and no attempt was made to claim the full sum she had received.

[70] [1999] 4 All ER 513 (HL).

not for the purchaser to establish a defence which would defeat it.'[71] Lord Hoffmann, with whom the whole House agreed, appeared to imply that the fact that the power is good against third-party holders of the *res* is not because it is a right *in rem* good against any recipient other than a bona fide purchaser for value but for some other reason, as, for instance, because of misbehaviour proved against the third party, although a volunteer cannot be brought within that notion simply because he gave no value. However, this is highly contentious and was not necessary for the decision. Clearly, if Lord Hoffmann's view were accepted, it would not be possible to place this power among proprietary interests which create a sufficient connection between a plaintiff in unjust enrichment and a remote recipient.

Equally problematic is *Ministry of Health v. Simpson*.[72] The next of kin successfully brought a restitutionary action against charities who ought never to have received any Diplock money. The charities had received from a third hand. This case was explained above as an interceptive subtraction: the money was destined as a matter of law to go to the next of kin; the charities, through no fault of their own, came between the executors and the next of kin. Smith's objection – that the executors remained as liable to pay the next of kin after the event as before it – was noted but not accepted.

Another explanation is based on the proprietary connection between the next of kin and the charities: the charities received money in which the next of kin held a proprietary interest. Against this Smith has pointed out that, unlike the beneficiaries under a trust, legatees have no proprietary interest in the estate but only a personal entitlement against the executors to have the estate administered according to the terms of the will.[73] However, it is not clear that the courts took that point. One indicator that they did not is that they upheld not only the personal claims of the next of kin but also their proprietary claims. It is not obvious that the next of kin could have rights *in rem* in the assets received by the legatees if they were not thought to have some proprietary right in the estate itself. It remains to be seen whether this puzzle can be solved. It may be that rightful legatees do after all have an inchoate but sufficient property in the estate itself, in that they can protect the integrity of the estate and control misdirections of the assets by injunction.

---

[71] *Ibid.* at 519 *per* Lord Hoffmann.
[72] [1951] AC 251 (HL). See 508, above.
[73] So held in *Commissioner for Stamp Duties v. Livingston* [1965] AC 694 (PC), discussed in Smith, 'Three-party Restitution'.

(b) Is this genuine leapfrogging?

Supposing that there is a sufficient proprietary connection, is the leapfrogging apparent or real? Even those who believe strongly in a requirement of privity or directness are content to accept the long reach of the proprietary argument.[74] Underlying this consensus is the fact that, like agency, this is not a genuine example of leapfrogging. A remote recipient of another's money is as direct a recipient from that other as the first recipient. Thus, if I find your wallet it makes no difference whether I am the first recipient or the second or the twenty-second. Suppose a pickpocket took it and, in alarm, threw it down, and then I found it. My position in that case would be the same as in the case in which your wallet fell from your pocket into the road without your noticing its loss. The mechanism does not matter: a receipt of your money is a receipt directly from you. Similarly, if I use your bicycle for a month, it does not matter whether you were or were not in possession immediately before me. My user is taken from you, because the bicycle is yours. The model from which their Lordships worked in *Lipkin Gorman v. Karpnale* cannot be used to support the proposition that true leapfrogging is permissible. The property argument looks as though it supports leapfrogging the first direct recipient but it actually only establishes what might be called sequential directness.

These conclusions can be confirmed from German law, where benefits acquired by the use or consumption of property belonging to another provide the central case for the *Eingriffskondiktion*, the claim in respect of enrichment obtained by encroachment on the rights of another. This claim is likewise indifferent to the number of hands between claimant and defendant. In one case cattle were stolen from their owner. They were later sold to the defendant. No exception to *nemo dat* operated. The cattle remained the property of the claimant until the buyer slaughtered and processed them, at which point, by *specificatio*, he became the owner of the resulting manufactured products. The owner was allowed to leapfrog the thief and recover their value from the innocent buyer. For the reasons just given, this was a factual leapfrog but in the eye of the law the buyer was immediately enriched from the owner, by his *Eingriff* upon the latter's

---

[74] Burrows, *Law of Restitution*, 48–9; Tettenborn, 'Lawful Receipt', 5; Virgo, *Principles*, 108, where, true to the structure produced by his analysis, he says this is vindication of property, not unjust enrichment, and therefore not a true exception to the privity rule which applies in the law of unjust enrichment.

property rights.[75] Again, on facts essentially identical to those of *Lipkin Gorman v. Karpnale*, the Federal Court held that a casino which had bona fide received money that had been misappropriated from the claimants was bound to make restitution to the claimants. In that case the facts were such that the casino did acquire title to the claimants' money but, because it could not be regarded as having given value for the money and therefore had to be regarded as having received gratuitously, it was bound to make restitution.[76]

3. The causation argument

The causation argument, if it works, does support genuine leapfrogging. There is genuine leapfrogging when the plaintiff can make out his case in unjust enrichment against a first recipient but wants to leap over that first recipient to attack a second or subsequent recipient. The causal argument cuts in at that point: but for the unjust enrichment of the first recipient, the second would not have received the thing. Andrew Tettenborn puts this case:

> C inadvertently overpays his creditor A by £1000; A, pleasantly surprised on reading his next bank statement but entirely unsuspicious, ... proceeds to give £1000 from his other account to his son B ... A can almost certainly plead change of position as a defence. Hence the potential significance of a direct claim by C against B; can C say (in effect): 'I have paid money by mistake; but for this B would not have been enriched; therefore B has been unjustifiably enriched at my expense and ought to refund.'[77]

Ought he to refund? His answer is no. In German law it is certainly yes, at least in this very case, which is provided for in the second sentence of § 816(1) BGB. It would be somewhat shocking if the answer were not yes in English law too and, with great respect to Professor Tettenborn, I think it is yes.

---

[75] BGHZ 55, 176; English translation in Markesinis *et al.*, *Law of Contracts*, 786. It is noteworthy that in holding the buyer liable in unjust enrichment for their value, the Federal Court declined to take into account his outlay in acquiring the cattle, which the Court said was recoverable by the buyer only from the thief. Cf. Dawson, 'Indirect Enrichment', 815: 'This is not usually thought to infringe the requirement of directness.'

[76] BGH 37, 363, 366. Here the contract between the dishonest gambler and the casino was illegal and void because the law debarred local residents from gambling in the casino. Contrast the otherwise identical BGHZ 47, 393, where the gambling contract was valid and the claim against the casino was defeated. For a full discussion of these cases, see Carsten Zülch, 'Bona fide Purchase, Property and Restitution: *Lipkin Gorman v. Karpnale* in German Law', in: Swadling, *Limits of Restitutionary Claims*, 106–40.

[77] Tettenborn, 'Lawful Receipt', 1–2.

The validity of the proposition that a second or subsequent recipient can be reached on the basis of the causal argument rests partly on the real state of things in *Lipkin Gorman v. Karpnale*, which differed from the model on which their Lordships relied. The House of Lords tried to bring the facts within the model of a proprietary connection between the firm and the casino. A proprietary connection satisfies and does not infringe the requirement of directness. However, the real situation in that case was quite different.

(a) **The true situation in** *Lipkin Gorman v. Karpnale*
The money which the gambling solicitor gave to the casino was his own, not the firm's. He was an authorised signatory to draw on the client account and it was expressly decided that the money which he drew out became his. The property had passed to him. The firm was indeed contemplated as having a power to revest it, and such a power may, as seen, suffice to create a proprietary connection. However, unless the title in the gambler was from the beginning voidable, which was not said but may have been assumed, it is difficult to explain how they acquired that power.

Traceability does not in itself confer rights.[78] Suppose I give you a gold coin which you sell for £500, with which you buy a painting. Through these substitutions I can trace the value of the gold coin into the painting. But if, at the moment you received the gold coin, I had no proprietary interest in it whatever, the successful tracing exercise will give me no rights in the painting. Let it be that I gave you the coin for your birthday. I can trace to satisfy my curiosity, but successful tracing will give me no rights. It would be utterly absurd to assert that the mere fact of substitution could create property rights in the substitute greater than and unrelated to property rights in the original. So here, to explain the firm's power to revest the money which traceably went into the coffers of the casino, it is necessary to know that it had a proprietary interest in the money at the moment at which the gambler received it. And that is not said.

It may therefore be that this case will ultimately be seen as explicable only on the basis that it is possible to reach a secondary recipient on a purely causal basis: the casino would not have received the money but for the enrichment by subtraction from the firm of the primary recipient, the gambling solicitor.

[78] L. D. Smith, *The Law of Tracing* (1997), 10-14, 299-300.

(b) Supporting case law

A reinterpretation of one major case would not suffice if the causal argument were not rooted in other decisions too. It has a good root, though somewhat overgrown with weeds. There is a group of cases, lucidly explained by Charles Mitchell,[79] in which mistaken payments have been recovered from subsequent recipients on proof that the enrichment did come through to them. Where these cases are difficult, it is usually not because the doctrine is itself suspect, but because of doubts as to whether the second recipient has indeed been enriched. The particular problem is generally the question whether money employed by the first recipient to discharge the obligations of the second recipient has indeed effected a legal discharge, for without that discharge it cannot be said that the money has been, in the Latin phrase, *in rem versum*, turned to his advantage. A more general difficulty has been the want of understanding of the law of unjust enrichment. As Mitchell shows, some cases have taken wrong turnings, for want of any map.

In *Bannatyne v. D. & C. MacIver* the London agents of the defendant firm borrowed money for them without authority. The plaintiff lenders mistakenly believed that they did have authority. The Court of Appeal upheld the claim against the firm to the extent that the money had been turned to their advantage. Romer LJ said:

> Where money is borrowed on behalf of a principal by an agent, the lender believing that the agent has authority, though it turns out that his act has not been authorised, or ratified, or adopted by the principal, then, although the principal cannot be sued at law, yet in equity, to the extent to which the money borrowed has in fact been applied in paying legal debts and obligations of the principal, the lender is entitled to stand in the same position as if the money had originally been borrowed by the principal.[80]

This is the same doctrine as underlies *B. Liggett (Liverpool) Ltd v. Barclays Bank Ltd*,[81] a decision of Wright J which was interpreted by the Court of Appeal in *Re Cleadon Trust Ltd*.[82] In that case a bank had laid out money believing that it had the authority of a company which was its customer, when in fact it had only the authority of one director of the company. It

---

[79] Charles Mitchell, *The Law of Subrogation* (1994), chap. 9, especially 124–9, 133–5. Cf. Whitty, 'Indirect Enrichment', 215, 251–2.

[80] [1906] 1 KB 103 (CA) at 109. In *Reid v. Rigby & Co.* [1894] 2 QB 40 recovery was allowed at law, the facts being materially identical.

[81] [1928] 1 KB 48.

[82] [1939] Ch 286 (CA), discussed by Mitchell, *Law of Subrogation*, 127–8, 162–5.

was allowed to debit the company's account. The explanation of the case, in the reinterpreted version later offered by the majority of the Court of Appeal, was that the money must be regarded as a mistaken advance to that one director applied by him to the discharge of the company's debts, which were indeed discharged because, though the director had no authority to draw on the company's account, yet he did have authority to discharge the company's debts.[83]

Butler v. Rice,[84] though in some respects confusing, is factually more straightforward. Butler, who had been misled by Mr Rice, mistakenly thought that Mr Rice owned a house subject to a charge and made a loan to him thinking he was lending to discharge that charge. Mr Rice had no such interest and in fact used the money to discharge a mortgage on property belonging to his wife. Mrs Rice, who had not known of her husband's doings, regarded herself as entitled to a windfall, leaving Butler to his remedy against her husband. But Warrington J held that Butler was entitled to be subrogated to the claim and security which had been paid off. In other words Mrs Rice, as second recipient, had to surrender the enrichment which she would not have received but for the unjust enrichment of the first recipient.

In *Agip (Africa) Ltd v. Jackson*[85] the plaintiff company's account with a bank in Tunisia was debited with large sums on the basis of forged payment warrants. The defendants were accountants who were ultimately made liable for the wrong of assisting the fraud. Another claim against the remote recipients as recipients rather than wrongdoers ultimately fell foul of a defence, but it was held in principle to lie. It is difficult to see why Agip was allowed to maintain this restitutionary claim.[86] The bank would appear to have lost its own money. However, if the bank is treated as having enriched itself without Agip's consent by insisting on debiting Agip's account, the rest follows: because of that enrichment of the first recipient, Agip was able to go after those who, but for that receipt, would not themselves have been enriched. Just possibly *Ministry of Health v. Simpson* (*Re Diplock* in the courts below)[87] might also be explained in this way.

---

[83] [1939] Ch 286 at 318 (Scott LJ) and 326 (Clauson LJ).   [84] [1910] 2 Ch 277.
[85] [1990] Ch 265, affirmed [1991] Ch 547 (CA).
[86] E. McKendrick, 'Tracing Misdirected Funds', [1991] *Lloyd's Maritime and Commercial Law Quarterly* 378-90 observes that no adequate explanation was given, the courts having accepted, somewhat mysteriously, that the bank being Agip's agent, Agip could avail itself of its mistake.
[87] [1948] Ch 465 (CA); [1951] AC 251 (HL).

(c) Restrictions

Bearing in mind the operation of defences, one should not jump to the conclusion that the causal argument needs to be heavily restricted. However, the largely illusory requirement of 'privity' inevitably encourages a suspicious or at best restrictive attitude to it. Tettenborn's example from which this discussion began turned on a situation in which the claimant's rights against the first recipient had been extinguished as a matter of law, for to the extent that the immediate enrichee had in turn enriched the remoter payee he himself had an indubitable defence of change of position. Identical in this respect is the case covered in the German Civil Code.[88] A requirement of extinction of the immediate enrichee's liability would be extreme. A milder requirement would be that remedies against the first recipient must have been exhausted. In *Agip (Africa) Ltd v. Jackson* it appears that Agip had tried and failed to get its bank to reinstate its account.[89]

It is impossible at the moment to say whether some such restrictive precondition will be insisted upon. A different and very severe precondition would be traceability. This can be ruled out, except in an evidential role. Successful tracing can certainly sometimes support the difficult factual finding that the remoter recipient would not have received but for the earlier receipt by the first recipient. The fact that the gambler traceably gave the casino the money which he obtained from the firm can be seen as helping to show that there was no other way that he could have indulged his habit.[90] However, traceability cannot be a necessary precondition of leapfrogging on the basis of the causation argument. Tettenborn's example is carefully constructed to exclude it. The father's gift to his son came from a separate account; the money that went to the son was definitely not traceably the money which the father mistakenly received.

(d) Where leapfrogging is not allowed, and why

It is necessary at the end to revisit the cases that were looked at earlier where C validly contracts with X to confer a benefit on D.[91] For example, C, a bank, contracts with its customer to lend the customer money and to send that money to D; or C, a garage, agrees with an insurance company to repair D's car at the insurance company's expense. In those cases C cannot leapfrog its contractual counterparty in order to bring a claim in

---

[88] Above, 518. [89] Above, n. 85.
[90] The invocation of tracing in *Baroness Wenlock v. River Dee Co.* (1887) 19 QBD 155 should be explained in the same way.
[91] Above, 502.

unjust enrichment against D. The valid contract between C and X makes the crucial difference.

It will be observed that in these cases C has a cause of action against the contractual counterparty X not only in contract but also in unjust enrichment. The reason why C wants to leapfrog X is precisely that he has suffered a repudiatory breach and a failure of consideration. It might at first be supposed that C must therefore be within the doctrine which allows him to show that the remote D would not have received but for the unjust enrichment of the immediate enrichee. The doctrine says that one who has a cause of action in unjust enrichment against the first recipient is, subject to unsettled restrictions as to exhaustion of remedies against that first recipient, entitled to proceed in unjust enrichment against such subsequent recipients as (a) would not have received but for the enrichment and (b) are not protected by the defences of bona fide purchase or change of position.

However, there is no question of allowing C to leapfrog his contractual counterparty. C, having dealt validly with X, has to take the risk of X's bad behaviour or insolvency. The point made earlier was that C cannot say that D is a direct or first recipient because in these cases it is not at C's immediate expense that D receives. C is the means chosen by X, and D receives immediately at the expense of X. At this point the concern is with the different question whether D can none the less be attacked as a subsequent recipient. He cannot. D is, remotely, enriched at C's expense, but he cannot on these facts be reached by C.

The policy reason still stands in the background: C must accept the risks of dealing with his chosen contractual counterparty. The insolvency regime would be subverted if C could find ways of leapfrogging an insolvent X. However, it might also be argued that C is anyhow not strictly within the causal doctrine which reaches remote recipients. That argument requires that the second or subsequent recipient would not have been enriched but for the unjust enrichment of the first recipient. In these cases that causal requirement might be said not to be satisfied. For here D, as second or remoter recipient, would have received anyway. The contract between C and X envisaged a benefit conferred on D. It is only by reason of a later breakdown in the relationship between C and X that D appears *ex post* in the guise of a subsequent recipient of an unjust enrichment. If this is right, there is no second avenue of attack. D is not a first recipient, and he is not a second recipient either. That is, he is not a person who would not have been enriched but for the unjust enrichment of the first recipient.

Peter Watts says that the best explanation of the denial of the leapfrogging claim against D in these cases is that, vis-à-vis D, C can point to no unjust factor. In performing the contract with X he voluntarily – neither mistakenly nor conditionally – confers the benefit on D.[92] Although that is true, it misses the point of the causation argument. The causation argument does not require the claimant to establish an unjust factor in relation to the remote recipient. It merely asserts that, subject to bona fide purchase and change of position, an unjust enrichment in the immediate recipient is an unjust enrichment in one who received through the immediate recipient and because of his receipt. That being the ground rule allowing recovery from the remote recipient, one needs a different kind of reason to explain why a claimant sometimes cannot rely on it. He cannot rely on it to leapfrog an initially valid contract. Why?

Putting aside the technical causal deficiency just noticed, Burrows comes nearer to the mark when he says that the law of unjust enrichment must not be allowed to undermine contracts.[93] That has to be filled out by repetition of the points on which German writers always insist, namely that nobody should be allowed to evade either defences arising in relation to a contract or the consequences of the insolvency of the chosen contractual counterparty.[94] It is for these reasons that there can be no leapfrogging over contractual counterparties. The remote recipient in such cases is enriched, and he is enriched at the expense of the claimant, but he is beyond reach.

V. Conclusion

This has been an exploration of the range of the law of unjust enrichment, as controlled by the phrase 'at the expense of the plaintiff'. In English law this means pushing out on almost unknown seas. A summary of the position is essentially this. In the law of unjust enrichment it cannot be used in the sense of 'by doing a wrong to'. It has to be used in the subtractive sense – the 'from' sense. 'From' might be understood narrowly or broadly. It looks as though English law is moving to a broad interpretation. That

---

[92] P. Watts, 'Does a Subcontractor have Restitutionary Rights against the Employer?', [1995] *Lloyd's Maritime and Commercial Law Quarterly* 398, 401.

[93] A. S. Burrows, 'Restitution from Assignees', [1994] *Restitution LR* 52, 55–6.

[94] Meier, 'Mistaken Payments', 571. The last paragraph of her article appears to suggest that leapfrogging in this situation might after all be possible, as though *Re Diplock* [1948] Ch 465 provided a springboard. Whatever else it might support, that case cannot dent the absolute bar against leapfrogging contractual counterparties.

means not insisting on a minus to the plaintiff and, broader still, accepting the possibility of interceptive subtraction freed from that restrictive requirement. Interceptive subtraction shorn of a requirement of loss and based on a logical extension of the attribution theory used in German law gives the law of unjust enrichment a range which the common law has not fully explored but to which it appears to have committed itself.

Finally, it is not true to say that the defendant's enrichment must be directly from the plaintiff, whether interceptively or otherwise. In different and more unsuitable language, it is not true that there is a strict requirement of privity between the parties. On the contrary, it is possible to reach over an immediate enrichee to others who would not have received if the immediate enrichee had not been unjustly enriched at the expense of the claimant. It cannot yet be said whether the courts will encourage leapfrogging claims, nor can it be foreseen what restrictions they will place on them if they do. But the foundations are in place, and the anxieties that inhibit the development are less substantial than has at times been thought.

The remoter recipients who are vulnerable are, however, rather few. They will not be bona fide purchasers or claimants through bona fide purchasers, and they will not have innocently disenriched themselves because of their receipt. Furthermore, one kind of leapfrogging which will never be allowed is the attempt to jump over a party to a valid contract with a view to attacking someone who received a benefit from the performance of that contract. The valid contract makes all the difference. One who makes a contract with another has to take the risk of that other's insolvency. Otherwise the statutory insolvency regime would be seriously eroded, and its impact would become open to the charge of needless arbitrariness.

19 Searches for silver bullets: enrichment in three-party situations

Daniel Visser

I. Introduction

The approach to 'indirect' or 'three-party' enrichment situations differs greatly from country to country. There is no clear fault-line between civilian and common-law systems, but generally speaking it seems to have emerged more patently as a problem in civilian systems. At the one end of the spectrum is Germany, where Peter Schlechtriem has called them the 'nightmare of the law of enrichment',[1] while Reinhard Zimmermann and Jacques du Plessis noted that they constitute 'an almost impenetrable jungle of dispute and uncertainty'.[2] At the other end is England, where Peter Birks's remark that it is hard even 'to discover the English equivalent to the "triangular relationship" and "indirect enrichment"', illustrates how utterly differently legal systems are able to view the same fact situations.[3] Between these extremities there are a number of legal systems where the problems associated with these situations are recognised, but where the solutions are far too simplistic or, at best, not fully developed. Among these we may count, aptly, the mixed jurisdictions of

---

[1] P. Schlechtriem, *Schuldrecht: Besonderer Teil* (1987), n. 685.
[2] R. Zimmermann and J. du Plessis, 'Basic Features of the German Law of Unjustified Enrichment', [1994] *Restitution LR* 14, 31.
[3] See his paper in the present volume. See generally in regard to third-party enrichment in English law, Kit Barker, 'Restitution and Third Parties', [1994] *Lloyd's Maritime and Commercial Law Quarterly* 305; R. J. Sutton, 'What Should be Done for Mistaken Improvers', in: P. D. Finn (ed.), *Essays on Restitution* (1990), 241; Lionel D. Smith, 'Three-party Restitution: A Critique of Birks's Theory of Interceptive Subtraction', (1991) 11 *Oxford JLS* 481 and Peter Watts, 'Does a Sub-contractor have Restitutionary Rights against the Employer?', [1995] *Lloyd's Maritime and Commercial Law Quarterly* 398.

South Africa[4] and Scotland[5] (but perhaps also France[6] and the various jurisdictions of the United States).[7] Why these situations should cause so much dogmatic distress in one system, while seeming to be of such little import in another, is not immediately obvious, but there are certain clues.

First, the general understanding of three-party situations has suffered, depending on which legal system one is concerned with, from either underanalysis or overanalysis. Germany, for instance, has examined these problems in great detail and has sought to lay down a clear rule for every conceivable instance of three-party enrichment. As is seen below, German law employs a specific dogmatic construction, namely the concept of *Leistung* or 'performance', as a 'silver bullet', which, when fired at appropriate triangular problems, is supposed to produce a clear answer. However, the problems in this area are so varied that this has not proved to be a fully realisable project. The result is an almost unbelievably complex set of rules, which, nevertheless, does not in the end produce for every situation an answer that can simply be 'read off' by placing the dogmatic grid over the facts in question.[8] One must pause here to state that there should be no doubt that the solutions that German law provides for these kinds of problems have been, and continue to be, refined to a degree that

---

[4] The classic studies in South Africa regarding three-party enrichment are by Honoré, Scholtens and de Vos. See A. M. Honoré, 'Third Party Enrichment', [1960] *Acta Juridica* 236; J. E. Scholtens, 'Enrichment at Whose Expense?', (1968) 85 *SALJ* 371–9; also his 'Unjustified Enrichment', (1968) *Annual Survey of South African Law* 150–2; Wouter de Vos, 'Enrichment at Whose Expense? A Reply', (1969) 86 *SALJ* 227–30; also his *Verrykingsaanspreeklikheid in die Suid-Afrikaanse Reg* (3rd edn, 1987), 339–53; also his 'Aspekte van Verrykingsaanspreeklikheid', [1970] *Acta Juridica* 231, 236–41; also his 'Retensieregte weens Verryking', (1970) 33 *Tydskrif vir Hedendaagse Romeins-Hollandse Reg* 357–68.

[5] See here the groundbreaking study of Niall R. Whitty, 'Indirect Enrichment in Scots Law', [1994] *JR* 200.

[6] See generally John Bell, Sophie Boyron and Simon Whittaker, *Principles of French Law* (1998) 410–11.

[7] See generally J. P. Dawson, 'Indirect Enrichment', in: Ernst von Caemmerer, Sonia Mentschikoff and Konrad Zweigert (eds.), *Ius Privatum Gentium: Festschrift für Max Rheinstein* (1969), vol. II, 789.

[8] See the trenchant criticism of Berthold Kupisch, 'Rechtspositivismus im Bereicherungsrecht', 1997 *JZ* 213, 214 (in which his earlier work in this regard is also referred to) and, most recently, his essay 'Der Gedanke "als ob": Zur wirtschaftlichen Betrachtungsweise bei der Anweisung, romanistisch und zivilistisch', in: Reinhard Zimmermann, Rolf Knütel and Jens Peter Meincke (eds.), *Rechtsgeschichte und Privatrechtsdogmatik* (2000), 431 ff.

no other legal system can remotely match. The disappointment is only that after so much effort it does not provide all the answers, while at the same time being so complex that no other legal system is likely to have the stomach to duplicate it.[9] And let there be no doubt either about the extremely involved nature of the German approach. When German professors argue heatedly in the pages of the prestigious *Neue Juristische Wochenschrift* about a rumour (albeit probably a spurious one) that certain examining authorities have considered three-party enrichment problems as being too complicated to be included in the State Law Examinations,[10] this much must be true: the situation cannot possibly be altogether simple. In England, on the other hand, the project to give shape to the law of unjust enrichment in the wake of *Lipkin Gorman (a Firm) v. Karpnale Ltd*[11] has not, for obvious reasons, been able to attend to all the details of systematisation and the problems associated with three-party situations have been given only slight attention.

Secondly, the degree to which three-party enrichment is seen as a single problem in a particular legal system may exacerbate the difficulties experienced by that system. Thus one suspects that the very fact that German law so specifically identifies three-party situations as a generic problem has contributed much to the law having to be stated in such a complex way. Perhaps an analogy is best suited to make this thought clear: throughout the law, whenever more than two parties are involved, all kinds of problems arise that inevitably make it more difficult to find solutions than would have been the case if only two persons were in the picture. But if we were, for example, to lump together in criminal law the problems of accessories after the fact, accomplices as well as other instances of multiple causation and then seek a solution, the situation will appear to be infinitely more complicated than if they were addressed separately.

---

[9] Although the orthodox position is hardly questioned in Germany and those who do venture to oppose it are studiously ignored, the criticism of the small band of commentators who have challenged the 'herrschende Meinung' is cogent and one cannot but imagine that the day will come when the limitations of the current doctrine are more generally questioned. Among the foremost critics are Berthold Kupisch, *Gesetzespositivismus im Bereicherungsrecht* (1978), 11 ff. (see also his 'Rechtspositivismus') and Manfred Lieb, in: *Münchener Kommentar zum Bürgerlichen Gesetzbuch* (2nd edn, 1986), vol. III, § 812, n. 25.

[10] See Horst Heinrich Jakobs, 'Die Rückkehr der Praxis zur Regelanwendung und der Beruf der Theorie im Recht der Leistungskondiktionen', 1992 NJW 2524 and, in response, Michael Martinek, 'Die venanlasste Drittleistung oder "Haare in der Suppe"', 1992 NJW 3134 and Claus-Wilhelm Canaris, 'Überforderte Professoren?!', 1992 NJW 3134.

[11] [1991] 2 AC 548 (HL).

The emphasis on the fact that it is a multi-party situation creates, to a certain extent, a false problem. Therefore, since English law has not positively conceptualised 'three-party enrichment' as a generic problem, its difficulties are fewer because it has avoided the extra layer of complexity produced by the use of a too widely conceived *genus*. But this problem is a bit like the fruit of the tree which was in the midst of the Garden. Once one tastes it the truth is revealed and the inevitable result is banishment from Eden. Since English law has begun to nibble, it cannot but realise that there are common fact patterns in three-party situations that are an important aid to finding a proper solution in this kind of situation. And so there will be no turning back.

Whatever the reasons why different systems approach the question of three-party enrichment in such different ways, one common tendency is discernible in every country: the basic principles of enrichment liability are neglected in the search for answers. Solutions have often tended towards a 'single-solution' model. Thus Germany's current approach to three-party enrichment is not its first attempt at finding a simple, straightforward answer to this kind of problem. Earlier the dogma had been that a 'direct transfer' between the enriched and the impoverished in three-party situations was necessary to found an enrichment claim. But this formula, like the modern approach based on the principle of performance, could not 'furnish an unambiguous answer as to who would be liable to return the enrichment in a three-party situation'.[12] South Africa, too, attempted to formulate a single answer to three-party enrichment situations by latching on to the German notion of 'direct' enrichment,[13] and it is only recently that this approach has been begun to be seriously questioned.[14] I shall argue that if legal systems generally are to progress to a proper understanding of three-party enrichment, there needs to be a reversal of the trend not to examine separately the individual elements of enrichment liability in each case. For in the principled application of these elements lies, I believe, the key to solving (though rarely without hard thinking) the many problems that arise in this context.[15] In my attempt to demonstrate that this is so I shall use a number of examples, but because the focus of this contribution is on the *process* of solving this kind of problem rather than on the actual solutions, I will make no attempt to deal exhaustively

---

[12] See generally Zimmermann and Du Plessis, 'Basic Features', 31.
[13] *Gouws v. Jester Pools (Pty) Ltd* 1968 (3) SA 563 (T).
[14] *ABSA Bank t/a Bankfin v. C. B. Stander t/a C. A. W. Paneelkloppers* 1998 (1) SA 939 (C); *Buzzard Electrical (Pty) Ltd v. 158 Jan Smuts Investments (Pty) Ltd* 1996 (4) SA 19 (A).
[15] This is, I believe, also the essence of the approach of Smith, 'Three-party Restitution'.

with all the different factual situations that may qualify to be included under the rubric of three-party enrichment. Nevertheless, it is my view that the approach that I advocate is of general validity for all three-party situations.

II. A possible approach to the analysis of three-party enrichment situations

1. The relevant policy considerations

A considered application of the general principles of enrichment liability involves three separate but interlocking steps:

In any three-party enrichment situation, the first step is to identify the decisive element of enrichment liability around which that particular factual constellation is likely to turn, be it (a) whether the defendant has been enriched (and, in many systems – outside enrichment for wrongs – whether the plaintiff has been impoverished), (b) whether the enrichment is unjust(ified),[16] or (c) whether it is at the expense of the plaintiff. (The modern German approach purports to do away with the necessity of establishing separately at least the last two elements in cases of enrichment brought about by a performance.[17] However, as is shown below, the formula intended to make this possible does not produce clear answers in a number of difficult situations.) Any of these elements may feature as the crucial element and, on occasion, the determination of different elements might shade into one another. The question whether, for example, a particular enrichment is unjustified can sometimes not easily be distinguished from the question whether that enrichment was at the expense of the claimant – much as the duty issue and the remoteness issue sometimes tend to run into one another in the law of tort. It is important, too, to understand the entire compass of each element. For instance, it must be kept in mind that the 'at the expense of' requirement embodies not only the question of factual causation but also that of legal causation.

[16] In this contribution I shall use the term 'unjust' when referring to common-law systems and the term 'unjustified' when referring to civilian systems or mixed systems in which the law of enrichment has a predominantly civilian character. To use the term 'unjust' in civilian systems (in this context) is considered to be imprecise in that it might be taken to denote a general notion of fairness or justice, whereas 'unjustified' is a term of art. However, in the common law 'unjust' in the context of enrichment law is as much a technical term as its equivalent in civilian systems and it seems artificial to impose the civilian usage when discussing the common law.

[17] See the (critical) explanation of Kupisch, 'Rechtspositivismus', 220.

Once it has been established which element or elements are likely to be determinative of the outcome of the case, the second step must be taken, namely to identify the relevant policy factors that are likely to influence the parameters of that element or elements.[18] Some of the policy factors that most often arise in the context of three-party enrichment are the following:

(i) The exact nature of the contractual or other legal relationship between the parties involved. In some legal systems (such as, for example, that of Germany), this factor plays an overt and structured role, while in others (for example, that of South Africa) it appears as a factor in certain cases, but is not taken into account as a matter of course – at least not consciously. For Scots law Niall Whitty,[19] basing his argument on Barry Nicholas,[20] has made a fourfold division of three-party enrichment situations on the basis of the legal relationship between the parties and has made a good case for this to form the bedrock of the solution of these kinds of problems.[21] (In certain legal systems – and here South African law is a good example – the legal relationship between the parties can operate in specific situations as more than a mere policy factor and can underlie inflexible rules in the determination of three-party situations.)

---

[18] See generally D. P. Visser, 'The Role of Judicial Policy in Setting the Limits of a General Enrichment Action', in: Ellison Kahn (ed.), *The Quest for Justice: Essays in Honour of Michael McGregor Corbett, Chief Justice of the Supreme Court of South Africa* (1995), 342. I accept Bell's definition of policy arguments as being '[s]ubstantive justifications to which judges appeal when the standards and rules of the legal system do not provide a clear resolution of the dispute' (John Bell, *Policy Arguments in Judicial Decisions* (1983), 22–3). It is also accepted by Cora Hoexter, 'Judicial Policy in South Africa', (1986) 103 *SALJ* 436 and Annél van Aswegen, 'Policy Considerations in the Law of Delict', (1993) 56 *Tydskrif vir Hedendaagse Romeins-Hollandse Reg* 171. Van Aswegen's version of Bell's definition is as follows (at 174): 'Policy considerations are substantive reasons for judgments reflecting values accepted by society. They consist in moral or ethical values, valuable in themselves, or in desirable goals of collective societal welfare, but there is no reason why these two types of consideration should not overlap. A decision determined by such considerations – a policy decision – comprises a balancing of the various values, and thus a value judgment by the decision-maker.' The specific policy factors enunciated by judges often rest on even deeper values that are not directly articulated, such as the general socio-economic ethos of the society in question. See generally Hanoch Dagan, *Unjust Enrichment: A Study of Private Law and Public Values* (1997), 1 ff.

[19] Whitty, 'Indirect Enrichment', 208.

[20] 'Unjustified Enrichment in the Civil Law and Louisiana Law', (1962) 36 *Tulane LR* 605, 632–3.

[21] The division is as follows: (a) a valid juridical act between the pursuer (i.e. the claimant (C)) and the third party (T), and between T and the defendant (D); (b) a valid juridical act between C to T, but not between T and D; (c) no valid juridical act between C and T, but a valid juridical act between T and D; and (d) a valid juridical act neither between C and T, nor between T and D.

(ii) Flowing from this basic consideration are a number of related policy factors, namely:
   (a) that a contracting party should normally bear the business risks of entering into a contract;
   (b) that a party should not run the risk of having to pay a debt twice;
   (c) that a party should not be in a position to claim twice for the same debt;
   (d) that a party to a contract should not be unjustifiably deprived of the right to rely on his or her contractual defences against their contracting partner; and
   (e) that the security of receipts should generally be encouraged.
(iii) A further major policy factor is whether or not – and if so to what degree – an enrichment claim should be treated as being subsidiary to any possible contractual claim that may exist in the circumstances. Both Italian law and French law adhere to some degree to the principle of subsidiarity.[22] The principle that an enrichment action is not available where the impoverished person is able to bring another action to make good his or her loss is quite strictly applied in Italian law, but in French law a more flexible approach is adopted, whereas German law has retreated from its original favourable attitude towards the subsidiarity principle.[23]

From this basic consideration flow, once again, a number of further policy factors, namely:
   (a) whether the claimant has availed him- or herself of any possible alternative remedies, and, in conjunction therewith,
   (b) the reasons why the claimant's contractual claim against the third party is not enforceable or not worth enforcing.
(iv) In addition there are also general policy factors relating to this situation such as:
   (a) that the principle of equality of the creditors (*paritas creditorum*) should be preserved and
   (b) the economic consequences of respectively allowing or disallowing a claim.

Policy considerations are openly invoked in many jurisdictions when this type of issue arises, but more often than not they are mentioned as being relevant to the problem without any explanation as to how they play

---

[22] Barry Nicholas, 'Unjust Enrichment and Subsidiarity', in: S. Passarelli and M. Lupoi (eds.), *Scintillae Iuris: Studi in Memoria di Gino Gorla* (1994), vol. III, 2037–45 and also his 'Modern Developments in the French Law of Unjustified Enrichment', in: Paul W. L. Russell (ed.), *Unjustified Enrichment: A Comparative Study of the Law of Restitution* (1996), 77, 87 ff.

[23] See Zimmermann and Du Plessis, 'Basic Features', 36–8.

out in the specific circumstances of the facts at hand. It is important that this kind of problem should not be solved by merely reciting all the policy factors that could possibly prevent an indirect enrichment claim and then declaring any such claim to be untenable on the basis of these platitudes. Rather, the specific factors that could be relevant in the circumstances should be identified as precisely as possible.

Thereafter the third step is to determine how each of these factors influence the existence of the specific element or elements relevant in the factual situation. Of course, policy can be invoked at varying levels of generality: it is possible for a legal system to decide that if a certain combination of policy factors arises, the enrichment in question will be regarded as unjustified or not (as the case may be) without specific inquiry into the actual influence of those factors in the specific circumstances of the case. The argument upon which a legal system could justify adopting this approach might be, for instance, that it is not an efficient use of resources to inquire more closely in such instances because of the very small likelihood that a detailed examination of the influence of the individual factors would produce any other result. This kind of policy decision is the equivalent of general policy decisions in other areas of the law such as whether harm caused by nervous shock or pure economic loss should be actionable. If the answer indicated by the relevant policy factors is 'no', the matter rests there and it need not be reviewed each time a case of that nature comes before the court. If the answer is 'yes', the next level of policy decision comes to the fore. The facts of the case at hand must be analysed to determine whether other policy considerations that are more specifically relevant in the circumstances point towards or away from liability by confirming or denying the existence of one of the core elements.

The next section turns to an illustration of how this approach could work in practice, but first a disclaimer: the approach is not put forward in order to argue that this is the only possible way of dealing with these problems, nor that it provides all the answers to the many difficult problems that arise in this context; rather, it is offered as an approach which can, on the one hand, provide systems in which there is a highly sophisticated set of rules to deal with three-party enrichment problems with a perspective that reminds them of the principles and policies that underlie those rules; and, on the other, provide systems that have not yet developed an extensive jurisprudence around this issue with a tool to begin to work towards a fuller analysis of this kind of problem.

2. Cases where enrichment (or its corollary, impoverishment) is the determining element

(a) The South African case law

Mistaken payments made by banks after the countermand of an instruction by their clients provides a convenient vehicle to illustrate how a three-party situation may turn on the question whether or not the claimant has actually been enriched (or the defendant impoverished in systems where that is a relevant consideration). Take for example the South African case of *Govender v. The Standard Bank of South Africa Ltd.*[24] This case primarily involved the questions whether the defendant had been enriched and the plaintiff impoverished.

A certain Saaiman had hired a bus from Govender. He then drew a cheque for the agreed amount on the Standard Bank, with which he had an account, and handed it to Govender. Subsequently, however, Saaiman gave written notice countermanding the payment of the cheque.[25] The notice was given on the standard form supplied by the bank, which contained the proviso that the countermanding order is given 'on the understanding that I have no claim against the bank in the event of such document being inadvertently paid by the bank', which is exactly what happened in this instance. When Saaiman queried the payment of the cheque the bank reversed the debit on his account and later sued Govender in an action based on unjustified enrichment.

After a magistrates' court had upheld the bank's claim it was dismissed on appeal to the Provincial Division. The court decided that the defendant's own performance (or his readiness to perform) should be taken into account – evidently as constituting a detrimental side-effect[26] – in determining the defendant's enrichment.[27] It was held that the performance was equivalent to the value placed thereon by the contract (i.e. the contract price) and that the defendant therefore cannot be held to have been enriched 'since the payment prima facie is balanced out by his performance'.[28] The court further held that the plaintiff-bank was in any

---

[24] 1984 (4) SA 392 (C).

[25] This he did because he had been informed by one of the passengers that cheaper transport had been arranged and that the contract with Govender had been cancelled. In fact it had not been cancelled and Govender's bus was available on the agreed date to transport the passengers.

[26] See J. C. Stassen, 'Countermanded Cheques and Enrichment – Some Clarity, Some Confusion', [1985] *Modern Business Law* 15, 17.

[27] 1984 (4) SA 392 (C) at 406 E-G.

[28] *Ibid.* See in regard thereto (critically) Stassen, 'Countermanded Cheques', 17, who agrees that the plaintiff was not enriched, but prefers to formulate the reason for

event not impoverished, as a result of the indemnity signed by its client, in terms of which it was empowered to debit the client's account in spite of having ignored the countermand. This aspect of the judgment is, in my view, the essential reason why the outcome of the case is correct.

First National Bank v. B. & H. Engineering[29] took the debate a step further. The facts of *B. & H. Engineering* (which was brought before the court *a quo* in the form of a stated case) were as follows. A cheque for R16,048 was drawn on First National Bank by its client, Sapco, in favour of the defendant. When drawing the cheque Sapco's intention was to pay for certain goods manufactured for it by B. & H. Engineering, but subsequently it countermanded payment of the cheque by written notice. However, it did so without signing an indemnity in favour of the bank in case the latter should fail to carry out the order to stop payment. The bank mistakenly paid out to the defendant's collecting banker. Thereupon the plaintiff bank instituted an enrichment action against the recipient, B. & H. Engineering, and the court of first instance allowed the action. The crucial difference between the facts of this case and those of *Govender* was that in this case the drawer had not signed an indemnity and the bank was therefore indeed impoverished by its payment of the cheque. If the court had been content to follow the decision in *Govender*, it would have found that the payment had, in spite of the countermand, extinguished the debt of Sapco towards B. & H. Engineering.

This, however, the court was not prepared to do. It held as follows, with reference to the writings of D. V. Cowen[30] and June Sinclair.[31] First, the payment of a cheque which has not been countermanded will extinguish a debt of the drawer to the payee, not because the bank pays as agent of the drawer (for, unlike the situation in England, it does not), but because when paying a debt by cheque there is an agreement between the drawer and the payee stipulating conditional payment, the condition being that the bank will obey its mandate. When the bank pays a duly drawn

---

this state of affairs as being that 'the bank simultaneously brings the amount of the cheque into the payee's estate and removes his contractual claim for the same amount against the drawer from his estate, leaving the net position the same'. The need to establish that the recipient was in fact enriched when a drawee reclaims a payment made on a cheque or bill of exchange from such recipient is emphasised by J. C. Stassen and A. N. Oelofse, 'Terugvordering van foutiewe wisselbetalings: Geen verrykingsaanspreeklikheid sonder verryking nie', [1983] *Modern Business Law* 137.

[29] 1993 (2) SA 41 (T).
[30] D. V. Cowen, 'A Bank's Rights to Recover Payments made by Mistake: *Price v. Neal* Revisited', (1983) 16 *Comparative and International Law Journal of Southern Africa* 1, 23-4.
[31] J. Sinclair, 'Unjustified Enrichment', in: *Annual Survey of South African Law* (1984), 385.

cheque this condition is satisfied and the debt discharged. Secondly, however, should the mandate to pay cease to exist by virtue of a countermand, as was the case here (or where it never existed at all, such as where the instrument had been forged), the condition can obviously no longer be fulfilled because there is no mandate to obey. A prerequisite for a valid payment of a debt is that there has to be a valid debt-extinguishing agreement, which presupposes a continuing intention to pay on the part of the drawer and a continuing intention to receive payment on the part of the payee. Since the countermand removed the intention to pay, this prerequisite for a valid payment was no longer present. The recipient (defendant) was therefore enriched by the payment – he received the amount of the debt, but because the payment did not extinguish the debt he was (unjustly) enriched thereby. In coming to this decision the court followed the English case of *Barclays Bank Ltd v. W. J. Simms, Son and Cooke (Southern) Ltd*.[32]

On appeal the Appellate Division[33] disagreed with this approach and ruled that a debt owed by the drawer is indeed discharged in these circumstances – that is to say, the defendant is not enriched by the receipt.[34] Although the Appellate Division confirmed that a debt-extinguishing agreement is a condition for a valid payment of a debt, it differed from the court of first instance on a crucial point. A debt-extinguishing agreement, it said, is normally to the effect that even an unauthorised payment by the bank would discharge the debt and therefore does not assume a continuing intention to pay on the part of the payer. Thus any attempt by the payer to stop the payment is irrelevant as far as the extinguishing of the debt is concerned.

The policy behind this thinking may be summarised in the following way. First, since a cheque itself is discharged when a bank pays that cheque – even if the payment is unauthorised – the approach of the court *a quo* would mean that the payee would not only have to return the

[32] [1980] QB 677. The facts of the case were that C drew a cheque on bank T and sent it to its contractual partner, the defendant D (a building company), as a progress payment after receiving the customary architect's certificate that the requisite stage of building had been reached. Almost immediately thereafter D went into liquidation and C stopped payment of the cheque, as it was entitled to do in terms of its contract. The bank overlooked the stop-order and paid the cheque when it was presented by the liquidator of D who had no knowledge of the stop-order. The bank claimed the amount of the payment from D and the court allowed the claim.

[33] The former Appellate Division of the Supreme Court of South Africa is now known as the Supreme Court of Appeal. In this contribution I refer to it as it was known at the time of the decision under discussion.

[34] *B. & H. Engineering v. First National Bank of South Africa Ltd* 1995 (2) SA 279 (A).

amount of the cheque, but at the same time he or she would no longer have the advantage of a liquid document, with its procedural and other advantages; and the fact of obtaining a liquid document after all ameliorates the risk of non-payment that a creditor runs when accepting payment by cheque. Good commercial practice demands, therefore, that a continuing authorisation should not be held to be part of an ordinary debt-extinguishing agreement. Secondly, commercial convenience further demands that the payee not be drawn into the question as to whether the cheque had been properly countermanded.

But there is, of course, another side to the coin. First, there is a price to pay in terms of the clarity of the general principles of South African law regarding a valid payment. It is not at all certain that the Appellate Division is correct when it says that the content of the debt-extinguishing agreement is normally to the effect that the original intention to pay is irrevocable, as an application of the 'interested bystander' test to the facts of this case demonstrates. Secondly, the Appellate Division might have overstated the commercial convenience of its own approach. The court acknowledges that the payee is exposed to the risk that, if payment is countermanded, the bank is not under a duty to pay and will normally not do so. It now seeks to protect the drawee from an additional risk, namely that the amount of the cheque may be claimed back if it had been mistakenly paid by the bank after a countermand and, consequently, to have to enforce the debt owing to him or her by a more cumbersome procedure than would have been the case if the countermand had been observed by the bank. But this argument can also be turned around. What if, for instance, the drawer had a valid counterclaim which could be set off against the debt of the payee? Does commercial convenience not demand that the bank should be able to correct its mistake and restore the situation to what it would have been if the error had not occurred? This approach would allow the parties to readjust their respective positions in the same way that they would have done if the bank had not erred, with the only exception that the payee cannot sue on the cheque, but has to rely on the original agreement. The Appellate Division's approach, on the other hand, leads to a situation where the drawer not only loses the advantage of any bargaining that he or she might have wanted to do, but the bank is placed in the position of having to proceed against its own client after having inconvenienced him or her by ignoring the countermand.

Be that as it may, the Appellate Division decided that the debt was extinguished and therefore that the defendant was not enriched by the receipt. This corresponds with the view of the Uniform Commercial Code in the

United States.[35] However, whether one is inclined towards the Uniform Commercial Code approach or whether one supports the view of the *Barclays Bank v. Simms* case (as adopted by the Court *a quo* in the *B. & H. Engineering* case), the most important problem which has to be solved here is whether the defendant *is considered to be enriched* by the receipt of the payment. Indeed Andrew Kull, writing about the situation in the United States, argues forcefully that an important difficulty in cases such as these is that the courts do not pay sufficient attention to the question whether the element of enrichment has been established. Thus he opines that the *Barclays Bank v. Simms* case stated its rule too widely and that its effect could be to impose liability on a defendant who was not enriched in the circumstances,[36] while in other cases, such as the New York case of *Banque Worms v. BankAmerica International*,[37] which involved a mistaken wire transfer that had been countermanded, inattention to the element of enrichment led to the defendants not being held liable even though they were in fact enriched.[38]

---

[35] Uniform Commercial Code, § 3-418 (1990).

[36] A. Kull, 'Rationalizing Restitution', (1995) 83 *California LR* 1191, 1229: 'On the facts of the case, it appears entirely possible that *Simms* imposed liability in restitution on a defendant who was not unjustly enriched by the plaintiff's mistake. [See note 32 above for the facts of *Simms*.] Because the check represented a progress payment based on an architect's certificate, it is reasonable to assume that the amount of the check had been earned and was owed to the payee under the building contract. Assuming that the owner's attempt to stop payment was contractually justified, in that the owner had a right to suspend payments pending an accounting and a set-off of costs incurred by reason of the builder's receivership, the owner's liability to pay the builder was not otherwise discharged (except to the extent that such costs might in fact be incurred). Under such circumstances, it is most unlikely that the builder would be unjustly enriched – by comparison with its contractual entitlement – if the owner made one more scheduled payment before asserting its rights of set-off.'

[37] 570 NE 2d 189 (1991).

[38] Kull, 'Rationalizing Restitution', 1237 ff. The facts of *Banque Worms* were as follows: Spedley Securities ('Spedley'), in response to a demand from Banque Worms, instructed Security Pacific International Bank ('Security Pacific') by telex to make a wire transfer of almost $2 million to Banque Worms, a bank in France with which it had a revolving credit facility. A few hours later, however, Spedley countermanded the instruction by means of a second telex, but Security Pacific mistakenly disregarded the countermand. Banque Worms used the funds thus received to expunge the debt owed to it by Spedley. Within a short time Spedley went into liquidation and Security Pacific instituted a restitution claim against Banque Worms to recover the amount of the mistaken transfer. The claim was not successful, the New York Court of Appeals upholding Banque Worms's plea of 'discharge for value', which it justified, among other reasons, with the 'policy goal of finality in business transactions' (570 NE 2d 189 (1991) at 296 and see Kull, 'Rationalizing Restitution', 1238). Kull (at 1239) does not, however, agree with this outcome and explains his

(b) The German approach

In German law, too, the question whether the defendant has actually been enriched looms large. In order to set out the position in German law it is necessary to outline briefly the basic tenets of that country's approach to enrichment in this kind of situation. In German enrichment law the principal division is between the *Leistungskondiktion* (the action based on a performance) and the *Nichtleistungskondiktionen* (actions not based on a performance of any kind).[39] The key element of the *Leistungskondiktion* is the *Leistungsprinzip* (the principle of performance) and it is said to encompass within itself the determination of the element of unjustifiedness as well as the causal question.[40] Subsuming these elements under the concept of 'performance' was the product of historical development:[41] The older theory had defined a performance simply as the 'conscious increase of another's patrimony'; the newer theory defines performance as the 'conscious and *purpose-oriented* increase in another's patrimony',[42] while the *Leistungskondiktion* is defined as being designed to a reverse a performance, the purpose of which has not been achieved. Thus, whenever a performance does not achieve its (objectively established) purpose, the *Leistungskondiktion* will be available. In other words, the concept of performance was developed to indicate – automatically, so to speak – in both bilateral and three-cornered situations, between which persons there are legally relevant performances that have to be reversed.[43]

---

view thus: 'The bank that has applied a mistaken payment in satisfaction of a third party's pre-existing obligation points to its release of the debt as *offsetting* value: the bank denies, in other words, that it has been enriched by the transaction when viewed as a whole. The force of this contention – as in the case of restitution between successive fraud victims – depends on what we identify as the baseline for measuring enrichment and the balance of justice between the parties.' In Kull's view the mistaken payment by Security Pacific should not have been seen as discharging the debt of Spedley but should rather have been held to have 'caused the unjust enrichment of Banque Worms to the same extent as if $2 million had been directly but involuntarily contributed the assets of the recipient bank'. His contention is that if one allows a payment such as this to discharge the debt, one is in effect allowing 'one bank's clerical error . . . [to lead to it having] to bear another bank's credit loss' (at 1240). After all, he points out, Banque Worms voluntarily assumed the credit risk of Spedley, while Banque Worms had not agreed to extend credit at any stage (at 1239).

[39] This is part of the famous 'Wilburg/von Caemmerer' typology, which forms the basis of the modern law of enrichment in Germany. See Dieter Reuter and Michael Martinek, *Ungerechtfertigte Bereicherung* (1983), 32 ff.; Dieter Medicus, *Bürgerliches Recht* (17th edn, 1996), n. 664.
[40] See generally in this regard Zimmermann and Du Plessis, 'Basic Features', 24 ff.
[41] Ulrich Loewenheim, *Bereicherungsrecht* (2nd edn, 1997), 24.
[42] BGHZ 58, 184, 188.   [43] See Kupisch, 'Rechtspositivismus', 214.

In the case of countermanded cheques the theory runs as follows. The relationship between the bank (T) and its client (C) is known as the *Deckungsverhältnis* (cover relationship) and that between the client and his or her contractual partner (D) as the *Valutaverhältnis* (the 'underlying debt relationship').[44] Where C instructs T to pay D (an example of a so-called *Anweisungsfall*, that is to say an instance of an order to pay a third party), there is a three-cornered situation:[45] the payment by T (bank) to D (payee) as directed by C (client) is seen (in the case of a valid order) as constituting two performances. C performs *vis-à-vis* D, and T performs his obligation as banker *vis-à-vis* his client, C.[46] If it turns out, however, that the underlying debt relationship did not exist (that is, C did not owe D anything) the resultant position is obviously in need of adjustment. In terms of orthodox theory one would not expect a direct claim by T against D (referred to as a *Durchgriffskondiktion* – 'a claim that reaches through') to be available. T did not make a performance *vis-à-vis* D (because his intention was to perform to his client, C) and thus the *Leistungskondiktion* against D is not available to him. Generally speaking, T should also not have any other action against D. This is because German law decrees that where a performance has been identified between two parties, but the *Leistungskondiktion* is for any reason not available against the person to whom the performance has been made, the actions which do not rely on a performance[47] are not available in a subsidiary way against a third party.[48] However, in the case of a countermanded payment by a bank, a *Durchgriffskondiktion* is recognised. If D, the recipient, *knew* of the countermand, the position is that the payment (both from C and D's perspectives) cannot constitute a performance of C to D; that means that C is not freed of his obligation towards D, and C is thus not enriched by the bank's payment. Thus the bank (T) cannot sue

---

[44] The English equivalents of the German terms were taken from Zimmermann and Du Plessis, 'Basic Features', 33.
[45] Which in German law is to be distinguished from a situation where T is merely a 'conduit pipe'. In the case of a bank paying a third party on the instruction of its client, it is transferring money of which it is owner and is therefore more than a conduit. On the exact technical meaning of *Anweisung* in German law, see *ibid.*, 33, n. 150.
[46] This situation needs to be distinguished from the so-called performance-chain (*Leistungskette*) cases, i.e. where C transfers money or other property to T, who in turn transfers it to D. In such a case the one transfer follows the other, whereas in the instance of a bank paying on the instruction of its client, there is one transfer with more than one legal effect. See generally *ibid.*, 32–3.
[47] *Bereicherung in sonstiger Weise* ('enrichment in another way') as provided for in § 812(1), first sentence, BGB.
[48] See B. S. Markesinis, W. Lorenz and G. Dannemann, *The German Law of Obligations*, vol. I, *The Law of Contracts and Restitution: A Comparative Introduction* (1997), 732.

the client (C), but is nevertheless allowed to sue the payee (D), even though this goes against the general 'non-subsidiarity' rule outlined above.[49] If D *did not know* of the countermand, however, then the payment appears to D as a performance by C and he is protected in his reliance. The bank cannot now sue D, but it is permitted to look to its client C in this case, who has been freed of his obligation and is thus enriched.[50]

The decision to protect D is a policy matter and thus it is clear that all these rules are not generated merely by using the principle of performance and therefore that that principle is not in itself sufficient to establish whether a claim exists or not.[51] Nevertheless, the principle of performance does focus the inquiry in a very useful way. The fact that the purpose with which a performance was made has failed is clearly an important indication that there might be a situation which the law of enrichment will be required to correct. Therefore, even though it does not produce the instant solution for three-party situations that it was once thought to do, the concept of a performance does provide a useful tool with which to attempt the solution of this kind of problem. In a very apt simile, Basil Markesinis, Werner Lorenz and Gerhard Dannemann liken the *Leistungsprinzip* to a compass and the relevant policy considerations to a map and observe that 'compass and map are usually complementary rather than irreconcilable methods for finding the path'.[52]

In all the jurisdictions considered above, the decisions in cases of three-party enrichment involving payments by banks in spite of a countermand can be said to revolve around the element of enrichment. That does not mean that the other elements cannot ever be determinative in this kind of situation. It merely indicates that this type of factual situation *primarily*

---

[49] In this regard Zimmermann and Du Plessis, 'Basic Features', 35 remark as follows: 'Uncertainty surrounds this type of enrichment claim ... It is obviously not the *Leistungskondiktion* (the bank did not pursue any specific purpose in terms of the *Leistungsbegriff* as far as [the payee] is concerned, but rather wanted to comply with what it assumed to be the instructions of its client) ... It would therefore seem that we are dealing with an enrichment "in any other way".'

[50] BGHZ 89, 376. (For a discussion and a translation (by Gerhard Dannemann) of this case, see Markesinis, Lorenz and Dannemann, *Law of Contracts*, 734–5 and 794–8.) As to the basis of the enrichment in this instance, see the (critical) appraisal of Kupisch, 'Rechtspositivismus', 214–15.

[51] That policy considerations play an important role in determining whether or not the retention of the enrichment by the claimant should be regarded as unjust appears from Claus-Wilhelm Canaris, 'Der Bereicherungsausgleich im Dreipersonenverhältnis', in: Gotthard Paulus, Uwe Diederichsen and Claus-Wilhelm Canaris (eds.), *Festschrift für Karl Larenz* (1973), 824; Zimmermann and Du Plessis, 'Basic Features', 34–5; Markesinis, Lorenz and Dannemann, *Law of Contracts*, 732–3.

[52] Markesinis, Lorenz and Dannemann, *Law of Contracts*, 733.

triggers a consideration of the question whether the retention of the benefit amounts to enrichment and that the other elements are normally not in dispute here. In other factual situations, however, the existence of enrichment might be obvious but one or both of the remaining elements need to be positively established. The next section gives an example where the outcome is usually decided by the element of unjust(ified)ness.

3. Cases where the unjust(ified)ness of the enrichment is the main determining factor

Emblematic of this kind of case is the situation where a sub-contractor is unable to claim successfully in contract from the main contractor and then seeks to claim in enrichment from the owner who received the benefit of the sub-contractor's performance in terms of the contract between himself and the main contractor. The outcomes of sub-contractor enrichment cases differ dramatically from country to country, but a constant in regard to them all is that more often than not that outcome (whether it is to allow the action or to refuse it) turns on a decision (though not always overtly expressed) about whether the enrichment may be regarded as unjustified. Let us survey the landscape by moving from those countries where an action is most adamantly refused to those where it is routinely recognised.

(a) South African law

In South Africa a sub-contractor is very firmly denied an action against the owner. This was unequivocally decided in *Buzzard Electrical (Pty) Ltd v. 158 Jan Smuts Investments (Pty) Ltd.*[53] The facts of this case were as follows: the respondents (D) had contracted with a company (T) to develop a tract of land in Johannesburg, and that company in turn engaged the appellants (C) as sub-contractors to do part of the electrical work. After the appellants had completed this work, but before they were paid, the company which had engaged them was liquidated. The work done by the appellant qualified as useful and/or necessary expenses and the value of the respondent's property was accordingly enhanced. The appellant claimed a lien over the property, but thereafter agreed to give up the property to the owner on the understanding that this action would not prejudice the appellant in any way. The appellant then instituted an enrichment action against the respondents, who raised an exception to the particulars of claim on the basis that they had not been unjustifiably enriched because they were

[53] 1996 (4) SA 19 (A).

obliged, in terms of their contract with the developing company (T), to pay for all work done, including the electrical work. The court of first instance upheld the exception and an appeal was noted. The Appellate Division dismissed the appeal. The reasoning of Van Heerden JA, delivering the judgment of the court, was as follows.

First, the learned judge put forward two examples for consideration. (a) Landowner D enters into a contract with T to erect a house on his property for a consideration of R500,000. T had always had in mind to have the work done by a sub-contractor, but discovers later that he had miscalculated the amount of his tender. The only possibility for him is to enter into a sub-contract with C in terms of which the latter will build the house at a price of R700,000. C completes the project but refuses to vacate the premises because T did not pay him due to his insolvency. The value of the property had risen by more than R700,000, and his costs amounted to more than that amount. (b) The owner of a house, D, has for many years had the intention of adding an extra room to that house, but realised that he could not afford it. His friend, T, who is aware of his wish, offers to have the room built as a gift. The owner gratefully accepts this offer. T thereupon enters into a contract with C in terms of which the latter will effect the addition to the house at a cost of R100,000. C performs his obligations in terms of the contract, but since, as a result of his uninsured factory burning to the ground, T has fallen insolvent, A is unable to recover any part of the contract price from T or his insolvent estate. Once again the value of the property had risen by at least R100,000 and C's costs were not less than that amount.

In regard to both these hypothetical situations – and, indeed, in regard to any case where the performance of work done by C in pursuance of a contract with T can be traced to a contract between the owner and T stipulating that exactly that work had to be done by T – the court held as follows:[54]

In all cases of [this] ... type of liability the owner contracted with [T] on a specific basis, and it would be unfair that his counterperformance, if any, were to increase in effect or that he should incur an obligation which did not arise out of the contract with [T], simply because [T] had engaged [C] to comply with his contractual obligations. There was no contractual relationship between [C] and the owner and, when [C] performed the work, he complied with his obligations towards [T]. At the same time, however, [C] also gave effect to [T]'s obligation to the owner and thus also performed indirectly with respect to the owner.

[54] I cite here (in slightly modified form) from the headnote on page 22 of the report, since the case is reported in Afrikaans.

The agreement between the owner and [T] was the primary source of the performance of the work and any possible enrichment of the owner; the owner received no more as a result of [C]'s performance than that which he had contracted for with [T]. For that reason the enrichment was not *sine causa*. On the contrary, his agreement with [T] was the cause of his enrichment. [C] could enforce his contractual rights against [T] and, if they turned out to be illusory because [T] was insolvent, it was an unhappy coincidence which did not render the owner's enrichment unjustified.[55]

(b) The German and Scottish approaches

This rather rigid approach – relying exclusively on the nature of the obligation between the parties – is strongly reminiscent of (but not identical to) the German solution to sub-contractor cases. It is therefore useful briefly to state how this problem would be approached in Germany before moving to an evaluation of the South African position.[56] The purpose of the work done by the sub-contractor (C in Van Heerden JA's example) is to fulfil the contractual obligation that he has *vis-à-vis* the main contractor (T). In that example C's purpose *vis-à-vis* T was fulfilled and he therefore cannot bring a *Leistungskondiktion* against T. (C does, of course, have a contractual action, which unfortunately is useless in the circumstances.) But the question is whether C could claim against the owner on the basis of one of the *Nichtleistungskondiktionen*, say the action based on outlays (the '*Verwendungskondiktion*'). The answer is, again, no – at least in cases where it is clear that A's purpose was to perform *vis-à-vis* T. As seen, German law employs a general rule of 'non-subsidiarity' in regard to the *Leistungskondiktionen*. If a 'performance' (in the technical sense described above) can be identified as existing in a particular situation, the only possible remedy is the *Leistungskondiktion*, the parties being indicated by the performance. If, for some reason, the *Leistungskondiktion* cannot successfully be relied upon, an alternative action based on enrichment 'in another way' (*Bereicherung in sonstiger Weise*) is not available. Unfortunately, however, there are instances where a *Leistung* can be identified but it does not automatically indicate whether an action is appropriate and, if it is, at whose instance it lies. This happens in cases where it is uncertain who made the performance. A case in which this kind of uncertainty existed was the famous *Elektrogerätefall* ('the case of the electrical appliances'),[57] in which the owner of land (D)

---

[55] 1996 (4) SA 19 (A) at 28G–H and 29D–H. I have changed the letters used in the judgment to maintain consistency in this contribution for ease of reading.
[56] In regard to the following see generally Zimmermann and Du Plessis, 'Basic Features', 36 ff. and Loewenheim, *Bereicherungsrecht*, 42 ff.
[57] BGHZ 40, 272.

contracted with a building concern (T) to build several homes on his property. T, in turn, sub-contracted with C to supply the electrical appliances for the houses. C supplied the appliances, but was not paid by T. D had become the owner of the appliances when they were built into the houses and was accordingly sued in enrichment by C (C had sent a 'confirmation of order' letter to D, who had responded that he had not placed any order and that C should contact T).

In this situation the notion of 'performance' does not identify conclusively who the claimant should be, for the question is: 'Who made the performance?' From C's (that is, the claimant's) point of view, he made the performance to D, but from D's point of view, T made the performance in terms of their contract. Whose view should prevail? Formerly the view was that the perspective of the person making the performance should prevail. The newer theory favours the perspective of the recipient. Thus in the *Elektrogerätefall* an approach which favours the defendant[58] was adopted by the court and accordingly C's claim was not allowed. Ulrich Loewenheim argues that the correct approach is that neither should necessarily prevail, but that policy reasons should indicate whether or not an enrichment claim by C should be recognised.[59] He indicates that the relevant considerations are: (i) that the risk of insolvency should be correctly allocated; (ii) that the defendant should not be exposed to the risk of double payment; and (iii) that the defendant who wishes to be solely in a relationship with the person with whom he contracted should not be forced to have to be involved in the contractual obligations that arise between C and T.[60]

Although German law has thus adopted the policy that normally a subcontractor cannot claim because the enrichment is not regarded as unjustified, there is nevertheless some awareness that, although this policy has hardened into a principle, there are circumstances in which a different policy may prevail and thus where an exception to the principle can be contemplated. This is not unlike the position in Scotland. Scots law's basic position is that a sub-contractor cannot claim directly from the owner on the basis of enrichment. The policy factors which Whitty indicates as dictating this outcome are very much in line with those mentioned in regard to German law.[61] He makes it clear, however, that there might be exceptions, for instance where 'T induces [C]'s performance by fraud and [D] benefits gratuitously or in bad faith'.[62] Like Loewenheim,

[58] Loewenheim, *Bereicherungsrecht*, 45.   [59] Ibid.   [60] Ibid.
[61] Whitty, 'Indirect Enrichment', 245.   [62] Ibid.

Whitty is therefore saying, essentially, that although the policy considerations against allowing an action by a sub-contractor against the owner are almost unassailable – thus enabling the rule to be stated in a robust way – this is not invariably so.

Neither the German commentators nor Whitty deal in any detail with the exact element to which these policy factors go. As far as German law is concerned it could hardly be otherwise, for the dogma pertaining to this situation subsumes the inquiries as to whether the enrichment is unjustified and whether a causal link exists under the alternative inquiry into whether the purpose of the sub-contractor's performance has been fulfilled. In regard to Scots law, too, it is understandable: in all three-party situations the inquiries into the elements of enrichment and unjustifiedness often shade into one another, and this is no less true in sub-contractor cases. If one asks whether any one or all of the typical policy factors[63] should prevent the sub-contractor (C) from claiming from the owner (D) one could, in effect, be taken to be simultaneously asking whether D's enrichment is unjustified *vis-à-vis* C *and* whether the causal link between C's loss and D's benefit is sufficiently close in law. The important point to remember, however, is that both German and Scots law, as interpreted by Loewenheim and Whitty, at least contemplate the possibility that the owner's enrichment could be unjustified *vis-à-vis* the sub-contractor. This approach is very different from that of the South African Appellate Division. In South African law the fact that there is a valid legal relationship between both (i) the impoverished person (the sub-contractor) and the third party, and (ii) between the third party and the enriched person (the owner) rules out all possibility of the enrichment being regarded as unjustified or *sine causa*. The German and Scots legal systems, however, are to the effect that this fact is merely a very strong indicator that it not be so regarded. As shown above, the view taken by the Appellate Division in the *Buzzard Electrical* case[64] was based on the argument that D receives only what he has bargained for in terms of his contract with T and therefore the receipt of the benefit is of necessity *cum causa*; indeed, because C performs no more than that which he has undertaken to do in terms

---

[63] For example: (i) the fact of the existence of contracts between the sub-contractor and the main contractor and between the main contractor and the owner, (ii) that the risk of insolvency should be correctly allocated, (iii) that the *paritas creditorum* rule should be preserved, (iv) that no one should be deprived of any defences that he might otherwise have had and (v) that no one should be required to pay the same debt twice.

[64] 1996 (4) SA 19 (A).

of his contract with T, he is not unjustifiably impoverished, and accordingly parts with the benefit *cum causa*. However, underlying the German and Scottish positions is the assumption that the question whether D's retention of the benefit received is *sine causa* is a relational one. Vis-à-vis T it could never be *sine causa* because T has a specific contractual obligation to transfer exactly that benefit. Vis-à-vis C it will also normally not be *sine causa* – and in this regard the fact that D received it as a result of a contract between himself and T will be a very important factor – but it could, in exceptional circumstances, be *sine causa*, if there are other factors present which make it desirable to hold the retention to be so classified *vis-à-vis* C.[65]

(c) The position in England

The situation in English law is less certain, but it too seems to be more or less in the middle bracket with German and Scots law: in principle the sub-contractor cannot claim, but a small opening seems to be left to accommodate unusual cases. Peter Watts[66] formulates the approach to sub-contractors' claims in common-law countries as follows: 'It is suggested that, in the absence of special features, such as a direct undertaking or inducement by the employer, there is properly no restitutionary

---

[65] Whitty cites the example where T induces C's performance by fraud and D benefits gratuitously or in bad faith (Whitty, 'Indirect Enrichment', 245). A central difficulty that J. C. Sonnekus would have with this approach is that it would, in his view, give C two claims. He argues thus ('Ongeregverdigde verryking en ongeregverdigde verarming vir kondikering in drieparty-verhoudings', 1996 *TSAR* 8; my translation of the Afrikaans original): 'There can never simultaneously be both a claim based on contract *and* a claim based on unjustified enrichment in respect of the same performance. The sources of the two claims would be mutually exclusive. After all, no one would claim that [a sub-contractor] ... should be able at the same time to institute a contractual action for the agreed remuneration and an enrichment claim for the same performance against the main contractor. Why then ostensibly allow him two claims solely because the owner of the property appears behind the main contractor?' The answer to this is, first, that, in general it *is* possible for there to be situations in which a claimant has either a claim in contract or a claim based on enrichment (see, e.g., the facts of *ABSA Bank Ltd v. De Klerk* 1999 (1) SA 861 (W)) and, secondly, that when that occurs the claims are not cumulative, but in the alternative. There are techniques to ensure that the owner does not suffer double jeopardy nor the sub-contractor benefit twice. These include (i) subrogating the claim of the sub-contractor against the main contractor to the owner, which would allow the owner to raise it by way of set-off against any claim by the main contractor and (ii) allowing a direct claim by the sub-contractor only after his remedies against the main contractor have been exhausted.

[66] 'Does a Subcontractor have Restitutionary Rights?', 399.

claim available to the sub-contractor against the employer.' A variety of policy and other reasons are given by Watts to justify this approach. He mentions: (i) that 'a direct claim would unduly complicate the legal position between both the employer and its head contractor and also the head contractor and the sub-contractor'; (ii) that 'other creditors of the head contractor may have been relying on the head contractor's being the sole person entitled to receive payment for work done for the employer'; (iii) that 'in essence, at least, the employer is a *bona fide* purchaser of the work performed by the sub-contractor'; and (iv) that 'in relation to the defendant the plaintiff will not usually be able to establish any ground for restitution'. Watts does not find all these reasons equally convincing. The final consideration he holds to be the most important reason why a sub-contractor's enrichment claim should not be allowed, thus confirming, I would argue, that the solution to this type of claim is to be found essentially in the element of unjustness. It is important to note that Watts does not state the rule in an absolute way and he clearly accepts that in certain circumstances the employer may be enriched *vis-à-vis* the sub-contractor – as do, it would seem, at least some Law Lords.[67]

An illustration of the approach of the House of Lords is *Pan Ocean Shipping Co. Ltd v. Creditcorp Ltd (The Trident Beauty)*,[68] which is not a sub-contractor situation, but is strongly analogous to it. Pan Ocean chartered a ship from Trident, the hire payable fifteen days in advance. Trident assigned its right to receive payment from Pan Ocean to Creditcorp (as security for a loan). At Trident's request one payment was made directly to Creditcorp by Pan Ocean, but, as luck would have it, Trident did not perform the charterparty in respect of which the advance payment was made. Pan Ocean validly terminated the charter and then sought to recover their payment from Creditcorp. The House of Lords, confirming the decision of the Court of Appeal, refused the claim.

The case was argued under two heads.[69] The burden of the first was whether liabilities could be assigned in the same way as rights, but this part of the judgment is not of primary importance for the present discussion. The second was based on enrichment, the argument being that, quite apart from any contractual claims which flow from the contract between Trident and Pan Ocean, Pan Ocean had a direct enrichment claim against Creditcorp based on total failure of consideration. This argument

---

[67] See the speech of Lord Goff, [1994] 1 WLR 161 at 166E and Barker, 'Restitution and Third Parties', 306.
[68] [1994] 1 All ER 470; [1994] 1 WLR 161.
[69] See Andrew Burrows, 'Restitution from Assignees', [1994] *Restitution LR* 52.

was rejected by both Lord Woolf (delivering the judgment of the majority) and by Lord Goff (with whom Lord Lowry agreed). Lord Woolf's reasoning was that the claim could in his view be brought only against the party responsible for the failure of consideration and that Pan Ocean should not, merely because Trident assigned their right to receive payment to Creditcorp, have the right to sue Trident or Creditcorp in the alternative.[70] This approach contains a privity of contract fallacy analogous to that which was once present in the law of tort, and it does not come to terms with the fact that, if any enrichment claim existed, it would have an entirely separate foundation.[71] Lord Goff had a keener appreciation that the direct claim was separate and he left open the possibility that there could be such a claim.[72] Nevertheless, he allowed the contractual relationship between Trident and Pan Ocean to influence the decision whether there should be a claim in the present instance: because Pan Ocean would not have been able to establish a claim in enrichment against Trident (due to the contract between them regulating repayment) it could also not have a claim in restitution against Creditcorp.

Although one might not agree with his policy of allowing an enrichment claim by Pan Ocean against Creditcorp to depend so directly on the relationship between Pan Ocean and Trident, the fact is that it is a legitimate approach.[73] In my view the question here was essentially whether the enrichment was unjust and in making that value judgment different considerations may be relevant. For instance, Andrew Burrows opines that the real reason for not allowing the claim in the present case is to be found in the fact that Creditcorp had, through the contract of assignment, in effect purchased the right to the payment of the hire and was therefore not in the position of a mere donee.[74] Watts disagrees, insisting that there is no reason why a donee should be in a worse position than someone who is in a position akin to a bona fide purchaser.[75] Using an example similar to that which Van Heerden JA used in South Africa's *Buzzard Electrical* case – 'an aunt, as a welcome gift to a nephew, asks a contractor to do work

---

[70] [1994] 1 All ER 470 at 479–80.
[71] See Burrows, 'Restitution from Assignees', 54.   [72] At 166.
[73] Barker, 'Restitution and Third Parties', 306 is, however, of the opinion that it is not a defensible position to take, saying that Lord Goff's reasoning 'wholly misconstrues the basis of the restitutionary cause of action in cases of failure of consideration'. My answer to this view is that, yes, the contract between Pan Ocean and Trident should not automatically determine whether Pan Ocean has an enrichment claim against Creditcorp, but that does not prevent the fact of its existence from functioning as a policy consideration in coming to the decision whether such an action should be recognised.
[74] 'Restitution from Assignees', 55.   [75] 'Does a Subcontractor have Restitutionary Rights?'

on her nephew's house' – he argues that the nature of the contractual relationship between the employer and the contractor should not make a difference and that therefore also in this case the contractor should not be able to claim directly against the nephew.[76] Kit Barker, again, would allow the claim.[77] But whatever the right answer is, the important point for present purposes is that that answer is a policy-based value judgment about whether the enrichment is unjust.[78]

(d) American law

Although at first blush it does not seem to be the case, American law occupies the opposite end of the spectrum on which South African law is at the one end and German and Scots law in the middle. One often comes across general statements in textbooks that in principle a sub-contractor is not entitled to a restitution claim, but closer examination shows that in fact, subject to certain important qualifications, sub-contractors are regularly allowed a direct claim. Indeed, when it is allowed it seems to be done much more matter-of-factly than anywhere else. The rule that applies in many parts of the United States has been stated thus: '*Apart from unjust enrichment* or any special statutory rights or remedies, a subcontractor who has furnished labor or materials for the construction or repair of some form of improvement on the lands of another has no right to a personal judgment against the landowner where there is no contractual relationship between them.'[79] This rule states the general position, but it must be remembered that there are jurisdictions in which the contractor is denied even a claim based on unjustified enrichment.[80] Where it is

---

[76] I am not sure that accepting that Watts is correct (in saying that the contractor should not be able to claim from the donee nephew) is incompatible with a view that someone in a position similar to that of a bona fide purchaser should be especially protected.

[77] Barker, 'Restitution and Third Parties', 305.

[78] Thus Goff and Jones rightly treat the *Trident Beauty* situation as part of the question of unjustness under the heading of 'Limits to a restitutionary claim based on another's unjust enrichment'. See Lord Goff of Chieveley and Gareth Jones, *The Law of Restitution* (5th edn, 1998 by Gareth Jones), 46 and 58 ff.

[79] See *Pendelton v. Sard* (1972) 297 A 2d 889 (Maine); 62 ALR 3d 277; J. R. Kemper, 'Building and Construction Contracts: The Right of Subcontractor who has Dealt Only with Primary Contractor to Recover against Property Owner in Quasi Contract', 62 ALR 3d (1975), § 2 (293).

[80] See *Custer Builders Inc. v. Quaker Heritage Inc.* (1973) 41 App Div 2d 448; 334 NYS 2d 606 (discussed by Kemper, 'Building and Construction Contracts', § 4 (300 ff.)); *Dales Service Co. v. Jones* 96 Idaho 662; 534 P 2d 1102; *Indianapolis Raceway Park Inc. v. Curtiss* (1979) 386 NE 2d 724 (Indiana CA). (See in regard to these and similar cases ALR 3d, August 1998 Supplement to volume 62, § 4 (54).)

allowed, the most important matter is, as in other jurisdictions, once again the question whether the enrichment is unjust or not. Tacitly contained in the American approach is the principle that, although C performed the work in terms of a contract with T, and although D received the benefit in terms of a contract with T, D can nevertheless be unjustifiably enriched *vis-à-vis* C. To establish whether this is so in any particular case, the courts take into account policy factors such as (i) whether the sub-contractor had taken the trouble to avail himself of alternative remedies (for example, a statutory mechanic's lien, if such is available in the jurisdiction), (ii) whether he had exhausted his remedies against the general contractor and (iii) any other equitable consideration.[81] A subsidiarity principle is therefore operative and in terms thereof the sub-contractor's claim is restricted to situations where the possible remedies against his contractual partner have been exhausted. This, incidentally, is very much how the subsidiarity principle operates in France – if the sub-contractor has a claim against the main contractor, but it is for all practical purposes useless, he can proceed against the owner – about which more below.[82] These kinds of considerations can be relevant only to the element of unjustness and therefore, even though the cases and commentary do not overtly localise the relevant policy factors within this element, that is clearly where the solution is to be found.

Once again it must be emphasised that the fact that the question of unjustness is the most important one in this situation does not mean that other elements never arise in this context. Thus the requirement of enrichment itself may be the focus of the inquiry, as it was in *Commerce Partnership 8098 LP v. Equity Contracting Co.*[83] There a sub-contractor (Equity) (who had made improvements in terms of a contract with the general contractor on the land of Commerce, but had not been paid) brought an action to recover the contract price from Commerce.[84] The issue that arose was whether Commerce could present evidence about amounts that it had

---

[81] See Kemper, 'Building and Construction Contracts', § 2 (294–5); *Guldberg v. Greenfield* (1966) 259 Iowa 873; 146 NW 2d 298; *Bishop v. Flood* 133 Ga App 804; 212 SE 2d 443; *Crockett v. Sampson* (1969) 439 SW 2d 355 (Texas Civil Appeals); *Commerce Partnership 8098 LP v. Equity Contracting Co.* (1997) 695 So 2d 383 (Florida CA).

[82] See the *Boudier* case (Req. 15 June 1892, S 1893.1.281 note Labbé, DP 1892.1.596); Nicholas, 'Unjust Enrichment', 2037 ff.; Eltjo J. H. Schrage, 'Unjustified Enrichment: Recent Dutch Developments from a Comparative Perspective', (1999) 46 *Netherlands International Law Review* 22.

[83] (1997) 695 So 2d 383.

[84] It should be noted that the contract price does not necessarily represent the enrichment of the owner, although this basic truth is sometimes neglected in the cases. See Kemper, 'Building and Construction Contracts', § 1 (c).

paid directly to other sub-contractors. The court of first instance excluded this evidence, but its ruling was reversed on appeal, the Florida Court of Appeals indicating that evidence about all payments to either the main contractor or sub-contractors was admissible. Commenting on this case Kull remarks as follows:

> The court makes it clear that an owner will be liable in restitution when it has paid no part of the price attributable to an improvement: this is a 'windfall benefit, something for nothing'. It is likewise clear that the owner cannot be liable in restitution if it has paid the full contract price, even if the subcontractor received nothing. The opinion gives no explicit direction for the most likely case – partial payment for the work of the unpaid contractor, in some knowable proportion – but seemingly leaves the trial court to determine the extent, if any, to which the owner has been enriched by the claimant's work.[85]

As has been alluded to above, the argument that particular fact situations tend to reveal themselves as soluble within the parameters of a particular element of liability does not seek to establish an absolute position. It merely appeals to the natural logic inherent in this situation. If legal systems generally accept the three basic elements as the cornerstones of enrichment liability, and given the fact that there are obvious policy factors that are relevant in every situation, it is very likely (if one accepts, as I believe one must, that there is a commonality to legal reasoning in Western legal systems) that similar *patterns* of solutions will emerge from the various systems. That this is so has been borne out by both examples considered thus far – countermanded cheques and sub-contractor situations. The various legal systems have all – either explicitly or implicitly – dealt with the one under the element of enrichment and with the other under the element of unjust(ified)ness. They have not all come to the same answer (which should not be surprising because the actual solution depends on the weight that a given legal systems attaches to each of the relevant policy factors), but the important thing is that an approach with a common core is discernible in those systems.

This brings us to the question whether this evaluation also holds for factual situations in which the last element of enrichment liability plays a prominent role.

---

[85] Andrew Kull, 'USA' [1997] *Restitution LR* § 208. See also *Crockett v. Sampson* (1969) 439 SW 2d 355 (Texas Civil Appeals); *Re Williamson Shaft & Slope Co.* 20 BR 73 (1982, BC SD Ohio): *Mandell-Vasquez Inc. v. University of Toledo* 67 Ohio Misc 2d 24 (1993, Ohio Ct Cl); 664 NE 2d 740; *Blum v. Dawkins Inc.* 683 So 2d 163 (Florida Districts CA, 5th District 1996).

4. Cases where the 'at the expense of' requirement is the determining factor

(a) English law: the causal decisions obscured

In order to be able to evaluate the role of the 'at the expense of' requirement in three-party situations let us again survey the general approach to this element in various countries, beginning with England. In their excellent casebook on restitution, Andrew Burrows and Ewan McKendrick explain the 'at the expense of' requirement in terms of the Birksian divide between unjust enrichment by subtraction and unjust enrichment by wrongdoing. In the former instance the defendant's benefit must represent a loss to the plaintiff, to be 'at his expense'; in the latter the plaintiff must establish that 'the defendant has committed a wrong ... against the plaintiff'.[86] Questions that immediately arise are: 'how must it be determined whether the loss of the plaintiff and the defendant's benefit are linked?' and 'is a factual connection enough, or can policy factors influence the decision whether the factual connection is recognised?' and 'how is one to deal with the peculiar difficulties that must inevitably arise when more than two parties are involved?'. These are the bread-and-butter issues of any causal situation in the law and yet the authors do not touch upon them at all.[87]

Why is this so? In my view it is at least partly due to the fact that English law has not consciously classified the problems that arise here. If it had, for instance, overtly conceptualised this problem as one of causation, it would immediately have drawn on the tools for dealing with causal problems that have been developed elsewhere in the law. (The development of causal theory was a painful enough process for any new discipline not to want to start afresh.) This problem runs even deeper in certain areas of the law when the authors turn their attention to tracing and proprietary restitution.[88] They remark that '[i]t is extremely difficult to pinpoint precisely what tracing is concerned with and what its role is within the law of restitution'.[89] They then argue that 'the essential role of tracing *in the law of restitution* is that it enables the plaintiff to establish that property retained or received by the defendant is retained, or was

---

[86] A. Burrows and E. McKendrick, *Cases and Materials on the Law of Restitution* (1997), 89.
[87] A. Burrows, *Understanding the Law of Obligations: Essays in Contract, Tort and Restitution* (1998), 60-1, does mention that particular difficulties may arise in regard to the 'at the expense of' requirement in three-cornered situations, but does not elaborate. Certain specific difficulties of three-cornered situations are sometimes discussed by authors, but often they do not bring them under the rubric of 'at the expense of' or any other element; but see Smith, 'Three-party Restitution', 481 ff.
[88] *Cases and Materials*, 663 ff.   [89] *Ibid.*, 663.

received, "at the expense of" the plaintiff'.[90] I believe that they are correct, but the fact that it is uncertain in English law what the ubiquitous tracing is all about shows very clearly how much the 'at the expense of' requirement is in need of sharper definition. The causal decisions that are at the heart of both tracing and, more generally, the 'at the expense of' requirement, are thus well and truly obscured in English law. But English law is not alone in this. The causal element in German law is similarly hidden.

(b) German law: the causation issue similarly obscured

As seen above, the *summa divisio* of German law is that between the 'action based on a performance' (which covers a large number of instances that would fall under the Birksian category of subtractive enrichment) and the 'actions not based on a performance', of which the most prominent categories are the *Eingriffskondiktion* ('action based on an encroachment', which, broadly speaking, approximates to 'enrichment by wrongdoing') and the *Verwendungskondiktion* ('action based on outlays'). Also, in the case of the action based on a performance the elements of unjustifiedness and causality were both subsumed under the concept of 'performance', which was developed to indicate in both bilateral and three-cornered situations who the persons are between whom there are legally relevant performances that have to be reversed (that is, to indicate the necessary causal link). In solving three-party situations, the German law's subsumption of causal questions under the element of performance has led to causal questions being discussed in 'non-causal' terminology. This can only exacerbate the problems around a concept which is already intrinsically extremely complex. For example, because the performance concept concerns itself exclusively with factual causation, the broader policy considerations such as the economic consequences of a particular decision cannot play a role.[91] Therefore Berthold Kupisch argues that the 'at the expense of' requirement should be reinstated as an overt part of the *Leistungskondiktion*.[92] In South Africa and Scotland, too, the theory around the 'at the expense of' requirement is unsatisfactory (although Niall Whitty's theoretical reorganisation of the Scottish case law has done much to place Scotland on a more considered path).

---

[90] *Ibid.*, 664 (emphasis in original).
[91] Kupisch, 'Rechtspositivismus', 215 and 218. See also Leib in: *Münchener Kommentar*, n. 2.
[92] Kupisch, 'Rechtspositivismus', 219.

(c) The causation issue in bilateral situations

Because this element is so ill defined in all legal systems, the difficulty of solving problems that naturally reside under causation is even greater than in the case of problems falling under the previous two elements. I would therefore like first to demonstrate the simple, but very important, fact that in ordinary bilateral situations, questions that are categorised under the 'at the expense of' requirement fall into either those relating to factual causation or those relating to what is known as 'legal causation' or 'remoteness' in other areas of law. A recent US case involving a bilateral situation (but one which is similar to a three-party situation), *Goldberg v. Bank of Alice Brown (Re Goldberg)*,[93] is convenient for this purpose. The Goldbergs entered into a contract with Citation Homes to purchase a residence in Stockton, California, making a down-payment of $17,000, which was held in escrow by Stewart Title. The Goldbergs, however, failed to secure financing and the sale was cancelled, whereupon both Citation and Stewart (the latter by mistake) issued cheques of $17,000 in refund of their deposit. Stewart assigned its rights to the Bank of Alice Brown, who filed a complaint to recover the money and impose a constructive trust on a house on which the Goldbergs had made a $15,000 down-payment soon after receiving the double refund. The Goldbergs did not appear, but before a default judgment had been applied for by the bank, the Goldbergs filed for bankruptcy. A trial was eventually conducted in the bankruptcy court, which ruled in favour of the bank. Franklin Goldberg appealed. The issue before the court was whether the bankruptcy court, with its broad and equitable remedial powers as a federal court, had 'abused its discretion in imposing a constructive trust on the Goldbergs' subsequently purchased home'.[94] The court described a constructive trust as 'an equitable remedy [imposed] to prevent unjust enrichment and enforce restitution'. It entails that a person who wrongfully acquires property of another holds it involuntarily as a constructive trustee and the trust extends to property 'acquired in exchange for that wrongfully taken'. Imposing a constructive trust is then just another way of saying that enrichment liability exists on the part of the defendant *vis-à-vis* the plaintiff.

In urging that a constructive trust should not be imposed Goldberg raised, amongst others, an argument that is in essence founded upon causation. He contended that he had commingled the refund with his personal funds and that the residence was bought with his personal funds,

---

[93] (1994) 168 BR 382 (Bankr 9th Cir). [94] *Ibid.* at 384.

while his expenses were paid with the funds subject to the bank's constructive trust (if indeed such trust were held to exist by the court). In cases of insolvency, he argued, 'strict tracing' (as opposed to 'liberal tracing') is required. To this the court responded as follows: 'Generally, it is true that where a constructive trust is sought to be imposed against the property of an insolvent debtor, strict tracing is required. The purpose of the rule is to treat all creditors equally.[95] However, it is not an abuse of discretion to allow liberal tracing when no creditors will be harmed.'

(d) Factual and legal causation

Strict and liberal tracing relate essentially to causation. The questions, I suggest, that had to be answered were first 'was $15,000 of the overpayment paid off on the house?' and, secondly, 'accepting that it was, were there any policy reasons why it should not be regarded as too remote from the plaintiff to be countenanced?' or, put differently, 'were both factual and legal causation satisfied?'. The division of causation into factual and legal causation is traditional, but it is important that one does not misunderstand what it is about. First, consider 'factual causation'. Many legal systems apply what is commonly known as the 'but for' test to determine factual causation – that is to say, they ask: 'would the result have occurred but for the alleged cause?'. If the answer is no, the alleged cause is held to be a factual cause.

It must be remembered, however, that this so-called test is nothing more than a structured thought-process and not a test at all. The first tell-tale sign of this is that we know which cause to eliminate in our 'but for' test, which indicates that we are in fact determining the factual connections by other means. And indeed there is no magical formula by which to determine causation: we have to rely on our experience of causal processes to make a decision about the existence or otherwise of a causal connection. The decision can mostly be no more precise than saying 'on a balance of probabilities A caused B', and the degree of probability that is acceptable is of necessity a matter of policy and convention.[96] Thus determining factual causation is not – as Basil Markesinis and Simon Deakin, speaking of causation in a delictual setting, rightly point out – merely 'a technical and evidentiary one, from which policy factors are absent, in contrast to an apparently more evaluative and normative second stage

---

[95] Here the court referred to *Re Esgro Inc.* 645 F 2d 794 at 797–8.
[96] See generally B. S. Markesinis and S. F. Deakin, *Tort Law* (3rd edn, 1994), 163 ff.; A. M. Honoré, 'Causation and Remoteness of Damage', in: A. Tunc (ed.), *International Encyclopaedia of Comparative Law* (1983), vol. II, chap. 7, § 4.

[i.e. of determining legal causation] when policy comes to the fore'.[97] In enrichment matters the same kind of policy considerations exist in regard to factual causation. In an ordinary case of funds of A and B being commingled and then spent on projects C and D (in the absence of any specific indicators such as, for example, instructions to a bank to use fund A to pay for project C) it cannot be determined whether fund A or B was used wholly, partially or at all for projects C and D. Experience of causal processes can indicate only that there is a possibility that fund A was used for project C and therefore one has to resort to policy to determine whether A should be regarded as having been spent on C. Not to decide the matter on the basis of policy would be on a par with, say, a court refusing to hold any one member of a firing squad liable for wrongfully and culpably executing a person because the 'but for' test, applied to each member of the squad individually, cannot be satisfied. The court simply has to grapple with this difficult factual problem so as not to leave the door wide open to abuse and the only possible solution is a policy-based decision.[98]

But once the factual link has been established in delict cases – to continue the analogy – one needs to determine whether the link in not too tenuous to be recognised in law. Asking this question in the law of delict allows, once all the elements of liability have been established, a final check that, in spite of each element being individually satisfied, one is not faced with an unacceptable result. This decision is again to a large extent based on policy considerations,[99] which are, of course, different from those employed to establish factual causation. The same question must be asked in enrichment cases: if one is satisfied that a definite factual causal link exists between the plaintiff's loss/injury and the benefit unjustly retained by the defendant, one has then to ask whether finally, in the circumstances of the case at hand, liability should really be imposed. As in the case of delict or tort, this is a different policy decision from the one involved in establishing factual causation. There the policy decision is only to break the deadlock produced by the limits of causal thinking; here it is to prevent unusual and unacceptable results from occurring that might come about if the elements of enrichment are viewed in isolation and not in the light of the combined result that they produce.

The court in the *Goldberg* case did not, as might be expected, work with causal terminology and conventions. In fact it conflated these two inquiries, using the notions of 'strict' and 'liberal' tracing. Translated into

---

[97] Markesinis and Deakin, *Tort Law*, 165.   [98] *Ibid.*
[99] For South Africa, see *Smit v. Abrahams* 1994 SA 1 (A).

the approach and terminology outlined above, the decision was as follows. Using ordinary causal thinking one cannot determine whether factually the enrichment benefit in question was transferred to the house account. However, resorting to policy, it will be presumed that it was (that is, liberal tracing). But this cannot be the end of the matter, because there might be policy-based reasons why the result produced in this way would not be acceptable. For instance, the principle of *paritas creditorum* has to be preserved in the case of insolvency and thus, if the defendant happened to be insolvent and the creditors could have been harmed, the policy in regard to the parity of creditors would have had to prevail and the decision would have been that, due to the unacceptable result, the causal link must be held not to be satisfied (that is, strict tracing). In this case the funds were invested in exempt property (that is, the residence of the defendant) and therefore unsecured creditors had no claim against that property, which means that liberal tracing could be allowed, since the policy consideration that creditors should not be treated unequally was irrelevant in the circumstances.[100]

(e) The causation issue in three-party situations

I now consider the question of causation in a typical three-party situation arising in practice. A very useful example of three-party enrichment liability being determined by the 'at the expense of' requirement is the following. C enters into a contract with T in terms of which the former will effect an improvement to the property of D in circumstances where D is unaware of that fact; C then performs his obligations under the contract with T (there being no contract between C and D, nor between T and D) and the value of D's property is enhanced; T then does not pay C and C seeks to claim the amount by which D had been enriched from him. In this situation, because D has so obviously been enriched and because there is no contract between D and T to cause one to doubt whether the enrichment is unjustified, the issue is clearly whether the 'at the expense of' element has been satisfied. (However, as in the case of the earlier examples, the courts often do not locate the policy considerations specifically within this element.)

(i) *Legal systems opposed to allowing a claim*

Again a spectrum of views comes to the fore in different countries. Scotland may be taken as an example of a legal system which is opposed to

---

[100] Andrew Kull, 'USA', [1994] *Restitution LR* § 282.

allowing a claim in this kind of case. Whitty cites *Thomson, Jackson, Gourlay, Taylor v. Lochead*[101] and *Kirklands Garage (Kinross) Ltd v. Clark*[102] as evidence that a contract between C and T itself is regarded as a complete bar to a claim by C against D. (The first of those two cases concerned a claim by C – an accountant – against D, in circumstances where C had entered into a contract with T to prepare a settlement between T and D; the claim was refused. The second case dealt with a situation where C – the owner of a garage – contracted with T – an insurance company – for the repair of a car, which belonged to D and where C's claim against D – after T had gone into liquidation – was similarly refused.) Neither of these cases can, however, be described as very strong authority. The former is a very old case and the claim in the latter was framed in contract (although the court remarked that the claimant's argument seemed to be partly based on enrichment and then said that it doubted whether an enrichment action was available if a contract existed between C and T).

(ii) Legal systems which, in principle, allow a claim

English law is probably in the same category as Scots law,[103] but at the other end of the spectrum is French law. There the whole matter is determined by the policy that a claim is allowed as long as the subsidiarity principle has been satisfied. Both Italian law and French law adhere to some degree to the principle of subsidiarity. Article 2024 of the Italian Civil Code decrees that an enrichment action is not available where the impoverished person is able to bring another action to make good his or her loss. Barry Nicholas[104] explains that this provision is capable of a 'concrete' and an 'abstract' meaning:

The concrete meaning is that the action for unjustified enrichment is excluded only when, in the circumstances of the particular plaintiff, the other action will in fact enable him to make good his loss. In other words, the plaintiff cannot bring the enrichment action when he has another effective remedy, but if, in the particular circumstances of the case, the other action will not be effective, the enrichment action is open. The abstract meaning is that the enrichment action is excluded whenever the other action is in principle available, or could have been available, even if, in the circumstances of the particular case, the plaintiff will derive no benefit from it. For example, the defendant may be insolvent or the period of prescription may have expired, or the plaintiff may be unable to find

---

[101] (1889) 16 R 373.   [102] 1967 SLT (Sh Ct) 60.
[103] See Watts, 'Does a Subcontractor have Restitutionary Rights?', 402.
[104] Nicholas, 'Modern Developments', 87–8.

the evidence required by law to support the other action. It should be noticed that the abstract meaning leaves little or no scope for the enrichment action.

Italian law adopts the abstract approach, but French law opts for a more concrete interpretation, as is evidenced by the *Boudier* decision[105] and the cases that followed its lead. In the *Boudier* case a seller of manure to a tenant of a farm could not recover the price from the tenant, who became insolvent and cancelled the tenancy, transferring the harvest to the owner. The seller therefore proceeded against the owner and was allowed to recover the latter's enrichment that resulted from the application of the manure to the land. The reason why the enrichment action was brought was not that 'in the abstract sense no other action was available to [the plaintiff] – there was a valid contract between him and the tenant – but that in the concrete sense a contractual action against the tenant would have been fruitless because of the tenant's insolvency'.[106]

The apparent unconcern of French law for the parity of creditors is unlikely to be duplicated in other legal systems, but in general the deployment of subsidiarity as one of the relevant policy considerations in this context (as in the context of sub-contractors) is obviously very useful. If the claimant has first exhausted his or her remedies against the other party to the contract, certain of the policy considerations that would otherwise militate against allowing a claim against the third party assume a smaller significance. In such a situation there is no chance of double recovery and the other party to the contract cannot be deprived of any defences that he or she might have. This approach must be distinguished from that where an enrichment claim is allowed only in an 'abstract' subsidiary capacity as an absolute rule and about which there is quite rightly a great deal of scepticism.[107] For instance, Italian law seems to lay down such an absolute rule and in *The Trident Beauty* Lord Goff's judgment likewise amounts to an absolute approach to subsidiarity.[108] However, the arguments routinely advanced in favour of such an approach are not very convincing.[109]

---

[105] Req. 15 June 1892, S 1893.1.281 note Labbé, DP 1892.1.596.
[106] Nicholas, 'Modern Developments', 88. It should be noted, however, that even though French law essentially adopts the concrete approach, it does not do so without qualification. A distinction is made between those instances where the basic, non-enrichment action 'is excluded by an obstacle of law and those where it is excluded by an obstacle of fact', lack of the necessary evidence being classified as an obstacle of law and insolvency as an obstacle of fact (*ibid.*, 90).
[107] See generally Schrage, 'Unjustified Enrichment', 78 ff.
[108] [1994] 1 WLR 161. See Schrage, 'Unjustified Enrichment', 79.
[109] See Nicholas, 'Modern Developments', 91 ff.

(iii) The German approach

Germany's solution to this kind of situation is quite unusual. In an ordinary two-party case German law provides a regime of alternativity between two actions. The ordinary law of enrichment is brought into play by § 951 BGB, which provides that anyone who has lost ownership in a thing by virtue of its attachment to the property of another[110] may claim compensation from the person thus benefited in terms of 'the rules regarding the disgorgement of an unjustified enrichment' (in other words, in terms of the provisions contained in §§ 812 ff. BGB). The relevant action is the so-called 'action for outlays'. The special rules in §§ 994 ff. BGB, on the other hand, allow a possessor to claim compensation for expenditure on the property of another. There are those who see the rules in §§ 994 ff. BGB as amounting merely to a somewhat modified enrichment law, but the better view is that the two kinds of claims differ in important respects.[111] In three-party situations the enrichment claim does not hold, but the §§ 994 ff. BGB claim does. Take, for instance, a garage-repair situation such as that presented in the Scottish case of *Kirklands Garage (Kinross) Ltd v. Clark*.[112] When the garage (C) performs its side of the bargain with T (the person giving the instruction to repair the car), German law's by now familiar argument is that it does so with the purpose of discharging its contractual obligation *vis-à-vis* T. C will therefore not have an enrichment claim based on a performance against T, because the purpose of the performance has been achieved. But it will also not have a claim based on outlays against the owner (D). This is so because the principle of no subsidiarity, as it applies in German law, decrees that if the claimant has made a performance in circumstances where the action based on a performance is – for whatever reason – not available, a claim based on enrichment 'in another way' will not be available instead.[113] But here the provisions of §§ 994 ff. BGB create the possibility of bypassing enrichment law and suing the owner directly, for § 994 decrees that any possessor (except a lawful possessor)[114] may demand from the owner compensation for necessary

---

[110] In the garage-repair situation § 947 BGB specifically would be relevant. It states that where a moveable is attached to another moveable (which can be regarded as the principal thing) in such a way that the two components form a unitary object, the owner of the principle object becomes owner of the new thing.

[111] See Dirk A. Verse, *Verwendungen im Eigentümer-Besitzer-Verhältnis* (1999), 43 ff. and the summary at 54.

[112] 1967 SLT (Sh Ct) 60.

[113] Verse, *Verwendungen*, 141 ff. The leading case is BGHZ 100, 95. See Verse, *Verwendungen*, 154 for a discussion of this case.

[114] See in this regard the discussion by Verse, *Verwendungen*, 49, of BGHZ 34, 122.

expenses made in respect of a thing. § 996 expands this right to useful expenses, but only for bona fide possessors;[115] and in terms of § 1000 the possessor has a right of retention until his claim for compensation is satisfied. Because of the difference in approach to subsidiarity, that part of the law designated as enrichment law in Germany produces the opposite of the position in French law, but achieves the same through the backdoor of the §§ 994 ff. BGB principles.

(iv) South African law

As happened in the examples employed to illustrate how the elements of enrichment and unjustifiedness could determine the outcome of three-party cases, this example reveals very different solutions across legal systems. Is it possible once again, in spite of the diversity of actual answers to this problem, to identify a dominant element through which the relevant policy factors may be focused? The courts and writers are even more reticent than usual when it comes to identifying the element of enrichment on which the solution should hinge. Some clues emerge, however, from South African law, which has moved right through the spectrum in a period of about thirty years. It started out being very strict about not allowing a claim in such a situation. In 1968 the Transvaal Provincial Division held, in *Gouws v. Jester Pools (Pty) Ltd*,[116] that the enrichment in such a case was not 'at the expense' of the owner, because, in essence, the test of legal causation had not been satisfied. This test would be satisfied, the court held, only where there was a direct transfer from the impoverished to the enriched, that is, without the transfer taking place via the estate of a third party. (In coming to this conclusion the court followed the now discredited earlier approach of German law, namely that a claim in a three-party situation would be allowed only if the enrichment was 'direct'.[117]) Thus the judgment placed the factual outcome in this situation on a par with that where the improver or preserver is a sub-contractor, a situation in regard to which

---

[115] If C is a lawful possessor, that is to say if D allowed T to contract with C for the repair of the vehicle, C will not be allowed to claim in terms of §§ 994 ff. BGB. It should be noted that if C was a lawful possessor when the car was repaired, but an unlawful possessor at the time that the owner claims back his car, §§ 994 ff. BGB will be applicable.
[116] 1968 (3) SA 563 (T).
[117] But see Kupisch, 'Rechtspositivismus', 219, who would like to reintroduce the notion of 'directness', but in a completely different guise.

the authorities have always been unanimous that a claim should not be allowed.

Although the decision had many supporters,[118] other commentators did not think it to be the correct approach.[119] The clearest indication that this approach was not generally accepted was that the Appellate Division began to erode the rule. Although it refused to overrule *Gouws*, it held, in *Brooklyn House Furnishers (Pty) Ltd v. Knoetze and Sons*,[120] that there was ample authority to allow a lien in these circumstances: T had bought, on hire-purchase, certain furniture from D, so D remained owner until the final instalment was paid. The hire-purchase agreement contained, furthermore, a condition that T would not store the furniture without the express approval of D. In spite of this arrangement, however, T contracted with C for the storage of the furniture without informing D. When T disappeared, D, having found out that the furniture was stored with C, sued C for the return of the furniture and it was held that C had an enrichment lien over D's property. This approach was subsequently confirmed in a garage-repair case, *Standard Kredietkorporasie v. JOT Motors (Edms) Bpk h/a Vaal Motors*.[121]

However, a lien and an action are, of course, merely different ways of enforcing a right, the one a shield, the other a sword, and logically both must be available whenever there is an underlying right.[122] This anomaly was finally addressed in *Buzzard Electrical (Pty) Ltd v. 158 Jan Smuts Investments (Pty) Ltd*,[123] encountered above in the discussion of sub-contractor cases. In this case Van Heerden JA made a distinction between sub-contractor cases and instances where improvements are made to property by a contractor in terms of a contract with a third party, without these improvements being traceable to an agreement between the owner and a third party to make them. The essential difference between the two, the judge said, was the absence of a contract between the owner and the third party for the specific work that was done. Since he did not have to make a decision

---

[118] See, for example, Sonnekus, 'Ongeregverdigde verryking', 12–13, who agrees with the outcome, if not the reasoning.
[119] See, for example, the famous discussion of this case by Scholtens, 'Enrichment at Whose Expense?', 372.
[120] 1970 (3) SA 264 (A).   [121] 1986 (1) SA 223 (A).
[122] But see the thought-provoking decision in the German case reported as BGHZ 51, 250. There it was held that if a garage voluntarily gives up possession of the repaired vehicle before having received the contract price, it is taken thereby to give unsecured credit and consequently must bear the resulting risk. Verse, *Verwendungen*, 152: if the contractor gives up possession, he is no longer worthy of protection.
[123] 1996 (4) SA 19 (A).

about this kind of situation, he merely stated that he assumed that an action would be available, thereby implicitly overruling the *Gouws* case.[124]

The Cape Provincial Division of the High Court very soon thereafter used the opportunity to overrule *Gouws* explicitly in *ABSA Bank t/a Bankfin v. C. B. Stander t/a C. A. W. Paneelkloppers*.[125] A car dealer, Motortown, sold a car to Georgina Kent subject to a reservation of title clause in terms of which ownership of the vehicle would only pass to her once all the instalments had been paid. Motortown thereafter ceded its ownership to the financier of the sale, ABSA Bank. Meanwhile Kent lent the car to Bezuidenhout who subsequently crashed it. Bezuidenhout then delivered the vehicle to Stander for repairs. Bezuidenhout, however, disappeared before making payment to Stander. Eventually ABSA instituted a *rei vindicatio* against Stander,[126] who themselves counterclaimed for the amount by which they alleged ABSA had been enriched by the repairs made to the car. The facts may be summarised as follows: D (ABSA) was in a contractual relationship with X (Kent), who was in a contractual relationship with T (Bezuidenhout) who in turn was in a contractual relationship with C (Stander).[127]

When the matter came to trial before the court of first instance, ABSA's claim for the return of the vehicle had already been granted. Accordingly, only Stander's counterclaim was in issue.[128] The court *a quo* upheld Stander's (C's) counterclaim on the basis that ABSA (D) had been unjustifiably enriched at their expense.[129] ABSA appealed. Mr Justice Van Zyl (with Burger AJ concurring) dismissed the appeal and held that ABSA (D) had indeed been enriched at Stander's (C's) expense, to the extent of the difference in the value of the car before and after the repairs had been effected.[130]

---

[124] But cf. contra J. C. Sonnekus, 'Ook verrykingsretensieregte behoef bewese ongeregverdigde vermoënsverskuiwing', 1996 *TSAR* 583, 585 and 590–1.
[125] 1998 (1) SA 939 (C).
[126] The *rei vindicatio* was instituted on the basis that Stander, the garage owner, was in unlawful possession of the vehicle owned by ABSA. *ABSA Bank t/a Bankfin v. C. B. Stander t/a C. A. W. Paneelkloppers* 1998 (1) SA 939 (C) at 941F.
[127] More particularly there was an instalment sale between D and X, a loan (*commodatum*) between X and T and a contract for the letting and hiring of work (*locatio conductio operis*) or mandate (*mandatum*) as between T and C. The interposition of T as between X and C is a variation on the classic fact scenario that usually occurs in garage-repair cases.
[128] 1998 (1) SA 939 (C) at 941J.   [129] *Ibid.* at 942A.
[130] The court *a quo* accepted the evidence of Stander's insurance assessor that the vehicle was valued at R2,000 before the repairs and R6,200 afterwards. The quantum of the Stander's enrichment claim was, accordingly, R4,200, being the difference between the two. This amount was accepted by the full bench as being 'fair and equitable' and could not be challenged. *Ibid.* at 942G and 956J–957D.

There are strong indications that the court considered the question of causation or the 'at the expense of' requirement as one of the crucial elements in this kind of situation.[131] Here too, however, the elements of unjustifiedness and causation are not easily separable and a particular situation might easily be decided with reference to one or other.[132] Mr Justice Van Zyl accordingly does not single out causation as the only element that could play a role in deciding this kind of case.[133] That is, of course, completely correct, but I would nevertheless argue that in a situation such as this the real question is not whether the owner has been unjustifiably enriched, but whether he is unjustifiably enriched *vis-à-vis* the claimant. The fact that the owner has received the benefit gratuitously, coupled with the fact that he is not exposed to a contractual claim from the person who instructed the work to be performed (as he would be in a sub-contractor situation) makes the probabilities very high that he has been unjustifiably enriched. The question is just whether there is a sufficient link between him and the person who performed the work. Normally the factual link, too, would be quite obvious in this context and the essential question that remains is whether the link is close enough in law. Mr Justice van Zyl indicated that various policy considerations could play a role here.[134] It appears that the following policy factors particularly influenced his conclusion that ABSA's enrichment was at Stander's expense: (i) the fact that Stander's contractual claim against

---

[131] Ibid. at 949H–950D.

[132] This is reflected in various passages from the judgment: *ibid.* at 949C–950D, 953B–D and 956F–G.

[133] Thus he states (at 953B–D): 'If the contractual action should be useless or academic, the plaintiff should not be allowed to suffer an irrecoverable loss and the defendant to derive an unassailable benefit for which he does not pay. The fact that, on the face of it, he might not have (strictly) complied with the causal requirement should not, in circumstances such as these, deprive him of an action which is based on the undeniably equitable principle that no one should be unjustifiably enriched at the expense of another. If A's contractual action against B is valueless and if C has, as a result of A's conduct or performance, received a benefit for which he has not paid, this equitable principle demands that A should be able to have redress against C, at least for his necessary and useful expenses, on the basis that C's retention of the benefit would be regarded as unjustified and at the expense of A.' It is important to note here that the statement that the claimant should be allowed to claim even if 'on the face of it, he might not have (strictly) complied with the causal requirement' should be read in the context of the whole judgment. It is not, in my view, intended to signify that causation may be dispensed with, but rather that the causal element is one of many facets and that whether it can be considered to have been established depends on a variety of factors; see the judgment at 950B–G.

[134] Ibid. at 950D.

Bezuidenhout was valueless (Bezuidenhout having disappeared)[135] – echoing the French approach to subsidiarity – and (ii) the fact that there was no question of Bezuidenhout's insolvency having any bearing on the case.[136] In making this last point the judge stressed that the policy considerations should not be considered out of context and that the question whether a particular policy factor influences the decision at hand can only be determined with reference to the actual facts and circumstances of that case.[137]

III. Conclusion

By establishing, first, which element can best be employed to solve a particular three-party situation and, secondly, which policy factors are actually (as opposed to possibly) relevant in that situation, a legal system can produce a flexible system which is nevertheless able to predict outcomes with reasonable certainty. It is important that the system be flexible because three-party situations are just too varied and complex for simple, hard-and-fast rules to be able to provide adequately for their solution. We have here, we might say, the law's equivalent of the difference between linear and non-linear mathematics. Not unlike the way in which linear mathematics can cope very adequately with simple structures such as planets in a stable orbit around a star, but non-linear chaos theory is necessary to explain the eddies that form in the water flowing under a bridge, and in the same way that the former seeks precise prediction while the latter attempts to describe the general pattern or character of a system's behaviour, two-party situations in law can often be solved with direct, clear rules whereas the best we can do in three-party situations is to lay down the general pattern along which a solution should proceed.

From the various situations discussed above it is clear that such patterns can be identified. There are certain policy factors that are often relevant in multi-party enrichment cases and if one views them through the lenses of the three basic elements of enrichment liability they become manageable. Indeed, in the three situations discussed above similar problems tend to be solved within the confines of the same element in different legal systems, although the actual solutions differ. If the pattern of the solution can be recognised, the difference in outcome is not perplexing because we know

---

[135] *Ibid.* at 953A. This accords with the subsidiarity approach that has come up several times in the discussion above.
[136] *Ibid.* at 954I.   [137] *Ibid.* at 954I–955B.

how the answer was reached. A legal system which approaches three-party problems in this way will over time be able to refine its understanding of the patterns by learning from other systems which policy considerations might be relevant and by building a growing corpus of case law that demonstrates how these policy factors are best combined to produce a specific result. In this way it can build a system far more sophisticated than if it were to continue the fruitless search for a single 'right answer'.

PART XI

Proprietary issues

20 Proprietary issues

George Gretton

I. Introduction

In much of enrichment law, the question of 'proprietary restitution' can hardly arise. If P renders medical services to D, without a contract, P's claim will be a simple personal claim.[1] Moreover, the civil-law tradition generally rejects 'proprietary restitution' in any circumstances. So is there really any value in discussing the matter from a comparative standpoint? I think that there is. Possibly a lawyer from a mixed system is well placed for the task. On the other hand, it may be that the task is impossible, especially since the English law in this area is complex, controversial and changing, and, of course, has that difficult dimension: equity.

II. 'Proprietary'

'Proprietary' is a term not generally used in Scots law. In Scots law rights are (following the *ius commune*[2]) divided into real and personal. 'Real' and 'proprietary' do not coincide: the latter is broader than the former. Equitable rights *in rem* are proprietary in English law, but such rights are not real rights from the civilian standpoint.[3]

---

[1] But one kind of emergency assistance has a proprietary angle: salvage.
[2] Scots property law forms an almost perfect *ius commune* system. An eighteenth-century lawyer from Cologne, Paris or Milan would have felt immediately at home in twentieth-century Scots property law. Perhaps Scots property law should be preserved as a sort of World Heritage Site.
[3] This question is too complex to be entered into here, so it will have to rest on assertion. I will merely mention *Webb v. Webb* [1994] ECR I-1717 (Court of Justice Case C-294/92), where it was held that when Art. 16 of the Brussels Convention speaks of *droits réels* that excludes an English equitable right *in rem*.

A difficulty lies in the fact that in the common-law tradition a specifically enforceable claim to a thing is itself normally proprietary so that the claimant already has an equitable right *in rem*. That equity regards as done that which ought to have been may be a tired maxim but is still good law (or equity). If P has a right against D for the specific performance of an obligation to convey an identifiable thing, P will be considered the equitable owner. But for the civil lawyer, such a right is a textbook example of a purely personal right, namely the *ius in personam ad rem acquirendam*. Thus in English law a personal right to the conveyance of an identifiable thing seems to be a pigeonhole in logical space in which there is no pigeon, or at least normally no pigeon.[4]

In this area the problems of communication between the two great legal traditions are so great as to tempt one to the sin of despair. Let me quote a lawyer of the highest eminence, Lord Millett:

A has power to deal with B's property, and wrongfully transfers legal title to the property to C. In such a case B sues to recover his own property: in civil law terms, he vindicates his title. German law locates such cases in the law of property, not unjust enrichment.[5]

Alas, this is not right. If 'legal title' means ownership, then C has ownership, and if C has ownership then B does not. The civil-law tradition is unititular: if X owns something at a given time, then Y does not.[6] In the example, if C is owner, B's remedy cannot be a vindication, for vindication is possible only if the claimant is the owner. German law locates such cases in the law of unjustified enrichment, not in the law of property.[7]

---

[4] Sometimes there is a pigeon. For instance, one can have a purely personal right to acquire ownership of a chattel pursuant to a contract of sale.

[5] 'The Law of Restitution: Taking Stock', (1994) 14 *Amicus Curiae: Journal of the Society for Advanced Legal Studies*. I am indebted to Niall Whitty for this reference.

[6] Unless, of course, they are co-owners. The civil-law tradition has, indeed, sometimes departed to some degree from unititularism, but these wobbles have always tended to be regarded as exceptional in their nature. For an interesting discussion see A. J. van der Walt and D. G. Kleyn, 'Duplex Dominium', in: D. P. Visser (ed.), *Essays on the History of Law* (1989), 213 ff. And see (1999) 6 *European Review of Private Law* 407 for an interesting discussion, from a German standpoint, by Ralf Michaels of the celebrated Scottish case *Sharp v. Thomson* 1997 SLT 636; 1997 SCLR 328.

[7] It is, of course, unfair to quote a small passage merely to expose its errors, and I should not like my own writings to be treated in such a manner. My purpose is a good one: if even so great a figure as Lord Millett can fall into this error, what hope is there for the rest of us?

III. Vindication based on retained ownership is not an enrichment action

It is a truism nowadays that if P has never lost ownership, his action against D is not an enrichment action.[8]

You own a dragon. There is a muddle about this dragon. You deliver it to me, and I mistakenly believe it to be mine. Am I enriched? I am enriched only to the extent that I have had the benefits arising out of the possession (lighting the barbecue, smiting my enemies, etc.), but I am not enriched any further than that. It is not as if I had wrongfully acquired ownership, and must now transfer ownership back again. I have not acquired ownership at all. And, by the same token, you are not impoverished as to the thing itself, because you began the story as the owner of the dragon and have continued as owner throughout. You may be impoverished as to your temporary loss of possession, and you may have a claim against me on that score, but that is all. What is the nature of your right? If it is not a claim in unjustified enrichment, what is it? The answer is, of course, that it is *rei vindicatio*. I may have been enriched by possession, but I have not been enriched by title.[9] That is an important point, and I do not wish to controvert it. But why is an action of this sort not an enrichment action?

IV. No one is enriched

In the example, I was not enriched, but why? One answer which suggests itself is that it is because my estate, my patrimony, was not enlarged. I had no more than I had before, apart from possession and the benefits which possession may have brought to me.

Very well. But now suppose that, instead of delivering to me a physical object, you deliver to me money, which, by some muddle, I spend as my own, in a manner which will (let us suppose, for simplicity) not result in any traceable proceeds. The money has gone, so that on any view of matters your claim against me is simply a personal claim. This is a claim in unjustified enrichment, unlike the case of the dragon. But have I been enriched? Is my estate, my patrimony, larger than it was before I had the money? The answer is no: as in the previous case, my patrimony is not

---

[8] For English law see, e.g., Peter Birks, 'Misnomer', in: W. R. Cornish *et al.* (eds.), *Restitution: Past, Present and Future* (1998), 1. For Scots law see Kenneth Reid, 'Unjustified Enrichment and Property Law', [1994] JR 167.

[9] To use the terminology of Kenneth Reid (see previous footnote).

enlarged, because when I got the money I acquired an asset, but I also acquired a matching and identical liability. My net estate was unchanged. And the same is true, conversely, for you. You were not impoverished, because when you handed the money over to me you lost one asset but immediately acquired another, namely your claim against me. Actually our positions are not quite mirror images of each other: in my patrimony I have an extra asset and also an extra, matching, liability, but in your patrimony the liability side is untouched, and what has happened is that on the asset side of the patrimony one asset (the money) has been replaced by another asset (your claim against me). When we think of enrichment we think of actions, but actions arise out of rights, rights that already exist, and a claim is a very good sort of asset: my money in the bank is, juridically speaking, an asset of the same sort as your enrichment claim against me.

Thus in the example of the money, it is not enough to say that the reason I am not enriched is because I have gained nothing. In enrichment law the defender *never* gains anything. Indeed, one may observe that when a person *is* indeed unjustifiably enriched that is precisely the case where the law gives *no* remedy. Those authors who describe this area of law as *preventing* unjustified enrichment are thus more accurate than those who describe it as *redressing* unjustified enrichment.

V. In some cases a vindicatory action can be an enrichment action ('proprietary restitution')

Thus the reason why a vindicatory action based on retained ownership is not an enrichment action is *not* that the defender is not enriched. So what is the reason? Is it perhaps because the claim of the plaintiff/pursuer is *real*?

The answer is no. If a legal system says that Jack is the *owner* of some asset that is in the *possession* of Jill, that fact does not necessarily imply that Jack's right is not an enrichment right, for the proprietary right might be *conferred* by the legal system as a means of preventing unjustified enrichment. This has been well brought out by a number of English authors. The point is this: a legal system could create a new proprietary right in favour of Jack over some asset in Jill's possession. Thus the law of Utopia might say that if Jack makes a mistaken payment to Jill, then a *pro indiviso* share (corresponding to the value of the mistaken payment) of any dragon owned by Jill henceforth belongs to Jack.[10] In that case, Jack would have

---

[10] This might happen *ipso facto* or by order of the court – the distinction between 'institutional' and 'remedial' constructive trusts.

a proprietary right, just as you had in the earlier case, but it would be genuinely an *enrichment* right – genuinely 'proprietary restitution'.

Thus 'vindication' and 'enrichment' are not necessarily opposed, for in the case just given, Jack can vindicate. Jack can vindicate because ownership almost always gives rise to a right of vindication, even if the ownership has arisen by reason of enrichment law. The question is whether the ownership that is vindicated is a *retained* ownership or an ownership that has been *conferred* to prevent unjustified enrichment.

VI. So why is vindication through retained ownership not an enrichment action?

If the discussion so far is right, the reason why vindication through retained ownership is not an enrichment action is that the claimant's right has not changed form.

VII. 'Proprietary restitution' in English law

The example above about Utopian law may seem fanciful (except, of course, to Utopian lawyers), but something very like it exists in Anglo-American law. Or does it? It appears that in English law (to say nothing of other systems) there is a debate to what extent the authorities (for example, *Lipkin Gorman v. Karpnale*[11]) that give to P a proprietary right are based on (i) the idea that P somehow had a proprietary right *all along*, a right which has, perhaps, survived all sorts of transformations, or (ii) the idea that a *new* proprietary right is raised up in P's favour. As an outsider I can offer no view on this debate. But nevertheless I have some reflections.

If it is true that an original proprietary right survives through all transformations, then that is a sort of proprietary right which is not merely unfamiliar but wholly alien to the civilian outlook. Take an example given by William Swadling.[12] Jack acquires possession of Jill's handkerchiefs. Jill is still the owner. Jack sells the handkerchiefs and uses the money to buy a horse. Swadling says that in English law the horse belongs to Jill, not Jack. In any civilian system of property law, that would be impossible. Jack intended to acquire the horse for himself. The seller intended to convey the horse to Jack. The seller did not convey the horse to Jill. The horse was the seller's. So Jack is now the owner. Full stop. That must be the case

---

[11] *Lipkin Gorman (a Firm) v. Karpnale Ltd* [1991] 2 AC 548.
[12] 'Property and Unjust Enrichment', in: J. W. Harris (ed.), *Property Problems from Genes to Pension Funds* (1997), 130 ff.

even where (as here) the property is not held on any written title. The case will be a fortiori if, instead of a horse, Jack buys land or registered shares.[13]

Swadling, in the valuable paper just mentioned, argues that English law should follow the civilian systems in rejecting 'proprietary restitution' – at least in most types of case.[14] It is not for me to express any views about which way English law should move, but I would suggest that the gap between the English and the civilian approaches would remain a wide one even if English law did move in this direction. If 'proprietary restitution' – which is to be killed off or at least cut down – is so defined as to exclude cases where the current proprietary right arises out of an earlier 'proprietary base', and (conversely) if cases where there is a 'proprietary base' that survives are defined as not being true enrichment cases, then a large area remains which (whatever you call it) is baffling to the civilian.

Take *Attorney-General for Hong Kong v. Reid*.[15] Here the Privy Council held that money given by way of bribes was the property of the Crown, in the sense that the actual banknotes were the Crown's property. That established a 'proprietary base' so that the land which (eventually) represented the value of the notes was deemed to be owned by the Crown. My point is this: one can decide to label the case as not involving enrichment law because the rogue never owned the notes and, later, never owned the land, but that does not bring about any real degree of convergence with the civilian approach. To the civilian, the official might have an obligation to pay the Crown. He might even have an obligation to convey the land to the Crown. (Actually I doubt if any civilian system would so hold, but at least one could imagine that possibility.) But the Crown would not (without a conveyance) own that land.

Roman law itself was perhaps not clear about this. There is a famous case at *Digest* 12, 1, 31. D bought a slave, but it turned out that his title was bad, and that the slave's true owner was P. The slave had with him a substantial sum of money, and this was used by D to buy another slave. It was held that P had a *condictio* against D in respect of the second slave. Perhaps one can regard this as yet another striking illustration of how

---

[13] As opposed to bearer shares, which would be like the horse.
[14] 'Civilian systems maintain a complete opposition between property and unjust enrichment ... The thesis of this chapter is that it is highly desirable that, so far as possible, this should also be the position in English law': Swadling, 'Property and Unjust Enrichment', 130.
[15] [1994] 1 AC 324 (New Zealand case).

Roman law and English law are often nearer each other than either is to the modern civilian systems.[16] Medieval law seems to have adopted this doctrine to some extent,[17] but later it faded away.

VIII. Real subrogation possible only for special patrimonies

Real subrogation corresponds roughly to tracing, but real subrogation, in the modern civilian tradition, can generally happen only in relation to a patrimony or a patrimonial mass (a special patrimony[18]). The English trust estate is a classical example of a special patrimony, and of course if the trustees of a trust sell BP shares and bank the money in the trust bank account and later use the money to buy British Airways shares, there is real subrogation, each asset replacing the one before as a trust asset. But, as Marie Malaurie remarks, 'ce n'est que dans les restitutions portant sur une universalité ou un ensemble...que la subrogation serait le plus facilement admise'[19].

IX. Subrogation -- cessio legis

Most (all?) legal systems recognise a possibility which in civilian systems is often called *cessio legis* and in common-law systems subrogation. Thus if Jack harms Jill's property, and Jill is insured, and the insurance company pays Jill, then Jill's delictual claim against Jack is deemed to be assigned to the company.[20] This could be regarded as a 'proprietary' remedy for preventing the unjustified enrichment of Jack. But it could also be regarded as an implied-in-law term of the contract of insurance. Another example of *cessio legis*, which again exists in most legal systems, whether common law, civilian or mixed, is where a wrongdoer (tortfeasor) is insured but is also bankrupt: here what happens is that there is a *cessio legis* to the

---

[16] I am no Romanist, but I would note that the purchase of the second slave, though done with the first slave's money, was also done by the first slave himself. On the basis that the benefit of a purchase by a slave benefited his master, who was P, not D, the new slave would belong to P without need for 'tracing'. Using inappropriate modern language, the first slave was an agent for his true owner. I am not suggesting that this is the only correct view of *D.* 12. 1. 31, but it seems to me a possible reading, though there is the difficulty that the action was a *condictio* not a *vindicatio*.

[17] For the history see J. P. Dawson, *Unjust Enrichment* (1951), chap. II.

[18] *Sondervermögen*.

[19] Marie Malaurie, *Les Restitutions en Droit Civil* (1991), 115. (Subrogation will readily be admitted only in cases of restitution involving universalities or collectivities.)

[20] Whether this is truly a deemed 'assignment' is an issue which each legal system will address in its own way.

victim of the wrongdoer's right of indemnity against the insurer. But it is doubtful whether it is helpful to regard this as a proprietary response to enrichment. At no stage, whether before or after bankruptcy, is the wrongdoer enriched at anyone's expense.[21]

X. Liens and hypothecs

A right of restitution may simply be a right to be paid money, but that of itself does not mean that it cannot also be 'proprietary' in some sense of that term. A salvor's right is a right to money, but most (all?) legal systems confer on the salvor a hypothec[22] over the saved ship, in security of the salvage debt. Whether salvage falls under the law of enrichment or under the law of *negotiorum gestio* need not be discussed here: if it is neither then at least it is in a closely related category. And there are similar cases. In Roman law a bona fide possessor could, sometimes at least, have a right of *retentio* for the value of his improvements.[23] Whether this was a true real right (valid against third parties) or whether it was merely a two-party right to retain is unclear. Scots law has taken the second view[24] whilst South African law has taken the first.[25] The common-law equitable charge is a hypothec of a sort, though not fully real in the civilian sense.

An interesting possibility is that the celebrated *Boudier* case[26] should be classified as a hypothec case. Here X sold and delivered manure to a tenant farmer. The latter became bankrupt before paying, and lost the lease. It

---

[21] Compare art. 122 of the Loi no. 85-98 of 25 January 1985, as amended by the Loi no. 94-475 of 10 June 1994, which covers the case where A sells to B, subject to retention of title, and B, before payment, and thus before acquisition of ownership, sells to C: the unpaid price of the good can be vindicated, that could, at a pinch, be conceptualised as a 'proprietary' remedy.

[22] Using this in the Ulpianic (and Scottish) sense of a security where the creditor does not have possession; D. 13, 7, 9, 2: 'Proprie pignus dicimus, quod ad creditorem transit; hypothecam, cum non transit nec possessio ad creditorem' [Pledge properly so called involves delivery to the creditor, but with hypothec possession does not pass to the creditor.] In contrast, I will use the term 'lien' to mean a possessory security.

[23] See, e.g., Iul. D. 12, 6, 33 *in fine*. There are various other texts bearing on this question, such as Inst. II, 1, 30.

[24] *Beattie v. Lord Napier* (1831) 9 S 639. But the area is undeveloped and *Beattie* may not be the last word. See also K. G. C. Reid, *The Law of Property in Scotland* (1996), § 173.

[25] See, e.g., C. G. van der Merwe and M. J. de Waal, *Law of Things and Servitudes* (1993), § 93. For the law in Ceylon (Sri Lanka), which is, of course, similar to South African law, see G. L. Peiris, *Some Aspects of the Law of Unjust Enrichment in South Africa and Ceylon* (1972), 44 ff. For the Louisiana law see the Civil Code, art. 529 (as revised 1979), which, interestingly, give a lien even to mala fide improvers. For Quebec see art. 963 of the new *Code Civil*.

[26] Req. 15 June 1892, S 1893.1.281 note Labbé, DP 1892.1.596.

was held that the supplier could recover from the owner of the land under the *actio de in rem verso*. This looks rather like an improvement hypothec over the land, but the better view is that it was merely a personal right against the current owner.[27] At all events, it was not a real right over any asset of the bankrupt's and so, whilst it gave the creditor a priority, it was not a priority at the expense of the other creditors.

XI. Property restitution may be purely personal

Just as (at least in theory) vindication may exist within the law of enrichment (though this does not happen in civilian systems), so property restitution may be purely personal (though this will not normally be the case in common-law systems). Jack transfers assets to Jill. To prevent unjustified enrichment the law says that Jill must transfer the assets back to Jack. English equity will tend to make Jack the equitable owner of the assets, but in the civil-law tradition Jack's right is a *ius in personam ad rem acquirendam*, and is simply a personal right. If 'proprietary' means 'real' in the civilian sense, this is not a proprietary right. For convenience I call it 'property restitution'.

XII. A table

Time for systematisation.

Class	Short title	Enrichment right?	Real right? (a)	Civil law? (b)	Common law? (c)
I	Original direct property restitution (d)	No	Yes	Yes	Yes
II	Original traced property restitution (e)	No? (f)	Yes	No	Yes
III	Conferred direct property restitution (g)	Yes	Yes	No	Yes? (h)
IV	Conferred traced property restitution (i)	Yes	Yes	No	Yes? (j)
V	Property restitution (direct or traced) (k)	Yes	No	Yes	No (l)
VI	Monetary restitution (direct or traced) (m)	Yes	No	Yes	Yes
VII	Monetary restitution and security (n)	Yes	Yes	Yes	Yes

---

[27] An interesting possibility is that it was an obligation *propter rem*.

XIII. Notes to the table

(a) 'Real right' is here used loosely, so as to include equitable rights *in rem*. As I said earlier, I do not actually think that an equitable right *in rem* can be glossed as a civilian real right. But that is another story.

(b) and (c) 'Civil law' and 'common law' are used here as broad-brush terms.

(d) Meaning the case where P has retained ownership of the very thing of which he seeks the return – classical vindication.

(e) Meaning the case where D has converted the thing into something else, and the legal system regards P as being the owner of this. For instance, the rogue sells the dragon and buys a basilisk. In general, civilian (and mixed) systems do not recognise this possibility.

(f) Whether cases of this sort should not be classified as enrichment cases is an English debate in which I am unqualified to express a view.

(g) This is the case where, to redress unjust enrichment, the legal system confers on P ownership of a thing which was, previously, the property of D. This will include reduction in Scots law. The right to reduce is not real, but the right after reduction is real.[28]

(h) I say 'yes' but I may be quite wrong. In the conference in which this book had its origins, Swadling said that 'I am not aware of the possibility of property rights being generated by unjust enrichment, at least in English law.'

(i) The same as the last class, but where ownership is conferred in a substitute asset

(j) See note (h).

(k) A personal claim to a particular thing. Normally it will be direct, as where P mistakenly transfers shares to D and seeks their retransfer. But in theory it might also be a traced claim, as where D has sold the shares and traceably bought something else with the money. I stress 'in theory' because I doubt whether any system actually has this approach. In the civilian and mixed systems the tendency will be to say that if D has sold, his liability is purely monetary, while in the common-law systems the tendency will be to say that P has a proprietary traced right – either Class II or Class III.

(l) On the basis that a specifically enforceable right to a thing is normally 'proprietary' in English law.

(m) Here there is a simple claim for money. This is perhaps the paradigmatic case of an enrichment claim.

(n) Here the claim is a monetary one, but P has a hypothec over some asset, in security of the claim. This is the equitable lien of the common-law tradition. As mentioned earlier, the civil-law and mixed traditions have something similar in some types of case.

---

[28] See below, 582–4.

XIV. Multiple claims

There are probably several possibilities which the table fails to reflect. One of them is that in English law P may have more than one type of claim open to him. Lionel Smith writes that 'every substitution offers a choice between tracing into a new asset in the same hands, or following the old asset into new hands'.[29] There are, however, obvious conceptual difficulties as to how this can be. How can P be able to claim from D *both* a thing *and* its value? Swadling has commented that 'in *Attorney-General for Hong Kong v. Reid* the plaintiff had both an equitable debt and an equitable property right. This is logically inconsistent. The problem is that the plaintiff is in the same breath saying that the defendant both owes a certain sum to him and that the plaintiff owns that sum in the defendant's hands.'[30]

Civil-law systems can occasionally have multiple claims, but the multiplication of rights *in rem* is unknown to them.[31]

XV. Can rescission have real effect? The pistol and the rope

This section deals chiefly with Scots law. I do not wish to say much about the details of Scots law, but I would like to mention one issue which is as important as it is problematic. 'Reduction' is a decree setting something aside as invalid. Reductions are common enough, but the substantive law on the subject is curiously undeveloped. (We need a book on the law of reduction.) In the context of this article, the interest in reduction is as an enrichment remedy,[32] and the key question is whether, and in what sense, reduction can have real effect. By that I mean real effect by force of the decree in and of itself. If it has, or can have, real effect, then it looks like Class III – conferred direct property restitution. A closely connected question concerns rescission – that is, an extrajudicial act setting aside a previous juridical act of the rescinder.

Reduction and rescission can be aimed at many kinds of juridical acts. In so far as they are aimed at contracts, they will not have real effect. A contract has no real effect, so the rescission or reduction of a contract has no real effect. Scots property law in general adheres to the 'abstraction

---

[29] *The Law of Tracing* (1997), 131.
[30] Swadling, 'Property and Unjust Enrichment', 144. I have said something similar in 'Constructive Trusts', [1997] 1 *Edinburgh LR* 281, 304.
[31] And (subject to some qualifications) unknown to Scots law.
[32] I take it as uncontroversial that immoveable property is as subject to the law of enrichment as moveable property is. But I am not aware that anyone expressly asserted this until Kenneth Reid did so in 1994: 'Unjustified Enrichment', 174.

principle'. Thus, for instance, if R[ogue] by a fraudulent deception induces P to sell and deliver a car to him, rescission of the contract of sale by P does not revest ownership in him, even if the rescission happens while R still has possession of the car. The rescission will bring about an obligation on R to reconvey and redeliver the car. But that obligation is personal.[33]

Swadling has argued that English law, too, accepts the abstraction principle.[34] But I would suggest that *Car & Universal Finance Co. Ltd v. Caldwell*,[35] commonly regarded as a leading case, is not easy to reconcile with the abstraction principle.[36] What if reduction or rescission is aimed at the conveyance itself? First rescission. Scots law seems to be that a juridical act of conveyance cannot be rescinded. The contract inducing it can be rescinded, thereby generating an obligation to reconvey, but that is all.

The fact that a contract can be set aside either by rescission or reduction, but a conveyance can be set aside only by reduction, may at first sight seem surprising. But a contract is like a knot, which can be undone, whereas a conveyance is like the firing of a pistol. You can unsqueeze the trigger but the bullet will not come back.

What about reduction of a conveyance? I begin with moveables. The general view is that reduction is appropriate only for written titles, so in the case of the car reduction would not be available, but it will be available for incorporeal moveables. Here the practice seems, however, to be to aim the reduction at the contract rather than the conveyance. Thus in *Spence v. Crawford*[37] a sale of shares was reduced, but the reduction was only of the contract, and the decree, after reducing the contract, proceeded with an order directed at the defender to execute and deliver a stock transfer deed. This was personal only.[38]

---

[33] The only case I can think of where rescission has real effect is where goods are sold but not delivered, but title has passed, and the seller rescinds. In this case ownership almost certainly revests. This is not a case covered by the common law, for at common law ownership would not have passed anyway. The buyer's title to undelivered goods is statutory: Sale of Goods Act 1979, s. 17.

[34] He founds on an Australian case, *Ayers v. South Australian Banking Co.* (1878) LR 3 PC, and a Malaysian case, *Singh v. Ali* [1960] AC 167, and also on *Westdeutsche Landesbank Girozentrale v. Islington LBC* [1996] AC 669.

[35] [1965] 1 QB 525.

[36] Which Swadling seems to accept: see Swadling, 'Property and Unjust Enrichment', 133. His statement that the result of the *Caldwell* case would be the same in Scots law (his footnote 17) is not correct. The principle, which he quotes, that 'fraud passes against creditors' is applicable to unsecured creditors, such as a creditor executing against the car. (If, in this article, I sometimes differ from Swadling, I must stress that that I have found his writing of the highest value.)

[37] 1939 SC (HL) 52.

[38] But if a defender defies an order of court to execute and deliver a document the court can authorise the Clerk of Court to do so in his stead.

That approach can also be taken in the case of immoveable property (*Scottice* heritable property), and sometimes it is taken.[39] It might be better if it were always taken. In practice, reductions are commonly aimed at conveyances themselves, and the general understanding is that, by common law, such decrees have real effect as soon as they have become final, without even the need for registration, though statute has intervened to a limited degree by requiring registration before the effect becomes real.[40]

So reduction has, or can have, real effect. However, the position is not simple. A decree of reduction is of effect only against those who are called as defenders, and against those in right of the parties so called. If the action calls all parties having an interest, the decree will genuinely have real effect, but otherwise it will be a limping decree, of no effect against those not called but having an interest. For example, D defrauds P into disponing land to him. D then grants a security to S. P raises an action of reduction but does not call S. Decree is granted. P is now owner again, but S's real right remains in place.[41] If P had called S he could have included a conclusion for reduction of the security, too. But such a conclusion would (in my opinion) be likely to fail. It would succeed only if S were in bad faith, so even if P calls all parties, his reduction may not achieve full restitution.

It is commonly said that reduction will be granted only if *restitutio in integrum* is possible. How far this doctrine goes is uncertain. In the example just given, it seems unlikely that this defence could be pled by D. As for S, he has no interest to oppose the reduction of the disposition, provided his security remains unreduced.

It is sometimes said that a contract cannot be reduced if third parties have acquired real rights. The meaning of this is unclear. It may be just one aspect of the more general doctrine (itself of uncertain scope) about *restitutio in integrum*. But at all events its interest is very limited, for whether or not a *contract* can be reduced is of little significance for real rights. Real rights arise abstractly, not causally. If A sells to B and B sells

---

[39] I am indebted to James Wolffe for pointing out to me that in that classic case *York Buildings Co. v. Mackenzie* (1795) 3 Paton 378 the decision of the House of Lords seems to have been to set aside the sale as a contract, but not as a conveyance. The defender was ordered to reconvey. In my view that was the right approach – as it was also the right approach in *Spence v. Crawford* 1939 SC (HL) 52.

[40] Conveyancing (Scotland) Act 1924, s. 46. However, the wording is strange, and it is evident that the draftsman did not grasp what he was about. What he should have done was to provide that the decree has real effect when it is registered. But what he actually did was to preserve the (alleged) common-law rule but take away most of its effect. In the growing number of cases where the Land Registration (Scotland) Act applies, reduction without registration has no real effect.

[41] See *Heron v. Stewart* (1749) 3 Ross LC 243 for an example of the principle in action.

to C, it may perhaps be true that C's real right bars a reduction by A of his contract with B, but if so, the doctrine does not exist to protect C. Even if the A–B contract *were* reduced, that could not impact on C's real right. C's real right does not rest, directly or even indirectly, on the A–B contract.

One of the myriad problems about reduction is whether it is available (so as to produce real effect) after D's sequestration (or insolvent liquidation). I think that the principle is this: that if the reduction is based on D's fraud, it is available (so as to produce real effect) after D's sequestration, on the footing that 'fraud passes against creditors'. But otherwise probably not. The issue also arises with diligence, and indeed (from the standpoint of Scots common law) this is a purer form of the question. Let P dispone to D. Let C, a creditor of D, adjudge. P now seeks to reduce the disposition to D. He calls C. In my view, the adjudication will fall if the reduction is for fraud, but not otherwise.

Cases of real reduction would seem to fall into Class III in the table. But not all Class III cases are cases of reduction. D acquires P's money in some way and buys property with it. If a legal system says that P owns the property (in law or in equity) that is a Class III case,[42] but no question of real reduction could arise here. Class III ought to be subdivided, but there are too many classes already.

I assume, in all these cases, that the nullity pled by P is not an absolute one, for instance a nullity caused by forgery, or force and fear. I am also restricting my discussion to common law. Where the Land Registration (Scotland) Act 1979 applies there is an extra layer of complication and confusion.

XVI. Constructive trusts

I have expressed most of my thoughts on constructive trusts in a fairly recent article,[43] and I do not repeat myself here. In Scots law if 'proprietary restitution' were to arrive to any large extent it would have to be through

---

[42] In some circumstances (and some legal systems) it might be analysed as a Class II case.

[43] 'Constructive Trusts', 281 and 408. Earlier in this article I had the misfortune to disagree with Lord Millett. I will make restitution by quoting here an admirable passage from his writings: 'There is no branch of the law in which so much difficulty has been caused by semantic and conceptual confusion. Much of this centres on the expression "constructive trust". What do equity lawyers mean by this? And what part does it, or should it, play in the law of restitution? I shall suggest that the answer to the first question should be "Too much" and the answer to the second should be: "Very little"': Sir Peter Millett, 'Restitution and Constructive Trusts', in: Cornish *et al.*, *Restitution*, 199; also printed at (1998) 114 *LQR* 399.

the mechanism of the constructive trust. In my view our law has recognised the constructive trust but only in a marginal way, and has in general proved resistant to it. One judge has remarked that the constructive trust is 'a concept not familiar in Scots law'[44] while another has confessed to 'an almost instinctive abhorrence' of the idea.[45] That unfamiliarity, and that horror, show a healthy system. I was happy to see that in *Shilliday v. Smith*[46] no attempt was made to argue that the pursuer had some sort of 'proprietary' right in the house itself. The case was pled and won on the *condictio causa data causa non secuta*, a purely personal action.

Many distinguished English lawyers now question the wisdom of proprietary restitution, because of its unfairness to other creditors,[47] and some say that the approach of the civil-law tradition is preferable. So I too believe, but I would say here what I have said above, which is that the gap between common law and civil law is broader than might appear. Once tracing is allowed to any significant extent, it is possible to say that many cases of proprietary enrichment are really cases of vindication or quasi-vindication, that is to say, they are really cases where P has never lost his right *in rem*. If that approach is taken, the result is still something uncivilian, and something which is still dubious on policy grounds.

Is it not repugnant that a person should not receive what he is legally and morally due? Of course it is. But the same can be said on behalf of all claimants. Bankruptcy is injustice: the demands of law and morals are defeated. There is only so much to go round. To point out that to give more to one is to give less to others may be glaringly obvious: it is an obviousness to which many are oblivious. Justifying special treatment in bankruptcy[48] is always easy, and usually specious. Attempts have been made to claim a priority for enrichment creditors on various grounds.

---

[44] Lord Coulsfield in *Bank of Scotland v. MacLeod Paxton Woolard & Co.* 1998 SLT 258.

[45] Lord Johnston in *Mortgage Corporation v. Mitchells Roberton* 1997 SLT 1305.

[46] 1998 SC 725.

[47] One puzzle is whether the priority effect was of the essence, or whether it was merely accidental. J. P. Dawson took the first view, writing of proprietary restitution that 'its purpose was always plain enough, to promote the creation of preferences': *Unjust Enrichment: A Comparative Analysis* (1951), 29. The second view seems to be taken by Roy Goode, who comments that 'in almost every reported case D's solvency has not been in doubt and the reason for P's assertion of a proprietary interest has been to capture value added': 'Proprietary Restitutionary Claims', in: Cornish *et al.*, *Restitution*, 63, 65. This puzzle would be worth studying: it might reveal much about how and why the law has reached its present position, and, indeed, much about what that present position actually is.

[48] The debate is always couched in terms of bankruptcy, or of insolvency processes in general, such as liquidation. But (in Scots law at least) it arises equally in the law of execution.

One is that they are involuntary creditors – but, as has often been pointed out, so are many others, including tort/delict creditors. Another is that their contribution has 'swollen' the assets of the bankrupt – but many other creditors can claim precisely the same thing.[49] Another is that if proprietary enrichment rights are unfair, so what? *All* proprietary rights are unfair. To which the answer is that *not* all proprietary rights are unfair.

Shipwreck is unfair. Within that unfairness some attempt is made at fairness. First-class passengers have no priority for the lifeboats. Bankruptcy is unfair. But, within that unfairness, the law has always striven to achieve some fairness. There is a hallowed expression for such fairness within unfairness, and it is *paritas creditorum*. In all systems it is subject to exceptions, and these hungry exceptions can eat up the rule: German lawyers have a neat expression: the 'bankruptcy of bankruptcy'.[50] There is always pressure on the principle. In Germany the 'bankruptcy of bankruptcy' has arisen chiefly because the courts have been so willing to recognise security rights *praeter legem*. And here I come to a lifelong theme: who speaks for the ordinary unsecured creditor? Where is his lobby? At the doors of Parliament organised and well-funded pressure groups secure for themselves special legislative preferences. Who speaks for him in the courts? If there is no insolvency he is normally unrepresented, and the courts can hand down decisions that will cause mayhem in bankruptcy cases. Even in a bankruptcy case the ordinary unsecured creditor is represented by a trustee or liquidator who is reluctant to litigate. Moreover, the ordinary unsecured creditor is faceless (like the taxpayer). Faced with a clamorous claimant, who, like all queue-jumpers, is utterly convinced of the justice of his cause, the courts too easily cave in.

There are wider issues here. 'Proprietary restitution' cannot be examined (from a policy standpoint) without looking at the whole law of insolvency. All I will say here is that if it is true (and it is true) that there are many priorities in bankruptcy whose justification is questionable, and if it is true (and it is true) that a certain element of arbitrariness is unavoidable in bankruptcy, that does not mean that we should abandon all attempt at a reasoned and equitable division of the inadequate bankrupt estate. The fact that any proprietary right will lead to unequal treatment

---

[49] The law-and-economics thinkers have argued that even tort creditors are often in this position, for tort liability represents the price that a business must pay for an element of cost-externalisation.

[50] Which the new *Insolvenzordnung* (in force 1 January 1999) addresses, but in my view inadequately.

in bankruptcy is sufficient to refute the argument that proprietary restitution should be rejected because it leads to inequality,[51] but the central issue remains: to determine when the *paritas creditorum* should be adhered to and when departed from. There are no good answers, but some answers are less bad than others.

---

[51] This I take to be the point made eloquently by Smith, *Law of Tracing*, 303 ff. His 'principle of unfairness' is that 'the specificity of property rights guarantees inequality of treatment among claimants'. But inequality is not necessarily unfair. Some inequalities are unfair but others fair; the task is to decide which.

21 Property, subsidiarity and unjust enrichment

Lionel Smith

I. Introduction

If someone were asked, as I was, to write a paper dealing with 'proprietary issues' in the law of unjust enrichment, he or she would most naturally think of proprietary consequences: that is, the extent to which unjust enrichments can be reversed by proprietary as opposed to obligationary responses. This of, course, would be an interesting study, although it might lack a certain promise as a comparative work, due to the well-known refusal of civilian systems to have any truck with such odd and uncontrollable devices as the constructive trust.[1] Instead I have chosen to consider the interaction between the law of property and the law of unjustified enrichment from the other end: that is, the extent to which the existence of a proprietary claim affects the availability of a claim in unjustified enrichment. Or, at least, I chose so to begin; for the study grew, as such things will, and in the end it has become a wider look at how and why the availability of unjustified enrichment is conditioned by the existence of other kinds of claims. The focus is on the common law, German law and the law of Quebec.

It can be described, then, as a comparative study of devices for controlling the scope of liability in unjust enrichment; but it must be emphasised

---

I would like to thank Dr Simon Whittaker for his thoughtful comments, although any remaining errors are my own. I acknowledge with gratitude the financial assistance of the Arts and Humanities Research Board, and also the kind hospitality of the Faculty of Law, McGill University, where much of the research for this paper was done and a working version presented. I am grateful for the helpful suggestions I received at that time.

[1] 'In the very short space of seventy-five years we have created a monster': J. P. Dawson, *Unjust Enrichment: A Comparative Analysis* (1951), 30.

that it is a study of only some such devices. The grounds on which claims can be made, the meaning of enrichment, the available defences: all of these could be described as devices for controlling the scope of liability, and so a comprehensive study of such devices would amount to a book on the subject. This attempt is obviously more limited in its ambitions, but it bears remembering that a restrictive approach taken by a system in one context can be offset by a more liberal approach in another.

II. Property

The threshold question is whether a plaintiff is allowed to make a claim in unjustified enrichment in respect of the transfer of some asset, in the case where the plaintiff remains the owner of the asset in question. A simple case will illustrate the point: if a thief steals my horse, can I sue the thief in unjustified enrichment?[2]

1. Common law

The position in the common law is not definitively settled. One reason may be that it seems to have little practical implication. The common law protects property in moveables through the law of wrongs, and in particular through the tort of conversion, which is a tort of strict liability. It is also a tort which does not admit of the defence of change of position. The tort claim being wider than the unjustified enrichment claim, there is no incentive to bring the latter. Even a defendant who came into possession of my horse in good faith is liable in conversion. There may, however, be some relevance where the plaintiff's proprietary right is an Equitable rather than a legal one.[3] The reason is that claims for interference with a plaintiff's Equitable proprietary rights are not strict but are fault-based.[4] If the plaintiff were allowed to deploy an unjustified enrichment claim

---

[2] Throughout this chapter, I expressly exclude the case where the first transferee has gone on to transfer the thing to some other person, gratuitously or for some exchange value. Such a possibility complicates the analysis considerably. Other chapters in this volume address the matter.

[3] Since later in the chapter I will have occasion to refer to 'equity' in the civilian sense, I have used 'Equity' and 'Equitable' where the reference is to that system of law. Although many consider this inelegant, I make no apologies for following the example of such as Professor F. W. Maitland and Sir George Jessel MR.

[4] *Citadel General Assurance Co. v. Lloyds Bank Canada* [1997] 3 SCR 805; 152 DLR 4th 411, required a showing of carelessness. See now *Twinsectra Ltd v. Yardley* [1999] Lloyd's Rep Banking 438 (CA), §§ 101–11, apparently assuming that liability depends upon a showing of dishonesty.

instead, the scope of liability might be wider.[5] It is also true that such things as limitation periods and the outcome of choice of law rules might differ depending upon what type of claim the plaintiff is able to deploy.[6]

It has been suggested that in such a case there is no room for an unjustified enrichment claim. One argument is that the defendant is not enriched in the requisite sense if the plaintiff retains his proprietary rights in the transferred asset.[7] Under this view, the non-availability of a claim in unjustified enrichment arises as a matter of logical necessity. The argument is that the elements of unjustified enrichment are simply not satisfied.

In order to evaluate this argument, a word must first be said about the measure of recovery. Assume that the thief stole my horse one year before the time of trial. If my claim were calculated so as to represent the recovery of the value of one year's use of the horse, it would be hard to deny it. That value has clearly been transferred from me to the defendant; and presumably, such a claim would leave untouched my ownership of the horse. The more difficult question is whether I can have an enrichment claim measured by the value of my ownership. Here the objection makes sense, and indeed has a certain logical attraction: if my ownership has not been transferred, how can I say that the defendant was enriched by the value of my ownership? On the other hand, the objection ignores the common law's tendency to multiply remedies, preventing excess recovery by requiring the plaintiff to elect between them.[8] For example, if I were to sue the horse thief in conversion, the normal measure of damages would reflect the full ownership of the horse, even though I remained the owner. Upon recovery of the full judgment, the ownership would be transferred by operation of law to the defendant.[9] There is no reason why this system,

---

[5] It would be wider if the unjust enrichment claim did not require the proof of any level of knowledge on the part of the defendant. This position is advocated in P. B. H. Birks, 'Misdirected Funds: Restitution from the Recipient', [1989] *Lloyd's Maritime and Commercial Law Quarterly* 296; Lord Nicholls of Birkenhead, 'Knowing Receipt: The Need for a New Landmark', in: W. Cornish et al. (eds.), *Restitution: Past, Present and Future* (1998), 231, and J. Martin, 'Recipient Liability after *Westdeutsche*', [1998] *Conveyancer and Property Lawyer* 13. It has not yet been adopted judicially. It is arguable that even if a claim in unjust enrichment may arise upon the defendant's interference with the plaintiff's Equitable proprietary rights, a level of knowledge on the part of the defendant must be established: L. D. Smith, 'Property, Unjust Enrichment and the Structure of Trusts' (2000) 116 *LQR* 412.

[6] See *Macmillan Inc. v. Bishopsgate Investment Trust plc* [1996] 1 WLR 387 (CA).

[7] W. Swadling, 'A Claim in Restitution?', [1996] *Lloyd's Maritime and Commercial Law Quarterly* 63, 65.

[8] *Kleinwort Benson Ltd v. Lincoln City Council* [1998] 4 All ER 513 at 542h; [1999] 2 AC 349 per Lord Goff.

[9] *Sadler v. Scott* [1947] 1 DLR 712 (BCCA); L. D. Smith, *The Law of Tracing* (1997), 291–2.

which was necessitated by the lack of any ability to vindicate a moveable thing, could not operate in unjustified enrichment claims. That is, the enrichment claim could also be measured by the value of full ownership of the horse and, upon payment of the judgment, title would pass. So it is strongly arguable that the enrichment claim is available at common law.

2. Roman law

Roman law provided for the reversal of unjustified enrichment through a set of actions called *condictiones*. These were personal claims for the transfer of a specific thing, or of a fixed amount of money or some other fungible asset. The form of words used in these claims asked for relief should it appear to the judge that the defendant 'ought to give' to the plaintiff that which was the object of the claim. In this context, at least in classical Roman law if not earlier, these words were understood to imply that the object of the claim belonged to the defendant. So on the face of it, no *condictio* could logically be used in the case of the stolen horse with which this discussion is concerned.

But the position was not governed entirely by logic. One of the *condictiones* was the *condictio ex causa furtiva*, and Gaius observed that it could be used against a defendant guilty of *furtum* even though he did not become owner of the stolen thing:

This distinction between real and personal actions means that we definitely cannot seek something of our own from another by a pleading – 'if it appears that he has a duty to give'. For what we own cannot be given to us, because 'give' is to be understood as meaning giving so that it may become ours. What is already ours cannot be made more so. No doubt it was from hatred of thieves, to multiply their liabilities, that the law came to allow against them not only the claims for twofold or fourfold penal damages [*actio furti*] but also the pleading – 'if it appears that they have a duty to give' – even though the real action [*rei vindicatio*], by which we claim what is ours, is also competent against them.[10]

Clearly Gaius viewed the claim as anomalous. The reason he gives – the hatred of thieves – is not the only one which has been suggested.[11] If it is taken as correct, it means that hatred of thieves leads to the allowance of an anomalous claim in order to make it easier for the plaintiff to recover,

---

[10] Gai. IV, 4. This text appears in Justinian's *Institutes* IV, 6, 14.

[11] R. Zimmermann, *The Law of Obligations: Roman Foundations of the Civilian Tradition* (1990, paperback edn 1996), 941, n. 152, suggests that the *condictio* was extended to *furtum* at a time when the words *dare oportere* ('ought to give') had not acquired a technical meaning confined to a duty to transfer ownership. Similarly, *Institutes of Gaius*, Part II (commentary by F. de Zulueta, 1953), 229.

or to recover more. If, regarding the recovery of what was stolen or its value,[12] the plaintiff were confined to his *rei vindicatio*, then he would need to prove that the defendant still had the stolen thing. He would also need to prove his 'quiritary ownership' of the thing. Moreover, the value would be assessed at the time of the commencement of proceedings, whereas under the *condictio ex causa furtiva* it was taken to be the highest value since the commission of the theft.[13] Finally, the *condictio* could be brought against an heir of the thief, unlike a delictual action.[14] It may be noted that the *condictio*, measured by the value of ownership of the thing, was alternative and not cumulative to the *rei vindicatio*; similarly to the common-law position, the enrichment claim effectively transferred a kind of title to the defendant.[15]

But if allowing this claim was anomalous, it must be that the 'normal' position was that no *condictio* was available where the plaintiff remained the owner; only the *rei vindicatio* could be brought. Although the concept of *furtum* was much wider than our modern idea of theft,[16] none the less it was possible for the defendant to acquire the plaintiff's horse in circumstances which did not amount to *furtum*; he might find it, or purchase it in good faith. In such a case, it seems, the Roman law position was that there was no enrichment remedy, but only the *rei vindicatio*.[17] If one asks why this was, it is tempting, perhaps, to say that the concepts used by the Roman lawyers were not sufficiently fine-grained to distinguish enrichment by use from enrichment by a transfer of ownership. In general terms, such an idea would clearly be incorrect. The possibility of theft

---

[12] The *actio furti* for damages was available in any case, and could be cumulated with one of (i) the *rei vindicatio*, (ii) the *condictio ex causa furtiva*, or (iii) a contractual action, which might lie if, for example, the stolen thing had been deposited with the thief. See Zimmermann, *Law of Obligations*, 942–3.

[13] *Ibid.*, 942; J. A. C. Thomas, *The Institutes of Justinian: Text, Translation and Commentary* (1975), 295.

[14] *Institutes of Roman Law by Gaius* (trans. and commentary by E. Poste, 4th edn by E. A. Whittuck, 1904), 450; this was true whether or not the heir could be shown to have been enriched: P. Pauw, 'Historical Notes on the Nature of the Condictio Furtiva', (1976) 93 *SALJ* 395, 397. The only disadvantage of the *condictio* was that it could not be brought against a thief who was not free: *Ibid.*, 396.

[15] Zimmermann, *Law of Obligations*, 943. Election occurred earlier in Roman law than in the common law, and the mere bringing of the *condictio* would eliminate any prospect of vindication.

[16] *Ibid.*, 922–30.

[17] *Ibid.*, 836, n. 20: 'The condictio ex causa furtiva survived as the only application of a condictio which could be brought by the owner.' The contrary position is taken in D. Liebs, 'The History of the Roman *Condictio* Up to Justinian', in: N. MacCormick and P. Birks (eds.), *The Legal Mind: Essays for Tony Honoré* (1986), 163, 165 ff.

of possession was recognised; if an owner pledged a thing with a creditor and then took it away without the latter's consent, this was *furtum*.[18] Moreover, there are cases in which it seems the *condictio ex causa furtiva* was available to a plaintiff who was a non-owner in possession, and whose possession was taken by the defendant.[19] So, at least against a thief, a transfer of possession could support a *condictio*, whether or not the plaintiff was the owner. And it has been argued that even in the absence of *furtum*, a plaintiff who was and remained the owner could use a *condictio* against a good-faith finder of property.[20]

This brings the discussion back to the anomaly of *furtum*. Gaius suggests that it was anomalous in the sense that the claim was allowed even though the facts did not really fit the words of the formula, the defendant not being the owner. If it was possible for the owner to use a *condictio* even in the absence of *furtum*, then it was not so anomalous. But it may be that the anomaly lay in the measure of recovery. Clearly, the *condictio ex causa furtiva* allowed recovery measured by the full value of ownership, and was a non-cumulative alternative to the *rei vindicatio*. It is less clear what might be the measure of recovery in the case of a *condictio* brought by an owner in the absence of *furtum*, but one possibility would be that recovery would be measured only by the value the defendant had derived by use. This would leave the plaintiff's ownership, and his *rei vindicatio*, intact.

3. German law

Most of the *condictiones* of Roman law were codified in the BGB, but that code also added a general enrichment action.[21] The doctrine that

---

[18] Gai. III, 200.
[19] Zimmermann, *Law of Obligations*, 840 notes that a *condictio* could be used by a possessor of land who was evicted. See also Liebs, 'Roman Condictio', 170. The designation of this type of claim based on loss of possession as *condictio possessionis* clearly shows the focus on possession, although it is not clear whether it sheds light on the question whether the *condictio ex causa furtiva* was the only *condictio* available where title did not pass. The reason is that the *condictio possessionis* was arguably a sub-category of the *condictio ex causa furtiva*: Zimmermann, *Law of Obligations*, 840, n. 40.
[20] In particular, Liebs, 'Roman Condictio', 171 suggests that an owner could bring a *condictio* against a finder of property. Note also the final words of Gai. II, 79, indicating that a *condictio* is available against 'thieves and certain other types of possessor' (sc.: defendants who are not owners but who have not committed *furtum*). Again, Zimmermann, *Law of Obligations*, 840 appears to take the view that such claims were sub-categories of the *condictio ex causa furtiva*.
[21] For the history, see R. Zimmermann and J. du Plessis, 'Basic Features of the German Law of Unjustified Enrichment', [1994] *Restitution LR* 14, 14–20.

has grown up around this part of the BGB is complicated indeed.[22] But the law governing the point dealt with in this article seems fairly clear. Where the plaintiff remains owner of a thing which is in the possession of the defendant, the defendant not having a right to retain possession, the provisions on unjustified enrichment in §§ 812–22 do not govern. Rather, the situation is governed by an 'owner–possessor relationship' (*Eigentümer-Besitzer-Verhältnis*) and certain provisions of the law of property apply (§§ 987 ff.). These provide for the restitution to the owner of any benefits derived from the thing by the possessor, including fruits but also use value. They also provide for the recovery from the owner of any necessary expenditures. The extent of recovery turns in large part on whether the possessor was in good faith.[23]

Generally, then, unjustified enrichment claims do not lie for use value. Or at least, claims which are sourced in the unjustified enrichment provisions of the BGB do not lie. If one were to ask why it is that a plaintiff can claim for the use value under §§ 987 ff., it would seem that the answer is that otherwise the defendant would be unjustly enriched.[24] The use value, which belonged to the plaintiff, was enjoyed by the defendant, and so there was a transfer of wealth without a legal basis. But the measure of recovery does not include the value of ownership, and the *rei vindicatio* is preserved. This was the position suggested for Roman law, in the absence of *furtum*. The parallel is heightened by the fact that in those cases where title does not pass but none the less the 'owner–possessor relationship' does not govern, an unjustified enrichment claim under § 812 is allowed for the value of possession, and indeed modern German lawyers still refer to it as the *condictio possessionis*.[25]

4. Quebec law

In the Civil Code of Lower Canada, as in the French Civil Code, there was no general action for unjustified enrichment. There was a regime governing the management of the business of another (*negotiorum gestio*), and there was a claim for reception of a thing not due (*réception de l'indu*),

---

[22] *Ibid.*, 15, quotes Detlef König: 'The terminology is confusing, almost each statement is disputed, the solution of trivial questions is becoming ever more complicated, and there is a grave danger of a loss of perspective.'

[23] See generally B. S. Markesinis, W. Lorenz and G. Dannemann, *The German Law of Obligations*, vol. I, *The Law of Contracts and Restitution*, (1997), 741–3.

[24] §§ 988 and 993 cross-refer to the provisions on unjustified enrichment.

[25] Markesinis *et al.*, *Law of Contracts*, 769.

reflecting one of the Roman *condictiones*, the *condictio indebiti*.[26] However, in Quebec, as in France, a general action was recognised by the courts under the rubric of the *actio de in rem verso*.[27] The general action is now codified in the Civil Code of Quebec, articles 1493–6.

There are provisions in the code that perform a similar function to those in the BGB on the 'owner–possessor relationship'. Articles 928 ff. deal with the effects of possession, and generally regulate the position of a possessor who is not the owner. On the other hand, articles 1699–707 govern 'restitution of prestations'.[28] Their applicability is set out in article 1699 and via certain other provisions;[29] the effect is that someone such as a finder or a thief of property would be subject to articles 931–2, but one to whom the property had been transferred by the plaintiff would be subject to articles 1699–707. Either way, the possessor must, of course, return the property if possible;[30] and both regimes require a bad-faith possessor to render account of the fruits and revenues of the property.[31] Fruits and revenues do not, however, include use value.[32] Under article 1704, the defendant must account for use value if he was in bad faith, or if use was the primary object of the prestation, or if the property was subject to rapid depreciation.

---

[26] Dawson, *Unjust Enrichment*, 96, laid the blame for this over-simplification on Robert-Joseph Pothier. The same view is expressed in K. Zweigert and H. Kötz, *Introduction to Comparative Law* (trans. by T. Weir, 3rd edn, 1998), 545–6.

[27] In France, in 1892 in the *Boudier* decision, Req. 15 June 1892, S 1893.1.281 note Labbé, DP 1892.1.596; in Quebec, not definitively until *Cie Immobilière Viger Ltée v. Laureat Giguère Inc.* [1977] 2 SCR 67. The *actio de in rem verso* was not one of the condictiones; it was originally applicable only to a narrow range of cases. For the history of how it came to be used as a general enrichment claim, see Zimmermann, *Law of Obligations*, 878–84.

[28] A prestation is the object of an obligation (art. 1373); it is that which the debtor is bound to render to the creditor.

[29] Arts. 1422, 1491 (*réception de l'indu*), 1606, 1694, 1838. The regime in arts. 1699–707 does not appear to govern where the general unjustified enrichment claim of arts. 1493–6 applies because (i) there is no cross-reference to arts. 1699–707 from arts. 1493–6, as there is from other provisions; (ii) the regime in arts. 1699–707 is inconsistent with arts. 1493–6. For example, art. 1495 in general excuses restitution to the extent that the enrichment has fallen away, but art. 1702 in general does not; and (iii) on facts which give rise to a claim under arts. 1493–6 the benefit received by the defendant cannot generally be seen as a prestation.

[30] Arts. 953 and 1700.   [31] Arts. 931 and 1704.

[32] See the definitions in art. 910. This is in contrast to the position in German law, where the provisions on the 'owner–possessor relationship' refer to *Nutzungen*, translated as 'emoluments' by Markesinis *et al.*, *Law of Contracts*. The term is defined in § 100 so as to include fruits (itself defined in § 99 to include revenues) and also (as translated by Markesinis *et al.*) 'the advantages which the use of the thing or right affords'.

Articles 931–2 are silent on the matter. Hence there appears to be a gap where the defendant has derived some significant use value, but the thing was not transferred as a prestation; for example, if someone has stolen my horse and used it for a year. It would be natural for this gap to be filled by a general enrichment action. G. S. Challies, relying on French decisions and commentators, thought that an enrichment by use value could support the *actio de in rem verso*.[33] So it appears that the Quebec position is quite similar to the Roman and German positions, allowing an enrichment claim for use value only, while preserving the ability to vindicate.

5. Conclusion

In these systems, outside *furtum* in Roman law, it seems you cannot measure an enrichment claim by the value of ownership where ownership has not passed. The enrichment claim is not permitted to supplant the *rei vindicatio*. But *furtum* shows the possibility of another solution, one which is arguably adopted by the common law. That is, through the use of appropriate doctrinal tools to avoid overcompensation, it is possible to create a relationship of elective concurrence between the enrichment claim and the *rei vindicatio*. So the question becomes, why has this possibility been resisted? Why is the relationship instead one of subsidiarity?

III. Subsidiarity

This section provides a brief comparative overview of some different kinds of subsidiarity applicable to unjustified enrichment claims in different systems. In the next section, an attempt will be made to understand the phenomenon of subsidiarity. It is, however, necessary to begin with definition and differentiation, because subsidiarity is a concept with different meanings. One understanding of it is as a kind of opposite to concurrent liability. On this approach, subsidiarity is a relationship between different types of claims such that one type of claim is disallowed by the presence of another claim.[34] If unjustified enrichment were subsidiary in this way to the *rei vindicatio*, then if the *rei vindicatio* were available, a claim in unjustified enrichment would not lie even if all of its elements were established. If, on the other hand, the *rei vindicatio* could not be made out, the claim in unjustified enrichment would be permitted. As seen in previous sections, this appears to be the law of Quebec and of Germany.

---

[33] G. S. Challies, *The Doctrine of Unjustified Enrichment in the Law of the Province of Quebec* (2nd edn, 1952), 63.
[34] Dawson, *Unjust Enrichment*, 106.

Then there is a much stronger idea of subsidiarity, which denies the availability of a claim in unjustified enrichment due to the applicability of some other set of legal principles, even if, according to those principles, no claim will lie. An example will assist. Assume that an occupier of land, who is not the owner, has made improvements to the land. If a codified system has a set of provisions which deal specifically with such improvements, and if, according to those provisions, the occupier has no claim, then a court would probably also deny a claim based on a general principle against unjustified enrichment.[35] The important point is that here the plaintiff has no claim at all. Weak subsidiarity, as discussed in the previous paragraph, only directs a plaintiff to the correct claim; strong subsidiarity can deny the plaintiff any claim. It can also be said that while weak subsidiarity is a relationship between claims, strong subsidiarity is better understood as a relationship between legal dispositions or sets of rules.

It will be argued below that each of the systems under consideration makes unjustified enrichment strongly subsidiary in some circumstances. It would be possible for a system to make unjustified enrichment claims weakly subsidiary to all other claims, and indeed it appears that this is the law of Quebec. It would not, however, make sense for a system to make unjust enrichment strongly subsidiary to all other rules of law. The effect would be that there could never be a claim in unjustified enrichment.[36] This can be illustrated by a recent French case, in which the plaintiff sought recourse by an action of guarantee as well as an action *de in rem verso*.[37] The action of guarantee was rejected since no fault was shown on the part of the defendant, but the claim in unjustified enrichment was allowed. The defendant appealed on the ground that this ignored its subsidiary character, but the Cour de cassation rejected the appeal. One might view the decision as an occasion for dispensing entirely with subsidiarity;[38] but it can be understood more narrowly, as holding that there was no strong subsidiarity between the action of guarantee and the action in unjustified enrichment. In that light, it does not touch the possibility of a general weak subsidiarity, nor the need for strong subsidiarity in some cases.[39]

---

[35] *Gagné v. Tremblay* [1989] RJQ 1619 (Que Ct).
[36] As observed in H. Mazaud et al., *Leçons de Droit Civil*, tome II, vol. I; F. Chabas, *Les Obligations* (8th edn, 1991), § 709.
[37] Civ. (1) 3 June 1997, JCP 1998.II.10102, note Viney. I am grateful to Jean-Pascal Chazal, Université Jean Monnet (Saint Etienne), for drawing this case to my attention.
[38] As does Viney in his note, *ibid*.
[39] Some French writers have recognised the difference between strong and weak subsidiarity: for example Chabas, *Les Obligations*, §§ 706–9.

1. Strong subsidiarity

The first step will be to examine strong subsidiarity. In what circumstances do other legal regimes exclude the possibility of a claim in unjustified enrichment, even where the elements of the claim are present, and even where the plaintiff has no other claim against the enriched defendant?

(a) Excluding claims due to the relationship between plaintiff and defendant

Strong subsidiarity often operates based on the legal relationship between the plaintiff and the defendant. There are a number of examples.

(i) Illegal, void or unenforceable transactions

Consider the case where some statutory provision comes into play to deny the plaintiff a right which it would otherwise have. Take the case of an illegal contract under which the plaintiff has conferred a benefit upon the defendant. A rule of law operates to take away the plaintiff's ability to sue for contractual performance; can the plaintiff none the less sue in unjustified enrichment to recover the benefit it has conferred? All legal systems have struggled with this question.[40] It can also arise where the contract is made merely unenforceable or void, rather than illegal. It is a question of trying to determine the intention of the legislator: would allowing the enrichment claim subvert the goals of the rule that made the contract illegal or unenforceable?[41] It is clear that, in any system, an unjust enrichment claim must be excluded by any legislative provision which implicitly denies it.

(ii) Different types of unjustified enrichment claims

The same reasoning can apply to the case in which a system provides more than one type of claim for unjustified enrichment. It might be that

---

[40] For Quebec, see for example *Nadeau v. Doyon* [1994] RJQ 2267 (Que Ct), citing Quebec and French doctrine. For Germany, Zimmermann and Du Plessis, 'Basic Features', 22-4. For the common law, G. Virgo, 'The Effect of Illegality on Claims for Restitution in English Law', in: W. Swadling (ed.), *The Limits of Restitutionary Claims: A Comparative Analysis* (1997), 141 ff.; Law Commission Consultation Paper No. 154, *Illegal Transactions: The Effect of Illegality on Contracts and Trusts* (1999), Part II.

[41] Dawson took the view that this is not subsidiarity as such: Dawson, *Unjust Enrichment*, 106; but that is understandable since he was using the term in the sense which in this paper is denoted by 'weak subsidiarity'. See also B. Nicholas, 'Unjust Enrichment and Subsidiarity', in: F. Santoro Passarelli and M. Lupoi (eds.), *Scintillae iuris: studi in memoria di Gino Gorla* (1994), 2037, 2044. Still, courts in France (Req. 15 June 1892, S 1893.1.281 note Labbé, DP 1892.1.596; Civ. 12 May 1914, S 1918.1.41 note Naquet; Civ. (3) 29 April 1971, GP 1971.2.554) and Quebec (*Bédard v. Bédard Transport Co.* [1960] CS 472) have described this as subsidiarity.

a plaintiff will not be allowed a free choice among them, even where the facts of the case satisfy more than one claim. Such a doctrinal rule could be justified where a general unjustified enrichment claim is provided along with other unjustified enrichment claims that apply only to particular fact patterns. For example, in Quebec there is a general enrichment action and also the action for *réception de l'indu*. It was held, under the Civil Code of Lower Canada, that the general claim is not appropriate where the facts fit the claim for *réception de l'indu*, even though the latter claim could not succeed.[42] Another example is provided by articles 955 ff., which govern the position relating to a landowner's obligation to pay for improvements to land; there is no room for the general enrichment action where these provisions are apt to decide the case, even if no claim lies under them.[43] Similarly, in German law the provisions governing the 'owner–possessor relationship' expressly exclude any other enrichment remedy on facts within that relationship.[44] In both of these systems, where a plaintiff can claim his expenses for managing the business of another, unjustified enrichment is excluded.[45] This kind of subsidiarity does not seem to be relevant in the common-law system, which does not have a general enrichment claim alongside more specific ones.[46]

(iii) Unjustified enrichment and contracts
Unjustified enrichment claims are not allowed where the matter in issue is dealt with by a subsisting contract between the parties. In that case, it is said, the contract governs, and only if it can be disposed of in some

---

[42] *Willmor Discount Corp. v. Vaudreuil (City)* [1994] 2 SCR 210 at 227. This conclusion can be expected to remain true under the Civil Code of Quebec. Because the action for reception of a thing not due had prescribed, however, the conclusion could rest on weak subsidiarity: see 608–9.
[43] *Gagné v. Tremblay* [1989] RJQ 1619 (Que Ct).
[44] § 993(1), last half-sentence. In German law if the plaintiff has an enrichment claim based on a 'performance', he may not bring any other kind of enrichment claim against that defendant. For further discussion, see below, 604.
[45] In Quebec, the general enrichment action is subsidiary to all claims, as discussed in the next section. For Germany, see Markesinis *et al.*, *Law of Contracts*, 768 (noting that claims *against* the manager may attract concurrent liability under both regimes).
[46] Note, however, the suggestion in A. S. Burrows, 'Free Acceptance and the Law of Restitution', (1988) 104 *LQR* 576, 599, that if the common law allows claims based on 'free acceptance', these should not be available except where no other basis for a claim exists. The suggestion is adopted in P. B. H. Birks, 'In Defence of Free Acceptance', in: A. Burrows (ed.), *Essays on the Law of Restitution* (1991), 105, 144–5. This, however, would probably be weak subsidiarity.

way is a claim in unjustified enrichment available.[47] An initial reaction might be to see this as an example of weak subsidiarity, on the view that rights in unjust enrichment are subsidiary to the parties' contractual rights. On a closer examination, however, it appears that the governing principle is strong subsidiarity.

It is not true to say that claims in unjustified enrichment are subsidiary to claims in breach of contract, because in all of the systems under consideration such claims are alternatives. If a contract is cancelled for breach (and conceptualisations of 'cancelled' vary in different systems), the non-breaching party is allowed to choose to recover the benefits it conferred, as an alternative to seeking damages valued by performance. A system may view this claim to recover benefits either as a contractual one or as founded on unjustified enrichment.[48] The claim is not one which can be understood as enforcing any contractual promise, and it is arguable that wherever the claim may appear in a civil code, its function is to prevent unjustified enrichment.[49]

One might try to formulate the relevant principle by saying that enrichment claims are weakly subsidiary to primary contractual rights. This would reflect the general position that there can be no enrichment claim

---

[47] That is, the plaintiff must show that the contract was void or unenforceable *ab initio*, or has been avoided or terminated. German law: Markesinis *et al.*, *Law of Contracts*, 45. Quebec law: Challies, *Doctrine of Unjustified Enrichment*, 95–6; J. Pineau, D. Burman and S. Gaudet, *Théorie des Obligations* (3rd edn, 1996), 305–6, 601–2. Common law: *Pan Ocean Shipping Co. Ltd v. Creditcorp Ltd (The Trident Beauty)* [1994] 1 WLR 161 at 164F (HL) per Lord Goff; *Singh v. Singh* (1992) 71 BCLR 2d 336; [1993] 2 WWR 59 (CA); *337965 B.C. Ltd v. Tackama Forest Products Ltd* (1992) 67 BCLR 2d 1; 91 DLR 4th 129 (CA), leave to appeal refused [1993] 1 SCR v; *Building Design 2 Ltd v. Wascana Rehabilitation Centre* [1992] 6 WWR 343 (Sask QB); *Hesjedal v. Granville Estate* (1993) 117 Sask R 2d 111; 109 DLR 4th 353 (QB); *Scott v. Noble* (1994) 99 BCLR 2d 137 (CA); *Luscar Ltd v. Pembina Resources Ltd* (1994) 24 Alta LR 3d 305; [1995] 2 WWR 153 (CA), §§ 111–22, leave to appeal refused [1995] 3 SCR vii; *Windisman v. Toronto College Park Ltd* (1996) 28 OR 3d 29; 132 DLR 4th 512 (Gen Div).

[48] R. Zimmermann, 'Restitution After Termination for Breach of Contract in German Law', [1997] *Restitution LR* 13, 17–18: the idea that the relevant provisions in the BGB are a special kind of enrichment claim is no longer accepted by most German jurists. Recovery in French law is usually understood as based on the claim for reception of a thing not due: J. Flour and J.-L. Aubert, *Droit Civil: Les Obligations* (6th edn by J.-L. Aubert, 1994), vol. II, 26; J. Bell, S. Boyron and S. Whittaker, *Principles of French Law* (1998), 421; even if the basis is said to be theoretically different, it is conceded that this is the practical outcome: M. Malaurie, *Les Restitutions en Droit Civil* (1991), 35. In Quebec, the provisions on 'restitution of prestations' in arts. 1699–707 were added in the new Civil Code for just this type of situation. In the plan of the code, they belong neither to unjust enrichment nor to contract.

[49] Zimmermann, 'Restitution After Termination', 18, apparently disagreeing with the majority view; D. P. Visser, 'Rethinking Unjustified Enrichment: A Perspective of the Competition between Contractual and Enrichment Remedies', [1992] *Acta Juridica* 203, 209–10.

so long as there is a subsisting contract between the parties. Of course, this covers the case where there has been no breach of the contract; but it also deals with the position where there has been a breach, so long as the breach does not lead to cancellation of the contract. Even this, however, does not appear to be quite wide enough. Sometimes, unjustified enrichment is excluded even where there are no primary rights. This can be illustrated by *Rillford Investments Ltd v. Gravure International Capital Corp*.[50] The plaintiff's business was to broker mergers and acquisitions. The defendant wanted to be acquired and it entered into a contract with the plaintiff providing for the payment of a healthy commission to the plaintiff, should the plaintiff arrange for the acquisition of the defendant by another corporation. The terms of the contract provided that the arrangement would end after sixty days, but that the fee would be payable if the defendant were acquired within 365 days by a company introduced by the plaintiff. The plaintiff introduced a potential buyer, Graphic Corp., but no sale was agreed. Two-and-a-half years after the agreement was executed, Graphic Corp. acquired the defendant. The plaintiff sued, relying on implied contract and unjust enrichment, but the claim was rejected. Although the contract said nothing about liability in unjustified enrichment, the Court held that it 'contemplated the possibility that the plaintiff would receive no compensation if the defendant was enriched by virtue of the sale of his business beyond the time of the expiry of the agreement'.[51] By the time all of the facts had occurred which allegedly generated an unjustified enrichment, there was no contract; there were no primary or secondary obligations. And yet somehow the contract excluded the enrichment claim. The decision was made under the common law, but one could expect a similar holding in each of the systems under consideration. If so, it follows that the unavailability of unjust enrichment in the contractual context cannot be understood through weak subsidiarity. Rather, the existence of a relevant distribution of risks and rewards between plaintiff and defendant excludes unjustified enrichment, even though the plaintiff has no other claim. This is strong subsidiarity.

At this point it must be observed that Stephen Smith has now argued that, for the common law, there should be concurrent liability in contract and unjustified enrichment just as there is between contract and tort.[52] The gist of the argument is the same as that which eventually prevailed in the debates about contract and tort: that is, the only question is whether the elements of the different causes of action can be established, and if

---

[50] (1997) 118 Man R 2d 11; [1997] 7 WWR 534 (CA).   [51] *Ibid.*, § 30.
[52] S. Smith, 'Concurrent Liability in Contract and Unjust Enrichment', (1999) 115 *LQR* 245. See also Visser, 'Rethinking Unjustified Enrichment', 231–6.

they can, then both types of claim are available. Clearly, this argument depends on the absence of any governing principle of subsidiarity, and it must be assessed in the light of the justifications for this principle, which are discussed below.

(b) Excluding claims due to relationships involving third parties

Where there is a relevant distribution of risks and rewards between plaintiff and defendant, enrichment claims are in general excluded. Here we need to consider some slightly more complex situations, namely where there is no contract between plaintiff and defendant, but there is a contract between one or the other of them and some third party.

(i) *Plaintiff's contract with a third party*

Consider first the case in which the plaintiff has a contract with some third party. This can be illustrated by the facts of the *Boudier* decision,[53] the case in which the Cour de cassation recognised the *actio de in rem verso* as a general enrichment remedy. The plaintiff contracted with a lessee of land to fertilise the land, and did so. The plaintiff was unable to recover the price because the lessee was insolvent. The plaintiff sued the lessor, who by that time had taken possession of the land. Recovery in that situation on the basis of unjustified enrichment raises certain difficulties. The plaintiff entered into a legal relationship with the lessee which provided for the payment for the fertiliser, and, with his right to payment still intact (albeit impaired by the lessee's insolvency), he was allowed to recover from another defendant. The policies will be discussed further below,[54] but it may be observed here that Challies noted that in two cases in 1939 the Cour de cassation disallowed claims in similar fact patterns.[55] The Civil Code of Quebec seems clearly to deny recovery such a case, as article 1494 provides: 'Enrichment or impoverishment is justified where it results from the performance of an obligation.' There is no stipulation that it has to be an obligation owed to the person who was enriched.[56] If the plaintiff was performing an obligation, his impoverishment was justified, and under Quebec law (as in France) the claim lies only if both the enrichment and the impoverishment were unjustified.[57]

---

[53] Req. 15 June 1892, S 1893.1.281 note Labbé, DP 1892.1.596.   [54] At 616.
[55] Challies, *Doctrine of Unjustified Enrichment*, 30.
[56] Contrast art. 1494, which establishes a relationship of weak subsidiarity between claims in unjustified enrichment and other claims: see below, 607–8.
[57] Art. 1493. Surprisingly, however, it is suggested in Pineau *et al.*, *Théorie*, 406–7, that a claim in unjustified enrichment would be available in this situation. Cf. *Pavage Rolland Fortier Inc. v. Caisse Populaire Desjardins de la Plaine* [1998] RJQ 1221 at 1227 (SC), although citing French doctrine.

The common law does not seem to have found its way to any firm doctrinal rule, but most cases deny recovery in this type of situation. Canadian cases sometimes cite the plaintiff's contract with a third party as the 'juristic reason' for the defendant's enrichment.[58] Lord Goff has suggested that 'the existence of a remedy in restitution in such circumstances must still be regarded as a matter of debate', but that 'serious difficulties arise if the law seeks to expand the law of restitution to redistribute risks for which provision has been made under an applicable contract'.[59] John Dawson said that the denial of recovery was 'almost unchallenged' in US law.[60] He said 'almost' because he noted a line of cases in which lawyers were allowed to recover from those whom their work had benefited when they were unable to enforce their contractual claims. He was not overly impressed by the 'success of American lawyers in escaping their self-imposed limitations';[61] but Canadian lawyers seem to have taken up the torch. In *Giffen, Lee & Wagner v. Zellers Ltd*,[62] Zellers was sued in negligence by another party. The action was taken over by its liability insurers, who retained the plaintiff law firm. The plaintiffs arranged a tentative settlement and sent an account for $3,220 to the insurer, which by then had become insolvent. The law firm successfully sued Zellers for this amount in unjust enrichment. To be fair, there is at least one recent case allowing recovery where the plaintiff was not, so far as can be discovered, a lawyer.[63]

In Peter Birks's contribution to this volume, he takes the view that the reason the plaintiff cannot recover in a case like this is that the defendant's enrichment is not at the expense of the plaintiff. On the assumptions of

[58] *Harris v. Nugent* (1996) 193 AR 113; 141 DLR 4th 410 (CA); *Toronto-Dominion Bank v. Carotenuto* (1997) 154 DLR 4th 627 (CA). See also *Nicholson v. St Denis* (1975) 8 OR 2d 315; 57 DLR 3d 699 (Ont CA), leave to appeal to SCC refused. This case refused recovery on the unhelpful ground that there was no 'special relationship' between plaintiff and defendant; but it is still often cited, and the facts are functionally those of *Boudier*. For other cases denying recovery, but with a slight factual twist on this basic pattern, see below, n. 77.
[59] *Pan Ocean Shipping Co. Ltd v. Creditcorp Ltd (The Trident Beauty)* [1994] 1 WLR 161 at 166E–F (HL).
[60] J. P. Dawson, 'Indirect Enrichment', in: E. von Caemmerer, S. Mentschikoff and K. Zweigert (eds.), *Ius Privatum Gentium: Festschrift für Max Rheinstein* (1969), vol. II, 789, 805, with citations to US authority; see also J. P. Dawson, 'The Self-serving Intermeddler', (1974) 87 *Harvard LR* 1409, 1444–50.
[61] Dawson, 'Indirect Enrichment', 805. The special treatment of lawyers was the jumping-off point of Dawson's important article 'The Self-serving Intermeddler', and Dawson returned to the theme in 'Lawyers and Involuntary Clients: Attorney Fees from Funds', (1974) 87 *Harvard LR* 1597 and 'Lawyers and Involuntary Clients in Public Interest Litigation', (1975) 88 *Harvard LR* 849.
[62] (1993) 15 OR 3d 387 (Gen Div).
[63] *Taylor (SA) Building Ltd v. Von Muenchhausen* (1995) 165 NBR 2d 219; 424 APR 219 (CA).

the current chapter, though, the plaintiff can prove all of the elements of his enrichment claim against the defendant, and it is only the presence of the plaintiff's contract with another party which bars the claim. In other words, saying that the enrichment was not at the plaintiff's expense is just a conclusion of law which is reached by applying a principle additional to the basic one that requires only that the plaintiff conferred the enrichment on the defendant.[64] The present chapter is attempting to analyse this additional principle.

Consider the position on this point in Germany, where the law is absolutely clear: there can be no claim in unjustified enrichment where the enrichment was conferred pursuant to a contract between the plaintiff and some other party. As a matter of doctrinal development of the words of § 812 BGB, German law distinguishes between cases where the enrichment can be described as a 'performance' (*Leistung*), and cases of enrichment in any other way. In this context, a performance means an enlargement of another's estate which is brought about intentionally and with a specific purpose in mind.[65] 'The concept of *Leistung* serves as a compass in this territory; once one has found who has performed to whom, one will normally know the right plaintiff and the right defendant for an action in unjustified enrichment.'[66] The German rule of subsidiarity is that whenever there has been a performance, there can be no claim based on enrichment in any other way.[67] If the plaintiff enriched the defendant pursuant to the plaintiff's obligations under a contract with a third party, then there has been a performance between the plaintiff and the third party. Any enrichment claim by the plaintiff against the defendant is excluded.[68]

(ii) Defendant's contract with a third party
What if it is the defendant who is in a contractual relationship with some third party, and that relationship contemplates provision of the

---

[64] This is supported by the contributions to this volume of Daniel Visser and Niall Whitty, both of whom note that the 'at the expense of' requirement permits the imposition of additional policy-driven constraints upon the claim.
[65] Zimmermann and Du Plessis, 'Basic Features', 25; Markesinis *et al.*, *Law of Contracts*, 720. The translation 'performance' is that of Markesinis *et al.*; Zimmermann and Du Plessis translate *Leistung* as 'transfer'.
[66] Markesinis *et al.*, *Law of Contracts*, 719.
[67] Zimmermann and Du Plessis, 'Basic Features', 37, discussing possible exceptions at 37–8; Markesinis *et al.*, *Law of Contracts*, 723.
[68] The German rule operates to exclude the claim even if the plaintiff's contract with the third party was void, because the concept of performance does not depend on the existence of an underlying contract.

enrichment by the plaintiff? One feature of this type of case is that even in the absence of any rule of subsidiarity, the claim may fail as the plaintiff may be unable to prove that the defendant was enriched. The defendant will be liable to pay, or will already have paid, the third party under the contract.[69] On the other hand, in the common law at least, a defendant's attempt to deny its enrichment on the basis of dealings with a third party is usually understood as a matter of defence.[70] This is parallel to the case of the plaintiff's contract with a third party;[71] the denial of recovery can be explained on the basis that the defendant's enrichment was not 'at the expense of' the plaintiff, but the reasoning behind that conclusion must be unearthed.

Even though the assumption here is that the plaintiff was not bound contractually to anyone, this does not mean that the claim against the defendant is the plaintiff's only possible recourse. Why might the plaintiff have enriched the defendant? Although there are other possibilities, it is most likely that the plaintiff was attempting to fulfil its obligations under a contract with some other party which turns out to be void or unenforceable.[72] This might be the same third party with whom the defendant contracted, or a fourth party. Under German law, since in this case the plaintiff was making a performance toward his contractual counterparty, his only claim will be an enrichment claim against that counterparty. Quebec law appears to generate the same conclusion. Liability for unjustified enrichment under article 1493 is defeated if either the defendant's enrichment or the plaintiff's impoverishment is justified; under article 1494, '[e]nrichment or impoverishment is justified where it results

---

[69] This point is taken in Dawson, 'The Self-serving Intermeddler', 1446-7.
[70] See, however, *Turf Masters Landscaping Ltd v. TAG Developments Ltd* (1995) 143 NSR 2d 275; 411 APR 275 (CA), leave to appeal refused (1996) 151 NSR 2d 240; 440 APR 240 (SCC). This was a 'combination' case as discussed in the next section: the plaintiff and the defendant both had contracts with the same third party (but not with each other); the Court's denial of the claim was based on the non-enrichment of the defendant.
[71] Above, 602-4 and n. 64.
[72] It seems just possible that a plaintiff might, by mistake, perform the prestation owing to the defendant under the defendant's contract with the third party. Assume that the third party was contractually bound to shovel the snow from the defendant's driveway, and the plaintiff, meaning to shovel his own driveway, cleared the defendant's. If the defendant is still liable to pay the third party, then presumably there can be no claim against the defendant, but rather the plaintiff could succeed against the third party whose contract the plaintiff performed. Alternatively the plaintiff's actions might have frustrated the contract between the defendant and the third party, leaving the way clear (so to speak) for an action against the defendant. Cf. Markesinis *et al.*, *Law of Contracts*, 731-2.

from the performance of an obligation'. So in this case of defendant's contract with a third party, it could be argued that the defendant's enrichment is justified, since it resulted from the performance of the obligation of the third party.[73] There is no stipulation that the obligation must be owed by the plaintiff. In the common law, there does not appear to have emerged any trend toward denying the plaintiff an enrichment claim against the defendant, but there are very few cases which are not also 'combination' cases.[74]

(iii) Combinations

Many cases involve a combination of the plaintiff's contract with a third party and the defendant's contract with a third party. It might be that the plaintiff and the defendant each have a contract, but each has contracted with a different party. More likely, the plaintiff and the defendant have each contracted with the same third party, as where a building project involves a general contractor and sub-contractors. The owner of the site contracts with the general contractor, and the general contractor contracts with sub-contractors. If the general contractor becomes insolvent, can the sub-contractors sue the owner in unjustified enrichment? There will often be legislative solutions to assist the sub-contractors, such as the possibility of registering a real security interest in the land, or a statutory trust fund of payments made by the owner to the general contractor which is for the benefit of sub-contractors. Such solutions are motivated by policies aimed at protecting the sub-contractors, and cannot be seen as reflecting the general law.[75] Moreover, such remedies cannot affect the enrichment claim except in a system with a wide-ranging subsidiarity principle.[76]

Since this combination involves both a plaintiff's contract with a third party and a defendant's contract with a third party, it follows that if

---

[73] As noted in Simon Whittaker's contribution to this volume, however, in the French legal tradition obligations are viewed as personal to the parties; while the plaintiff can perform the prestation owing under another's obligation, it is not clear that the plaintiff can perform another's obligation as such. None the less, note that in discussing the position under the Civil Code of Lower Canada (and in French law), Challies, *Doctrine of Unjustified Enrichment*, 104–12, was of the view that no claim could be made in such a case.

[74] *Friesen (P. H.) Ltd v. Cypress Colony Farms Ltd* (1993) 87 Man R 2d 250 (QB) suggests that the defendant's contract with a third party is not a bar.

[75] Dawson, *Unjust Enrichment*, 125. See also his 'Indirect Enrichment' 802–3 and 'The Self-serving Intermeddler', 1450–7.

[76] In order to deny a claim in unjustified enrichment where the statutory protection was unavailable, it would also have to be a strong subsidiarity principle.

either of those configurations denies the plaintiff its enrichment claim, there can be none. Some recent common-law cases seem to support this view.[77] Unfortunately, the simple denial of recovery in such a case does not make clear which of the two contracts is keeping the plaintiff from recovering.[78]

2. Weak subsidiarity

The widest possible principle of weak subsidiarity would provide that a claim in unjustified enrichment was unavailable where the plaintiff had any other claim against some defendant. For example, if the plaintiff could establish all of the elements of an enrichment claim against the defendant, but it transpired none the less that the plaintiff held a tort claim against some third party, the enrichment claim would be disallowed. No system seems to have a principle as wide as this. An argument along these lines was made and rejected for Quebec law under the Civil Code of Lower Canada.[79]

The widest possible version of weak subsidiarity operating *inter partes* would say that if the plaintiff has any other claim against the defendant, unjustified enrichment cannot be used. This appears to be the law of Quebec, in respect of the general enrichment action, because article 1494 of the Civil Code of Quebec provides that enrichment or impoverishment is justified where it results 'from the failure of the person impoverished to exercise a right of which he may avail himself or could have

---

[77] *Pan Ocean Shipping Co. Ltd v. Creditcorp Ltd* [1994] 1 WLR 161 (HL); *Turf Masters Landscaping Ltd v. TAG Developments Ltd* (1995) 143 NSR 2d 275; 411 APR 275 (CA), leave to appeal refused (1996) 151 NSR 2d 240; 440 APR 240 (SCC); *Hussey Seating Co. (Canada) Ltd v. Ottawa (City)* (1997) 145 DLR 4th 493 (Gen Div) affirmed (1998) 41 OR 3d 254 (CA). Writing particularly of the three-party building contract cases in US law, Dawson, *Unjust Enrichment*, 1447 said that '[t]he decisions, old and new, are lined up in an unbroken phalanx against restitution recovery'.
[78] In *Pan Ocean Shipping Co. Ltd v. Creditcorp Ltd* [1994] 1 WLR 161 (HL), Lord Goff was of the view that it was the fact that the plaintiff had conferred the benefit under a contractual obligation to do so; interestingly, in his comment on the case, Burrows seems to prefer the view that it was the defendant's contract that was decisive: 'Restition from Assignees', [1994] *Restitution LR* 52, 55.
[79] *Cie Immobilière Viger Ltée v. Laureat Giguère Inc.* [1977] 2 SCR 67 at 84. The words of art. 1494, Civil Code of Quebec, that enshrine the weak subsidiarity principle seem designed to codify this ruling: enrichment or impoverishment is justified where it results 'from the failure of the person impoverished to exercise a right of which he may avail himself or could have availed himself *against the person enriched*' (emphasis added). This interpretation finds favour in J.-L. Baudouin, *Les Obligations* (5th edn, 1998), 442.

availed himself against the person enriched'.[80] A general doctrine of weak subsidiarity of unjustified enrichment would explain the non-availability of an enrichment claim where the *rei vindicatio* subsists, the phenomenon observed for Germany and Quebec in section II of this article. An argument has been made that the common law takes a similar line.[81]

It would appear that the German version of subsidiarity is not as wide as that prevailing in Quebec. The reason is that a generalised weak subsidiarity must make unjustified enrichment claims unavailable where there is a claim based on a wrong. If, as is suggested by the language of article 1494, this is the law of Quebec, then it would be another reason for disallowing an enrichment claim in the case of the stolen horse under Quebec law.[82] But in German law, unjustified enrichment is not subsidiary to the law of wrongs.[83] Nor has it been suggested, to my knowledge, that there is any such subsidiarity in the common law. In these systems, therefore, a narrower principle applies.

A final point can usefully be addressed before attempting to understand the reasons for subsidiarity. It relates to prescription. Assume that an unjustified enrichment claim is subsidiary to another claim; make it a claim for breach of contract, where the contract has not been terminated by the breach. Now assume that the contractual claim is prescribed by the passage of time. Does it still preclude the enrichment claim? The principle in all systems appears to be that it does.[84] This might be thought to

---

[80] Note, however, that it was held in *Willmor Discount Corp. v. Vaudreuil (City)* [1994] 2 SCR 210 that a claim for reception of a thing not due is not subsidiary to a claim based on fault, and there is no reason to think this is not still true under the Civil Code of Quebec, where reception of a thing not due is codified separately from the general unjustified enrichment claim, and without any language giving rise to subsidiarity.

[81] R. B. Grantham and C. E. F. Rickett, 'Restitution, Property and Ignorance – A Reply to Mr Swadling', [1996] *Lloyd's Maritime and Commercial Law Quarterly* 463, 465; see also J. H. Baker, 'The History of Quasi-contract in English Law', in: Cornish *et al.*, *Restitution*, 37 ff., 52.

[82] See Pineau *et al.*, *Théorie*, 404 (my translation): 'the action *de in rem verso* is not available where the plaintiff has an action arising from a contract, from extra-contractual fault, from management of the business of another, or from payment of a thing not due'.

[83] Markesinis *et al.*, *Law of Contracts*, 768.

[84] Art. 1494 of the Civil Code of Quebec seems clear on this point; the claim in unjustified enrichment is denied if the situation arises from the failure of the plaintiff to exercise a right 'of which he may avail himself or could have availed himself'; this is in line with what the law was understood to be under the Civil Code of Lower Canada; *Cie Immobilière Viger Ltée v. Laureat Giguère Inc.* [1977] 2 SCR 67; *Loungnarath v. Centre Hospitalier des Laurentides* [1996] RJQ 2498, per Chamberland J. Common-law authority on the point goes the same way: *Luscar Ltd v. Pembina Resources*

indicate a relationship of strong subsidiarity, since the claim in unjustified enrichment is denied even though the other is unavailable. Conversely it might be thought to be inconsistent with a relationship of weak subsidiarity; that only operates when there is another viable claim. It does, however, seem possible to reach this result even if the relationship is one of weak subsidiarity. This involves treating the case of a prescribed claim in the same way as a viable claim, rather than treating it like the situation where the substantive elements of the claim cannot be established.[85] It appears therefore that conclusions about the nature of the subsidiarity relationship cannot be drawn from the treatment of prescribed claims.

IV. Understanding subsidiarity

1. A model of subsidiarity

The preceding comparative study suggests that subsidiarity is a general feature of the law of unjust enrichment, although the strength of the subsidiarity principle varies widely from system to system and even within each system. This section is an attempt to understand what might justify this variation in subsidiarity. This chapter is not primarily concerned with the way in which subsidiarity is worked out in doctrinal terms. A claim may be denied in one system due to a recognised principle of subsidiarity; in another, it may be denied because the defendant's enrichment is said not to be at the plaintiff's expense. The concern here is with making sense of the results, in terms of principle.

It does not appear that strong subsidiarity can be justified by a desire for orderliness in general legal categories. If claims exist, it is presumably to meet the demands of justice, and therefore any principle which will deny an otherwise existing claim must be one with more normative weight than this.[86] It might be possible to understand weak subsidiarity in this way, since weak subsidiarity only orders claims and cannot exclude them. Even here, however, substantive rights are affected and one would hope for a better justification.[87]

Ltd (1994) 24 Alta LR 3d 305; [1995] 2 WWR 153 (CA), §§ 117, 120, leave to appeal refused [1995] 3 SCR vii. See also E. Schrage, 'Restitution in the New Dutch Civil Code', [1994] *Restitution LR* 208, 220–1.

[85] Art. 1494, cited in the previous note, arguably does exactly this.
[86] Nicholas, 'Unjust Enrichment', 2039–40.
[87] Rights are affected in some sense when a claim in unjustified enrichment is barred even if another claim is available. Moreover, even weak subsdiarity can prevent a claim in unjustified enrichment when the other claim has prescribed (above, 608–9), which obviously has a substantial effect on the plaintiff's legal position.

Another possible justification might be the general principle that the specific overrides the general. This certainly comes to mind when considering how codified systems make the general unjustified enrichment claim strongly subsidiary to a more specific regime. This result can be seen to derive directly from the implied intention of the legislature; but the same principle could be deployed in a wider way, if unjustified enrichment claims could somehow be understood as more general in their application than such things as the terms of a specific contract. A well-known feature of the French legal tradition is its refusal to allow concurrent liability in contract and in delict, which may be understood as based on a philosophy that the specific terms of a particular contract should govern in preference to a general law of fault, especially one so general as is usual in the French tradition. But this understanding would explain too much and too little at the same time. It would explain too little, because there are elements of strong subsidiarity for unjustified enrichment claims even in systems, such as German law and the common law, which have no general aversion to concurrent liability. It would explain too little, because in the French legal tradition unjustified enrichment claims are subsidiary (albeit weakly so) even to delictual claims, and it is difficult to see how this could be explained on the basis that the delictual claim is somehow more specific than the claim in unjustified enrichment.

What seems to be needed is a conviction that unjustified enrichment claims serve a corrective role.[88] In the common law, some parts of unjust enrichment come from Equity, such as the resulting trust. But even those parts of the law which are rooted solely in the common law can be said to be derived not from Equity, but from equity. So said the great common-law judge, Lord Mansfield;[89] and civilian lawyers, who have nothing to do with Equity, also view unjustified enrichment as based on equity. In both France and Quebec, the need for this corrective was so strongly felt that a whole head of liability was created by the courts outside the civil codes, and the basis for this step was *équité*.[90] The impetus for the

---

[88] Nicholas, 'Unjust Enrichment', 2041–3.

[89] *Moses v. Macferlan* (1760) 2 Burr 1005; 97 ER 676 (KB). See also Baker, 'History of Quasi-contract', 48–9; M. Macnair, 'The Conceptual Basis of Trusts in the Later 17th and Early 18th Centuries', in: R. Helmholz and R. Zimmermann (eds.), *Itinera Fiduciae: Trust and Treuhand in Historical Perspective* (1998), 207, 218.

[90] J. E. C. Brierley and R. A. Macdonald (eds.), *Quebec Civil Law* (1993), 464, suggest that this was the most important extra-codal development under the Civil Code of Lower Canada. See also Baudouin, *Les Obligations*, 441 (my translation): 'The action *de in rem verso* exists to remedy unforeseen situations and not to replace existing dispositions or agreements.'

inclusion of a general enrichment action in the BGB came from Otto von Gierke, who viewed it as equitable in nature.[91] This only means that it is corrective.

The idea of one part of the law operating so as to correct other parts of the law is a slightly curious one. It makes sense in relation to laws which are of different orders, as where a statute is declared void due to its inconsistency with some constitutional principle. This may be why some German jurists have, in the past, viewed unjustified enrichment as a kind of higher law.[92] But paradoxically, to the extent that it is subsidiary, it is a kind of lower law. In fact, 'correction' by a disposition of a higher legal order is just the natural outcome of that hierarchical structure; the higher order governs the lower. It is when the parts of the law in question are of the same order that correction is more difficult to conceptualise.

What follows from the conceptualisation of unjustified enrichment as corrective of other parts of the law, while yet being of the same order as those other parts? There is a parallel in that other great corrective system, Equity. One of the 'maxims of Equity' was (or is, depending on one's view of such things) that 'Equity supplements but does not contradict the common law.' This is, at the same time, fundamentally important and completely false. It is false inasmuch as any supplementation amounts to a kind of contradiction. There is no point in having a second, supplementary set of rules unless it changes the outcome which the first set would give. On the other hand, the maxim is fundamentally important in the sense that it was the whole basis for the creation of Equity. When the first chancellors enforced the first uses against legal title-holders, the suggestion that they were contradicting the common law would have appalled them. They were merely requiring those people to behave according to good conscience (and telling them what good conscience required). Of course, Equity developed into a set of legal rules, but the same reasoning holds: having a second set of rules only makes sense if the second set 'supplements but does not contradict' the first set. If one wanted to contradict the first set, one would just change it. How can the circle be squared? For one legal regime to correct another, without possessing the authority of belonging to a higher legal order, it must in a sense go to a lower level; it must defer, at least nominally, to that which it corrects. Equity corrects the common law, but it cannot correct too much, or too obviously; the

---

[91] B. Dickson, 'The Law of Restitution in the Federal Republic of Germany', (1987) 36 ICLQ 751, 770–1. See also Zweigert and Kötz, *Introduction*, 561–2.

[92] See Zimmermann and Du Plessis, 'Basic Features', 24; Dawson, 'Indirect Enrichment', 796–7.

correction cannot lay itself open to the charge of being a contradiction.[93] So, down the centuries to the present day, there are those who want Equity to do more, and those who want it to do less. Among the latter, there are concerns about containing it. Another consequence of the corrective nature of Equity is that it is very difficult to define it in any positive way: you cannot understand what it is without understanding that it is a corrective, and without having at least some grasp of what it corrects.[94]

The parallels with unjustified enrichment are striking. It is a corrective and, just as in the case of Equity, this makes it difficult to define positively.[95] It can only be understood in the light of that which it corrects. Furthermore, since this corrective regime does not stand higher in the legal order than that which it corrects, it must not correct so much as to contradict. Moreover, the concerns with containing unjust enrichment liability are always to the fore.[96] So the question becomes, what are the limits? When will correction amount to contradiction? The main difficulty here is what might be called 'negative implication'. This name is borrowed from a doctrine (its status now uncertain) of Canadian constitutional law.[97] Sometimes it is possible for a provincial legislature and the federal Parliament both to pass legislation which overlaps in its effects, each level of government being able to point to jurisdictional powers to justify the

---

[93] Upon the institution of the Judicature Act system, consolidating the two legal regimes into a single court, it was enacted that in the case of any conflict between law and Equity, Equity should prevail; and this disposition remains operative in every jurisdiction which possesses the Judicature Act system. To the modern lawyer this might seem to indicate that Equity belongs to a higher legal order. Viewing the matter in a historical light, as captured by the maxim about supplementing without contradicting, Maitland took the view that this provision is 'practically without effect'; apparent conflicts resolve themselves into cases of supplementation. See F. H. Maitland, *Equity: A Course of Lectures* (revised by J. Brunyate, 1936), 16-19. By contrast, if one takes the other perspective, that any alteration of the final result amounts to contradiction, then Equity is constantly contradicting the law: see W. N. Hohfeld, 'The Relations Between Equity and Law', (1913) 11 *Michigan LR* 537, 543-4.

[94] Maitland famously gave up on any positive definition: 'we are driven to say that Equity now is that body of rules administered by our English courts of justice which, were it not for the operation of the Judicature Acts, would be administered only by those courts which would be known as Courts of Equity. This, you may well say, is but a poor thing to call a definition' (Maitland, *Equity*, 1).

[95] Zweigert and Kötz, *Introduction*, 538.

[96] Zimmermann and Du Plessis, 'Basic Features', 24, on interpretation of the BGB; Dawson, *Unjust Enrichment*, 104, 106 on French law and subsidiarity. Subsidiarity as an adequacy test provides another parallel to Equity. Containment is a constant concern in unjustified enrichment, more so than in other fields. See Baudouin, *Les Obligations*, 441; K. Barker, 'Unjust Enrichment: Controlling the Beast', (1995) 11 *Oxford JLS* 457.

[97] See P. W. Hogg, *Constitutional Law of Canada* (3rd edn, 1992), 423-9.

act which it has passed. If the two pieces of legislation conflict, the federal legislation prevails under another doctrine called 'paramountcy'.[98] But do they conflict? This is where negative implication might have a role to play. Here is a simple example.[99] The federal Parliament, under its power over banking, passed legislation that provided rules for taking and enforcing a kind of security interest. The provincial legislation, under its power over property and civil rights in the province, passed legislation that required formal notice to the debtor before property subject to a security interest could be seized. The two regimes did not conflict, because it was perfectly possible for a bank to comply with both the federal and the provincial rules. But the doctrine of paramountcy was held to apply. In passing its legislation, the federal Parliament implied certain things, including that seizure could not be made more difficult by a notice requirement. The provincial legislature must avoid conflict not only with what the federal Act says, but with what it implies is not to have anything said about it. It is as though the federal Act casts a shadow beyond its express provisions, which the province must not enter. One expression sometimes used is that the federal Parliament has 'occupied the field'.

If this framework can be used to understand subsidiarity, then to different extents, corresponding to different conceptions of subsidiarity, the law of unjustified enrichment is not supposed to contradict the effects of other legal institutions. Weak subsidiarity sees a contradiction only where another recourse actually exists. Strong subsidiarity incorporates the idea of 'negative implication', so that in assessing whether or not there is a contradiction, one must determine the extent to which other legal institutions cast shadows which unjustified enrichment cannot enter. Unjustified enrichment must yield to the positive dispositions and also to the negative implications of those other legal institutions.

2. Implications of the model

First, apply this concept to the phenomenon, discussed earlier, of the exclusion of unjustified enrichment claims by statutory implication. A statute makes a contract unenforceable. Can the plaintiff claim in unjust enrichment for benefits transferred? The question here is whether the policy that made the contract illegal or unenforceable excludes the enrichment claim. In other words, do the provisions which nullify the contract cast a shadow over the law of unjustified enrichment as well?

---

[98] The provincial legislation is still valid, because by assumption it was competent to the provincial legislature; but its effects are suspended.

[99] Based on *Bank of Montreal v. Hall* [1990] 1 SCR 121; 65 DLR 4th 361.

Have they occupied the field? Here the relationship between the statute and the enrichment claim is clear, because these dispositions are of different legal orders. In other areas the matter may be less clear.

(a) Unjust enrichment and contract law

The comparative study above suggested that all legal systems make unjustified enrichment strongly subsidiary to the law of contract: the existence of a contractual regime can exclude an enrichment claim, even where there is no contractual claim. On the present analysis, this means that unjustified enrichment is viewed as in some sense corrective of contract. Or, perhaps more precisely, unjustified enrichment is corrective of something with which contract tends to deal; so that if contract *does* deal with it, there is no room for correction. Can this case be made? There are many ways of understanding what contract is about. Maybe it is about keeping promises, maybe it is about wealth maximisation, maybe it is about reasonable reliance. But on any view, it seems, contract is about the transfer of benefits, in the sense that what people do, or promise to do, under contract is thought by the other party to the contract to be of some benefit. Unjustified enrichment, at least over much of its range, is about the reversal of non-consensual transfers of benefits.[100] If contract law deals with the consensual transfer of benefits, it makes sense that unjustified enrichment, dealing with defective or non-consensual transfers, should stand in a corrective and subsidiary role to contract.[101]

Clearly, between the parties to the contract, the contract casts a long shadow. It occupies the field relating to the transfer of benefits within the contractual framework. The length of the shadow which is cast is a matter of interpreting the contract to decide whether or not it dealt with the benefit in issue, even if only in a negative way. In *Hoffman v. Sportsman Yachts Inc.*,[102] the plaintiff was buying a boat from the defendant

---

[100] In the framework developed by P. B. H. Birks, *An Introduction to the Law of Restitution* (revised edn, 1989), reasons why enrichments are unjustified fall into three categories. In most cases it is because the plaintiff's consent to the transfer was impaired in some way. In some cases it is because the defendant's receipt was unconscientious, and in some others it is because of a reason of policy which does not depend on the position of either party to the transfer. In the other systems there is no doctrinal framework of 'unjust factors', but it is true (although it may be a matter of defence) that there can be no recovery if the plaintiff had an unimpaired desire to make the transfer: § 814 BGB; Civil Code of Quebec, art. 1494, closing words.

[101] In *Pan Ocean Shipping Co. Ltd v. Creditcorp Ltd* [1994] 1 WLR 161 at 164F, Lord Goff used language which strongly suggested that the law of unjustified enrichment and the parties' contract are on different legal orders: 'as between shipowner and charterer, there is a contractual regime which *legislates* for the recovery of overpaid hire' (emphasis added).

[102] (1992) 89 DLR 4th 600.

for $174,345. There was a term which provided for the price to rise, and on delivery the defendant relied on this and demanded $202,500. The plaintiff paid but then sued to recover the difference of $28,155, arguing that the term was not enforceable. For reasons that are immaterial here, the judge agreed that the contract had to be read without this term. So amended, the contract had nothing to say about the extra $28,155. One of the things which the contract was very much about was the price of the boat. But, without the disputed term, the $28,155 was not referable to the price even though it was paid as part of the price. It was therefore recoverable. If that result seems obvious, recall *Rillford Investments Ltd v. Gravure International Capital Corp.*[103] The plaintiff conferred a benefit long after the contract between the parties had ended, but the Court held that the contract 'contemplated the possibility that the plaintiff would receive no compensation if the defendant was enriched by virtue of the sale of his business beyond the time of the expiry of the agreement'. This is clearly an example of negative implication.

So sometimes a claim in unjustified enrichment may be denied even where there is no continuing contractual tie between the parties. The consensual distribution of risks and benefits can continue to govern, excluding unjustified enrichment, even when the contract has ceased to operate. Conversely, there might be cases where a claim would be allowed even though the matter was governed by a contract. If the plaintiff owed the defendant £50 for work done, and the plaintiff paid when the defendant threatened him with personal violence, it might well be that the money would be recoverable. The matter is governed by a contract, but the consensual distribution of risks and benefits did not contemplate personal violence, and so the unjustified enrichment claim is not excluded.

It begins to appear that unjustified enrichment is not actually subsidiary to contract law. Rather, it is excluded by an operative distribution of risks and benefits. To say that there can be no claim in unjustified enrichment so long as there is a subsisting contract is to make a slightly inaccurate generalisation by aiming at a false target. A subsisting contract usually corresponds to an operative distribution of risks and benefits, but the examples above show that it does not always do so. What implications does this understanding have for the situations discussed above, where the contract is not between plaintiff and defendant but between one (or both) of them and some other party? Can the bargain cast a shadow on third parties? The case of the plaintiff's contract with a third party seems to be within the principles being discussed here. The plaintiff is party to

---

[103] (1997) 118 Man R 2d 11; [1997] 7 WWR 534 (CA).

a regime governing the conferral and receipt of benefits, and that regime remains in force. An enrichment claim against a third party would contradict that regime if the contract is understood in this way: in providing for some counterperformance for what the plaintiff had done, the contract negatively implies that there is to be no other right of payment. The common law may therefore be on the right track in moving, as it seems to be, towards a rule excluding enrichment claims in this situation. The common law has a strong commitment to privity of contract: to say that a contract between the plaintiff and a third party affects the legal position between the plaintiff and the defendant, who is not a party to the contract, might be thought to contradict that. In fact, the privity argument cuts both ways: nobody should have to pay for benefits conferred under a contract to which he was not a party.[104] But in the end privity seems to be irrelevant, since it is about controlling contractual liability.

The question has been examined most carefully by German jurists: in German law contracts cast shadows over third parties. The doctrinal reason is that where the plaintiff has rendered a performance (Leistung), no enrichment claim can be brought except against the person who received the performance. Thus, where the plaintiff enriched the defendant pursuant to the plaintiff's contract with a third party, the plaintiff has no enrichment claim. Moreover, in German law this applies even if the plaintiff's contract is void. His actions still count as a performance and have the same effect. The applicable policies have been elucidated by German jurists, in particular Claus-Wilhelm Canaris. He formulated three principles governing the availability of third-party enrichment claims in a contractual context.[105] These are said to apply where two parties have tried to contract, successfully or not. One principle is that the parties should bear the risk of insolvency of their chosen counterparty. Moreover, the parties should be able to rely upon, and to be bound by, the defences they have against one another. These are the reasons why plaintiffs are not allowed to make claims against third parties. Such claims would be a way of avoiding the effects of the insolvency of their chosen counterparty, or of avoiding his defences. While this learning is very instructive, it is inconsistent with the view which appears to be emerging in the common law, to the effect that void contracts can have no influence on the law of unjust enrichment.[106] The difference between the two systems can be

---

[104] Dawson, Unjust Enrichment, 104–5.
[105] Discussed in Markesinis et al., Law of Contracts, 732–3.
[106] See, for example, Rover International Ltd v. Cannon Films Sales Ltd (No. 3) [1989] 1 WLR 912 (CA).

understood in this way. German law gives effect to the parties' transaction as creating and distributing certain risks in relation to the transfer of a benefit, even if the transaction fails to create a contract; and these effects are sufficient to exclude the corrective law of unjust enrichment. The common law takes the voidness of the contract to exclude any legal effects whatsoever.

The German approach might well be considered more sophisticated in this regard. It was noted above that, even within the common law, it is inaccurate to say that unjust enrichment claims are excluded by contract. That statement is, in extreme cases, both too wide and too narrow. The point can be further tested by recalling the example of the building project. The owner contracts with the general contractor, and the general contractor contracts with the sub-contractor. Can the sub-contractor sue the owner in unjustified enrichment? Surely not, if both contracts are valid; and the same result must follow if both were valid, but are now terminated by complete performance on both sides. By imagining that one or both of the contracts is void it is possible to test what really bars the action. German law will reply that the sub-contractor can never sue the owner in unjustified enrichment even if both contracts are void; and the theoretical underpinnings for that position seem formidable.

The position in Quebec makes an interesting contrast. Under the Civil Code of Lower Canada, following French law, it would appear that the plaintiff who had a contract with a third party could not prima facie sue the defendant in unjustified enrichment. This result was superseded, however, in the case in which it mattered most: when the third party was insolvent. This was the situation in the root case of the whole body of jurisprudence.[107] It was sometimes explained doctrinally by saying that the action *de in rem verso* was not subsidiary to another claim if there was a factual obstacle to that other claim.[108] To the extent that the insolvency policies discussed above are accepted, however, this result seems difficult

---

[107] The *Boudier* decision, Req. 15 June 1892, S 1893.1.281 note Labbé, DP 1892.1.596.
[108] This was opposed to a legal obstacle, such as prescription or inability to make out the elements of the other claim. See P. Drakidis, 'La "subsidiarité", caractère spécifique et international de l'action d'enrichissement sans cause', (1961) 59 *Revue trimestrielle de droit civil* 577, 586–7, 613. For recovery in Quebec in the same situation, see Challies, *Doctrine of Unjustified Enrichment*, 139. Italian law followed the French law in this regard: Zweigert and Kötz, *Introduction*, 550; Nicholas, 'Unjust Enrichment', 2038–9. Nicholas notes that Italian writers distinguish between an 'abstract' and a 'concrete' understanding of subsidiarity; the 'concrete' understanding allows the claim in unjustified enrichment where the other claim is useless due to insolvency or prescription.

to justify. The wording of article 1494 of the Civil Code of Quebec appears apt to alter this result for the future in providing that '[e]nrichment or impoverishment is justified where it results from the performance of an obligation'.[109]

The analysis based on a consensual distribution of risks can also be used to deal with another point. In *Kleinwort Benson Ltd v. Lincoln City Council*,[110] the House of Lords allowed a claim based upon mistake of law, even though the swaps transaction under which the payments had been made was fully executed. One of the arguments by which the defendants tried to resist payment was based upon the logic of mistake. It was said that in such a case, the force of the mistake was spent.[111] The argument in those terms was rejected, as it had been in earlier litigation where the claim was based on failure of consideration.[112] In other words, the 'executed transaction' defence does not seem to work when it is tied into the logic of unjust factors. A mistake is a mistake, and a failure of consideration remains one, even where the transaction is fully executed. If it is recognised that unjust enrichment is excluded by the existence of an operative distribution of risks and rewards, that could be used to build an independent principle which excluded claims in such cases. The distribution of risks was fully realised, leaving no room for unjust enrichment. This, of course, would also depend on following the German lead in recognising that such an effect can occur even where the contract embodying the distribution is void.

This argument is not intended to imply that *Kleinwort Benson* itself was wrongly decided, but the result may turn on the fact that the defendant was a public body which lacked capacity to enter into the transaction. Allowing restitution can be seen as necessary to give full legal effect to that lack of capacity, which is imposed as a protection for the defendant's constituents.[113] This permits a final point to be made. The argument in

---

[109] Some commentators and judges, however, appear to take the view that the distinction between factual and legal obstacles remains relevant: Pineau *et al.*, *Théorie*, 406–7; *Pavage Rolland Fortier Inc. v. Caisse Populaire Desjardins de la Plaine* [1998] RJQ 1221 at 1227, citing French doctrine.

[110] [1999] 2 AC 349; [1998] 4 All ER 513.

[111] The argument was built on points made in P. B. H. Birks, 'No Consideration: Restitution After Void Contracts', (1993) 23 *University of Western Australia LR* 195, 230, n. 137.

[112] *Guinness Mahon & Co. Ltd v. Kensington and Chelsea Royal LBC* [1999] QB 215 (CA).

[113] See Lord Goff at [1998] 3 WLR 1126–7; Lord Hope at 1153H. Birks himself has now made this point: P. B. H. Birks, 'Restitution at the End of an Epoch', (1999) 28 *University of Western Australia LR* 13, 37–9; see also L. D. Smith, 'Restitution for Mistake of Law', [1999] *Restitution LR* 148, 157.

this section has been that subsidiarity in the context of contracts turns on the idea that a relevant consensual distribution of risks and rewards ousts unjustified enrichment, to the extent that the latter is based on non-consensual transfers of benefits. The discussion of *Kleinwort Benson Ltd v. Lincoln City Council* emphasises that, in some cases, liability in unjustified enrichment is not based on the defective consent of the plaintiff to the transfer of wealth in question.[114] If this argument is correct, then in exactly those cases one should expect to find that the existence of any consensual distribution of risks and rewards cannot exclude liability in unjustified enrichment.

(b) Unjust enrichment and property law

This section turns to the interaction between the law of unjustified enrichment and actions which vindicate property rights. The earlier analysis suggested that enrichment claims are subsidiary to the *rei vindicatio* in German and Quebec law. As was mentioned above, unjustified enrichment, in the widest sense, is about the reversal of defective transfers of value. Some such transfers are by way of services, but many are by way of transfers of property. It therefore seems justifiable to say that one function of unjustified enrichment is as a corrective of property transfers, which would suggest that unjustified enrichment would be subsidiary to actions that vindicate property rights. As was mentioned above, this has been suggested as the common-law position, but the matter is far from clear.[115] It is complicated by the absence of any *rei vindicatio* for moveables in the common-law system. Property in moveables is protected by the law of wrongs, and it is not suggested that unjust enrichment is subsidiary to the law of wrongs. On the other hand, there is a *rei vindicatio* for immoveables, and it may well be that a claim in unjust enrichment, measured by the value of ownership of an immoveable, would not lie where the plaintiff still held ownership of the immoveable.[116] Similarly, Equity can provide the equivalent of a *rei vindicatio* in the form of a declaration of trust and consequential orders, and it has been held that no claim in unjust enrichment lies where the plaintiff retains his Equitable ownership of the transferred asset.[117] In other words, wherever a *rei vindicatio* is potentially available, its actual availability seems to preclude unjust enrichment.

---

[114] See n. 100.   [115] Grantham and Rickett, 'Reply to Swadling', 465.
[116] Baker, 'History of Quasi-contract', 52.
[117] *Portman Building Society v. Hamlyn Taylor Neck* [1998] 4 All ER 202 (CA).

Is the subsidiarity strong or weak? Although unjustified enrichment can be understood as corrective of property dispositions, their interaction does not seem to generate the same concerns about 'negative implication' as does the interaction of unjustified enrichment and contracts. The presence of a *rei vindicatio* may exclude an enrichment claim – this is weak subsidiarity – but the *absence* of any claim that vindicates property will not generally do the same. In other words, the fact that property has passed to the defendant does not, by itself, generally exclude an enrichment claim. While a contract creates a regime for the consensual transfer of benefits, a property transfer is not so much a regime as it is an event, albeit one which may occur within a contractual regime. As a result, a transfer of property does not in itself cast a shadow that excludes unjustified enrichment; any such shadow is cast by the context in which the transfer is made. A transfer of property made outside any contractual context is commonly the very occasion for an unjustified enrichment claim, aimed at the recovery of the property or its value.

If unjustified enrichment is generally only weakly subsidiary to property transfers, there is one apparent exception. Assume that the plaintiff transfers possession of a thing to another party, X, while retaining ownership. X then transfers possession to the defendant, in circumstances which give the defendant ownership of the thing, without the plaintiff's consent. Here the plaintiff has lost ownership, and the defendant has acquired it; but any claim in unjustified enrichment will be excluded.[118] The rule by which the defendant acquired ownership here casts a shadow which negatively implies that there may be no enrichment claim. But this exception is more apparent than real. The acquisition of ownership by the defendant in such a case is not merely an event; it is also part of a transaction between the defendant and X. This activates the considerations discussed in the previous section. The rule that gives ownership to the defendant is designed to protect the transaction between the defendant and X, and this protection ousts the plaintiff's enrichment claim.

The position in the common law (understood broadly so as to include Equity) is also complicated by the existence of trusts raised to reverse

[118] For the common law, see Smith, 'Unjust Enrichment, Property and the Structure of Trusts', (2000) 116 *LQR* 412–44; for German law, K. Zülch, '*Lipkin Gorman* in German Law', in: W. Swadling (ed.), *The Limits of Restitutionary Claims: A Comparative Analysis* (1997), 106, 116–19. In Quebec the same result must follow from the requirement (art. 1493) that a claim will not lie if either the plaintiff's impoverishment or the defendant's enrichment is justified; here the defendant's enrichment would be justified by the rule of law giving him ownership.

unjustified enrichment. On the face of it, this phenomenon seems clearly inconsistent with any relationship of subsidiarity between unjust enrichment and claims protecting property. But on further examination, this does not appear to be the case. If an asset is transferred at common law in circumstances which amount to an unjustified enrichment of the defendant, the common law will allow a personal claim to recover the value. The common law, viewed on its own, is like a civilian system in this regard; the law of unjust enrichment may step in to correct (but not to contradict) the property transfer, by creating an obligation. There is no difficulty about subsidiarity, because there is no *rei vindicatio*. Equity, however, adds another layer of correction to the analysis. It has long been established that the principle of non-contradiction which operates between common law and Equity does not prohibit interfering with common-law ownership; that is the basis of all uses and trusts. Nor does it prohibit the addition of Equitable proprietary rights to common-law personal rights. Unjust enrichment as it operates through Equity has different tools at its disposal from unjust enrichment operating through common law.

(c) Unjust enrichment and wrongs

Finally, the law of wrongs. In the German system and the common law, there is no general subsidiarity principle between wrongs and unjustified enrichment. The inference is that, for these systems, there is no sense in which unjustified enrichment stands in a corrective relationship to the law of wrongs; they do not deal with the same kind of matter.[119] Wrongs are not, in general, concerned with transfers of benefits. But this brings us to the widest subsidiarity principle, which applies to the general enrichment action in Quebec. If the plaintiff has a claim based on extra-contractual fault, or even used to have one which has now prescribed, it appears that there can be no general enrichment action. The generally subsidiary character of the general unjustified enrichment claim in Quebec law suggests that its relationship to all other parts of the legal system is conceived as a corrective one.

It is difficult to understand how it can be thought to have this relationship to the law of wrongs, but a historical explanation seems best. The general enrichment action in the form of the *actio de in rem verso* was an extra-codal development. This lent it a generally subsidiary air; in

[119] Nicholas, 'Unjust Enrichment', 2043–4.

a system with a general civil code, an extra-codal liability, created judicially, exists almost in a different legal order from the provisions of the code.[120] This historical explanation fits with the observation that the action for the reception of a thing not due, which was always in the code, is not subsidiary to the law of wrongs.[121] It also fits with the observation of other jurisdictions.[122] The difference between the general action and the action for the reception of a thing not due is otherwise puzzling, since on any view the latter is a special case of the former.[123] If this is right, one might question the choice made for the new Civil Code of Quebec, to codify the general subsidiarity of the general unjustified enrichment claim.[124]

---

[120] Ibid., 2040–1. Challies, *Doctrine of Unjustified Enrichment*, 125 was not enthusiastic about this argument as a *justification* for general subsidiarity, but it may still function as an explanation for the current law.

[121] *Willmor Discount Corp. v. Vaudreuil (City)* [1994] 2 SCR 210.

[122] In French law, the *actio de in rem verso* developed extra-codally (and still is so), and is generally subsidiary. On the other hand, the action for reception of a thing not due was always in the code, and it is not subsidiary: Chabas, *Les Obligations*, § 653; Bell, Boyron and Whittaker, *Principles*, 410, 416–17. In Italy, the *actio de in rem verso* appeared first as an extra-codal development and, when it was codified, it kept its subsidiary character, just as in Quebec. By contrast, German law never knew unjustified enrichment as an extra-codal development; there has been a general action from the time of codification. Similarly, in the Netherlands, there was no general extra-codal enrichment claim under the old code, and the new code, in adding one, did not make it subsidiary: E. Schrage, 'Restitution in the New Dutch Civil Code', [1994] *Restitution LR* 208, 216, 220. See also D. H. van Zyl, 'The General Enrichment Action is Alive and Well', [1992] *Acta Juridica* 115, 128–30.

[123] In *Willmor Discount Corp. v. Vaudreuil (City)* [1994] 2 SCR 210 at 227, Gonthier J referred to the action for the reception of a thing not due as 'the only action for unjust enrichment' available in that case.

[124] The *travaux préparatoires* for the new code show an attempt to codify the law of unjustified enrichment as it was understood; they do not reveal any critical examination of the general subsidiarity of the general enrichment claim. See Québec (Ministère de la Justice), *Commentaires du ministre de la Justice: le Code civil du Québec* (1993), 917 (my translation): 'This article [i.e. art. 1493] will therefore give legislative effect to these doctrinal and jurisprudential developments in unjustified enrichment.' Challies, *Doctrine of Unjustified Enrichment*, was of the view that the *actio de in rem verso* was not generally subsidiary: he states this explicitly at 143, and the section of his book which addresses the matter is entitled not 'Subsidiarity' but 'No indirect contravention of imperative rules of law'. The Nahum Gelber Law Library at the Faculty of Law, McGill University, holds the unpublished manuscript of Challies' third edition, dated 1970; this shows that he planned to change this title to 'Absence of other possible action – or – No indirect contravention of imperative rules of law'. No doubt this was due to the accumulation of cases accepting subsidiarity in the intervening years.

V. Conclusion

The relationship between unjustified enrichment and other claims is complex. Understanding it depends not only upon an understanding of the overall function of the law of unjustified enrichment, but also upon the history and philosophy underlying the structure of private law in a particular system. The common law does not know 'subsidiarity' by that name, but elements of that relationship appear to be embedded in the law. As the common law of unjust enrichment develops, it can be expected that the policies discussed here will need to be addressed, and their impact on unjust enrichment liability analysed.

PART XII

Taxonomy

22 Taxonomy: does it matter?

Ewan McKendrick

> Some parts of the subject are very interesting, and here and there it seems, though I may be wrong, that the law is still unsettled even on rudimentary points, and in such matters one feels the excitement of an explorer.

One might be forgiven for thinking that this statement was made by a lawyer writing about the law of restitution. Indeed, references can be found in modern writings on the law of restitution to the 'sense of excitement that comes from working as a pioneer'.[1] But in fact the statement was written towards the end of the nineteenth century by Sir William Anson (as he was later to become) in a letter to Lord Justice Thesiger, his former pupil-master, on the publication of the first edition of his pathbreaking book on the law of contract.[2] Today, the word 'explorer' would not readily jump into one's mind if asked to describe a contract lawyer. The contours of the subject are now well defined. The modern contract lawyer is no longer thought of as an architect; rather, he or she resembles a plumber trying to repair the many leaks in the system and the leaks seem to increase as the system becomes ever more antiquated.

Yet in many ways Pollock and Anson were explorers. From the forms of action and the mass of detailed case law, they sought to deduce principles that were of general application. In the same way, it can be argued that restitution lawyers in this generation have sought to deduce general principles from the case law and from the forms of action and build an analytical framework for the modern law. To draw such an analogy with the work of Anson might strike some (perhaps many) scholars as less than

---

[1] Lord Goff in his foreword to A. Burrows (ed.), *Essays on the Law of Restitution* (1991), vi.
[2] The letter is to be found inside the first edition of Anson's *Law of Contract*, which is deposited in the library of the Institute of Advanced Legal Studies in London. I am grateful to Roger Halson for drawing the existence of this letter to my attention.

flattering. The structure that Anson developed for the law of contract is now the subject of challenge. Doctrines such as consideration and privity, which he articulated as principles of general application, are now the subject of substantial criticism and, in the case of privity, subject to recent, substantial qualification.[3] Will the same happen in the case of the law of restitution? Are modern writers guilty of deducing principles of general application which later generations of writers will look back upon as simplistic over-generalisations that elevate to the status of principle points which belong in the realm of fact? Is a taxonomic exercise of the type carried out, most notably, by Professor Birks,[4] one that is inevitably doomed to failure and, further, is it an enterprise which is wholly alien to the traditional pragmatic development of English law? Are modern restitution lawyers no more than closet civilian lawyers seeking to import into English law techniques that do not truly belong?

I. The importance of taxonomy

It is important at the outset of this article to consider whether taxonomy is important or not. It cannot be assumed that it is. Many English lawyers operate happily and profitably without giving much thought to questions of taxonomy. If you ask a practising lawyer whether a particular claim is a restitutionary claim or a proprietary claim, he or she would in all likelihood ask you why you want to know. The question is not obviously an important one in its own right. The law of tort and the law of trusts have developed without attaching much, if any, significance to the question of taxonomy. Indeed the English law of tort is, in all probability, incapable of being analysed within a single classificatory framework given the extent to which the torts intersect and cut across each other's boundaries.[5] Provided

---

[3] As a result of the Contracts (Rights of Third Parties) Act 1999. The Act has not abolished the doctrine of privity; in the words of the Law Commission, 'our proposed statute carves out a general and wide-ranging exception to the third party rule but it leaves the rule intact for cases not covered by the statute' (*Privity of Contract: Contracts for the Benefit of Third Parties*: Law Com No. 242, 1996, § 5.16).

[4] See, for example, P. Birks, 'Equity in the Modern Law: An Exercise in Taxonomy', (1996) 26 *University of Western Australian LR* 1; also his 'Property and Unjust Enrichment: Categorical Truths', [1997] *New Zealand LR* 623; also his 'Definition and Division: A Meditation on *Institutes* 3.13', in: P. Birks (ed.), *The Classification of Obligations* (1998), 1; also his 'Misnomer', in: W. Cornish, R. Nolan, J. O'Sullivan and G. Virgo (eds.), *Restitution: Past, Present and Future* (1998), 1; and his 'The Law of Restitution at the End of an Epoch', (1999) 28 *University of Western Australia LR* 13.

[5] See, for example, *Spring v. Guardian Assurance plc* [1995] 2 AC 296, where the House of Lords had to grapple with the intersection of the tort of negligence and the tort of defamation.

that all understand the relevant rules of law, are aware of the fact that individual torts do intersect and deal openly with the difficulties which arise at the point of intersection, it can be argued that no harm is done. And if tort lawyers and trusts lawyers can survive and prosper without agonising over the development of an appropriate taxonomy for their subject, why can restitution lawyers not do likewise?

Indifference to taxonomy cannot be confined to practising lawyers. It also extends to academic lawyers. Legal education attaches little, if any, significance to issues of taxonomy. Law students are required to study subjects in individual units but the relationship between the units is rarely, if ever, explored.[6] Academic lawyers themselves specialise in increasingly narrow areas of law and the ability to see the connections, or lack of them, between different areas of the law is slowly being lost. At the same time the demand for specialist postgraduate options pulls more and more full-time teachers away from 'core' undergraduate subjects with the result that the latter courses do not receive the attention that they deserve. This relative neglect of the core is likely to result in the production of legal practitioners who have at best a partial understanding of core subjects, such as the law of obligations.

II. Why has English law traditionally been indifferent to taxonomy?

A number of reasons can be advanced in an attempt to explain the traditional indifference of English law to matters of taxonomy. In the first place English law has often prided itself on its pragmatic development. What matters is that the law works, not that it looks good. The point has been well put by Graham Virgo in the following terms:

[T]he law of restitution is not a work of art; something to be looked at and admired. It is a body of law which must operate in the real world. Elegance and function do not always go together. Far better that the body of law works, even if it has some rough edges.[7]

Consistent with this pragmatic approach, the traditional emphasis of the English courts has been on the incremental and analogical development

---

[6] There are exceptions. Concurrent liability as between contract and tort is, I would imagine, studied in many universities in the aftermath of *Henderson v. Merrett Syndicates Ltd* [1995] 2 AC 145. But concurrent liability between restitution and contract or between restitution and tort is probably examined in rather fewer institutions.

[7] G. Virgo, *The Principles of the Law of Restitution* (1999), viii.

of the law.[8] Judges are generally content to leave the law to develop on a case-by-case basis. What is required is an educated response to the facts of the individual case, not the production of a legal principle which will hold good for all time. The emphasis is therefore on evolution, not revolution. One further consequence of this evolutionary development is the reluctance of the courts to cast aside the language of the past. While it would be an overstatement to claim that the forms of action continue to rule us from their graves, there is no doubt that they continue to influence the shape of the modern law.[9]

Secondly, and relatedly, the function of the judge is seen by many to be to achieve 'practical' justice on the facts of the case. It is a noticeable feature of leading restitution cases, such as *Lipkin Gorman (a Firm) v. Karpnale Ltd*[10] and *Woolwich Equitable Building Society v. Inland Revenue Commissioners*,[11] that they invoke the language of unjust enrichment but do not identify with any great precision the reason or reasons which made the enrichment unjust. Rather, one finds rather vague references to the 'simple call of justice'[12] or to 'common justice'.[13] This is not to say that in these cases the success of the restitutionary claim was generally a 'matter of discretion for the court'.[14] On the contrary, Lord Goff was at pains in *Lipkin Gorman* to state that, where a restitutionary claim succeeds, it does so 'as a matter of right' and that where it fails the claim is 'denied on the basis of legal principle'.[15] Nevertheless, the fact that the reason for restitution is identified in a rather imprecise fashion lends support to the view that the concern of the court is simply to do what it perceives to be justice on the facts of the case and not to fit the reason for ordering restitution within some typology of 'unjust factors' or 'reasons for restitution'.

Thirdly, it has been argued that the facts of individual cases are too complex or too varied to be accommodated within detailed principles beyond some abstract statement which is so broad as to be practically useless.[16]

---

[8] The classic modern example has been the incremental and analogical development of the tort of negligence; see, for example, *Caparo Industries plc v. Dickman* [1990] 2 AC 605 at 617–18.

[9] The classic example is the distinction between money claims and non-money claims. The distinction is vitally important in terms of the forms of action but, as a matter of principle, its relevance to the reason for restitution is not at all obvious. See further notes 23–7 and associated text.

[10] [1991] 2 AC 548.   [11] [1993] AC 70.   [12] *Ibid.* at 172C *per* Lord Goff.   [13] *Ibid.* at 172B.

[14] *Lipkin Gorman v. Karpnale* [1991] 2 AC 548 at 578.   [15] *Ibid.*

[16] See, for example, B. Dickson, 'Unjust Enrichment Claims: A Comparative Overview', (1995) 54 *CLJ* 100, esp. 109–11.

Thus it has been argued that the result of theorising about the basis of the law of restitution is a 'straightjacket which cannot accommodate all the various species of liability'.[17] Jane Stapleton has rejoiced in the 'richness and sensitivity of the common law' and she has decried 'reformist zeal to "simplify" the law by constructing an artificially seamless web of general principles'.[18] There seem to be two distinct points being made here. The first is the implicit assumption that advocates of a principled approach to the development of the law are somehow insensitive to the importance of the facts of individual cases. Thus I have been accused of regarding it as 'some kind of fraud, when the court has to delve deeply into the facts to resolve these issues'.[19] To my knowledge I have never said any such thing. There can be no doubt that it is of the first importance that the facts of an individual case be established carefully and accurately. Indeed, a large percentage of the work of a barrister and of a court is concerned with establishing the facts of the case. But belief in the importance of principles is not inconsistent with a belief in the importance of the fact-finding process. It is perfectly possible to believe, as I do, in the importance of both. The facts must be established with care and the role of legal principle is to help in the task of working out, from the morass of facts, which are important and which are unimportant.

The second point is that the facts are simply too varied to be accommodated within some analytical framework. There is no doubt that many commercial disputes today concern factual situations which are extremely complex and which require a great deal of hard graft to master.[20] Yet the function of the analytical framework is to seek to reduce the complexity, not add to it. It helps to reduce the complexity by enabling the lawyer and the court to identify the relative importance and unimportance of certain facts. An example might help to illustrate the point. Assume that a claimant pays money to a defendant as a result of pressure applied by the defendant. The claimant sues to recover the money so paid on the ground that it was paid under duress. Is the basis of the claim to

---

[17] S. Hedley, 'Unjust Enrichment', (1995) 54 *CLJ* 578.
[18] 'A New "Seascape" for Obligations: Reclassification on the Basis of Measure of Damages', in: Birks, *Classification of Obligations*, 193, 213.
[19] S. Hedley, 'Work Done in Anticipation of a Contract which does not Materialise: A Response', in: Cornish *et al.*, *Restitution*, 195, 196.
[20] In this sense there may be a temptation to retreat into general principle in order to avoid having to wrestle with the facts. This temptation must be resisted. The facts must be established and the legal principle applied to them; the legal principle should not be applied to facts which have only been partially established or to an assumed state of facts which bears no relationship to reality.

recover the money the fact that the defendant behaved unconscionably or illegitimately, the fact that the claimant did not consent to the payment or some combination of these two facts? Once a legal system has answered this question as a matter of principle, the lawyer is then in a position to know the type of evidence which must be led in court and the facts which must be established if the claim is to succeed. Without any guiding principle it is difficult if not impossible to know what type of evidence to lead.

The fourth reason for the lack of interest in taxonomy in recent years may be the rise of post-modernism, which has poured scorn on attempts to produce order out of chaos. Post-modernism has had little or no effect on the courts but it has had an impact on academic writers and it may offer some explanation for their relative lack of interest in taxonomic issues. A reaction to the rise of post-modernism has, however, set in. Thus William Twining has recently stated that 'without concepts we cannot think'[21] and, when constructing his modern Benthamite jurist, he noted that he or she would today fight for a revival of analytical jurisprudence, that is 'the elucidation, refinement, and construction of key concepts'.[22] The focus on taxonomy is no more than an attempt to elucidate, refine and construct the key concepts which together make up the law of restitution.

III. Why does taxonomy matter?

There are at least six reasons that can be advanced in support of the proposition that the taxonomy of the law of restitution is a matter of first importance. Indeed, it can be argued that taxonomy is a matter of importance for the legal system as a whole, not just the law of restitution. The first is that it is a vital part of ensuring that like cases are treated alike, which in turn is a fundamental aspect of justice. If we have no more than a wilderness of individual instances, it becomes much more difficult for us to be sure that we are in fact treating like cases alike. Cases can still be found which, upon careful examination, concern very similar fact patterns but the relationship between them has not been noted because they are discussed in separate books or, for some other reason, their similarity has never been noted. The failure to notice the similarity is often caused by the tricks played by the historical divide between law and equity. Here it will suffice to provide two examples.

---

[21] W. Twining, 'Imagining Bentham: A Celebration', [1998] *Current Legal Problems* 1, 34.
[22] *Ibid.*

TAXONOMY: DOES IT MATTER? 633

The first is taken from cases concerned with the not uncommon situation in which work is done in anticipation of a contract which fails to materialise. On what basis and in what circumstances can the party who has done the work bring a claim against the person for whom the work was done? This has proved to be a surprisingly difficult and contentious question to answer. In some cases claimants have advanced a restitutionary claim against the defendant;[23] in other cases the claim has been made on the basis of estoppel.[24] In other cases it is not at all clear on what basis the claim was advanced or the case decided.[25] In this confused state of affairs there is a real possibility that the courts will not have their attention drawn to all of the relevant authorities[26] and so the prospect of inconsistency becomes ever greater. What is required is a clear conceptual understanding of the basis of the claim advanced in each case (for example, is it a basis of the claim to recover the claimant's reliance loss or is it one to reverse an unjust enrichment that the defendant has obtained at the claimant's expense?) and the relationship, if any, between the different claims.[27]

The second example is provided by the 'knowing receipt' and 'knowing assistance' cases, which for many years were confined to the books on equity.[28] Broadly speaking, 'knowing receipt' cases concern the liability of a recipient of trust property who is not an express trustee but who, for example, receives trust property knowing that it is trust property and that the transfer to him was in breach of trust, while 'knowing assistance'

---

[23] See, for example, *William Lacey (Hounslow) Ltd v. Davis* [1957] 1 WLR 932, *British Steel Corporation v. Cleveland Bridge and Engineering Co. Ltd* [1984] 1 All ER 504 and *Regalian Properties plc v. London Docklands Development Corp.* [1995] 1 WLR 212.

[24] See, for example, *Attorney-General of Hong Kong v. Humphreys Estate Ltd* [1987] AC 114 and *Salvation Army Trustee Co. Ltd v. West Yorkshire Metropolitan County Council* (1981) 41 P & CR 179.

[25] An example in the latter category is provided by *Sabemo Pty Ltd v. North Sydney Municipal Council* [1977] 2 NSWLR 880. The focus on the facts rather than legal categories has been applauded in some quarters: see, for example, J. D. Davies, 'What's in a Title?', (1981) 1 *Oxford JLS* 301.

[26] This may in fact have happened in *Regalian Properties plc v. London Docklands Development Corp.* [1995] 1 WLR 212 where no reference was made to *Attorney-General of Hong Kong v. Humphreys Estate Ltd* [1987] AC 114, notwithstanding the fact that they were both concerned with work done on a 'subject to contract' basis.

[27] One difficulty which arises here is that there are a number of different conceptual schemes on offer. What should a court do when faced with conflicting analytical frameworks or taxonomic schemes? The question whether or not we should all adopt the same taxonomy is considered in more detail at notes 85–91 below and associated text.

[28] See, for example, *Snell's Principles of Equity* (29th edn, 1990), 193.

cases concern the liability of a person who does not actually himself receive the trust property but who knowingly assists in the breach of trust by the trustee. The use of the word 'knowing' in both categories clearly conveyed the impression that liability in both cases could not be strict; it was based on the knowledge of the defendant (although the extent of the knowledge required before liability could be imposed was a matter of debate). The close proximity of these two doctrines in the textbooks[29] also implied that there was some kind of close relationship between the two. At least two fundamental points remained largely undetected as a consequence. The first was that the relationship between the knowing receipt cases and the law of restitution was never explored, so that the existence of factually similar lines of authority went unnoticed for many years.[30] But the relationship (or possible relationship) between these lines of authority was to prove to be of fundamental importance because it raised issues of considerable significance for the basis upon which liability is imposed. Prior to the recognition of any link, support had been building up in equity for the proposition that the liability of the recipient was fault based[31] or was based on dishonesty.[32] Cases such as *Re Diplock*,[33] which favoured the imposition of strict liability, had been effectively marginalised.[34] However, the proposition that there was a restitutionary basis to these claims added considerable strength to the argument that the liability of the recipient was, subject to defences, strict and that case was further strengthened by the decision of the House of Lords in

---

[29] They are discussed in consecutive paragraphs in *Snell's Principles of Equity* (29th edn, 1990), 193. However in the thirtieth edition, published in 1999, the editor has retitled knowing assistance 'dishonest assistance' and states that the claim 'on the basis of knowing receipt or dealing has been described as a restitutionary claim' (§§ 9-43). The different juridical bases of the two doctrines has now been noted, although they are still discussed in consecutive paragraphs (§§ 9-42–9-43).

[30] In hindsight it is clear that the vital turning point was the work of Birks, commencing with his article 'Misdirected Funds: Restitution from the Recipient', [1989] *Lloyd's Maritime and Commercial Law Quarterly* 296. The advances which have been made since that article was written are substantial. The issues, and the likely future path of the law, has been set out with great clarity and insight by Lord Nicholls, writing extra-judicially in 'Knowing Receipt: The Need for a New Landmark', in: Cornish *et al.*, *Restitution*, 231 ff.

[31] See, for example, *Selangor United Rubber Estates Ltd v. Cradock (No. 3)* [1968] 1 WLR 1555; *International Sales and Agencies Ltd v. Marcus* [1982] 3 All ER 551 and *Westpac Banking Corp. v. Savin* [1985] 2 NZLR 41.

[32] *Re Montagu's Settlement Trusts* [1987] Ch 264.

[33] [1948] Ch 465. A further example of strict liability was provided by *G. L. Baker Ltd v. Medway Building & Supplies Ltd* [1958] 1 WLR 1216.

[34] Thus *Re Diplock* was regarded for many years as being confined in its application to the administration of estates and was not recognised as a case of general application.

Lipkin Gorman (a Firm) v. Karpnale Ltd,[35] where the liability at law of the recipient of money which traceably belonged at law to the claimant was held to be strict, subject to defences. The second point, which remained largely undetected, was that 'knowing receipt' and 'knowing assistance' claims are analytically distinct. Knowing receipt cases are, it is suggested, part of the law of restitution,[36] whereas the knowing assistance cases are properly part of the law of civil wrongs, a point now recognised by the Privy Council in *Royal Brunei Airlines Sdn Bhd v. Tan*.[37] While the liability of an accessory is now clearly based on dishonesty in equity, there is as yet 'no clear picture of the law of intentionally assisting other wrongs'.[38] A limitation which confines the *Tan* principle to cases concerned with dishonest assistance in a breach of trust will tempt the courts artificially to extend the ambit of the wrong of breach of trust.[39] Much better is to undertake the more difficult task of seeking to integrate the knowing assistance cases with the economic torts, particularly the tort of interfering with contractual relations.[40] Yet such a task can only be safely undertaken with a secure taxonomy.

Secondly, taxonomy is important because it can expose anomalies or inconsistencies in the present set of rules. In the words of Peter Birks, 'neglect of taxonomy leads to errors and confusion'.[41] An example here might be the rule that a failure of consideration must be total in order to ground a restitutionary claim. The authorities cited in support of this rule[42] appear increasingly vulnerable and may not withstand further judicial scrutiny.[43] The argument that money paid should be recoverable

---

[35] [1991] 2 AC 548.
[36] It must, however, be conceded that this proposition is a contentious one. It has been argued that *Lipkin Gorman* is not an example of a restitutionary claim at all but a property claim where the claimant was seeking to vindicate his property rights: see, for example, W. Swadling, 'Restitution and Bona Fide Purchase', in: W. Swadling (ed.), *The Limits of Restitutionary Claims: A Comparative Analysis* (1997), 79, esp. 96–104. It is not possible to explore this issue within the confines of this chapter.
[37] [1995] 2 AC 378.   [38] Birks 'Equity in the Modern Law', 48–9.
[39] As indeed happened in *Bank Tejarat v. Hong Kong and Shanghai Banking Corp. Ltd* [1995] 1 Lloyd's Rep 239.
[40] The link was noticed by Lord Nicholls in his speech in *Tan* ([1995] 2 AC 378 at 387) and work had in fact begun prior to the decision itself (see, for example, Philip Sales, 'The Tort of Conspiracy and Civil Secondary Liability', (1990) 49 *CLJ* 491 and Sir Leonard Hoffmann, 'The Redundancy of Knowing Assistance', in: P. Birks (ed.), *The Frontiers of Liability* (1994), 27), but relatively little has been achieved since then.
[41] Birks, 'Equity in the Modern Law', 4.
[42] Such as *Giles v. Edwards* (1797) 7 TR 181; 101 ER 920; *Hunt v. Silk* (1804) 5 East 449; 102 ER 1142 and *Whincup v. Hughes* (1871) LR 6 CP 78.
[43] See, in particular the speech of Lord Goff in *Goss v. Chilcott* [1996] AC 788 at 798.

upon a partial failure of consideration might be strengthened if an analogy could be drawn with cases involving goods or services and it could be shown that the law permitted the provider of goods and services to recover the value of the goods or services upon a partial failure of consideration. If the law allows recovery on a partial failure in the case where the claimant provides goods and services, why not also in the case where the claimant pays money to the defendant? Thus the vital question becomes: can an analogy be drawn between the money cases on the one hand and the goods and services cases on the other? The traditional answer is 'no'. The claim to recover upon a total failure of consideration is a money claim which has no application to non-money claims. This divide between money and non-money claims has the consequence that an appeal to non-money cases has little, if any, analogical force. Yet, analytically, it can be argued that the distinction between a money claim and a non-money claim is relevant only to the existence or otherwise of an enrichment. It can have no relevance to the reason for restitution which, in both cases, it has been argued is to be located in the failure of the expected consideration for the payment or the work done.[44] If this argument is correct, it follows that the non-money cases (where it is clear that the failure of consideration need not be total because receipt of part-payment of the contract price does not operate to bar the restitutionary claim by the provider of the goods or services[45]) can be used to attack the total failure of consideration requirement which still prevails in the case of money claims. In this way a concern for taxonomy can assist in the exposure of anomalies in the current corpus of rules and, hopefully, lead to their elimination.

Thirdly, a proper emphasis on taxonomy will help to keep the legal system on the right track. Andrew Kull has graphically described the decline of the law of restitution in the United States, in terms of scholarly writings, teaching within law schools and consequent awareness of the issues by practitioners.[46] It has also been claimed that the law of restitution has receded from American legal scholarship to the extent that 'few law professors teach the material, fewer still write in the area, and no one

---

[44] See A. Burrows, 'Free Acceptance and the Law of Restitution', (1988) 104 *LQR* 576.
[45] See, for example, P. Birks, *An Introduction to the Law of Restitution* (1985), 242–4 and A. Burrows, *The Law of Restitution* (1993), 260–1.
[46] A. Kull, 'Rationalizing Restitution', (1995) 83 *California LR* 1191. See also J. Langbein, 'Scholarly and Professional Objectives in Legal Education: American Trends and English Comparisons', in: P. Birks (ed.), *Pressing Problems in the law*, vol. II, *What are Law Schools For?* (1996), 1 and J. Langbein, 'The Later History of Restitution', in: Cornish et al., *Restitution*, 57, 60–2.

even agrees what the field comprises anymore'.[47] Kull concludes that 'no legal topic can long survive this degree of professional neglect' and states that the 'loss to American law, measured in terms of its ability to yield coherent and reasoned adjudication, has already been very great, and the outlook is not encouraging'.[48]

Fourthly, taxonomy is important to the extent that it results in the production of a clearer, more accessible body of law. Thus Andrew Burrows has argued that the rule of law demands accurate, clear and simple language and that 'fictions and obscure jargon in the law are an abomination and must be sought out and excised'.[49] The force with which this view is expressed may occasion some surprise. Yet it can be argued that the law of restitution has had more than its fair share of obscure and misleading terminology, which has hindered the development of the law. The uncertainty generated by this obscure terminology has had practical as well as academic consequences. Thus Lord Nicholls, writing extra-judicially, criticised the current state of the law on knowing receipt and knowing assistance on the ground that 'the law does not yet exhibit the degree of certainty which the business community is entitled to expect'.[50] This was particularly so in relation to knowing receipt liability where the need for clarification was 'particularly pressing' because 'those who operate in the financial markets need to be able to evaluate the risks of proposed transactions'.[51] It would be going too far to claim that an interest in taxonomy will eliminate these uncertainties, but it should help to reduce them.

Fifthly, taxonomy is important for reasons of economy. If the structure of the law is clear then it should be much easier to find. This assists both practitioners of the law (in that it makes it easier to find the law and hence reduces the likelihood of mistakes being made) and litigants (in that it should take practitioners less time to find the law and so their fees should be reduced accordingly). Finally, taxonomy may be important for reasons of elegance. This is the weakest argument of the six. It can be

---

[47] M. Heller and C. Serkin, 'Revaluing Restitution: From the Talmud to Postsocialism', (1999) 97 *Michigan LR* 1385, 1386, although it is only fair to point out that the authors are rather more optimistic about the future of the subject as a result of the publication of Haroch Dagan's book *Unjust Enrichment: A Study of Private Law and Public Values* (1997).

[48] Kull, 'Rationalising Restitution', 1196.

[49] A. Burrows, 'Restitution: Where Do We Go From Here?', [1997] *Current Legal Problems* 95, 98.

[50] Lord Nicholls, 'Knowing Receipt', 232.   [51] *Ibid.*

argued that elegance in the law is a value in and of itself.[52] The difficulty with this argument is that it is open to challenge on the ground that the law is concerned with resolving practical problems and that therefore what matters is that it works and not that it looks good.[53] Perhaps this argument should be understood as simply a more refined way of saying that the law ought to be clear. In so far as it suggests that the law ought to be elegant as well as clear, the merits of the argument are less than obvious.

IV. For whom does taxonomy matter?

The answer to the question whether or not taxonomy is a matter of importance may well depend upon the perspective of the person who is asked the question. At least three different perspectives can be adopted, namely the jurist (or academic lawyer), the judge and the legislator.[54] The significance attached to taxonomy is likely to vary between the three different perspectives (indeed, it is likely to vary within them).

1. The jurist

In my view taxonomy is of primary significance for the jurist or the academic lawyer. The principal function of the jurist is to analyse, expound and teach the law. Each of these functions is likely to be assisted by a secure taxonomy. Yet it must be conceded that English academics and English law schools have traditionally placed little, if any, emphasis on taxonomy (especially in the way in which the law degree programme is structured). Some modern scholarship on the law of restitution stands out against this indifference to taxonomy. Indeed, its principal feature is probably its concern, some would say obsession,[55] with questions of classification or taxonomy. This concern manifests itself both internally and externally; that is to say, writers have devoted considerable effort to developing the internal structure of the law of restitution and at the same time have sought to attend to its external relationship with other compartments of the law, notably the law of contract, the law of tort, the law of property and, more broadly, equity.[56]

---

[52] See, for example, Birks, 'Misnomer', 1–2.   [53] See Virgo, *Principles*, viii.
[54] Other perspectives could be adopted. For example, the perspective of the individual citizen could be employed but his or her interest in the issue is likely to be confined to the requirement that the law be clear, accessible and fair.
[55] See, for example, S. Hedley in his review of A. Burrows, '*Understanding the Law of Obligations*', [1999] *Lloyd's Maritime and Commercial Law Quarterly* 578.
[56] See, for example, the work of Peter Birks, 'Equity in the Modern Law'.

It can be argued that, in so far as taxonomy has any significance, it is only for jurists. This view has recently been articulated by Peter Cane. He has argued that, while classification is useful for teaching or expounding the law, it should not be given any greater role. In his view, 'the categories of the law of obligations, namely tort, contract, equity and restitution, should be recognized for what they are, namely expository devices. They should not be given any dispositive significance.'[57] On this view classifications are helpful in so far as they 'make it easier to understand, expound and teach the law' and so 'make it more user-friendly for lawyers seeking to solve real-life problems for clients'.[58] But, at the same time, classification has its limitations; in particular, Cane argues that categories should not be used 'for dispositive purposes to decide cases'.[59] Dispositive classification, in his view, should be based on a separate analytical scheme,[60] apparently because it 'affects remedies'.[61] While expository classifications may be allowed to 'track'[62] dispositive classifications they should not be allowed to trespass any further. In the view of Cane, categories such as 'contract, tort and equity are lawyers' inventions' and it is 'important that lawyers should remain the masters of their own categories and not become servants of such conceptualism'.[63] The difficulty with this view lies in the distinction which it draws between exposition and disposition. If the categories we use make the law more 'user-friendly' to the practising lawyer seeking to 'resolve real-life problems', why should they not be used by the courts when deciding these cases? If the aim of taxonomy is to deduce a set of principles which will help to eliminate anomalies and inconsistencies in the law and to ensure that like cases are treated alike, it is difficult to see why taxonomy should be a matter of indifference to the courts. On the other hand it does not follow from the proposition that the courts should not be indifferent to issues of taxonomy that they should attach the same significance to it as jurists (should) do. For a number of reasons the courts must be much more cautious than jurists in their approach to questions of taxonomy.

---

[57] P. Cane, *The Anatomy of Tort Law* (1997), 201. For a similar view see Dickson, 'Unjust Enrichment Claims', 109–10.
[58] Cane, *Anatomy*, 198.   [59] *Ibid.*, 199.
[60] The scheme that Cane advocates is based on the interplay of the interests which the law of tort protects, the conduct which it sanctions or penalises and the remedies which it affords. The analysis is introduced at 10–18 of the book and developed in subsequent chapters. It is important to note that Cane does not object to classification as such; he simply distinguishes between disposition and exposition in terms of the production of an analytical scheme.
[61] Cane, *Anatomy*, 202.   [62] *Ibid.*, 202.   [63] *Ibid.*, 198.

2. The courts

The courts are constrained by a number of factors. The first of these is that the function of the judge is to do justice according to law for the parties who appear before him or her; hence the emphasis on 'practical justice'[64] which can be found in a number of judgments. The judge must answer the questions of law which divide the parties; it is not necessary (or even in most cases desirable) for him or her to seek to resolve similar but related issues which have not arisen on the facts. Secondly, and relatedly, the range of issues raised by the case may be limited (for example, the dispute may relate to the basis of the claimant's cause of action but not to the defences or vice versa). Thirdly, the judge is likely to be constrained by the nature of the arguments that have been advanced by counsel. The aim of the barrister who is arguing the case is to win, not to render the law more elegant or more consistent, and this will have an impact on the nature and the scope of the argument presented to the judge. Fourthly, the judges (especially, it would seem, in the Court of Appeal) are constrained by a lack of time and resources. They simply do not have the time to analyse each and every issue exhaustively. They are under pressure to get their judgments out quickly and this often necessitates the adoption of a narrow approach which focuses only on the essential issues raised by the facts of the case. Fifthly, the judge must consider the consequences which may follow from the adoption of a rule (or, even worse, a classificatory scheme) that subsequent developments reveal to have been flawed. It is one thing for an academic lawyer to recant on views previously expressed;[65] it is rather more difficult when the author is a judge writing a speech in an appellate court. It may take some time and considerable expense to 'innocent' litigants before the judge, or a subsequent court, is given the opportunity to recant and set the law back on its proper course. For a judge caution is often necessary. Finally, the judge is constrained by precedent. At all levels in the judicial hierarchy (but particularly at first instance and in the Court of Appeal) judges are likely to find that it is not possible for them to iron out the inconsistencies

---

[64] The emphasis on the need to do 'practical justice' has been a feature of the speeches of Lord Goff in the House of Lords: see, for example, *Frost v. Chief Constable of South Yorkshire Police* [1999] 2 AC 455 at 475; *Kleinwort Benson Ltd v. Lincoln City Council* [1999] 2 AC 349 at 372F, 377H; *Airbus Industrie GIE v. Patel* [1999] 1 AC 97 at 132, 133; *Westdeutsche Landesbank Girozentrale v. Islington London Borough Council* [1996] AC 669 at 682, 685, 687; *White v. Jones* [1995] 2 AC 207 at 259, 260, 263, 264, 265, 268, 269; *Spiliada Maritime Corporation v. Cansulex Ltd* [1987] AC 461 at 483; *Smith v. Littlewoods Organisation Ltd* [1987] AC 241 at 280.

[65] A not uncommon feature of modern restitutionary scholarship.

in the cases which have been cited to them. They have to do the best they can 'under adverse conditions'[66] with the material they have: they do not start with a clean sheet.

The more limited role of the courts in developing a taxonomy of the law of restitution is perhaps best illustrated by reference to the decision of the House of Lords in *Lipkin Gorman v. Karpnale Ltd*.[67] The case positively bristles with taxonomic issues but their Lordships passed them all by. The first is that the appeal was confined to the claimant's common-law claim. The House of Lords was not asked to consider, and did not consider, what the position would have been if the claim had been brought in equity.[68] Yet, from a taxonomic perspective, the relationship between the claim at law and the claim in equity is a matter of some considerable importance,[69] on which it would be very helpful to have had the view of the House of Lords. Secondly, the defendants conceded that the claim at law was not defeated by the fact that the partner who misappropriated the money may have mixed it with his own money before he gambled it away at the defendants' club.[70] This concession may have been 'inexplicable'[71] and the rule that mixing defeats the ability to trace at common law may stand in need of reconsideration,[72] but the effect of the concession was to deprive their Lordships of the opportunity to carry out that re-examination on the facts of *Lipkin Gorman*. Thirdly, their Lordships did not identify the 'unjust factor' or the reason for restitution with any precision. In particular no mention was made of 'ignorance' as a possible unjust factor,[73] whether the claim was in a fact a proprietary claim,[74] or whether it was a restitutionary claim based upon the vindication of the

---

[66] Per Lord Hoffmann in *Frost v. Chief Constable of South Yorkshire Police* [1999] 2 AC 455 at 511C.

[67] [1991] 2 AC 548.   [68] *Ibid.* at 572.

[69] The argument being that if liability is strict, subject to defences, at law, should liability in equity not also be strict? Alternatively, if there is to be a difference in treatment between law and equity, what is the basis or justification for this difference? The conflict in the authorities is noted in slightly more detail at notes 28–40 above and associated text.

[70] [1991] 2 AC 548 at 572.

[71] W. Swadling, 'Some Lessons from the Law of Torts', in: P. Birks (ed.), *The Frontiers of Liability* (1994), vol. I, 41, 45.

[72] See, for example, L. D. Smith, *The Law of Tracing* (1997), 162–74.

[73] On which see P. Birks, 'The English Recognition of Unjust Enrichment', [1991] *Lloyd's Maritime and Commercial Law Quarterly* 473 and E. McKendrick, 'Restitution, Misdirected Funds and Change of Position', (1992) 55 MLR 377. Contrast E. Bant, '"Ignorance" as a Ground of Restitution – Can it Survive?', [1998] *Lloyd's Maritime and Commercial Law Quarterly* 18.

[74] As argued by Swadling, 'Restitution and Bona Fide Purchase'.

claimant's proprietary interest.[75] As far as their Lordships were concerned, the claim fell legitimately within the scope of the money had and received claim that had been advanced by the claimant and that, effectively, was that.

Finally, while their Lordships took the vital step of recognising the existence of the defence of change of position, it is a noticeable feature of the case that they were not concerned to identify the juridical basis or even the precise scope of the defence. Rather, they were content to leave it to develop on a case-by-case basis.[76] It has since continued to develop on a case-by-case basis and few if any issues of principle have been resolved by the courts.[77] This is in large part attributable to the way in which cases are argued in the appellate courts. Unlike the jurist who is concerned with taxonomic issues, counsel are not concerned first to establish the principle underlying the defence and then to seek to apply that principle to the facts of the case. Generally speaking, counsel are concerned only with the application of the defence to the facts of the particular case. The focus is different and this has a significant impact on the form of argument employed in the courts. It is important to recognise this difference. A failure to do so can result in confusion and misunderstanding between the jurist and the practitioner. Take the illustration sometimes used in the academic literature of money which is mistakenly paid over to the defendant but which is destroyed in a fire shortly after receipt.[78] Does such a defendant have a defence of change of position? Statements by practitioners that this illustration is 'commercially unrealistic' miss the point, which is not to mimic commercial reality but to assist in the location of the principle that underpins the defence. In particular, does the defence require that the defendant alter his position in reliance upon the receipt of the enrichment (in which case it can be argued that the

---

[75] As argued by G. Virgo, 'Reconstructing the Law of Restitution', (1996) 10 *Trust Law International* 20.

[76] [1991] 2 AC 548 at 580.

[77] One issue of principle, namely whether or not the defence can be invoked in the case of pre-receipt expenditure, has been the subject of conflicting dicta: contrast Clarke J in *South Tyneside MBC v. Svenska International plc* [1995] 1 All ER 545 at 565–6 (defence cannot be invoked, save in exceptional cases) with *Kleinwort Benson v. Birmingham City Council* [1997] QB 380 at 394 (defence may possibly be invoked). In New Zealand the defence appears to have assumed a discretionary form which is resistant to explanation in principled terms: see *National Bank of New Zealand Ltd v. Waitaki International Processing (NI) Ltd* [1999] 2 NZLR 211, which is noted in critical terms by R. Grantham and C. Rickett, 'Change of Position and Balancing the Equities', [1999] *Restitution LR* 158.

[78] See, for example, Burrows, *Law of Restitution*, 427; P. Birks, 'Change of Position and Surviving Enrichment', in Swadling, *Limits of Restitutionary Claims*, 36, 50–1.

defence would not be applicable) or does it suffice that the defendant's enrichment has been dissipated or destroyed through no fault of his own (in which case the defence could apply)? If the latter view is adopted then it can be argued that the defence is one which relates to the erasure of the enrichment[79] or, possibly, the interest of the defendant in the stability of his receipts, whereas if the former view is adopted the defence may still be rooted in the defendant's interest in the stability of his receipts but the interest which is protected is much narrower in scope. Although the immediate purpose of the 'burnt notes' illustration is not to solve practical problems, the answer given to it may reveal different conceptions of the defence which in turn will have practical consequences.

If one of the tasks of the jurist is to ascertain the principles on which the law is based and the task of practising lawyers and the courts is to resolve particular cases, what should be the relationship between academic writing (and, in particular, academic writing that is committed to developing a taxonomy of the law of restitution) and the courts? It can be argued that there should be none. But this would be to go too far. Academic writing on taxonomy can assist the judge in that it can expose and hopefully help to eliminate anomalies in the law or enable the judge to rationalise a group of cases which hitherto had been scattered. In the words of Gareth Jones, the function of the jurist is to 'assist the judge in finding principle which may lie buried in a morass of case law and to consider the wider implications of the acceptance or rejection of that principle'.[80] But jurists should not expect their work immediately to be absorbed and reproduced by counsel and the courts. There should be a time lag (possibly a considerable one) between academic writings and their reception by the courts. This enables the work of the jurist to be absorbed, explored and tested before finding its way formally into the law. The constraining factors which have been noted limit the ability of the courts to take a leading role in the development of an appropriate taxonomy.

3. Legislators

Finally taxonomy may be important for the legislator. In England today legislative intervention in the heartland of the law of obligations largely

---

[79] If this view is correct then the task which lies ahead is to work out when an particular enrichment has, or is deemed to have, disappeared. This could either be done impressionistically by the courts or they could devise a set of rules or presumptions (rather like the present tracing rules) which could be applied to work out whether or not a particular enrichment has disappeared.

[80] G. Jones, '"Traditional" Legal Scholarship: A Personal View', in: Birks, *Pressing Problems in the Law*, vol. II, *What are Law Schools For?*, 9, 10.

takes the form of remedial surgery. The role of the Law Commission is now confined largely to important but piecemeal law reform.[81] Codification of private law is no longer on their agenda.[82] The same cannot be said for Europe, where interest in codification and unification (or harmonisation) of private law is increasing rapidly. An important question to be answered is: if we believe in taxonomy, should it take the form of a code or not? This is a huge question which cannot be answered within the scope of this essay. The advantages of a code are obvious if the code results in the production of a clear, concise and coherent statement of the law. But the danger of a code is that it may freeze the law at an inconvenient point and further development may be difficult because of the problems inherent in amending a code. There is also a question whether or not a code gives too much power to the framers of the code.[83] But, given that the Code, if it is to become law, must be approved by a democratically elected national Parliament, the democratic deficit inherent in a code is not at all obvious. As a practical matter English law is not yet ready to receive a code given that even the present limited legislative intervention in the law of restitution is the subject of some controversy,[84] but the day will come when a code will be drawn up[85] and the decision will have to be made whether or not to embrace it. The decision should ultimately turn on the quality of the code that has been produced and not on some abstract decision for or against codification.

V. Should we all adopt the same taxonomic scheme?

In an ideal world we should all probably adopt the same taxonomic scheme and that scheme should be rational, clear and not consist of intersecting categories. The difficulty, of course, is that this is not an ideal

---

[81] See, for example, the Contracts (Rights of Third Parties) Act 1999.
[82] A possible exception is the creation of a Commercial Code: see M. Arden, 'Time for an English Commercial Code?', (1997) 56 *CLJ* 516.
[83] A reservation expressed by Birks, 'Equity in the Modern Law', esp. 97–9 and his rather harsh reference to 'insufficiently humble codifiers' who appear to be open to the charge of failing to honour the 'democratic bargain'.
[84] The competing arguments are carefully considered by J. Beatson, 'Should There be Legislative Development of the Law of Restitution?', in: Burrows, *Essays*, 279 ff.
[85] A draft code has already been drawn up for Scotland prepared by Dr Eric Clive at the Scottish Law Commission. The code is produced as an Appendix to the Scottish Law Commission Discussion Paper No. 99: *Judicial Abolition of the Error of Law Rule and its Aftermath* and in: F. D. Rose (ed.), *Blackstone's Statutes on Contract, Tort and Restitution* (10th edn, 1999), 494. See discussion in chap. 23, 691 ff., below.

world and no legal system in the world starts with a clean sheet. Every system has evolved over a number of years and has had to learn a number of (often painful) lessons both in the courts and the national Parliaments. The law in some areas – and the areas will differ between national legal systems – may be thought by some to be less than satisfactory, but at least it is settled. And, even where it is neither settled nor satisfactory, the courts and Parliaments tend to be unwilling to throw out years of learning and start all over again unless the advantages of so doing are clear and overwhelming. A court may, in the light of experience elsewhere, modify existing rules of law but it is unlikely to wish to engage in wholesale reconstruction of the law. Comparative law enables a lawyer to learn from another system and then to look at his or her own system with fresh eyes; it has, in the words of Lord Steyn, the 'inestimable value of sharpening our focus on the weight of competing considerations [and] it reminds us that the law is part of the world of competing ideas markedly influenced by cultural differences'.[86] But comparative law also has its limitations. In the first place, a judge, having looked at the development of the law in another jurisdiction, may conclude that it is simply too late for one system to borrow extensively from another.[87] Secondly, legal transplants[88] are fraught with difficulty. For example, a legal system which borrows from another system a broad ground of restitution without also borrowing the corresponding checks and balances is bound to create substantial difficulties for itself in the future.[89] Comparative law may assist in the incremental development of the law and in the resolution of particular issues, but it is unlikely, at least in the short run, to lead to radical restructuring of the law by the judiciary.

Thus a legal system which does not start out with a sound taxonomy is unlikely to develop one as a result of the occasional intervention of the judiciary in the development of the law. The legacy of history and the

---

[86] *McFarlane v. Tayside Health Board* [1999] 3 WLR 1301 at 1317.

[87] A good example in this context might be the decision of the House of Lords in *White v. Jones* [1995] 2 AC 207, where extensive reference was made by Lord Goff in his speech to German law although, in the final analysis, he was unable to transplant German doctrines into English law and had to content himself with developing English law in a very pragmatic way (albeit that such an approach is not consistent with the development of a sound taxonomy).

[88] Or, if one prefers, 'legal irritants': see G. Teubner, 'Legal Irritants: Good Faith in British Law or How Unifying Law Ends Up in New Divergences', (1998) 61 *MLR* 11.

[89] These difficulties may arise if English law borrows 'absence of legal ground' from Germany: see P. Birks, 'Mistakes of Law', [2000] *Current Legal Problems* 205–36, where it is pointed out that Commonwealth jurisdictions presently lack 'a science of nullity' and so lack the 'essential infrastructure' that is a feature of German law.

practical constraints to which the courts are subject are likely to inhibit the development of a sound taxonomy. The impetus to develop a sound taxonomy must therefore come from elsewhere, either the legislature or jurists. In England the likelihood of parliamentary intervention is remote. It therefore falls to the academic community to develop a sound taxonomy of the law of restitution. But, when seeking to do so, academic writers cannot expect their work immediately to be incorporated into the law. Nor should they necessarily expect the production of a taxonomy which receives universal acclaim. If taxonomy is important because of the need to ensure that like cases are treated alike and because of the assistance which it provides in terms of the elimination of anomalies then it does not necessitate the adoption of one particular taxonomy to the exclusion of others provided that we understand what we are doing and, in the event of our taxonomies intersecting, that we realise that they intersect and deal sensibly with them at the point of intersection.[90] It is only in the unlikely event of a taxonomy achieving widespread acceptance[91] after substantial debate that it should be formally received into the law. Until that time comes, incremental development of the law of restitution and the gradual elimination of anomalies is likely to be the fruit of academic writing on the subject of taxonomy.

VI. Some current taxonomic issues

The fact that the influence of taxonomy is likely to be confined to the incremental development of the law and the elimination of anomalies does not mean that there are no taxonomic issues of any consequence to be explored. On the contrary there are a number of taxonomic issues that remain to be resolved. Here there is only room to sketch out some of the more important issues. What the sketch reveals is how much

---

[90] Obviously a taxonomy which does not intersect is preferable to one which does but, given the legacy of history, the likelihood of us being able to agree a single taxonomy which can then be implemented by the courts or by Parliament appears remote. On the other hand a greater emphasis on efficiency and elegance as the virtues of taxonomy might lead to an intolerance of intersection. But the more dogmatic approach exemplified by, for example, W. Swadling in 'What is the Law of Restitution About? Four Categorical Errors', in: Cornish *et al.*, *Restitution*, 331, is unlikely to appeal to the English legal mind and, given the differences of opinion which exist in the academic community, is unlikely to command widespread support.

[91] Which is not the case yet in England. Indeed, there is still a very long way to go in terms of achieving a taxonomy that commands substantial if not universal acceptance.

uncertainty there is in relation to the scope and the essential ingredients of the subject.

1. Restitution or unjust enrichment?

Start with the title of the subject: is it the law of restitution, the law of unjust(ified) enrichment or simply enrichment law? Indeed, does it matter what the subject is called as long as it is understood what is meant by the label attached to it? The label obviously helps. Were the subject to be called 'the law of hocus pocus' we would have to explain every time we used these words what we meant by them. A word or a phrase which accurately encapsulates the essence of a subject is obviously preferable to one which does not. Until recently, accepted usage in English law was the 'law of restitution'. Books have been written on the subject, the *Restitution Law Review* has emerged in recent years and the phrase is increasingly working its way into the vocabulary of practising lawyers. But, just as English lawyers were beginning to come to grips with an independent law of restitution, Birks has announced that the law of restitution is a 'misnomer'[92] and the subject should henceforth be known as the law of unjust enrichment. Why seek to make this change at such a crucial stage in the development of the law? Will it not cause unnecessary confusion?

The change of label advocated by Birks has some validity in the sense that restitution is a response rather than an event and unjust enrichment, being an event, aligns rather better with contract and tort (or wrongs). Although the point is not beyond dispute,[93] restitution can be a response to events other than unjust enrichment; the most obvious example being as a response to the commission of a wrong. But, given that restitution was generally being used as shorthand for the law of restitution based on the principle that unjust enrichments must be reversed, what is the point in causing so much trouble simply to change the label?

The answer may lie in the instability of the word 'restitution'. It can be argued that 'restitution' was always an inappropriate term, which conceals more than it reveals. The origins of the current use of the word by lawyers can be traced back to the Restatement of Restitution in 1938 but, even here, it is apparent that the use of 'restitution' was a result of a last-minute amendment (the drafts bore the title 'Restatement of Restitution

---

[92] Birks, 'Misnomer', 1 ff.
[93] See M. McInnes, 'Restitution, Unjust Enrichment and the Perfect Quadration Thesis', [1999] *Restitution LR* 118.

and Unjust Enrichment')[94] and that Warren Seavey, one of those responsible for the Restatement, later thought better of the change of name.[95] Andrew Kull has gone so far as to label the choice of restitution a 'serious blunder'.[96] It is a blunder because the word 'restitution' bears different meanings in both common parlance and legal debate. For example, it can be used of the criminal who must make restitution to his victim, of the tortfeasor who must make 'reasonable restitution'[97] to the claimant, of the tortfeasor who must hand over to the claimant the gains he has made as a result of the commission of a tort,[98] and of the fiduciary who, by virtue of his breach of fiduciary duty, must restore the party to whom the fiduciary duty was owed to his former state of affairs.[99] While objection may be taken to the use of the word 'restitution' in some or all of these contexts,[100] the basis of the objection cannot be that the word 'restitution' is not capable of bearing any of these meanings. It is. The objection can only be that these different usages are likely to lead to confusion, either because the sense in which the word is being used in a particular context might not be immediately apparent or because of a lack of awareness of the different senses in which the word can be used.

But the task of straightening out this conflicting use of terminology is not going to be easy: as Guenter Treitel has pointed out, 'there is probably no change in the law which is harder to achieve than one of terminology'.[101] Yet restitution lawyers have not always heeded this warning. Rather, they have sought to introduce their own terminology into the law, most of which is foreign to English practitioners. Thus we have 'unjust factors', 'incontrovertible benefit', 'change of position', 'passing on' and 'restitution for wrongs', to name but a few. Even well-known doctrines such as subrogation,[102] tracing[103] and resulting trusts[104] have been subjected to fresh analysis, much of which challenges received wisdom

---

[94] See Kull, 'Rationalising Restitution', 1213, n. 67.
[95] W. Seavey, 'Problems in Restitution', (1954) 7 *Oklahoma LR* 257.
[96] Kull, 'Rationalising Restitution', 1214.
[97] A recent example of this usage is to be found in the speech of Lord Clyde in *McFarlane v. Tayside Health Board* [1999] 3 WLR 1301 at 1339–40. See to similar effect the speech of Lord Steyn at 1318H.
[98] See, for example, *Ministry of Defence v. Ashman* [1993] 2 EGLR 102 at 105 (Hoffmann LJ).
[99] See, for example, *Swindle v. Harrison* [1997] 4 All ER 705 at 713–14 (Evans LJ) and 733 (Mummery LJ).
[100] See, for example, P. Birks and W. Swadling, 'Restitution', [1997] *All ER Annual Rev* 385–7.
[101] G. Treitel, '"Conditions" and "Conditions Precedent"', (1990) 106 *LQR* 185, 192.
[102] C. Mitchell, *The Law of Subrogation* (1996).   [103] Smith, *Law of Tracing*.
[104] R. Chambers, *Resulting Trusts* (1998).

in fundamental ways. In part the new terminology has been introduced because of the misleading or obscure nature of the old terminology. The problem here is, essentially, one of striking a balance between the need for appropriate terminology and the need for stable terminology.[105] The balance is a delicate one. A legal system requires secure terminology if it is to avoid undue upheaval. This suggests the need for caution. On the other hand, it is hard to avoid the conclusion that 'restitution' is presently used in too many different senses and that its use must be refined if confusion is to be avoided. The risk of confusion would be reduced if 'unjust enrichment' were used to describe the cause of action to reverse an unjust enrichment,[106] 'compensation' to describe the making good of a loss suffered by the claimant and 'disgorgement' to describe the process of requiring a defendant to give up to the claimant gains made as a result of the commission of a wrong.[107] Yet even here it must be conceded that the risk of confusion will only be reduced if we manage to agree on a common terminology and, it must be conceded, that agreement among academic writers on the subject appears still to be a long way off.

2. The future of the 'unjust factors'

At first sight English law appears to stand out from other legal systems because of its requirement that the claimant prove the existence of a specific reason for restitution. Thus one can draw up a list of factors that render an enrichment unjust. Professor Zimmermann has argued that English law's insistence on the identification of a specific 'unjust factor' is inelegant, uncertain and fragmentary and that it leads to an unnecessary duplication of problems;[108] in his view the civilian 'focus on the single issue of "transfer without legal ground"'[109] is preferable. In the light of the decision of the House of Lords in *Kleinwort Benson Ltd v. Lincoln City*

---

[105] The difficulty is evidenced by the range of views expressed in the literature. The balancing exercise carried out by individual authors can also appear questionable: for example, Birks, in 'Misnomer', objects to the change from 'restitutionary damages' to 'disgorgement damages' on the ground, *inter alia*, that it 'would disrupt a usage only now settling down' (at 13) but advocates the change from the law of restitution to the law of unjust enrichment notwithstanding the fact that usage of the law of restitution is only now settling down.

[106] As in fact is advocated by Birks (ibid.).

[107] As advocated by Lionel Smith, 'The Province of Restitution', (1992) 71 *Canadian Bar Review* 672.

[108] R. Zimmermann, 'Unjustified Enrichment: The Modern Civilian Approach', (1995) 15 *Oxford JLS* 403, 416.

[109] Ibid.

Council[110] and the breadth of the notion of mistake of law there employed by their Lordships it may be said that English law is beginning to move in the direction of German law.[111] It is possible that the broad notion of mistake embraced by the House of Lords will in time become the functional equivalent of *ohne rechtlichen Grund* in German law. But English law has not yet reached the position of formally adopting a ground of restitution known as 'transfer without legal ground' and may never do so. All that has happened so far is that the courts have adopted a broad interpretation of mistake. And there is much to be said for the retention[112] of the specific unjust factors in English law.

In the first place such recent experience as English law has had with broad general principles has not been a happy one. A useful illustration is provided by the rise and fall of Lord Wilberforce's two-stage test for the existence of a duty of care in the tort of negligence.[113] Its demise shows that English judges on the whole prefer to develop the law incrementally and by analogy with the established precedents.[114] General principles lend themselves to invocation by English legal practitioners in a loose fashion in what is often a last-ditch attempt to subvert established precedents or principles of law. A recent example of this phenomenon is provided by the argument of counsel in *Lloyds Bank plc v. Independent Insurance Co. Ltd*,[115] where reliance was placed on the five-stage approach to restitutionary claims adopted by Lord Millett, writing extra-judicially,[116] in a vain attempt to establish a restitutionary claim where none had previously been

---

[110] [1999] 2 AC 349 at 455.

[111] See, for example, S. Meier and R. Zimmermann, 'Judicial Development of the Law, *Error Juris* and the Law of Unjustified Enrichment – A View from Germany', (1999) 115 LQR 556.

[112] It is an altogether different question whether the unjust factors should be exported to another system. While the incremental development of the law via the gradual expansion of the unjust factors may suit the English legal mind, it does not follow that it should be exported to Scotland (see the objections to its export given by Niall Whitty, below).

[113] As set out in his speech in *Anns v. Merton LBC* [1978] AC 728 at 752–3.

[114] This view was classically expressed by Lord Bridge in his speech in *Caparo Industries plc v. Dickman* [1990] 2 AC 605 at 617–18.

[115] [1999] 2 WLR 986 at 997–1000 (Waller LJ) and 1003–5 (Peter Gibson LJ). A further example of this phenomenon, this time drawn from the tort of negligence, is provided by *Leigh and Sillivan Ltd v. Aliakmon Shipping Co. Ltd* [1986] AC 785, where the House of Lords refused to allow Lord Wilberforce's two-stage test to be used to find a duty of care in a factual situation in which the existence of a duty of care had repeatedly been held by previous courts not to exist.

[116] Sir Peter Millett, 'Restitution and Constructive Trusts', in: Cornish et al., *Restitution*, 199, 208.

recognised.[117] Of course it is true that the use of broad general principles need not (and should not) result in a lack of respect for existing case law but the relative unfamiliarity of English lawyers with broad general principles means that there is real risk that they will be used in just such a loose fashion. English law is generally much more secure when it develops in an incremental fashion.

Secondly, and relatedly, the more precise grounds of restitution adopted by English law express the reasons for granting restitution in clearer terms than can be found in the abstraction 'transfer without legal ground'. Thirdly, there are some cases in English law where a transfer is made without legal ground and yet we would not, for good reasons, currently allow a restitutionary claim. Thus the sudden introduction of 'transfer without legal ground' into English law might have unintended consequences. An obvious example is the case of illegal contracts where, presumably, 'transfer without legal ground' would have to give way to other considerations.[118] Similarly, when declaring a contract to be void, the courts or Parliament in the past have not taken into account the consequence that restitution will automatically follow. Subsequently to introduce an automatic right to restitution in such cases might produce results which would not have been desired by the court that declared the contract void or by those responsible for drafting the legislation that rendered the contract void. There is a need for caution in the development of the law and that can best be done by a gradual expansion of the existing grounds of restitution rather than by the recognition of a broad new ground of restitution. Too much can be made by critics of the fragmentary nature of the development of English Law. The courts are unlikely to develop a never-ending list of unjust factors. When the list threatens to become unmanageable the courts may abandon the specific list and move to a higher level of abstraction when articulating the reasons for restitution. But that point has not yet come and the courts should not be too willing to anticipate it.

3. The meaning of enrichment

Difficulties also arise in deciding whether or not a defendant has been enriched, particularly where the alleged enrichment takes the form of

---

[117] The cases which stood in the way of the success of the restitutionary claim were *Aiken v. Short* (1856) 1 H & N 210; 156 ER 1180 and *Kerrison v. Glyn, Mills, Currie & Co.* (1911) 81 LJKB 465. The Court of Appeal refused to allow them to be subverted by means of Lord Millett's five-stage approach.

[118] Discussed in more detail by Swadling and Dannemann in this volume (chapters 10 and 11).

services.[119] The difficulty is compounded by the fact that the courts tend to treat the enrichment issue in an impressionistic manner,[120] thereby giving ammunition to those who decry attempts to rationalise the law in unjust enrichment terms.[121] Yet, if the law of restitution is in fact based on the principle that unjust enrichments must be reversed, then it must be possible to identify the existence of an enrichment in order to establish whether or not a claim should succeed on a particular set of facts and in order to work out the limits of the subject. The boundary between claims to reverse a defendant's unjust enrichment and claims to protect the claimant's reliance loss can be notoriously indistinct, especially in services cases, for example work done in anticipation of a contract that fails to materialise.[122] In some of the cases it has been argued that 'the restitutionary claim for benefits conferred conceals a claim for reliance loss'[123] and, in the view of some writers,[124] protection of the reliance interest is a legitimate function of the law of restitution. In my view it is not. Protection of the reliance interest in such cases must rest on some other principle, yet to be identified in the case law.[125] A secure taxonomy should be able to identify the test to be applied in any given case to determine whether or not a defendant has been enriched and to distinguish between claims to reverse unjust enrichments and claims to protect reliance losses.

4. *Negotiorum gestio*

English law remains reluctant to recognise the existence of a doctrine of *negotiorum gestio*.[126] In refusing to recognise the existence of such a

---

[119] These difficulties are well illustrated by the improvement cases discussed by Wolffe and Kull above (chapters 14 and 15).

[120] See, for example, *Greenwood v. Bennett* [1973] 1 QB 195, discussed in more detail by E. McKendrick, 'Restitution and the Misuse of Chattels – The Need for a Principled Approach', in: N. Palmer and E. McKendrick (eds.), *Interests in Goods* (2nd edn, 1998), 897 ff.

[121] See, for example, S. Hedley, 'Restitution: Contract's Twin?', in: F. D. Rose (ed.), *Failure of Contracts: Contractual, Restitutionary and Proprietary Consequences* (1997), 247, esp. 270–1.

[122] See generally E. McKendrick, 'Work Done in Anticipation of a Contract which does not Materialise', in: Cornish *et al.*, *Restitution*, 163 ff.

[123] Lord Goff of Chieveley and Gareth Jones, *The Law of Restitution* (5th edn, 1998), 21.

[124] Most notably *ibid.* and J. Beatson, 'Benefit, Reliance, and the Structure of Unjust Enrichment', in: J. Beatson, *The Use and Abuse of Unjust Enrichment* (1991), 21.

[125] The most convincing attempt at providing a rationale for the protection of the reliance interest is provided by M. Spence, *Protecting Reliance: The Emergent Doctrine of Equitable Estoppel* (1999).

[126] The principal cases which are hostile to such a claim are *Nicholson v. Chapman* (1793) 2 H Bl 254; 126 ER 536 and *Falcke v. Scottish Imperial Insurance Co.* (1886) 34 Ch D 234. But

doctrine English law appears to stand out from its civilian counterparts. Yet if English law were to recognise such a doctrine how should it be classified? In truth it would appear to be a functional category which consists of three distinct claims. It has a contractual aspect, in that the intervener, once he has intervened, must complete the provision of the service so far as it is necessary and reasonable for him to do so. Secondly it has a tortious aspect, in that the intervener is under a duty to provide the service with reasonable care. Finally, there is the active right of the intervener against the recipient of the service. How should the latter claim be rationalised? Is it a restitutionary claim or not? The difficulty with explaining these cases in restitutionary or unjust enrichment terms is that in some of the cases the claim has succeeded notwithstanding the fact that the recipient of the service does not appear to have benefited in any way from the receipt of the service (for example, because the intervention was unsuccessful).[127] Yet if it is not a restitutionary claim, what is it? Is there some claim known to the law as 'unjust sacrifice',[128] which entitles an intervener to recover the value of the services that he has provided in situations of necessity (and, possibly, in other situations)? The answer to this question is obviously beyond the scope of this chapter. It suffices to note that the answer involves not only issues of policy (should we allow interveners to sue?) but also issues of taxonomy (if we do, how should we classify the claim?).

5. Restitutionary or disgorgement damages

Suppose that a defendant commits a tort and the gain that the defendant makes from the commission of the tort exceeds the loss that the claimant suffers. Can the claimant recover the gain that the defendant has made or is she confined to a claim for the loss that she has suffered? This question raises two issues of principle for English law. The first is whether or not the claimant is entitled to recover the gain made by the

---

the cases are not all one way. There are cases which recognise the existence of a claim by a party who intervenes in a situation of necessity and these cases could be used to construct a more generalised recovery. These cases are gathered together by A. Burrows and E. McKendrick, *Cases and Materials on the Law of Restitution* (1997), 480–508.

[127] A good example is provided by *Matheson v. Smiley* [1932] 2 DLR 787, where the claim was brought by a surgeon who unsuccessfully tried to save the life of a person who had made a suicide bid.

[128] See S. Stoljar, 'Unjust Enrichment and Unjust Sacrifice', (1987) 50 *MLR* 603 and G. Muir, 'Unjust Sacrifice and the Officious Intervener', in: P. Finn (ed.), *Essays on Restitution* (1990), 297.

defendant[129] and the second is, if she is, how is that claim to be classified? It is the second question that is important for taxonomic purposes. Is the claim one in autonomous unjust enrichment or is it a claim based on the tort committed by the defendant in which the claimant elects to recover damages measured by reference to the defendant's gain rather than her loss? English law has so far not produced a clear answer to this question.[130] Yet it is an important question to answer because the answer to it can have important consequences for limitation purposes,[131] for concurrent liability[132] and for the taxonomy of the law of obligations.

6. What is it that makes a particular enrichment 'unjust'?

Lurking beneath the surface is an awkward question that needs to be answered by jurists: what is it that makes a particular enrichment unjust? It is a question which has not been answered in modern writing on the law of restitution. Indeed, most modern writing on the law of restitution is notable for its apparent indifference to theoretical issues. What is the notion of justice which underpins the law and its development? If this area of law is to be restyled the law of unjust enrichment, surely it cannot avoid openly addressing questions that relate to the conception of justice which underpins the law? Writers avoid the issue: for example, unjust 'does not look up to an abstract notion of justice but down to the cases and statutes'.[133] But when we look at what has happened in the last ten years we find that restitution lawyers have looked down at the cases, not liked what they have seen and advocated change. Indeed, it has been argued that one of the virtues of the recognition of the unjust enrichment principle is that it 'can be expected to lead to some differences in the results of cases'.[134] And one can see this in the cases, most obviously in the following three developments: the recognition of the defence of

---

[129] For many English lawyers, damages are inevitably compensatory in nature. For such lawyers there is no such thing as restitutionary damages. One difficulty with this view is that it leaves out of account punitive damages. The better view would appear to be that there are different measures of damages, namely compensatory, restitutionary (or disgorgement) and punitive damages.

[130] See generally McKendrick, 'Restitution and the Misuse of Chattels', 908–17.

[131] See, for example, *Chesworth v. Farrar* [1967] 1 QB 407.

[132] If there are two different causes of action (unjust enrichment and tort) then the rules governing concurrent liability laid down by the House of Lords in *Henderson v. Merrett Syndicates Ltd* [1995] 2 AC 145 should be applied, whereas if there is one cause of action (the tort) but two remedial responses (compensatory damages and restitutionary or disgorgement damages) then the applicable rules should be those laid down by the Privy Council in *Personal Representatives of Tang Man Sit v. Capacious Investments Ltd* [1996] AC 514.

[133] Birks, *Introduction*, 99.   [134] Burrows, 'Restitution: Where Do We Go From Here?', 98.

change of position,[135] the creation of the right to recover money paid pursuant to an ultra vires demand for tax[136] and the realisation that mistake of law can give rise to a restitutionary claim.[137] What was it that enabled counsel and writers to persuade the judges that it was right to take these three steps?

One answer is to say that this is simply a working out of the incremental and analogical development of the common law. But, with respect, this will not do. How are we to decide whether an analogy is an appropriate one or not? Surely there must be some theory which tells us whether or not an analogy is appropriate or inappropriate? There have been some calls for greater consideration of these broader, theoretical issues[138] but the call has received a lukewarm reception in some quarters[139] on the ground that restitution scholars might cross the line from 'practical to impractical scholarship'.[140] Yet is it really 'impractical' to seek to articulate the conception of justice that underpins the law?

Take the following example. A young, inexperienced man is persuaded to pay money to his financial adviser as part of a pension plan. The financial adviser does not tell the young man any lies, nor does he subject him to undue pressure. The deal is simply a bad one from the perspective of the young man and the financial adviser knows it but does not tell the young man because of the substantial commission he will earn from the sale of the pension plan. Can the young man obtain restitution of the sums paid under the contract? This is not a value-neutral question and it should be possible to articulate the conception of justice which leads to our answer. Is it based on corrective justice or some broader notion of distributive justice? If judges in negligence cases can speak openly about the conception of justice which leads them to a particular conclusion[141] should restitution lawyers not do so also, the more so if the subject is to be retitled 'unjust' enrichment? A secure

---

[135] In *Lipkin Gorman (a Firm) v. Karpnale Ltd* [1991] 2 AC 548.
[136] In *Woolwich Equitable Building Society v. Inland Revenue Commissioners* [1993] AC 70.
[137] In *Kleinwort Benson Ltd v. Lincoln City Council* [1999] 2 AC 349.
[138] See, for example, K. Barker, 'Unjust Enrichment: Containing the Beast', (1995) 15 *Oxford JLS* 457.
[139] See, for example, Burrows, 'Restitution: Where Do We Go From Here?', 109–11 and 115–16. Particularly influential on Burrows is the essay by H. Edwards, 'The Growing Disjunction between Legal Education and the Legal Profession', (1992) 91 *Michigan LR* 34. Similar views to those expressed by Burrows can be found in Jones, '"Traditional" Legal Scholarship', 14.
[140] Burrows, 'Restitution Where Do We Go From Here?', 116.
[141] See, for example, *Frost v. Chief Constable of South Yorkshire Police* [1999] 2 AC 455 at 503–4 (Lord Hoffmann) and *McFarlane v. Tayside Health Board* [1999] 3 WLR 1301 at 1319 (Lord Steyn).

taxonomy of unjust factors should be grounded in a coherent conception of justice.[142]

7. Other taxonomic issues

There are numerous other taxonomic issues to be resolved. For example, how does one distinguish between the law of restitution (or the law of unjust enrichment) and the law of property? Where is the line to be drawn between the law of contract and the law of restitution? Is, for example, rescission a contractual remedy or a restitutionary remedy? Should two- and three-party cases[143] be aligned? And what about remedies? A notable feature of some recent academic writing has been the emphasis that it places on remedies.[144] This discussion of remedies must in turn be located within the context of a broader discussion of remedies which emphasises the 'progressive divorce of remedy from doctrine'[145] and the consequent importance of the role of discretion in giving to the courts the power to award the most appropriate remedy on the facts of the case. The latter school of thought together with the more flexible approach to unjust enrichment adopted by the Supreme Court of Canada[146] represents a serious challenge to the case for taxonomy presented in this article.

VII. Conclusion

The aim of this chapter has not been to defend a particular taxonomy of the law of restitution or the law of unjust enrichment. English law has not reached the stage of having to choose between different taxonomies of the law of restitution because it is not yet convinced of the importance of the quest to establish a secure taxonomy of the law. English law still prides itself on its pragmatism and its incremental and analogical

---

[142] Another important question is: who bears the burden of proof of showing that a particular enrichment was unjust? English law places that burden squarely on the claimant. But in other systems the onus would appear to be on the defendant (see the discussion of this particular issue in the speech of Lord Hope in *Kleinwort Benson Ltd v. Lincoln City Council* [1999] 2 AC 349 at 408–9).

[143] On which see the contributions by Daniel Visser and Lionel Smith in this volume (chapters 19 and 21).

[144] See, for example, K. Barker, 'Rescuing Remedialism in Unjust Enrichment Law: Why Remedies are Right', (1998) 57 *CLJ* 301 and G. Virgo, 'What is the Law of Restitution About?', in: Cornish *et al.*, *Restitution*, 305.

[145] P. Finn, 'Equitable Doctrine and Discretion in Remedies', in: Cornish *et al.*, *Restitution*, 251, 260.

[146] On which see Justice B. McLachlin, 'Restitution in Canada', in: Cornish *et al.*, *Restitution*, 275.

development. But this pragmatic development is not in itself incompatible with a concern for taxonomy. This is because, on the view put forward in this paper, taxonomy is of primary significance for the jurist as he or she analyses case law and legislation. Taxonomy is a vital part of the quest to eliminate anomalies and inconsistencies in the law and to ensure that like cases are treated alike. As these anomalies are eliminated, in line with the incremental development of the law, so the case for the judicial or legislative adoption of the taxonomy which has been used to eliminate these anomalies will become stronger. But jurists still have a long way to go in terms of producing a taxonomy that enjoys a substantial measure of agreement. This is not to suggest that the work on producing a taxonomy of the law should be abandoned. On the contrary, it should continue but jurists should not expect their writing to have an immediate impact on the courts. In the vast majority of cases the courts can dispense justice to litigants without concern for taxonomy. It is in the difficult borderline case that taxonomy assumes significant practical importance. Here it is to be hoped that judges will refer to academic writing on taxonomy in an effort to ensure that the law is developed in a coherent and systematic fashion. In this way, and over a period of time, a consensus may emerge (in the traditional English fashion) in relation to the adoption of an appropriate taxonomy of the law of restitution.

23 Rationality, nationality and the taxonomy of unjustified enrichment

Niall R. Whitty

In an institute of law, or of any other science, the analyzing it into its constituent parts, and the arranging every article properly, is of supreme importance. One could not conceive, without experience, how greatly accurate distribution contributes to clear conception... No work of man is perfect: it is good, however, to be on the mending hand; and in every new attempt, to approach nearer and nearer to perfection. To compile a body of law, the parts intimately connected and every link hanging on a former, requires the utmost effort of human genius.

        Lord Kames, *Principles of Equity* (3rd edition, 1773), Introduction.

I. Setting the scene

1. The brief of this chapter

As Lord President Rodger has recently remarked, references to 'taxonomy' are 'very much à la mode in discussions of enrichment law'.[1] The reason is well known. The English legal system accidentally overlooked its law of unjust enrichment for several centuries and has just rediscovered it. English lawyers are now busy exploring and developing it. The resultant outburst of intellectual creativity displays the awesome strength of English legal culture. The English enrichment law revolution has had a moderately galvanising effect in Scotland.[2]

---

[1] A. Rodger, 'The Use of the Civil Law in Scottish Courts', in: D. L. Carey Miller and R. Zimmermann (eds.), *The Civilian Tradition and Scots Law* (1997), 225, 229, n. 26, commenting on Lord Cullen's dictum in *Morgan Guaranty Trust Company of New York v. Lothian Regional Council* 1995 SC 151 at 173H: 'The taxonomy of the quasi-contractual remedies which are afforded by the law of Scotland is not in a wholly satisfactory state.'

[2] Lord Rodger of Earlsferry, 'Savigny in the Strand', (1993-5) 28-30 *Irish Jurist* 1, 15.

Certainly before Robert Goff and Gareth Jones's *Law of Restitution* broke the English ice in 1966,[3] there was in Scotland a complacent tendency to believe that Scots enrichment law with its *Cantiere* case[4] was much more advanced than the English law with its 'Coronation' cases[5] and the implied contract fiction in *Sinclair v. Brougham*.[6] We now recognise that we have much work to do. As befits a mixed system, in Scotland there has been a debate (still unresolved) as to what route we should take (English, civilian or indigenous) and by what vehicle (common law or statute). 'Statute' includes a reference to an Act of the Scottish Parliament which, apart from refunds of central government taxes, has power to regulate Scots enrichment law.[7] In the absence of legislation, which seems unlikely in the near future,[8] progress will have to be made through a good textbook which succeeds in reconciling the cases and putting them into the context of an overall theoretical structure. This chapter considers what that overall theoretical structure should be.

2. Comparative law and legal transplants; ideology and legal science

The modern history of the Scots law of unjustified enrichment began in 1985 with two pioneering articles by Peter Birks.[9] Scots lawyers are greatly indebted to him for highlighting the subject's crisis of identity. Birks thought that the primary division of the Scottish taxonomy[10] was based on the type of benefit received; that the worst consequence of such a division was to give the false impression that the causes of action differ depending on the type of benefit received; and that the solution lay in unifying the subject under the principle of unjustified

---

[3] R. Goff and G. Jones, *The Law of Restitution* (1st edn, 1966).
[4] *Cantiere San Rocco SA v. Clyde Shipbuilding & Engineering Co.* 1923 SC (HL) 105.
[5] *Krell v. Henry* [1903] 2 KB 740; *Chandler v. Webster* [1904] 1 KB 493.
[6] [1914] AC 398 (HL). [7] See Scotland Act 1998, especially section 126(4), quoted below.
[8] The Scottish Law Commission (Report on *Unjustified Enrichment, Error of Law and Public Authority Receipts and Disbursements* (1999), Scot Law Com No. 169) stated (at § 5.16) that their involvement with enrichment law should now come to an end at least for the time being.
[9] P. Birks, 'Six Questions in Search of a Subject – Unjust Enrichment in a Crisis of Identity', [1985] JR 227; P. Birks, 'Restitution: A View of the Scots Law', (1985) 38 *Current Legal Problems* 57. These have been endorsed by Lord President Rodger, e.g. A. Rodger, 'Roman Law in Practice in Britain', (1993) 12 *Rechtshistorisches Journal* 261, 266, 267; *Shilliday v. Smith* 1998 SC 725 at 727. Birks's taxonomy was commended for Scots law by W. J. Stewart, *The Law of Restitution in Scotland* (1992).
[10] See 684–6, below.

enrichment.[11] However, Birks's proposal to replace the Roman categories with his own system of unjust factors provoked considerable opposition.[12] The ensuing debate goes to the roots of Scots law. In the context of Scottish opposition to his proposals, Birks contends: 'Considered commitments apart, the national is enemy of the rational.'[13] This rationalism is very attractive but has limitations. First, as Hume explained, reason does not determine action but only shows the means of reaching the desired aim.[14] Secondly, comparative law is a rational discipline but the decision whether to accept or reject legal transplants is quite different and not entirely a rational matter.[15] There are costs in change.[16] There is a national interest to consider and (according to Lord Rodger) even legitimate national pride.[17] Thirdly, between legal systems there are differences in *mentalité* and scale: organisation of voluminous case materials by numerous 'unjust factors' may suit the English legal mind but be unsuitable and even unworkable in a small legal system. Fourthly, the assumptions one makes before applying reason can make a big difference. Purist opposition by English academics to the intrusion of the civilian concept of *sine causa* into English

---

[11] 'A View of the Scots Law', 63, commended in *Dollar Land (Cumbernauld) Ltd v. CIN Properties Ltd* 1998 SC (HL) 90 at 98D, E *per* Lord Hope.

[12] For an excellent review of the literature see R. Evans-Jones and P. Hellwege, 'Some Observations on the Taxonomy of Unjustified Enrichment', (1998) 2 *Edinburgh LR* 180.

[13] P. Birks, *Against Codification and Against Codification of Unjust Enrichment* (unpublished paper delivered at Edinburgh, October 1994), § 3: 'Law differs from moral philosophy in that in some matters on which reasonable philosophers may differ the law must make a considered choice. Considered commitments apart, the national is enemy of the rational. It cannot be of any importance whether a rule or classification has a Roman, English, Scots or German pedigree.' *Ibid.*, 7: '"Procul profani" means "Codifiers and juridical nationalists keep out".' Cf. P. Birks, 'The Foundation of Legal Rationality in Scotland', in: R. Evans-Jones (ed.), *The Civil Law Tradition in Scotland* (1995), 81. For comments thereon, see J. du Plessis, 'The Promises and Pitfalls of Mixed Legal Systems: The South African and Scottish Experiences', (1998) 9 *Stellenbosch LR* 338, 344 ff.

[14] David Hume, *A Treatise of Human Nature* (1748), Book II, Part III, Section III: 'Reason is and ought only to be the slave of the passions and can never pretend to any other office than to serve and obey them.'

[15] E. M. Clive, unpublished seminar paper on 'Unjustified Enrichment – A Code for Scotland?', October 1994: '[I]t is not necessary to be a juridical nationalist to think that national differences are of some importance. First, indiscriminate borrowing of rules or classifications from another system, particularly one with a very different intellectual tradition, can lead to confusion and incoherence. Secondly, there are costs in change and good reasons for keeping changes to the minimum necessary to achieve the desired result. Unless the desired result includes an element of conformity to supra-national or international norms, a solution which builds on familiar existing law has to be preferred to an imported solution which is as good but no better.'

[16] *Ibid.*   [17] See, e.g., Rodger, 'Roman Law in Practice', 262.

law[18] can be justified on the ground of its inconsistency with the English case materials. That justification assumes, however, that these materials have to be accepted as authoritative whereas legal science might dictate that they impede true progress and should be swept away.

Fifthly, in mixed systems, there are different views as to whether or how far the sources and pedigrees of rules and classifications should affect legal development. Some have downplayed their importance.[19] By contrast, Jacques du Plessis argues that a new rule must not only be rational but fit in the context or structure of related rules.[20] It follows that in developing mixed systems, 'it is desirable that we should as far as possible take into account the character of the specific area of law within which the development is going to take place. It requires that we should determine the historical foundations of that area of law, and then build on these foundations to maintain the integrity of the structure.'[21] The need for equipoise in a mixed legal system suggests to me that Du Plessis is right. Scots lawyers should look to a civilian model to improve our mainly civilian enrichment law.

II. Obligations to redress unjustified enrichment in the masterplan of Scots private law

While there is no binding masterplan of Scots private law, the Justinianic institutional scheme – persons, things (obligations and property), actions – not only inspired the Scottish institutional writers who followed it with their own modifications[22] but has recently entered our constitutional law. The Scotland Act 1998, section 126(4), provides:

References in this Act to Scots private law are to the following areas of the civil law of Scotland –

 (a) the general principles of private law (including private international law),
 (b) the law of persons (including natural persons, legal persons and unincorporated bodies),
 (c) the law of obligations (including obligations arising from contract, unilateral promise, delict, unjustified enrichment and *negotiorum gestio*),[23]

---

[18] See 711–13, below.
[19] A. Rodger, 'Thinking About Scots Law', (1996) 1 *Edinburgh LR* 3, 24.
[20] 'Promises and Pitfalls', 344.   [21] Ibid.
[22] J. W. Cairns, 'Institutional Writings in Scotland Reconsidered', (1983) 3 *Journal of Legal History* 76.
[23] The original precursor of paragraph (c) carried an impure classification, namely: 'voluntary and conventional obligations, obligations of restitution, and obligations of reparation'. See Scotland Bill, cl. 111(3) (b) (House of Commons, Bill 104; print of 17 December 1997).

(d) the law of property (including heritable and moveable property, trusts and succession), and
(e) the law of actions (including jurisdiction, remedies, evidence, procedure, diligence, recognition and enforcement of court orders, limitation of actions and arbitration)

and include references to judicial review of administrative action.

There is a separate definition of 'Scots criminal law'[24] but none of 'public law'. No reference is made to fiduciary obligations. The system is unitary, abjuring equity.

To set obligations for the redress of unjustified enrichment within the masterplan of Scots law, five taxonomic levels may be considered, as shown in Table 23.1. A cross-cutting common law/equity divide, at each of levels three to five, would have to be inserted in the application of the tree to English law.

III. Preliminary matters: levels one and two

1. Level one: civil law and criminal law

In English law it is disputed whether restitution of benefits from crimes is part of the private law of restitution for wrongs or unjust enrichment.[25] It is difficult to refute Andrew Burrows's argument that 'a crime cannot in itself be a relevant restitution-yielding wrong because a crime is a "wrong" against the state and is not "at the expense of" any particular person'.[26] No special taxonomic pigeonhole is set aside for restitutionary claims arising out of a crime. In both English and Scots law the victim of a crime must found on a specific ground for redress of unjustified enrichment.[27] In English law, however, arguably enrichment law has strayed into the sphere of the criminal law. Where there is no victim of the crime or the victim suffers no loss, should the criminal's enrichment go as a windfall benefit to a third party under enrichment law or to the state under the criminal law? Probably *Attorney-General for Hong Kong v. Reid*[28] gives the wrong answer. A public prosecutor accepted bribes for not

---

[24] Scotland Act 1998, s. 126(5).
[25] The topic is included in Lord Goff of Chieveley and G. Jones, *The Law of Restitution* (5th edn, 1998), chap. 38; and P. D. Maddaugh and J. D. McCamus, *The Law of Restitution*, chap. 22. Its inclusion is criticised in A. Burrows, *The Law of Restitution* (1993), 380.
[26] Burrows, *Law of Restitution*, 380.
[27] For English law, see G. Virgo, 'The Law of Restitution and the Proceeds of Crime: A Survey of English Law', [1998] *Restitution LR* 34.
[28] [1994] 1 AC 324 (PC).

Table 23.1. *Taxonomy of Scots law*

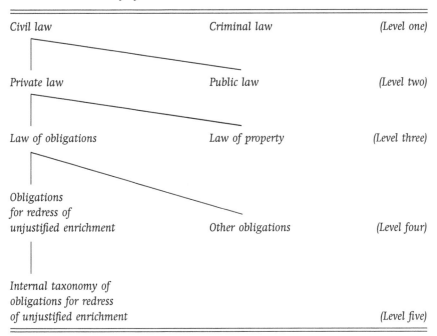

prosecuting and was convicted. His employer was held to be entitled to the bribe. In principle that seems wrong. The prosecutor's enrichment was not 'at the expense of' his employer nor was there any encroachment on the employer's patrimonial rights. Eric Clive has argued powerfully[29] that a Scottish court in a similar case should exercise its criminal jurisdiction to order the proceeds of the crime to be confiscated by the state.[30] An example of an intrusion the other way (by criminal law into enrichment law) was the error of law rule (recently banished from enrichment law),[31]

---

[29] Clive, 'A Code for Scotland?' He points out: 'It so happened that in *Reid* the employer was the Crown. So the result seems acceptable. But suppose that the employer of a corrupt official is an agency or other body with an interest in making money. Is it not dangerous to give such an employer an incentive to allow corrupt profits to accumulate so that it can reap the benefit?'

[30] Cf. Scottish Law Commission, Report on *Confiscation and Forfeiture* (1994), Scot Law Com No. 147.

[31] E.g. *Willis Faber Enthoven (Pty) Ltd v. Receiver of Revenue* 1992 (4) SA 202 (A); *Morgan Guaranty Trust Co. of New York v. Lothian Regional Council* 1995 SC 151; *Kleinwort Benson Ltd v. Lincoln City Council* [1999] 2 AC 349 (HL).

which was in part founded on a so-called 'duty to know the law' inaptly imported from criminal law.[32]

2. Level two: private law and public law

In civil-law systems, there are special public-law regimes for the refund of overpaid taxes.[33] In the United Kingdom, special statutory regimes regulate refund of overpayments of the main types of taxes.[34] The common law fills any gaps. In Scotland traditionally at common law the same rules of restitution apply to public- and private-sector debts and litigants.[35] The English common law on refund of overpaid taxes has fluctuated[36] but in 1993 the *Woolwich* case[37] introduced in English law a new automatic ground of restitution of undue payments of taxes made to public authorities pursuant to an *ultra vires* demand. It gave little guidance as to the type of public debts to which the new ground of recovery (or 'unjust factor') should apply and its scope is uncertain.[38] A somewhat uncivilian view in

---

[32] *Dixon v. Monkland Canal Co.* (1831) 5 W & S 445 at 451–2 *per* Lord Brougham; *Glasgow Corporation v. Lord Advocate* 1959 SC 203 at 233 *per* Lord President Clyde. Cf. W. M. Gloag, *The Law of Contract* (2nd edn, 1929), 62, n. 4; Scottish Law Commission, Discussion Paper No. 95, *Recovery of Benefits Conferred Under Error of Law* (1993), vol. I, §§ 2.79, 2.80; J. P. Dawson, *Unjust Enrichment: A Comparative Analysis* (1951), 130–1.

[33] I. England, 'Restitution of Benefits Conferred Without Obligation', in: *International Encyclopedia of Comparative Law* (1991), vol. X, chap. 5, §§ 30–1.

[34] See Law Commission, *Restitution: Mistakes of Law and Ultra Vires Public Authority Receipts and Payments* (1994), Law Com No. 227, parts VI–XVI; Scottish Law Commission, Report on *Unjustified Enrichment, Error of Law and Public Authority Receipts and Disbursements* (1999), Scot Law Com No. 167, part 3.

[35] *Glasgow Corporation v. Lord Advocate* 1959 SC 203.

[36] Up to the 1880s a series of English cases (from *Newdigate v. Davy* [1693] 1 Ld Raym 742 to *Hooper v. Exeter Corporation* (1887) 56 LJQB 457) supported a constitutional right to recovery. Then Dicey, *Introduction to the Study of the Law of the Constitution* (1st edn, 1885; 2nd edn, 1886) appeared. Soon thereafter, refunds of overpaid tax and levies were made to depend on the ordinary, private-law grounds of restitution: *Slater v. Burnley Corporation* (1888) 59 LT 636; *William Whiteley Ltd v. R.* (1910) 191 LT 741; *National Pari-Mutuel Association v. R.* (1929) 46 TLR 594; *Twyford v. Manchester Corporation* [1946] Ch 236. This line of cases was followed in *Glasgow Corporation v. Lord Advocate* 1959 SC 203.

[37] *Woolwich Equitable Building Society v. IRC* [1993] AC 70 (HL affirming CA); reversing [1989] 1 WLR 137.

[38] See, e.g., Burrows, *Law of Restitution*, 354: if the payment demand falls within the public-law doctrine of ultra vires and hence is susceptible to judicial review, the *Woolwich* rule applies; otherwise not. Contrast J. Beatson, 'Restitution of Taxes, Levies and Other Imposts: Defining the Extent of the *Woolwich* Principle', (1993) 109 *LQR* 401, 417–18: it applies to taxes, duties and imposts levied ultra vires (i.e. unlawfully) by three categories of payee, namely: (1) governmental bodies; (2) other public bodies whose authority to charge is subject to public-law principles; and (3) other bodies whose authority to charge is solely the product of statute and thus limited. Cf.

Scotland holds that introducing the private/public dichotomy into enrichment law would give rise to great uncertainty and invidious distinctions which are best avoided.[39] The justifications for the *Woolwich* rule apply well enough to recovery from the mighty Inland Revenue but seem inapt when applied to a statutorily licensed, single taxi-cab operator with no de facto monopoly. The fact that a completely new unjust factor had to be invented to solve a straightforward case like *Woolwich* may suggest that something is wrong with the taxonomic structure of the English system of unjust factors.

IV. The boundary between the law of obligations and property law

1. The civilian approach and English law

Civil-law systems draw a relatively sharp and clear line between enrichment law and property law.[40] Enrichment law concerns obligations for the redress of unjustified enrichment and is therefore classified as part of the law of obligations. Apart from constructive trusts imported raggedly from England, in Scots law it is only in isolated cases that a personal right to redress unjustified enrichment is secured by a tacit hypothec,[41] or converted into a real right.[42] Furthermore, Scots law laid great emphasis on the parity of creditors: for example, the hypothec of a law agent (unlike the English solicitor's lien) did not apply to property preserved or recovered in litigation for his client.[43] In civil law and mixed systems, the parity of general creditors is also protected by the *numerus clausus* of real

---

P. Birks: the basis is 'transactional inequality' ('The English Recognition of Unjust Enrichment', [1991] *Lloyd's Maritime and Commercial Law Quarterly* 473, 498; also his 'Restitution from the Executive – A Tercentenary Footnote to the Bill of Rights', in: P. D. Finn (ed.), *Essays on Restitution* (1990), 164, 175, 176); basis is the need to confine public authorities within their powers (P. Birks, '"When Money is Paid in Pursuance of Void Authority..." – A Duty to Repay?', [1992] *Public Law* 580, 587).

[39] A judicial dictum states (1995 SC 151 at 165B-C) that the decision in *Morgan Guaranty* achieved the same result as *Woolwich* but independently 'by reference to the principles of Scots law'.

[40] K. G. C. Reid, 'Unjustified Enrichment and Property Law', [1994] *JR* 167 at 167-8; K. G. C. Reid, 'Obligations and Property: Exploring the Border', in: D. Visser (ed.), *The Limits of the Law of Obligations* (1997), 225 (reprinted from [1997] *Acta Juridica* 225).

[41] I.e. a security without possession, imposed by operation of law.

[42] One example is a maritime lien securing a claim for general average.

[43] G. J. Bell, *Principles of the Law of Scotland* (10th edn, 1899), § 1388; G. J. Bell, *Commentaries on the Law of Scotland and the Principles of Mercantile Jurisprudence* (7th edn, 1870), Vol. II, 35; *Halsbury's Laws of England* (4th edn, 1983), vol. XLIV, § 236; N. R. Whitty, 'Indirect Enrichment in Scots Law', [1994] *JR* 200 (part I) at 224 and 239 (part II).

rights[44] (the very antithesis of the remedial constructive trust) and the rules restricting redress of indirect enrichment.[45] The clarity of the property/obligations boundary in civil-law systems should not be exaggerated, however: in some systems (notably French law), it is to some extent transgressed by the expansionist tendencies of enrichment law. An *actio de in rem verso* by one creditor of an insolvent against another of his creditors or his debtor, though couched in the terminology of obligations, is in substance a claim for a preference in insolvency[46] and to that extent operates as a proprietary right. This demonstrates the truth of William Swadling's proposition that 'unjust enrichment is an event and property the response to an event...There is no logical reason why the event of unjust enrichment should not meet the response of rights *in rem*.'[47] So maintenance of this vital taxonomic boundary depends on policy considerations about which legal systems can and do differ.

By contrast with civil-law systems, in English law enrichment law shades into and overlaps with property law. In many situations English law creates new proprietary rights and remedies in response to unjust enrichment.[48]

---

[44] Cf. K. G. C. Reid, *The Law of Property in Scotland* (1996), § 5, n. 1.

[45] See as to German law, R. Zimmermann and J. du Plessis, 'Basic Features of the German Law of Unjustified Enrichment', [1994] *Restitution LR* 14, 31–6; B. S. Markesinis, W. Lorenz and G. Dannemann, *The German Law of Obligations* (1997), vol. I, *The Law of Contracts*, 731–5; J. P. Dawson, 'Indirect Enrichment', in: Ernst von Caemmerer, Soia Mentschikoff and Konrad Zweigert (eds.), *Ius Privatum Gentium, Festschrift für Max Rheinstein* (1969), vol. II, 789; for the French system, see B. Nicholas, 'Unjustified Enrichment in the Civil Law and Louisiana Law', (1962) 36 *Tulane LR* 605, 626–33; also his 'Modern Developments in the French Law of Unjustified Enrichment', in: P. W. L. Russell (ed.), *Unjustified Enrichment: A Comparative Study of the Law of Restitution* (1996), 77, 77, 78, 95; for South African law, see Daniel Visser's contribution to this volume; W. de Vos, Liability arising from Unjustified Enrichment in the Law of the Union of South Africa', [1960] *JR* 125 and 236 at 244–50; for Scots law, see Whitty, 'Indirect Enrichment'; as to the civil-law historical background, see Dawson, *Unjust Enrichment*, 70 ff.

[46] As in French law, notably the famous *Boudier* decision, Req. 15 June 1892, S 1893.1.281, see, e.g., Nicholas, 'Modern Developments', 95: the *Boudier* case 'can be said to perpetrate a fraud on the law by overriding the rules governing insolvency'.

[47] W. J. Swadling, 'Property and Unjust Enrichment', in: J. W. Harris (ed.), *Property Problems from Genes to Pension Funds* (1997), 130.

[48] A. Burrows, 'Restitution: Where Do We Go From Here?', (1997) 50 *Current Legal Problems* 95, 113, gives the following examples: (1) constructive trusts imposed by gains made by equitable wrongs, as in *Boardman v. Phipps* [1967] 2 AC 46 and *Attorney-General for Hong Kong v. Reid* [1994] 1 AC 324; (2) examples of subrogation: e.g. Mercantile Law Amendment Act 1856, s. 5; *Boscawen v. Bajwa* [1996] 1 WLR 328; *Lord Napier and Ettrick v. Hunter* [1993] AC 713; (3) the equitable lien of the mistaken improver: *Cooper v. Phibbs* (1867) LR 2 HL 149; (4) a rescission of a contract revesting

The courts have invented the 'process' of tracing (or real subrogation) and the 'restitutionary proprietary' remedies of the equitable lien and the constructive trust. The last may include the 'remedial' constructive trust under which 'no creditor will know with certainty whether his interests will be protected until the court has so determined'.[49] These rights or remedies, aided by tracing, are effective in three situations where civil-law personal rights to redress of unjustified enrichment are not, namely:

(a) where the recipient of the claimant's money is insolvent and there are competing creditors;
(b) where money or property has changed form, as where the claimant's money has been spent by the recipient to buy property, or the claimant's property has been sold and transformed into money by the recipient (real subrogation or 'intra-patrimonial' tracing); and
(c) where money or property has been transferred by the original recipient to a third party, and perhaps by him to a fourth party, and so on down the links in an enrichment chain ('inter-personal' tracing).[50]

To a non-English lawyer, these are astonishing privileges. Among mixed systems which accommodate the trust, constructive trusts have been rejected in South Africa.[51] They have gained a shaky foothold in Scotland but are highly controversial,[52] filling one Scottish judge recently with 'almost instinctive abhorrence'.[53] There are only two categories.[54] George Gretton demonstrates that since a true constructive trust must rest on a finding binding the fiduciary's creditors in insolvency proceedings, only

---

proprietary rights to goods or land transferred under the contract: e.g. *Car and Universal Finance Company Ltd v. Caldwell* [1965] 1 QB 525; and (5) equitable proprietary remedies awarded following equitable tracing.

[49] Goff and Jones, *Law of Restitution*, 202.
[50] Cf. P. Gallo, 'Unjust Enrichment: A Comparative Analysis', (1994) 40 *American Journal of Comparative Law* 431, 444. Tracing can also apply to personal rights.
[51] E. Cameron, 'Constructive Trusts in South African Law: The Legacy Refused', (1999) 3 *Edinburgh LR* 341; A. M. Honoré and E. Cameron, *The South African Law of Trusts* (4th edn, 1992), 110.
[52] For magisterial criticism, see Gretton, (1997) 1 *Edinburgh LR* 281 and 408; cf. P. Hood, 'What is so Special About Being a Fiduciary?' (2000) 4 *Edinburgh LR* 308.
[53] *Mortgage Corporation v. Mitchells Roberton* 1997 SLT 1305 (OH) at 1310 *per* Lord Johnston. See also *Bank of Scotland v. MacLeod Paxton Woolard & Co.* 1998 SLT 258 (OH) at 274E–F *per* Lord Coulsfield ('a concept not familiar in Scots law').
[54] W. A. Wilson and A. G. M. Duncan, *Trusts, Trustees and Executors* (2nd edn, 1995), § 6–61: namely '(1) Where a person in a fiduciary position gains an advantage by virtue of that position. (2) Where a person who is a stranger to an existing trust is to his knowledge in possession of property belonging to the trust.'

about four cases qualify in the first category and that the second category turns out to be illusory.[55]

It is widely held that the most difficult question in the English law of restitution is the exact circumstances in which a proprietary restitutionary remedy will be available to a restitutionary claimant.[56] The boundary between restitution and property has been recently described as 'at best soggy',[57] 'still largely unmapped'[58] and a 'continuing mystery'.[59] Hence, for example, the continuing debate on whether in *Lipkin Gorman (a Firm) v. Karpnale Ltd*[60] the plaintiff's successful claim, based on the proposition that the defendant received what was traceably the plaintiff's property, was (i) a 'pure proprietary' claim, (requiring the plaintiff to establish legal title but no unjust factor); or (ii) a 'restitutionary proprietary claim' (requiring the plaintiff to establish not only legal title by tracing but also an unjust factor); or (iii) a restitutionary personal claim (also requiring the plaintiff to establish not only legal title by tracing, to satisfy causation, but also an unjust factor).[61] Hence also the controversy over whether a mistaken payment of money is recoverable by a proprietary claim by the payer against the payee.[62] There are many variables depending on hotly debated distinctions[63] which are described in three different technical vocabularies (namely traditional common law, traditional equity and newly minted restitution language). In Lord Millett's view, in no branch of English law has so much difficulty been caused by semantic and conceptual confusion.[64] The view that this jungle should be transplanted to Scots law is controversial; we have difficulties enough of our own.

---

[55] G. Gretton, 'Constructive Trusts', (1997) 3 *Edinburgh LR* 281–316 and 408–19. Of only two apparent cases in the second category – *Southern Cross Commodities Property Ltd v. Martin* 1991 SLT 83 (OH); *Huisman v. Soepboer* 1994 SLT 682 (OH) – it turns out that neither was binding on competing creditors.

[56] See e.g. P. J. Millett (Lord Millett), 'Restitution and Constructive Trusts', (1998) 114 *LQR* 399; cf. his 'The Law of Restitution: Taking Stock', (1999) 14 *Amicus Curiae: Journal of the Society for Advanced Legal Studies*.

[57] D. Ibbetson, Book Review, (1997) 1 *Edinburgh LR* 270, 272.

[58] W. Swadling, 'A New Role for Resulting Trusts?', (1996) 16 *Legal Studies* 110.

[59] Burrows, 'Restitution', 112.

[60] [1991] 2 AC 548.   [61] Goff and Jones, *Law of Restitution*, 77, 78, 177.

[62] *Chase Manhattan Bank NA Ltd v. Israel-British Bank (London) Ltd* [1981] Ch 105 disapproved in *Westdeutsche Landesbank Girozentrale v. Islington LBC* [1996] AC 669 at 714, 715 per Lord Browne-Wilkinson; Goff and Jones, *Law of Restitution*, 200 ff.

[63] E.g. the various meanings of 'constructive trust' (cf. Millett, 'Restitution and Constructive Trusts'); the distinctions between legal and equitable titles, rights and remedies; proprietary and personal rights and remedies; 'pure proprietary rights' and 'restitutionary proprietary rights'; institutional and remedial constructive trusts; and vindicatory and enrichment restitution.

[64] Millett, 'Restitution and Constructive Trusts', 408.

The differences between civil-law and common-law systems extend beyond formal differences in taxonomic structure to differences in approach and *mentalité*. As a German scholar states:[65]

the German law first looks to see how title behaves in a given transaction. All questions of restitutionary claims depend on that primary question, and restitution itself is never proprietary. To the mind of an English lawyer, the German approach, especially the strict separation of property and restitution, may seem very formal and rigid. In English law it is often less clear who is the owner of a certain value at any given point in time; English law seems to be concerned rather with ensuring that, in the end result, every party gets what it should get, and creates proprietary rights where it seems appropriate to do so.[66]

Kenneth Reid places Scots property law in the civil-law camp.[67]

2. Distinguishing 'vindicatory restitution' and 'enrichment restitution'

The slippery label 'restitution' can cause extreme taxonomic confusion because it can have reference both to the real right to vindicate property, which is part of property law, and the personal right to redress of unjustified enrichment, which is part of the law of obligations. There can be different views on whether the obligation to restore possession of a thing to the true owner should be treated (a) as an obligation to redress unjustified enrichment (a very outdated misconception); or (b) as a non-enrichment restitutionary obligation belonging in the residual category of obligations *ex variis causarum figuris*; or (c) as a remedy ancillary to the *rei vindicatio* and lying outside the substantive law of obligations.

In English law it seems now to be generally agreed that enrichment law does not cover 'pure proprietary claims' (equivalent to the *rei vindicatio*)

---

[65] C. Zülch, 'Bona Fide Purchase, Property and Restitution: *Lipkin Gorman v. Karpnale* in German Law', in: W. Swadling (ed.), *The Limits of Restitutionary Claims: A Comparative Analysis* (1997), 106, 139, 140. He continues: 'Despite the appeal which such a flexible system has, there are two things to be said in favour of the German approach. First, it is beneficial for legal and commercial certainty and reliability that there are clear and simple rules as to property, and the German rules try to take into account the fact that in commercial transactions it will often be impossible to investigate questions of title. Secondly, the law of restitution becomes clearer and easier to grasp if, at the very least, the question of title is settled. In particular, the question whether a certain person is enriched is straightforward once there are clear rules on the behaviour of title in transactions, given that in most cases the supposed enrichment can only be the consequence of a transfer of value from one party to the other.'

[66] Citing as an illustration *Chase Manhattan Bank NA Ltd v. Israel-British Bank (London) Ltd* [1981] Ch 105.

[67] Reid, 'Unjustified Enrichment', 168.

but does cover proprietary remedies creating new proprietary rights in response to the defendant's unjust enrichment at the plaintiff's expense.[68] Despite Scottish claims to have a clear boundary, the Scottish Institutional writers[69] (except Hume[70]) subsumed vindicatory remedies as well as personal enrichment rights under the head of 'restitution' and at least one unreconstructed modern text even subsumes vindication under the head of 'unjust enrichment'.[71] It is only recently that the vindicatory and enrichment-remedy roles of 'restitution' are coming to be clearly differentiated.[72] The right of the owner of property to vindicate it from someone who has no right to retain it does not derive from the law of unjustified enrichment. Clive makes three points.[73] First, if a man can simply claim delivery of his own property by relying on his right of ownership, he does not need to use a law on unjustified enrichment because he can rely on property law. Secondly, the law of unjustified enrichment would become incoherent if it had to cover non-enrichment cases. Thirdly, Clive argues that to allow the true owner to rely on the law of unjustified enrichment to recover possession would involve a distortion of the idea of enrichment. The possessor is not enriched by the mere fact that someone else's property has fallen temporarily into his possession.[74] Reid, however, contends that there can be enrichment by possession and that is true of German law.[75] Birks[76] regards 'the obligation which activates the *vindicatio*' as a non-enrichment, restitutionary obligation belonging in the

---

[68] See Burrows, 'Restitution', 112, 113; A. Burrows and E. McKendrick, *Cases and Materials on the Law of Restitution* (1997), 724, correcting Burrows, *Law of Restitution*, chap. 13.

[69] Viscount Stair, *Institutions of the Law of Scotland* (ed. by D. M. Walker, 1981), Book I, Title 7 pr. defines 'restitution' as the 'natural or obediential' obligation 'whereby men are holden to restore the proper goods of others'.

[70] Baron David Hume's *Lectures on the Law of Scotland*, vol. III, 228-42.

[71] *Stair Memorial Encyclopaedia* (1996), vol. XV, §§ 44-52; compare the careful distinction drawn in W. R. Wilson, A. Forte et al. (eds.), Gloag and Henderson, *The Law of Scotland* (10th edn, 1995), § 29.9.

[72] See Reid, 'Unjustified Enrichment'; E. M. Clive, *Draft Rules on Unjustified Enrichment and Commentary* (1994), 93 (an Appendix to Scottish Law Commission, Discussion Paper No. 99 on *Judicial Abolition of the Error of Law Rule and its Aftermath* [1996]), reprinted in F. D. Rose (ed.), *Blackstone's Statutes on Contract, Tort and Restitution* (7th edn, 1996), 400 ff.

[73] Clive, *Draft Rules*, comment on rule 11, 87.   [74] *Ibid*.

[75] Reid, 'Unjustified Enrichment', 170 on 'enrichment by possession' (remediable by a decree for restoration of possession and an accounting for the profits of the defender's period of possession). For German law see Markesinis, Lorenz and Dannemann, *Law of Contracts*, 741-3, 749-50.

[76] P. Birks, 'Misnomer', in: W. R. Cornish et al. (eds.), *Restitution: Past, Present and Future, Essays in Honour of Gareth Jones* (1998), 1, 21-6.

residual category of obligations *ex variis causarum figuris*.[77] He finds support for this view in Stair.[78] In modern Scots law, however, it is thought that the obligation of delivery of a corporeal moveable, or of a document of title to heritable or incorporeal moveable property, pursuant to a *rei vindicatio*, is best classified as remedial – that is to say, an obligation consequential upon, or ancillary to, that remedy.[79] It seems undesirable and unnecessary to clutter up the substantive law of obligations with rules designed to give effect to property-law remedies.

3. Tracing in English law: one regime or two?

In English law the process of tracing or combined tracing and following[80] in indirect enrichment cases postulates a transmission chain with at least two transactional links and involves the issue of the imputation of the ultimate recipient's obligation towards the dispossessed original owner or, in remedy-based language, the original owner's title to sue the ultimate recipient. The original owner must show that the ultimate recipient was enriched at his expense and not, or not merely, at the expense of the first recipient in the transmission chain (or third-party intermediary) through whose estate the traceable value passed on its way to the ultimate recipient. 'The effect of a successful tracing exercise is to confer on the parties the same rights and obligations *mutatis mutandis* as they or their predecessors in title had to the original asset.'[81] Many English lawyers believe that the dispossessed original owner should become entitled to trace at common law into and through a mixed fund just as he can do in equity.[82] In English law, there are questions (i) whether there are two regimes of tracing rules, one for common law and the other for equity, or one regime;

---

[77] I.e. in a fourfold taxonomy of obligations including contract, delict and unjustified enrichment, the fourth category is miscellaneous: *D*. 44, 7, 1 pr.
[78] Stair, *Institutions*, Book I, Title 7, 2.
[79] Where the property is shares in a company registered in a putative owner's name, for example, and the true owner has vindicated his real right by a declarator (declaration) of ownership, the court may grant one or more of a range of remedies in lieu of, and equivalent to, a transfer by the putative owner back to the true owner. This range of remedies includes a decree of reduction (setting aside) both of the share transfer and its registration; a court order requiring the clerk of court (in lieu of the putative owner) to sign and deliver a share transfer back; a self-executing judicial adjudication vesting the title in the true owner; or in the case of performance error (e.g. where the claimant has paid too much or to the wrong person), judicial rectification of the conveyance: Law Reform (Miscellaneous Provisions) (Scotland) Act 1985, s. 8; Reid, 'Unjustified Enrichment', 171.
[80] L. D. Smith, *The Law of Tracing* (1997), 6–10.
[81] Millett, 'Restitution and Constructive Trusts', 409.   [82] E.g. Burrows,'Restitution', 112.

and (ii) if one regime, whether it requires a fiduciary relationship between the third-party intermediary and the original owner. The leading monograph on tracing argues that there already is only one regime and that it does not require a fiduciary relationship,[83] but others think that English law has not yet gone that far.[84] At least three options for dealing with the dualism have been identified.[85] It seems that one regime may yet be evolved by the English courts.

4. Taxonomic implications of common-law/equity dualism and tracing: 'ignorance' as an unjust factor

In sorting out the intricate problems of indirect enrichment, German enrichment law generally applies the concepts of transfer (*Leistung*) or encroachment on rights (*Eingriff*) to each of the distinct transactional links in enrichment 'chains' and 'triangles'. Though lacking these concepts Scots law has instinctively adopted a similar approach.[86] It acknowledges, however, an exceptional liability in indirect enrichment based on the principle of no knowing or gratuitous benefit at the pursuer's expense from another's fraud or breach of trust (derived partly from the civilian tradition and partly from 'knowing receipt' in English equity).[87] Nobody in Scotland argues that this species of liability for three-party cases should be replaced by strict liability in order to align it with two-party cases. By contrast, some English lawyers have formulated two new unjust factors, namely 'ignorance' and 'powerlessness', which are designed to apply both to two-party cases and three-party, transmission-chain cases and this is said to be necessary if the English law on unjust factors is to be coherent.[88] Thus where an insolvent rogue misappropriates the plaintiff's money and transfers it, the plaintiff's claim against the transferee is said to be based on 'ignorance'. It is difficult for one not bred in English law to understand

---

[83] Smith, *Law of Tracing*, 162–74 (common law can trace through a mixed fund); 342–7 (no fiduciary relationship necessary).

[84] E.g. R. Nolan, Book Review, (1998) 114 *LQR* 331, 332.

[85] N. H. Andrews and J. Beatson, 'Common Law Tracing: Springboard or Swansong', (1997) 113 *LQR* 21, 26: '(a) to keep common law and equity in parallel, but to eliminate differences of technique or analysis (notably the mixing rules); (b) to draw upon equity to supplement the common law's deficiencies or limitations (the theory of a robust "auxiliary jurisdiction"); (c) to elide both systems and thus create a unified set of rules and a common phraseology.'

[86] Cf. Whitty, 'Indirect Enrichment'.

[87] See, e.g., as to the civil law Ulp. D. 44, 4, 4, 27 and 29; Stair, *Institutions*, Book I, Title 9, 10; Whitty, 'Indirect Enrichment', 256.

[88] P. Birks, *An Introduction to the Law of Restitution* (1985, revised edn 1989) 140–6; Burrows, *Law of Restitution*, chap. 4.

this emphasis on the alignment of two-party and three-party unjust factors.

It is tentatively suggested that the answer may lie in two highly distinctive aspects of English property law which bring the parties at the opposite ends of a transmission chain together into a direct relationship, so that the ultimate recipient is treated as receiving the original owner's property. The first is the dualism of law and equity and in particular the bi-titular character of the English concept of ownership. This has the consequence that the legal title can move down the transactional links in a transmission chain while equitable ownership remains vested in the first owner at the beginning of the chain. The second aspect is tracing. Under the theory of tracing, an abstract entity, called 'value', with a changing content (which may consist at different times of amounts of money, or items of property, or both) moves down the transmission chain until it is acquired by the ultimate recipient.[89] The fact that, by reason of bi-titularity or tracing or both, the ultimate recipient is treated as receiving the original owner's property[90] seems to have encouraged the belief that if the English law is to be coherent, the unjust factors in indirect (or third-party) enrichment cases must belong to the same series as the unjust factors in two-party enrichment cases. This in turn may explain the emergence of 'ignorance' and strict liability in some taxonomies.[91]

In civil-law systems, since equitable ownership is not found, and tracing (real subrogation) only to a limited extent,[92] the same direct relationship and the same encouragement does not exist.

5. Ownership of money, tracing, vindication and enrichment

In transmission chains initiated by the wrongful misappropriation by an intermediary of money, Scots law allows a claim for redress of indirect enrichment in order to stop an ultimate recipient from benefiting knowingly or gratuitously from the intermediary's wrong. There must be a causal link between the dispossessed owner's loss and the ultimate recipient's enrichment but the tests of causation (for example, tracing, or 'but for' causation) require exploration. The ultimate recipient is not generally treated as receiving money belonging to the dispossessed original owner.

---

[89] Smith, *Law of Tracing*.

[90] See e.g. Lord Nicholls, 'Knowing Receipt: The Need for a New Landmark', in: Cornish et al., *Restitution* 231, 236, characterising the mischief struck at by 'knowing receipt' as 'the receipt by a third party of property belonging in equity to another person'; 'the presence or absence of fault is unsatisfactory as the sole criterion of whether a recipient must restore or may keep a benefit to which he was not entitled'.

[91] See Section VIII. [92] Smith, *Law of Tracing*, 18, n. 32.

Following the civilian tradition,[93] there are two exceptions to the *nemo dat* rule affecting money (which is a fungible and consumable), both of which involve an original mode of acquisition. First, an original title of ownership of another's money may be acquired by mixing (*commixtio*) with one's own.[94] Secondly, 'consumption' of another's money by spending it confers a new title of ownership on the bona fide recipient. So even stolen money becomes the property of a non-owner to the extent that he can confer good title on 'any singular successor by commerce'.[95] Where therefore the ultimate recipient acquires a title to misappropriated funds by commixtion or transfer, the dispossessed person is not treated, by reason of tracing, as owner of the money entitled to a vindicatory remedy but (at best) as having a personal right of recompense for the redress of unjustified enrichment.[96]

It is because the real right of ownership of money can be so easily lost that the temptation arises to import from English law the rules of tracing money into its surrogates and intermixtures. But while rules on changes in the ownership of money through mixing and spending are essential for every legal system, the rules of tracing (real subrogation) of money are almost peculiar to common-law systems and an optional extra for a legal system.

In German law, in a transmission chain, the dispossessed original owner of money very rarely has any personal right or real right against the

[93] P. J. Thomas and A. Boraine, 'Ownership of Money and *Actio Pauliana*', (1994) 57 *Tydskrif vir die Hedendaagse Romeins-Hollandse Reg* 678.

[94] D. 46, 3, 78, cited by Stair, *Institutions*, Book II, Title 1, 34: 'Commixtion of money is esteemed as consumption'; Lord Bankton, *An Institute of the Law of Scotland* (1751–3, and reprinted as vols. 41–3 of the Stair Society series), Book I, Title 24, 14; *Crawfurd v. Royal Bank* (1749) Mor 875. This rule differs from the general rule on *commixtio* of fungibles other than money under which common (*pro indiviso*) ownership in proportion to the constituents results: *Stair Memorial Encyclopaedia*, (1993), vol. XVIII, § 564 (W. M. Gordon), citing Stair, *Institutions*, Book II, Title 1, 36 and 37; J. Erskine, *An Institute of the Law of Scotland* (8th edn, 1871), Book II, Title 1, 17; Bell, *Principles*, § 1298(2). Consumption destroys the previous owner's real right.

[95] Stair, *Institutions*, Book II, Title 1, 34; *Crawfurd v. Royal Bank* (1749) Mor 875; see also Bankton, *Institutes*, Book I, Title 8, 34 and Book I, Title 24, 14; Bell, *Principles*, § 528. It is misleading to say that ownership of money passes with possession. Where physical possession of stolen money is acquired in bad faith or gratuitously and the money is still 'earmarked' or identifiable and unmixed with other funds, ownership has not been acquired by the possessor and so may be vindicated by the dispossessed true owner in an action *ad factum praestandum* for delivery without pecuniary conclusions: *Henry v. Morrison* (1881) 8 R 692 at 693.

[96] *Bank of Scotland v. MacLeod Paxton Woolard & Co.* 1998 SLT 258 (OH) at 271L–272A *per* Lord Coulsfield.

ultimate recipient of the money or its product.[97] A *rei vindicatio* under § 985 BGB requires, *inter alia*, that the ultimate recipient has the actual coins or notes of which the original owner was dispossessed. A claim by the original owner for redress of the ultimate recipient's unjustified enrichment generally requires, *inter alia*, that the original owner was still owner when the intermediary transferred it to the ultimate recipient. Both cases are rare because ownership of money is lost as soon as it is either mixed with other money[98] or acquired by another in good faith.[99] If a rogue intermediary takes another's money and pays it to the ultimate recipient who takes it in good faith and for value then the ultimate recipient is not liable to the dispossessed owner; the latter's remedy is against the intermediary.[100] If the rogue intermediary pays the misappropriated money into his own bank account, the bank becomes owner of the coins and notes. The dispossessed owner can use an *Eingriffskondiktion* to acquire the right to the intermediary's personal right against the bank.[101] If the rogue intermediary takes the money from his account and pays to the ultimate recipient, the dispossessed owner has various personal claims against the intermediary.[102] In principle the dispossessed owner has no claim against the ultimate recipient except in limited circumstances under § 822 BGB,[103] which applies only if the intermediary was in good faith. If the intermediary was in bad faith – the common money-laundering case – the ultimate recipient is never directly liable to the dispossessed original owner even if he likewise was in bad faith. In this respect, Scots law differs from German law and is more in line with the English law by which it has been influenced. It is for consideration whether here German law is too restrictive in allowing the ultimate recipient to benefit from the intermediary's fraud. In civil-law systems generally, real subrogation is limited to property and does not extend to money.[104]

---

[97] I am grateful to Dr Sonja Meier for guidance on the German law.
[98] §§ 947(2), 948 BGB; or there is co-ownership §§ 947(1), 948 BGB. [99] §§ 932, 935(2) BGB.
[100] § 816(1), first sentence, BGB.
[101] § 812(1), first sentence, BGB. The original owner can also claim damages for loss of property: §§ 989, 992, 832(1) BGB.
[102] E.g. an enrichment claim (§ 812(1), first sentence, BGB) for (a) the amount of the money; or (b) (in rare cases) any claim by the intermediary against the ultimate recipient to redress a transfer made *sine causa*; (c) any consideration which the ultimate recipient gave to the intermediary.
[103] Here the dispossessed owner has an enrichment claim against the ultimate recipient if he acquired the money gratuitously and if the intermediary's liability is excluded through loss of enrichment: § 818(3) BGB.
[104] Smith, *Law of Tracing*, 18, n. 32.

In Scotland tracing has been criticised, whether employed in aid of constructive trusts[105] or of obligations to redress unjustified indirect enrichment.[106] Nevertheless in the battle against money laundering it may be too useful to abrogate. This subject is dealt with below, in Section VIII.

6. Bankruptcy, 'proprietary' rights, 'preferred' or 'protected' personal rights, trustee's two patrimonies

In English law a 'legal' or 'equitable' right having priority in or excluded from bankruptcy proceedings is treated as operating '*in rem*' and therefore as 'proprietary'.[107] In Scots law matters are not quite so simple. First, a personal right to reduce a transfer voidable for fraud, or to recover a payment induced by fraud, is recognised in the debtor's bankruptcy under the doctrine known as *tantum et tale* and is best characterised, not as a 'proprietary right', but as a 'protected' or 'preferred' personal right.[108] Secondly, Scots law accommodates the trust in a civilian system of property law by affirming the theory that the trustee has ownership (*dominium*) of two patrimonies (estates), his personal patrimony and his trust patrimony.[109] Property owned by the trustee in one capacity (the trustee always has '*dominium*') is not attachable for debts owed by him in the other capacity.[110] Thirdly, there are also older cases characterising a trust beneficiary as 'true owner' and the trustee as 'apparent owner', but that theory is wrong, alien and incoherent.[111] Fourthly, if the theory of two patrimonies applies to express trusts, it should apply also to constructive trusts. But their nature and role is uncertain in Scots law.[112] Fifthly, Scots law recognises resulting trusts.[113] Since they arise by operation of law[114] they may be

---

[105] Gretton, 'Constructive Trusts', 291, 292 and 413.   [106] *Ibid.* (part II), 418, 419.
[107] Burrows, *Law of Restitution*, 28.   [108] Bell, *Commentaries*, vol. I, 299, 309–11.
[109] See e.g. G. L. Gretton, 'Trust and Patrimony', in: H. L. MacQueen (ed.), *Scots Law into the 21st Century* (1996), 182; K. G. C. Reid, 'National Report for Scotland', in: D. J. Hayton, S. C. J. J. Kortmann and H. L. E. Verhagen (eds.), *Principles of European Trust Law* (1999), 67, 68.
[110] Bankruptcy (Scotland) Act 1985, s. 31(1)(b). Last century the trust beneficiary's right to have trust property excluded from the sequestration in bankruptcy of the trustee in his personal capacity was explained by reference to the *tantum et tale* doctrine (e.g. Bell, *Commentaries*, vol. I, 300) but the two patrimonies theory is a better explanation. In South Africa, the beneficiary has 'a protected right *in personam*' in the trustee's bankruptcy: Honoré and Cameron, *South African Law of Trusts*, 474.
[111] *Inland Revenue v. Clark's Trs* 1939 SC 11; Wilson and Duncan, *Trusts* chap. 1.
[112] Gretton, 'Constructive Trusts'.   [113] Wilson and Duncan, *Trusts*, §§ 6-40–6-58.
[114] They result on the failure of the trust purposes to exhaust the trust estate.

explained as based upon unjustified enrichment,[115] but the matter awaits exploration.

7. Unjustified enrichment and bankruptcy

Legal systems will generally not allow an enrichment claim to prevail over the right of a bona fide purchaser for value from the enrichment-debtor but may sometimes allow an enrichment claim to prevail over the enrichment-debtor's creditors on his bankruptcy.[116] Bankruptcy involves at least two transactional links in a transmission chain. The first link involves a benefit passing from an unsecured creditor to the bankrupt by the creditor's transfer or the bankrupt's wrongful misappropriation. The second link involves the sequestration or adjudication in bankruptcy transferring the bankrupt's assets to the trustee for the creditors.

Where a creditor has a personal right against the bankrupt, say for the unpaid price of goods or services, he cannot claim in the debtor's bankruptcy for a preference for his claim on the ground that the general creditors have been unjustifiably enriched by their sequestration or attachment in the bankruptcy proceedings of the goods or the product of the services.[117] This is consonant with the principle of the parity of the general creditors of an insolvent and the fact that the vesting in the trustee in bankruptcy is not *sine causa*.[118]

Much more frequently litigated is the question whether a right to the redress of unjustified enrichment in the first transactional link should have a priority or preference in the enrichment-debtor's subsequent bankruptcy in competition with his general, unsecured creditors. This should depend on which specific ground of redress ('unjust factor') of the bankrupt's unjustified enrichment (through the first transactional link) is relied on by the enrichment-creditor.[119] English lawyers speak of the need to examine

---

[115] Cf. R. Chambers, *Resulting Trusts* (1997), who contends that in English law resulting trusts reverse unjust enrichment.

[116] Why the difference? Two traditional reasons are that the general creditors when extending credit rely on the bankrupt's personal credit not on his ownership of any asset, and, when bringing or claiming in bankruptcy proceedings, do not give new consideration. E.g. *Heritable Reversionary Co. Ltd v. Millar* (1892) 19 R (HL) 43 at 47–8 *per* Lord Watson. The same reasoning applies to a bankrupt's donee.

[117] Here there is a contract in the first transactional link (between the creditor and the bankrupt) and an enrichment claim in the form of a claim for a preference arising out of the second link (the sequestration in bankruptcy). *Mess v. Sime's Tr* (1898) 1 F (HL) 22; affirming 25 R 398; [1899] AC 233.

[118] *Ibid.*   [119] For the Scots law, see Whitty, 'Indirect Enrichment', 267–9.

all the unjust factors from this standpoint.[120] This is discussed below when considering indirect enrichment in Section VIII.

V. Obligations to redress unjustified enrichment distinguished from other categories of obligations

The label 'unjustified enrichment' invokes the measure of recovery as the criterion determining the scope of the types of obligations which it describes. Several legal doctrines are concerned to some extent with the redress of unjustified enrichment, so the boundaries between enrichment law and other legal categories are not always clear.[121]

1. The interface with contract law

The English enrichment law revolution has rescued the subject from the fringes of contract law and destroyed the implied contract fiction. The fiction was never the basis of the civil-law and mixed systems. They characterise obligations to redress enrichment as obediential (arising by operation of law) and so springing from a different source than obligations assumed voluntarily by contract or promise. In Scots law, demarcation disputes can arise on the boundary between enrichment law and contract law[122] but in principle the distinction is clear.

2. The interface with fiduciary obligations in Scots law

Views may differ on how the category of fiduciary obligations fits into the masterplan of the Scottish law of obligations which ought in principle to be unitary. For several reasons, however, it is probably better to

---

[120] E.g. Swadling, 'New Role?'; Smith, *Law of Tracing*, chap. 8 on 'Proprietary claims'.
[121] As regards remedies, it might be helpful if Scots law were to adopt Lionel Smith's lucid and precise distinction between (i) 'disgorgement' whereby D surrenders (i.e. gives *up*) his enrichment to P; (ii) 'compensation' or 'reparation' whereby D pays P the amount of P's loss; and (iii) 'restitution' whereby D surrenders (i.e. gives *back*) his enrichment to P to compensate P for his loss. Restitution (iii) is a combination of disgorgement (i) and compensation (ii). See L. D. Smith, 'The Province of the Law of Restitution', (1992) 71 *Canadian Bar Review* 672 at 695-7. In Scots law (unlike English law) 'damages' always has reference to compensatory damages. In this perspective, the term 'restitutionary damages' (fashionable in English law) is a misnomer because it is a synonym for 'disgorgement' and is therefore neither 'damages' in the Scottish sense nor 'restitutionary' in the normal or natural sense. The verb 'disgorge' is sometimes found in older Scots cases. The older Scottish synonym for 'to disgorge' was 'to make furthcoming', still used in the law of diligence.
[122] See H. L. MacQueen, 'Contract, Unjustified Enrichment and Concurrent Liability: A Scots Perspective', [1997] *Acta Juridica* 176.

classify fiduciary obligations to account for and surrender unauthorised gains separately from obligations under the general law for the redress of unjustified enrichment. For example, the fiduciary's enrichment is not necessarily 'at the expense of' the constructive beneficiary: rather, it arises from a wrong against him (breach of fiduciary obligation) even in the absence of mirror loss on his part.[123] Moreover, the rationale is different.[124] Arguably the law on the special obligations of fiduciaries differs from the law on unjustified enrichment in that the policy behind it is not so much to redress an imbalance as to encourage high standards of probity. The status of a fiduciary obligation is unclear and it may be that it only arises within the context of some already existing branch of law.[125] Again, a breach of fiduciary obligation[126] attracts the privileges of a constructive trust and tracing, which are not normally available for breaches of obligations to redress unjustified enrichment.

3. The interface with delict

The big question here is whether there is a category of enrichment from wrongs, 'or whether that category is redundant, and perhaps incoherent, if a category such as "enrichment from invasion of rights" is recognised'.[127] German law has chosen a category of 'encroachment on rights' (the *Eingriffskondiktion*).[128] Stemming from the old doctrine of 'waiver of tort',[129] the dominant English view is that an enriched person is liable to redress an enrichment arising from his own act only if (a) the act is a tort or equitable wrong and (b) the wrong is one of those for which restitution lies.[130] The role of enrichment law is to add the remedy of disgorgement (surrender of enrichment without mirror loss) to the usual remedy of

---

[123] See J. Blackie, 'Enrichment and Wrongs in Scots Law', [1992] Acta Juridica 23.
[124] See Clive, *Draft Rules*, 93. [125] Gretton, 'Constructive Trusts', 290.
[126] Or the mala fide or gratuitous acquisition of 'trust property' from a fiduciary in breach.
[127] J. Blackie, 'Enrichment, Wrongs and Invasion of Rights in Scots Law', [1997] Acta Juridica 284 reprinted in: Visser, *Limits of the Law of Obligations*, 284. It is convenient to address this question here, though 'wrongs' might include not only torts/delicts but also breaches of contract or of trust.
[128] See Gallo, 'Unjust Enrichment', 449; Zimmermann and Du Plessis, 'Basic Features', 28–39; Markesinis, Lorenz and Dannemann, *Law of Contracts*, 710 ff.; R. Zimmermann, 'Unjustified Enrichment: The Modern Civilian Approach', (1995) 15 Oxford JLS 403, 418–21.
[129] I.e. the rule under which the plaintiff may elect to sue in restitution to recover the defendant's unjustified enrichment rather than in tort for damages.
[130] D. Friedmann, 'Restitution for Wrongs: The Basis of Liability', in: Cornish et al., *Restitution*, 133.

damages compensating for loss.[131] This 'parasitic' theory has been attacked.[132] Within enrichment law the concept of 'encroachment on rights' differs from the notion of wrong because liability may arise even though the mental element (malice, intent or negligence) required for wrongfulness is missing. It may be that English law can work with 'restitution for wrongs' only because some English torts (for example, conversion) attract strict liability. On that view Scots law, which has not received these torts, cannot with advantage take over the English concept.[133] It is thought that Scots law does and should allow redress of unjustified enrichment arising out of encroachments on patrimonial rights independently of delict. The existence of a category of encroachment on rights wider than delict has taxonomic implications explored below.[134] A claim for disgorgement of profits arising from a delict encroaching on patrimonial rights (for example, wrongful use of another's property or confidential information) would not be inconsistent with the rule against punitive damages: 'there is no public policy against allowing unjustified enrichments to be redressed – quite the reverse – and it therefore seems that the policy against punitive damages is based on upholding the purity of the idea that damages are for the compensation of loss and resisting the idea that the civil courts should have a broad discretion to punish for conduct of which they disapprove'.[135]

4. Other excluded or doubtful categories

Some other categories of obligations concerned with restoring or surrendering enrichments[136] have rules of their own and do not fall under the general law of obligations for the redress of unjustified enrichment, namely rights of relief of cautioners and co-obligants;[137] subrogation of

---

[131] Ibid., 133, 134.

[132] J. Beatson, 'The Nature of Waiver of Tort', in: J. Beatson, *The Use and Abuse of Unjust Enrichment* (1990), 206; S. Hedley, 'The Myth of Waiver of Tort', (1984) 100 *LQR* 653; N. J. McBride and P. McGrath, 'The Nature of Restitution', (1995) 15 *Oxford JLS* 33 at 44, 45 (arguing that claims in respect of the defendant's unauthorised use of the plaintiff's property involve a wrong but the wrong is incidental to, and not the basis of, the plaintiff's claim); Friedmann 'Restitution for Wrongs' (arguing that, under his 'independent claim theory', liability is founded on the defendant's enrichment by the 'invasion or appropriation' of the plaintiff's 'protected interest' as defined by enrichment law not tort law).

[133] I am indebted to Dr Sonja Meier for this observation.   [134] Section VII, 3, below.

[135] Clive, *Draft Rules*, comment on rule 11(1), page 82. In its report on *Breach of Confidence* (Scot Law Com No. 90, 1984, § 4.98) the Scottish Law Commission recommended that the remedy of an accounting for profits should be available in respect of a knowing and deliberate breach of an obligation of confidence.

[136] Clive, *Draft Rules*, comment on rule 12, 92.

[137] In actions of relief, there is no defence of change of position.

insurers or of those who have paid an indemnity;[138] the rules derived from the case of *Walker v. Milne*;[139] and general average or salvage. In *negotiorum gestio*, unjustified enrichment provides neither the ground of action, nor the measure of recovery, in the gestor's claim (the *actio negotiorum gestorum contraria*). The *gestio* must have been useful but in principle 'initial utility' suffices[140] so that the *dominus* may be liable though not enriched. Further, apart from certain isolated cases,[141] the measure of recovery is limited to the gestor's expenses (if initially useful) and outlays and does not extend to the full enrichment of the *dominus*.[142] *Negotiorum gestio* is separately regulated in all the codes.[143]

VI. The internal taxonomy of obligations to redress unjustified enrichment

1. Overview

In enrichment law, the complexities of three-party situations present especially difficult legal problems and some of them attract rules of their own, which are examined in Section VIII. This section is mainly confined to two-party cases. With the breakdown of its centuries-old system of classifying obligations for redress of unjustified enrichment, Scots law has to reorganise its principles and rules in accordance with a new taxonomy. This section first places Scots enrichment law in its comparative context. It belongs in the same tradition as civil-law systems, which distinguish between enrichment by transfer (the modern successor of the *condictio indebiti*) and other modes of acquiring enrichment. The main English taxonomies are

---

[138] Now regarded in England as a remedy to redress unjust enrichment: Goff and Jones, *Law of Restitution*, chap. 3, 120 ff.

[139] (1823) 2 S 379; (1824) 3 S 123; (1825) 3 S 478 (whereby loss suffered or expenditure incurred in the expectation of a contract may in certain circumstances be recovered).

[140] R. D. Leslie, '*Negotiorum Gestio* in Scots Law: The Claim of the Privileged Gestor', [1983] JR 12, 15, 16, 28-32; D. H. van Zyl, *Negotiorum Gestio in South African Law* (1985), 40-6; S. J. Stoljar, '*Negotiorum Gestio*', in: *International Encyclopedia of Comparative Law* (1984), vol. X, chap. 17, §§ 49-54, 99-102; N. R. Whitty, '*Negotiorum Gestio*', in: Stair Memorial Encyclopaedia (1996), vol. XV, §§ 117-20; Stair, *Institutions*, Book I, Title 8, 3.

[141] Stoljar, '*Negotiorum Gestio*', § 171; van Zyl, '*Negotiorum Gestio*', 84-118; Whitty, '*Negotiorum Gestio*', §§ 137-41.

[142] Stoljar, '*Negotiorum Gestio*', 52; van Zyl, '*Negotiorum Gestio*'; Whitty, '*Negotiorum Gestio*', § 121.

[143] E.g. France, *Code civil* (1804), arts. 1372-5; Netherlands, *Burgerlijk Wetboek* (1992), arts. 6:198-6:202; Germany, BGB (1900), §§ 677-87; Italy, *Codice civile* (1942), arts. 2028-32; Switzerland, OR (1912), §§ 419-24; Austria, ABGB (1811), §§ 1035-40; Civil Code of Quebec (1991), arts. 1482-90; Louisiana Civil Code (revised articles inserted in 1996), arts. 2292-7. For a comparative survey of codal provisions in 1985, see van Zyl, '*Negotiorum Gestio*', chap. 6.

unsuitable models for Scots law, though that of Birks has some Scottish supporters. All these approaches provide that an enrichment at another's expense is 'unjustified if' certain grounds are established. On Clive's alternative approach, an enrichment at another's expense is 'unjustified unless' it is justified by a legal cause or public policy. The section then argues in more detail that the Wilburg/von Caemmerer plan of German enrichment law would fit the Scottish legal terrain and accord best with the natural development of the Scots law.

2. The existing laws and models: civilian and mixed systems

(a) Transfer (repetition of the undue) and enrichment without cause

Many European legal systems draw a distinction between repetition of an undue transfer and a residual category of redress of enrichment without cause or unjustified enrichment. Repetition of the undue stems by direct lineage from the *condictiones* of the Roman law. These regulated restitution of property and money transferred by the claimant directly to the enriched party without legal cause. Two limitations were important which have left marks on the modern law.[144] First, the *condictiones* reversed the transfer (*datio*) of money or a thing and did not provide recompense for the value of services (a *factum*) performed without legal ground.[145] This limitation remains in some codes requiring separate articles or supplement outside the codes[146] and distinguishes restitution from recompense in Scots law.[147] Secondly, for any of the relevant *condictiones* to lie, there had to be a direct legal transaction (*negotium*) between the parties[148] so that such a *condictio* could not redress 'indirect enrichment' – for example, enrichment arising from a contract between two others. The residual category of unjustified enrichment derives from scattered texts and forms of action of Roman law, as developed by the *ius commune*[149] or even by post-codal judicial decisions as, famously, in France.[150]

---

[144] De Vos, 'Liability arising from Unjustified Enrichment', 131, 137. [145] *Ibid.*, 131.
[146] See the codes in France, Italy, Quebec and Louisiana described below.
[147] Stair, *Institutions*, Book I, Title 7 (restitution); Book I, Title 8 (recompense).
[148] Celsus D. 12, 1, 32; De Vos, 'Liability arising from Unjustified Enrichment', 131; R. Zimmermann, *The Law of Obligations: Roman Foundations of the Civilian Tradition* (paperback edn, 1996), 853–4, 874, 880–1; J. Hallebeek, 'Developments in Mediaeval Roman Law', in: E. J. H. Schrage (ed.), *Unjust Enrichment: The Comparative Legal History of the Law of Restitution* (1995), 59, 108–11.
[149] Especially the *actio de in rem verso*; the action against the pupil (the *actio in quantum locupletior factus est*); and the *actio negotiorum gestorum contraria* in its role as an enrichment action.
[150] *Boudier* decision, Req. 15 June 1892, S 1893.1.281.

(b) From *indebitum solutum* to 'enrichment by transfer'

French law deals with *paiement de l'indu* in the Code civil (1804)[151] and developed the *actio de in rem verso* by judicial decisions as a remedy for *l'enrichissement sans cause* outside the code in the late nineteenth century.[152] In Italian law, following the French pattern and influence, the first national code of 1865 catered for *pagamento dell'indebito* leaving a judicial remedy for 'enrichment without cause' (*arrichimento senza causa*) to be developed outside the code.[153] The *Codice civile* of 1942 expressly recognised the latter and enacted separate provisions on both.[154] The very recent codal revisions in Quebec[155] and Louisiana,[156] the two main mixed systems within the French tradition, have done the same. The Dutch Civil Code of 1838, while recognising the *condictio indebiti* and some other specific enrichment cases, lacked a general enrichment obligation.[157] The new Civil Code (*Burgerlijk Wetboek*) of 1992, after regulating 'undue performance' in nine articles, introduces a statutory general obligation for redress of unjustified enrichment separately in another article.[158] A similar distinction is made by the Swiss Code of Obligations[159] and the Austrian General Civil

---

[151] Arts. 1376–81.

[152] Dawson, *Unjust Enrichment*, 98–107; Nicholas, 'Unjustified Enrichment', 622 ff.

[153] P. Gallo, 'Remedies for Unjust Enrichment in the History of Italian Law and in the Codice Civile', in: Schrage, *Unjust Enrichment* 275, 275–8.

[154] Ibid., 278 ff. For *pagamento dell'indebito*, see arts. 2033–40; for *arrichimento senza causa*, see arts. 2041, 2042.

[155] Quebec Code Civil (1991), Book 5 (Obligations), Title 1 (Obligations in general), chapter IV (Other sources of obligations), Section II (Reception of a thing not due), arts. 1491, 1492; Section III (Unjust enrichment), arts. 1493–6; (art. 1492 applies the rules on prestation of payments in arts. 1699–707).

[156] Louisiana Civil Code (1995), art. 2298 (enrichment without cause: compensation); arts. 2299–305 (payment of a thing not owed). See C. L. Martin, 'Louisiana State Law Institute Proposes Revision of *Negotiorum Gestio* and Codification of Unjust Enrichment', (1994) 69 *Tulane LR* 181; P. Birks, 'Obligations Arising Without Agreement Under the Louisiana Civil Code', [1997] *Restitution LR* 222.

[157] In the leading case of *Quint v. Te Poel*, NJ 1959, 546, the Hoge Raad 'held that in unjust enrichment cases for which there is no express statutory basis, an action for recovery may nonetheless be awarded if this fits in "the system of law" and if it can be linked with cases which have been expressly dealt with by statute': H. L. E. Verhagen and N. E. D. Faber, 'A Trace of *Chase Manhattan* in the Netherlands', [1998] *Restitution LR* 165.

[158] Book 6 (General part of the law of obligations), Title 4 (Obligations from a source other than delict or contract), Section 2 (Performance not due), arts. 6:203–6:211; Section 3 (Unjustfied enrichment), art. 6.212. See E. J. H. Schrage, 'The Law of Restitution: The History of Dutch Legislation', in: Schrage, *Unjust Enrichment*, 323; E. Schrage, 'Restitution in the New Dutch Civil Code', [1994] *Restitution LR* 208; also published with modification in P. W. L. Russell (ed.), *Unjustified Enrichment: A Comparative Study of the Law of Restitution* (1996), 9.

[159] *Code des Obligations*, arts. 62 II and 63 I.

Code (ABGB).[160] In South African law, the *condictiones* survive[161] and are supplemented by other forms of action.[162] A general enrichment action existed in classical Roman-Dutch law and there is pressure to reintroduce it in South African law, but as yet without success.[163]

Showing its age, the French code is relatively narrow. Following the Roman *condictiones*, it does not cover recompense for services, which still falls under the judge-made 'enrichment without cause'. Following 'a systematic idiosyncrasy of Domat', it does not cover the restoration of benefits conferred under an invalid contract.[164] It appears that Italian law is getting rid of these restrictions.[165] The new Dutch version of the *condictio indebiti* provides (in article 6:203) not only for restitution of money and property but also in respect of other benefits – for example, services. On the other hand, the Quebec and Louisiana versions of the *condictio indebiti*[166] do not apply to services which are governed by the articles on enrichment without cause.[167] In South African law it is disputed whether a *condictio* lies for services.[168]

(c) Scots law

At least until very recently, the uncodified mixed system in Scotland belonged in the same tradition, distinguishing between restitution and

---

[160] §§ 1431 ff. ABGB.

[161] De Vos, 'Liability arising from Unjustified Enrichment', 236; G. Lotz (rev. A. de W. Horak), 'Enrichment' in: W. A. Joubert (ed.), *The Law of South Africa* (first reissue), vol. IX; D. P. Visser, 'Unjustified Enrichment', in: D. Hutchison (ed.), *Wille's Principles of South African Law* (8th edn, 1991), chap. XXXVIII; S. Eiselen and G. Pienaar, *Unjustified Enrichment: A Casebook* (2nd edn, 1999).

[162] Notably the action against a person of limited capacity; the action for work done or services rendered; the action for improvements to another's property; and the enrichment action of the *negotiorum gestor*: see previous note.

[163] In *Nortje v. Pool* 1966 (3) SA 96 (A) the majority of the Appellate Division (Rumpff JA dissenting) held that a general enrichment action did not yet exist; see Visser, 'Unjustified Enrichment', 630, 631; R. Zimmermann, 'A Road Through the Enrichment Forest?' (1985) 18 *CILSA* 1; D. H. van Zyl, 'The General Enrichment Action is Alive and Well', [1992] *Acta Juridica* 115; R. Feenstra, 'Grotius' Doctrine of Unjust Enrichment as a Source of Obligation: Its Origin and its Influence in Roman-Dutch law', in: Schrage, *Unjust Enrichment*, 197; Eiselen and Pienaar, *Unjustified Enrichment*, 10 ff.; D. P. Visser, 'Unjustified Enrichment', in: R. Zimmermann and D. Visser (eds.), *Southern Cross: Civil Law and Common Law in South Africa* (1996), 523, 549–55; see also *Kommissaris van Binnelandse Inkomste v. Willers* 1994 (3) SA 283 (A); comment by D. P. Visser, 'Not the General Enrichment Action', [1994] *Tydskrif vir die Suid-Afrikaanse Reg* 196.

[164] Zimmermann, 'Unjustified Enrichment', 409.

[165] Engłard, 'Restitution of Benefits', § 37.

[166] Quebec Code Civil, art. 1491; Louisiana Civil Code, art. 2299.

[167] Quebec Civil Code, arts. 1493–1496; Louisiana Civil Code, art. 2298.

[168] *Nortje v. Pool* 1966 (3) SA 96 (A) *per* Rumpff JA (dissenting); *contra Gouws v. Jester Pools (Pty) Ltd* 1968 3 SA 563 (T) at 575 *per* Jansen J, criticised by Eiselen and Pienaar, *Unjustified Enrichment*, 108.

Table 23.2. *Taxonomy of Scots enrichment law (up to 1998)*

1. Repetition (money)	1.1 *condictio indebiti*
	1.2 *condictio causa data causa non secuta*
	1.3 *condictio ob turpem vel iniustam causam*
	1.4 *condictio sine causa*; miscellaneous innominate claims
2. Restitution (property)	2.1 *condictio indebiti*
	2.2 *condictio causa data causa non secuta*
	2.3 *condictio ob turpem vel iniustam causam*
	2.4 *condictio sine causa*; miscellaneous innominate claims
3. Recompense (services, expenditures, etc.)	3. general; *actio de in rem verso*; [*actio in quantum locupletior factus est*]; miscellaneous innominate claims

repetition (based on the *condictiones* and indigenous innominate heads of claim) and recompense (based in part on the *actio de in rem verso* and the pupil's action as developed in the *ius commune*) – see Table 23.2.[169] The basis of the distinction between these categories (the three Rs) was much disputed[170] but may have turned on whether the content of the obligation to redress enrichment concerned the return of a *certum* (as in restitution and repetition) or redress in respect of an *incertum* (recompense).[171]

The courts, however, have recently transposed the three Rs from the domain of substantive law (where they denoted the main categories of obligations redressing unjustified enrichment) to the law of remedies; characterised the *condictiones* as merely labels for particular 'fact situations' grounding recovery; extended the *condictiones* beyond their traditional boundaries of restitution of money and property to recompense for expenditures; and at the same time affirmed the existence of a unitary system of specific grounds applying to all types of benefit conferred (money, property, services and expenditures) – see Table 23.3.[172]

Some supporters of a 'pure' general enrichment action regard the taxonomic split between enrichment by transfer and other cases as

---

[169] See e.g. Gloag and Henderson, *Law of Scotland*, chap. 29.
[170] See the thorough overview of the debates in Evans-Jones and Hellwege, 'Some Observations', 180.
[171] Ibid., 181, 182, 187–9; 194, 205, 207, 208.
[172] *Shilliday v. Smith* 1998 SC 725 (1st Division); *Dollar Land (Cumbernauld) Ltd v. CIN Properties Ltd* 1998 SC (HL) 90.

Table 23.3. *New taxonomy of Scots enrichment law (1999)*

Principle of unjustified enrichment
(applicable to money, property, services, expenditures)
condictio indebiti
condictio causa data causa non secuta
condictio ob turpem vel iniustam causam
condictio sine causa
miscellaneous innominate claims; *actio de in rem verso;*
[actio in quantum locupletior factus est]

outmoded.[173] Yet it is deeply embedded in the civilian approach. It is found everywhere including recent codal revisions.[174]

(d) Transfer; interference; obtruding benefit (Wilburg/von Caemmerer taxonomy)

The BGB states the general principle against enrichment at another's expense by transfer or in another way without legal ground (§ 812(1), first sentence, combining the *condictiones indebiti* and *sine causa*) and provides separately for other *condictiones*.[175] It has been observed that,[176] although § 812 BGB *ex facie* introduces a general enrichment obligation, its wording as interpreted by Walter Wilburg in 1934[177] preserved the distinction between a 'transfer' (that is, a performance or *Leistung* being the pursuer's intentional or conscious conferment of a benefit in money, goods or services on the defender[178]) and other modes of acquiring enrichment. Then

---

[173] See e.g. the criticism of the split in the 1995 revision of the Louisiana Civil Code, between art. 2298 and arts. 2299–305, by Birks, 'Obligations Arising Without Agreement', 228. See also Clive, *Draft Rules* (see 691–3, below).

[174] In Quebec (1991), the Netherlands (1995) and Louisiana (1995).

[175] § 812(1), second sentence, BGB (*condictiones ob causam finitam* and *causa data causa non secuta*) and § 817, first sentence, BGB (*condictio ob turpem vel iniustam causam*).

[176] In describing German law, the following works are relied on: Gallo, 'Unjust Enrichment'; Markesinis, Lorenz and Dannemann, *Law of Contracts*, 710 ff.; E. von Caemmerer, 'Problèmes fondamentaux de l'enrichissement sans cause', (1966) 18 *Revue internationale de droit comparé* 573; Zimmermann, 'A Road through the Enrichment Forest?'; also his 'Unjustified Enrichment'; also his *Law of Obligations*, 889–91; Zimmermann and Du Plessis, 'Basic Features'; K. Zweigert and H. Kötz, *Introduction to Comparative Law* (trans. T. Weir, 3rd edn, 1998), chaps. 38 and 39.

[177] W. Wilburg, *Die Lehre von der ungerechtfertigten Bereicherung nach österreichischem und deutschem Recht* (1934).

[178] See 694 ff., below.

in 1954 Ernst von Caemmerer elaborated a typology of the classes of enrichment created otherwise than by transfer.[179] The resulting taxonomy is the accepted orthodoxy in German law. Its primary division has four categories of claim classified by the mode of acquiring the enrichment, namely claims arising: (i) from 'transfer' (*Leistungskondiktion*); (ii) from the defender's unauthorised encroachment on or interference with the pursuer's patrimonial rights (*Eingriffskondiktion* or 'interference action'); (iii) from the pursuer's unauthorised improvements of the defender's property in the erroneous belief that it is his own (*Verwendungskondiktion* or 'expenditure action'); and (iv) from the pursuer's discharge of the defender's debt or performance of the defender's obligation (*Rückgriffskondiktion* or 'recourse action').

While recognising the need to study the *ius commune* background,[180] Lord President Rodger has warned that 'even if the Court of Session were one day tempted to adopt some version of the German analysis which figures prominently in modern academic writing, this could not alter the simple fact that in the existing cases the Scottish courts had not adopted an analysis of that kind'.[181] So the case has still to be made out. The claim of German enrichment law to be a model for Scots law lies mainly in two considerations. First, as a matter of legal history the German law has grown directly from the same Roman and *ius commune* sources as Scots enrichment law. Much of its value for mixed systems such as South African law and Scots law is that it 'represents a continuation of the civilian tradition'.[182] It has travelled several stages further down the very same historic path on which the Scots law is and has been travelling. It follows that adapting the German taxonomy would be in tune with the natural development of our law. Secondly, the German law is probably the most highly developed of the civilian systems of unjustified enrichment. And it is increasingly accessible to monoglot Anglophones, though any borrowing can only be at a general level.

---

[179] E. von Caemmerer, 'Bereicherung und unerlaubte Handlung', in: H. Dölle, M. Rheinstein and K. Zweigert (eds.), *Festschrift für Ernst Rabel* (1954), vol. I, 333. See also von Caemmerer, 'Problèmes fondamentaux'.

[180] Cf. H. L. MacQueen and W. D. H. Sellar, 'Unjust Enrichment in Scots Law', in: Schrage, *Unjust Enrichment*, 289.

[181] Rodger, 'Use of the Civil Law', 230.

[182] J. E. du Plessis, *Compulsion and Restitution: A Historical and Comparative Study of the Treatment of Compulsion in Scottish Private Law with Particular Emphasis on its Relevance to the Law of Restitution or Unjustified Enrichment* (1997) (unpublished Ph.D. thesis for the University of Aberdeen), 236.

3. The competing taxonomies in English law
(a) The taxonomies of Birks and Burrows

Since Peter Birks has suggested that Scots law should 'receive' his taxonomy, it might be prudent to check whether it is generally accepted in English law. Poles apart is Jack Beatson's chapter in Chitty (27th edition, 1994),[183] which, following John Munkman,[184] adopts a splendidly unreconstructed, old-fashioned taxonomy described modestly as 'a pragmatic classification... with some attempt to follow a logical pattern'.[185] Its four categories (restitution, reimbursement, liability to account to the plaintiff, and recompense) are mainly remedy-based and since it therefore resembles the old remedy-based classification which the Court of Session has just rejected,[186] it could not be transplanted to Scots law. It was criticised by Goff and Jones as unrevealing and harmful.[187] Goff and Jones (5th edition, 1998) adopt at the top level a tripartite classification depending on which party caused the enrichment, namely: (a) the act of the plaintiff; (b) the act of a third party for which the defendant must account to the plaintiff; and (c) the defendant's wrongful act.[188] There is some similarity with the Wilburg/von Caemmerer taxonomy.[189] This too differs from Birks's taxonomy.

Birks proposes a five-tiered taxonomy. The facts which trigger claims are in the first place divided into two broad categories, namely 'A. Enrichment of D (the defendant) by subtraction from P (the plaintiff)' and 'B. Enrichment of D by wrongdoing to P'. Given subtraction from P's patrimony or wrongdoing, a *prima facie* cause of action is perfected by adding an 'unjust factor'. The 'map' of the unjust factors grounding restitution, as explained by Birks in 1985,[190] may be presented in tabular form, following his own numbers and letters (Table 23.4). There is a qualification: at any level there must be added a residual category of 'other possible cases'.

Burrows's textbook (1993), which uses much of the distinctive terminology coined by Birks, follows Birks in adopting as its primary division the

---

[183] J. Beatson, 'Restitution' in: A. G. Guest *et al.* (eds.), *Chitty on Contracts* (27th edn, 1994), chap. 29.
[184] J. Munkman, *The Law of Quasi-contracts* (1950).   [185] Beatson, 'Restitution', § 20-015.
[186] *Shilliday v. Smith* 1998 SC 725; 684–6, above.
[187] Goff and Jones, *Law of Restitution*.   [188] *Ibid.* 73–5.
[189] Compare (a) with the *Leistungskondiktion* and (c) with the *Eingriffskondiktion*. The resemblance has been recognised by German authors: see Zimmermann, 'Unjustified Enrichment', 415, n. 77.
[190] In Birks, 'View of the Scots Law', 65–7. Birks now argues that category B (Enrichment of D by wrongdoing to P) is part of the law of wrongs not unjust enrichment: see P. Birks, 'Misnomer', in: Cornish *et al.*, *Restitution*, 1.

Table 23.4. *Birks's taxonomy*

A. Enrichment of D by subtraction from P

A.1 *Non-voluntariness*
    A.1.1 vitiation
        A.1.1.1: *ignorance*: P wholly unaware that D acquiring
        A.1.1.2: *mistake*:
            A.1.1.2.1: spontaneous mistake
            A.1.1.2.2: induced mistake.
        A.1.1.3: *compulsion*:
            A.1.1.3.1: coercion (i.e. duress or actual undue influence);
            A.1.1.3.2: compulsion by legal process;
            A.1.1.3.3: moral compulsion (i.e. arising from others' need);
            A.1.1.3.4: circumstantial compulsion.
        A.1.1.4: *inequality* (i.e. P was, in circumstances, not up to making a judgment as to the transfer to D);
            A.1.1.4.1: relational (i.e. rising from the nature of the relation between P and D);
            A.1.1.4.2: transactional (i.e. arising from the nature of the transaction in question);
            A.1.1.4.3: personal (i.e. arising from personal defect or disadvantage in P).
    A.1.2 Qualification
        A.1.2.1: specification of a requirement for contractual reciprocation;
        A.1.2.2: specification of a condition other than contractual reciprocation.

A.2 *Free acceptance*, i.e. D chose to accept value in the knowledge that it was not being offered gratuitously.

A.3 *A policy motivation requiring restitution to be made.*

B. Enrichment of D by wrongdoing to P

B.1 Deliberate exploitation of wrongdoing for profit;

B.2 An anti-enrichment policy behind the wrong itself;

B.3 A prophylactic determination to apply a sanction to a wrong even before, or without asking whether, it has damaged victim.

---

distinction between (A) 'unjust enrichment by subtraction' and (B) 'unjust enrichment by wrongdoing'. Burrows subdivides 'unjust enrichment by subtraction' into a series (which is not necessarily closed) of ten (formerly eleven) types of 'autonomous unjust factor' (or specific ground), each having a chapter to itself:[191]

1. Mistake
2. Ignorance
3. Duress
4. Exploitation
5. Legal compulsion
6. Necessity
7. Failure of consideration
8. Incapacity
9. Illegality
10. Ultra vires fiscal demands
[11. Retention of property.]

The last-mentioned category is now omitted as truly part of property law. For the undernoted reasons Burrows rejects the intermediate tiers of Birks's taxonomy[192] and, unlike Birks, continues to regard enrichment by wrongdoing as part of unjust enrichment.[193]

(b) Criticism of these taxonomies

The English system of unjust factors is not the product of a considered commitment at any point in time. Its undue complexity reflects its haphazard historical development. In order to provide a remedy redressing a transfer without legal ground, as many as eleven unjust factors have already been created and there are more to come. There are too many debatable borders and not enough settled territory. This compares with the small number of tests for redressing enrichment by transfer without legal ground in civil-law systems. One can understand that systematisation of the unjust factors is a stage through which English law must pass. Less intelligible is the fact that radical simplification has not, or not yet, been recognised as a desirable ultimate aim by English jurists. The English system can only progress by adding new unjust factors to the existing canon incrementally or by expanding the scope of the existing factors. This increases the fragmentation. Birks's superstructure may explain, but it scarcely simplifies, the law on unjust factors. It may actually divert attention away from proper reform by appearing to modernise a

---

[191] Burrows, *Law of Restitution*, chaps. 3–13; modified by Burrows and McKendrick, *Cases and Materials*, 724

[192] Burrows, *Law of Restitution*, 21, 22. The category of 'factors negativing voluntariness' (A.1), and its offshoots (A.1.1 and A.1.2) are rejected, as is 'policy-motivated restitution' (A.3).

[193] A. S. Burrows, 'Quadrating Restitution and Unjust Enrichment: A Matter of Principle', [2000] *Restitution LR* 257.

system which in substance remains fundamentally flawed. Moreover, by providing a framework for the proliferation of new unjust factors, it could make the basic problem worse.

4. 'Unjustified unless': general enrichment obligation with no primary division of grounds (Clive's draft code)

(a) A new approach

A bold and radical alternative has been suggested by Eric Clive, in his *Draft Rules on Unjustified Enrichment and Commentary*.[194] He regards the distinction between repetition of the undue and the redress of unjustified enrichment (or enrichment without cause) as historical rather than functional. He rejects two functional reasons for the distinction,[195] and also the Wilburg/von Caemmerer taxonomy and the English primary division between enrichment by wrongdoing and by subtraction.[196] In his view, since there are elements common to all types of unjustified enrichment and enrichment by transfer or by subtraction is just one type, it is undesirable to use the distinction in the primary division.

In Clive's view the best solution is to have no primary division but to begin the code provisions with a general obligation to redress unjustified enrichment. His rules have a simple structure: one general principle (elegantly drafted)[197] whose three elements – enrichment, at the expense of, unjustified – are then explained, followed by ancillary rules on the measure of recovery, three-party situations, judicial power to modify awards, defences and bars to proceedings, scope and interpretation.[198] The basic principle of Clive's rules is that an enrichment at the expense of another is 'unjustified unless' it is justified either by a legal cause (such as a statute or a contract) or by a consideration of public policy (for example, that the claimant conferred the benefit 'incidentally', or knowingly took the risk that the enriched would not pay for it).[199]

---

[194] See n. 73, above. An abbreviated and simplified version of the rules is set out in E. Clive, 'Restitution and Unjustified Enrichment', in: A. Hartkamp *et al.* (eds.), *Towards a European Civil Code* (2nd edn, 1998), Appendix to chap. 25, 393-4.

[195] First, that the measure of recovery has to be different in the two cases, and second, that it is convenient to deal separately with repetition of the undue and the redress of unjustified enrichment.

[196] See 686-90, above.

[197] *Draft Rules*, rule 1: 'A person who has been enriched at the expense of another person is bound, if the enrichment is unjustified, to redress the enrichment.'

[198] Rule 4 contains the basic principle that an enrichment is unjustified (i.e. recovery is allowed) unless it is justified by a statutorily defined legal cause (rule 5, subject to exceptions in rule 7) or public policy (rule 6). In other words recovery is allowed for all enrichments unless a justification specified in rules 5 to 7 excludes recovery.

[199] *Draft Rules*, comment on rule 4, 44.

Clive outlines four advantages of his 'unjustified unless' approach.

(i) It avoids the risk of confining the general principle more than is necessary.
(ii) It avoids some problems of definition which arise when specific grounds for recovery are set out.[200]
(iii) It avoids the danger of an unprincipled proliferation of specific grounds as more and more cases are discovered where redress for unjustified enrichment would be appropriate.
(iv) It makes for easier drafting.

One difficulty with an 'unjustified if' approach is that it is still necessary to provide for the possibility that an enrichment unjustified because of a specific ground may none the less be justified by a legal cause. The specific ground may be necessary but may not be sufficient to found a claim for unjustified enrichment.[201] A general principle that an enrichment at another's expense is 'unjustified unless' justified by a 'legal cause' is that, for this purpose, the concept of 'legal cause' is too narrow. It would allow redress in circumstances where the enriched person should keep his enrichment.[202] Clive meets this objection head on by proposing a rule[203] providing that an enrichment is justified in certain broadly defined classes of case where the enriched person cannot point to any specific *legal cause* justifying his retention of the enrichment, such as a valid contract, but where there is some good reason of *public policy* for not treating the enrichment as unjustified.

---

[200] For example, if error is a ground for recovery of a payment or transfer, what is meant by error? If compulsion is a ground for recovery, what is meant by compulsion?

[201] For example, the fact that I pay in error, thinking that the payment is due under a contract when it is in fact not due under the contract, does not necessarily mean that the enriched person's enrichment is unjustified. He may be entitled to the payment anyway under a statute or court decree or even another contract which has superseded the one under which I thought I was paying. Similarly, the fact that I think I am improving my own property when I am in fact improving someone else's does not necessarily mean that the other person's enrichment is unjustified. I may be bound to effect the improvement anyway under a contract or statute. In short, an enrichment which is unjustified by a ground or factor is only *prima facie* unjustified and never necessarily absolutely unjustified.

[202] Zimmermann, 'A Road through the Enrichment Forest?', 11 (footnotes omitted): '[T]he enrichment may be due to the display of particular skill in (lawful) competition or to acquisitive or extinctive prescription. It can also be due to reflexive effects. Somebody builds a dam and the neighbours who have refused to participate in the expenses, also benefit from its construction. This benefit accrues to them without specific contractual or legal reason. Nevertheless they are not unjustifiedly enriched, a claim for unjustified enrichment does not lie.'

[203] Rule 6.

(b) Assessment of 'unjustified unless' approach

Some features of the 'unjustified unless' approach may stand in the way of its acceptance. First, control of the situations where recovery is allowed is not left to the courts' gradual and incremental expansion of specific 'grounds' of redress but rather to judicial interpretation of certain of the vaguer enrichment-justifications denying redress.[204] Secondly, the code makes a large shift from emphasis on non-recovery to emphasis on recovery, not dissimilar to the shift in negligence once effected by *Anns v. Merton London Borough Council*[205] but later departed from. It creates a general enrichment obligation (or action) which has to be disapplied (or barred) in certain cases. Judges often prefer that the extension of enrichment obligations to new cases should be incremental. Thirdly, since the 'unjustified unless' approach is novel, the changes in the scope of recovery effected by the code would not be easily measured. By contrast, the test of failure of purpose in an enrichment-by-transfer claim is sufficiently broad and has been well tried and tested in civil-law systems. Fourthly, the disadvantage of a general ground of redress is that difficult problems of definition can arise in relation to the categories of 'legal cause' and more especially 'public policy'.[206] Fifthly, in a competitive capitalist society, it may be that (as at present) enrichment at another's expense should remain where it arises unless the case for its reversal is established rather than (as under Clive's code) that it should be redressible unless the enriched party can justify its retention. In short, Clive's rules have been rightly called 'superb',[207] but it is by no means clear whether they will win acceptance.

VII. The internal taxonomy continued: the modern civilian approach and Scots law

1. A model of the modern civilian approach

In Scots law, recent decisions have swept away the old primary division of the three Rs[208] and with it classification by the type of benefit received or by the content of the obligation.[209] What precisely will replace it is unclear. Assuming that the courts will persevere with an 'unjustified if' approach, this section argues that the modern civilian version of that approach based

---

[204] E.g. the novel and original concept of 'lawful endeavour' in rule 6(a) and the residual 'some other cause' in rule 6(g).
[205] [1978] AC 728 (HL).   [206] Mentioned in rules 5 and 6 respectively.
[207] Burrows, 'Restitution', 115.   [208] See 684-6, above.   [209] Table 23.2, above.

Table 23.5. *The modern civilian approach (Wilburg/von Caemmerer taxonomy)*

First level (modes of acquiring enrichment)
1. Transfer (intentional and purpose-oriented act of payment, conveyance or performance; *dare* or *facere*).
2. No transfer
    2.1 Interference with patrimonial rights
    2.2 Payment of another's debt
    2.3 Bona fide possessor's improvements.

Second level (types of transfer, classified by their purpose)
   1.1 To implement an existing or future obligation (*solvendi causa*) *condictiones indebiti; ob causam finitam; ob turpem vel iniustam causam; sine causa (specialis)*
   1.2 To encourage the transferee to act in a certain way (*ob rem*) *condictio causa data causa non secuta*
   1.3 To impose an obligation on the transferee (*obligandi causa*)
   1.4 to make a gift (*donandi causa*)
   1.5 By way of yielding to improper compulsion or threat (*condictio ob turpem vel iniustam causam*).

---

on the Wilburg/von Caemmerer taxonomy should be followed in Scots law in preference to the unjust factors scheme of the English law as developed, for example, by Birks or Burrows. As Lord President Rodger pointed out,[210] Birks was right to warn against too facile an acceptance of Roman law terminology.[211] However, the relevant comparison is not with classical or Justinianic Roman law but with the modern civilian approach.[212] In theory a 'mixed' or compromise approach would also be possible in which the primary division at the top level (following Wilburg/von Caemmerer) would classify by mode of acquisition[213] and, within the category of 'transfer', there would be subsumed specific grounds of redress similar to the unsystematised innominate claims, *condictiones* and other forms of action received in Scots law or South African law[214] or the English system of unjust factors. But such a solution is not recommended since it would not solve the main problems of Scots law concerning enrichment by transfer.

---

[210] 'Roman Law in Practice'.   [211] 'View of the Scots Law'; 'Six Questions'.
[212] See e.g. Zimmermann, 'Unjustified Enrichment'; Evans-Jones and Hellwege, 'Some Observations'.
[213] i.e. transfer, interference, payment of another's debt, mistaken improvements of another's property.
[214] Visser, 'Unjustified Enrichment'; Eiselen and Pienaar, *Unjustified Enrichment*.

The Wilburg/von Caemmerer taxonomy, the German version of the modern civilian approach (see Table 23.5), may be taken to have two taxonomic levels.

2. Enrichment by transfer

(a) The definition of transfer

The first step in adopting the modern civilian approach would be the recognition of a category of enrichment obligations having the concept of 'transfer' or 'performance' (*Leistung*) as its unifying element. By 'transfer' is meant 'an intentional and purpose-oriented enlargement of another person's assets'.[215] Three advantages have been claimed for this concept.[216] In summary:

(i) '[I]t supplies a relatively simple and straightforward test as to whether an enrichment is unjustified.'[217]
(ii) It determines who are the proper parties to an obligation to redress unjustified enrichment. So it is said that it 'determines to whom restitution is due',[218] and that it defines 'who is enriched by the performance and should therefore be the right defendant'.[219] This is particularly important in the complex three-party cases.[220]
(iii) It synchronises the law of unjustified enrichment with the law of contract and other branches of the law of obligations.[221]

The definition of 'transfer' includes a definition of what amounts to an enrichment of the transferee. Since a claim to redress enrichment by transfer or performance 'tries to undo a performance which was actually not due, it is only logically consistent that anything which can be the object of an obligation can amount to an enrichment'.[222] So the notion of transfer widens the scope of enrichment beyond economic benefits. The recipient, however, is protected from liability for unwanted or valueless 'benefits' by the rules on measuring enrichment, subjective devaluation, tracing and change of position.[223]

---

[215] Markesinis, Lorenz and Dannemann, *Law of Contracts*, 720; Zimmermann, 'Unjustified Enrichment', 405, n. 9.
[216] Zimmermann, 'Unjustified Enrichment', 406. See also Zimmermann and Du Plessis, 'Basic Features', 25–7.
[217] 'Unjustified Enrichment', 406.
[218] *Ibid.*   [219] Markesinis, Lorenz and Dannemann, *Law of Contracts*, 722.
[220] See Section VIII below.   [221] Zimmermann, 'Unjustified Enrichment', 406.
[222] Markesinis, Lorenz and Danemann, *Law of Contracts*, 720.   [223] *Ibid.* 722.

(b) Transfer to implement a non-existent obligation

Detlef König's draft rules for revising the BGB[224] provide:

A person who has transferred something to another in order to fulfil an existing or future obligation can reclaim what he has transferred from the putative creditor (the recipient) a) if the obligation does not exist, does not come into existence, or later on ceases to exist or b) if the right to claim is barred by a defence on account of which enforceability is excluded permanently.[225]

This category of transfer is the lineal descendant of the *condictio indebiti*, the *condictio ob turpem vel iniustam causam*, the *condictio ob causam finitam* and the *condictio sine causa (specialis)*. Paragraph a) neatly captures the essence of these *condictiones*. In the *ius commune* when the restricted Roman contracts law was replaced by the idea that 'every paction produceth action'[226] the scope of the *condictio indebiti* expanded while the scope of the *condictio ob turpem vel iniustam causam*, the *condictio ob causam finitam* and the *condictio sine causa (specialis)* contracted.[227]

Until recently it was generally assumed that proof of error was an essential requirement of the *condictio indebiti*. In Gloag and Henderson's *Introduction to the Law of Scotland* (1994), all the cases cited under *condictio indebiti* are cases of error.[228] This narrow focus is, however, made much less damaging than it otherwise would have been by the acceptance of the *condictio ob turpem vel iniustam causam* and the *condictio sine causa (specialis)*.[229] Indeed it is difficult to see how the error of law rule and the requirement of inexcusable error could have been part of Scots law if error had not been a ground of repetition or restitution. The *Morgan Guaranty* case swept away these two rules but may have left 'error' as a requirement at least for the meantime.[230] In recent years, Robin Evans-Jones and others have argued indomitably that the *condictio indebiti* has in Scots law the same objective character and wide role as in German law and other

---

[224] D. König, 'Ungerechtfertigte Bereicherung', in: Bundesminister der Justiz (ed.), *Gutachten und Vorschläge zur Überarbeitung des Schuldrechts* (1981), vol. II, 1519 ff. These rules were prepared by the late Professor Detlef König at the request of the Federal German Ministry of Justice; translation in Zimmermann, 'Unjustified Enrichment', 425–9.

[225] Translation in Zimmermann, 'Unjustified Enrichment', 425, 426.

[226] Stair, *Institutions*, Book I, Title 10, 7.   [227] See e.g. Zimmermann, *Law of Obligations*, 857 ff.

[228] Gloag and Henderson, *Law of Scotland*, §§ 29.4 and 29.10.

[229] *Ibid.*, §§ 29.6, 29.7, 29.11.

[230] *Morgan Guaranty Trust Co. of New York v. Lothian Regional Council* 1995 SC 151 at 165D-F per Lord President Hope. But cf. *Dollar Land (Cumbernauld) Ltd v. CIN Properties Ltd* 1998 SC (HL) 90 at 98H, I per Lord Hope: 'In general terms it may be said that the remedy [of recompense] is available where the enrichment lacks a legal ground to justify the retention of the benefit. In such circumstances it is held to be unjust.'

modern civilian systems.[231] There is an argument that in Scots law the *condictio indebiti* absorbed the *condictio ob turpem vel iniustam causam* and that the plea of *turpis vel iniusta causa* is now available only as a defence.[232] If the *condictio indebiti* were confined to error, this absorption would not be possible.

(c) The change from 'error' as ground to knowledge as defence

Restitution of a mistaken payment is governed in English law by the separate category of 'mistake',[233] which has reference to the payer's state of mind and is therefore subjective. In civil-law systems it is usually governed by the broader categories derived from the *condictio indebiti* – 'payment of the undue' in France and Italy and 'transfer without legal ground' in Germany – all of which lay down objective requirements. In Europe there is a trend towards a solution accepted in German law under which error as to the existence of a legal ground is not a specific ground of redress but knowledge of the absence of legal ground is a defence to an action.[234] Paolo Gallo states that this European 'tendency is to be encouraged' and that the reversal of the burden of proof solution 'seems to be the most efficient and rational one. In effect between a payor who tries to avoid a loss and a recipient who tries to hold on to an improper benefit, the former is to be preferred.'[235] In France and Italy the codes expressly require error only in cases of mistaken payment of another's debt[236] (where payment may discharge the debt) and not in normal two-party cases.[237] In Italy it is enough to prove the absence of a duty to pay.[238] In France the issue is debated but the requirement has been weakened and some leading authors affirm that in *la répétition de l'indu objectif* proof of error is

---

[231] R. Evans-Jones, 'Some Reflections on the *Condictio Indebiti* in a Mixed Legal System', (1994) 111 *SALJ* 759; also his 'From "Undue Transfer" to "Retention without a Legal Basis" (The *Condictio Indebiti* and the *Condictio ob Turpem vel Iniustam Causam*)', in: R. Evans-Jones (ed.), *The Civil Law Tradition in Scotland* (1995), 213. See also J. E. du Plessis and H. Wicke, '*Woolwich Equitable v. IRC* and the *Condictio Indebiti* in Scots Law', 1993 *SLT* (News) 303; R. Evans-Jones and P. Hellwege, 'Swaps, Error of Law and Unjustified Enrichment', (1995) 1 *Scottish Law and Practice Quarterly* 1.

[232] R. Evans-Jones and D. McKenzie, 'Towards a Profile of the *Condictio ob Turpem vel Injustam Causam* in Scots Law', [1994] *JR* 60; Evans-Jones, 'From "Undue Transfer"', 213, 243–6.

[233] Within the broader 'action for money had and received'.

[234] § 814 BGB; Markesinis, Lorenz and Dannemann, *Law of Contracts*, 736–8.

[235] Gallo, 'Unjust Enrichment', 444.   [236] *Code civil*, art. 1377; *Codice civile*, art. 2036.

[237] *Code civil*, art. 1376; *Codice civile*, art. 2033.

[238] Gallo, 'Unjust Enrichment', 443. Strict formalities are required to establish donation so error is not required to disprove donation.

not required.[239] The new Dutch code has dropped the requirement[240] and the claim is not even barred by proof of the transferor's knowledge at the time of transfer.[241] Even in England, proof of error is no longer required at common law to recover overpaid tax.[242] Moreover, the recent abrogation of the mistake of law rule has raised the question whether 'restitution for mistake of law may not, after all, be restitution for vitiated intention but a disguised form of restitution for invalidity of the contract'.[243] In Europe, the requirement of error is now seen as 'an outdated historical quirk'.[244]

Error is the main key to the future of Scots enrichment law. Realising this, Evans-Jones and others[245] have argued cogently that in Scots law liability under the *condictio indebiti* does and should depend on an objective test of transfer (or retention) without legal ground;[246] that it does not and should not require affirmative proof of error;[247] but that proof of the transferor's knowledge that the transfer was undue is a defence. These arguments are of very great importance. Whatever the present law may be, unless the Scottish courts can effect a clear change from 'error as a ground' to 'knowledge as a defence to a claim based on transfer without legal ground', Scots law is likely to assimilate error to the English 'mistake' and end up replicating the English system of unjust factors. Some might seek to justify such a retrograde development on the basis of cross-border legal unionism but it certainly could not be justified on the basis of legal

---

[239] B. Starck, H. Roland and L. Boyer, *Droit Civil, Obligations* (2nd edn, 1986), vol. II, n. 2064: 'L'obligation de restitution s'explique par l'idée de l'absence de cause'; H. Mazeaud, L. Mazeaud, J. Mazeaud and F. Chabas, *Leçons de Droit Civil*, tome II, premier volume, *Obligations théorie générale* (8th edn, 1991), n. 658; I. Defrénois-Souleau, 'La répétition de l'indu objectif', (1989) 88 *Revue trimestrielle de droit civil* 243.

[240] New Dutch Civil Code, art. 6:203 (which took effect in 1992). The repealed code of 1838 art. 1395 had required error but this had been eroded by the Hoge Raad: see E. Schrage, 'Netherlands', [1994] *Restitution LR* 208, 209, 210.

[241] Zimmermann, 'Unjustified Enrichment', 410, 411.

[242] *Woolwich Equitable Building Society v. IRC* [1993] AC 70 (HL).

[243] R. Zimmermann and S. Meier, 'Judicial Development of the Law, *Error Iuris*, and the Law of Unjustified Enrichment – A View from Germany', (1999) 115 *LQR* 556 at 564 commenting on *Kleinwort Benson Ltd v. Lincoln City Council* [1999] 2 AC 349 and suggesting that that case may have achieved 'the (re-)introduction of the *condictio indebiti* through the back door of mistake of law'.

[244] Zimmermann, 'Unjustified Enrichment', 410.   [245] See n. 232, above.

[246] Or failure to implement an obligation.

[247] Evans-Jones, 'From "Undue Transfer"', 231 cites *Carrick v. Carse* (1778) Mor 2931 for the proposition (at 2933) that 'when payment is made *sine causa*, it will be presumed to have proceeded from error, and not donation, unless the contrary can be proved'. Cf. *Miller v. Campbell* 1991 GWD 26-1477 (Extra Division) (payer pursuer must aver and prove error).

science. No doubt legal unionism should be given effect in many areas of Scots law, but this is not one of them.

(d) Transfer to encourage the transferee to act in an agreed way
The rump of the *condictio causa data causa non secuta* left after its emasculation by the expansion of European contract law[248] is captured in this provision of the König draft rules:

A person who transfers something to another, not in order to fulfil an obligation, but with the intention, noted by the latter, to induce him to act in a certain way, may reclaim the benefit if that action does not in fact take place.[249]

Evans-Jones and others argue that the scope of the Scottish version of the *condictio causa data causa non secuta* ought to be, and is, similarly circumscribed[250] except for its application to frustration of contract.[251]

(e) Transfer to impose obligation or make donation
What if a transfer is made not to implement an obligation but either to impose an obligation (*obligandi causa*) or to make a valid donation (*donandi causa*) and fails to achieve its object?[252] In Roman law innominate *condictiones* lay to redress such a transfer.[253] These unusual *condictiones* were not mentioned by the Scottish Institutional writers, perhaps because they did not have their own Digest title.[254] Moreover, in Scots law a loan to an *incapax* (for example, a pupil child) was redressible not by a *condictio obligandi causa* but by an action of recompense against the *incapax* based

---

[248] See e.g. Zimmermann, *Law of Obligations*, 861; Zimmermann, 'Unjustified Enrichment', 407, 408.

[249] Zimmermann, 'Unjustified Enrichment', 426, § 1.2(1). See e.g. *Grieve v. Morrison* 1993 SLT 852; *Shilliday v. Smith* 1998 SC 725.

[250] R. Evans-Jones, 'Unjust Enrichment, Contract and the Third Reception of Roman Law in Scotland', (1993) 109 *LQR* 663; J. A. Dieckmann and R. Evans-Jones, 'The Dark Side of *Connelly v. Simpson*', [1995] *JR* 90; G. D. MacCormack, 'The *Condictio Causa Data Causa Non Secuta*', in: R. Evans-Jones (ed.), *The Civil Law Tradition in Scotland* (1995), 253; R. Evans-Jones, 'The Claim to Recover what was Transferred for a Lawful Purpose outwith Contract (*Condictio Causa Data Causa Non Secuta*)', [1997] *Acta Juridica* 139 reprinted in: D. Visser (ed.), *The Limits of the Law of Obligations* (1997), 139.

[251] *Cantiere San Rocco SA v. Clyde Shipbuilding & Engineering Co.* 1923 SC (HL) 105.

[252] Evans-Jones, 'From "Undue Transfer"', 235. For an example of what in effect was a transfer *obligandi causa* see *ELCAP v. Milne's Executor* 1998 SLT 58 (OH) at 62E (company provided community-care service to *incapax* with the intention, known to his curator, to charge for it; held relevant case of recompense).

[253] Iul. D. 12, 1, 19, 1. An example is a loan to an *incapax*.

[254] Evans-Jones, 'From "Undue Transfer"', 235.

on the *actio in quantum locupletior factus est*.[255] Lord President Rodger, however, has recently shown that the *actio* was only appropriate to the case of the 'limping contract' (*negotium claudicans*) – that is, a contract between a party with full capacity and an *incapax* binding the former but not the latter.[256] Evans-Jones remarks that '[n]othing is known in modern [Scots] law of the classifications *obligandi* and *donandi causa*. It is only when we return to early case law that we find that the gift which fails is treated as recoverable on the ground that it is held without a legal basis.'[257]

(f) Transfer yielding to improper compulsion or threat

It is clear that persons induced to make a transfer by the pressure of improper compulsion or threat do so to relieve the pressure rather than to satisfy an obligation. This is recognised in the König draft:

> A person who transfers something to another, not in order to fulfil an obligation, but on account of compulsion or threat, may reclaim the benefit, unless the recipient proves that he had a right to the benefit.[258]

Du Plessis contends that 'within the context of the Scots law of unjustified enrichment, it is undesirable to regard compulsion as an "unjust factor" or ground for recovery'.[259] He proposes instead 'that the recoverability of compelled transfers should rather be determined by asking whether they are retained without a legal ground. If undue, the transfer in principle should be recoverable.'[260] Doubting the last limb of the König rule, Du

---

[255] The *actio* was extended to a loan by a bank to a local authority borrowing ultra vires in *Magistrates of Stonehaven v. Kincardineshire CC* 1939 SC 760; N. R. Whitty, 'Ultra Vires Swap Contracts and Unjustified Enrichment', 1994 *SLT* (News) 33.

[256] A. Rodger, 'Recovering Payments under Void Contracts in Scots Law', in: W. Swadling and G. Jones (eds.), *The Search for Principle: Essays in Honour of Lord Goff of Chieveley* (2000), 1. In a limping contract, since the pupil *incapax* had no obligation to repay sums paid under the contract, a *condictio indebiti* or *condictio sine causa* could not lie against him. Instead the pupil was liable in recompense to the extent of his enrichment under the *actio*. In Scotland limping contracts with pupils were abolished by the Age of Legal Capacity (Scotland) Act 1991.

[257] Evans-Jones, 'From "Undue Transfer"', 237.

[258] Zimmermann, 'Unjustified Enrichment', 426, § 1.3.

[259] Du Plessis, *Compulsion and Restitution*, 236. Du Plessis shows that the Scots law on redress of enrichment arising from compulsion, though underdeveloped, is sufficiently rich in principle to cover a wide range of cases of compulsion.

[260] *Ibid*. He continues: 'Recovery should only be excluded if, amongst others, the transferor acted in a way which indicated that the recipient could keep the transfer, or (in the case of an illegal or immoral transfer) if both parties were tainted by turpitude. Compulsion then plays the limited role of being but one consideration which indicates that these rules should not apply. If due, the transfer in principle should not be recoverable. Recovery should only be allowed if the compulsion was so serious that the transfer cannot be regarded as a valid act of fulfilment.'

Plessis questions whether due transfers should never be recoverable on grounds of improper compulsion.[261]

(g) Synchronising enrichment law with contract law

'The main work of quasi-contract', said Dawson, 'is done in the field of express contract, awarding value restitution of performances rendered in actual or supposed conformity with contractual obligations'.[262] In German law, this central task of synchronisation with contract law is performed by the concept of enrichment by transfer (*Leistung*) with far greater economy than is attained by the English unjust factors. The difference is very striking as comparative lawyers emphasise. So Markesinis, Lorenz and Dannemann remark:

> The general *Leistungskondiktion* simply leaves it to other areas of the law (and in particular to contract law) to decide whether or not the enrichment is unjustified. By this *Leistungskondiktion*, German law has therefore covered most of what Professor Birks [*Introduction*, 21] calls 'unjust factors' in English law, namely mistake, deceit, duress, undue influence, illegality, acting ultra vires, as well as many cases of legal compulsion and incapacity. If the law of contract tells us that the underlying contract was void for any of the above list of reasons, there is no *causa*, and the enrichment must be given up.[263]

English law does not lay down general rules governing restitution of benefits conferred under a contract which is void *ab initio*[264] or is voidable[265] and has been avoided, or has been discharged through frustration. So, for example, an obligation void *ab initio* is treated as non-existent. But the invalidity or non-existence is not per se a ground of redress of unjustified enrichment: the claimant has to establish an unjust factor.[266] So the rules on restitution differ depending on the particular defect which is the cause of the invalidity. Konrad Zweigert and Hein Kötz observe that this adaptability, which enables the common law to regulate the effects of invalidity in accordance with the relevant interests, is 'purchased at the price of a very considerable casuistic diversity which makes it bewildering

---

[261] See Du Plessis, above, 213ff.   [262] Dawson, *Unjust Enrichment*, 23.
[263] Markesinis, Lorenz and Dannemann, *Law of Contracts*, 718.
[264] E.g. by reason of operative mistake, incapacity, illegality or statute (e.g. the Gaming Act 1845).
[265] E.g. for fraud, or duress. See D. Friedmann, 'Valid, Voidable, Qualified, and Non-Existing Obligations: An Alternative Perspective on the Law of Restitution', in: A. Burrows (ed.), *Essays on the Law of Restitution* (1991), 247.
[266] E.g. mistake (P believed the void contract to be valid): *Rover International Ltd v. Cannon Films Sales Ltd* [1989] 1 WLR 912 (CA). The fact that the benefit was requested by the recipient defendant may be a ground of redress: *British Steel Corporation v. Cleveland Bridge and Engineering Co. Ltd* [1984] 1 All ER 504.

to the Continental observer, since it is almost impossible to state any general rules at all'.[267]

In Scots law (and South African law) in the case, for example, of a void contract, Hector MacQueen points out that 'there is generally no need to point to "unjust factors" requiring the enrichment to be reversed... [I]t is usually enough that a transfer was made under a contract which was void. The legal cause of the transaction does not exist and retention of enrichment is ipso facto unjustified.'[268] This view may be too optimistic since the *Morgan Guaranty* case suggests that proof of error is necessary in repetition of sums paid under a contract void for incapacity or ultra vires.[269] There are debates on what enrichment remedy lies in particular cases, for example in the case of illegal contracts,[270] underlining 'the need for Scots law to move forward from its traditional distinctions between different forms of action and concentrate instead upon the identification and application of general principles of unjustified enrichment'.[271] The general principle of transfer without legal ground should satisfy that need. Likewise Clive's rules require mutual restitution, if either party claims it, under an executed void contract,[272] unless one of the defences or bars applies. Enrichment law should not do the same work as contract law all over again. As Clive explained, 'the law on unjustified enrichment assumes that if a contract is void on a substantive ground[273] there is a good reason for this. It just picks up the pieces.'[274]

There are, however, qualifications. The application of enrichment law to benefits conferred under a void contract should be so restricted as to ensure that it does not infringe the policy underlying the rule invalidating the contract.[275] So, after all, enrichment law cannot ignore the reasons

---

[267] Zweigert and Kötz, *Introduction*, 556, 557. See also Dawson, *Unjust Enrichment*, 113 ff.; Gallo, 'Unjust Enrichment', 445–8; cf. Zimmermann, 'Unjustified Enrichment', 416.
[268] MacQueen, 'A Scots Perspective', 186, 187.
[269] *Morgan Guaranty Trust Co. of New York v. Lothian Regional Council* 1995 SC 151: see nn. 231 and 232, above.
[270] The candidates being the *condictio indebiti*, the *condictio ob turpem vel iniustam causam* and recompense: see, e.g., Evans-Jones and McKenzie, 'Towards a Profile'; Gloag and Henderson, *Law of Scotland*, §§ 29.6, 29.15.
[271] MacQueen, 'A Scots Perspective', 187, 188.   [272] *Draft Rules*, rule 2(3).
[273] There is a special rule for merely formal invalidity in rule 6(1) (d). In any event, in the case of *executed* contracts, any formal invalidity would often have been cured by *rei interventus*.
[274] Clive, 'A Code for Scotland?' He continues: 'It does mean that the legislature has to be careful in using the sanction of nullity, but that is in itself a good thing'.
[275] MacQueen, 'A Scots Perspective', 187: König rules, rule 1.1(2)(d): 'Restitution is excluded... insofar as the restitution of what was transferred to fulfil an invalid contract would frustrate the purpose of the unvalidating rule': see Zimmermann, 'Unjustified Enrichment', 427.

for invalidity of contracts. Moreover, Markesinis, Lorenz and Dannemann remark that the *Leistungskondiktion* only dovetails with German contract law because the latter provides several mechanisms enabling it to do so, and that since English law would find it difficult to provide these mechanisms, the English courts are justified in rejecting 'restitution for no consideration' following performance of a void contract.[276] Scots law, by contrast, would not have the same difficulty.

(h) Defences to enrichment by transfer claim
In striking the balance between the policy against unjustified enrichment and the policy of protecting the security of receipts, defences – for example, 'change of position', or loss of enrichment – as well as grounds of redress have to be weighed.[277] If all undue transfers without legal ground were to become *prima facie* recoverable, defences would assume much greater importance. The wide ground of recovery in German law is balanced by a wide defence of loss of enrichment.[278] This has been criticised as unduly discriminating against claimants.[279] By contrast English law provides multiple, closely defined grounds of recovery and only recognised a general defence of change of position in 1991.[280] Its incidents have yet to be clarified by case law.[281] Scots law recognised a general defence of change of position in the *condictio indebiti* centuries ago[282] but it seems to be rarely invoked and also requires clarification. The defence of

---

[276] Five are identified at *ibid.*, 726, 727: (i) gratuitous contracts; (ii) contracts which are invalid through a defect in form but which attain validity upon performance so that though future performance cannot be required, an executed performance cannot be claimed back; (iii) gaming, betting or marriage-broking contracts which are unenforceable but performance cannot be claimed back; (iv) abstract acknowledgements of debt; and (v) compromises which carry their own *causa*.

[277] For a comparison of the Roman, Roman-Dutch, German and English law approaches to erased enrichment, see D. P. Visser, 'Responsibility to Return Lost Enrichment', [1992] *Acta Juridica* 175.

[278] § 812(1), second and third sentences, BGB; Visser, 'Responsibility to Return', 175: 'essentially, that as long as the enrichment-debtor is bona fide, the recipient can plead loss of enrichment'.

[279] E.g. Visser, 'Responsibility to Return', 187; J. P. Dawson, 'Erasable Enrichment in German Law', (1981) 61 *Boston University LR* 271, 272; Zimmermann, *Law of Obligations*, 898.

[280] *Lipkin Gorman (a Firm) v. Karpnale Ltd* [1991] 2 AC 548 (HL) at 580 *per* Lord Goff: '[T]he defence is available to a person whose position has so changed that it would be inequitable to require him to make restitution, or alternatively to make restitution in full.'

[281] See Goff and Jones, *Law of Restitution*, 739–45; Burrows, *Law of Restitution*, 421–31.

[282] Scottish Law Commission, Discussion Paper No. 95, vol. II, §§ 2.63–2.65. The defender must reasonably believe the receipt to be his and, acting on that belief, so alter his position as to make repetition unjust: *Credit Lyonnais v. George Stevenson and Co. Ltd* (1901) 9 SLT 93.

'submission to an honest claim' is not part of Scots law. Indeed it is difficult to understand why an unfounded claim for an undue debt should found a defence to an action of repetition by the unjustifiably impoverished payer. It should be treated as a factor favouring repetition rather than a factor negating it. The defence of *res judicata* is much narrower in Scots law than in English law.

It might be thought that the relatively narrow definition of the English unjust factors emphasises the policy of protecting the security of receipts more than a general enrichment by transfer claim. However, mistake in English law does not require to be by the payer as to liability; it suffices to show that the mistake caused the payment in the sense that but for the mistake the claimant would not have made the payment.[283] So the English unjust factors are in some respects wider than the German concept of transfer without legal ground. But generally they seem narrower than that concept. The policy of security of receipts may be invoked by some English lawyers to justify the non-recovery of some common types of undue transfers, such as payments under protest and payments under doubt as to the payer's liability.[284] In the latter case, for example, the argument would be that doubt is not compatible with the existence of mistake and that the payer should satisfy himself that he is liable before making a payment lest it raise false expectations in the payee. That is a possible approach. To my mind, however, it is too restrictive for it gives insufficient weight to the principle against unjustified enrichment. Narrowly defined unjust factors have the effect that cases where recovery should be allowed may fall between them.[285] I agree with those who argue that an undue payment made without legal ground, including payments under doubt or protest, should normally be *prima facie* recoverable and that the protection of the security of receipts is better achieved by the defence of change of position and other defences (such as the payer's knowledge that

---

[283] *Barclays Bank Ltd v. W. J. Simms Son & Cooke (Southern) Ltd* [1980] QB 677; S. Meier, 'Mistaken Payments in Three-party Situations: A German View of English Law', (1999) 58 *CLJ* 567, 574, 575; see also S. Meier in her contribution to this volume. See also *Nurdin & Peacock plc v. D. B. Ramsden & Co. Ltd* [1999] 1 WLR 1249 (in addition to mistake being 'but for' cause of payment, it must relate directly and closely to the payment and the relationship between payer and payee) criticised by G. Virgo, 'Recent Developments in Restitution of Mistaken Payments', (1999) 58 *CLJ* 478: '[T]he case for extending the test of mistake beyond liability mistakes is still unproven.'
[284] *Twyford v. Manchester Corporation* [1946] Ch 236 (payment under protest); *Maskell v. Horner* [1915] 3 KB 106 (CA) (payment in doubt as to liability); England, 'Restitution of Benefits', §§ 12–14.
[285] E.g. *CTN Cash and Carry v. Gallaher Ltd* [1994] 4 All ER 714 (CA); *Slater v. Burnley Corporation* (1888) 59 LT 636.

the payment was undue) rather than by the narrow definition of unjust factors.

3. Enrichment by act of the enriched person encroaching on patrimonial rights

(a) General

In connection with the boundary between enrichment law and delict, reference was made above[286] to the important distinction between enrichment by the claimant's transfer and enrichment by the enriched party's own act. In French and Italian law, still reflecting the thinking of Charles Aubry and Charles-Henri Rau,[287] there is no equivalent to the German *Eingriffskondiktion* or the English enrichment by wrongs: the enrichment must arise out of the claimant's loss and, under the doctrine of subsidiarity, a cause of action in delict excludes an enrichment remedy. The view that tort/delict and contract remedies suffice seems incorrect because there are situations where unjustified enrichment without mirror loss (for example, use of intellectual property) calls for redress. Gallo remarks that the different configuration of the enrichment remedy (dispensing with mirror loss and subsidiarity) explains its vitality in German and Anglo-American law.[288]

In Scots law the *condictio furtiva* was not received[289] and a general obligation arising from the enriched party's encroachment on the pursuer's patrimonial rights was not recognised by the Institutional writers[290] though it has to some extent been recognised by some modern secondary sources on recompense[291] and restitution.[292] Recent articles have begun to develop

---

[286] 679–80, above.
[287] C. Aubry and C. Rau, *Cours de droit civil francais* (4th edn, 1871), vol. IV, 725 (correlation between enrichment and loss); vol. IX, 355 (subsidiarity); cited by Gallo, 'Unjust Enrichment', 449, nn. 67 and 68.
[288] Gallo, 'Unjust Enrichment', 449.
[289] Bankton, *Institutes*, Book I, Title 8, 33; *Dawson v. Stirton* (1863) 2 M 196 at 202 (pursuer's argument).
[290] See, e.g., Bell, *Principles*, § 538, defining recompense as a redress of gain 'by the lawful act of another'; quoted by A. J. M. Steven, 'Recompense for Interference in Scots Law', [1996] JR 51, 64.
[291] See Gloag, *Law of Contract*, 329; Lord Wark, 'Recompense', in: *Encyclopaedia of the Laws of Scotland* (1931), vol. XII, § 728; Gloag and Henderson, *Law of Scotland*, 484: 'Where the defender uses the pursuer's property in the knowledge that the pursuer does not intend to give him the use gratuitously, the defender is liable to pay a reasonable sum for it.'
[292] See, e.g., Gloag *Law of Contract*, who says that the rule 'rests...in some cases on the obligation of restitution' (at 329) and cites (at n. 9) *Monro v. Findlay* (1698) Mor 1768.

the category.[293] Andrew Steven has shown that the pattern of Scottish cases resembles the typology of the *Eingriffskondiktion*[294] though the law has developed piecemeal.[295] The owner of valuable property is entitled to recover from its possessor a reasonable payment in respect of the possession, and liability rests on unjustified enrichment (recompense) if the owner did not consent to the possession or implied contract if he did.[296] The measure of recovery is the same whether the possession is unauthorised or authorised on a non-gratuitous basis.[297] Despite the varied roots of the various categories, and the pockets of confusion, Steven concludes that 'there is much to be said for Scots law recognising the notion of an "interference action"'.[298] John Blackie identifies obstacles to its recognition but considers them surmountable.[299]

(b) Rationale underlying D's liability for unauthorised interference with P's patrimonial rights

It has been suggested[300] that von Caemmerer's rationale of the principles underlying the unauthorised interference category fitted and explained

---

[293] J. Blackie, 'Enrichment and Wrongs in Scots Law', [1992] *Acta Juridica* 23; Reid, 'Unjustified Enrichment', 171-3, 184-9; Steven, 'Recompense for Interference', 52; J. Blackie, 'Enrichment, Wrongs and Invasion of Rights in Scots Law', [1997] *Acta Juridica* 284, republished in: Visser, *Limits of the Law of Obligations*, 284. On other mixed systems, see B. Nicholas, 'The Louisiana Law of Unjustified Enrichment through the Act of the Person Enriched', (1991/2) 6/7 *Tulane Civil Law Forum* 3; D. H. van Zyl, 'Enrichment and Wrongs in South African Law', [1997] *Acta Juridica* 273 republished in: Visser, *Limits of the Law of Obligations*, 273.

[294] Steven, 'Recompense for Interference', 52.

[295] Steven, 'Recompense for Interference', 63. (1) D's unauthorised use of P's property; (2) D's profit on a bona fide sale of P's property; (3) consumption or destruction of P's moveable property in good faith; (4) D's act causing himself or a third party to gain title to the property of P via original acquisition; (5) D's misappropriation of P's funds; (6) miscellaneous cases. Steven points out that the first category (D's unauthorised use of P's property) has developed in unhealthy unison with the law on implied contract and a basic distinction between two types of cases has been ignored. One is where D without P's permission makes use of P's property: D actively interferes while P is passive, e.g. *Earl of Fife v. Wilson* (1867) 3 M 323; *Chisholm v. Alexander & Son* (1882) 19 SLR 835. In the other type of case, D actively allows P to possess or to make use of his (D's) property but does not intend the possession or use to be gratuitous: e.g. *Glen v. Roy* (1882) 10 R 239; *Mellor v. William Beardmore & Co.* 1927 SC 597; *Broun v. Mitchel* (1630) 1 BS 68. Steven argues (at 52-3) that P's claim of recompense here does not rest on enrichment by D's interference action but rather on enrichment by transfer.

[296] See *Shetland Islands Council v. BP Petroleum Development Co. Ltd* 1990 SLT 82 (OH); 1989 SCLR 48 (OH).

[297] Steven, 'Recompense for Interference', 56.   [298] *Ibid.*, 64.

[299] Blackie, 'Enrichment, Wrongs and Invasion of Rights'.

[300] Scottish Law Commission, Discussion Paper No. 95, vol. I, § 3.115.

the Scottish cases well. The right of property or ownership carries with it the exclusive rights of use, consumption and disposal (*ius utendi, fruendi, abutendi*). Any enrichment which any other person acquires by exercising these rights without the owner's authority is therefore, in principle, unjustified. It follows that that person must restore to the owner the value which he would have had to pay if he had bargained for the benefits in question. In such a case the defender's enrichment is unjustified because it contradicts the objectives pursued by the law of property. In this category of case a claim for unjustified enrichment 'forms an appendix to the rules on the protection of ownership and of other rights'.[301]

(c) Encroachment on rights, 'ignorance' and 'powerlessness' in two-party cases

In English law by contrast, the main textbooks subsume the equivalent of encroachment cases partly under the defendant's 'wrongdoing'[302] (B in Birks's map at Table 23.4, above) and partly under 'defective transfer' categories based on the plaintiff's reasoning processes; for example, in Birks's taxonomy, sub-categories of non-voluntariness (A.1 in Birks's map) such as 'ignorance' (A.1.1.1) or 'powerlessness' (an extreme form of 'duress' or coercion) (A.1.1.3.1).[303] These two new categories cut untidily and confusingly across two-party cases of transfer or encroachment and three-party indirect enrichment cases; they have never been recognised by the English courts. In two-party enrichment by transfer cases, the High Court of Australia[304] and Goff and Jones assert that 'ignorance' is subsumed within mistake[305] even in cases of mechanical error.[306] 'Ignorance' may not mop up all the cases left by confining enrichment by the act of the enriched to cases of wrongs but may leave an undistributed middle. What if the enrichment claimant is not ignorant of the enriched party's

---

[301] K. Zweigert and D. Muller-Gindullis, 'Quasi-contracts', in: *International Encyclopedia of Comparative Law*, vol. III, chap. 30, § 35.
[302] See, e.g., Goff and Jones, *Law of Restitution*, 709–814 ('Where the defendant has acquired a benefit through his own wrongful act'); Birks, *Introduction*, chap. X, 313–57 ('Restitution for wrongs'); Burrows, *Law of Restitution*, chap. 14, 376–419 ('Unjust enrichment by wrongdoing').
[303] Birks, *Introduction*, 140–2, 174; see also Burrows, *Law of Restitution*, chap. 4, 139–60.
[304] *David Securities Pty Ltd v. Commonwealth Bank of Australia* (1992) 175 CLR 353 at 369 and 374: '[T]he concept [of mistake] includes cases of sheer ignorance as well as cases of positive but incorrect belief'.
[305] E.g. Goff and Jones, *Law of Restitution*, 175–7.
[306] E.g. a payment through the malfunction of a computer; *Ibid.*, 176: '[I]n such a case, the payer or his agent or employee may have caused the computer to make the payment, at least in the sense of failing to stop it doing so, in the mistaken belief that the computer is functioning well.'

unauthorised use of his (the claimant's) property nor powerless to prevent it but has simply not got round to dealing with the matter? Are we to add other unjust factors to cover the various possible objective positions or subjective states of mind of the enrichment creditor during the period when the enriched party was invading his property rights, for example 'reasonable preoccupation with other matters'? This could get silly: what about 'dilatoriness' or perhaps 'slothfulness'? 'Ignorance' and 'powerlessness' are two of the oddest products of the English enrichment revolution and are not ripe for export to Scots law.

4. Obtruding benefits

The last two of the four categories in the Wilburg/von Caemmerer taxonomy concern principles of civilian origin which are recognised in Scots law as well as German law but are not recognised in the same form in English law, *inter alia* because they infringe a basic policy of English law against obtruding benefits on another against his will.

(a) Recompense for bona fide possessor's mistaken improvements of another's property

The first of these categories is recompense for mistaken repairs and improvements by the bona fide *possessor rei alienae*: the 'expenditure action' or *Verwendungskondiktion*.[307] In German law, the scope of the *Verwendungskondiktion* is very limited because of special rules in the code governing the claim of the bona fide possessor.[308] At one time this was regarded in Scots law as 'the strongest case for a plea of recompense'[309] and as 'the best and most familiar example' of recompense.[310] Historically, English law resisted the claim because of the policy against obtruding unwanted benefits on a person, though the difference with the civil law is slowly being eroded, at least in the case of moveables.[311] Birks's taxonomy makes no separate niche in the primary division for the bona fide possessor's claim for mistaken improvements but (because in English law virtually every causal mistake triggers restitution) subsumes the claim under 'mistake'.[312]

---

[307] See Gallo, 'Unjustified Enrichment', 452–5; Markesinis, Lorenz and Dannemann, *Law of Contracts*, 752, 753; von Caemmerer, 'Problèmes fondamentaux'; Zimmermann, 'Unjustified Enrichment', 421, 422; Zweigert and Kötz, *Introduction*, 540 ff.; D. A. Verse, 'Improvements and Enrichment: A Comparative Analysis', [1998] Restitution LR 85.

[308] §§ 994 ff. BGB; Markesinis, Lorenz and Dannemann, *Law of Contracts*, 752.

[309] Gloag, *Law of Contract*, 324.

[310] Lord Wark, 'Recompense', § 725 echoing Lord President Inglis in *Stewart v. Steuart* (1878) 6 R 145 at 149.

[311] *Greenwood v. Bennett* [1973] 1 QB 195. [312] Birks, *Introduction*, 155.

On the modern civilian approach, the *condictio indebiti* or *sine causa* cannot apply because the improvements are not a transfer made *solvendi donendi eunt obligendi causa*.

In Scots law, though modern cases are unusual, it is thought that the claim of the bona fide possessor for mistaken improvements should be recognised in the primary division as a category having rules of its own. First, in Scotland the law on the subject has threatened to distort the law applicable in other types of case. For example all the judicial dicta[313] (now controverted[314]) that error is essential in all cases of recompense, were pronounced in cases involving improvements to another's property. Secondly, the claim is distinct from enrichment by transfer.[315] Like recompense for payment of another's debt, it relates exclusively to an enrichment which ensues from the pursuer's act without the defender's collaboration.[316] As von Caemmerer observed,[317] the bona fide possessor has enriched the owner-defender entirely by his own conduct. He did not obtain any payment or other prestation from the defender because he did not act to fulfil a contractual or other legal obligation. He desired to act only in his own interest. If he had known the true facts, he would be denied an enrichment claim because he would have assumed the risk of being paid. The error which he makes does not relate to any obligation to pay but is rather a bona fide but erroneous belief that he (or a third party[318]) is the true owner of the property which he has improved,[319] or that he has a contractual right to become owner,[320] or that he possesses under a title equivalent to ownership.[321]

---

[313] *Buchanan v. Stewart* (1874) 2 R 78 at 81; *Rankin v. Wither* (1886) 13 R 903 at 908; *Soues v. Mill* (1903) 11 SLT 98; *Newton v. Newton* 1925 SC 715 at 723; *Gray's Exor v. Johnston* 1928 SC 659.

[314] See the dicta to the effect that in recompense error is essential in some cases but not others: *Varney (Scotland) Ltd v. Lanark Town Council* 1974 SC 245 at 252, 256, 260; *Lawrence Building Co. Ltd v. Lanark County Council* 1978 SC 30 at 53, 54; *Horne v. Horne's Executors* 1963 SLT (Sh Ct) 37 at 39.

[315] Von Caemmerer, 'Problèmes fondamentaux', 584, 585.

[316] B. Dickson, 'The Law of Restitution in the Federal Republic of Germany: A Comparison with English Law', (1987) 36 ICLQ 751, 780.

[317] 'Problèmes fondamentaux', 584 and 585.

[318] *Duff, Ross and Co. v. Kippen* (1871) 8 SLR 299; *McDowel v. McDowel* (1906) 14 SLT 125 (OH).

[319] See, e.g., *York Buildings Co. v. Mackenzie* (1795) 3 Paton 378; (1797) 3 Paton 579; *Magistrates of Selkirk v. Clapperton* (1830) 9 S 9; *Douglas v. Douglas' Trs* (1864) 2 M 1379; *Morrisons v. Allan* (1886) 13 R 1156; *Newton v. Newton* 1925 SC 715; *Wood v. Gordon* (1935) 51 Sh Ct Rep 132.

[320] *Yellowlees v. Alexander* (1882) 9 R 765.

[321] *Clarke v. Brodie* (1801) Hume 548; *McKay v. Brodie* (1801) Hume 549; (tenure described as 'kindly tenancy').

(b) Recompense from a debtor for payment of his debt or performance of his obligation

Recompense for payment of another's debt is the last of the four main categories of the Wilburg/von Caemmerer taxonomy to be considered. Alone of the four, it relates exclusively to three-party situations. It is called the 'recourse action' (*Rückgriffskondiktion*). By contrast, payment of another's debt does not appear as a separate category in Birks's taxonomy because it is primarily based on grounds of redress, and in English law payment discharging another's debt is not by itself an unjust factor. So Birks treats payment of another's debt under such grounds-based topics as 'legal compulsion' (A.1.1.3.2 in his map, Table 23.4, above), and 'free acceptance' (A.2).[322] There are several reasons why payment of another's debt should be classified separately. First, the complexity of three-party situations raises special problems and rules.[323] Secondly, the grounds of redress in enrichment by transfer presuppose that something has gone wrong with the transfer which has therefore enriched the recipient unjustifiably. By contrast in payment of another's debt, recovery is allowed *even if* the transaction achieves its purpose (discharge of the other's debt). Indeed, where the pursuer intended to discharge the defender's debt, recovery is *not* allowed *unless* the transaction has achieved its purpose, because unless the debt is discharged, the debtor is not enriched.[324] Thirdly, it is thought that in Scots law (like German law and other civilian systems),[325] assuming that

---

[322] In Scots law, though there are dicta to the effect that rights of relief (*Anglice* contribution) between co-obligants are founded on unjustified enrichment, it is thought that this is loose usage and that relief is a distinct category of obligations. The defence of change of position is not available in an action of relief between co-obligants.

[323] See D. Friedmann and N. Cohen, 'Payment of Another's Debt', in: *International Encyclopedia of Comparative Law* (1991), vol. X, chap. 10, § 1: 'Payment does not move directly from the payor to the debtor. It is made to the creditor but it may affect the creditor–debtor relations as well as those of the payor–debtor and those of the payor–creditor.'

[324] Markesinis, Lorenz and Dannemann, *Law of Contracts*, 769 observe: 'German law could learn from English law that cases of subtractive enrichment and, perhaps, mistake, ought to be treated together as far as possible, and thus see in particular the *Rückgriffskondiktion* as an exception to the principles under which the right defendant is found for performance-related restitution, rather than as a non-performance case.' However, in payment of another's debt the payer may recover from the person whose debt he has discharged even though he paid not under error but deliberately to discharge the person's debt. It seems to have affinity with a *datio obligandi causa*, a payment to constitute an obligation.

[325] Friedmann and Cohen, 'Payment of Another's Debt', § 9; also § 3; Meier, 'Mistaken Payments', 568–70.

the conditions of the third party's entitlement to discharge another's debt without the debtor's authority are satisfied (that is, the creditor agrees),[326] the mere fact of the discharge arguably entitles the third party to recompense from the debtor.[327] Fourthly, payment of another's debt (like the bona fide possessor's claim for mistaken improvements and *negotiorum gestio*)[328] relates to an enrichment arising from the payer's act entirely without the enriched party's collaboration.[329]

5. System of specific grounds mere product of haphazard development?

A century ago the German general enrichment action was based on a conscious policy decision by the compilers of the BGB. It had in effect to be supplemented by specification of broad grounds of recovery based on a typology which is prescriptive and not merely explanatory or descriptive. A comparison between the single broad concept of 'enrichment by transfer' or *Leistungskondiktion* with the English series of unjust factors (see Table 23.4, above) may suggest that the latter is unduly complex. It is true that if the English unjust factors are compared with the sub-categories of types of transfer classified by their purpose in the König rules (see Table 23.5, second level) the contrast is much less marked though it is still significant. The complexity of the English system is clearly the product of a long history of haphazard, incremental development.[330] The recognised grounds are too numerous with more to come.[331] A new unjust factor has recently been added by the courts[332] and legal scholars are bidding for others to be recognised.[333]

---

[326] See Bankton, *Institutes*, Book I, Title 24, 2; Bell, *Principles*, § 557; *Reid v. Lord Ruthven* (1918) 55 SLR 616 at 618 (admittedly an unsatisfactory case), all citing (or in Bell's case misciting) Justinian's *Institutes* III, 29 pr. For a different view see Kames, *Principles of Equity* (5th edn, 1825), 330, 331; Hume, *Lectures*, 70), vol. III, 16, 17. See generally Scottish Law Commission Discussion Paper No. 95, vol. II, §§ 2.158 ff.

[327] See Scottish Law Commission, Discussion Paper No. 95, vol. I, § 3.105.

[328] The discharge of debts due by the *dominus negotii* is a well-recognised category of *negotiorum gestio* entitling the gestor to recover from the *dominus*: Stair Memorial Encyclopaedia (1996), vol. XV, § 97; *Graham's Executors v. Fletcher's Executors* (1870) 9 M 298; *Reid v. Lord Ruthven* (1918) 55 SLR 616 at 618 *per* Lord Anderson.

[329] Zimmermann, 'Unjustified Enrichment', 423, 424.

[330] For a general overview, see D. J. Ibbetson, *A Historical Introduction to the Law of Obligations* (1999), chap. 14.

[331] Burrows, *Law of Restitution*, 21: '[T]he list should not be regarded as closed.'

[332] *Woolwich Equitable Building Society v. IRC* [1993] AC 70 (HL).

[333] E.g. ignorance and powerlessness (see n. 303, above); as to 'unconscionability' see Goff and Jones, *Law of Restitution*, 45, 46.

A very important question for legal science generally, and in particular for Scots law at its crossroads, is whether development on the English pattern by way of the ever-increasing recognition and extension of specific grounds or unjust factors is the hallmark of a mature system of restitution, especially of undue transfers. On the one hand, the approach of the German *Leistungskondiktion* suggests a negative answer. On the other hand, there is as yet no sign that English commentators are dissatisfied with the basic approach of the English law. On the contrary, when in particular cases the English courts do not identify an unjust factor as in *Lipkin Gorman*, or when they recognise 'transfer without legal ground' by another name ('no consideration') as in *Westdeutsche* (in the courts *a quo*)[334] or in dicta in *Woolwich*,[335] the English jurists swiftly protest.[336] Such cases are not seen as an opportunity to start making the change towards a better and more highly developed system based on transfer without legal ground. They are stigmatised rather as a dangerous straying from the path of virtue. So Birks observes:

[I]t does not do to have a ground of restitution which cannot be fitted within any of the families of unjust factors. The intelligibility of the law requires either that such a ground be eliminated or that the family tree be extended in some convincing manner. Then, there is a particular danger that if expressions such as 'no consideration' and 'absence of consideration' are, so to say, left lying casually around, they may yet cause great and uncontrollable changes in the structure of the law of unjust enrichment.

The reason for regarding 'no consideration' with respect and suspicion is that it creates a standing invitation to alter the language of our law of unjust enrichment in such a way as to make it resemble more closely that of civilian systems. Canada has already taken a large step in that direction. In handling cases in unjust enrichment it now regularly looks for an enrichment to one side, a corresponding deprivation in the other and the absence of a sufficient juristic

---

[334] *Westdeutsche Landesbank Girozentrale v. Islington LBC* [1994] All ER 890 (QBD and CA). Also *Kleinwort Benson v. Lincoln City Council* [1999] 2 AC 349 (HL) and n. 243, above.

[335] *Woolwich Equitable Building Society v. IRC* [1993] AC 70 (HL and CA) at 166 *per* Lord Goff; at 197-8 *per* Lord Browne-Wilkinson.

[336] On *Lipkin Gorman*, see E. McKendrick, 'Tracing Misdirected Funds', [1991] *Lloyd's Maritime and Commercial Law Quarterly* 378; also his 'Restitution, Misdirected Funds and Change of Position', (1992) 55 *MLR* 377. On *Westdeutsche*, see P. Birks, 'No Consideration: Restitution after Void Contracts', (1993) 23 *University of Western Australia LR* 195; W. Swadling, 'Restitution for No Consideration', [1994] *Restitution LR* 73; A. Burrows, 'Swaps and the Friction between Common Law and Equity', [1995] *Restitution LR* 15. On *Woolwich*, see Birks, 'No Consideration', 232, 233. On *Kleinwort Benson*, see Birks, 'Mistakes of Law'.

reason for the transfer. The 'unjust' enrichment at a plaintiff's expense thus becomes the enrichment 'without sufficient juristic reason'. Absence of reason is no more than the Latin 'sine causa', the French 'sans cause' and the German 'ohne rechtlichen Grund'.[337]

This is the language of purism.[338] One can sympathise because *sine causa* could indeed bring the whole structure of English unjust factors crashing down and Birks's own newly formed superstructure with it. Elsewhere he has said that drawing English law into a much more German configuration should not be 'the inescapable result of our long labours' because 'it would not make the best of our materials'.[339] The proposition that *sine causa* does not fit the English case-law materials is no doubt true. Given the understandable loyalty of the English profession to their case-law heritage, that proposition may rule out the reception of *sine causa*. But as a matter of legal science the proposition is neutral. It may be that something is wrong with the English case materials and that they are now impeding progress. In short, the English purist approach may well be an example of the national blocking the rational.[340] Further, if *sine causa* is incompatible with the English system of unjust factors, it is difficult to see why the civilian Scots enrichment law should adopt that system.

VIII. Third-party enrichment

1. Preliminary

One test of the true worth of any taxonomy of enrichment law is the extent to which it successfully caters for the complexities of three-party situations.[341] In some areas it is possible to analyse three-party situations as a combination of two-party situations governed by the ordinary rules of enrichment liability applying as between two parties. But other

---

[337] Birks, 'No Consideration', 231, 232, cf. 233. Also his 'Mistakes of Law', 230 ff.
[338] Cf. Lord Cooper, *The Scottish Legal Tradition* (1949; 4th revised edn, 1977), 24: 'Either oil or water is preferable to the unsatisfactory emulsion which results from attempts to mix the two.'
[339] P. Birks, 'Against Codification and Against Codification of Unjust Enrichment' (unpublished paper delivered at Edinburgh, October 1994), 7.
[340] See n. 13, above.
[341] For an excellent analysis of the problems in English law, see Burrows, *Law of Restitution*, 45-54.

three-party situations attract rules of their own which as a matter of preference, if not necessity, should be separately classified.

Apart from recompense from a debtor for payment of his debt or performance of his obligation considered above, there are other categories of three-party situations. These include: (i) innominate claim for repetition at the instance of a creditor redressing his debtor's erroneous payment to a third-party defender; (ii) subrogation of an insurer or indemnifier to the rights and remedies of the insured or indemnified person; and (iii) 'indirect enrichment' (that is, enrichment of a person arising out of a transaction between two or more other persons).

2. Creditor's claim against putative creditor enriched by erroneous payment

Where a debtor pays the wrong person, the unpaid true creditor normally has no right of action against the wrongly paid putative creditor. Such claims are exceptional since normally only the payer has a title to sue for repetition.[342] It may be that some of these exceptional claims are *sui generis*, forming a category with rules of its own allowing the true creditor to sue the payee putative creditor direct in circumstances where the debtor's payment, though made to the wrong person, has liberated the debtor from liability to the true creditor, for example (a) where the true creditor's title to sue the debtor is cut off by the defence of bona fide payment[343] and (b) where the unpaid creditor of a deceased debtor sues for repetition from a wrongly paid beneficiary (after unsuccessfully claiming against the executor).[344] There is an analogy with § 816(2) BGB.[345] On the other hand, where the debtor's erroneous payment to the putative creditor does not cut off the true creditor's right to sue the debtor, the true

---

[342] See Scottish Law Commission, Discussion Paper No. 95, vol. I, §§ 3.56–3.67.

[343] E.g. D assigns T's debt to P; in good faith, T pays D; P intimates the assignation to T and demands payment; T refuses to pay P relying on the defence arising from his bona fide payment to D; P may sue D for the debt: see Stair, *Institutions*, Book IV, Title 40, 33, approved in *Stewart's Trs v. Evans* (1871) 9 M 810 at 813; Kames, *Principles of Equity* (5th edn), 349; Scottish Law Commission, Discussion Paper No. 95, vol. I, § 3.59, head (i).

[344] See the cases from *Robertsons v. Strachans* (1760) Mor 8087 to *St Andrews Magistrates v. Forbes* (1893) 31 SLR 225 cited in Scottish Law Commission Discussion Paper No. 95, vol. I, § 3.59, head (vi).

[345] See B. Dickson, 'The Law of Restitution in the Federal Republic of Germany: A Comparison with English Law', (1987) 36 *ICLQ* 751, 777, 778.

creditor's innominate repetition action against the putative creditor[346] is dependent on the debtor's right of repetition against the putative creditor, is subject to the same limitations and defences, and has procedural safeguards since the debtor must be called. Such cases might be treated as special cases of a debtor's *condictio indebiti* but one brought at the instance of the true creditor.

In Birks's taxonomy, these claims appear to be subsumed under 'ignorance' (A.1.1.1 in his map, Table 23.4, above) and form a special subcategory of 'ignorance' called by Birks 'interceptive subtraction'.[347] This latter doctrine is inconsistent with the Scots rules on title to sue. If one takes away from Birks's category of 'ignorance' transfers, unauthorised interference, interceptive subtraction and indirect enrichment,[348] there seems to be nothing much left.

3. Indirect enrichment

'Indirect enrichment' concerns the enrichment of a person arising out of a transaction between two or more other persons. The present Scots law is governed by: (i) the 'delegation theory' in the *condictio indebiti*;[349] and (ii) recompense as the lineal descendant of the post-Justinianic *actio de in rem verso* in its original distinctive role as a remedy redressing indirect enrichment.[350]

(a) Overview: ultimate recipient's obligation based on fault or gratuitous title with burden of proof on enrichment-creditor

The argument of this section on indirect enrichment may be summarised briefly.

(i) The general rule is no liability for indirect enrichment. In other words in three-party, indirect enrichment cases, the norm is not strict liability as in two-party direct enrichment cases but non-liability.[351]

---

[346] E.g. to avoid circuity of action (unpaid true creditor sues debtor; debtor sues wrongly paid putative creditor), as in *Countess of Cromertie v. Lord Advocate* (1871) 9 M 988, or to overcome a trustee's refusal to sue the wrongly paid putative creditor, as in *Armour v. Glasgow Royal Infirmary* 1909 SC 916.

[347] See Birks, *Introduction*, 142–5, 133–9; and comments thereon by L. D. Smith, 'Three-party Restitution: A Critique of Birks's Theory of Interceptive Subtraction', (1991) 11 *Oxford JLS* 481 and by Burrows, *Law of Restitution*, 45 ff.

[348] See 715 ff., below.

[349] R. Evans-Jones, 'Identifying the Enriched', 1992 *SLT* (News) 25; and see also Scottish Law Commission, Discussion Paper No. 95, vol. II, §§ 2.168 ff.

[350] See Whitty, 'Indirect Enrichment'.   [351] See 717–18, below.

(ii) There are sound and widely acknowledged reasons of policy and principle for this general rule.[352]
(iii) Exceptionally, under the general principle of 'no enrichment from another's fraud', the ultimate recipient in a transmission chain will be liable to redress indirect enrichment acquired from a fraudulent intermediary if he either knew of the fraud or acquired the benefit on a gratuitous title.[353]
(iv) Liability is (as it ought to be) based on (a) the existence of fraud on the part of the intermediary, coupled with (b) either the bad faith (notice of the fraud) of the ultimate recipient or his gratuitous title.[354] These concepts reflect the transactional links in the transmission chain and form the specific grounds justifying redress.
(v) Scots law ought not to adopt 'ignorance' as the specific ground for redress of indirect enrichment.[355]
(vi) The same rules should apply where the intermediary committed a wrong comparable to fraud.[356] But the rules do not apply where the claimant's transfer in the first transactional link was made under error or other defect of consent not implying fault on the part of the intermediary.[357]
(vii) The onus of proof lies, as it ought to lie, on the claimant to establish the specific grounds.[358] It follows that liability for indirect enrichment is not, and ought not to be, strict.

---

[352] In summary, where P in pursuance of a contract with T provides money, goods or services benefiting D, P's claim against D is normally rejected for any of a number of sound reasons. First, P's reliance on T's faith and credit precludes P's enrichment claim against D, because P assumes the risk of T's insolvency. In other words, P's contract with T bars P's enrichment claim against D. Secondly, where T's payment to D, using money obtained by T from P, extinguishes T's debt to D, D is not enriched: *suum recepit*. Thirdly, D must be protected from double liability, for example to T in contract and to P in an enrichment claim. Fourthly, if P were allowed an enrichment claim against D, defences which D has in a question with his contractor T would be unjustifiably denied to D. Fifthly, where P and D are both creditors of T and T is insolvent (as he usually is), P's claim against D would violate the principle of the parity of the general creditors on T's insolvent estate. Sixthly, it is a general rule (at least in Scots law) that a creditor cannot recover his debt from his debtor's debtor but must first constitute his debt against his debtor and then arrest or garnish in the hands of his debtor's debtor. Of these justifications, all but the first could apply also where in the first relation T misappropriates P's money. For more details see Whitty, 'Indirect Enrichment', 224, 239. Gretton, 'Constructive Trusts', 418, 419 contends that redress of indirect enrichment is (i) arbitrary because it depends on tracing; (ii) unnecessary because the *actio pauliana* (now the statutory power of the bankrupt's trustee to set aside the bankrupt's gratuitous alienations) does the same job; (iii) incoherent because it conflicts with the trustee's claim; and (iv) unjust because either the debtor should pay if solvent or the *actio Pauliana* should apply.
[353] See below, 717–18 and 722–3.   [354] Below, 722–3.   [355] Below, 719–22.
[356] Below, 724.
[357] See *Mansfield v. Walker's Trs* (1833) 11 S 813; affirmed (1825) 1 Sh & MacL 203.
[358] Below, 722–3.

(b) General rule: no liability for indirect enrichment

The following fourfold typology of indirect enrichment cases[359] may help to focus the issues:

(i) a valid, juridical act between P and T, and T and D;
(ii) a valid, juridical act between P and T, but not between T and D;
(iii) no valid juridical act between P and T, but a valid juridical act between T and D; and
(iv) a valid juridical act neither between P and T, nor between T and D (the 'double fault' category, a term derived from tennis).

The transactional link between P and T may be referred to as the 'first relation' and that between T and D as the 'second relation'.[360] The general rule is that P has no claim against D.

(i) Where there is a valid juridical act in both relations (the most common case), P has generally no claim to redress D's indirect enrichment.[361] In particular cases, the principle or policy reason is sometimes found in the first relation, sometimes in the second, and sometimes in both relations.
(ii) Non-recovery is also the general rule in the second category (where there is a valid, juridical act in the first relation but not the second).[362]
(iii) The third category (valid juridical act in the second relation but not the first) is probably the most commonly litigated. It includes, for example, most money-laundering cases. Typically T, a rogue often in a fiduciary position, by a wrong of dishonesty misappropriates P's money

---

[359] Borrowed with modifications from a famous article by Professor Barry Nicholas, 'Unjustified Enrichment in the Civil Law and Louisiana Law', (1962) 36 *Tulane LR* 605.
[360] In German law, the relation between P and T is known as the 'cover relation' and the relation between T and D as the 'value relation'. See Friedmann and Cohen, 'Payment of Another's Debt', 50; Meier, 'Mistaken Payments', 570.
[361] Where P, acting under contract with D's insurance company T, repairs D's car and T goes into liquidation, P cannot recover the cost of the repairs from D: *Kirklands Garage (Kinross) Ltd v. Clark* 1967 SLT (Sh Ct) 60; *Express Coach Finishers v. Caulfield* 1968 SLT (Sh Ct) 11. Then take the very common sub-contractor cases. P, a sub-contractor under contract with T, the principal contractor, builds with his own materials on the land of T's employer D. The building belongs to D by accession. T becomes insolvent. P cannot recover from D the price of his labour and materials: *J. B. Mackenzie (Edinburgh) Ltd v. Lord Advocate* 1972 SC 231; see also *Robertson v. Beatson McLeod & Co.* 1908 SC 921.
[362] *Ellis v. Fraser* (1840) 3 D 264. P, on the instructions of an election agent T, erected hustings for the nomination of the famous historian Thomas Babington Macaulay as a member of Parliament. D1 and D2, the mover and seconder of another candidate, took the benefit of T's hustings without T's consent. P sought to recover the expense of erecting the hustings from T and also from D1 and D2 on the ground that their use of the hustings was *in rem versum* of them (i.e. had enriched them). P's claim against D1 and D2, however, was rejected on the ground that it was excluded by P's contract with T.

or induces P to part with it to him. T then pays the money to a third party D, or applies it for D's benefit, in order to satisfy T's obligations to D or to obtain some reciprocal benefit from D or as a gift. P has no claim against D if D did not know of the wrong or gave consideration (*suum recepit*). It is very important to note that this category of liability is exceptional.[363]

(iv) In the fourth category (no valid juridical act in either the first or second relation), legal systems vary. Some legal systems, possibly including Scots law, will sometimes allow P to recover from D.[364] In German law, where there is no valid juridical act in either relation, nevertheless P must sue T and T must sue D.[365] In services cases, both the result and the justifications of the Scottish cases arrive independently at a similar solution to German law (namely that where, under contract with T, P performs services which, in terms of T's contract with D, benefit D, P's single physical performance is treated as two legal performances, namely from P to T and from T to D); and the remedy of each legal performer lies only against the legal recipient.

(c) The English strict liability theory in redress of indirect unjustified enrichment

As regards the grounds of redress of indirect enrichment (unjust factors), in English law there is an inconsistency between common law and equity. At common law the restitutionary liability is strict.[366] So where P's money has been transferred by T to D without P's knowledge, D is strictly liable to P subject to restitutionary defences (for example, change of position or bona fide purchase). It is said that this strict liability is necessary because ignorance (in three-party cases) must cohere with mistake (in two-party cases) where there is also no requirement that the recipient must have known of the mistaken nature of the payment.[367] In equity, the orthodox rule is that where the ultimate recipient receives trust property, he is liable for 'knowing receipt'.[368]

---

[363] See 724–5, below.
[364] *Extruded Welding Wire (Sales) Ltd v. McLachlan and Brown* 1986 SLT 314: for example, P paid a debt to T when he should have paid X. D wrongfully took the money from T and appropriated it in settlement of fees due by T to him. It was held that P could recover payment from D. But this is an exceptional case.
[365] Zimmermann and Du Plessis, 'Basic Features', 34; Meier, 'Mistaken Payments', 571.
[366] *Banque Belge pour L'Étranger v. Hambrouck* [1921] 1 KB 321; *Agip (Africa) Ltd v. Jackson* [1991] Ch 547 (CA); *Lipkin Gorman (a Firm) v. Karpnale Ltd* [1991] 2 AC 548 (HL).
[367] *Kelly v. Solari* (1841) 9 M & W 54.
[368] See, e.g., S. Gardner, 'Knowing Assistance and Knowing Receipt: Taking Stock', (1996) 112 *LQR* 56.

Under a theory first adumbrated by Birks,[369] liability is, or should be, strict upon the view that the claim is part of the law on autonomous unjust enrichment; that claims to redress unjust enrichment are based on an absence of intention by the claimant to transfer the property; and that therefore they do not depend on fault.[370] This theory has now gained widespread support in England and Wales[371] including support from equity lawyers.[372] On the other hand, according to Lionel Smith, the English 'judiciary have not warmed to the idea of strict liability. Case after case affirms the contrary.'[373] It is submitted that from the standpoint of Scots law, the analogy with two-party direct enrichment cases is false and that the theory is contrary to the sound and well-established principles of Scots law derived from both the Romanistic and English traditions.

(d) Criticism of 'ignorance' as an unjust factor in indirect enrichment cases in English law

The use by English academics of 'ignorance' to explain three-party cases has been criticised.[374] In Lord Millett's view, for example, 'it is important... to distinguish between the two-party and three-party cases because they are governed by different rules'.[375] It seems to me that the criticisms are justified.

[369] P. Birks, 'Misdirected Funds: Restitution from the Recipient', [1989] *Lloyd's Maritime and Commercial Law Quarterly* 296; also his 'The English Recognition of Unjust Enrichment', [1991] *Lloyd's Maritime and Commercial Law Quarterly* 473; also his *Introduction*, 140–6; also his 'Trusts in the Recovery of Misapplied Assets: Tracing, Trusts and Restitution', in: E. McKendrick (ed.), *Commercial Aspects of Trusts and Fiduciary Obligations* (1992), 149; also his, 'Persistent Problems in Misdirected Money: A Quintet', [1993] *Lloyd's Maritime and Commercial Law Quarterly* 218.

[370] Birks, 'Persistent Problems', 222.

[371] Burrows, *Law of Restitution*, chap. 4, 139–60; Burrows and McKendrick, *Cases and Materials*, chap. 4, 149–94; P. Millett, 'Tracing the Proceeds of Fraud', (1991) 107 *LQR* 71, 85; E. McKendrick, 'Tracing Misdirected Funds', [1991] *Lloyd's Maritime and Commercial Law Quarterly* 378; also his 'Restitution, Misdirected Funds and Change of Position', (1992) 55 *MLR* 377; Lord Nicholls, 'Knowing Receipt: The Need for a New Landmark', in: Cornish et al., *Restitution*, 231.

[372] E.g. C. Harpum, 'The Basis of Equitable Liability', in: P. Birks (ed.), *The Frontiers of Liability* (1994), 9; D. J. Hayton, *Underhill and Hayton: Law of Trusts and Trustees* (15th edn, 1995), 409, 415, 416.

[373] L. Smith, 'W(h)ither Knowing Receipt?', (1998) 114 *LQR* 394, 394.

[374] See, e.g., W. Swadling, 'A Claim in Restitution?', [1996] *Lloyd's Maritime and Commercial Law Quarterly* 63; E. Bant, '"Ignorance" as a Ground of Restitution – Can it Survive?', [1998] *Lloyd's Maritime and Commercial Law Quarterly* 18; Lord Millett, 'Law of Restitution', 4; cf. R. Grantham and C. E. F. Rickett, 'Restitution Property and Ignorance – A Reply to Mr Swadling', [1996] *Lloyd's Maritime and Commercial Law Quarterly* 465.

[375] Lord Millett, 'Law of Restitution', 4.

(i) Consider a two-party case in which D steals £100 from P without P's knowledge. Burrows[376] states that in this case the unjust factor is P's ignorance. Further (he argues) where T steals £100 from P without P's knowledge and passes that £100 to D, the unjust factor should likewise be ignorance. 'In principle', he says, 'the unjust factor should not change just because the benefit has been conferred by a third party rather than by the plaintiff.' With respect this seems unconvincing. In the first example, since the theft was D's act, the ground of redress should be D's interference with P's rights, not P's ignorance. It is quite true that logically a legal system which accepts error as a ground of restitution of property transferred by the claimant must a fortiori accept ignorance as a ground of restitution of property so transferred.[377] This follows from the fact that error is defective knowledge and ignorance is absence of knowledge. But although the claimant's error is a ground of restitution of property acquired by a transferee through the claimant's transfer, it does not follow that the claimant's ignorance must be a ground of restitution of property acquired through the unauthorised act of the acquirer. That would be a *non sequitur*. Ignorance is an extrapolation from error and therefore an example of defective transfer theory, so it should not be applied to acts which are not transfers.

(ii) The type of ignorance which in law vitiates a transfer is not ignorance of the transfer but ignorance of a pertinent fact, enactment or rule of law. Ignorance as used by Birks and Burrows may be ignorance of the transfer (or other mode of transmission) itself.

(iii) Again, the supporters of 'ignorance' as an unjust factor rely heavily on the analogy with 'mistake'. But in cases of indirect enrichment the analogy is false because mistake by itself is not a ground for restitution of indirect enrichment.

(iv) In three-party cases, Burrows[378] concedes that the English courts have tended to regard the unjust factor as being D's interference with P's ownership rather than P's ignorance, but argues in favour of the latter on several grounds. For example:

Ignorance clearly belongs to the same series as the well-recognised unjust factors triggering personal restitution, such as mistake, duress and failure of

---

[376] Burrows, *Law of Restitution*, 139.
[377] Ibid., 141: 'Logic necessitates that if one is willing to recognise an unjust factor of mistake one must be willing to recognise ignorance.'
[378] Ibid., 140, 141.

consideration. Interference with ownership is a different animal in that it does not identify facts relevant to the plaintiff's reasoning process.[379]

The answer is that in cases of interference with ownership, the law is concerned with enrichment of the enriched party through his own act or the acts of a third-party intermediary and therefore not with defective transfers. All the unjust factors mentioned by the learned author are examples of defective transfer theory and inapplicable to acts other than transfers. In the case of such acts the reasoning process of the enrichment-creditor seems irrelevant to the ground of liability, though it may set up a defence of authorisation. Other arguments favouring 'ignorance' also take insufficient account of the point that the interference in question is not the act of the claimant.

For example: (v) the argument that to recognise interference with ownership means that in principle one ought to back-track over the ground covered by the standard unjust factors so as to recognise an alternative restitutionary claim whenever title in the property transferred did not pass to the defendant.[380]

(vi) Then it is said: 'In practice there is no indication that the courts have reasoned in terms of interference with ownership in standard two party personal restitution cases, such as those dealing with mistake or duress.'[381] Again one would not expect that in two-party cases of defective transfer by the claimant, the courts would invoke an unjust factor appropriate to an act of the enriched party or a third party. The argument continues: 'And in other cases interference with ownership clearly cannot have any relevance.'[382] That is true, but interference with ownership rights is needed to cater for cases where the interference is not a tort/delict and where a proprietary or possessory remedy is either unavailable or insufficient.

(vii) Finally Burrows states:

Although personal restitution is in issue, the emphasis on the unjust factor being that, without the plaintiff's consent, the defendant received property that

---

[379] Ibid., 141.
[380] Ibid., 141. He continues: 'For example, if P pays D £100 by a fundamental mistake of fact, one would need to recognise two unjust factors triggering an action for money had and received: mistake and receipt of property that, at the time of receipt, belonged to the plaintiff.'
[381] Ibid., 141.
[382] Ibid., 141; he continues: 'For example, title to money passes to the defendant despite a total failure of consideration: and restitution for services rendered plainly cannot rest on the plaintiff owning the benefit when received by the defendant'.

at the time of receipt belonged to the plaintiff, may lead to confusion with [the case] where a proprietary restitutionary remedy is sought for *retention* of the plaintiff's property without his consent.[383]

That may be so in English law, but in legal systems that distinguish clearly between the law of obligations and the law of property this should not be a problem.

(e) Scots law: no gratuitous or mala fide profit from another's fraud or breach of trust: onus on claimant

Scots law borrowed tracing rules uncertainly and untidily from English law (mainly from equity though Scots law is unitary) and uses them mainly in connection with constructive trusts (likewise borrowed shakily from England).[384] Scots law also allows a form of tracing (without using that name) where D knowingly or gratuitously takes a benefit from T's fraud against P.[385] D then comes under a personal obligation to recompense P. Where the recipient in the first (P–T) relation has acquired money or property from its original owner through fraud or breach of trust and transferred it, the transferee in the second (T–D) relation is only liable to redress his indirect enrichment at the original owner's expense on the principle that no one is entitled to profit gratuitously or knowingly from another's fraud or breach of trust.[386] That principle is firmly rooted in the case law and it has civil-law and common-law ancestry.[387] In applying that principle to recompense for unjustified indirect enrichment, the Scottish courts have for a very long time paid respectful regard to English decisions on 'knowing receipt'.[388] In Scots law it is undoubted that the onus rests on

---

[383] *Ibid.*, 141 (emphasis in original). He continues: 'Lord Templeman's judgment in *Lipkin Gorman v. Karpnale Ltd* [1991] 2 AC 548 exhibits this kind of confusion.'

[384] Gretton, 'Constructive Trusts', 408.

[385] See, e.g., *Bank of Scotland v. MacLeod Paxton Woolard & Co.* 1998 SLT 258 (OH) at 271I–272A *per* Lord Coulsfield.

[386] *Ibid.* at 272B and 277G *per* Lord Coulsfield. See also *Taylor v. Forbes* (1830) 4 W & S 444; *Clydesdale Bank v. Paul* (1877) 4 R 626; *Gibbs v. British Linen* noted (1875) 4 R 630; *Thomson v. Clydesdale Bank* (1893) 20 R (HL) 59; *New Mining and Exploring Syndicate v. Chalmers and Hunter* 1912 SC 126; *Smith v. Liquidator of James Birrell Ltd* 1968 SLT 174; *Extruded Welding Wire (Sales) Ltd v. McLachlan and Brown* 1986 SLT 314 at 316; *Style Financial Services Ltd v. Bank of Scotland* 1997 SCLR 633 (OH) at 657–8; 1996 SLT 421 (2nd Division) at 426E–F; *Bank of Scotland v. Junior* 1999 SCLR 284 (Extra Division); Gloag, *Law of Contract*, 332, 333; Whitty, 'Indirect Enrichment', 252–9.

[387] See, Ulp. D. 44, 4, 4, 29; Whitty, 'Indirect Enrichment', 256, n. 17.

[388] See, e.g., *Eyre v. Burmester* (1864) 4 De G & J 435, cited in *Gibbs v. British Linen Co.* (1875) 4 R 630 at 634 ff.; *Bank of Scotland v. MacLeod Paxton Woolard & Co.* 1998 SLT 258 (OH) at 274 ff.

the pursuer to prove that the defenders received the property or money either gratuitously or in the knowledge, actual or constructive, of the fraud or breach of trust.[389] It is submitted that this is the correct approach to the burden of proof. The onus of proof of fraud lies on the claimant in a question with the fraudster.[390] It would therefore be anomalous if the incidence of onus were different in a question with the fraudster's mala fide or gratuitous successor, especially since in theory the successor's bad faith (knowing receipt) makes him *particeps fraudis*. If strict liability were to take over 'knowing receipt' in English law[391] I earnestly hope that the Scots law would not change. The liability is an exception to the general rule in three-party cases of non-liability for indirect enrichment. There is no case for moving from non-liability to strict liability. In English law equitable ownership or tracing or both may make parties at the opposite ends of an enrichment chain appear to be in a direct relationship similar to a two-party case. But that is an optical illusion.

(f) Remedies: priority in enrichment-debtor's bankruptcy and the context and vehicle for reform

A key taxonomic fallacy can spawn other fallacies. Accepting 'ignorance' as the specific ground of redress of indirect enrichment (unjust factor) would mask or displace the true reasons of principle explaining why, exceptionally, an enrichment creditor may have priority in the intermediary's bankruptcy,[392] that is that the general creditors cannot profit at another's expense from the bankrupt's fraud or breach of trust.[393] If there were to be a comprehensive and systematic inquiry into the 'proprietary' or priority-yielding consequences of specific unjust factors,[394] the proper

---

[389] *Thomson v. Clydesdale Bank* (1893) 20 R (HL) 59 at 61 *per* Lord Watson; *M. & I. Instrument Engineers Ltd v. Varsada* 1991 SLT 106 (OH); *Universal Import Export GmbH v. Bank of Scotland* 1995 SC 73; 1995 SLT 1318 (2nd Division) at 1323 *per* Lord Morison; *Style Financial Services Ltd v. Bank of Scotland* 1997 SCLR 633 (OH) at 657; *Bank of Scotland v. MacLeod Paxton Woolard & Co.* 1998 SLT 258 (OH).

[390] Cf. *Sodden v. Prudential Assurance Co. Ltd* 1999 SCLR 367 (2nd Div.); *Royal Bank of Scotland v. Holmes* 1999 SCLR 297 (OH).

[391] As predicted by Burrows, 'Restitution', 112.

[392] The bankruptcy proceedings operate as an involuntary transmission to the trustee in bankruptcy for distribution of his estate to all of his pre-bankruptcy proceeding creditors in accordance with their respective rights and preferences.

[393] See 722–3, above.

[394] Called for by Swadling, 'New Role?', 110; also his 'Property and Unjust Enrichment', in: Harris, *Property Problems* 130.

starting point should be that principle. The view that, among the specific grounds of redress, 'ignorance' has the strongest claim to priority,[395] would get the inquiry off on the wrong foot.

If the specific ground is 'no *mala fide* or gratuitous benefit from fraud (or a comparable wrong)', it is arguable that that principle should continue to override both the policy restricting redress of indirect enrichment and the related principle of the parity of the general creditors: 'fraud passes against creditors'.[396] Breach of trust is also a ground for redress of indirect enrichment and trust property is excluded from the trustee's personal insolvency proceedings.[397] The difficult question (on which the Anglo-American literature is large and growing[398]) is: what other grounds of redress do and should attract the privilege of a priority by exclusion, or a preference, in bankruptcy having regard to *paritas creditorum*, which is for other reasons already greatly endangered?[399] It is not a simple seesaw situation in which failure to uphold the enrichment-creditor's claim will benefit the general creditors, for in ranking creditors on an insolvent estate it is likely to be statutory preferred creditors and any floating charge-holder who take all.

Mistaken payments or conveyances are not at all comparable to fraud. Scots law had its equivalent to *Chase Manhattan*[400] in the 1830s and decided it on sound principles the other way. The case was *Mansfield v. Walker's*

---

[395] Smith, *Law of Tracing*, 301: 'There is some disagreement as to when proprietary restitution is appropriate; but if it is ever appropriate, it will be so where the defect in the transfer from plaintiff to defendant is the plaintiff's ignorance of the transfer. That is the strongest defect of all, and it is generally applicable to each step in the typical tracing exercise' (footnote omitted). In this very fine work, the learned author accepts 'ignorance' as part of English law. But why?

[396] Bell, *Commentaries*, vol. I, 310.   [397] But see Gretton, 'Constructive Trusts', 408.

[398] E.g. E. L. Sherwin, 'Constructive Trusts in Bankruptcy', (1989) *University of Illinois LR* 297; D. M. Paciocco, 'The Remedial Constructive Trust: A Principled Basis for Priorities over Creditors', (1989) 68 *Canadian Bar Review* 315; R. Goode, 'Property and Unjust Enrichment', in: Burrows, *Essays*, 213, 234, 244; Smith, *Law of Tracing*, 303 ff.; Swadling, 'Property and Unjust Enrichment', concludes (at 145): '[W]ith the sole exception of maritime salvage, no good reason has yet been advanced for treating restitutionary plaintiffs differently from the defendant's other unsecured creditors.'

[399] Cf. the Report of the *Review Committee on Insolvency Law and Practice* (1982; Cmnd 8558) (chairman: Sir Kenneth Cork), which found that the injustice suffered by unsecured creditors on the bankruptcy of their common debtor was the most pressing problem in the reform of bankruptcy law. The problem is still acute.

[400] *Chase Manhattan Bank NA Ltd v. Israel-British Bank (London) Ltd* [1981] Ch 105 disapproved in *Re Goldcorp Exchange* [1995] 1 AC 74; *Westdeustche Landesbank Girozentrale v. Islington London Borough Council* [1996] AC 669.

Trs,[401] which involved a conveyancing error.[402] Lord Craigie[403] observed that 'there are no equities in competitions among creditors'.[404] Rights are upheld for the vigilant not those asleep, and although no one ought to be enriched from another's loss, yet in avoiding loss, 'everyone is entitled to avail himself of the blunders of those whose interests are opposed to his'.[405] The justifications vary slightly. Sometimes it is said that the general creditors are not enriched because they cannot receive more than their debt and a creditor is never enriched merely by receipt of his debt.[406] Sometimes it is said that, far from being enriched, the general creditors are 'striving to avoid loss'.[407] Sometimes it is said that the general creditors are enriched but justifiably, the justification being the principle of the parity of the general creditors of an insolvent.[408]

Gretton is surely right to affirm that the question of priorities for constructive trust beneficiaries and indirect enrichment claimants should be made in the context of a study of insolvency law, and not (or not merely) enrichment law.[409] His point is that other classes of creditor may have a better claim to priority than enrichment creditors.[410] Such a study should address the perceived injustice that the general creditors are ousted from bankruptcy by the prior claims of preferential creditors and floating charge-holders.[411]

---

[401] *Mansfield v. Walker's Trs* (1833) 11 S 813; affirmed (1835) 1 Sh & MacL 203; 3 Ross LC 139.
[402] A party lent a sum of money on the security of a property which he was led to believe extended to ninety-five acres but which in fact only extended to five acres. The borrower was sequestrated before the error was corrected. It was held that there was no fraud on the part of the borrower to affect the trustee and the general creditors: error did not suffice.
[403] (1833) 11 S 813 at 828.
[404] Referring to *Duke of Norfolk v. York Building Co. Annuitants' Trs* (1752) Mor 7062, in which a company granted bonds of annuity and in security of these disponed their estates to a trustee. Some annuitants renewed their bonds in ignorance of the fact that they thereby lost the benefit of the security for the annuity. The security subjects were then adjudged by third parties who recorded their adjudications. Despite the annuitants' error, the Court of Session preferred the adjugers and this was upheld by the House of Lords.
[405] (1833) 11 S 813 at 828.
[406] '*Suum recepit*': e.g. Gloag and Henderson, *Law of Scotland*, § 29.13: 'The other creditors are not *lucrati* merely because the dividend on their debts is larger'; *Universal Import Export GmbH v. Bank of Scotland* 1995 SC 73 at 93 *per* Lord Caplan.
[407] '*Certantes de damno evitando*': Hume, *Lectures*, vol. III, 168; Gloag, *Law of Contract*, 331.
[408] Whitty, 'Indirect Enrichment', 225, 226.   [409] Gretton, 'Constructive Trusts', 412.
[410] 'Those who make bids to a committee must present their bids with other bids': *Ibid*.
[411] Cork Report (n. 399).

Now voices are being raised against allowing any priority to any type of enrichment claim.[412] If that policy were accepted, it would go some way towards harmonising English law with German law. Alternatively, in this age of money-laundering, should we regard the German law of tracing and indirect enrichment as unduly weak and underdeveloped? Few policy questions affecting the structure of enrichment law are more difficult than these. In the United Kingdom, it seems to me that it is the legislatures, not the judges and their academic allies, who should decide them.

IX. Conclusions

1. Preliminary

(i) With the breakdown of its centuries-old system of classifying obligations for redress of unjustified enrichment, Scots law has to reorganise its principles and rules in accordance with a new taxonomy.[413]

2. Synchronising enrichment law with other branches of law

(ii) Civil-law and common-law systems differ in the way in which they synchronise obligations redressing unjustified enrichment with other branches of the law and this can affect the content and internal taxonomy of enrichment law.[414]

(iii) Property law. As between civil-law and common-law systems, there are large differences in formal taxonomic structure and in conceptual approach to the boundary between property law and enrichment law.[415] Civil-law systems draw a sharp and clear line between property law and enrichment law. Enrichment law redresses transfers without legal ground and encroachments on rights. The role (if any) of enrichment law is always obligational and never, in itself, 'proprietary'. In sharp contrast, in common-law systems enrichment law shades imperceptibly into and overlaps with property law (including bankruptcy). The law uses proprietary remedies – the constructive trust and equitable lien – in response to unjustified enrichment.

Scots law does not acknowledge equitable ownership but has some difficult demarcation problems of its own, for example as to the scope of the rule that fraud passes against creditors and as to the extent and nature

---

[412] Gretton, 'Constructive Trusts', goes very near to that view; Swadling, 'Property and Unjust Enrichment', takes that view except for salvage (which in the eye of Scots law is probably not an enrichment claim but a reward system more akin to, yet different from, *negotiorum gestio*).

[413] 658–61 and 684–6, above. [414] Sections II to V, above. [415] Section IV, above.

of the reception of the constructive trust (but not yet the equitable lien) and tracing.

(iv) Contract law. The main questions here seem to be whether or how far the grounds of redress under enrichment law can refer questions of the invalidity and other defects in failed contracts to contract law (as in civil-law systems) or whether enrichment law must do the work of contract law when determining whether an unjust factor exists (as in common-law systems). In my view the civil-law approach is preferable for Scots law.

(v) Delict/tort. Next there is the question of enrichment arising from the act of the enriched person.[416] A choice lies between a category of enrichment from wrongs or a category of 'encroachment on rights'. The dominant common-law view is that an enriched person is liable to redress an enrichment arising from his own act only if (a) the act is a tort or equitable wrong and (b) the wrong is one of those for which restitution lies. The main alternative, found in some (not all) civil-law systems, and contended for by some common law jurists is a category of 'encroachment on (patrimonial) rights' within enrichment law having rules of its own determining liability independently of delict/tort (or equitable wrongs). In such a category it is easier to hold that liability may arise even though the mental element required for wrongfulness is missing. Scots law is underdeveloped but it may and probably should follow the second alternative.

3. The internal taxonomy of obligations for redress of unjustified enrichment

(vi) Three main options have been suggested for reorganising the internal taxonomy, namely:

- the 'unjustified unless' approach proposed by Dr Clive;
- the English system of specific grounds of redress ('unjust factors'); and
- the modern civilian approach, in particular the Wilburg/von Caemmerer taxonomy of German law.

Clive's elegant code seems much preferable for Scots law to the common-law system of unjust factors. It may turn out to be too radical and untested to win acceptance on a Scottish or European level. It is thought that the modern civilian approach is also much preferable to the common-law system of unjust factors as a model for Scots law, however suitable it may be for common-law systems.

(vii) The English system of specific grounds of redress (unjust factors) is not a suitable model for Scots law.

---

[416] Section V, 3, above.

First, it relies too much on the formulation of narrow and detailed grounds of recovery to protect the security of receipts when it should rely instead on appropriate defences, notably change of position.

Secondly, the English system of unjust factors is not the product of a considered commitment at any point in time; it is just the product of historical growth. Its undue complexity reflects its haphazard historical development. In order to provide a remedy redressing a transfer without legal ground, as many as ten unjust factors have already been created. This compares with the small number of tests for redressing enrichment by transfer without legal ground in civil-law systems. Systematisation of the unjust factors is a stage through which English law must pass.

Thirdly, the English system can only progress by adding new unjust factors to the existing canon incrementally or by expanding the scope of the existing factors. This increases the fragmentation.

Fourthly, the trend in Europe suggests that error as to the existence of the legal ground of a transfer should not be a specific ground of redress but rather knowledge of the absence of legal ground should be a defence to an enrichment-by-transfer claim.[417] It is submitted that Scots law should follow this European trend. Undue transfers in doubt or under protest should likewise be prima facie recoverable. Generally the test should be failure to achieve the purpose of the transfer whether the purpose was to implement, or (exceptionally) to create, an obligation, or to make a donation. Undue transfers under compulsion or threat are not made for any such purpose and should form a distinct sub-category of the enrichment-by-transfer claim.

Fifthly, Scots law should not recognise 'ignorance' or 'powerlessness' as specific grounds of redress.[418] The material in these categories should be subsumed under other categories such as mistake (in English law) or transfer without legal ground, encroachment on rights, or the tests for redress of indirect unjustified enrichment.

Sixthly, the experience of the civil-law systems seems to indicate that, in transfer cases, the test (or tests) of transfer without legal ground would not open the floodgates to too much restitution.

Seventhly, the unjust factors duplicate the work of contract law, again causing unnecessary complexity.[419]

For these reasons I respectfully agree with Reinhard Zimmermann's conclusion that 'it is hardly conceivable that a legal system engaged with the task of rationally reorganising its law of unjustified enrichment should

---

[417] 697–9, above. [418] 707–8 and 719–22, above. [419] Section VII, 4.

take its lead from English jurisprudence. Scots law... has all the less reason to do so, since the Institutional writers have implanted in it the germ of the modern enrichment-by-transfer claim: the *condictio indebiti*.'[420]

(viii) Encroachment by the enriched party on another's rights, dealt with at (v), should appear in the primary division of the taxonomy.[422]

(ix) In Scots law, which recognises *negotiorum gestio*, two closely related enrichment law categories allowing recompense for obtruding a benefit on another without his consent (that is, the bona fide possessor's claim for mistaken improvements of another's property, and payment discharging another's debt) should also appear in the primary division of the taxonomy.[422] They do not fit well under transfer (there is no failure of purpose) or encroachment on rights (the enriching act is not that of the enriched party).

4. Indirect enrichment

(x) In Scots law, in three-party, indirect enrichment cases, the norm is not strict liability as in two-party direct enrichment cases but non-liability for very good reasons, including the parity of general creditors.[423] Exceptionally, under the general principle of 'no enrichment from another's fraud', the ultimate recipient in an enrichment chain may be liable. Liability is based on (a) the existence of fraud on the part of the intermediary, coupled with (b) either the bad faith of the ultimate recipient (notice of the fraud) or his gratuitous title. These concepts reflect the transactional links in the enrichment chain and form the specific grounds justifying redress. Therefore Scots law ought not to adopt 'ignorance' as the specific ground. The same rules should probably apply where the intermediary committed a wrong comparable to fraud. In Scots law these rules neither do nor should apply where, in the first transactional link, the claimant made a transfer under error. Error is not comparable to fraud. The analogy of some two-party enrichment cases (where liability is strict) is false. The intermediary's liability for fraud is not strict, and his onerous transferee's liability is dependent on his knowledge of the intermediary's fraud. Moreover, the rule is an exception to a rule in three-party cases of non-liability for indirect enrichment. There is no case for moving from non-liability to strict liability.

(xi) In Scots law, however, constructive trusts and tracing are trickling in, arousing one judge's 'instinctive abhorrence',[424] and soon the cursed dualism may be upon us with what results nobody knows.

[420] 'Unjustified Enrichment', 416.   [421] Section VII, 3, above.
[422] Section VII, 4, above.   [423] Section VIII, 3, above.
[424] *Mortgage Company v. Mitchells Roberton* 1997 SLT 1305 at 1310.

Index

The text under consideration, by its nature, has much overlapping of concepts and variation of terminology and approach. The index normally adopts the terminology in use at any given moment coupled with a liberal use of cross-references to indicate where alternative approaches are to be found.

References to countries are subsumed in the subject headings either as subheadings or (where the references are many) as part of a main heading. To avoid unwieldy and repetitious lists, cross-references usually omit this country element. Equally to avoid unwieldiness and repetition, references to countries are omitted where this would seem not to add significant information.

actio de in rem verso, 444, 513, 520, 578–9, 595–7, 602, 617–18, 621–2, 666, 682 n. 149, 683
actio in quantum locupletior factus est, 248, 682 n. 149, 700
actio quod metus causa, 202–3
agency. See fiduciary obligations, restitutionary damages for breach
Anweisungsfall, 540
assignatus utitur iure auctoris, 461
aufgedrängte Bereicherung, 312

bad faith
  See also good faith
  condictio causa data causa non secuta and, 141–2, 145
  England, 123–4, 141–3, 155–6, 169–70, 176, 506
  France, 444
  Germany, 142 n. 42, 169–70, 179, 595, 675
  Quebec, owner/possessor relationship and, 595
  Roman law, 142 n. 43
  Scotland, 141 n. 41, 142, 145–6, 155–6, 392, 396–404, 722–3

  South Africa, 396 n. 49
Bereicherung in sonstiger Weise, 4, 540, 544
betterment acts, 376–8
betting debt, 43–4, 72
bona fide purchase for value, 311–12
bonus iudex varie ex personis causisque constituet, 370
breach of contract. See contract, restitutionary damages for breach; frustration or fundamental breach of contract as ground for restitution
burden of proof
  civil law, 126–7
  England, 23, 92, 97, 99–100, 126–7
  Germany, 79, 85, 213
  Netherlands, 208
  Scotland, 390 n. 26, 482, 722–3
  South Africa, 212–13

casum sentit dominus/res perit domino, 133, 273–4
causation
  See also three-party situations; tracing
  'at the expense' requirement
    England, 553–4

Germany, 554
  South Africa, 562
 constructive trusts
  Scotland, 584–7, 665–8
  United States, 555–6
  delict/tort and, United States, 557
  factual/legal, 556–8
  insolvency and, United States, 555–6
  parity of creditors and
   England, 559–60
   France (*Boudier*), 560
   Scotland, 558–9, 723–6, 729
   South Africa, 565
  two-party situations, United States, 555–8
cessio legis, 577–8
change of position
  restitutio in integrum and, 243–85
  restitution without enrichment and, 227–42
  unwinding of contract and, 24, 259–60, 282–5
change of position (England), 642–3, 654–5, 703
  bad faith and, 506
  defendant, 23–4, 51, 164, 168–74
  devaluation of counter-restitution and, 187
  estoppel/personal bar distinguished, 24, 275
  plaintiff, 180–2
  tort/unjust enrichment claims distinguished, 589
  undue influence and, 24, 170–1, 174
change of position (Germany)
  on basis of contract with incompetent party, 233–4
  defendant, 23–4, 164, 168–74, 179
  enrichment, relevance, 227–42
  plaintiff, 179–80
  three-party situations, 522
  undue influence and, 24, 74, 170–1
  unwinding of contract and, 259–60
change of position (Scotland)
  condictio indebiti and, 703
  estoppel/personal bar distinguished, 24, 275
change of position (United States)
  on basis of contract with incompetent party, 233–4
  enrichment, relevance, 227–42

Clive Code (1996), 26–7, 482–5, 644, 660 n. 15, 670, 691–3, 702
coactus volui principle, 17, 221
commodum eius esse debet, cuius periculum est, 274
compulsion, 210, 446–7, 700–1
condictio causa data causa non secuta
  condictio ob causam finitam distinguished, 144
  England, 67, 129–35, 153, 154–6
  Germany, 40–1, 67, 73, 142, 156
  Roman law, 67, 142
  Scotland, 26, 129–35, 143–4, 145, 154–5, 254, 386, 387–8, 404–6, 467 n. 29, 699
condictio ex causa furtiva, 591–3, 705–6
condictio indebiti
  civil law, 135–6
  England, 4, 38–9, 65, 73–4, 76, 92–3, 98, 136–7, 139
  Germany, 38, 40–1, 55, 206, 207–8, 212–13, 258
  Italy, 683
  Louisiana, 683
  Netherlands, 683
  Quebec, 683
  Roman law, 37–8
  Scotland, 42 n. 15, 73, 75, 136, 213 n. 80, 249 n. 14, 386, 387–8, 390 n. 26, 406–7, 414, 464–5, 467, 476–7, 696–7, 703–4
  South Africa, 212–13, 683
condictio ob causam finitam, 135, 136–7, 144
condictio ob turpem vel iniustam causam, 135, 217–18, 467, 696–7
condictio obligandi/donandi causa, 135, 137
  Scotland, 699–700
condictio possessionis, 594
condictio sine causa, 30, 38, 136–7, 143–6, 217–18, 712–13
  Scotland, 142–6, 386, 387–8, 696–7
  separability of *causa*, 147–8
condictio sine causa specialis, South Africa, 217–18
condictiones
  fraud/duress and, 202
  retention without a legal basis (*sine causa*) as underlying principle, 135–6
  unjust factors compared, 135–6
consent of plaintiff. *See* fraud/duress as ground for rescission, vitiation/qualification of plaintiff's consent

732 INDEX

consideration in English law
  See also failure of consideration
  as *causa*, 16, 139, 147–9, 154–6
  as condition governing transfer of benefit, 105, 120–1, 128–9, 139–40
  benefit to claimant, 104
    without performance, 105
  condictio causa data causa non secuta and, 129–35
  contractual and restitutionary meanings distinguished, 69, 103–5, 128–9, 151–6
  'Coronation' cases, 128–9
  Fibrosa, 129, 133–4
  performance without benefit to claimant, 104–5, 187–8
constructive trusts
  England, 667–8
  Scotland, 584–7, 665–8, 676, 722–3, 729
  South Africa, 667
  United States, 555–6
contract
  See also contract, restitutionary damages for breach; failure of consideration as ground for restitution (England); frustration or fundamental breach of contract as ground for restitution; illegality of contract; rescission; restitution in case of void transactions; unwinding of contract
  equality of parties, 356–9
contract (England)
  allocation of risk, 10, 110–11, 112–13, 131, 139, 274
  non-operative
    as requirement for remedy of restitution, 10, 109–11, 131
    civil law distinguished, 110
    determination as, 109
    measure of enrichment and, 10, 110–11
  separability of interest and capital, 114–15
  termination
    for breach, 255–6
    judicial, 247–8
contract (France), termination by court (article 1184 of Civil Code), 451–4
contract (Germany)
  allocation of risk, 274
  casum sentit dominus/res perit domino, 273–4
  mutuality, 178–9, 259, 271–3
  Synallagma, 271 n. 79
  normative Kraft des Faktischen, 272–3
  reliance principle, 272
  termination
    for breach, 66, 260
    judicial, 248 n. 10
  will of the parties, relevance, 271–2
  Willenserklärung, 200–1
contract, restitutionary damages for breach (England), 10–11, 327–47, 678. See also encroachments, restitutionary liability; measure of enrichment/damages
  Attorney-General v. *Blake*, 10–11, 327, 330–4
  criticisms of, 337–47
  City of New Orleans v. *Firemen's Charitable Association*, 337–9
  contract/property right distinction, 355
  defective compensatory measures and, 334–7, 354
  displacement of contractual remedies (*Adras*), 332–4, 354
  in lieu of injunction, 328–9
  loss to claimant, relevance, 11, 337–9, 354
  measure
    'consumer surplus', 335, 341–2
    contractual basis, 328–9
    restitution/compensation divide, 329, 342–7
  mitigation of loss requirement, 332–4
  performance interest and, 334–7
  skimped performance, 337–42
contract, restitutionary damages for breach (Israel), 354–9
  Adras Building Material Ltd v. *Harlow and Jones GmbH*, 332–4, 354
  measure
    market value, 355–9
    profits accruing to defendant, 354–9
contract (Scotland)
  allocation of risk, 274
  condictio sine causa in case of breach, 142–6
counter-restitution, See also measure of enrichment/damages; restitution; *Saldotheorie*
counter-restitution (England), 116–17
  as *restitutio in integrum*, 173, 256, 271
  bad faith and, 176

contractual mistake and, 46–7
equity/common law distinguished, 116–17
incontrovertible benefit and, 185–6
liability mistake and, 46–7
partial failure of consideration and, 16, 116–17, 277–8
rescission in case of impossibility, 40, 174–8, 182, 203–5, 204 n. 46, 209, 258, 260, 262–3, 272, 312 n. 12
restoration of *status quo ante*, as object, 180 n. 80
slow development of concept, 116
subjective devaluation, 187
third party as beneficiary, relevance, 187–8
counter-restitution (Germany), 174–5, 261
counter-restitution (Scotland)
reduction in case of impossibility, 204 n. 46, 252–5, 272, 407–9
void transactions and, 267–8
culpa in contrahendo, 221

damages for breach of contract. See contract, restitutionary damages for breach (England)
datio ob rem, 206 n. 57
debt. See betting debt; insolvency; payment of another's debt without authorisation; performance of another's obligation
Deckungsverhältnis, 540
defences
 See also change of position; estoppel/personal bar; fraud/duress as ground for rescission; illegality as defence; limitation periods; mistake; restitution without enrichment
 enrichment by transfer and, 703–5
defences (England)
 detrimental reliance on payment, 55
 discharge of obligation, 19, 53–4
 failure to comply with legal formalities, 71–2
 knowledge of claimant, 58–9, 73–4, 165–6
 moral/natural obligation, 56
 payment under unenforceable promise, 98
 'submission to an honest claim', 58–62, 120 n. 53
defences (Germany), 88–90
 aufgedrängte Bereicherung, 312

 bona fide purchase for value, 311–12
 failure to comply with legal formalities, 71–2, 88–9
 fulfilment of moral duty, 56
 good faith of defendant, 18, 59, 322
 knowledge of claimant, 38–9, 58–9, 73, 204–5
  bad faith and, 169
  fraud/duress and, 213
  mistake of law and, 55
  unjust factors and, 192–3
  venire contra factum proprium, 204
 natural obligation, 56, 90
 valid contract, 39, 65–7
defences (Netherlands), knowledge of claimant, 213
defences (Scotland)
 knowledge of claimant, 73 n. 127
 'submission to an honest claim', 703–4
delict (Germany), unjustified enrichment remedies distinguished, 12, 220–2
delict/tort
 causation/tracing and, 557
 interface with unjust/unjustified enrichment, 12–13, 177, 220–2, 510–12, 589–93, 653–4, 679–80, 705–6, 727
disgorgement, 11, 678 n. 121, 679–80
dolo facit qui petit quod redditurus est, 216
dolus, 195 n. 5, 199. See also fraud/duress
Durchgriffskondiktion, 540
duress. See fraud/duress

EC Directive on the Protection of Consumers in respect of Distance Contracts, 426
Eingriffskondiktion, 4, 12 n. 35, 162, 206, 311 n. 8, 467, 510–11, 517–18, 554, 675, 679, 705–6
encroachments, restitutionary liability
 See also *Eingriffskondiktion*
 diversity of measures, 351–2
 'encroachment', 349 n. 2
 measure
  compensation for harm to plaintiff, 351–2
  market value, 352
  profits accruing to defendant, 351–2
 mixed public/private basis, 348–65
 Olwell v. Nye & Nissen, 348–50, 352

734   INDEX

encroachments, restitutionary (cont.)
  on patrimonial rights (Scotland), 680, 705–7
  three-party transactions and, 517–18
  unauthorised alienation/unauthorised use distinguished, 352–3
enrichessement sans cause, 441–2, 444–5, 448, 454
enrichment. See unjust/unjustified enrichment
equitable considerations (England), 589–90, 610–13, 672–3
  counter-restitution, 116–17
  property rights, 294–8
equitable considerations (United States), 551–2
estoppel/personal bar, 312 n. 12
  change of position distinguished, 24, 275
  restitutio in integrum/counter-restitution distinguished, 275
ex turpi causa non oritur actio, 298, 312–13, 315–16
exceptio doli, 276, 405
exécution en nature, 449–50
exécution forcé en nature, 449
exploitation. See fraud/duress

faculté de remplacement, 449–50, 452, 454–5
failure of consideration as ground for restitution (England)
  See also frustration or fundamental breach of contract as ground for restitution; mistake as ground for restitution (England)
  acceptance by other party, need for, 142–3
  as unjust factor, 15–16, 77, 81–3, 91–2, 93, 94, 97–8, 108–9, 135–6, 155–6
  bad faith and, 123, 141–3
  breach of contract and, 66–7, 107
  broad-ranging nature, 136–40
  Coronation cases, 131
  failure of condition, 155–6
  frustration and, 256–7
  mistake as cause of action distinguished, 39–40, 41–3, 44–6, 137–41
  partial failure as basis for restitution, 16, 147–9, 154–6
    advantages, 16, 117–18, 127

  counter-restitution and, 16, 116–17, 277–8
  exceptions to 'total failure' requirement and, 115
  setting-aside of contract and, 148–9
  proprietary consequences, 107–8
  Quistclose trust, 108
  restitution in absence of failure
    insurance contracts, 71–2
    minors' contracts, 70–1
  separability of contract and, 132
  swaps litigation and, 14–15, 68–9, 81–3, 107–8, 118–22, 139–40, 152–4, 618
  total failure requirement, 16, 111–12, 131, 133–5, 146–9, 256, 257
    collateral benefit and, 113, 115
    condictio causa data causa non secuta and, 132, 153–6
    contract as determining factor, 113
    counterclaims and, 132–3
    'entire contract' and, 112–13
    historical context, 117
    separability of contract and, 114–15, 132
  ultra vires demands and, 64–5, 82–3, 107–8, 118–22
  unjust enrichment arising from, 108–9, 111, 123
  valid contract and, 93, 155–6
  vitiation/qualification of plaintiff's consent and, 140–3
  void contract as result of failure, 67–72, 78, 310
  void contract causing, 76, 105–6, 118–20, 121
failure of consideration as ground for restitution (Germany), as unjust factor, 260
failure of consideration as ground for restitution (Scotland)
  See also restitution in case of frustration or fundamental breach of contract, Scotland
  breach of contract and, 143–6
  total failure requirement, Cantiere, 132–3, 154–5
fault, examples, 382. See also bad faith
fiduciary obligations, interface with unjust/unjustified enrichment, 11, 360–4, 395–6, 408–9, 672, 678–9

INDEX 735

fiduciary obligations, restitutionary
  damages for breach, 360-4
  deterrence and, 361-3
  enrichment, relevance, 363
  inequality of parties, 362
  measure, profits accruing to defendant, 361-4
  Snepp v. United States, 360-4
  voidable nature of transaction, 408-9
fraud/duress. *See* change of position; fraud/duress as ground for rescission; fraud/duress, definitions; fraud/duress, effect on; rescission; restitution without enrichment (*Wegfall der Bereicherung*); *Saldotheorie*; unwinding of contract
fraud/duress as ground for rescission (England), 159-93
  alternative 'unjust factors', 210-11
  as independent cause of action, 17-18
  as unjust factor, 4, 17-18, 77, 164-6, 209-10
  bad faith and
    defendants', 169
    minors, 169-70
  by third party, 165-6
  compulsion and, 210
  constructive fraud/exploitation
    constructive notice, 161
    misrepresentation, 161, 168, 197-8
    O'Brien doctrine, 165, 167-8, 172-4, 187-8, 504
    unconscientious receipt, 166-7
  unconscionability, 161, 168-9, 170 n. 46
  undue influence, 161, 167-8, 170-2, 174, 198
  due legal process as, 78
  in pari delicto rule and, 301
  unconscientious procurement, 166
  vitiation/qualification of plaintiff's consent and, 164, 165
fraud/duress as ground for rescission (Germany)
  remedies, 258-60
  right of rescission, 258
  three-party situations, 675
fraud/duress, definitions 196-200. *See also* fraud/duress as ground for rescission
  compulsion or threat, 210, 700-1
  duress, 198-200
    civil law, 199-200

  common law concept, 198
  England, 210
  Germany, 198-9
  Netherlands, 198-9
  South Africa, 199
  undue influence distinguished, 198
duress, fraud and exploitation, 164-8
fraud/fraudulent misrepresentation
  common law concept, 196
  England, 197-8
  Germany (*arglistige Täuschung*), 196, 198
  Netherlands (*bedrog*), 196-7, 198
  South Africa, 197
fraud/duress, effect on
  remedies (civil law), 200-24
    as delicts, 220-2
    basis of restitution obligation, 222
    due transfers and, 213-18
  remedies (England),
    vitiation/qualification of plaintiff's consent and, 164
  remedies, (Germany)
    as delicts, 221-2
    bad faith and, 169-70
    declaration of intent and, 164, 214-16
    due transfers and, 214-18, 231
    lack of legal cause/ground and, 17, 192-3
    Leistungskondiktion and, 207-8
  remedies (Roman-Dutch law), due transfers and, 214
  remedies (South Africa), as delicts, 221
  transfer of ownership
    civil law, 218-20, 222-3
    Germany, *Verpflichtungsgeschäft/ Verfügungsgeschäft* distinction, 218-19
    Netherlands, 220
    South Africa, 219-20
    rei vindicatio, 219-20
frustration or fundamental breach of contract as ground for restitution (England), 65-7, 107, 109, 265-6. *See also* failure of consideration as ground for restitution (England)
  breach of contract and invalidity *ab initio* distinguished, 112, 265-6
  in case of valid contract, 65-7
  condictio causa data causa non secuta, relevance, 67, 129-35

frustration or fundamental (*cont.*)
  consideration/expectation of
    counterperformance and, 16, 66–72,
    77, 106, 107, 153
  frustrating event as invalidation of
    obligation to pay, 66–7
  payments outstanding at time of
    frustration, 66
  payments prior to frustration, 66
  requirements
    non-operation of contract, 10, 109–11,
      123–4, 155
    total failure of consideration
      requirement, 115, 256–7
  statutory basis, 115
frustration or fundamental breach of
  contract as ground for restitution
  (Germany), 65–6
  condictio causa data causa non secuta,
    relevance, 67
  rescission affecting terms of contract as
    basis, 66
  unjust enrichment as basis, 15,
    66
  other than on grounds of unjust
    enrichment, 12
frustration or fundamental breach of
  contract as ground for restitution
  (Scotland), 265–6
  bad faith and, 141 n. 41
  breach of contract and invalidity *ab
    initio* distinguished, 265–6
  condictio causa data causa non secuta,
    132–3, 143–4, 154–5, 254, 699
  fault and, 141 n. 41, 145–6
  total failure of consideration
    requirement and, 143–6, 254–5
furtum, 591–3, 594
fundamental breach of contract as ground
  for restitution, *See* frustration or
  fundamental breach of contract as
  ground for restitution

Gestaltungsrecht, 247
gestion d'affaires, 441–5, 454, 488
gifts
  England
    mistake as ground for restitution,
      47–8, 52, 54
    nature of obligation, 44–5
  Germany, as binding contract, 44

good faith
  See also bad faith
  Germany
    illegality and, 322
    venire contra factum proprium and,
      274–6
  Israel, contract, 332 n. 26
  Netherlands, illegality and, 322

ignorance as unjust factor, 77 n. 7, 91,
  672–3, 707–8, 719–22, 728
illegality as cause of action (England), 290,
  300–9
  in pari delicto potior est conditio defendentis,
    301–2
  'protected class' cases. *See* vitiated
    consent distinguished *below*
  'repentance' cases, 305–9
  ultra vires acts of public authorities,
    62–5
  vitiated consent distinguished, 300–5,
    308–9
    duress, 301
    inequality of parties, 302–3
    non-voluntary transfer, 301–2
illegality as defence
  discretionary approach
    Israel, 321
    Netherlands, 321–4
    New Zealand, 321
  justification, 312–15
    deterrence/punishment, 313–15
    *nemo auditur turpitudinem suam
      allegans*, 24–5, 312–13, 315–16
    payment of costs as middle way, 324
    Roman law basis, 310
illegality as defence (England), 290, 291–9
  cause of action distinguished, 290, 306
  common law, 292–4, 296–8
  discretionary approach, 322
  equity, 294–8
  ex turpi causa non oritur actio, 298, 315–16
  in pari delicto potior est conditio defendentis,
    298–9, 316
  property rights not generated by unjust
    enrichment
    common law, 292–8
    equity, 294–8
  restitution of unjust enrichment, 298–9
illegality as defence (Germany), 311 n. 4
  discretionary approach, 321–3

good faith and, 322
in pari turpitudine melior est causa possidentis, 316–21
mutual performance, 320–1
nemo auditur turpitudinem suam allegans, 311 n. 4, 315–16
quantum meruit action and, 316–21
unilateral performance, 317–20
illegality of contract
England
  effect, 289, 303
  examples, 289–90
Germany, whether justifying restitution, 86–8
improvement of another's property as ground for restitution
England
  absence of remedy, 369 n. 1
  US law distinguished, 369–71
France, right to require removal, 416 n. 128
Germany, 22, 371 n. 9
  forced exchange, duty in tort to mitigate damages compared, 381
Italy, right to require removal, 416
Roman law, 21–2
South Africa, voluptuary expenses, 394 n. 38, 427
improvement of another's property as ground for restitution (Scotland)
accession, 392, 413–17
  other than by accession, 393, 417–21
bad faith and, 392
Bankton's *Institutions*, 393–4
basis of owner's liability
  condictio causa data causa non secuta, 404–6
  condictio indebiti, 406–7, 709
  implied contract, 411
  lack of legal cause/ground, 402–3
  unjust use, 411
donation and, 392, 405 n. 87
EC Directive on the Protection of Consumers in respect of Distance Contracts, 426
English law distinguished, 411
examples, 384
male fide improvers, 396–8
measure of enrichment, 413
  mode of enrichment, relevance, 412–13

objective approach, 424–6
quantum meruit, 407 n. 98, 429–30
saved expense, 403, 418, 428–9
subjective devaluation, 421–4
where value of improvement realized through sale or lease, 423–5
mistake, relevance, 398–404
necessary, profitable and voluptuary expenses, relevance, 394
Newton v. *Newton*, 398–400, 424–5
recoverable 'enrichment', 419–21
remedies
  diversity, 22, 386–9
  forced exchange, 414
  money equivalent, 414
  recompense, 398, 708–9
  retention, 393–4
  right of removal (*ius tollendi*), 394, 415–16
  right to require removal, 416–17
  waiver, 417 n. 131
Shilliday v. *Smith*, 385–9, 404–5, 427, 465–6, 585
Stair's *Institutions*, 387–9, 391–3
tenant's right, 392
title/possession, relevance, 398–402
unnecessary improvements, 398–401
void contract and, 406–7
voidable contract and
  Adamson v. *Glasgow Corporation Water-Works Commissioners*, 409
  Boyd & Forrest v. *Glasgow & South Western Railway*, 407–11
  York Buildings Co. v. *Mackenzie*, 394–6, 419, 424
improvement of another's property by mistake as ground for restitution (United States)
alternative remedies, 22–3, 370, 375–6
betterment acts, 376–8
deferred relief, 375
English law distinguished, 369–71
fault, relevance, 382, 383
measure of enrichment, 22–3, 371–83
  fault/relative hardship and, 373
  incontrovertible benefit to owner/cost to improver dichotomy, 12, 22–3, 372–3
  liquidity and, 373–5
  market value, 381–2
  owner's own revaluation, 374–5

738 INDEX

improvement of another's property (*cont.*)
  saved expense, 374
  remedies
    forced exchange, 22, 375–6, 378–81
    lien, 22
    tender to improver at unimproved value, 22
    Restatement of Restitution (1936), 371 n. 8, 375 n. 16, 381–2
in pari delicto potior est conditio defendentis/in pari turpitudine melior est causa possidentis, 298–9, 301–2, 316–21
incompetence of contracting party
  See also minors
  Germany
    change of position and, 233–4
    void transaction, 260
  Scotland, 699–700
  United States, change of position, 233–4
indebitum solutum, 683–4. *See also condictio indebiti*
inequality of parties, 57, 64–5, 167–8, 231–2, 301–3, 356–7, 362
insolvency
  constructive trusts, Scotland, 584–7, 665–8, 722–3, 729
  interface with unjust/unjustified enrichment, Scotland, 677–8, 723–6
  parity of creditors (*paritas creditorum*)
    France, 560
    Scotland, 723–6
    United States, 558, 586, 723–6
  proprietary restitution and, 577–8, 584–7
  subrogation/*cessio legis*, 577–8, 665–8
  tracing, United States, 555–6
insurance contracts, 71–2, 577, 680–1
interest
  England, delay in payment of debt and, 455
  France (article 1153 of Civil Code), 454–5
ius in personam ad rem acquirendam, 579
ius tollendi, 394, 415–16

just factors (Germany). *See* defences (Germany)

knowledge of claimant defence. *See* defences, knowledge of claimant

lack of legal cause/ground (Germany), 5, 14–15, 17–18, 37, 38, 79. *See also* performance/transfer without legal basis (*Leistungskondiktion*)
  condictiones, 135–6
  duress and. *See* fraud/duress
  unjust enrichment and, 311, 494
  unjust factors, relevance, 18, 192–3, 649–50
laesio enormis, 231
leapfrogging. *See* three-party situations
Leistung/Leistungskondiktion
  England, 82, 92–3, 702–3
  Germany, 4, 5, 17, 40–1, 162, 205–8, 224, 467–9, 479, 539–41, 544–7, 554, 616–17, 701. *See also* performance/transfer without legal basis (*Leistungskondiktion*) (Germany)
  Scotland, 467–9
Leistungskette, 540 n. 46
Leistungsprinzip, 539, 541
liens and hypothecs, proprietary restitution in case of, 578–9, 665
limitation periods
  England
    failure of consideration, 83, 125–6
    mistake, 125–6
    right to payment, 56–8
  Germany, 56, 90
  subsidiarity and, 608–9

mandament van spolie, 216 n. 99
mandat, 441, 442–3, 445
measure of enrichment/damages
  See also contract, restitutionary damages for breach; encroachments, restitutionary liability; improvement of another's property as ground for enrichment; *quantum lucratus*; *quantum meruit/quantum valebat*; *restitutio in integrum*
  in absence of unjust factor, 185–6
  compensation for harm to plaintiff, 351–2
  'consumer surplus', 335, 341–2
  contract as determinant, 10–11, 110, 184–5, 327–9
  non-operative contract, 10, 110–11
  defendant's enrichment, 183–5
  difficulty in case of non-money benefits, 373–4

disgorgement, 11, 678 n. 121, 679–80
fault/relative hardship and, 373
incontrovertible benefit to owner/cost to improver dichotomy, 12, 22–3, 372–3
law of delict as determinant, 12
liquidity and, 373–5
market value, 352, 355–9, 381–2
mode of enrichment, relevance, 412–13
mutual restitution in money and, 177–8, 182–3
non-contractual situation, 184
objective approach, 182–3, 424–6
owner's own revaluation, 374–5
plaintiff's enrichment, 185–6
policy-motivated, 13
profits accruing to defendant, 351–2, 361–4, 653–4
punitive damages, 654 n. 129
quantum meruit, 407 n. 98, 428–30
restitution/compensation divide, 329, 342–7
saved expense, 374, 403, 418, 428–9
subjective devaluation, 421–4, 485
unjust factors, relevance, 168, 182–3, 185–6
where value of improvement realized through sale or lease, 423–5
metus, 195 n. 5, 199
metus reverentialis, 199
minors
See also incompetence of contracting party
England
bad faith, 169–70
failure of consideration as ground for restitution, 70–1
Germany
bad faith, 169–70, 179
unwinding of contract, 260
Scotland, unwinding of contract, 253, 281
mise en demeure, 450–1
misrepresentation (England), 161, 168, 197–8
mistake as ground for restitution (England), 37–62, 73–4, 120, 311
as 'unjust factor', 15–16, 21, 72, 77, 93, 94, 504, 704–5
causal mistake, 49–53, 73–4, 125
neglect of recipient's interests, 53
contractual mistake, 46–7

counter-restitution and, 46–7
degrees of mistake, relevance, 48, 52
failure of consideration
as cause of action distinguished, 125, 136–40, 618
as ground, 125, 136–40, 618
formation of intention/absence of legal ground distinguished, 46, 311
gift, 47–8, 52, 54
'legal ground' approach and, 5, 27–8, 43, 48, 53–4, 58, 65, 75
liability mistake, 38–40, 45, 46–7
contractual mistake distinguished, 39–40, 41–3, 44–6, 137–41
mistaken assumption of valid contract, 68
unenforceable obligation and, 46
limitation period, 125–6
mistake of fact, 38–9, 50, 124–6
mistake of law, 16–17, 29, 55–8, 59–60, 72–5, 83–5, 97, 107 n. 15, 124–6, 508, 655, 663–4
judicial change in the law and, 28, 74–5, 83–5, 93
non-liability mistake, 43–54
as origin of remedy, 46–7
objective approach, 5
right of rescission, 40, 258
unenforceable obligation and, 41–8
mistake as ground for restitution
Germany, as 'unjust factor', 85–6
Roman law, 37–8
mistaken assumption of liability (Scotland)
condictio indebiti, 42 n. 15, 73, 75, 136, 213 n. 80, 249 n. 14, 696–7
mistake, need for, 696–9
mitigation of damages (England), 456–7
breach of contract, 332–4
duty in tort, 381
reasonableness test, 456–7
money
bad faith and, 675
tracing, 673–6
mora creditoris, 438, 446
mutual restitution. *See* counter-restitution; mutual restitution; restitution; *Saldotheorie*

nam hoc natura aequum est neminem cum alterius detrimento et iniuria fieri locupletiorem, 3

negotiorum gestio
  civil/common law compared, 652-3
  classification, 652-3, 681
  England, 652-3
  Germany, 19, 98 n. 58, 459-60, 511 n. 61
  Quebec, 594
  Scotland, 462-3, 472-4, 476, 487-9, 681, 729
    agency of necessity distinguished, 463
    improvements to another's property, 398 n. 58
nemo auditur turpitudinem suam allegans, 312-13, 315-16
Nichtleistungskondiktion, 496, 499-500, 511-12
normative Kraft des Faktischen, 272-3

obligations de faire, 454-5

paiement, 434-5, 441, 454
paritas creditorum, 558, 585-6
parity of creditors
  causation and, 558-60, 723-6, 729
  hypothec, 665
  insolvency and, 558, 560, 586, 677-8, 723-6
payment of another's debt without authorisation, civil/common law compared
  assignability of debt, 461-2
  consent of creditor, need for, 461
  Scots law lessons, 485-9
  'unjust factor' requirement, 462
payment of another's debt without authorisation (England), 19-20, 28-9, 50 n. 28
payment of another's debt without authorisation (France), 19-20, 28-9
payment of another's debt without authorisation (Germany), 50 n. 28
  as special category of enrichment, 468-9
  creditor's right of refusal, 471-2
  negotiorum gestio, 19, 459-60, 468
  Rückgriffskondiktion, 19, 467-9, 480, 488, 710-11
payment of another's debt without authorisation (Scotland), 462-72
  basis of liability, 715-18
  by mistake, 477-82
  Clive Code, 482-5
  creditor's right of refusal, 484-5

  discharge of debt, 469-72, 481-2, 486-7, 710-11
  right of
    recompense, 474-6, 710-11, 715
    recovery on basis of *negotiorum gestio*, 472-4, 487-9
    repetition (*condictio indebiti*), 476-7, 481-2, 714-15
  Rückgriffskondiktion, 467-9, 480, 488, 710-11
  subrogation, 463 n. 16
payment of another's debt without authorisation (South Africa)
  discharge of debt, 536-8
  First National Bank v. B & H Engineering, 478-9, 535-8
  Govender v. The Standard Bank of South Africa, 478-9, 481-2, 534-5
performance of another's obligation, *See also* payment of another's debt without authorisation
performance of another's obligation (England)
  as 'vicarious performance', 445-6, 457
  by mistake, 477-82, 504
  creditor's right of refusal, 445-6, 460-1
  'officious intermeddling', 447-8, 460
  discharge of debt, 19, 446-7
    intervention under compulsion of law, 446-7
    necessity, 447
  loan at interest, 455-7
    as mitigation of damage, 456-7
  right of recovery, 447
  subrogation, 447 n. 70
  substitute performance, 455-7
  tender of due performance, effect, 446
performance of another's obligation (France)
  action in de rem verso, 444 n. 55
  bad faith and, 444
  by interested third party, 439-40, 448, 454
  by non-interested third party, 440-4
    enrichessement sans cause, 441-2, 444-5, 448, 453-4
  gestion d'affaires, 441-5, 448, 454
  mandat, 441, 442-3, 445
  right of recovery, 441-4
  Civil Code
    article 1142, 448-55

article 1144, 433, 435, 443, 448–57, 461 n. 6
article 1236, 433, 436, 439–45, 454
article 1237, 436–8
consent of creditor, need for, 437–9
right of refusal, 438–9, 445
English law distinguished, 445–8, 455–7
judicial authorisation of performance at debtor's expense, 433, 448–57, 461 n. 6
exécution en nature, 449–50
exécution forcé en nature, 449
faculté de remplacement, 449–50, 452, 454–5
judicial discretion and, 451–5
mise en demeure, 450–1
obligations de faire, 454–5
subrogation, 19, 439–42, 445, 463 n. 16
terminology, 433–5
débiteur, 434
paiement, 434–5, 441, 454
prestation, 434, 437–9
performance/transfer without legal basis
condictiones, 135–6
duress and. See fraud/duress
relevance of other factors, 18, 192–3
unjust enrichment and, 311
performance/transfer without legal basis (Leistungskondiktion) (Germany), 4, 17, 40–1, 205–8, 467–9. See also undue transfers
duress/fraud and, 207–8, 213, 215, 224
failure of purpose, relevance, 206–7, 215–16, 224
Leistungsprinzip, 539, 541
Nichleistungskondiktion, 496, 539, 544
unenforceable obligations, 40–1
performance/transfer without legal basis (Leistungskondiktion) (Scotland), 693–713
'transfer', 694–5
personal bar. See estoppel/personal bar
powerlessness as unjust factor, 672, 707–8
prestation, 434, 437–9
promises in English law
enforceability, 41–3
restitution distinguished, 42–3
payment under unenforceable promise, 98
proportionality, England, counter-restitution and, 177–8
proprietary basis for unwinding of contracts, 268–70

proprietary restitution, 268–70. See also subrogation/cessio legis
definitions
property, 352–3
proprietary, 571–2, 676–7
insolvency and, constructive trusts, 584–7, 665–8
interface with unjust/unjustified enrichment, 12–14, 268–70, 290–1, 292–8, 392, 588–96, 665–71, 705–8, 726–7
liens and hypothecs, 578–9, 665
personal rights and, 579
property rights, 707
rei vindicatio. See vindicatory remedies/vindicatio
vindicatory action as enrichment action, 574–5

quantum lucratus, 244, 428–9
quantum meruit/quantum valebat, 25, 244, 313–14
England, 122–3, 177, 312 n. 11
Germany, 316–21
Scotland, 407 n. 98, 429–30
Quistclose trust, 108

réception/répétition de l'indu, 434 n. 6, 594–5, 599, 682–3
Rechtsgeschäft, 200–1
rechtshandeling, 201
recompense (Scotland)
as general remedy, 464–9
mistake, relevance, 398 n. 59, 474–6, 708–9
relevance of term, 428–9
remedy/liability distinguished, 389–90
unauthorised payment of another's debt, 474–6, 710–11
reduction of contract (Scotland), 248 n. 10, 267–268, 427
impossibility of restitution/counter-restitution and, 204 n. 46, 252–5, 267, 272, 407–9, 583–4
real/personal effect, 581–4
third party rights and, 270
void contract, 267
reduction of contract (Scotland). See reduction of contract (Scotland)
relief as unjust enrichment remedy (Scotland), 387 n. 7, 428, 463 n. 15, 680

repetition (Scotland)
  condictio indebiti and, 464-5, 476-7
  mistake, need for, 464-5
  restitution distinguished, 388-9, 405 n. 84
res perit domino, 133, 273-4
rescission (England)
  See also counter-restitution; fraud/duress as ground for rescission (England); restitution
  in case of worthless contract, 180 n. 81
  classification of remedy, 250-1
  contract/unjust enrichment interface, 161
  German law distinguished, 86, 137 n. 21, 174-7, 250
  impossibility of restitution/ counter-restitution and, 40, 174-8, 182, 204 n. 46, 258, 260, 262-3, 272, 312 n. 12
  partial rescission, 173-4, 186-7, 189-91
  restitution as consequence, 40, 86, 161, 163
  termination distinguished, 262-5
  third party rights and, 270
rescission (Germany) (*Anfechtung*)
  classification of remedy, 250
  English law distinguished, 86, 137 n. 21, 174-7, 250
  grounds, 86, 258
  impossibility of restitution/ counter-restitution and, 203-5, 258, 260, 261
  rendering contract void *ab initio*, 86
  restitution on basis of underlying ground for rescission, 86
  right of, 247, 258
  termination distinguished, 263-5
  vertragsähnliches Recht, 137 n. 21
rescission (Netherlands), impossibility of restitution/counter-restitution and, 204, 209
rescission (Scotland)
  See also reduction of contract
  termination distinguished, 265
Restatement of Contracts (Second), 233
Restatement of Restitution, 371 n. 8, 375 n. 16, 381-2, 506 n. 43, 647-8
restitutio in integrum, 24. See also measure of enrichment/damages
  arguments in favour of principle, 270-7, 281-5

  as contractual concept, 203, 221
  change of position and, 24, 243-85
  England
    in case of, 265-6
    transactions, 267-8
  counter-restitution as, 173, 256, 271
  definition, 281-2
  Germany, 203-5, 261
    void transactions, 267
  rescission and, 202-5
  Roman law, 202-3
  Scotland
    in case of, 265-6
    transactions, 267-8
  definition, 281-2
  frustration, 265-6
  improvements to another's property, 407-9, 427-8
  limitation to rescission of legal act, 253
  South Africa, 203, 221
  unwinding of contract and, 24, 243-77
restitution
  See also contract, restitutionary damages for breach; failure of consideration as ground for restitution (England); frustration or fundamental breach of contract as ground for restitution; frustration or fundamental breach of contract as ground for restitution; improvement of another's property as ground for restitution; mistake as ground for restitution; proprietary restitution; *restitutio in integrum*; restitution without enrichment; subsidiarity; ultra vires acts of public authorities (England)
  history, 227-9
  private/public law régimes, *ultra vires* acts, 664-5
  scope of remedy, 41-2, 312 n. 12
  unjust enrichment, equivalence, 3, 497, 647-9
  variety of meanings, 647-8
restitution (civil law), bad faith and, *condictio causa data causa non secuta*, 141-2
restitution (England)
  alternative grounds/remedies, 124-6, 135-6, 581, 590-1, 653-4, 703
  limitation periods and, 83, 125-6
  basis, vitiation of consent, 49, 140-3

INDEX 743

in case of
  moral obligation, 41–2, 312 n. 12
  unenforceable obligation, 47–8, 55–8, 70–2
civil law distinguished, 76
counterclaims and, 133–4
evolving system, 127
monetarization, 174–8, 182
mutual, 177–82
policy-motivated, 55–9, 61, 78–9, 84, 93–8, 170–1, 176–7
  court's discretion in respect of illegal transactions, 94–5
  Insolvency Act, 1986 93–5
  Law of Property (Miscellaneous Provisions) Act, 1989 95–7
  time-barred claim, 55
proportionality, 177–8
proprietary nature, 175–6
requirements
  enrichment. *See* restitution without enrichment
  non-operation of contract, 10, 109–11, 123–4, 155
  unjust factors, 76
rescission and. *See* rescission
restoration of parties to previous position as objective, 116
scope of remedy, 106–7
  benefit to claimant as basis, 106–7
  failure of consideration, relevance, 107–9
restitution (France), 436
restitution (Germany)
  alternative grounds/remedies, 594
  policy-motivated, 59
  secondary enrichment, 182–3
restitution (Quebec), alternative grounds/remedies, *negotiorum gestio*, 594
restitution (Scotland)
  in case of wrong of third party, 673–4
  linkage with unjust enrichment, *condictio causa data causa non secuta*, 26, 386, 404–6
  repetition distinguished, 388–9, 405 n. 84
restitution in case of void transactions (England), 67–9, 76, 78–9, 82–3, 84–5, 95–7, 109, 237–8, 616–17, 701–2
  betting debt, 43–4, 72
  breach of contract distinguished, 112

  consideration/expectation of counterperformance and, 67–72, 105–6, 109, 118–22
  illegal transaction, 289, 303, 310
  impossibility of restitution/counter-restitution and, 267–8
  lack of clarity of concept, 72, 267–8
  mistake of law and, 45, 72–5, 84–5, 92–3, 107 n. 15
  remedy in tort, 256–7
  unjust factor, need for, 701
  void/unenforceable distinction, 70
  void/voidable distinction, 94, 201 n. 37, 267–8
  without failure of consideration, 69–72
restitution in case of void transactions (Germany), 80, 86–6. *See also* lack of legal cause/ground (Germany)
  avoidance of *nichtig* where right to restitution not intended, 87–8, 93, 99
  clarity of concept, 72, 267–8
  condictio causa data causa non secuta, relevance, 67 n. 98, 73
  consideration/expectation of counterperformance and, 67 n. 98
  illegal transactions as, 86–8, 310
  impossibility of restitution/counter-restitution and, 267–8
  incompetence of party, 260
  intended discharge of contract as basis of payment, 67
  rescission (*Anfechtung*) giving rise to, 86, 268
  restitution without enrichment (*Wegfall der Bereicherung*) and, 235–8
  right to claim back transferred goods, 260
  void/voidable distinction, 267–8
restitution in case of void transactions (Netherlands), void/voidable distinction, 201 n. 37
restitution in case of void transactions (Scotland), 254, 406–11, 702
  impossibility of restitution/counter-restitution and, 267–8
restitution in case of void transactions (United States), void/unenforceable distinction, 70

restitution without enrichment, 227–42.
  See also change of position; contract,
  restitutionary damages for breach;
  fraud/duress, effect on, transfer of
  ownership; frustration or fundamental
  breach of contract as ground for
  restitution; proprietary restitution;
  restitutio in integrum
restitution without enrichment
  fiduciary relationship, 363
  improvement of another's property and,
    381–3
  retained ownership and, 573–5
restitution without enrichment (England),
  void transactions, 237–8
restitution without enrichment (Germany)
  (*Wegfall der Bereicherung*), 229–42
  cases outside doctrine
    bona fide purchaser, 230
    change of position on basis of contract
      with incompetent party, 233–4
    exploitation, 231–2
    liability for actions of sub-contractor,
      238–9
    void transactions, 235–8
    wrongful appropriation of benefit, 232
restitution without enrichment (United
  States), 239–42
  cases outside doctrine
    change of position on basis of contract
      with incompetent party, 233–4
    liability for actions of sub-contractor,
      238–9
    void transaction, 236–7
    wrongful appropriation of benefit,
      232–3
restitutionary damages for breach of
  contract. *See* contract, restitutionary
  damages for breach
right of recovery, 447
risk, allocation of, 10, 110–11, 112–13, 131,
  139, 273–4. *See also res perit domino*
  splitting the loss, 280–1
Rückgriffskondiktion
  Germany, 4, 19, 467–9, 480, 488
  Scotland, 19, 467–9, 710–11
Rücktrittsrecht, 260, 263

Saldotheorie, 178–80, 188, 205, 234–5,
  258–61, 267, 279
  description, 178–9

  displacement, 179, 205
  Zweikondiktionenlehre and, 179, 192, 205,
    258
solutio, 214
specificatio, 517
subcontractors. *See* restitution without
  enrichment; three-party situations
subrogation/*cessio legis*
  See also tracing
  insolvency and, 577–8
    Scotland, 665–8
  insurance contracts, 577, 680–1
  payment of another's debt without
    authorisation, 463 n. 16
  performance of another's obligation
    England, 447 n. 70
    France, 19–20, 439–42, 445, 463 n. 16
  special patrimonies/trusts, 577
  trusts, 577
subsidiarity, 596–623
  actio de in rem verso and, France, 597,
    602, 617, 622 n. 122, 666
  applicability of different set of legal
    principles, 597–607
  availability of alternative remedies, 581,
    596, 607–9
    Quebec, 607–8
  in case of
    contractual remedy, 599–602
    defendant's contract with third party
      Germany, 605
      Quebec, 605–6
    illegal, void or unenforceable
      transactions, 598
    plaintiff's contract with third party
      Canada, 603–4
      France, 602
      Germany, 604
      Quebec, 602–3
    range of unjustified enrichment
      remedies, 598–9
    tort/delict
      France, 705
      Germany, 608
  justification, 609–13
  Leistung and, Germany, 599, 604
  potential for conflict, 612–13
  prescription and, 608–9
  in three-party situations, 558–66, 602–7,
    617 n. 108
    England, 559

France, 560
Germany, 561–2
Italy, 559–60, 617 n. 108
Scotland, 558–9
South Africa, 562–6
weak subsidiarity, Quebec, 597
swaps litigation (England)
   See also ultra vires acts of public authorities
   description of problem, 80–1, 149–51
   failure of consideration and, 14–15, 68–9, 81–3, 107–8, 118–22, 139–40, 152–4, 618
   interrupted swap, 81–2
Synallagma, 271 n. 79

tantum et tale doctrine (Scotland), 676
taxonomy
   See also unjust factors; unjust/unjustified enrichment, definitions; unjust/unjustified enrichment, interface with *and under separate subject headings*
   Birks, 4–5, 39–40, 49, 164–6, 659–60, 670–1, 688, 691, 693–4, 715
   Burrows, 688–91, 693–4
   Clive Code (1996) (Scotland), 26–7, 482–5, 644, 644 n. 85, 660 n. 15, 670, 691–3, 702
   codification and, 643–4
   common law/equity dualism, 672–3
   harmonisation, scope for, 659–61
   importance, 632–44
   lack of attention to (England), 628–57
   Lipkin Gorman, 630, 641–3, 668
   liability/remedy, 388–90, 412–13
   'proprietary rights', 'personal rights', trusts, 676–7
   'restitution', 'recompense', 'repetition' and 'relief' (Scotland), 427–30, 464–9, 474, 682, 684–6, 691
   the 'three Rs' (Scotland), 427–30, 693
   Wilburg/von Caemmerer, 4, 91–2, 539 n. 39, 686–7, 693–713. See also performance/transfer without legal basis (*Leistungskondiktion*)
taxonomy (Scotland), confusion of terminology, 26–7
third party rights, 187–8, 270, 336. See also performance of another's obligation

three-party situations
   See also causation; insolvency; payment of another's debt; performance of another's obligation; subsidiarity; tracing
   diversity of approach, 526–30, 542, 562
   fraud/duress and, 675
   other than payment of another's debt, 20
   policy considerations underlying liability, 530–3, 557–8, 566–7
   sub-contractor's rights against beneficiary of performance, 20, 542–52, 561–6, 606–7
three-party situations (England)
   agency, 513–14
   alignment with two-party situations, 672–3
   causation, leapfrogging, 518–24
   change of position defence, 522
   interceptive subtraction, 506–12
   leapfrogging, 493, 504, 512–24
   proprietary connection and, 515–19
   Lipkin Gorman, 514–15, 517–19, 528, 575, 668
   other than payment of another's debt, 20
   restitution based on 'encroachment', 517–18
   sub-contractor's rights against beneficiary of performance, 20, 547–50
   The Trident Beauty, 548–50, 560
   third party beneficiary of contract, 501–6
   putative contract, 504–6, 510–12
   valid contract, 502–4
   traceability, 519
three-party situations (France)
   actio de in rem verso, 513, 578–9, 602, 682 n. 149, 683
   Boudier, 560, 578–9, 602, 682
three-party situations (Germany)
   actio de in rem verso, 513
   Canaris principles, 20, 616
   change of position defence, 522
   compensation for necessary expenses (Civil Code provision (*BGB*) (ss 944ff)), 561–2
   enrichment, need for, 539–42
   interceptive subtraction, 512
   Leistungskondiktion and, 527–8, 539–41, 544–7, 554, 616–17

746 INDEX

three-party situations (Germany) (cont.)
  sub-contractor's rights against beneficiary of performance, 20, 544–7, 561–2
    Elektrogerätefall, 544–5
  third party beneficiary of contract, putative contract, 504–6, 510–12
three-party situations (Scotland)
  bad faith and, 722–3
  divergence from two-party transactions, 672
  strict liability, 729
  sub-contractor's rights against beneficiary of performance, 546–7
    contract with contractor as bar, 20, 558–9
three-party situations (South Africa)
  enrichment, need for
    First National Bank v. B & H Engineering, 535–8
    Govender v The Standard Bank of South Africa, 534–5
  sub-contractor's rights against beneficiary of performance, 562–6
    ABSA, 564–6
    Buzzard Electrical, 542–4, 546–7, 563–4
  unjust(ified)ness of enrichment, relevance, 542–4
three-party situations (United States)
  enrichment, need for, 537–8
  strict liability, 718–19
  sub-contractor's rights against beneficiary of performance, 550–2
    Commerce Partnership 8098 LP v. Equity Contracting Co., 551–2
  third party beneficiary of contract, putative contract, 504
tracing of money or other property, 13–14, 553–4, 667, 671–6. *See also* subrogation
transfer of ownership. *See* fraud/duress, effect on; undue transfers; unwinding of contract
trusts
  See also constructive trusts
  Scotland, 676–7
  subrogation, 577

ultra vires acts of public authorities (England), 62–5, 107–8, 118–22, 655, 664–5. *See also* swaps litigation
  illegality of demand, 62–5
  public authority liability in Germany distinguished, 62
  unjust factors and, 4, 27–8, 62–5, 664–5
    failure of consideration, 64–5, 82–3, 107–8, 118–22
undue influence (England), 24, 170–1, 174, 198
undue influence (Germany), 24, 74, 170–1, 198–9
undue transfers
  See also performance/transfer without legal basis (*Leistungskondiktion*)
  mistake, relevance, 697–9, 728
undue transfers (France), *répétition de l'indu*, 434 n. 6, 683, 697–8
undue transfers (Netherlands)
  See also performance/transfer without legal basis (*Leistungskondiktion*) (Germany)
  unjust enrichment/undue payment distinguished, 194–5
  fraud/duress and, 208–9, 224
undue transfers (Scotland), 682
  compulsion and, 700–1
undue transfers (South Africa), *condictio indebiti* and, 212–13
unjust factors
  See also failure of consideration as ground for restitution; fraud/duress; fraud/duress as ground for rescission; illegality as cause of action (England); inequality of parties; lack of legal cause/ground (Germany); measure of enrichment/damages; mistake as ground for restitution; performance/transfer without legal basis (*Leistungskondiktion*); ultra vires acts of public authorities
  advantages of system, 160–1, 191–3, 649–51
  lack of legal ground and, 18, 192–3, 649–51
unjust factors (England)
  condictio indebiti and, 38–9, 65, 73–4, 76, 92–3, 98, 139
  condictiones compared, 135–6
  exploitation of claimant's weakness, 77–8, 185–6
  ignorance, 77 n. 7, 91, 672, 707–8, 719–22, 728

lack of coherent system, 5–6, 135,
    159–60, 162–3, 649–51, 665, 672–3,
    690–1
need for, 58–9
powerlessness, 672, 707–8, 728
unjust factors (Germany)
    illegality, 88
    immorality, 88
    mistake, 85–6
    relevance of concept, 159–64,
        192
unjust factors (Scotland),
    non-voluntariness, 211
unjust/unjustified enrichment
    as corrective, 610–12, 619–21
    definitions, 3–8, 647–9
        'enrichment', 651–2
        loss, relevance, 500–1
    by wrong/enrichment 'by subtraction'
        distinguished, 4–5, 164, 497–9,
        524–5, 553
    /possession distinction and, 573
    ownership remains unchanged, 578,
        589–96
    'unjust', 654–6
    unjust enrichment/restitution,
        equivalence, 3, 497, 647–9
    'unjust'/'unjustified' distinguished, 79,
        530 n. 16
    'unjustified unless', 691–3
    'enrichment', corresponding loss,
        relevance, 11, 500–1, 509–12
    general action, 192, 593–4, 595–6,
        617–18, 621–2, 686–7
    history of concept, 8–9, 227–9
    interface with
        contract law, 9–12, 202–9, 262–4,
            497–9, 524–5, 543–4, 546–7,
            598–607, 614–19, 678, 701–3,
            727
        criminal law, 663–4
        delict/tort, 12–13, 177, 220–2, 510–12,
            589–93, 653–4, 679–80, 705–6,
            727
        /duress, 220–2
        as defence, 312–13
        fiduciary obligations, 11, 360–4,
            395–6, 408–9, 672, 678–9
        insolvency law, 677–8, 723–6
        law of wrongs, 12, 608, 619, 621–2
        property law, 12–14, 268–70, 290–8,
            392, 588–96, 619–21, 665–71, 705–8,
            726–7
        /possession/transfer of property,
            13–14, 398–402
    remedies, 574–5, 669–71
    repetition of the undue, 682
    trusts, 676–7
    where ownership remains unchanged,
        Scotland, *condictio ex causa furtiva*,
        705–6
unjust/unjustified enrichment (England)
    as independent source of rights and
        obligations, 9
    burden of proof, 126–7
    'enrichment'
        'at the expense of', 493–525, 553–4,
            562, 565
        subtraction, 506–12
        by performance/other than by
            performance, 496, 499–500
        causation, 553–4
        corresponding loss, relevance, 11,
            500–1, 509–12
        unjust(ified)ness, relevance, 547–50
    failure of consideration giving rise to,
        108–9, 111
    non-monetary enrichment, 122–3
    measure of enrichment. *See* measure of
        enrichment/damages
    property rights distinguished, 290–1,
        292–8, 575–7, 666–71, 707–8
    quantum meruit/quantum valebat actions
        and, 122–3, 177
    'unjust', 110, 111
    'unjust factors, relevance, 77
unjust/unjustified enrichment (France),
    'enrichment', corresponding loss,
        relevance, 705
unjust/unjustified enrichment (Germany)
    See also restitution without enrichment
    'at the expense of', causation, 554
    Civil Code provision (*BGB*) (s 812(1)), 4,
        79, 496, 561, 593–4
    condictio indebiti/condictio sine causa and,
        38, 40–1, 55
    proposed revision, 696
    sweeping nature, 79–80, 88, 93,
        205
    codification of law, effect, 194
    'enrichment'
        'at the expense of', 493–4, 496

unjust/unjustified enrichment (cont.)
  by performance (Leistung)/other than by performance (Nichtleistung), 80, 91, 496, 499–500, 511–12, 539, 604, 686–7
  incurred by claimant (Verwendungen), 4, 554
  corresponding loss, relevance, 496 n. 12, 500–1, 510–12
  'in another way' (Bereicherung in sonstiger Weise), 4, 544
  general action, 192, 593–4, 686–7
  where ownership remains unchanged, 593–4
  condictio possessionis, 594
unjust/unjustified enrichment (Netherlands), general action, 683
unjust/unjustified enrichment (Quebec)
  Civil Code provisions, 594–6
  general action, actio de in rem verso as, 595–6, 617–18, 621–2
  réception de l'indu, 594–5, 599, 608 n. 80
  where ownership remains unchanged, 594–6
unjust/unjustified enrichment (Roman law)
  where ownership remains unchanged, 591–3
  condictio ex causa furtiva, 591–3
unjust/unjustified enrichment (Scotland)
  See also improvement of another's property as ground for restitution (Scotland)
  Clive Code (1996), 26–7, 482–5, 644, 660 n. 15, 670, 691–3, 702
  delict/contract, 498–9
  diversity of remedies, 387–9, 488
  encroachment on claimant's property (Eingriff), 680, 705–7
  'enrichment', 411–13, 417–21, 651–2
    'at the expense of', 554
    and, 663–4
    by performance/other than by performance, 684–6, 694–705
    'transfer', 694–5
    unjust(ified)ness, relevance, 545–7
  'unjustified unless', 691–3
  where ownership remains unchanged, liens and hypothecs, 578
unjust/unjustified enrichment (South Africa)
  'enrichment'
    'at the expense of', 554, 562, 565
    corresponding loss, relevance, 534–8
    unjust(ified)ness, relevance, 542–4, 546–7
  general action, 684
unjust/unjustified enrichment (United States)
  'enrichment'
    'at the expense of', 493
    unjust(ified)ness, relevance, 550–2
unwinding of contract
  change of position defence and, 24, 259–60, 282–5
  effect on
    contract, 244, 252–70
    possession, 245
    transfer of property, 244–5
  failure of consideration and, 260, 262–3
  methods
    automatic, 248, 266
    classification of remedy, 250–70
    effect on contract, 252–70
    exceptio against plaintiff, 248
    judicial, 247–8
    obligational, 247, 266
    proprietary basis, 268–70
    reasons, 248–50
  terms to be avoided, frustration, 244–6
  unified system, desirability, 262–70
unwinding of contract (England)
  breach of contract, 256
  defective goods, 255
  frustration, 256–7
  mistake, fraud, force or fear, 255
  where transfer of property rendered void, 257–8
unwinding of contract (Germany), 258–60
  breach of contract, 260
  minority, 260
  mistake, fraud, force or fear, 258–60
  rescission/termination distinction, 263–5
  splitting the loss, 261, 280–1
  Zweikondiktionenlehre, 261, 278–9
unwinding of contract (Scotland)
  minority, 253, 281
  mistake, fraud, force or fear, 252–3

Valutaverhältnis, 540
venire contra factum proprium, 204, 274–6. See also estoppel/personal bar
Verfügungsgeschäft, 218–19

Verpflichtungsgeschäft, 218–19
vertragsähnliches Recht, 137 n. 21
Verwendungskondiktion, 4, 467, 554
'vicarious performance', 445–6, 457
vindicatory remedies/*vindicatio*, 13–14, 573–5, 596, 619–21, 669–71, 675
  England, 13, 591
  Germany, 218–20, 249, 250–1, 268–9, 594
  interface with unjust/unjust enrichment, 574–5, 669–71
  Roman law, 591–3
  South Africa, 219–20, 564
vitiation/qualification of plaintiff's consent. *See* failure of consideration as ground for restitution (England); fraud/duress as ground for rescission; illegality as cause of action (England)
void/voidable transactions
  See also restitution in case of void transactions
  right to claim back transferred goods, 260
  subsidiarity in case of, 598
Vorleistungsfälle, 137 n. 25

Wandelung, 247
Wegfall der Bereicherung, 227–42
Willenserklärung, 200–1

Zuweisungsgehalt eines Rechts, 511
Zweikondiktionenlehre, 179, 192, 205, 258, 261, 278–9

For EU product safety concerns, contact us at Calle de José Abascal, 56–1°, 28003 Madrid, Spain or eugpsr@cambridge.org.

www.ingramcontent.com/pod-product-compliance
Ingram Content Group UK Ltd.
Pitfield, Milton Keynes, MK11 3LW, UK
UKHW040413060825
461487UK00006B/492